The Oxford Compa

—TO—

Consciousn

Tim Bayne, Ph.D. (University of Arizona, 2002), is Philosophy, School of Social Sciences, University of Manchester. He is the author of *The Unity of Consciousness* (OUP, 2012) and *Thought: A Very Short Introduction* (OUP, 2013), and has edited a number of volumes in the philosophy of mind and cognitive science. A native of New Zealand, he has taught at Canterbury University, Macquarie University and the University of Oxford.

Axel Cleeremans, Ph.D. (Carnegie Mellon, 1991), is a Research Director with the Fonds de la Recherche Scientifique and a professor of cognitive psychology at the Université Libre de Bruxelles, where he heads the Center for Cognition & Neurosciences. His research is dedicated to exploring the differences between information processing with and without consciousness, particularly in the domain of learning and memory. A member of the Royal Academy of Belgium, Cleeremans is Field Editor-in-Chief of Frontiers in Psychology and a member of the board of the Association for the Scientific Study of Consciousness.

Patrick Wilken, Ph.D. (University of Melbourne, 2001) is the founder and former director of the Association for the Scientific Study of Consciousness, as well as founder of the electronic interdisciplinary consciousness studies journal *Psyche*. As a vision scientist, while working at the California Institute of Technology, he developed a novel probabilistic model of visual short-term memory with his collaborator Weiji Ma. After leaving academia, he was subsequently employed as an editor for the journals Trends in Cognitive Science, Trends in Neuroscience, and Neuron, before leaving to work for the Berlin School of Mind and Brain at Humboldt University, Germany.

The Oxford Companion
—TO—
Consciousness

EDITED BY

TIM BAYNE
AXEL CLEEREMANS
PATRICK WILKEN

Great Clarendon Street, Oxford, OX2 6DP,
United Kingdom

Oxford University Press is a department of the University of Oxford.
It furthers the University's objective of excellence in research, scholarship,
and education by publishing worldwide. Oxford is a registered trade mark of
Oxford University Press in the UK and in certain other countries

First Edition published in 2009

First published in paperback 2014

Impression: 1

Published in the United States of America by Oxford University Press
198 Madison Avenue, New York, NY 10016, United States of America

British Library Cataloguing in Publication Data
Data available

Library of Congress Cataloging in Publication Data
Data available

ISBN 978–0–19–856951–0 (hbk.)
ISBN 978–0–19–871218–3 (pbk.)

Printed in Great Britain by
CPI Group (UK) Ltd, Croydon, CR0 4YY

We dedicate this to our fathers: Andrew Bayne, Raf Cleeremans, and David Wilken

Preface

A companion is a comrade, a consort, and a partner, and our hope in putting together this volume was to create such a guide and friend for students of consciousness. As such, this volume aims to provide a comprehensive account—a map, if you like—of current work on consciousness. Our approach has been an inclusive one. Some of the entries found herein form the mainstay of consciousness research (e.g. consciousness and attention; the neural basis of consciousness; consciousness in animals); others concern topics that are perhaps less central to the study of consciousness but—we think—no less interesting (e.g. the rubber hand illusion; the experience of *déjà vu;* the neuroscience of orgasm). In adopting this somewhat eclectic approach to our topic we have taken our cue from Richard Gregory's *Oxford Companion to the Mind*, to which we are much indebted.

Some readers may discern an emphasis on scientific approaches to consciousness and to that we plead guilty: without wishing to diminish in any way the importance of philosophical perspectives on consciousness, in our view, a full understanding of consciousness will be reached—if at all—only with the methods of science. After many dark decades, the science of consciousness is in a state of rude health, and we have attempted to capture some of its exuberance and vitality within this volume. Whether you come to this book as a seasoned consciousness expert in need of background on an unfamiliar topic, or as a general reader looking for diversion on a rainy day, we hope that you will find what you seek here.

We have incurred numerous debts in putting this volume together. First and foremost we would like to thank our authors. Not only did a great many researchers find time in their busy schedules to write entries for us, they have also shown significant patience in waiting for those entries to appear in print.

We are also deeply indebted to the Association for the Scientific Study of Consciousness (ASSC). The ASSC was the vehicle through which we recruited many of our authors, and indeed the initial construction of the book's keyword list started with a careful analysis of ten years' worth of ASSC meeting reports. This volume would have been unthinkable without the existence of the ASSC; indeed, the current state of the science of consciousness, as well as our own research careers, would undoubtedly have been much the poorer without it.

We are also indebted to a number of individuals at Oxford University Press. Our editor Martin Baum supported us through our many editorial ups and downs; Carol Maxwell provided us with invaluable administrative expertise; Marionne Cronin guided us safely though the production process; and Kathleen Lyle did a wonderful job of copy-editing the manuscript. Our heartfelt thanks to them all.

As individual editors we are also indebted to a number of institutions and persons. Midway through this project Tim Bayne moved from a position in the Philosophy Department at the University of Macquarie (Sydney) to a position at the University of Oxford. He would like to thank both institutions for their support. Axel Cleeremans would like to thank the Université Libre de Bruxelles and the Fonds National de la Recherche Scientifique for their continued support. Patrick Wilken was working at the University of Magdeburg during the early stages of the book, and would like to thank Jochen Braun for his patience and encouragement during this period, and Joseph Dial and the Mind-Science Foundation for kindly stepping in at a critical juncture with a short-term grant when he was transitioning out of academia to work as a journal editor at Cell Press. Finally, we would like to thank our spouses: Nishat, Nathalie, and Kristina. They have provided us with unremitting support throughout this volume's long gestation, and our gratitude to them is immeasurable.

Tim Bayne
Axel Cleeremans
Patrick Wilken
January 2009

Contents

Contributors

Ralph Adolphs, Division of Humanities and Social Sciences, California Institute of Technology, Pasedena

Michael T. Alkire, Center for the Neurobiology of Learning and Memory, University of California, Irvine

Rhiannon Allen, Department of Psychology, University of British Columbia, Vancouver

John Allman, Division of Biology, California Institute of Technology, Pasadena

Torin Alter, Department of Philosophy, University of Alabama, Tuscaloosa

Michael S. Ambinder, Department of Psychology, University of Illinois at Urbana-Champaign

Jackie Andrade, School of Psychology, University of Plymouth

Stuart Anstis, Department of Psychology, University of California, San Diego

Murat Aydede, Department of Philosophy, University of British Columbia, Vancouver

Bernard J. Baars, Neurosciences Institute, San Diego

Paul Bach-y-Rita, Departments of Orthopedics and Rehabilitation Medicine, and Biomedical Engineering, University of Wisconsin, Madison

Alan Baddeley, Department of Psychology, University of York

Sylvain Baillet, Cognitive Neuroscience and Brain Imaging Laboratory, Centre National de la Recherche Scientifique, Université Pierre & Marie Curie, Paris and Department of Neurology, Medical College of Wisconsin, Milwaukee

Mahzarin R. Banaji, Department of Psychology, Harvard University, Cambridge MA

William Banks, Department of Psychology, Pomona College, Claremont

Tim Bayne, Philosophy, School of Social Sciences, University of Manchester

Marc Bekoff, Ecology and Evolutionary Biology, University of Colorado, Boulder

José-Luis Bermúdez, Philosophy–Neuroscience–Psychology Program, Washington University in St Louis

Anna Berti, Dipartimento di Psicologia, Università di Torino

Ravi Bhat, Goulburn Valley Area Mental Health Service, Shepparton

John Bickle, Department of Philosophy, University of Cincinnati

Emmanuel Bigand, Institut Universitaire de France, Le Laboratoire d'Etude de l'Apprentissage et du Développement-Centre National de la Recherche Scientifique, Université de Bourgogne, Dijon

Yitzchak M. Binik, Department of Psychology, McGill University, Montreal

Susan Blackmore, Visiting Professor at the Department of Psychology, University of Plymouth

Mark Blagrove, Department of Psychology, Swansea University

Randolph Blake, Department of Psychology, Vanderbilt University, Nashville

Sarah-Jayne Blakemore, Institute of Cognitive Neuroscience, University College London

Olaf Blanke, Laboratory of Cognitive Neuroscience, Brain Mind Institute, Swiss Federal Institute of Technology, Lausanne

Mélanie Boly, Coma Science Group, Cyclotron Research Centre and Neurology Department, University of Liège

Yoram S. Bonneh, Center for Brain and Behavior Research, University of Haifa

Stephen E. Braude, Department of Philosophy, University of Maryland Baltimore County, Baltimore

Jochen Braun, Institute of Biology, University of Magdeburg

Bruno G. Breitmeyer, Department of Psychology, University of Houston

Davina Bristow, Institute of Cognitive Neuroscience, University College London

Gordon M. Burghardt, Departments of Psychology and Ecology and Evolutionary Biology, University of Tennessee, Knoxville

Darren Burke, Department of Biological Sciences, Macquarie University, Sydney

John Campbell, Department of Philosophy, University of California, Berkeley

Marisa Carrasco, Psychology and Neural Science, New York University

Wallace Chafe, Department of Linguistics, University of California, Santa Barbara

C. Richard Chapman, Pain Research Center, Department of Anesthesiology, University of Utah, Salt Lake City

Louis C. Charland, Departments of Philosophy and Psychiatry and Faculty of Health Sciences, University of Western Ontario, London, Ontario

James A. Cheyne, Department of Psychology, University of Waterloo

Ron Chrisley, Centre for Research in Cognitive Science, Department of Informatics, University of Sussex

Philippe Chuard, Department of Philosophy, Southern Methodist University, Dallas

Marvin M. Chun, Department of Psychology, Yale University, and Department of Neurobiology, Yale School of Medicine, New Haven

Robert E. Clark, Department of Psychiatry, University of California, San Diego

Axel Cleeremans, Séminaire de Recherche en Sciences Cognitives, Université Libre de Bruxelles

Jonathan Cole, Poole Hospital and Centre of Postgraduate Medical Research and Education, University of Bournemouth
Max Coltheart, Macquarie Centre for Cognitive Science, Macquarie University, Sydney
Richard P. Cooper, School of Psychology, Birkbeck, University of London
Nelson Cowan, Department of Psychological Sciences, University of Missouri, Columbia
Alan Cowey, Department of Experimental Psychology, University of Oxford
Tim Crane, Faculty of Philosophy, University of Cambridge
Barry Dainton, Department of Philosophy, University of Liverpool
Thanh Dang-Vu, Cyclotron Research Centre, University of Liège
Lars De Nul, Centre for Philosophical Psychology, Department of Philosophy, Universiteit Antwerpen
Frédérique de Vignemont, Institut Jean-Nicod, EHESS—Ecole Normale Supérieure—Centre National de la Recherche Scientifique, Paris
Jean Decety, Department of Psychology, University of Chicago
Stanislas Dehaene, Collège de France, Paris
Sergio Della Sala, Human Cognitive Neuroscience, Department of Psychology, University of Edinburgh
Daniel C. Dennett, Centre for Cognitive Studies, Tufts University, Medford
Arnaud Destrebecqz, Université Libre de Bruxelles
Zoltán Dienes, School of Psychology, University of Sussex, Brighton
Michael J. Dixon, Department of Psychology, University of Waterloo
Donelson E. Dulany, Department of Psychology, University of Illinois, Urbana-Champaign
David M. Eagleman, Departments of Neuroscience and Psychiatry, Baylor College of Medicine, Houston
H. Henrik Ehrsson, Department of Neuroscience, Karolinska Institutet, Stockholm
Howard Eichenbaum, Center for Memory and Brain, Boston University
Andreas K. Engel, Department of Neurophysiology and Pathophysiology, University Medical Center, Hamburg-Eppendorf
Manfred Fahle, Department of Human Neurobiology, University of Bremen, and Henry Wellcome Laboratory for Vision Sciences, City University, London
Martha J. Farah, Center for Cognitive Neuroscience and Department of Psychology, University of Pennsylvania, Philadelphia
Bill Faw, Psychology, Division of Social and Behavioral Sciencens, Brewton Parker College, Georgia
Justin S. Feinstein, Department of Neurology and Department of Psychology, University of Iowa, Iowa City
Dominic H. ffytche, Institute of Psychiatry, King's College London
Cordelia Fine, Centre for Applied Philosophy and Public Ethics, Department of Philosophy, University of Melbourne
Ione Fine, Department of Psychology, University of Washington, Seattle
Kit Fine, Department of Philosophy, New York University
J. Randall Flanagan, Department of Psychology and Centre for Neuroscience Studies, Queen's University, Kingston, Ontario
Robert M. French, Le Laboratoire d'Etude de l'Apprentissage et du Déviloppement—Centre National de la Recherche Scientifique, Dijon
Chris D. Frith, Wellcome Trust Centre for NeuroImaging, University College London
Steffen Gais, Cyclotron Research Centre, University of Liège
Shaun Gallagher, University of Central Florida, Orlando and University of Hertfordshire, Hatfield
Vittorio Gallese, Dipartimento di Neuroscienze, Università di Parma
Giorgio Ganis, Department of Radiology, Harvard Medical School, Boston, and Department of Psychology, Harvard University, Cambridge MA
Helena Hong Gao, Division of Chinese, Nanyang Technological University, Singapore
Brie Gertler, Department of Philosophy, Southern Methodist University, Dallas
Fernand Gobet, Centre for the Study of Expertise, School of Social Sciences, Brunel University, Uxbridge
Alvin I. Goldman, Department of Philosophy, Rutgers University, New Brunswick, NJ
Juan-Carlos Gómez, School of Psychology, University of St Andrews
Melvyn A. Goodale, Department of Psychology, University of Western Ontario, London, Ontario
Patrick Haggard, Institute of Cognitive Neuroscience and Department of Psychology, University College London
Francesca Happé, MRC Social, Genetic and Developmental Psychiatry Centre, Institute of Psychiatry, King's College London
Larry S. Hauser, Philosophy, Alma College
Bernd Heinrich, Department of Biology, University of Vermont, Burlington
Benj Hellie, Department of Philosophy, University of Toronto
Louis M. Herman, University of Hawaii and The Dolphin Institute, Honolulu
Michael H. Herzog, Laboratory of Psychophysics, Brain Mind Institute, Ecole Polytechnique Fédérale de Lausanne
Charles Heywood, Department of Psychology, University of Durham
Christopher S. Hill, Department of Philosophy, Brown University, Providence
William Hirstein, Department of Philosophy, Elmhurst College
Jakob Hohwy, School of Philosophy and Bioethics, Monash University, Clayton
Jess Scon Holbrook, Seattle, Washington
Owen Holland, School of Computer Science and Electronic Engineering, University of Essex, Colchester
Anthony G. Hudetz, Department of Anesthesiology, Medical College of Wisconsin, Milwaukee
Nicholas K. Humphrey, Centre for Philosophy of Natural and Social Sciences, London School of Economics
Russell T. Hurlburt, University of Nevada, Las Vegas
Daniel D. Hutto, School of Humanities, University of Hertfordshire, Hatfield
Jonathan Ichikawa, Arché Philosophical Research Centre, University of St Andrews

Larry L. Jacoby, Department of Psychology, Washington University in St Louis
Kimberly A. Jameson, Institute for Mathematical Behavioral Sciences, University of California, Irvine
Graham A. Jamieson, School of Behavioural Cognitive and Social Sciences, University of New England, Armidale
Yuhong Jiang, Department of Psychology, University of Minnesota, Minneapolis
Sabine Kastner, Department of Psychology, Center for the Study of Brain, Mind and Behavior, Princeton University
Julian Paul Keenan, Department of Psychology, Montclair State University
Robert W. Kentridge, Department of Psychology, University of Durham
Stephen W. Kercel, Endogenous Systems Research Group, New England Institute, University of New England, Portland
John F. Kihlstrom, Department of Psychology, University of California, Berkeley
Alice S. N. Kim, Department of Psychology, University of Toronto, and Rotman Research Institute at Baycrest, Toronto
Daniel Kimball, Department of Psychology, University of Texas at Arlington
Amy Kind, Department of Philosophy, Claremont McKenna College, Claremont
Daniel Kiper, Institute of Neuroinformatics, University of Zurich, and ETH Zurich
David Kirsh, Department of Cognitive Science, University of California, San Diego
Stanley Klein, School of Optometry, University of California, Berkeley
Bernard W. Kobes, Department of Philosophy, Arizona State University, Tempe
Stephen M. Kosslyn, Department of Psychology, Harvard University, Cambridge MA
Gabriel Kreiman, Children's Hospital Boston, Harvard Medical School, and Center for Brain Science, Harvard University, Cambridge MA
Uriah Kriegel, Department of Philosophy, University of Arizona, Tucson
Monisha Anand Kumar, Department of Psychology, Montclair State University
Victor A. F. Lamme, Department of Psychology, University of Amsterdam
Cara Laney, School of Psychology, University of Leicester
Steven Laureys, Coma Science Group, Cyclotron Research Centre and Neurology Department, University of Liège
Joseph LeDoux, Center for Neural Science, New York University
David A. Leopold, Unit on Cognitive Neurophysiology and Imaging, Laboratory of Neuropsychology, National Institute of Mental Health, National Institute of Health, Bethesda
Joseph Levine, Department of Philosophy, University of Massachusetts at Amherst
David E. J. Linden, School of Psychology, University of Wales, Bangor
Dan Lloyd, Department of Philosophy and Program in Neuroscience, Trinity College, Hartford
Elizabeth F. Loftus, Psychology and Social Behavior, University of California, Irvine
Robert H. Logie, Human Cognitive Neuroscience, University of Edinburgh
E. Jonathan Lowe, Department of Philosophy, University of Durham
Antoine Lutz, Laboratory for Functional Brain Imaging and Behavior, Waisman Center, University of Wisconsin, Madison
William G. Lycan, Department of Philosophy, University of North Carolina, Chapel Hill
Jay L. McClelland, Department of Psychology and Center for Mind, Brain, and Computation, Stanford University
Colin M. MacLeod, Department of Psychology, University of Waterloo
E. M. Macphail, Department of Psychology, University of York
Fiona Macpherson, Department of Philosophy, University of Glasgow, and Philosophy Program, Research School of Social Sciences, Australian National University, Canberra
Kenneth Mah, Behavioural Sciences and Health Research Division, Toronto General Hospital
Alexander Maier, Unit on Cognitive Neurophysiology and Imaging, Laboratory of Neuropsychology, National Institute of Mental Health, National Institute of Health, Bethesda
Bertram F. Malle, Department of Psychology, Brown University, Providence
Joseph R. Manns, Department of Psychology, Emory University, Atlanta
Pierre Maquet, Cyclotron Research Centre, University of Liège
Olivier Massin, Department of Philosophy, University of Geneva
David Milner, Cognitive Neuroscience Research Unit and Department of Psychology, University of Durham
Yuri Miyamoto, Department of Psychology, University of Wisconsin, Madison
Cathleen M. Moore, Department of Psychology, University of Iowa, Iowa City
Timothy E. Moore, Department of Psychology, Glendon College, York University, Toronto
Agnes Moors, Department of Psychology, Ghent University
Alain Morin, Department of Psychology, Mount Royal College, Calgary
Michael C. Mozer, Department of Computer Science and Institute of Cognitive Science, University of Colorado, Boulder
Erik Myin, Centre for Philosophical Psychology, Department of Philosophy, University of Antwerp
Lionel Naccache, Clinical Neurophysiology and Neurology Departments and INSERM (UMRS 975) Neuropsychology and Neuroimaging Team, Hôpital de la Pitié-Salpêtrière, Paris
Yujin Nagasawa, Department of Philosophy, University of Birmingham
Yoshio Nakamura, Pain Research Center, Department of Anesthesiology, University of Utah, Salt Lake City
Dirk Neumann, Emotion and Social Cognition Laboratory, California Institute of Technology, Pasedena

David E. Nichols, Department of Medicinal Chemistry and Molecular Pharmacology, Purdue University, Lafayette
Romi Nijhawan, Department of Psychology, University of Sussex, Falmer
Elisabeth Norman, Faculty of Psychology, University of Bergen, and Haukeland University Hospital, Bergen
Brian A. Nosek, Department of Psychology, University of Virginia, Charlottesville
Gerard O'Brien, Discipline of Philosophy, University of Adelaide
Casey O'Callaghan, Philosophy Department, Rice University, Houston
J. Kevin O'Regan, Laboratoire Psychologie de la Perception, Centre National de Recherche Scientifique, Institut de Psychologie, Centre Universitaire de Boulogne, Paris
Jon Opie, Discipline of Philosophy, University of Adelaide
Thomas U. Otto, Laboratory of Psychophysics, Brain Mind Institute, Ecole Polytechnique Fédérale de Lausanne
Elisabeth Pacherie, Institut Jean-Nicod, Centre National de la Recherche Scientifique, Département d'Etudes Cognitives, Ecole Normale Supérieure, Paris
Stephen E. Palmer, Department of Psychology, University of California, Berkeley
Jaak Panksepp, College of Veterinary Medicine, Washington State University, Pullman
Adam Pautz, Department of Philosophy, University of Texas at Austin
Josef Perner, Department of Psychology, University of Salzburg
Thomas Pink, Department of Philosophy, King's College, London
Guy Pinku, Philosophical Department, University of Haifa
Thomas W. Polger, Department of Philosophy, University of Cincinnati
Mary C. Potter, Department of Brain and Cognitive Sciences, Massachusetts Institute of Technology, Cambridge MA
Mark C. Price, Faculty of Psychology, University of Bergen
V. S. Ramachandran, Department of Psychology, University of California, San Diego
Jane Raymond, School of Psychology, Bangor University
Arthur S. Reber, Department of Psychology, Brooklyn College of City University of New York
Geraint Rees, Institute of Cognitive Neuroscience, University College London
Eyal M. Reingold, Department of Psychology, University of Toronto at Mississauga
Antti Revonsuo, School of Humanities and Informatics, University of Skövde
Georges Rey, Department of Philosophy, University of Maryland, College Park
Lynn C. Robertson, Veterans Administration, Martinez, CA, and University of California, Berkeley
William S. Robinson, Department of Philosophy and Religious Studies, Iowa State University, Iowa City
Kenneth Rockwood, Centre for Health Care of the Elderly and Department of Medicine (Geriatric Medicine and Neurology), Dalhousie University, Halifax, Nova Scotia
Tiger C. Roholt, Assistant Professor of Philosophy, Montclair State University
David M. Rosenthal, Philosophy and Cognitive Science, Graduate Center, City University of New York
Mark Rowlands, Department of Philosophy, University of Miami, Coral Gables
Eric Salmon, Cyclotron Research Centre, University of Liège
Manuel Schabus, Cyclotron Research Centre, University of Liège
Daniel L. Schacter, Department of Psychology, Harvard University, Cambridge MA
Jonathan W. Schooler, Department of Psychology, University of California, Santa Barbara
William Seager, Department of Philosophy, University of Toronto at Scarborough
John R. Searle, Department of Philosophy, University of California, Berkeley
Ladan Shams, Department of Psychology, University of California, Los Angeles
Heather Sheridan, Department of Psychology, University of Toronto at Mississauga
Gordon M. Shepherd, Department of Neurobiology, Yale University School of Medicine, New Haven
Susanna Siegel, Department of Philosophy, Harvard University, Cambridge MA
Mauricio Sierra, Institute of Psychiatry, King's College London
Charles Siewert, Department of Philosophy, University of California, Riverside
Michael Silberstein, Department of Philosophy, Elizabethtown College
Daniel J. Simons, Department of Psychology, University of Illinois at Urbana-Champaign
Jonathan Smallwood, School of Psychology, University of Aberdeen
Daniel Smilek, Department of Psychology, University of Waterloo
J. David Smith, Department of Psychology and Center for Cognitive Science, University at Buffalo, the State University of New York
Thomas R. Smith, Department of English, Penn State, Abington
Michael Snodgrass, Department of Psychiatry, University of Michigan Medical Center, Ann Arbor
Ernest Sosa, Department of Philosophy, Rutgers University, New Brunswick, NJ
Sean A. Spence, Academic Clinical Psychiatry, University of Sheffield
Petra Stoerig, Institute of Experimental Psychology, Heinrich-Heine University, Düsseldorf
Daniel Stoljar, Philosophy Program, Research School of Social Sciences, Australian National University, Canberra
Richard Sylvester, Institute of Cognitive Neuroscience, University College London
Niels A. Taatgen, Department of Psychology, Carnegie Mellon University, Pittsburgh, and Department of Artificial Intelligence, University of Groningen
Charles Taliaferro, Philosophy Department, St Olaf College
Catherine Tallon-Baudry, Laboratoire de Neurosciences Cognitives & Imagerie Cérébrale, Paris
Brad Thompson, Department of Philosophy, Southern Methodist University, Dallas
William L. Thompson, Department of Psychology, Harvard University, Cambridge MA

Caroline Tomiczek, Department of Psychology, Macquarie University, Sydney
Frank Tong, Department of Psychology, Vanderbilt University, Nashville
Giulio Tononi, Department of Psychiatry, University of Wisconsin, Madison
Janet P. Trammell, Department of Psychology, University of Virginia, Charlottesville
Daniel Tranel, Department of Neurology and Department of Psychology, University of Iowa, Iowa City
Colwyn Trevarthen, Department of Psychology, The University of Edinburgh
Manos Tsakiris, Department of Psychology, Royal Holloway, University of London
Endel Tulving, Department of Psychology, University of Toronto, and Rotman Research Institute at Baycrest, Toronto
Joseph Tzelgov, Achva Academic College and Ben-Gurion University of the Negev, Beer-Sheva
Robert Van Gulick, Philosophy Department, Syracuse University
Thomas Van Vleet, Veterans Administration, Martinez CA
Vincent Walsh, Institute of Cognitive Neuroscience and Department of Psychology, University College London
Xiaoang Irene Wan, Department of Psychology, University of Illinois at Urbana-Champaign
Daniel Wegner, Department of Psychology, Harvard University, Cambridge MA
Larry Weiskrantz, Department of Experimental Psychology University of Oxford
Stephen L. White, Associate Professor, Department of Philosophy, Tufts University, Medford
Kenneth Williford, Department of Philosophy, St Cloud State University
Daniel T. Willingham, Department of Psychology, University of Virginia, Charlottesville
E. Samuel Winer, Department of Psychology, University of Illinois at Chicago
Daniel M. Wolpert, Department of Engineering, University of Cambridge
David Woodruff-Smith, Department of Philosophy, University of California, Irvine
Dan Zahavi, Center for Subjectivity Research, Department of Media, Cognition and Communication, University of Copenhagen
Nick Zangwill, Philosophy Department, Durham University
Semir Zeki, Wellcome Laboratory of Neurobiology, Department of Cell and Developmental Biology, University College London
Philip David Zelazo, Institute of Child Development, University of Minnesota, Minneapolis
Adam Zeman, Cognitive Neurology Research Group, Peninsula Medical School, Exeter

Note to the reader

Entries are arranged in strict alphabetical order of their headword. Cross-references between entries are indicated either by an asterisk (*) in front of the word to be looked up, or by 'See' or 'See also' followed by the entry title in SMALL CAPITALS.

absent qualia See INVERTED SPECTRUM; QUALIA; ZOMBIES

access consciousness The term 'access consciousness' was introduced by Ned Block to capture a functional notion of consciousness. In Block's original formulation, a state is access conscious exactly when it is 'poised for free use in reasoning and for direct "rational" control of action and speech' (Block 1995:231). Although Block's characterization of access consciousness has changed over the years—recent formulations have downplayed the centrality of verbal report—the notion has retained its exclusively functional character. Access consciousness, or *A-consciousness* as it is often known, is contrasted with phenomenal consciousness, or *P-consciousness*. Whereas A-consciousness is a function notion, P-consciousness is defined in terms of phenomenal character or '*what it's likeness'.

Placed alongside P-consciousness, A-consciousness is relatively unproblematic. The attempt to understand how physical systems might enjoy states with phenomenal character comes up against the infamous *explanatory gap, but no such challenge confronts the attempt to understand how physical systems can contain information that is poised for the rational control of thought and action. Nonetheless, many of the deepest questions surrounding P-consciousness can be—and often have been—formulated as questions about the relationship between P-consciousness and A-consciousness. This entry examines three such questions: (1) How are the *concepts* of A-consciousness and P-consciousness related? (2) How are the *properties* of A-consciousness and P-consciousness related? (3) How is the *study* of P-consciousness related to that of A-consciousness?

The concept of access consciousness

The concept of A-consciousness is somewhat 'open-ended' one; as Block puts it, A-consciousness is a cluster concept. What exactly is it for the content of a state to be poised (or available) for free use in reasoning and for direct 'rational' control of action and speech? One notion that bears scrutiny here is that of *poisedness* or *availability*. At one end of the spectrum there is content that can be consumed by cognitive and motor systems with some time and effort; at the other end of the spectrum there is content that is actually deployed for cognitive and behavioural control. In between these two points lies content that is positioned on the boundaries of consuming systems—available for cognitive consumption should it be attended to. Just where on this spectrum of 'poisedness' a state must lie in order to qualify as A-conscious is not settled. Also in need of clarification is the notion of rational control of action and speech. Could primitive creatures with little in the way of reasoning or executive systems possess states whose contents are directly available for the rational control of thought and action? Could cognitively sophisticated creatures with reasoning and executive systems that are temporarily offline—perhaps due to the effects of drugs or brain damage—possess states whose contents are directly available for the rational control of thought and action? Block's characterization of A-consciousness does not dictate answers to these questions.

How ought these questions to be answered? Here, we need to ask whether the concept of A-consciousness is a purely nominal one that can be refined by stipulation, or whether it is meant to pick out a real kind—that is to say, a natural kind—that we should be attempting to discover. Opinions will differ. One approach to this issue is to think of A-consciousness as picking out the functional content of the folk concept of consciousness. In fact, Block introduces the notion of A-consciousness in just this way. He holds that the folk psychological term 'consciousness' equivocates between two concepts, a third-person or functional concept (his A-consciousness) and a first-person—'what it's like'—concept (P-consciousness). Another approach is to treat A-consciousness as referring to the functional correlate of P-consciousness, whatever exactly that might turn out to be. As Chalmers has pointed out, one of the most interesting projects in this area is that of determining whether there is a kind of A-consciousness that correlates perfectly with P-consciousness (Chalmers 1997). (If there is such a notion, we might even be tempted to think of phenomenal consciousness as forming its categorical ground.) For many purposes it is useful to think of A-consciousness as encompassing a family of closely related concepts rather than as a unitary notion with well-demarcated boundaries.

Let us leave to one side the question of exactly how A-consciousness should be construed and turn to the relationship between the concepts of A-consciousness and P-consciousness. Block holds that the concepts of A-consciousness and P-consciousness are distinct, in the sense that there is no conceptual incoherence in the thought that a mental state could be A-conscious without being P-conscious or vice-versa. In support of this position one might argue that it is possible to conceive of A-consciousness in the absence of P-consciousness and vice versa. The apparent conceivability of *zombies—creatures that are functionally identical to normal human beings but lacking in P-conscious states—suggests that the concept of A-consciousness does not entail that of P-consciousness. And the apparent conceivability of 'bare experiences'—phenomenal states to which the subject has no form of cognitive access—lends support to the idea that the concept of P-consciousness does not entail that of A-consciousness. However, it should be noted that these claims are extremely controversial. Those who deny that A-consciousness and P-consciousness are conceptually distinct either reject the apparent conceivability of these scenarios or argue that apparent conceivability is a poor guide to the structure of our concepts.

A certain kind of access demands special mention in this context—namely, *introspective access. According to Block's characterization, the fact that a state is A-conscious does not imply that one is able to form an introspective judgement to the effect that one is in the state in question. Nonetheless, introspective access is clearly within the orbit of A-consciousness, broadly construed. And here it appears to be particularly difficult to drive a wedge between P-consciousness and A-consciousness (Clark 2000). Being able to tell whether one is aware of a certain property via touch or via vision arguably demands that there be a distinctive phenomenal character to one's representation of that property, and if that is so then certain sorts of A-consciousness demand—of conceptual necessity—certain sorts of P-consciousness. In short, there might be certain kinds of access to representational content that are conceptually connected to P-consciousness, even if the notions of P-consciousness and A-consciousness as such are conceptually independent.

The property of access consciousness

It is one thing to grant that there are two *concepts* of consciousness but it is quite another to hold that there are two *properties* of consciousness. Many of those who grant that the concepts are distinct resist the thought that they pick out distinct properties. However, a number of theorists—including Block himself—suggest that we should take seriously the possibility that the property of P-consciousness is distinct from that of A-consciousness.

One line of argument for this view appeals to *conceptual thought. Take the thought 'Democracy is the least worst form of government'. It is clear that this state can be A-conscious, for its content can be poised for the direct rational control of thought and action. But is this thought phenomenally conscious? There are some who would say no. According to phenomenal conservatives, cognitive states such as thoughts, intentions, and desires do not possess proprietary phenomenal character—they might be accompanied by phenomenal states of various kinds (such as images), but the thoughts themselves do not enjoy phenomenal character. If the conservatives are right, then it is possible for a state to be A-conscious without being P-conscious. Of course, phenomenal conservatism is controversial. Proponents of cognitive phenomenology hold that thoughts do possess proprietary phenomenal character, and thus they will not see conscious thought as providing any wedge between A-consciousness and P-consciousness.

Rather than concern himself with the question of whether A-consciousness might be possible in the absence of P-consciousness, Block has focused on whether P-consciousness might be possible in the absence of A-consciousness. Consider an unnoticed perceptual event, such as the background ticking of a clock. Block (1995) suggests that such states might be P-conscious but not A-conscious. The thought here is that although the representation of the ticking becomes A-conscious when one notices or attends to it, it was not A-conscious prior to that point, even though it was—so Block suggests—P-conscious. Although some are convinced by such cases, many claim that one is P-conscious of the ticking of the clock only when one notices it, and hence that such scenarios give us no reason to suppose that P-consciousness can dissociate from A-consciousness.

A more influential reason for thinking that A-consciousness can dissociate from P-consciousness can be found in Block's 'overflow argument' (Block 2007). The argument appeals to experiments conducted by Sperling and others, in which subjects are presented with a matrix of 3 × 4 alphanumeric figures for a brief period, and asked to report as many of the items as they can (see MEMORY, ICONIC). On average, subjects who are asked to report the contents of the entire matrix can report only 4.5 of the 12 items, but when directed immediately after presentation of the matrix to report just one of the 3 rows they can report 3.3 of the 4 items in that row. This suggests that in the full report condition subjects had been aware of more than the 4.5 items that they reported. Although the interpretation of this data is highly controversial, Block suggests that it provides evidence that the capacity of P-consciousness can 'overflow' that of A-consciousness.

Whether or not the overflow argument succeeds depends, of course, on just how A-consciousness is construed. Arguably, the argument shows that A-consciousness can dissociate from P-consciousness according to the letter of the act, for subjects seem to be P-conscious of the identity of 9 or so of the 12 items, even though all 9 items were not, as such, A-conscious. But the argument does not give us any reason to think that P-consciousness can dissociate from a less demanding notion of A-consciousness, according to which A-consciousness requires only that the subject have *some* form of high-level (personal, executive) access to the information in question. After all, subjects do report that they identified each of the items in the matrix, despite being unable to report them all. Of course, 'access consciousness' is Block's term, and he might well object that 'some form of high-level access' does not constitute A-consciousness as he defined it. Fair enough, but in a sense the issue is precisely how A-consciousness is to be defined. Indeed, we might use Sperling's results (and others like them) to home in on a notion of A-consciousness that it correlates more closely with P-consciousness.

Access consciousness and the study of consciousness
The third of our three questions concerned the relationship between the *study* of P-consciousness and that of A-consciousness. Many of those who grant that A-consciousness and P-consciousness could be distinct properties nonetheless insist that we cannot study P-consciousness without studying A-consciousness, and thus that we could never have good reason to think that A-consciousness and P-consciousness can dissociate even if they are, in fact, distinct.

The key question here is whether P-consciousness is—or must be—operationalized in terms of A-consciousness. Although certain theorists regard verbal report as the gold standard of consciousness, many (most?) of us are willing to ascribe P-consciousness on the basis of something akin to A-consciousness (minus verbal report). For example, we are inclined to think that infants and other non-linguistic animals are conscious of their bodies and environment, despite the fact that they may be unable to produce any form of metacognitive commentary on the objects of their experience. Arguably, we are inclined to regard such animals as conscious because they have representations whose contents can be freely deployed for use in reasoning and the rational control of action. In other words, we do seem to take A-consciousness—or something very much like it—as an intuitive marker of P-consciousness.

Of course, it is one thing to hold that P-consciousness is operationalized in terms of A-consciousness, but it is another thing to hold that P-consciousness can be detected only via A-consciousness. Are there principled reasons for thinking that we could never have reason to posit P-consciousness in the absence of A-consciousness and vice versa? Block (2007) has recently argued that converging evidence from psychology and neuroscience might give us reason to posit P-conscious states that are not A-conscious. Block's specific suggestion is that recurrent loops of neural activation between fairly specific neural regions (such as MT) and earlier visual areas might form the neural correlate of particular experiences (such as visual motion). Block suggests that since not all such local loops are selected for global broadcasting, we have here some evidence that it is possible for a state to be P-conscious without being A-conscious. But Block's more important point is a methodological one: we should not rule out the possibility that developments in neuroscience and psychology will provide us with ways of detecting P-consciousness that do not involve A-consciousness.

Block's arguments have met with a mixed response (see Block 2007). Evaluating their prospects goes beyond the ambit of this entry, but what does seem clear is that this will be a central issue of discussion for some years to come. Our ability to sever the methodological tie between A-consciousness and P-consciousness would be enhanced if we had a model of how consciousness arises out of the neural or representational properties of the mind–brain, but we have no such theory, nor does there seem to be any such theory on the horizon. In the absence of such a theory we are, arguably, stuck with something like A-consciousness as our measure of P-consciousness, albeit one that may be less demanding than Block's full-blooded notion.

TIM BAYNE

Block, N. (1995). 'On a confusion about a function of consciousness'. *Behavioral and Brain Sciences*, 18.
Block, N. (2001). 'Paradox and cross purposes in recent findings about consciousness'. *Cognition*, 1–2.
Block, N. (2005). 'Two neural correlates of consciousness'. *Trends in Cognitive Sciences*, 9.
Block, N. (2007). 'Consciousness, accessibility and the mesh between psychology and neuroscience'. *Behavioral and Brain Sciences*, 30.
Burge, T. (1997). 'Two kinds of consciousness'. In Block, N. et al. (eds) *The Nature of Consciousness*.
Chalmers, D. (1997). 'Availability: the cognitive basis of experience?' *Behavioral and Brain Sciences*, 20.
Clark, A. (2000). 'A case where access implies qualia?' *Analysis*, 60.

achromatopsia, cerebral Cerebral achromatopsia is a type of acquired colour blindness in which it is not possible to perceive colours, correctly name colours, or tell the difference between two grossly different coloured patches that have the same brightness.

Towards the end of the 19th century several neurologists (Brill, Wilbrand, Verrey), working independently of each other, described rare patients who had suffered a stroke that damaged the lingual and posterior fusiform gyri on the ventromedial aspect of the occipital and temporal lobes. The conspicuous feature of the patients' visual symptoms was acquired colour blindness. Although it was given little attention at the time, the remarkable nature of the phenomenon became clear almost a century later when the anatomical and physiological basis of normal colour vision was finally elucidated in the eye and its connections to the primary visual cortex (*V1) at the back of the brain. There was no evidence that the stroke had affected the eyes or these initial connections to the brain in the achromatopsic patients, and this was a puzzle.

What is it like to have cerebral achromatopsia? The condition is often described as if the patient perceived the world in shades of grey, like watching an old black and white film, but that apart from that, vision is more or less normal. There are two ways in which this is inaccurate. First, patients with cerebral achromatopsia usually have other perceptual disorders, notably object *agnosia, and, often conspicuously, agnosia for faces (*prosopagnosia*). Second, they behave as if colour did not exist, rather than as if they remembered everything about colour as they experienced it before their brain damage but could no longer see it. These two provisos are sufficiently important to warrant discussion.

First, the common association of achromatopsia with object and face agnosia should not surprise us. Modern *functional magnetic resonance imaging (fMRI) of the brain, a technique dating only from the mid 1990s, has repeatedly shown that different parts of the ventromedial aspect of the posterior temporal lobe change their pattern of blood flow when subjects look at displays of colours or faces or inanimate objects, and that these regions correspond to areas damaged in patients with different patterns of agnosia. As these areas are adjacent and/or overlap it is not surprising that so-called *pure perceptual deficits*, where only colour or form vision is impaired, are exceedingly rare if they exist at all. This association of deficits does not disprove the idea that there is regional functional specialization for different aspects of visual perception. However, the extent of the functional separation is disputed. Some achromatopsic patients have impaired but not destroyed colour vision and they tend to have smaller lesions, suggesting that some conscious colour processing is taking place elsewhere. In contrast, patients with seemingly complete abolition of colour vision have larger lesions, usually extending further forward into the temporal lobe, also suggesting a wider involvement of temporal lobe cortex in colour processing, well beyond the region pinpointed as the 'colour area' by functional brain imaging.

The second point concerns the nature of phenomenal perceptual awareness. *Hemiachromatopsia*, where the patient loses colour vision in only one side of the visual field, contralateral to the damage restricted to one side of the brain, does not cause the patient to be constantly and distressingly aware of the difference between the normal and the colour-blind half-fields. They seem to be so inattentive to the colour-blind side that they do not notice the difference. Furthermore, patients with bilateral achromatopsia often seem puzzled by questions about their colour vision, as if their conceptual knowledge about colour had been impaired. Perhaps they can use information provided by colour without experiencing and thinking about colour itself, as described next.

The possibility that even in dense cerebral achromatopsia the eyes and brain are still processing information about the wavelength of light, which is what determines our ability to discriminate between different wavelengths or stimuli of different mixed wavelengths, has been intensively investigated in recent years. After all, the brain damage does not involve the primary visual cortex and its surrounding visual areas, where many investigations of the visual areas of monkeys show that millions of cells respond selectively to light of different colours. If such brain cells survive in patients with cerebral achromatopsia, perhaps their selectivity to different colours could be demonstrated even though they no longer have access to whatever leads to the visual experience of colour. That, paradoxically, the loss of phenomenal colour vision does not prevent the segmentation of a visual scene on the basis of colour differences was shown with the much-studied patient M. S. Although unable to read the Ishihara colour-blindness plates at conventional reading distance, he could do so when they were presented 2 metres away. The test requires the identification of a hidden number which is defined by coloured dots embedded in similar but grey dots of varying lightness. At normal reading distance, the coloured border which outlines the numeral is masked by the luminance contours of individual dots. At a distance where the latter can no longer be resolved, or when the display is optically blurred, he can now detect the dominant coloured boundary and correctly read the concealed but still colourless number. In a further test he was presented with two rows of coloured patches, each patch having the same brightness. In each row the colours touched each other, but in one row they were in chromatic order, from short to longer wavelengths, and in the other they were jumbled. M. S. could easily tell the difference between jumbled and ordered arrays, presumably by detecting and distinguishing the salience of coloured boundaries. In the jumbled array, adjacent colours were often more widely separated in colour space and the greater colour contrast presumably made their outlines more obvious to the brain. The borders between two abutting and equally bright colours are therefore visible to M. S. even when the two colours cannot be told apart. When all the colours were moved a few millimetres apart, creating a conspicuous white border between adjacent colours, he was totally unable to discriminate the ordered from the disordered series, showing that what he was discriminating was the difference between conspicuous and inconspicuous borders (Heywood and Cowey 1999, 2003, Kentridge et al. 2004).

Patient M. S. and others like him have now been tested on a variety of visual displays in which wavelength must be processed in order to spot the target in the display. For example, when presented with a chequerboard in which one of the several hundred squares is coloured and all the others are shades of grey, he can point to the coloured one which, he says, stands out from the others. If several squares have the same colour but vary in luminance, like the grey squares, and are arranged in a simple figure like a cross, he can identify the cross. And if he inspects a display in which coloured bands move in one direction he readily perceives their direction of motion even though to do so requires that their wavelength (colour) must be processed by the brain. His spatial attention can also be directed by motion that is defined purely by chromatic information. However, and tellingly, in the chequerboard test he confuses the coloured target with very dark or very bright grey squares when the latter have strong luminance contrast with squares surrounding them. This shows that he treats strong colour contrast and strong luminance contrast as if they were the same.

Cerebral achromatopsia is sometimes described as the consequence of destroying a visual area, called V4 in monkeys, in which many of the cells certainly code wavelength. This is the proverbial beautiful idea destroyed by an ugly fact. Monkeys in which V4 has been removed are not achromatopsic. Only when more anterior areas of the temporal lobe are removed, as in patient M. S., is the performance of monkeys anything like that of achromatopsic patients (Heywood and Cowey 1999, 2003).

What does cerebral achromatopsia tell us about phenomenal consciousness? It is sometimes described as being like *blindsight for colour, blindsight being the ability to localize and discriminate visual targets presented in a region of total blindness caused by damage to the primary visual cortex under conditions of forced-choice guessing. But patient M. S. cannot discriminate colours by forced-choice guessing, and he is aware of the visual stimuli. Instead, achromatopsia is a deletion of conscious awareness of one visual quality, namely colour, and resembles the condition of cortical motion blindness. Both of them are important pieces of evidence that conscious awareness of different stimulus attributes can be regionally segregated.

ALAN COWEY

Heywood, C. A. and Cowey, A. (1999). 'Cerebral achromatopsia'. In Humphreys, G. W. (ed.) *Case Studies in the Neuropsychology of Vision*.

—— —— (2003). 'Colour vision and its disturbances after cortical lesions'. In Fahle, M. and Greenlee, M. (eds) *The Neuropsychology of Vision*.

Kentridge, R. W., Heywood, C. A., and Cowey, A. (2004). 'Chromatic edges, surfaces, and constancies in cerebral achromatopsia'. *Neuropsychologia*, 42.

acquaintance Acquaintance is an intimate way of being in a subject's perspective.

In every familiar case, a conscious subject has a perspective on the world. From time to time, various things are brought within this perspective: when one sees a mockingbird, or entertains a thought about Tony Blair, the mockingbird—or Blair—comes within one's perspective. Upon reflection, it seems that not all entries into a subject's perspective are on a par: the mockingbird when seen seems to be in some sense more intimately within one's perspective than is Blair when merely thought about. This suggests—and a number of philosophers have found theoretical utility in supposing—that there may be a maximally intimate way of being in a subject's perspective.

One of these philosophers was Bertrand Russell, who influentially labelled this maximally intimate connection 'acquaintance' (Russell 1912). Russell was renaming his teacher James Ward's notion of *presentation*, arguably adapted in turn from Kant's *intuition*, itself an adaptation of still older notions.

1. Russell on acquaintance
2. Acquaintance in contemporary perspective
3. Objects of acquaintance
4. Philosophical applications of acquaintance

1. Russell on acquaintance

It will aid understanding to briefly sketch Russell's discussion of acquaintance. His paradigm case of acquaintance emerged out of a discussion of perceptual experience: given that such an experience brings acquaintance with something—Russell called this thing a *sense-datum*—he wondered what this thing is. Suppose one walks around a square table one sees: the object of one's acquaintance changes shape, Russell thought (here one is aware of a diamond, there one is aware of a trapezoid). Since the table does not change shape, it follows that the sense-datum is something other than the table, and indeed, not in the external world but rather somehow inside one: in Russell's view, an entity in one's brain.

This discussion raises two questions: first, why suppose perceptual experience brings acquaintance with something? Arguably, this claim, quite persistent in the tradition, may be accepted because of the way such experience strikes one upon introspective reflection (Martin 2001). And second, why suppose the sense-datum changes shape? Certainly such an experience seems to involve awareness of a changing shape, but it also involves awareness of a constant shape-like property: the square shape of the table. Still, the changing shapes are arguably aspects under which the constant shape is perceived; in this sense, awareness of the changing shapes is more intimate than awareness of the constant shape. (In addition to brain entities and their features presented in perception, Russell's list of objects of acquaintance extended—with perhaps more tenuous motivation—to include remembered such objects, and 'universals' or features grasped by 'abstraction' from repeated instances.)

Russell endorsed a famous 'principle of acquaintance'—loosely, that one can only refer to, or think directly about, objects of one's acquaintance. One can in a sense think about Blair, but not refer to him: such a thought is about Blair only indirectly or 'by description', as the entity associated in a certain way with certain sense-data.

2. Acquaintance in contemporary perspective

Recent literature has developed a number of notions which help to clarify the metaphor of *maximal intimacy*. First, acquaintance can be thought of as a prime psychological relation (Williamson 2000). That is to say, when one is acquainted with an entity, this is a psychological matter; and it is not composed out of a psychological feature one has in oneself, leaving the object out, together with a non-psychological condition the object has. The existence of prime psychological relations is at odds with a popular view expressed in the slogan '*intentionality is the mark of the mental' (see also CONTENTS OF CONSCIOUSNESS; REPRESENTATIONALISM). Arguably, for something to be intentional is for it to be directed at a goal specified with a certain condition; directedness is arguably a matter of how something is in itself, rather than in relation to other things. So if all psychological features are a matter of directedness, as the slogan suggests, no psychological features can be prime relations. The very existence of acquaintance, on this analysis, is a matter of controversy. Primeness is required for intimacy, since the object is a participant in the psychological fact, rather than external to it.

Second, acquaintance can be thought of as involved with phenomenal consciousness (see CONSCIOUSNESS, CONCEPTS OF). An entity with such-and-such features being an object of my acquaintance can be part of what my experience is like for me—relations of acquaintance can be phenomenal characters—rather than beyond my conscious ken.

Third, although Russell's paradigm of acquaintance was perception, rather than thought, acquaintance can still be thought of as having a special status in relation to thought. For instance, whenever so-and-so is an object of acquaintance, one should be in a position to think about it. Still stronger connections could be embraced. For one, perhaps what is sometimes called an *epistemic rigidity* condition could be imposed, according to which there is a way of thinking about the object of acquaintance guaranteed to eliminate reasonable mistakes about which thing it is (by contrast, I could be mistaken about who I am, if due to a knock on the head I come to think that I am Hume). For another, perhaps there is a way of thinking about the object of acquaintance which brings the object into the thought: an idea sometimes expressed by calling such thoughts *quotational*—after the manner in which putting quotation marks around a word provides a way of talking about that word (Chalmers 2003; see EPISTEMOLOGY OF CONSCIOUSNESS).

3. Objects of acquaintance

What sorts of entities can be objects of acquaintance? Was Russell correct to think that physical objects outside one's body are never objects of acquaintance? Perhaps this question can be answered indirectly, by assessing which features can be objects of acquaintance, then determining which entities can have those features.

The epistemic rigidity condition may prove useful for determining which features can be objects of acquaintance, on a case-by-case basis. Is there a way of thinking about the feature *being made of water* guaranteed to latch on to that specific feature? Plausibly, thinking of it in terms of its being clear, drinkable, and abundant would not do the trick: something other than water, with a different chemical composition, could mimic these features (Putnam 1975). What about thinking of it as the substance whose molecules are composed of two hydrogen atoms and an oxygen atom? Maybe some deeper substance could mimic our way of thinking about oxygen? However, it is plausible to suppose that we have a way of thinking about the particular phenomenal character of seeing something red which cannot be mimicked, so perhaps this phenomenal character is an object of acquaintance (Chalmers 2003).

So, while psychological entities continue to seem to be good candidate objects of acquaintance, the jury is still out on whether—contradicting Russell—acquaintance with the external world is possible.

4. Philosophical applications of acquaintance

Acquaintance may play a role in the theory of reference. Russell's view that one can only refer to an object of one's acquaintance is not especially plausible (Kripke 1972). But if all reference is under an aspect or 'mode of presentation' (Frege 1892), the Russellian idea that aspects must be objects of acquaintance might still have a significant place in the theory of reference.

Acquaintance may play a role in the theory of consciousness. On the widely discussed '*higher-order representation' theory of consciousness, for an experience to have a certain feature—say, being uncomfortable—as its phenomenal character (for it to be uncomfortable for its subject) is for the experience to be represented to its subject as having that feature (see PHILOSOPHY AND THE STUDY OF CONSCIOUSNESS). The theory is popular because it captures the idea that one cannot be utterly blind to one's phenomenal characters: they must be present to one's perspective. One version of the high-order representation theory involves a so-called 'inner sense', according to which what it is for an experience to have a certain feature as its phenomenal character is for the subject to have an inner perception of the experience as having that feature. Now, if inner sensing is like outer sensing, it can go wrong: just as a red thing can look green, one's experience could be of something's looking red, but be sensed as—and therefore have as its phenomenal character—a case of something's looking green. This might seem to beggar comprehension, and is sometimes given as a reason to reject higher-order representation views (Byrne 1997). But suppose the experience's being a certain way is present to one's perspective by being an object of acquaintance. Since acquaintance is a prime relation, there can be no possibility of absence of its object, and thus no error can arise (Hellie 2007).

Acquaintance may play a role in the theory of perception. A lively debate in the contemporary literature concerns whether perception essentially involves acquaintance, or mere intentionality; if it involves acquaintance rather than intentionality, whether the object of acquaintance can ever be in the external world; and if so, how to square this with the possibility of perceptual aspect and error (Martin 2006).

BENJ HELLIE

Byrne, A. (1997). 'Some like it HOT'. *Philosophical Studies*, 86.

Chalmers, D. J. (2003). 'The content and epistemology of phenomenal belief'. In Jokic, A. and Smith, Q. (eds) *Consciousness: New Philosophical Essays.*

Frege, G. (1892). 'Uber Sinn und Bedeutung'. *Zeitschrift fur Philosophie und philosophische Kritik*, 100.

Hellie, B. (2007). 'Higher-order intentionality and higher-order acquaintance'. *Philosophical Studies*, 134.

Kripke, S. A. (1972). *Naming and Necessity.*

Martin, M. G. F. (2001). 'Beyond dispute'. In Crane, T. and Patterson, S. (eds) *History of the Mind–Body Problem.*

—— (2006). 'On being alienated'. In Gendler, T. S. and Hawthorne, J. (eds) *Perceptual Experience.*

Putnam, H. (1975). 'The meaning of "meaning" '. In Gunderson, K. (ed.) *Language, Mind, and Knowledge.*

Russell, B. (1912). *The Problems of Philosophy.*

Williamson, T. (2000). *Knowledge and its Limits.*

action, philosophical perspectives Until quite recently, the phenomenology of *agency* received surprisingly little attention from action theorists, theorists of consciousness, and epistemologists alike. To a large extent, the exact nature of the experiences associated with action, their contents, and the role they play are still to be elucidated. Yet, the significance of this investigation extends beyond the phenomenological to issues pertaining to the metaphysics of action and agency and to epistemology.

1. Consciousness of action: metaphysical and epistemological issues
2. The phenomenology of agency: aspects and components
3. Sources of the phenomenology of agency
4. Veridicality and causal efficacy

1. Consciousness of action: metaphysical and epistemological issues

According to Malle and Knobe (1997), awareness is an important component in the folk-conception of intentional action: we think that an action cannot qualify as intentional unless the agent is aware of what she is doing while doing it. In philosophical action theory, a similar awareness requirement is often implicitly assumed although less often explicitly stated. For instance, Anscombe (1957) argues that it is a necessary condition for an action under a description to qualify as intentional that its agent be aware that he is performing that very action. Yet, most action theorists have had surprisingly little to say as to what exactly this awareness amounts to and as to why indeed such an awareness requirement should hold.

Philosophers have also been interested in the sense of agency as a form of self-consciousness. When you are voluntarily lifting your index finger, your experience is quite different from what it would be if that finger was lifted by someone pulling a string attached to it. Although the finger movement may be the same in both cases, you feel active in the first case, passive in the second. Your experience of actively moving your finger is also quite different from the experience you may have when watching someone else lifting their finger. Although in the latter case, you may be aware that an action of finger lifting is being performed, you do not experience yourself as the agent of that action. Philosophers often assume that that there is a constitutive link between being aware of an action one is performing and experiencing oneself as the agent of that action. They may hold that our awareness of the action always includes the agent of the action as part of its content: this content is not just 'finger lifting', it is either 'my lifting my finger' if I am performing the action myself, or 'your lifting your finger', if I am observing you performing it. Or, alternatively, they may hold that the identity of the agent is fixed by the mode of access we have to the content of actions, where actions I am aware of from the inside and not just by observation can only be mine. Yet, empirical evidence suggests that awareness of action and sense of agency can sometimes come apart (see ACTION, SCIENTIFIC PERSPECTIVES). It therefore remains to be seen whether the normal link between these two kinds of experience is necessary or only contingent.

It is often held that awareness from the inside provides a distinctive form of knowledge of at least certain aspects of our own actions. But what form of knowledge is that and which aspects of our actions does it concern? Traditionally, knowledge from within has been equated with introspective knowledge, the only possible objects of which are inner mental states or events. But then, knowledge from within could only be knowledge of our intentions and volitions, not of our bodily actions per se. Some philosophers have wanted to go further and claim that we have knowledge from within of our bodily actions themselves and not just their mental antecedents. Thus, Anscombe claims that we have non-observational knowledge of the intentional actions we are currently performing. According to her, we know of our current actions not on the basis of observation nor on the basis of introspection, but because we have non-observational knowledge of our practical reasons and our actions are the upshot of our practical reasoning. Although they grant that there are important connections between action control and knowledge of action, many philosophers reject her account of this connection. Instead (e.g. Peacocke 2003), they consider our knowledge from within of our actions as grounded on our experience of acting, and a proper delimitation of this knowledge as requiring a clear determination of the contents of this experience and of its relation to action control.

Clearly, resolving these metaphysical and epistemological issues depends in part on how we conceive of the phenomenology of action and of its relation to action specification and action control mechanisms.

2. The phenomenology of agency: aspects and components

The now growing literature on the content and sources of the phenomenology of first-person agency highlights the fact that the phenomenology of agency is multifarious. Some distinctions are in order.

First, one should distinguish between physical actions and mental actions and their respective phenomenologies. Typically, physical actions involve the production of causal effects in the external world through movements of the body of the agent, while mental actions, such as attending to something or trying to remember someone's name, do not. A distinctive component of the phenomenology of physical actions is a sense of oneself as a physical agent producing physical effects in the world via its bodily interactions with it. In what follows, I focus on physical actions.

A second important distinction is between a *long-term sense of agency* and an *occurrent sense of agency*. The former may be thought to include both a sense of oneself as an agent apart from any particular action, i.e. a sense of one's capacity for action over time, and a form of self-narrative where one's past actions and projected future actions are given coherence by being integrated into a set of overarching goals, motivations, projects, and general lines of conduct. The latter is the sense of agency one experiences at the time one is performing, or preparing to perform, a particular action.

A third distinction is between detached and immersed awareness. *Immersed awareness* is the kind of non-reflective experience one has when one is fully engaged in an activity, while *detached awareness* requires a form of reflective consciousness, where the agent, so to speak, mentally steps back and either observes himself acting or introspects what he is doing.

The occurrent, immersed sense of agency is not monolithic but includes a number of distinguishable aspects. A non-exhaustive list of components would include: awareness of a goal, awareness of an intention to act, awareness of initiation of action, awareness of movements, sense of activity, sense of mental effort, sense of physical effort, sense of control, experience of authorship, experience of intentionality, experience of purposiveness, experience of freedom, and experience of mental causation.

A preliminary regimentation of this profusion of states would distinguish between them on the basis of their contents. Some aspects of the phenomenology of agency concern the action itself, what is being done, while others concern the agent of the action, her awareness that she is acting or that she is the agent of the action. The former aspects, constituting what we may call *awareness of action*, themselves subdivide into that, what, and how, i.e. awareness of active movement as opposed to passive or mechanical movement, awareness of the goal pursued, and awareness of the means employed to attain this goal. The latter aspects of the phenomenology of agency, the sense of agency proper, may itself be subdivided into a sense of intentionality or intentional causation, a sense of initiation, and a sense of control.

Note that this preliminary regimentation leaves open a number of questions: How are these various components of the phenomenology of agency related? To what extent are they dissociable? Are some more basic than others? Where does their content come from? Are they veridical? Do they play a causal role, and if so what role?

3. Sources of the phenomenology of agency

To make progress on these issues, one also needs to understand what the sources of the components of the phenomenology of action are and how they relate to action production and control mechanisms. In the recent literature we find two contrasting approaches. According to one approach, championed by Daniel Wegner (2002) and close in spirit to Dennett's general views on consciousness, the phenomenology of agency, or what he calls the *experience of the conscious will*, is the result of interpretative processes, distinct and separate from the processes involved in the specification and control of the action. The experience of agency arises primarily when there is a match between an action and a prior thought. More precisely, we believe our thoughts have caused our action when we have thoughts that occur just before the action, when these thoughts are consistent with the action, and when potential other causes of the action are not present. On this view, the phenomenology of agency is an inferentially mediated reconstruction.

Several critics have pointed out that Wegner's three criteria of priority, consistency, and exclusivity are not sufficient for us to experience our normal sense of agency. For physical action at least, sensorimotor experiences of our body and its movements would seem to be necessary as well. Conversely, one may also doubt that these three conditions are necessary. We often experience ourselves as the authors of our well-rehearsed routine actions, even when we experience no immediately preceding conscious thoughts to perform the specific behaviours involved. More generally, Wegner's model of the phenomenology of agency has been criticized as over-simplistic and as failing to do justice to its various component elements. Although the interpretive processes Wegner appeals to may contribute to agentive experience, they do not provide a complete story (see Bayne and Pacherie 2007).

A different approach, advocated by Patrick Haggard, is based on the assumption that the processes through which the phenomenology of agency is generated have strong connections with the processes involved in action specification and control. More specifically, the latter processes have a causal/teleological quality in the sense that representations of action goals cause general preparation, then progressive specification, then physical movement. The component representations that lead to action evolve over measurable time, and can be distinguished from each other by the time of their activation as well as their functional and content properties. Finally, these component representations are differentially accessible to consciousness and can be the source of various aspects of agentive experience.

Crucial to this approach are three main ideas. First, action specification and action rely on internal models of two kinds: inverse models that compute the motor programs and commands needed to achieve a desired state given one's current state, and forward models that predict the sensory consequences of executing these motor commands. Second, action and movement control depend in a large part on the coupling of inverse and forward models through a series of comparators that compare desired, predicted, and actual states at various levels of specification and use the results of these comparisons for various forms of regulation. Third, it is proposed that some of the representations thus computed and compared form the basis of our awareness of action.

Like Wegner's, this approach is a kind of matching model of the experience of doing. Yet, in contrast to it, it does not conceive of this experience as arising simply from the comparison of prior thoughts and observed actions. Rather, it should be seen as a multilevel and multi-matching model. Some aspects of the phenomenology of action may arise from the comparison and binding of representations of desired and predicted states at various levels of specification and thus be the outcome of pre-constructive rather than reconstructive processes; others arise from comparisons of representations of predicted and actual states and thus involve both pre-constructive and reconstructive elements, and still others arise from comparisons of representations of desired and actual states. Even the latter need not be thought to reduce to reconstructions in Wegner's sense, for the representations of agency that Haggard posits have much more fine-grained contents than the representations posited by Wegner.

4. Veridicality and causal efficacy

Wegner thinks his model provides evidence for the claim that the conscious will is an illusion, by which he seems to mean both that our experiences are often non-veridical—they misrepresent the agent and the structure of their actions—and that they are *epiphenomenal—they play no causal role in the production of the action they are experiences of. Both the non-veridicality and the epiphenomenality of our experiences are deemed consequences of the fact that the processes through which the phenomenology of agency is generated are quite separate from the processes involved in action-specification and control. As regards non-veridicality, Wegner seems to think that our experiences of acting could only be veridical if they had some direct link to their objects. Their being theoretically mediated would make them illusory. Yet, it is quite unclear why inferential mediation should be incompatible with reliability. As regards epiphenomenality, if our conscious experiences are actually post hoc reconstructions then they are obviously epiphenomenal with respect to the actions they are about, since they arise after these actions have taken place. Of course—as Wegner points out—this would not prevent them from possessing long-term causal efficacy, in that they could contribute to the development of our long-term sense of agency, which would in turn inform the processes that determine what we will do.

In contrast, the multi-matching model suggests that the processes through which the phenomenology of agency is generated are closely tied to the processes involved in action-specification and control. On this model, different varieties of conscious experiences would tap component representations constructed at various stages in the process of action specification; some would be pre-constructions, others reconstructions, and still others would involve both pre-construction and reconstruction. Given this diversity, it is not sure we should aim at giving a unique answer to the question whether the phenomenology of agency is veridical or at providing a unitary account of its reliability (or lack thereof).

Arguing that the processes involved in action specification are tightly coupled with those responsible for the various facets of the experience of doing keeps open the possibility that conscious experience plays a causal role in the production and control of action. Yet, it should not lead one to automatically embrace the view that our experience of doing in all its aspects systematically plays a role in the production, guidance, and control of action. Rather than try and defend an all-or-none view, we should be open to the idea that some but not all of the processes of action production and control depend on conscious experiences and be ready to acknowledge the complexity of cognitive–experiential interactions.

ELISABETH PACHERIE

Anscombe, G. E. M. (1957). *Intention.*

Bayne, T. J. and Levy, N. (2006). 'The feeling of doing: deconstructing the phenomenology of agency'. In Sebanz, N. and Prinz, W. (eds) *Disorders of Volition.*

Bayne, T. J. and Pacherie, E. (2007). 'Narrators and comparators: the architecture of agentive self-awareness'. *Synthèse*, 159.

Frith, C. D. (2005). 'The self in action: lessons from delusions of control'. *Consciousness and Cognition*, 14.

Haggard, P. and Johnson, H. (2003). 'Experiences of voluntary action'. *Journal of Consciousness Studies*, 10.

Horgan, T., Tienson, J., and Graham, G. (2003). 'The phenomenology of first-person agency'. In Walter, S. and Heckmann, H.-D. (eds) *Physicalism and Mental Causation: The Metaphysics of Mind and Action.*

Jeannerod, M. (2006). *Motor Cognition.*

Malle, B. F. and Knobe, J. (1997). 'The folk concept of intentionality'. *Journal of Experimental Social Psychology*, 33.

Marcel, A. (2003). 'The sense of agency: awareness and ownership of action'. In Roessler, J. and Eilan, N. (eds) *Agency and Self-awareness.*

Nahmias, E. (2005). 'Agency, authorship and illusion'. *Consciousness and Cognition*, 14.

Pacherie, E. (2007). 'Sense of control and sense of agency'. *Psyche*, 13.

Pacherie, E. (2008). 'The phenomenology of action: a conceptual framework'. *Cognition*, 107.

Peacocke, C. (2003). 'Action: awareness, ownership, and knowledge'. In Roessler, J. and Eilan, N. (eds) *Agency and Self-awareness.*

Roessler, J. and Eilan, N. (eds) (2003). *Agency and Self-awareness.*

Searle, J. (1983). *Intentionality.*

Wegner, D. M. (2002). *The Illusion of Conscious Will.*

action, scientific perspectives A number of recent studies have suggested that, in healthy subjects, the predicted sensory consequences of movement are available to awareness whereas the actual sensory consequences of movement are not.

1. Awareness of action in healthy subjects
2. Forward models and prediction of action
3. Awareness of action in pathology
4. Awareness of action: brain basis
5. Conclusion

1. Awareness of action in healthy subjects

There are a number of demonstrations in healthy subjects that many aspects of action can occur without awareness (see Frith et al. 2000 for more details). In one experiment, subjects were required to point at a visual target. During a saccade they occasionally displaced the target by several degrees. Although the displacement of the target went unnoticed by the subjects, they nevertheless adjusted the trajectory of their moving hand to the new target position. In this case, subjects were aware neither of the sensory information that elicited the movement correction nor of the change in the motor programme that was elicited (Goodale et al. 1994). Similarly, Castiello et al. (1991) found that awareness (as measured by subjects' verbal responses) of an unexpected target jump occurred more than 200 ms after the motor system had initiated an appropriate movement correction.

Evidence that sensations associated with actual movements are unavailable to awareness comes from a study in which the sensory consequences of movement were made to deviate from subjects' expectations (Fourneret and Jeannerod 1998). In this study, the subjects' task was to draw a straight line on a computer screen. Subjects could not see their arm or hand and were given false feedback about the trajectory of their arm movement. Thus they had to make considerable deviations from a straight movement in order to achieve their goal. Verbal reports indicated that subjects were unaware that they were making deviant movements—they claimed to have made straight movements. These results suggest that subjects were aware of the movements they intended to make (the sensory consequences of which were predicted) rather than the movements they actually made.

A rather different experiment that altered the correspondence between movement and its sensory consequences provides further evidence that subjects are unaware of the actual consequences of movement. In this study, subjects moved a robotic arm with their left hand and this movement caused a second foam-tipped robotic arm to move across their right palm. Without the subjects' knowledge, delays of 0, 100, 200, and 300 ms were introduced between the movement of the left hand and the tactile stimulus on the right palm. Delays are not predicted and therefore produce increasing levels of discrepancy between the sensory prediction and the actual sensory feedback from movement. This results in less perceptual attenuation with increasing delays. Subjects rated the sensation of the tactile stimulation in each condition, and although there was a striking correlation between delay and the perceived tickliness of the stimulus, when asked afterwards none of the subjects claimed to have noticed the delays (Blakemore et al. 1999). This demonstrates that although delays, because they are not predicted, result in less cancellation of the sensory signal, subjects are unaware of sensory discrepancies between the predicted and actual sensory consequences of movement.

On the basis of these experiments, Frith and colleagues (2000) proposed that there is only limited awareness of the actual state of the motor system whenever it has been successfully predicted in advance. It has been suggested that, under normal circumstances, we are aware only of the predicted sensory consequences of movements. Further evidence for this proposal comes from studies by Libet demonstrating that subjects are aware of initiating a movement about 200 ms before the actual movement occurs (Libet et al. 1983, Haggard et al. 1999). Thus the awareness of initiating a movement must depend on the predicted sensory consequences of the movement, which is available before the sensory feedback from the movement. These studies suggest that we may only be aware of the actual sensory consequences of our movements when they deviate from what we expect. As long as actions more or less correspond to intentions (and therefore sensory prediction is accurate), subjects are not aware of the actual action and its consequences.

2. Forward models and prediction of action

These phenomena can be explained by referring to the properties of forward models of action. It has been proposed that the recognition of action is achieved by predicting the sensory consequences of motor commands whenever movements are made (Frith et al. 2000). One way that the brain predicts the consequences of movement is by using an internal *forward model. Based on the efference copy produced in parallel with motor commands, the forward model predicts the sensory consequences of motor commands whenever movements are made (see Fig. A1). Forward models make two types of prediction. First, they predict the actual outcome of the motor command and compare this to the desired outcome and they predict the sensory consequences of movement and compare this with the actual feedback. The prediction of the outcome of the motor command is used to estimate the state of the motor system, which is not directly observable by the central nervous system.

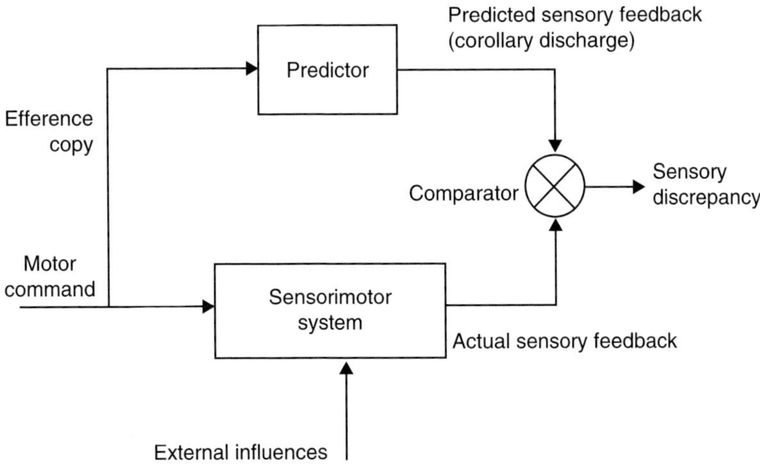

Fig. A1. Forward model.

The second type of prediction is of the sensory consequences of movement, and can be used to filter sensory information, attenuating the component that is due to self-movement from that due to changes in the outside world. This is achieved by comparing the predicted and actual sensory feedback from the movement. When there is little or no discrepancy between the predicted and actual sensory consequences of a movement, the sensory consequences of movement can be attenuated relative to external sensory events (see TICKLING).

3. Awareness of action in pathology

In the remainder of this entry, I will briefly describe two examples of neurological experiences (the results of parietal lesions and phantom limbs) and an example of a psychiatric symptom (delusion of control/passivity) in which awareness of action is somehow changed. Further examples can be found in Frith et al. (2000).

Parietal lobe lesions. Damage to the parietal lobe often causes problems with the control and awareness of action. These cases suggests that the parietal lobe plays a role in producing a sense of agency and the conscious representation of actions, a proposal that has been supported by neuroimaging experiments (Frith et al. 2000). A paradigm that has been used extensively to investigate self-movement recognition involves subjects viewing the visual consequences of their own hand movements, which can be manipulated so that the ownership of the hand is ambiguous (Sirigu et al. 1999). The subject sees on a television screen a hand that is either their own or that of the experimenter performing movements that are either congruent or incongruent with the subject's own hand movements. Using this paradigm, Sirigu and colleagues showed that patients with left parietal lobe damage tend to confuse their hand movements with those of another agent.

It has been proposed that forward model-like prediction underlies the ability to prepare and imagine movements. Parietal lesions impair the ability to use mental motor *imagery. Parietal patients are unable to predict the time necessary to perform finger movements and visually guided pointing gestures using their imagination. Normally imagined and executed movement times are highly correlated, Fitts' law accounting equally well for both types of movement. This was found to be true for a patient with motor cortex damage, whereas in patients with parietal lesions actual movement execution was modulated by target size but motor imagery was not (Sirigu et al. 1996).

Delusions of control/passivity experiences associated with schizophrenia. Certain psychiatric symptoms are characterized by an inability to distinguish self- and externally produced actions. Many patients with *schizophrenia describe 'passivity' experiences in which actions, thoughts, or emotions are made for them by some external agent rather than by their own will. The experience of passivity might arise from a lack of awareness of the predicted limb position (Frith et al. 2000). The idea is that the forward model prediction somehow does not reach awareness in these patients. In the presence of delusions of control, the patient is not aware of the predicted consequences of a movement and is therefore not aware of initiating a movement. In parallel, the patient's belief system is faulty so that he interprets this abnormal sensation in an irrational way.

Several studies have shown that patients with delusions of control confuse self-produced and externally generated actions. Using the paradigm in which subjects see feedback of their own hand movement or that of the experimenter's hand making similar movements, Daprati and her colleagues (1997) found that schizophrenic patients with delusions of control are more likely than control subjects to confuse their hand with that of the experimenter. These patients have difficulty distinguishing between correct visual feedback about the position of their hand and false feedback when the image of the hand they see is in fact that of another person attempting to make the same movements as the patient. One explanation for this is that the patients only have proprioceptive and visual feedback to rely on for recognition, whereas normal control subjects are able additionally to compare the sensory prediction with the sensory feedback from the movement.

Evidence that this confusion between self and other in patients with delusions of control is a consequence of an abnormal sensory prediction comes from studies based on the finding that, normally, because a movement is predicted, its sensory consequences can be perceptually attenuated relative to external sensations (Blakemore et al. 1999). Patients with delusions of control do not show this perceptual attenuation of self-produced sensory stimulation (Blakemore et al. 2000). If delusions of control are associated with an impairment in sensory prediction, we would expect to see no attenuation of the activity in sensory regions. This was precisely the result of a study in which schizophrenic patients with and without delusions of control were scanned while they performed a movement task (Spence et al. 1997). The presence of delusions of control was associated with overactivity in right inferior parietal cortex. Moreover, activity in this region returned to normal levels when the patients were in remission. Overactivity of the inferior parietal cortex might reflect a heightened response to the sensory consequences of the movements the patients were making during scanning, contributing to the feeling that movements are externally controlled.

Phantom limbs. After amputation of a limb many patients experience a *phantom limb: they still feel the presence of the limb although they know it does not exist (Ramachandran and Rogers-Ramachandran 1996). It has been suggested that neural plasticity plays a role in the experience of phantom limbs. Some patients report being able to move their phantoms voluntarily, while others experience their phantom as paralysed and can not move it even with intense effort. If the limb was paralysed before amputation, the phantom normally remains paralysed. If not, then typically immediately after amputation patients feel that they can generate movement in the phantom. However, with time they often lose this ability. It has been suggested that the estimated position of a limb is not based solely on sensory information, but also on the stream of motor commands issued to the limb muscles. On the basis of these commands the forward model can estimate the new position of the limb before any sensory feedback has been received. If these commands lead to the prediction of movement, then the phantom will be experienced as moving. However, the motor system is designed to adapt to changing circumstances. Since the limb does not actually move there is a discrepancy between the predicted and the actual consequences of the motor commands. With time the forward models will be modified to reduce these discrepancies—the prediction will be altered so that no movement of the limb is predicted even when motor commands to move the limb are issued. Such adaptation in the forward models could explain why patients eventually lose the ability to move their phantoms.

Such adaptation of the forward models would also explain how Ramachandran and Rogers-Ramachandran (1996) were able to reinstate voluntary movement of the phantom by providing false visual feedback of a moving limb corresponding to the phantom. This was achieved by placing a mirror in the midsagittal plain. With the head in the appropriate position it was possible for the patient to see the intact limb at the same time as the mirror reflection of this limb. For most patients, moving their hand in this mirror box rapidly leads to the perception that they are now able to move the phantom limb again. It has been suggested that the false visual feedback supplied by the mirror box allowed the forward models to be updated (Frith et al. 2000). In consequence, efference copy produced in parallel with the motor commands now generated changes in the predicted position of the missing limb corresponding to what the patient had seen in the mirror.

4. Awareness of action: brain basis

It is well established that the parietal lobe is involved in predicting actions. Recent *functional neuroimaging studies in healthy subjects have demonstrated a role for parietal cortex in sensory prediction. For example, the parietal lobe is involved in the cancellation of self-produced sensory stimulation. Activity in the bilateral parietal operculum (secondary somatosensory cortex), amongst other regions, was higher during externally produced tactile stimulation of the palm than during self-produced tactile stimulation (Blakemore et al. 1998). This relative attenuation of parietal opercular activity during self-produced sensory stimulation requires the sensory consequences of movement to be predicted accurately. The parietal lobe also seems to play a role in movement imagery. A recent fMRI study that directly compared movement execution with movement imagination demonstrated that imagining a movement activates the left posterior and inferior parietal lobe to a greater extent than executing the same movement (Gerardin et al. 2000).

5. Conclusion

In this entry, I have summarized how the predicted sensory consequences of movement are available to awareness while the actual sensory consequences of movement are not, and how this might be related to forward models of action. Two examples of neurological symptoms that are characterized by changes in the prediction process are the experiences after damage to the parietal lobe and phantom limbs in amputees. A delusion of control or passivity symptom is a psychiatric symptom that has been characterized by an impaired forward model sensory prediction process. Functional neuroimaging studies have suggested that sensory prediction involves activity in the parietal cortex.

SARAH-JAYNE BLAKEMORE

Blakemore, S.-J., Wolpert, D. M., and Frith, C. D. (1998). 'Central cancellation of self-produced tickle sensation'. *Nature Neuroscience*, 1.

——, Frith, C. D., and Wolpert, D. M. (1999). 'Spatiotemporal prediction modulates the perception of self-produced stimuli'. *Journal of Cognitive Neuroscience*, 11.

——, Smith, J., Steel, R., Johnstone, E., and Frith, C. D. (2000). 'The perception of self-produced sensory stimuli in patients with auditory hallucinations and passivity experiences: evidence for a breakdown in self-monitoring'. *Psychological Medicine*, 30.

Castiello, U., Paulignan, Y., and Jeannerod, M. (1991). 'Temporal dissociation of motor responses and subjective awareness. A study in normal subjects'. *Brain*, 114.

Daprati, E., Franck, N., Georgieff, N. et al. (1997). 'Looking for the agent: an investigation into consciousness of action and self-consciousness in schizophrenic patients'. *Cognition*, 65.

Fourneret, P. and Jeannerod, M. (1998). 'Limited conscious monitoring of motor performance in normal subjects'. *Neuropsychologia*, 36.

Frith, C. D., Blakemore S.-J., and Wolpert, D. M. (2000). 'Abnormalities in the awareness and control of action'. *Philosophical Transactions of the Royal Society of London Series B: Biological Sciences*, 355.
Gerardin, E., Sirigu, A., Lehericy, S. et al. (2000). 'Partially overlapping neural networks for real and imagined hand movements'. *Cerebral Cortex*, 10.
Goodale, M. A., Jacobson, L. S., Milner, A. D., Perrett, D. I., Benson, P. J., and Hietanen, J. K. (1994). 'The nature and limits of orientation and pattern processing visuomotor control in a visual form agnosic'. *Journal of Cognitive Neuroscience*, 6.
Haggard, P., Newman, C., and Magno, E. (1999). 'On the perceived time of voluntary actions'. *British Journal of Psychology*, 90.
Libet, B., Gleason, C. A., Wright, E. W., and Pearl, D. K. (1983). 'Time of conscious intention to act in relation to onset of cerebral activity (readiness potential): the unconscious initiation of a freely voluntary act'. *Brain*, 106.
Ramachandran, V. S. and Rogers-Ramachandran, D. (1996). 'Synaesthesia in phantom limbs induced with mirrors'. *Proceedings of the Royal Society of London Series B: Biological Sciences*, 263.
Sirigu, A., Duhamel, J. R., Cohen, L., Pillon, B., Dubois, B., and Agid, Y. (1996). 'The mental representation of hand movements after parietal cortex damage'. *Science*, 273.
——, Daprati, E., Pradat-Diehl, P., Franck, N., and Jeannerod, M. (1999). 'Perception of self-generated movement following left parietal lesion'. *Brain*, 122.
Spence, S. A., Brooks, D. J., Hirsch, S. R., Liddle, P. F., Meehan, J., and Grasby, P. M. (1997). 'A PET study of voluntary movement in schizophrenic patients experiencing passivity phenomena (delusions of alien control)'. *Brain*, 120.

ACT-R architecture ACT-R (Adaptive Control of Thought, Rational) is an architecture of cognition created by John Anderson in 1991 (Anderson et al. 2004 describe the latest version). It is used to simulate and explain human performance and learning in a wide range of tasks, from typical psychological experiments to complex, dynamic tasks. The architecture follows Anderson's earlier work on ACT architectures, most notably ACT* (Anderson 1983).

ACT-R has three categories of scientific goals. The first are *functional* goals: the architecture should be capable of producing intelligent behaviour at the same level as humans, for example in models that can perform complex dynamic tasks (e.g. Taatgen 2005), or models that can interpret natural language (e.g. Lewis and Vasishth 2005). The second are *behavioural* goals: the architecture should be able to predict the outcomes of human experiments, including details like error rates, response times, and eye movements, which fall outside the scope of a purely functional model. Models of memory, like list learning, fall into this category (Anderson and Matessa 1997). The third are *neuropsychological* goals: components of the architecture should correspond to areas in the brain, and patterns of activation found in neuroimaging experiments should correspond to what the architecture would predict. An example of this is a model that can successfully predict brain activity during algebraic problem solving (Anderson 2005).

Architectures of cognition operate on a level of abstraction intermediate between the brain and what Newell called the *knowledge level*, the level of intelligent behaviour. As a consequence, many common psychological terms that characterize human cognition do not have a one-to-one mapping to either the level of the cognitive architecture or the brain. Concepts like attention, intelligence, intention, and also consciousness are not defined directly in terms of components of the architecture, but are instead *emergent properties. ACT-R has no direct theory of consciousness, but is nevertheless able to shed light on the issue by modelling tasks and phenomena associated with consciousness. We will look at two aspects in detail: which parts of the knowledge representation are open to awareness, and how the distinction between implicit (unconscious) and explicit (conscious) learning can be understood.

1. Awareness in ACT-R
2. Implicit vs explicit learning
3. Conclusion

1. Awareness in ACT-R
ACT-R is made up of several modules (visual, manual, intentional, declarative, procedural, and others) that can all operate independently (see Fig. A2). These modules communicate through buffers, each of which can hold a single piece of information. The system can be considered 'aware' of the contents of all these buffers, i.e. it is aware of the currently attended visual stimulus, it is aware of the current action that is being taken, it is aware of the current goal, and of the currently active fact in declarative memory. A central part of the theory is taken by two long-term *memory systems: procedural and declarative. *Declarative memory* is open to inspection, meaning that when the system successfully retrieves knowledge from declarative memory it becomes aware of it. *Procedural knowledge*, on the other hand, is not open to direct conscious inspection. The awareness status of the other modules is currently undefined. Nevertheless, awareness in ACT-R can be seen as a function of communication between systems made explicit in the buffers, whereas processing both in the central production system and in the modules is unconscious.

ACT-R's notion of awareness is close to Baars' *global workspace (GW) theory (Baars 1997). According to GW theory, people are aware of the contents of the global workspace itself, which is 'an architectural capability for system-wide integration and dissemination of information'. The other constructs in GW theory,

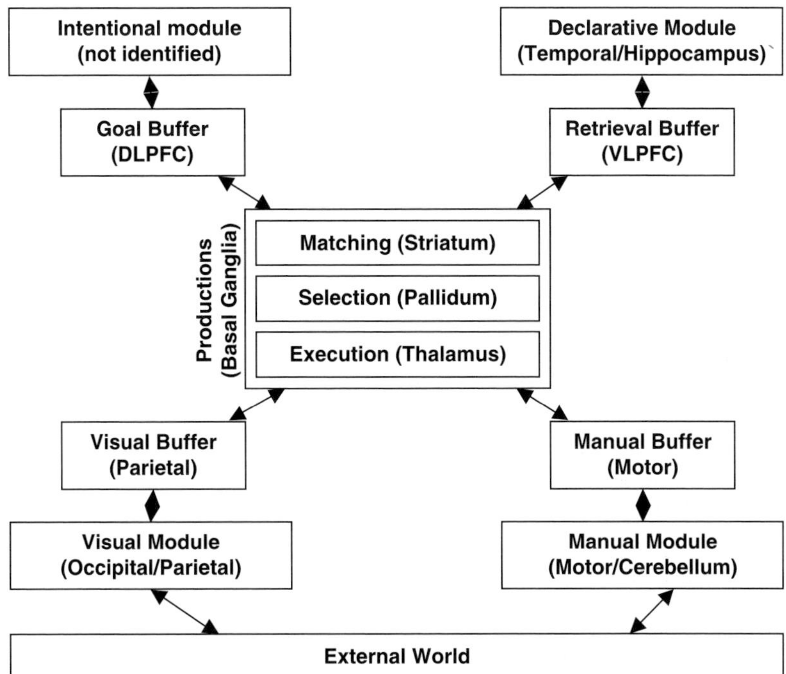

Fig. A2. Overview of the ACT-R architecture.

specialized processors and contexts, are unconscious. The global workspace concept itself maps very well onto ACT-R's buffers, and the specialized processors onto ACT-R's modules. The concept of contexts, 'unconscious factors that shape conscious contents', has a less clear mapping, because it has correspondence both to ACT-R's subsymbolic contextual activation processes and to procedural memory.

The notion that consciousness mainly plays out in the ACT-R buffers implies that the intensity of buffer use corresponds to the level of awareness. This is the case in models of skill acquisition in ACT-R (Anderson et al. 2004, Taatgen 2005). The assumption of these models is that knowledge for a new task is initially stored in declarative memory. In order to use this knowledge it has to be retrieved into the retrieval buffer and then be interpreted by the appropriate production rules. With practice, declarative knowledge is gradually transformed into procedural knowledge, making it no longer necessary to hold the information in the retrieval buffer. This process explains both the increase of performance with practice, and the decrease of awareness that is associated with expert and automated behaviour.

2. Implicit vs explicit learning

The difference between implicit (unconscious) and explicit (conscious) *learning is traditionally explained by assuming separate memory systems for implicit and explicit *knowledge (Tulving et al. 1982). Although this seems to map well onto ACT-R's notions of procedural and declarative memory, it is not consistent with the way ACT-R learns from experience. Many ACT-R models of implicit learning use storage and retrieval of examples in declarative memory (instance theory) to explain that performance improves without participants being able to extract an explicit rule. Instead of abstracting a rule, they rely on retrieving a past experience that best fits the current situation. In these models there is no representation of a rule at all, either conscious or unconscious. Examples are models of implicit learning in the Sugar Factory task (Taatgen and Wallach 2002) and *sequence learning tasks (Lebiere and Wallach 2001).

The ability to model memory phenomena in detail can also help to show that certain dissociations that show up in memory experiments do not necessarily have to be explained by separate memory systems. In an experiment by Tulving et al. (1982), participants had to learn a list of words, and were tested after an hour and then after a week explicitly (by being asking whether a particular word was on the list) and implicitly (through a word-completion task in which words were sometimes from the list and sometimes not). Performance on the explicit task turned out to decrease after a week, but performance on the implicit task remained constant. Tulving et al. interpreted this as evidence for separate implicit and explicit memory systems. However, an ACT-R model showed that the task can be modelled by just using declarative memory. The explicit task requires the creation of a separate declarative memory element to record that a word has been studied in the context of the experiment, while the implicit task only relies on the word having received extra activation by studying it. The experimental results can be explained by the fact that the new declarative memory elements that represent the study episode decay quickly and cannot be recalled after a week, but the extra activation still gives the word chunks an edge in the competition with other words.

3. Conclusion

ACT-R's set of buffers form the centre of awareness of the architecture, corresponding to what in other theories might be called *working memory. The extent to which buffers are used in performing a task can be seen as an indication of level of awareness. Phenomena of implicit learning can often be explained by the fact that knowledge that helps performance improvements is not represented in the form of rules, but as examples. The fact that ACT-R can also show a dichotomy between implicit and explicit memory is not necessary to explain the results of Tulving's experiment.

NIELS A. TAATGEN

Anderson, J. R. (1983). *The Architecture of Cognition.*

—— (2005). 'Human symbol manipulation within an integrated cognitive architecture'. *Cognitive Science*, 29.

—— and Matessa, M. P. (1997). 'A production system theory of serial memory'. *Psychological Review*, 104.

Anderson, J. R., Bothell, D., Byrne, M., Douglass, S., Lebiere, C., and Qin, Y. (2004). 'An integrated theory of cognition'. *Psychological Review*, 111.

Baars, B. J. (1997). *In the Theater of Consciousness: The Workspace of the Mind.*

Lebiere, C. and Wallach, D. (2001). 'Sequence learning in the ACT-R cognitive architecture: empirical analysis of a hybrid model'. In Sun, R. and Gilles, C. L. (eds) *Sequence Learning: Paradigms, Algorithms, and Applications.*

Lewis, R. L. and Vasishth, S. (2005). 'An activation-based model of sentence processing as skilled memory retrieval'. *Cognitive Science*, 29.

Taatgen, N. A. (2005). 'Modeling parallelization and flexibility improvements in skill acquisition: from dual tasks to complex dynamic skills'. *Cognitive Science*, 29.

—— and Wallach, D. (2002). 'Whether skill acquisition is rule or instance based is determined by the structure of the task'. *Cognitive Science Quarterly*, 2.

Tulving, E., Schacter, D. L., and Stark, H. A. (1982). 'Priming effects in word-fragment completion are independent of recognition memory'. *Journal of Experimental Psychology: Learning, Memory, and Cognition*, 8.

acute confusional state See DELIRIUM

aesthetic experience Aesthetic experience is a common and important part of our lives. Yet it is puzzling, and there are many questions that we might want to ask about it. For example, we might want to investigate aesthetic experience empirically, or we might wonder how aesthetic experiences can ground judgements that aspire to correctness. But before we think about these ambitious questions we need a good grasp of what we are talking about. This is not a mere luxury or an annoying detail that delays pushing forward more interesting frontiers and the pursuit of more fundamental questions. It is an essential prerequisite. There is no point trying to penetrate, explain, and justify something if we lack a clear idea of the target. We need an adequate and relatively uncontroversial description of what aesthetic experience is before we can graduate to further questions, otherwise our further enquiries are likely to lack a clear content and our efforts will be inconclusive.

One problem with fixing a target is that the words 'aesthetic experience' lack a fixed common meaning among philosophers or anyone else. They can mean and have meant many different things, and they need to be given a useful meaning or interpretation before any fruitful empirical investigation or philosophical reflection can take place.

One way to give them meaning that we should avoid like the plague would be to say that aesthetic experiences are those that we have in response to works of art. For one thing this replaces one terminological vagueness with a different one, and for another thing, it is not plausible that there is any one type of experience that we typically have or should have in response to works of art. Works of art are many and varied, and so are the responses that they typically invite.

A more profitable avenue is to find some characteristic of the experiences themselves, rather than their objects, which makes them aesthetic. Only some experiences of works of art are aesthetic, and aesthetic experiences are also had in response to the perception of nature.

There is a central intellectual current that finds elaborate expression in Kant's *Critique of Judgement* that can help us (Kant 1928). This is complex work. But the basic conception of the aesthetic is one that Kant draws from his British predecessors, especially Hume (Hume 1985). Kant focused on what he called 'judgements of taste', i.e. judgements of beauty or ugliness, and he claimed that such judgements are 'subjectively universal'. By this he meant (a) that judgements of taste are based on feelings of pleasure or displeasure; and (b) that they also lay claim to 'universal validity'. That is, on the one hand such judgements derive from feelings and are not beliefs about the world that might be true or false in virtue of that world; and on the other hand, there are some judgements that we ought to have and others that we ought not to have, some are correct, others incorrect—at least, some such judgements are better than others. In these two respects, judgements of beauty and ugliness contrast with various other judgements. They contrast with what Kant calls judgements of the agreeable, such as judgements of the niceness and nastiness of food and drink. They contrast with judgements of goodness, such as judgements of prudential and moral goodness. And they contrast with ordinary empirical judgements, such as judgements about the physical and sensory properties of things. Judgements of beauty and ugliness are like judgements of the agreeable in being subjective, but unlike them in claiming universal validity, and they are like moral and empirical judgements in claiming universal validity but unlike them in being subjective (see Kant 1928:sections 1, 6–9, 22, 32–34; pp. 40–41, 50–60, 85–89, 136–142).

Kant did not talk in terms of 'aesthetic experience' as we do today. For Kant, 'aesthetic' judgements include both judgements of taste or beauty as well as judgements of the agreeable, since both have 'subjective' grounds, in the sense that they are grounded on feelings of pleasure and displeasure. But we can translate Kant's framework into the modern idiom if we say an aesthetic experience is an experience of beauty or ugliness, where it is essential to such an (aesthetic) experience to ground a judgement of taste or beauty—one based on a feeling of pleasure or displeasure yet which claims validity. The fact that aesthetic experience grounds a judgement with such a claim to validity is essential to what it is to be an aesthetic experience or a pleasure in the beautiful. This gives us a useful grip on the notion of aesthetic experience, which can then be the basis for philosophical speculation or empirical investigation.

In the 20th century aestheticians have wanted to broaden the notion of the aesthetic to include other judgements besides judgements of beauty and ugliness, such as judgements of daintiness, dumpiness, delicacy, and elegance (Sibley 2001, especially Chs 2 and 3). My own view is that we can broaden the account to capture these other kinds of judgements by accepting the traditional account of the judgement of beauty and ugliness and then saying that the other judgements describe ways of being beautiful or ugly (Zangwill 2001:Chs 1 and 2).

Thus far we have been considering what it is that distinguishes aesthetic judgements and experiences from other kinds of judgements and experiences. But there are of course further questions to be asked about the nature of aesthetic judgements and experiences. In particular, two such further projects might be their justification (their 'possibility', in Kant's sense), and the empirical investigation of aesthetic judgements and experiences.

Let us move on, then, to consider the justification of the aesthetic judgements that we base on aesthetic experiences. The two features—*subjectivity* and *universal validity*—seem to be in tension. It is difficult to see how a judgement could have both of these characteristics. Hume and Kant both tried to solve this problem and tried to legitimize aesthetic judgements. And the debate continues today. *Aesthetic realism* is a more recent position that would explain the aspiration to validity of aesthetic judgements by saying that it has its source in reality—in mind-independent aesthetic facts (see for example Zemach 1997). On this view, aesthetic judgements are beliefs about aesthetic facts, and when true are true in virtue of them. But most aestheticians would like to explain the aspiration to validity without positing an aesthetic reality and beliefs about them. The trouble is that this does not seem easy to do. Hume gives a sentimentalist account: he thinks that aesthetic judgements are, or express, sentiments such as pleasure or displeasure, which do not represent aesthetic facts. Hume has a sophisticated account of how some sentiments might be more apt than others, even lacking a 'reality check'. Hume's account invokes an 'ideal critic' to which actual critics may aspire but also fall short. But many find problems with Hume's account. For instance, Jerrold Levinson argues that Hume cannot explain why we should strive to be like ideal critics (Levinson 2002). Kant's own justification of aesthetic judgement is very hard to understand. Like Hume, Kant appeals to pleasure and displeasure. But it turns out to be a strange kind of pleasure—a certain kind of 'free play of the cognitive faculties' (Kant 1928:sections 9, 35–40; pp. 57–60, 142–154). He thinks that those faculties must be shared by all cognizers, as he thinks he has shown in earlier work (the famous *Critique of Pure Reason*, Kant 2003). This means that pleasures in the beautiful are open to all. But it does not seem to explain why free play should be of one sort rather than another (see also Malcolm Budd's critique in Budd 2001). Contemporary non-realist accounts do not seem more promising than Hume's or Kant's. One suggestion that is more promising than many has been made by Roger Scruton, who appeals to *imaginative experiences*; these are cognitive states that are not beliefs. (This account may be similar in some ways to Kant's.) Scruton hopes to explain the aspiration to validity by connecting some kinds of imaginative experiences with morality (Scruton 1974, last chapter; Scruton 1979, last chapter). The problem with this is that morality and aesthetics often place opposing demands on us; so it is difficult to see how morality can help us to capture the aspiration to correctness that we deploy in our aesthetic judgements. This area of philosophical aesthetics is very much open now.

What about the empirical investigation of aesthetic experience? The idea of an empirical approach to understanding aesthetic experience was proposed in a spirited yet subtle paper of the great philosopher Moritz Schlick (1909). His approach was this:

> ... the whole field of aesthetics would have been dealt with, from the philosopher's point of view, if an answer could be given to the one basic question: 'Why does anything whatsoever appear beautiful?' The 'why' here must be taken to be asking for a real causal explanation; so it is not a matter of specifying the properties in virtue of which an object becomes a beautiful one, but rather of discovering the causes that lead to these properties actually having such an effect.

This interesting statement is silent about justificatory issues; either Schlick is ignoring those issues or else he thinks that explanation would be justification. But surely we might explain an error. It seems that justificatory issues needs to be separately addressed. Nonetheless, the explanation of our aesthetic life would be interesting and important even if there are other philosophical questions, such as the issue of justification, which it does not address. Perhaps we can separate explanatory and justificatory questions.

However, the idea that we can decouple the explanatory and justificatory projects is not uncontroversial. It might be maintained that the issue of whether our aesthetic life is empirically tractable, and if so how, turns on what justifies the practice of making aesthetic judgements. Perhaps we need not only a good account of what distinguishes aesthetic experiences and judgements, but also a deep account of how aesthetic judgements are 'possible' (i.e. justified), before we can know whether empirical investigation of them is possible and if so what form it will take. That would yield a strong 'first-philosophy' view. The contrary view would be that once we have a philosophically adequate description of our aesthetic lives, empirical evidence could be brought to bear on the justificatory question, because it would tell us whether the state of mind involved in aesthetic experience and judgement is a belief (as realists think), or a sentiment (as Hume thinks), or an imaginative state (as Scruton and possibly Kant think).

Some might be attracted to the strong position that aesthetic experience lies beyond the grasp of the science of empirical psychology, being part of the *Lebenswelt*, rather than the objective world that science investigates (Scruton 1989). The idea would be that only by falsifying aesthetic experience can it be made empirically tractable. Others would be more open to such an investigation. Aesthetic experiences, they might say, are after all psychological events, so it is difficult to see why they cannot be empirically investigated.

Sociologists and brain scientists have tried to draw conclusions about aesthetic experience from empirical data. The results thus far have not been inspiring. For example, the sociologist Pierre Bourdieu correlates judgements of taste with social class, and then draws sceptical conclusions about the notion of the aesthetic, in a move that is completely unexplained (Bourdieu 1984). Moreover he operates with a very odd notion of the aesthetic, one that no one has ever deployed (certainly not Kant).

Some brain scientists have been tempted to speculate about the 'experience of art' in the light of information about the brain. For example, Semir Zeki investigates brain activity during the experience of art (Zeki 1999). He claims that 'great' art involves ambiguity. This is a dubious general claim about art that is not at all supported by his brain data. Like Bourdieu, he leaps to all sorts of surprising conclusions that seem to bear little relation to the evidence cited. Another brain scientist who is interested in art is V. S. Ramachandran, who thinks that art has the function of distorting reality (Ramachandran and Herstein 1999). This is an equally dubious general claim (it suffers an avalanche of counter-examples). Furthermore, both Zeki and Ramachandran seem to take as their target the experience of art, which is obviously not a promising target for empirical investigation, since it is not a unitary phenomenon. And it is never made clear how exactly the facts about the brain tell us about 'the experience of art'. (For further discussion, see Hyman 2006.)

What seems to have gone wrong in these cases is that the target for explanation was not adequately described, and the relation of the evidence to the target is obscure. Clarifying an adequate notion of aesthetic experience is essential if empirical investigation of the phenomenon is meaningful. That does not mean that we must know the essence of such states before we can investigate them empirically; only that we have an adequate description of the kind of states that we are investigating. We must have some fix on what it is that we are trying to explain. Otherwise the pursuit will be premature. It will be a wild goose chase. We need a good idea of what kind of beast we are hunting.

However, I do not wish to be over-sceptical about the possibility of empirical research into aesthetic experience. Vladimir Konecni and his associates have pursued more conceptually nuanced empirical investigation (see Konecni 2005, Konecni et al. 2008; and see Konecni 2003 for some critical reflections on empirical research on music appreciation). There is surely some scope for empirical research. It would be odd if there were not. There are likely to be interesting findings in the future. But that will require (1) that researchers operate with a concept of the aesthetic that allows them to distinguish aesthetic experiences from other experiences; and (2) that there is shrewd experimental design that is sensitive to the features of aesthetic experience that distinguish it from other kinds of experience.

Schlick's own explanatory approach, in the early 20th century, was more nuanced and interesting than many contemporary accounts. He pursued an evolutionary account of aesthetic experience. He wonders why the capacity to have such experiences has evolved. Schlick distinguishes direct and indirect evolutionary approaches: *direct* approaches show how having aesthetic experiences themselves is adaptive, whereas *indirect* approaches show how aesthetic experiences are connected with, or are a by-product of, something else that is adaptive. Schlick favours the latter approach. Contemporary empirical approaches to aesthetic experience have tended to turn to sociology, brain science, or cognitive science, and there has been less exploration of evolutionary issues. But the evolutionary approach is a promising avenue for research, and may prove more fruitful than sociology or brain science. Moreover, such an approach echoes Kant's theory, since Kant was also concerned with the function or purpose of our aesthetic faculties. Perhaps a teleological explanatory approach allows us to ask the normative question: what would be wrong with someone who lacked an aesthetic sensitivity?

NICK ZANGWILL

Bordieu, P. (1984). *Distinction.*
Budd, M. (2001). 'The pure judgement of taste as an aesthetic reflective judgement'. *British Journal of Aesthetics*, 41.
Hume, D. (1985). 'Of the standard of taste'. In Miller, E. (ed.) *Essays: Moral, Political and Literary.*
Hyman, J. (2006). 'Art and neuroscience'. Art and Cognition Workshops, http://www.interdisciplines.org/artcognition, January.
Kant, I. (1928). *Critique of Judgement*, transl. J. C. Meredith.
Kant, I. (2003). *Critique of Pure Reason*, transl. N. Kemp-Smith.
Konecni, V. (2003). 'Review of Patrik Juslin and John Sloboda (eds) *Music and Emotion: Theory and Research*'. *Music Perception*, 20.
—— (2005). 'The aesthetic trinity: awe, being moved, thrills'. *Bulletin of Psychology and the Arts*, 5.
—— Brown, A., and Wanic, R. A. (2008). 'Comparative effects of music and recalled life events on emotional states'. *Psychology of Music*, 36.
Levinson, J. (2002). 'Hume's standard of taste: the real problem'. *Journal of Aesthetics and Art Criticism*, 60.
Ramachandran, V. S. and Herstein, W. (1999). 'The science of art: a neurological theory of aesthetic experience'. *Journal of Consciousness Studies*, 6.
Schlick, M. (1909/1978). 'The fundamental problems of aesthetics, seen in an evolutionary light'. In Mulder, H. L. and van Velde-Schlick, B. F. B. (eds) *Philosophical Papers I, 1909–1922.*
Scruton, R. (1974). *Art and Imagination.*
—— (1979). *The Aesthetics of Architecture.*
—— (1989). 'Contemporary philosophy and the neglect of aesthetics'. *The Philosopher on Dover Beach.*
Sibley, F. (2001). *Approach to Aesthetics.*
Zangwill, N. (2001). *The Metaphysics of Beauty.*
Zeki, S. (1999). *Inner Vision.*
Zemach, E. (1997). *Real Beauty.*

after-effects, perceptual Exposure to a sensory stimulus can produce illusory perceptual experiences immediately following this exposure period. The period of initial stimulation is typically called the *adaptation period* and the resulting alteration in perception is termed an *adaptation after-effect.* The duration of adaptation can range from a few seconds or less up to several hours. The resulting after-effect, too, can vary in duration, with some lasting for days or even weeks.

After-effects can be generated in any of the sensory modalities. To give a few examples: (1) after running your hand over a convex surface for a minute or so, a flat surface will feel distinctly oblong in shape (*haptic* after-effect); (2) after listening to broadband 'noise' containing a small gap in its frequency spectrum, you will subsequently hear an illusory tone in the absence of any acoustic stimulation, with the tone's pitch corresponding to the gap frequency in the adaptation noise (*auditory Zwicker tone*); (3) after viewing a set of lines tilted counterclockwise, you visually perceive a set of vertical lines to be tilted slightly clockwise (*visual tilt* after-effect). One familiar type of adaptation after-effect is a *visual afterimage*, the illusory spot of light one sees after staring at a bright light or viewing an intense flash of light. Afterimages involve adaptation of neural cells in the retina, whereas most other visual after-effects are thought to arise from adaptation occurring within the visual cortex.

Perceptual after-effects can be expressed by temporary changes in sensory threshold (*reduced sensitivity*) or by temporary changes in the experienced quality of a clearly detectable stimulus (*altered perception*); whether experienced as reduced sensitivity or altered perception, after-effects are typically limited to stimuli similar to the adapting stimulus. To illustrate the various forms after-effects may take, consider the visual consequences of adaptation to an array of high-contrast dots moving rightwards within a circular aperture (Fig. A3). Immediately following adaptation, three after-effects may be experienced depending on the 'test' stimulus viewed immediately following adaptation: (1) low-contrast dots

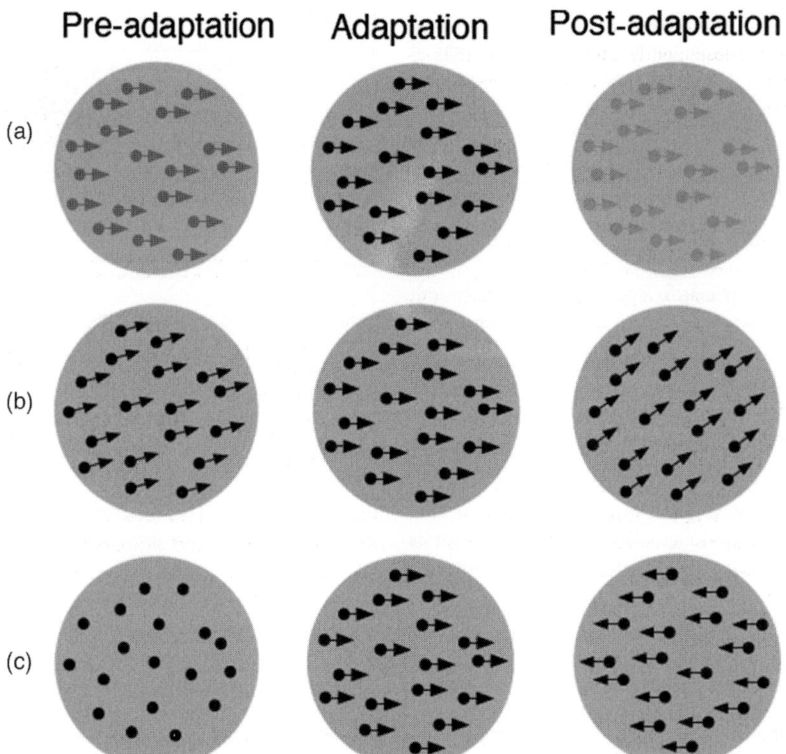

Fig. A3. After-effects of adaptation to visual motion. Schematic showing three visual after-effects produced by adaptation to motion in a given direction (rightward in this example). (a). Ordinarily visible low-contrast dots moving rightwards (pre-adaptation) are more difficult to see and, in the limit, may be rendered temporarily invisible (post-adaptation) following adaptation to high contrast dots moving rightward (adaptation). (b). Dots moving slightly up and to the right (pre-adaptation) appear to move even more upward (post-adaptation) following adaptation to dots moving rightwards (adaptation). (c). Stationary dots (pre-adaptation) appear to move leftwards (post-adaptation) following adaptation to rightward moving dots (adaptation). This third after-effect is what is usually referred to as the motion after-effect or the waterfall illusion.

moving in the same direction become more difficult to see (reduced sensitivity); (2) the perceived direction of motion of high-contrast dots may be distorted away from the direction experienced during adaptation (altered perception); (3) stationary dots can appear to drift in a direction opposite to that experienced during adaptation (altered perception). In contemporary parlance, this third after-effect is typically called the *motion after-effect* or, sometimes, the waterfall illusion in recognition of its having been observed and described by Robert Addams in 1834 after staring at the Falls of Foyers in Scotland. Earlier, suggestive accounts of the motion after-effect can be found in the writings of Aristotle (*c.*330 BC) and of Lucretius (*c.*56 BC).

Most, but not all, visual after-effects dissipate in less than a minute unless one postpones viewing the test stimulus by closing the eyes immediately following adaptation. With eyes closed, an ordinarily brief after-effect can survive an unusually long post-adaptation period and still be experienced. This survival in the absence of stimulation is called *storage*, and it implies that recovery from adaptation is an active process and not simply passive recovery from neural fatigue caused by prolonged stimulation. Some after-effects, specifically those involving the conjunction of visual attributes such as form and colour, can persist for days or even weeks following adaptation. Best known of these contingent after-effects is the *McCollough effect*, in which prolonged exposure to, say, red horizontal contours and green vertical contours subsequently causes achromatic horizontal and vertical contours to appear greenish and reddish, respectively.

A number of perceptual after-effects, including the motion after-effect, are characterized by an opponent quality, meaning that a neutral stimulus temporarily takes on the quality of a stimulus opposite in character to the one experienced during adaptation. A classic example of an opponent after-effect is the temperature illusion described by John Locke in his *Essay Concerning Human Understanding*: after immersing your hand in cool (warm) water for a period of time, water of neutral temperature will feel warm (cool) to that hand. In vision, a white surface can look yellowish following exposure to a genuinely blue surface; another example of after-images, these illusory colours tend to be fleeting but compelling (Fig. A4A). Opponent after-effects can be induced not only by adaptation to colour and to motion but also by adaptation to more complex visual forms (Rhodes et al. 2004). Thus, for example, exposure to a picture of a male face causes a subsequently viewed gender-neutral face briefly to resemble a female face (Fig. A4B).

Perceptual after-effects are frequently deployed to infer the response properties of neural 'channels' responsive to the adaptation stimulus. Used for this purpose, adaptation after-effects can be characterized as the psychologist's microelectrode (Frisby 1979), since adaptation is being used to probe the neural representation of sensory information. In vision, for example, after-effects produced by adaptation to gratings (patterns comprising parallel light and dark bars) are strongest when the grating viewed during adaptation is similar or identical to the grating viewed during testing. The selectivity of after-effects associated with grating adaptation presumably reflects the involvement of neurons selectively sensitive to contour size and contour orientation. Many after-effects, grating after-effects included, also transfer between the eyes, meaning that adaptation can be confined to one eye and, yet, the after-effect can be observed using the other, non-adapted eye. This after-effect characteristic, called *interocular transfer*, points to a central, binocular site of adaptation. Moreover, some visual after-effects, including the motion after-effect, are especially strong when attention is maintained on the adaptation stimulus; conversely, distracting attention away from an adapting stimulus can produce a weak, shorter-lived after-effect.

Perceptual after-effects could be construed as evidence implicating design flaws in sensory processing, flaws leading to misperception of objects or events in the world. In fact, however, perceptual after-effects are probably side effects of an adaptive process whereby sensory systems continuously adjust their dynamic ranges, allowing sensitivity and discrimination to be optimized for prevailing stimulus conditions. Viewed in this light, perceptual after-effects are useful tools for examining the nature of perceptual coding schemes employed by the human brain (Leopold et al. 2001).

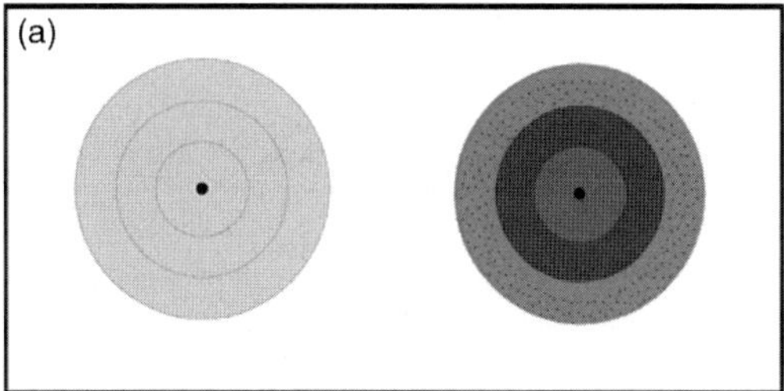

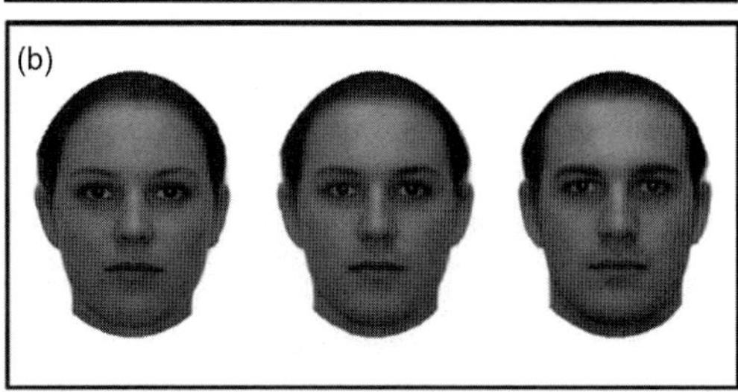

Fig. A4. Opponent visual after-effects. (a) Colour afterimages. The three concentric circles on the left are identical in colour. To colour these circles, stare for 20 s at the small black dot in the middle of the three coloured circles on the right, holding your fixation as steady as possible. At the end of this adaptation period, shift your gaze to the black dot in the centre of the uncoloured figure on the left. The illusory colours you experience should be the complements to the real colours in the adaptation figure. (b) Face adaptation. The middle photograph constitutes a gender-neutral face, and the two photographs on either side of the neutral face are versions biased toward female (left) and toward male (right). Maintain fixation on the right-hand photograph for 20 s or so and then look at the middle photograph—for the first few seconds, it should look more 'female'. Next, adapt for 20 s to the left-hand photograph and notice how the appearance of the gender-neutral face now looks more 'male' (see Colour Plate 1). Photographs courtesy of Tamara Watson and Colin Clifford, University of Sydney.

Perceptual after-effects may also be used to study the neural concomitants of perceptual awareness, based on the following line of reasoning. Most after-effects are stronger following longer periods of adaptation. Thus, for example, 60 s of adaptation to visual motion produces a more vivid, long-lasting motion after-effect than does 30 s of adaptation. Now suppose one adapts to motion for 60 s, but during that adaptation period one is unaware of the motion for a substantial portion of the time. (Awareness of an adapting stimulus can be abolished by any of several means, including *binocular rivalry, *motion-induced blindness, or visual crowding—see Kim and Blake 2005.) Now, following adaptation without continuous awareness, we measure the strength of the resulting after-effect. If the after-effect is reduced in magnitude relative to the condition where awareness was continuous, then we conclude that the absence of visual awareness of the motion was accompanied by a reduction in the effective neural strength of that adapting stimulus. The site of adaptation, in other words, resides somewhere within the visual nervous system beyond a point where neural signals involved in awareness are being registered. But if an after-effect grows to full strength despite interrupted awareness of the adaptation stimulus, we are led to conclude that the underlying neural adaptation transpires within brain areas that precede those critical for visual awareness. This logic has been applied to a number of different adaptation after-effects, and the results vary depending on the complexity of the visual adaptation stimulus. Thus, for example, the face adaptation after-effect described above occurs only when an observer is consciously aware of seeing the face during adaptation; when the face is erased from conscious awareness, the after-effect is abolished (Moradi et al. 2005). On the other hand, the tilt after-effect generated by adaptation to simple, oriented gratings occurs even when the adaptation pattern is suppressed from awareness. For further discussion of the use of adaptation after-effects as a tool for identifying neural *correlates of consciousness, see Blake and He (2005).

RANDOLPH BLAKE

Blake, R. and He, S. (2005). 'Visual adaptation as a tool for studying the neural correlates of conscious visual awareness'. In Clifford, C. and Rhodes, G. (eds) *Fitting the Mind to the World*.

Frisby, J. P. (1979). *Seeing: Illusion, Brain and Mind*.

Kim, C. Y. and Blake, R. (2005). 'Psychophysical magic: rendering the visible "invisible"'. *Trends in Cognitive Sciences*, 9.

Leopold, D. A., O'Toole, A. J., Vetter, T., and Blanz, V. (2001). 'Prototype referenced shape encoding revealed by high-level after-effects'. *Nature Neuroscience*, 4.

Moradi, F., Koch, C., and Shimojo, S. (2005). 'Face adaptation depends on seeing the face'. *Neuron*, 45.

Rhodes, G., Jeffery, L., Watson, T. L., Jaquet, E., Winkler, C., and Clifford, C. W. G. (2004). 'Orientation-contingent face after-effects and implications for face-coding mechanisms'. *Current Biology*, 14.

afterimage See AFTER-EFFECTS, PERCEPTUAL

agnosia Historically, the study of ventral visual agnosia is often associated with Lissauer's description of *Seelenblindheit*, or 'psychic blindness', in 1890. Agnosia (a term later coined by Sigmund Freud) is a relatively rare neuropsychological disorder characterized by an inability to recognize and/or identify visual items that are nevertheless detected. Agnosia can be limited to one sensory modality such as vision or hearing, to one feature such as shape or colour, or to particular categories such as faces or words. It can occur in the absence of deficits in elementary sensory processing or other cognitive/intellectual abilities. For example, a person with agnosia may have difficulty recognizing an object as a clock or identifying a sound as a sneeze, but retain the ability to copy a picture of a clock or mimic the sound of a sneeze. Agnosia can result from a number of neurological events such as stroke, *dementia, or anoxia and is usually caused by damage to the occipital, temporal, or parietal areas of the brain (see BRAIN DAMAGE).

Agnosia is defined as the conscious awareness of an item or its features but without conscious awareness of its identity. The study of this syndrome has revealed several intriguing findings that have relevance for questions about *binding in conscious awareness (see also BALINT'S SYNDROME AND FEATURE BINDING). In the present entry we will limit our discussion to visual agnosias produced by ventral cortical involvement, areas that are believed to process 'what' is present.

No standard taxonomy or universal agreement exists for distinguishing differences within and/or between distinct types of agnosia. However, broad classifications are generally accepted. Most neuropsychologists would agree that agnosia can be classified according to Lissauer's distinction: either *apperceptive* or *associative*. That is, individuals with apperceptive agnosia are impaired in their ability to perceptually integrate or organize incoming information (above the level of an elementary sensory impairment; sometimes called *visual form agnosia*—see Benson and Greenberg 1969 and Farah 2004—while individuals with associative agnosia retain the ability to integrate sensory information normally but suffer from problems of attribution or association ('a normal percept stripped of its meaning'—Teuber). Both types are produced by bilateral occipital–temporal lesions, although unilateral damage can produce some variants.

Humphreys and Riddoch (1987) have further divided the agnosias into five sub-classes: (1) *shape agnosia*, in which contours in the visual field are fragmented by minute cortically induced scotomas obscuring the continuity of contours (although see Vecera and Gilds 1998, who have shown that normal observers easily resolve stimuli that simulate these scotomas, suggesting that mechanisms that normally integrate fragments into contours may not be operating in shape agnosia); (2) *integrative agnosia*, an intermediate visual problem in which primary vision is intact and contours and other object features are accurately seen but accurate integration is disrupted; (3) *transformation agnosia*, in which perceptual integration of an object is intact, but the object cannot be matched from different views; (4) *semantic agnosia*, in which perceptual integration of the object is intact but the memory representation that supports knowledge of an object's function and meaning are damaged; and (5) *semantic access agnosia*, in which both the perceptual and memory representations are intact but have been isolated from one another through disconnection of processing pathways.

There are also other more specific agnosias that affect categories of visual stimuli, such as *prosopagnosia* (face blindness) and *topographical agnosia* (place blindness). Pure *alexia* or *word form agnosia* has also been placed in this category (Farah 2004). In such cases patients can only read words in a letter-by-letter fashion even though they can write out complete sentences (which then must be read letter-by-letter at a later time). In addition, perception of features associated with ventral encoding can be disrupted separately, such as orientation, colour, and size.

The main thread running through all of these agnosias is that they cannot be attributed solely to primary visual loss or the absence of perceiving sensory information in the visual field. Rather, they change the contents of perceptual awareness by disrupting some form of integration, whether integration of parts into unitary shapes (apperceptive) or integration of form and function (associative).

Shape agnosia and integrative agnosia demonstrate that perception of individual parts of a stimulus that are normally seen as a self-contained, whole unit need not emerge into a unitary shape in awareness. It is important to note that patients with these agnosias have no difficulty with spatially locating or tracing these parts, so it is not the case that a normally unified set of parts has become spatially distinct or transformed. Rather, a mechanism that produces an integrated global form, normally working in parallel with local processing of parts, seems to be disrupted. There is also no indication that the global and local forms are integrated at a preconscious level in this type of agnosia, since unlike normal observers no interference from one level of perceptual organization on responses to the other has been found. Thus, it does not appear that parts are integrated before awareness and that only the parts enter awareness in such cases. This may be the case in ventral simultanagnosia, word form agnosia, and prosopagnosia as well (see Bentin et al. 2007), in which configural processing deficits have been demonstrated.

Feature agnosias appear to be quite different, however. Even though the orientation or colour of an object may be perceptually absent in these types of agnosia, there is evidence that they are nevertheless coded implicitly (although at least partially separate). For instance, patient D. F. studied by Milner and Goodale (1995) could not accurately match the orientation and size of lines and objects by sight but was able to use these features to guide hand movements. Likewise, a patient with colour agnosia reported by Heywood and Cowey (1999) could discriminate isoluminant objects above chance levels but did not explicitly report seeing colour (see ACHROMATOPSIA, CEREBRAL).

Associative agnosia also has relevance for the study of integration mechanisms. Normally, once perception of an object occurs, its meaning is automatically registered. But the associative agnosias demonstrate that this need not be the case. The perception of an object does not automatically 'afford' its function (contrary to claims of theories of direct perception by the influential vision scientist James Gibson and his contemporaries). Whether the semantics of a shape are disrupted due to direct damage to memory representations that contain functional information (*semantic agnosia*) or due to a disconnection between intact perceptual and memory representations (*semantic access agnosia*), the consequences are the same: object function and object perception are independent and require integration to account for normal visual experience.

It is also revealing that even when semantic access agnosia is severe, object representations can influence early visual processing. In a study reported by Peterson et al. (2000) a patient with a nearly complete loss of object identity and function was nevertheless influenced by objects in a figure/ground segmentation task. A series of black and white stimuli were presented. On a subset of trials, unknown to both the patient and a group of normal controls, one side of the contour that divided these regions was the lines forming an object (e.g. the silhouette of the right side of a lamp). All participants were simply asked to choose which colour (black or white) appeared more as the figure against a background defined by the other colour. The colour with the object contour was more likely to be chosen as figure compared to contours that were not associated with an object, and equally likely to be chosen as figure by both normals and the agnosia patient. These findings demonstrate that intact memory representations of objects can continue to influence early visual processing even in a person with associative agnosia. Thus, the ascending pathways from object perception to object memory can be disconnected without affecting the descending pathways from object memory to perceptual organization.

In sum, the evidence from the study of visual agnosia has helped to isolate certain features, categories, and concepts that are in need of integration in order to account for the seemingly automatic perception that normal observers attain of a unified visual world. They also demonstrate that intact detection of items in a visual display, including their proper locations, sizes, and orientations is not sufficient to produce either an integrated perceptual representation or semantic knowledge of that representation. Something more must be added to account for the unity of visual experience, namely integration mechanisms that bind together different information into an organized and useful conscious mosaic.

THOMAS VAN VLEET AND LYNN C. ROBERTSON

Benson, D. F. and Greenberg, J. P. (1969). 'Visual form agnosia'. *Archives of Neurology*, 20.

Bentin, S., DeGutis, J. M., D'Esposito, M., and Robertson, L. C. (2007). 'Too many trees to see the forest: performance, ERP and fMRI manifestations of integrative congenital prosopagnosia'. *Journal of Cognitive Neuroscience*, 19.

Farah, M. J. (2004). *Visual Agnosia*.

Heywood, C. A. and Cowey, A. (1999). 'Cerebral achromatopsia'. In Humphreys, G. W. (ed.) *Case Studies in the Neuropsychology of Vision*.

Humphreys, G. W. and Riddoch, M. J. (1987). *To See But Not To See*.

Milner, A. D. and Goodale, M. A. (1995). *The Visual Brain in Action*.

Peterson, M. S., de Gelder, B., Rapcsak, S. Z., Gerhardstein, P. C., and Bachoud-Levi, A.-C. (2000). 'Object memory effects on figure assignment: conscious object recognition is not necessary or sufficient'. *Vision Research*, 40.

Vecera, S. P. and Gilds, K. S. (1998). 'What processing is impaired in apperceptive agnosia? Evidence from normal subjects'. *Journal of Cognitive Neuroscience*, 10.

akinetopsia Akinetopsia refers to the loss of visual motion perception as a result of *brain damage (Zeki 1991). Electrophysiological recording from *single cells, *functional brain imaging techniques, and the study of the consequences of brain damage have led to considerable success in understanding the neural underpinnings of visual motion perception. The discovery, in 1974, of cortical area MT in the monkey brain provided strong evidence for regional specialization for motion vision (Zeki 2004). The selectivity of neurons in this region to the direction of visual motion led to it being dubbed the 'motion area'. Thereafter, the first case of a patient with a relatively selective and profound deficit in the perception of visual motion, namely cerebral akinetopsia, was reported (Zihl et al. 1983).

Patient L. M., a 43-year-old woman, had suffered bilateral cerebral infarctions in the middle temporal, lateral occipital, and angular gyri, as a result of a superior sagittal sinus thrombosis. Her chief complaint was that she no longer saw movement; moving objects appeared 'restless' or 'jumping around'. Although she could see objects at different locations and distances, she was unable to find out what happened to them between these locations. She was severely handicapped in her daily activities, e.g. she had substantial difficulty in pouring drinks into a cup or glass, because the fluid appeared 'frozen like a glacier'; she could not see the fluid rising and was unable to judge when to stop pouring. Detailed examination found no evidence of motor or somatosensory deficits. Verbal and non-verbal memory performance was in the lower normal range; topographical memory was normal. She ascribed difficulties in copying, drawing from memory, and writing to the discomfort she felt when tracking the trajectory of her own right hand. Visual fields were full for light, colour, and form targets, and there were no signs of visual neglect or impaired simultaneous vision. Visual acuity, stereopsis, spatial and temporal contrast sensitivity, colour vision, and form perception were normal. Visual identification and recognition of objects, faces, and places were preserved. Formal testing of motion vision indeed suggested that L. M. suffered from a selective loss of movement vision.

Motion processing is multifaceted and includes deriving the speed and direction of moving targets, judging the direction of motion by a moving observer from optic flow signals, and extracting shape boundaries from motion signals. Its ubiquitous role in vision suggests it is unsurprising that akinetopsic observers display a number of motion-related deficits.

Motion vision can be assessed with conventional grating patterns. These are sinusoidally, spatially modulated luminance patterns with varying contrast and periodicity. L. M.'s chief impairment was in the ability to discriminate the properties of motion, e.g. the direction or speed of a moving grating. Although L. M. has been dubbed 'motion-blind', she retains rudimentary movement vision, e.g. she can discriminate speed and direction of motion of high-contrast gratings at low speeds. However, the minimum contrast at which normal observers detect the presence of a grating is comparable to that needed to discriminate its direction of motion. When an akinetopsic observer can detect the motion of a grating pattern, a 20-fold increase in contrast may be required before the direction in which it is moving can be judged correctly.

A further standard psychophysical stimulus to assess motion vision is the random dot kinematogram in which a group of randomly distributed dots are displaced coherently against a background of spatially and temporally uncorrelated dots which constitute noise. Even at relatively high level of noise, normal observers have no difficulty in detecting the overall direction of motion. L. M. requires a considerably higher proportion of coherently moving dots to judge the direction of motion reliably. Furthermore, when kinetic boundaries were produced by differential motion of adjacent groups of dots, L. M. was impaired at extracting the shape defined by such boundaries, i.e. at perceiving structure-from-motion.

This ubiquitous nature of motion vision is also reflected in surprising dissociations following brain damage that have been reported between different aspects of motion processing, suggesting that several varieties of the disorder may exist. For example, despite the severity of L. M.'s disorder, she is able to perceive some complex forms of motion normally. Thus, when a moving pattern of dots, created by attaching small lights to the joints of an actor filmed in the dark, defines 'biological motion' such as running, squatting, and jumping (so-called Johansson figures), L. M. has no difficulty in readily identifying the action. Deficits in motion perception have now been reported in a number of patients, yet L. M. remains the most extensively studied case. How can we account for such a pattern of impairments?

Cells in early visual areas, such as area *V1, are tuned to the spatial and temporal properties of visual stimuli and respond better to moving than to stationary stimuli. However, a region located in the posterior bank and floor of the caudal superior temporal sulcus of the macaque monkey has been described with a strikingly high proportion of cells that preferentially respond to the direction and speed of stimulus motion. This region, known as area MT (or V5) appears to play a central role in the processing of visual movement. Moreover, neuroimaging of human brains has identified a region, hMT+, located at the temporoparietal–occipital junction. This region is activated by stimuli which also activate area MT of the monkey, suggesting a close functional resemblance. Cells in MT respond to more complex characteristics of motion than those in area V1, which are responsive to the component parts of a complex pattern. In MT, cells respond to the vector sum of the motion of the component parts and thus code global rather than local pattern motion. Similarly, in people, hMT+ adapts to motion of complex patterns while lower visual areas adapt to motion of the components (Huk and Heeger 2001). Both MT and hMT+ respond to illusory afterimages of visual motion and the latter is also activated when observers view 'implied motion', where motion is represented by static pictorial cues. Moreover, the perceptual after-effects are abolished when *transcranial magnetic stimulation (TMS) is applied to hMT+. In the monkey, microstimulation of area MT during the viewing of a display of moving dots influenced judgements of the direction of their motion. Similarly, hMT+ is active during the viewing of moving dot displays. Activity is greater for coherent, compared with random and incoherent, motion and the increases linearly as the coherence of the dots increases.

There is thus considerable evidence that activity of hMT+ parallels both the response properties of single neurons in MT of the monkey and perception. In other words, hMT+ is a likely candidate for the neural *correlate of phenomenal consciousness and its ablation leads to the clinical condition of cerebral akinetopsia. Further evidence that this is so is provided by the effects of experimental ablation of area MT in the monkey. As with L. M., early studies showed that neither contrast sensitivity nor the ability to saccade to a moving target were impaired by lesions to MT. However, the ability to detect structure-from-motion and shearing motion are substantially impaired. In addition, monkeys with MT lesions have difficulty in detecting the direction of motion of coherently moving dots in an otherwise random dot display even when the proportion of correlated dots is considerably increased. Their thresholds, as measured by the minimum coherence required for consistently accurate judgement of direction of motion, are comparable with that of patient L. M.

Nevertheless, unlike L. M., impairments in monkeys are generally short-lived and followed by rapid recovery to essentially normal levels of performance. A possible reason for this is that L. M.'s lesions are the result of a cerebrovascular accident and are likely to invade territory which surrounds the location of the putative human MT area. This will include other areas known to process motion, e.g. those that show selectivity to radial and circular motion patterns, crucial perhaps for the processing of optic flow. Certainly, the perception of biological motion appears to involve an area located within the ventral bank of the occipital extent of the superior temporal sulcus (STS) which is selectively activated during viewing of light-point-defined moving figures.

In conclusion, akinetopsia provides a clear example of selective loss of phenomenal consciousness for visual motion. Patient L. M. lost the phenomenal experience of motion and her ability to discriminate the presence and direction of motion was severely impaired. She also lost the ability to perceive shapes defined by motion, but she retained the ability to use biological motion cues which are probably processed by brain areas distinct from those concerned with processing motion of rigid bodies and global motion of a scene.

CHARLES HEYWOOD AND ROBERT W. KENTRIDGE

Huk, A. C. and Heeger, D. J. (2001). 'Pattern-motion responses in human visual cortex'. *Nature Neuroscience*, 5.

Zeki, S. (1991). 'Cerebral akinetopsia (visual motion blindness): a review'. *Brain*, 114.

—— (2004). 'Thirty years of a very special visual area, area V5'. *Journal of Physiology*, 557.

Zihl, J., von Cramon, D., and Mai, N. (1983). 'Selective disturbance of movement vision after bilateral brain damage'. *Brain*, 106.

alien hand See ANARCHIC HAND

alien voices See SCHIZOPHRENIA

alloscopy See OUT-OF-BODY EXPERIENCE

altered state of consciousness The notion of altered states seems intuitively obvious; we are familiar with ourselves and other people falling asleep, waking up, or getting drunk, and it seems obvious that their consciousness is altered in some way. In this everyday sense of the term altered states of consciousness (ASCs) include naturally occurring states such as deep *sleep and *dreaming, pathological states such as mania or coma, and states induced by drugs, *hypnosis, *meditation, and other mental practices.

However, the concept is notoriously difficult to define. If 'consciousness' itself were clearly defined we might start by asking how it is altered, but there is no generally agreed definition of consciousness. When we ask what is altered in an ASC we find that memory, attention, learning, arousal, and other familiar variables are altered; we cannot find something called 'consciousness' that can be measured to see how far it has changed. Nor is there any agreed way of defining and measuring normality, or a normal state of consciousness from which ASCs might differ. People may be confident that they know what is a normal state for them but we do not know whether normal states are the same for everyone, the same for a given person over time, or how far their state has to be altered to count as an ASC.

Attempts to define ASC have nevertheless been made and they fall into two categories. *Objective* definitions rely on observations of the person's physiology or behaviour, or on the method of induction. For example, states can be categorized according to how they were induced (e.g. by a certain drug or a hypnotic procedure). The problem here is that the same drug may have different effects on different people, or a different effect on the same person at different times; a hypnotic procedure may put some people into a deep trance while others are unaffected. This might suggest that it would be better to measure the person's behaviour (e.g. whether they can walk in a straight line, or how responsive they are) or to take physiological measurements (e.g. heart rate, emotional arousal, or brain scans). The problems here are that very few states are associated with discrete physiological changes, and states that are subjectively very different may look similar to an outside observer. For example, someone having a dramatic out-of-body experience may appear to others to be asleep, quietly relaxing, or even carrying on with their normal waking behaviours.

The alternative is to define ASCs *subjectively*, and this is the more common approach (Farthing 1992, Blackmore 2003). Charles Tart, who coined the phrase ASC, defines it as 'a qualitative alteration in the overall pattern of mental functioning, such that the experiencer feels his consciousness is radically different from the way it functions ordinarily' (Tart 1972:1203).

Definitions of this kind seem to capture the basic idea of ASCs but raise problems of their own. For example, experiencers may be quite sure that their consciousness is 'radically different from the way it functions ordinarily' but this is only useful as a definition if they can tell other people about it, at which point the spoken words become another kind of objective data. Is this kind of data preferable? It may be, but there are cases of obvious conflict with how things appear from the outside—think of the staggering drunk with slurred speech who claims to be perfectly sober and about to drive his car, or the first-time marijuana user who grins uncontrollably and giggles at the feeblest joke while claiming to feel no effect. In these cases we may think that an objective definition would be more useful.

Even in cases where the person's own words seem the best guide there are problems. For example some states, such as mystical experiences, are said to be ineffable—that is, no words can really capture how they felt—indeed, this is said to be one of their defining characteristics. This is very curious, because people can agree with each other that they have had similar experiences and insights, without being able to say anything coherent about what it is they have seen. Other states may seem to be describable at the time, but are disrupted by any attempt to speak and are impossible to remember later. This leaves experiencers with the frustrating feeling that they knew at the time how to describe their state but could never do so. Others, such as states induced by *hallucinogenic drugs, may change so quickly that memory is overwhelmed and speech cannot keep pace.

One possible solution is to develop better techniques for communicating from ASCs. For example, in the mid 1960s Timothy Leary and his colleagues developed the 'experiential typewriter' which recorded sensations, emotions, colours, and many other variables, but produced masses of data that was hard to use. Another approach is to train people to become better at exploring and observing their own states. Highly experienced explorers of ASCs are sometimes called *psychonauts* (literally, 'sailors of the psyche'). They may become adept at entering trances, becoming lucid during dreams, using psychedelic drugs, or moving from one state to another, but typically they are more interested in their own personal development than in communicating the results of their explorations to others. At present, drug prohibition makes it difficult to do scientific research with psychonauts, although a great deal of informal research is done and is reported on websites such as www.erowid.org.

One aim of such research might be to map out the universe of possible ASCs and the routes that can be taken between them. There have been many attempts to describe ASCs in terms of multidimensional spaces. An early example is Tart's (1975) space which used the two dimensions of irrationality and ability to hallucinate to describe ordinary dreaming, lucid dreaming, and waking. A more recent example is Hobson's (1999) three-dimensional space, or AIM model, which uses activation energy, internal or external information source, and cholinergic/aminergic balance to position different ASCs. Although useful for some purposes, these models are highly simplified and cannot capture the complexity of state space. The trouble is we have no idea even how to think about this hypothetical multidimensional space. Apart from its unknown size, dimensionality, and complexity there are two interesting questions that need answering. One is whether all areas of the theoretical space can be occupied, or whether some are forbidden. Tart thought that large areas of his space were uninhabitable or unstable so that a person's state would always end up in one of the recognized clusters. He called these 'discrete states of consciousness'. Just how many states are like this we still do not know. Another unanswered question concerns the possible routes between states. We do not know whether it is possible to move from any state to any other state, whether there are multiple routes between states, or whether some states are effectively isolated from each other.

Given all these problems, Tart (1972) argued that normal science might be unable to understand ASCs using conventional methods and that we need a new kind of 'state-specific science' in which scientists work and communicate with each other while in various ASCs. Although no such science has developed formally, it is possible that psychonauts are carrying out such work informally.

The most extreme doubts about the concept of ASCs are expressed by those who argue that certain states are not ASCs at all. For example, there have been lengthy debates between 'state' and 'non-state' theories of hypnosis. Proponents of non-state theories argue that the behaviours seen during hypnosis are best explained in terms of compliance and role-playing and that no altered state is involved at all, even though some hypnotic subjects are convinced that they enter a completely different state of consciousness from their normal one. Others have argued that dreams are not ASCs or are not even experiences. One reason is that, upon waking, all we have is the memory of a dream that has already ended. Another reason depends on the definition of an ASC. On that given above, an experiencer must 'feel his consciousness is radically different', but in normal dreams we do not realize this. Only during lucid dreams do we realize that we are dreaming and therefore that our consciousness is different from normal.

The concept of an ASC, which seems so obvious on first acquaintance, turns out to be yet another aspect of consciousness that is fraught with paradoxes and unknowns.

SUSAN BLACKMORE

Blackmore, S. (2003). *Consciousness: An Introduction.*

Farthing, G. W. (1992). *The Psychology of Consciousness.*

Hobson, J. A. (1999). *Dreaming as Delirium: How the Brain Goes Out of its Mind.*

Tart, C. T. (1972). 'States of consciousness and state-specific sciences'. *Science*, 176.

—— (1975). *States of Consciousness.*

amnesia The study of amnesia has played an important part in research on the role of conscious awareness in memory, in particular through the concept of implicit memory.

1. Types of amnesia
2. Explicit and implicit memory
3. Psychogenic amnesia
4. Amnesia and consciousness

1. Types of amnesia

In the early years of the 20th century, the Swiss doctor Claparède (1911) conducted a simple experiment on one of his densely amnesic patients. On one occasion, when conducting his morning round and shaking hands with this patient, he secreted a pin in his hand. On the next day, the lady in question refused to shake hands, although she did not know why. She appeared to have memory, but no conscious awareness. To place this in context we need to discuss more recent research on amnesia, which is of two distinct kinds, *organic amnesia* which results from *brain damage, and *functional amnesia* which is typically of emotional origin. Organic amnesia itself is of two types, *retrograde amnesia* in which the patient loses access to earlier memories, and *anterograde amnesia* where the problem is one of establishing new memories. Functional amnesias are more varied and can involve either.

Retrograde amnesia commonly results from brain trauma such as might occur in a road traffic accident. The patient typically knows who they are, but loses access to information leading up to the accident, with the gap sometimes extending to many years before. The extent of the amnesia may shrink as the patient recovers, indicating that the memories are still stored, but cannot be accessed. However, the few moments before the accident are typically not recovered, probably because this memory trace never adequately consolidated, and hence was rapidly lost (Levin and Hanten 2004).

Anterograde amnesia occurs when the patient is unable to retain memory of new events or experiences, a process known as *episodic memory* which allows what Endel Tulving refers to as 'mental time travel', the capacity to 'relive' an event and use that information to plan the future. The classic case of amnesia is that of H. M. who was treated for intractable *epilepsy. It is often possible to alleviate epileptic seizures by removing scar tissue within the brain that triggers the epileptic attack. In H. M.'s case the damage involved both the left and right hemispheres in the region surrounding the hippocampus, a structure that plays an important role in memory. Although his epilepsy was relieved, he became densely amnesic. You could talk with him all morning and he would not recognize you in the afternoon. He could not commit verbal or visual material to memory, and had great difficulty learning the way around his new house, and learning where various objects were kept. He could read the same magazine repeatedly without finding it familiar, and was unable to keep track of a film or a sports game, or to know whether his favourite team was doing well or badly that season. Public events left no trace, so he did not know who the current President of the United States was (Milner 1966). While it remains controversial as to precisely what areas are involved in long-term *memory, it is clear that the hippocampus and surrounding regions play a crucial role in forming new memories, while the temporal lobes of the brain are important for storage, and the *frontal lobes for encoding and retrieving memories (see Tranel and Damasio 2002 for a more detailed account).

Neurosurgeons now take great care to ensure that they do not produce another H. M., but unfortunately there are many other causes of amnesia (O'Connor and Verfaellie 2004). These include alcoholic Korsakoff syndrome, in which alcohol abuse leads to thiamine deficiency resulting in a confusional state and subsequently amnesia. Another source of dense amnesia is encephalitis resulting from brain infection, as in the case of Clive Wearing, a very talented musician and expert on early music, who had the misfortune to develop encephalitis as a result of infection by the herpes simplex virus, a virus that many people carry, but which rarely leads to anything more serious than cold sores. However, very occasionally it can cross the blood–brain barrier with potentially disastrous consequences. Clive became so densely amnesic that he could not remember anything extending over more than seconds, and was perpetually convinced he had just woken up. He had lost access to much of his general knowledge; e.g. he did not know who had written *Romeo and Juliet*, and failed to recognize the Cambridge college where he had studied for four years. His musical skills were, however, remarkably preserved. He could conduct his choir and could read a musical score, singing and accompanying himself on the harpsichord, providing a very dramatic illustration of the fact that memory is an alliance of separable components rather than a single unitary system (Wilson et al. 1995).

Patients often suffer from both anterograde and retrograde amnesia. One such case involved a distinguished academic who had written his autobiography shortly before an amnesic episode, resulting from alcoholic Korsakoff syndrome. His retrograde amnesia was reflected in the fact that he could remember the events of his early life well, but had very few recent memories, even though he had written them down from memory shortly beforehand.

2. Explicit and implicit memory

Despite Claparède's informal experiment with a pin, it was not until the 1970s that it began to be widely appreciated that even densely amnesic patients were capable of showing normal learning on certain tasks. Elizabeth Warrington and Lawrence Weiskrantz (1968) showed their amnesic patients a list of words and tested for learning in a number of different ways. They found that their patients were very poor at recalling or recognizing the words when tested shortly afterwards, but when given the first few letters and asked to 'guess' what the word was, the patients were likely to produce a word they had seen, even though they had no recollection of seeing it earlier. Clearly something had been learned. This method of testing for learning by observing its impact on a later task is known as **priming*, and has been demonstrated many times using both pictures and words with visual and auditory presentation. Priming also occurs with more complex tasks. For example, if the patient is required to read out a list of words, some of which are animals, and then asked to produce as many animal names as possible, the previously presented names are more likely to be evoked, even though the patient has no recollection of having read that word (Schacter and Tulving 1994).

Other instances of the capacity to demonstrate learning from something that cannot be consciously recollected are provided in the case of motor skills, where practice on a task leads to a normal rate of learning, even though the patient thinks on each occasion that the task is being performed for the first time (Brooks and Baddeley 1976). Pleasure and pain can also show evidence of learning, as Claparède's pinprick demonstration indicates. In another study, people were presented with melodies in an unfamiliar style, Korean, and asked to judge their pleasantness. People initially find such melodies unpleasant, but increasing familiarity leads to enhanced pleasantness—an effect that also occurred in amnesic patients, who had no recollection of ever having encountered such a melody before (Johnson et al. 1985).

There is controversy as to whether this wide range of learning effects should be regarded as depending on a single mechanism or system that is preserved in amnesic patients. It seems unlikely, however, that tasks as disparate as the acquisition of a skill such as riding a bicycle, the priming of a word in a category, and *conditioning a response to pain or pleasure can usefully be regarded as representing a single system. What they do have in common, however, is that they do not depend on the episodic memory system that is impaired in amnesia, the system that allows us to retrieve individual memories and to use them to recollect our past and plan our future.

3. Psychogenic amnesia

A theme beloved of writers of stories and film-makers is the man who has 'lost his memory'. This person usually resembles, more or less closely, a case of psychogenic amnesia, a form of amnesia that is associated with stress and the attempt of the mind to deal with it. Its classic form is the *fugue state* which, as its name suggests, implies that the patient is fleeing, usually from some major source of stress. Such patients do not seem to know who they are or where they come from, and while this information is often recovered relatively quickly, the amnesia can sometimes extend for weeks or months. In a review of this disorder, Kopelman (2002) notes that it is often the case that such patients have had some form of organic memory disturbance earlier, although forgetting who you are very rarely occurs in patients whose amnesia is purely organically based.

The fact that psychogenic patients are typically escaping some form of emotional trauma raises the question as to whether the amnesia is 'genuine' or whether the patient is simply malingering; are they unable to recollect their past, or simply unwilling? Some light is thrown on this question by another form of psychogenic amnesia, whereby a violent criminal has no memory for the crime, a situation that is particularly likely to occur in the case of crimes of passion. Kopelman describes the case of a man who discovered that his wife was having an affair with a musician. This led to a furious row with his wife, during which he threatened to kill the musician. He subsequently remembered going to kiss his children goodnight that evening, then nothing until the police arrived in response to a telephone call he had made, confessing that he had stabbed his wife.

The amnesia in this and a number of other similar situations seems unlikely to be motivated by a desire to conceal the crime. In most cases the offenders report a memory loss that lasts only during the time of the offence. Similar memory gaps are sometimes observed in people who are eyewitnesses of a violent incident, for which there is no reason for wilful concealment, thus supporting the view that extreme emotion can cause amnesia for an event. Paradoxically, such an experience can also have the opposite effect, as in *post-traumatic stress disorder* (PTSD) in which the patient suffers from extremely vivid and frightening flashbacks of the traumatic experience. It seems likely that both these, and the amnesic episodes associated with violent crime, are ways in which we try to deal with the effects of extreme emotion.

4. Amnesia and consciousness

What are the implications of amnesia for the nature of consciousness? The amnesias in their various forms can be regarded as disturbances in our capacity to become consciously aware of our past. In the case of a pure anterograde amnesia, the patient may retain conscious access to memory of events up to the onset of the disease, but fail to create consciously accessible new memories of any form; although implicit, unconscious aspects of memory may be normal. In the case of retrograde amnesia, the patient loses access to aspects of the past that have already been acquired. The amnesia can often be patchy, with islands of memory, and may decrease with time, indicating that the problem is not the loss of memories but the loss of access. Psychogenic amnesias are also disturbances of access to earlier memories, in this case depending on emotional factors whereby the patient may be defending themselves from the awareness of a stressful past event. All these tell us something about the way in which our memories become conscious, or in some cases remain unconscious.

ALAN BADDELEY

Baddeley, A. (2002). *Your Memory: A User's Guide.*

Brooks, D. N. and Baddeley, A. D. (1976). 'What can amnesic patients learn?' *Neuropsychologia*, 14.

Claparède, E. (1911). 'Recognition et moïté'. *Archives de Psychologie*, 11.

Johnson, M. K., Kim, J. K., and Risse, G. (1985). 'Do alcoholic Korsakoff syndrome patients acquire affective reactions?' *Journal of Experimental Psychology: Learning, Memory and Cognition*, 11.

Kopelman, M. D. (2002). 'Psychogenic amnesia'. In Baddeley, A. D. et al. (eds) *Handbook of Memory Disorders*, 2nd edn.

Levin, H. S. and Hanten, G. (2004). 'Post traumatic amnesia and residual memory deficit after closed head injury'. In Baddeley, A. D. et al. (eds) *The Essential Handbook of Memory Disorders for Clinicians.*

Milner, B. (1966). 'Amnesia following operation on the temporal lobes'. In Whitty, C. W. M. and Zangwill, O. L. (eds) *Amnesia.*

O'Connor, M. and Verfaellie, M. (2004). 'The amnesic syndrome: overview and subtypes'. In Baddeley, A. D. et al. (eds) *The Essential Handbook of Memory Disorders for Clinicians.*

Schacter, D. L. and Tulving, E. (1994). 'What are the memory systems of 1994?' In Schacter, D. L. and Tulving, E. (eds) *Memory Systems.*

Tranel, D. and Damasio, A. R. (2002). 'Neurobiological foundations of human memory'. In Baddeley, A. D. et al. (eds) *Handbook of Memory Disorders*, 2nd edn.

Warrington, E. K. and Weiskrantz, L. (1968). 'New methods of testing long-term retention with special reference to amnesic patients'. *Nature*, 217.

Wilson, B. A., Baddeley, A. D., and Kapur, N. (1995). 'Dense amnesia in professional musician following herpes simplex virus and encephalitis'. *Journal of Clinical and Experimental Neuropsychology*, 17.

anaesthesia and consciousness

Everybody wants to have a hand in a great discovery. All I will do is to give you a hint or two as to names, or the name, to be applied to the state produced and the agent. The state should, I think, be called 'Anaesthesia' [from the Greek word *anaisthēsia*, 'lack of sensation']. . . . The adjective will be 'Anaesthetic.' Thus we might say the state of Anaesthesia, or the anaesthetic state.

Oliver Wendell Holmes, 21 November 1846

This quotation is from a letter to William Thomas Green Morton, who is credited with the first public demonstration of the use of ether surgical anaesthesia at the Massachusetts General Hospital, 16 October 1846.

1. Anaesthesiology: a practical need to understand consciousness
2. Cellular basis of anaesthesia
3. Anaesthesia meets neuroanatomy: towards multiple sites and multiple mechanisms
4. Neural correlates of loss of consciousness (LOC)
5. Consciousness is information integration
6. Conclusions

1. Anaesthesiology: a practical need to understand consciousness

The job of the anaesthetist (or the anesthesiologist, in the USA) involves rendering patients unconscious for surgery. Anaesthetics are molecules that have three fundamental properties: (1) low doses cause *amnesia; (2) moderate doses cause unconsciousness; and (3) higher doses cause immobility to painful surgical stimulation. Patients are considered unconscious during surgery when they fail to move in response to a verbal stimulation, or to a good shake. They are considered adequately anaesthetized when they fail to move in response to surgical stimulation. Much research is directed toward understanding the mechanisms by which anaesthetics prevent movement in response to a painful stimulation. Such studies investigate the end-point of relatively deep surgical anaesthesia, which is known as the *MAC response*. In essence, this measure of anaesthetic potency determines the minimum alveolar (i.e. lung) concentration (MAC) of an inhaled anaesthetic agent needed to prevent movement in 50% of subjects in response to a painful surgical stimulation. This standard of anaesthetic potency was developed by Eger et al. in 1965 (see Sonner et al. 2003).

The clinical definition of anaesthetic-induced unconsciousness can fail miserably if the anaesthetic technique involves the commonplace use of drugs that cause muscle paralysis. Paralysed patients are rendered unable to move and thus can appear anaesthetized, yet can (on rare occasions) remain conscious. This awareness during anaesthesia is often the most traumatic and horrific experience of a person's life (see ANAESTHESIA, AWARENESS UNDER). Thus, anaesthetists would like to have a monitor of consciousness.

Currently, the gold standard for assessing consciousness during surgery is the *isolated forearm technique* (IFT). In this technique, a tourniquet is placed on a person's arm before a muscle relaxant is given. Then, during surgery, the anaesthetist can simply ask the patient to move their hand if they are awake. As effective as the IFT is, however, it is infrequently used because it is relatively labour intensive. Thus anaesthetists would prefer a consciousness monitor that can be placed on the patient and forgotten about until it alarms to indicate an inadvertent return to consciousness. Such a monitor does not yet exist. Many commercial monitors have been developed to inform the anaesthetist about how drugs are affecting the brain. However, these devices tend to be poor at detecting the exact transition between conscious and unconscious. They perform poorly when compared directly with the IFT. It is hoped, therefore, that elucidating the nature of human consciousness will greatly accelerate the development of an effective clinical monitor of consciousness.

2. Cellular basis of anaesthesia

In 1901 two German scientists (working independently) discovered that the amount of an anaesthetic molecule dissolved in olive oil correlated with a particular agent's ability to block the swimming of tadpoles. This observation became known as the *Meyer–Overton hypothesis*. It suggested the logic that if anaesthetic potency correlates with an agent's ability to dissolve in olive oil (a lipid), then clearly anaesthesia must work by affecting lipid membranes of the brain and spine. This thinking is a classic example of the scientific blunder where one assumes that correlation implies causation. The Meyer–Overton hypothesis dominated thinking in mechanism of anaesthesia research for nearly a century and numerous lipid-based theories of anaesthetic action evolved from this correlation.

However, in 1984 Nicholas P. Franks and William R. Lieb demonstrated a similar correlation between anaesthetic potency and the ability of an agent to competitively inhibit firefly luciferase, a pure soluble protein (i.e. no lipids involved). This seminal observation suggested anaesthetics might work through specific interactions with cellular protein channels, such as those that control neurotransmission, rather than through some non-specific disturbance of cell membranes. A plethora of studies detailing anaesthetic inhibition and enhancement of numerous ligand gated ion channels (proteins) have since been forthcoming.

The cellular targets most closely linked with anaesthetic mechanisms involve anaesthetic-induced enhancement of inhibitory currents mediated by gamma-aminobutyric acid (GABA) and glycine protein channels, anaesthetic-induced reductions of excitatory currents mediated by glutamate and acetylcholine protein channels, and most recently anaesthetic-induced enhancement of background potassium leak currents (causing intracellular hyperpolarization, an effect which reduces a cell's chances of firing an action potential). These are generally considered the most plausible cellular mechanisms accounting for anaesthetic action, although alternative hypotheses still exist. For instance, anaesthetics affect numerous G-protein-coupled receptors, which can change the modulatory state of the brain. Anaesthetics change the shear stress factors within the lipid membrane and thus may affect multiple membrane bound proteins. Anaesthetics affect voltage-gated ion channels as well as mitochondrial complex proteins and could thus affect cellular energy states. Anaesthetics also affect gap junctions and so interfere with fast electrical cell-to-cell communication, perhaps stopping long-range synchrony.

3. Anaesthesia meets neuroanatomy: towards multiple sites and multiple mechanisms

For years a unitary theory of anaesthetic action was sought. The unitary theory proposed that anaesthetics exert their effects by dose-dependently interacting with a singular site within the central nervous system (CNS) through a singular mechanism (such as the lipid membrane). Thus many attempted to discover '*the* mechanism of anaesthesia'. However, in 1994, Ira Rampil discovered that the dose of anaesthesia needed to prevent a rat from moving in response to a painful stimulation was the same in normal and decerebrate rats. Rampil thus proved that the site mediating the MAC response, the standard of anaesthetic potency, was the spine and not the brain! This finding established that a unitary site of anaesthetic action could not exist and that anaesthetic mechanisms of action must be understood relative to the specific neuroanatomy being affected by the drugs and relative to the specific anaesthetic end-point being examined.

Another example of anaesthetics exerting their specific behavioural effects through interactions with specific CNS sites comes from studies of long-term *memory for aversive learning. Evidence implicates the basolateral amygdala, a brain site involved in memory consolidation and emotional processing, as being important for the long-term memory blocking effect of a number of anaesthetic agents including the benzodiazepines, propofol, sevoflurane, and nitrous oxide. In fact, animals with small bilateral lesions of the basolateral amygdala fail to show the expected long-term memory impairment usually caused by systemically delivered anaesthetic agents.

Today, the multiple manifestations of the anaesthetic state are considered to occur because anaesthetics act at multiple sites in the CNS and these site-specific effects are likely mediated through a multitude of various different cellular mechanisms. These components of anaesthesia correspond to clinical end-points such as the loss of memory, loss of consciousness, loss of spontaneous movement, and suppression of reflexes. Research attention has been directed toward understanding how each of these various components of anaesthesia might work. These components can be dissociated somewhat and studied individually because anaesthetics can be titrated to precise low sub-anaesthetic doses. Thus, to study the consciousness-ablating effects of anaesthetics, one can give anaesthetics at low consciousness-blocking doses and compare results between conditions where consciousness is just allowed to be present and where it is just taken away with the anaesthetic.

4. Neural correlates of loss of consciousness (LOC)

A basic understanding of how anaesthesia affects human cerebral blood flow and cerebral metabolic rate is now readily available as common textbook material. In general, most anaesthetic agents decrease global cerebral metabolism in a dose-dependent manner with variable effects on global cerebral blood flow. The level of the metabolic depression at LOC (globally around 30–60%) is comparable to that found with sleep and the persistent vegetative state (see BRAIN DAMAGE). Inasmuch as consciousness is an energy-dependent process, then LOC with anaesthesia may simply be due to the ability of most anaesthetic agents to suppress global brain metabolism below some critical threshold that is required to maintain a conscious waking state. Even if this is true, the question still remains: what is the last critical circuit that 'turns off' when consciousness is lost as a dose of anaesthesia increases?

An answer to this question may be approached with human brain imaging studies of anaesthesia. The regional effects of a number of anaesthetic agents have been studied with *functional brain imaging in humans at doses near to, or just more than, those required to produce unconsciousness.

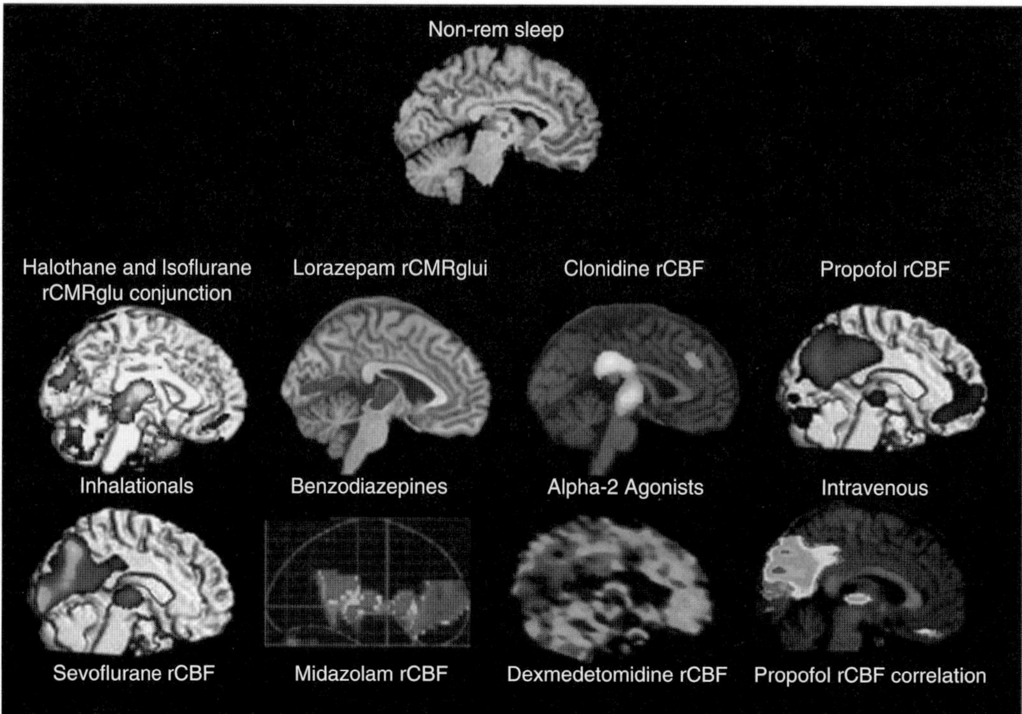

Fig. A5. The regional effects of anaesthetics on brain function are shown in humans who were given various anaesthetic agents at doses that caused, or nearly caused, a loss of consciousness. The data are from eight different groups of investigators and encompass the study of eight different agents and normal non-REM sleep (as detailed in Alkire and Miller 2005). The agents studied were halothane and isoflurane, lorazepam, clonidine, propofol, sevoflurane, midazolam, dexmedetomidine, and sleep. The regional effects were measured using techniques based on either blood flow or glucose metabolism. The images were reoriented, and resized to allow for easy comparisons between studies. The original colour scales were used. Nevertheless, all images show regional decreases of activity caused by anaesthesia (or sleep) compared to the awake state, except the propofol correlation image, which shows where increasing anaesthetic dose correlates with decreasing blood flow. The figure identifies that the regional suppressive effects of anaesthetics on the thalamus is a common finding associated with anaesthetic-induced unconsciousness and sleep (see Colour Plate 2).

Figure A5 shows data from human studies where anaesthetics are given at or near a LOC end-point. Despite the technical differences between studies, when consciousness is lost with *sleep or anaesthesia, or is nearly lost with anaesthesia, there is a relative decrease in thalamic activity. The relative thalamic effect implies that there is a minimal amount of regional thalamic activity that may be necessary to maintain consciousness and the thalamus or thalamocortical networks thus emerge as potentially important components of the neural *correlate of consciousness.

This commonality between agents led to the development of the *thalamic consciousness switch* hypothesis of anaesthetic-induced unconsciousness. This hypothesis suggests that a dose-related anaesthetic-induced hyperpolarization occurs in thalamocortical network cells (i.e. thalamocortical, corticothalamic, and reticulothalamic cells) that switches these network cells from a tonic firing mode to a burst firing pattern during the transition to unconsciousness. Unconsciousness occurs when a sufficient proportion of network cells switch to the burst firing pattern. This switch is hypothesized to effectively diminish sensory information processing in thalamic and cortical regions, especially layer V of the cortex, and block the long-range secondary corticothalamo-cortical sensory processing likely necessary to generate a conscious percept.

If the thalamus plays a fundamental role in consciousness, then one would expect that impairments of consciousness should occur not only if the thalamus is 'turned off' with anaesthetics, but also if it were lesioned. In fact, impairments of consciousness are known to occur with even relatively small lesions of the thalamus, especially those involving the intralaminar nuclei (ILN). The resolution of the human brain imaging techniques used to date precludes the precise anatomic localization within the thalamus of the thalamic-anaesthesia effect. Nevertheless, the anaesthesia imaging results are consistent with Joseph E. Bogen's (1997) idea about how 'the central core of consciousness is engendered by neuronal activity in and immediately around the ILN of each thalamus'.

The ILN is thought to be an extension of the ascending reticular activating system (ARAS). Anaesthetic effects on the ARAS have long been hypothesized to mediate anaesthetic effects on consciousness, and suppression of activity in brainstem regions is a well-known component of the neuropathology of coma. However, for anaesthesia, suppression of the brainstem is likely not the whole answer. Alemà and colleagues (1966) found that injection of barbiturate into the vertebral arteries, which supply the brainstem, did not result in LOC in humans or in the loss of response to auditory or visual evoked responses. This prompted the authors to conclude, 'In man the most important subcortical structures ultimately responsible for maintenance of the level of consciousness are located rostral to the brainstem, perhaps in the diencephalon.' Nevertheless, these early observations do not necessarily rule out a role for lower brain centres in the control of cortical arousal and anaesthetic effects. Indeed, Devor and Zalkind (2001) found a zone in the mesopontine tegmentum that caused analgesia, atonia, and a loss of consciousness with slow-wave *electroencephalograph (EEG) patterns in rats when this area was microinjected with minute infusions of a barbiturate.

Ultimately, the overlapping regional effect of anaesthetics on the thalamus may be shown to be mediated through the direct effects anaesthetics have on normal sleep pathways. Such an idea would seem to provide a reasonable explanation as to why the regional metabolic suppression of anaesthesia closely parallels the pattern of the regional metabolic suppression seen with non-REM sleep. Alternatively, direct anaesthetic suppression of cortical activity might cause thalamic suppression by blocking corticothalamic feedback.

However, not all anaesthetics suppress global cerebral metabolism and cause a regionally specific effect on thalamic activity. Ketamine, a so-called *dissociative* anaesthetic agent, increases global cerebral metabolism in humans at doses associated with LOC. Thus, some other mechanism or some additional process must be at work to cause LOC with dissociative agents. Nevertheless, a thalamocortical mechanism may still apply to ketamine, if ketamine simply scrambles the signals associated with normal neuronal network reverberant activity.

5. Consciousness is information integration

According to Giulio Tononi's theory, 'consciousness corresponds to the capacity of a system to integrate information' (Tononi 2004). This **information integration* process of consciousness is thought to occur in a system of sufficient complexity that it allows differentiation of one state from a repertoire of a near-infinite number of possible states. The neuroanatomy best suited for rapid effective integration of a massive amount of information is thought to exist in the mammalian thalamocortical system. Tononi's theory raises the question of whether anaesthetic agents produce unconsciousness by disrupting the effective integration of information in thalamocortical systems.

Empirical support for this idea comes from both human and animal studies. E. Roy John and colleagues showed that LOC during surgical anaesthesia was accompanied by reductions in both interhemispheric and frontal–occipital intrahemispheric connectivity, as measured by the coherence of EEG *gamma waves. Whereas other EEG bands were also affected with anaesthesia, only gamma coherence disappeared and returned with the anaesthetic-induced change in level of consciousness. John summarized his observations in a review and hypothetical model of anaesthetic effects on consciousness (John and Prichep 2005).

In animals, where spatially more precise measurements can be made with implanted electrodes, one can examine information transfer across brain regions using various EEG measurements of entropy. There are several types of EEG entropy, including cross-approximate entropy and transfer entropy. *Cross-approximate entropy* quantifies the independence of EEG recorded from two regions. When derived from the EEG of the frontal lobes, cross-approximate entropy is reduced under halothane and isoflurane anaesthesia suggesting altered interhemispheric coupling. The entropy reduction can be reversed by a pharmacological activation of the brain using cholinergic agents and this reversal coincides with animals regaining consciousness. *Transfer entropy* provides a directional measure of information flow, so that one can estimate the extent region A affects region B and the extent region B affects region A, independently. Anthony Hudetz's group examined transfer entropy when the visual system was stimulated with discrete light flashes during inhalational anaesthesia (see Hudetz et al. 2003). They found directional information transfer was asymmetrical near the LOC end-point. In particular, feedback information transfer between the frontal cortex and the parietal and occipital cortices was reduced more than the corresponding feedforward information transfer. At deeper levels of anaesthesia, information transfer in both directions was reduced. These effects are summarized in Fig. A6.

What this finding indicates is that although sensory brain activation progresses hierarchically in a feedforward manner, the top-down signals that are assumedly required for contextual interpretation of sensory data are suppressed by anaesthesia at LOC. Perception depends crucially on context presented top-down. Many have argued for a role of cortico-cortical back-projections in perceptual integration. When such recurrent information transfer is prevented by anaesthesia, conscious perception is no longer possible. The failure of conscious perception under a sufficient depth of anaesthesia may thus be interpreted as 'information received but not perceived'.

White and Alkire (2003) examined the functional and effective connectivity in the human brain with LOC induced by inhalational anaesthesia. Using a path analysis approach on positron emission tomography (PET) data, it was determined that anaesthetic-induced LOC is associated with a functional change in effective thalamocortical and cortico-cortical connectivity (see Fig. A7).

Another demonstration that anaesthetics change functional connectivity was reported by Peltier and colleagues (2005). They showed with fMRI data that a decrease in cortico-cortical functional interactions occurs with increasing anaesthetic dose, though they did not specifically investigate if the connectivity changes were directly related to LOC per se.

The hypothesis that unconsciousness occurs with anaesthesia because of a blockade of effective information integration receives additional support from studies of sleep and the vegetative state. Massimini et al. (2005) found that propagating brainwaves induced by TMS of the premotor cortex were extinguished and failed to reach distant brain areas during non-REM sleep, indicating a breakdown in cortical effective connectivity in slow-wave sleep. Laureys et al. (2000) found that loss and recovery of consciousness of vegetative state patients was associated with the loss and return of thalamocortical and cortico-cortical functional connectivity. The commonalities among neural changes in anaesthesia, non-REM sleep, and coma (Baars 2005) may represent a promising approach towards understanding the neurophysiology of unconsciousness and thus, by inference, consciousness.

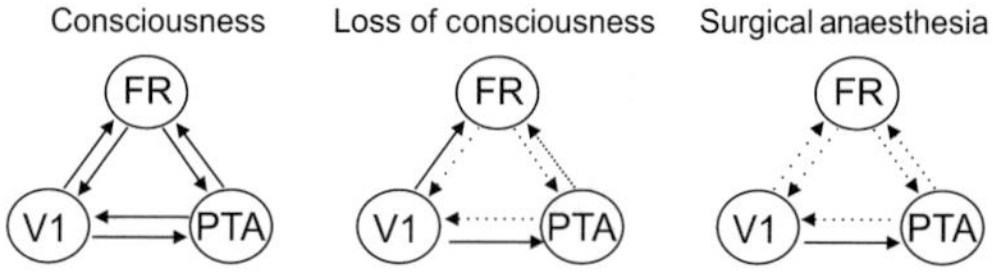

Consciousness — Loss of consciousness — Surgical anaesthesia

Fig. A6. Schematic summary of anaesthetic effects on feedforward (V1FR, PTAFR, V1PTA) and feedback (V1FR, PTAFR, V1PTA) information transfers at high gamma frequency (40–50 Hz) as generalized to two anaesthetics, halothane and isoflurane. The schematic reflects principal changes in feedforward and feedback information transfers at anaesthetic-induced loss of consciousness and in surgical anaesthesia from the conscious-sedated state. The arrows indicate the direction of information flow. The following conclusions can be drawn: (1) both feedforward and feedback information transfers were balanced during consciousness; (2) the anaesthetic agents upon loss of consciousness produced a stronger depression of the feedback than of the feedforward information transfer, especially between frontal and posterior sensory cortices; (3) in surgical anaesthesia, both feedforward and feedback information transfers were depressed below the conscious baseline. These findings suggest that a preferential decrease in feedback information transfer at high gamma frequencies between frontal and posterior cortices is a possible neural correlate of anaesthetic-induced unconsciousness. Modified from Imas et al. (2005).

6. Conclusions

A convergence of evidence points towards the thalamus, thalamocortical, and cortico-cortical interactions as being involved with mediating not only anaesthetic-induced unconsciousness, but also with mediating other forms of altered states of consciousness. The study of the effects of anaesthetics on consciousness is only just beginning. Current work suggests pharmacological manipulations in humans coupled with brain imaging techniques and theory-directed (i.e. consciousness is information integration) experimentation may be one empirical path out of the consciousness quagmire.

MICHAEL T. ALKIRE AND ANTHONY G. HUDETZ

Alemà, G., Perria, L., Rosadini, G., Rossi, G. F., and Zattoni, J. (1966). 'Functional inactivation of the human brain stem related to the level of consciousness. Intravertebral injection of barbiturate'. *Journal of Neurosurgery*, 24.

Alkire, M. T. and Miller, J. (2005). 'General anesthesia and the neural correlates of consciousness'. *Progress in Brain Research*, 150.

Baars, B. J. (2005). 'Global workspace theory of consciousness: toward a cognitive neuroscience of human experience'. *Progress in Brain Research*, 150.

Bogen, J. E. (1997). 'Some neurophysiologic aspects of consciousness'. *Seminars in Neurology*, 17.

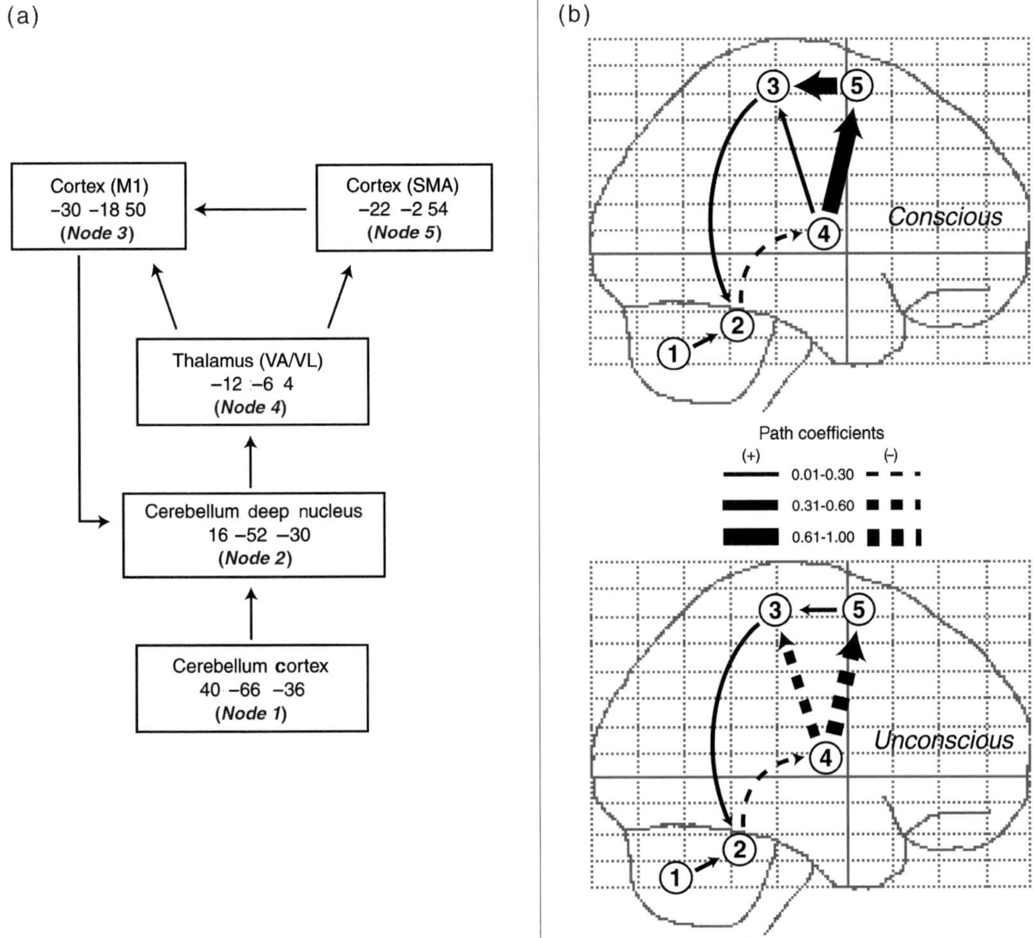

Fig. A7. Effective connectivity changes with anaesthetic-induced unconsciousness in the human lateral cerebello-thalamocortical network (White and Alkire 2003). Part (a) of the figure shows the network nodes, with their Talariach coordinates, and their modelled interactions. Structural equation modelling of this limited corticothalamic network (b) reveals that effective connectivity dramatically changes within this network, especially involving the thalamocortical and cortico-cortical interactions, depending on the presence or absence of consciousness. Such a connectivity analysis approach can reveal network interactions and regional effects that might otherwise be missed with more traditional analysis techniques.

Devor, M. and Zalkind, V. (2001). 'Reversible analgesia, atonia, and loss of consciousness on bilateral intracerebral micro-injection of pentobarbital'. *Pain*, 94.

Drummond, J. C. and Patel, P. (2000). 'Cerebral blood flow and metabolism'. In Miller, R. D. (ed.) *Anaesthesia*.

Franks, N. P. (2006). 'Molecular targets underlying general anaesthesia'. *British Journal of Pharmacology*, 147 Suppl 1.

Hudetz, A. G., Wood, J. D., and Kampine, J. P. (2003). 'Cholinergic reversal of isoflurane anesthesia in rats as measured by cross-approximate entropy of the electroencephalogram'. *Anaesthesiology*, 99.

Imas, O. A., Ropella, K. M., Ward, B. D., Wood, J. D., and Hudetz, A. G. (2005). 'Volatile anesthetics disrupt frontal–posterior recurrent information transfer at gamma frequencies in rat'. *Neuroscience Letters*, 387.

John, E. R. and Prichep, L. S. (2005). 'The anesthetic cascade: a theory of how anesthesia suppresses consciousness'. *Anaesthesiology*, 102.

Laureys, S., Faymonville, M. E., Luxen, A., Lamy, M., Franck, G., and Maquet, P. (2000). 'PET scanning and neuronal loss in acute vegetative state'. *Lancet*, 355.

Massimini, M., Ferrarelli, F., Huber, R., Esser, S. K., Singh, H., and Tononi, G. (2005). 'Breakdown of cortical effective connectivity during sleep'. *Science*, 309.

Peltier, S. J., Kerssens, C., Hamann, S. B., Sebel, P. S., Byas-Smith, M., and Hu, X. (2005). 'Functional connectivity changes with concentration of sevoflurane anesthesia'. *NeuroReport*, 16.

Sonner, J. M., Antognini, J. F., Dutton, R. C. et al. (2003). 'Inhaled anesthetics and immobility: mechanisms, mysteries, and minimum alveolar concentration'. *Anesthesia and Analgesia*, 97.

Tononi, G. (2004). 'An information integration theory of consciousness'. *BMC Neurosci*, 5.

White, N. S. and Alkire, M. T. (2003). 'Impaired thalamocortical connectivity in humans during general-anaesthetic-induced unconsciousness'. *Neuroimage*, 19.

anaesthesia, awareness under Awareness under anaesthesia appears to be an uncommon event when measured conventionally, i.e. as recall by the patient of events that happened during surgery. Sebel et al. (2004) found an incidence of awareness during general anaesthesia of 0.13%, just over one per thousand adult patients, or approximately 26 000 cases per year in the United States. The incidence of awareness is higher in children, at 0.8% (Davidson et al. 2005).

Awareness under anaesthesia can be devastating, especially when accompanied by pain. A common theme in patients' recollections is terror that something is wrong and that they are helpless to prevent the situation degenerating further into intolerable pain, coma, or death. Post-traumatic stress disorder is a common consequence of awareness during anaesthesia, with symptoms including flashbacks to the event, insomnia, avoidance of hospitals, and persistent general anxiety (Osterman et al. 2001).

Research on awareness under anaesthesia highlights the point that consciousness is not an all-or-none phenomenon and raises the question of how to measure consciousness. Achieving the right level of unconsciousness, or depth of anaesthesia, is a matter of balancing the hypnotic effects of the anaesthetic against the arousing effects of surgery. Depth of anaesthesia is affected by variations in surgical stimulation and individual differences between patients, as well as by the dose of anaesthetic. Measuring where a patient is on this continuum during surgery is not straightforward. Conventionally, anaesthetists have monitored vital signs such as blood pressure and sweating but these are unreliable indicators of impending awareness, particularly in patients receiving neuromuscular blockers to ensure paralysis (Moerman et al. 1993). Research into techniques for measuring depth of anaesthesia has focused on *electroencephalogram (EEG) measures of brain activity. There are two ways of using the EEG as an index of consciousness. One is to measure the general level of cortical brain activity by recording the raw EEG. Of the raw EEG measures, the most widely used at present is the commercially marketed *bispectral index*, a composite of several variables within the EEG signal. The alternative method is to provoke brain activity with auditory stimuli (clicks or tones) and record the latency and amplitude of the EEG response to those stimuli—the *auditory evoked response*. Research using evoked response techniques has shown that the brainstem remains responsive to sounds even during deep anaesthesia. Late cortical responses, reflecting activity in frontal and association areas of the brain, are mainly abolished before loss of consciousness. The mid-latency waves, arising from the thalamus and primary auditory cortex, are most useful for distinguishing consciousness from unconsciousness during anaesthesia (Thornton and Sharpe 1998). Careful EEG monitoring of anaesthetic depth substantially reduces intraoperative awareness but does not completely abolish it (Myles et al. 2004).

There are two problems with the techniques for assessing awareness discussed so far. The EEG measures are probabilistic, indicating the likelihood that a particular patient is unconscious rather than giving an absolute measure of their state of consciousness. Patients' self-reports of awareness are prone to forgetting due to inadequate encoding of the salient information, amnestic effects of anaesthetic drugs, and changes in context between the awareness episode and recollection. An *online measure of awareness, in the form of purposeful responses to command, avoids these problems. This *isolated forearm technique* (IFT) involves inflating a cuff around the patient's forearm just before injection of neuromuscular blockers, leaving that arm free to move even when the rest of the body is paralysed. Patients are repeatedly asked to 'squeeze my fingers' if they are awake, and any positive responses are verified by repeating the command. Studies using the IFT have shown much higher incidences of awareness during anaesthesia than are indicated by patients' postoperative recollections of surgery. For example, using a modern anaesthetic technique associated with a low incidence of recollections of surgery, Russell and Wang (2001) found positive isolated forearm responses in 7 out of 40 patients. None recollected details of surgery when interviewed afterwards. Such findings show that measures of patients' recall of surgery underestimate the incidence of awareness during anaesthesia. The impact of forgotten episodes of awareness on patients' recovery is not known.

As a tool for manipulating consciousness, anaesthetics provide a means of addressing some important questions about consciousness. One such question relates to the functional *correlates of consciousness: what are the cognitive and brain processes that consistently accompany consciousness and are inactive in the absence of consciousness? *Functional brain imaging studies of anaesthetic effects suggest activity in thalamocortical networks as a neural correlate of consciousness (Alkire and Miller 2005), while *working memory function is a potential cognitive correlate of consciousness (Andrade 1996). A second question is: what cognitive functions persist in the absence of awareness? Studies that combine monitoring of anaesthetic depth with testing of implicit memory for words presented during surgery suggest that some memory function persists even during deep anaesthesia (Deeprose and Andrade 2006). There is evidence for perceptual *priming in unconscious patients. Presenting a word during surgery activates the mental representation of that word and so enhances processing of that word on subsequent encounters. For example, presenting words during anaesthesia increases the chance of patients using those words to complete word stems, even if they have no explicit recall of those words. There is no clear evidence for more extensive cognitive processing in the form of conceptual priming, i.e. the activation of related items in memory during anaesthesia.

Practical and theoretical issues require further research. Individual variations in response to anaesthetics are not well understood; improved understanding could help develop tools for measuring anaesthetic depth more accurately in individual patients. Little attention has so far been paid to monitoring anaesthetic depth and awareness in children. It is not known how long an episode of awareness is needed to produce postoperative recall, or whether perceptual priming during anaesthesia affects patients' well-being on recovery. Even this limited cognitive function may be sufficient for operating room comments to exacerbate patients' anxieties about their condition. Better integration of cognitive and neurobiological research should help to explain more fully why anaesthetic action on the brain causes loss of consciousness.

JACKIE ANDRADE

Alkire, M. T. and Miller, J. (2005). 'General anesthesia and the neural correlates of consciousness'. *Progress in Brain Research*, 150.

Andrade, J. (1996). 'Investigations of hypesthesia: Using anaesthetics to explore relationships between consciousness, learning and memory'. *Consciousness and Cognition*, 5.

Davidson, A. J., Huang, G. H., Czarnecki, C. et al. (2005). 'Awareness during anesthesia in children: a prospective cohort study'. *Anesthesia and Analgesia*, 100.

Deeprose, C. and Andrade, J. (2006). 'Is priming during anesthesia unconscious?' *Consciousness and Cognition*, 15.

Moerman, N., Bonke, B., and Oosting, J. (1993). 'Awareness and recall during general anesthesia—facts and feelings'. *Anesthesiology*, 79.

Myles, P. S., Leslie, K., McNeil, J., Forbes, A., and Chan, M. T. V. (2004). 'Bispectral index monitoring to prevent awareness during anaesthesia: the B-Aware randomised controlled trial'. *Lancet*, 363.

Osterman, J. E., Hopper, J., Heran, W. J., Keane, T. M., and van der Kolk, B. A. (2001). 'Awareness under anesthesia and the development of post traumatic stress disorder'. *General Hospital Psychiatry*, 23.

Russell, I. F. and Wang, M. (2001). 'Absence of memory for intra-operative information during surgery with total intravenous anaesthesia'. *British Journal of Anaesthesia*, 86.

Sebel, P. S., Bowdle, T. A., Ghoneim, M. M. et al. (2004). 'The incidence of awareness during anesthesia: a multicenter United States study'. *Anesthesia and Analgesia*, 99.

Thornton, C. and Sharpe, R. M. (1998). 'Evoked responses in anaesthesia'. *British Journal of Anaesthesia*, 81.

anarchic hand Anarchic hand (AH) refers to the occurrence of complex movements of one hand that are apparently directed to a goal and are smoothly executed although, according the people affected, they are unintended. These unwanted movements may interfere with the desired actions carried out by the other hand. The patients are bewildered and dismayed by the experience and disown the actions, but never deny that this capricious hand is their own and not a robotic counterfeit; they are aware of the bizarre and potentially hazardous behaviour of their hand but fail to inhibit it. They often refer to the feeling that their AH behaves as if it has a will of its own.

Examples of AH behaviour include a woman throttling herself with some left-over fishbones that her left hand tried to shovel into her throat; grabbing someone else's ice cream; selecting unwanted TV channels; snatching the experimenter's packed lunch; and seizing other people's objects irrespective of social rules. In all these instances the patients, embarrassed and distressed, tried to control their AH's wayward behaviour by talking to it in anger and frustration or by hitting it violently. Hence the popular press label of 'Dr Strangelove's syndrome'.

We tend to take for granted that what we do is the result of a choice. After all, we can inhibit whatever gesture, action, or behaviour we are about to undertake. Sometimes people can perform actions for which they are not technically responsible, e.g. if threatened or if affected by a severe psychiatric condition. However, even if courage fades, one could still make a choice; and when acting under a schizophrenic urge the conflict between wanted action and performed action is unbearable. People affected by AH, on the other hand, have no choice but to perform actions they do not want to carry out, and often should not be carrying out. The condition demonstrates that self-ownership of actions can be separated from awareness of actions.

AH is often referred to in the literature as 'alien hand'. This term came into use due to a misinterpretation of an early 1970s paper written in French describing the feeling of non-belonging of an arm associated with damage to the posterior part of the corpus callosum and thought of as a partial hemisomatognosia, i.e. a unilateral loss of the knowledge or sense of one's own body (Marchetti and Della Sala 1998). Alien hand is therefore a sensory deficit, AH a motor one. AH has also been often used as an example to support a dichotomous consciousness in the human brain. The idea that 'Man is not truly one, but truly two' (like Stevenson's Jekyll and Hyde), perhaps half good and half bad as in Italo Calvino's Cloven Viscount, is entwined with the history of humanity, and is certainly fascinating from the artist's point of view. However, scientifically it is rather simplistic, and as an interpretation for AH it proved wrong (Della Sala 2005).

AH is a syndrome associated with lesions to the *frontal lobe of the brain, and could be interpreted as intrahemispheric disconnection syndrome. It results from an imbalance between the damaged premotor medial system, centred on the supplementary motor area (SMA), and the spared lateral motor system centred on a region sometimes referred to as premotor cortex (Fig. A8). The two systems carry out different functions and have different phylogenetic origin. The medial system is responsible for inner-driven actions and for the inhibition of automatic responses. The lateral system is considered to be responsible for actions generated in response to external stimuli. Although the theory is not universally accepted, several experiments indicate that the control of movements may vary as a function of whether the action is internally or externally guided. Mushiake et al. (1991) trained monkeys to press buttons in a given sequence. In one condition, the *external condition*, lights told the monkeys which button to press (it was a visually guided sequence). In the other condition the monkeys performed the sequence from memory with no external cues; this was the *internal condition*. The movements made by the monkeys were identical. Yet the SMA cells were more active during the internal condition and the premotor cells were most active during the external, visually guided condition. This and other similar experiments indicate that the control of movements may vary as a function of whether the action is internally or externally guided.

An account of AH could be given as a phenomenon resulting from the imbalance of this complex mechanism within the frontal lobe of the brain: a lesion of the medial system would leave the contralateral hand at the mercy of external stimuli that operate through the premotor lateral system. The damaged medial system

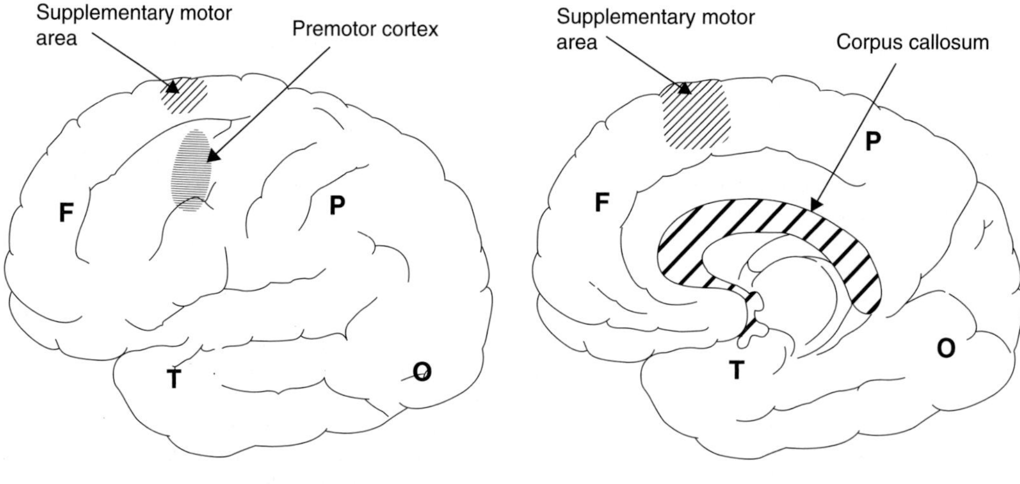

Fig. A8. An anatomical sketch of the respective localization of the premotor cortex and the supplementary motor area within the frontal lobe (F) as seen in the lateral and medial view of the left human hemisphere. O, occipital lobe; P, parietal lobe; T, temporal lobe.

would be unable to inhibit the automatic provoked responses. This hand would therefore show 'anarchic' behaviour. The 'frontal' account of anarchic hand makes sense if one considers the basic role of the frontal lobes in the human brain: to allow humans to interact with the environment.

If damage to one SMA results in AH, damage to both SMAs elicits utilization behaviour (Boccardi et al. 2002). In both cases the affected patients will perform inappropriate actions. The environment triggers the actions performed by patients showing utilization behaviour, exactly as it does those of people with AH syndrome. However, the patients with utilization behaviour are not aware that their behaviour is inappropriate, and do not show any conflict between wanted and unwanted actions. It may well be that the lack of awareness observed in these patients comes from the complete impairment of the medial system.

Think about a possible scenario that could apply to us all. One Saturday morning while driving to the country for the weekend you cross the usual road to your office. Absent-mindedly, you may turn and find yourself driving to the office for a while before recognizing your error. The environment provided a trigger strong enough for you to initiate an *automatic behaviour, which you had to inhibit to go back to your intended plan. You would have performed an action that you did not mean to do. This is what often happens to people affected by utilization behaviour who lack the capacity to inhibit behaviour triggered by environment.

AH is a clear example of uncontrolled behaviour triggered by the environment caused by a lesion to a sub-region of the frontal lobes. Are the anarchic actions still intentional? Whose will are they responding to? It would be possible to maintain that this epistemological problem springs from the conflict between stated will and performed action.

AH epitomizes the inability to inhibit actions triggered by the environment. The syndrome suggests that conscious will could only veto some undesired actions. From this perspective it looks as if our brain may have laid away a free 'won't' rather than a free will. The only control we would have over our actions is a negative control; the possibility of inhibiting them. To achieve the (desired?) aim, the motor system makes non-stop refinements, of which we are usually not aware. These include inhibition of actions triggered by environmental affordances. AH is the result of the lack of such inhibition, due to a lesion of the mainly inner driven medial–frontal motor system.

SERGIO DELLA SALA

Boccardi, E., Della Sala, S., Motto, C., and Spinnler, H. (2002). 'Utilisation behaviour consequent to bilateral SMA softening'. *Cortex*, 38.

Della Sala, S. (2005). 'The anarchic hand'. *Psychologist*, 18.

—— and Marchetti, C. (2005). 'The anarchic hand syndrome'. In Freund, H.-J. et al. (eds) *Higher-Order Motor Disorders: from Neuroanatomy and Neurobiology to Clinical Neurology*.

Marchetti, C. and Della Sala, S. (1998). 'Disentangling the alien and anarchic hand'. *Cognitive Neuropsychiatry*, 3.

Mushiake, H., Masahiko, I., and Tanji, J. (1991). 'Neuronal activity in the primate premotor, supplementary, and precentral motor cortex during visually guided and internally determined sequential movements'. *Journal of Neurophysiology*, 66.

animal consciousness Consciousness has periodically been a pressing issue in the scientific study of non-human animals, and we are currently in one of these periods. As with humans, discussions of consciousness in other species are often inconclusive; however, recent conceptual clarifications and empirical observations are facilitating new perspectives. Here we focus primarily, but not exclusively, on the importance of ethological studies for gaining essential insights into animal mentality and its evolution. Knowledge about what animals do in various situations (e.g. interacting socially, foraging, and avoiding predation) is of critical importance in learning about animal minds and how they operate (Allen and Bekoff 1997).

There are five primary issues in the study of animal consciousness (see Allen and Bekoff 2007): (1) What is consciousness, and how many kinds or levels are there? (2) How can we determine if other species are conscious? (3) Which species have which type(s) of consciousness (the distribution question)? (4) What can we know about the nature of the private or subjective experiences of other species (the *qualia question)? and (5) How and why has consciousness *evolved? We will consider all five with varying degrees of brevity.

For ethologists, who study the natural behaviour of animals from an evolutionary perspective in both the field and the laboratory, the issue of consciousness is valuable insofar as it helps us understand how and why animals behave the way they do. Ethologists assume that all features of animals have some continuity with some ancestral population or process. Thus, we must ask why various levels of consciousness have evolved in species showing different life-history strategies. Philosophical analysis and neuroscience data thus inform, but do not drive, comparative behavioural studies. Baars (2005) reviews the history of animal consciousness and concludes that consciousness is a 'fundamental biological adaptation'. The scientific literature on animal consciousness is now voluminous (e.g. Baars 2005, Merker 2007). Typically, however, most treatments discuss only some of the most widely reported cognitive accomplishments of select species (e.g. dolphins, birds, and non-human primates, especially the great apes—see the following entries).

More specifically, the aims of ethology are typically viewed as: to understand (1) the proximate sensory, learning, and physiological mechanisms underlying behavioural performance; (2) the development (ontogeny) of behaviour; (3) the adaptiveness of behaviour (especially in a species' natural habitat); and (4) the evolution and phylogenetic history of behaviour (Tinbergen 1963). Conspicuously absent from 'classical' ethology were issues involving consciousness. Thus, in ethology as well as in behaviouristic experimental and comparative psychology, questions of animal consciousness and related ones involving emotion and subjective experiences in general became largely taboo. To recognize a broadened view of ethology that encompassed cognitive, emotional, and conscious processes, Burghardt (1997) added a fifth aim, the study of private experience.

The eminent scientist Donald Griffin (1976, 1992) tirelessly promoted the field of cognitive ethology for the study of such topics as animal thinking, awareness, mentality, and consciousness. Although frequently criticized for advancing some questionable claims (Bekoff and Allen 1997), Griffin had considerable impact in reviving the search for mental abilities in non-human animals. Increased interest outside ethology, psychology, and philosophy in issues of animal conservation and animal rights and welfare (including the treatment of laboratory and agricultural animals) also helped foster interest in cognitive ethology (e.g. Dawkins 1992). It turns out that the subjective lives of non-human, as well as human, animals might not be as private as used to be thought, and that the privacy-of-mind argument (no one has access to another individual's mental states) is invoked too rapidly when studying such phenomena as consciousness (Burghardt 1997, Bekoff 2007).

Careful observation of animals in naturalistic contexts is an essential feature of ethology and a benchmark for evaluating claims for animal mentality. Rare, often serendipitous, observations by informed observers can allow glimpses into the inner life of animals and inspire formal studies as well as help us to evaluate and extend laboratory-based phenomena.

1. Current stances on animal consciousness
2. The study of animal consciousness
3. The origins of consciousness
4. The need for broad interdisciplinary research

1. Current stances on animal consciousness

As a result of renewed interest in animal awareness and consciousness, many popular and scientific books and articles are making strong and sometimes questionable claims about animal mentality, raising again the problem of anthropomorphic interpretations of behaviour. On the other hand, many biomedical and behavioural scientists refuse to acknowledge any essential similarity in the mental lives and experiences of human and non-human animals. Yet many creative scientists, when developing research questions, essentially put themselves in the animal's 'shoes'. To provide some guidelines for doing this, Burghardt (1985) suggested the employment of a 'critical anthropomorphism' that utilizes both our own stance as sentient problem-solving creatures and the careful incorporation of scientific knowledge about a species (e.g. ecology, neuroscience, perceptual abilities) in developing testable hypotheses about the private experiences of other species. An explicit critical anthropomorphism needs to be adopted because humans have a natural propensity to attribute human psychological attributes to both living and non-living entities, including the weather (a 'violent' storm). We seem to be programmed to see human-type mentality in events where it cannot possibly be involved.

An associated issue is that some of the severest critics of the study of animal mentality are sociobiologists, behavioural ecologists, and selfish-gene theorists who view the detailed study of animal mental abilities as irrelevant, yet often use anthropomorphic terms in discussing the wants, desires, and needs of genes, animals, and groups. Although these researchers typically assert that such terminology is just useful shorthand, the use of this double standard (Bekoff 2007) has the effect of making the endeavour to determine the actual status of animal mentality more problematic, and lessens interest by evolutionary biologists.

Additionally, in ethology and comparative psychology it is common to discuss 'mind' in animals while omitting any discussion of consciousness, as was true of much early cognitive psychology (Burghardt 1985). While acknowledging that animals have minds, and that we can study aspects of them and how they may work, it basically ignores the issue of what having a mind means, experientially, to the animals themselves. It is basically the study of the problems animals can solve, and relies on behavioural means alone. This is fine, but we can also try to test more experientially inferential questions about consciousness as well as those inferring cognitive processes from behaviour. As we will see, neuroscience is becoming relevant as well.

2. The study of animal consciousness

Clearly, the conception one has of consciousness influences whether one accepts that it is nearly universal in all living things, or at least vertebrates; present in at least some other species; possibly present in some but not yet firmly established; or impossible to ever determine in other species (or, in an extreme mode, people other than oneself). That almost all scholars accept the existence of various kinds or levels of consciousness compounds the problem, in that all are covered by the same word. Views of consciousness may range from being awake, alert, or responsive to being able to reflect on one's own experiences and 'intentionally' communicate them to other beings. For some writers, behavioural expressions of emotional states such as pain, rage, or pleasure are important markers of consciousness.

How can we effectively characterize and study the mentality and private experiences of other species, and especially their evolution? We can begin by parsimoniously accepting that if consciousness occurs in people it has adaptive counterparts and homologues in other species, a view perfectly in line with evolutionary continuity of morphology, brain, and behaviour expressed by Charles Darwin. The focus should be on the specific mechanisms, evolution, and development of continuity, not whether or not it exists. Baars (2005) argues that grounded inference from both behavioural and brain studies strongly suggests that non-human animals, especially mammals with 'human-like brains and behavior', have subjective experiences. Here Baars invokes two venerable methods, *subjective analogical inference* and *neural analogical inference* (Burghardt 1985).

Typologies of consciousness that go beyond mere wakefulness and responsiveness to stimuli in the environment vary, but all require these first two most basic types of consciousness. *Phenomenal consciousness* is often used to refer to subjective, qualitative, or experiential aspects of consciousness and incorporates emotions, feelings, qualia, and sentience in general (Allen and Bekoff 2007). Here the focus is both on attempting to determine which animals have such consciousness (the distribution question) and also on trying to gain some knowledge of what such conscious experiences are like for other species (Burghardt 1997). How do other species perceive and experience the external world and their own bodies? Basically, the best we can do is comparable to how we answer this question about other people, except that we need to use behavioural and neural methods and inference grounded in a critical anthropomorphism. For example, our anthropocentric inclinations harbour the danger of minimizing attributions of pain in species that do not show distress in ways we are programmed to view empathically, such as screams or whines. This almost guarantees a confounding of biological relatedness or similarity with our concept of consciousness.

The Cartesian view, that human-style language is necessary for consciousness to occur, and thus is absent from all animals, is still encountered. In this approach, studying animal consciousness besides the obvious awake/alert sense can only follow discovering of human types of communication in other species. This is a high bar, and was basically used to deny the need to explore consciousness in other species. More useful is the acceptance that there are a group of types of conscious experiences in which animals may use their experiences to make more or less rational (adaptive?) decisions. This has been called *access consciousness* by Block (1995). While access consciousness does not require language to exist, it does make animals more like intentional actors than mere passive responders.

Much current interest centres on **self-consciousness*, also referred to as self-awareness, self-cognizance, or reflective consciousness (thinking about one's thoughts). *Mirror self-recognition, developed by Gordon Gallup, was one of the first methods to test a sense of self in other species, but there have been criticisms of how this approach has been employed (Bekoff 2007). While definitive answers on the general issue of self-awareness remain elusive, progress can be made by clarifying the terms listed above, perhaps by arranging a continuum of levels such as self-cognizance, self-referencing, self-awareness, self-consciousness, and reflective consciousness, each with differing behavioural markers based on long-term observations of social interactions (Bekoff and Sherman 2004). In any event, researchers need to produce and largely agree upon a standardized vocabulary and consider modalities other than our anthropocentric emphasis on vision.

Those who focus on reflective consciousness often invoke the **theory of mind*, the idea that being able to posit mental states in others (e.g. anger, knowledge of where food is hidden), including 'intentional' deception, is the key issue. Brüne and Brüne-Cohrs (2006) argue that theory of mind originated in non-human primates and evolved from the need for 'social intelligence' based on living in large groups. They even identify putative neural locations involved in these mechanisms.

Finally, another type of advanced consciousness is *episodic memory*, the ability to construct or represent a simple narrative (Terrace and Metcalfe 2005). If animals can show recall of the sequential order of past events (mental time travel), then perhaps this involves consciousness as well. Monkeys have shown this ability repeatedly in experimental research, and rats may show it too (Babb and Crystal 2006). Field observations of animals have often suggested such abilities, and evidence is accumulating in birds and other vertebrates as well.

3. The origins of consciousness

Although we know that human abilities differ in many ways from those of other species, we still want to uncover the origins of cognitive abilities and subjectivity, both those accentuated in human beings as well as those less developed in us, such as many perceptual, sensory, and memory abilities. We should not keep raising the bar for what we accept as evidence of consciousness or 'private' experiences as animals continue to show unexpected abilities that are very difficult or impossible to explain without invoking the presence of subjective experiences using existing criteria. Indeed, cognitive arguments appealing to consciousness, intentions, expectations, and beliefs might be more useful, even more parsimonious, than complex reductionist behaviourist explanations. Those who favour such behaviourist explanations often cannot offer evidence that their views are better for understanding and predicting behaviour than the views they eschew (Bekoff 2007).

As noted above, the type of conscious experience (or mental capacity) invoked will impact views of its existence in other species. There is a tendency to arrange these varying types of consciousness in a hierarchy, with some animals reaching one level and others that level and more advanced ('higher') ones (e.g. Merker 2007). Usually this is tied to a linear hierarchy of mental abilities, with 'higher' animals such as chimpanzees having more complex abilities than monkeys, who have more complex abilities than dogs, who have more complex abilities than rats, and so on. This 'ladder' approach, still widely accepted (see Merker 2007 and comments thereon), is incompatible with a more modular view of brain and behavioural organization, and with modern evolutionary theory. The continued popularity of such simplistic views suggests that they may be as endemic to human nature as naive anthropomorphism. Other recent approaches focus on relative brain size, but this trait can be independently evolved as well (e.g. in whales, bears, ravens, parrots, and squirrels). Rarefied abilities on arbitrary tasks, cognitive modules, or relative brain size and neural development should not be the sole markers confirming consciousness.

If the continuity position is most reasonable from an evolutionary perspective, plausible phylogenetically testable scenarios for its origin are necessary. Baars (2005) accepts that consciousness evolved in early mammals and is probably found in birds, but he is more reserved about reptiles and cephalopods. Merker, beginning with an analysis of peripheral sensory feedback in earthworm locomotion, identifies the origins of consciousness in the evolution of central representations that allow a 'distinction between self and something else *within one representational space*, short of which it cannot embody even a minimal criterial definition of consciousness' (Merker 2005:107–108). This is a property that arose from the demands for mobility and integrating diverse sensory information. More recently he has developed a theory that places consciousness in brainstem mechanisms and basal ganglia, with brain cortex involved primarily in influencing and refining the more advanced types of consciousness (Merker 2007).

A rather different approach to the evolution of consciousness is taken by Cabanac (1999) who, on the basis of several behavioural and physiological measures of emotion and preference, argues that consciousness arose somewhere between the evolution of amphibians and reptiles. His data show that reptiles, but not amphibians, experience emotional fever (e.g. ectotherms increase their preferred temperature by choosing warmer locations), illness-induced food aversions, and other traits showing response to internal states accompanied by emotion in other species, and thus he concludes that emotional private experiences do not exist in amphibians, fish, and invertebrates. Although this is intriguing, more species in these groups need be studied before accepting this major evolutionary leap in animal consciousness. Note also that in this scheme consciousness does, however, have adaptive consequences.

4. The need for broad interdisciplinary research

From various perspectives, then, there is much agreement that animals other than humans are conscious and have subjective experiences that rely on some degree of consciousness (Bekoff 2007). Nonetheless, questions about the taxonomic distribution of different kinds of consciousness remain unanswered. We must broaden our taxonomic interests beyond non-human primates as it becomes increasingly clear that we and our relatives are not the only species in which consciousness (not necessarily 'human'-type consciousness) has evolved. Primatocentric speciesism ignores many of the interesting questions about the evolution of consciousness and animal minds and its relationship to various life-history strategies. We also need to incorporate diverse perceptual and neural systems underlying these strategies. To learn more about animal consciousness we need interdisciplinary integrative research on diverse species living in conditions in which individuals are free to express a full (or natural) behavioural repertoire, especially in social conditions that reflect those in which they evolved or currently live. Comparative and developmental behavioural data from ethological studies are crucial to our learning more about animal consciousness and how and why it evolved.

GORDON M. BURGHARDT AND MARC BEKOFF

Allen, C. and Bekoff, M. (1997). *Species of Mind. The Philosophy and Biology of Cognitive Biology*.

—— —— (2007). 'Animal consciousness'. In Velmans, M. and Schneider, S. (eds) *Blackwell Companion to Consciousness*.

Baars, B. J. (2005). 'Subjective experience is probably not limited to humans: the evidence from neurobiology and behavior'. *Consciousness and Cognition*, 14.

Babb, S. J. and Crystal, J. D. (2006). 'Episodic-like memory in the rat'. *Current Biology*, 16.

Bekoff, M. (2007). *The Emotional Lives of Animals: A Leading Scientist Explores Animal Joy, Sorrow, and Empathy—and Why They Matter*.

—— and Allen, C. (1997). 'Cognitive ethology: slayers, skeptics, and proponents'. In Mitchell, R. W. et al. (eds) *Anthropomorphism, Anecdotes, and Animals*.

—— and Sherman, P. (2004). 'Reflections on animal selves'. *Trends in Ecology and Evolution*, 19.

Block, N. (1995). 'On a confusion of consciousness'. *Behavioral and Brain Sciences*, 18.

Brüne, M. and Brüne-Cohrs, U. (2006). 'Theory of mind—evolution, ontogeny, brain mechanisms and psychopathology'. *Neuroscience and Biobehavioral Reviews*, 30.

Burghardt, G. M. (1985). 'Animal awareness: current perceptions and historical perspective'. *American Psychologist*, 40.

—— (1997). 'Amending Tinbergen: a fifth aim for ethology'. In Mitchell, R. W. et al. (eds) *Anthropomorphism, anecdotes, and animals*.

Cabanac, M. (1999). 'Emotion and phylogeny'. *Journal of Consciousness Studies*, 6.

Dawkins, R. (1992). 'Higher and lower animals: a diatribe'. In Fox-Keller, E. and Lloyd, E. (eds) *Keywords in Evolutionary Biology*.

Griffin, D. R. (1992a). *Animal Consciousness*.

—— (1992b). *Animal Minds*.

Merker, B. (2005). 'The liabilities of mobility: a selection pressure for the transition to consciousness in animal evolution'. *Consciousness and Cognition*, 14.

—— (2007). 'Consciousness without a cerebral cortex: a challenge for neuroscience and medicine (includes commentaries)'. *Behavioral and Brain Sciences*, 30.

Terrace, H. S. and Metcalfe, J. (eds) (2005). *The Missing Link in Cognition: Origins of Self-reflective Consciousness*.

Tinbergen, N. (1963). 'On aims and methods of ethology'. *Zeitschrift für Tierpsychologie*, 20.

animal consciousness: dolphins Researchers interested in animal consciousness face the daunting task of designing experiments that can address this elusive concept. For the researcher, *consciousness* may be approached experimentally by defining tasks that can reveal the animal's *awareness of self*. An early task of this type was the **mirror self-recognition task* (MSR). This task, originally created by Gallup (1970), asked whether chimpanzees recognize themselves in a mirror. Animals characteristically fail to recognize that the reflection in the mirror is itself. To test whether MSR might develop with experience, Gallup placed a mirror in a chimpanzee's cage and noted that after a long period of exposure the chimp began to attend to its mirror image in ways that suggested it understood that it was viewing its own image and not that of another chimpanzee. Gallup's definitive test was to place a coloured mark on the forehead of a chimp while it was under anaesthesia. When the chimp recovered and once again approached the mirror, it attempted to wipe the mark off of its forehead, thereby demonstrating MSR. Until recently, the only animals that passed the mark test were the great apes. Lesser primates failed this test, as did all other species examined. Marten and Psarakos (1994) were among the first to attempt a mark test with dolphins. These researchers placed zinc oxide or some other bright substance on parts of the dolphin's body not visible without a mirror. The results were suggestive of MSR but, unfortunately, the study had two major weaknesses. First, the dolphins did not have prolonged exposure to mirrors prior to the test, so that initial reactions suggesting they perceived the image to be another dolphin were not extinguished. Second, there was no control condition where the tactile components of marking occurred, but no mark was actually applied (*sham marking*). Similar limitations occurred in a dolphin mark study by Marino et al. (1994). Reiss and Marino (2001) published the first definitive study showing that dolphins (bottlenosed dolphins *Tursiops truncatus*) could in fact pass the mark test. Two dolphins, with long exposure to mirrors in their pool, were either marked with temporary black ink on body parts not visible without a mirror, or were sham-marked with a water-filled marker. Thus, the tactile sensations were the same for real marking and for sham marking. Both dolphins spent significantly more time at a mirror, or other reflective surface, examining themselves when real-marked than when sham-marked. Importantly, the dolphins turned in ways that enabled them to view the parts of their body that had been marked. Reiss and Marino concluded that the dolphins perceived the mirror image as themselves and that mirror-self recognition by great apes and by dolphins may be attributable to the high degree of 'surplus' brain tissue (*encephalization*) and general cognitive ability shared in common by these otherwise very evolutionarily divergent species.

Consciousness, operationalized as 'self-awareness' (see SELF-CONSCIOUSNESS), is best viewed as a multidimensional phenomenon, with self-recognition but one facet. Researchers at the University of Hawaii examined two other facets. The first was a test for the dolphin's awareness of its own behaviours, and the second a test for its awareness of its own body parts. To test for behavioural awareness, defined as conscious awareness of its own recent behaviours, the investigators created and trained two distinct symbolic gestural commands. One gesture required the dolphin to do again the behaviour it just did, i.e. to repeat it. The second gesture required the dolphin to do a different behaviour than that just performed, i.e. to not repeat it. A set of five different behaviours were selected, each controlled by a unique gestural command and each behaviour to be carried out on an object floating in the dolphin's pool. The gestural behavioural commands were: *go over, go under, touch with the tail, touch with the pectoral fin*, and *bite* the object. The dolphin was first given one of these commands and after carrying it out was either given the 'repeat' command or the 'don't repeat' command. In the latter case, the dolphin was to choose one of the four remaining behaviours. For example, if the dolphin was initially instructed to jump over the object, did so, and then was given the don't-repeat command, it could choose either to go under the object, bite it, or touch it with the tail or the pectoral fin. The dolphin was not only successful at repeating or not repeating the initial behaviour, but could also respond successfully to a string of successive commands. For example, a four-item sequence might be *go under, repeat, don't repeat, repeat,* in which case the dolphin, after swimming under the object, is expected to swim under it again, then choose a different behaviour, and finally repeat that latter self-selected behaviour. The dolphin was highly successful at carrying out various four-item sequences of this type in all possible three-way permutations of 'repeat' and 'don't repeat'. In order to perform at this level, the dolphin must retain a representation in memory of the behaviour it just did, process and carry out the subsequent instruction to repeat it or not, and update its memory of what it just did for each successive behaviour performed. The findings of high levels of performance in this task reveal conscious awareness by the dolphin of its own recent behaviours (see Mercado et al. 1998 and summaries in Herman 2006).

Conscious awareness of one's own body parts is easily measured in young children by their ability to identify and point to their own body parts, when asked, by their caregiver, e.g. 'where is your nose, your eye, your foot', and so forth. Children as young as 2 years can identify as many as 20 different body parts, and can also respond appropriately to action requests, such as 'push the ball with your foot'. The young child's ability to do this follows a developmental progression and reveals the emergence of a **body image* that allows for conscious awareness and conscious control of his or her own body parts. As adults, we take this capability for granted, but there are certain types of brain lesions that destroy this capability. In *autotopagnosia*, for example, the patient is unable to point to a body part on request. The patient has thus lost conscious awareness of these body parts. Herman et al. (2001) demonstrated that a bottlenosed dolphin could understand symbolic gestural references to its own body parts, by either showing the referenced body part, shaking it, or using it to either touch or toss a referenced object in her pool. Further, the dolphin was able to use a referenced body part in unique, novel ways, on request by the experimenter. For example, when given for the first time the three-item gestural sequence glossed as *'frisbee + dorsal fin + touch'*, the dolphin swam to the frisbee floating in her pool (there were five different objects floating in the pool), turned on her side, and laid her dorsal fin precisely on top of the frisbee. This was a behaviour that this dolphin or other dolphins would not likely do spontaneously. Results like this showed that the dolphin had a body image that allowed for conscious awareness and conscious control of its own body parts as well as an understanding of symbolic references to those body parts.

The dolphin's awareness of its own body image and own body parts also manifests itself in its remarkable ability to imitate the motor behaviours of human demonstrators. The dolphin is arguably the best behavioural imitator among non-humans. In the wild, dolphins are naturally synchronous, e.g. as shown in their leaps through the air in close synchrony with one or more companions. In the laboratory, as shown by further studies of Herman and colleagues, bottlenosed dolphins can mimic the behaviour of a human demonstrator who may, for example, be performing a pirouette, leaning over backwards, or raising a leg in the air (Herman 2002). For the latter behaviour, the dolphin raises its tail in the air, in effect analogizing a relation between its tail and our leg. Thus, the dolphin is relating directly or by analogy its body image to the human body plan, even though the two body plans are so different. Further, the dolphin is able not only to imitate human behaviours demonstrated live, but also behaviours appearing on a television screen displayed behind an underwater window, revealing that it recognizes abstract or degraded images of the human form (Herman et al. 1990).

Finally, self-awareness in dolphins is also suggested by a study of meta-cognition—awareness of one's own state of knowledge. Smith et al. (1995) tested a bottlenosed dolphin in a psychophysical task requiring it to discriminate between a high and a low tone, but the low tone was of variable frequency that at times closely approached the frequency of the high tone. The dolphin had available separate levers for judging 'high' or 'low', as well as a third lever that it could use as an 'escape' when uncertain. Five human subjects were tested in an equivalent task. The humans and the dolphins each evidenced small thresholds, a narrow interval of uncertainty, and used the escape response similarly. Smith et al. concluded that the 'uncertain' task taps cognitive self-awareness while tasks like MSR may tap body self-awareness.

There are many other questions about consciousness that await further study, including, for example, the dolphin's awareness of 'self' in others. There is no doubt, however, that dolphins, especially the well-studied bottlenosed dolphin, are highly intelligent, rivalling their 'cognitive cousin', the chimpanzee, in that capacity, particularly when intelligence is measured by the species' flexibility in developing new behaviours or in adapting effectively to new challenges in its natural world or in the very different world of the aquarium or laboratory.

LOUIS M. HERMAN

Gallup Jr., G. G. (1970). 'Chimpanzees: self-recognition'. *Science*, 167.

Herman, L. M. (2002). 'Vocal, social, and self-imitation by bottlenosed dolphins'. In Nehaniv, C. and Dautenhahn, K. (eds) *Imitation in Animals and Artifacts*.

—— (2006). 'Intelligence and rational behaviour in the bottlenosed dolphin'. In Hurley, S. and Nudds, M. (eds) *Rational animals?*

——, Matus, D. S., Herman, E. Y., Ivancic, M., and Pack, A. A. (2001). 'The bottlenosed dolphin's (*Tursiops truncatus*) understanding of gestures as symbolic representations of its body parts'. *Animal Learning and Behavior*, 29.

——, Morrel-Samuels, P., and Pack, A. A. (1990). 'Bottlenosed dolphin and human recognition of veridical and degraded video displays of an artificial gestural language'. *Journal of Experimental Psychology: General*, 119.

Marino, L., Reiss, D., and Gallup Jr., G. G. (1994). 'Mirror recognition in bottlenose dolphins: implications for comparative investigations of highly dissimilar species'. In Parker, S. T. et al. (eds) *Self-Awareness in Animals and Humans: Developmental Perspectives*.

Marten, K. and Psarakos, S. (1994). 'Evidence of self-awareness in the bottlenosed dolphin (*Tursiops truncatus*)'. In Parker, S. T. et al. (eds) *Self-Awareness in Animals and Humans: Developmental Perspectives*.

Mercado III, E., Murray, S. O., Uyeyama, R. K., Pack, A. A., and Herman, L. M. (1998). 'Memory for recent actions in the bottlenosed dolphin (*Tursiops truncatus*): repetition of arbitrary behaviors using an abstract rule'. *Animal Learning and Behavior*, 26.

Reiss, D. and Marino, L. (2001). 'Mirror self-recognition in the bottlenose dolphin: a case of cognitive convergence'. *Proceedings of the National Academy of Sciences of the USA*, 98.

Smith, J. D., Schull, J., Strote, J., McGee, K., Egnor, R., and Erb, L. (1995). 'The uncertain response in the bottlenosed dolphin (*Tursiops truncatus*)'. *Journal of Experimental Psychology: General*, 124.

animal consciousness: great apes Great apes (chimpanzees, gorillas, orangutans, and bonobos) are evolutionarily the closest relatives to humans. They engage in a variety of intelligent behaviours, such as tool use and tool manufacture; they present cultural variations in such behaviours (e.g. under similar ecological conditions, some communities use stones as hammers to break open hard nuts, whereas other communities use sticks to exploit ant and termite resources), and in captive conditions they learn to use manual gestures or artificial symbols in what, according to some, might amount to a rudimentary language (Gómez 2004).

Because of this cognitive complexity and their closeness to humans, great apes are specially interesting candidates for showing consciousness in the animal kingdom. A number of behaviours have been highlighted as indicators of consciousness in apes.

1. Mirror self-recognition
2. Tests of metacognition
3. Metacognition of others' mental states

1. Mirror self-recognition

A manifestation of self-awareness is the ability to recognize that the image reflected by a mirror corresponds to oneself. When great apes are confronted with mirrors, initially they show social responses, treating their mirror image as a conspecific. However, as they have experience with the mirror, in a matter of days, social reactions disappear and, instead, they show self-inspecting behaviours, especially directed at parts of their bodies that are not directly visible to them, such as their faces or the inner parts of their mouths. In contrast, the vast majority of other animals, including all non-ape primates, such as macaque monkeys, continue to give social responses to the mirror image; or end up ignoring it, but never make the transition to use the mirror for self-inspection or self-contemplation (Parker et al. 1994). This suggests that apes, but not monkeys and other animals, have the ability to self-recognize.

To formally test this suggestion, Gordon Gallup developed the mirror test (Gallup et al. 2002; see MIRROR TEST). At its most stringent, this test requires the subject to be anaesthetized and, while sleeping, marking an invisible (for the subject) part of its body, for example, the eyebrow, with odourless dye. When the subject wakes up, its behaviour without a mirror is quantitatively compared with its behaviour when a mirror is available. If the painted mark is inspected only or preferentially in front of the mirror, using the reflection as a guide, then the conclusion is that the subjects indeed recognize the image in the mirror as a reflection of themselves, and therefore show the ability for self-awareness.

Chimpanzees, orangutans, and bonobos typically pass the mirror test, provided they have had at least a few days' experience with mirrors prior to the test, and provided they have not been reared in isolation. Another variable affecting their performance is age: younger and older chimpanzees are less likely to pass the test, and some may lose the ability as they age (Gallup et al. 2002). In contrast, the first gorillas tested failed the mirror test. Only a few gorilla individuals are reported to pass some version of this test (the first and most proficient being Koko, a 'linguistically' trained gorilla), or engage in mirror self-inspection suggestive of self-recognition (Patterson and Cohn 1994, Posada and Colell 2007). The relatively poor performance of gorillas as a species in mirror self-recognition remains a puzzle. It is still contentious if this is due to performance problems (e.g. shyness, aversion to mirrors) or competence factors (e.g. they may have lost or lessened the ability for self-awareness during their own evolution diverging from the other great apes). One possibility is that mirror self-recognition does not directly reflect *one* ability, but is an emergent result of the combination of several skills, which in gorillas are more rarely combined, maybe only under unique rearing conditions such as those enjoyed by Koko, the linguistically trained gorilla. For example, in language training experiments, great apes have been taught to use artificial symbols (manual gestures or geometric shapes) to refer to objects and events in the world. Among the 'words' they have been trained to use are symbols to refer to themselves, such as their own names or pointing gestures directed to themselves. In one case (the orangutan Chantek), a relationship has been reported between the progressive learning of such symbols and the emergence of mirror self-recognition (Parker et al. 1994).

In contrast to the generally good performance of apes, a robust result is that no other non-human primates pass the mirror test even after intensive exposure and training with mirrors. Monkeys initially react to their mirror image as if it were a conspecific, and although eventually they learn that it is not a real monkey, they show no sign of recognizing themselves: neither passing the mark test nor engaging in self-inspecting behaviours. Surprisingly, however, they show good evidence that they understand the mechanism of the mirror in relation to other objects; thus, they can accurately use mirrors to find hidden objects or objects behind themselves. They can find anything with the help of a mirror, except themselves (Anderson 2001). An interpretation is that this inability reflects the absence of a notion of themselves as individuals—an inability to be aware of themselves as objects of their own attention.

Methodological objections to the mirror test have proved unfounded. For example, the suggestion that monkey species fail because eye-contact with their own image is so arousing that they cannot process correctly the information or perform the necessary behaviours has been disproved by using mirrors placed in an oblique position, such that eye contact with the reflected image is impossible. No improvement in monkey performance has been detected with this procedure (Anderson 2001).

This sharp and robust phylogenetic divide within primates between monkeys and apes in mirror self-recognition (with the possible exception of gorillas) has prompted speculation that the mirror test captures some key cognitive difference closely related to the human ability for *self-consciousness. The fact that only our closest relatives pass this test would suggest that it is diagnostic of some key cognitive step towards humanness (Parker et al. 1994). Gallup's original suggestion was that it implied a complex form of metacognition, or awareness of mental states. However, critics suggest that it might rather measure an ability to represent body schemas, rather than cognitive schemas; i.e., awareness of oneself as a physical entity rather than awareness of oneself as a psychological entity (Gallup et al. 2002).

A recent, partial challenge to the phylogenetic divide singling out apes and humans comes from studies with dolphins and elephants claiming that some individuals of these species are capable of passing the mirror test (see ANIMAL CONSCIOUSNESS: DOLPHINS). The argument is that the type of self-awareness measured with mirrors could be linked to some ability for *empathy that would have evolved independently in different species where empathetic skills were selected for (Plotnik et al. 2006). Among primates this would have happened only in some apes and humans.

2. Tests of metacognition

Other approaches to primate self-awareness have tried to address directly the issue of awareness of one's own mental states, avoiding the confusion with awareness of one's own body. Two main paradigms dominate the field.

In the so-called *optional test paradigm* (Hampton 2005, Smith 2005), participants can choose whether or not to take a test on the basis of whether they know or do not know the correct response. It is therefore supposed to require the ability to evaluate one's own state of knowledge. In a typical optional test, a monkey learns that he will receive a reward when among two or more images on a computer screen he chooses the one that is identical to a sample shown a few moments before. This is a test of recognition memory for the sample image. Monkeys typically respond correctly in 80–90% of trials when the delay between sample and choice is under 30 s. With longer delays, their performance progressively deteriorates, getting close to chance level with more than 2 min delay, when they seem to forget the sample.

In a *metacognitive test*, after seeing the sample, the monkey is allowed to decide whether or not he wants to proceed to the final phase (where he will get a preferred reward if correct, or nothing plus a time-out period if incorrect). If he wants to proceed, he touches a pattern on the computer screen, and then the test images appear; if he declines the test, he touches a different pattern, and gets a low-quality reward (a small piece of his usual monkey food). With delays slightly over 30 s (where performance in forced tests is about 70%), monkeys frequently decline to take the test and go for the low-quality reward. But their performance when they do choose to take the test is about 85% correct, significantly higher than in forced tests. This has been taken to indicate that rhesus monkeys are aware of whether or not they remember the sample, and decide to take or decline the test on the basis of this meta-knowledge.

Support for this notion comes from two additional results. First, when monkeys are given no sample (and therefore have no information to guide their choice), they are much more likely to use the decline option, in some cases in 100% of the trials. Second, as the delay between sample presentation and option increases, so the probability of choosing not to take the test increases. This suggests that declining the test is indeed related to the probability of having forgotten the sample. Rhesus monkeys pass this test, whereas pigeons fail. To date, this test has not been given to great apes, but the prediction is that they would pass.

Great apes (chimpanzees and orangutans) have received a second metacognitive test—the *looking to know* test (Call 2005). In this test, a piece of food is inserted into one of a number of hollow tubes that are then presented in horizontal position to the ape, in such a way that, if the ape wishes, she can bend down and look inside the tubes before choosing one. When apes see the baiting process and therefore know which tube the food is in, they typically (75% of times) reach directly for the tube without bothering to first look inside. However, if a 5 s delay is introduced before they are allowed to make a choice, their looking behaviour (during the delay) may increase to 50%. When the apes are not allowed to see which tube the food is placed in during baiting, looking behaviour significantly increases to 60% with immediate choice and up to 85% with the 5 s delay. This suggests that the apes are aware of whether or not they know the location of the food, and take appropriate action in the latter case. All four species of apes—chimpanzees, orangutans, bonobos, and gorillas—perform similarly in this test. Moreover, in a proportion of occasions, the apes chose the baited tube after having looked only into the other, empty tube: i.e. they inferred the presence of the food in the other tube from its absence in the one they had checked. This reveals that the looking strategy is not an automatic or reflex-like reaction (grab the food that you see), but part of a flexible problem-solving strategy (mentally establishing the location of the food). The suggestion is that in order to act like that, apes need to be metacognitively aware of their lack of knowledge

Rhesus monkeys and 2-year-old human children behave like the apes in this test (although the monkeys require preliminary training to learn to look through the tubes). However, domestic dogs fail an adapted version of this test: they do not take the opportunity of visually or olfactorily inspecting boxes before making a decision, thereby revealing an apparent lack of awareness of their lack of knowledge (Call 2005).

As in the optional test paradigm, the issue here is to what extent an explicit metacognitive representation of 'knowing' vs 'not knowing' is necessary to perform well, or it suffices some implicit computation of whether a target for action is or is not present. Primates are used to visually guided reaching and tracking of targets. If the slot for the target in their mental scheme is empty or underdetermined, this may inhibit action until the slot is filled, prompting the primates to try and find the whereabouts of the target. Rather than consciously categorizing their state in terms of knowing or not knowing, primates may simply aim at finding the missing element of their well-practised reaching schemas. But it could be argued that even this lower-level explanation may reflect a primitive, implicit type of metacognitive self-awareness—an ability to act in response to the state of internal representations rather than directly in response to external stimuli.

3. Metacognition of others' mental states

Consciousness has been related to the ability to attribute mental states to others. Indeed some models of *theory of mind propose that mental state attribution is achieved through a process of simulation or mental perspective-taking in which one uses awareness of one's own mental states to imagine others' mental states. After a period of scepticism about great apes' abilities to attribute even such simple mental states as 'attention' or 'seeing' to others, recent evidence suggests that chimpanzees and other apes may understand what others can or cannot see and even what others have or have not seen in the past (amounting to attributing knowledge and ignorance to others), especially when they are tested with conspecifics in competitive contexts. For example, subordinate chimpanzees prefer to retrieve pieces of food that are not visible to other, dominant chimpanzees, or that were hidden when the dominants were not present. Skills like these might amount to having some components of theory of mind (Tomasello et al. 2003). However, it is unclear that the attribution of visual access and knowledge in these experiments requires a conscious simulation of mental states. A simpler interpretation is that primates may be coding intentional relations between agents and targets, without explicit representations of subjective mental states (Gómez 2004). Recent experiments with rhesus monkeys suggest that they perform similarly to chimpanzees in competitive tests that require attribution of vision and knowledge to others (Santos et al. 2007). However, neither chimpanzees nor rhesus have been able to pass tests of false-belief attribution (predicting the behaviour of agents that do not just ignore, but *misrepresent* the whereabouts of a target). These might require more complex metacognition (e.g. a so-called 'meta-representational theory of mind') that might be more closely related to consciousness. The performance of chimpanzee and rhesus monkeys in theory of mind tests therefore roughly mirrors their performance in self-metacognitive tests.

When comparing the mirror test with both individual and social metacognitive tests, we are left with a paradoxical situation: the experimental test that best discriminates phylogenetic proximity to humans (mirror self-recognition) is theoretically argued to be less demanding in cognitive terms (it may reflect bodily awareness rather than metacognitive awareness), whereas the tests that theoretically seem to require more complex cognition (awareness of mental states) do not discriminate within primates (but they may do between primates and other animals). There remains the possibility, therefore, that metacognitive tests tap basic cognitive skills that may be necessary but not sufficient for human forms of consciousness, whereas the mirror test is diagnostic of something, as yet unidentified, that is closer to human consciousness.

JUAN-CARLOS GÓMEZ

Anderson, J. R. (2001). 'Self and others in nonhuman primates: a question of perspective'. *Psychologia*, 44.

Call, J. (2005). 'The self and other: a missing link in comparative social cognition'. In Terrace, H. S. and Metcalfe, J. (eds) *The Missing Link in Cognition: Origins of Self-reflective Consciousness*.

Gallup Jr., G. G., Anderson, J. H., and Shillito, D. J. (2002). 'The mirror test'. In Bekoff, M. et al. (eds) *The Cognitive Animal*.

Gómez, J.-C. (2004). *Apes, Monkeys, Children, and the Growth of Mind*.

Hampton, R. R. (2005). 'Can rhesus monkeys discriminate between remembering and forgetting?' In Terrace, H. S. and Metcalfe, J. (eds) *The Missing Link in Cognition: Origins of Self-reflective Consciousness*.

Parker, S., Boccia, M., and Mitchell, R. (eds) (1994). *Self-recognition and Awareness in Apes, Monkeys and Children*.

Patterson, F. and Cohn, R. (1994). 'Self-recognition and self-awareness in Lowland gorillas'. In Parker, S. et al. (eds) *Self-recognition and Awareness in Apes, Monkeys and Children*.

Plotnik, J. M., Waal, de. F., and Reiss, D. (2006). 'Self-recognition in an Asian elephant'. *Proceedings of the National Academy of Sciences of the USA*, 103.

Posada, S. and Colell, M. (2007). 'Another gorilla (*Gorilla gorilla gorilla*) recognizes himself in a mirror'. *American Journal of Primatology*, 69.

Santos, L. R., Flombaum, J. I., and Webb, P. (2007). 'The evolution of human mindreading'. In Platek, S. M. et al. (eds) *Evolutionary Cognitive Neuroscience*.

Smith, J. D. (2005). 'Studies of uncertainty monitoring and metacognition in animals and humans'. In Terrace, H. S. and Metcalfe, J. (eds) *The Missing Link in Cognition: Origins of Self-reflective Consciousness*.

Tomasello, M., Call, J., and Hare, B. (2003). 'Chimpanzees understand psychological states—the question is which ones and to what extent'. *Trends in Cognitive Sciences*, 7.

animal consciousness: raven The common raven, *Corvus corax*, has the widest geographical and ecological range of any native bird in the world and is prominent in the mythology of many different cultures within that range. It has been variously described as a trickster, a creator, and an omen of death. The raven has for centuries given the impression that it possesses uncommon intelligence. In recent decades its often-enigmatic behaviour has finally come under scientific scrutiny. Recent research on ravens provides reasonable inferences that meet the criteria of 'knowing'. Ravens accomplish not only physical but also social tasks that indicate at least rudimentary mental sophistication resembling that demonstrated for humans, great apes, and some other corvid birds.

1. Insight
2. Social behaviour

1. Insight

Any specific behaviour is likely the result of an ever-changing mix of the relative roles of pre-programmed behaviour, maturation, learning, and conscious insight. Modifications of the ravens' responses occur through learning as well as maturation. Consciousness may be common, but demonstrating what is 'in the head' of another who cannot use words may be next to impossible under most circumstances. Proof requires that the major distinguishing characteristic of the behaviour is neither innate nor learned. As a consequence, the test for consciousness involves exhibition of a behaviour that the animal does not normally perform yet does so proficiently at first try. The following sets of experiments, involving strings and a piece of hard salami, come fairly close to those requirements.

In one set of experiments, adult captive ravens with no experience of strings approached a metre-long string tied to a branch, from which dangled a piece of meat. They reached down, grasped the string with their bill, pulled up, placed the string on the branch, stepped on to the string and held it down on the branch, then let go of the string, reached down again and pulled up another length of string, and then repeated the precise sequence 6–10 times until reaching the food. Furthermore, while naive birds unhesitatingly attempted to fly off with food while it was still tied to a string, those who had pulled up food did not attempt to leave with it when they were startled. Significantly, this behaviour of letting go of the meat occurred following the first pull-up. When two strings were crossed with only one holding meat and the other a rock, some birds nevertheless (on their first trial) first contacted the string with food, while others initially gave a brief yank on the wrong string, which was directly below them (as on previous straight pull-ups). Apparently then noticing that the rock and not the meat moved, they then quickly switched their attention to the other string and pulled up the meat. Repeated trials did little to change the individuals' initial mistake of contacting the wrong string, as though trial-and-error learning had no or little effect. Apparently some individual birds did not know that the strings were crossed and so they persisted in what 'made sense' according to what they thought they knew. On the other hand, these same birds almost instantly corrected their mistake when they saw it. To test further whether concepts do play a role in the string-pulling behaviour, in another test other similarly aged ravens in the same aviary set-up were confronted with the illogical situation of a looped string that had to be pulled down to make the meat come up. These birds were unable to reach the meat and soon lost interest in trying.

Other potential means of reaching the meat on string include flying at it, trying to rip off the string, twisting it off, pecking it, using a twig as a tool to pull, etc. The effects of any and all of these potential responses could be either learned or acquired through maturation. Once gained, they could be tried sequentially by mental pictures, and eliminated in favour of the best option. Juvenile ravens applied most of these options overtly, presumably because they lacked accurate metal images. In 6 minutes (on average) they 'learned' that most options did not work, and they then narrowed in on the 'right' solution. Some adults, in contrast, hit on the right solution in as little as 30 seconds after contacting string and without overtly going through the repertoire of possible choices.

Ravens almost routinely exhibit behaviour that suggests they 'look ahead' or fill in beyond what is proximally available to their vision. Adult birds who have experience with a metre-long horizontal tube, and are then for the first time confronted with the tube placed at an angle, search for food they see dropped in to slide down, not where they last see it (at the entrance) but at ground level where it has slid down but is not visible. They routinely stash surplus food next to them, to then pick it up all in one packet, but only when competitors (who would pick up loose food) are absent. They effectively slice hard suet by pecking it in directed lines, to then haul off chunks suitable for carrying (Comstock 2006).

2. Social behaviour

Ravens' social dependency lasts throughout their lives. The reliance of the offspring on their parents extends for 1–3 months after the young fledge. The non-breeders and young then become gregarious and often gather into non-kin groups. These groups commonly feed on temporary food bonanzas such as large animal carcasses, and to gain access to this meat they must contend both with dominant resident pairs that try to monopolize the resource and also with dangerous carnivores. By the age of about 3 years they form stable, lifelong partnerships. Pairs stay together year-round.

Numerous tactics have been identified that relate to social manipulation. First, as a counter-strategy to the dominant adults, the juveniles recruit conspecifics from communal nocturnal roosts and thereby gain access to clumped and defended food by swamping the dominant's defences. However, after the crowd has gained access, the individuals within it engage in a competition to haul off meat and hide it out of sight of their competitors. Thus, the same behaviours that give them access to the food also create competitors that take it away. Numerous complex cognitive problems and opportunities arise from the conflicts at locally abundant but ephemeral food.

The meat that the birds haul off for later use is tucked into crevices or is buried and camouflaged with debris, so that it is invisible. Ravens remember the locations not only of their own food caches, but also of those they see others make (Heinrich 1995). As a counter-tactic, birds attempt to cache in private and may use visual obstructions to screen the sight of their cache. As a counter-counter-strategy, potential cache-raiders remain hidden and approach another's cache when the owner is absent. If (under experimental conditions) the cache-makers have the potential audience of a viewer while another nearby bird is hidden behind an obstruction, they attempt to repel the viewer when it later comes near the cache but ignore non-viewers (Bugnyar and Heinrich 2005). These results suggest that the birds can attribute knowledge to others. An alternative explanation, that the 'knower' may have divulged its knowledge of the cache, via subtle behavioural cues when near it, is not supported by empirical evidence. When experiments were repeated with a human as a cacher, and observing and non-observing birds were pitted against each other by simultaneously allowing both into the caching area, observing birds pilfered the cache ten times faster when they were in the presence of another bird (who also had had a view of the cache-making) than in the presence of a non-observer (Bugnyar and Heinrich 2006). In the latter case, when paired with a non-observer they did not hurry in cache-recovery, nor did they attempt to repel non-observers that wandered near the cache. This provides evidence that observing birds have an internal representation of other birds' mental states regarding the existence and location of the cache.

Ravens not only appear to know about others' knowledge, they also gauge others' behaviour and ascertain unknowns that could be relevant to them. Cueing begins with the young following their parents. The young fearlessly approach objects (such as carcasses) near their parents. After leaving their parents they learn about new objects (such as carcasses to feed from, or sleeping predators) by behaviour that functions to elicit responses from these objects. Supine bodies are approached from the rear and the birds then make conspicuous 'jumping jacks', and/or they keep visiting the 'carcass' at intervals of minutes or hours before venturing near it.

The intentions and capabilities of moving predators are tested by gradually approaching and tweaking the tails of these animals. Within minutes the birds then learn the animal's reaction speeds, pursuit tendencies, and capabilities. Such knowledge becomes useful when they are required to feed alongside tested animals, such as wolves, bears, cats, and eagles. The ravens' pronounced *neophobia* of large objects, combined with apparent playful curiosity associated with dangerous predators attending food bonanzas, allow them to exploit a great diversity of food. Similarly, the young ravens' *neophilia* permits them to discover a great diversity of small food items, such as berries, eggs, insects and other invertebrates, human refuse, etc.

An individual raven's responses are greatly modulated by social considerations. If one raven in a crowd is alarmed it flies up quickly and leaves without vocalizing. Almost in the same instant all the rest then fly up and leave as well, even though the alarm object is totally out of view from them. Apparently the raven's flight behaviour is a sufficient cue to the others. Similarly, captive ravens use the gaze direction of their keeper (who feeds them) as a behavioural cue that guides their attention. They co-orient with the human's look-ups and may even reposition themselves to follow the experimenter's gaze around a visual barrier (Bugnyar et al. 2004).

Ravens live in the context of a social unit of other individuals for at least part of their lives. Perhaps they have uniquely sophisticated abilities relative to other birds because they must contend not only with conspecific associates and competitors, but also with dangerous predators whose reactions they need to anticipate in order to feed in their near proximity without being killed.

BERND HEINRICH

Bugnyar, T. and Heinrich, B. (2005). 'Ravens, *Corvus corax*, differentiate between knowledgeable and ignorant competitors'. *Proceedings of the Royal Society of London Series B: Biological Sciences*, 272.

—— —— (2006). 'Ravens, *Corvus corax*, alter pilfer behaviour according to social context and identity of competitors'. *Animal Cognition*, 9.

——, Stoewe, M., and Heinrich, B. (2004). 'Ravens, *Corvus corax*, follow gaze direction of humans around obstacles'. *Proceedings of the Royal Society of London Series B: Biological Sciences*, 271.

Comstock, C. (2006). 'Suet carving to maximize foraging efficiency by common ravens'. *Wilson Journal of Ornithology*, 119.

Heinrich, B. (1995). 'An experimental investigation of insight in common ravens, *Corvus corax*'. *The Auk*, 112.

—— (1999). *Mind of the Raven: Investigations and Adventures with Wolf-birds*.

—— and Bugnyar, T. (2005). 'Testing problem solving in ravens: string-pulling to reach food'. *Ethology*, 111.

Marzluff, J. M., Heinrich, B., and Marzluff, C. S. (1996). 'Raven roosts are mobile information centers'. *Animal Behaviour*, 51.

Range, F., Bugnyar, T., Schloegl, C., and Kotrschal, K. (2006). 'Individual learning ability and coping styles in ravens'. *Behavioural Processes*, 73.

animal metacognition and consciousness Humans monitor their states of knowing and remembering, of certainty and doubt, and respond appropriately to these states by rethinking and seeking help or information when necessary. These responses ground the literatures on uncertainty monitoring and metacognition (i.e. thinking about thinking—Nelson 1992). Researchers take humans' metacognitive behaviours to show hierarchical levels of *cognitive control, cognitive *self-consciousness, and declarative consciousness (i.e. conscious mental states that are reportable to others). Because metacognition is one of humans' most sophisticated cognitive capacities, it is an important question whether animals (i.e. non-human animals) have this capacity as well. Indeed, the sophistication of the metacognitive capacity could let it rival tool use and language in revealing continuities or discontinuities between the mind and consciousness of animals and humans.

Accordingly, since 1995 researchers have investigated a new area of comparative inquiry considering whether animals have a capacity for cognitive monitoring (Cowey and Stoerig 1995, Smith et al. 1995). Researchers have used tasks in which a mix of easy and difficult trials are presented, and in which animals are allowed—in addition to the primary discrimination responses—to decline to complete any trials they choose. If animals can monitor cognition accurately, they should identify difficult trials as error-risking and decline those trials selectively. Indeed, this is what some animals do; producing data patterns in cognitive-monitoring tasks that are like those produced by humans (Smith et al. 2003). The logic of these comparative experiments—which evaluate metacognition using a non-verbal, behavioural task—has natural extensions to the ongoing study of metacognition in young human children.

In one of the original comparative studies, monkeys performed a visual discrimination task in which they were asked to make a 'Dense' response if a cued area on a computer monitor contained exactly 2950 illuminated pixels, and alternatively a 'Sparse' response if any fewer pixels were presented. A third, uncertainty response was allowed that enabled monkeys to decline difficult trials. The results are shown in Fig. A9a. When the discrimination involved easier Sparse and Dense trials, monkeys primarily used the perceptual Sparse and Dense responses, and generally did so correctly. Interestingly, the uncertainty response was used most in the region of maximum uncertainty, at the point where these two response curves cross, and where it would be maximally beneficial to respond 'Uncertain'. Thus, monkeys correctly assessed when they were at risk for error and declined those trials selectively and adaptively. Humans did so, too (Fig. A9b). Humans attributed their uncertainty responses to their mental state (e.g. 'when I wasn't sure'; 'when I couldn't tell'). Although monkeys can make no explicit attribution of their internal state, there is a clear isomorphism between the uncertainty responses of the two species. In related work using an auditory discrimination task, Smith et al.

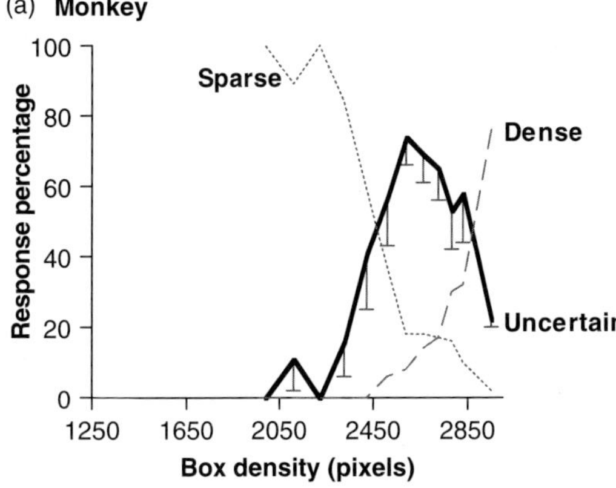

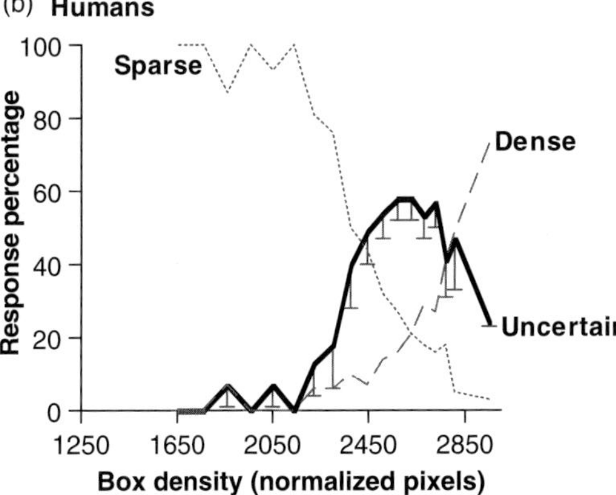

Fig. A9. Visual discrimination performance by a monkey (a) and humans (b). The horizontal axis in each graph gives the pixel density of the box, and the vertical axis indicates the percentage of trials ending with each possible response. The 'dense' response (dashed lines) was correct for boxes with 2950 lit pixels; all other densities deserved the 'sparse' response (dotted lines). Participants could also choose the uncertainty response (solid lines). The error bars show the lower 95% confidence limits. To clarify the human results by equating discrimination performance across human participants, their perceptual thresholds were aligned through a normalization procedure so that each crossover of the two primary responses lay at about 2700 pixels. The graph in (a) is from Smith et al. (1997). Copyright 1997 by Elsevier. Reprinted with permission. The graph in (b) is from Smith et al. (2003). Copyright 2003 by Cambridge University Press. Reprinted with permission.

(1995) showed that humans and dolphins make use of uncertainty responses equivalently to decline those trials that are likely to lead to error. The dolphin in this study produced various auxiliary behaviours that would be interpreted as outward signs of uncertainty in human participants (e.g. hesitation and wavering), and the strength of these behaviours predicted whether the dolphin would respond 'Uncertain' on any particular trial.

Subsequent research has made it clear that low-level explanations grounded in conditioning or stimulus control cannot explain what animals do in these tasks. Various issues have been resolved concerning the uncertainty response and the positive contingencies accidentally granted it in some studies (e.g. some researchers directly rewarded the Uncertain response, which compromised its uncertainty interpretation). Monkeys have now been shown to respond Uncertain in a number of different experimental paradigms: when facing difficult same–different judgements that are abstract and removed from the stimuli that might exert behavioural control (Shields et al. 1997); when facing difficult numerosity judgements (Beran et al. 2006); when asked in a memory task whether an item has previously been presented (Smith et al. 1998), or whether, even in the absence of any choice stimuli, they remember a previously presented sample (Hampton 2001). An example of this can be seen in Fig. A10a, which shows the performance of a monkey asked to judge whether a probe picture had previously appeared in a list of pictures. The crucial result was that the animal correctly assessed when his memory about a probe was problematic or ambiguous and he declined those trials. His uncertainty responding was the mirror image of his performance when he tried to answer the memory question on other occasions, and it was the mirror image of the predictable strength of memory traces at different positions in the list. Human observers perform this task similarly (Fig. A10b). Finally, monkeys are even able to respond Uncertain when in new tasks they are denied trial-by-trial feedback so that they have to self-construe the task and self-instruct their performance within it. This makes it impossible for conditioning processes to operate, and so in this case one knows that uncertainty responses are cognitive, decisional, and high level, not conditioned and low level (Smith et al. 2006).

Interestingly, research has failed to demonstrate equivalent high-level uncertainty responding by either rats or pigeons (Foote and Crystal 2007, Inman and Shettleworth 1999, Sutton and Shettleworth 2008). Of course caution attends null results like these—positive results might await different methods or more dogged training. Nonetheless, it is an exciting possibility that these cross-species studies are gradually drawing the map of the phylogenetic spread and distribution of metacognition and cognitive self-awareness.

Comparative metacognition researchers have naturally approached cautiously the issue of declarative consciousness in animals. There is agreement that animals in these tasks are showing a capacity—for knowing when they know or remember—that is associated with conscious cognition in humans. Thus, animals are showing functional parallels to human conscious metacognition, though they may not experience everything that accompanies conscious metacognitive experience in humans. For that matter, human metacognitive experience may not always be perfectly conscious, either. There is also an active consideration of whether animal metacognition has implications regarding animals' self-consciousness. It remains open to debate and experiment whether and how an organism must feel like a self in order to monitor the content of the self's mental states.

Nonetheless, the comparative findings on uncertainty monitoring and metacognition bring a constructive new perspective to considerations of animal consciousness. Previously, interest had focused on the intriguing idea that animal consciousness and awareness had a social origin, by which animals evolved self-awareness of mood, state, and motivation so as to model and predict the mood, state, and motivation of the conspecific (Humphrey 1978). Consciousness, in the view of Humphrey and others, was an adaptation to social living that increased social intelligence.

However, comparative metacognition research demonstrates why consciousness might have an independent adaptive role and an independent evolutionary origin. Animals frequently encounter ambiguity, impoverished inputs, threshold detection conditions, novel contexts, complex situations, and so forth. They likely have the need for a higher-level cognitive-regulatory system wherein cognitive close calls can be refereed and adjudicated. A working consciousness would be an ideal information-processing locus for the decisional assemblage that conducts such adjudication.

In fact, it has been a recurrent idea in cognitive science that cognitive difficulty and indeterminacy elicit higher-level and more conscious modes of cognitive processing. James (1890/1952:93) noted that consciousness provides extraneous help to cognition when nerve processes grow hesitant—'Where indecision is great, as before a dangerous leap, consciousness is agonizingly intense.' Tolman agreed that conscious awareness and ideation arise mainly at times of conflicting signals and predictions. In fact, in a claim remarkable for its time, Tolman (1927) suggested that animals' uncertainty behaviours—for example, the hesitation and wavering the dolphin showed in Smith et al. (1995)—could operationalize consciousness for the behaviourist. The claim—that uncertainty and difficulty are uniquely associated with higher and more conscious forms of cognitive self-regulation—is potentially an inclusive claim that has no necessary reason or way to include only human minds and exclude animal minds. Certainly, animals' success in uncertainty-monitoring paradigms encourages the extension of the claim to them.

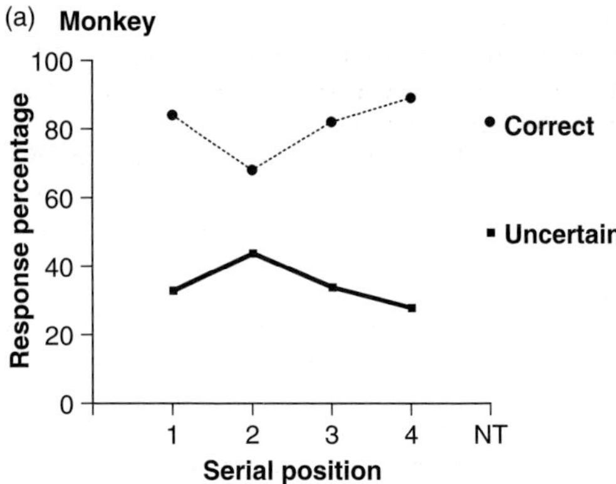

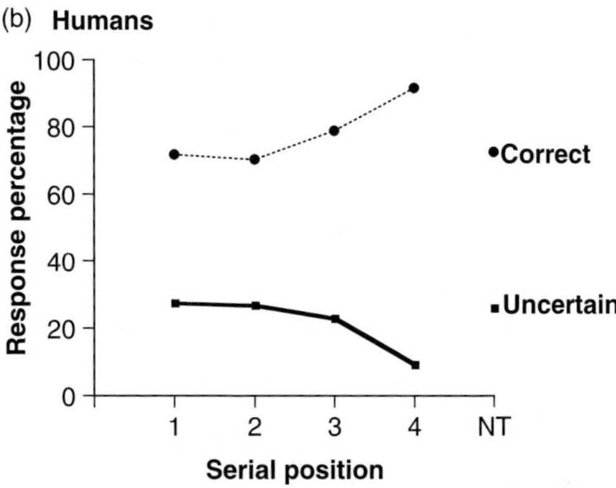

Fig. A10. Memory performance by a monkey (a) and humans (b). The horizontal axis in each graph indicates the serial position of the probed picture; 'NT' ('Not There') denotes trials on which the probe picture had not been in the preceding list of pictures. Each graph shows the percentage of total trials that received the uncertainty response (solid lines), along with the percentage correct when participants chose on other occasions to accept the memory test (dotted lines). From Smith et al. (1998). Copyright 1998 by the American Psychological Association. Reprinted with permission.

Comparative metacognition research joins related research on animals' bodily self-awareness as explored using the *mirror test (Gallup 1982) in which some animals inspect dye marks on their bodies after discovering the marks when looking in a mirror. This intriguing paradigm rightly remains a component of the discussion about animal awareness. However, the paradigm has been beset by methodological concerns (e.g. confounds with the recovery cycle from anaesthesia during which the mark is applied). Moreover, the theory behind the paradigm has been partially disconfirmed (i.e. the theory holds that only apes and humans should show mirror awareness, but dolphins and elephants have recently shown that awareness). Finally, it remains unclear just what aspect of consciousness and self-awareness is necessarily confirmed when an animal inspects a body mark in a mirror. Given these concerns, the advent of the metacognition approach is welcome for providing complementary methods and perspectives in this area, and in particular for providing paradigms that test directly animals' capacity for cognitive self-awareness and their ability to make behavioural reports of that awareness. The metacognition approach has also been valuable for moving the comparative scientific study of consciousness beyond the idea that only a common ancestor of apes and humans experienced the evolutionary flashpoint of aware mind, and toward the idea that consciousness may be broadly adaptive, and so evolved and maintained within the evolutionary history of many species.

J. DAVID SMITH

Beran, M. J., Smith, J. D., Redford, J. S., and Washburn, D. A. (2006). 'Rhesus macaques (*Macaca mulatta*) monitor uncertainty during numerosity judgments'. *Journal of Experimental Psychology: Animal Behavior Processes*, 32.

Cowey, A. and Stoerig, P. (1995). 'Blindsight in monkeys'. *Nature*, 373.

Foote, A. and Crystal, J. (2007). 'Metacognition in the rat'. *Current Biology*, 17.

Gallup, G. G. (1982). 'Self-awareness and the emergence of mind in primates'. *American Journal of Primatology*, 2.

Hampton, R. R. (2001). 'Rhesus monkeys know when they remember'. *Proceedings of the National Academy of Sciences of the USA*, 98.

Humphrey, N. K. (1978). 'The social function of the intellect'. In Bateson, P. P. G. and Hinde, R. A. (eds) *Growing Points in Ethology*.

Inman, A. and Shettleworth, S. J. (1999). 'Detecting metamemory in nonverbal subjects: a test with pigeons'. *Journal of Experimental Psychology: Animal Behavior Processes*, 25.

James, W. (1890/1952). *The Principles of Psychology*.

Nelson, T. O. (ed.) (1992) *Metacognition: Core Readings*.

Shields, W. E., Smith, J. D., and Washburn, D. A. (1997). 'Uncertain responses by humans and rhesus monkeys (*Macaca mulatta*) in a psychophysical same-different task'. *Journal of Experimental Psychology: General*, 126.

Smith, J. D., Schull, J., Strote, J., McGee, K., Egnor, R., and Erb, L. (1995). 'The uncertain response in the bottlenosed dolphin (*Tursiops truncatus*)'. *Journal of Experimental Psychology: General*, 124.

——, Shields, W. E., Schull, J., and Washburn, D. A. (1997). 'The uncertain response in humans and animals'. *Cognition*, 62.

——, ——, Allendoerfer, K. R., and Washburn, D. A. (1998). 'Memory monitoring by animals and humans'. *Journal of Experimental Psychology: General*, 127.

——, ——, and Washburn, D. A. (2003). 'The comparative psychology of uncertainty monitoring and metacognition'. *Behavioral and Brain Sciences*, 26.

——, Beran, M. J., Redford, J. S., and Washburn, D. A. (2006). 'Dissociating uncertainty states and reinforcement signals in the comparative study of metacognition'. *Journal of Experimental Psychology: General*, 135.

Sutton, J. E. and Shettleworth, S. J. (2008), 'Memory without awareness: pigeons do not show metamemory in delayed matching-to-sample'. *Journal of Experimental Psychology: Animal Behavior Processes*, 34.

Tolman, E. C. (1927). 'A behaviorist's definition of consciousness'. *Psychological Review*, 34.

anosognosia The term 'anosognosia' indicates the denial of one's own disease or deficit. It can be observed in association with many different kinds of pathological conditions, ranging from *schizophrenia (Pia and Tamietto 2006) to neurological and cognitive disorders. In these latter cases, patients may be unaware of their reading, language, or memory problems (Prigatano and Schacter 1991) or may even resolutely deny the contralesional sensorimotor impairments resulting from localized *brain damage. Patients may deny being blind or paralysed, and their false beliefs are strong and often intractable.

1. Historical development
2. Denial behaviour in anosognosia for hemiplegia
3. Theories of anosognosia
4. Anosognosia for hemiplegia as a disturbance of motor self-awareness

1. Historical development

Historically, the first 'description' of anosognosia can be found in Seneca (Liber V, Epistula IX in Bisiach and Geminiani 1991). In a letter to his friend Lucilius, Seneca reported the puzzling case of a woman who suddenly became blind, most probably after a stroke affecting the posterior parts of the brain (where the areas devoted to the processing of visual information are located):

> You know that Harpestes, my wife's fatuous companion, has remained in my home as an inherited burden.... This foolish woman has suddenly lost her sight. Incredible as it might appear, what I am going to tell you is true: *she does not know she is blind*. Therefore, again and again she asks her guardian to take her elsewhere because *she claims that my home is dark.... It is difficult to recover from a disease if you do not know yourself to be ill.*

Seneca's description was very insightful because it identified the three main characteristics of ansognosia. First, the denial of the primary illness (in Seneca's case the denial of blindness) and the consequent false believe of being 'normal'; second, the confabulation that patients may produce in order to justify their problems (for instance the claim that the house was dark); and third, the negative impact that denial has on recovery (now experimentally demonstrated, e.g. Gialannella and Mattioli 1992).

In the neurological literature, the term anosognosia was first used by Babinski (1914) to denote the puzzling behaviour of right-brain-damaged patients, who, after having developed contralesional hemiplegia, deny that there is anything wrong with their limbs (*anosognosia for hemiplegia*, AHP).

2. Denial behaviour in anosognosia for hemiplegia
The denial behaviour seen in hemiplegic patients affected by AHP is one of the most studied and is paradigmatic: when asked about their potential capability for performing actions, either with the right or with the left hand, or bimanually, they claim that they can perform any kind of movement equally well. The false conviction of being still able to move remains unchanged even when, after they are requested to actually perform different kinds of actions, sensory and visual evidence from the motionless affected side should suggest that no movement has been performed. For instance, patients asked to clap their hands may lift their right hand and put it in the position of clapping, perfectly aligned with the trunk midline, moving it as if it is being clapped against the left hand. They usually appear perfectly satisfied with their performance, never admitting, in the most severe cases, that the left arm did not participate in the action. This despite the fact that the patients can see that the left hand did not clap against the right hand and that they can hear that the typical noise of clapping is not produced. As in Seneca's case, they can generate verbal *confabulations such as 'I never produce noise' or 'I'm not clapping my hands because we aren't at the theatre' or even 'My left hand has gone for a walk' (Berti et al. 1998).

Patients affected by AHP (usually right-brain-damaged patients) may show different degrees of awareness of their physical conditions, ranging from a resolute and intractable unawareness of the neurological symptoms to attenuated forms of unawareness such as emotional indifference (*anosodiaphoria*), in which the motor problems may be admitted but without concern (Critchley 1953), and *dim knowledge* (Anton 1899), in which the patient's behaviour suggests that at some level in the cognitive system the presence of a deficit is recorded, but it is not accessible to the awareness system. For instance, patients who do not admit their paralysis may not object to being bedridden, and do not comment on, and do not ask questions about, their stay in hospital (Bisiach and Geminiani 1991). However, other patients who verbally admit their motor impairment may attempt to stand and walk or to use tools they are completely unable to handle. It has also been shown that anosognosic patients who verbally deny their motor deficit, when asked to rate their capacity to carry out a number of activities involving the use of the left limbs may give very low scores to their potential ability of performing left limb movements (Berti et al. 1996, Marcel et al. 2004), whereas other patients, who are not considered anosognosic on the basis of their verbal report, can give very high scores to their motor capabilities. Some authors have suggested considering these different forms of anosognosia as indicating *dissociations* between awareness verbally reported (i.e. where the phenomenal experience is directly expressed in first-person discourse), and awareness non-verbally demonstrated (i.e. in a condition where the phenomenal experience is not directly reported by the subject), rather than different degrees of awareness (e.g. Bisiach and Geminiani 1991, Berti et al. 1998). A counter-intuitive dissociation is observed when, in the presence of multiple neurological/neuropsychological impairments, the denial is confined only to one of them. For instance, patients with motor impairment of the left limbs may be aware of the paresis of the upper limb, but not that of the lower limb; and patients with multiple physical and cognitive deficits (e.g. contemporary presence of hemiplegia and hemianestesia, as in Marcel et al. 2004, or hemiplegia and reading and drawing disorders, as in Berti et al. 1996) may deny the presence of one disorder while admitting the others.

3. Theories of anosognosia
The theories that consider anosognosia either a consequence of a psychodynamic reaction against the illness (e.g. Weinstein and Kahn 1955) or a disturbance caused by the impossibility of discovering the disease due to the concomitant presence of other neurological (sensory deficits) and neuropsychological disorders (e.g. neglect and cognitive impairment; e.g. Levine et al. 1991) are insufficient to explain the multifaceted aspect of the anosognosic disturbance. For instance, they do not predict the counter-intuitive dissociations found in AHP of the kind just described (for a review, see Berti et al. 2007).

It has been suggested (e.g. Heilman et al. 1998, Frith et al. 2000, Berti et al. 2007) that anosognosia can be conceptualized as (1) a *specific* disorder of **self-consciousness*, that is an impairment of awareness that does not affect the processing of all kinds of stimuli and events, but that is confined to the monitoring of a particular (motor) condition of the self; and (2) a *selective, domain-specific* self-awareness disorder, i.e. an awareness impairment that may affect only one aspect of the patient's pathological condition and not another, and may manifest itself depending on the response modality and task demands. The observation of double dissociations in the patients' attitude towards the illness, triggered by different response modalities, suggests the existence of different streams of awareness in relation to the same pathological event, causing the puzzling effect of a mind that, at a given time, can offer two different interpretations of the same event. The selectivity of unawareness for a specific neurological symptom, when multiple concomitant deficits are present, discloses the multi-component structure of conscious processes. Studies on anosognosia suggest that, although phenomenal experience, as we infer it from normal subject behaviour and from our own experience, has the quality of *unity, mental states at a given time can be kept separate from one another within the flow of consciousness. This separateness allows a brain injury to affect a single *stream of consciousness, leaving the others intact or quasi-intact.

4. Anosognosia for hemiplegia as a disturbance of motor self-awareness

The denial of hemiplegia is in most cases associated with the delusional belief of being able to produce meaningful action with the plegic limbs. One question we need to answer (Pacherie et al. 2006) is whether the delusion encodes, in linguistic form, the real content of the perceptual experience (*endorsement account*). In this case, the phenomenal experience of an anosognosic patient, although not veridical, might be very similar to the motor experience we normally have. Alternatively, does the verbal delusion represent an attempt to explain or make sense of an unusual experience (*explanationist account*)? In this case the phenomenal experience should be odd and contradictory with respect to the previous acquired knowledge of being able to move. Although it might be that a comprehensive account of delusions will contain both endorsement and explanationist components (see below), a recent account of anosognosia seems to favour the endorsement position, at least for explaining the illusion of movement (e.g. Berti and Pia 2006, Berti et al. 2007). This account refers to a model for motor control and motor awareness (Wolpert et al. 1995, Haggard 2005) according to which, once the appropriate motor commands are selected and sent to muscles for the execution of the desired movement, a prediction of the sensory consequences of the movement is formed and would be successively matched with the feedback associated with the actual execution of the intended movement by the activity of a comparator (see Fig. A11). This prediction, based on the efference copy of the programmed motor act (i.e. on signals that, once that we have programmed a movement, are sent to sensory and motor structures that are responsible for adjustments in perception and posture required by that movement), constitutes, according to Blakemore et al. (2002), the signal on which motor awareness is constructed. This may appear counter-intuitive because the prediction (and, therefore, the motor awareness) is formed before the actual execution of the movement. However, it has been demonstrated (Libet et al. 1983) that when neurologically intact subjects have to estimate the time at which they become aware of a voluntary movement (the so called *M judgement*) they indicate a moment that precedes the actual initiation of the movement by 50–80 ms. Thus, Libet et al.'s findings demonstrated that motor awareness is not simply constructed on the sensory feedback coming from the moving muscles, but instead emerges before the afference of any sensory proprioceptive input. It is worth noting that such a model would imply that, whenever the system makes sensory predictions about a certain programmed movement, we may construct the belief that that movement is actually performed (see Berti and Pia 2006). The comparator would then match the congruency between the belief of the intended movement and the representation of the actual status of the system. When, in a normal subject, the motor act corresponds to the representation of the intended movement, motor awareness is *veridically* constructed. When the peripheral event does not correspond to the prediction, the comparator should detect the discrepancy. On the basis of this model, it has been proposed (Berti et al. 2006, 2007) that in *hemiplegic patients without anosognosia* the comparator is still able to detect the mismatch between the prediction and the actual condition and as a result constructs a (non-veridical) experience of motor awareness. As a consequence, when hemiplegic patients without anosognosia are asked to move their affected limb, they acknowledge their motor failure. On the contrary, *hemiplegic-anosognosic patients* with damage to the comparator component of the forward model of the motor system cannot detect the mismatch between the predictions and the feedback, and are not able to distinguish between a purely intended action and the real movement execution. This would lead to the construction of a *non-veridical* motor awareness and, therefore, to the false belief of being able to move. On this view, the delusion reflects the patient's movement experience that arises from the normal or quasi-normal functioning of the prediction/awareness system of the model. Therefore, anosognosic patients may experience the movement they intend to perform. According to this explanation, the activity of the areas involved in motor intentionality (such as the supplementary motor area, SMA) should be spared by the lesion, whereas the areas involved in the comparator activity (such as premotor areas) should be affected. This has been shown in clinical anatomic studies (Berti et al. 2005, Karnath et al. 2005).

A dramatic consequence of being paralysed is that the conditions of the external world cannot be changed by the execution of a purposeful action. Hemiplegic/non-anosognosic patients who admit their paralysis

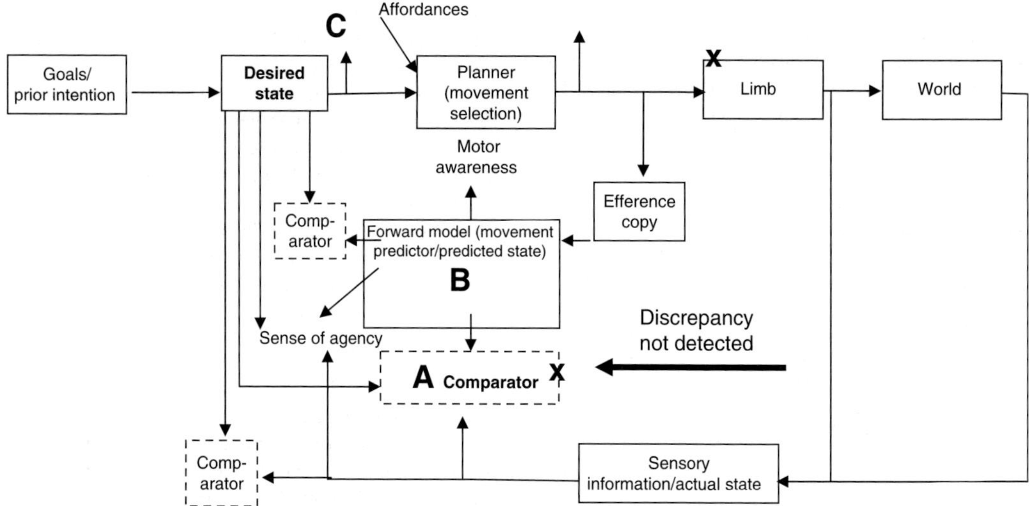

Fig. A11. A version of the forward model of motor production and motor control (modified from Haggard 2005 and Berti and Pia 2006). The 'X' indicates the locus of the brain damage, and the lesion obviously affects the motor capacity of the contralesional limb (the patient is plegic). A is the comparator damaged by the lesion; B is the predictor; C is the locus of emergence of intention to move. According to the model, anosognosia is due to a damage in A, and the false belief of anosognosic patients are due to the normal functioning of both the intentional system (C) and the predictor (B), unmonitored by the damaged comparator (A).

do not encounter any contradiction between their beliefs and the sensory events, and therefore do not need to confabulate to explain the reality. On the other hand, ansognosic patients who experience the illusion of movement might construct complex verbal confabulations because they need to explain the contradiction between the claim of being able to move and the evidence that the pretended movement has not affected the condition of the external world. On this view, the confabulation may be an attempt to make sense of an unusual experience (the fact that despite the 'execution of the movement' nothing has changed in the environment).

It is worth noting that, as Seneca pointed out, anosognosia represents a severe impediment for rehabilitation (Gialannella and Mattioli 1992, Gialannella et al. 2005). Indeed, it is extremely difficult to motivate patients to regain an ability they do not know is lost. As a consequence, patients do not compensate for their motor disturbances and may also refuse rehabilitation treatment because they are convinced that they do not need it. The outline of a plausible theoretical model for explaining anosognosia may help in finding a useful methodological approach for treating the denial disturbance and consequently for improving the motor condition of hemiplegic/anosognosic patients.

Anosognosia has become an important field of neurobiological research, for both theoretical and clinical reasons. From a theoretical point of view, anosognosia represents a powerful lesional model for studying the structure of conscious processes and, in particular, the mechanisms of motor self-awareness, as discussed above. From a clinical point of view its presence negatively affects the patient's attitude towards the illness and constrains the design of rehabilitation programmes and the guideline for future research.

ANNA BERTI

Anton, G. (1899). 'Über die Selbstwahrnehmung der herderkrankungen des gehirnes durch den kranken bei indenblindheit und rindentaubheit'. *Archiv für Psychiatrie und Nervenkrankheit*, 32.

Babinski, J. (1914). 'Contribution à l'étude des troubles mentaux dans l'hémiplégie organique cérébrale (anosognosie)'. *Revue Neurologique*, 27.

Berti, A. and Pia, L. (2006). 'Understanding motor consciousness through normal and pathological motor behaviour'. *Current Directions in Psychological Sciences*, 15.

——, Làdavas, E., and Della Corte, M. (1996). 'Anosognosia for hemiplegia, neglect dyslexia and drawing neglect. Clinical findings and theoretical consideration'. *Journal of the International Neuropsychological Society*, 2.

——, ——, Stracciari, A., Giannarelli, C., and Ossola, A. (1998). 'Anosognosia for motor impairment and dissociations with patient's evaluation of the disorder: theoretical considerations'. *Cognitive Neuropsychiatry*, 3.

——, Bottini, G., Gandola, M. et al. (2005). 'Shared cortical anatomy for motor awareness and motor control'. *Science*, 309.

——, Spinazzola, L., Pia, L., and Rabuffetti, M. (2007). 'Motor awareness and motor intention in anosognosia for hemiplegia'. In Haggard, P. et al. (eds) *Attention and Performance XXII, Sensorimotor Foundations of Higher Cognition*.

Bisiach, E. and Geminiani, G. (1991). 'Anosognosia related to hemiplegia and hemianopia'. In Prigatano, G. P. and Schacter, D. L. (eds) *Awareness of Deficit after Brain Injury*.

Blakemore, S.-J., Wolpert, D. M., and Frith, C. D. (2002). 'Abnormalities in the awareness of action'. *Trends in Cognitive Sciences*, 6.

Critchley, M. (1953). *The Parietal Lobe*.

Frith, C. D., Blakemore, S.-J., and. Wolpert, D. M. (2000). 'Abnormalities in the awareness and control of action'. *Philosophical Transactions of the Royal Society of London Series B: Biological Sciences*, 355.

Gialannella, B. and Mattioli, F. (1992). 'Anosognosia and extrapersonal neglect as predictors of functional recovery following right hemisphere stroke'. *Neuropsychological Rehabilitation*, 2.

——, Monguzzi, V., Santoro, R., and Rocchi, S. (2005). 'Functional recovery after hemiplegia in patients with neglect: the rehabilitative role of anosognosia'. *Stroke*, 36.

Haggard, P. (2005). 'Conscious intention and motor cognition'. *Trends in Cognitive Sciences*, 9.

Heilman, K. M., Barrett, A. M., and Adair, J. (1998). 'Possible mechanisms of anosognosia: a defect in self-awareness'. *Philosophical Transactions of the Royal Society of London Series B: Biological Sciences*, 353.

Karnath, H. O., Baier, B., and Nagele, T. (2005). 'Awareness of the functioning of one's own limbs mediated by the insular cortex?' *Journal of Neuroscience*, 25.

Levine, D. N., Calvanio, R., and Rinn, W. E. (1991). 'The pathogenesis of anosognosia for hemiplegia'. *Neurology*, 41.

Libet, B., Gleason, C. A., Wright, E. W., and Pearl, D. K. (1983). 'Time of conscious intention to act in relation to onset of cerebral activity (readiness-potential). The unconscious initiation of a freely voluntary act'. *Brain*, 106.

Marcel, A. J., Tegnèr, R., and Nimmo-Smith, I. (2004). 'Anosognosia for plegia, specificity, extension, partiality and disunity of bodily unawareness'. *Cortex*, 40.

Pia, L. and Tamietto, M. (2006). 'Unawareness in schizophrenia: neuropsychological and neuroanatomical findings'. *Psychiatry and Clinical Neurosciences*, 60.

Pacherie, E., Green, M., and Bayne, T. (2006). 'Phenomenology and delusions: who put the "alien" in alien control?' *Consciousness and Cognition*, 15.

Prigatano, G. P. and Schacter, D. L. (1991). *Awareness of Deficit after Brain Injury*.

Weinstein, E. K. and Kahn, R. L. (1955). *Denial of Illness. Symbolic and Physiological Aspects*.

Wolpert, D. M., Ghahramani, Z., and Jordan, M. I. (1995). 'An internal model for sensorimotor integration'. *Science*, 269.

apperceptive agnosia See AGNOSIA

apraxia Apraxia is a deficit of voluntary movement. The term, which is from the Greek meaning 'inaction', was first used by the German neurologist Hugo Liepmann (1900/1977). The deficit is characterized by difficulties in copying someone else's movements (imitation), gesturing movements on verbal command (pantomime), and sometimes in handling familiar objects (tool use). The deficit is a fairly common consequence of damage to the parietal or frontal areas of the left side of the brain, generally following stroke (see BRAIN DAMAGE), and cannot be explained as arising from motor weakness or sensory problems. Traditionally there are two main sub-types of apraxia: ideomotor and ideational apraxia.

1. Ideomotor apraxia
2. Ideational apraxia

1. Ideomotor apraxia

This includes impaired imitation and pantomime. This particular deficit is evident only in voluntary movements, while *automatic movements of daily life are preserved. For example, patients who are unable to pantomime the use of a toothbrush on verbal command tend to use the toothbrush correctly when brushing their teeth in the bathroom. Similarly, patients who are unable to imitate the gesture of waving goodbye may do so spontaneously when the examiner leaves the room. In these context-dependent forms of apraxia, the patient can carry out spontaneous and automatic acts, but is impaired in performing to command, suggesting intact motor plans and programmes that cannot be wilfully employed. Patients with this form of apraxia know exactly what they are supposed to do, but are incapable of calling on the movement schemata needed to execute the movements. These patients are unimpaired in daily life.

2. Ideational apraxia

In contrast, ideational apraxia is characterized by the failure to handle objects correctly. This form of apraxia is not context dependent and does disable patients in activities of daily living. They no longer know what to do with familiar objects such as a pair of scissors or a knife. These patients know what the object is for, and may even know what they want to achieve with it, but the idea of how to put the movement together, the *ideation*, is no longer intact. When handed an object these patients are puzzled about how to use it, making vague and inappropriate attempts to do so. Typically, established movement sequences are also affected. Patients may put the teabag in the kettle and the sugar in the teapot. This second form of apraxia is relatively rare.

It should be noted that, in both forms of apraxia, unaffected as well as impaired movements are typically smooth and coordinated. Although ideomotor apraxia is only evident when you look for it and is of limited clinical significance, it is of interest to research scientists who study people with brain damage to examine what can be learned from these patients about the workings of the normal brain (for reviews on apraxia see Halsband 1998 and Buxbaum 2001). The fact that ideomotor apraxia is selective to voluntary movements may provide a window into important aspects of the human condition such as the nature of the will. The essence of voluntary action is the translation of thought into a performed action. What distinguishes voluntary from automatic movements is that voluntary movements are willed (or intended) action. Understanding how the ability to perform voluntary actions can break down, therefore, can inform our understanding of the nature of the will.

MELVYN A. GOODALE

Buxbaum, L. J. (2001). 'Ideomotor apraxia: a call to action'. *Neurocase*, 7.

Halsband, U. (1998). 'Brain mechanisms of apraxia'. In Milner, A. D. (ed.) *Comparative Neuropsychology*.

Liepmann, H. (1910/1977). 'The syndrome of apraxia (motor asymboly) based on a case of unilateral apraxia'. In Rottenberg, D. A. and Hochberg, F. H. (eds) *Neurological Classics in Modern Translation*.

arousal vs awareness There is at present no satisfactory, universally accepted definition of consciousness. For the purposes of clinical neurosciences, consciousness consists of two basic components: *arousal* (i.e. wakefulness, vigilance, or level of consciousness) and *awareness of environment and of self* (i.e. *contents of consciousness; Laureys 2005a; see Fig. A12). The interpretation of this delineation depends on the clinical, neuroscientific, or philosophical approach of the authors. Hereinafter operational definitions are proposed as they are employed in neurology. Consciousness is a multifaceted concept and the proposed neurological definitions do not necessarily overlap with those used by philosophers or basic neuroscientists elsewhere in this volume.

Arousal refers to the behavioural continuum that occurs between *sleep and wakefulness. This is not an on–off mechanism as it can show rapid fluctuations in response to external stimulation (e.g. to intense, unexpected, or novel stimuli), called orienting reaction or vigilance. Clinically, arousal is assessed by the presence of prolonged periods of spontaneous or induced opening of the eyes.

Awareness refers to the thoughts and feelings of an individual. The operational definition is limited to an appraisal of the potential to perceive the external world and to voluntarily interact with it (also called *perceptual awareness*). In clinical practice this can be done by careful and repeated examination of spontaneous motor behaviour and of the subject's capacity to formulate reproducible, voluntary, purposeful, and sustained behavioural verbal or non-verbal responses to auditory, visual, tactile, or noxious stimuli. Compared to awareness of the environment, self-awareness is an even more complex and ill-defined concept, requiring a representation of self vs other (see SELF-CONSCIOUSNESS). In non-communicative patients the estimation of awareness requires the interpretation of several clinical signs. Patients in a vegetative state (see BRAIN DAMAGE) illustrate a complete dissociation between awareness (which is abolished) and arousal (which is preserved). Bedside evaluation of awareness in vegetative and minimally conscious patients is difficult because it relies on inferences made from observed spontaneous or stimulation-induced motor responses.

Figure A12 shows that, in normal physiological states (underlined), level of arousal and content of consciousness (environmental and self) are positively correlated. You need to be awake in order to be aware (REM sleep being a notorious exception). Patients in pathological or pharmacological coma (i.e. general *anaesthesia) are unconscious because they cannot be awakened. The vegetative state is a dissociated state of consciousness (i.e. patients being seemingly awake but lacking any behavioural evidence of 'voluntary' or 'willed' behaviour).

Neuroanatomically, arousal and awareness have different neuronal correlates. Arousal is supported by several brainstem neuronal populations (formerly termed the *ascending activating reticular system*) that project to both non-specific (intralaminar) thalamic nuclei and cortical neurons (Kinomura et al. 1996). These are shown in green in Fig. A13, upper left corner area. Depression of either brainstem or both cerebral hemispheres may cause reduced wakefulness. Clinically, the assessment of brainstem reflexes is a key to the evaluation of the functional integrity of the brainstem arousal system. According to UK guidelines, the death of the brainstem (as clinically assessed by the absence of all brainstem reflexes) equals the death of the person (for review see Laureys 2005b).

Awareness is thought to be dependent upon the functional integrity of the cerebral cortex and its reciprocal subcortical connections; each of its many aspects resides to some extent in anatomically defined regions of the *brain. As discussed below, recent *functional neuroimaging studies in pathological states of wakeful unawareness converge to the critical role of a frontoparietal network (which has been termed the *neuronal global workspace) subserving awareness (Dehaene et al. 1998, Baars et al. 2003, Laureys 2005a).

Positron emission tomography (PET) studies modulating arousal—and hence awareness—by means of

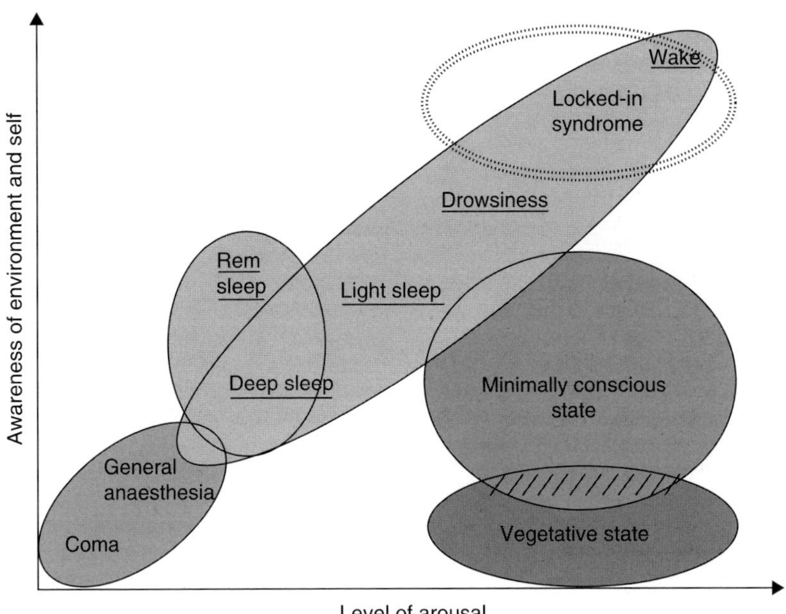

Fig. A12. Graphical illustration of the two major components of consciousness: wakefulness or arousal (i.e. the level of consciousness) and awareness of environment and self (i.e. the content of consciousness). In normal physiological states (underlined) arousal and awareness are positively correlated (with the exception of the oneiric activity during REM sleep). The vegetative state illustrates the dissociation between arousal and awareness (see text).

anaesthetic drugs have shown a drop in global brain metabolism to around half of normal values. Similar global decreases in metabolic activity are observed in deep sleep, while in REM sleep metabolism returns to normal waking values. In the vegetative state, that is in 'wakefulness without awareness', also, global metabolic activity decreases to about 50% of normal levels. However, in some patients who subsequently recover awareness from the vegetative state, global metabolic rates for glucose metabolism do not show substantial changes. Moreover, some awake healthy volunteers have global brain metabolism values comparable to those observed in some patients in a vegetative state. Inversely, some well-documented vegetative patients have shown close to normal global cortical metabolism. Hence, the relationship between global levels of brain function and the presence or absence of awareness is not absolute.

Voxel-based statistical analyses have identified dysfunction in a wide frontoparietal network encompassing the polymodal associative cortice—bilateral lateral frontal regions, parietotemporal and posterior parietal areas, mesiofrontal, posterior cingulate, and precuneal cortices (Fig. A13), when the vegetative state is contrasted to the conscious resting state in healthy controls (Laureys 2005a). This network is also known to be the most active 'by default' in resting non-stimulated conditions (see CONSCIOUS RESTING STATE). Awareness seems not exclusively related to the activity in the frontoparietal network but, as importantly, to the functional connectivity within this network and with the thalami. Long-range cortico-cortical and corticothalamo-cortical 'functional disconnections' have been identified in the vegetative state and recovery is paralleled by a functional restoration of the frontoparietal network and part of its cortico-thalamocortical connections.

Studies using external stimulation such as auditory or noxious stimuli in vegetative patients have shown activation in primary sensory cortices, disconnected from the frontoparietal network, thought to be required for awareness. Such activation in primary cortices in awake but unaware patients confirms Crick and Koch's (1995) hypothesis (based on visual perception and monkey histological connectivity) that neural activity in primary cortices is necessary but not sufficient for awareness.

Other examples of dissociation between awareness and arousal can be observed in some cases of *epilepsy and parasomnia. Absence seizures are brief episodes (5–10 s) of staring and unresponsiveness, often

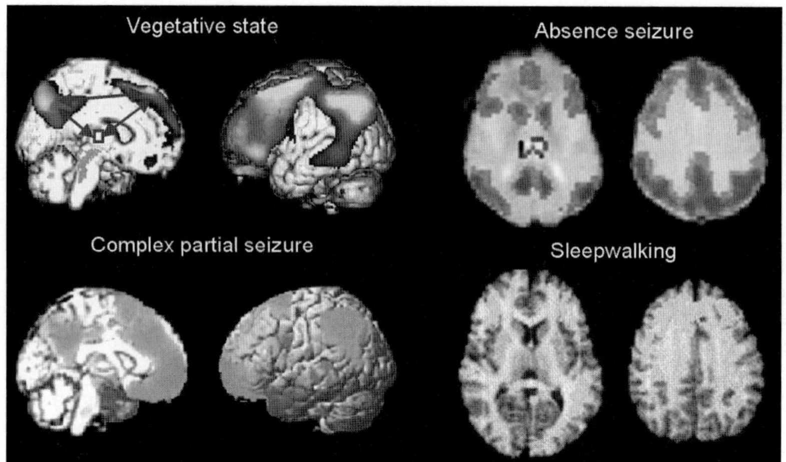

Fig. A13. The neuronal global workspace underlying awareness in pathological dissociations of awareness and arousal. The common hallmark of the vegetative state is a metabolic dysfunctioning of a widespread cortical network encompassing medial and lateral prefrontal and parietal multimodal associative areas. This is due to either direct cortical damage or to cortico-cortical or cortico-thalamo cortical disconnections (shown by blue arrows). The arousal systems in the brainstem and mesencephalon remain intact (green). Recent functional imaging studies in similar, albeit much more transient, dissociations between wakefulness and awareness resulting in 'automatic' unwilled action have shown decreased blood flow in this frontoparietal network when patients suffer from complex partial seizures (in green), absence seizures (in blue), and sleepwalking (in yellow). (See Colour Plate 3.)

accompanied by eye-blinking and lip-smacking. fMRI studies have shown widespread deactivations in fronto-parietal associative cortices during these absences. Temporal lobe seizures may also impair awareness (they are than classified 'complex partial', whereas if they terminate without impaired consciousness they are called 'simple partial'). Loss of responsiveness in complex partial seizures usually persists for up to several minutes and patients may show oral and manual automatisms (e.g. picking, fumbling, cycling). Contrasting ictal with interictal conditions again revealed marked bilateral deactivation in frontal and parietal association cortex. In contrast, temporal lobe seizures in which consciousness was spared were not accompanied by these widespread changes.

Finally, somnambulism or sleepwalking, a parasomnia occurring during deep sleep, is a further example of transient non-responsiveness with partially preserved arousal and semi-purposeful behaviour such as ambulation. In one patient, the only one studied so far, large areas of frontal and parietal association cortices remained deactivated during sleepwalking. All these studies confirm the critical role of the frontoparietal network underlying awareness in humans.

STEVEN LAUREYS

Baars, B., Ramsoy, T., and Laureys, S. (2003). 'Brain, conscious experience and the observing self'. *Trends in Neurosciences*, 26.

Crick, F. and Koch, C. (1995). 'Are we aware of neural activity in primary visual cortex?' *Nature*, 375.

Dehaene, S., Kerszberg, M., and Changeux, J. P. (1998). 'A neuronal model of a global workspace in effortful cognitive tasks'. *Proceedings of the National Academy of Sciences of the USA*, 95.

Kinomura, S., Larsson, J., Gulyas, B., and Roland, P. E. (1996). 'Activation by attention of the human reticular formation and thalamic intralaminar nuclei'. *Science*, 271.

Laureys, S. (2005a). 'The neural correlate of (un)awareness: lessons from the vegetative state'. *Trends in Cognitive Science*, 9.

Laureys, S. (2005b). 'Science and society: death, unconsciousness and the brain'. *Nature Reviews Neuroscience*, 6.

artificial grammar learning A grammar is a way of specifying how elements should be ordered. One sort of grammar is a *finite state grammar*, as illustrated in Fig. A14. It contains a finite number of states, represented by circles, connected by arrows showing allowable transitions. A grammatical sequence or 'string' can be produced by entering the network and changing states until the network is exited. So, for example, according to the grammar shown in the figure, XMMXM is grammatical.

In the 1960s Arthur Reber asked people to look at strings of letters generated by a finite state grammar (which was *artificial* in that it did not correspond to any natural language structure). Only then did he inform his participants that the order of letters obeyed a complex set of rules. He showed people a new set of letter sequences, half of which obeyed the rules and half of which did not, and asked people to classify the sequences. He found people could classify with about 60–80% accuracy even though they found it very difficult to report knowledge of the rules of the grammar. Reber realized that such artificial grammar learning could be used as a method for investigating what he termed *implicit learning*, i.e. the acquisition of implicit (unconscious) knowledge (see LEARNING, EXPLICIT VS IMPLICIT). In general, artificial grammar learning is investigated by any experimental method involving learning the structure of sequences of elements and would include, for example, the serial reaction time task (see SEQUENCE LEARNING). We will deal here with studies closely modelled on Reber's original; parallel conclusions can be drawn from the other paradigms. Research has addressed both what people learn and whether or not such knowledge is unconscious. We consider each in turn.

1. What is learned
2. Is knowledge conscious?

1. What is learned

Initially, inspired by work in linguistics at the time, Reber believed people learned the syntactic structure of the grammar as such. As evidence, Reber showed that people asked to look at strings of letters generated by a grammar could later classify strings of completely different letters generated by the same grammar (e.g. if trained on strings using the letters M, T, V, R, and X, they could be tested on strings made up of the letters B, C, F, G, and L). That is, there was knowledge that could be used when the grammar was the same but its concrete embodiment different.

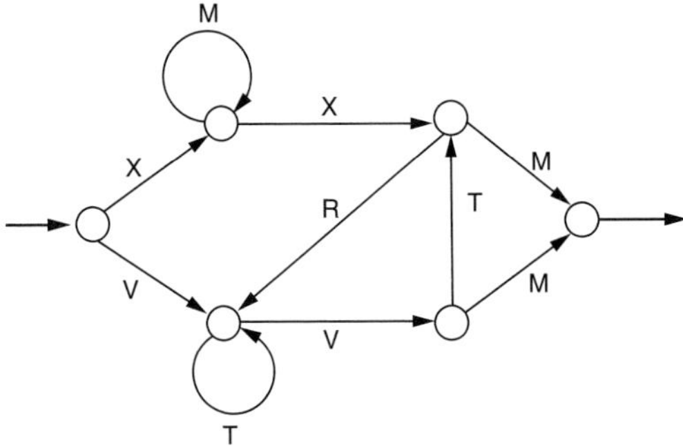

Fig. A14. Example of a finite-state grammar.

The first person to challenge the view that knowledge was of the grammar per se was Lee Brooks (1978), who showed how people could memorize whole strings and classify by *analogy* to these remembered exemplars (e.g. MTTVT is very similar to MTTXT). People need not have learned any general rules, just specific exemplars. Even when letter sets have changed, a test string MTTVT could be seen as abstractly similar to a training exemplar BFFCB, and correctly classified above chance without people inducing the rules of the grammar. According to this view, much of human implicit or intuitive learning is based on retrieving relevant specific past cases ('case-based reasoning'), perhaps together with associated irrelevant aspects of context. Another view is that people learn *chunks*, e.g. of two successive letters (bigrams, e.g. MT) or three successive letters (trigrams, e.g. TTV), or, in general, *n* successive letters (*n*-grams). There is considerable evidence that people do indeed learn which chunks are allowable in a range of implicit learning paradigms. Both the above views (analogy to specific exemplars and chunking) are in principle consistent with the knowledge being conscious or unconscious. A third view is that people's knowledge is embedded in the weights of a *neural network* and can thus fall along a continuum of concreteness or abstraction, depending on the details of the network (see CONNECTIONIST MODELS). One neural network commonly used in the literature for simulating artificial grammar learning results is Elman's *simple recurrent network*, which can learn chunks as well as long-distance dependencies. The view that the knowledge is embedded in weights fits naturally with the finding that the knowledge is hard to report verbally.

2. Is knowledge conscious?

The initial evidence for the unconscious nature of knowledge acquired in artificial grammar learning was that people's freely stated rules could not account for the level of classification performance achieved. But critics have been unhappy with free report as an indicator of unconscious knowledge. Conscious knowledge may not be freely reported merely because the person is not completely sure of it, has momentarily forgotten it, or does not believe it is the sort of knowledge the experimenter is looking for. One solution is to conjecture what properties of strings people have learned and administer forced-choice tests concerning those properties. The use of forced-choice tests ensures people do not hold back from using any knowledge they may have. For example, if it is conjectured that people have simply learned bigrams (e.g. that MT can occur in grammatical strings), then they can be asked to discriminate legal from illegal bigrams. People are good at this discrimination task, which has been taken to indicate that their knowledge is conscious. The problem is that both conscious and unconscious knowledge would in principle allow such discrimination.

Another method for determining the conscious status of knowledge states is to ask participants to report or discriminate not states of the world (e.g. 'can this bigram occur in the grammar?') but the relevant mental states involved in classification (see OBJECTIVE VS SUBJECTIVE MEASURES OF CONSCIOUSNESS). Unconscious knowledge is knowledge a person is not aware of. Thus, we need to determine whether or not the person knows that they know in order to determine if the knowing is conscious. For example, confidence ratings can be elicited after each classification decision. According to the *guessing criterion*, unconscious knowledge is shown when the participant says they are purely guessing but they are in fact performing above baseline. According to the *zero correlation criterion*, knowledge is unconscious if the person cannot discriminate between when they are guessing and when they have knowledge, i.e. there is no relationship between confidence and accuracy. Both criteria have indicated unconscious knowledge, though a typical pattern is for there to be evidence of both conscious and unconscious knowledge.

The guessing criterion has been criticized because of the bias problem: when people *say* they are guessing, they might *think* that they are not. (Note that the existence of an adjustable bias for *thinking* one is guessing vs knowing is not in itself a problem for the guessing criterion.) A response to the objection has been to indicate evidence that people's reports of whether or not they are guessing distinguish knowledge types that differ in ways predicted by a theory of consciousness (e.g. resilience to a secondary task). The zero correlation criterion is less susceptible to the bias problem.

The guessing and zero correlation criteria measure the conscious status of *judgement knowledge*: i.e. knowing that this string is grammatical. That leaves open the question of whether the person's *structural knowledge* (knowledge of the structure of the training strings) is conscious or unconscious. To address the latter, the experimenter can ask people after each classification decision whether they based their answer on random responding or intuition (unconscious structural knowledge) or rules or memory (conscious structural knowledge). This subjective method indicates that people typically use both conscious and unconscious structural knowledge.

People trained on two grammars in different contexts can choose which of the grammars to use in the classification phase (when the content of their structural knowledge is sufficient for discrimination between the grammars; see MEMORY, PROCESS-DISSOCIATION PROCEDURE). That is, like bilinguals, people can choose which language to use; in that sense, grammatical knowledge is not applied automatically. Further, people trained on one grammar in one context do not apply it in a test phase in a different context unless told of the connection between the contexts. Such intentional control of the use of the knowledge often coexists with lack of awareness of what the knowledge is by the guessing criterion. That is, a person does not need to be aware of controlling their knowledge, nor of what the knowledge is, in order to control it.

A common argument for there being unconscious knowledge learned in artificial grammar learning is that other primates and human babies as young as two months can learn statistical structures in sequences. The assumption made in this argument is that such creatures do not consciously test hypotheses nor do they have fully fledged episodic memory. Further, people with *amnesia caused by damage to the temporal lobes learn artificial grammars almost as well as normal adults. But none of these facts entail that the corresponding learning mechanism in normal human adults produces unconscious knowledge. Moreover, the mere fact that a person has impaired episodic memory does not entail they do not use conscious knowledge, either judgement or structural (e.g. rules). However, these studies on different populations can be very informative about the basis of implicit learning in adults, when its implicit nature is established by other means.

ZOLTÁN DIENES

Dienes, Z. (2008). 'Subjective measures of unconscious knowledge'. In Banerjee, R. and Chakrabarti, B. (eds) *Models of Brain and Mind: Physical, Computational and Psychological Approaches.*

Gómez, R. L. (2006). 'Dynamically guided learning'. In Munakata, Y. and Johnson, M. (eds) *Attention and Performance XXI: Processes of Change in Brain and Cognitive Development.*

Pothos, E. M. (2007). 'Theories of artificial grammar learning'. *Psychological Bulletin*, 133.

Reber, A. S. (1993). *Implicit Learning and Tacit Knowledge: an Essay on the Cognitive Unconscious.*

Shanks, D. R. (2005). 'Implicit learning'. In Lamberts, K. and Goldstone, R. (eds) *Handbook of Cognition.*

artificial intelligence and the study of consciousness Artificial intelligence (AI), in its broadest sense, is any attempt to design and create artefacts that have mental properties, or exhibit characteristic aspects of systems that have such properties. Despite the name, such properties include not just intelligence, but also those having to do with e.g. perception, action, emotion, creativity, and consciousness.

1. Varieties of AI
2. Symbolic AI
3. AI and understanding consciousness
4. Difficulties
5. Unexplored possibilities

1. Varieties of AI

Although the last half-century or so has seen various approaches to AI, including connectionism/neural networks, dynamical systems engineering, embodied/situated robotics, and artificial life, the term is often used more narrowly to refer to approaches that emphasize symbolic computation. Indeed, it was this particular approach that was dominant among those who first used the term to describe their work (John McCarthy coined the term in 1956), a situation that arguably continues to this day. To avoid confusion in what follows, the term *symbolic artificial intelligence* (or *symbolic AI*) will be used to refer to this specific approach, and *artificial intelligence* (or *AI*) to the general endeavour.

Another distinction can be made between two related, but distinct, goals in pursuing AI. *Engineering AI* is primarily concerned with creating artefacts that can do things that previously only naturally intelligent agents could do; whether or not such artificial systems perform those functions in the way that natural systems do is not considered a matter of primary importance. *Scientific AI*, however, is primarily concerned with understanding the processes underlying mentality, and the technologies provided by engineering AI, however impressive, are only considered of theoretical relevance to the extent that they resemble or otherwise illuminate the mental processes of interest.

Within scientific AI, further distinctions can be made concerning the relation that is believed to hold between the technology involved in an AI system and the mental phenomena being explained. Adapting terminology from Searle (1980), *weak AI* is any approach that makes little or no claim of a relation between the technology and modelled mentality. This would be a use of AI technology in a way similar to the use of computational simulations of hurricanes in meteorology: understanding can be facilitated, but no one supposes that this is because hurricanes are themselves computational in any substantive sense. At the other extreme, *strong AI* is any approach that claims that instantiations of the technologies involved are thereby instantiations of the mental phenomena being explained/modelled. For example, strong symbolic AI maintains that an appropriately programmed computer actually understands, believes, knows, is aware, etc. Between these two poles is what might be termed *moderate AI*. This view, unlike weak AI, claims that the modelling relation holds as a result of deeper, explanatory properties being shared by the AI technology and the mental phenomena being explained/modelled. However, unlike strong AI, moderate AI does not go on to claim that instantiating these common properties is alone sufficient for instantiating those mental phenomena—something else might be required (e.g. in the case of symbolic AI, proper historical/environmental situatedness, or 'symbol grounding'; implementation in living matter as opposed to dead metal and silicon, etc.).

Since a consideration of all the combinations of these approaches is not possible here, the focus will be on the prospects for symbolic, strong, scientific AI with regard to mentality in general. Some perceived limitations of the symbolic approach and proposed alternatives will be discussed before considering the specific issues that arise concerning AI and the understanding of consciousness in particular.

Attempting to use AI to instantiate or explain consciousness is sometimes called **machine consciousness*; see Holland (2003) and the entry for that topic for further discussion, and for some specific examples of work in this area. Other notable examples of AI models of consciousness include the symbolic of Johnson-Laird (1983); the connectionsist of Churchland (1995), Lloyd (1995), and Sun (1999); and the embodied/situated robotics of Dennett (1994).

2. Symbolic AI

The emphasis of symbolic AI is on the processing of representations, specifically symbols. At the heart of the symbolic approach are two features: (1) a sharp distinction between semantic and non-semantic (syntactic) properties; and (2) context-invariant atoms that can be composed, usually concatenatively like language, into complex structures whose syntax and semantics depend systematically on those atoms and their mode of composition.

The programming of digital computers, although thoroughly symbolic, is not in itself a reliable indicator of the symbolic approach to AI, since other approaches often use such technology merely as a means of creating or modelling systems that are (or are claimed to be) non-symbolic or even non-computational.

There have been several motivations for the symbolic approach. One derives from some results in computability theory that pre-date AI and computer technology itself. Turing (1950) introduced a set of formal models of digital, algorithmic computation called *Turing machines, automata that are given a symbol string (usually interpreted as an integer) as an input, and produce a symbol string (also usually interpreted as an integer) as the output for that input. In this way such machines could be understood to be computing functions over the integers. Turing proved that there exist universal Turing machines that can simulate the action of any other Turing machine. Such machines can therefore be seen to be capable of computing any Turing-computable function. This, coupled with the assumption that if any function can be computed at all, it can be computed by a Turing machine (the *Church–Turing thesis*), yields the result that a universal machine can be seen to be capable of computing anything that is computable at all. In particular, many take this to establish that a universal machine can compute any function a human can compute. If one then adds the assumption that human behaviour, or at least the mental processes that give rise to it, can be conceptualized as mathematical functions of the relevant sort, then it follows that any universal machine can, in principle, be programmed to exhibit behaviour functionally equivalent to that of any human being.

In some sense, this is enough of an existence proof for the purposes of engineering AI, but motivating this approach for scientific AI requires a behaviourist assumption to establish that any such simulation of human behaviour would have, or at least would model, mentality. Since, the Turing test notwithstanding, symbolic AI has anti-behaviourist roots, a different motivation is usually given for scientific applications of symbolic AI: *cognitivism* (or *computationalism*). This is the claim that cognition (more narrowly: thinking; more broadly: all mentality) actually is a kind of (symbolic) computation. It follows from this claim that implementing certain kinds of computation is sufficient for reproducing or modelling cognitive phenomena. Cognitivism is the idea that mentality, in particular thinking, is at root a formal activity: unlike, say, a rainstorm, if you computationally simulate thinking, you actually recreate it. Furthermore, since the steps involved in thinking are, it is assumed, accessible to the thinker, it is in general possible for a thinker to write those steps down, turn them into a set of instructions for a computer, and thereby create a system that reproduces, or at least models, any particular instance of thinking.

3. AI and understanding consciousness

Modelling, in particular computational modelling, confers several benefits on scientific investigation (Sloman 1978), including allowing one to: (1) state theories precisely; (2) test theories rigorously; (3) encounter unforeseen consequences of one's theories; (4) construct detailed causal explanations of actual events; and (5) undergo conceptual change through direct, interactive experience with the phenomena under investigation.

Thus, even at its weakest, AI offers these benefits to the understanding of mentality. Moving from mere simulation toward strong AI (cf. section 1) presumably multiplies these benefits, especially (2) and (3) (cf. Brooks 1991).

There are three ways the AI methodology is usually applied to explaining consciousness. One can attempt to model the physical system underlying consciousness, at a particular level of abstraction (e.g. a connectionist model is pitched at a lower, more hardware-dependent level of abstraction than is a typical symbolic model). One can attempt to model conscious processes directly, by using introspection to note their causal structure, and them implementing this structure in a (usually symbolic) AI system. Or one can attempt to model the behaviour of a system known or believed to be conscious, without any direct knowledge of the underlying physical or phenomenological structure, in the hope that reproducing both actual and counterfactual behaviour is sufficient to ensure that the same consciousness-producing causal structure is thereby implemented.

Central to applying AI methodology to understanding mentality is belief in the multiple realizability of mental states, itself motivated by, e.g., thought experiments concerning creatures ('Martians') that behave just like humans, but have a very different physiology. Since it would be politically incorrect in the extreme to deny mental states to these Martians, it must be a mistake to think that mental states can only be implemented in biological states like those of humans and animals on Earth. The question then arises: what do Martians and Earthlings have in common by virtue of which they both enjoy mental lives? Again, since AI arose out of an anti-behaviourist tradition, the commonality is not believed to be behaviour, but abstract causal organization, something that is describable using computational formalisms such as Turing machines. The belief that it is abstract causal organization that identifies mental states is called *functionalism*; if functionalism is true, then not only is it possible to investigate mentality with non-neural hardware, but also (some would say) it is a mistake to spend much time investigating neurophysiology to explain mentality. Doing so would be like trying, for example, to understand flight by looking at birds' feathers under a microscope. Instead, the analogy continues, we only came to understand natural flight by achieving artificial flight, and we only succeeded in doing that once we stopped trying to copy slavishly the superficial characteristics of biological flyers. Similarly, AI allows one to specify and test the *virtual machine* that, it is proposed, provides the proper level of analysis for explaining mentality.

4. Difficulties

There are several reasons why one might think that AI cannot contribute to the understanding of consciousness.

First, there are the problems shared by all naturalistic approaches. For example, it seems that phenomenal states can be observed directly only by the subject of those states, yet objective or at least inter-subjective observation and verification is thought to be at the very heart of scientific method. There is also the *explanatory gap (Levine 1983), or *hard problem (Chalmers 1996): it seems that naturalistic, non-phenomenal properties of a system do not explain, or at least do not imply, the phenomenal properties of that system. The applicability of these problems to AI explanations of consciousness is most clear in the case of strong AI (cf. section 1): how could one ever know if one has succeeded in creating an artificial consciousness, since one cannot directly observe its purported conscious states? For any AI system that is supposedly conscious, one can always imagine it being built and behaving the same way and yet not being conscious, so what exactly has been explained? Some have argued that these are not the insurmountable problems they seem to be, but there is little consensus on the matter. One constraint can be noted, however: in arguing that we would not be able to know that an AI system is conscious, we should be careful not to set the epistemological bar so high that we call into question our knowledge that other humans are conscious.

Next, there are doubts concerning the ability of AI systems to model cognition/mentality in general. These vary depending on the AI approach; the development of some AI approaches can be seen as attempts to overcome the general limitations of another (usually the symbolic) approach. For example, it is argued that symbolic AI cannot provide an accurate model of human cognition, since in such AI systems, millions of serially dependent operations must be performed to, say, recognize an object, but this is done in the brain in fewer than a hundred such steps. Connectionist AI is then offered as an approach that does not suffer from this problem. Another example of a purported obstacle to symbolic AI in general is the *frame problem* (cf. e.g. Pylyshyn 1987).

Third, there are specific doubts concerning the inability of AI (in particular) to explain consciousness (in particular). These are often aimed specifically at symbolic AI, but there is at least one argument against an AI account of consciousness that applies independently of approach. This argument finds an incompatibility between the possibility of being conscious and at the same time being an artefact in any interesting sense. To be considered artificial, it would seem an AI system would have to be not just the results of our labour (children are that), but also designed by us. But this means that any purpose, meaning, or intentionality in the system is not its own, but rather derivative from our design of it. Yet consciousness, it seems, is autonomous, exhibiting original, non-derivative intentionality. As with all the objections to AI presented here, this argument can be resisted. A sign that it might be too strong is that it would imply that I might not be conscious, since it might be that I was created by design (divine or mundane). Yet surely this is not a possibility I can countenance! It would be odd indeed if the details of my origins, usually believed to be an empirical matter, could be known by me a priori.

Perhaps the most well known of the specific objections to symbolic AI accounts of consciousness is Searle's *Chinese room argument (Searle 1980). Searle argues against the claim that a computer could understand solely by virtue of running the right program. To do this, he exploits the subjective, conscious nature of understanding, and the formal, implementation-independent nature of symbolic computation and programs. Since he can himself implement any purported understanding-endowing program, and presumably would not come to understand anything thereby, he refutes the strong AI claim he targets, or at least appears to do so. It is not necessary here to rehearse the various replies and counter-replies that have been given. But it is of note that what was referred to above as 'moderate AI' (cf. section 1) is immune to this argument. The Chinese room may show that computation is not *sufficient* for conscious understanding, but it does not show that it is not *necessary* for it, nor does it show that computation cannot play an explanatory role with respect to consciousness. And of course the argument does not apply in general to alternative approaches to AI that do not place as much emphasis on implementing formal programs.

Another famous objection to symbolic AI is the *diagonal argument*. This dates back to Gödel and Turing, but was developed philosophically by Lucas (see Lucas 1996 for a retrospect) and, more recently, Penrose (1994). It can be shown that no Turing machine can compute the non-halting function. Enumerate all the Turing machines. Now consider this function: 'For all n, halt if and only if the nth Turing machine does not halt when given input n'. No Turing machine that is sound with respect to this function can halt when given its own number k in the enumeration as an argument (it must halt on k if and only if it does not halt on k). Furthermore, I just proved to you that any such sound Turing machine k does not halt when given input k. Thus you and I can answer this question (compute this function?) correctly for all n, while no Turing machine can. So we can do more than Turing machines. The explanation Penrose offers for this fact is that we are conscious, and can use our consciousness to jump out of the algorithmic 'system', see patterns that are not classically computable, etc. Thus, symbolic AI cannot even match the performance of a conscious system, let alone explain it or re-instantiate it. As with the Chinese room, there are too many replies and counter-replies to consider them here. But some similar observations can be made; specifically, 'moderate AI' (cf. section 1) is again immune to this argument. Even if there are aspects of consciousness that are non-computational, this does not show that computation of some sort is not necessary/explanatory for those aspects of consciousness. Nor does it show that all aspects or instances of consciousness have non-algorithmic components. Like the Chinese room, the argument does not apply in general to alternative approaches to AI that do not place algorithms centre stage. And one may wonder: even if computers cannot recreate human consciousness, is halting-problem-defying human consciousness the only kind of consciousness possible in this universe? If not, then AI (even symbolic AI) explanations of these other kinds of consciousness have not been shown to be impossible.

5. Unexplored possibilities

It could very well be that there are more possibilities for using AI to understand consciousness than we have yet envisioned. For example, an aspect of AI that had more prominence in the field's early years than it does now is AI as prosthesis: 'artificial intelligence' as a parallel construction to 'artificial leg' rather than 'artificial light'.

Ross Ashby, a venerated pioneer in the field of dynamical AI, proposed a 'design for an intelligence amplifier' (Ashby 1956). Perhaps AI could contribute to our understanding of consciousness as much by systematically altering or extending it as by replicating it. Technologies based on AI may also be required to help us mine and process the enormous quantities of data we anticipate to acquire concerning the operation of the brain over the next decades. If so, AI will have a perhaps more prosaic, though no less crucial, role to play in understanding consciousness.

RON CHRISLEY

Ashby, R. (1956). 'Design for an intelligence-amplifier'. In Shannon, C. E. and McCarthy, J. (eds) *Automata Studies*.

Bechtel, W. (1993). 'Consciousness: perspectives from symbolic and connectionist AI'. *Neuropsychologia*, 33.

Brooks, R. (1991). 'Intelligence without reason'. MIT AI Lab Memo 1293.

Chrisley, R. (ed.) (2000). *Artificial Intelligence: Critical Concepts*. (Many of the earlier references are reprinted here.)

Chalmers, D. J. (1996). *The Conscious Mind: In Search of a Fundamental Theory*.

Churchland, P. M. (1995). *The Engine of Reason, the Seat of the Soul: a Philosophical Journey into the Brain*.

Dennett, D. C. (1994). 'The practical requirements for making a conscious robot'. *Philosophical Transactions of the Royal Society Series A: Physical Sciences*, 349.

Pylyshyn, Z. (ed.) (1987). *The Robot's Dilemma: the Frame Problem in Artificial Intelligence*.

Holland, O. (ed.) (2003). *Machine Consciousness*.

Johnson-Laird, P. N. (1983). *Mental Models*.

Levine, J. (1983). 'Materialism and qualia: the explanatory gap'. *Pacific Philosophical Quarterly*, 64.

Lloyd, D. (1995). 'Consciousness: a connectionist manifesto'. *Minds and Machines*, 5.

Lucas, J. (1996). 'Minds, Machines and Gödel: a Retrospect'. In Millican, P. J. R. and Clark, A. (eds) *Machines and Thought: the Legacy of Alan Turing*.

Penrose, R. (1994). *The Shadows of the Mind: a Search for the Missing Science of Consciousness*.

Searle, J. (1980). 'Minds, brains and programs'. *Behavioral and Brain Sciences*, 3.

Sloman, A. (1978). *The Computer Revolution in Philosophy*.

Sun, R. (1999). 'Accounting for the computational basis of consciousness: a connectionist approach'. *Consciousness and Cognition*, 8.

associative agnosia See AGNOSIA

attentional blink The attentional blink (AB) is a temporary state of poor awareness of current stimuli, lasting about half a second, that is induced by focusing attention and becoming consciously aware of a relevant stimulus object that has just previously been briefly presented.

The concept of the AB was originally developed to describe a phenomenon uncovered in a series of laboratory experiments in which normal human adults were required to report the presence of two different target letters (T1 and T2) that had been embedded within a series of other briefly presented letters, each seen for about 100 ms (Raymond et al. 1992; see Fig. A15a). Although the probability of reporting both targets was found to be very high if the interval (or lag) between their presentations was greater than about 500 ms, the ability to report the second target (T2) dropped precipitously when intervals between 200 and 500 ms were used. In these, and many other studies, it was found that if the T2 item appeared immediately after the T1 item (with no intervening item), no deficit in reporting T2 occurred. This effect has been called *lag-1 sparing*. Figure A15b shows the now classic U-shaped function that relates performance on the T2 task to the T1–T2 interval. The T1–T2 interval has no effect on T1 performance. Critically, if T1 is simply ignored even though it is still presented, no AB (dip in T2 performance) is seen. This is why the effect was called the *attentional blink*: 'attentional' because it is induced by attention to a prior target and 'blink' because it is a normal and temporary period of apparent insensitivity.

Of theoretical interest is the observation that the effect depends on the presentation of a second (or ('*masking') stimulus immediately after T1 and T2; the AB disappears completely when there is more time to complete processing of each of the two targets, a point that argues against the idea that a simple bottleneck limits how quickly two simple detection task can be performed in succession. Phenomenally, the AB 'feels' as if a consciously perceived event in the world is slipping from mental grasp. The T2 stimulus is either retained sufficiently to report it or it is not; poor or fuzzy visibility is not typically experienced.

The AB is a robust phenomenon and has been found with visual presentation of words, letters, digits, symbols, faces, imaginary objects, and scenes. It has been reported to occur for auditory stimuli including spoken syllables, spoken letters and digits, and non-verbal musical tones. It has also been reported for tactile stimuli and can, under some circumstances, be found when T1 and T2 demand different sense modalities. It has been studied in numerous abnormal populations including people with *brain lesions, dyslexia, *schizophrenia, depression, anxiety, and *synaesthesia.

The AB is important to the understanding of consciousness for at least two reasons. First, it demonstrates elegantly that conscious awareness of stimuli depends vitally on central brain resources and is not an obligatory process driven simply by the presence of sensory information or processing by the sense organs. Second, it offers a method for inducing a precise and well-defined lapse of consciousness and so provides a helpful tool for empirical studies of consciousness. The AB is also fertile ground for people interested in mathematical modelling of mental processes, especially consciousness.

Cognitive psychologists have developed several different theories to account for the AB. Most theories agree that conscious reporting of T2 requires activation of both an early stage of perceptual processing and a second, later stage that involves short-term or working memory and consciousness (Shapiro et al. 1997). The former stage appears to operate very quickly and can handle large amounts of information whereas the second stage is limited in its capacity to deal with information and is necessary to create durable representations of information that makes it available for conscious experience and subsequent report. When T2 stimuli are presented within the critical interval and are not reported (i.e. they are *blinked*), it is assumed that they have not been processed properly by the second stage for some reason. In different views, T2's early-stage perceptual representation is thought to decay before it can access the second stage; to be overwritten by succeeding information; or to become confused with other information in the second stage before it can be reported. Observations that the AB can be induced only when new objects are attended supports the general notion that the temporal limitations on consciousness reflected by the AB result from the mental construction of whole-object representations rather than the processing of stimulus attributes.

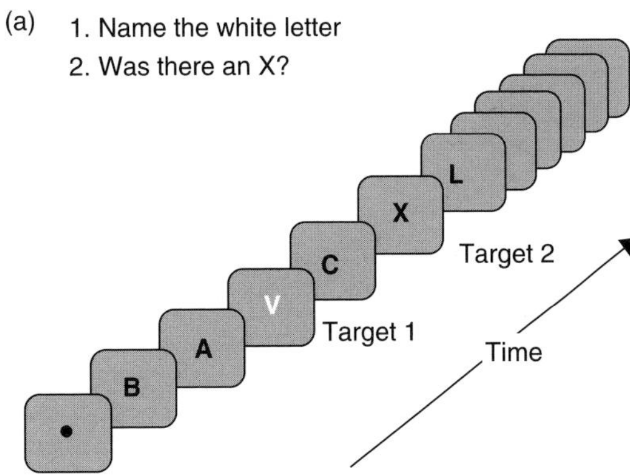

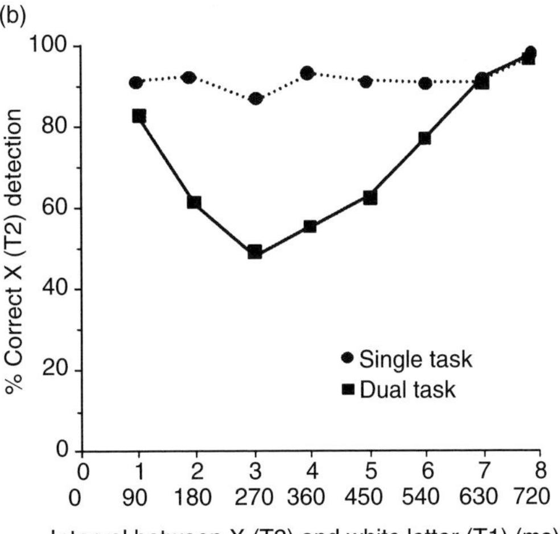

Fig. A15. (a) An illustration of the stimuli used in the original attentional blink experiments (Raymond et al. 1992). Each letter was presented 90 ms after the onset of the preceding letter. There were between 16 and 24 items in each trial. (b) A typical attentional blink results. Percentage correct T2 detection is plotted as a function of the interval between the onset of T1 and the onset of T2. The squares represent data on trials in which both T1 and T2 tasks were required (and T1 was correct). The circles represent trials in which only the T2 task was required. The difference between the two curves describes the attentional blink.

Studies of the underlying neural mechanisms have shown that even when a T2 stimulus is blinked, the brain processes it at a reasonably high level (Luck et al. 1996). Several studies using the AB procedure (i.e. a rapid successive series of stimuli in which two targets are embedded) have examined brain responses when T2 is unsuccessfully reported and compared this to brain responses measured when T2, presented with the same timing, is successfully reported. These comparisons reveal that when T2 reaches consciousness, a very distinct pattern of brain activation results that suggests the presence of long-range communication of many different brain areas (Gross et al. 2004). To the extent that the AB reflects the absence and presence of consciousness, these studies of the AB's neural correlates provide exciting glimpses into how the brain might create and control our conscious experience of the world.

JANE RAYMOND

Gross, J., Schmitz, F., Schnitzler, I. et al. (2004). 'Modulation of long-range neural synchrony reflects temporal limitations of visual attention in humans'. *Proceedings of the National Academy of Sciences of the USA*, 101.

Luck, S. J., Vogel, E. K., and Shapiro, K. L. (1996). 'Word meaning can be accessed but not reported during the attentional blink'. *Nature*, 383.

Raymond, J. E., Shapiro, K. L., and Arnell, K. M. (1992). 'Temporary suppression of visual processing in an RSVP task: an attentional blink?' *Journal of Experimental Psychology: Human Performance and Perception*, 18.

Shapiro, K. L., Arnell, K., and Raymond, J. E. (1997). 'The attentional blink: a view on attention and a glimpse on consciousness'. *Trends in Cognitive Science*, 1.

attention and awareness In normal perception, attention and awareness are hand in glove and thus almost impossible to tell apart. The precise relation between these two psychologically defined processes is nevertheless an empirical question of some consequence. Is attention required to bring stimuli to our awareness? Can we attend to stimuli without becoming aware of them? Can we be aware of unattended stimuli? The answer to these questions matters both for understanding the nature of attention and awareness and for identifying their respective mechanistic and neuronal underpinnings. This entry summarizes experimental findings that bear most directly on the relation between attention and awareness. It will focus exclusively on the visual domain, where attention and awareness have been studied most thoroughly.

Current opinion on the relation between attention and awareness is divided: some authors see attention and awareness as distinct and dissociable processes, while others view attention as a necessary precondition for awareness. Of course, the experimental tools for manipulating and diagnosing states of attention and awareness are anything but straightforward. As different authors use different tools, they tend to form different conceptualizations of attention and awareness and, consequently, they may reach different conclusions about the relation between attention and awareness. Before addressing the main topic, we therefore need to consider briefly which operational definitions are currently available and accepted for both attention and awareness.

1. Attention
2. Awareness
3. Relation between attention and awareness
4. Awareness without attention
5. Attention without awareness
6. Conclusion

1. Attention

Roughly speaking, attention is the ability to rapidly match sensory processing to current behavioural goals. In operational terms, the defining characteristics of attention are *selectivity* and *limited capacity*: goal-related information is processed more thoroughly than goal-unrelated information, as long as the total amount of thoroughly processed information does not exceed a certain limit (Pashler 1999). Ideally, therefore, experimental manipulations of attention combine physically identical stimulation with alternative behavioural goals (e.g. alternative cues or task instructions), and document both an increase of visual performance on goal-related and a decrease of visual performance on goal-unrelated information.

Neural correlates of attentional 'selectivity' are discussed elsewhere in this volume (see ATTENTION, NEURAL BASIS). The neural basis of attention's 'limited capacity' remains unclear. Computational models suggest that pervasive inhibitory interactions place an upper bound on the amount of neuronal activity and force different stimuli to compete with each other for visual responses (Itti and Koch 2001). Perceptually, competitive interactions between stimuli are well established and reveal themselves, for example, in lateral masking, in crowding effects, and in the context-dependence of saliency.

2. Awareness

The best indication that a stimulus has reached awareness remains a positive subjective report. Unfortunately, subjective report understates the contents of awareness, as the reporting of multiple elements from a complex scene is limited also by short-term memory. A more inclusive criterion for awareness is provided by Sperling's iconic memory paradigm, in which a complex scene is presented and the elements to be reported are indicated only afterwards (see MEMORY, ICONIC). Of course, it is hard to know whether awareness of potentially reportable but unreported elements is fully equivalent to awareness of actually reported elements (see ACCESS CONSCIOUSNESS).

In practice, the most widely used measure of awareness is a voluntary discrimination between predefined stimulus classes. In studies of this type, the observer becomes highly familiar with the display layout and knows precisely which specific attributes he or she is expected to report. Typically, this induces the observer to focus attention on the attributes in question. Accordingly, voluntary discrimination tends to measure awareness of stimuli that are selected by attention.

3. Relation between attention and awareness

In many situations, the voluntary discrimination of stimulus alternatives is found to require attention. In these instances, discrimination performance deteriorates to chance level when attentional capacity is exhausted or rendered unavailable by means of a concurrent task, an *attentional blink (e.g. Sergent et al. 2005), *inattentional blindness (Mack and Rock 2000), or *change blindness.

As a neural correlate of the voluntary discrimination of an attended stimulus, one finds increased activity in parietal, premotor, and prefrontal cortices (e.g. Sergent et al. 2005). However, this neural activity seems likely to confound the host of covert processes that presumably accompany voluntary discrimination, among them attention, awareness, short-term memory, response planning, and others. Accordingly, paradigms such as attentional blink, inattentional blindness, or change blindness are unlikely (without further ado) to reveal specific neural correlates of either attention or awareness.

Near the threshold of visibility, physically identical stimuli sometimes reach awareness and sometimes not. Several studies have taken advantage of this variability and have compared the neural activity evoked when a stimulus becomes visible and when it does not (e.g. Rees et al. 2002). However, the reservations mentioned above hold also for this situation: when a stimulus crosses the threshold of visibility, it may not merely gain access to awareness but, in addition, may be selected by attention, enter short-term memory, activate associated action plans, and so on. Thus it is again difficult to unambiguously attribute the neural activity that correlates with visibility.

In a number of situations, therefore, attention and awareness are tightly coupled. This is why many authors consider attentional selection a necessary precondition for awareness and voluntary report (e.g. Dehaene et al. 2006). In this view, the allocation of attention determines the extent of conscious awareness, which in turn limits voluntary reports (Fig. A16a). An alternative position (Lamme 2003) is that conscious awareness extends to both unattended and attended stimuli, but that only attended stimuli are available for voluntary report. This position retains the tight link between attentional selection and voluntary report, but downplays the link between attentional selection and conscious awareness (Fig. A16b). Yet another view (Koch and Tsuchiya 2007) holds that the link between attention and awareness is contingent rather than necessary. In this latter view, conscious awareness is needed for voluntary report, but extends to both attended and unattended stimuli. In other words, even unattended stimuli may (at times) reach conscious awareness and become available for voluntary report (Fig. A16c).

To decide between these possibilities, we need to know the extent to which attention and awareness may become dissociated from each other. Indeed, there seem to be several experimental situations, some natural and some more contrived, in which such dissociations may occur. The remainder of this entry will summarize these situations, which have generated considerable interest in recent years. Note that these situations may also be particularly revealing about the respective neural bases of attention and awareness, as they may allow us to distinguish between correlates of attention on the one hand and correlates of awareness on the other.

4. Awareness without attention

Natural scenes. It is well known that natural visual scenes are perceived easily and rapidly. Scene gist and presence of certain object classes (animals, faces) are reported correctly after approximately 120 ms. Our subjective experience even suggests (misleadingly) that we become immediately and completely aware of simple visual scenes. In fact, awareness of natural scenes may be possible without attention and thus may escape the limitations of attentional capacity.

For instance, natural scenes seem immune to inattentional blindness: when such a scene is flashed briefly and unexpectedly, observers correctly report scene gist (Mack and Rock 2000). In dual-task experiments, natural scene objects are classified reliably (e.g. animals vs distractors, vehicles vs distractors, animals vs vehicles), although the observer's attention is engaged elsewhere in the visual field by a second task (Li et al. 2002). Further experiments with the same paradigm show that observers can distinguish male and female faces, and even famous and non-famous faces, in the absence of attention.

The results with natural scenes contrast sharply with seemingly much simpler discriminations of shapes or colour arrangements (e.g. T vs L shape, red–green vs green–red targets), the performance of which deteriorates to chance level in the absence of attention (e.g. Li

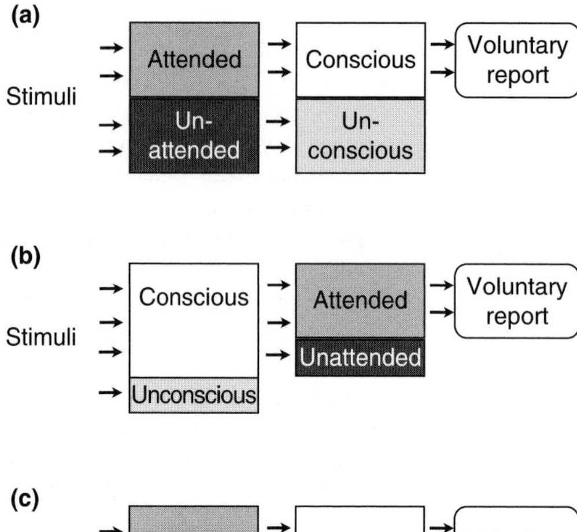

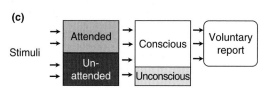

Fig. A16. Three possible relations between attention and awareness. (a) Only attended stimuli reach conscious awareness and become available for voluntary report. (b) The distinction between conscious and unconscious stimuli is independent of attention. However, only attended stimuli are available for voluntary report. (c) All attended and some unattended stimuli reach conscious awareness and thereby become available for voluntary report. Modified from Lamme 2003.

et al. 2002). The reasons for this astonishing discrepancy between the discrimination of natural and artificial stimuli are unclear.

In complex natural scenes, many aspects of detail can be reported only with attention, as demonstrated strikingly by the change blindness paradigm. An exception to this rule are objects that are salient in the context of a particular scene, i.e. objects that differ prominently from the background in at least one elementary attribute (form, colour, motion, depth, or texture). Objects that are salient in this way tend not to be subject to change blindness, and thus appear to reach awareness without particular assistance from attention.

Salient stimuli. That there exists a link between saliency and relative independence from attention is one of the key lessons from the enormous body of work on visual search and texture segregation, which ultimately led to computational models of stimulus competition and saliency (Itti and Koch 2001). When attention is compromised by either a concurrent task or a lesion in visual area V4, visual search for salient targets is still performed well whereas visual search for non-salient targets deteriorates to chance. Whether visual search for salient targets is entirely independent of attention, or whether a residual amount of attention is still required, has been debated vigorously. However, there is agreement that the amount of residual attention required (if any) is comparatively small, certainly less than 10%. Thus, it is safe to say that awareness of salient targets (as judged by search performance) is comparable in the full presence and in the near absence of attention.

More recently, the approach of using a second task elsewhere in the visual field to draw attention away from a salient target has been extended to visual performance near threshold (Braun et al. 2001). The results established good sensitivity for luminance and chromatic contrast, for visual orientation, spatial frequency, and visual motion of salient targets even in the near absence of attention. In the full presence of attention, sensitivity was generally higher, but not inordinately so (approximately 30%).

It nevertheless remains true that numerous visual discriminations cannot be performed at all in the near absence of attention (Braun et al. 2001). The picture that emerges is thus rather mixed, with some types of information being almost normally discriminable and other types of information not being discriminable at all. Interestingly, these disparities become apparent only in the near absence of attention. In the full presence of attention, the discriminations in question seem quite comparable.

In summary, visual awareness of stimuli well outside the current attention focus (i.e. in the near absence of attention) appears to be considerable. It includes simple attributes of salient stimuli and suffices to extract scene gist and to identify certain object classes such as animals, vehicles, and faces. Not included in this 'ambient' awareness are non-salient objects and more complex attributes of salient objects. The latter type of information requires attention in order to reach awareness.

Ambiguous patterns. Ambiguous stimulus patterns often evoke seemingly spontaneous alternations of awareness (e.g. *binocular rivalry, *multistable perception). Several studies have used various methods to dissociate these fluctuations of awareness from attention. Attending to one particular appearance of an ambiguous pattern does not arrest alternations of awareness. Alternations of awareness continue also when attention is compromised to some degree, although the alternation rate is lower than when attention is fully available. Finally, alternations of awareness continue also under the dual-task situation mentioned above, that is, in the near absence of attention.

That attention increases alternation rates is expected and consistent with the known effects of attention on visual responses (i.e. alternation rates increase also when visual responses are boosted in other ways). In the present context, the implication of interest is that visual awareness undergoes transitions that are uncoupled from attention.

Neural correlates. So far, there appears to have been only one attempt to identify neural *correlates of awareness in the absence of attention (Tse et al. 2005). The study uses visual masking to manipulate the visibility of targets presented in the peripheral visual field. Observers attend to a different task at the centre of the visual field, ignoring the peripheral targets, which are therefore presumed to be unattended. In this situation, the authors observe visibility-correlated differences in fMRI activations exclusively in extrastriate visual cortex (see FUNCTIONAL BRAIN IMAGING). An otherwise similar study, which did not dissociate attention and awareness in that observers reported on (and therefore presumably also attended to) the peripheral targets, observed visibility-correlated activations in a wider network of areas (extrastriate visual cortex and fusiform cortex; Haynes and Rees 2005). It is tempting to speculate that this wider pattern of activations reflected neural correlates of both awareness and attention.

While further studies are required before firm conclusions can be drawn, these first results demonstrate both the feasibility and the promise of dissociating attention from awareness.

5. Attention without awareness

The notion of 'attention without awareness' may at first appear paradoxical. In what sense may a stimulus be said to be 'attended', when it does not reach awareness? As long as attention is viewed in terms of 'selection for awareness', it is indeed difficult to conceive of 'attention without awareness'. When one adopts a neurobiological perspective, however, the idea acquires some credibility. For even though a neural response may not suffice for visual awareness, it seems possible that such a response would increase or decrease depending on behavioural goals. In other words, it is conceivable that attention might modulate a neural response that does not contribute to awareness.

Invisible stimulation. We know of several kinds of stimulation that evoke neuronal responses but do not reach awareness. Among the better-known examples are high spatial and temporal frequencies, anti-correlated binocular disparity, and stimuli rendered invisible by *masking or by interocular competition.

In some cases, the invisible stimulation even causes *after-effects or *priming effects that, in turn, alter subsequent conscious perceptions. Interestingly, these delayed effects on awareness tend to be obtained when attention is directed at the location of the invisible stimulation. Such an attention-dependence has been reported for orientation-specific after-effects, for word priming, and for attention cueing by invisible images of male and female nudes.

Two recent studies are of particular interest, in that invisible stimuli elicit neural activity in higher areas of visual cortex. In the first study, low-contrast images of tools were presented to one eye but rendered invisible by high-contrast, dynamic images presented to the other eye (Fang and He 2005). In spite of their invisibility, the tool images produced almost normal levels of fMRI activation in dorsal visual areas along the intraparietal sulcus. No such activation was observed in ventral visual cortex, consistent with the view that visual awareness is supported by ventral (not dorsal) visual cortex (see VISUAL STREAMS: WHAT VS HOW).

In the second study, invisible tool images were presented in the peripheral visual field while attention was engaged to different degrees by either a simple or a complex task in the central visual field (Bahrami et al. 2007). Without these tasks, attention would presumably have been held by the flashing peripheral images that concealed the invisible tool images. Indeed, the fMRI activation by invisible tool images proved higher when some attention remained available to the periphery (simple task in the centre) than when attention was effectively removed from the periphery (complex task in the centre). These results demonstrate clearly that a neural response that does not contribute to awareness may nevertheless be modulated by attention.

Implicit selection. Presumably, attention is limited not only in capacity but also in precision. The ideal of enhancing all goal-related information and only goal-related information cannot be reached by a physical system. In fact, there are reports of attentional 'mistakes', such as attention lowering rather than raising task performance and attention modulating goal-unrelated information. The latter set of observations concerns situations where a task-relevant attribute (e.g. direction of visual motion) is enhanced not only for the task-relevant stimulus, but also for other task-irrelevant stimuli elsewhere in the visual field. It looks as if the attentional enhancement of the task-relevant attribute spreads counter-productively across the entire visual field.

There is evidence to suggest that these collateral effects of attention extend to unconscious processes, i.e. to neural activity that does not contribute to awareness

(Kanai et al. 2006). For example, attending to the colour of a target stimulus enhances the priming effect of a subliminal (not consciously perceived) and task-irrelevant stimulus elsewhere in the visual field, provided that the latter stimulus shares the attended colour ('implicit selection'). Similarly, attending to the orientation of a target stimulus enhances after-effects from a task-irrelevant stimulus rendered invisible by interocular suppression, but only if the latter stimulus shares the attended orientation.

These results dissociate attention's impact on awareness from its effect on neural responses. Only a subset of the neural representations modulated by attention contributes to awareness and becomes available for voluntary report. In short, the neural 'footprint' of attention seems to be larger than that of awareness.

6. Conclusion

If attention is defined in terms of limited capacity, the relation between awareness and attention becomes an empirical question that must be decided by suitable experiments. In the past decade, numerous relevant experiments have been conducted and plenty of evidence has been amassed. For example, there is now overwhelming evidence that attention is not the only route by which visual information may reach awareness. In addition to their awareness of the current attention focus, observers enjoy an ambient awareness of salient objects elsewhere in the visual field, especially in natural scenes. Thus, there is awareness without attention. There also is increasing evidence that attention modulates neural processes that do not contribute to awareness. At least at the level of neural correlates, therefore, one may also speak of attention without awareness.

In conclusion, conscious visual experience is not produced by a 'magic wand' called attention. The respective neural correlates of awareness and attention are fundamentally distinct, although there may well be considerable overlap. More and more experimental paradigms are being devised that successfully dissociate attention from awareness.

JOCHEN BRAUN

Bahrami, B., Lavie, N., and Rees, G. (2007). 'Attentional load modulates responses of human primary visual cortex to invisible stimuli'. *Current Biology*, 17.

Braun, J., Koch, C., and Davis, J. (2001). *Perceptual Consequences of Multilevel Selection. Visual Attention and Cortical Circuits*.

Dehaene, S., Changeux, J. P., Naccache, L., Sackur, J., and Sergent, C. (2006). 'Conscious, preconscious, and subliminal processing: a testable taxonomy', *Trends in Cognitive Science*, 10.

Fang, F. and He, S. (2005). 'Cortical responses to invisible objects in the human dorsal and ventral pathways'. *Nature Neuroscience*, 8.

Haynes, J. D. and Rees, G. (2005). 'Predicting the orientation of invisible stimuli from activity in human primary visual cortex'. *Nature Neuroscience*, 8.

Itti, L. and Koch, C. (2001). 'Computational modelling of visual attention'. *Nature Reviews Neuroscience*, 2.

Kanai, R., Tsuchiya, N., and Verstraten, F. (2006). 'The scope and limits of top-down attention in unconscious visual processing'. *Current Biology*, 16.

Koch, C. and Tsuchiya, N. (2007). 'Attention and consciousness: two distinct brain processes'. *Trends in Cognitive Science*, 11.

Lamme, V. A. (2003). 'Why visual attention and awareness are different'. *Trends in Cognitive Science*, 7.

Li, F. F., VanRullen, R., Koch, C., and Perona, P. (2002). 'Rapid natural scene categorization in the near absence of attention'. *Proceedings of the National Academy of Sciences of the USA*, 99.

Mack, A. and Rock, I. (2000). *Inattentional Blindness*.

Pashler, H. E. (1999). *The Psychology of Attention*.

Rees, G., Wojciulik, E., Clarke, K., Husain, M., Frith, C., and Driver, J. (2002). 'Neural correlates of conscious and unconscious vision in parietal extinction'. *Neurocase*, 8.

Sergent, C., Baillet, S., and Dehaene, S. (2005). 'Timing of the brain events underlying access to consciousness during the attentional blink'. *Nature Neuroscience*, 8.

Tse, P. U., Martinez-Conde, S., Schlegel, A. A., and Macknik, S. L. (2005). 'Visibility, visual awareness, and visual masking of simple unattended targets are confined to areas in the occipital cortex beyond human V1/V2'. *Proceedings of the National Academy of Sciences of the USA*, 102.

attention, neural basis Natural visual scenes are cluttered and contain many different objects. However, the capacity of the visual system to process information about multiple objects at any given moment in time is limited. Hence, attentional mechanisms are needed to select relevant information and to filter out irrelevant information from cluttered visual scenes. Even though not all information that we attend to ultimately reaches awareness, selectively attending to sensory information is often a necessary step in order to gain access to conscious processing (but see ATTENTION AND AWARENESS for an alternative account). Given the intimate relationship of visual attention and awareness it is possible that these cognitive abilities share many common neural resources. This entry will serve to review some basic findings on the neural basis of visual attention, as obtained from monkey physiology and human neuroimaging.

There is converging evidence from *single-cell physiology studies in non-human primates and *functional brain mapping studies in humans that selective attention modulates neural activity at multiple stages of visual processing, from the lateral geniculate nucleus of the thalamus to areas in ventral and dorsal extrastriate cortex. The modulatory processes affecting the visual system appear to be controlled by a higher-order frontoparietal network of brain areas. Below, we will briefly describe the major components within this widely distributed system of areas subserving visual attention and their possible functional roles in the selection process.

1. The lateral geniculate nucleus: an early 'gatekeeper'
2. Visual cortex: spatial filtering of distractor information in areas V4 and TEO
3. Frontal and parietal cortex: sorting out sources and sites
4. Conclusion

1. The lateral geniculate nucleus: an early 'gatekeeper'

The lateral geniculate nucleus (LGN) is the thalamic station in the retinocortical projection and has traditionally been viewed as the gateway to the visual cortex (Sherman and Guillery 2001). In addition to retinal afferents, the LGN receives input from multiple sources including striate cortex, the thalamic reticular nucleus (TRN), and the brainstem. The retina itself does not receive feedback projections. The LGN therefore represents the first stage in the visual pathway at which cortical top-down feedback signals could affect information processing. It has proven difficult to study attentional response modulation in the LGN using single-cell physiology due to the small receptive field (RF) sizes of LGN neurons and the possible confound of small eye movements. Several single-cell physiology studies have failed to demonstrate attentional modulation in the LGN supporting a notion that selective attention affects neural processing only at the cortical level. This view has recently begun to change due to human fMRI studies demonstrating attentional modulation as well as neural correlates of conscious perception in the LGN (e.g. O'Connor et al. 2002).

It was found that, just as in visual cortex, selective attention affected visual processing in three different ways in the LGN. First, neural responses to attended visual stimuli were enhanced relative to the same stimuli when unattended (attentional enhancement, Fig. A17a, d; e.g. Moran and Desimone 1985). Importantly, this effect was shown to be spatially specific, indicating that it was due to selective attention rather than to unspecific arousal. Second, neural responses to unattended stimuli were attenuated depending on the load of attentional resources engaged elsewhere (attentional suppression, Fig. A17b, e; e.g. Rees et al. 1997). And third, directing attention to a location in the absence of visual stimulation and in anticipation of the stimulus onset increased neural baseline activity (attention-related baseline increases, Fig. A17c, f; e.g. Kastner et al. 1999). In visual cortex (*V1), the magnitude of all attention effects increased from early to more advanced processing levels along both the ventral and dorsal pathways. This is consistent with the idea that attention operates through top-down signals that are transmitted via cortico-cortical feedback connections in a hierarchical fashion. Thereby, areas at advanced levels of visual cortical processing are more strongly controlled by attention mechanisms than are early processing levels. This idea is supported by single-cell recording studies, which have shown that attention effects in area TE of inferior temporal cortex have a latency of approximately 150 ms, whereas attention effects in V1 have a longer latency of approximately 230 ms. According to this account, one would predict smaller attention effects in the LGN than in striate cortex. Surprisingly, it was found that all attention effects tended to be larger in the LGN than in striate cortex (O'Connor et al. 2002). This finding suggests that attentional response modulation in the LGN is unlikely to be due solely to corticothalamic feedback from striate cortex, but may

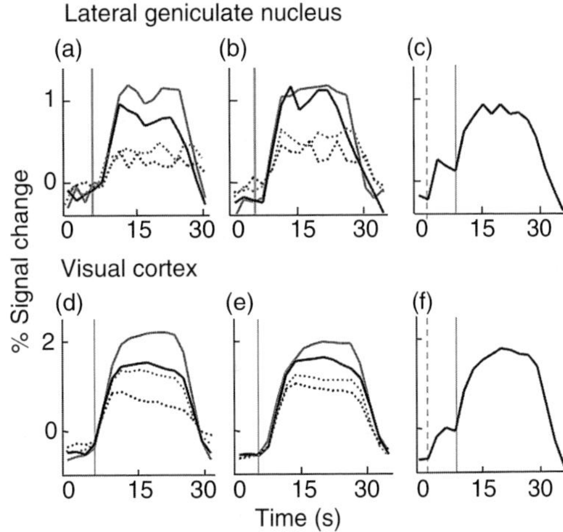

Fig. A17. Attentional modulation in the LGN and in visual cortex. Time series of fMRI signals (n = 4). (a), (d) Attentional enhancement. During directed attention to the stimuli (grey curves), responses to both the high-contrast stimulus (100%, solid curves) and low-contrast stimulus (5%, dashed curves) were enhanced relative to an unattended condition (black curves). (b), (e) Attentional suppression. During an attentionally demanding 'hard' fixation task (black curves), responses evoked by both the high-contrast stimulus (100%, solid curves) and low-contrast stimulus (10%, dashed curves) were attenuated relative to an easy attention task at fixation (grey curves). (c), (f) Baseline increases. Baseline activity was elevated during directed attention to the periphery of the visual hemifield in expectation of the stimulus onset (darker grey shaded areas). The lighter grey shaded area indicates the beginning of stimulus presentation periods. From O'Connor et al. 2002.

be further influenced by additional sources of input such as the TRN.

In summary, the LGN appears to be the first stage in the processing of visual information that is modulated by attentional top-down signals. These findings indicate the need to revise the traditional view of the LGN as a mere gateway to the visual cortex. The LGN may, in fact, serve as a gatekeeper to amplify gain, thereby increasing neural signals relative to background noise. The nature of the mechanism by which attention controls neural gain at the level of the thalamus remains to be explored. At the cortical level, one important function of attention is to filter out another type of noise that is induced by the vast majority of visual information: the unwanted information from distractors. Evidence from single-cell physiology and lesion studies in monkeys and fMRI studies in humans suggests that areas V4 and TEO are important sites where relevant information is selected and irrelevant information is filtered out, as reviewed in the next section.

2. Visual cortex: spatial filtering of distractor information in areas V4 and TEO

Because of the limited processing capacity of the visual system, multiple objects present at the same time in visual scenes compete for neural representation. Single-cell physiology studies suggest that such neural competition occurs at the level of the RF of neurons in extrastriate cortex, where the RFs are sufficiently large to encompass multiple stimuli. In physiology studies, neural responses to a single visual stimulus presented alone in a neuron's RF have been compared to the responses evoked by the same stimulus when a second stimulus was presented simultaneously within the same RF. The responses to paired stimuli were found to be smaller than the sum of the responses evoked by each stimulus individually and turned out to be a weighted average of the individual responses (Reynolds et al. 1999). This result suggests that when multiple stimuli are presented at the same time within a neuron's RF, the stimuli are not processed independently, but interact with each other in a mutually suppressive way, in a competition for neural representation. Similarly, in fMRI studies, it has been found that multiple simultaneously presented (i.e. competing) stimuli evoked weaker responses than the same stimuli presented sequentially (i.e. in a non-competing fashion) in visual areas V1, V2/VP, V4, and TEO, suggesting mutual suppression among the competing stimuli (Fig. A18a; Kastner et al. 1998). The magnitude of the suppression effect was smallest in V1 and increased toward extrastriate areas V4 and TEO, indicating that the competitive interactions were scaled to the increase in RF size of neurons within these areas and occurred most strongly at the level of the RF.

In single-cell recording studies, it has been shown that spatially directed attention influences the competition among multiple stimuli in favour of the attended stimulus by modulating competitive interactions. When a monkey directed attention to one of two competing stimuli within a RF, the responses in extrastriate areas V2, V4, and MT were as large as those to that stimulus presented alone, thereby eliminating the suppressive influence of the competing stimulus (Reynolds et al. 1999). A similar mechanism appears to operate in the human visual cortex (Kastner et al. 1998). It was shown that directed attention leads to greater increases of fMRI signals for simultaneously presented stimuli, than for sequentially presented stimuli, in areas V4 and TEO (Fig. A18b). The magnitude of this attention effect scales with the magnitude of the competitive interactions among stimuli, with the strongest reduction of competition occurring in ventral extrastriate areas V4 and TEO, suggesting that the effects scaled with RF size. These findings support the idea that directed attention enhances information processing of stimuli at the attended location by counteracting suppression induced by nearby stimuli, which compete for limited processing resources. This may be an important mechanism by which attention filters out information from nearby distractors (Desimone and Duncan 1995).

The spatial filtering of distractor information can be achieved not only by resolving competitive interactions among multiple stimuli through top-down mechanisms, but also through bottom-up mechanisms. For example, if a salient stimulus is present in a cluttered scene (*pop-out effect*), it will be effortlessly and quickly detected independent of the number of distractors (Treisman and Gelade 1980), suggesting that competition is biased in favour of the salient stimulus. Pop-out is an example of a contextual effect that depends on factors present in the stimulus and surrounding items, including simple feature properties such as the colour of the stimulus, perceptual grouping of stimulus features by *gestalt principles, and the dissimilarity between the stimulus and nearby distractors. Neural correlates of pop-out have been found as early as in area V1, where neural responses to a single item presented in a RF surrounded by a homogeneous array of items presented outside the RF were stronger when the surround differed from the RF stimulus than when it was identical to it, suggesting that neural responses depended on the context in which the stimuli were shown (Knierim and Van Essen 1992). In fMRI studies, it was shown that competitive interactions among multiple stimuli were eliminated in extrastriate areas V2 and V4, when

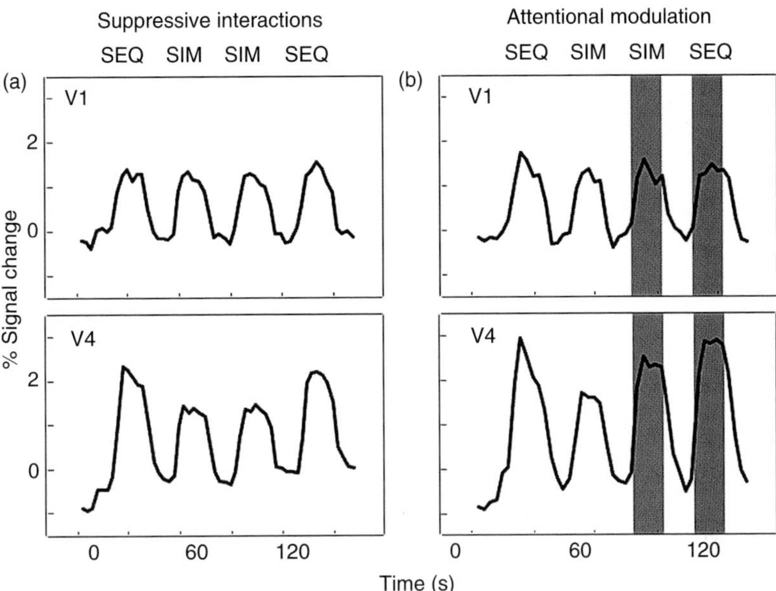

Fig. A18. Competitive interactions and attentional modulation in visual cortex. (a) Suppressive interactions in V1 and V4. Simultaneously presented stimuli evoked less activity than sequentially presented stimuli in V4, but not in V1, suggesting that suppressive interactions were scaled to the RF size of neurons in visual cortex. (b) Attentional modulation of suppressive interactions. The suppression effect in V4 was replicated in the unattended condition of this experiment, when the subjects' attention was directed away from the stimulus display (unshaded time series). Spatially directed attention (shaded time series) increased responses to simultaneously presented stimuli to a larger degree than to sequentially presented ones in V4. Adapted from Kastner et al. 1998.

they were presented in the context of pop-out displays, in which a single item differed from the others, but not in heterogeneous displays, in which all items differed from each other (Fig. A19; Beck and Kastner 2005). As in non-human primates, the pop-out effects appeared to originate in early visual cortex and were independent of attentional top-down control, suggesting that stimulus context may provide a powerful influence on neural competition in human visual cortex. Moreover, visual salience may be just one example of a number of bottom-up contextual effects, instrumental in scene segmentation and guiding attention to object-based selections that may operate by influencing competition for neural representation in visual cortex.

3. Frontal and parietal cortex: sorting out sources and sites

There is evidence from studies in patients suffering from attentional deficits due to *brain damage and from functional brain imaging studies in healthy subjects performing attention tasks that attention-related modulatory signals are not generated within the visual system, but rather derive from higher-order areas in parietal and frontal cortex and are transmitted via feedback projections to the visual system (Kastner and Ungerleider 2000). This network includes the frontal eye field (FEF), supplementary eye field (SEF), and regions in the superior parietal lobule (SPL) and has been found to be activated in a variety of visuospatial attention tasks, suggesting that it constitutes a rather general attention network that operates independent of the specific requirements of the visuospatial task (Fig. A20a, b). The notion of a general attention network has been further corroborated by studies demonstrating its involvement in the control of attention shifts between spatial locations, stimulus features, object representations, and sensory modalities (Serences and Yantis 2006).

Neuroimaging and physiology studies suggest that this network reflects the top-down sources that generate attentional feedback signals, which in turn modulate

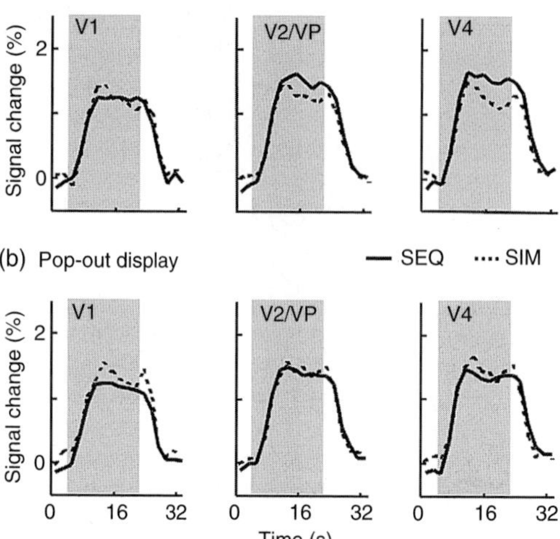

Fig. A19. Pop-out as a bottom-up factor in biasing competitive interactions in visual cortex. Time series of fMRI signals in areas V1, V2/VP, and V4 (n = 10). Solid curves indicate activity evoked by sequential presentations and dashed curves that evoked by simultaneous presentations. (a) For heterogeneous displays, sequentially presented stimuli evoked more activity than simultaneously presented stimuli in areas V2/VP and V4. In V1, there was no difference between sequentially and simultaneously presented heterogeneous stimuli. (b) Pop-out displays did not induce significant response differences between simultaneously and sequentially presented stimuli in areas V2/VP and V4. In area V1, the difference in responses evoked by sequential and simultaneous presentations was reversed. From Beck and Kastner 2005.

visual processing at 'sites' in sensory cortex. In fMRI studies, neural activity related to the attentional operations themselves were dissociated from modulatory effects on visual stimuli by probing the effects of spatially directed attention in the presence and in the absence of visual stimulation (Kastner et al. 1999). Subjects were cued to direct attention to a peripheral target location and to expect the onset of visual stimuli, which occurred with a delay of several seconds after which subjects indicated the detection of target stimuli at the attended location. It has been shown in visual cortex, as illustrated for area V4 in Fig. A20c, that fMRI signals increase during the expectation period (textured epochs), before any stimuli are present on the screen. This increase of baseline activity is followed by a further increase of activity evoked by the onset of the stimulus presentations (grey-shaded epochs). This baseline increase is found in all visual areas with a representation of the attended location, indicating that it is topographically specific. These results are in accordance with single-cell recording studies showing that spontaneous (baseline) firing rates were 30–40% higher for neurons in areas V2 and V4 when an animal is cued to attend covertly to a location within the neuron's RF before the stimulus is presented there (Luck et al. 1997). In parietal and frontal cortex, the same distributed network for spatial attention is activated during directed attention in the absence of visual stimulation as during directed attention in the presence of visual stimulation, consisting of the FEF, the SEF, and the SPL (Fig. A20a, b). As in visual cortical areas, there is an increase in activity in these frontal and parietal areas

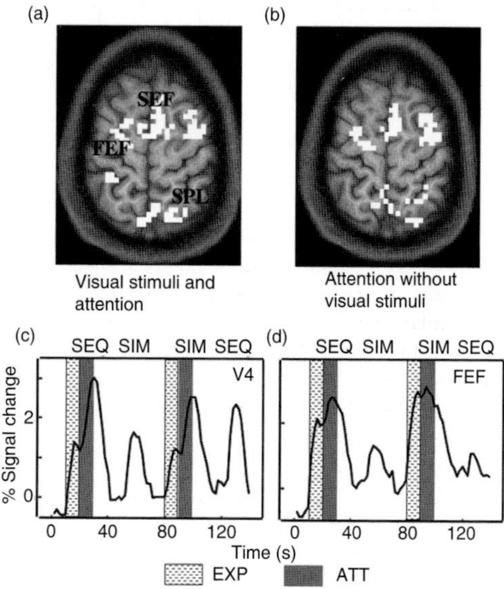

Fig. A20. Frontoparietal network for spatial attention. Axial slice through frontal and parietal cortex. (a) When the subject directed attention to a peripheral target location and performed a discrimination task, a distributed frontoparietal network was activated including the SEF, the FEF, and the SPL. (b) The same network of frontal and parietal areas was activated when the subject directed attention to the peripheral target location in expectation of the stimulus onset. (c) Time series of fMRI signals in V4. Directing attention to a peripheral target location in the absence of visual stimulation led to an increase of baseline activity (textured blocks), which was followed by a further increase after the onset of the stimuli (grey shaded blocks). Baseline increases were found in both striate and extrastriate visual cortex. (d) Time series of fMRI signals in FEF. Directing attention to the peripheral target location in the absence of visual stimulation led to a stronger increase in baseline activity than in visual cortex; the further increase of activity after the onset of the stimuli was not significant.

due to directed attention in the absence of visual input. However, (1) this increase in activity is stronger in SPL, FEF, and SEF than the increase in activity seen in visual cortex (as exemplified for FEF in Fig. A20c), and (2) there is no further increase in activity evoked by the attended stimulus presentations in these parietal and frontal areas. Rather, there is sustained activity throughout the expectation period and the attended presentations (Fig. A20c). These results from parietal and frontal areas suggest that this activity reflects the attentional operations of the task and not visual processing per se. These findings therefore provide the first evidence that these parietal and frontal areas may be the sources of feedback that generates the top-down biasing signals seen in visual cortex. This notion has been strongly corroborated by physiology studies in monkeys showing that microstimulation of the FEF can mimic the modulatory effects of attention in downstream area V4 (Moore and Armstrong 2003).

4. Conclusion

The overall view that emerges from these studies is that visual attention affects neural processing at multiple stages of processing. At the thalamic level, attention appears to act by controlling neural response gain. At early cortical processing stages, attention affects contextual modulation of neural responses, which may serve important functions in basic mechanisms of scene segmentation and grouping (Ito and Gilbert 1999). At intermediate cortical processing stages, attention mediates the spatial filtering of unwanted information. These multilevel modulatory processes appear to be controlled by a higher-order frontoparietal network of brain areas that may coordinate its function with the pulvinar nucleus of the thalamus (Fig. A22). Together, these brain systems cooperate to generate attentional functions that enable us to select relevant visual information for further processing in memory and other cognitive systems to guide actions. In this respect, visual selective attention can be described as a multilevel selection process that operates by coordinating information processing in several parallel distributed cortical and subcortical networks.

SABINE KASTNER

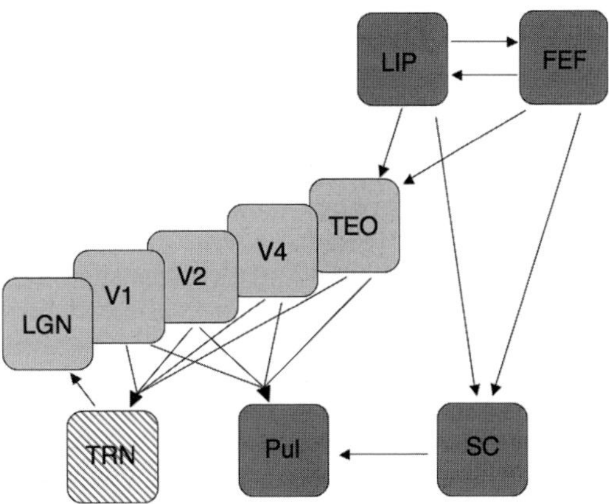

Fig. A21. Neural architecture of visual attention. The diagram illustrates the widely distributed network of brain areas that subserves visual attention and operates across various processing levels. The LGN is the first stage at which visual processing is modulated by attention; this modulation may be under control of the thalamic reticular nucleus (TRN), which operates as a local integrator of visual information. Intermediate cortical areas such as V4 and TEO act as filter sites to reduce the amount of unwanted information (only areas along the ventral stream are shown for reasons of simplification). Higher-order areas in the parietal (LIP) and frontal (FEF) cortices integrate information from the visual system and provide top-down attentional control via feedback connections. Furthermore, the pulvinar (Pul) may act as an additional integrator receiving information from both the visual system and the higher-order areas via the superior colliculus (SC). The connectivity of these brain systems is indicated in simplified form and does not reflect the complexity of the known anatomical connections. It should be noted that most, if not all, of the connections are reciprocal.

Beck, D. M. and Kastner, S. (2005). 'Stimulus context modulates competition in human extrastriate cortex'. *Nature Neuroscience*, 8.

Desimone, R. and Duncan, J. (1995). 'Neural mechanisms of selective visual attention'. *Annual Review Neuroscience*, 18.

Ito, M. and Gilbert, C. D. (1999). 'Attention modulates contextual influences in the primary visual cortex of alert monkeys'. *Neuron*, 22.

Kastner, S. and Ungerleider, L. G. (2000). 'Mechanisms of visual attention in the human cortex'. *Annual Review of Neuroscience*, 23.

——, De Weerd, P., Desimone, R., and Ungerleider, L. G. (1998). 'Mechanisms of directed attention in the human extrastriate cortex as revealed by functional MRI'. *Science*, 282.

——, Pinsk, M. A., De Weerd, P., Desimone, R., and Ungerleider, L. G. (1999). 'Increased activity in human visual cortex during directed attention in the absence of visual stimulation'. *Neuron*, 22.

Knierim, J. J. and Van Essen, D. C. (1992). 'Neuronal responses to static texture patterns in area V1 of the alert macaque monkey'. *Journal of Neurophysiology*, 67.

Luck, S. J., Chelazzi, L., Hillyard, S. A., and Desimone, R. (1997). 'Neural mechanisms of spatial selective attention in areas V1, V2, and V4 of macaque visual cortex'. *Journal of Neurophysiology*, 77.

Moore, T. and Armstrong, K. M. (2003). 'Selective gating of visual signals by microstimulation of frontal cortex'. *Nature*, 421.

Moran, J. and Desimone, R. (1985). 'Selective attention gates visual processing in the extrastriate cortex'. *Science*, 229.

O'Connor, D. H., Fukui, M. M., Pinsk, M. A., and Kastner, S. (2002). 'Attention modulates responses in the human lateral geniculate nucleus'. *Nature Neuroscience*, 5.

Rees, G., Frith, C. D., and Lavie, N. (1997). 'Modulating irrelevant motion perception by varying attentional load in an unrelated task'. *Science*, 278.

Reynolds, J. H., Chelazzi, L., and Desimone, R. (1999). 'Competitive mechanisms subserve attention in macaque areas V2 and V4'. *Journal of Neuroscience*, 19.

Serences, J. T. and Yantis, S. (2006). 'Selective visual attention and perceptual coherence'. *Trends in Cognitive Sciences*, 10.

Sherman, S. M. and Guillery, R. W. (2001). *Exploring the Thalamus*.

Treisman, A. M. and Gelade, G. (1980). 'A feature-integration theory of attention'. *Cognitive Psychology*, 12.

attention psychophysical approaches Attention is the mechanism that allows us to selectively process the vast amount of information that we receive and to guide our behaviour. Visual spatial attention can be deployed overtly, accompanied by eye movements to the relevant location, or covertly, without eye movements (Helmholtz 1910/1925, Posner 1980). There are two types of covert attention: *sustained attention* refers to the voluntary, endogenous directing of attention to a location in the visual field, and *transient attention* refers to the automatic, exogenous capture of attention to a location, brought about by a sudden change in the environment (Nakayama and Mackeben 1989, Posner 1980).

Following a procedure devised by Posner (1980), whereby observers are cued to attend to specific locations while keeping their gaze at a central fixation point, many studies have characterized the effects of covert attention on perception. Attention improves performance (higher accuracy and shorter reaction times) on many tasks, involving several dimensions of early vision (contrast sensitivity and spatial resolution), such as detection, discrimination, localization, and visual search. Moreover, attention increases the haemodynamic response, an index of neural activity, in visual areas (for reviews see Reynolds and Chelazzi 2004, Carrasco 2006).

1. Attention and appearance
2. Attention alters spatial vision: perceived contrast, spatial frequency, gap size and object size, and saturation (but not hue)
3. Attention alters temporal vision: perceived flicker rate, motion coherence, and speed
4. Ruling out alternative explanations of the cueing effect
5. Conclusion

1. Attention and appearance

Psychologists, physiologists, and philosophers have debated the phenomenology of attention since the late 19th century. Does attention alter our subjective experience of the visual world? Which aspects of our visual experience does attention affect? Can attention make a visual pattern seem more detailed, or a colour more vivid? Studies on the phenomenological correlates of attention, which are relevant to the topic of subjective experience and awareness, show that attention alters appearance of basic spatial (contrast, spatial resolution, colour saturation, object size) and temporal (flicker rate, motion coherence, speed) visual dimensions.

Whether and how attention affects appearance has been systematically investigated only recently. This may be due to the difficulty in objectively testing and quantifying the subjective experience of perceived stimuli and changes in such experience with attention. The phenomenology of selective attention has been a subject of debate among pioneers in experimental psychology such as Mach, Fechner, von Helmholtz, Wundt, and James (see James 1890/1950, Wundt 1902). Much of this early work was *introspective, and conflicting conclusions were often drawn from such subjective methods of investigation. On the disagreement among investigators about whether attention increases the perceived intensity of a stimulus, James concluded: 'The subject is one which would well repay exact experiment, if methods could be devised' (James 1890/1950:426).

A psychophysical paradigm that assesses the phenomenological correlate of attention, by manipulating transient attention via uninformative spatial cues, makes it possible to study subjective experience and visual awareness more objectively and rigorously (Luck 2004, Treue 2004). This paradigm quantifies the observer's subjective perception using a task contingent upon a comparative judgement between two stimuli on a particular feature (Carrasco et al. 2004; Fig. A22). Observers are shown two stimuli and asked to 'report property *x* of the stimulus that is greater/lesser in property *y*'. That is, the perceived relative values of property *y*—the primary interest of the experiment (e.g. contrast)—is an indicator of which stimulus to report on property *x* (e.g. orientation). The critical manipulation is that observers are not asked to directly rate their subjective experience on property *y*, but to make a decision about stimulus property *x*. This paradigm allows us to simultaneously measuring the effect of attention on appearance and performance. This paradigm coupled with control experiments for cue bias (see below) rule out response bias (Luck 2004, Treue 2004).

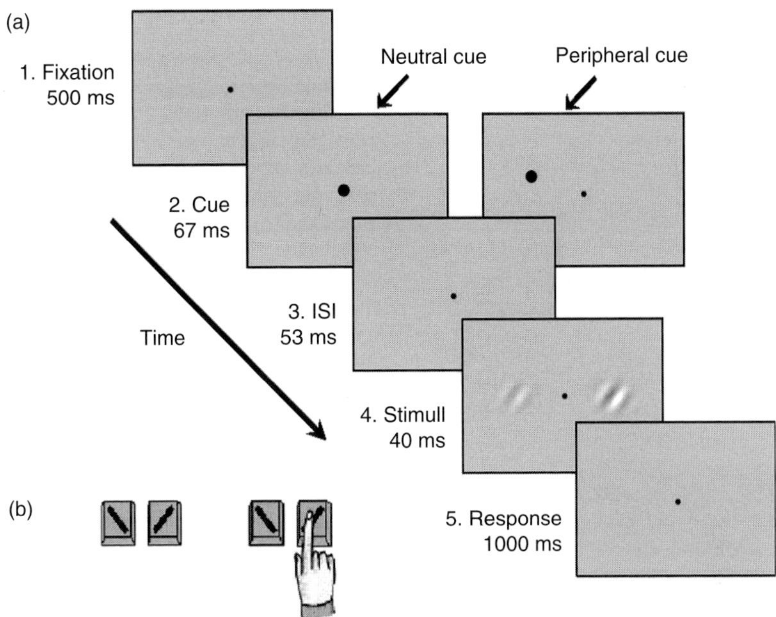

Fig. A22. Sequence of events in a single trial. (a) Each trial began with a fixation point followed by a brief neutral or peripheral cue. The peripheral cue had equal probability of appearing on the left- or right-hand side, and was not predictive of the stimulus contrast or orientation. The timing of this sequence maximized the effect of transient attention and precluded eye movements. (b) Observers performed a two-by-two forced-choice (2 × 2 AFC) task: they were asked to indicate the orientation (left vs right) of the higher-contrast stimulus. After Carrasco et al. 2004; Figure 1.

2. Attention alters spatial vision: perceived contrast, spatial frequency, gap size and object size, and saturation (but not hue)

Attention increases perceived contrast. Contrast, a fundamental dimension of vision, is a natural candidate for understanding the relation between attention and appearance. Psychophysical and neurophysiological studies indicate that attention increases contrast sensitivity, and suggest that attention may also increase perceived contrast (for reviews see Reynolds and Chelazzi 2004, Carrasco 2006).

To investigate the effects of attention on perceived contrast, observers are presented with two Gabor patches, one to the left and one to the right of fixation, and asked to report the orientation of the higher-contrast stimulus. These instructions emphasize the orientation judgement, when in fact the main interest is in the contrast judgements. On each trial, the 'standard' Gabor had a fixed contrast, whereas the contrast of the 'test' Gabor was randomly chosen from a range of contrasts sampled around the standard contrast. The orientation of each Gabor was chosen randomly. By assessing observers' responses, the psychometric function describing the probability of choosing the test patch relative to the standard, as a function of their contrast, was obtained. The test contrast at which this function reaches 50% is the *point of subjective equality* (PSE). These functions were measured when transient covert attention was automatically captured to the cued location, via a peripheral cue, and when it was distributed across the display, via a neutral cue. The peripheral cue was uninformative in terms of both stimulus orientation and contrast. Observers were told that the peripheral cue had equal probability of appearing either to the left or right of fixation and over the higher or lower contrast stimulus. This eliminated the possibility of observers giving more weight to the information at the cued location and hence a decisional explanation for an attentional effect.

Transient attention significantly increased perceived contrast (Fig. A23a). In the neutral condition the PSE occurred at physical equality. When the test patch was cued the PSE shifted to lower test contrasts; conversely, when the standard patch was cued the PSE shifted to higher test contrasts. The effects are similar for low- and high-contrast stimuli. Because observers perform an orientation discrimination task contingent upon appearance, an objective index shows that the cue improved performance in the discrimination task. The results further argue against response bias, as it should not produce a change in discrimination performance. In sum, when observers' attention was drawn to a stimulus location, observers reported that stimulus as being higher in contrast than it actually was, thus indicating that attention changes appearance.

Schneider (2006) reported that peripheral cues increase perceived brightness only at levels near detection threshold, more so for white than black cues, and he predicted that reversing the cue's luminance polarity should lead to differential cueing effects. However, when this prediction was tested, both black and white cues increased the apparent contrast to the same degree, thus confirming that the cue effect is due to attention, not to sensory factors (Ling and Carrasco 2007).

Tsal et al. (1994) reported that attention reduces perceived brightness contrast, whereas Prinzmetal et al. (1997), using a dual task, reported that attention does not change stimulus appearance in a number of perceptual domains (e.g. frequency, hue); rather, it only reduces response variance, rendering a more veridical percept. However, methodological concerns limit both findings: in Tsal's study, observers were asked to make a comparison judgement between the target and one of four test patterns held in memory, thus forcing observers to rely on a possibly biased categorical memory representation to make their responses. In Prinzmetal's studies, a concurrent task paradigm was used in which attention allocation is not properly controlled, making it difficult to isolate the source of possible processing differences. Moreover, because observers were given an unlimited response time, eye movements between the simultaneously presented target and the response palette were possible, thus confounding results attributed to covert attention with overt eye movements, which could underlie the veridicality of their judgements. The conclusions of these studies are further limited because observers were asked to make appearance judgements directly, and there was no objective index of the effectiveness of the attention manipulation (e.g. Carrasco et al. 2004, Treue 2004).

It is likely that the appearance enhancement (Carrasco et al. 2004, Ling and Carrasco 2007) accompanies the increased contrast sensitivity observed in previous psychophysical studies. The conclusion that attention increases apparent contrast supports a linking hypothesis, which states that the attentional enhancement of neural firing is interpreted as if the stimulus has a higher contrast. Converging evidence from neurophysiological, psychophysical, and neuroimaging studies support this proposal (Luck 2004, Reynolds and Chelazzi 2004, Treue 2004, Carrasco 2006).

Attention increases perceived spatial frequency, gap size, and object size. Using the appearance paradigm described above, it has been shown that attention increases apparent spatial frequency and apparent gap size, which are both related to spatial resolution (Gobell and Carrasco 2005). This result is consistent with the finding that in a gap-localization task, attention increases the perceived distance between the ends of the two line stimuli, making the gap bigger and easier to localize (Shalev and Tsal 2002). Both studies lend support to the proposal that attention increases spatial resolution by contracting a neuron's effective receptive field around the attended stimulus. Furthermore, because spatial tuning of visual neurons provides the basis for perceiving spatial relations, attention might distort perceived spatial relation and object sizes by shifting receptive fields. The appearance paradigm was used to test this hypothesis. Consistent with the finding that attention is mediated by dynamic shifts of visual receptive fields, attention increased the perceived size of moving visual patterns (Anton-Erxleben et al. 2007).

Attention increases perceived saturation, but does not alter perceived hue. The appearance paradigm also revealed that attention increases perceived saturation consistently for three separated equiluminant regions of colour space (red, blue, and green). The same paradigm, however, revealed no effect on apparent hue (Fig. A24a). The existence of the effect for saturation, but not for hue, is notable in light of the fact that attention improves orientation discrimination for both hue and saturation stimuli, which validates cue effectiveness. This dissociation shows that the presence of an attentional enhancement of behavioural performance does not lead to, or require, a corresponding change or enhancement in appearance. Thus, the cueing effect on saturation appearance cannot be explained by response bias or cue bias—response bias towards the cued item. This finding is strong evidence that it is a genuine phenomenal effect and not a cognitive effect that is not driven by phenomenology (Fuller and Carrasco 2006).

A useful distinction in this context is that of metathetic vs prothetic perceptual dimensions. Saturation, contrast, spatial frequency, and flicker rate are prothetic dimensions having meaningful zero values and inherent directionality. Hue is metathetic; our percepts of red and blue are qualitatively different. Attention may increase the appearance of prothetic dimensions because increased contrast and saturation make it easier to discriminate the signal from the background, and facilitate the discrimination of the features of the signal.

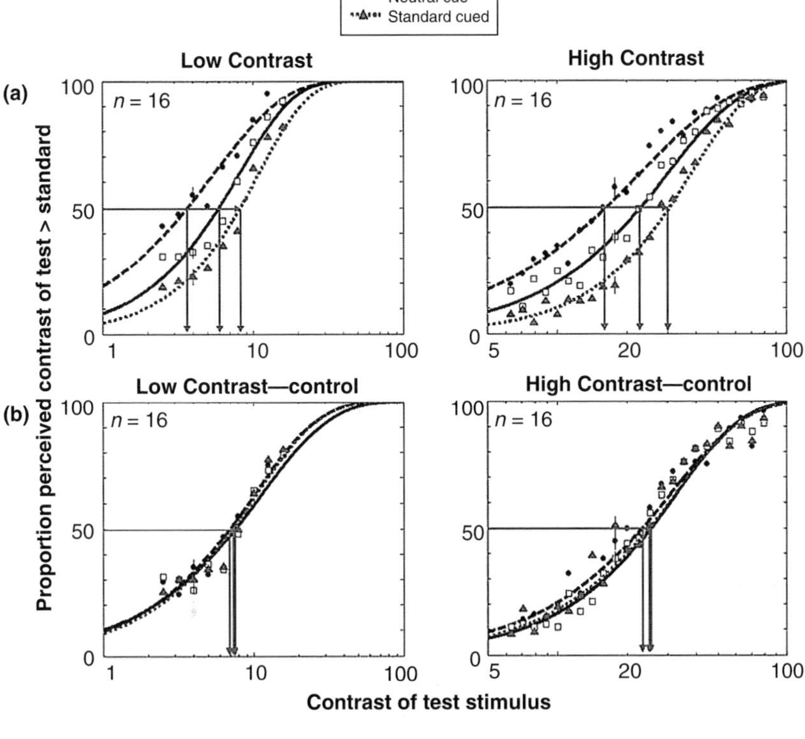

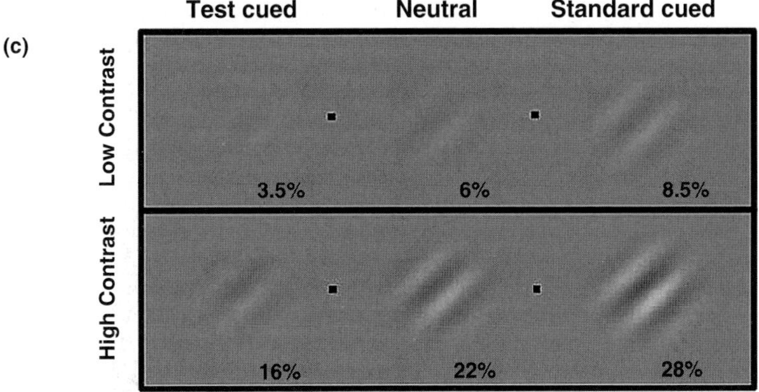

Fig. A23. Contrast appearance. (a) Psychometric functions (proportion of responses in which observers reported the contrast of the test patch as higher than the standard patch as a function of the test patch's physical contrast) for the neutral and peripheral conditions (test cued and standard cued). The standard was 6% contrast (left panel) for the low-contrast condition and 22% contrast (right panel) for the high-contrast condition. The horizontal line intersecting both fits indicates the contrasts necessary for the test and standard stimuli to attain subjective equality (50%; see (c)). (b) Control experiment: lengthened interval between cue and target. When transient attention is extinguished via a longer timing interval, results are the same when the test is peripherally or neutrally cued. Error bars correspond to the average ± 1 s. e. for each condition. (c) Effect of covert attention on apparent contrast. If you were looking at one of the four fixation points (black dot), and the grating to the left of that fixation point that was cued, the stimuli at both sides of fixation would appear to have the same contrast. Top: With attention, a 3.5% contrast stimulus appears as if it were 6% contrast. Similarly, a cued 6% contrast stimulus appears as if it were a more clearly discriminable 8.5% contrast stimulus. Bottom: Likewise, with high-contrast stimuli when a 16% contrast grating is cued it appears as if it were 22% contrast, and a cued 22% contrast grating appears as if it were 28%. After Carrasco et al. 2004; figures 2, 4, and 5.

However, there is no a priori reason why attention should affect apparent hue in one direction or another.

3. Attention alters temporal vision: perceived flicker rate, motion coherence, and speed

The appearance paradigm was used to assess a phenomenological correlate of attention for temporal vision, asking whether and how transient attention affects perceived flicker rate. In each trial, two suprathreshold Gabor stimuli were counter-phase modulated at either the same or different temporal frequencies. Observers were asked to report the orientation of the stimulus that flickered faster. Directing attention to a stimulus location increased its perceived flicker rate. Attention could affect the activation pattern across temporal frequency channels by increasing the contribution or weight of the highest temporal frequency channel to the total output. This would result in an overestimation of perceived flicker rate in the attended compared with the neutral condition (Montagna and Carrasco 2006).

To assess the effect of attention on the appearance of motion, observers viewed pairs of moving dot patterns and were asked to report the motion direction of the pattern with higher coherence. Directing attention to a stimulus location increased its perceived coherence level and improved performance on a direction discrimination task. These results are consistent with neurophysiological studies showing that attention modulates motion-sensitive areas MT/hMT+ in monkeys and humans respectively, and provide evidence of a subjective perceptual correlate of attention with a concomitant effect on performance (Liu et al. 2006).

The appearance paradigm has also revealed that directing attention to a stimulus location increased its perceived speed, although, according to the author, this may occur despite a lack of change in visual awareness (Turatto et al. 2007).

4. Ruling out alternative explanations of the cueing effect

Several control experiments rule out alternative explanations of the appearance results, namely cue or response bias.

Reversing the direction of the question. When observers were asked to report the orientation of the stimulus of lower, rather than higher, apparent contrast, they chose the cued test stimulus less frequently. Had results been due to cue bias, observers would have chosen the cued stimulus more often than the other stimulus regardless of the direction of the question. Reversing the instructions has been a successful control in appearance studies of colour saturation (Fuller and Carrasco 2006; see Fig. A19b), contrast (Carrasco et al. 2004, Ling and Carrasco 2007), spatial frequency (Gobell and Carrasco 2005), flicker rate (Montagna and Carrasco 2006), size of a moving object (Anton-Erxleben et al. 2007), and speed (Turatto et al. 2007).

Lengthening the interval between the cue and target. Because of the ephemeral nature of transient attention (*c.*120 ms), a lengthened interval between the cue and target should eliminate any effect that it may have on perception, and any residual effect would be attributed to a cue bias. When the cue preceded the stimuli by 500 ms, neutral and peripheral conditions did not differ. Appearance studies of contrast appearance (Carrasco et al. 2004, Ling and Carrasco 2007; see Fig. A18b), motion coherence (Liu et al. 2006), and speed (Turatto et al. 2007) show that when transient attention was no longer active, stimulus appearance is not altered.

Post-cue vs pre-cue. When observers were asked to report the stimulus followed by a post-cue rather than preceded by a pre-cue, the pre-cue increased perceived spatial frequency (Gobell and Carrasco 2005) or object size (Anton-Erxleben et al. 2007), but the post-cue did not alter appearance, although the spatial and temporal contiguity between cue and stimulus were the same. These results are consistent with an fMRI study investigating the neural basis of transient attention, in which pre-cueing, but not post-cueing, the target location increased stimulus-evoked response in corresponding retinotopic striate and extrastriate areas (Liu et al. 2005).

Performance. Appearance and orientation discrimination performance have been concurrently assessed (Carrasco et al. 2004, Fuller and Carrasco 2006, Liu et al. 2006, Anton-Erxleben et al. 2007, Ling and Carrasco 2007). Improvements in such performance-based tasks indicate that exogenous attention has been engaged to a peripheral location. Because cue location and stimulus orientation are uncorrelated, concurrent improvements at the cued locations and impairments at the uncued locations further show that the appearance results are not due to response bias.

5. Conclusion

Using this appearance paradigm, it has been found that attention alters our subjective impression of many dimensions of spatial and temporal vision, mediated by the ventral and dorsal streams, respectively: contrast (Carrasco et al. 2004, Ling and Carrasco 2007), spatial frequency and gap size, both related to spatial resolution (Gobell and Carrasco 2005), colour saturation (but not hue; Fuller and Carrasco 2006) and perceived size of moving visual patterns (Anton-Erxleben et al. 2007),

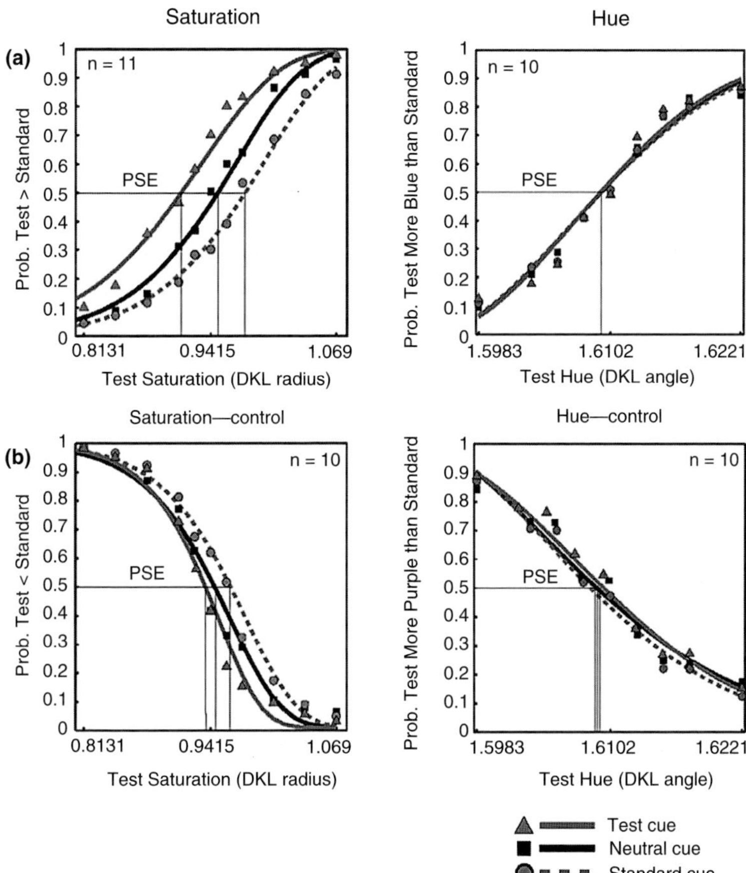

Fig. A24. Colour appearance psychometric functions. (a) Left panel: saturation functions (proportion of responses when observers were asked to report the orientation of the 'redder' stimulus in which observers reported the saturation of the test patch as higher than the standard as a function of the test patch's physical saturation) for the neutral and peripheral conditions (test cued and standard cued). The intersection of the horizontal and vertical lines indicates the saturation necessary for the test and standard stimuli to attain subjective equality (50%). Right panel: hue functions (proportion of responses in which observers reported the 'bluer' stimulus of each pair as higher than the standard as a function of the test patch's physical hue) for the neutral and peripheral conditions (test cued and standard cued). The intersection of the horizontal and vertical lines indicates the hue necessary for the test and standard stimuli to attain subjective equality (50%). (b) Control experiments: reversed instructions functions when observers were asked to report the orientation of the 'less red' stimulus (saturation; left panel) or the 'purpler' stimulus (hue; right panel). Attention altered the appearance of saturation (left panels) but not of hue (right panels). After Fuller and Carrasco 2006, figures 5 and 7.

as well as flicker rate (Montagna and Carrasco 2006), motion coherence (Liu et al. 2006), and perceived speed (Turatto et al. 2007).

By showing that the spatial deployment of attention leads to a change in phenomenological experience, these studies confirm the intuition of William James that attention and awareness are intertwined. We conclude that covert attention can intensify the sensory impression of a stimulus. Attention not only affects how we perform in a visual task—it also affects what we see and experience.

MARISA CARRASCO

Anton-Erxleben, K., Henrich, C., and Treue, S. (2007). 'Attention changes perceived size of moving visual patterns'. *Journal of Vision*, 7.

Carrasco, M. (2006). 'Covert attention increases contrast sensitivity: psychophysical, neurophysiological and neuroimaging studies'. *Progress in Brain Research*, 154.

——, Ling, S., and Read, S. (2004). 'Attention alters appearance'. *Nature Neuroscience*, 7.

Fuller, S. and Carrasco, M. (2006). 'Exogenous attention and color perception: performance and appearance of saturation and hue'. *Vision Research*, 46.

Gobell, J. and Carrasco, M. (2005). 'Attention alters the appearance of spatial frequency and gap size'. *Psychological Science*, 16.

Helmholtz, H. L. F. von (1910/1925). *Helmholtz's Treatise on Physiological Optics*, Vol. 3, ed. and trans. J. P. C. Southhall.

James, W. (1890/1950) *The Principles of Psychology*.

Ling, S. and Carrasco, M. (2007) 'Transient covert attention does alter appearance: a reply to Schneider (2006)'. *Perception and Psychophysics*, 69.

Liu, T., Fuller, S., and Carrasco, M. (2006). 'Attention alters the appearance of motion coherence'. *Psychonomic Bulletin and Review*, 13.

——, Pestilli, F., and Carrasco, M. (2005). 'Transient attention enhances perceptual performance and FMRI response in human visual cortex'. *Neuron*, 45.

Luck, S. J. (2004). 'Understanding awareness: one step closer'. *Nature Neuroscience*, 7.

Montagna, B. and Carrasco, M. (2006). 'Transient covert attention and the perceived rate of flicker'. *Journal of Vision*, 6.

Nakayama, K. and Mackeben, M. (1989). 'Sustained and transient components of focal visual attention'. *Vision Research*, 29.

Posner, M. I. (1980). 'Orienting of attention'. *Quarterly Journal of Experimental Psychology*, 32.

Prinzmetal, W., Nwachuku, I., Bodanski, L., Blumenfeld, L., and Shimizu, N. (1997). 'The phenomenology of attention. 2. Brightness and contrast'. *Consciousness and Cognition*, 6.

Reynolds, J. H. and Chelazzi, L. (2004). 'Attentional modulation of visual processing'. *Annual Review of Neuroscience*, 27.

Schneider, K. (2006). 'Does attention alter appearance?' *Perception and Psychophysics*, 68.

Shalev, L. and Tsal, Y. (2002). 'Detecting gaps with and without attention: further evidence for attentional receptive fields'. *European Journal of Cognitive Psychology*, 14.

Treue, S. (2004). 'Perceptual enhancement of contrast by attention'. *Trends in Cognitive Science*, 8.

Tsal, Y., Shalev, L., Zakay, D., and Lubow, R. E. (1994). 'Attention reduces perceived brightness contrast'. *Quarterly Journal of Experimental Psychology A*, 47.

Turatto, M., Viscovi, M., and Valsecchi, M. (2007). 'Attention makes moving objects be perceived to move faster'. *Vision Research*, 47.

Wundt, W. (1902). *Outlines of Psychology*, trans. C. H. Judd.

attitude, implicit The world is a complicated place. To live in it successfully, humans need ways to simplify it. One ability that comes in handy is forming preferences—is this thing good or bad?—and having a mechanism for storing them. That way, instead of entering every new situation as a blank slate, preferences developed from previous experience can used to guide behaviour. An efficient system would accomplish these operations *automatically, without requiring deliberate effort or even conscious thought, serving as a quick and intuitive guide for responding. Deliberate, conscious thinking could then be reserved for situations when such automatic preferences are not available. Or, if prior experience does not apply, conscious deliberation could override, adjust, or regulate the expression of automatically generated preferences. Such mental operations provide tools for comprehending the situation, evaluating the relevant concepts, and motivating behaviour without having to think about it much, sometimes without really thinking at all.

An *attitude* is an association between a concept and an evaluation—an assessment of whether something is good or bad, positive or negative, pleasant or unpleasant. A familiar way to assess an attitude is to ask, 'Do I like this?' Positive and negative evaluations of this kind require introspection about one's feelings about the concept. The end result, e.g. 'I like this very much', is an *explicit attitude*. Explicit attitudes are deliberate, intentional, and available to conscious awareness. They are often obtained using language to reveal an internal state.

The notion of an implicit attitude is less familiar. Implicit attitudes were defined by psychologists Anthony Greenwald and Mahzarin Banaji (1995) as 'introspectively unidentified (or inaccurately identified) traces of past experience that mediate favorable or unfavorable feeling, thought, or action toward a social object [concept]'. This is quite different from the conception of explicit attitudes. Implicit attitudes are not accessed by *introspection, and may exist outside conscious awareness. Implicit attitudes are thought to derive from the basic mental operations of seeing relationships between concepts and evaluations in everyday experience and accumulating those associations into summary assessments. Such associations can influence how humans see, think, and react to the world, even without the individual having awareness of their existence, activity, or influence.

Having two types of attitude—one implicit and one explicit—introduces the possibility that they can conflict. Explicit attitudes reflect values, beliefs, and deliberate assessments of the world. Implicit attitudes reflect positive and negative associations accumulated through experience. There are a variety of circumstances that might lead these evaluations to differ. For example, somebody who prizes the quality of being egalitarian may hold equally positive explicit attitudes toward members of all ethnicities (e.g. toward Arabs and white Europeans). But such a person also possesses implicit attitudes that have also been obtained from experience in a given culture. The implicit version of attitude may not reveal the even-handedness of the explicit attitude; it may in fact show more positivity toward Europeans than Arabs. It is interesting that a single individual can hold both types of attitudes in one mind. Such differences between explicit and implicit attitude are referred to as *dissociations*. Dissociations do not suggest that either one or the other attitude is the real or true attitude. Both provide information about the individual, and both can guide behaviour. When an individual is tired, preoccupied, or under pressure, it may be more difficult to retrieve the explicit response and regulate behaviour accordingly. In these circumstances, action may be influenced more by the implicit attitude. On the other hand, when an individual is alert, motivated, and aware of the situation, explicit attitudes can be recruited and these may be a stronger influence on behaviour. Dissociations of this form illustrate that humans possess multiple ways of expressing their likes and dislikes and social circumstances and the person's state will determine which one is likely to dominate.

It is easy to imagine how to measure an explicit attitude—ask respondents how they feel. An implicit attitude, however, is not measured by introspection. The varieties of methods used for implicit attitude measurement do not depend on the respondent's ability to self-report their attitude. One such implicit attitude measure is the Implicit Association Test (IAT). Imagine sorting a deck of playing cards as fast as possible into two piles. Instead of four suits this deck has four other categories: items with pleasant meaning (e.g. joyful), items with unpleasant meaning (e.g. terrible), items representing England (e.g. Tower Bridge), and items representing the USA (e.g. Statue of Liberty). You sort these cards twice, each time with different sorting rules. For the first sorting, all of the pleasant words and English images go in one pile, and unpleasant words and American images go in the other. For the second sorting, all of the pleasant words and American images go in one pile, and unpleasant words and English images go in the other. The speed of sorting is an indication of the association strengths between the national concepts and evaluation. In this example, it is likely that Americans would sort the cards faster in the second task and English people would sort faster in the first task, because nationals are likely to have more positive associations with their home country than with the other. You can try the IAT yourself by visiting https://implicit.harvard.edu/.

This approach to measuring attitudes is fundamentally different from asking for a self-report of one's feelings. The only task is to sort cards into groups as quickly as possible; respondents do not consider how they feel about the concepts. Despite this unusual approach, the IAT and related measures have been applied successfully to many topics including social groups, political candidates, food, consumer products, health, and pop culture.

Current research on implicit attitudes is investigating a variety of questions including: (1) How do implicit attitudes form? (2) When will implicit attitudes be similar to and different from explicit attitudes? (3) How stable are implicit attitudes? (4) How do implicit attitudes change? (5) When do implicit attitudes influence behaviour more or less than explicit attitudes? (6) What psychological processes influence performance on implicit attitude measures? These are lively research areas, and the emerging evidence suggests that multiple factors influence the relationship between implicit and explicit attitudes—such as the desire not to express unpopular ideas (social desirability) and the amount of practice or time thinking about the topic (elaboration). Also, while implicit attitudes show some stability over time, they show flexibility in expression based on the immediate social circumstances. And, finally, both implicit and explicit attitudes are related to behaviour, sometimes independently.

Research on implicit attitudes tells us that much of our mental work happens outside conscious awareness, conscious control, without intention, and without requiring self-reflection. Implicit attitudes facilitate heuristic, rapid assessment of the social context. Simultaneously, getting evidence of our implicit attitudes can sometimes surprise us because they do not fit with the way in which we view ourselves. Such situations can provoke and challenge us to think about how we might understand our attitudes and align our implicit and explicit attitudes, goals, and intentions.

BRIAN A. NOSEK AND MAHZARIN R. BANAJI

Fazio, R. H. and Olson, M. A. (2003). 'Implicit measures in social cognition research: their meaning and use'. *Annual Review of Psychology*, 54.

Greenwald, A. G. and Banaji, M. R. (1995). 'Implicit social cognition: attitudes, self-esteem, and stereotypes'. *Psychological Review*, 102.

——, McGhee, D. E., and Schwartz, J. L. K. (1998). 'Measuring individual differences in implicit cognition: the Implicit Association Test'. *Journal of Personality and Social Psychology*, 74.

Nosek, B. A. (2007). 'Implicit–explicit relations'. *Current Directions in Psychological Science*, 16.

——, Greenwald, A. G., and Banaji, M. R. (2006). 'The Implicit Association Test at age 7: a methodological and conceptual review'. In Bargh, J. A. (ed.) *Social Psychology and the Unconscious: the Automaticity of Higher Mental Processes*.

——, Smyth, F. L., Hansen, J. J. et al. (2007). 'Pervasiveness and correlates of implicit attitudes and stereotypes'. *European Review of Social Psychology*, 18.

Poehlman, T.A., Uhlmann, E., Greenwald, A. G., and Banaji, M. R. (2006). 'Understanding and using the Implicit Association Test: III. Meta-analysis of predictive validity'. Unpublished MS.

Wilson, T. D., Lindsey, S., and Schooler, T. Y. (2000). 'A model of dual attitudes'. *Psychological Review*, 107.

attractor networks Artificial neural networks (ANNs), sometimes referred to as **connectionist networks*, are computational models based loosely on the neural architecture of the brain. Since the late 1980s, ANNs have proven to be a fruitful framework for modelling many aspects of cognition, including perception, attention, learning and memory, language, and executive control. A particular type of ANN, called an *attractor network*, is central to computational theories of consciousness, because attractor networks can be analysed in terms of properties—such as temporal stability, and strength, quality, and discreteness of representation—that have been ascribed to conscious states. Some theories have gone so far as to posit that attractor nets are the computational substrate from which conscious states arise.

1. Artificial neural networks
2. Attractor dynamics
3. Relationship between attractor states and conscious states
4. Attractor networks and theories of consciousness

1. Artificial neural networks

ANNs consist of a large number of simple, highly interconnected neuron-like processing units. Each processing unit conveys an *activation level*, a scalar that is usually thought to correspond to the rate of neural spiking. Typically, activation levels are scaled to range between 0 (no spiking) to 1 (maximal spiking), and might represent the absence or presence of a visual feature, or the strength of belief in some hypothesis. For example, if the processing units—*units* for short—are part of a model of visual information processing, activity of a particular unit might denote the presence of the colour red at some location in the visual field. If the units are part of a model of memory, activity of individual units might instead denote semantic features of an item to be recalled.

Each unit receives input activation from a large number of other units, and produces output—its activation level—that is a function of its inputs. A typical function yields an output that grows monotonically with the weighted sum of the inputs. The weights, or strength of connectivity, can be thought of as reflecting the relationship among features or hypotheses. If the presence of feature A implies the presence of feature B, then the weight from A to B should be positive, and activation of A will tend to result in activation of B; if A implies the absence of B, the weight from A to B should be negative.

Units in an ANN can be interconnected to form two basic architectures: feedforward and recurrent. In a *feedforward architecture* (Fig. A25a), activity flows in one direction, from input to output, as indicated by the arrows. A feedforward network performs associative mappings, and might be used, for instance, to map visual representations to semantic representations. In a *recurrent architecture* (Fig. A25b), units are connected such that activity flows bidirectionally, allowing the output activity of a unit at one point in time to influence its activity at a subsequent point in time. Recurrent networks are often used to implement content-addressible memories.

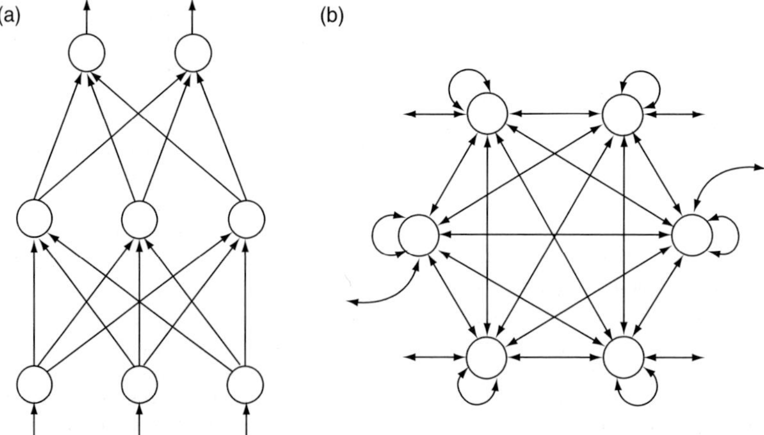

Fig. A25. (a) Feedforward architecture in which activity flows from the bottom layer of units to the top layer. (b) Recurrent architecture in which activity flows in cycles.

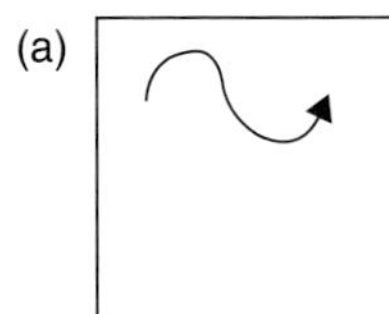

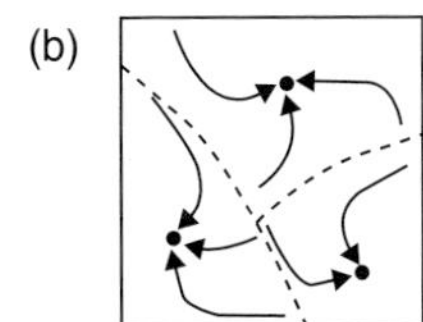

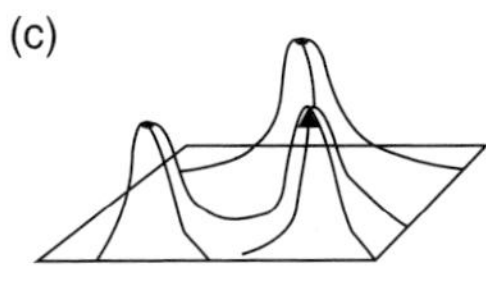

Fig. A26. (a) The activation state of a two-unit recurrent network can be depicted as a point in a two-dimensional space. If activation is bounded, e.g. to lie between 0 and 1, then the state lies within a box. The solid curve depicts the time-varying trajectory of the state, where the arrow represents the forward flow of time. (b) A state space with three attractors carved into attractor basins (dotted lines). (c) A harmony landscape over the state space with three attractors.

The network is first trained on a set of items, and then, when it is presented with a partial featural description of one item, network dynamics fill in the missing features. Both feedforward and recurrent networks can perform cued retrieval, but recurrent networks are more flexible in that they allow any subset of features to serve as a cue for the remaining features.

The activation state of a network with *n* units can be characterized as a point in an *n*-dimensional space, and temporal dynamics of a recurrent network can be described as a time-varying trajectory through this state space (Fig. A26a). An attractor network is a recurrent ANN whose dynamics cause the network state to converge to a fixed point. That is, given an input—which might represent a stimulus to be processed, or the output of another ANN—the dynamics of the network will cause the state to evolve over time to a stable value, away from which the state will not wander.

2. Attractor dynamics

The states to which the net might evolve are called *attractors*. The attractors are typically sparse in the state space. (Technically, attractors can also be limit cycles—non-static, periodic trajectories—but attractor net dynamics ordinarily produce only point attractors.)

The state space of an attractor net can be carved up into *attractor basins*, regions of the state space in which all starting points converge to the same attractor. Figure A26b depicts a state space with three attractor basins whose boundaries are marked by dotted lines, and some trajectories that might be attained within each attractor basin.

Attractor dynamics are achieved by many neural network architectures, including Hopfield networks, harmony networks, Boltzmann machines, adaptive resonance networks, and recurrent back-propagation networks. To ensure attractor dynamics, these popular architectures require symmetry of connectivity: the connection weight from processing unit A to unit B must be the same as the weight from B to A. Given this restriction, the dynamics of the networks can be characterized as performing local optimization—minimizing energy, or equivalently, maximizing harmony. Consider the attractor state space of Fig. A26b, and add an additional dimension representing harmony, a measure of the goodness of a state, as shown in Fig. A26c.

The attractors are at points of maximum harmony, and the network dynamics ensure that harmony is non-decreasing. Because the net is climbing uphill in harmony, it is guaranteed to converge to a local optimum of harmony. The input to an attractor net can either specify the initial state of the net, or it can provide biases—fixed input—to each unit; in the latter case, the biases reshape the landscape such that the best-matching attractor has maximum harmony, and is likely to be found for a wide range of initial network states.

The connection strengths (including biases) in the network determine the harmony landscape, which in turn determines the attractors and the shape of the attractor basins. When a set of attractor patterns are stored in a net, gang effects are typically observed: the shapes of attractor basins are influenced by the proximity of attractors to one another (Zemel and Mozer 2001).

In traditional attractor nets, the knowledge about each attractor is distributed over the connectivity pattern of the entire network. As a result, sculpting the attractor landscape is tricky, and often leads to spurious (undesired) attractors and ill-conditioned (e.g. very narrow) attractor basins. To overcome these limitations, a localist attractor net has been formulated (Zemel and Mozer 2001) that consists of a set of state units and a set of attractor units, one per attractor. Each attractor unit draws the state toward its attractor, with the attractors closer to the state having a greater influence. The localist attractor net is easily configured to obtain a desired set of attractors. The dynamics of a localist attractor net, like its distributed counterpart, can be interpreted as climbing uphill in harmony.

Attractor nets can also be conceptualized from a probabilistic perspective. If the net has intrinsically stochastic dynamics (e.g. Boltzmann machines, or back-propagation networks with added noise), each point in the state space can be characterized in terms of the probability of reaching each attractor from that point—a discrete probability distribution over attractors. The points far from any attractor have a nearly uniform distribution (maximum entropy), whereas the attractors themselves are represented by a distribution with probability 1.0 for the attractor and probability 0.0 for any other attractor (minimum entropy). This conceptualization allows for one to abstract away from neural net representations and dynamics, and to characterize the dynamics as entropy minimization (Colagrosso and Mozer 2005).

3. Relationship between attractor states and conscious states

Theorists have identified certain properties that are claimed to be prerequisites or characteristics of conscious mental states. Attractors share these properties, as we elaborate here.

Conscious perceptual states have been conceived of as interpretations of noisy or ambiguous sensory input (Marcel 1983). For example, the Necker cube admits two possible interpretations, and perceptual awareness flips between these interpretations (see MULTISTABLE PERCEPTION). Searle (1992) focuses on interpretation in terms of pre-existing categories. One can conceive of attractors as interpretations or learned categories, and the dynamics of an attractor net as mapping a noisy or partial input to the most appropriate interpretation. Attractor dynamics are highly non-linear: two similar initial states may lead to distant attractors. This type of non-linearity allows two similar inputs to yield distinct interpretations. The Necker cube is an extreme case in which a single input—lying on the boundary between two attractor basins—can lead to two different interpretations. (Many attractor nets assume intrinsic noise to break symmetry for ambiguous inputs.)

Conscious states have been characterized as high-quality representations (Farah 1994, Munakata 2001). The notion of quality is ill defined, but essentially, a high-quality representation should be capable of triggering the correct representations and responses further along the processing stream; in the terminology of the consciousness literature, such a representation is *accessible*. Quality is not an intrinsic property of a representation, but comes about by virtue of how that representation affects subsequent processing stages, which in turn is dependent on whether past learning has associated the representation with the appropriate effects. From this definition, attractors are high quality. Attractors come into existence because they correspond to states the system has learned about in the past. An attractor net cleans up a noisy input, yielding a pattern that corresponds to a previously experienced state. Because of this past experience, later stages of processing receiving input from the attractor net are likely to have learned how to produce appropriate responses to attractor states. When cognitive operations involve multiple steps, the quality of a representation is critical: without the sort of clean-up operation performed by an attractor net, representations degrade further at each step (Mathis and Mozer 1995).

Temporal stability of neural states is often associated with consciousness (e.g. Taylor 1998). Attractors have the property of temporal stability. Once the dynamics of the attractor net lead to an attractor, the state of the network persists until the network is reset or is perturbed by a different input.

Conscious states are generally considered to be *explicit* (e.g. Baars 1989, Dehaene and Naccache 2001), meaning that they are instantiated as patterns of neural activity, in contrast to *implicit* representations, which are patterns of connectivity. An attractor net encodes its attractors implicitly, but the current attractor state is explicit.

Conscious states might arise at the interface between sub-symbolic and symbolic processing (Smolensky 1988, Cleeremans and Jiménez 2002). From a connectionist perspective, perceptual processes are intrinsically sub-symbolic, but yield representations of object identities and categories that subserve subsequent symbolic processing. This view fits in well with the fact that attractor nets typically map a continuous activation space to a discrete set of alternatives (Fig. A26b), which can be viewed as a mapping from sub-symbolic to symbolic representations. If conscious states are indeed symbolic, then they should be all-or-none. Studies have indeed suggested discrete, all-or-none states of consciousness (Sergent and Dehaene 2004), although others consider consciousness to be a graded phenomenon (Farah 1994, Munakata 2001, Cleeremans and Jiménez 2002).

4. Attractor networks and theories of consciousness

Grossberg's *adaptive resonance* theory, proposed in 1976, describes an attractor network that achieves resonant states between bottom-up information from the world and top-down expectations. Grossberg (1999) subsequently made the claim that conscious states are a subset of resonant (attractor) states. From *functional brain imaging data, evidence is also consistent with the notion that conscious states arise from resonant circuits linking temporal, parietal, and prefrontal cortical areas (Lumer and Rees 1999).

Many computational theories of consciousness have argued that attractors have the right functional characteristics to serve as the computational *correlate of consciousness. Rumelhart et al. (1986) and Smolensky (1988) first proposed that conscious mental states may correspond to stable states of an attractor network. Like subsequent theorists, they envision an attractor net defined over multiple cortical regions thereby able to capture global cortical coherence. Farah et al. (1993) describe attractor nets as allowing stimuli to be integrated into a global information-processing state which corresponds with consciousness. Other theorists are less explicit in describing attractor nets, yet focus on key properties of attractor nets, such as self-sustaining activation patterns (Dehaene and Naccache 2001), dynamic competitions among coalitions of neurons (Crick and Koch 2003), and non-linear bifurcations in neural activity (Sergent and Dehaene 2004). Although many theories simply postulate that stable, high-quality representations—such as attractors—are associated with awareness, some models show that accessibility and reportability is an emergent property of such representations (Mathis and Mozer 1996, Colagrosso and Mozer 2005).

MICHAEL C. MOZER

Baars, B. (1989). *A Cognitive Theory of Consciousness.*

Cleeremans, A. and Jiménez, L. (2002). 'Implicit learning and consciousness: a graded, dynamic perspective'. In French, R. M. and Cleeremans, A. (eds) *Implicit Learning and Consciousness.*

Colagrosso, M. D. and Mozer, M. C. (2005). 'Theories of access consciousness'. In Saul, L. K., Weiss, Y., and Bottou, L. (eds) *Advances in Neural Information Processing Systems*, 17.

Crick, F. and Koch, C. (2003). 'A framework for consciousness'. *Nature Neuroscience*, 6.

Dehaene, S. and Naccache, L. (2001). 'Towards a cognitive neuroscience of consciousness: basic evidence and a workspace framework'. *Cognition*, 79.

Farah, M. J. (1994). 'Visual perception and visual awareness after brain damage: a tutorial overview'. In Umiltà, C. and Moscovitch, M. (eds) *Attention and Performance XV: Conscious and Nonconscious Information Processing.*

——, O'Reilly, R. C., and Vecera, S. P. (1993). 'Dissociated overt and covert recognition as an emergent property of a lesioned neural network'. *Psychological Review*, 100.

Grossberg, S. (1999). 'The link between brains, learning, attention, and consciousness'. *Consciousness and Cognition*, 8.

Lumer, E. D. and Rees, G. (1999). 'Covariation in activity in visual and prefrontal cortex associated with subjective visual perception'. *Proceedings of the National Academy of Sciences of the USA*, 96.

Marcel, A. J. (1983). 'Conscious and unconscious perception: an approach to the relations between phenomenal experience and perceptual processes'. *Cognitive Psychology*, 15.

Mathis, D. A. and Mozer, M. C. (1995). 'On the computational utility of consciousness'. In Tesauro, G. et al. (eds) *Advances in Neural Information Processing Systems*, 7.

—— —— (1996). 'Conscious and unconscious perception: a computational theory'. In Cottrell, G. (ed.) *Proceedings of the Eighteenth Annual Conference of the Cognitive Science Society.*

Munakata, Y. (2001). 'Graded representations in behavioral dissociations'. *Trends in Cognitive Sciences*, 5.

Rumelhart, D. E., Smolensky, P., McClelland, J. L., and Hinton, G. E. (1986). 'Schemata and sequential thought processes in PDP models'. In Rumelhart, D. E. et al. (eds) *Parallel Distributed Processing: Explorations in the Microstructure of Cognition*, Vol. 2.

Searle, J. R. (1992). *The Rediscovery of the Mind.*

Sergent, C. and Dehaene, S. (2004). 'Is consciousness a gradual phenomenon? Evidence for an allornone bifurcation during the attentional blink'. *Psychological Science*, 15.

Smolensky, P. (1988). 'On the proper treatment of connectionism'. *Behavioral and Brain Sciences*, 11.

Taylor, J. G. (1998). 'Cortical activity and the explanatory gap'. *Consciousness and Cognition*, 7.

Zemel, R. S. and Mozer, M. C. (2001). 'Localist attractor networks'. *Neural Computation*, 13.

autism The term 'autism', from the Greek word meaning self, was first applied to children with notably abnormal social development by Leo Kanner (1943) and Hans Asperger (1944)—who took the term from Bleuler's (1911) description of withdrawal and self-absorption in *schizophrenia.

Autism is a neurodevelopmental disorder diagnosed by the presence of qualitative social and communicative impairments and restricted and repetitive interests and activities, manifest before age three. A child with autism may be silent and socially aloof, and line up toys repetitively; an adult with high-functioning autism may be verbally fluent in a pedantic monologuing way, socially over-eager in a gauche way, and repetitive in his narrow interest in, say, electricity pylons. Since the range of manifestations of this 'triad' of impairments varies with age and ability, the notion of *autism spectrum disorders* (ASD) has become popular. This spectrum includes *Asperger's syndrome*, in which the key features of autism are present but there is no general intellectual or language delay. ASDs are not as rare as once thought; perhaps as many as 1 in 1000 individuals may have autism, and almost 1 in 100 may have an ASD. The majority of affected individuals are male, and many people with autism also have general intellectual impairment. Search for the causes of ASD continues; while there is a strong genetic component (autism is among the most highly heritable psychiatric disorders), no specific genes or brain basis have as yet been identified.

Prominent among psychological accounts of the distinctive behavioural impairments in ASD is the idea of deficits in **theory of mind* or *mentalizing*: the everyday ability to attribute beliefs, desires, and other mental states to self and others in order to explain and predict behaviour. There is now overwhelming evidence from a variety of simple tests that most people with ASD have difficulty knowing what others think and feel (reviewed in Baron-Cohen et al. 2000). For example, they will assume someone else will act according to the real state of affairs rather than according to their, perhaps mistaken, belief. In everyday life this 'mind-blindness' (which may vary in degree) shows itself in an inability to understand lying, to tell when someone is joking or being sarcastic, to make or keep secrets, or to impart new information, as well as in a fundamental difficulty connecting with other minds in conversation or friendship.

The lack of awareness of other minds has been enthusiastically researched and has had a major impact on educational interventions and even early diagnostic screening for ASD, but much less attention has been paid to the possible implications for *self*-awareness in autism. While there is debate as to how we understand other minds, it seems clear that we need to represent who and how someone is representing the world, e.g. 'He thinks it will rain' vs 'I hope it is sunny'. Representing thoughts, one's own or others', has been suggested to require a common representational format (*metarepresentation*). Might people with ASD, then, have as much difficulty reading their own minds as they do reading others' minds? This is not to suggest that people with ASD do not have beliefs and desires, as well as strong emotions, but that they may be unable to *reflect* on these inner states. This has been relatively little researched, but appears an important possibility on a number of grounds.

First, despite an intuitive belief that we have 'privileged' access to our own mental states, evidence from typically developing young children suggests that the recognition of one's own false beliefs and those of others emerges at around the same age. Thus, for example, when asked what they (mistakenly) believed was inside a Smarties tube—instantly recognizable to British children as the container for a well-known brand of sweets—before they saw the real (surprising) contents, e.g. pencils, ordinary three-year-olds will wrongly claim they knew the contents were pencils, even though they in fact guessed Smarties. At the same age, these children also expect another child to guess 'pencils' even before the tube is opened. These findings suggest that the ability to reflect on one's own thoughts develops alongside the ability to represent the thoughts and feelings of others.

Second, people with autism appear to have difficulty monitoring their own thoughts, e.g. knowing whether they know or merely guess what is inside a box. They are no better at this task than at telling whether someone they have seen look (or not look) into a box knows (vs guesses) the contents. Other experimental evidence that people with ASD may have reduced awareness of their own mental states includes their difficulty recalling the intended target of an action, relatively poor memory for own actions and own traits, and relative difficulty reporting current thoughts (reviewed in Happé 2003). Problems in planning (imaginative rehearsal 'in your head') may also relate to impoverished access to own mental states. Poor planning, along with difficulty monitoring performance and switching tasks (so-called *executive functions*), contribute to the rigid and repetitive behaviour in ASD, and difficulty coping in novel situations.

Third, *functional imaging studies using techniques such as fMRI, which track activity in the brain during specific psychological tasks, suggest that similar brain regions are used when we think about our own inner states and when we try to understand what someone else is thinking. For example, when asked to monitor our own intended speech or emotional reaction to pictures, areas of the medial prefrontal cortex are activated (over and above activity during control tasks)—these same regions are active when we try to deduce what a story character is intending, a cartoon character is misunderstanding, or an animated shape is wanting (see Amodio and Frith 2006 for review). Preliminary studies also suggest these brain regions are less active in volunteers with ASD when they attempt to mind-read, and that there may be structural brain changes in these parts of the medial prefrontal cortex in ASD.

Inability to (meta)represent mental states may result in impaired self-consciousness in autism. However, there is considerable debate about the necessary role of theory of mind for (one or more types of) self-awareness (Raffman 1999, McGeer 2004). It remains an empirical challenge to tap self-awareness in autism through psychological tests. After all, we know how efficiently it is possible to operate without conscious self-awareness; think of automatic actions, like driving home and arriving barely aware of the journey, while appearing to any outside observer a competent, sentient being. A promising experimental design would be to explore tasks where *self-consciousness could *impair* performance; it is said, for example, that asking someone to explain exactly how their golf swing works is the best way to put them off the shot.

In recent years, and with the recognition of ASD in highly intelligent and verbal individuals, many autobiographies have been written describing autism or Asperger's syndrome first-hand. Some of these, while by their existence attesting to the ability and self-reflection of at least this talented minority among those with ASD, provide hints at a different type of self-awareness (discussed by Frith and de Vignemont 2005). Temple Grandin, for example, writes, 'As a child, I often talked out loud because it made my thoughts more "concrete" and "real"' (Grandin 1992:122). Donna Williams also describes a sense of lack of access to inner states:

'Like someone sleep-walking or sleep-talking, I imitated the sounds and movements of others—an involuntary compulsive impressionist' (Williams 1994:3); and '. . . autism lets me speak my own words without knowing what I am saying or even thinking' (Williams 1994:233).

Other aspects of consciousness in ASD, such as bodily and perceptual self-awareness, have yet to be researched, despite a large number of anecdotal and autobiographical reports of, e.g., unusual sensory sensitivities and reduced pain responses. Awareness of own emotional states appears to be reduced in many individuals with ASD, at least according to self-report using questionnaire measures of so-called *alexithymia*. Other theoretical accounts of ASD, such as those focusing on enhanced processing of details, may have relevance for understanding self-awareness, but have yet to be developed in this direction.

Although it is never possible to know with certainty what another person's inner experience is like, it seems probable that people with autism and ASD may have a fundamentally different sense of self.

FRANCESCA HAPPÉ

Amodio, D. M. and Frith, C. D. (2006). 'Meeting of minds: the medial frontal cortex and social cognition'. *Nature Reviews Neuroscience*, 7.

Asperger, H. (1944). 'Die "Autistischen Psychopathen" im Kindesalter'. *Archiv für Psychiatrie und Nervenkrankheiten*, 117.

Baron-Cohen, S., Tager-Flusberg, H., and Cohen, D. J. (eds) (2000). *Understanding Other Minds: Perspectives from Autism*, 2nd edn.

Frith, U. (2003). *Autism: Explaining the Enigma*, 2nd edn.

—— and Happé, F. (1999). 'Theory of mind and self consciousness: what is it like to be autistic?' *Mind and Language*, 14.

—— and de Vignemont, F. (2005). 'Egocentrism, allocentrism and Asperger syndrome'. *Consciousness and Cognition*, 14.

Grandin, T. (1992). 'An inside view of autism'. In Schopler, E. and Mesibov, G. B. (eds) *High Functioning Individuals with Autism*.

Happé, F. (2003). 'Theory of mind and the self'. *Annals of the New York Academy of Sciences*, 1001.

Kanner, L. (1943). 'Autistic disturbance of affective contact'. *Nervous Child*, 2.

McGeer, V. (2004). 'Autistic self-awareness'. *Philosophy, Psychiatry and Psychology*, 11.

Raffman, D. (1999). 'What autism may tell us about self-awareness; a commentary on Frith and Happé'. *Mind and Language*, 14.

Williams, D. (1994). *Somebody Somewhere: Breaking Free from the World of Autism*.

automaticity The term *automatic* has been used in cognitive psychology to describe behaviour and the processes underlying behaviour. One question that automaticity researchers try to answer is how to diagnose whether a behaviour or process is automatic. Another question is how to explain the development toward automaticity (i.e. automatization). Both questions are discussed in turn. In the final section, I focus on the relation between automatic and unconscious as it is construed from the various views of automaticity discussed.

1. Diagnosis of automaticity
2. Explanation of automatization
3. Relation between automatic and unconscious

1. Diagnosis of automaticity

Usually, the diagnosis of a phenomenon is closely related to how it is defined. I therefore briefly consider some prominent views of automaticity here. Most theories of automaticity are feature-based, defining automaticity as an umbrella term for a number of features such as unintentional, uncontrolled, unconscious, efficient, and/or fast. The concept *non-automatic* covers the opposites of these features. Different feature-based theories vary with regard to the features they select as the crucial ones, as well as with regard to the degree of coherence they assume among features. Features have been clustered into two modes (dual-mode view), into three modes (triple-mode view), or have been considered to be entirely independent (e.g. decompositional view). Before discussing these views, I briefly consider definitions of the most recurring features in automaticity literature (see Moors and De Houwer 2006 for a detailed justification of these definitions).

Definitions of automaticity features. I start with a discussion of the features *controlled* and *intentional*. To say that a process is controlled implies that one has a goal regarding the process and that this goal actually causes the end state put forward in the goal. Processing goals can be of the promoting type (i.e. the goal to engage in the process) or of the counteracting type (e.g. the goals to alter, stop, or avoid the process). In the case of a promoting goal, the end state is the actual occurrence of a process. In the case of a counteracting goal, the end state is a change, the interruption, or the prevention of a process. To say that a process is uncontrolled can have different meanings. It can refer to the fact that one has a goal about the process but the desired effect is absent. It can also mean that the state of a process alters (i.e. that the process occurs, changes, is interrupted, is prevented) in the absence of the goal to achieve it. For instance, a process can be called *uncontrolled* in the sense that it is interrupted even when the person did not have the goal to interrupt it. A more subtle meaning of the term 'uncontrolled' refers to a situation in which both the goal and the desired effect are present, but the effect was not caused by the goal.

To say that a process is intentional means that one has the goal to engage in a process and that this goal results in the occurrence of the process. Note that 'intentional' is identical to 'controlled' in the promoting sense. Intentional processes are thus a subset of controlled processes. Unintentional processes are also a subset of uncontrolled processes.

The next feature to discuss is *(un)conscious*. It is notoriously difficult to define the concepts *conscious* and *unconscious*. Many theorists have distinguished two aspects of consciousness: an *aboutness* aspect and a *phenomenal* aspect. The aboutness aspect refers to the fact that consciousness is about something, that it has content; the phenomenal aspect is subjective feeling. The first depends on attention whereas the second escapes attention. Some theorists have even argued that both aspects can be separated, thus arguing for two types of consciousness (Block 1995). It is important to keep in mind that the concepts 'conscious' and 'unconscious' can be used as a predicate of several things (Bargh 1994). They can be applied to (a) the stimulus input of the process, (b) the output of the process, and (c) the process itself (i.e. the relation between input and output). Many unconscious processes require conscious input in order to operate. For example, in several implicit learning tasks, participants seem to unconsciously pick up patterns in stimulus material that is itself consciously perceived (because it is presented supraliminally).

Another correlate of (non)automaticity is the feature *(non)efficient*. A process is efficient when it consumes little or no attentional capacity. Attention can be said to have two aspects: quantity and direction. Efficiency is related to the quantity aspect. Efficient processes operate without or with very little of this quantity. Efficiency is usually investigated using dual-task paradigms. The final feature in the list is *fast* (*slow*). A fast process is one with a short duration. The duration of a process should not be confounded with the duration of the stimulus input on which the process operates. For example, slow processes may be triggered by briefly presented stimuli.

Views of automaticity. According to the *dual-mode view*, also called the *all-or-none view*, processes are either automatic or non-automatic. Automatic processes hold all automatic features; non-automatic processes hold all non-automatic features. It has become clear, however, that the dual-mode view is incorrect. Studies have demonstrated that most processes possess a combination of automatic and non-automatic features. Evidence from *Stroop studies, for instance, suggests that the processing of word meaning is automatic in that it does not depend on intention, but at the same time occurs only when attention is directed toward the word. This and other evidence led researchers (e.g. Bargh 1989, Shiffrin 1988) to abandon the dual-mode view. Despite the fact that many researchers now openly reject this view, it seems that it is difficult to shake off.

I first discuss five sources that have contributed to the creation and/or the persistence of the dual-mode view, and I consider whether there are ways to escape the dual-mode view. After that, I discuss four alternative views. Two historical research traditions have been appointed as responsible for the creation of the dual-mode view (Bargh 1994). The first tradition is the capacity view of attention (Shiffrin and Schneider 1977), a view that originated in early research on skill development and dual tasks (see review by Shiffrin 1988). This tradition was also inspired by James's (1890) writings on habit formation. The *capacity view* of attention defines an automatic process as an efficient one. As a process becomes more automatic due to practice it requires less and less attention. Although this view started out as a gradual view (efficiency is a gradual notion, after all), it developed into a dual-mode view. The second research tradition is the *New Look* programme in perception research (e.g. Bruner 1957). The original focus in this tradition was on the constructivist nature of perception, i.e. the interaction between personal variables (needs, expectancies, values, knowledge) and information from the environment. Because of the hidden character of the influence of personal variables on perception, the focus shifted toward unconscious perception. Dual-mode models that developed from this tradition put more emphasis on the features 'unintentional' and 'unconscious'.

A third element that has contributed to the persistence of the dual-mode view is the fact that this view is based on the computational metaphor of cognition. In many computational models, there is one single entity, e.g. a central executive, that is charged with both processing (which comes down to the manipulation of symbols) and the conscious interpretation of outputs of processing. In most models this executive is also charged with directing the attention window. This explains why the features 'controlled', 'conscious', and 'efficient' are often mentioned in the same breath. Connectionist models, on the other hand, do not have a central executive and therefore are less prone to group together features of automaticity.

A fourth source of the dual-mode view is that people assume conceptual *overlap* among features. Both laymen and scientists define features in such a way that there is overlap among them. This means that the definitions of features share ingredients. For example, it is often assumed that there is overlap among the feature 'controlled' (in the promoting and counteracting sense) and the feature 'conscious'. Consciousness is often considered an ingredient of the definition of 'controlled'. It might seem reasonable to assume that being in control asks for a conscious subject. However, recent research has convincingly demonstrated that unconsciously activated goals to engage in or counteract a process can also be causally effective. For example, Moskowitz et al. (1999) showed that unconscious activation of a (pre-established) goal to be egalitarian led participants to successfully, but unconsciously, counteract stereotype activation. Hence, one can have control without being aware of it.

The fifth source of the dual-mode view is that people assume what I call *modal relations* among features. This means that one feature is considered a necessary or sufficient condition for another. For example, in addition to the assumption that consciousness is an *ingredient* of control, many researchers hold that consciousness is also a *necessary condition* for control. It seems plausible that to control a process in the promoting sense, the person should be aware of the stimulus input (e.g. to intentionally evaluate a job candidate, information about the candidate must be consciously available), and that to control a process in the counteracting sense, the person should be aware that the process is taking place (e.g. to counteract activating stereotypes, one must be aware that one is susceptible to activating stereotypes). However, the above assumptions may be true only when control is understood in the sense of *conscious* control. It is quite possible that unconscious control in the promoting sense is possible when the stimulus input is unconscious and that unconscious control in the counteracting sense is possible when the process is unconscious (see Moskowitz et al. 1999).

Another illustration of modal overlap is that among the features *efficient* and *unconscious*. It is often assumed that attention is both necessary and sufficient for consciousness. However, some theorists have argued that there is a type of consciousness that can occur outside of the focus of attention (Block 1995). According to these authors, attention is not necessary for consciousness. Further, subliminal priming studies indicate that attention is not sufficient for consciousness either. Other necessary factors are stimulus strength and duration. When a stimulus is too weak or occurs too briefly, the stimulus may not be accessible to consciousness, despite adequate focusing of attention. Finally, attention may not even be exclusive for consciousness. Indeed, recent evidence suggests that unconscious processing may also depend on attention (e.g. Naccache et al. 2002).

The above discussion indicates that there are ways to avoid conceptual overlap among features and that there are no one-to-one modal relations among features. Thus, it is desirable and feasible to abandon the dual-mode view. Below, I describe four alternatives to the dual-mode view and examine their viability.

Alternative views. A first alternative to the dual-mode view is the triple-mode view. Several authors have distinguished between two types of automatic processes (bottom-up ones, and overlearned top-down ones) in addition to the non-automatic mode (e.g. Carver and Scheier 2002). Both types of automatic processes come about at different stages in the evolution of a process. This evolution has been described as follows. In an initial phase, emergent, bottom-up processes are triggered by stimulus input alone and they are so weak that they remain hidden to consciousness (i.e. bottom-up automatic phase). When processes become stronger due to repetition, they become recognizable to a conscious processor which uses them as a guide to behaviour (i.e. non-automatic phase). With more top-down use, these processes become so well established and accurate that control is no longer required and as a result they drop out of consciousness again (i.e. overlearned top-down automatic phase).

The triple-mode view is likely to run into the same problems as the dual-mode view. For one thing, a strong modal relation is assumed between consciousness and control. Indeed, it is assumed that when a process is recognizable to a conscious processor it can be controlled. It is also assumed that when control of a process is no longer required, the process drops out of consciousness.

A second alternative to the dual-mode view is to choose one feature as the one that is shared by all automatic processes. Automatic processes can differ with regard to all features except the chosen one. Bargh (1989) adopted this approach and appointed the feature *autonomous* as the one common to all automatic processes. He defined an autonomous process as one that runs to completion without the need for conscious guidance, regardless of whether it was started intentionally or unintentionally. The main problem with this approach is that the choice of one minimal feature is an arbitrary matter.

A third proposal is to investigate features separately in their own right and to abandon the automaticity concept. This would indeed be a viable option. A fourth, more cautious, approach is to also investigate features separately, but to hold on to the concept of automaticity and to conceive of it as a gradual concept (i.e. decompositional and gradual approach; Shiffrin 1988, Moors and De Houwer 2006). The notion of 'gradual' applies to two things. First, processes can be automatic with regard to more or fewer features. The more features of automaticity a process has, the more automatic it is. Second, each of the automaticity features discussed can itself be considered as a gradual notion. This is most obvious for the features *fast* and *efficient*, but it also goes for the features *conscious* (cf. gradual views of consciousness) and *controlled* (a goal about a process can match the effect to a greater or lesser extent).

2. Explanation of automatization

In addition to the question of how to diagnose automaticity, researchers have tried to answer the question of how to explain the development toward automaticity (i.e. automatization). Starting from the observation that many processes and behaviour become automatic as a result of practice, researchers have asked which learning mechanism could be responsible for this development. According to Logan (1988), automatization of behaviour is explained by a shift in the underlying mechanism. Skills that are initially based on a complex procedure become automatic after practice when the complex procedure is replaced by the mechanism of direct memory retrieval.

For example, when children learn to add pairs of digits, they initially count the units of both digits. Once a sufficiently strong association is formed in memory between the pair of digits and their sum, children may retrieve the sum from memory, circumventing the complex procedure of counting the units. Logan stated that direct memory retrieval is the only mechanism that can be automatic. He consequently *defined* automaticity as direct memory retrieval and proposed *diagnosing* automaticity by investigating whether the performance was based on direct memory retrieval instead of by looking at features. Other theorists (e.g. Anderson 1992) explained automatization not as a shift from one type of mechanism to another, but rather as a change in the *same* underlying mechanism. They emphasized the strengthening of procedures as the main mechanism underlying automatization of skills. The procedure-strengthening view hypothesizes that the same mechanism responsible for the non-automatic stage of performance is responsible for the automatic stage of performance, but that, in the latter stage, the mechanism is executed faster and more efficiently. Hence, automatic and non-automatic processes and behaviour differ only with regard to the features (fast, efficient) they possess. Still other theorists (e.g. Tzelgov et al. 2000) advocated a reconciling approach, maintaining that both mechanisms of procedure strengthening and a shift toward direct memory retrieval are equivalent mechanisms underlying automatization.

3. Relation between automatic and unconscious

The terms 'unconscious' and 'automatic' have sometimes been equated. Within feature-based views of automaticity, however, the feature *unconscious* is regarded as only one among several features of automaticity. Proponents of a strict all-or-none view consider each feature of automaticity to be necessary, including the feature 'unconscious'. Moreover, the feature 'unconscious' is often regarded as a strong indication of automaticity. This probably has to do with the assumption that there is conceptual and modal overlap among the feature 'unconscious' and other features such as *controlled* and *efficient* (see above). Several other feature-based views have regarded the feature 'unconscious' as an optional feature. Indeed, the gradual, decompositional, view and the view that automatic processes share one particular feature (autonomy) leave room for automatic processes that are not unconscious.

In addition to the position that not all automatic processes are unconscious, there is a position that not all unconscious processes are automatic. For example, Shiffrin and Schneider (1977) left room for non-automatic processes that are unconscious (they call them the *veiled controlled processes*). For another example, Cleeremans and Jiménez (2002) have distinguished two types of unconscious processes, bottom-up ones and overlearned top-down ones (as do proponents of the triple-mode view), but they have reserved the term 'automatic' exclusively for the latter type (in contrast with proponents of the triple-mode view). The latter authors side with the view that the concepts 'conscious' and 'unconscious' refer to two separate modes of processing (rather than to features of processes) and that automaticity is to be regarded an optional feature of the unconscious mode.

AGNES MOORS

Anderson, J. R. (1992). 'Automaticity and the ACT* theory'. *American Journal of Psychology*, 105.

Block, N. (1995). 'On a confusion about a function of consciousness'. *Behavioral and Brain Sciences*, 18.

Bargh, J. A. (1989). 'Conditional automaticity: varieties of automatic influence in social perception and cognition'. In Uleman, J. S. and Bargh, J. A. (eds) *Unintended Thought*.

—— (1994). 'The four horsemen of automaticity: awareness, intention, efficiency, and control in social cognition'. In Wyer, R. S. and Srull, T. K. (eds) *Handbook of Social Cognition*, Vol. 1.

Bruner, J. S. (1957). 'On perceptual readiness'. *Psychological Review*, 64.

Carver, C. S., and Scheier, M. F. (2002). 'Control processes and self-organization as complementary principles underlying behaviour'. *Personality and Social Psychology Review*, 6.

Cleeremans, A. and Jiménez, L. (2002). 'Implicit learning and consciousness: a graded, dynamic perspective'. In French, R. M. and Cleeremans, A. (eds) *Implicit Learning and Consciousness*.

James, W. (1890). *The Principles of Psychology*.

Logan, G. D. (1988). 'Toward an instance theory of automatization'. *Psychological Review*, 95.

Moors, A. and De Houwer, J. (2006). 'Automaticity: a theoretical and conceptual analysis'. *Psychological Bulletin*, 132.

Moskowitz, G. B., Gollwitzer, P. M., Wasel, W., and Schaal, B. (1999). 'Preconscious control of stereotype activation through chronic egalitarian goals'. *Journal of Personality and Social Psychology*, 77.

Naccache, L., Blandin, E., and Dehaene, S. (2002). 'Unconscious masked priming depends on temporal attention'. *Psychological Science*, 13.

Shiffrin, R. M. (1988). 'Attention'. In Atkinson, R. C. et al. (eds) *Stevens' Handbook of Experimental Psychology*, Vol. 2.

—— and Schneider, W. (1977). 'Controlled and automatic human information processing: II. Perceptual learning, automatic attending and a general theory'. *Psychological Review*, 84.

Tzelgov, J., Yehene, V., Kotler, L., and Alon, A. (2000). 'Automatic comparisons of artificial digits never compared: learning linear ordering relations'. *Journal of Experimental Psychology: Learning, Memory, and Cognition*, 26.

automatisms In the ordinary way, we are aware of actions that we perform; remember them afterwards, if only briefly; and are prepared to acknowledge that we intended them, even if we had not explicitly articulated the intention to ourselves previously. *Automatisms* are exceptions to these typical cases in which we are unaware of what we have done, are unable to remember it, and lack the normal sense of agency. They have been defined as 'complex behaviour in the absence of conscious awareness or volitional intent'.

Automatisms can occur as a result of clear-cut brain—or other medical—disorder (see BRAIN DAMAGE), but also occur in a variety of non-medical contexts (Fenwick 1990). They are of great interest to the study of awareness and volition, as they challenge the assumption that complex behaviour requires their guidance. In cases in which only one or two of the normally linked trio of awareness, memory, and volition are disrupted it can be difficult to decide whether the concept of 'automatism' applies. In the medical sphere, the most familiar automatisms are those occurring as a result of *epilepsy and during *parasomnias*, disorders of experience and behaviour during *sleep.

Hughlings Jackson, the father of British neurology, referred to 'all kinds of doings after epileptic fits' under the rubric of automatisms. Contemporary epileptologists recognize five categories of epileptic automatism, 'more or less coordinated adapted involuntary motor activity occurring during the state of clouding of consciousness . . . and usually followed by amnesia for the event': (1) *oropharyngeal*, for example lip-smacking or chewing movements; (2) expression of *emotion*, most often fear; (3) *gestural*, such as tapping, rubbing, fidgeting, or flag-waving movements; (4) *ambulatory*, including walking, running, or bicycling movements; and (5) *verbal*, usually single words or short phrases (Oxbury et al. 2000). As a rule, patients cannot interact with others, or report their behaviour at the time, and appear to be unaware of these behaviours—though this is not always the case.

When patients behave in highly complex ways during seizures—e.g. making a correct diagnosis of pneumonia, like Hughlings Jackson's epileptic patient Dr Z. (Hughlings Jackson 1888)—the explanation is likely to be that the seizure specifically disabled memory without impairment of awareness. A similar deficit of memory, not caused by epilepsy, presumably often underlies the common experience of arriving at a destination with no recollection of the route along which one has driven. Whether such episodes of conscious but unremembered behaviour deserve the name 'automatism' is doubtful. The observation that epileptic activity can disable some but not other psychological capacities complicates our understanding of automatisms: for example, a focal *frontal lobe seizure might selectively impair decision-making capacities, interfering with 'volitional intent'. Would a resulting crime be an 'automatism'?

Automatisms in sleep occur mostly in people who sleepwalk, and in the much more recently recognized REM sleep behaviour disorder (RSBD; Schenck and Mahowald 2002). Sleepwalking is common, affecting around 15% of children on at least one occasion and sometimes continuing into adolescence and even adult life. It results from partial arousal from deep 'slow wave' sleep. The intuitive notion that the brains of people who sleepwalk are in a twilight state between sleep and waking has been borne out by a recent *functional imaging study demonstrating activity at waking levels in regions of the brain controlling movement while activity in other regions of the cortex, particularly frontal cortex, remains at sleeping levels (Bassetti et al. 2000). Sleepwalkers can evade obstacles but sometimes come to grief, falling from windows or balconies. A patient awoke in her car, frustrated by her unsuccessful efforts to start it with the back-door key. As this suggests, moderately complex behaviour, though generally rather poorly coordinated, can occur during sleepwalking, including sleep eating and sleep sex. In a well-known recent case a Canadian man was acquitted of the murder of his mother-in-law, an act he had committed after driving 12 km to his in-laws' home, on the grounds that he was sleepwalking (Broughton et al. 1994). People who sleepwalk tend to recall little if any of the episode on awakening, in keeping with the paucity of mental activity in slow wave sleep. In RSBD, by contrast, sufferers enact their dreams. These often have a violent content, and sleeping partners are at risk of becoming the victim of assaults launched against an assailant in their partner's dream. The underlying pathology is loss of the atonia, or paralysis, that normally comes into play during our dreams to prevent just such dream enaction. RSBD is often a precursor of Parkinson's disease.

While automatisms occurring in epilepsy or during sleep usually involve a primary disturbance of awareness, a third type of neurological disorder may result from a primary disturbance of the sense of agency, linking neurological automatisms with those occurring in everyday life. In *psychogenic movement disorders* (see ALIEN HAND), sufferers appear to be performing actions—e.g. making their hands shake—without any acknowledged act of will (Hallett et al. 2006). If one accepts that such people are, at least sometimes, telling the truth as best they can, the implication is that we can be mistaken about what we are doing: we can misinterpret our *volitional intent*.

Several non-pathological examples illustrate the possibility of engaging in 'apparently voluntary behaviour that one does not sense as voluntary' to which the term 'automatism' is sometimes applied. Automatic writing, the movement of a hand across a ouija board, and the tilting of dowsing rods are all likely to be actions under the agent's control but divorced from the normal sense of agency. Dan Wegner has argued that such cases support the—perhaps startling—general conclusion that our actions are not in fact caused by our acts of will (Wegner 2002). On this view, our actions, and our awareness of our intentions, are linked but separate outcomes of the neural processes governing behaviour. Under certain circumstances one can occur without the other, so that we can be tricked into believing that we are not the authors of actions we are performing, or that we are responsible for acts that, in fact, are not of our doing.

The concept of automatism has legal significance. A criminal act, *actus reus*, committed as a result of an automatism does not involve a *mens reus*, a criminal mind. Both elements are required for criminal conviction. Therefore if one can prove that a crime was committed during, or just after, a seizure by someone whose awareness of what he was doing was impaired, or by someone who was sleepwalking or dreaming, acquittal is likely, though compulsory treatment and supervision might be considered wise. The more subtle criterion for automatism suggested by the kinds of case mentioned in the last paragraph, lack of 'a sense of agency', would probably not suffice to tip the legal balance, as it is likely that it would be widely claimed!

DANIEL WEGNER

Bassetti, C., Vella, S., Donati, F., Wielepp, P., and Weder, B. (2000). 'SPECT during sleepwalking'. *Lancet*, 356.

Broughton, R., Billings, R., Cartwright, R. et al. (1994). 'Homicidal somnambulism: a case report', *Sleep*, 17.

Fenwick, P. (1990). 'Automatism, medicine and the law'. *Psychological Medicine Monograph Supplement*, 17.

Hallett, M., Fahn, S., Jankovic, J., Lang, A. E., Cloninger, C. R., and Yudofsky, S. C. (2006). *Psychogenic Movement Disorders: Neurology and Neuropsychiatry*.

Hughlings Jackson, J. (1888). 'On a particular variety of epilepsy (intellectual aura), one case with symptoms of organic brain disease'. *Brain*, 11.

Oxbury, J., Polkey, C., and Duchowny, M. (2000). *Intractable Focal Epilepsy*.

Schenck, C. H. and Mahowald, M. W. (2002). 'REM sleep behavior disorder: clinical, developmental, and neuroscience perspectives 16 years after its formal identification in SLEEP'. *Sleep*, 25.

Wegner, D. M. (2002). *The Illusion of Conscious Will*.

autonoetic consciousness Autonoetic consciousness (or *autonoesis* for short) is a mind–brain capacity that enables individuals to become aware of their personal experiences from times other than the present. It is one of the three defining features of episodic memory, *self* and *subjective time* being the other two. It contrasts with *noetic consciousness*, which allows awareness of the world here and now. Noetic consciousness is associated with semantic memory, and it can be thought of as the default conscious state of an awake individual.

The concepts of autonoetic and noetic consciousness emerged from the development of the theory of *episodic memory*, and therefore receive their meaning and significance from the roles they play in that theory. Episodic memory differs from semantic memory in that it makes possible 'mental time travel' into the past and into the future: a brain–mind feat that transcends the capabilities of semantic memory. Autonoetic consciousness provides the window through which the travelling self becomes aware, as it were, of the sights and sounds of such travels. It is autonoetic consciousness that confers a special phenomenal flavour to remembering, distinguishing remembering from other forms of mental experiences, such as seeing apples, hearing waves, feeling an aching tooth, smelling a rose, imagining dinosaurs roaming the Earth, dreaming of a white Christmas, or daydreaming of fame and fortune. When we remember an event, we have an image of its ingredients, and we also know that we are remembering, and not perceiving, or imagining, or dreaming. We do so automatically and effortlessly, seldom wondering how such a marvellous capability can arise from a physical object, albeit a very complex one, i.e. the *brain. Whereas semantic memory provides the 'message' of remembered events, i.e. a description of what happened, episodic memory, through autonoetic consciousness, furnishes the experiential 'medium' that carries the message.

Autonoetic consciousness, like all other forms of consciousness, is based on what the brain does. Certain kinds of *brain damage can result in highly selective impairment in a patient's ability to become consciously aware of personal past experiences and personal future happenings in the absence of any other intellectual or cognitive impairment. One such patient, when asked to describe what his mind is like when he is trying to think about what he might do 'tomorrow', said simply, 'Blank, I guess'. Although it is not yet known which brain regions are especially critical for autonoetic consciousness, the prefrontal cortex is among the more prominent candidates.

The possibility that conscious awareness of one's personal past and future experiences may be lost without any impairment of one's ability to function normally within the range allowed by noetic consciousness was appreciated by some students of the brain–mind a long time ago, when amnesic patients were described as 'living in permanent present'. But it was not until a formal distinction was made between episodic and semantic memory, and applied to *amnesia, that the idea became more generally accepted, and its implications seriously pursued. Thus we now find numerous reports in the literature suggesting that autonoesis develops late in children, that it is more likely to be deleteriously affected by normal ageing than noetic consciousness, that it is among the first mental faculties to fade in clinical *dementia, and that it is readily identifiable in psychiatric conditions such as *schizophrenia.

The differences between autonoetic and noetic consciousness in normal, healthy people have been extensively explored with a simple procedure known as the *remember/know method*. Its logic is derived from episodic theory. According to this theory, episodic memory evolved 'out of' semantic memory, and, correspondingly, autonoetic consciousness evolved as a refinement of noetic consciousness, in no way replacing the already existing forms of consciousness, but rather elaborating and embellishing them. (The same evolutionary logic applies, as already mentioned, to ontogenetic development.) Beings that do not have the capability of autonoetic memory—young children, certain severely brain-damaged individuals, non-human animals—are by no means oblivious of their past. They are perfectly capable of learning from their past and 'knowing' the past. Such knowledge need not be only non-conscious, as it is in forms of implicit *learning and implicit memory, it can also be fully conscious, but noetically, not autonoetically, conscious. What beings without autonoesis cannot do is 'remember', or consciously re-experience their past life events as previously experienced.

Thus, according to theory, healthy individuals can consciously access their own past in two ways—by noetically *knowing* it or autonoetically *remembering* it. In reality, of course, there is no such dichotomy: the two forms of consciousness, like almost everything else in living nature, constitute a smooth continuum. But the dichotomy serves as a useful heuristic for studying and describing the continuum.

In memory experiments employing the remember/know method, subjects encounter 'miniature events': the presentation of individual stimulus items, such as unrelated common words. Then, when they are given the memory test—to recall or recognize the studied items—and they correctly identify such an item, they are also asked to make a judgement about the phenomenal nature of their knowledge of the correctness of their response. The subjects have to judge whether they actually *recollect the event* of the item's appearance in the study list ('remember') or whether they just 'know' that they had encountered the item in the study list without remembering the experience of the encounter. (In more recent studies the subjects are also given an additional choice of a 'guess'.)

The results of a large number of studies using the remember/know method have shown (a) that the request, even if it may sound odd at first blush, makes sense to most subjects, in that the two categories of judgements, *remember* vs *know*, produce regular patterns of data, and (b) that the exact behaviour of the two categories varies systematically with manipulated independent variables. The remember/know method has also been successfully employed in the study of conscious awareness accompanying successful memory retrieval in clinical and developmentally defined populations. In addition, direct electrophysiological recording from, and *functional imaging of, the brain has provided a good deal of evidence in support of differences in neural correlates of autonoetic and noetic consciousness as captured by the remember/know judgements.

Although the idea of autonoetic consciousness originated in the study of memory, and therefore was directed at the past, it was soon extended to cover mental time travel into the future as well. This extension was motivated by the observation, already mentioned, that amnesic individuals have difficulties not only with their personal, actually lived past but also with their personal, imagined future. One reason that amnesics have difficulty imagining themselves doing something in the future may lie in their inability to remember what they did in the past, the problem of the 'faulty message'. Another reason may lie in their lack of the kind of conscious capability that is required for any mental travel away from the present, the problem of the 'faulty medium'. In any given situation, of course, both factors may be effectively present. To acknowledge the possibility of the existence of the 'missing medium', the concept of *chronaesthesia* (sense of time) has recently been proposed as a label for the (hypothetical) brain–mind capability that endows the possessor of episodic memory and autonoetic consciousness with awareness of, and control over, subjectively experienced time.

In conclusion, two related but separable forms of consciousness, autonoetic and noetic, allow individuals to subjectively experience their personal past and projected future in somewhat different ways. Noetic consciousness, the evolutionarily and developmentally earlier form, allows one to contemplate what one can find in the universe, including oneself, not only 'here' but somewhere else as well. Autonoesis enhances this noetic awareness of one's continued existence and identity in Isaac Newton's fourth dimension, serving as a sine qua non of mental time travel.

ENDEL TULVING AND ALICE S. N. KIM

Gardiner, J. M. (2001). 'Episodic memory and autonoetic consciousness: a first-person approach'. *Philosophical Transactions of the Royal Society of London*, 356.

Klein, S. B., Loftus, J., and Kihlstrom, J. F. (2002). 'Memory and temporal experience: the effects of episodic memory loss on an amnesic patient's ability to remember the past and imagine the future'. *Social Cognition*, 20.

Perner, J. (2001). 'Episodic memory: essential distinctions and developmental implications'. In Moore, C. and Lemmon, K. P. (eds) *Self in Time: Developmental Perspectives*.

Piolino, P., Desgranges, B., Belliard, S. et al. (2003). 'Autobiographical memory and autonoetic consciousness: triple dissociation in neurodegenerative diseases'. *Brain*, 126.

——, ——, Manning, L., North, P., Jokic, C., and Eustache, F. (2007). 'Autobiographical memory, the sense of recollection and executive functions after severe traumatic brain injury'. *Cortex*, 43.

Tulving, E. (1985). 'Memory and consciousness'. *Canadian Psychology*, 26.

—— (2002). 'Chronesthesia: awareness of subjective time'. In Stuss, D. T. and Knight, R. C. (eds) *Principles of Frontal Lobe Functions*.

Wheeler, M., Stuss, D. T., and Tulving, E. (1997). 'Toward a theory of episodic memory: the frontal lobes and autonoetic consciousness'. *Psychological Bulletin*, 121.

B

Balint's syndrome and feature binding Balint's syndrome is a rare disorder that can occur with lesions to both parietal lobes of the human brain (specifically inferior parietal and dorsal occipital cortex) and characterizes the most severe spatial deficit observed in neuropsychology (Balint 1909/1995). It results in what Balint termed *functional blindness*, meaning that even when primary visual areas (*V1) are functionally intact patients behave as if they are blind in their daily life. The spatial information of the external world is all but lost, while perception of personal body space remains intact (e.g. determining right limb from left). However, the relationship between the patient's body and objects and/or features in the external world are absent (Robertson et al. 1997). Clinically, one of the syndrome's defining features is the inability to perceive more than one object at any given time, accompanied by an inability to reach in the correct location (*optic ataxia*) and a fixated gaze (*optic apraxia*). The perception of only one object is more than simply an inability to apprehend the whole from a set of parts (both are often called *simultanagnosia*, but this refers to very different phenomena). Rather, the patient may see a pencil in an examiner's hand, but will not perceive the hand that holds it. Note that the parts of the pencil itself appear to be integrated (which remains a puzzle). However, its location is unknown. While the perceived item may be large or small, complex or simple, or appear within foveal or peripheral vision, it cannot be localized accurately above chance levels (either by naming, pointing, reaching, or gesturing). As a result, nearly constant care is required to accomplish basic everyday tasks. For example, without seeing both a plate and a fork on the dinner table, or knowing where the fork is relative to the body, it is nearly impossible for these individuals to feed themselves. Fortunately, some of the most severe aspects of Balint's syndrome tend to improve slowly over time, although the symptoms reappear under time limited conditions even after years after the insult (Robertson et al. 1997).

1. Property binding and parietal damage

For the purposes of this entry, we will focus on another prominent perceptual dysfunction in individuals with Balint's syndrome: namely, a deficit in *binding basic features (e.g. size, colour, motion, shape) together in perception. The features that produce binding errors have been associated with specialized neural populations of the primate brain. This form of binding has been termed *property binding* by Treisman (1996), and can be distinguished from other types of binding (e.g. binding parts to form a shape or binding properties to location). Although the parts of a single object may be bound together and identified accurately (i.e. the four lines and corners of a square), without an accurate spatial map of the external world, basic features that are properties of an object such as size and colour are not bound accurately to the perceived shape (Freidman-Hill et al. 1995, Humphreys et al. 2000). In fact, features from other items in a display can be incorrectly attached to the shape that one sees (e.g. a display containing a blue T and green X may be seen as a green T or blue X). This type of error is known as an *illusory conjunction*, and in Balint's patients can occur even under free viewing conditions in which no time limitations are imposed. It is also consistent with reports by Balint's patients themselves about their perceptual experiences in everyday life (e.g. a house by a busy street appearing to move even when the patient denies seeing any vehicles or even a street).

Despite the loss of spatial awareness in Balint's patients, there is now substantial evidence that they can detect basic feature properties with relative ease. For example, a patient with a classic case of Balint's syndrome due to bilateral parietal/occipital lesions (R. M.) was able to detect a unique feature target among related distractors in a visual search display (e.g. a red X among a number of green O and green X distractors). Furthermore, his ability to detect a feature was independent of the number of distractors in the display, a well-known perceptual phenomenon called *pop-out* in which a unique feature is detected without the necessity for a serial attentional search through the items in the display. However, when a target contained features shared by the distractors in the search display (e.g. a red X among red O and green X distractors; conjunction search display), R. M. was unable to detect the target any better than chance. This problem in property binding occurred in displays with as few as one, three, or five distractors (Robertson et al. 1997), and again was observed under free viewing conditions. Thus, unique features (at least those associated with specialized neural populations) capture attention even when the external representation of space is lost, but the ability to voluntarily search for a conjunction of two features (which requires serial search for the properly bound item) is severely impaired. In either case, Balint's patients are unable to spatially locate the item they report seeing. Spatial deficits can be so severe that even reporting whether a target is located to the left or right of central fixation on a computer monitor can be at chance levels (Friedman-Hill et al. 1995), Robertson et al. 1997).

These deficits are consistent with attentional theories proposing that feature and conjunction processing are qualitatively different. While feature detection does not require spatial attention and is often considered *preattentive* (Treisman and Gelade 1980), detection of conjunctions requires accurate binding of features in multi-item arrays through spatial attention. Balint's syndrome extends this conclusion to consciousness by showing that properties of objects of which the patient is unaware can migrate to an object of which the patient is aware, as shown in the case of illusory conjunctions.

The perceptual deficits evident in Balint's syndrome support the hypothesis that dorsal stream spatial processes are critically involved in binding properties such as colour and shape that are encoded in the ventral stream of the human brain (Treisman 1996, Robertson 2003). They further show that this binding process (the binding of properties to the shapes of the objects themselves) appears to rely critically upon perceptual awareness of space itself.

2. Property binding and consciousness

One of the most challenging questions of consciousness is how and why it came to be. But another issue is whether consciousness has a role to play in cognition, or is simply the end product of a massive amount of preprocessing that precedes it. Mechanistic views posit (whether explicitly or implicitly) that consciousness is an *epiphenomenon that reflects the underlying biological and/or cognitive processes.

While not denying underlying biological processing, the case of Balint's syndrome suggests that accurate binding (at least of features on dimensions such as colour and shape) requires conscious awareness of the space in which features coexist. Thus, consciousness seems to play a role in properly binding biologically distributed properties in a way that reflects the spatially segregated structure of the external world. Balint's syndrome demonstrates that without awareness of the dimension of space, binding between non-spatial properties is altered. In this way Balint's syndrome suggests that one job of consciousness is to individuate objects (in this case in space) in order for the features in a scene to be properly bound together. Objects that disappear from conscious awareness when dorsal spatial maps are damaged nevertheless continue to supply feature information that drives neural encoding of their properties. However, the brain has no place to put them without a spatial map, resulting in the random selection of features for perception. The implications for normal consciousness are that it has a crucial role in cognition (or at least in perception) in establishing and maintaining segregation of features and their proper location.

3. Summary

In sum, the evidence from patients with Balint's syndrome is consistent with a central role for spatial awareness in accurately binding features that are properties of objects. When this breaks down, features from objects that are outside awareness can intrude on objects of awareness. These features have been associated with ventral coding, suggesting a network for binding that includes interactions between ventral and dorsal posterior areas of the cortex. Spatial maps that guide controlled spatial attention appear necessary to accurately bind at least some types of features together in conscious perceptual awareness.

LYNN C. ROBERTSON AND THOMAS VAN VLEET

Balint, R. (1909/1995). 'Seelenlahmung des 'Schauens', optische Ataxie, raumliche Storung der Aufmerksamkeit'. *Monatshrift fur Psychiatrie und Neurologie*, 25; transl. *Cognitive Neuropsychology*, 12.

Friedman-Hill, S., Robertson, L. C., and Treisman, A. (1995). 'Parietal contributions to visual feature binding: evidence from a patient with bilateral lesions'. *Science*, 269.

Humphreys, G. W., Cinel, C., Wolfe, J., Olson, A., and Klempen, N. (2000). 'Fractionating the binding process: neuropsychological evidence distinguishing binding of form from binding of surface features'. *Vision Research*, 40.

Robertson, L. C. (2003). 'Binding, spatial attention and perceptual awareness'. *Nature Reviews Neuroscience*, 4.

——, Treisman, A., Friedman-Hill, S., and Grabowecky, M. (1997). 'The interaction of spatial and object pathways: evidence from Balint's syndrome'. *Journal of Cognitive Neuroscience*, 9.

Treisman, A. M. (1996). 'The binding problem'. *Current Opinion in Neurobiology*, 6.

—— and Gelade, G. (1980). 'A feature-integration theory of attention'. *Cognitive Psychology*, 12.

Bereitschaftspotential See READINESS POTENTIALS AND HUMAN VOLITION

bicameral mind The term 'bicameral mind' was coined by psychologist and archaeologist Julian Jaynes (1920–1997) in a controversial book (Jaynes 1976). His hypothesis was that early humans, and even the ancient Greeks, were not conscious in the way we are now; they had a two-part or 'bicameral' (literally meaning 'two-chambered') mind, and consciousness arose only in the last few thousand years when this two-part structure broke down, long after the evolution of language and with the development of modern language and thought. This means that Jaynes's theory puts the origin of consciousness as far more recent than almost all other theories.

Jaynes argued that the earliest text from which we can deduce the nature of mind was the *Iliad*, an epic story of revenge, blood and tears, written about 900 or 850 BC. He explores the question 'What is mind in the *Iliad*?' and answers that 'There is in general no consciousness in the *Iliad*' (Jaynes (1976:69)). He bases this conclusion on the fact that he can find no words in the *Iliad* that can be translated directly as 'consciousness', and no descriptions of mental acts either; words such as *psyche* or *thumos*, which later came to mean 'mind' or 'soul', usually referred to concrete things like blood or breath. There is also no word for 'will', and no concept of free will. Most curiously, when the heroes of the *Iliad* carry out their great acts of revenge, abduction, deception, or generosity they are not described as having their own plans and intentions, or even reasons and motives, but as hearing the gods telling them what to do.

Although this sounds very strange to the modern mind it is, claims Jaynes, just what we should expect from a bicameral mind. One chamber deals with action (including volition, planning, and initiative), while the other deals with perception. These are not integrated into one whole and so when the action system decides what to do the perception system hears this in the form of voices. We modern humans would call these *hallucinations, but for the early Greeks they were the voices of the gods. The voices were obeyed, and had to be obeyed, because bicameral man could not work out what to do by himself.

To try to imagine what this is like, Jaynes points out that we can easily drive a car without awareness, doing all sorts of complex actions in response to events in the outside world, while our conscious self is busy with something else. Bicameral man was even more split than that and without a conscious self; unconsciously hearing voices and unconsciously obeying them.

According to Jaynes, the bicameral mind began to break down when language led to the use of analogies and metaphors. Modern consciousness, he claims, operates by way of constructing an analogue space with an analogue 'I' that can observe that space and move metaphorically within it. The whole thing is an invented world with an invented self, built on analogies with both the outside world and observed behaviours. We may feel as though we are a continuous self having conscious experiences but according to Jaynes 'The seeming continuity of consciousness is really an illusion' (1976:24). This is a modern illusion. Bicameral man had 'no awareness of his awareness of the world, no internal mind-space to introspect upon', no self, no free will, and no subjectivity.

Evidence to support the theory includes the importance of hallucinations, oracles, and divination in contemporary bicameral societies, the role of idols and burial practices found in archaeology, the changing use of words in literature and linguistics, and the neuropsychology of hallucinations and religious behaviour.

The theory has been described as preposterous (indeed Jaynes himself uses this word) and has been controversial since its first publication (Cavanna et al. 2007). Nevertheless it continues to be widely read and cited. A second edition was published in 1990, the book has been reprinted many times, and there is even a Julian Jaynes Society.

SUSAN BLACKMORE

Cavanna, A. E., Trimble, M., Federico, C., and Monaco, F. (2007). 'The 'bicameral mind' 30 years on: a critical reappraisal of Julian Jaynes' hypothesis'. *Functional Neurology*, 22.

Jaynes, J. (1976). *The Origin of Consciousness in the Breakdown of the Bicameral Mind*.

binding problem Binding, in the most general sense of the word, refers to a process or an underlying mechanism of integration that results in the overall unity of an entity, or to the emergence of its holistic features.

1. Binding and consciousness
2. Binding in neuroscience
3. Binding in cognitive science
4. Local and global unity of consciousness
5. Different approaches to the phenomenal binding problem
6. Cognitive and neural theories of binding mechanisms
7. Conclusion

1. Binding and consciousness

The contents of conscious experience are unified. An object visually perceived, such as a red ball rolling towards you, is experienced as a unified package of visual features, where motion, colour, and form are coherently bound together. Binding is thus required for the *unity of consciousness. Some believe that a solution to the binding problem is the key to solving the entire problem of consciousness, because consciousness is taken to be fundamentally unified. Others argue that binding and consciousness are two different and dissociable problems and therefore a solution to one does not necessarily shed any light to the other.

There are many varieties of binding and therefore also many different binding problems. When it comes to consciousness, one variety of binding is the process or mechanism that brings about the unity of *phenomenal consciousness or the holistic features of subjective phenomenal experience (phenomenal unity, phenomenal binding). Thus, the *phenomenal binding problem* is the problem of explaining how exactly the unity of consciousness is brought about in the brain or the mind. The problem is considered difficult and persistent because it is not at all obvious how it could be solved, or whether it will be solved at all. The phenomenal binding problem deals purely with the unity of subjective experience and is therefore in principle independent of external physical stimuli or brain responses to them. Thus, the phenomenal binding problem applies equally well to externally evoked percepts as to internally generated images such as *dreams (Revonsuo and Tarkko 2002).

2. Binding in neuroscience

In neuroscience and cognitive science, the binding problem has been formulated in ways that do not refer to the phenomenal unity of consciousness. In neuroscience, binding is the neural process or mechanism that integrates the activities of single neurons to functional groups and neural assemblies. The problem here stems from the fact that any stimulus object appearing in the visual field will activate a huge number of neurons across a wide range of spatially separated cortical areas. Although the response properties of *single neurons in the visual cortex are relatively well known, it remains unclear how thousands or even millions of spatially separate neurons in the cortex interact to form a functionally unified group when they all simultaneously respond to different features of the same object.

This *neural binding problem* as such thus deals with purely neurophysiological unity: the mechanisms of the holistic features of neural activity that represent an external stimulus as a coherent object. Whether or not such activity is correlated with conscious experience is largely irrelevant. In fact many experiments exploring the mechanisms of neural binding have been conducted by using anaesthetized, unconscious animals as subjects. It is possible to present visual stimuli for an unconscious animal and to detect neural responses in the animal's visual cortex. Although the animal is unconscious, coherent large-scale neural activity elicited by the stimulus in the animal's visual cortex may still reflect the holistic properties of the stimulus and covary with the appearance of such properties in the visual field. This kind of coherent neural activities may be the solution to the purely neural binding problem, but they do not address the phenomenal binding problem directly, as no phenomenal experiences, unified or non-unified, exist for the anaesthetized animal during the experiment.

3. Binding in cognitive science

In cognitive science, the binding problem has been formulated in terms of the integration of representation or information processing. As cognitive systems, humans have several modular input systems that process sensory information independently of each other, in an isolated manner. Thus, within the input systems, sensory information originating in a single stimulus object is mostly represented in a non-unified manner. The different features of the object, such as its shape, colour, motion, location, and sound, are handled by separate processing modules, in parallel, at least in the early stages of input processing. By contrast, in the more central systems dealing with selective attention, decision-making, declarative memory, and the control of our interactions with the environment, object representations are complex and holistic, unifying information within and across the modular input systems. At those stages of processing, complex and integrated representations of the world must be formed, because they are required to control and guide coherent behaviour. The *cognitive binding problem* thus is to explain how the widely distributed, isolated, independently processed streams of modular input information become bound together to integrated representations of the world. The cognitive binding problem deals with purely cognitive unity. The question whether the representations or streams of information being bound together are at some point accompanied by subjective experience or consciousness is largely irrelevant. Thus, the cognitive binding problem is considered to be no different in non-conscious information-processing systems such as robots or machine vision systems from what it is in conscious humans beings.

4. Local and global unity of consciousness

Although consciousness is largely irrelevant to the neural and the cognitive binding problems, cognitive and neural mechanisms are highly relevant when it comes to the phenomenal binding problem. Thus, it may be that some specific types of cognitive and neural binding in the conscious human brain might in fact underlie phenomenal unity and therefore solve the phenomenal binding problem. But in fact phenomenal unity itself is rather complex and comes in different forms (Revonsuo 1999, Bayne and Chalmers 2003). Before we explore the underlying mechanisms of phenomenal binding in more detail, we need to take a closer look at phenomenal unity itself.

Roughly, the phenomenal unity of consciousness may be divided to two different varieties: local and global. First, consider the *local* unity of particular contents of consciousness. A paradigmatic example of this is a unified visual percept where a number of different parts and visual features such as colour, shape, and motion are integrated to form a single well-defined phenomenal object. A concrete example: when tracking a flying bird or a colourful butterfly with your gaze, the visual experience caused by the stimulus constitutes a locally integrated percept where all the separate visual parts and features are bound coherently together in a single well-defined region in the subjective visual field.

Second, there is the *global* unity of consciousness. This refers to the entire phenomenal field where all simultaneous experiences, such as the phenomenal body image, phenomenal visual field, phenomenal auditory space, and the rest of our external sense experiences and internal images and thoughts, form a single experiential space. All simultaneously present phenomenal contents are thus fundamentally interrelated with each other within a unified spatiotemporal context. A concrete example of this is the intuitive feeling of *being one single person within one single world*, as the philosopher Thomas Metzinger (2003) has put it. The global unity of consciousness forms the constant phenomenal background unity that pervades all subjective experience.

5. Different approaches to the phenomenal binding problem

In consciousness research the binding problem is the problem of explaining how the phenomenal unity of consciousness comes about. What kind of underlying process or mechanism could bring about locally unified phenomenal experiences, where a number of different phenomenal parts or features of an experience hang coherently together, or the globally unified phenomenal field that underlies our all-embracing experience of being constantly present within a unified world? The difficulty with this problem lies in the fact that the processes and mechanisms that could, even in principle, account for phenomenal unity remain unknown.

Three different directions in which a solution to the phenomenal binding problem has been sought can be identified.

Elimination of phenomenal unity. According to this line of thought, the phenomenal unity of consciousness is an illusion. The most radical version argues that there is no definable time and space in the brain (or anywhere else) where phenomenal events happen or phenomenal features come together in a 'Cartesian theatre'. Phenomenal consciousness does not exist, therefore phenomenal unity is an illusion and phenomenal binding is unnecessary, because there is nothing there to be bound together for a unified phenomenal presentation to a subject, and moreover there are no known mechanisms in the brain that could account for such binding. This line of thought can be found e.g. in Daniel Dennett's work. Typically, empirical data from *change blindness and *inattentional blindness experiments are invoked to support the idea that we are simply mistaken about the unity of consciousness. A somewhat less radical version argues that phenomenal consciousness does exist, but in a non-unified manner. Semir Zeki has defended this line of thought under the label of **microconsciousness theory* (Zeki 2003). According to this, the different features of phenomenal experience come about in an isolated manner in different parts of the cortex: each functionally specialized module produces its own microconsciousness (e.g. phenomenal colour or motion), but whether and to what extent these isolated phenomenal features ever become integrated anywhere in the brain remains doubtful.

Purely phenomenological description of phenomenal unity. According to this line of thought, to investigate the experiential unity of consciousness, we need not assume that anything external to the experiences themselves exist. Thus, data from neuroscience, brain anatomy, or experimental psychology is irrelevant to the task. This approach has been advocated by Barry Dainton (2000), who argues that the unity of consciousness can be described and explained by an experiential relation of synchronic co-consciousness. Experience is self-unifying, in that to understand the unity we find within experience, we need not go beyond experience itself.

Mechanistic explanation of phenomenal unity. According to this line of thought, phenomenal unity must be taken seriously as a real feature of experience. In order to explain the holistic features of phenomenal consciousness, the underlying cognitive and neural mechanisms of binding must be exposed and described (Revonsuo 2006). The difficulty of solving the binding problem in this manner arises from the disunity of the input mechanisms and cortical sensory representations of stimulus information. The different features of a stimulus object are separately represented in a number of specialized cortical areas and maps, but there seems to be no brain area or mechanism that would put all the information back together again, resembling the manner in which the information is experienced as phenomenally unified. There are, however, a number of theoretical ideas about the potential cognitive and neural mechanisms suggested to account for phenomenal unity. Most of them refer to a large-scale integration of information that could take place within the densely interconnected thalamocortical system in the brain (e.g. Llinás 2001).

6. Cognitive and neural theories of binding mechanisms

The *feature integration theory* (FIT; Treisman 1996) proposes the following cognitive mechanism to account for the binding of different perceptual features together. In addition to the input modules that process information representing the separate features of the stimulus, there is a *master map of locations*, representing the entire perceptual space, and a *window or spotlight of attention*, scanning the location map. The stimulus features that fall within the spotlight of attention and are connected to the same location become bound together. They form a single unified package of information called an *object file*. Outside the window of attention bindings may also happen, but only randomly and temporarily. Empirical evidence that can be interpreted to support FIT (but is consistent with other binding theories as well) comes from *Balint's syndrome (Robertson 2003): patients with this neuropsychological syndrome have bilateral damage in the posterior parietal cortex and therefore the master map of locations is deficient. Consequently, patients with Balint's syndrome report seeing random and rapidly changing illusory bindings of features, not knowing which feature in reality belongs together with which others. Coherent, stable visual objects cannot be held together in the absence of the required cognitive mechanisms.

According to Treisman (2003:103), 'attention provides a window for consciousness through which we become aware of a small subset of real bindings among a throng of illusory phantom objects'. Thus, the cognitive binding mechanism proposed in FIT may account for the local unity of visual consciousness, as the mechanism is supposed to produce coherent object representation that emerge into consciousness.

The neural mechanism that typically has been proposed to underlie perceptual binding is *temporal coding* or the *synchronicity of neural activity*. The basic idea is that spatially separated neurons that all respond to the same stimulus object will start to fire in temporal synchrony so that the same rhythm of activity is shared by all the neurons representing that object, and the rhythm is also unique to the neurons representing that object. Thus, the spatially distributed neural assembly becomes a higher-level coherent functional entity defined by its unique synchronous activity pattern. There is a growing body of empirical evidence from animal and human experiments that neural synchronicity correlates with the perception of coherent visual objects and with the *gestalt principles of perceptual grouping (Singer and Gray 1995). Human electroencephalography (EEG) studies have shown that there is a transient increase in high-frequency or *gamma-band power around 300 ms after stimulus onset, and that this response is larger for coherent visual objects, even when the coherence is merely illusory, not present in the physical stimulus (Tallon-Baudry 2003).

In a now classic paper, Crick and Koch (1990) first put forward the idea that there may be a connection between neural binding through synchronization and the phenomenal unity of objects in visual consciousness. According to their hypothesis there is an attentional mechanism that temporarily binds the relevant neurons together by synchronizing their spikes in 40 Hz oscillations, and this results in a coherent object representation in consciousness. Engel and Singer (2001) developed the synchronicity hypothesis further. They propose that synchronization may be the neural mechanism of several different aspects of consciousness, such as arousal, perceptual organization, the short-term stability of the contents of focal attention and working memory, and even the global unity of the self and the world (Engel and Singer 2001).

Whereas the above neural synchronicity theories mostly deal with potential cortical mechanisms of neural synchrony, Rodolfo Llinás (2001) suggests that the key mechanisms of binding consist of the *bidirectional loops of thalamocortical connectivity*. His theory describes two different types of thalamocortical loops: the *specific loop* is assumed to be responsible for the binding of distributed sensory fragments into single coherent objects, and the *non-specific loop* is assumed to provide the overall context or the conscious state where the individual objects are related to each other. The interaction between the two loops through synchronous oscillatory activity around 40 Hz is proposed to bind all the simultaneous contents into one coherent experience. Thus, this theory attempts to give an account of both local and global phenomenal binding. It furthermore develops into a more general neural theory of consciousness. Llinás (2001:126) suggests that our subjectivity is generated by the dialogue between the thalamus and the cortex, a temporally coherent sphere of activity: *'It binds, therefore I am'*.

7. Conclusion

Overall, the problems related to binding and the unity of consciousness have not yet been solved. During the brief history of modern consciousness research, at least some progress has been made in understanding what the problem is all about. We now see that the term 'binding' refers to several different processes at different levels of description (phenomenal, cognitive, neural). Therefore, the binding problem is a whole group of related problems. We also understand that the unity of consciousness is an enormously complex achievement, and that there are many different kinds of unity—as well as many different kinds of disunity—of consciousness. The theories proposed to solve the binding problem are still quite speculative, but at least empirically testable. To some extent the currently available data support the idea that high-frequency neural synchronization is correlated with some aspects of phenomenal unity. More detailed theories as well as new empirical data directly testing such theories are required before we can expect to understand how the phenomenal unity of consciousness is brought about by neurocognitive mechanisms in the brain.

ANTTI REVONSUO

Bayne, T. and Chalmers, D. J. (2003). 'What is the unity of consciousness?' In Cleeremans, A. (ed.) *The Unity of Consciousness*.

Crick, F. and Koch, C. (1990). 'Towards a neurobiological theory of consciousness'. *Seminars in the Neurosciences*, 2.

Dainton, B. (2000). *Stream of Consciousness*.

Engel, A. K. and Singer, W. (2001). Temporal binding and the neural correlates of sensory awareness. *Trends in Cognitive Sciences*, 5, 16–25.

Llinás, R. (2001). *I of the Vortex*.

Metzinger, T. (2003). *Being No One*.

Revonsuo, A. (1999). 'Binding and the phenomenal unity of consciousness'. *Consciousness and Cognition*, 8.

—— (2006). *Inner Presence*.

—— and Tarkko, K. (2002). 'Binding in dreams'. *Journal of Consciousness Studies*, 9.

Robertson, L. C. (2003). 'Binding, spatial attention and perceptual awareness'. *Nature Reviews Neuroscience*, 4.

Singer, W. and Gray, C. M. (1995). 'Visual feature integration and the temporal correlation hypothesis'. *Annual Review of Neuroscience*, 18.

Tallon-Baudry, C. (2003). 'Oscillatory synchrony as a signature for the unity of visual experience in humans'. In Cleeremans, A. (ed.) *The Unity of Consciousness*.

Treisman, A. (1996). 'The binding problem'. *Current Opinion in Neurobiology*, 6.

—— (2003). 'Consciousness and perceptual binding'. In Cleeremans, A. (ed.) *The Unity of Consciousness*.

Zeki, S. (2003). 'The disunity of consciousness'. *Trends in Cognitive Sciences*, 7.

binocular rivalry Binocular rivalry refers to a perceptual phenomenon that occurs when very different visual patterns are presented to each eye simultaneously. In normal vision, the two eyes receive corresponding views of the world from slightly different perspectives, yet the visual system successfully interprets and synthesizes them into a coherent, stable perceptual experience. However, under certain (often artificial) circumstances, retinal projection patterns can be beyond the integrative capacity of the brain. This can be demonstrated by showing differently oriented or coloured patterns, directions of motion, or even different photographs to each eye in isolation. In these cases the brain proves incapable of arriving at a stable and satisfying interpretation of the retinal input. Perhaps surprisingly, the result is not a transparent superposition of the dissimilar patterns, but rather an unstable and wavering perception, with one eye's view dominating for a few seconds before being replaced by its rival from the other eye. Accordingly, an observer will typically experience a sequence of stochastic alternations that proceeds as long as the sensory conflict is present.

Binocular rivalry has fascinated humans throughout the centuries. The first known written account of the phenomenon was from Neapolitan polymath Giambattista della Porta, who in 1593 bemoaned the fact that he was unable to read more than one book at a time by using each eye independently. Subsequent centuries witnessed further anecdotal references to the rivalry phenomenon. When Charles Wheatstone introduced the mirror stereoscope in the 1830s, the systematic testing of binocular rivalry became possible, and from this point on binocular rivalry became the subject of intense scientific research. Up to this day, several dozens of studies on binocular rivalry are published each year, either exploring the phenomenon itself or using it as a research tool to study conscious perception.

While the experience during binocular rivalry is often characterized as a simple switching between the right eye's and left eye's views, which might produce a percept similar to opening and closing each eye in succession, this is a considerable oversimplification of what subjects actually observe. Particularly with larger and more complex visual stimuli, rivalry perception can proceed as a fluid sequence of ever-changing mosaics (so-called *piecemeal percepts*), consisting of an interleaved patchwork of portions of the two eyes' views. Several studies have revealed that the structure of this patchwork at each point in time is determined by a combination of local inter-ocular competition, *gestalt grouping principles, and waves of ocular dominance that are likely to reflect coherent spatiotemporal activity patterns in the visual cortex. Also, when competing rivalry patterns are both very low in their contrast, perception can be marked by a superposition of the two eyes' views, something that is never observed when one or both of the patterns are of higher contrast. Likewise, very short presentations of conflicting stimuli are frequently perceived as being fused.

When rivalry suppression does occur, the suppressed area is rendered completely invisible. At the same time, suppression is surprisingly superficial when measured psychophysically, since the threshold for detecting test probes presented to the non-dominant eye is only minimally elevated by suppression. Moreover, the temporal dynamics of rivalry alternations are determined by the characteristics of the suppressed, rather than dominant, stimulus. At each point in time the expected dominance duration is predicted by the strength (i.e. contrast, speed, brightness) of the suppressed pattern. These findings suggest that unperceived stimuli in the suppressed eye are still processed to a large extent by the visual system and not simply blocked at an early processing stage. It is for this reason that binocular rivalry became a primary research tool for investigators interested in the differential effects of consciously perceived and suppressed visual stimuli.

Initial studies on the brain mechanisms underlying binocular rivalry were focused on the activity of *single neurons in monkey visual cortex. It was found that isolated neurons throughout visual cortex change their firing rate whenever the percept changes during rivalry. It turned out the proportion of neurons that do so differs drastically between visual cortical areas. While only few cells modulate their activity with perceptual alternations in primary visual cortex (*V1), there is an increasing frequency of neurons with percept-related activity as one goes up the classical visual hierarchy. Recordings in both monkeys and humans showed that at the latest stages of visual processing, the majority of neurons alter their activity during perceptual switches. This activation pattern is not explainable by a fixed network of neurons with a closer link to perception than other cells, since different stimuli elicit perceptual modulation among different neuronal populations.

Human *functional brain imaging (fMRI) studies agree that there are widespread activity changes throughout the brain at the moment of a spontaneous perceptual reversal, particularly in the *frontal and parietal lobes. Activity in higher cortical areas (such as that responsible for face processing) is modulated so consistently during rivalry that it can be used to read out the actual perception of an observer. It has also been shown that the unperceived, perceptually suppressed stimuli are not entirely erased form processing at these stages since their impact is still measurable. Disagreement exists, however, between imaging and single-unit data on the participation of the earliest stages of cortical processing in the formation and maintenance of a perceptual state during rivalry. While single neurons in monkeys show minimal correspondence with the perceptual state, human neuroimaging studies demonstrated that the fMRI signal in primary visual cortex is closely coupled with the visibility of a pattern during rivalry. Recent findings hint at a resolution of this conflict by suggesting that the fMRI signal is more related to the synaptic membrane currents than local spiking activity, and perceptual suppression has a profound impact on the first but not the latter. How much primary visual cortex contributes to binocular rivalry remains an important question to explore.

Putative evidence for the involvement of other cortical areas in binocular rivalry is its close relationship to the bistable perception induced by other ambiguous geometrical patterns that give rise to more than one valid perceptual solution. The temporal dynamics of rivalry alternations are nearly identical with that of the famous Necker cube, whose structure similarly appears to change spontaneously every few seconds (see MULTISTABLE PERCEPTION). Most attempts to simulate binocular rivalry in neuronal networks can be generalized to other bistable stimuli. These models generally assume mutual inhibition between neuronal populations as the ultimate cause of perceptual instability (further assuming that a population being more active is somehow causing one of the alternative percepts). This simple 'flip-flop' circuitry is the easiest way to generate oscillations in a model. The randomness of the perceptual state changes then are explained by 'noise' that is added to the system. Other models assume more complex mechanisms related to dynamical systems theory such as local minima in an abstract energy space or chaotic fluctuations in a self-organized system.

Another indication for a common mechanism of perceptual alternation is that the temporal dynamics of binocular rivalry and other bistable visual phenomena are all connected to several cognitive variables. In particular, the switching frequency can vary by an order of magnitude between observers but is consistent within an observer over multiple testing sessions, declining slowly with age. A large number of studies have attempted to link IQ and personality type to alternation rate with bistable figures, with limited success. While voluntary control over alternation is limited, observers can improve their ability to control reversal with practice, but never learn to inhibit it altogether. Neurostimulants, mood disorders, *meditative states, and *brain damage, particularly to the right frontal cortex, can all impact the rate of reversal. While the connection between these factors and rivalry is by no means clear, these findings support the assumption that perceptual switching is induced or at least influenced by modulating factors outside the sensory domain.

Binocular rivalry also appears to be closely related to spontaneous fluctuations observable in some dim visual patterns, where two components of the pattern can alternate in their visibility—a phenomenon misleadingly termed *monocular rivalry*. Despite these similarities, binocular rivalry appears to be unique in its generality among different stimuli, as well as in the completeness of its perceptual suppression. It is possible that these unique qualities are related to its relevance in natural vision. Binocular vision in a cluttered three-dimensional environment involves zones of inter-ocular discrepancy, including a vast zone outside of Panum's fusional area where there is no interocular correspondence at all. Under these conditions, the brain is often forced to choose one eye's view while completely suppressing the other's. This commonplace suppression may be directly related to that observed in binocular rivalry.

Binocular rivalry has always attracted students of diverse disciplines. It has been used as a tool to study the human unconscious, to assess cognitive abnormalities, and to learn more about binocular vision and perception in general. Thus, it has served as an unlikely common ground for philosophers, biologists, psychologists, and physicists, who all seem captivated by the implications for subjective experience. While a great deal is known about rivalry, it is, perhaps surprisingly, the big picture questions that are the still the most contentious. With technical advances in neuroscience, passive-correlational approaches are slowly being complemented by causal manipulations. Such interventions may ultimately provide a clearer picture of the neuronal mechanisms underlying perceptual alternation and visual suppression during rivalry. Understanding the neuronal mechanisms causing binocular rivalry may have direct implications for our understanding of how a percept gets established and supported in the brain. It thus has been and continues to be a vital and fascinating paradigm for the scientific study of visual awareness.

ALEXANDER MAIER AND DAVID A. LEOPOLD

Blake, R. and Logothetis, N. K. (2002). 'Visual competition'. *Nature Reviews Neuroscience*, 3.

Crick, F. and Koch, C. (1998). 'Consciousness and neuroscience'. *Cerebral Cortex*, 8.

Leopold, D. A. and Logothetis, N. K. (1996). 'Activity changes in early visual cortex reflect monkeys' percepts during binocular rivalry'. *Nature*, 379.

Logothetis, N. K. and Schall, J. D. (1989). 'Neuronal correlates of subjective visual perception'. *Science*, 245.

Lumer, E. D., Friston, K., and Rees, G. (1998). 'Neural correlates of perceptual rivalry in the human brain'. *Science*, 280.

Sheinberg, D. L. and Logothetis, N. K. (1997). 'The role of temporal cortical areas in perceptual organization'. *Proceedings of the National Academy of Sciences of the USA*, 94.

Tong, F., Nakayama, K., Vaughan, J. T., and Kanwisher, N. (1998). 'Binocular rivalry and visual awareness in human extrastriate cortex'. *Neuron*, 21.

Wilson, H. R., Blake, R., and Lee, S.-H. (2001). 'Dynamics of travelling waves in visual perception'. *Nature*, 412.

biological naturalism Biological naturalism is an account of the relation of consciousness, as well as other mental phenomena, to the brain and the rest of the body. It rejects both *dualism and materialism (see PHYSICALISM), while attempting to preserve what is true in each. The theory begins with a common-sense definition of 'consciousness', one that is intended to identify the target rather than try to provide a scientific or philosophical analysis of the sort that can only come at the end of the investigation. 'Consciousness' is defined as those qualitative states of sentience or feeling or awareness that typically begin in the morning when we wake from a dreamless *sleep, and continue throughout the day until we fall asleep again or otherwise become unconscious. *Dreams, on this definition, are a form of consciousness. Consciousness, so defined, does not necessarily imply a higher order level of *self-consciousness. Humans and many species of animals are conscious, but we do not yet know how far on the phylogenetic scale consciousness goes.

The first feature to notice about consciousness is that there is a qualitative feel or character to every conscious state, a 'what it feels like', or '*what it is like' aspect of consciousness. You can see this by reflecting on the difference between, for example, drinking wine and listening to a string quartet. These may occur simultaneously, but they have a different *qualitative* character. A second feature of consciousness is that it is *subjective* in the ontological sense that it can only exist when experienced by a human or animal subject. Its subjective, first-person ontology makes it differ from other features of the world such as mountains, molecules, and tectonic plates, that have an objective, or third-person, ontology. Third, any conscious state, such as feeling of pain or thinking about one's income tax, can only exist as part of a *unified, conscious field*. You do not just think about your income tax, feel a pain, and taste the wine you are drinking, but you have all of these experiences as parts of one large experience that constitutes your entire conscious field at this very moment. These three features of consciousness—qualitativeness, *subjectivity, and *unity—appear to be distinct from each other, but if we reflect on them we can see that in fact each implies the next. There is no way that a state could be qualitative in the sense described without it being subjective, and there is no way that it could be subjective without occurring as part of a unified conscious field.

About consciousness so defined and so characterized, biological naturalism makes the following four claims:

1. *Consciousness is real.* It is a real part of the biological world and cannot be reduced to something else, nor eliminated by any kind of reduction. It cannot be reduced to any third-person phenomena because it has a first-person or subjective ontology, and this ontological feature would be lost if we reduced consciousness to neuron firings or any other such third-person phenomena.

2. *Consciousness is entirely caused by neuronal processes.* We do not know the exact mechanisms that cause consciousness, but we are sure, beyond a reasonable doubt, that these are neurobiological mechanisms in the brain, and perhaps parts of the rest of the central nervous system. Consciousness so defined is thus causally reducible but not ontologically reducible to brain processes. It is causally reducible because there is no feature of consciousness which is not causally explained by neuronal behaviour, but it is not ontologically reducible because the first-person ontology of consciousness prevents it from being reduced to a third-person ontology of the rest of neurobiology.
3. *Consciousness is entirely realized in the brain as a higher-level or system feature.* Though a state of consciousness is caused by the behaviour of neurons, individual neurons and synapses by themselves are not conscious. Just as individual H_2O molecules are not liquid or solid, and yet the behaviour of the molecules accounts for liquidity and solidity as features of systems of molecules, so individual neurons are not conscious, yet the behaviour of the neurons accounts for the existence of consciousness as a feature of a system of neurons. You cannot point to a single neuron and say: 'This one is conscious', any more than you can point to a single water molecule and say: 'This one is wet'.
4. *Consciousness functions causally in producing behaviour.* You consciously decide to raise your arm, for example, and then your intention-in-action causes your arm to go up. Consciousness, like other real features of the real world, stands in cause and effect relationships to other phenomena.

Biological naturalism can best be understood by comparing it with dualism and materialism, the two traditionally most widely accepted theories of mind–body relationships. According to the biological naturalist it is possible to preserve what is true in both of these theories, while discarding with what is false.

Materialists say truly that the universe consists entirely of physical particles (or whatever entities the ultimately true physics comes up with) in fields of force, and these are typically organized into systems, and on our Earth some carbon-based systems have evolved into the present human animal and plant species. But, according to the biological naturalist, materialists claim falsely that there are no irreducible mental phenomena in the world. Consciousness really does exist, so it cannot be eliminated, but it has a first-person ontology and therefore cannot be reduced to something that has a third-person ontology.

Dualists say truly that consciousness really does exist as part of the universe and cannot be eliminated or reduced to anything else. Dualists say falsely that recognition of the irreducible character of consciousness commits us to the existence of two distinct realms of being, the realm of the physical and the realm of the mental. According to the biological naturalist, once we discard the Cartesian heritage of talking about the mental and the physical as distinct metaphysical realms, we can see that the so-called mental is really just a higher level of biological, and therefore physical, feature of neurobiological systems. But in order to say that, we have to abandon the traditional usage of the Cartesian heritage according to which anything irreducibly mental must be in a different metaphysical realm from anything physical. According to the biological naturalist, if we just state the facts as they are stated in propositions 1–4, we can see how it is possible to perceive the true claim of dualism with the true claim of materialism, while abandoning the false claims in each.

In light of this comparison with the traditional views, let us now consider the four defining propositions of biological naturalism:

1. *The reality and irreducibility of consciousness.* In our philosophical tradition there is supposed to be a distinction between **eliminative reductions* that show that the reduced phenomena never existed, at all, and non-eliminative reductions that show that the phenomenon does exist, but it is nothing but something else, the reducing phenomenon. An example of an eliminative reduction is the reduction of rainbows which shows that they do not really exist as arches in the sky. A non-eliminative reduction is water to H_2O molecules which shows that water consists of H_2O molecules, but does not show that it does not exist. The problem with attempting to do a non-eliminative reduction of consciousness is that it turns out to be eliminative because any attempt to reduce something that has an essential first-person ontology to something with a third-person ontology will eliminate the essential trait. So to grant the existence of consciousness is already to grant that it cannot be reduced or eliminated by the standard reductive methods.
2. *The neurobiological causation of consciousness.* Many writers in the dualist tradition think it is impossible that we should ever be able to explain how the brain causes consciousness, or, at least, that we cannot possibly explain it with our present conceptual apparatus. To the biological naturalist this is unwarranted pessimism. We now know, for a fact, that brain processes do cause consciousness, and though we are still struggling to figure out exactly how they do it, there has been a remarkable amount of progress in neurobiology in the past several decades and it is not at all unlikely that in this century we will have an

explanation of how brain processes cause consciousness. But whether we get a scientific explanation or not is in a sense beside the point. We know that in fact it happens. There is no doubt that all of our conscious states are entirely caused by neuronal processes, and in that sense consciousness is *causally* reducible to brain processes.

3. *Realization in the brain of consciousness*. We know that consciousness exists, we know that it is a real phenomenon. Where is it? Where is it in real space-time? All of our conscious states exist between our ears. To understand this point we have to see that consciousness does not exist on the level of neurons and synapses, much less at the level of atoms and electrons, but at a much higher systemic level. There are lots of features of nature that are like that. Consider liquidity and solidity, for example. Individual water molecules are neither liquid nor solid, it is only the system of which the individual molecule is a component that can be liquid or solid.
4. *The causal functioning of consciousness*. A normal person intends to raise her arm and then she does so intentionally. Her conscious intention-in-action causes the arm to raise. Indeed, in that particular context, we can suppose that the intention-in-action was causally sufficient for the arm to go up. But we know independently that in order for her arm to go up, there has to be a series of purely physical causal factors such as the secretion of acetylcholine at the axon end-plates of her motor neurons. It is sometimes presented as an objection to biological naturalism that it appears to be causal overdetermination. On the one hand, the arm going up is caused by her intention; on the other, it is caused by neuronal electrochemical processes. The objection is that this leaves us with too many causes. This would be a case of causal overdetermination. To the biological naturalist, however, this seems to strengthen his position, because it shows us, indeed offers us implicitly a proof that the conscious intention-in-action is part of a complex neuronal event that also has chemical properties. In fact, we can prove this point by simple deduction: (1) The conscious intention-in-action causes the arm to go up. (2) Anything that caused the arm to go up must have the necessary chemical and electrical properties (enough to contract the arm muscles). (3) Therefore the conscious intention-in-action must have these properties.

The existence of a complex event that can be described causally at higher and lower levels is not at all unusual in the real world. Consider, for example, the operation of a car engine. We can describe the operation of the car engine either at the level of the passage of electrons between the electrodes of the spark plug, or we can describe the same operation in terms of the explosion of the fuel mixture in the cylinder; one event, different levels of description. In the same way, we can describe the one event of my intentionally raising my arm in terms of the conscious intention-in-action or in terms of the lower-level biochemical features.

Biological naturalism is a form of naturalism because it insists on the fact that consciousness and other mental properties are parts of the natural world. It is biological in the sense that it insists that the peculiarity of consciousness is that it is caused by certain sorts of biological systems, and it exists in those biological systems. It is a natural property of humans and certain animal species, and thus is a natural, biological property.

JOHN R. SEARLE

blindness, recovery from In 1688 William Molyneax sent a letter to John Locke asking whether a man, born blind, who had learnt to distinguish a globe and cube by touch, would be able to distinguish them by vision alone if sight were ever restored. This question, known as Molyneax's problem, played an important role in the seventeenth and eighteenth century development of the empiricist argument that perceptual concepts are not present from birth but require the presence of sensory experience. Empiricists such as Locke were well aware that our sensations have a complex and occasionally indirect relationship to the physical world. However, Locke believed that the sensations of shape and distance involved in seeing a cube were primary sensations that originated more directly from the object than secondary sensations such as those of colour. Locke therefore believed that a sight-recovery patient would have the same visual *sensations* as a person with normal visual experience (Locke 1690), but would not know that these sensations were of the same 'cube' objects for which he had previous tactile experience.

Fifty years later, Cheselden's (1728) publication of a sight-recovery case study revealed that his patient had acute difficulty interpreting his two-dimensional retinal image as a three-dimensional world. Condillac (1746) and Diderot (1749) questioned whether the blind man would even have the same visual sensations as someone with a normal visual history. Both philosophers emphasized the role of active experience in making sense of vision. For example, Diderot, in his *Letter on the Blind*, suggested that some visual sensations (such as those of shape) might need to be disambiguated by tactile experience to be understandable. Later, Reid (1764) made the distinction between sensations (e.g. 'feeling a smooth surface') which belong to a particular sense, and *perceptions*, an awareness of external objects that could be mediated by more than one sense: one can 'perceive a cube' through either touch or vision. According to Reid, perceptions were innate ideas about the external world that were awakened by sensations. This is of course very similar to the nativist tradition originally rejected by Locke. Thus, as far as the epistemological issue of how our sensations, perceptions, and cognitive constructs might be related to the outside world, within a hundred years Molyneux's question had led philosophers full circle.

However, the study of Molyneux's question did lead philosophers to make increasingly fine distinctions between different types of internal psychological events, such as sensations, perceptions, and cognitive constructs. These distinctions were often based on prescient behavioural observations and played a significant role in guiding later experimental research. Condillac, in discussing the development of understanding in a statue progressively provided with smell, hearing, touch, and sight, recognized that intentional action is crucial in relating sensations to external objects. Diderot, considering how a three-dimensional world is inferred from the two-dimensional retinal image, suggested that the development of certain sensations, such as those of shape and size, may be acquired in a developmental process that depends on tactile experience. Both of these observations have since been supported by infant development studies suggesting that the understanding of three-dimensional shape develops in parallel with grasping behaviour between four and six months of age (Piaget 1952). For a comprehensive description of the philosophical issues raised by Molyneux's question, see Morgan (1977).

This philosophical debate has not been seriously troubled by an overabundance of empirical data. Although the first report of recovery from blindness was in AD 1020 and the first clinical study of sight recovery after long-term blindness was carried out in 1728 (Cheselden 1728), only sporadic cases have been studied over the last three centuries: e.g. S. B. (Gregory and Wallace 1963), H. S. (Valvo 1971), H. B. (Ackroyd et al. 1974), Virgil (Sacks 1995), and M. M. (Fine et al. 2003). None of these cases should be considered as examples of 'pure' sight recovery as defined by no light perception from birth to adulthood, and in many cases the patients were only studied some months after sight recovery had occurred. Nonetheless, some consensus has gradually emerged about the restored visual abilities of those who have lost their sight early in childhood.

Most sight-recovery patients can name colours easily once they have learned the correct colour names, and can distinguish fine differences in hue (Ackroyd et al.'s patient H. B. had difficulty with colour naming, but her English, though fluent, was a second language). Colour processing for M. M. was essentially normal. Similarly, motion processing also appears to be relatively spared. It was said of S. B. 'His only signs of appreciation were to moving objects, particularly the pigeons in Trafalgar Square.' Similarly, for H. B., 'She could see the pigeons as they alighted in Trafalgar Square but she said that they appeared to vanish as they came to rest.' M. M. had no difficulty on motion tasks that included identifying the direction of motion of simple and complex plaids (see Fig. B1), the barber's pole *illusion, segregating textured fields based on motion, and using motion cues to compute the three-dimensional shape of a rotating cube. M. M. was also sensitive to biological motion, recognizing a point-light Johansson figure (a dynamic representation of a walking person represented by dots of light at the walker's joints, see Fig. B1), and was even able to make sense of the fine motion cues that differentiate male and female gaits.

Sight-recovery patients also have few difficulties with recognizing two-dimensional shapes. M. M. could segment texture patterns based on luminance contrast, could identify whether a field of line contours contained a sequence of nearly collinear line segments, and could discriminate Glass patterns from random noise (see Fig. B1). The only two-dimensional task M. M. had difficulty with might be considered a three-dimensional one: though he recognized outlined two-dimensional shapes, he could not identify the same shapes in Kanisza illusory contours.

In contrast, sight-recovery patients seem to have little understanding of three-dimensional shape. It was reported of Sacks' patient Virgil, 'Sometimes surfaces of objects would seem to loom ... when they were still quite a distance away; sometimes he would get confused by his own shadow ... [Steps] posed a particular hazard. All he could see was a confusion, a flat surface of parallel and crisscrossing lines'. H. S. described his initial experiences after sight recovery: 'I had no appreciation of depth or distance; street lights were luminous stains stuck to window panes, and the corridors of the hospital were black holes.' (H. S. was not deprived of sight until the age of 15, and recovered his ability to interpret the world in three dimensions over a matter of months postoperatively.) M. M. could exploit occlusion cues but not shading, transparency, or perspective. He could not identify wire drawings of stationary Necker cubes or pyramids, describing the cube as 'a square with lines'. M. M. was also immune to illusions based on perspective cues such as the Shepard tables.

Presumably as a consequence of these difficulties in constructing a three-dimensional percept, sight-recovery patients have trouble recognizing even 'familiar' objects and faces. Cheselden (1728) describes this confusion in his patient: 'Having often forgot which was the cat and which the dog, he was ashamed to ask, but catching the cat which he knew from feeling, he was observed to look at her steadfastly and then ... have said, So puss, I shall know you another time.'

Why is it that colour, two-dimensional shape, and motion perception are relatively unaffected by

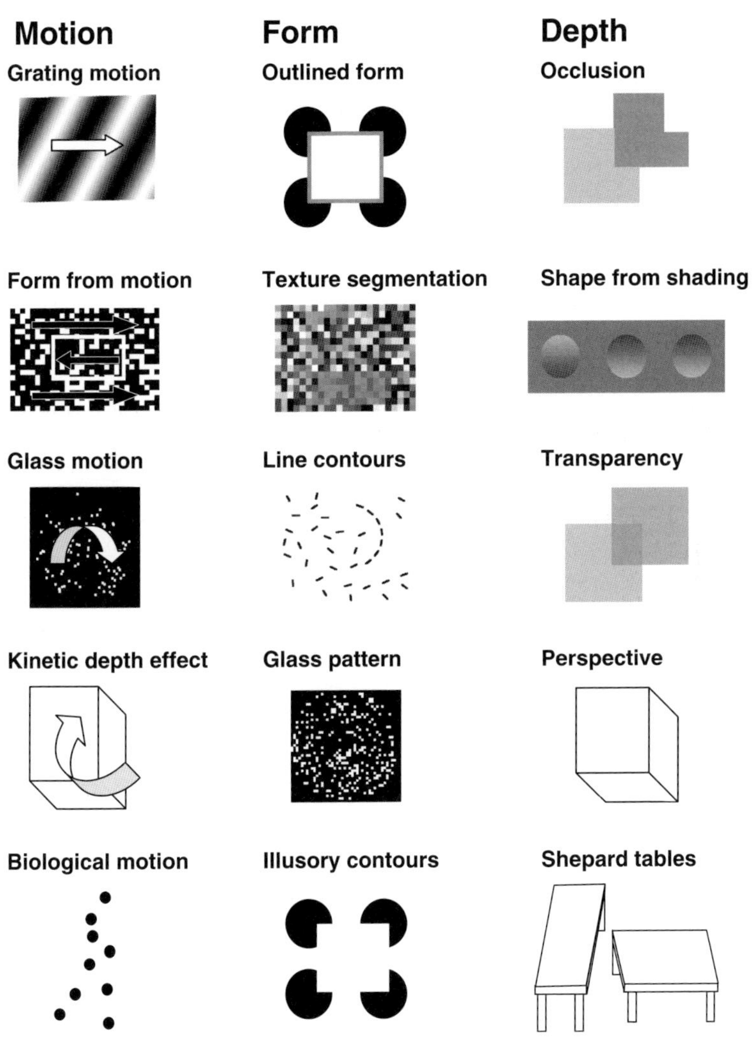

Fig. B1. Tasks and illusions.

deprivation, while three-dimensional processing is dramatically impaired? One hypothesis is that some abilities might be more innate, as evidenced by developing early in infancy, and might therefore be more robust to deprivation (Lewis and Maurer 2005). However, two-dimensional tasks such as contour integration develop relatively late in infancy, yet remain relatively undisturbed by deprivation. Another suggestion is that non-spatial temporal information (flicker), which has been preoperatively available to all the sight-recovery patients studied to date, results in a sparing of motion pathways. But chromatic and two-dimensional form processing also seem to be spared from the effects of visual deprivation. Spared chromatic and two-dimensional form processing is also left unexplained by the hypothesis that ventral 'what/recognition' pathways are more affected by deprivation than dorsal 'where/action' pathways, since chromatic and two-dimensional information is thought to be predominantly processed within 'what' pathways (see VISUAL STREAMS: WHAT VS HOW). It has been suggested that sight-recovery patients might only have the ability to understand those sensations for which there is a tactile equivalent: yet they have no difficulty discriminating colours. One intriguing possibility is that almost the opposite is true. As suggested by Diderot, and confirmed by later infant development studies, the development of some visual perceptions such as those of shape may depend on tactile experience.

Perhaps sight-recovery patients have no difficulties with purely visual sensations (colour, two-dimensional shape, and motion) but, without the developmental experience of disambiguating visual experience with the help of touch, find it impossible to construct a three-dimensional world from a two-dimensional retinal image.

IONE FINE, CORDELIA FINE, AND KIT FINE

Ackroyd, C., Humphrey, N. K., and Warrington, E. K. (1974). 'Lasting effects of early blindness. A case study'. *Quarterly Journal of Experimental Psychology*, 26.

Cheselden, W. (1728). 'An account of some observations made by a young gentleman, who was born blind, or who lost his sight so early, that he had no remembrance of ever having seen, and was couch'd between 13 and 14 years of age'. *Philosophical Transactions of the Royal Society of London*, 35.

de Condillac, E. B. (1746). *Essai sur l'origine des connaissances humaines*.

Diderot, D. (1749). *Lettre sur les aveugles*.

Fine, I., Wade, A., Boynton, G. M. B., Brewer, A., May, M., Wandell, B., and MacLeod, D. I. A. (2003). 'The neural and functional effects of long-term visual deprivation on human cortex'. *Nature Neuroscience*, 6.

Gregory, R. L. and Wallace, J. G. (1963). *Recovery from Early Blindness: a Case Study*. Experimental Psychology Society Monograph No. 2

Lewis, T. L. and Maurer, D. (2005). 'Multiple sensitive periods in human visual development: evidence from visually deprived children.' *Developmental Psychobiology*, 46.

Locke, J. (1690). *An Essay Concerning Human Understanding*.

Morgan, M. J. (1977). *Molyneux's Question: Vision, Touch and the Philosophy of Perception*.

Piaget, J. (1952). *The Origins of Intelligence in Children*.

Reid, T. (1764). *An Inquiry into the Human Mind on the Principles of Common Sense*.

Sacks, O. (1995). 'To see and not to see'. In *An Anthropologist on Mars*.

Valvo, A. (1971). *Sight Restoration After Long-Term Blindness: the Problems and Behavior Patterns of Visual Rehabilitation*.

blindsight Blindsight is an oxymoron—surely one cannot be blind and sighted at the same time? But if not all sight is conscious, and 'blind' refers to a lack of conscious sight, visual functions would be possible although one would not experience oneself as seeing. This occurs in patients with fields of cortical blindness caused by lesions of the primary visual cortex (*V1, striate cortex). Their ability to detect, localize, and discriminate between visual stimuli they avow not to see demonstrates that sight can indeed be blind. The term 'blindsight' captures this dissociation (Weiskrantz et al. 1974) which 'knocked the stuffing out of the "obvious" assumption that awareness of a signal is necessary for an intentional response to that signal' (Churchland 1984:45–46). The phenomenon has intrigued neuroscientists, psychologists, and philosophers who try to understand its implications for conscious and unconscious vision, their function(s) and neuronal bases.

Lesions that destroy or denervate the primary visual cortex cause cortical blindness in the region of the visual field that was represented in that area. Complete cortical blindness results from bihemispheric destruction of V1 and is fortunately rare; most patients suffer unilateral damage that affects the same region of the contralateral visual hemifield in both eyes. V1 lesions induce widespread degeneration in the neuronal structures that lose their connections to the damaged region. Nevertheless, visual input from the blind field still reaches the retinorecipient nuclei, and these transmit it, directly or via other nuclei, to visual cortical areas beyond V1 (Fig. B2). Physiological recordings in monkeys whose V1 was

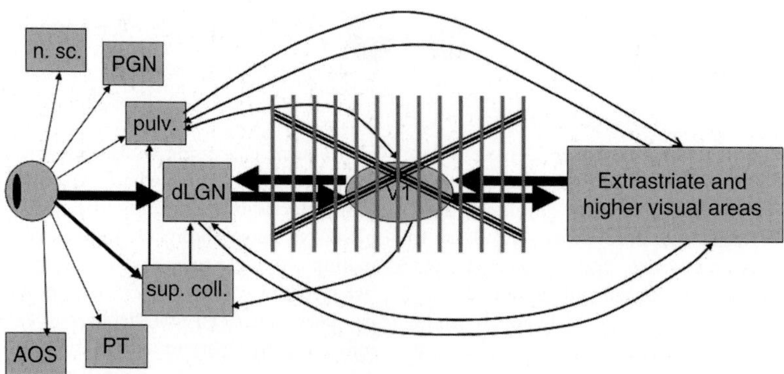

Fig. B2. A simplified schema of the visual system shows that only the extra-geniculostriate projections, from and to parts of the thalamus, escape the effects of the V1 lesion indicated by vertical grey bars. Both the affected hemiretina and its projection to the dorsal lateral geniculate nucleus also undergo partial degeneration (n. sc., suprachiasmatic nucleus; PGN, pregeniculate nucleus; pulv., pulvinar nuclei; sup. coll., superior colliculus; PT, pretectal nuclei; AOS, accessory optic system).

ablated or cooled revealed that neurons in the occipitoparietal (dorsal) visual processing stream respond more vigorously to stimuli presented to the affected visual field (see Bullier et al. 1994 for review) than those in the occipitotemporal (ventral) stream (see VISUAL STREAMS: WHAT VS HOW). The lesion's anatomical and functional repercussions depend on the age at lesion; earlier lesions cause more degeneration, but at the same time induce more plastic alterations which are expressed in unusual anatomical pathways and close-to-normal neuronal responses in extrastriate visual cortical areas. The information on the neuroanatomical and neurophysiological consequences of V1 lesions in animals has been confirmed and extended by pathological and, more recently, structural and *functional neuroimaging studies of patients.

The neuronal pathways that survive destruction of V1 support a variety of visually guided behaviours. This was first clearly shown by Heinrich Klüver's studies of monkeys with bilateral removal of occipital cortex; investigators who include the Pasiks, Weiskrantz, Humphrey (see HELEN, 'A BLIND MONKEY WHO SAW EVERYTHING'), Cowey, Keating, Mohler, and Wurtz have followed in his footsteps. The visual functions they have demonstrated include detection, manual localization, and saccadic localization as well as visually guided navigation, but also discrimination of total contour, shapes, patterns, and chromatic differences (for reviews, see Pasik and Pasik 1982, Stoerig and Cowey 1997).

The monkeys' visual capacities have always and necessarily been tested with non-verbal behavioural methods, and were interpreted in terms of residual conscious sight because the majority of human patients with striate cortical damage consistently declared that they did not see anything in their blind field. In humans, but not monkeys, conscious sight thus depended on the integrity of V1. The apparent contrast between sight in monkeys and blindness in humans was regarded as evidence for stronger corticalization: only in humans, it was posited, is cortex required for conscious vision. This hypothesis ruled as long as the patients were asked only whether they were aware of stimuli presented within their blind field. But it was undermined when behavioural methods previously only used on monkeys 'forced' the patients to respond to targets presented within their blind field. Although the patients claimed to be 'just guessing', they performed much better than expected by chance (Pöppel et al. 1973, Weiskrantz et al. 1974). The reports on unconscious vision in humans met with surprise bordering on disbelief. They also sparked methodological critiques attributing human 'blindsight' to eye movements, stray light falling on to the normal parts of the retina, and near-threshold vision (Campion et al. 1983). However, despite careful experimental control measurements that excluded artefacts, e.g. by showing that the same stimuli failed to elicit better-than-chance performance when they were presented so as to fall on to the receptor-free optic disc (the natural blind spot), visual functions continued to be demonstrated in the cortically blind field. In addition to saccadic and manual localization of blind-field targets, they include detection and discrimination of stimuli differing in flux, contour, orientation, motion, spatial frequency, shape, and wavelength (for review see Weiskrantz 1996, Stoerig and Cowey 1997). Humans and monkeys thus show largely similar visual functions in their cortically blind fields.

Together with the similar functional neuronanatomy of the human and simian visual systems, this raised the question of whether monkeys, like the human patients, have blindsight rather than the residual conscious sight originally attributed to them. To tackle this question, three monkeys with complete unilateral V1 ablation and a control monkey were first tested in a target localization task, where they manually localized small visual stimuli that could appear briefly in any one of the four corners of a touch-sensitive monitor at better than 90% correct in *both* hemifields. Then the paradigm was changed so as to allow the possibility of signalling 'no target'. This was done by introducing blank (no light) trials which were presented unpredictably among target trials. Whenever a blank trial occurred, the correct response was to touch a constantly outlined 'no target' area on the screen. Having this option did not affect responses to good-field targets which remained close to perfect. It did, however, radically alter the responses to the targets presented in the hemianopic field: despite their excellent localization performance, the monkeys now treated these stimuli as 'no target' (Cowey and Stoerig 1995). The results thus suggested that the monkeys had blindsight rather than (possibly poor) conscious sight, a hypothesis strengthened when the same combination of forced-choice localization and signal detection tasks subsequently differentiated between blind and poor sight in human patients. In line with their reporting awareness of a percentage of targets presented to the relatively blind region, the 'poor-sight' patients not only performed well in the localization but in the detection task as well (see Fig. B3). Conversely, patients tested in regions of absolute blindness performed well in the localization task, but indicated 'no target' whenever a blind-field target was presented in the signal detection test (Stoerig et al. 2002). Like the monkeys, the patients with blindsight thus showed a behavioural difference in their responses to blind-field targets that depended on whether or not the response options included a 'no-target' one. Offering this option thus appeared to capture the dissociation between localization performance and stimulus unawareness.

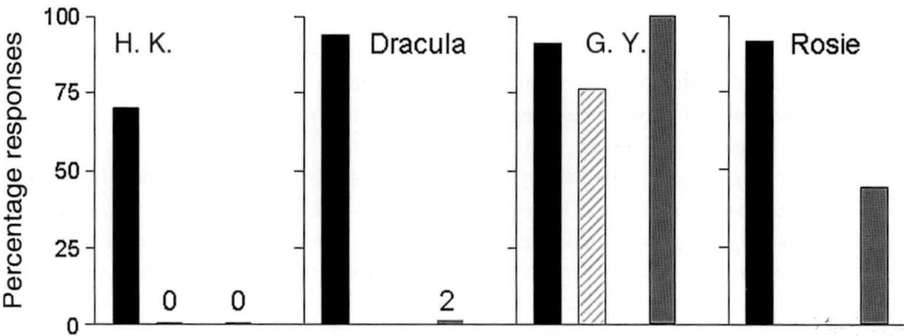

Fig. B3. Percentage correct localization (black), percentage aware responses (striped), and percentage correct detection of targets presented within the affected hemifield (grey). H. K. was tested in his absolutely blind hemifield, and like monkey Dracula performed well in the localization, but indicated 'no target' on almost all trials in the detection task. In contrast, monkey Rosie more resembled G. Y. who was tested in his relatively blind field, and eventually detected a sizeable proportion of the blind-field targets she localized so accurately.

Interestingly, Rosie, a hemianopic monkey who also participated in the latter experiment, correctly localized 6% of the blind-field targets even when she had the option to signal 'no target'. Her behaviour thus somewhat resembled that of the human patients who were tested in regions of relative blindness; more strikingly, with continued testing she eventually raised the proportion of blind-field trials to which she responded by signalling a target instead of a blank stimulus to about 50%. Does this indicate that she learned to discriminate unseen stimulus and blank trials in her blind field? Or that she recovered some conscious sight in her hemianopic field?

Both options are possible. That blindsight requires and improves with practice has been documented in simian (Humphrey 1974) and human subjects (e.g. Stoerig 2006), and is important in several ways. First, it shows that the prevalence of blindsight, higher in monkeys and varying widely in humans, depends not only on factors including extent and type of lesion, age at lesion, and the precise task to be performed, but also on whether subjects have had sufficient practice; monkeys, by virtue of the training required to inform them what to do, generally have much more practice. Second, by furthering the capacities of the blind field, training of blindsight may improve subjects' functional outcome, opening a route to rehabilitation. Third, the evidence for learning through practice shows that blindsight is not simply the sum of functions that remain when conscious vision is lost, but develops slowly and for a long time as long as it continues to be challenged (Humphrey 1974). The alternative option, recovery of conscious sight, was already suggested when repeated visual field perimetry in monkeys who participated in studies of blindsight revealed a shrinkage or filling-in of the blind field (Cowey 1967). More recently, Moore et al. (1996) interpreted the excellent localization performance of their infant-lesion hemianopic monkeys as indicative of conscious sight, because, unlike that of their adult-lesion brethren, it persisted even when no central and visible cue announced the presentation of a target. That the younger system's greater plasticity enables better recovery from occipital lesions was also found in a longitudinal study of veterans with fields of cortical blindness. Those who had suffered their lesions in their teens were much more likely to recover sight spontaneously than those injured later in life. Nevertheless, spontaneous recovery from cortical blindness can also occur in subjects who suffered their lesions later in life. As this opportunity is restricted to a period of up to six months after injury, during which recovery is attributed to the particular lesion's at least partially transient effects, it cannot account for the changes in the size and/or density of the field defect that occur long after this period.

Nevertheless, such changes continue to be documented in cases where the blind field's capacities are persistently challenged. Practice thus not only improves blindsight performance, it can also provoke pronounced reductions in the size and/or the density of the blind field of monkeys (Cowey 1967) and patients (Zihl and von Cramon 1985, Sahraie et al. 2006, Stoerig 2006). Although an early age at lesion is likely to promote them, such changes have also been found in older lesion subjects. They may thus have contributed to the marked reduction in 'no target' responses made by our monkey Rosie, who was 4 years at lesion, to stimuli presented to the hemianopic field; they may also have contributed to the improved performance a different adult lesion monkey eventually showed in the uncued localization task of Moore and colleagues (1996). They make it easy to confound poor sight and blindsight, a task not made simpler by the improvements in performance that can occur with and without any stimulus awareness.

Blindsight recruits the parts of the visual system that escape the effects of the V1 lesion. These may include V1 neurons that survive next to or even within the damaged region, but blindsight does not depend on these. Histology carried out on monkeys has only occasionally shown that lesions were less complete than intended; more often they were total or extended beyond V1. As far as can be judged from functional neuroimaging studies that repeatedly failed to reveal any activation within the lesion, the same is true for human patients. Instead of demonstrating a necessity for V1 neurons surviving in the damaged region, such studies have consistently revealed that visual information from the blind field can activate intact extrastriate visual cortical areas, implying that blindsight is not blind by virtue of relying exclusively on subcortical processes. Moreover, by also revealing that areas in the occipitotemporal processing stream may respond to colours and objects presented to the blind field, they have shown that in practised patients blindsight invokes occipitoparietal areas which are known to be important for visuomotor behaviour. It is noteworthy that stimulation of fields of recovered, albeit sometimes poor, sight yielded similar activation patterns regardless of whether the recovery occurred spontaneously or in response to practice. If a failure to reveal evidence for activation with functional imaging indicates an absence of possibly weak responses from within the lesion, extrastriate cortical activation is sufficient to mediate not only blindsight but also the conscious sight that can remain or recover in fields of cortical blindness (Kleiser et al. 2001, Schoenfeld et al. 2002).

What are the implications of blindsight research? Regarding the quest for the neuronal correlates of conscious sight, it seems that destruction of the primary visual cortex disables the mysterious transition from neurochemical and electrical events to visual *qualia not because the computations V1 normally performs are indispensable, but because this area gates the vast majority of retinal input to the higher visual cortical areas. In this scenario, blindsight is blind because the retinal input from the blind field that informs visually guided responses fails to activate these areas sufficiently effectively to enable even poor conscious sight. If blindsight training induces changes that increasingly engage these cortical areas, training-induced recovery of varying degrees of conscious sight would result once the extrastriate cortical activation reached a critical level and/or pattern. The pronounced extrastriate cortical activation observed in patients who recovered sight spontaneously (Schoenfeld et al. 2002) or, more painstakingly, in the course of extended practice (Kleiser et al. 2001) support this conjecture. Support of a different kind comes from the visual *hallucinations that patients with fields of absolute cortical blindness can experience in their blind fields. They may appear as vague moving shapes, geometric patterns, or scenes, and are attributed to strong endogenous activation of higher visual cortices. In addition to showing that blind but veridical and conscious but non-veridical sight are also dissociable, they indicate that extrastriate areas can retain the capacity to generate non-veridical conscious vision in the absence of V1. Recovery of veridical conscious sight in fields of cortical blindness should result when sufficient retinal input informs higher visual cortical areas.

Does blindsight imply that conscious vision is *epiphenomenal, because monkeys and patients with destruction of V1 can learn to initiate non-reflexive visually guided actions in the absence of a phenomenal representation (Churchland 1984)? Careful observation of blindsight-guided behaviour shows it to be distinct from that displayed by sighted individuals. It resembles the fast motor responses we know from sports, where balls are hit precisely although they move too fast to allow conscious perception, and often deteriorates when responses are pondered. While 'unseen' information is sufficient to initiate a variety of responses (manual, saccadic, verbal, navigational), it is insufficient for recognition and for considered, representational responses. Normal-sighted monkeys are clearly capable of such responses, but like human patients lose this capacity through destruction of primary visual cortex. In addition, animals and humans show closely similar visual functions in the affected fields. Both may respond effectively to stimuli they indicate non-verbally are invisible when given this option; both improve with practice; and both may eventually stop signalling 'no target' on every blind-field trial. Although only the patients can verbally report concomitant stimulus awareness or unawareness, the overwhelming similarities between human and simian blindsight and the way it differs from conscious sight at least to us appear very difficult to reconcile with views that deny conscious sight to normal monkeys.

See also HELEN, 'A BLIND MONKEY WHO SAW EVERYTHING'

PETRA STOERIG AND ALAN COWEY

Bullier, J., Girard, P., and Salin, P.-A. (1994). 'The role of area 1 in the transfer of information to extrastriate visual cortex'. In Peters, A. and Rockland, K. S. (eds) *Cerebral Cortex*, Vol. 10.

Campion, J., Latto, R., and Smith, Y. M. (1983). 'Is blindsight an effect of scattered light, spared cortex, and near-threshold vision?' *Behavioural and Brain Sciences*, 6.

Churchland, P. M. (1984). *Matter and Consciousness*.

Cowey, A. (1967). 'Perimetric study of field defects in monkeys after cortical and retinal ablations'. *Quarterly Journal of Experimental Psychology*, 19.

—— and Stoerig, P. (1995). 'Blindsight in monkeys'. *Nature*, 373.

Humphrey, N. K. (1974). 'Vision in a monkey without striate cortex: a case study'. *Perception*, 3.

Kleiser, R., Wittsack, J., Niedeggen, M., Goebel, R., and Stoerig, P. (2001). 'Is V1 necessary for conscious vision in areas of relative cortical blindness?' *Neuroimage*, 13.

Moore, T., Rodman, H. R., Repp, A. B., Gross, C. G., and Mezrich, R. S. (1996). 'Greater residual vision in monkeys after striate cortex damage in infancy'. *Journal of Neurohysiology*, 76.

Pasik, P. and Pasik, T. (1982). 'Visual function in monkeys after total removal of visual cerebral cortex'. *Contributions to Sensory Physiology*, 7.

Pöppel, E., Held, R., and Frost, D. (1973). 'Residual visual function after brain wounds involving the central visual pathways in man'. *Nature*, 243.

Sahraie, A., Trevethan, C. T., MacLeod, M. J., Murray, A. D., Olson, J. A., and Weiskrantz, L. (2006). 'Increased sensitivity after repeated stimulation of residual spatial channels in blindsight'. *Proceedings of the National Academy of Sciences of the USA*, 103.

Schoenfeld, M. A., Noesselt, T., Poggel, D. et al. (2002). 'Analysis of pathways mediating preserved vision after striate cortex lesions'. *Annals of Neurology*, 52.

Stoerig, P. (2006). 'Blindsight, conscious vision, and the role of primary visual cortex'. *Progress in Brain Research*, 155.

—— and Cowey, A. (1997). 'Blindsight in man and monkey'. *Brain*, 120.

——, Zontanou, A., and Cowey, A. (2002). 'Aware or unaware? Assessment of cortical blindness in four men and a monkey'. *Cerebral Cortex*, 12.

Weiskrantz, L. (1996). *Blindsight: a Case Study and its Implications*, 2nd edn

——, Warrington, E. K., Sanders, M. D., and Marshall, J. (1974). 'Visual capacity in the hemianopic field following a restricted occipital ablation'. *Brain*, 97.

Zihl, J. and von Cramon, D. (1985). 'Visual field recovery from scotoma in patients with postgeniculate damage. A review of 55 cases'. *Brain*, 108.

blind spot See FILLING-IN

blinking Humans blink spontaneously about 15 times per minute. Voluntary, spontaneous, and reflex blinks all have similar stereotyped kinematics, though voluntary blinks tend to be slightly greater in amplitude than spontaneous or reflex blinks. Blink duration ranges from 200 to 400 ms. The down-phase of a blink, when the eyelids close, typically lasts half as long as the up-phase, when the eyelids reopen, and the maximum velocity of the down-phase is twice as fast as that of the up-phase. During blinks the pupil is fully occluded by the eyelid for 100–140 ms.

Although blinks occur frequently in normal vision, they are rarely noticed, even though external darkening of the visual scene of similar durations is readily apparent. Continuity of conscious vision during blinks does not depend on continuous activity in early visual areas, as *single neurons in monkey early visual cortex show rapid and significant decreases in firing during a blink (Gawne and Martin 2002). These reductions in firing may even exceed the reduction caused by an equivalent external darkening. Interestingly, a significant minority of early visual cortex neurons show a strong transient response to the shutting off of visual input, whatever its cause. Some of these neurons respond differently depending on what caused the visual stimulus to disappear. Continuity of conscious vision during blinking may therefore rely on the suppression of these neuronal transients, which otherwise signal that the visual stimulus has disappeared.

Responses of the human visual system during blinks have been investigated using an ingenious device that bypasses the physical consequences of eyelid closure, by stimulating the retina via a fibre-optic cable placed in the mouth (Volkmann et al. 1980; see Fig. B4). This illuminates the retina via the palatine bone and allows retinal stimulation to be maintained during a blink, permitting measurement of visual sensitivity unconfounded by the purely mechanical effects of eyelid closure. In such circumstances, visual sensitivity is

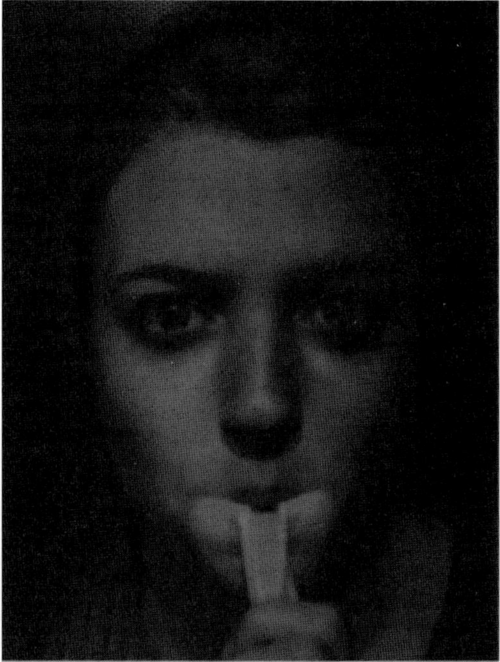

Fig. B4. Technique devised by Volkmann et al. (1980). Light is passed into the mouth via a fibre-optic cable and transilluminates the retina via the palatine bone (see Colour Plate 4).

nevertheless reduced about tenfold during a blink; and this reduction commences just before the descent of the eyelid (Volkmann 1986). This indicates an active suppression of visual sensitivity associated with the motor commands underpinning eyelid closure. The loss of visual sensitivity mainly affects the magnocellular visual pathway that carries information about changes in luminance and responds to low spatial frequency, high temporal frequency, low contrast, and achromatic stimuli (Ridder and Tomlinson 1993). This suggests that visual suppression that occurs during blinks has evolved to minimize our ability to detect the eyelid descending across the pupil, a low spatial frequency stimulus, and the reduction in visual input, a change of luminance, that occur during blinks. This loss of visual sensitivity is thought to be caused by a neural signal from the motor regions controlling blinking (an efferent copy or corollary discharge) produced in parallel with the motor commands that cause the blink, and sent to the visual system causing the reduction in sensitivity and allowing the blink to go unnoticed.

Consistent with these psychophysical studies, non-invasive *functional brain imaging using a very similar experimental apparatus to stimulate the retina shows that the response to visual stimulation in early visual cortex is reduced during blinking (Bristow et al. 2005a, 2005b). This reduction of activity is especially apparent in retinotopic area V3, which has a very strong magnocellular input. In contrast, enhanced signal can be measured in visual cortex when blinking occurs in darkness. This pattern of effects of blinking on activity in visual cortex is very similar to that seen during saccadic eye movements, with suppression of visually evoked activity and an enhanced signal in darkness (Sylvester et al. 2005). The activation in darkness may reflect a motor signal associated with blinking (and saccades), perhaps a form of 'corollary discharge' that accompanies the motor command.

In addition to finding effects of blinking on early visual cortex, areas of prefrontal and parietal cortex also show significant reductions in activity during blinking when visual stimulation was held constant. These changes in activity in higher cortical areas may simply reflect the reduced output of earlier visual areas feeding forward. However, activation of similar *frontal and parietal regions is also reliably associated with changes in the *contents of consciousness (see FUNCTIONAL BRAIN IMAGING). Thus, reduction in the activity of such areas during blinking may indicate suppression of structures required to consciously register changes in the content of consciousness, preventing awareness of loss of visual continuity during a blink.

DAVINA BRISTOW AND GERAINT REES

Bristow, D., Frith, C., and Rees, G. (2005a). 'Two distinct neural effects of blinking on human visual processing'. *Neuroimage*, 27.

Bristow, D., Haynes, J. D., Sylvester, R., Frith, C. D., and Rees, G. (2005b). 'Blinking suppresses the neural response to unchanging retinal stimulation'. *Current Biology*, 15.

Gawne, T. J. and Martin, J. M. (2002). 'Responses of primate visual cortical neurons to stimuli presented by flash, saccade, blink, and external darkening'. *Journal of Neurophysiology*, 88.

Ridder, W. H. and Tomlinson, A. (1993). 'Suppression of contrast sensitivity during eyelid blinks'. *Vision Research*, 33.

Sylvester, R., Haynes, J. D., and Rees, G. (2005). 'Saccades differentially modulate human LGN and VI responses in the presence and absence of visual stimulation'. *Current Biology*, 15.

Volkmann, F. C. (1986). 'Human visual suppression'. *Vision Research*, 26.

——, Riggs, L. A., and Moore, R. K. (1980). 'Eyeblinks and visual suppression'. *Science*, 207.

body image and body schema The terms *body image* and *body schema* are used in a variety of disciplines, including psychology, neurology and medicine, philosophy, and psychoanalysis, to explain how the body maintains spatial orientation, controls movement, and organizes somatosensory information and body awareness. The origins of these concepts can be traced to 19th-century neurology. Various neurologists postulated the existence of 'images' or 'schemas' stored in the sensorimotor cortex for the spatial awareness of the body and the control of movement. Henry Head (1920) proposed the concept of a body schema as a postural model that actively organizes sensory impressions to dynamically represent current body position with reference to previous position. These postural schemas are not conscious images but non-conscious functions, generated and controlled by cortical representations that register postural changes, in the service of motor control. The same neural activations, however, may generate a conscious sense of bodily position and movement.

Terminological and conceptual confusions soon developed around these concepts. Paul Schilder (1935), for example, claims to be in agreement with Head, yet equates body schema with the *conscious* sensation of position and uses the terms 'body image' and 'body schema' interchangeably. Confused usage of these terms continues, despite some justified criticisms and attempts at conceptual reform (e.g. Poeck and Orgass 1971). The fact that these terms continue to be used in various literatures, despite the confusion, suggests that they can be useful tools for understanding the dynamics of bodily movement and experience (De Preester and Knockaert 2005, Gallagher 2005; see Tiemersma 1989 for a good review of the literature).

From both behavioural and neurological perspectives, body image and body schema can be understood, respectively, as two different, albeit closely related, interactive and coordinated systems. As such, the *body image* is characterized as a system of inconstant perceptions, feelings, and beliefs where the object of such intentional states is one's own body. The *body schema*, in contrast, consists of a system of sensorimotor capacities designed for motor and postural control without awareness or the necessity of perceptual monitoring. Just as having a perception of one's body is different from having a capacity to move one's body, so a body image is different from a body schema. Most of the time the body schema functions when the intentional object of perception is something other than one's own body. For example, when I reach to open the door, I may consciously perceive the doorknob, or I may be attending to my reason for opening the door, or to the person I expect to see on the other side, but I am not attending to, and in most cases, I am not aware of my hand, the specific details of its grasp or my reach, or the posture that I take (Campbell 1995, O'Shaughnessy 1995).

Although perceptual consciousness of one's own movement (or someone else's movement) can be interrelated with one's actions, so that processes connected with body image may be interrelated with body-schematic processes, there is good empirical support for the conceptual distinction. In some cases of unilateral neglect, for example, body-schematic processes for the neglected side of the body may remain intact despite the disruption of the body image for the neglected side. In contrast, in cases of deafferentation, subjects who have lost tactile and proprioceptive input from the neck down are able to control their limb movements only by visual guidance (see PROPRIOCEPTION). They use their body image in a unique way to compensate for the loss of body-schematic function (Cole and Paillard 1995). Such dissociations provide empirical reasons for thinking that the conceptual distinction between body image and body schema points to a real difference.

The conceptual distinction is also useful for understanding recent findings in neuroscience, which themselves help to explain how body image and body schema interact on the behavioural level. Areas of the brain responsible for motor control are activated not only when we engage in intentional action (serving body-schematic functions) but also when we observe others act, or when we imagine ourselves acting (which involves the body image). On the behavioural level we may exploit our body image to learn new movements, or to correct movements when things go wrong, in which case the body image clearly informs or modifies the body schema.

There is a substantial amount of literature on pathologies that involve the body image. There is general agreement, for example, that *anorexia nervosa* involves distortions of the body image, although there continues to be some debate about whether the distortions are affective or perceptual in nature, or to what extent such distortions are connected with cultural and socially determined ideals of acceptable body shape. *Body dysmorphic disorder* (BDD) is defined as a disturbance of body image that involves an extreme dissatisfaction with the appearance of one's body. BDD can manifest in compulsive mirror checking, social withdrawal, excessive plastic surgeries, or even voluntary amputation.

Disorders that involve degrees of disembodied experience manifest themselves as an ambiguous presence of the body as object. The body may appear as something alien or as something to consciously control, although these feelings of alienation from the body do not advance to the point where the subject fails to acknowledge it as his or her own body. *Cotard's syndrome* involves a delusional belief about various states of one's body, e.g. that it is dead, rotting, or missing certain internal organs. Other disorders involve disruptions of the body image in which there is no sense of presence or ownership, as in the case of unilateral neglect mentioned above. In some neglect subjects there are complications from paralysis and they may also misidentify their arm or leg. Such patients famously complain that there is a strange leg in their bed, or that they cannot understand whose hand it is that is lying next to them (this is not to be confused with *anarchic hand syndrome; see below). In most cases of neglect, however, subjects pay no attention to the affected side of their body, and it seems not to belong to their embodied self-image. *Anosognosia often accompanies neglect and involves a lack of awareness of any problem with the body. The anosognosic patient will claim that he is indeed using the limb when in fact it is paralysed and he cannot move it (Berti et al. 2005). Autotopagnosia (somatotopagnosia) is another form of body-image related agnosia that involves the inability to name or point to various parts of one's body on command.

Body-schematic functions in motor control normally tend to be non-conscious or tacit, and the body-in-action tends to efface itself phenomenologically. In *schizophrenia, however, it is sometimes the case that the normally tacit aspects of automatic body-schematic processes become explicit (what Sass 1998 calls a 'hyperreflexive' awareness of one's body). In some cases, a disruption in processes of action preparation (corresponding to neurological problems in the generation of motor commands and efference copy) may disrupt the normal sense of agency for such action and motivate delusions of control, involving misattributions of agency to some other person. *Anarchic hand syndrome*, due to lesions in the supplementary motor area (SMA), involves a similar loss of the sense of agency, although the subject does not misattribute agency to someone else (Della Sala et al. 1994). Body-schematic motor control of the hand is neurologically disconnected from intentional control mechanisms, yet the hand makes complex purposive movements that are not intended by the subject. Environmental affordances likely elicit the hand's behaviour and the subject is unable to inhibit it.

SHAUN GALLAGHER

Berti, A., Bottini, G., Gandola, M. et al. (2005). 'Shared cortical anatomy for motor awareness and motor control'. *Science*, 309.

Campbell, J. (1995). 'The body image and self-consciousness'. In Bermúdez, J. L., Marcel, A., and Eilan, N. (eds) *The Body and the Self.*

Cole, J. and Paillard, J. (1995). 'Living without touch and peripheral information about body position and movement: studies with deafferented subjects'. In Bermúdez, J. L. et al. (eds) *The Body and the Self.*

Della Sala, S., Marchetti, C., and Spinnler, H. (1994). 'The anarchic hand: a fronto-mesial sign'. In Boller, F. and Grafman, J. (eds) *Handbook of Neuropsychology*, Vol. 9.

De Preester, H. and Knockaert, V. (eds) (2005). *Body Image and Body Schema: Interdisciplinary Perspectives on the Body.*

Gallagher, S. (2005). *How the Body Shapes the Mind.*

Head, H. (1920). *Studies in Neurology*, Vol. 2.

O'Shaughnessy, B. (1995). 'Proprioception and the body image'. In Bermúdez, J. L. et al. (eds) *The Body and the Self.*

Poeck, K. and Orgass, B. (1971). 'The concept of the body schema: a critical review and some experimental results'. *Cortex*, 7.

Sass, L. (1998). 'Schizophrenia, self-consciousness and the modern mind'. *Journal of Consciousness Studies*, 5.

Schilder, P. (1935). *The Image and Appearance of the Human Body.*

Tiemersma, D. (1989). *Body Schema and Body Image: an Interdisciplinary and Philosophical Study.*

brain Although several scientists and philosophers used to think otherwise a long time ago, consciousness is *in the brain*. The possibility to acquire information about the world from the senses, the capability to experience feelings, the complexities of language and motor output as well as many other facets of conscious experience can and should be attributed to activity in the brain (Crick 1994, Koch 2005). Therefore, an important focus of the scientific research efforts to elucidate a mechanistic explanation for consciousness is the search for the *neural *correlates of consciousness* (NCC). The simple observation that consciousness needs to be accounted for in terms of brain processes embodies the difficulties involved in explaining consciousness and at the same time points to the road towards an eventual possible solution. The mystery arises because the brain is a physical system; a complex physical system indeed, but a physical system nonetheless. Therefore, phenomena related to consciousness need to be ultimately linked to a material substrate to provide a scientific explanation. The laws of physics, chemistry, and biology, through molecules and neurons, need to produce *qualia and the mind.

In order to explain consciousness, scientists need to decipher the inner workings of the brain. In spite of major progress in neuroscience in recent years, the brain remains one of the most challenging and fascinating objects of scientific study. The human brain, for example, contains about 10^{11} neurons (Kandel et al. 2000). Brains of other species such as non-human primates, mice, and dogs show an approximately similar complexity. There are organisms with a much smaller nervous system that play a pivotal role in the development of neuroscience; one such example is the *C. elegans* worm where all neurons can be counted and identified. Unfortunately, the usefulness of such species for the study of consciousness remains highly unclear (see EVOLUTION OF CONSCIOUSNESS). Most neurons communicate with other neurons through connections called *synapses*. There are thousands of synapses per neuron. In contrast to modern computers where the circuit diagram is clearly known (by design), the sheer number of synapses in the primate brain makes the task of mapping the connectivity pattern a daunting one.

There are many different types of neurons in the brain (Koch 1999, Kandel et al. 2000). A basic distinction can be made between so-called *pyramidal neurons* and *interneurons*; these two classes of neurons can be distinguished based on their morphology, the type of neurotransmitters they release, their connectivity properties, and their firing patterns. The codes that neurons and networks of neurons use to represent information are still not fully understood (Kreiman 2004). Both the number of spikes and the pattern of spikes fired by each neuron seem to matter for conveying information. There are also network properties including synchronization and *gamma-band oscillations that can play important roles in information transmission across and within brain areas (Engel and Singer 2001, Bichot et al. 2005). Deciphering the signatures or codes that neuronal networks use to represent information in general may provide important insights into the study of consciousness. It is possible that specific firing patterns or network properties are particularly relevant for representing the contents of consciousness (Koch 2005).

The brain has two hemispheres and four main lobes: the occipital lobe, the parietal lobe, the *frontal lobe, and the temporal lobe. The two hemispheres communicate with each other at several points, the most prominent of which is the *corpus callosum*. In some patients with severe *epilepsy, neurosurgeons may need to conduct a resection of one or more of the connections across hemispheres. This procedure may lead to a failure of information transmission between the two hemispheres. These *commissurotomy (split-brain) patients can show remarkable properties and, under appropriate circumstances, they can be shown to function as if they had two independent brains (Sperry 1982).

Over the years, it has become clear that functions are specialized within different regions of the brain. Scientists have mapped the approximate locations for many different functions. For example, parts of the cerebral cortex may be specialized for processing auditory information; other parts are specialized in processing olfactory information. Yet other areas, such as the *hippocampus*, are necessary to transfer short-term memories into long-term *memories (Zola-Morgan and Squire 1993). Within the visual system, investigators have discovered that there are about twenty or more distinct areas that process different aspects of visual information and are segregated into two main *visual streams (Felleman and Van Essen 1991). Therefore, in the same way that distinct brain regions may be specialized to process information from different sensory modalities, different behaviours, or different cognitive processes, it is conceivable that different parts of the brain may play very distinct roles with respect to the representation of conscious information (Koch 2005).

Several different tools are used to study the brain (Kreiman 2004). These different tools span wide ranges of spatial and temporal resolutions. At the smaller spatial scales, scientist study, for example, the structure and function of specific ion channels at the angstrom resolution (10^{-10} of a metre). At the larger spatial scales, several studies make inferences about the function of the brain as a whole or use tools with very coarse special resolution such as the scalp *electroencephalogram (EEG) or *magnetic encephalography (MEG). At the faster temporal scales, electrophysiological measurements including EEG, MEG, and also neuronal spike recordings can analyse activity at the sub-millisecond level. At the other extreme other tools such as *functional magnetic resonance imaging (fMRI) provide information with a resolution of seconds. In other cases, scientists may be interested in the effects of learning or ageing across months or years.

What the appropriate spatial and temporal scale to study consciousness should be is not necessarily trivial. In terms of temporal scales, the subjective impression is that conscious percepts are continuous in time. Even though this notion has been challenged (Dennett 1991, Chalmers 1996, Koch 2005), it still seems that high temporal resolution will be important to study the neuronal dynamics that give rise to consciousness. A scale of seconds or minutes may be too slow for us to be able to comprehend how consciousness arises from the activity of networks of neurons. In terms of spatial scales, the more detailed mechanistic and quantitative description of brain phenomena are typically rooted at the level of single neurons or small networks of neurons. Coarser techniques that average the activity of multiple neuronal types and across large areas may fail to unveil some key aspects of how conscious percepts arise. The devil is in the detail. The difficulty arises from two methodological aspects: the technological challenge of studying large ensembles of neurons at the single-neuron level and the invasive nature of the single-neuron studies. The invasive nature of single-neuron electrophysiology generally makes it necessary to study animal models such as the *single-cell studies in monkeys. Under special circumstances, including the study of patients with intractable epilepsy and patients with Parkinson's disease, it has been possible to study *single-neuron activity in the human brain.

In addition to the many tools used to measure brain activity, another important piece of evidence relating to the function of a given brain area has been the study of lesions. In animal models, scientists can induce rather specific brain lesions in order to understand the function of specific circuits. In humans, these studies are limited to naturally occurring lesions (see BRAIN DAMAGE). The study of lesions has provided the first demonstrations of functional specialization in the brain, going back to the initial studies in Broca's language area (Broca 1861, Finger 2000). Other important insights into the nature of consciousness that came through the studies of lesions or other brain abnormalities include the research into *blindsight, neglect (see ANOSOGNOSIA), *schizophrenia, and epilepsy. In the future, it is likely that tools that rely on molecular biology may be used to induce reversible and high-resolution microlesions in specific circuits in animal models including primates. These high-resolution and reversible microlesion studies may eventually help provide a link between the correlative physiological measurements and the neuronal causes of consciousness.

Lesion studies provide support to assess whether specific brain areas may be necessary for consciousness. Questions about sufficiency are extremely hard to ask in the context of consciousness. For example, is the activation of neurons in inferior temporal cortex sufficient for the perception of complex visual objects? The closest one can get to answers to such questions comes from studies that use brain stimulation tools including *transcranial stimulation (TMS) and electrical neural stimulation. Several studies in animal models have shown that electrical microstimulation of relatively small clusters of neurons can bias or even induce specific percepts (Salzman et al. 1990, Romo et al. 1998, Brecht et al. 2004). Electrical stimulation in human epileptic patients also suggests that specific and transient sensory experiences can be elicited by direct stimulation of the brain (Penfield, 1937, Ojemann and Mateer 1979).

The brain is perhaps one of the body parts that have been subject to very strong evolutionary selective pressure. It is therefore not surprising to find important changes across species in brain function and structure. Still, there are also strong similarities between the brains of non-human primates and humans. For example, many visually selective brain areas in the macaque monkey brain have a corresponding homologue region in the human brain. A detailed study of the way in which the brain evolved over long periods of time and the important differences that distinguish humans from other species may yield important insights into the evolution of consciousness.

At any given time, many brain areas show intense activity, even in the absence of concomitant sensory input. Most neurons in the brain have a sustained level of spontaneous activity which can be modulated dependent on the time of day and other environmental circumstances. What this spontaneous activity represents (if anything at all) is still strongly debated. What is clear is that even under conditions with no sensory input, many brain areas can be strongly activated. Examples of such situations include *sleep and *anaesthesia. It can be argued that brain activity during non-dream sleep and anaesthesia is not correlated with conscious percepts. Thus, the study of brain activation during these states can provide interesting insights into the neuronal correlates of consciousness. In general, these studies (and many other such studies) show that humans are not aware of a large fraction of the activity in their brains.

Given that many brain processes may be uncorrelated with conscious perception, an important focus of research in the search for the neuronal correlates of consciousness has been the attempt to elucidate which brain areas correlate with subjective perception. The use of situations where perception is dissociated from sensory input allows us to distinguish between input-related activation and subjective activation. One important experimental paradigm that follows this idea is the study of *binocular rivalry where two different images are shown to the two eyes. Under these circumstances, perception alternates in a seemingly random fashion between the two images. At the level of the retina, activity should be essentially constant given that the sensory input is constant where the competition between the two images for conscious perception takes place in higher visual areas.

GABRIEL KREIMAN

Bichot, N. P., Rossi, A. F., and Desimone, R. (2005). 'Parallel and serial neural mechanisms for visual search in macaque area V4'. *Science*, 308.

Brecht, M., Schneider, M., Sakmann, B., and Margrie, T. (2004). 'Whisker movements evokes by stimulation of single pyramidal cells in rat motor cortex'. *Nature*, 427.

Broca, M. (1861). 'Remarques sur le siège de la faculté du langage articule, suivies d'une observation d'aphémie (perte de la parole)'. *Bulletin de la Société Anatomique*, 6.

Chalmers, D. (1996). *The Conscious Mind: in Search of a Fundamental Theory*.

Crick, F. (1994). *The Astonishing Hypothesis*.

Dennett, D. (1991). *Consciousness Explained*.

Engel, A. and Singer, W. (2001). 'Temporal binding and the neural correlates of sensory awareness'. *Trends in Cognitive Sciences*, 5.

Felleman, D. J. and Van Essen, D. C. (1991). 'Distributed hierarchical processing in the primate cerebral cortex'. *Cerebral Cortex*, 1.

Finger, S. (2000). *Minds Behind the Brain. A History of the Pioneers and Their Discoveries*.

Kandel, E., Schwartz, J., and Jessell, T. (2000). *Principles of Neural Science*, 4th edn.

Koch, C. (1999). *Biophysics of Computation*.

—— (2005). *The Quest for Consciousness*.

Kreiman, G. (2004). 'Neural coding: computational and biophysical perspectives'. *Physics of Life Reviews*, 1.

Ojemann, G. and Mateer, C. (1979). 'Human language cortex: localization of memory, syntax, and sequential motor-phoneme identification systems'. *Science*, 205.

Penfield, W. (1937). 'The cerebral cortex in man. I. The cerebral cortex and consciousness'. *Archives of Neurology and Psychiatry*, 40.

Romo, R., Hernandez, A., Zainos, A., and Salinas, E. (1998). 'Somatosensory discrimination based on cortical microstimulation'. *Nature*, 392.

Salzman, C., Britten, K., and Newsome, W. (1990). 'Cortical microstimulation influences perceptual judgements of motion direction'. *Nature*, 346.

Sperry, R. (1982). 'Some effects of disconnecting the cerebral hemispheres'. *Science*, 217.

Zola-Morgan, S. and Squire, L. R. (1993). 'Neuroanatomy of memory'. *Annual Review of Neuroscience*, 16.

brain damage Progress in intensive care efforts has increased the number of patients who survive severe acute brain damage. The most frequent causes of coma are traumatic or ischaemic brain damage. Although most of these patients recover from coma within the first days after the insult, some permanently lose all brain function (brain death), while others evolve to a state of 'wakeful unawareness' (vegetative state, VS). Those who recover, typically progress through different stages before fully or partially recovering consciousness

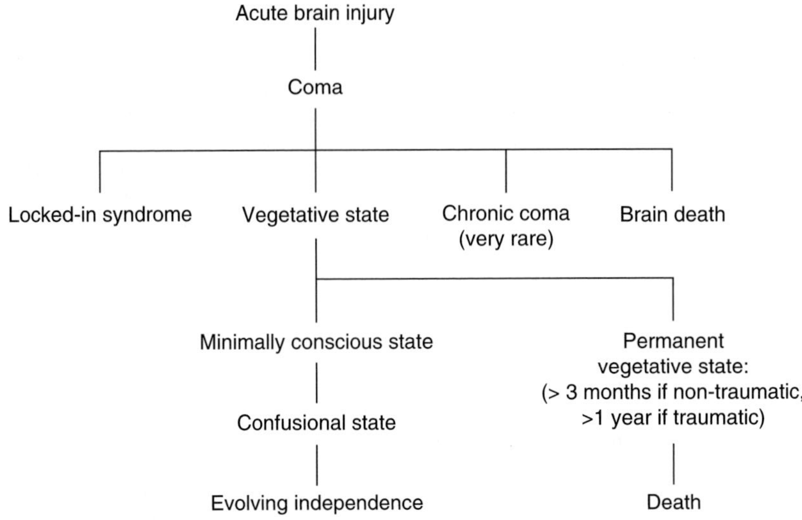

Fig. B5. Flowchart of the different conditions that follow a cerebral insult. Classically vegetative state follows a coma; after 1 month the term *persistent vegetative state* is used; after 3 months (non-traumatic insult) or 1 year (traumatic insult) some authors use the term *permanent vegetative state* which implies no chance of recovery.

(minimally conscious state, MCS; see Fig. B5). Bedside evaluation of residual brain function in severely brain-damaged patients is difficult because motor responses may be very limited or inconsistent. In addition, consciousness is not an all-or-none phenomenon and its clinical assessment relies on inferences made from observed responses to external stimuli at the time of the examination. We here review the major clinical entities of altered states of consciousness following severe acute brain damage.

1. Brain death
2. Coma
3. Vegetative state
4. Minimally conscious state
5. Locked-in syndrome

1. Brain death

The concept of brain death as defining the death of the individual is largely accepted. Most countries have published recommendations for the diagnosis of brain death, but the diagnostic criteria differ from country to country. Some rely on the death of the brainstem only, others require death of the whole brain including the brainstem. However, the clinical assessments for brain death are very uniform and based on the irreversible loss of all brainstem reflexes and the demonstration of continuing apnoea in a persistently comatose patient. Since the first definition of the neurological criteria of death in the mid 1960s, no patient in apnoeic coma properly declared brain (or brainstem) death has ever regained consciousness.

*Functional imaging using cerebral perfusion tracers and single-photon emission computed tomography (SPECT) or cerebral metabolism tracers and positron emission tomography (PET) typically show a 'hollow skull phenomenon' in brain death patients, confirming the absence of neuronal function in the whole brain.

Some authors have proposed that death be defined by the permanent cessation of the higher functions of the nervous system that demarcate humans from the lower primates. This *neocortical* or *higher brain death* definition has been mainly developed by philosophers and its conceptual basis rests on the premise that consciousness, cognition, and social interaction, not the bodily physiological integrity, are the essential characteristics of human life. On the basis of this definition, vegetative patients following an acute injury or chronic degenerative disease and anencephalic infants are considered dead. This neocortical definition of death has never convinced either medical associations or courts (for a recent review see Laureys 2005).

2. Coma

Coma is characterized by the absence of arousal and thus also of consciousness. It is a state of unarousable unresponsiveness in which the patient lies with the eyes closed and has no awareness of self and surroundings. The patient lacks the spontaneous periods of wakefulness and eye-opening induced by stimulation that can be observed in the VS. Coma can result from diffuse bihemispheric cortical (e.g. after cardiac arrest) or white matter damage secondary to diffuse neuronal or axonal injury (e.g. after deceleration traffic accidents), or from focal brainstem lesions that affect the pontomesencephalic tegmentum and/or paramedian thalami bilaterally (e.g. after stroke or haemorrhage). To be clearly distinguished from syncope, concussion, or other states of transient unconsciousness, coma must persist for at least one hour. In general, comatose patients who survive begin to awaken and recover gradually within 2–4 weeks. This recovery may go no further than VS or MCS, or these may be stages (brief or prolonged) on the way to more complete recovery of consciousness.

The prognosis of coma survivors following brain anoxia is worse than following trauma. Clinically, absent or stereotyped motor responses and absent pupillary reflexes often indicate bad outcome. Paraclinically, isoelectrical ('flat') or 'burst suppression' *electroencephalogram (EEG) and the bilateral absence of somatosensory evoked potentials (SEPs) in primary cortex (called N20 potential) are strong indicators of death or irreversible VS. In contrast, auditory oddball evoked potentials showing an intact *mismatch negativity* (MMN) effect predicts an outcome better than death or VS.

In patients with coma of traumatic or hypoxic origin, PET studies show that, on average, grey matter metabolism is 50–70% of normal values. Cerebral metabolism

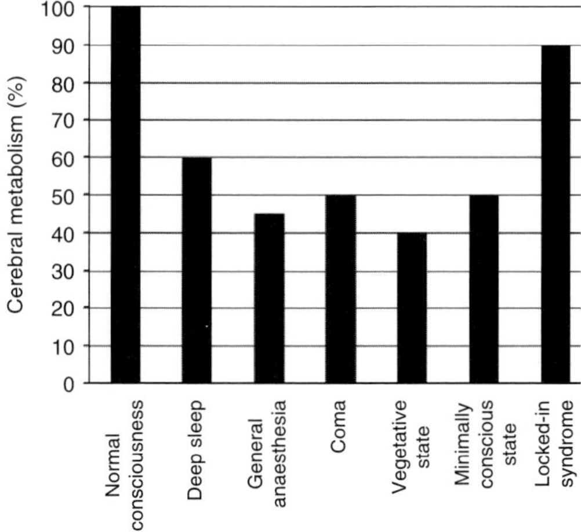

Fig. B6. Overall cortical metabolism in coma, VS, MCS, and LIS as compared to slow-wave sleep and anaesthesia.

has been shown to correlate poorly with the level of consciousness, as measured by the Glasgow Coma Scale, in mild to severely brain-damaged patients. A global depression of cerebral metabolism is not unique to coma. When different *anaesthetics are titrated to the point of unresponsiveness, the resulting reduction in brain metabolism is similar to that observed in comatose patients. Another example of transient metabolic depression can be observed during deep *sleep (stages III and IV). In this daily physiological condition, cortical cerebral metabolism can drop to nearly 40% of normal values (Fig. B6; Laureys et al. 2004).

3. Vegetative state

Patients in a VS are awake but are unaware of self or of the environment. Bryan Jennett and Fred Plum cited the *Oxford English Dictionary* to clarify their choice of the term 'vegetative': to vegetate is to 'live merely a physical life devoid of intellectual activity or social intercourse' and vegetative describes 'an organic body capable of growth and development but devoid of sensation and thought'. *Persistent VS* has been arbitrarily defined as a vegetative state still present one month after acute traumatic or non-traumatic brain damage, but does not imply irreversibility. *Permanent VS* denotes irreversibility. Current UK medical guidelines consider that 6 months following a non-traumatic brain damage and 12 months after traumatic injury, the condition of VS patients may be regarded as 'permanent' (Jennett 2005).

The terms *apallic syndrome* and *neocortical death* have previously been used to describe patients in a VS. However, as discussed below, functional imaging studies have shown that vegetative patients are not apallic—that is, they still may show preserved activation in islands of functional 'pallium' or cortex.

It has been shown that more than one out of three patients initially diagnosed as being in a VS in fact shows some signs of awareness when carefully examined. Although these studies on the misdiagnosis of the VS are distressing, they also show that more careful examinations by skilled clinicians can identify very subtle signs of awareness in severely brain-damaged patients who remain unable to communicate verbally or nonverbally. To reliably make the diagnosis of the vegetative or minimally conscious state, especially adapted standardized consciousness scales should be employed (reviewed in Majerus et al. 2006). The chances of recovery from VS are better in children than in adults; better after traumatic than non-traumatic brain injury; and worse as the time spent in VS passes. Neither clinical nor complementary tests such as EEG, event-related potentials (ERP), structural or functional imaging alone can reliably predict the individual patient's potential for recovery. At present, no treatment has been shown to increase the chances of recovery from VS (or MCS).

In the VS the brainstem is relatively spared, whereas the grey and/or white matter of both cerebral hemispheres are widely and severely damaged. Overall cortical metabolism of vegetative patients is 40–50% of normal values. Characteristic of VS patients is a relative sparing of metabolism in the brainstem (encompassing the pedunculopontine reticular formation, the hypothalamus, and the basal forebrain). The functional preservation of these structures allows for the preserved arousal and autonomic functions in these patients. The other hallmark of the vegetative state is a systematic impairment of metabolism in the polymodal associative cortices (bilateral prefrontal regions, Broca's area, parietotemporal and posterior parietal areas and precuneus; see also AROUSAL VS AWARENESS). These regions are known to be important in various functions that are closely related to consciousness, such as attention, memory, and language. It has long been controversial whether the observed metabolic impairment in this large frontoparietal cortical network reflects an irreversible structural neuronal loss, or functional and potentially reversible damage. However, in the rare cases where VS patients recover awareness of self and environment, PET shows a functional recovery of metabolism in these same cortical regions. Moreover, the resumption of long-range functional connectivity between these associative cortices and between some of these and the intralaminar thalamic nuclei parallels the restoration of their functional integrity. The cellular mechanisms which underlie this functional normalization remain putative: axonal sprouting, neurite outgrowth, and cell division (known to occur predominantly in associative cortices in normal primates) have been proposed as candidate processes. The challenge is now to identify the conditions in which, and the mechanisms by which, some vegetative patients may recover consciousness.

In addition to measuring resting brain function and connectivity, neuroimaging studies have identified which brain areas still 'activate' during external stimulation in vegetative patients. In cohort studies of patients unequivocally meeting the clinical diagnosis of VS, noxious somatosensory and auditory stimuli have shown robust activation of primary sensory cortices and lack of activation in higher-order associative cortices from which they were functionally disconnected. For example, high-intensity noxious electrical stimulation activated midbrain, contralateral thalamus, and primary somatosensory cortex in each and every one of the 15 VS patients studied, even in the absence of detectable cortical evoked potentials (Laureys et al. 2002). However, the rest of the 'pain matrix' (encompassing secondary somatosensory, insular, posterior parietal, and anterior cingulate cortices) failed to show activation. Moreover, the activated primary somatosensory cortex was shown to exist as an island, functionally disconnected from the higher-order associative cortices in VS. Similarly, auditory stimuli activated bilateral primary auditory cortices in VS patients, but hierarchically higher-order multimodal association cortices were not activated. Moreover, a cascade of functional disconnections was observed along the auditory cortical pathways, from primary auditory areas to multimodal and limbic areas (Laureys et al. 2000). These studies suggest that the observed residual cortical processing in the VS does not lead to integrative processes which are thought to be necessary for awareness.

4. Minimally conscious state

The clinical criteria for MCS, formally proposed only in 2002, subcategorize patients above VS but unable to communicate consistently. To be considered as *minimally conscious*, patients have to show limited but clearly discernible evidence of consciousness of self or environment, on a reproducible or sustained basis, by at least one of the following behaviours: (1) following simple commands; (2) gestural or verbal yes/no response (regardless of accuracy); (3) intelligible verbalization; and (4) purposeful behaviour (including movements or affective behaviour that occur in contingent relation to relevant environment stimuli and are not due to reflexive activity). The emergence of MCS is defined by the ability to use functional interactive communication or functional use of objects (Giacino et al. 2002). Further improvement is more likely than in VS patients. However, some patients remain permanently in MCS.

Akinetic mutism is an outdated term that is better avoided and is now considered to be a subcategory of MCS. The term was first introduced in 1941 to describe a condition characterized by severe poverty of movement, speech, and thought without associated arousal disorder or descending motor tract impairment. Typical for akinetic mutism is the complete or near-complete loss of spontaneity and initiation so that action, ideation, speech, and emotion are uniformly reduced. The absence of internally guided behaviour allows attention to be passively drawn to any environmental stimulus that the patient is exposed to. The preservation of spontaneous visual tracking and occasional, albeit infrequent, speech and movement to command, help differentiate akinetic mutism from VS.

Because criteria for the MCS have only recently been introduced, there are still few functional imaging studies of patients in this condition. Overall cerebral metabolism is

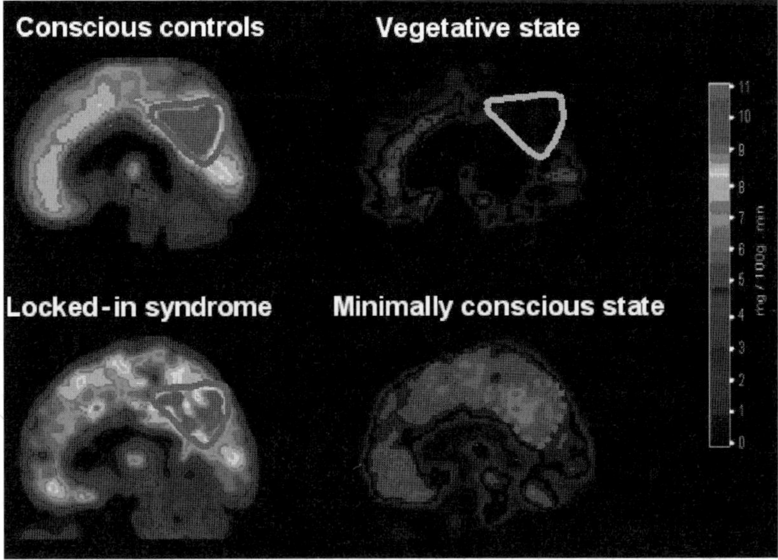

Fig. B7. In normal conscious waking, the medial posterior cortex (encompassing the precuneus and adjacent posterior cingulate cortex, delineated by a red line) is the metabolically most active region of the brain; in waking vegetative patients, this same area (delineated by a blue line) is the metabolically least active region. In the locked-in syndrome, no supratentorial brain region shows significant decreases in metabolism. In the minimally conscious state, the precuneus and posterior cingulate cortex shows an intermediate metabolism, higher than in vegetative patients, but lower than in conscious controls. We hypothesize that this region represents part of the neural network subserving (human) consciousness (see Colour Plate 5). Reproduced from Laureys et al. (2004).

decreased to values slightly higher but comparable to those observed in the VS. Metabolic activity in the medial parietal cortex (precuneus) and adjacent posterior cingulate cortex seems to best differentiate minimally conscious from vegetative patients. Interestingly, these areas are among the most active brain regions in conscious waking and are among the least active regions in *altered states of consciousness such as general *anaesthesia, *sleep, *hypnotic state, *dementia, and Wernicke–Korsakoff's or post-anoxic *amnesia. It has been suggested that this richly connected multimodal posteromedial associative area is part of the neural network subserving human awareness (Fig. B7).

Simple auditory stimulation has been shown to induce a more widespread activation in minimally conscious than in vegetative patients. In the former, activation encompassed not only primary but also higher-order associative areas, suggesting a more elaborate level of processing. Moreover, cortico-cortical functional connectivity is more efficient in the MCS, compared to the VS, between auditory cortex and the frontoparietal '*global neuronal workspace' considered critical in awareness. Such findings encourage ongoing developments of neuromodulatory and cognitive revalidation therapeutic strategies in MCS patients.

In response to natural language stimuli (e.g. meaningful sentences), fMRI activation patterns of MCS patients exhibiting command-following were examined by Schiff et al. (2005) during presentation of forward and backward narratives read in a familiar voice and containing personally meaningful content. Components of the cortical language networks showed selective activation compared to baseline conditions. Presentation of the narratives time-reversed (played backward), which shared most of the physical properties of the sounds, activated the same networks as forward narratives in the normal control subject, but failed to activate the networks in the MCS patients. These findings correlate with low resting metabolic activity and suggest that a residual capacity to activate large integrative networks may remain in some MCS patients. Preservation of large-scale networks in MCS patients may underlie rare instances of late recoveries of verbal fluency in such patients.

5. Locked-in syndrome

The term *locked-in syndrome* (LIS) was introduced by Fred Plum and Jerome Posner in 1966 to reflect the quadriplegia and anarthria brought about by the disruption of corticospinal and corticobulbar pathways respectively. It is defined by (1) the presence of sustained eye opening (bilateral ptosis should be ruled out as a complicating factor); (2) preserved awareness of the environment; (3) aphonia or hypophonia; (4) quadriplegia or quadriparesis; and (5) a primary mode of communication that uses vertical or lateral eye movement or blinking of the upper eyelid to signal yes/no responses (Plum and Posner 1983).

Classically, structural brain imaging (MRI) may show isolated lesions (bilateral infarction, haemorrhage, or tumour) of the ventral portion of the basis pontis or midbrain. According to some authors, electroencephalography (EEG) and evoked potentials do not reliably distinguish the LIS from the VS. PET scanning has shown significantly higher metabolic levels in the brains of patients in a LIS compared to patients in the VS. Voxel-based statistical analyses show that no supratentorial cortical areas show a significantly lower metabolism in LIS patients when compared to healthy controls. These findings emphasize the need for speed both in making the diagnosis and in recognizing the terrifying situation of patients with intact awareness of self and environment in acutely locked-in immobile bodies. Health-care workers should adapt their bedside behaviour and consider pharmacological anxiolytic therapy, taking into account the intense emotional state acute LIS patients go through. With appropriate medical care, life expectancy may be several decades and even if the chances of motor recovery are very limited, computer-based communication methods have drastically improved the quality of life of chronic LIS patients (Laureys et al. 2005).

STEVEN LAUREYS AND MÉLANIE BOLY

Giacino, J. T., Ashwal, S., Childs, N. et al. (2002). 'The minimally conscious state: definition and diagnostic criteria'. *Neurology*, 58.

Jennett, B. (2005). '30 years of the vegetative state: clinical, ethical and legal problems'. In Laureys, S. (ed.) *The Boundaries of Consciousness: Neurobiology and Neuropathology*.

Laureys, S. (2005). 'Science and society: death, unconsciousness and the brain'. *Nature Reviews Neuroscience*, 6.

Laureys, S. and Boly, M. (2008). 'The changing spectrum of coma'. *Nature Clinical Practice Neurology*, 4.

——, Degueldre, C. et al. (2000). 'Auditory processing in the vegetative state'. *Brain*, 123.

——, ——, Peigneux, P. et al. (2002). 'Cortical processing of noxious somatosensory stimuli in the persistent vegetative state'. *Neuroimage*, 17.

——, Owen, A. M., and Schiff, N. D. (2004). 'Brain function in coma, vegetative state, and related disorders'. *Lancet Neurology*, 3

——, Pellas, F., Van Eeckhout, E. et al. (2005).'The locked-in syndrome: what is it like to be conscious but paralyzed and voiceless?' *Progress in Brain Research*, 150.

Majerus, S., Gill-Thwaites, H., Andrews, K., and Laureys, S. (2006). 'Behavioral evaluation of consciousness in severe brain damage'. In Laureys, S. (ed.) *The Boundaries of Consciousness: Neurobiology and Neuropathology*.

Owen, A. M., Coleman, M. R., Boly, M., Davis, M. H., Laureys, S., and Pickard, J. D. (2006). 'Detecting awareness in the vegetative state'. *Science*, 313.

Plum, F. and Posner, J. B. (1983). *The Diagnosis of Stupor and Coma*, 3rd edn.

Schiff, N. D., Rodriguez-Moreno, D., Kamal, A. et al. (2005). 'fMRI reveals large-scale network activation in minimally conscious patients'. *Neurology*, 64.

brain death See BRAIN DAMAGE

capacity limits and consciousness Capacity limits refer to limits in how much information an individual can process at one time.

1. A brief history
2. Objective and subjective sources of evidence of capacity limits and consciousness
3. Capacity limits, type 1: information processing, attention, and consciousness
4. Capacity limits, type 2: working memory, primary memory, and consciousness
5. Reconciling limits in attention, primary memory, and consciousness

1. A brief history

Early in the history of experimental psychology, it was suggested that capacity limits are related to the limits of conscious awareness. For example, James (1890) described limits in how much information can be attended at once, in a chapter on *attention; and he described limits in how much information can be held in mind at once, in a chapter on *memory. In the latter chapter, he distinguished between *primary memory*, the trailing edge of the conscious present comprising the small amount of information recently experienced and still held in mind; and *secondary memory*, the vast amount of information that one can recollect from previous experiences, most of which is not in conscious awareness at any one time. Experimental work supporting these concepts was already available to James from contemporary researchers, including Wilhelm Wundt, who founded the first experimental psychology laboratory. In modern terms, primary and secondary memory are similar to **working memory* and *long-term memory* although, according to most investigators, working memory is a collection of abilities used to maintain information for ongoing tasks and only part of it is associated with consciousness.

In the late 1950s and early 1960s, the concepts of capacity limits began to receive further clarification with the birth of the discipline known as *cognitive psychology*. Broadbent (1958) in a seminal book described some work from investigators of the period indicating tight limits on attention. For example, individuals who received different spoken messages in both ears at the same time were unable to listen fully to more than one of these messages at a particular moment. Miller (1956) described work indicating limits on how long a list has to be before people can no longer repeat it back. This occurs in adults for lists longer than 5–9 items, with the manageable list length within that range depending on the materials and the individuals involved. One of the most important questions we must address is how attention and primary memory limits are related to one another. Are they different and, if so, which one indicates how much information is in conscious awareness? This will be discussed.

2. Objective and subjective sources of evidence of capacity limits and consciousness

Philosophers worry about a distinction between *objective* sources of information used to study capacity limits, and *subjective* sources of information used to understand consciousness. For objective information, one gives directions to research participants and then collects and analyses their responses to particular types of stimuli, made according to those directions. The only kind of subjective information is one's own experience of what it is like to be conscious (aware) of various things or ideas. People usually agree that it is not possible to be conscious of a large number of things at once, so it makes sense to hypothesize that the limits on consciousness and the limits on information processing have the same causes. However, logically speaking, this need not be the case.

Certain experimental methods serve as our bridge between subjective and objective sources of information. If an experimental participant claims to be conscious of something, we generally give credit for the individual being conscious of it. Often, we verify this by having the participant describe the information. For example, it is not considered good methodology to ask an individual, 'Did you hear that tone?' One could believe one is aware of a tone without really hearing the intended tone. It is considered better methodology to ask, 'Do you think a tone was presented?' On some trials, no tone is presented and one can compare the proportion of 'yes' responses on tone-present and tone-absent trials. Nevertheless, an individual could be conscious of some information but could still say 'no', depending on how incomplete information is interpreted.

3. Capacity limits, type 1: information processing, attention, and consciousness

There seem to be solid demonstrations that individuals can process some information outside the focus of attention and, presumably, outside conscious awareness. One demonstration is found, for example, in early work on selective listening (Broadbent 1958). Only one message could be comprehended at once but a change in the speaker's voice within the unattended message (say, from a male to a female speaker) automatically recruited attention away from the attended message and to the formerly unattended one. The evidence was obtained by requiring that the attended message be repeated. In that type of task, breaks in repetition typically are found to occur right after the voice changes in the unattended message, and participants in that situation often note the change or react to it and can remember it.

There has been less agreement about whether higher-level semantic information can be processed outside attention. Moray (1959) found that people sometimes noticed their own name when it was included in the unattended message, implying that the name had to have been identified before it was attended. However, one important question is whether the individuals who noticed actually were focusing their attention steadily on the message that they were supposed to repeat. When Conway et al. (2001) examined this for individuals in the highest and the lowest quartiles of ability on a working memory span task (termed high- and low-span, respectively), they found that only 20% of the high-span individuals noticed their names, whereas 65% of the low-span individuals noticed their names. This outcome suggests that the low-span individuals may have noticed their names only because their attention often wandered away from the assigned message, or was not as strongly focused on it as in the case of high-span individuals, making attention available for the supposedly unattended message. This tends to negate the idea that one's name can be automatically processed without attention, in which case high-span individuals would be expected to notice their names more often than low-span individuals.

There are some clear cases of processing without consciousness. In *blindsight, a particular effect of one kind of brain damage, an individual claims to be unable to see one portion of the visual field but still accurately points to the location of an object in that field, if required to do so (even though such patients often find the request illogical). Processing without consciousness of the processed object seems to occur.

In normal individuals, one can find *priming effects in which one stimulus influences the interpretation of another one, without awareness of the primed stimulus. This occurs, for example, if a priming word is presented with a very short interval before a masking pattern is presented, and is followed by a target word that the participant must identify, such as the word 'dog'. This target word can be identified more quickly if the preceding priming word is semantically related (e.g. 'cat') than if it is unrelated (e.g. 'brick'), even on trials in which the participant denies having seen the priming word at all and later shows no memory of it.

The question arises as to how much can be processed not only without conscious awareness, but also without attention. In the above cases, participants attended to the location of the stimulus in question, even when they remained unaware of the stimulus itself. As in the early work using selective listening procedures, work on vision by Ann Treisman and others has suggested that individuals can process simple physical features automatically, whereas attention is needed to process combinations of those features. This has been investigated by presenting arrays in which participants had to find a specific target item (e.g. a red square) among other, distracting items with a common feature distinguishing them from the target (e.g. all red circles, or all green squares) or among distracting items that shared multiple features with the target (e.g. some red circles and some green squares on the same trial). In the former case (a common distinguishing feature), searching for the target is rapid no matter how many distracting objects are included in the array. This suggests that participants can abstract physical features from many objects at once, and that an item with a unique feature automatically stands out (e.g. the only square or the only red item in the array). However, when the target can be distinguished from the distracting objects only by the particular conjunction of features (e.g. the only red square), searching for the target occurs slowly and depends on how many distracting objects are present. Thus, it takes focused attention, and presumably conscious awareness, to find an object with a particular conjunction of features. This attention must be applied relatively slowly, to just one object or a small number of objects at a time. Further research along these lines (Chong and Treisman 2005) suggests that it is possible for the brain automatically to compute statistical averages of features, such as the mean size of a circle in an array of circles of various sizes.

An especially interesting procedure that illustrates a limit on attention and awareness is *change blindness. If one views a scene and it cuts to another scene, something in the scene can change and, often, people will not notice the change. For example, in a scene of a table setting, square napkins might be replaced with triangular napkins without people noticing. This appears to occur because only a small number of objects can be attended at once and unattended objects are processed to a level that allows the entire scene to be perceived and comprehended in some holistic sense, but not to a level that allows individual details of most objects to be registered in memory.

4. Capacity limits, type 2: working memory, primary memory, and consciousness

The previous discussion implies that attention is closely related to conscious awareness (although for differences between the two see ATTENTION AND AWAREDNESS). Next, consider the other main faculty of the mind that may be linked to consciousness, namely primary memory. Here, the case may not be as straightforward as one would think. Miller (1956) showed that people can repeat lists of about seven items, but are they conscious of all seven at once? Not necessarily. Miller also showed that people can improve performance by grouping items together to form larger units called *chunks*. For example, it may be much more difficult to remember a list of nine random letters than it is to remember the nine letters *IRS–FBI–CIA*, because one may recognize acronyms for three prominent United States agencies in the latter case and therefore may have to keep in mind only three chunks. Once the grouping has occurred, however, it is not clear if one is simultaneously aware of all of the original elements in the set, in this example including *I, R, S, F, B, C,* and *A*. Miller did not specifically consider that the seven random items that a person might remember could be memorable only because new, multi-item chunks are formed on the spot. For example, if one remembers the telephone number *548-8634*, one might have accomplished that by quickly memorizing the digit groups *548*, *86*, and *34*. After that there might be simultaneous awareness of the three chunks of information, but not necessarily of the individual digits within each chunk.

People have a large number of strategies and resources at their disposal to remember word lists and other stimuli, and these strategies and resources together make up working memory. For example, they may recite the words silently to themselves, and this covert rehearsal process may take attention only for its initiation (Baddeley 1986). Rehearsal might have to be prevented before one can fairly measure the conscious part of working memory capacity (i.e. the primary memory of William James). The chunking process also may have to be controlled so that one knows how many items or chunks are being held. A large number of studies appearing to meet those requirements seem to suggest that most adults can retain 3–5 items at once (Cowan 2005). This is the limit, for example, in a type of method in which an array of coloured squares is briefly presented, followed after a short delay by a second array identical to the first or differing in the colour of one square, to be compared to the first array (Luck and Vogel 1997). A similar limit of 3–5 items occurs for verbal lists when one prevents effective rehearsal and grouping by presenting items rapidly with an unpredictable ending point of the list, or when one requires that a single word or syllable be repeated over and over during presentation of the list in order to suppress rehearsal.

What is essential in such procedures is that the research participant has insufficient time to group items together to form larger, multi-item chunks (Cowan 2001). Another successful technique is to test free recall of lists of multi-item chunks that have a known size because they were taught in a training session before the recall task. Chen and Cowan (2005) did that with learned pairs and singletons, and obtained similar results (3–5 chunks recalled).

A limit in primary memory of 3–5 items seems to be analogous to the limits in attention and conscious awareness. The latter are assumed to be general in that attention to, and conscious awareness of, stimuli in one domain detracts from attention and awareness in another domain. For example, listening intently to music would not be a good idea while one is working as an air traffic controller because attention would sometimes be withdrawn from details of the air traffic display to listen to parts of the music. Similarly, in the case of primary memory, Morey and Cowan (2004) found that reciting a random seven-digit list detracted from carrying out the two-array comparison procedure of Luck and Vogel that has just been described, whereas reciting a known seven-digit number (the participant's telephone number) had little effect.

It is not clear where the 3–5-chunk working memory capacity limit comes from, or how it may help the human species to survive. Cowan (2001, 2005) summarized various authors' speculations on these matters. The capacity limit may occur because each object or chunk in working memory is represented by the concurrent firing of neurons signalling various features of that object. Neural circuits for all objects represented in working memory must be activated in turn within a limited period and, if too many objects are included, there may be contamination between the different circuits representing two or more objects. Capacity limits may be beneficial in highlighting the most important information to guide actions in the right direction; representation of too much at once might result in actions that were based on confusions or were dangerously slow in emergency situations. Some mathematical analyses suggest that forming chunks of 3–5 items allows optimal searching for the items. To acquire complex tasks and skills, chunking can be applied in a reiterative fashion to encompass, in principle, any amount of information.

5. Reconciling limits in attention, primary memory, and consciousness

A major question that remains is how to reconcile the different capacity limits of attention vs primary memory. People generally can attend to only one message at a time, whereas they can keep several items at once in primary memory. Can these somehow represent compatible limits on conscious awareness? Perhaps so. There are several possible resolutions of the findings with attention vs primary memory. It might be that only a single message can be attended and understood because several ideas in the message must be held in primary memory at once, long enough for them to be integrated into a coherent message. Alternatively, the several (3–5) ideas that can be held in primary memory at once may have to be sufficiently uniform in type to be integrated into a coherent scene, in effect becoming like one message. According to this account, one would have difficulty remembering, say, one tone, one colour, one letter, and one shape at the same time because an integration of these events may not be easy to form. The more severe limit for paying attention, compared to the primary memory limit, might also occur because the items to be attended are fleeting, whereas items to be held in working memory theoretically might be entered into attention one at a time, or at least at a limited rate, and must be made available long enough for that to happen (Cowan 2005).

We at least know that individuals who can hold more items in primary memory seem to be many of the same individuals who are capable of carrying out difficult attention tasks. Two such tasks are (1) to go against what comes naturally by looking in the direction opposite to where an object has suddenly appeared, called *anti-saccade eye movements* (Kane et al. 2004); and (2) efficiently to filter out irrelevant objects so that only the relevant ones have to be retained in working memory (e.g. Conway et al. 2001). However, one study suggests that the capacity of primary memory and the ability to control attention are less than perfectly correlated across individuals (Cowan et al. 2006), and that both of these traits independently contribute to intelligence. It may be that the focus of attention and conscious awareness need to be flexible, expanding to apprehend a field of objects or contracting to focus intensively on a difficult task such as making an anti-saccade movement. If so, attention and primary memory tasks should interfere with one another to some extent, and this seems to be the case (Bunting et al. in press). There may also be additional skills that help primary memory but not attention, or vice versa. The present field of study of memory and attention and their relation to conscious awareness is exciting, but there is much left to learn.

See also AUTOMATICITY; GLOBAL WORKSPACE THEORY

Acknowledgement

This chapter was prepared with funding from NIH grant number R01-HD 21338.

NELSON COWAN

Baddeley, A. D. (1986). *Working memory.*

Broadbent, D. E. (1958). *Perception and communication.*

Bunting, M. F., Cowan, N., and Colflesh, G. H. (2008). 'The deployment of attention in short-term memory tasks: tradeoffs between immediate and delayed deployment'. *Memory and Cognition*, 36.

Chen, Z. and Cowan, N. (2005). 'Chunk limits and length limits in immediate recall: a reconciliation'. *Journal of Experimental Psychology: Learning, Memory, and Cognition*, 31.

Chong, S.C. and Treisman, A. (2005). Statistical processing: computing the average size in perceptual groups'. *Vision Research*, 45.

Conway, A. R. A., Cowan, N., and Bunting, M. F. (2001). 'The cocktail party phenomenon revisited: the importance of working memory capacity'. *Psychonomic Bulletin and Review*, 8.

Cowan, N. (2001). 'The magical number 4 in short-term memory: a reconsideration of mental storage capacity'. *Behavioral and Brain Sciences*, 24.

—— (2005). *Working Memory Capacity.*

——, Fristoe, N. M., Elliott, E. M., Brunner, R. P., and Saults, J. S. (2006). 'Scope of attention, control of attention, and intelligence in children and adults'. *Memory and Cognition*, 34.

James, W. (1890). *The Principles of Psychology.*

Kane, M. J., Hambrick, D. Z., Tuholski, S. W., Wilhelm, O., Payne, T. W., and Engle, R. W. (2004). 'The generality of working-memory capacity: a latent variable approach to verbal and visuospatial memory span and reasoning'. *Journal of Experimental Psychology: General*, 133.

Luck, S. J. and Vogel, E. K. (1997). 'The capacity of visual working memory for features and conjunctions'. *Nature*, 390.

Miller, G. A. (1956). 'The magical number seven, plus or minus two: some limits on our capacity for processing information'. *Psychological Review*, 63.

Moray, N. (1959). 'Attention in dichotic listening: affective cues and the influence of instructions'. *Quarterly Journal of Experimental Psychology*, 11.

Morey, C. C. and Cowan, N. (2004). 'When visual and verbal memories compete: evidence of cross-domain limits in working memory'. *Psychonomic Bulletin and Review*, 11.

Cartesian dualism See DUALISM

cerebellum See BRAIN

change blindness Change blindness, a term coined by Ronald Rensink and colleagues (Rensink et al. 1997), refers to the striking difficulty people have in noticing large changes to scenes or objects. When a change is obscured by some disruption, observers tend not to detect it, even when the change is large and easily seen once the observer has found it. Many types of disruption can induce change blindness, including briefly flashed blank screens (e.g. Rensink et al. 1997), visual noise or 'mudsplashes' flashed across a scene (O'Regan et al. 1999, Rensink et al. 2000), eye movements (e.g. Grimes 1996), eye blinks (O'Regan et al. 2000), motion picture cuts or pans (e.g. Levin and Simons 1997), and real-world occlusion events (e.g. Simons and Levin 1998). It can also occur in the absence of a disruption, provided that the change occurs gradually enough that it does not attract attention (Simons et al. 2000).

Change blindness is interesting because the missed changes are surprisingly large: a failure to notice one of ten thousand people in a stadium losing his hat would be unsurprising, but the failure to notice that a stranger you were talking to was replaced by another is startling. People incorrectly assume that large changes automatically draw attention, whereas evidence for change blindness suggests that they do not. This mistaken intuition, known as *change blindness blindness*, is evidenced by the finding that people consistently overestimate their ability to detect change (Levin et al. 2000).

The phenomenon of change blindness has challenged traditional assumptions about the stability and robustness of internal representations of visual scenes. People can encode and retain huge numbers of scenes and recognize them much later (Shepard 1967), suggesting the possibility that people form extensive representations of the details of scenes. Change blindness appears to contradict this conclusion—we fail to notice large changes between two versions of a scene if the change signal is obscured or eliminated. The phenomenon has led some to question whether internal representations are even necessary to explain our conscious experience of our visual world (e.g. Noë 2005).

Change blindness has received increasing attention over the past decades, in part as a result of the advent of readily accessible image editing software. Limits on our ability to detect changes have been investigated using simple stimuli since the 1950s; most early studies documented the inability to detect changes to letters and words when the changes occurred during an eye movement. More recent change blindness research built on these paradigms, but extended them to more complex and naturalistic stimuli. In a striking demonstration, participants studied photographs of natural scenes and then performed a memory test (Grimes 1996). While they viewed the images, some details of the photographs were changed, and if the changes occurred during eye movements, people failed to notice them. Even large changes, such as two people exchanging their heads, went unseen. This demonstration, coupled with philosophical explorations of the tenuous link between visual representations and visual awareness, sparked a resurgence of interest in change detection failures as well as paradigms to study change blindness.

The *flicker task* is perhaps the best-known change blindness paradigm (Rensink et al. 1997). In this task, an original image and a modified image alternate rapidly with a blank screen between them until observers detect the change. The inserted blank screen makes this task difficult by hiding the change signal. Most changes are found eventually, but they are rarely detected during the first cycle of alternation, and some changes are not detected even after one minute of alternation. Unlike earlier studies of change blindness, the flicker task allows people to experience the extent of their change blindness. That is, people can experience a prolonged inability to detect changes, but once they find the change, the change seems trivial to detect. The method also allows a rigorous exploration of the factors that contribute to change detection and change blindness in both simple and complex displays.

Change blindness also occurs for other tasks and with more complex displays, even including real-world interactions (see Rensink 2002 for a review). For example, in one experiment an experimenter approached a pedestrian (the participant) to ask for directions, and during the conversation, two other people interrupted them by carrying a door between them. Half of the participants failed to notice when the original experimenter was replaced by a different person during the interruption (Simons and Levin 1998). Change blindness has also been studied using simple arrays of objects, complex photographs, and motion pictures. It occurs when changes are introduced during an eye movement, a flashed blank screen, an eye blink, a motion picture cut, or a real-world interruption.

Despite the generalizability of change blindness from simple laboratory tasks to real-world contexts, it does not represent our normal visual experience. In fact, people generally do detect changes when they can see the change occur. Changes typically produce a detectable signal that draws attention. In demonstrations of change blindness, this signal is hidden or eliminated by some form of interruption or distraction. In essence, the interruption 'breaks' the system by eliminating the mechanism typically used to detect changes. In so doing, change blindness provides a tool to better understand how the visual system operates. Just as visual *illusions allow researchers to study the default assumptions of our visual system, change blindness allows us to better understand the contributions of attention and memory to conscious perception.

In the absence of a change signal, successful change detection requires observers to encode, retain, and then compare information about potential change targets across views. Successful change detection requires having both a representation of the pre-change object and a successful comparison of it to the post-change object. If any step in the process fails—encoding, representation, recall, or comparison—change detection fails. Evidence for change blindness suggests that at least some steps in this are not automatic—when the change signal is eliminated, people do not consistently detect changes. A central question in the literature is which part or parts of this process fail when change blindness occurs.

Change blindness has often been taken as evidence for the sparseness or absence of internal representations. If we lacked internal representations of previously viewed scenes, there would be no way to compare the current view to the pre-change scene, so changes would go unnoticed due to a representation failure. However, it is crucial to note that change blindness does not logically require the absence of representations. Change blindness could occur even if the pre-change scene were represented with photographic precision, provided that observers failed to compare the relevant aspects of the scene before and after the change. In fact, even when observers represent both the initial and changed version of a scene, they sometimes fail to detect changes (Mitroff et al. 2004).

The completeness of our visual representations in the face of evidence for change blindness remains an area of extensive investigation. Some researchers use evidence of change blindness to support the claim that our visual experience does not need to rely on complete or detailed representations. In essence, our visual representations can be sparse, provided that we have just-in-time access to the details we need to support conscious experience of our visual world. Others argue that our representations are, in fact, fairly detailed. Such detailed representations might underlie our long-term memory for scenes, but change blindness occurs either due to a disconnection between these representations and the mechanisms of change detection, or because of a failure to compare the relevant aspects of the pre- and post-change scenes. The differences in these explanations for change blindness have implications both for the mechanisms of visual perception and representation and for the link between representations and consciousness (see Simons 2000, Simons and Rensink 2005 for detailed discussion of these and other possible explanations for change blindness).

In addition to spurring research on visual representations and their links to awareness, change blindness has also yielded interesting insights into the relationship between *attention and awareness. In the presence of a visual disruption, the change signal no longer attracts attention and change blindness ensues. Even when observers know that a change is occurring, they cannot easily find it and have to shift attention from one scene region to another looking for change. Once they attend to the change, it becomes easy to detect. This finding, coupled with evidence that changes to attended objects (e.g. the 'centre of interest' of the scene) are more easily detected, led to the conclusion that attention is necessary for successful change detection. However, attention to an object does not always eliminate change blindness. Observers may fail to detect changes to the central object in a scene. Thus, attention to the changing object may not be sufficient for detection.

In the past several years, the phenomenon of change blindness also has attracted the attention of neuroscientists who have used *functional brain imaging techniques to investigate the neural underpinnings of change blindness and change detection. Most of these studies suggest a role for both *frontal and parietal (particularly right parietal) cortex in change detection (e.g. Beck et al. 2006). Other imaging studies have examined the role of focused attention in change detection as well as the correlation between conscious change perception and neural activation. Such neuroimaging measures hold promise as a way to explore the mechanisms of change detection by providing additional measures of change detection even in the absence of a behavioural response or a conscious report of change. In that way, they might help determine the extent to which visual representation and change detection occur in the absence of awareness.

In summary, change blindness has become increasingly central to the field of visual cognition, and through its study we can improve our understanding of visual representation, attention, scene perception, and the neural correlates of consciousness.

XIAOANG IRENE WAN, MICHAEL S. AMBINDER, AND DANIEL J. SIMONS

Beck, D. M., Muggleton, N., Walsh, V., and Lavie, N. (2006). 'Right parietal cortex plays a critical role in change blindness'. *Cerebral Cortex*, 16.

Grimes, J. (1996). 'On the failure to detect changes in scenes across saccades'. In Akins, K. (ed.) *Vancouver Studies in Cognitive Science: Vol. 5. Perception*.

Levin, D. T. and Simons, D. J. (1997). 'Failure to detect changes to attended objects in motion pictures'. *Psychonomic Bulletin and Review*, 4.

——, Momen, N., Drivdahl, S. B., and Simons, D. J. (2000). 'Change blindness blindness: the metacognitive error of overestimating change-detection ability'. *Visual Cognition*, 7.

Mitroff, S. R., Simons, D. J., and Levin, D. T. (2004). 'Nothing compares 2 views: change blindness results from failures to compare retained information'. *Perception and Psychophysics*, 66.

Noë, A. (2005). 'What does change blindness teach us about consciousness?' *Trends in Cognitive Sciences*, 9.

O'Regan, J. K., Rensink, R. A., and Clark, J. J. (1999). 'Change-blindness as a result of "mudsplashes"'. *Nature*, 398.
——, Deubel, H., Clark, J. J., and Rensink, R. A. (2000). 'Picture changes during blinks: looking without seeing and seeing without looking'. *Visual Cognition*, 7.
Rensink, R. A. (2002). 'Change detection'. *Annual Review of Psychology*, 53.
——, O'Regan, J. K., and Clark, J. J. (1997). 'To see or not to see: the need for attention to perceive changes in scenes'. *Psychological Science*, 8.
——, ——, —— (2000). 'On the failure to detect changes in scenes across brief interruptions'. *Visual Cognition*, 7.
Shepard, R. N. (1967). 'Recognition memory for words, sentences and pictures'. *Journal of Verbal Learning and Verbal Behavior*, 6.
Simons, D. J. (2000). 'Current approaches to change blindness'. *Visual Cognition*, 7.
—— and Levin, D. T. (1998). 'Failure to detect changes to people during a real-world interaction'. *Psychonomic Bulletin and Review*, 5.
—— and Rensink, R. A. (2005). 'Change blindness: past, present, and future'. *Trends in Cognitive Sciences*, 9.
——, Franconeri, S. L., and Reimer, R. L. (2000). 'Change blindness in the absence of a visual disruption'. *Perception*, 29.

Charles Bonnet syndrome The natural scientist and philosopher Charles Bonnet (1720–93) wrote on topics as diverse as parthenogenesis, worm regeneration, metaphysics, and theology. Influencing Gall's system of organology and the 19th century localizationist approach to cerebral function, Bonnet viewed the brain as an 'assemblage of different organs', specialized for different functions, with activation of a given organ, e.g. the organ of vision, responsible not only for visual perception, but also visual imagery and visual memory—a view strikingly resonant with contemporary cognitive neuroscience. His theory of the brain and its mental functions was first outlined in his 'Analytical essay on the faculties of the soul' (Bonnet 1760), in which passing mention was made of a case he had encountered that was so bizarre he feared no one would believe it. The case concerned an elderly man with failing eyesight who had experienced a bewildering array of silent visions without evidence of memory loss or mental illness. The visions were attributed by Bonnet to the irritation of fibres in the visual organ of the brain, resulting in *hallucinatory visual percepts indistinguishable from normal sight. Bonnet was to present the details of the case in full at a later date but never returned to it other than as a footnote in a later edition of the work identifying the elderly man as his grandfather, the magistrate Charles Lullin (1669–1761).

Bonnet's description of Lullin, although brief, was taken up by several 18th and 19th century authors as the paradigm of hallucinations in the sane. However, it would likely have become little more than a historical curiosity, were it not for the chance finding of Lullin's sworn, witnessed testimony among the papers of an ophthalmological collector and its publication in full at the beginning of the 20th century (Flournoy 1902). In 1756, three years after a successful operation to remove a cataract in his left eye, Lullin developed a gradual deterioration of vision in both eyes which continued despite an operation in 1757 to remove a right eye cataract (his visual loss was probably related to age-related macular disease). The hallucinations occurred from February to September of 1758 when he was aged 89. They ranged from the relatively simple and mundane (e.g. storms of whirling atomic particles, scaffolding, brickwork, clover patterns, a handkerchief with gold disks in the corners, and tapestries) to the complex and bizarre (e.g. framed landscape pictures adorning his walls, an 18th century spinning machine, crowds of passers-by in the fountain outside his window, playful children with ribbons in their hair, women in silk dresses with inverted tables on their heads, a carriage of monstrous proportions complete with horse and driver, and a man smoking—recognized as Lullin himself). Some 250 years on, it has become clear that experiences identical to Lullin's are reported by *c*.10% of patients with moderate visual loss.

In 1936, Georges de Morsier, then a recently appointed lecturer in neurology at the University of Geneva, honoured Bonnet's account of Lullin's hallucinations by giving the name 'Charles Bonnet syndrome' to the clinical scenario of visual hallucinations in elderly individuals with eye disease (de Morsier 1936). However, de Morsier made it clear that eye disease was incidental, not causal, and in 1938 removed it entirely from the definition. In his view, Lullin's hallucinations, and those of patients like him, were the result of an unidentified degenerative brain disease which did not cause dementia as it remained confined to the visual pathways. While the idea of honouring Bonnet was widely embraced by the medical community, de Morsier's definition of the syndrome was not. Parallel uses of the term have emerged, some following de Morsier, others describing complex visual hallucinations with insight (ffytche 2005). Yet the use of the term that has found most favour describes an association of visual hallucinations with eye disease, reflecting mounting evidence for the pathophysiological role played by loss of visual inputs (see Burke 2002). While arguments continue over the use of the term, what is beyond dispute is that visual hallucinations are relatively common and occur in patients able to faithfully report their hallucinated experiences without the potential distortion of memory loss or mental illness. As foreseen by Bonnet, the hallucinations in such patients, and their associated brain states, provide important insights into the neural correlates of the contents of consciousness.

DOMINIC. H. FFYTCHE

Bonnet, C. (1760). *L'Essai analytique sur les facultés de l'âme.*
Burke, W. (2002). 'The neural basis of Charles Bonnet hallucinations: a hypothesis'. *Journal of Neurology, Neurosurgery and Psychiatry (London)*, 73.
de Morsier, G. (1936). 'Les automatismes visuels. (Hallucinations visuelles rétrochiasmatiques)'. *Schweizerische Medizinische Wochenschrift*, 66.
ffytche, D. H. (2005). 'Visual hallucinations and the Charles Bonnet syndrome'. *Current Psychiatry Reports*, 7.
Flournoy, T. (1902). 'Le cas de Charles Bonnet: hallucinations visuelles chez un vieillard opéré de la cataracte'. *Archives de Psychologie (Geneva)*, 1.

Chinese room argument John Searle's Chinese room argument goes against claims that computers can really think; against 'strong *artificial intelligence' as Searle (1980a) calls it. The argument relies on a thought experiment. Suppose you are an English speaker who does not speak a word of Chinese. You are in a room, hand-working a natural language understanding (NLU) computer program for Chinese. You work the program by following instructions in English, using data structures, such as look-up tables, to correlate Chinese symbols with other Chinese symbols. Using these structures and instructions, suppose you produce responses to written Chinese input that are indistinguishable from responses that might be given by a native Chinese speaker. By processing uninterpreted formal symbols ('syntax') according to rote instructions, like a computer, you pass for a Chinese speaker. You pass the *Turing test for Chinese. Still, it seems, you would not know what the symbols meant: you would not understand a word of the Chinese. The same, Searle concludes, goes for computers. And since 'nothing depends on the details of the program' or the specific psychological processes being 'simulated', the same objection applies against all would-be examples of artificial intelligence. That is all they ever will be, simulations; not the real thing.

In his seminal presentations, Searle speaks of 'intentionality' (1980a) or 'semantics' (1984), but to many it has seemed, from Searle's reliance on 'the first person point of view' (1980b) in the thought experiment and in fending off objections, that the argument is really about consciousness. The experiment seems to show that the processor would not be *conscious* of the meaning of the symbols; not that the symbols or the processing would be *meaningless* . . . unless it is further assumed that meaning requires consciousness thereof. Searle sometimes bridles at this interpretation. Against Daniel Dennett, for example, Searle complains, 'he misstates my position as being about consciousness rather than about semantics' (1999:28). Yet, curiously, Searle himself (1980b, in reply to Wilensky 1980) admits he equally well 'could have made the argument about pains, tickles, and anxiety', when pains, tickles, and undirected anxiety are not intentional states. They have no semantics! The similarity of Searle's scenario to 'absent *qualia' scenarios generally, and to Ned Block's (1978) Chinese nation example in particular, further supports the thought that the Chinese room concerns consciousness, in the first place, and *intentionality only by implication (insofar as intentionality requires consciousness). What the experiment, then, would show is that hand-working an NLU program for Chinese would not give rise to any *sensation* or *first-person impression* of understanding; that no such computation could impart—not meaning itself—but phenomenal consciousness thereof.

Practical objections to Searle's thought experiment concern whether human-level conversational ability can be computationally achieved at all, by look-up table or otherwise; and if it could be, whether such a program could really be hand-worked in real time, as envisaged. Such objections raise questions about computability and implementation that do not directly concern consciousness. More theoretical replies—granting the 'what if' of the thought experiment—however, either go directly to consciousness themselves; or else Searle's responses immediately do.

The *systems reply* says the understander would not be the person in the room, but the whole system (person, instruction books, look-up tables, etc.). Even if meaning does require consciousness, according to this reply, from the fact that the person in the room would not be conscious of the meanings of the Chinese symbols, it does not follow that the *system* would not be; perhaps the system, consequently, understands. Many proponents of this reply, additionally, however, would not grant the supposition that meaning requires consciousness. According to *conceptual role semantics*, inscriptions in the envisaged scenario get their meanings from their inferential roles in the overall process. If they instance the right roles, they are meaningful; unconsciousness notwithstanding. The *causal theory of reference* (inspiring the *robot reply*), on the other hand, says that inscriptions acquire meaning from causal connections with the actual things they refer to. If computations in the room were caused by real-world inputs, as in perception; and if they caused real-world outputs, such as pursuit or avoidance (put the room in the head of a robot); then the inscriptions and computations would be about the things perceived, avoided, etc. This would give the inscriptions and computations semantics, unconsciousness notwithstanding.

Searle responds to the systems and robot replies, initially (1980a), by tweaking the thought experiment.

Suppose you internalize the system (memorize the instructions and data structures) and take on all the requisite conceptual roles yourself. Put the room in a robot's head to supply causal links. Still, Searle argues, this would not make the symbols meaningful to *you, the processor*, so as to give them 'intrinsic intentionality' (Searle 1980b) besides the 'derived' or 'observer relative intentionality' they have from the conventional Chinese meanings of the symbols. Derived intentionality, Searle explains, exists 'only in the minds of beholders like the Chinese speakers outside the room': this too is curious. Inferential roles and causal links are not observer-relative in this way. Inferential roles are system-internal by definition. On the other hand, if I avoid real dangers to myself (in the robot head) by heeding written warnings in Chinese, the understanding would effectively seem to be *mine* (or the robot's) independently of any outside observers. Searle's response in either case is to take the 'in' of 'intrinsic' to mean, not just objectively contained, but subjectively experienced; not just physically in but metaphysically inward or 'ontologically subjective': to take it in a way that seems to suppose meaning requires consciousness thereof. Searle's later advocacy of 'the Connection Principle' (1990b) can be viewed as an attempt to discharge this supposition.

According to Searle's Connection Principle, 'ascription of an unconscious intentional phenomenon to a system implies the phenomenon is in principle accessible to consciousness'. As he goes on to explain it, unconscious psychological phenomena do not actually have meaning while unconscious 'for the only occurrent reality' of that meaning 'is the shape of conscious thoughts' (1992). Searle, however, remains vague about what these 'shapes' are and how their subjective and qualitative natures (on which he insists) could be meaning constitutive in ways that objective factors like inferential roles and causal links (as he argues) cannot be. Nor is this the only reason Searle's Connection Principle has won few adherents. Psychological phenomena such as 'unconscious *priming' (e.g. subjects previously exposed to the word-pair 'ocean–moon' being subsequently more likely to respond 'Tide' when asked to name a laundry detergent) seem to show that unconscious mental states and processes do have intentionality while unconscious, since they are subject to semantic effects while unconscious. Furthermore, the supposition of unconscious intentionality has proved scientifically fruitful. 'Cognitive' theories such as Noam Chomsky's theories of language and David Marr's theories of vision suppose the existence of unconscious representations (e.g. language rules, and preliminary visual sketches) which are intentional (about the grammars they rule, or scenes preliminarily sketched) but not accessible to introspection as Searle's Connection Principle requires. In contrast, the view of the mental that Searle endorses in accord with his Principle—according to which 'the actual ontology of mental states is a first-person ontology' and 'the mind consists of qualia, so to speak, right down to the ground' (1992)—seems, to many, scientifically regressive; seeming to 'regress to the Cartesian vantage point' (Dennett 1987) of dualism.

Of the Chinese room, Searle says, the 'point of the story is to remind us of a conceptual truth that we knew all along' (1988), that *'syntax is not sufficient for semantics'* (1984). But the insufficiency of syntax in motion (playing inferential roles), and in situ (when causally connected) are hardly conceptual truths we knew all along; they are empirical claims the experiment has to support (Hauser 1997). The support offered would seem to be the intuition that such processing would not make the processor conscious of the meanings of the symbols. But, of course, it is supposed to be an *understanding* program, not a *consciousness thereof* (or introspective access) program: if the link between intentionality and consciousness his Connection Principle articulates were not already being presupposed, it seems Searle's famous argument against 'strong AI' would go immediately wrong. However much Searle might like his Chinese room example to make a case against AI that stands independently of this 'conceptual connection' (Searle 1992), then, it seems extremely doubtful that it does.

See also, COGNITION, UNCONSCIOUS; CONSCIOUSNESS, CONCEPTS OF; DUALISM; INTENTIONALITY; QUALIA; SUBJECTIVITY

LARRY. S. HAUSER

Block, N. (1978). 'Troubles with functionalism'. In Savage, C. W. (ed.) *Perception and Cognition: Issues in the Foundations of Psychology*.

Dennett, D. (1987). *The Intentional Stance*.

Hauser, L. (1997). 'Searle's Chinese box: debunking the Chinese room argument'. *Minds and Machines*, 7.

Preston, J. and Bishop, M. (eds) (2001). *Views into the Chinese Room: New Essays on Searle and Artificial Intelligence*.

Searle, J. R. (1980a). 'Minds, brains, and programs'. *Behavioral and Brain Sciences*, 3.

Searle, J. R. (1980b). 'Intrinsic intentionality'. *Behavioral and Brain Sciences*, 3.

Searle, J. R. (1984). *Minds, Brains and Science*.

Searle, J. R. (1988). 'Minds and brains without programs'. In Blakemore, C. (ed.) *Mindwaves*.

Searle, J. R. (1990a). 'Is the brain's mind a computer program?' *Scientific American*, 262(1).

Searle, J. R. (1990b). 'Consciousness, explanatory inversion, and cognitive science'. *Behavioral and Brain Sciences*, 13.

Searle, J. R. (1992). *The Rediscovery of the Mind*.

Searle, J. R. (1999). *The Mystery of Consciousness*.

Wilensky, R. (1980). 'Computers, cognition and philosophy'. *Behavioral and Brain Sciences*, 3.

cocktail party effect See ATTENTION; CAPACITY LIMITS AND CONSCIOUSNESS

cognition, unconscious The unconscious mind was one of the most important ideas of the 20th century, influencing not just scientific and clinical psychology but also literature, art, and popular culture. Sigmund Freud famously characterized the 'discovery' of the unconscious as one of three unpleasant truths that humans had learned about themselves: the first, from Copernicus, that the Earth was not the centre of the universe; the second, from Darwin, that humans are just animals after all; and the third, ostensibly from Freud himself, that the conscious mind was but the tip of the iceberg (though Freud apparently never used this metaphor himself), and that the important determinants of experience, thought, and action were hidden from conscious awareness and conscious control.

In fact, we now understand that Freud was not the discoverer of the unconscious (Ellenberger 1970). The concept had earlier roots in the philosophical work of Leibniz and Kant, and especially that of Herbart, who in the early 19th century introduced the concept of a *limen*, or threshold, which a sensation had to cross in order to be represented in conscious awareness. A little later, Helmholtz argued that conscious perception was influenced by unconscious inferences made as the perceiver constructs a mental representation of a distal stimulus. In 1868, while Freud was still in short trousers, the Romantic movement in philosophy, literature, and the arts set the stage for Hartmann's *Philosophy of the Unconscious* (1868), which argued that the physical universe, life, and individual minds were ruled by an intelligent, dynamic force of which we had no awareness and over which we had no control. And before Freud was out of medical school, Samuel Butler, author of *Erewhon*, drew on Darwin's theory of evolution to argue that unconscious memory was a universal property of all organized matter.

Nevertheless, consciousness dominated the scientific psychology that emerged in the latter part of the 19th century. The psychophysicists, such as Weber and Fechner, focused on mapping the relations between conscious sensation and physical stimulation. The structuralists, such as Wundt and Titchener, sought to analyse complex conscious experiences into their constituent (but conscious) elements. James, in his *Principles of Psychology*, defined psychology as the science of mental life, by which he meant *conscious* mental life—as he made clear in the *Briefer Course*, where he defined psychology as 'the description and explanation of states of consciousness as such'. Against this background, Breuer and Freud's assertion, in the early 1890s, that hysteria is a product of repressed memories of trauma, and Freud's 1900 topographical division of the mind into conscious, preconscious, and unconscious systems, began to insinuate themselves into the way we thought about the mind.

On the basis of his own observations of hysteria, fugue, and hypnosis, James understood, somewhat paradoxically, that there were streams of mental life that proceeded outside conscious awareness. Nevertheless, he warned (in a critique directed against Hartmann) that the distinction between conscious and unconscious mental life was 'the sovereign means for believing what one likes in psychology, and of turning what might become a science into a tumbling-ground for whimsies'. This did not mean that the notion of unconscious mental life should be discarded; but it did mean that any such notion should be accompanied by solid scientific evidence. Unfortunately, as we now understand, Freud's 'evidence' was of the very worst sort: uncorroborated inferences, based more on his own theoretical commitments than on anything his patients said or did, coupled with the assumption that the patient's resistance to Freud's inferences were all the more proof that they were correct—James's 'psychologist's fallacy' writ large. Ever since, the challenge for those who are interested in unconscious mental life has been to reduce the size of the tumbling-ground by tightening up the inference from behaviour to unconscious thought.

Unfortunately, the scientific investigation of unconscious mental life was sidetracked by the behaviourist revolution in psychology, initiated by Watson and consolidated by Skinner, which effectively banished consciousness from psychological discourse, and the unconscious along with it. The 'cognitive revolution' of the 1960s, which overthrew behaviourism, began with research on *attention, short-term memory, and imagery—all aspects of conscious awareness. The development of cognitive psychology led ultimately to a rediscovery of the unconscious as well, but in a form that looked nothing like Freud's vision. As befits an event that took place in the context of the cognitive revolution, the rediscovery of the unconscious began with cognitive processes—the processes by which we acquire knowledge through perception and learning; store knowledge in memory; use, transform, and generate knowledge through reasoning, problem-solving, judgement, and decision-making; and share knowledge through language.

The first milestone in the rediscovery of the unconscious mind was a distinction between **automatic* and *controlled processes*, as exemplified by various phenomena of perception and skilled reading. For example, the perceiver automatically takes distance into account in inferring the size of an object from the size of its retinal image (this is an example of Helmholtz's 'unconscious inferences'). And in the *Stroop effect, subjects automatically process the meaning of colour words, which makes it difficult for them to name the incongruent colour of the ink in which those words are printed. In contrast to controlled processes, automatic processes are inevitably evoked by the appearance of an effective stimulus; once evoked, they are incorrigibly executed, proceeding to completion in a ballistic fashion; they consume little or no attentional resources; and they can be performed in parallel with other cognitive activities. While controlled processes are performed consciously, automatic processes are unconscious in the strict sense that they are both unavailable to introspective access, known only through inference, and involuntary.

It is one thing to acknowledge that certain cognitive processes are performed unconsciously. As noted earlier, such a notion dates back to Helmholtz, and was revived by Chomsky, at the beginning of the cognitive revolution, to describe the unconscious operation of syntactic rules of language. But it is something else to believe that cognitive **contents*—specific percepts, memories, and thoughts—could also be represented unconsciously. However, evidence for just such a proposition began to emerge with the discovery of spared *priming and source *amnesia in patients with the amnesic syndrome secondary to damage to the hippocampus and other subcortical structures. This research, in turn, led to a distinction between two expressions of episodic memory, or memory for discrete events: *explicit memory* entails conscious recollection, usually in the form of recall or recognition; by contrast, *implicit memory* refers to any effect of a past event on subsequent experience, thought, or action (Schacter 1987; see AUTONOETIC CONSCIOUSNESS).

Preserved priming in amnesic patients showed that explicit and implicit memory could be dissociated from each other: in this sense, implicit memory may be thought of as unconscious memory. Similar dissociations have now been observed in a wide variety of conditions, including the anterograde and retrograde amnesias produced by electroconvulsive therapy, general *anaesthesia, conscious sedation by benzodiazepines and similar drugs, *dementias such as Alzheimer's disease, the forgetfulness associated with normal ageing, posthypnotic amnesia, and the 'functional' or 'psychogenic' amnesias associated with the psychiatric syndromes known as the dissociative disorders, such as 'hysterical' fugue and *dissociative identity disorder (also known as multiple personality disorder).

Implicit memory refers to the influence of a *past* event on the person's subsequent experience, thought, or action in the absence of, or independent of, the person's conscious *recollection* of that event. This definition can then serve as a model for extending the cognitive unconscious to cognitive domains other than memory. Thus, *implicit perception* refers to the influence of an event in the *current* stimulus environment, in the absence of the person's conscious *perception* of that event (Kihlstrom et al. 1992). Implicit perception is exemplified by so-called subliminal perception (see PERCEPTION, UNCONSCIOUS), as well as the *blindsight of patients with lesions in striate cortex. It has also been observed in conversion disorders (such as 'hysterical' blindness); in the anaesthesias and negative *hallucinations produced by hypnotic suggestion; and in failures of conscious perception associated with certain attentional phenomena, such as unilateral neglect, dichotic listening, parafoveal vision, *inattentional blindness, repetition blindness, and the *attentional blink. In each case, subjects' task performance is influenced by stimuli that they do not consciously see or hear—the essence of unconscious perception.

Source amnesia shades into the phenomenon of *implicit *learning*, in which subjects acquire knowledge, as displayed in subsequent task performance, but are not aware of what they have learned. Although debates over unconscious learning date back to the earliest days of psychology, the term *implicit learning* was more recently coined in the context of experiments on *artificial grammar learning (Reber 1993). In a typical experiment, subjects were asked to memorize a list of letter strings, each of which had been generated by a set of 'grammatical rules'. Despite being unable to articulate the rules themselves, they were able to discriminate new grammatical strings from ungrammatical ones at better-than-chance levels. Later experiments extended this finding to concept learning, covariation detection, *sequence learning, learning the input–output relations in a dynamic system, and other paradigms. In source amnesia, as an aspect of implicit episodic memory, subjects have conscious access to newly acquired knowledge, even though they do not remember the learning experience itself. In implicit learning, newly acquired semantic or procedural knowledge is not consciously accessible, but nevertheless influences the subjects' conscious experience, thought, and action.

There is even some evidence for unconscious thought, defined as the influence on experience, thought, or action of a mental state that is neither a percept nor a memory, such as an idea or an image (Kihlstrom et al. 1996). For example, when subjects confront two problems, one soluble and the other not, they are often able to identify the soluble problem, even though they are not consciously aware of the solution itself. Other research has shown that the correct solution can generate priming effects, even when subjects are unaware of it. Because the solution has never been presented to the subjects, it is neither a percept nor a memory; because it has been internally generated, it is best considered as a thought. Phenomenologically, *implicit thought* is similar to the *feeling of knowing someone we cannot identify further, or the experience when words seem to be on the tip of the tongue; it may also be involved in intuition and other aspects of creative problem-solving.

With the exception of implicit thought, all the phenomena of the cognitive unconscious are well accepted, although there remains considerable disagreement about their underlying mechanisms. For example, it is not clear whether explicit and implicit memory are mediated by separate brain systems, or whether they reflect different aspects of processing within a single *memory system. The theoretical uncertainty is exacerbated by the fact that most demonstrations of implicit perception and memory involve repetition priming that can be based on an unconscious perceptual representation of the prime, and the extent of unconscious semantic priming, especially in the case of implicit perception, has yet to be resolved. One thing that is clear is that there are a number of different ways to render a percept or memory unconscious; the extent of unconscious influence probably depends on the particular means chosen.

Occasional claims to the contrary notwithstanding, the cognitive unconscious revealed by the experiments of modern psychology has nothing in common with the dynamic unconscious of classic psychoanalytic theory (Westen 1999). To begin with, its contents are 'kinder and gentler' than Freud's primitive, infantile, irrational, sexual, and aggressive 'monsters from the Id'; moreover, unconscious percepts and memories seem to reflect the basic architecture of the cognitive system, rather than being motivated by conflict, anxiety, and repression. Moreover, the processes by which emotions and motives are rendered unconscious seem to bear no resemblance to the constructs of psychoanalytic theory. This is not to say that emotional and motivational states and processes cannot be unconscious. If percepts, memories, and thoughts can be unconscious, so can feelings and desires. Of particular interest is the idea that stereotypes and prejudices can be unconscious, and affect the judgements and behaviours even of people who sincerely believe that they have overcome such attitudes (Greenwald et al. 2002).

Mounting evidence for the role of automatic processes in cognition, and for the influence of unconscious percepts, memories, knowledge, and thoughts, has led to a groundswell of interest in unconscious processes in learning and thinking. For example, many social psychologists have extended the concept of *automaticity to very complex cognitive processes as well as simple perceptual ones—a trend so prominent that automaticity has been dubbed 'the new unconscious' (Hassin et al. 2005). An interesting characteristic of this literature has been the claim that automatic processing pervades everyday life to the virtual exclusion of conscious processing—'the automaticity of everyday life' and 'the unbearable automaticity of being' (e.g. Bargh and Chartrand 1999). This is a far cry from the two-process theories that prevail in cognitive psychology, and earlier applications of automaticity in social psychology, which emphasized the dynamic interplay of conscious and unconscious processes. Along the same lines, Wilson has asserted the power of the 'adaptive unconscious' in learning, problem-solving, and decision-making (Wilson 2002)—a view popularized by Gladwell as 'the power of thinking without thinking' (Gladwell 2005). Similarly, Wegner has argued that conscious will is an illusion, and that the true determinants of conscious thoughts and actions are unconscious (Wegner 2002). For these theorists, automaticity replaces Freud's 'monsters from the Id' as the third unpleasant truth about human nature. Where Descartes asserted that consciousness, including conscious will, separated humans from the other animals, these theorists conclude, regretfully, that we are automatons after all (and it is probably a good thing, too).

The stance, which verges on *epiphenomenalism, or at least conscious inessentialism, partly reflects the 'conscious shyness' of psychologists and other cognitive scientists, living as we still do in the shadow of functional behaviourism (Flanagan 1992)—as well as a sentimental attachment to a crypto-Skinnerian situationism among many social psychologists (Kihlstrom 2008). But while it is clear that consciousness is not necessary for some aspects of perception, memory, learning, or even thinking, it is a stretch too far to conclude that the bulk of cognitive activity is unconscious, and that consciousness plays only a limited role in thought and action. 'Subliminal' perception appears to be analytically limited, and earlier claims for the power of *subliminal advertising were greatly exaggerated (Greenwald 1992). Assertions of the power of implicit learning are rarely accompanied by a methodologically adequate comparison of conscious and unconscious learning strategies—or, for that matter, a properly controlled assessment of subjects' conscious access to what they have learned. Similarly, many experimental demonstrations of automaticity in social behaviour employ very loose definitions of automaticity, confusing the truly automatic with the merely incidental. Nor are there very many studies using techniques such as Jacoby's process-dissociation procedure to actually compare the impact of automatic and controlled processes (Jacoby et al. 1997; see MEMORY, PROCESS-DISSOCIATION PROCEDURE).

So, despite the evidence for unconscious cognition, reports of the death of consciousness appear to be greatly exaggerated. At the very least, consciousness gives us something to talk about; and it seems to be a logical prerequisite to the various forms of social learning by precept, including sponsored teaching and the social institutions (like universities) that support it, which in turn make cultural evolution the powerful force that it is.

JOHN F. KIHLSTROM

Bargh, J. A. and Chartrand, T. L. (1999). 'The unbearable automaticity of being'. *American Psychologist*, 54.

Ellenberger, H. F. (1970). *The Discovery of the Unconscious: the History and Evolution of Dynamic Psychiatry.*

Flanagan, O. (1992). *Consciousness Reconsidered.*

Gladwell, M. (2005). *Blink: the Power of Thinking Without Thinking.*

Greenwald, A. G. (1992). 'New Look 3: Unconscious cognition reclaimed'. *American Psychologist*, 47.

——, Banaji, M. R., Rudman, L. A., Farnham, S. D., Nosek, B. A., and Mellott, D. S. (2002). 'A unified theory of implicit attitudes, stereotypes, self-esteem, and self-concept'. *Psychological Review*, 109.

Hassin, R. R., Uleman, J. S., and Bargh, J. A. (eds) (2005). *The New Unconscious.*

Jacoby, L. L., Yonelinas, A. P., and Jennings, J. M. (1997). 'The relation between conscious and unconscious (automatic) influences: a declaration of independence'. In Cohen, J. and Schooler, J. (eds) *Scientific Approaches to Consciousness.*

Kihlstrom, J. F. (2008). 'The automaticity juggernaut'. In Baer, J. et al. (eds) *Psychology and Free Will.*

——, Barnhardt, T. M., and Tataryn, D. J. (1992). 'Implicit perception'. In Bornstein, R. F. and Pittman, T. S. (eds) *Perception Without Awareness: Cognitive, Clinical, and Social Perspectives.*

——, Shames, V. A., and Dorfman, J. (1996). 'Intimations of memory and thought'. In Reder, L. M. (ed.) *Implicit Memory and Metacognition.*

Reber, A. S. (1993). *Implicit Learning and Tacit Knowledge: an Essay on the Cognitive Unconscious.*

Schacter, D. L. (1987). 'Implicit memory: history and current status'. *Journal of Experimental Psychology: Learning, Memory, and Cognition*, 13.

Wegner, D. M. (2002). *The Illusion of Conscious Will.*

Westen, D. (1999). 'The scientific status of unconscious processes: is Freud really dead?' *Journal of the American Psychoanalytic Association*, 47.

Wilson, T. D. (2002). *Strangers to Ourselves: Discovering the Adaptive Unconscious.*

cognitive control and consciousness In a forced-choice reaction time task, responses are slower after an error. This is one example of dynamic adjustment of behaviour, i.e. control of cognitive processing, which according to Botvinick et al. (2001) refers to a set of functions serving to configure the cognitive system for the performance of tasks. We focus on the question whether cognitive control requires conscious awareness. We wish to emphasize that the question refers not to the awareness of all aspects of the world surrounding the performing organism, but to the conscious awareness of the control process itself, i.e. consciousness of maintaining the task requirements, supporting the processing of information relevant to the goals of the current task, and suppressing irrelevant information (van Veen and Carter 2006).

During the last quarter of the 20th century, the term *control* was contrasted with **automaticity* (e.g. Schneider and Shiffrin 1977). Automatic processes were defined as being effortless, unconscious, and involuntary, and the terms *unconscious* and *automatic* were used by some interchangeably, leading to the conclusion that control should be viewed as constrained to conscious processing. However, it was shown that phenomena considered to be examples of automatic processing, such as the flanker effect and the *Stroop effect, showed a dynamic adjustment to external conditions, corresponding to the notion of control. In particular, some (e.g. Gratton et al. 1992) showed an increase in the flanker effect after an incompatible trial, while others (e.g. Logan et al. 1984) showed sensitivity of the Stroop effect to the various trial types. Consequently, Tzelgov (1997) proposed to distinguish between *monitoring* as the intentional setting of the goal of behaviour and the intentional evaluation of the outputs of a process, and *control*, referring to the sensitivity of a system to changes in inputs, which may reflect a feedback loop.

According to these definitions, monitoring can be considered to be the case of conscious control, that is, the conscious awareness of the representations controlled and the very process of their evaluation. The *global workspace (GW) framework proposed by Dehaene et al. (1998) may be seen as one possible instantiation of the notion of monitoring in neuronal terms. Accordingly, unconscious processing reflects the activity of a set of interconnected modular systems. Conscious processing is possible due to a distributed neural system, which may be seen as a 'workspace' with long-distance connectivity that interconnects the various modules, i.e. the multiple, specialized brain areas. It allows the performance of operations that cannot be accomplished unconsciously and 'are associated with planning a novel strategy, evaluating it, controlling its execution, and correcting possible errors' (Dehaene et al. 1998:11). Within such a framework the anterior cingulate cortex (ACC) and the prefrontal cortex (PFC), two neural structures known to be involved in control, may be seen as parts of the GW and consequently, are supposed to indicate conscious activity.

In contrast, there are models of control that do not assume involvement of consciousness. For example, Bodner and Masson (2001) argue that the operations applied to the prime in order to identify and interpret it result in new memory *representations, which can later be used without awareness. Jacoby et al. (2003) referred to such passive control as 'automatic'. A computational description of *passive control* is provided by the conflict-monitoring model of the Stroop task (Botvinick et al. 2001), which includes a conflict detection unit (presumed to correspond to the ACC) that triggers the control-application unit (presumed to correspond to the PFC). To be more specific, consider a presentation of an incongruent Stroop stimulus, for example, the word 'BLUE' printed in red ink, with instructions to respond with the colour of the ink. This results in a strong activation to respond with the word presented, and in parallel, the instructions cause activation of the colour the stimulus is written in. The resulting conflict in the response unit is detected by the ACC, which in turn augments the activation of the colour unit in the PFC, leading to the relevant response. Notice that no conscious decisions are involved in this process.

Thus, the question of the relation between consciousness and cognitive control may be restated in terms of whether cognitive control requires conscious monitoring as implied by the GW and similar frameworks, or whether it can be performed without the involvement of consciousness, as hypothesized by the conflict-monitoring model. Mayr (2004) reviewed an experimental framework for analysing the consciousness-based vs consciousness-free approaches to cognitive control by focusing on behavioural and neural (e.g. ACC and ERN activity) indications of control. He proposed to contrast these indications under a condition of conscious awareness vs absence of awareness, of the stimuli presumed to trigger control by generating conflict. For example, in the study of Dehaene et al. (2003), the contrast is between an unmasked (high awareness) condition in which the participants can clearly see the prime, and a *masked (low awareness) condition. After reviewing a few studies that applied such a design, Mayr had to conclude that the emerging picture is still inconclusive. We agree that the proposed approach is very promising, yet some refinements are needed. First, in most cases discussed by Mayr, the manipulation of awareness was achieved by masking a prime stimulus. The critical assumption, that under masking conditions the participants are totally unaware of the masked stimulus and yet process it up to its semantic level, is still controversial (Holender 1986). Second, concerning the casual order: consider the case in which both behavioural and neuronal (i.e. ACC activity) markers of conflict are obtained only when the person is fully aware of the conflict-triggering stimulus. At face value, it seems to indicate that the causal link is from awareness to markers of conflict; however, it could be equally true that the causal link is from the markers of conflict to awareness. Mayr (2004:146) hints at this point by suggesting the 'possibility that rather than consciousness being a necessary condition for conflict related ACC activity, conflict related ACC activity might be the necessary condition for awareness of conflict'. Third, concerning the assumed notion of conscious control: what is supposed to be manipulated in the awareness-control design is the awareness of the conflict. Actually, however, what is manipulated is the awareness of the stimulus generating the conflict. Such awareness may be seen as a precondition for applying deliberate monitoring.

Thus, in order to advance answering the question whether cognitive control requires consciousness, future research should distinguish between awareness of the stimulus that causes the conflict, awareness of the conflict per se and awareness of the very process of control as implied by the notion of monitoring. Furthermore, such research should emphasize the distinction between consciousness as a condition for control processes and consciousness as a result of control processes.

JOSEPH TZELGOV AND GUY PINKU

Bodner, G. E. and Masson, M. E. J. (2001). 'Prime validity affects masked repetition priming: evidence for an episodic resource account of priming'. *Journal of Memory and Language*, 45.

Botvinick, M., Braver, T., Barch, D., Carter, C., and Cohen, J. (2001). 'Conflict monitoring and cognitive control'. *Psychological Review*, 108.

Dehaene, S., Kerszberg, M., and Changeux, J. P. (1998). 'A neuronal model of a global workspace in effortful cognitive tasks'. *Proceedings of the National Academy of Sciences of the USA*, 95.

——, Artiges, E., Naccache, L. et al. (2003). 'Conscious and subliminal conflicts in normal subjects and patients with schizophrenia: the role of the anterior cingulate'. *Proceedings of the National Academy of Sciences of the USA*, 100.

Gratton, G., Coles, M. G. H., and Donchin, E. (1992). 'Optimizing the use of information: strategic control of activation and responses'. *Journal of Experimental Psychology: General*, 121.

Holender, D. (1986). 'Semantic activation without conscious identification in dichotic listening, parafoveal vision, and visual masking: a survey and appraisal'. *Behavioral and Brain Sciences*, 9.

Jacoby, L. L., Lindsay, D. S., and Hessels, S. (2003). 'Item-specific control of automatic processes: Stroop process dissociations'. *Psychonomic Bulletin and Review*, 10.

Logan, G., Zbrodoff, N., and Williamson, J. (1984). 'Strategies in the color-word Stroop task'. *Bulletin of the Psychonomic Society*, 22.

Mayr, U. (2004). 'Conflict, consciousness and control'. *Trends in Cognitive Sciences*, 8.

Schneider, W. and Shiffrin, R. M. (1977). 'Controlled and automatic human information processing: I. Detection, search and attention'. *Psychological Review*, 84.

Tzelgov, J. (1997). 'Specifying the relations between automaticity and consciousness: a theoretical note'. *Consciousness and Cognition*, 6.

van Veen, V. and Carter, C. S. (2006). 'Conflict and cognitive control in the brain'. *Current Directions in Psychological Science*, 15.

cognitive feelings Cognitive feelings are a loose class of experiences with some commonality in their phenomenology, representational content, and function in the mental economy. Examples include *feelings of knowing, of familiarity, of preference, tip-of-the-tongue states, and the kinds of hunches that guide behavioural choice in situations ranging from implicit *learning paradigms to consumer choice. The concept overlaps with those of intuition, *metacognition, and *fringe consciousness, and probably has some degree of continuity with *emotional feeling.

Cognitive feelings play a monitoring and control function in the mental economy. They are *conscious* experiences in the sense that they can be reported, either verbally or in the form of predictive introspective ratings, and can be used to guide behaviour in a flexible and contextually appropriate manner (Price 2002). Specifically, the experiences provide us with *metacognitive* information about aspects of our mental processes that are otherwise rather inaccessible to consciousness. The inaccessibility of the non-conscious antecedents of the experience may be especially salient because, in other situations, similar experiences would be accompanied by conscious access to their antecedents. The feelings may also feel vague in the sense that their detailed nature may be difficult to describe and communicate verbally, whether to others or oneself.

Before discussing these characteristics of cognitive feelings further, we briefly summarize some classic examples of cognitive feelings that cut across the research domains of memory, perception, attention, language production, problem-solving, and decision-making.

1. Varieties of cognitive feeling
2. The defining characteristics of cognitive feelings
3. Fringe consciousness and the function of cognitive feelings
4. Cognitive vs emotional feelings
5. Neurocognitive basis
6. Shades of consciousness

1. Varieties of cognitive feeling

The *feeling of knowing* (FOK) state is usually studied by asking people to answer a set of questions about existing or newly learned knowledge. For questions that people cannot currently answer, introspective ratings of FOK nevertheless predict the likelihood that the correct answer will be picked out in a subsequent multiple-choice recognition test. In problem-solving tasks, FOK ratings of perceived closeness to the solution have been referred to as *warmth ratings*. For non-insight problems, these ratings again have some predictive accuracy, although this is not found for problems requiring insight.

The more naturally occurring *tip-of-the-tongue* (TOT) phenomenon can be considered as a variety of the FOK state where people feel that memory retrieval of a word is imminent, even though they are currently unable to retrieve it. The feeling of imminence, in the absence of full access to the word, is salient, verbally reportable, and predictive of the actual likelihood of future recall. The feeling also seems stronger and more emotional than illusory TOT states which are induced experimentally. This predictive quality shows that the TOT feeling veridically reflects aspects of the cognitive processes involved in the memory search.

Feelings of familiarity (FOF) refer to a sense of *knowing* one has encountered something before, despite being unable to explicitly *remember* the learning episode (Gardiner and Richardson-Klavehn 2000). Whether people rate a previously exposed item as remembered (R) vs just known (K, in this so-called *RK paradigm*) is known to be influenced by different variables. One explanation for FOF is that previously exposed stimuli seem subjectively more *perceptually fluent* since they are processed faster, and are therefore assumed to be familiar. Fluency seems to be a learned heuristic based on environmental contingencies. Enhancing perceptual fluency by, for example, increasing the orthographic regularity of non-word letter strings, makes it more likely that previously unseen stimuli are falsely rated as recognized. Manipulating perceptual fluency can bias a variety of intuitive judgements, including the felt truth of written statements.

People tend to prefer things they have encountered before. This *mere exposure effect* is at the heart of commercial advertising. *Feelings of preference* (FOP) for previously seen stimuli (e.g. random shapes) in laboratory experiments occur even when people cannot discriminate whether they have been shown the items before, and are even claimed for situations in which the exposure is conducted subliminally (Bornstein 1992). As with other examples of cognitive feelings, the FOP may therefore occur without awareness of its information processing antecedents (i.e. previous exposure). Intuitive decisions based on rapid FOP, rather than on deliberative analysis, are sometimes advantageous. For example, long-term satisfaction with wall posters increases when they are chosen quickly and intuitively in a non-deliberative manner (Wilson et al. 1993).

Cognitive feelings are probably important in many domains beyond the classic paradigms described above. For example, during implicit learning, complex regularities in our environment are encoded without full awareness of what has been learned, or sometimes even without awareness that learning has occurred at all. It has been proposed that such learning can nevertheless result in the development of intuitive feelings of rightness which help guide behaviour. For example, in the context of laboratory studies where artificial rule-governed sequences are learned without verbalizable knowledge of the nature of the sequences (see ARTIFICIAL GRAMMAR LEARNING), intuitive feelings of anticipation may help people to predict the next move in the sequence, and feelings of familiarity may allow rule-governed sequences to be distinguished from random novel sequences (Norman et al. 2006). In every-day life, cognitive feelings derived from implicit learning may underlie social intuitions such as gut feelings about people's intentions. When information becomes complex, consumer choice may also benefit more than ever from intuitive rather than deliberative judgements. Other varied examples of experiences that could be labelled as cognitive feelings include the intuitive hunches that drive the cognitive heuristics used in everyday decision-making, including stock market speculation.

2. The defining characteristics of cognitive feelings

These examples of cognitive feelings help to clarify the type of informational content carried by the feelings—which is what makes them cognitive. They also illustrate the nature of the interplay between conscious and unconscious processes involved in these experiences—which is what encourages us to label them as feelings.

Take the informational content first. TOT states, and feelings of knowing, familiarity or preference, all convey something about our cognitive processes, and are therefore examples of what has been called *online metacognition*, which refers to the monitoring and control of ongoing cognition. For example, we know that we are about to retrieve a word, or that we could recognize a currently unrecallable item, or that we have probably encountered an item before. However, in these examples we are only aware of the information conveyed by the feeling. We do not have conscious access to the antecedents of the feelings, such as the encoding episode that gives rise to the feeling of familiarity. Koriat (2000) uses the term *experience-based metacognitive judgements* to refer to this variety of online metacognition whose information-processing antecedents are not (or not yet) consciously accessible to the person, in contrast to *information-based metacognitive judgements* which are based on explicit inferential processes. This type of 'sheer metacognitive feeling' (Koriat 2000:163) is argued to be a 'direct unmediated experience' of the type that people sometimes refer to as 'an intuitive feeling, a hunch' (Koriat 2000:152).

It is this absence of cognitive transparency that makes it appropriate to apply the folk psychological label of *feeling* to these experiences. Dictionaries usually give many definitions of feelings, from the experience of physical sensation or emotion, to a sense of impression and intuitive understanding. Common to these various definitions is a phenomenology characterized by the relative absence of reasoned, analytical thought processes. For sensory feelings, the feelings may appear to stem directly from external perceptual receptors (e.g. a feeling of touch). For emotional feelings, they may seem to derive heavily from internal bodily sensations. But even if the dominant component of a conscious experience is some aspect of our thoughts rather than a perceptual or emotional sensation, the experience may still have the quality of a feeling if the antecedents of the mental state seem largely inaccessible. Hence we continue to talk metaphorically about a *gut feeling* that we prefer one picture over another without being able to express *why*. Feelings can therefore be cognitive, even if the term *cognitive feeling* seems initially self-contradictory, because feelings are often taken to be the antithesis of the rational and analytical cognitive end of the mental spectrum.

An additional criterion is useful in constraining the class of experiences that are regarded as cognitive feelings (Price 2002): the gap between the experience and its non-conscious antecedents is typically somewhat anomalous or unexpected. When we recognize a class of object, we do not find it curious that we are unaware of the antecedent information-processing stages of object recognition. Here we take it for granted that consciousness is the tip of the information-processing iceberg. However, when we intuitively prefer one painting over another, or experience the familiarity of a face despite no episodic recall of having met its owner before, our judgements have the character of feelings or intuitions to the extent that we notice the absence of conscious supporting evidence that could in principle be present.

3. Fringe consciousness and the function of cognitive feelings

This outline of cognitive feelings has much overlap with aspects of the Jamesian concept of fringe consciousness, as revived and elaborated by Mangan (2001). Fringe consciousness refers to all components of the stream of consciousness other than the *nucleus* of focally attended sensory information. The concept is particularly concerned with *feelings of relation* which provide a summary signal of the degree of fit or integration between this nucleus and its contextual background of largely non-conscious information processing. Although the range of experiences subsumed under the concept of fringe consciousness is considerably broader than just cognitive feelings, Mangan considers that the types of empirically studied cognitive feelings listed above are important examples of fringe consciousness, and suggests they are manifestations of a core relational feeling of rightness.

Mangan's proposed function for fringe consciousness in the cognitive economy is also similar to Koriat's (2000) suggested function for experience-based metacognitive feelings. Within both theoretical frameworks, the cognitive feeling has the monitoring role of summarizing aspects of currently unavailable non-conscious processing that are relevant to ongoing, conscious, mental tasks. By acting as an interface between non-conscious and conscious processing, this summary feeling then has a control role in directing behaviour—e.g. choosing the object which feels right or familiar or preferred—and in directing ongoing cognition—e.g. attempting to retrieve the non-conscious context information into consciousness, as during the 'tip of the tongue' state. The functional advantage of having a *conscious* feeling to do these jobs, rather than relying on non-conscious automatic processes, is that conscious processes are qualitatively more flexible. The owner of the feeling therefore benefits from a much higher level of behavioural choice.

According to Mangan, attempting to attend to a fringe feeling will often instantly retrieve its previously non-conscious antecedents into consciousness and the feeling will therefore have a very transient and fleeting nature. Norman (2002) argues that in situations where the background context information is relatively inaccessible, fringe consciousness has a 'frozen' sustained quality, allowing it to be attended and introspectively reported. Cognitive feelings, which are amenable to conscious introspection, correspond closely to this subclass of fringe consciousness.

More speculatively, the overlap between cognitive feelings and fringe consciousness may extend to other examples such as the general sense of understanding the text we are reading, which is argued by Mangan (2001) to be a variety of fringe feeling which expresses a global metacognitive impression of coherence and meaning.

4. Cognitive vs emotional feelings

There are several similarities between cognitive feelings and the affective feelings present during emotional experience. (1) Both may share phenomenological qualities such as descriptive vagueness or fleetingness. (2) As with cognitive feelings, emotions may be consciously experienced even if their antecedent causes are not consciously accessible, and act as a summary alarm system to warn us of the presence of the currently unavailable non-conscious information (Damasio 1994). (3) Cognitive feelings are by no means always affectively neutral, even if they are usually associated with less salient somatic responses than strong emotions. The positive or negative evaluative valence of feelings such as feelings of rightness, preference, familiarity, and so on has been commented on by many authors writing on fringe consciousness. (4) Just as theories of emotion such as Damasio's (1994) *somatic marker hypothesis* stress the crucial role of autonomic bodily signals in shaping the gut feelings of emotional experience, so it has been argued that cognitive feelings are often grounded in bodily sensations. For example, sensorimotor phenomenology may be integral to experiences such as TOT or even to abstract relational fringe feelings such as 'andness' (Epstein 2000), and feelings of rightness or wrongness may be rooted in postural maintenance systems, as suggested by everyday language such as making a 'solid' vs a 'shaky' argument, and having 'no leg to stand on' (Woody and Szechtman 2002). Somatic markers have been implicated in implicit learning paradigms by showing that skin-conductance measures of autonomic activity correlate with the accuracy of intuitively made judgements about implicitly learned perceptual patterns (Bierman et al., 2005).

The distinction between cognitive and emotional feelings therefore seems to be one of gradation, with the metacognitive vs emotional contents of a feeling both varying in an at least semi-independent fashion.

5. Neurocognitive basis

The extent to which various cognitive feelings share common neurocognitive processes remains an open question, especially as there is already disagreement over the processes underlying specific feelings such as the feeling of knowing. Attempts have been made to map fringe feelings to aspects of global cognitive architectures such as the *interactive cognitive subsystems* (ICS) model, and to formally model metacognitive feelings as higher-order representations of the state of neural networks. It has also been speculated that these feelings may involve the associative memory networks of the mediotemporal hippocampal system, which originally evolved to support external spatial navigation, but then came to support internal cognitive navigation of a less explicitly topographical nature by providing a summary sketch of critical relationships between thoughts, and by pointing to the potential availability of further information (Epstein 2000). This idea that the feelings are embodied in spatial representation systems has some resonance with evidence that implicit learning can influence moment-to-moment visuospatial orienting by guiding attention to the spatial locations where useful information is implicitly anticipated to lie.

Abnormalities of cognitive feelings among clinically abnormal or brain-damaged patients may also provide a useful future source of evidence for underlying processes. Some groups of patients illustrate the behavioural problems associated with the absence of cognitive feelings. People with Capgras syndrome seem not to experience the usual feelings of familiarity when meeting significant people in their life, and have the delusional belief that these people have been replaced by impostors. In a gambling task which involves learning simple predictive patterns, patients with damage to prefrontal cortex fail to experience the usual *hunch phase* in their learning, which in normals is characterized by behavioural signs of having implicitly learned the predictive pattern at an intuitive level while still unable to verbalize the predictive rule (Bechara et al. 1997). Later, the subset of patients who manage to eventually verbalize the rule are still unable to use it to guide their behaviour.

Conversely, other groups of patients illustrate the residual usefulness of isolated feelings. One patient with severe encephalitis, resulting in profound *amnesia and agnosia, experienced an intuitive feeling of preference for sweet over saline drinks in the absence of the usual antecedent taste experiences that would justify the preference (Adolphs et al. 2005). Some of the shades of consciousness reported by so-called *blindsight patients may also provide examples of intuitive cognitive feelings that guide behaviour in the absence of usual visual experiences.

6. Shades of consciousness

Cognitive feelings have a conscious phenomenology, even if sometimes vague, but are grounded in non-conscious processing. They can therefore seem to be a kind of halfway house between conscious and non-conscious mental representations, making people unsure which of these two categories to assign them to. This notion of a shady interface between the conscious and non-conscious is captured by the connotations of the folk psychological terms *hunch* or *intuition*. Confusion is further exacerbated in situations where there is dissociation between different operational criteria for whether mental representations are conscious, such as dissociation between subjective verbal report and more objective behavioural tests (Price 2002, Norman et al. 2006). However, by characterizing and measuring intermediate states of awareness, the empirical study of cognitive feelings can help resolve polarization in debates such as whether learning in so-called *implicit learning paradigms* is purely implicit or explicit. Some authors characterize such intermediate states in terms of the presence of some types of knowledge, such as meta-knowledge (or *judgement knowledge*), in the absence of other qualitatively different types of knowledge, such as detailed *structural* knowledge about learned information (Dienes and Scott 2005). Others see these intermediate states as occupying points on a more continuous gradation of consciousness. In either case, studying the variables that modulate these intermediate states may provide future insights into the dynamic construction of consciousness.

MARK C. PRICE AND ELISABETH NORMAN

Adolphs, R., Tranel, D., Koenigs, M., and Damasio, A. R. (2005). 'Preferring one taste over another without recognising either'. *Nature Neuroscience*, 8.

Bechara, A., Damasio, H., Tranel, D., and Damasio, A. (1997). 'Deciding advantageously before knowing the advantageous strategy'. *Science*, 275.

Bierman, D., Destrebecqz, A., and Cleeremans, A. (2005). 'Intuitive decision making in complex situations: somatic markers in an implicit artificial grammar learning task'. *Cognitive, Affective, and Behavioral Neuroscience*, 5.

Bornstein, R. F. (1992). 'Subliminal mere exposure effects'. In Bornstein, R. F. and Pittman, T. S. (eds) *Perception Without Awareness; Social, Clinical and Social Perspectives*.

Damasio, A. R. (1994). *Descartes' Error: Emotion, Reason, and the Human Brain*.

Dienes, Z. and Scott, R. (2005). 'Measuring unconscious knowledge: distinguishing structural knowledge and judgment knowledge'. *Psychological Research*, 69.

Epstein, R. (2000). 'The neural-cognitive basis of the Jamesian stream of thought'. *Consciousness and Cognition*, 9.

Gardiner, J. M. and Richardson-Klavehn, A. (2000). 'Remembering and knowing'. In Tulving, E. and Craik, F. I. M. (eds) *The Oxford Handbook of Memory*.

Koriat, A. (2000). 'The feeling of knowing: some metatheoretical implications for consciousness and control'. *Consciousness and Cognition*, 9.

Mangan, B. (2001). 'Sensation's ghost: the non-sensory "fringe" of consciousness'. *Psyche*, 7, http://psyche.cs.monash.edu.au/v7/psyche-7-18-mangan.html

Norman, E. (2002). 'Subcategories of "fringe consciousness" and their related nonconscious contexts'. *Psyche*, 8. http://psyche.cs.monash.edu.au/v8/psyche-8-15-norman.html

——, Price, M. C., and Duff, S. C. (2006). 'Fringe consciousness in sequence learning: the influence of individual differences'. *Consciousness and Cognition*, 15.

Price, M. C. (2002). 'Measuring the fringes of consciousness'. *Psyche*, 8, http://psyche.cs.monash.edu.au/v8/psyche-8-16-price.html

Wilson, T. D., Lisle, D. J., Schooler, J. W., Hodges, S. D., Klaaren, K. J., and LaFleur, S. J. (1993). 'Introspecting about reasons can reduce post-choice satisfaction'. *Personality and Social Psychology Bulletin*, 19.

Woody, E. and Szechtman, H. (2002). 'The sensation of making sense. Motivational properties of the "fringe" '. *Psyche*, 8(20). http://psyche.cs.monash.edu.au/v8/psyche-8-20-woody.html

colour, philosophical perspectives According to experience, tangerines are orange. According to science, tangerines are collections of colourless particles. There is some reason to think that the picture of the world provided by experience and the picture of the world provided by science are in conflict. This leads to perhaps the most central philosophical issue concerning colour, the issue of *realism* vs **eliminativism*. Realists hold that the pictures may be reconciled. Tangerines really are orange. By contrast, eliminativists hold that the two pictures cannot be reconciled. Tangerines

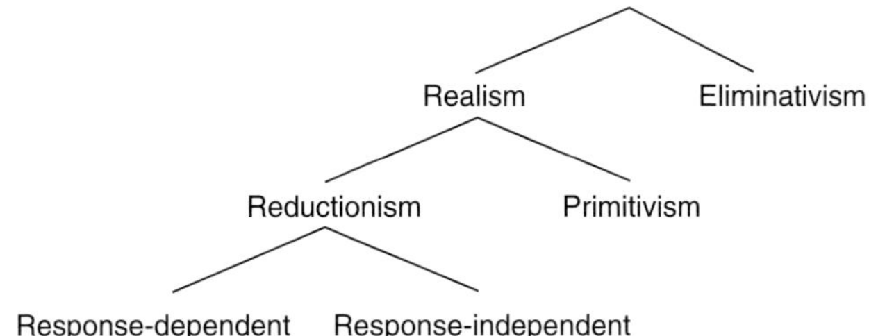

Fig. C1. Philosophical views on colour.

appear orange, but are not really orange: the appearances are misleading. This view, then, eliminates colours from the physical world. This was the view taken by Galileo, who held that colours are only 'in the mind'. Notice that no analogous issue arises for other properties that we experience, e.g. shapes. There is no evident conflict between the picture of shape provided by experience and that provided by science.

There is a second philosophical issue concerning colour. Many philosophers wish to reductively explain all the properties of the common sense world in physical terms. This is due to the popularity of physicalism, the view that everything is explainable in physical terms (see PHYSICALISM and REDUCTIONISM). Typically, the issue of reduction is discussed in connection with the mind, but the same issue arises in connection with colour. There are two views, *reductionism* and *primitivism*. Reductionists hold that colours can be reduced to physical properties. As we shall see, reductionism comes in two different versions. *Response-dependent reductionism* explains colours in terms of how objects affect perceivers. *Response-independent reductionism* explains colours in terms of physical properties of objects that are independent of perceivers, such as properties concerning how objects reflect light. By contrast to reductionists of either stripe, primitivists hold that colours cannot be reduced to physical properties. Primitivism is so called because it maintains that colours are basic or primitive properties that cannot be explained in other terms, much like fundamental physical properties such as *charge* and *mass*. So if one combines realism and primitivism, one takes the view that objects have colours *in addition* to their physical properties. This view, then, rejects reductive physicalism. It bears an obvious analogy to dualism because it recognizes a dualism of physical and chromatic properties at the surfaces of physical objects (see DUALISM). Notice that no analogous issue arises for other properties that we experience, for instance shapes. Shapes are obviously physical properties. There is no *explanatory gap here. By contrast, many believe that, just as there is an explanatory gap between states of consciousness and physical properties, there is also an explanatory gap between colours and physical properties. So it is not obvious that colours are physical properties.

These two issues create a decision tree (see Fig. C1). If one accepts realism, one faces the choice between reductionism and primitivism. If one accepts reductionism, one faces the additional choice between response-dependent reductionism and response-independent reductionism. Alternatively, in view of the difficulties with realist theories, one might accept eliminativism, banishing colours from the external world. Let us now examine the four views at the end points in the decision tree, moving from left to right. We begin with views that combine realism and reductionism, which are popular among philosophers.

1. Response-dependent reductionism
2. Response-independent reductionism
3. Realist primitivism
4. Eliminativism

1. Response-dependent reductionism

Response-dependent reductionism (McGinn 1983) maintains that the property of being orange is a *secondary quality* of external objects: it is defined in terms of the responses objects produce in human beings. In particular, the property of being orange is the property of being disposed to produce orange experiences in normal individuals under normal conditions. By an 'orange experience', I mean the kind of experience one has when one looks at orange objects. To put it crudely, on this view, if a tangerine is in the forest and no species exists to see it, the tangerine is not orange. On response-dependent reductionism, then, colour is a perceiver-dependent property, like being funny or being poisonous. Yet it is a form of realism, because it holds that tangerines really are orange: they are orange, because they are disposed to produce orange experiences in normal individuals under normal circumstances. It is also a form of reductionism, because the property of being disposed to produce orange experiences in normal individuals under normal conditions is a physical property of objects if orange experiences in turn may be identified with physical (e.g. neural) states of persons.

One argument for response-dependent reductionism derives from the possibility of *biological variation* in colour vision (McGinn 1983). Consider a hypothetical case (Pautz 2006). Maxwell and Mabel belong to different species. Owing to naturally evolved differences between their colour systems, a tangerine normally appears orange to the members of Maxwell's species but pure red to the members of Mabel's species. Who gets it right? One option is to say that both get it right. A second option is to say that one gets it right and the other gets it wrong: for instance, the tangerine is orange but not pure red. A third option is eliminativism: neither gets it right. The second option appears arbitrary, and the third flies in the face of experience and common sense. Therefore one might think that the first option—chromatic liberalism—is the best. Response-dependent reductionism secures this result. On this view, when Maxwell says 'the tangerine is orange', he attributes to the tangerine the disposition to normally produce orange experiences in members of his species. When Mabel says 'the tangerine is pure red', she attributes to the tangerine the disposition to produce pure red experiences in members of her species.

But there are problems with response-dependent reductionism. First, it is not clear that it has a sound motivation. Each of the above three options has a cost. True, the claim that only one individual gets it right appears arbitrary, and the claim that neither gets it right is contrary to common sense. But many would say that intuition goes against the verdict of response-dependent reductionism that both get it right. For Maxwell attributes the property of being orange to the tangerine and Mabel attributes the property of being pure red to the tangerine, and many have the intuition that a single object cannot be orange and pure red all over, contrary to response-dependent reductionism. So it is not obvious that this option is the best one. Indeed, in view of the problems with the various forms of realism, it may be that eliminativism is the best option. Second, many philosophers hold that response-dependent reductionism is phenomenologically implausible. Colours, they claim, do not look like dispositions to produce effects in us (Boghossian and Velleman 1989). Instead, they look like intrinsic, non-relational properties of objects on a par with shapes. Third, intuitively, to have an orange experience is to have an experience of the colour orange. The colour orange enters essentially into the specification of orange experiences. If so, then the response-dependent reductionist identifies the colour *orange* with the disposition to normally produce experiences of that very property, *orange*. This appears incoherent or circular (Boghossian and Velleman 1989).

2. Response-independent reductionism

By contrast to response-dependent reductionists, response-independent reductionists identify colours with response-independent properties of objects, that is, properties of objects that are completely independent of the responses objects produce in perceivers (Dretske 1995, Lycan 1996, Armstrong 1999, Tye 2000, Byrne and Hilbert 2003). On the most popular version of response-independent reductionism, colours are properties concerning the reflection of light, or *reflectance properties* for short. On this view, just as water is H_2O, the colour orange is a certain reflectance property. Like response-dependent reductionism, this view is both realist and reductionist. Colours are real properties of physical objects, and they are physical properties of physical objects.

On response-independent reductionism, by contrast to response-dependent reductionism, if a tangerine is in a forest and no species exists to see it, the tangerine is still orange, since the tangerine has the reflectance property that is identical with orange. Likewise, on response-independent reductionism, if we evolved a new colour vision system, so that tangerines came to look pure red rather than orange to us, then the tangerines themselves would remain orange, because they would retain the reflectance property that is identical with orange. By contrast, on a simple form of response-dependent reductionism, the correct description of this scenario is that tangerines change from orange to pure red (somewhat as a substance could go from being poisonous to being non-poisonous as a result of a change in our neurophysiology). In short, response-independent reductionism differs from response-dependent reductionism because it holds colour is an objective property like shape, rather than a perceiver-dependent property like being poisonous.

Typically, response-independent reductionists about colours accept a **representational theory* of our consciousness of colours. On this view, to be conscious of orange is simply to have an experience that represents or registers that something has the colour orange (which, on this view, is identical with a reflectance property). And, typically, they accept a *tracking theory* of sensory representation according to which the brain represents reflectance properties (on this view, colours) in the same way that a thermometer represents temperatures (see INTENTIONALITY). A pattern of neural firing represents or registers a certain reflectance property just in case it is caused by that reflectance property under optimal conditions (Tye 2000), or just in case it has the biological function of indicating that reflectance property (Dretske 1995). This philosophical view of colour fits well with the view in vision science that colour perception is a computational process whereby the reflectances and other properties of objects are recovered from the information arriving at the retina (Marr 1982).

What is the argument for response-independent reductionism? Like response-dependent reductionism, it is both realist and reductionist. So it agrees with experience and common sense, which have it that the world is coloured. And it agrees with physicalism, which seeks to explain everything in physical terms. At the same time, it avoids some of the difficulties with response-dependent reductionism. For instance, as noted above, many would say, against response-dependent reductionism, that colours do not look like dispositions to produce effects in us. Instead, they look like perceiver-independent of objects on a par with shapes. This is exactly what response-independent reductionism says colours are.

But there are also arguments against response-independent reductionism. First, what will the response-independent reductionist say about cases of biological variation, such as the case of Maxwell and Mabel? On a representational theory of colour experience, Maxwell represents the tangerine as *orange* and Mabel represents it as *pure red*. On response-independent reductionism, the represented properties *orange* and *pure red* are identical with different reflectance properties. Furthermore, response-independent reductionists hold that no surface can have *both* of these reflectance properties (Byrne and Tye 2006). Who then gets it right? One option for the response-independent reductionist is to say that the colour orange that Maxwell represents is identical with a reflectance property *R* that the tangerine does have, while the colour pure red that Mabel represents is identical with a different reflectance property *X* that the tangerine does not have (Byrne and Tye 2006). Call this *asymmetrical misrepresentation*. But there are two serious problems with this inegalitarian account of biological variation.

First, we may suppose that Maxwell and Mabel are alike at the receptoral level, so that their visual systems track exactly the same reflectance property *R* of the tangerine. They have different colour experiences because they naturally evolved different *postreceptoral* processing. So, when they view the tangerine and are put into different brain states, both of their visual systems are operating exactly as they were designed by evolution to operate. So, both brain states track *R* under optimal conditions, and both have the function of indicating *R*. So, given the stipulated basic physical facts of the situation, a tracking theory of representation predicts that both Maxwell and Mabel *accurately* represent the tangerine as having the reflectance property *R*. Thus, asymmetrical misrepresentation is incompatible with a tracking theory. In fact, no known theory of sensory representation supports this inegalitarian verdict. To underscore the problem, consider the following. According to asymmetrical misrepresentation, it is Maxwell who accurately represents the tangerine as having *R*, and it is Mabel who inaccurately represents it as having *X*. But if response-independent reductionism is correct, then another possibility is that it is Maxwell who inaccurately represents the tangerine as having *X*, and it is Mabel who accurately represents it as having *R*. (This option holds, contrary to the first option, that the orange colour that Maxwell represents is identical with *X*, and the pure red colour that Mabel represents is identical with *R*.) What could possibly make it the case that one of these possibilities obtains to the exclusion of the other? Apparently, the response-independent reductionist who favours asymmetrical misrepresentation must say that which of these possibilities actually obtains is a kind of primitive fact with no basis in the physical facts of the situation. In other words, he must give up on reduction. Yet achieving a reductive account was one of the motivations behind response-independent reductionism.

Second, the present account of biological variation may have the consequence that we cannot be said to know the colours of things. Maybe our own wiring, like Mabel's, makes us normally represent objects as having reflectance properties (colours) that they do not possess. Then our colour beliefs are false. If, on the other hand, our wiring, like Maxwell's, makes us normally represent objects as having reflectance properties that they do have, then this would seem to be a matter of luck. Either way, we cannot be said to know the colours of objects, which is contrary to common sense. So, given the account of biological variation under discussion, response-independent reductionism does not agree with the common-sense view of colour. Yet agreeing with common sense was one of its motivations.

A second argument against response-independent reductionism concerns *colour structure* (Hardin 1988). Blue resembles purple more than green does. Purple is a binary colour: every shade of purple is somewhat reddish and bluish. By contrast, green is a unitary colour. It does not contain a hint of any other colours. According to the opponent process theory of colour vision (see Hardin 1988 for an accessible account), we experience unitary and binary colours because of features of the colour vision system, although the neurobiological details remain poorly understood (see COLOUR, SCIENTIFIC PERSPECTIVES). But the belief that some colours are unitary while others are binary is justified on the basis of colour experience and experiments on colour naming. It does not stand or fall with any neurobiological theory of colour vision. Here now is the problem for response-independent reductionism. There is no obvious sense in which the blue-reflectance (the reflectance property the response-independent reductionist identifies with blue) resembles the purple-reflectance more than the green-reflectance. Nor is there any sense in which the purple-reflectance is binary, while the green-reflectance is unitary (Byrne and Hilbert 2003). So, the colours our colour experiences represent have structural features which are not possessed by the reflectance properties which normally cause those colour experiences. But then colours must be distinct from those reflectance properties.

A third argument against response-independent reductionism is based on the intuition that there is an explanatory gap: however closely the colour orange and the reflectance property *R* may be correlated, they are intuitively wholly distinct from each other, just as pain is intuitively wholly distinct from the correlated brain state.

3. Realist primitivism

Some philosophers are attracted to the realist view that external objects are coloured, because it agrees with experience and common sense. But, for the reasons we have discussed, they are dissatisfied with both response-dependent reductionism and response-independent reductionism. These philosophers accept realism but reject reductionism, and accept primitivism instead (Campbell 1993, McGinn 1996). This combination of views is called *realist primitivism*. It is realist because it holds that the tangerine has the property of being orange. It is primitivist because it holds that the property of being orange is an extra, primitive property of the tangerine that cannot be identified with its disposition to produce orange experiences or its reflectance property *R*. To highlight this feature of the view, we might call this property *primitive orange*. On this view, then, colours are fundamental properties of the world, like *charge* and *spin*. As noted in the introduction, this view bears an obvious analogy to dualism because it recognizes a dualism of physical and chromatic properties at the surfaces of physical objects.

Now, realist primitivists typically do not stop here. They typically say that the extra, primitive property of being orange 'supervenes on' or 'emerges from' some other properties of the tangerine (see EMERGENCE). On one version of this idea, the property of being orange emerges from the tangerine's disposition to produce orange experiences in perceivers (McGinn 1996). So if a tangerine is in a forest and no species exists to see it, the tangerine does not have the emergent property of being orange, because it does not have such a disposition. This view is analogous to response-dependent reductionism. The difference is that it is a primitivist view, rather than a reductionist view: it holds that the property of being orange is an extra, emergent property of the tangerine, over and above its disposition to produce orange experiences in perceivers. Call it *response-dependent primitivism*. On another version, the property of being orange emerges from the tangerine's reflectance property *R*. So if a tangerine is in a forest and no species exists to see it, the tangerine nevertheless has the emergent property of being orange, because it has the reflectance property *R*. This view is analogous to response-independent reductionism. Again, the difference is that it is a primitivist view, rather than a reductionist view: it holds that the property of being orange is an extra, emergent property of the tangerine, over and above its reflectance property *R*. Call it *response-independent primitivism*. So, although this is not represented in Fig. C4, primitivism as well as reductionism comes in response-dependent and response-independent versions.

What is the argument for realist primitivism of either variety? To begin with, it is a realist view, so it agrees with experience and common sense, which have it that external objects are coloured. At the same time, it avoids the problems with reductionism. For instance, it avoids Hardin's (1988) problem about colour structure. Even though reflectance properties are not unitary or binary, the colour properties that emerge from reflectance properties might be unitary or binary. And realist primitivism avoids the explanatory gap problem, because it endorses the intuition that colours are wholly distinct from reflectance properties.

But there are also problems with realist primitivism. First, one motivation behind realist primitivism is to accommodate common sense, but it is unclear that either response-dependent primitivism or response-independent primitivism accommodates common sense in its entirety. In fact, unsurprisingly, they share some of the problems of their reductive cousins, response-dependent reductionism and response-independent reductionism. Response-dependent primitivism (McGinn 1996) entails that, in the case of Maxwell and Mabel, the tangerine instantiates both primitive orange and primitive pure red, since it normally produces experiences of orange in members of Maxwell's species and it normally produces experiences of pure red in members of Mabel's species. This goes against the intuition that nothing can be both orange and pure red all over. And response-independent primitivism (Campbell 1993) may have the consequence that we cannot be said to know the colours of things. If this view is correct, then objects had response-independent primitive colours prior to the evolution of colour vision. Now, what colour vision system evolved (and hence what primitive colours objects look to have) in any given species was independent of the actual primitive colours of objects. Instead, it was determined by the peculiar set of selection pressures that operated on its ancestors: their habits, dietary needs, predators, and environments.

It follows that if a species happens to evolve a colour vision system that makes objects look to have the primitive colours that they actually do possess, this can only be an accident. This seems to imply that no species (including *Homo sapiens*) can be said to know the primitive colours of objects. What is the point of claiming that objects have primitive colours if we cannot be said to know what those primitive colours are?

A problem that attends both versions of realist primitivism is that they are complicated, as they are dualist views that hold that physical objects have 'extra' or 'emergent' colour properties over and above their physical properties. Therefore Occam's razor counts against both versions of realist primitivism.

4. Eliminativism

All forms of realism, then, face problems. These problems lend some support to eliminativism. On this view, a tangerine in the forest is not orange, even if someone is there to see it. On some versions, colours are 'only in the mind'. We evolved to experience objects as coloured, not because they really are coloured, but because experiencing objects as coloured enhances adaptive fitness. Philosophers today generally favour realism. But in the past many favoured eliminativism, including Galileo, Newton, Descartes, and Locke. And many contemporary vision scientists favour eliminativism. Thus, Zeki writes 'the nervous system... *takes what information there is in the external environment, namely, the reflectance of difference surfaces for different wavelengths of light, and transforms that information to construct colours*, using its own algorithms to do so' (Zeki 1983:746, emphasis original).

I have noted that realist theories come in reductionist and primitivist versions. The same is true of eliminativist theories, although this is not represented in Fig. C4. The eliminativist might hold that colours (or colour *qualia) reduce to neural properties of the brain, which we somehow mistakenly project onto external objects (Hardin 1988). Alternatively, he might hold that colours are primitive properties, which absolutely nothing has (Mackie 1976). On this view, colour properties only live in the contents of our experiences. Similarly, absolutely nothing has the property of being a winged horse: this property only lives in the contents of our thoughts.

The argument for eliminativism is that it provides the best overall account of the facts about colours. Consider, for instance, Maxwell and Mabel, who exhibit a case of biological variation. We have seen that some response-independent reductionists accept asymmetrical misrepresentation: the verdict that one gets it right and the other gets it wrong. The problem is that they cannot provide an explanation of why one gets it right and the other gets it wrong, rather than the other way around. On eliminativism, both get it wrong, so there is no need to decide. And, crucially, the eliminativist may provide an explanation of why both get it wrong, which appeals (among other things) to the claim that objects do not have the colours presented to us in colour experience. The eliminativist can also account for facts involving the unitary–binary character of the colours. If he holds that colours are neural properties of the brain, he can treat them as neural facts. If he holds that colours are primitive properties that nothing has, he can treat them as primitive facts about colours. Finally, because eliminativism banishes colours from the external world, it is much simpler than realist versions of primitivism.

An obvious argument against eliminativism is that it flies in the face of experience and common sense, which have it that the world is coloured. In reply, the eliminativist might point out that the all of the realist theories we have examined depart considerably from common sense at some points. This illustrates a general feature of the philosophical debate concerning colour: here as elsewhere, there is no perfect theory. The best we can do is to try to draw up a balance sheet and see where the balance of considerations tilts.

ADAM PAUTZ

Armstrong, D. M. (1999). *The Mind-Body Problem: an Opinionated Introduction*.

Boghossian, P. and Velleman, D. (1989). 'Colour as a secondary quality'. *Mind*, 98.

Byrne, A. and Hilbert, D. (2003). 'Color realism and color science'. *Behavioral and Brain Sciences*, 26.

—— and Tye, M. (2006). 'Qualia ain't in the head'. *Noûs*, 40.

Campbell, J. (1993). 'A simple view of colour'. In Haldane, J. and Wright, C. (eds) *Reality, Representation, and Projection*.

Dretske, F. (1995). *Naturalizing the Mind*.

Hardin, C. L. (1988). *Color for Philosophers: Unweaving the Rainbow*.

Lycan, W. (1996). *Consciousness and Experience*.

Mackie, J. L. (1976). *Problems from Locke*.

Marr, D. (1982). *Vision: a Computational Investigation into the Human Representation and Processing of Visual Information*.

McGinn, C. (1983). *The Subjective View: Secondary Qualities and Indexical Thoughts*.

—— (1996). 'Another look at color'. *Journal of Philosophy*, 93.

Pautz, A. (2006). 'Sensory awareness is not a wide physical relation'. *Noûs*, 40.

Tye, M. (2000). *Consciousness, Color and Content*.

Zeki, S. (1983). 'Colour coding in the cerebral cortex: the reaction of cells in monkey visual cortex to wavelengths and colours'. *Neuroscience*, 9.

colour, scientific perspectives The human visual system is sensitive to a narrow band of electromagnetic radiation with wavelengths between 400 and 700 nm. These wavelengths are those which pass, largely unattenuated, through the Earth's atmosphere and make up the *visible spectrum*, a term coined by Isaac Newton in

1671. Newton was also aware that colour sensation does not derive from a property of light; 'For the rays to speak properly are not coloured. In them there is nothing else than a certain power and disposition to stir up a sensation of this or that colour'. Here Newton correctly asserts in *Opticks* (1704) that colour is a product of our nervous system. Yet three centuries later, it is apparent that the task of elucidating the neural processes responsible for our chromatic world is far from straightforward. A naive description of the neural basis of colour vision may be caricatured as follows: the human retina contains distinct types of light-sensitive receptors, the retinal cones, adapted to detect light of specific wavelengths; different wavelengths thereby elicit different colour experiences. Nearly everything in this caricature is wrong. Misconceptions about colour perception range from erroneous assumptions about the functions of colour vision as a whole to subtle misunderstandings about the responses of specialized cells in the visual system. Advances in our understanding of the neurobiology of colour vision, often in conjunction with psychophysical studies, have resolved many of these issues and led to a clearer picture of the determinants of colour experience. It is, perhaps, easiest to understand the neurobiology of colour vision in the context of its function. We will initially consider the functions of colour vision, then summarize the mechanisms through which these functions might be realized, and then assess how our current understanding of the anatomy and physiology of the visual system might instantiate those mechanisms. Along the way we note how different aspects of colour-processing are related to the conscious experience of colour *qualia.

1. What is colour vision for?
2. Disentangling wavelength from intensity; disentangling surface reflectance from illumination
3. Anatomy and physiology of wavelength processing

1. What is colour vision for?

Colour perception is mediated by differential responses of the visual system to light of different wavelengths. It is, however, misleading to assume that colour perception has evolved for seeing the wavelength of light, or that different colour qualia simply reflect differences in the wavelength of light. Colour vision, in common with the rest of vision, appears adapted for seeing objects in the world, and objects are seen by virtue of the fact that they reflect light. The ability to respond differentially to the wavelength of light, over and above its intensity, provides a perceiver with additional information about the visual world. Different materials vary in the efficiency with which they reflect light of different wavelengths. Thus determining the relative reflectance of different wavelengths will specify the nature of the surface material of which an object is composed. Unfortunately, the light illuminating the world can vary considerably. The distribution of intensity at different wavelengths, a light's spectrum, differs markedly as sunlight changes over the day, the spectrum of skylight differs from horizon to zenith, and the spectrum of diffusely reflected light in shadows is influenced by the objects that have reflected it. The spectrum of light reaching our eyes from an object is therefore not just determined by the reflectance properties of the object's surface, but also by the spectrum of the light illuminating it. Our ability to see an object as having an invariant colour despite changes in its illuminant is called *colour constancy* and the visual system appears adapted to achieving it, albeit imperfectly (see e.g. Brainard 2003).

We might then propose that colour perception is really for establishing the reflectance properties of materials. Is there any evidence that this is the case? Are the reflectance properties of materials with particular evolutionary value to an organism especially well discriminated? From the seminal work of Allen (1879), a number of studies have addressed this question by comparing the spectral reflectance properties of materials with the sensitivities of the pigments within retinal photoreceptors which are the first stage in permitting an animal to discriminate wavelength. Candidates have included colour variation signalling the ripeness or esculence of major items in animals' diets (Regan et al. 2001) and sexual signals (Dixson 2000).

Is colour vision for anything other than perceiving the surface properties of objects? The ability to respond to lights of different wavelengths confers more potential abilities on an organism than estimating the reflectance properties of objects. If an object has a different reflectance function from its background, an organism can exploit this to segment the object from its background. Spectral differences may well provide better segmentation cues than light intensity (Sumner and Mollon 2000). Intensity variation resulting from direct lighting and shadows can break up the true contours of objects and provide less reliable information than spectral content. The use of wavelength information to segment an object from its background does not require any estimation of the nature of the light illuminating the visual scene and so does not depend on colour constancy. It is only necessary to signal that the reflectance properties of an object and its background are different. The neurological condition of cerebral *achromatopsia, where patients are rendered colour blind as a result of *brain damage, provides evidence that the perception of surface colour and the ability to use wavelength to segment objects from their backgrounds are independent of one another. Achromatopsic observers retain the latter but have no phenomenal experience of colour qualia.

Possessing multiple types of photoreceptors, sensitive to different wavelengths of light, may also be advantageous even if wavelength information is not extracted from their signals. Intensity information will be available over a wider range of wavelengths than would be possible using a single type of photoreceptor, and differently lit environments will be discriminable. The advantages multiple receptor types give for sight in differing lighting conditions provide a plausible mechanism for the earliest origins of colour vision as it does not depend upon the pre-existence of neural circuitry for disentangling wavelength from intensity signals (Pichaud et al. 1999).

2. Disentangling wavelength from intensity; disentangling surface reflectance from illumination

Using multiple receptor types to extend the usable spectrum over which intensity variation can be seen requires little computation—the outputs of the receptors can simply be added together. Disentangling wavelength variation from intensity variation is a little more complex. Estimating the reflectance properties of surfaces is even more difficult.

If receptors are tuned to a specific wavelength to which they are most sensitive, but nevertheless respond less effectively over a range of wavelengths, then responses will be inherently ambiguous. Changes in the response of a single receptor could equally well be caused either by shifts in the wavelength or by the intensity of the light falling upon it. It is only by comparing changes in the responses of receptors which differ in their spectral tuning that these two possibilities can be distinguished. If the stimulating light is composed of a mixture of wavelengths then, although comparisons of receptor responses will distinguish between spectral and intensity changes, a number of different mixtures of lights will, nevertheless, produce identical responses in both types of receptors and hence be indistinguishable (such indistinguishable mixtures are known as *metamers*). In humans, the consequence of possessing fewer receptor types than normal is that colour mixtures that would otherwise be discriminable are seen as identical. The overwhelming causes of colour blindness are genetically based failures to produce one of more photoreceptor pigments, or production of pigments which are abnormally close to one another in the wavelengths of their peak sensitivity. If the number of receptor types increases above the normal complement then otherwise indistinguishable mixtures become discriminable, provided relevant comparisons are computed (see COLOUR VISION, TETRACHROMATIC).

Simple comparisons of the responses of different receptor types therefore allow wavelength and intensity to be disentangled. There is, however, no means by which surface reflectance can be extracted from the information available to the visual system. The problem is that the wavelength composition of reflected light depends on the spectrum of the illuminant. Without knowing the latter, the visual system must rely on heuristics which provide good estimates in most circumstances.

One approach to determining the reflectance property of a surface, in the absence of information about the illuminant, is to select an *anchor*. Anchors are other surfaces in the scene about which one can make educated guesses of their reflectance properties. Various heuristics may be applied to selecting anchors. An object whose surface colour is known can provide a good anchor (a *memory colour*). Alternatively, one might assume that very light surfaces are white and therefore reflect all wavelengths with equal efficiency. The reflectance of any other surface can then be estimated in comparison to one of these anchors simply by computing the chromatic contrast between it and the anchor. If the surface to be estimated and the anchor are not adjacent they can still be compared simply by taking the product of all of the contrasts at the surface boundaries lying on the path between the anchor and the target surface. This scheme forms the core of the *retinex colour-constancy algorithm* developed by Edwin Land (Land and McCann 1971). Its success or failure depends upon two key factors: the accuracy with which the reflectances of the anchors are estimated and, in the case of multiple illuminants, the ability of the observer to determine which parts of a scene are illuminated by lights with different spectra.

There are many other cues which may be used heuristically to gauge the composition of an illuminant and so discount it in the computation of surface reflectances. These include specular highlights on shiny objects within a scene, the colouring of shadows between mutually illuminated objects, and covariations of wavelength and intensity statistics within a scene.

It should be clear that many aspects of colour constancy are likely to depend upon cognitive factors in the interpretation of a visual scene. Nevertheless, understanding the anatomy and physiology of wavelength processing provides us with substantial insights into the mechanism colour vision and the potential neural correlates of colour experience.

3. Anatomy and physiology of wavelength processing

Three different types of cone-shaped photoreceptors in the retina convert lights of differing wavelengths into neural signals (Fig. C2). Recently it has become possible to image, determine the type, and illuminate individual cones in the living human retina. One of

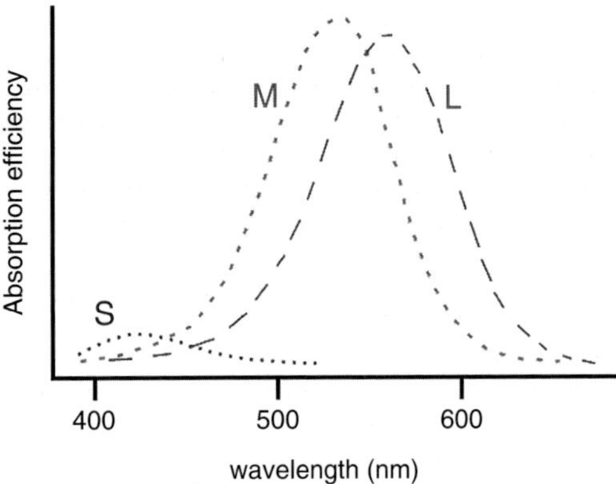

Fig. C2. The retina contains three types of daylight photoreceptors called *cones* . Each type contains a different light-sensitive pigment which absorbs light and produces neural signals in response. The three pigments are sensitive to short- (blueish), medium- (greenish), or long- (reddish) wavelength lights as shown above, and are hence referred to as S, M, and L cones (see Colour Plate 6).

the most remarkable findings of this work is that stimulating any type of cone can evoke any colour experience, demonstrating that colour experience is not determined by cone activations but by the way they are subsequently processed (Hofer et al. 2005). The three cone-types have peak sensitivities to lights with wavelengths of 560 nm, 530 nm and 430 nm, and are referred to as L, M, and S (long-, medium-, and short-wavelength sensitive) cones respectively (informally, red, green, and blue cones). The processes through which colour percepts are derived from wavelength information also begin in the retina but continue in dorsal lateral geniculate nucleus (dLGN) of the midbrain, striate cortex, and extrastriate areas beyond it.

In the retina three types of ganglion cells receive inputs from cones and extract information from them—they form the start of the M (luminance contrast), P (red–green), and K (blue–yellow) visual processing channels. All three ganglion cells have centre–surround receptive field organization. The types of cones feeding each ganglion cell-type and the manner in which stimulation of the centre and surround components of their receptive fields interact determine the nature of the information conveyed from them (Dacey 2000).

Parasol cells pit excitation from both L and M cones against inhibition, again from both (few if any S cones contribute). As a consequence of the symmetry between inhibitory and excitatory inputs, such cells fail to signal overall changes in the intensity of light filling their entire receptive field but are sensitive to differential illumination of centre and surround and can thus signal the presence of a luminance-varying edge falling in the receptive field. These cells form the start of the M-channel and might be seen as implementing the broadening of sensitivity to luminance across the spectrum by integrating signals form different receptors discussed earlier (Fig. C3a).

Both midget ganglion cells and small bistratified cells pit signals from cones of one type against signals from other types and hence convey wavelength information. Midget ganglion cells (the start of the P-channel) pit signals from L and M cones against one another (Fig. C3b). Small bistratified cells (the start of the K-channel) pit signals from S cones against combined L and M cone signals. In the periphery of the retina this opponent receptive field structure breaks down for midget ganglion cells.

As discussed above, in principle, chromatic opponency permits the separation of wavelength and intensity signals. Changes in intensity will act equally on the inhibitory and excitatory fields and hence produce little

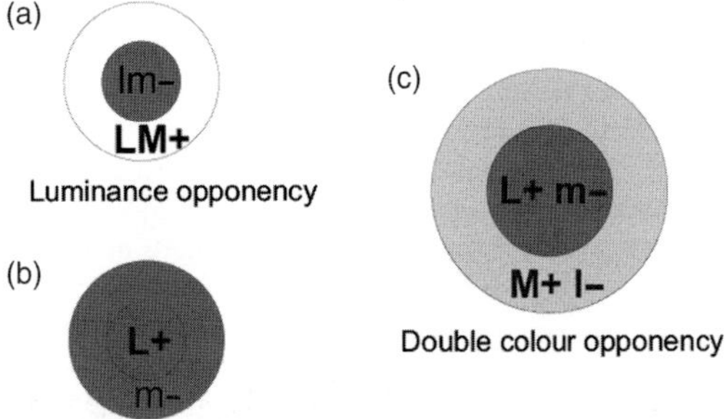

Fig. C3. Outputs from cones feed into cells further into the visual system with a 'centre–surround' spatial organization. (a) At the start of the M-channel combined L and M cone signals in one part of visual space inhibit a cell while the same combination in the surrounding part of space excite it (inhibition and excitation switch roles in other cells). The result is a cell which is sensitive to luminance contrast (edges). (b) At the start of the P-channel L and M cone signals are not combined but are themselves put into opposition. For example, L signals in one part of visual space excite a cell while the M signals in the surrounding part of space inhibit it (inhibition and excitation switch roles in other cells; there are also cells which have inputs from S cones). The result is a cell which is sensitive to variation in the wavelength of light but whose response does not change as luminance varies. (c) In primary visual cortex, combinations of cone signal with excitatory and inhibitory action are put into spatial opposition. Unlike the cells in (b) these 'double-opponent' cells are sensitive to chromatic contrast (see Colour Plate 7).

response. A change in wavelength will, however, elicit a response as it differentially influences the excitatory and inhibitory fields. Such cells can be seen as disentangling wavelength from intensity. They do not, however, signal chromatic contrast—stimulating their centre and surround fields with lights of differing wavelengths produces weak or non-existent responses. There is evidence, nevertheless, that L/M cone opponent signals might help animals detect food sources by wavelength even if determining the shape of the food items requires additional processing (Lovell et al. 2005).

In both the P- and K-channels the receptive field organization found in the retina is replicated in the LGN—in the parvocellular layers and in cells between layers respectively (although K-cells identified by cell-membrane chemistry are also found in the parvocellular layer, with a smaller number being found in the magnocellular layer). Both P- and K-channels project on to cells in the cytochrome-oxidase blobs of striate cortex (groups of cells identified by their membrane chemistry). Some K-cells also project directly to V2 and some P-cells also innervate *V1 interblobs.

There is recent evidence for cells in V1 that respond selectively to specific chromatic contrasts (Conway 2001, Johnson et al. 2001). Unlike the colour-opponent cells in the retina and LGN, these cortical cells have a *double-opponent* organization—their centre fields are both excited by one class of cone input and inhibited by another; in their surround fields the cones types exert the opposite influence (the central inhibitor is excitatory in the surround and vice versa; Fig. C3c). Activation of both the centre and surround fields of such cells will be modulated by changes in the wavelength, but not intensity, of light. The optimal stimulus will be one with different wavelengths in the centre and surround regions of the receptive field. These cells may have inputs from all three cone types, so cells selective for a wide range of contrasts, and for combinations of luminance and colour contrast, could exist. The cells, as has been demonstrated, respond well to borders between differently coloured areas of an image. Such cells could contribute both to the segmentation of visual scene on the basis of colour borders and to early stages of some colour constancy processes (Fig. C4).

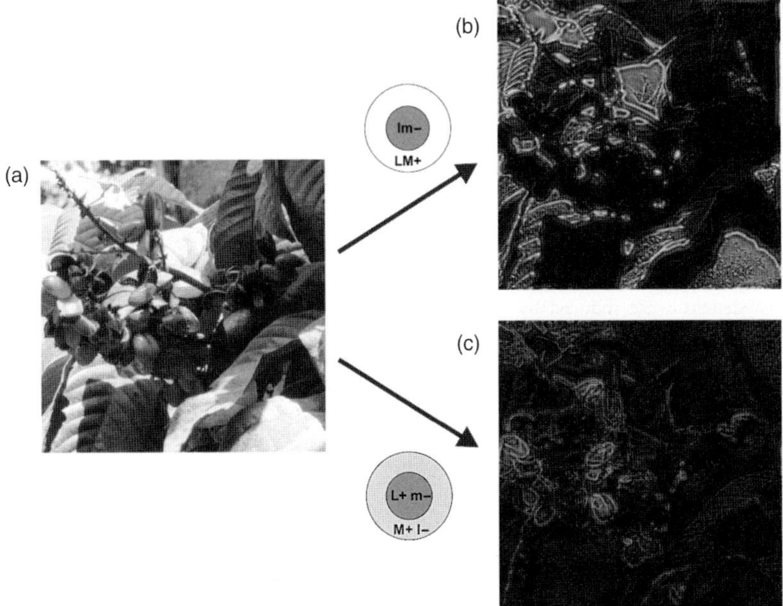

Fig. C4. Chromatic contrast can be more useful in detecting the edges of objects than brightness contrast, which is often due to lighting effects such as shadows. The cone activations elicited by the image (a) were used to compute areas of high brightness contrast (b) and high colour contrast (from L and M cone signals). Brightness contrast is detected by luminance opponent cells in the retina and LGN. Colour contrast is detected only by double opponent cells in striate cortex. The photograph and cone activation data were kindly supplied by Professor T. Troscianko and Dr P. G. Lovell, from Lovell et al. (2005). The image processing is by the author (RWK). (See Colour Plate 8).

Cells in V1 blobs project to the 'thin stripes' in V2. There is tentative evidence that the location of these cells within each stripe is organized in a systematic manner—in *colour maps* (Xiao et al. 2003). Combined with the likelihood that these cells are not responding to wavelength per se, but to the chromatic contrast of light in a particular location against its background, this raises the intriguing possibility that the location of neural activation in V2 thin stripes will correlate quite well with perceived colour.

The evidence for colour processing in V1 and V2 is quite recent; earlier work on cortical colour processing concentrated on extrastriate areas in ventromedial occipital cortex. The clinical condition of cerebral achromatopsia, in which patients lose the ability to perceive colour, not as a result of retinal abnormalities, but rather as a consequence of brain damage, provides strong evidence that brain areas specialized for colour perception exist beyond striate cortex. *Functional brain imaging studies have also shown increases in cerebral blood flow (implying increased brain activity) in these areas when normal subjects observed coloured, as opposed to monochrome, images. The area was therefore dubbed the *colour centre* (Lueck et al. 1989). Responses from single neurons in monkeys in cortical area V4 when the animals were presented with coloured stimuli suggested that the colour centre might correspond to cortical area V4. A number of problems arose with this interpretation. The selectivity of the response of neurons to particular characteristics of stimuli differs only in degree between brain areas. Some neurons in nearly all visual areas respond selectively to wavelength—the proportion in V4 is not comparatively large. In addition, damage to area V4 in monkeys does not result in deficits in discriminations based on wavelength, although deficits were induced by damage to areas anterior to V4 (Heywood et al. 1995).

Areas distinct from those involved in colour perception but associated with the storage of colour knowledge are activated when recalling objects' colours, or differentially activated when seeing objects in typical and atypical colours (Zeki and Marini 1998, Chao and Martin 1999). In addition to imaging studies which isolate areas lateral and anterior to the colour centre, the wide variety of colour-related pathologies resulting from brain damage suggests that different aspects of colour information are represented in anatomically distinct regions. Patients have been found who are unable to retrieve colour information about objects, but retain their ability to discriminate, name, and sort colours—just the deficit one might expect to result form damage to an area storing object–colour associations (Miceli et al. 2001). Other neurological conditions, in which colour discrimination is preserved, include those where colour-naming (Oxbury et al. 1969), short-term memory for colours (Davidoff and Ostergaard 1984), or colour-sorting are impaired (Beauvois and Saillant 1985). Although the functions lost in these disorders might contribute to colour experience through the role of cognitive factors in colour constancy, these functions cannot be necessary for the experience of colour qualia—patients with these deficits do not report any loss of colour experience. This can be contrasted with cerebral achromatopsia, in which colour experience is indeed lost. It has been suggested that the loss of colour experience in cerebral achromatopsia is related to failure of aspects of colour constancy and so, perhaps, the origin of colour experience arises out of the process of estimating the reflectance properties of surfaces (Kentridge et al. 2004).

Colour perception has been used as a favourite example in philosophical discussions of brain and consciousness (Jackson 1986). Although we now know many of its details, it is hard to see how even this knowledge could help us understand what it is like to see in colour even if we now know a lot more about how, and even why, we do so.

ROBERT W. KENTRIDGE AND CHARLES HEYWOOD

Allen, G. (1879). *The Colour Sense: Its Origin and Development.*

Beauvois, M. F. and Saillant, B. (1985). 'Optic aphasia for colors and color agnosia—a distinction between visual and visuoverbal impairments in the processing of colors'. *Cognitive Neuropsychology*, 2.

Brainard, D. H. (2003). 'Color constancy'. In Chalupa, L. M. and Werner, J. S. (eds) *The Visual Neurosciences.*

Chao, L. L. and Martin, A. (1999). 'Cortical regions associated with perceiving, naming, and knowing about colors'. *Journal of Cognitive Neuroscience*, 11.

Conway, B. R. (2001). 'Spatial structure of cone inputs to color cells in alert macaque primary visual cortex (V-1)'. *Journal of Neuroscience*, 21.

Dacey, D. M. (2000). 'Parallel pathways for spectral coding in primate retina'. *Annual Review of Neuroscience*, 23.

Davidoff, J. B. and Ostergaard, A. L. (1984). 'Colour anomia resulting from weakened short-term colour memory'. *Brain*, 107.

Dixson, A. F. (2000). *Primate Sexuality.*

Heywood, C. A., Gaffan, D., and Cowey, A. (1995). 'Cerebral achromatopsia in monkeys'. *European Journal of Neuroscience*, 7.

Hofer, H., Singer, B., and Williams, D. R. (2005). 'Different sensations from cones with the same photopigment'. *Journal of Vision*, 5.

Jackson, F. (1986). 'What Mary didn't know'. *Journal of Philosophy*, 83.

Johnson, E. N., Hawken, M. J., and Shapley, R. (2001). 'The spatial transformation of color in the primary visual cortex of the macaque monkey'. *Nature Neuroscience*, 4.

Kentridge, R. W., Heywood, C. A., and Cowey, A. (2004). 'Chromatic edges, surfaces and constancies in cerebral achromatopsia'. *Neuropsychologia*, 42.
Land, E. H. and McCann, J. J. (1971). 'Lightness and retinex theory'. *Journal of the Optical Society of America*, 61.
Lovell, P. G., Tolhurst, D. J., Párraga, C. A. et al. (2005). 'Stability of the color-opponent signals under changes of illuminant in natural scenes'. *Journal of the Optical Society of America A*, 22.
Lueck, C. J., Zeki, S., Friston, K. J. et al. (1989). 'The colour centre in the cerebral cortex of man'. *Nature*, 340.
Miceli, G., Fouch, E., Capasso, R., Shelton, J. R., Tomaiuolo, F., and Caramazza, A. (2001). 'The dissociation of color from form and function knowledge'. *Nature Neuroscience*, 4.
Oxbury, J. M., Oxbury, S. M., and Humphrey, N. K. (1969). 'Varieties of colour anomia'. *Brain*, 92.
Pichaud, F., Briscoe, A., and Desplan, C. (1999). 'Evolution of color vision'. *Current Opinion in Neurobiology*, 9.
Regan, B. C. et al. (2001). 'Fruits, foliage and the evolution of primate colour vision'. *Philosophical Transactions of the Royal Society of London, Series B: Biological Sciences*, 356.
Sumner, P. and Mollon, J. D. (2000). 'Catarrhine photopigments are optimised for detecting targets against a foliage background'. *Journal of Experimental Biology*, 203.
Xiao, Y., Wang, Y., and Felleman, D. J. (2003). 'A spatially organized representation of colour in macaque cortical area V2'. *Nature*, 421.
Zeki, S. and Marini, L. (1998). 'Three cortical stages of colour processing in the human brain'. *Brain*, 121.

colour vision, tetrachromatic The term *tetrachromacy* describes the physiological possession of four different classes of simultaneously functioning retinal photopigments (also called *weak tetrachromacy*). From an empirical standpoint, tetrachromatic colour vision (or *strong tetrachromacy*) additionally requires demonstrating that mixtures of four independent appropriately chosen primary lights will simulate all distinctions in appearance possible in visible colour space. Independence of the primary lights implies that no mixtures of any subset of these lights (or their intensity variants) will produce an identical match to any combination of mixtures of the remaining lights. By comparison, *trichromacy* empirically requires only three primaries to simulate all visible colours.

Established theory states that humans with normal colour vision are trichromats (as, primarily, are Old World monkeys and apes). The first element of trichromacy is the output from three simultaneously functioning retinal cone classes: short-, medium-, and long-wavelength sensitive (SWS, MWS, LWS) cones. Three cone classes alone do not establish a trichromat colour code, however. A postreceptoral code for three categories of signal is also needed. A standard assumption in vision science is that the postreceptoral recoding of cone outputs initiates the neural trivariant (or trichromatic) property of human colour perception, and the need for only three primary lights to match any test light.

1. Animal tetrachromacy
2. Potential human tetrachromacy
3. Empirical studies of human tetrachromacy
4. Tetrachromacy controversies

1. Animal tetrachromacy

Tetrachromacy is an early vertebrate characteristic, existing in fish and reptiles, and is evolutionarily more ancient than primate trichromacy. Essentially all diurnal birds have four retinal cone types (two SWS classes, plus a MWS and a LWS class) which neurally produce four-dimensional colour experience, or tetrachromatic colour vision. Such birds probably perceive a greater number of distinct colours than humans do, and many more colours than dichromat mammals. Generally, non-human Old World primates tend to be trichromatic and New World primates dichromatic. Recent studies have found that some New World monkeys—the squirrel monkey, spider monkey, marmoset, and dusky titi—are colour vision polymorphic species in which the base condition is dichromacy, although a considerable proportion of individuals are trichromats (Jacobs 1996, Jacobs and Deegan 2005). Many animal species (e.g. squirrels, rabbits, some fishes, cats, and dogs) are dichromatic (as are some colour-deficient humans); they possess only two functioning classes of cone photopigments and need only two primary lights to match the colour of any test light.

2. Potential human tetrachromacy

Physiological considerations of potential human tetrachromacy began in the 1940s with genetic studies of inherited colour vision deficiencies or *Daltonism*. Approximately 8% of Caucasion males exhibit some degree of colour vision deficiency caused by inheriting altered LWS and MWS photopigment genes on the X chromosome. Males, possessing a single X chromosome, are less likely to express both LWS and MWS retinal photopigments than are females, who have two X chromosomes. Furthermore, a female carrying altered photopigment genes may not experience colour vision deficiency, although her male offspring will likely inherit it. Photopigment gene deletions during expression (due to intergenic non-homologous recombination), and alterations (due to missense mutations, coding sequence deletions, or intragenic crossover between different genes) underlie Daltonism. Failure to express either the LWS or MWS photopigment produces a Daltonian form of dichromacy, and expression of altered photopigment genes can lead to colour vision anomalies.

For many years scientists have known that some fraction of human females inherit the genetic potential to produce four cone photopigment variants, and actually express these variants as distinct retinal cone classes with four different spectral sensitivity distributions. Certain females of 'heterozygous' genotypes can express both altered and 'normal' forms of photopigment genes thought to underlie colour matching differences. Retinal expression of four distinct cone classes requires random X-inactivation during embryonic development so that genes from both altered and normal pigment genes are alternatively expressed as photopigments across the retina's cone cell mosaic. The resulting mosaic may include a patchwork of usual SWS, MWS, and LWS cone types, plus, for example, a fourth long-wavelength class variant with peak sensitivity differing from the usual LWS class by 4–7 nm. Frequency estimates of Caucasian females who are potential tetrachromats range between 15% and 47% depending on the heterozygote genotypes considered. Less is known about the actual frequency of expressing four retinal cone classes.

While the potential for human tetrachromacy exists, the general theory suggests that humans process no better than a trivariant colour signal. Thus, four retinal cone classes are a necessary (but not a sufficient) condition for tetrachromatic colour perception, and for true tetrachromacy a tetravariant colour signal processing is also needed.

Some scientists conjecture that humans with four retinal photopigment classes might experience a dimension of perceptual experience denied to trichromat individuals (Jordan and Mollon 1993), implying that cortically humans might process four colour channels, or otherwise learn to use the additional information. New World primate trichromacy suggests a parallel: female spider monkeys possessing extra photopigment gene variants are trichromats, while both males and females without such variants experience only dichromat colour vision. Gene variants thereby allow some female monkeys to experience a dimension of colour experience that other females and males do not (Jordan and Mollon 1993).

3. Empirical studies of human tetrachromacy

Anomaloscope investigations. Typically, psychophysical anomaloscope 'colour-matching' investigations are used to study human tetrachromacy. In an anomaloscope task observers monocularly view a bipartite field of primary mixtures and adjust the primaries in one half-field until a 'colour match' with a fixed test light in the other half-field is obtained. Nagy et al. (1981) examined potential tetrachromacy using such a task with chromatic annulus-surround stimuli and a large-field Rayleigh match task variant. Jordan and Mollon (1993) used both large-field Rayleigh matching and a ratio-matching task where ratios of pairs of primary lights are mixed to match a test light. For evaluating signal processing mechanisms most anomaloscope investigations distinguish 'weak' and 'strong' forms of tetrachromacy to interpret mixture settings of potential tetrachromats. Weak tetrachromacy occurs if an observer has four different cone classes but lacks the post-receptoral capacity to transmit four truly independent colour signals. Nagy et al. (1981) demonstrated this form in potential tetrachromats who accepted trichromatic colour matches made in a context-free (black annulus) background condition, but did not exhibit the stability of such matches under different chromatic background conditions (unlike trichromats). The observation that matched fields become distinguishable in a coloured background clearly indicates weak tetrachromacy, suggesting that the kind of stimulus additivity found in trichromats fails for some potential tetrachromats, or that signals from the extra cone class produce perceptual differences when viewing is contextualized. Nagy et al. (1981) also imply that tetrachromat retinal mosaicism may be a contributing factor in their study.

Strong tetrachromacy arises from four different cone types plus the capacity to transmit four independent cone signals. Such observers would reject large-field trichromat colour matches and require four variables to match all colours. Jordan and Mollon (1993:1501) showed 8 out of 14 candidate tetrachromats refused large-field Rayleigh matches providing 'preliminary evidence for [the strong form of] tetrachromacy'. They also identified two subjects with precise matches in a ratio matching task (as would have been expected from a tetrachromat in their experiment), suggesting one subject's 'tetrachromacy is not of the form we initially envisaged' (1993:1503) although she 'remains in play as a candidate tetrachromat in the strong sense' (1993:1505). Jordan and Mollon (1993) nevertheless remain tentative concerning the existence of 'strong' human tetrachromacy.

Conservative interpretions of both Nagy et al. (1981) and Jordan and Mollon (1993) suggest weak tetrachromacy interferes with the ability of potential tetrachromats to repeat match mixture settings when producing mixtures with fewer than four variables. In this regard, at least, some potential tetrachromats differ from trichromats. Additional factors are likely to influence the empirical identification of human tetrachromats: complexity of colour experience will increase with scene, stimulus, and viewing complexity. Monocularly viewed stimuli used in anomaloscope investigations impose empirical constraints on the dimensionality of perceptual experience, whereas naturalistic binocular viewing of contextualized scenes is more likely to uncover tetrachromacy. Thus, the empirical detection of human tetrachromacy is more likely to occur under complex stimuli and viewing conditions (e.g. Bimler and Kirland 2009).

Non-anomaloscope investigations. Some investigations have employed increased stimulus complexity, examined more natural processing conditions and behaviours, and obtained human observer genotype information (Jameson et al. 2001, 2006, Sayim et al. 2005). These investigations used molecular genetic methods to identify potential retinal tetrachromats, and found differences in perceptual behaviours when a genetic potential existed for more than three photopigment classes. Behaviours that differentiated these potential tetrachromats from trichromat controls included perceiving more colours in diffracted spectra (Jameson et al. 2001); performance variation on a standardized test for trichromacy that was correlated with indices of richer colour experience (Jameson et al. 2006); and colour similarity and colour naming patterns showing cognitive colour processing variation among potential tetrachromats (Sayim et al. 2005). Although such investigations were not designed to address colour vision neural mechanisms or specify forms of 'weak' or 'strong' tetrachromacy, the results show that using empirical conditions that approximate more naturalistic viewing circumstances (e.g. binocular viewing and contextualized stimuli) makes tetrachromacy more apparent, and that the genetic potential to express more than three cone classes correlates with differences in colour categorization, naming, and colour similarity judgements. These findings are among the first to suggest human tetrachromat differences for such colour processing behaviours.

4. Tetrachromacy controversies

Despite the norm of human trichromacy, empirical support for human tetrachromacy exists, and other terrestrial species have evolved the neural hardware for tetrachromacy. Because the evolution of human colour vision capacities is not static, cortical rewiring for tetrachromacy could occur similar to the remapping seen in other visual processing types (e.g. *achromatopsia), suggesting that the assumed trivariant recoding of four retinal colour signals may be more a conservative theoretical constraint than an actual neural limitation. Other human sensory domains show specialization: gustatory 'supertasters' exhibit taste threshold differences linked to variation in taste sensor densities. Human colour vision abilities vary enormously across normal individuals and most of these differences have a genetic base, like the basis underlying tetrachromacy.

Anomaloscope results find a few 'strong' and 'weak' tetrachromat humans demonstrate subtle but reliable colour processing differences; thus, even under an assumed neural trivariance constraint, it is reasonable to expect some tetrachromat perceptual difference. Also, no radical hypotheses are needed for plausible human tetrachromacy given the prevalence of tetrachromacy in non-primate species, the precedents from New World primate trichromacy (Jacobs 1996), and primate diversity (Jacobs and Deegan 2005).

Exactly how the human visual system processes retinal signals to produce colour experience remains unknown. However, the visual system can inductively reconstruct information from the environment (often inferring more than that which is present in the signal alone), and processing extra dimensions of colour experience could be within the computational power of visual system neural circuitry.

Clearly, human tetrachromacy requires further empirical demonstration and discussion. Regardless of the frequency of occurrence of strong or weak tetrachromacy, the potential presence of retinal tetrachromats within a normal trichromat population provides additional opportunities to analyse relations between individual perceptual colour experience and colour-processing behaviours. Trichromacy allows humans to distinguish an estimated 2 million different colours. Even if retinal tetrachromacy produces only minor discriminable differences in a small proportion of human observers, these phenomena remain important from both a perceptual and an evolutionary modelling perspective. Given findings suggesting the possibility of human tetrachromacy, future research should clarify the nature of this potential variation in human perceptual experience.

KIMBERLY A. JAMESON

Bimler, D. and Kirkland, J. (2009). 'Colour-space distortion in women who are heterozygous for colour deficiency'. *Vision Research*, 49.

Jacobs, G. H. (1996). 'Primate photopigments and primate color vision'. *Proceedings of the National Academy of Sciences of the USA*, 93.

—— and Deegan II, J. F. (2005). 'Polymorphic new world monkeys with more than three M/L cone types'. *Journal of the Optical Society of America A*, 22.

Jameson, K. A., Highnote, S. M., and Wasserman, L. M. (2001). 'Richer color experience in observers with multiple photopigment opsin genes'. *Psychonomic Bulletin and Review*, 8.

——, Bimler, D., and Wasserman, L. M. (2006). 'Re-assessing perceptual diagnostics for observers with diverse retinal photopigment genotypes'. In Pitchford, N. J. and Biggam, C. P. (eds) *Progress in Colour Studies 2: Cognition*.

Jordan, G. and Mollon, J. D. (1993). 'A study of women heterozygous for colour deficiencies'. *Vision Research*, 33.

Nagy, A. L., MacLeod, D. I. A., Heyneman, N. E., and Eisner, A. (1981). 'Four cone pigments in women heterozygous for color deficiency'. *Journal of the Optical Society of America A*, 71.

Sayim, B., Jameson, K. A., Alvarado, N., and Szeszel, M. K. (2005). 'Semantic and perceptual representations of color: evidence of a shared color-naming function'. *Journal of Cognition and Culture*, 5.

coma See BRAIN DAMAGE

commissurotomy and consciousness Fifty years ago a surgical procedure for research with cats and monkeys initiated new research on cortical connections and consciousness. This commissurotomy or 'split-brain' procedure combined division of the commissures linking left and right cerebral cortices, including the massive corpus callosum, with an operation to the optic chiasma to separate the inputs from the two eyes.

1. Investigating the organ of consciousness
2. How animals act and know with a divided cortex
3. Manual dominance and antecedents of human cerebral asymmetry
4. Consciousness in the human split brain
5. Cerebral asymmetry, speaking, and knowing
6. Allocation of consciousness between the hemispheres

1. Investigating the organ of consciousness

Brains of animals that swim, fly, or walk map directions for movements in a body-related behaviour space, and they have sensory fields that take up awareness of the world to guide them in the same space. They are bisymmetric, with left and right halves at every level. Larger, longer-lived, more agile, and more intelligent animals have bigger brains, the area of the cortex of the two cerebral hemispheres being in proportion to how long they live and learn. Humans have the largest cortex, and injury or malfunction in it disturbs both intentions of moving and the consciousness of perceiving.

Medical scientists using anatomical studies and clinical accounts of the effects of restricted *brain damage have long tried to fathom how the cortex mediates consciousness, and what the rest of the brain (the limbic system, thalamus, basal ganglia, brainstem, and cerebellum), with many more neurons, contributes. In the 17th century some proposed that the *corpus callosum*, the conspicuous bridge of fibres that connects the cortices of the two hemispheres, is the seat of the soul, conferring an essential unity to consciousness. The innate asymmetry of the human brain became an exciting topic in the 19th century with evidence that lesions confined to the left hemisphere could cause loss of speaking or comprehension of speech, as well as one-sided problems with intentions of the hands. It seemed to some that this indicates that only that the language-aware hemisphere is conscious. The work of neurologists Carl Wernicke, Hugo Liepmann, Jules Dejerine, and Kurt Goldstein confirmed that left and right cortices are different, specifically in the cultivated functions of intelligence, and they concluded that the corpus callosum must contribute to normal integration of mental states, given that damage to it could render the left hand of a right-handed person incapable of obeying verbal instructions, though its manipulatory habits remained normal.

The commissurotomy procedure was further refined for medical use in development of an operation that, by sectioning parts of the commissures, helped children and adults with life-threatening epilepsy to live more normal lives. Roger Sperry received the Nobel Prize for Physiology and Medicine in 1981 for his contributions to this research clarifying cerebral functions of consciousness in animals and humans. Now there is a very large literature on the effects of commissurotomy on perception, learning, and motor coordination. The cerebral asymmetry of human consciousness, and its great variety, is better appreciated, as well as its relation to motivations and emotions that involve the whole brain asymmetrically. Great popular interest has been excited concerning how, and why, individuals come to use left and right brains differently.

2. How animals act and know with a divided cortex

In 1952 Sperry published an essay entitled 'Neurology and the mind–brain problem' in which he argued that speculations about the nature of consciousness are best inferred from patterns of *motor output*—from actions of the body generated by expectant 'motor images' or 'motor sets'—rather than from hypothetical 'processing' of *sensory input* by a disembodied intelligence. This theory guided Sperry's investigation of the mechanisms of consciousness over the next 40 years. He believed that axonal connections spanning long distances in cortical white matter mediate intentions and awareness, and he proposed this idea should be tested by surgical experiments.

Also in 1952, Ronald Myers, working with Sperry in Chicago, divided the optic chiasma so each eye of a cat was connected only to the cortex on the same side, and then trained the cat to choose between visual stimuli with one eye at a time. Myers proved, first, that learning transferred between the separated inputs of the eyes, then that transfer was abolished when the forebrain commissures were divided in a second operation. The chiasma–commissure sectioned 'split-brain' cats could even be trained to make opposite choices with the two eyes. Apparently their visual consciousness was divided. Nevertheless, when free they walked normally, showing no obvious clumsiness or confusion about how to see the world. Presumably the freely moving cat could distribute its brain activity to see with one cortex at a time to access conflicting memories. Was its 'will' still one? Were the two hemispheres equal in potential for perception and memory? Could any information be shared through subcortical bridges? These questions remained unanswered.

In 1954 Sperry took the Hixon Chair of Psychobiology at the California Institute of Technology, where, with Myers and other graduate students and postdoctoral workers, his work with split-brain cats showed that touch perception of shapes or textures felt by left and right paws were also disconnected. Split-brain research was extended to rhesus monkeys, which were more likely to reveal the part one-sided motor intentions of the hands could play in directing consciousness. In test boxes with fixed face masks to control which eye could see stimuli, and a sliding barrier to control which hand could push response levers or feel objects to obtain a food reward, it was demonstrated that monkeys with the optic chiasma and forebrain commissures divided had, like the operated cats, split awareness for objects seen or felt in the hand, and they, too, appeared normally coherent in movements and motivation when out of the test box, except for a loss of binocular depth perception in near central space and occasional confusions of bimanual control.

It became clear that the separated cerebral cortices of vision were not acting on their own and that other levels of seeing could perceive and learn. Experiments showed that certain stimuli could 'leak' learning between the eyes of a split-brain cat or monkey through a brainstem visuomotor system. These stimuli differed in intensity, complexity, size, colour, or brightness—like textures, shadows, and reflections in the world that have usefulness in guiding movement through the time/space gradients of self-related 'ex-proprioceptive' awareness. From my doctoral research with Sperry I concluded that monkeys have two visual systems, operating at different levels of consciousness to guide movement on different scales of moving. One is *ambient*, informing whole-body locomotion and posture change, orientation of the head, and reaching with the arms. The other is *focal*, engaging foveal attention for object identification, and for directing fast sequential manipulations of the hands. Ambient vision, involving subcortical visuomotor systems, is undivided by commissurotomy. The focal system, dependent on cortical analysis and cortico-cortical motor-perceptual links, is split.

3. Manual dominance and antecedents of human cerebral asymmetry

Using stimuli projected in horizontally and vertically polarized light to test for double awareness, Sperry and I obtained evidence that subhemispheric motor processes could channel visual consciousness when a split-brain monkey was using one hand. The monkeys viewed orthogonally polarized and conflicting stimulus pairs on response panels. With the chiasma and corpus callosum divided they could learn two mutually contradictory visual discrimination habits in the right and left half brains, confirming that the split brain could keep apart two realms of awareness and memory that could both be ready to guide actions. But this learning was not just an automatic impression from stimuli; it depended on which hand–eye combination was active. After learning the task with one hand, the split-brain monkeys knew the task with the eye on the opposite side, and they could not immediately change hands. When required to make reaching and grasping movements with the 'ipsilateral' limb (on the same side as the seeing hemisphere, i.e. with the eye on the same side), they were unwilling, and became clumsy, as if blind. Crossed, 'contralateral', pathways linking each half of the cortex to the opposite hand were much more effective for guiding, reaching to pick up objects, and fine exploratory movements of the fingers. John Downer found the same effects in split-brain monkeys, and in the 1970s their anatomical basis was clarified by Jacoba Brinkman and Hans Kuypers. The split-brain monkeys had two eye–hand systems and showed shifts of consciousness between the separated cortices correlated with intentions to move with one or other hand.

Research with split-brain baboons in Jacques Paillard's laboratory in Marseilles found that the animals showed a preference for using one hand for fine manipulations with visual guidance, as humans do, though the side of 'hand dominance' was not consistent for the baboons. Tests with a puzzle-box task requiring use of both hands proved that when the hands had learned complementary moves, the skill for timing and sequencing of the motor strategy was established in the hemisphere opposite the preferred hand, for both hands. These studies support the conclusion that cerebral dominance evolved in primates with manual skill. They related to what Peter MacNeilage, discussing the regulation of speech, called the 'frame and content' strategy of complex motor articulations, which might be the basis for elaboration of the semantic and syntactic motor programmes for mimesis and language in the left hemisphere of predominantly right-handed humans. The baboons learned how to feel the components of the puzzle-box in a succession of complementary moves with the two hands, just as the organs of vocalization and the articulation of speech learn to feel and hear their different moving parts in the uttering of syllables, words, and phrases of speaking. Indeed, speech and manual skill had proved to be the functions most affected by commissurotomy in human subjects.

4. Consciousness in the human split brain

Sectioning of the cerebral commissures, of varying completeness, was performed on human patients in the early 20th century, to remove life-threatening tumours beneath the corpus callosum, and to prevent brain damage caused by epilepsy, but the function of the commissures remained unclear. A series of commissurotomies by Van Wagenen and Herren and tests by Akelaitis in the early 1940s showed equivocal psychological effects, partly because in many cases the sections were not complete and partly because visual testing was not sufficiently controlled, but there were signs that consciousness of the hands was partly divided, and that the right hemisphere could not speak.

The first conclusive demonstrations of profound effects of commissurotomy for human consciousness were made at Caltech in the 1960s. Los Angeles neurophysiologist and neurosurgeon Joseph Bogen, seeing that split-brain animals retained conscious control of their whole body, proposed to Sperry that selected *epileptic patients would benefit from this surgery without serious mental loss. Between 1962 and 1968, nine complete commissurotomies were performed by Philip Vogel and Bogen with success in reducing fits. Psychological tests performed by Sperry and Bogen assisted by Michael Gazzaniga soon revealed that, while, after a variable time in which speech was lost and the hands showed dissociated activities, the general psychological state and behaviour was, in most cases, little affected, there was a profound separation in mental activities. Other studies with commissurotomy patients carried out since, in the USA, France, and Australia, have produced similar findings.

After the operation, immediate central awareness of what is being focused on by eyes or hands is in two. The shape of an object felt in the left hand out of sight cannot be matched to the same kind of object felt separately and unseen in the right hand. If the eyes are stationary, an object a few degrees to the left of the fixation point cannot be compared to one on the right side. Comparable divisions in olfactory and auditory awareness may be demonstrated. Furthermore, although sight and touch communicate normally on each side, left visual field to left hand or right visual field to right hand, the crossed two-hemisphere combinations fail, as if experiences of eye and hand were obtained by separate persons.

The division of sight for detail is sharp at the midline as long as the patient keeps the eyes fixated. When he or she is free to look to left and right and to see in both halves of vision what both hands are holding, the division of awareness ceases to be apparent. Moreover, outside the discriminating centre of awareness, division of consciousness is incomplete. With touch on arms, legs, face, or trunk, there is transfer of feeling between the sides. Large, long-lasting stimuli moving in the periphery of the left visual field can be described. Intuitive seeing of surroundings by 'ambient vision' (also called *blindsight to emphasize that it is a 'less conscious' level of awareness than categorical object awareness)—necessary for walking, for maintaining balance, and to locate off-centre targets of attention before eyes move to fixate—is not divided by commissurotomy. Each cerebral hemisphere can initiate eye movements to left and right, and can reach to left and right with either hand. This 'speculative' or 'expectant' peripheral awareness, in absence of clear contrary evidence, can generate 'false' or illusory notions, and can fail to register or 'neglect' stimuli.

5. Cerebral asymmetry, speaking, and knowing

The most significant finding of the early tests performed by Sperry, Bogen, and Gazzaniga was the failure of the right cerebral cortex to articulate words. When conscious of stimuli in the left visual field or left hand, the subjects were often speechless. If urged to reply, they reported some weak and ill-defined event, or else they *confabulated experiences, unable to apply a test of truth or falsity to spontaneously imagined answers to questions. With stimuli in the right field the subject could name, compare, and describe objects or the occurrence or non-occurrence of stimulus events.

Commissurotomy patients offered a direct approach to questions that have been debated in clinical neurology since the discovery, over a century ago, that muteness or disturbance of language comprehension can result from brain injury confined to the left hemisphere. Could the right hemisphere comprehend spoken or written language at all? Could it express itself in signs, by writing, or by gesture? Could it make any utterance? Could it reason and think? Was it really conscious?

In the past 40 years, Gazzaniga and his colleagues have made many tests of commissurotomy subjects, attempting to measure selective attention and perceptual information processing by cognitive modules. His 'cognitive neuroscience' approach popularizes the view that consciousness is a product of logical processes and dependent on 'interpretation' by language. It does not explain how consciousness evolved to guide animal movement and with the benefit of affective regulations, or how it develops in a child. It leaves obscure how immediate sympathetic awareness of intentions and emotions in action is possible between animal subjects, and between humans, infant or adult, and how such awareness might lead to language.

The tests performed at Caltech proved that some comprehension of spoken and written language was present in the mute right side of the brain. Information about how this hemisphere should perform a test could be conveyed by telling it what to do, and if the name of a common object was projected to the right cortex only, the patient could retrieve a correct example by hand, or identify a picture of it by pointing. The right hemisphere could solve simple arithmetic problems by arranging plastic digits, out of sight, with the left hand. Nevertheless, vocabulary and sentence meaning as well as powers of calculation of the right hemisphere were greatly inferior to these abilities in the left hemisphere of the same patient. Rarely, a patient could start an utterance with the right hemisphere, but the vigilance of the more competent left hemisphere blocked the initiative after the first syllable or letter. In general only the left hemisphere could (or would) speak or calculate. Written responses to left field stimuli were more complete than spoken ones, which, as Bogen emphasized, may indicate that symbolic communication by hand activity is more fundamental or more 'primitive' than speech.

Jerre Levy found that the right hemisphere was superior on certain tasks that tested for non-verbal intelligence, such as visual or touch perception of configurations, and on judgements involving exploration of shapes by hand or manipulative construction of geometric assemblies or patterns. Robert Nebes confirmed that the right hemisphere was better able to recognize familiar objects with incomplete pictorial data, and better able to perceive whole shapes from parts seen or that were felt in the hand. Bogen described the right hemisphere thought as 'appositional' and the left as 'propositional'.

Perceptual confabulations were prominent. With stimuli, pictures, drawings or words, crossing the vertical meridian both hemispheres gave 'false' responses showing perceptual 'completion' or 'neglect' in the ipsilateral field. Occasionally when the left hand attempted to touch an object perceived moving in the right field the subject said it 'disappeared' just as the move was started. This 'erasure' from consciousness appeared to delete apperceptions in both hemispheres at the moment when one hand was starting a movement to reach a goal object in the opposite side of the body.

6. Allocation of consciousness between the hemispheres

To further test intentional effects on consciousness, Levy, Trevarthen, and Sperry gave split-brain subjects a free choice of which hemisphere to use to respond in tests. Halves of two different pictures were joined together down the vertical midline to make a double picture or *stimulus chimera*. When presented to the split-brain patient with the join on the fixation point, information about each half is received in a different hemisphere. The tasks were designed so that in every trial a correct choice could be made using either left or right experience. Preference for one half of the chimera depends on one-sided intentions, or preparations to think, that arise in response to the test instructions. With this test, preferred modes of understanding of the hemispheres can be revealed, as well as functions that allocate interest and expectation between the two hemispheres. Tests showed that the right hemisphere cannot imagine the sound of a word for an object seen, so it cannot perform rhyming 'in the head' to match names for drawings (e.g. 'eye' matches 'pie'; 'key' matches 'bee'). Evidently the dominance of the left hemisphere for motor control of speaking involves a one-sided ability to predict *how words will sound*.

Preference for the right hemisphere in *matching appearances* becomes strong for unfamiliar complex shapes with no simple name, for colours, and for faces. With pictures restricted to the left hemisphere, face recognition by commissurotomy patients is poor and identification is achieved by a laborious checklist of details such as glasses, moustache, or hat that must be memorized and searched for. Dahlia Zaidel used comparison of pictures in tests of visual imagination and memory to confirm that there is a stark contrast in cognitive style, imagination, and memory strategies between the hemispheres.

Occasionally commissurotomy patients show activation of one or other side *independently of task requirements*. Sometimes the 'wrong' hemisphere attempts a task, and performance suffers. This *metacontrol*, biasing the link between expectations and intentions in disregard of the processing required, may contribute to habitual differences in the way normal individuals process cognitive problems. It may lie behind differences in mental abilities—e.g. leading one person to be skilled at, and prefer, visuo-constructive tasks while another is gifted at verbal rationalizations. Since the hemispheres of commissurotomy patients become progressively more alike by changes compensating for their separation, tests with them probably reveal only reduced forms of hemisphere specialization as these exist in intact brains where complementary activities cooperate.

Eran Zaidel developed a method for blocking off half of the visual field of one mobile eye of a commissurotomy patient so they could take part on much more natural 'narratives' of experience and share them with a researcher. He attaches a contact lens to the eye that carries a small optical system and screen. The patient can cast eyes over a test array while picking up visual information by only one hemisphere. These tests prove that each of the hemispheres can elaborate awareness of the meanings of words and pictures employing metaphor. Objects may be linked in awareness by their customary usefulness and social importance as well as by more obvious perceptual features. Names, colours, temperatures, and many other properties of things may be correctly identified from black and white pictures.

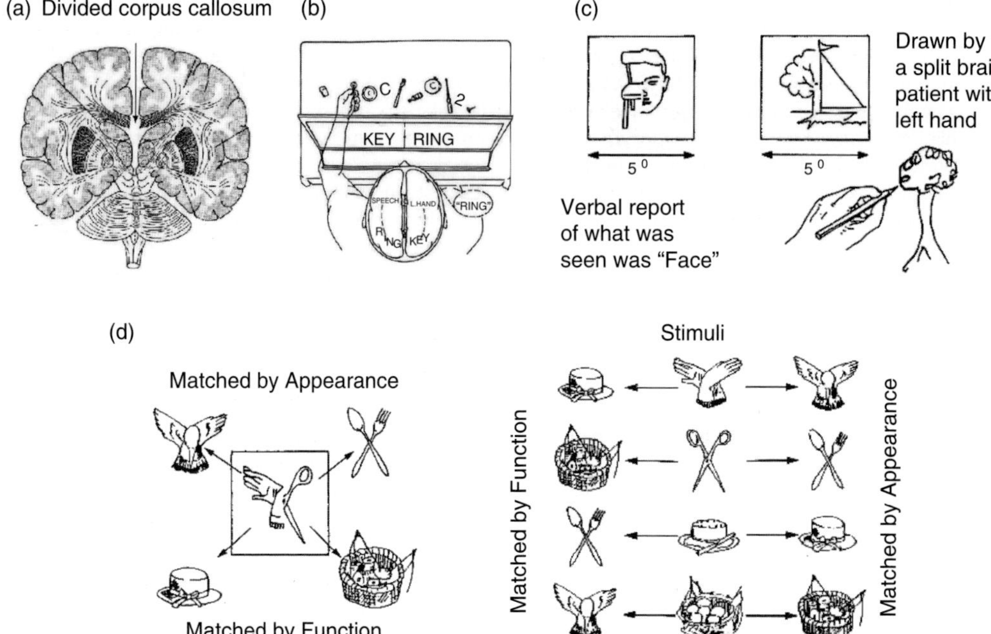

Fig. C5. Visual and haptic consciousness in the separated hemispheres of commissurotomy patients. (a) and (b), illustrations from Sperry's publications: (a), the divided corpus callosum; (b), the separation of word recognition reported verbally for the right visual field from recognition of an object in the left hand to match a word in the left field. (c) how chimeric stimuli are reported, by speech (left hemisphere—right visual field) and by drawing (right hemisphere—left visual field). (d) use of chimeric stimuli to demonstrate the different recognition systems of left and right hemisphere. The left hemisphere matches by 'function' or 'meaning', which can be easily verbalized. The right hemisphere matches readily by appearance or form.

The tests of Zaidel and Sperry have shown that both hemispheres of commissurotomy patients are capable of supporting personal consciousness. Each can exhibit a strong sense of the social and political meaning of pictures or objects that are being inspected while the other hemisphere is not seeing them. Comprehension of words, spoken or written, is surprisingly rich in the right hemisphere, but when words are combined in a proposition, the comprehension of the right hemisphere falls drastically. The linguistic abilities of the right hemisphere resemble those of a nursery-school child.

The human brain has *inherent motives* adapted to create and maintain a society and its culture by two complementary conscious systems, which differ not only in their cognitive achievements, the focus of most research studies, but also in their emotions and 'personality' or self–other regulation. As Donald Tucker has recorded, the two halves of the brain are adapted to guide the actions of the body with different emotions, the left being more 'assertive' or proactive and environment challenging, the right being more self-regulating and 'apprehensive'. These innate differences guide the development of attachments and cooperative understanding in early childhood when the functions of the cerebral hemispheres are growing rapidly and changing in response to experience gained intersubjectively—by shared consciousness.

Research with normal subjects inspired by split-brain research proves that individuals vary greatly in asymmetric cerebral functions and consciousness. Such diverse factors as sex, age, handedness, education, and special training correlate with psychological and physiological measures of cerebral lateralization and hemispheric activation. It is not hard to perceive advantages of such physical and psychological diversity in the most highly cooperative of animal beings, in whom bodies, minds, and the actions and the relational experiences of society and culture become inseparable.

Commissurotomy patients have helped us understand how consciousness, intention, and feelings are generated in activity *at different levels* of brain function. Regulation of intentional activity and phenomenal experience is a multi-layered phenomenon. It does not appear necessary to imagine that the 'self', which must maintain a unity, is split when the forebrain commissures are cut, although some of its activities and memories are depleted or dissociated after the operation. Most importantly, the complementary emotions that regulate personal experience and moral and cooperative awareness with others are not dissociated by commissurotomy, though the efficiency of their control may be diminished.

COLWYN TREVARTHEN

Bogen, J. E. (1993). 'The callosal syndromes'. In Heilman, K. M. and Valenstein, E. (eds) *Clinical Neuropsychology*.

Levy, J. and Trevarthen, C. (1976). 'Metacontrol of hemispheric function in human split-brain patients'. *Journal of Experimental Psychology: Human Perception and Performance*, 2.

Marks, C. (1981). *Commissurotomy, Consciousness and Unity of Mind*.

Nagel, T. (1971). 'Brain bisection and the unity of consciousness'. *Synthèse*, 22.

Sperry, R. W. (1974). 'Lateral specialization in the surgically separated hemisphere'. In Schmitt, F. O. and Warden, F. G. (eds) *The Neurosciences: Third Study Program*.

—— (1982). 'Some effects of disconnecting the cerebral hemispheres' (Nobel lecture). *Science*, 217.

—— (1984). 'Consciousness, personal identity, and the divided brain'. *Neuropsychologia*, 22.

Trevarthen, C. (1974). 'Analysis of cerebral activities that generate and regulate consciousness in commissurotomy patients'. In Dimond, S. J. and Beaumont, J. G. (eds), *Hemisphere Function in the Human Brain*.

—— (1990). 'Integrative functions of the cerebral commissures'. In Boller, F. and Grafman, J. (eds) *Handbook of Neuropsychology*, Vol. 4.

—— (ed.) (1990). *Brain Circuits and Functions of the Mind: Essays in Honour of Roger W. Sperry*.

—— and Reddy, V. (2007), 'Consciousness in infants'. In Velman, M. and Schneider, S. (eds) *A Companion to Consciousness*.

Zaidel, D. (1994). 'A view of the world from a split-brain perspective'. In Critchley, E. M. R. (ed.) *The Neurological Boundaries of Reality*.

Zaidel, E. and Iacoboni, M. (eds) (2003). *The Parallel Brain: the Cognitive Neuroscience of the Corpus Callosum*.

——, Iacoboni, M., Zaidel, D. W., and Bogen, J. E. (2003). 'The callosal syndromes'. In Heilman, K. M. and Valenstein, E. (eds) *Clinical Neuropsychology*.

Zangwill, O. L. (1974). 'Consciousness and the cerebral hemispheres'. In Dimond, S. J. and Beaumont, J. G. (eds) *Hemisphere Function in the Human Brain*.

complexity See INFORMATION INTEGRATION THEORY

concepts of consciousness Consciousness is a complex feature of our mental life, and the concepts we use to talk and think about it are correspondingly diverse. The terms 'conscious' and 'consciousness' are used in a variety of ways both in everyday speech and theoretical practice, none of which is specially privileged.

Indeed, the adjective 'conscious' varies not only in its meaning but also in the sorts of things to which it is applied. Sometimes it is used to attribute so-called *creature consciousness* to persons or organisms, and at other times to ascribe *state consciousness* to mental states or processes (Rosenthal 1986). Each in turn is interpreted in many ways. Thus it crucial to explicate these various concepts clearly, and then determine what links, if any, there may be among them.

1. Creature consciousness
2. State consciousness
3. Conceptual links and relations

1. Creature consciousness

A person, organism or other relevant system (e.g. a suitable robot) might be described as conscious in a number of different, though perhaps interrelated, respects.

Sentience. At minimum, a conscious creature might simply be one that is sentient, i.e. capable of sensing and responding to its environment (Armstrong 1981). Organisms vary in the quantity and quality of information to which they are sensitive, and it is not clear where to draw the threshold for being conscious in the relevant sense. Indeed such sensitivity varies by degree, as does the speed and flexibility with which organisms can respond, and there may be no sharp dividing line. Plants respond adaptively to changes around them, as do protozoa, but few would regard them as conscious or sentient in the relevant sense. Mammals, birds, and even lizards seem to qualify, but what about shrimp, grasshoppers, sea slugs, or anemones? In part we may not know enough about their actual sensory and behavioural capacities, but our difficulties also reflect a certain vagueness in the concept itself. What counts as 'sensing' or 'responding' is itself far from clear in marginal cases.

Wakefulness. Most sentient creatures exhibit multiple states of alertness. They vary over time in how sensitive or responsive they are to the world around them as well as in their level of core activity. One might regard a creature as conscious only when it is in a relatively high level of alertness and thus using its sensory and response capacities in an active way. Merely having such capacities would not suffice: only when they were being actively used would a creature count as conscious in the relevant sense. It would not qualify as such when it was *sleeping deeply, in a coma, or sedated. However, just where to draw the boundaries is unclear. How alert or wakeful must a creature to be to qualify? Should it count as conscious when it is dreaming, drowsing, emerging from *anaesthesia, or having an *epileptic absence? Wakefulness, like sentience, varies in degree along multiple dimensions, and there is no obviously right way to draw the boundaries for being conscious in the relevant sense.

Self-awareness. Some concepts of creature consciousness require a conscious creature to be aware not only of its surroundings but also of its own awareness of its world (Carruthers 2000). Such concepts treat consciousness as a form of self-awareness (see SELF-CONSCIOUSNESS). An automaton might be sentient and awake in so far as it actively responds to sensory inputs but not count as conscious in the *self-aware* sense because it lacked reflective inner-awareness of its own outer-awareness. That intuition is sometimes supported by appeal to cases such as that of the absent-minded long-distance highway driver (Armstrong 1981) or of the petit mal seizure patient who persists in an ongoing activity while 'absent' (Penfield 1975). They respond to their surroundings, but they are not conscious in the reflective sense because they are not aware of their of own awareness.

One may interpret the self-aware requirement in multiple ways, and the relevant concept of consciousness will vary correspondingly. One might demand explicit, fully conceptualized self-awareness, in which case many complex creatures such as dogs, cats, or even young children would fail to qualify. Indeed, such a requirement might exclude all non-linguistic creatures. Alternatively, if basic forms of implicit and non-conceptual self-awareness sufficed, the concept would apply to a far wider range of cases. Creatures incapable of explicit I-thoughts might nonetheless be reflectively aware of their own minds in an implicit and non-conceptual but nonetheless very real way. A dog watching the preparation of its dinner would seem to be aware of its own hunger and desire, even if it lacks explicit I-thoughts.

**What it is like.* Thomas Nagel (1974) famously defined a conscious creature as one that 'there is something that it is like to be'. Bats and horses are conscious in the Nagel sense just if there is something that it is like to experience the world from the bat or horse point of view. A conscious creature is one that has an experiential perspective or subjective point of view.

A system might be quite sophisticated in its sensory and response abilities yet lack a point of view in the relevant subjective experiential sense. We feel confident that there is something that it is like to be a pig, a pigeon, or a lemur. But anti-computationalists have denied that there is anything it is like to be a digital electronic computer, no matter how powerful or intelligent its responses may be (Searle 1992). Having a subjective point of view seems to require something of another sort, something other than mere intelligence or response abilities. But what it is or how it might be produced remains unclear.

The notion of a point of view may get a bit fuzzy at the margins. Is there anything it is like to be an iguana or a honeybee? It may be hard to decide or even to grasp what the issue comes to in such cases. However, there are plenty of clear central cases. We seem to know it when we see it, even if we cannot say just what it is we know is there. We just know that wolves and beavers are conscious in the 'what it is like' sense when they smell each other on the wind.

Subject of conscious states. If the notion of state consciousness could be defined in a way that made no essential appeal to creature consciousness, then conscious creatures might be non-circularly analysed as the subjects of such states. A conscious creature would simply be one that had conscious states in the relevant sense. Understood in that way, the concept of a conscious creature is secondary and derivative from a more basic concept of a conscious state. Thus what being such a subject would involve turns crucially on how the concept of state consciousness is itself understood.

Transitive consciousness. A distinction is commonly drawn between transitive and intransitive senses of consciousness. As well as predicating consciousness of creatures in various senses, we also speak in a relational way of creatures being *conscious of* something. The 'of' here is *intentional, and it involves being *directed at* an object, the object of which the creature is conscious. It is that object-directedness which supposedly distinguishes *transitive consciousness* from the various predicative concepts above, which might be classed as types of *intransitive consciousness*.

As a grammatical or logical fact, the transitive and intransitive concepts differ. We speak both of a creature's *being conscious* and of its *being conscious of* some *x*. The latter requires a direct object, some *x*, whether real or not, of which it is conscious. But one should be cautious about the psychological implications of grammatical distinctions. Many of the so-called intransitive concepts seem on analysis to involve intentional directedness as well. For example, a creature could not be sentient with respect to its surroundings nor self-aware without being intentionally directed at the relevant sorts of inner and outer objects. As a matter of grammar no direct object may be required, but as a matter of psychology an intentional object is entailed.

2. State consciousness

Concepts of state consciousness are equally diverse. Mental states and processes can be described or conceived of as conscious in a variety of distinct if interrelated senses.

State one is aware of. On one very common usage, a conscious mental state is simply a state one is aware of being in (Armstrong 1981). A conscious desire or memory is just a desire or memory that one is aware of having. An unconscious desire is transformed into a conscious one not by a change in the desire itself but by one's becoming aware of having that desire. Conceived of in this way, the conscious–unconscious division among our mental states simply tracks the extent and limits of our self-awareness.

So-called *higher-order theories are concerned most directly with conscious states in this sense. According to higher-order theory, a mental state *M* of subject *S* is conscious just if *S* is also in a simultaneous higher-order state—either perception-like (Lycan 1996) or thought-like (Rosenthal 1986)—whose content is that *S* is in *M*.

Qualitative state. Conscious states might be distinguished as those that involve so-called *qualia or experiential feels, such as the red associated with the visual experience of a ripe tomato, the taste of a pineapple, or the pain in a stubbed toe (Chalmers 1996). On this concept, a conscious state must do more than merely represent; it must do so in a way that involves the presence of experiential qualities or so called 'raw feels'. The nature of such qualia is matter of current controversy—as is their very existence. Thus one's concept of qualitative state consciousness will depend upon one's account of qualia.

Phenomenal state. The term *phenomenal property* is sometimes used interchangeably with *qualitative property*. However, if the two are distinguished, one might conceive of conscious states as states with a *phenomenal aspect that goes beyond the presence of experiential feels. Following a long tradition, going back at least to Immanuel Kant, the phenomenal has been understood to concern the overall structure of experience. It thus includes global organizing aspects such as the fact that our experience is structured as the unified continuous experience of an ongoing self set within a world of objects ordered in space, time and causality. Thus the presence of such aspects would be part of what is implied by the concept of a phenomenally conscious state (Husserl 1913/1931).

Subjective state. The term **subjective*, like 'phenomenal', is often interchanged with 'qualitative', but again it may useful to keep them distinct. The term 'subjective' can be understood as referring to important aspects of mind not captured by those other notions.

On an epistemic reading, a subjective state or feature might be one that can be known only in a certain way, perhaps only from the first-person experiential perspective (Jackson 1982, Van Gulick 1985). The subjective taste of a mango can be known or understood only from the perspective of those who have had that experience. On a more ontological reading, subjective features are those that can exist only as states of a subject, or only from the perspective of a subject. A pain that exists without being felt by anyone may be impossible. In this sense subjective states exist only as modes of experiential subjects. On either reading, a perspectival link is an essential element in the concept of a subjectively conscious state.

'What it is like' states. Thomas Nagel's (1974) notion of 'what it is like' might be used to define a conscious state as one that there is something that it is like to be in. A visual perception or memory is a conscious one in this sense just if there is something that it is like to have that perception or that memory. Nagel's concept has intuitive appeal, but what it involves is not so clear. It may be just a particularly first-person way of picking out the same features aimed at by the qualitative, phenomenal, and subjective concepts of a conscious state, or perhaps it is something more. But if so, it remains unclear what that extra element might be.

Access consciousness. From a more third-person perspective one might define conscious states in terms of the access they afford to other parts of the mind. Following Ned Block (1995), a state is *access conscious if its content is readily available for inference, application, and report. On this more functional concept, a visual perception's being access conscious is not a matter of qualia or raw feels, but of the degree to which its visual information is readily and flexibly available for use by other mental systems in guiding personal behaviour and making reports. If one can report and act in all the relevant ways on the information in that state, then it counts as a conscious perception in the access sense.

Narrative consciousness. Normal experience exhibits a narrative structure; it is the 'story' of the self. It forms an ongoing and relatively coherent history from the perspective of a more or less unified self, whether actual or merely virtual (Dennett 1991). Only a subset of one's states are included in that stream, and those that are might be counted as narratively conscious on that basis. The concept of a narratively conscious state is simply that of a state that appears in one's stream, i.e. in one's self-interpreted experiential narrative.

3. Conceptual links and relations

Given that there are so many concepts of creature consciousness and equally many or more of state consciousness, what relations might there among them? What links are there, either among those in each family or between the two families of concepts? The cross-product of possibilities is far too large to survey in any comprehensive way, but a few notable relations should be noted.

One might choose to treat either creature consciousness or state consciousness as primary, and analyse the other in terms of it. Conscious creatures might be conceived of derivatively as simply those that have conscious states. Or, working in the other direction, conscious states might be defined as those that occur in conscious creatures.

Alternatively, one might view the two conceptual families as interdependent and accord neither clear priority. The creature level and the state level might be two complementary ways of conceptualizing and viewing the overall nature and structure of conscious mentality. Our understanding of conscious states and processes may enhance our understanding of what it is to be a conscious creature. And, conversely, reflecting on the nature of conscious creatures, selves, and subjects may provide important insights for better conceptualizing conscious states and processes.

The division between creature and state concepts is cross-cut by that between so-called first-person and third-person concepts of consciousness. The former are concepts that are applied and understood from the 'inside', i.e. from within the experiential perspective. By contrast the latter are grounded in external factors such as behaviours, reports, and functional capacities.

Although the distinction between first-person and third-person concepts is ubiquitous in the literature, its application is less than clear in many cases. In general, it is not possible to sort the various concepts of consciousness into those that are first-person and those that are third. Most instead have a first-person and a third-person mode of use. For example, one might suppose that phenomenality is a paradigmatically first-person concept in so far as it concerns the structure and feel of experience. But one could also approach it from an external perspective, as by the method of **heterophenomenology* (Dennett 1991), which aims to inferentially construct a conscious being's 'phenomenal world' on the basis of its responses and reports. The same duality of use applies in general to our various concepts of consciousness. Each can be used in either a first-person or third-person mode, though one or the other method will dominate in many cases.

In terms of inter-family relations, there are obviously corresponding pairs among some state concepts and analogous creature concepts. The self-awareness concepts in each family involve a reflective aspect of inner-directed intentionality of the sort that higher-order theories aim to explain, and Nagel's 'what it is like' test might be used as a criterion both for conscious creatures and for conscious states.

Within the families, specific clusters of concepts appear to overlap or interpenetrate each other. The qualitative, phenomenal, and subjective notions of state consciousness offer somewhat different slants on the experiential dimension of consciousness, which is the aspect most closely associated with the so called **hard problem* and the supposed resistance of consciousness to explanation (Chalmers 1996). Although those three concepts are often used interchangeably with each other and with the 'what it is like' concept, it is useful to keep them distinct. They focus on different aspects of experiential consciousness, and thus provide the opportunity to articulate and explain its various aspects and their interrelations.

The notion of a point of view—whether subjective, narrative, or phenomenal—figures as well in multiple concepts of both state and creature consciousness. Others, such as the notion of access consciousness, may seem to be orthogonal, but even in those cases important interlinks may be involved. For example, the unified integration associated with phenomenal structure seems apt to support the richness of inferential connection and application associated with access conscious states. The fact that phenomenality and access consciousness so often co-occur is not likely mere coincidence. More explanatory links appear to be involved.

We use the noun 'consciousness' as well as the adjective 'conscious' in its various senses. However, that need not imply any commitment to consciousness as a thing or substance over and above conscious states and creatures, at least not any more that we are committed to the existence of redness or squareness as distinct entities over and above red objects and square objects. Consciousness in that respect is like life. Contemporary biologists do not regard life itself as something over and above living organisms. Life is not an extra substance or force that gets added into organisms. Similarly, the existence of conscious creatures and states need not involve the presence of consciousness as an extra ingredient or substance. Conscious creatures are different from non-conscious ones just as living systems are different from non-living ones, but in neither case need that difference be a matter of an added basic force or substance.

Given that states and creatures can be conceived of as conscious in so many different ways, care must be taken to avoid confusion and merely verbal disputes. One needs to be clear about which sense one intends and not to conflate one concept with another. However, the multiplicity of concepts need be no embarrassment. Nor does it provide any reason to disparage consciousness as ill defined. Given the complex nature of conscious mentality, a pluralistic diversity of concepts is just what we need to understand it and explain it in all its many aspects.

ROBERT VAN GULICK

Armstrong, D. (1981). 'What is consciousness?' In *The Nature of Mind*.
Block, N. (1995). 'On a confusion about the function of consciousness'. *Behavioral and Brain Sciences*, 18.
Carruthers, P. (2000). *Phenomenal Consciousness*.
Chalmers, D. (1996). *The Conscious Mind*.
Dennett, D. C. (1991). *Consciousness Explained*.
Husserl, E. (1913/1931). *Ideas: General Introduction to Pure Phenomenology*, transl. W. Boyce Gibson.
Jackson, F. (1982). 'Epiphenomenal qualia'. *Philosophical Quarterly*, 32.
Lycan, W. (1996). *Consciousness and Experience*.
Nagel, T. (1974). 'What is it like to be a bat?' *Philosophical Review*, 83.
Penfield, W. (1975). *The Mystery of the Mind: a Critical Study of Consciousness and the Human Brain*.
Rosenthal, D. (1986). 'Two concepts of consciousness'. *Philosophical Studies*, 49.
Searle, J. (1992). *The Rediscovery of the Mind*.
Van Gulick, R. (1985). 'Physicalism and the subjectivity of the mental'. *Philosophical Topics*, 13.

conceptual thought A central question about consciousness turns on a distinction between sensory and conceptual aspects of mind: does consciousness in the phenomenal sense extend to *both* aspects, or is it exclusively a sensory affair? The question, though central, is hard to frame because of obscurities both in the relevant sensory/conceptual distinction, and in the relevant notion of consciousness. But briefly we may say this. The relevant sensory aspect includes appearances of colour, shape, location, movement, sound, taste, and odour; bodily feelings of pain, pleasure, pressure, and warmth; and modality-specific *imagery (e.g. visualization). And the conceptual aspect comprises the exercise of capacities for inference, classification, and analogy—what is thus involved in using concepts. Finally, phenomenal consciousness has to do with consciousness in the '*what it's like' sense. There is, for example, some way it feels to you to be in pain, there are ways colours look to you, and quite generally, there are ways in which it seems to you to have the experiences you do—and there is, in every such case, something that it is like for you to have such experiences. What it is like for you is the phenomenal character of the experience, and phenomenally conscious states are just those which have phenomenal character in this sense. Now, the issue is roughly this. Are occurrences of non-sensory conceptual thought conscious in the phenomenal sense? Should we say they have phenomenal character that is not exhausted by that of whatever sensory experiences and imagery coincide with them?

Foundational issues about consciousness depend on whether we say phenomenal character is exclusively *sensory* (what we might label the *exclusive* view), or whether we find it extends to *conceptual* activity more generally (the *inclusive* view). For example, only if we are exclusive can we accept approaches to phenomenal consciousness (like Michael Tye's and Fred Dretske's) that propose to explain it as a species of sensory representation. Exclusivists and inclusivists would also obviously differ on whether a search for the neural basis of consciousness should be confined to whatever aspects of the brain are dedicated to sense perception and imagery. Further: only inclusivists can propose (as do Alvin Goldman and David Pitt) that our 'introspective' knowledge of mind can be generally accounted for in terms of some uniquely first-personal sensitivity to the phenomenal character of our experience. And the two camps will divide on the special value that attaches to consciousness in this sense. Exclusivists will see it bound up only with a special consideration due the sentient, while inclusivists will take it to concern also whatever distinctive value accrues to 'higher' faculties. Exclusive views have been defended in, e.g., Jackendoff (1987), Lormand (1996), Robinson (2005), Georgalis (2003), and Wilson (2003). Inclusive views are advocated in Horgan and Tienson (2002), Pitt (2004), Siewert (1998), and Strawson (1994).

Care must be taken not to misrepresent the views of either camp. Inclusivists need not claim that thoughts have distinctive sensation-like 'feels'. And they are not committed to saying that conscious episodes of non-imagistic thought and understanding could occur in isolation from the sort of general (e.g. inferential) abilities many would deem requisite for the possession of concepts. Exclusivists, for their part, need not simply deny conceptual thought is phenomenally conscious—they may say rather, that it is so only indirectly, through being accompanied by relevant sense experience or imagery (e.g. verbal imagery that expresses it). What, then, is the dispute? Most would accept that subjectively discernible differences occur in what and how we understand and think. And it will be granted that these are not just differences in how something appears to the senses, or in the modality or content of imagery. But consensus is more elusive on the question: do any such more-than-sensory differences count as **phenomenal*? This question need not be addressed only with an appeal to 'what it seems right to us to say' directly in response to it. There is a place here for reasoned consideration. Further attempts to clarify what is meant by 'phenomenal character' should be part of this. Also, we should examine arguments for inclusivism (like Pitt's) that hold we need to recognize differences in occurrent thought as phenomenal in nature to account for the immediacy with which we know our own minds. But we also need to consider argument from critical first-person reflection on actual cases.

At least two general kinds of cases seem pertinent: (1) unverbalized occurrences of non-imagistic thought; and (2) experiences of understanding.

Regarding (1): we should take note of occasions on which we have warrant for asserting: 'It just occurred to me that...'; 'I was just thinking of...'; or 'I just realized that...'. If there was something it was like for a thought to occur to us on such occasions, but we cannot recall having either formed an *image of* or *verbalized* what we were thinking at that earlier time, and yet, we have no reason to attribute this to a deficit in memory, then we have prima facie reason to be inclusive. For then there is phenomenal character to thought even when we lack evidence of anything sensory with which we can plausibly identify it.

Type (2) cases—'experiences of understanding'—are various. Consider the following. (1) You repeat a word or phrase until it becomes for you a 'meaningless sound'. (2) You *cease to follow* the meaning of a text (in a language in which you are fluent) and then you re-read it, *following* the meaning. (3) You are faced with a syntactically odd or complex sentence—at first it does not make sense to you, and then, suddenly, it does. (4) You encounter a sentence in a language you understand poorly or not at all—initially it means nothing to you, but subsequently you 'get' it. Finally, (5) consider instances of ambiguous phrases—first taken (or understood) one way, then another: cases of 'interpretive switch'. In each of (1)–(5), you may ask: (a) Is there a subjectively discernible change in what it is like for you to undergo the experiences involved? (b) If so, can you plausibly conceive of this change purely in sensory terms, without resort to what is thought, or understood by the utterance? Answering 'yes' to (a) and 'no' to (b) seems to give you reason to be inclusive.

An inclusive view must confront difficult questions that arise once we consider a distinction between *what* is thought (i.e. thought *content*) and *how* it is thought (i.e. its *mode*—as, e.g., a doubt, a supposition, or a judgement), and associated controversies over *externalist* and *internalist* views of content. Are the more-than-sensory differences in the phenomenal character of thought separable from thought-content and mode? It will seem not, if we have no way to conceive of what it is like for us to think, except in terms of thought-mode and content. But externalist views of thought content may seem to suggest an alternative. If, as externalism holds, having the right external causal connection to the world is essential to thought content, and the subjective character of experience could remain the same even when these connections were broken, might not a literally thought-less subject have experience with the very same phenomenal character as a conceptual thinker? Against this, one may argue that the thought experiments crucial to establishing externalism do not show this is possible, but, at most, only that some ways of identifying thought content would distinguish two subjects content-wise who were phenomenally the same. For example, in a standard externalist thought experiment, a (chemically uninformed) subject on Earth is thinking that 'there is water in a glass', while another, similarly ignorant and phenomenally type-identical subject (on Twin Earth) is thinking (not this, but) that 'there is twater in a glass'. ('Twater', we assume, names a Twin Earth substance superficially similar to, but microstructurally quite different from, Earth's H_2O.) But this leaves it open that two such subjects may still be *somehow* cognitively similar, insofar as the conception one has of *water* is no different from that the other has of *twater*. And if having what they share would be enough to make someone a thinker of thoughts, then externalism does not refute the idea that phenomenal character is sufficient for some kind of thought content.

CHARLES SIEWERT

Georgalis, N. (2003). 'The fiction of phenomenal intentionality'. *Consciousness and Emotion*, 4.

Horgan, T. and Tienson, J. (2002). 'The intentionality of phenomenology and the phenomenology of intentionality'. In Chalmers, D. (ed.) *Philosophy of Mind: Classical and Contemporary Readings.*

Jackendoff, R. (1987). *Consciousness and the Computational Mind.*

Lormand, E. (1996). 'Nonphenomenal consciousness'. *Noûs*, 30.

Pitt, D. (2004). 'The phenomenology of cognition, or, what is it like to think that P?'. *Philosophy and Phenomenological Research*, 69.

Robinson, W. (2005). 'Thoughts without distinctive non-imagistic phenomenology'. *Philosophy and Phenomenological Research*, 70.

Siewert, C. (1998). *The Significance of Consciousness.*

Strawson, G. (1994). *Mental Reality.*

Wilson, R. (2003). 'Intentionality and phenomenology'. *Pacific Philosophical Quarterly*, 84.

conditioning The word 'conditioning' has two different meanings, only one of which is uncontroversial. In common usage, even in the psychological literature, the word is used to refer to a *kind* (or *kinds*) of learning, but formally it refers only to two basic *procedures* that have been used to study learning; instrumental and Pavlovian conditioning. The question of what exactly is learnt under these procedures is very much a matter of ongoing debate. As will become apparent, this question is particularly important when we are considering the role that conscious awareness might play in 'conditioning'.

1. Instrumental conditioning
2. Pavlovian conditioning
3. Evaluative conditioning
4. The role of awareness in conditioning

1. Instrumental conditioning

Instrumental, or *operant, conditioning* is a procedure in which behaviours increase or decrease in frequency as a consequence of being followed by reinforcing (rewarding) or punishing outcomes. For example, Thorndike, who discovered instrumental conditioning, noticed that cats escaping from his 'puzzle boxes' initially seemed to behave in a largely random manner until they inadvertently 'solved' the puzzle, pushing a lever and releasing themselves from the box. He concluded that many sophisticated, apparently goal-directed behaviours may depend on an essentially blind mechanism that simply favours successful behaviours—those that happen to lead to reward. An implicit assumption was that the strengthening of successful behaviours was completely automatic and independent of conscious thought. *Pavlovian*, or *classical, conditioning* is a procedure in which a neutral stimulus (most famously, a bell) repeatedly predicts the arrival of a behaviourally important stimulus (like food), resulting in the previously neutral stimulus acquiring the ability to produce responses relevant to the behaviourally important stimulus (like preparatory salivation).

Both these procedures reliably produce learning in a very wide range of species—from ants to elephants (and humans)—which is usually taken to mean that the learning mechanisms engaged under these procedures are in some sense fundamental properties of neural activity and that they have been conserved over evolutionary time. Indeed, a major rationale for studying learning in rats and pigeons—still the main experimental subjects for such research—is that the conditioning mechanisms themselves are thought to be essentially identical, at least across the vertebrates, and so choice of species is largely a matter of convenience. If this view is valid, it implies that the learning in such circumstances should be very simple, automatic and independent of conscious control or interference. Interestingly, in the case of human learning, exactly the opposite view now dominates—that is, that conditioning does not occur in humans in the absence of awareness of the stimulus contingencies.

It had been almost universally assumed that conscious awareness was unnecessary (indeed irrelevant) for any kind of conditioning until three separate reviews of the evidence for conditioning in the absence of awareness each concluded that the accumulated evidence was, in fact, unconvincing (Brewer 1974, Dawson and Schell 1985, Shanks and St John 1994). This conclusion was subsequently reinforced by two more critical reviews (Lovibond and Shanks 2002, Shanks 2005). The reviews differ in their details, and are directed at different bodies of empirical data, since they span nearly 30 years, but the main thrust of the arguments have remained the same. In common with most of the research conducted in this area, the reviews concentrated on the possible role played by awareness of the *relationship* to be learnt in a conditioning situation, *while* that learning is taking place. There are clearly other things that learners may or may not be aware of (e.g. the stimuli being learned *about*), but these have been considered less critical or less interesting questions (Boakes 1989). As might be imagined, the difficult part of demonstrating conditioning without awareness is in devising a measure of awareness that captures all of the learner's relevant conscious knowledge without providing them with explicit information about the contingency they had been exposed to. The main criticisms of the awareness tests that have been used is that they were either too insensitive, and so simply failed to detect conscious knowledge possessed by the learners, or that they asked the wrong questions, failing to detect the conscious knowledge that actually helped in the learning task. As will be discussed below, these criticisms are important and frequently valid, but unless our default assumption is that conditioning does depend on awareness, it is equally important to be sure that awareness tests only measure conscious knowledge, without any contamination from unconsciously acquired information, and that claims of strong links between awareness and conditioned responding are held to the same high standards of evidence as alleged dissociations. In other words, reasons for doubting the evidence purporting to show conditioning without awareness are not, themselves, reasons for believing that conditioning depends on awareness. This is a separate claim, in need of independent empirical support.

Starting with Thorndike himself, a number of researchers have investigated whether instrumental conditioning can occur in the absence of awareness of the relationship between responding and its consequences. Many of those studies were criticized in Brewer's (1974) review, mostly on the grounds that the awareness tests used were too insensitive, and in many early cases they clearly were, but there are at least a few studies that have produced reasonably compelling evidence of instrumental responding without awareness. For example, Hefferline et al. (1959) showed that when termination of a loud, unpleasant noise was made contingent on a small movement of the subject's thumb (detected by an electrode), thumb twitches increased in frequency. Similarly, Liebermann et al. (1998) constructed a fake *extrasensory perception (ESP) task, in which feedback that the subject had selected the card the experimenter was 'thinking of' was actually contingent on the subject's voice volume, and produced both conditioned increases and decreases in volume, without subjects becoming aware of the contingency. In both these tasks the intention of the experiment was disguised by a convincing cover story that participants seem to have believed.

Unfortunately, despite these apparent successes, it is difficult to evaluate the extent to which instrumental conditioning can occur without awareness because there is an essentially infinite number of ways in which a response can increase or decrease in frequency, and so no way to be sure that even a very sensitive awareness test actually measures awareness of the particular 'response' reinforced in any given situation. For example, although Hefferline et al's subjects may, in fact, have been completely unaware of the relationship between their thumb movement and the offset of the loud noise, they *may* have been aware of the relationship between some correlate of the thumb movement and noise offset, about which they were not asked a specific question. Presumably a general increase in muscular tension, certain kinds of gross bodily movements, or even thinking about flicking switches might each produce small, inadvertent or incidental movements of the thumb, and so it may have been any of these (or a host of others) that were actually reinforced—and no sensitive, specific measure of awareness could hope to capture all of them. Equally plausible correlated hypotheses can be postulated to underlie the voice level effects found by Liebermann et al. Of course this is not to say that instrumental conditioning does not happen without awareness—the fact that it occurs in headless cockroaches strongly suggests that it can—just that it is, in practice, difficult to be sure that it has. For this reason, most of the research designed to test whether conditioning can occur without awareness has focused on classical or Pavlovian conditioning.

2. Pavlovian conditioning

Pavlovian conditioning was discovered around the same time as instrumental conditioning when Pavlov, a digestive physiologist, noticed that the dogs he was using in his experiments started salivating prior to the delivery of food. His research led him to believe that the anticipatory salivation occurred because the close temporal proximity of some neutral stimulus and the food had given the neutral stimulus the power to produce the same reflex normally elicited by the food. More modern research (starting with Rescorla 1967) has demonstrated that this kind of conditioning actually depends on the extent to which the previously neutral stimulus *predicts* the arrival of the behaviourally significant stimulus (the extent to which the predicted stimulus is *contingent* on the signal), although there is no reason to suspect that this more complex process is necessarily more likely to depend on conscious mechanisms. There are two main paradigms that have been used to study the role of awareness in classical conditioning—conditioning of psychophysiological responses (mainly eyeblinks and skin conductance) and evaluative conditioning.

In a typical human psychophysiological Pavlovian conditioning experiment, a participant is exposed to two or more neutral stimuli (usually sounds of different frequencies), one of which predicts the delivery of a puff of air to the eye (in some experiments) or a mild electric shock (in others). Puffs of air to the eyeball produce eyeblinks, measured by electrodes over the eye muscles, and electric shocks produce a range of physiological responses, but the most frequently measured is a change skin conductance level. These kinds of contingencies produce rapid conditioning, with changes in the psychophysiological measures usually detectable after just a few pairings, and reliably higher responding to the sound paired with the shock or air puff than to the other sounds after tens of pairings. Because the relationship to be learnt is so straightforward, and because it is completely under the control of the experimenter, it is easy to exhaustively test for awareness of the contingency participants are exposed to, and so these kinds of paradigms have formed the major testing ground for the role of awareness in conditioning. Of course, the relationship is so straightforward, and the predicted stimulus sufficiently aversive, that it is not really particularly surprising that there is typically a tight relationship between awareness and conditioning in such studies, as long as awareness is measured sensitively. The most sensitive awareness test developed is to have subjects turn a dial to continuously indicate the extent to which they expect to receive an electric shock (or an air puff), and the usual finding is that there is very little evidence of conditioning until there is also evidence of a conscious expectancy (although Perruchet 1985 collected data in which these two measures in fact dissociated). The normally tight relationship between expectancy and conditioning has been widely interpreted to mean that conditioned responding *depends* on developing an awareness of the contingency, but it is, of course, only a demonstration that conscious awareness of the contingency is *sufficient* to produce a 'conditioned' response. In order to demonstrate that conscious awareness is also *necessary* for conditioning it must be shown that there are no conditioning paradigms in which conditioned responding can occur in the absence of awareness of the contingency. Since this is logistically impossible (there will always be the possibility of an untested paradigm that would yield unconscious conditioning), it must at least be demonstrated that the evidence for a tight relationship between awareness and conditioning is equally strong in paradigms where the contingency is less obvious, and in which the learner's attention is not explicitly drawn to the contingency, as it almost certainly is when they are asked to continuously self-report their expectancy on a dial.

One way of making the contingency less obvious is to introduce a delay between the tone and the puff of air. Squire and colleagues (reviewed in Clark et al. 2002) used exactly this strategy, comparing the role of awareness in traditional forward conditioning, in which the tone starts before the air puff, but is still on when the air puff arrives, and in trace conditioning, in which the tone is over before the air puff arrives. As well as rendering the contingency less obvious, the trace conditioning procedure might be expected to draw on memory mechanisms, and the results of these studies are consistent with that expectation. The major findings are that in trace conditioning learning is apparent only in subjects classified as aware of the tone–puff contingency in a later questionnaire. Subjects who show no awareness of the contingency do not produce conditioned eyeblinks, and neither do amnesiac subjects, who have memory deficits resulting from damage to the hippocampus. All three groups show conditioned responding in normal, forward conditioning. While criticisms have been levelled at the adequacy of the awareness test used in these experiments (Lovibond and Shanks 2002), the fact that the results map perfectly onto findings from rabbit eyeblink conditioning, in which rabbits with hippocampal lesions learn in forward, but not trace, conditioning situations (whereas intact rabbits learn in both situations), suggests that there is a genuine dissociation between these procedures, and that awareness (requiring at least an intact hippocampus) is necessary only in the trace conditioning procedure. This implies that awareness is not, therefore, necessary for basic Pavlovian conditioning.

An alternative way to make the contingency in a Pavlovian conditioning paradigm less obvious is to avoid the use of an aversive stimulus by burying the to-be-learnt contingency in an innocuous (cued) reaction time task. This was the approach used by Burke and Roodenrys (2000), and they also concluded that basic conditioning can proceed in the absence of awareness of the contingency. In this task, learners are simply asked to respond as quickly as possible to two target shapes which appear in a continuous sequence of shapes, replacing each other every 250 ms. The order of the shape sequence is random except that one of the targets is always preceded by a cue shape. All subjects come to respond more quickly to cued than to uncued targets, including those identified as unaware in a post-learning awareness test designed to be as sensitive and specific as is possible without providing the subjects with awareness of the cue–target contingency that they did not possess during the task.

3. Evaluative conditioning

The other major human conditioning procedure that has been used to study the role of awareness is evaluative conditioning. In this procedure affective responses are transferred from a liked or disliked stimulus to a neutral stimulus it is paired with (for a review see De Houwer et al. 2005). For example, if a face rated as neutral (neither liked nor disliked) is presented in close temporal proximity before a disliked face, in a long string of faces, then the neutral face is subsequently rated as more disliked than it had been. The effect also works for liked stimuli. Since it is true that most people seem unable to account for many of the likes and dislikes they have, this kind of learning seemed particularly likely to proceed unconsciously, and, indeed, all of the early studies suggested that awareness was not involved in evaluative conditioning. More recently collected data, however (reviewed in Lipp and Purkis 2005), has resulted in a controversy that almost exactly parallels the earlier debate about whether traditional, psychophysiological conditioning can occur in the absence of awareness. The current consensus seems to be that evaluative conditioning is a genuine, if experimentally fragile, conditioning phenomenon, but that the issue of whether it can occur in the absence of awareness has not yet been conclusively resolved. Learned *synaesthesia (Stevenson and Boakes 2004), on the other hand, a conditioning phenomenon that shares many features with evaluative conditioning, has provided perhaps the clearest evidence yet collected of unconscious learning in a conditioning paradigm.

In a typical odour–taste learned synaesthesia experiment, participants first rate the sweetness (for example) of various sniffed odours, and are then exposed to the odours paired with tastes (in a sucrose solution, for example). Just as in an evaluative conditioning experiment, some of the properties of the taste stimulus transfer to the odour, so that an odour that has been paired with sucrose is subsequently rated as sweeter than it had been before conditioning. The awareness test used in these studies involves re-exposing subjects to the odours, immediately after the main experiment, and asking them to identify which taste each had been paired with. This is a very sensitive and specific technique, and it results in some subjects being classified as aware of (at least some of) the taste–odour pairing(s), and some being classified as unaware. There is no relationship between the size of the conditioning effect and conscious knowledge of the stimulus pairing, suggesting that in this paradigm, at least, awareness is not only unnecessary for conditioning, it is irrelevant.

4. The role of awareness in conditioning

In evaluating the evidence for the role of awareness in conditioning it is important to remember that Pavlovian and instrumental conditioning are only *procedures* for studying learning. In both paradigms, there is ample opportunity to learn a wide range of things, including, of course, whatever it is that enables people to become consciously aware of the contingency they have been exposed to. But given the wide range of species that do learn in conditioning situations, and the accumulated evidence from human studies suggesting that behaviour can change in these paradigms in the absence of awareness of the contingencies, it is likely that some of the things learned in conditioning paradigms do depend on awareness and some do not. If we are to ever understand the functional role of consciousness in learning, then the simplicity of conditioning paradigms makes them particularly attractive avenues for research.

DARREN BURKE AND CAROLINE TOMICZEK

Boakes, R. A. (1989). 'How might one find evidence for conditioning in adult humans?'. In Archer, T. and Nilsson, L. G. (eds) *Aversion, Avoidance and Anxiety: Perspectives on Aversively Motivated Behaviour.*

Brewer, W. F. (1974). 'There is no convincing evidence for operant or classical conditioning in adult humans'. In Weimer, W. B. and Palermo, D. S. (eds) *Cognition and the Symbolic Processes.*

Burke, D. and Roodenrys, S. (2000). 'Implicit learning in a simple cued reaction-time task'. *Learning and Motivation*, 31.

Clark, R. E., Manns, J. R., and Squire, L. R. (2002). 'Classical conditioning, awareness, and brain systems'. *Trends in Cognitive Sciences*, 6.

Dawson, M. E. and Schell, A. M. (1985). 'Information processing and human autonomic classical conditioning'. In Ackles, P. K. et al. (eds) *Advances in Psychophysiology.*

De Houwer, J., Baeyens, F., and Field, A. P. (2005). 'Associative learning of likes and dislikes: some current controversies and possible ways forward'. *Cognition and Emotion*, 19.

Hefferline, R. F., Keenan, B., and Harford, R. (1959). 'Escape and avoidance conditioning in human subjects without their observation of the response'. *Science*, 130.

Lieberman, D. A., Sunnucks, W. L., and Kirk, J. D. J. (1998). 'Reinforcement without awareness I: voice level'. *Quarterly Journal of Experimental Psychology*, 51B.

Lipp, O. V. and Purkis, H. M. (2005). 'No support for dual-process accounts of human affective learning to simple Pavlovian conditioning'. *Cognition and Emotion*, 19.

Lovibond, P. F. and Shanks, D. R. (2002). 'The role of awareness in Pavlovian conditioning: empirical evidence and theoretical implications'. *Journal of Experimental Psychology: Animal Behavior Processes*, 28.

Perruchet, P. (1985). 'Expectancy for airpuff and conditioned eyeblinks in humans'. *Acta Psychologica*, 58.

Rescorla, R. A. (1967). 'Pavlovian conditioning and its proper control procedures'. *Psychological Review*, 74.

Shanks, D. R. (2005). 'Implicit learning'. In Lamberts, K. and Goldstone, R. (eds) *Handbook of Cognition.*

—— and St John, M. F. (1994). 'Characteristics of dissociable human learning systems'. *Behavioral and Brain Sciences*, 17.

Stevenson, R. J. and Boakes, R. A. (2004). 'Sweet and sour smells: learned synesthesia between the senses of taste and smell'. In Calvert, G. et al. (eds) *The Handbook of Multisensory Processes.*

conditioning, delay vs trace Classical conditioning is a basic form of associative learning where the organism learns something about the causal fabric of the environment. In an experimental setting, stimuli are arranged such that one stimulus provides the organism with information concerning the occurrence of another stimulus. With repeated presentations (or pairings) of the stimuli, the organism makes an association between the two stimuli. This type of associative learning is most commonly referred to as classical conditioning, but is also often referred to as *Pavlovian conditioning* in honour of Ivan Petrovich Pavlov (1849–1936), the scientist who described and named all of the basic elements and procedures of classical conditioning. In classical conditioning the stimulus that predicts the occurrence of another stimulus is termed the *conditioned stimulus* (CS). The predicted stimulus is termed the *unconditioned stimulus* (US). The CS is a relatively neutral stimulus that can be detected by the organism, but does not initially induce a reliable behavioural response. The US is a stimulus that can reliably elicit a measurable response from the first presentation. The response that is elicited by the presentation of the US is termed the *unconditioned response* (UR). The term 'unconditioned' was chosen by Pavlov to indicate that the behaviour is not a learned response, but rather it is an innate or reflexive response to the US. With repeated presentations of the CS followed by US (referred to as *paired training*) the CS begins to elicit a conditioned response (CR). Here Pavlov chose the term 'conditioned' to indicate that the response is learned (Pavlov 1927).

Classical conditioning is an umbrella term that can refer to a variety of different types of classical conditioning procedures and paradigms. For example, different forms of classical conditioning paradigms can be identified based on the temporal arrangement and spacing of the CS and US. Delay conditioning and trace conditioning are without question the two most commonly studied forms of classical conditioning.

1. Delay and trace conditioning
2. Cerebral substrates of fear conditioning
3. Cerebral substrates of eyeblink conditioning
4. Awareness and eyeblink conditioning in humans

1. Delay and trace conditioning

In *delay conditioning* (Fig. C6a), the CS onset precedes the US onset. The termination of the CS occurs, either with the US onset, during the US, at the termination of the US, or at some point after the US. Pavlov termed this type of conditioning 'delay conditioning' because the onset of the US is delayed relative to the onset of the

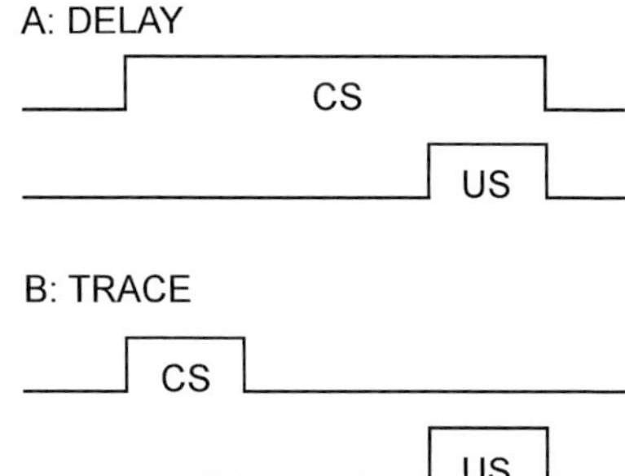

Fig. C6. Delay and trace conditioning.

CS. In *trace conditioning* (Fig. C6b), the CS is presented and terminated before the onset of the US. The interval separating the CS offset and the US onset is called the trace interval. This paradigm was named trace conditioning by Pavlov because in order for an association to be made between the CS and US, the organism must maintain a memory 'trace' of the CS at least until the US is presented. Despite the high degree of parametric similarity between delay and trace conditioning, in almost all cases, trace conditioning is more difficult to acquire and there is often a dramatic difference in the brain structures and cognitive processes that are necessary to support these two forms of classical conditioning. Examples will be taken for two of the most thoroughly researched and understood conditioning paradigms—*fear conditioning* and *eyeblink conditioning*.

2. Cerebral substrates of fear conditioning
In the laboratory, classical fear conditioning is generally studied in the rodent (Fanselow and Poulos 2005). The basic paradigm involves the presentation of a tone CS which is followed a few seconds later by an aversive electric shock to the paw delivered through a grid floor. After a few pairings (or even after a single pairing) of the CS and US, a fear CR is established and can be measured by the amount of freezing the rodent exhibits when the tone CS is presented. Rodents that exhibit a classically conditioned fear response show an increase in the amount of time they spend freezing compared to rodents that have not made the association between the CS and US. The standard paradigm is a form of delay classical conditioning where the CS is presented for a few seconds and then terminates with the presentation of the shock US. In this paradigm, the amygdala is essential for the acquisition and retention of the CR and this is true regardless of the CS modality (e.g. auditory, visual, olfactory). Lesions of the hippocampus, for example, do not impair fear conditioning using the delay paradigm. However, if the delay paradigm is changed to a trace paradigm by inserting a trace interval of several seconds, lesions to both the amygdala and the hippocampus severely impair the acquisition and retention of the fear CR.

3. Cerebral substrates of eyeblink conditioning
Eyeblink conditioning is the most widely studied form of associative learning in mammals (Thompson 2005). In the basic paradigm, a tone CS is paired with a reflex-eliciting US such as a puff of air to the cornea. Initially the CS does not elicit an eyeblink response. With repeated pairing of the CS and US an association is formed such that that presentation of the CS elicits an eyeblink CR in advance of the US. In general, it takes many more trials to establish a well-formed eyeblink CR than it does the non-specific freezing CR in fear conditioning. Extensive investigation into the neural substrates of eyeblink conditioning using most often rabbits, but also humans, monkeys, and rodents, has resulted in perhaps the most complete description of mammalian memory formation to date.

The acquisition and retention of delay eyeblink conditioning requires the cerebellum and associated brainstem structures. These structures are necessary and sufficient for the formation and storage of the CR. No forebrain structures, including the hippocampus, are required. For example, decerebrate rabbits with no remaining forebrain tissue (i.e. after removal of cerebral cortex, basal ganglia, limbic system, thalamus, and hypothalamus) exhibit normal retention of delay eyeblink conditioning. Findings in humans are completely consistent with the animal work. Thus, delay eyeblink conditioning is impaired in patients with cerebellar or brainstem lesions, but intact in amnesic patients with damage that includes the hippocampus (see BRAIN DAMAGE).

However, in eyeblink conditioning, changing delay conditioning to trace conditioning by inserting a trace interval as brief as 500–1000 ms substantially changes the brain substrates and cognitive processes required to support this form of conditioning. For example, successful trace eyeblink conditioning, like delay conditioning, requires the cerebellum. However, trace conditioning differs from delay conditioning in that it also requires the hippocampus and portions of neocortex. Thus, acquisition and retention of trace conditioning are severely disrupted in rabbits and rats when the hippocampus is damaged and trace conditioning is also disrupted by damage to portions of the prefrontal cortex. Again, findings in humans are consistent. In amnesic patients with damage that includes the hippocampus, trace eyeblink conditioning is mildly impaired with a trace interval of 500 ms, and severely impaired with a trace interval of 1000 ms.

4. Awareness and eyeblink conditioning in humans From a behavioural perspective, work with experimental animals is limited to examining the acquisition, storage, and generation of the CR. However, in humans it is also possible to determine if the participants have additionally developed an awareness that the CS comes before the US and is predictive of the US. Thus, humans have the potential to become aware of this contingency and to develop an expectation of the US following the presentation of the CS. The awareness and expectancy can then be related to the CR in both the delay and trace paradigms (Clark et al. 2002). In both delay and trace conditioning paradigms, individuals sometimes develop awareness regarding the stimulus contingencies and sometimes do not. For the most commonly studied forms of delay conditioning this awareness is superfluous to the acquisition of the CR, presumably because cerebellar and brainstem circuits can support performance. Trace conditioning is fundamentally different. Unlike delay conditioning, trace conditioning is strongly related to the awareness of the CS–US contingency and to the degree to which the US is expected.

It is possible that trace eyeblink conditioning may additionally require the hippocampus and the development of contingency awareness because the trace interval makes it difficult for the cerebellum to associate the CS and the US. In trace conditioning, because the US follows the CS by as much as 1000 ms the cerebellum may not be able to maintain a representation of the CS across the trace interval. If, however, the hippocampus and neocortex have represented the stimulus contingencies, then perhaps processed information concerning the CS can be transmitted to the cerebellum at a time during each trial that is optimal for cerebellar plasticity.

ROBERT E. CLARK

Clark, R. E., Manns, J. R., and Squire, L. R. (2002). 'Classical conditioning, awareness, and brain systems'. *Trends in Cognitive Science*, 6.

Fanselow, M. S. and Poulos, A. M. (2005). 'The neuroscience of mammalian associative learning'. *Annual Review of Psychology*, 56.

Pavlov, I. P. (1927). *Conditioned Reflexes; an Investigation of the Physiological Activity of the Cerebral Cortex*, transl. and ed. G. V. Anrep.

Thompson, R. F. (2005). 'In search of memory traces'. *Annual Review of Psychology*, 56.

confabulation 'Confabulation' as a technical term was first used by the German neurologists Bonhoeffer, Pick, and Wernicke in the early 1900s for false memory reports made by patients who suffered from a syndrome that later came to known as *Korsakoff's amnesia*. When asked what they did yesterday, these patients do not remember, but will report events that either did not happen, or happened long ago. During the remainder of the 20th century, the use of the term was gradually expanded to cover claims made by other types of patients, many of whom had no obvious memory problems, including patients who deny illness, *commissurotomy (split-brain) patients, patients with misidentification disorders (who make false claims about the identities of people), and patients with *schizophrenia, as well as children and normal adults in certain situations.

There are currently two schools of thought on the proper scope of the concept of confabulation, those who remain true to the original sense and so believe that the term should only be applied to false memory reports, and those who believe that the term can be usefully applied to a broader range of disorders. An examination of the etymology of the English word is not very helpful. When those German neurologists at the turn of the 20th century began using '*konfabulation*', they probably meant that their memory patients were creating fables when asked about their pasts. The patients were *fabulists*.

The technical definition of 'confabulation' the early neurologists coined has three components: (1) confabulations are false; (2) confabulations are reports; and (3) confabulations are about memories. There are significant problems with each of these three criteria, however. First, relying on falsity alone to characterize the problem in confabulation can produce arbitrary results. If a Korsakoff's syndrome patient, when asked what day of the week it is, happens to state correctly that it is Saturday, or an Anton's patient guesses correctly that the neurologist is holding up two fingers, we may still want to consider these to be confabulations. They are only true out of luck—simply made up, rather than the result of accurate tracking of the facts. Second, the idea that confabulations are reports, or stories, might be taken to imply that they are intrinsically linguistic in nature, in that they are always reports in the patient's natural language, such as German, and that hence confabulation is a strictly linguistic phenomenon. However, several researchers have categorized non-linguistic responses as confabulatory. One group had patients whose left hemispheres had been temporarily anaesthetized point to fabric samples with one hand to indicate which texture of fabric they had been stimulated with on the other hand. The patients also had the option of pointing to a question mark in trials in which they had not been stimulated, a non-linguistic version of answering 'I don't know'. Other researchers applied the term 'confabulation' to the behaviour of patients when they produced meaningless drawings as if they were familiar designs. Similarly, another group had patients reproduce from memory certain drawings they had seen, and referred to cases in which the patients added extra features to the drawings which were not actually present as confabulations. Finally, the problem with relating confabulations to memories is that, even in Korsakoff's syndrome, many confabulations are simply made up on the spot, and have little to do with any actual memories. That is, strictly speaking it is wrong to describe confabulations as memory reports. They are rather fictional fables, or at least false claims alleged to be memory reports.

Thus it seems that confabulations need not be false, may not be reports, and need not be about memories. If the original definition is problematic, that may be one reason why it was ignored by those who later described claims made by other, non-memory, patients. Patients who deny that they are paralysed have been claimed to confabulate when they provide reasons for why they cannot move ('My arthritis is bothering me', 'I'm tired of following your commands'). Another type of patient will deny blindness and attempt to answer questions about what he sees, producing what have been called confabulations ('It's too dark in here'). Misidentification patients have been said to confabulate when asked what the motives of the 'impostor' are, or why someone would go through all the trouble to impersonate someone else ('Perhaps my father paid him to take care of me'). Similarly, when the left hemispheres of split-brain patients attempt to answer questions without the necessary information (which is contained in their right hemispheres), this has also been called a confabulation.

This expansion forces several difficult questions about what had happened to the concept of confabulation. Has it expanded so much as to become meaningless? Do the new confabulation syndromes share anything significant with the classical memory cases? Some writers on confabulation have despaired of the fact that some of the confabulation syndromes involve memory (Korsakoff's, aneurysm of the anterior communicating artery), whereas others involve perception (denial of paralysis or blindness, split-brain syndrome, misidentification disorders). Since both memory and perception are knowledge domains, however, perhaps this indicates that the broader sense of 'confabulation' has to do with knowledge itself. According to this approach (Hirstein 2005), the brain's implementation of each knowledge domain—memory, perception, and introspection—is subject to characteristic confabulation syndromes.

1. Confabulations about memories

These are a defining characteristic of Korsakoff's syndrome and a similar syndrome caused by aneurysm of the anterior communicating artery (Kopelman 1987). Alzheimer's patients will often produce memory confabulations (see DEMENTIA), and children up to a certain age are also prone to reporting false memories, apparently because their brain's prefrontal areas have not yet fully developed, while the Alzheimer's patients prefrontal lobes have been compromised by the amyloid plaque lesions. All of these confabulators have an initial memory retrieval problem, coupled with a failure to check and correct their false 'memories' (Johnson and Raye 1998). In contrast, there exist many memory patients with damage only to more posterior parts of the memory system (e.g. to the hippocampus or other parts of the temporal lobes) who freely admit that they cannot remember, and are not at all prone to producing confabulations (see BRAIN DAMAGE).

2. Confabulations about perceptions

Vision. Anton's syndrome patients are at least partially blind, but insist that they can see. Their posterior damage typically involves bilateral lesions to the occipital cortex, causing the blindness, coupled with prefrontal damage, causing the inability to become aware of the blindness. Split-brain patients will also confabulate when asked in certain situations about what they perceived.

Somatosensation. The patients who deny paralysis have a condition referred to as **anosognosia*, meaning unawareness of illness. They typically have a loss of one or more somatosensory systems for the affected limb. Apparently, certain types of damage (e.g. to the right inferior parietal lobe) can cause both the somatosensory problem, and at least temporarily affect prefrontal functioning enough to cause the confabulated denials of illness (Berti et al. 2005). The nature of the connections between frontal areas and the right inferior parietal lobe are less well understood. One possible connection is that the high level prefrontal executive processes based in the orbitomedial cortex are heavily dependent on the high level perceptual processing housed in the right inferior parietal lobe.

Person perception. Perceptual confabulations are also issued by patients suffering from the misidentification syndromes (especially Capgras syndrome). These syndromes may be caused by a deficit in representing the mind of the person who is misidentified (Hirstein 2008), coupled with an inability to realize the implausibility of the impostor claim.

3. Confabulations about introspection

Confabulations about intentions and actions. Patients who have undergone a commissurotomy will tend to confabulate about actions performed by the right hemisphere. In a typical experiment, commands are sent to the right hemisphere only, but the left hemisphere, unaware of this, confabulates a reason for why the left hand obeyed the command. Similar sorts of confabulations can be elicited by brain stimulation. For example, the patient's cortex is stimulated, causing her arm to move. When asked why the arm moved, the patient claims she felt like stretching her arm. *Hypnotized people may also confabulate, e.g. the subject is given a hypnotic suggestion to perform a certain action, but then confabulates a different reason for it when asked.

There are many cases of confabulations about actions and intentions that do not involve the right hemisphere or any obvious lateral element (Wegner 2002). When Wilder Penfield electrically stimulated people's brains in the 1950s, he was able to cause them to make movements or emit sounds. Sometimes the patients would claim that Penfield was the cause of the movement. They responded with remarks such as, 'I didn't do that. You did' and, 'I didn't make that sound. You pulled it out of me' (Penfield 1975). In contrast, Hecaen et al. (1949) electrically stimulated a different area which caused the patients to perform 'pill-rolling' motions, or clench and unclench their fists. The patients claimed that they had done this intentionally, but were unable to offer a reason for the action. Delgado's brain stimulation patients also claimed they had performed the actions voluntarily, and confabulated a reason why. When Delgado (1969) stimulated yet another area, producing 'head turning and slow displacement of the body to either side with a well-oriented and apparently normal sequence, as if the patient were looking for something', and the patients were asked why they engaged in those actions, genuine confabulations seemed to result:

> The interesting fact was that the patient considered the evoked activity spontaneous and always offered a reasonable explanation for it. When asked 'What are you doing?' the answers were, 'I am looking for my slippers,' 'I heard a noise,' 'I am restless,' and 'I was looking under the bed'. (Delgado 1969).

Confabulations about emotions. False attributions of emotions can count as confabulations. For example, in one experiment, people were given an injection of adrenaline (epinephrine) without their knowledge, but attributed their inability to sleep to, e.g., nervousness about what they had to do the next day. We may all be guilty of confabulating about our emotions on occasion, perhaps due to the combination of our feeling responsible for giving coherent accounts of our emotions and the opacity of our emotions to cognition.

Classifying confabulation syndromes as malfunctions in different knowledge domains eliminates the problem with the falsity criterion. The problem is not so much the falsity of their claims, it is rather their overall unreliability, at least in the affected domain. Confabulation seems to involve two phases of error. First, a flawed memory or response is created. Second, even with plenty of time to examine the situation and with urging from doctors and relatives, the patient fails to realize that the response is flawed. Our brains create flawed responses all the time. If I ask you if you have ever been inside the head of the Statue of Liberty, for instance, your brain is happy to provide an image of a view from inside, even if you've never been near the statue. But you are able to reject this as a real memory, so you catch the mistake at the second phase.

The brain processes capable of checking and correcting or rejecting flawed representations are called *executive processes*. Most executive processes reside in the prefrontal lobes, including the dorsolateral frontal lobes, on the side of the brain, the ventrolateral frontal lobes below them, and the orbitofrontal lobes, located just above the eye sockets (Rolls 1999, Fuster 2002). The following situations require the intervention of executive processes: planning or decision-making is required; there are no effective learned input–output links; a habitual response must be inhibited; an error must be corrected; the situation is dangerous; we need to switch between two or more tasks; or, we need to recall something. In theory, given the brain's large number of knowledge sources, there are many more confabulation syndromes than those listed here, but they should all follow the same pattern: damage to a knowledge system (either perceptual or mnemonic), typically located in the temporal or parietal lobes, coupled with damage to prefrontal executive processes responsible for monitoring and correcting the representations delivered by that epistemic system.

4. The locus of damage in confabulation

There are several clues as to the nature and location of the neurological damage in confabulation patients. (1) Confabulation about paralysis of the left arm can occur with stroke damage restricted to the right inferior parietal cortex. (2) The patients with aneurysms of the anterior communicating artery—a tiny artery near the anterior commissure that completes the anterior portion of the circle of Willis—provide our best clue about the locus of the frontal problems in memory confabulation (DeLuca and Diamond 1995). (3) Split-brain patients confabulate about information perceived by the right hemisphere. The right hemisphere, or lack of communication with the right hemisphere, shows up in all of the perceptual confabulations. Given the right hemisphere's greater role in producing and perceiving emotions, there may be a lateral element to the neural locus of confabulations about emotions. The cerebral commissures, the corpus callosum, and the anterior commissure are the three connecting fibre bundles between the two hemispheres. There are important functional links between the posterior orbitomedial cortex and the corpus callosum. Given the existence of dense interconnections between the left and right orbitomedial cortices, cutting their commissures may have the same effect of lesioning them directly.

5. The broader sense of 'confabulation'

The following definition is based on the idea that confabulation syndromes involve malfunctions in different knowledge domains, coupled with executive system damage (Hirstein 2005):

Jan confabulates that *p* if and only if: (1) Jan claims that *p*. (2) Jan believes that *p*. (3) Jan's thought that *p* is ill-grounded. (4) Jan does not know that her thought is ill-grounded. (5) Jan should know that her thought is ill-grounded. (6) Jan is confident that *p*.

'Claiming' is broad enough to cover a wide variety of responses by subjects, including drawing and pointing. The second criterion captures the sincerity of confabulators. The third criterion refers to the problem that caused the flawed response to be generated. The fourth criterion refers to the failure of the second phase, the failure to reject the flawed response. The fifth criterion captures the normative element of our concept of confabulation. If the confabulator's brain was functioning properly, she would not make that claim. The last criterion refers to another important aspect of confabulators, the serene certainty they have in their communications, which may be connected to the frequent finding of low or abolished sympathetic autonomic activity in confabulating patients.

6. Confabulation and consciousness

Why does the anosognosic not notice what is missing? One message carried by the phenomena one encounters in a study of confabulation is that consciousness does not contain labels saying, 'an adequate representation of your left arm is missing' (denial); 'there is a gap in your memory here' (memory syndromes); 'you have no information about why your left arm just pointed at a picture of a cat' (split-brain syndrome); 'your representation of your father's mind is missing' (Capgras syndrome). The obvious hypothesis is that we confabulate because both the conscious data and the checker of that data are flawed.

Is confabulation then a type of *filling-in, comparable to the way that the brain's visual system fills in the optic blind spot? Confabulation might be considered filling-in at a higher, social level. It fills in social gaps in information: the doctor has asked for information, for example, so the patient supplies it. More sceptical writers seem to see consciousness itself as a massive confabulation, a *user illusion*. There may also be information here relevant to another question: What is the function of consciousness? The existence of confabulation supports the idea that consciousness functions as a testing ground, where thoughts and ideas can be checked, before they are allowed to become beliefs or participate in the causing of actions.

WILLIAM HIRSTEIN

Berti, A., Bottini, G., Gandola, M. et al. (2005). 'Shared cortical anatomy for motor awareness and motor control'. *Science*, 309.

Delgado, J. M. R. (1969). *Physical Control of the Mind: Toward a Psychocivilized Society*.

DeLuca, J. and Diamond, B. J. (1995). 'Aneurysm of the anterior communicating artery: a review of the neuroanatomical and neuropsychological sequelae'. *Journal of Clinical and Experimental Neuropsychology*, 17.

Fuster, J. (2002). *Cortex and Mind: Unifying Cognition*.

Hecaen, H., Talairach, J., David, M., and Dell, M. B. (1949). 'Coagulations limitées du thalamus dans les algies du syndrome thalamique: resultats thérapeutiques et physiologiques'. *Revue Neurologique (Paris)*, 81.

Hirstein, W. (2005). *Brain Fiction: Self-Deception and the Riddle of Confabulation*.

—— (2008). 'Confabulations about people and their limbs, present or absent'. In Bickle, J. (ed.) *Oxford Handbook of Philosophy and Neuroscience*.

Johnson, M. K. and Raye, C. L. (1998). 'False memories and confabulation'. *Trends in Cognitive Sciences*, 2.

Kopelman, M. D. (1987). 'Two types of confabulation'. *Journal of Neurology, Neurosurgery, and Psychiatry*, 50.

Penfield, W. (1975). *The Mystery of the Mind*.

Rolls, E. T. (1999). *The Brain and Emotion*.

Wegner, D. M. (2002). *The Illusion of Conscious Will*.

confidence judgement See SIGNAL DETECTION THEORY

connectionist models Connectionist models, also known as *parallel distributed processing* (PDP) models, are a class of computational models often used to model aspects of human perception, cognition, and behaviour, the learning processes underlying such behaviour, and the storage and retrieval of information from memory. The approach embodies a particular perspective in cognitive science, one that is based on the idea that our understanding of behaviour and of mental states should be informed and constrained by our knowledge of the neural processes that underpin cognition. While *neural network* modelling has a history dating back to the 1950s, it was only at the beginning of the 1980s that the approach gained widespread recognition, with the publication of two books (McClelland and Rumelhart 1986, Rumelhart and McClelland 1986), in which the basic principles of the approach were laid out, and its application to a number of psychological topics were developed. Connectionist models of cognitive processes have now been proposed in many different domains, ranging from different aspects of language processing to cognitive control, from perception to memory. The specific architecture of such models often differs substantially from one application to another, but all models share a number of central assumptions that collectively characterize the 'connectionist' approach in cognitive science. One of the central features of the approach is the emphasis it has placed on mechanisms of change. In contrast to traditional computational modelling methods in cognitive science, connectionism takes it that understanding the mechanisms involved in some cognitive process should be informed by the manner in which the system changed over time as it developed and learned. Understanding such mechanisms constitutes a significant part of current research in the domain (Elman et al. 1996; Mareschal et al. 2007a, 2007b).

Connectionist models take their inspiration from the manner in which information processing occurs in the brain. Processing involves the propagation of activation among simple units (artificial neurons) organized in networks, i.e. linked to each other through weighted connections representing synapses or groups thereof. Each unit then transmits its activation level to other units in the network by means of its connections to those units. The *activation function*, that is, the function that describes how each unit computes its activation based on its inputs, may be a simple linear function, but is more typically non-linear (e.g. a sigmoid function).

1. Representation, processing, and learning in connectionist networks
2. Connectionism and consciousness

1. Representation, processing, and learning in connectionist networks

Representation can take two very different forms in connectionist networks, neither of which corresponds to 'classical' propositional *representations. One form of representation is the pattern of activation over the units in the network. Units in some connectionist networks are specifically designated in advance by the modeller to represent specific items such as identifiable visual features, letters, words, objects, etc. Networks that employ such units for all cognizable entities of interest are called *localist* networks—the representation of an item is in a sense localized to the single unit that stands for it. Most networks, however, rely on *distributed* representation—the idea that an item, such as a word, object, or memory, is instantiated by a pattern of activation over a large ensemble of units. In such systems, each representation thus depends on the activation of many units, and each unit is involved in representing many different objects. Distributed representations in early models were assigned by the modeller, using for instance a set of primitive features as the components of the representation or, in multilayer networks with hidden units, allowing the patterns to be determined from an initial random starting place through a learning process.

The other form of representation in connectionist networks consists of the values of the *connection weights* linking the processing units. Such connection weights may be positive or negative real numbers. In some models they are set by hand by the modeller but in most cases they are set through a learning process, as discussed below.

Importantly for the relevance of connectionist models to the study of consciousness, neither the patterns of activation in a network nor the connection weights linking them are subject to direct inspection or manipulation by some other part of a connectionist system. Instead, activations in one part of a system simply directly influence the activation of connected units elsewhere. Thus, while it is possible to build connectionist networks that have weights that allow, e.g., patterns of activation on two sets of units to be compared, with another set of units then reporting the degree of sameness or difference, this is not necessary for processing to occur and indeed most connectionist networks do not embody such mechanisms. Connection weights, in contrast, are generally assumed to be completely inaccessible to any form of inspection. They can and do, however, encode associative relationships between arbitrary patterns (such as the association between a name and a face) and structured or lawful mappings between patterns (such as the relationship between the present tense form of a word and its past tense).

Another important feature of connectionist systems is the fact that the patterns of activation that are formed during processing are not subsequently stored in the system as memories. Instead, they are thought of as leaving a trace in the network through the adjustments they produce in the connection weights. These adjustments can then allow the pattern (or something like it) to be reconstructed at a later time, as a form of memory. Thus, long-term knowledge in connectionist networks is always encoded by the connection weights, whereas the temporary results of processing occur through activation patterns over units.

Processing in connectionist networks occurs through the propagation of activation signals among the processing units, via the weighted connections. The process is generally regarded as a continuous-time process subject to random variability. Thus, it is widely assumed that the state of activations of units evolves continuously over time, and is not completely deterministic so that the same input can give rise to different real-time trajectories. While in reality much of our experience consists of a fairly continuous flow e.g. of visual or auditory experience, many connectionist networks settle over time after the presentation of an input into what is called an *attractor state* (see ATTRACTOR NETWORKS)—a stable pattern of activity that tends to remain in place until some sort of reset occurs so that the next input can be presented. Such attractor states may be seen, perhaps, as representing the sequence of states a perceiver might enter into while making fixations on different points in a static scene, or experiencing a set of discrete items presented one after another in a sequence. In this respect, Rumelhart and McClelland (1986:39), reflecting on the implications of a connectionist approach to cognition and consciousness, noted for instance that 'consciousness consists of a sequence of interpretations—each represented by a stable state of the system'. This process is often further simplified as a simple, one-pass, feedforward process that allows the pattern of activation over a set of input units, together perhaps with an internal pattern left over from the last round of settling, to influence the next state of the network. Networks of this type—known as *simple recurrent networks*—have many of the essential properties of PDP models, and so have been a subject of fairly intensive study, particularly in the domains of language processing (e.g. Elman 1990) and implicit learning (e.g. Cleeremans and McClelland 1991).

Learning in connectionist models is the process of connection weight adjustment. In contrast to traditional models in cognitive science, most connectionist models learn through experience, i.e. through repeated exposure to stimuli from the environment. Two broad classes of learning mechanisms can be distinguished, based on whether adjustments to the connection weights are dependent on an error signal or not. In the former case, learning is said to be supervised for it is driven by the difference between the current response of the network and a target response specified by the environment. Such supervised learning (e.g. back-propagation) instantiates the computational objective of mastering specific input–output mappings (i.e. achieving specific goals) in the context of performing specific tasks. By contrast, unsupervised learning (e.g. Hebbian learning) instantiates the different computational objective of capturing the correlational structure of the stimulus environment, so enabling the cognitive system to develop useful, informative models of the world. Unsupervised learning procedures do not depend on the availability of a 'teacher' signal, but instead determine adjustments to the connection weights based on the simultaneous activation of connected units, so instantiating Hebb's (1949) notion that 'neurons that fire together wire together'—the same principle that is also observed in the neural process of long-term potentiation.

In simple models, the environment specifies the states of all units in the system, in which connection weights can be seen as establishing associative links between these units. In localist networks, individual connections mediate meaningful associative relationships. In distributed models, however, the situation is more complex. In such systems, if one wishes to associate, let us say, the sight of a rose with the smell of a rose, and if the sight and smell are each represented as a pattern of activation over a set of units, then the connection weight changes needed to store the association may in many cases impact all of the connections. It remains surprising to many people that many different associations can be stored in the same set of connection weights, especially if, as is often done, one or more layers of intermediate units is interposed between input and output. The consequence of this is to then introduce intermediate representations that can re-represent input patterns in new ways.

Connection adjustment schemes in connectionist networks are used both for processes usually thought of as 'learning' and also for processes usually thought of as 'memory'. In the former case, connectionist models generally rely on very gradual connection adjustment procedures to give rise to a set of connections that implement a learned skill such as reading (mapping patterns representing the sounds of words to other patterns representing their sound and meaning). One such learned skill is the ability to anticipate the successive elements of a sequence from preceding elements, as a result of prior experience with many such sequences.

In the case of memory for a particular episode or event, the event is by definition experienced only once. To store it effectively in memory it is generally assumed that relatively large changes to connection weights must be made at or very near the time of the actual experience. In many models, the elements of the experience are thought of as forming a single pattern of activation (perhaps spanning many brain areas) representing all different aspects of the experience. An architecture that may involve many layers of intermediate units with very easily modifiable connections then essentially allows all elements of the pattern to become inter-associated with all other elements. As a result, later presentation of a unique subset of the pattern can then allow the rest of the pattern to be reinstated over the units of the network.

2. Connectionism and consciousness

A starting place for consideration of the relevance of connectionist models and our concept of consciousness lies in the distinction, made above, between patterns of activation and the knowledge stored in connections. It is likely that the patterns of activation over some brain area are associated with states of conscious experience. Thus, you may experience a friendly beagle through the pattern of white and brown blotches of its fur, the yipping sounds it makes, and the excited frisking about that it does when it meets you, and this may be crucially dependent upon active patterns of activation in a relevant ensemble of brain areas. You may imagine or remember an experience with the beagle by activating (pale, incomplete, and likely distorted) versions of these patterns over the same units when the beagle is not physically present. Within the connectionist framework it is often imagined that not all aspects of these patterns are likely to be consciously experienced; those that are especially emphasized by control processes and persist in a relatively stable form as attractor states may, however, be more likely to be consciously experienced, both during the initial event itself, and during a subsequent episode of imagination or memory. Stability of representation has been proposed as a *computational *correlate of consciousness* by Mathis and Mozer (1995, see also attractor networks) and also by philosophers O'Brien and Opie (1999) in their 'vehicle theory of phenomenal experience'. Likewise, Koch (2004) and Kirsh (1991; see also KNOWLEDGE, EXPLICIT VS IMPLICIT) have also proposed that the distinction between implicit and explicit processing is best captured by the occurrence, in the latter but not in the former case, of activation patterns that directly code for a state of affairs, i.e. that involve low complexity in the computations that are necessary to recover their contents. Thus, a neuron that fires only when a picture of former American president Bill Clinton is presented (Kreiman et al. 2002) is explicitly representing the occurrence of Bill Clinton; whereas the connection weights that facilitate the processing of Bill Clinton's name in a *priming task, for instance, would constitute an implicit representation because such weights are not directly available for inspection and because such inspection would require many computational operations to retrieve the relevant information.

The fact that connectionist models rely on knowledge stored in connections is important for the study of consciousness since it makes it clear how processing can be guided by learned knowledge without that knowledge being accessible to inspection. A central feature of explicit representations is that one is, at least potentially, conscious of having them. However, the knowledge acquired by a trained connectionist network is stored in the form of connection weights between processing units. The information contained in the pattern of connectivity that characterizes a trained network can not be accessed directly by the network itself. Instead, this knowledge can only manifest itself by the influence it exerts on the activation level of the units of the network. In this sense, such weights are not representational: they do not constitute objects of representation in and of themselves. Indeed, Clark and Karmiloff-Smith (1993:504) have pointed out that in connectionist networks, 'knowledge of rules is always emergent. [These models] do not depend on symbolic expressions that stand for the elements of a rule. Instead, they exploit a multitude of subsymbolic representations whose complex interaction produces behaviour which, in central cases, fits the rule'. Clark and Karmiloff-Smith continue by noting that such networks have no '... self-generated means of analyzing their own activity so as to form symbolic representations of their own processing. Their knowledge of rules always *remains* implicit unless an external theorist intervenes' (1993:504).

Knowledge is thus always *implicit* in what Clark and Karmiloff-Smith (1993) called *first-order connectionist networks*. In contrast, knowledge in classical, symbolic systems always seems to be at least potentially *explicit*, to the extent that it is stored in a format (symbolic propositions) that makes it impossible for it to influence behaviour (i.e. to have causal powers) without being accessed or manipulated by an agent (i.e. the processor). In other words, information processing in classical systems always appears to entail access to stored representations in a way that is strikingly different from what happens in connectionist networks.

Finally, an important aspect of connectionist modelling is the use of some parts of a complex connectionist network to control the states of activation in other parts of the network. In this respect, a useful distinction is offered by O'Reilly and Munakata (2000)—the distinction between *weight-based* and *activation-based* processing. According to O'Reilly and Munakata, 'Activation-based processing is based on the activation, maintenance, and updating of active representations to influence processing, whereas weight-based processing is based on the adaptation of weight values to alter input/output mappings' (2000:380). The main advantage of activation-based processing is that it is faster and more flexible than weight-based processing. Speed and flexibility are both salient characteristics of high-level cognition. O'Reilly and Munakata further speculate that activation-based processing is one of the central characteristics of the frontal cortex, and suggest that this region of the brain has evolved specifically to serve a number of important functions related to controlled processing, such as *working memory, inhibition, executive control, and monitoring or evaluation of ongoing behaviour. To serve these functions, processing in the *frontal cortex is characterized by mechanisms of active maintenance through which representations can remain strongly activated for long periods of time so as it make it possible for these representations to bias processing elsewhere in the brain. This attentional modulation of activation may have important implications for what aspects of a visual scene become available for overt responding or storage in memory, and indeed, Dehaene et al. (2006) have proposed to distinguish between unconscious, preconscious, and conscious processing based precisely on interactions between top-down and bottom-up processing in the brain. Note that such interactions presuppose the existence of recurrent connections—another proposed correlate of consciousness (e.g. Lamme and Roelfsema 2000). Likewise, Maia and Cleeremans (2005) have proposed that many connectionist networks can be thought of as implementing a process of global constraint satisfaction whereby biased competition between neural coalitions results in the network settling on to the most likely interpretation of the current input. Importantly, this suggests a strong link between attention, working memory, cognitive control, and availability to conscious experience, for the mechanisms underlying each of these different aspects of information processing in the brain can be thought of as depending on the operation of the same computational principles.

JAY L. MCCLELLAND AND AXEL CLEEREMANS

Clark, A. and Karmiloff-Smith, A. (1993). 'The cognizer's innards: a psychological and philosophical perspective on the development of thought'. *Mind and Language*, 8.

Cleeremans, A. and McClelland, J. L. (1991). 'Learning the structure of event sequences'. *Journal of Experimental Psychology: General*, 120.

Dehaene, S., Changeux, J.-P., Naccache, L., Sackur, J., and Sergent, C. (2006). 'Conscious, preconscious, and subliminal processing: a testable taxonomy'. *Trends in Cognitive Sciences*, 10.

Elman, J. L. (1990). 'Finding structure in time'. *Cognitive Science*, 14.

——, Bates, E. A., Johnson, M. H., Karmiloff-Smith, A., Parisi, D., and Plunkett, K. (1996). *Rethinking Innateness: a Connectionist Perspective on Development*.

Hebb, D. O. (1949). *The Organization of Behavior*.

Kirsh, D. (1991). 'When is information explicitly represented?' In Hanson, P. P. (ed.) *Information, Language, and Cognition*.

Koch, C. (2004). *The Quest for Consciousness. A Neurobiological Approach*.

Kreiman, G., Fried, I., and Koch, C. (2002). 'Single-neuron correlates of subjective vision in the human medial temporal lobe'. *Proceedings of the National Academy of Sciences of the USA*, 99.

Lamme, V. A. F. and Roelfsema, P. R. (2000). 'The distinct modes of vision offered by feedforward and recurrent processing'. *Trends in Neurosciences*, 23.

Maia, T. V. and Cleeremans, A. (2005). 'Consciousness: converging insights from connectionist modeling and neuroscience'. *Trends in Cognitive Sciences*, 9.

Mareschal, D., Johnson, M. H., Sirois, S., Spratling, M. W., Thomas, M. S. C., and Westermann, G. (2007a). *Neuroconstructivism: How the Brain Constructs Cognition*, Vol. 1.

——, Sirois, S., Westermann, G., and Johnson, M. H. (2007b). *Neuroconstructivism: Perspectives and Prospects*.

Mathis, W. D. and Mozer, M. C. (1995). 'On the computational utility of consciousness'. In Tesauro, G. and Touretzky, D. S. (eds) *Advances in Neural Information Processing Systems*, Vol. 7.

McClelland, J. L. and Rumelhart, D. E. (1986). *Parallel Distributed Processing. Explorations in the Microstructure of Cognition. Volume 2: Psychological and Biological Models*.

O'Brien, G. and Opie, J. (1999). 'A connectionist theory of phenomenal experience'. *Behavioral and Brain Sciences*, 22.

O'Reilly, R. C. and Munakata, Y. (2000). *Computational Explorations in Cognitive Neuroscience: Understanding the Mind by Simulating the Brain*.

Rumelhart, D. E. and McClelland, J. L. (1986). *Parallel Distributed Processing: Explorations in the Microstructure of Cognition. Volume 1: Foundations*.

consciousness expansion Consciousness expansion, or *expanded awareness*, is a rather broad concept, usually referring to certain states of consciousness in which either self or the space around seem greatly enhanced or enlarged. These states can happen spontaneously in mystical experiences; they can be achieved deliberately through practices such as yoga, prayer, *meditation, and sensory deprivation and they can be induced by taking drugs, including psychedelics, *hallucinogens, and *anaesthetics. Such states are often described as higher, better, more spiritual, or more open to new experiences than ordinary states, and are sometimes linked with enhanced intuition and creativity. Characteristic features include the cessation or transcendence of logical thoughts and verbal concepts, slowing of perceived time, expansion of experienced space, and changes in or dissolution of personal identity (see also ALTERED STATES OF CONSCIOUSNESS).

The ultimate expansion of consciousness can occur in spontaneous mystical states in the form of a complete loss of self and a resulting oneness with the universe. In this state there is no individual awareness; rather, one's previously separate self seems to have merged with everything else. As William James (1902), among others, pointed out, such mystical experiences are difficult or impossible to describe, and come with a sense of passivity or surrender in the face of what seems to be true knowledge or insight.

Psychedelic drugs are often used to expand awareness (Jay 1999). Mescaline was said by Aldous Huxley (1954) to open the doors of perception, and many have linked the expansion of consciousness with a new appreciation of reality—claiming to see things more clearly or as they really are. The early psychonauts, including Timothy Leary and Richard Alpert (Baba Ram Dass), advocated using LSD to expand consciousness and to reach states of mind beyond space, time, self, or any words or concepts that can be thought about. They explicitly likened the process to a spiritual journey or awakening. Other drugs that can induce such states include psilocybin, dimethyltryptamine (DMT), and cannabis. Even some anaesthetics can induce states of oneness or expansion, including nitrous oxide, ether, and ketamine.

Many meditation techniques are claimed to expand awareness. Some emphasize practising non-judgemental awareness towards all sensory experiences, leading to a sense of an expanded space of possibilities. Others emphasize a withdrawal from the senses into inner space which can then seem to expand. Long-term meditators, and those who practise mindfulness in everyday life, describe the changes that take place as being a kind of awakening from illusion, or an expansion of consciousness.

If we had any usable maps of altered states of consciousness, or knew more about the neural *correlates of different states, it would be possible to place expanded consciousness into its psychological and biological context. As it is we cannot do so, and the concept remains vague. In popular literature it is often linked with theories and practices which have no basis in evidence, such as the chakra system derived from Hindu philosophy, the Chinese concept of chi energy, and the use of crystals and magical ceremonies.

SUSAN BLACKMORE

Huxley, A. (1954). *The Doors of Perception.*

James, W. (1902). *The Varieties of Religious Experience: a Study in Human Nature.*

Jay, M. (ed.) (1999). *Artificial Paradises: a Drugs Reader.*

consciousness, modern scientific study of Consciousness has elicited interest amongst philosophers, theologians, and scientists through the ages and across cultures, but the scientific study of consciousness is a relatively recent phenomenon. After a burst of sustained interest during the early 20th century, initiated by William James and, later, by the introspectionist movement, behaviourism brought with it a period of stagnancy in the study of consciousness. Scientific interest in consciousness was rekindled in the 1960s and 1970s, in part due to the influence of the counter-culture, but it was not until the 1990s that the scientific study of consciousness really took hold. This entry provides a one-eyed overview of some of the key events in this history, with a focus on developments since 1980.

1. The emergence of consciousness science
2. Basic themes in consciousness science
3. Neuroscience
4. Conclusion

1. The emergence of consciousness science

We can chart the rise of consciousness science by charting the development of its conferences and journals. To use Kuhn's term, we might think of the period 1980–94 as representing the transition from the *pre-paradigm* stage of consciousness science to a *normal science* stage. New journals such as *Journal of Mind and Behavior* (1980), *Imagination, Cognition and Personality* (1981), and *Philosophical Psychology* (1988) were launched, and a variety of one-off conferences and symposia were held. The second half of the period—from 1994 to 2008—constitutes what we might think of as an early phase of normal consciousness science. At the 10th annual conference of the Association for the Scientific Study of Consciousness (ASSC) in Oxford in 2006, co-founder Patrick Wilken noted that discussions of consciousness by journals like *Science* and *Nature* showed a steady increase from 1960 to 1990 and a sharp spike in the mid 1990s. This spike, Wilken suggests, is the best estimate we have for the start of the modern science of consciousness. Two conference–journal pairings dominated this period: Tucson conferences, which are paired with the *Journal of Consciousness Studies* (1994), and the Association for the Scientific Study of Consciousness (ASSC) conferences, with *Consciousness and Cognition* (1992) and *Psyche* (1993) as its journals. The *Journal of Consciousness Studies* (*JCS*) appeared immediately after the first Tucson conference (below) in 1994, with the avowed intent not to limit itself to science and Western philosophy but to cover consciousness 'in all its aspects', including those unique to the transpersonal and contemplative traditions, spiritual metaphysics, and altered states of consciousness. With its broad scientific and philosophical coverage, *Consciousness and Cognition* has been a mainstay of the consciousness studies field. *Psyche*, an electronic journal, has run some 40 symposia on a wide range of topics relating to consciousness. Another notable publication specifically dedicated to consciousness is John Benjamins' book series 'Advances in Consciousness Research', which has published about three dozen books since 1995. Most other major publishing houses have also produced books dealing with consciousness, with about a thousand titles now available.

With a long tradition of interest in consciousness, psychologists, philosophers, and pharmacologists at the

University of Arizona held a conference in 1994, under the title 'Toward a Science of Consciousness', with some 300 registrants. This led to the biennial Tucson conferences, which average about 700 attendees per conference and retain the original conference's title, as do various Tucson-inspired conferences in other countries. The reviewer of the first Tucson in *JCS* called it 'the first large-scale scientific conference to be devoted entirely to the study of consciousness' and prophetically predicted that it would become 'a seminal event for the future of consciousness studies'. Tucson conferences are known for their somewhat controversial inclusion of fringe or '1960s' topics, such as meditation, transpersonal psychology, psychoactive drugs, 'pure consciousness', *panpsychism, and parapsychology. An informal show of hands at one Tucson conference suggests that perhaps 20% of the participants relate passionately to these esoteric issues.

The ASSC began as a membership organization in 1994, immediately after Tucson-1, with the intent of organizing a second event dedicated to consciousness. Debate about the scope of this second event resulted in a split, with one group opting to continue with Tucson-style conferences (the second of which was organized in 1996) and the other founding the ASSC, which held its first conference in Claremont, California in 1997. For the first ten years ASSC meetings alternated between Europe and North America, but in 2008 the association moved to a three-year cycle that includes Asia. The meetings generally attract around 300–400 people, many of whom also attend the Tucson conferences. About one-third of the present 480 members of the ASSC are graduate students, a membership demography that prompted the ASSC to initiate an annual William James Prize which is awarded to junior consciousness researchers.

2. Basic themes in consciousness science

We now turn to a selective overview of the central themes on which the study of consciousness has focused.

Perceptual (un)consciousness. Perception is a central aspect of conscious experience, and it is no surprise that the study of perceptual experience has occupied a pre-eminent place in the scientific study of consciousness. The questions addressed in the study of perceptual consciousness are many. To what degree can perceptual stimuli be processed without consciousness? What differences are there between the processing of perceptual stimuli with and without awareness? What is the relationship between perceptual awareness and attention? How is perceptual experience related to memory and reportability? How many systems are involved in the generation of perceptual experience, and how do they interact? And so on.

There have been many important milestones in the recent history of the study of perceptual experience. Sperling's 1960s experiments on the reportability of briefly presented stimuli provided evidence for the existence of a rapidly decaying perceptual trace, the capacity of which exceeds one's ability to report its contents. Broadbent, Treisman, and Posner proposed contrasting models of how attention regulates consciousness ('early' and 'late' selection theories), and explored the mechanisms responsible for '*binding' perceptual features into coherent perceptual objects and scenes. In the early 1960s, Hubel and Wiesel traced early pathways in vision, recording cellular firing in anaesthetized animals. In 1980, Hubel and Livingston published similar work in awake animals and launched a major study of the role of *gamma-wave oscillations in consciousness. In the 1980s Ungerleider and Mishkin, followed by Goodale and Milner in the 1990s, did important work on the two *visual systems, showing that there is a 'ventral' cortical visual path which is involved in identifying and categorizing objects, and a 'dorsal' pathway which, depending on the view, is either involved in processing object-location or subserves online motor control.

As might be expected, scientists have employed a number of tools in their study of perceptual consciousness. A particularly important tool is *binocular rivalry. Binocular fusion can fail when very different stimuli are projected to each eye, with the result that the subject's visual experience spontaneously alternates between the stimulus presented to the left eye and that presented to the right eye. This allows theorists to identify the neural activity that correlates with the (unchanging) perceptual input and that which correlates with the (alternating) conscious percept. Logothetis and others have shown that early visual areas are activated by both conscious and unconscious stimuli, while later areas are activated mainly by the conscious stimulus.

Of course, binocular rivalry is only one of the tools used to study perceptual experience. Early 20th century *gestalt psychology employed ambiguous figures, optical *illusions, and after-images to explore the structure of conscious perception, and these phenomena still occupy centre stage in contemporary consciousness science. Also important are the phenomena of *attentional blink, *change blindness, and *inattentional blindness. Perhaps pride of place goes to subliminal *priming, a phenomenon in which briefly presented stimuli can nevertheless influence subsequent emotional, verbal, or motor responses in the absence of awareness. The British psychologist Marcel first demonstrated subliminal priming using modern methods in the 1980s, generating substantial controversy both about the implications of the work as well as about the methods (e.g. see Holender's 1986 scathing critique of the subliminal perception literature). More recently, Dehaene and colleagues rekindled interest in the exploration of priming to study consciousness through the use of brain imaging methods. Today, the domain remains rather controversial. While it is now clearly established that a stimulus may influence subsequent processing in the absence of awareness, significant debate remains about the extent of such priming and about the interpretation of positive findings. A substantial part of this debate is focused on which methods are most appropriate to establish information processing without awareness. There is thus a continuing need for the refinement of existing behavioural methods such as *signal detection theory or first-person methods such as confidence judgements or *introspection.

Cognitive (un)consciousness. Implicit *memory and implicit *learning suggest that people's behaviour can be influenced by events that they later fail to recollect. Implicit learning and implicit memory, in contrast to subliminal perception, typically involve supraliminal stimuli. Implicit learning differs from implicit memory in that it involves tasks that require sensitivity to the structural relationships between series of stimuli (e.g. strings of an artificial language—see ARTIFICIAL GRAMMAR LEARNING) rather than to specific items. The core phenomenon in both cases is priming, that is, the process through which processing one or a series of stimuli subsequently facilitates performance on identical or similar items. Crucially, in implicit learning and memory, this priming occurs in the absence of episodic recall of the relevant items (implicit memory) or in the absence of one's ability to report on the acquired knowledge (e.g. the structural relationships that define membership in a category).

Research on implicit *memory* was initiated by work with *amnesic patients (e.g. Claparèdes' observations; work with patient H. M.), whose episodic memory is severely impaired despite showing continued ability to learn new procedural skills. This work was regarded with some suspicion until Jacoby developed the process-dissociation method in the 1990s (see MEMORY, PROCESS-DISSOCIATION PROCEDURE). Implicit *learning* was first demonstrated by Ebbinghaus in the late 19th century, and explored anew in the 1960s by Reber, and later by Broadbent and others. Both domains continue to be characterized by lively and essential methodological debates (How do we best measure awareness? What is the most sensitive method? Do all measures tend to correlate?) and theoretical differences (Do implicit memory and explicit memory involve separate systems? Are implicit and explicit learning rooted in the same processes?). Despite this continuing questioning, it is now clearly established that behaviour can be influenced—often in profound ways—by information of which one is unaware. Many of the most striking demonstrations of this can be found in the domain of social cognition, where the 'cognitive unconscious' has taken central stage, through the work of authors such as Bargh, Wegner, and Dijksterhuis.

Interpersonal consciousness and introspection. In 1964, social psychologists Duvall and Wicklund launched an extensive research programme in *objective self-awareness*, showing that being put into 'second-person' situations (being observed or observing yourself in a mirror) triggers intense 'first-person introspection'; unfortunately, this research has been largely ignored by contemporary consciousness science. In 1977, Nisbett and Wilson published an important experimental critique of introspection, in response to which some researchers concluded that *introspection* is merely *retrospection* or rationalization for actions, whilst others sharpened their sense of what introspection can and cannot do. Recent discussion of introspection has focused on two issues. The first is Kornhuber and Deecke's finding, replicated by Libet, that there is an identifiable neural event—the *readiness potential*—which begins some 500 ms before conscious awareness of having made the decision to make a motor response. Many have argued that this research shows that our introspective awareness of consciously initiating agency is mistaken in some way. The second locus of recent discussion concerning introspection is the claim—made by Gazzaniga amongst others—that the verbal speech/thought network operates independently of the response-generation network, with the former being primarily an interpreter—rather than the instigator—of our actions.

**Animal and *infant consciousness.* The study of animal behaviour and mind (ethology) derives from Darwin's study of the expression of emotions in animals and humans (1871). Early ethologists made anthropomorphic assertions about animal minds, leading comparative psychologists such as Thorndike and Watson to limit their animal study to specific snippets of overt behaviour such as maze running and bar pressing. Since then, however, ethology has had a rich history of laboratory experimentation and field observation, leading to important findings concerning primate social life (Yerkes, Harlow) and language acquisition (Gardners, Rumbaughs). With particular reference to animal self-consciousness, Gallup developed the facial 'mark tests' (1968) to determine which creatures (higher apes, dolphins, and elephants) can recognize themselves in a mirror. Chimpanzees pass the *mirror test, as do orangutans; monkeys, regardless of species or length of exposure, do not. In many ways the study of animal self-consciousness is more advanced than the study of animal consciousness. There is some work (and much speculation) today on the nature and distribution of animal consciousness, but much of this literature is plagued by disagreement regarding criteria for the ascription of consciousness. What orders of animals are conscious? Of those animals that are conscious, what type of conscious states do they enjoy? These questions are of vital importance for the science of consciousness, but we are a long way from knowing the answers to them.

For the most part, developmental psychology has also focused on the ontogeny of *self-consciousness rather than that of consciousness per se. In 1968 Amsterdam created her own facial mark test to study the development of self-consciousness in children, finding that children are able to recognize themselves in a mirror at about 16–18 months. Continuing this line of research, Harter clocked a progression of ages at which various abilities distinctive of self-consciousness appear: being able to use a mirror to spot objects behind one; responding differentially to one's face in the mirror (or video); knowing one's physical and social traits; being able to self-ascribe thoughts; being able to refer to oneself in the first person. The study of self-consciousness within developmental psychology is often conducted in the context of **theory of mind* research. One of the lessons of this literature is that the acquisition of a theory of mind is gradual, with different components of folk psychology being acquired at different times.

Just as the study of animal consciousness has focused on self-consciousness rather than consciousness per se, so too has the study of infant and fetal consciousness. Although there is little consensus in this field, most would argue that the advent of consciousness per se pre-dates that acquisition of a theory of mind. In fact, Gopnik has recently suggested that babies are more conscious than adults, on the grounds that they have a much broader attentional focus than do adults. But the question of just when babies (or fetuses) become conscious is plagued by many of the same methodological and conceptual problems that are faced by the study of animal consciousness. We know an increasing amount about the neural and psychological development of the neonate, but we are still faced with problems about what to take as our markers of consciousness.

Disorders of consciousness. It is useful to group disorders of consciousness into two categories: focal disorders and global disorders. In the former case, some particular (fine-grained) class of conscious contents is lost from awareness. Many of the focal disorders of consciousness were well-known to the consciousness researchers of the 19th century: aphasia, associative and apperceptive *agnosia, prosopagnosia, *anosognosia, ataxia, loss of mental *imagery, and unilateral neglect. These syndromes, which continue to elicit much interest from students of consciousness, have been joined by disorders unknown in the 19th century, the most famous of which is *blindsight. Blindsight is a phenomenon that occurs in patients with regions of cortical blindness caused by lesions of the primary visual cortex. Although patients with blindsight claim that they cannot see stimuli in their blindfield, they retain the ability to detect, localize, and discriminate between visual stimuli in the affected regions of their visual field.

We can contrast these focal disorders of consciousness with the global disorders seen in such conditions as *delirium, *anaesthesia, certain forms of *schizophrenia, and *brain damage and *epilepsy. Rather than affecting particular contents within consciousness, these conditions target the subject's general level of consciousness. The subject's overall field of consciousness becomes clouded, disturbed, disorganized, and perhaps even disappears altogether. The study of these conditions, together with that of *dreaming, coma, and the persistent vegetative state, promises to shed much light on the enabling conditions of consciousness.

Another 'disorder' of consciousness that has been of much interest to consciousness researchers is the *commissurotomy (or split-brain) syndrome. Performed in order to restrict the spread of epileptic seizures, the commissurotomy operation involves severing the bundle of fibres (corpus callosum) that connects the two cerebral hemispheres. Split-brain patients suffer no significant impairments to everyday conscious experience, but careful experimentation has revealed a wide array of deficits caused by the procedure. Just what these deficits tell us about the structure of consciousness in the split-brain patient is very much an open question; some theorists claim that the split-brain patient has two streams of consciousness, one in each hemisphere, whereas others hold that consciousness remains fundamentally unified in the split-brain patient.

**Artificial intelligence (AI)* and **machine consciousness.* One of the ambitions harboured by many in the consciousness studies community is the creation of artificial or machine consciousness. Beginning with the work of Turing in the 1950s and furthered by the work of Newell and Simon in the 1960s and the appearance of *expert systems* in the 1970s, considerable effort has been extended in this general direction. This work has prompted not only technical developments in engineering and programming, but also vigorous philosophical debate about the nature of the mind and consciousness. Searle's *Chinese room argument famously aims to show that 'the mind is not a computer program', leading to a distinction between AI as an ensemble of methods to simulate human cognition (*weak AI*) and AI as a model of the human mind (*strong*

AI). Classical symbol-crunching models of intelligence dominated AI until the publication of Rumelhart and McClelland's *Parallel Distributed Processing* in the 1980s rekindled interest in neural network modelling methods, which had fallen into relative obscurity since the pioneering work of the 1950s. Parallel distributed processing (or *connectionism) takes it as a starting point that any attempt to simulate human cognition must be informed by how the brain works. This suggests massively distributed networks of simple computing elements (e.g. artificial neurons) rather than symbol manipulation.

Importantly, the problem of simulating human cognition is different from that of simulating human consciousness, for it seems possible for a system to exhibit intelligence (defined narrowly as, say, to ability to solve complex problems in flexible ways) yet lack awareness. Nevertheless, a number of authors (such as Kurzweil, Aleksander, Holland, and Franklin) have begun to reflect on the conditions in which an artificial system might exhibit some form of awareness. This emerging field is known as *machine consciousness*. It faces the daunting problem of establishing criteria for the presence of awareness—an issue that is perhaps best addressed in precisely the way that *Turing addressed the problem of establishing whether an artificial system exhibits 'intelligence', that is, by noting that one should conclude that the artificial agent is conscious if one cannot tell the difference between a human being and a conscious machine.

Altered, expanded and transpersonal consciousness. The counter-culture of the 1960s, with its interest in Eastern meditative traditions, New Age cosmology, and psychoactive drugs, displayed a 'romanticist' interest in bizarre extremes of conscious/unconscious *altered states. The *Journal of Altered States of Consciousness* was launched in 1975, with a grand mix of '1960s' topics and neuroscience. The *meditative tradition might be seen as an 'applied' component of modern consciousness science, in much the same way that surgery and counselling are applied components of their respective sciences. Benson has conducted electrophysiological studies of Tibetan meditators since the 1970s, and more recently Dunn and Lutz have used *functional brain imaging to study subjects during various meditative states involving 'focused attention', 'emptiness', and 'reflexive consciousness'.

Deriving from Brentano's act psychology, humanistic psychology emerged in the 1950s as a 'third way' reaction against deterministic psychoanalysis and the 'rat psychology' of behaviourism. Transpersonal psychiatry derived from Jung, with his concepts of the collective consciousness, and was furthered by Maslow. These paradigms were highly attuned to the 1960s counter-culture, with awareness-training groups, Esalen Institute, and EST. The *Journal of Transpersonal Psychology* made its debut in 1969, and the formation of the *Association for Transpersonal Psychology* followed three years later. The Institute of Noetic Science (founded in 1973 and with its own journal) has been a co-sponsor of Tucson conferences.

Motivational and affective (un)consciousness. Questions concerning the relationship between consciousness, motivation, and affect have been an integral part of consciousness studies since the work of Freud, Janet, and Charcot. Freud's three-part distinction between ego, id, and superego set the stage for discussion of the 'self' over the last century, and his notion of psychosexual stages opened up (with Anna Freud) work on infant bonding, object relations, and the development of self-awareness out of other-awareness. Janet's work on dissociation has played an important role in how the relationship between motivation and consciousness is understood, while Charcot's influence continues to be felt in the use of *hypnosis as a tool for the study of consciousness—work that has recently entered into the mainstream of consciousness research. An important development in recent years is the integration of psychological and neurological perspectives on these questions, with the rise of affective neuroscience and neuropsychiatry. In one study, Marshall and colleagues used functional neuroimaging to study a patient presenting with hysterical paralysis. They found evidence that the limbic/emotional frontal areas were preventing the motor-commanding frontal areas from lifting the 'paralysed' arm—a putative mechanism for Freud's repression. A further key development is the rise of models of consciousness that emphasize the importance of the primitive bodily registration of affect. Damasio's work on somatic markers and Panksepp's work on *core consciousness have been widely influential, not only for what they tell us about conscious emotion but also for what they tell us about unconscious emotion. One of the lessons to be learnt from this work parallels that gleaned from the study of conscious perception and cognition: much of mental processing takes place outside of consciousness awareness.

Consciousness and physics. There is much debate in consciousness science about whether 'Newtonian physics' can explain the evolution and existence of consciousness, or whether one must invoke the processes of non-classical quantum mechanics (Penrose), perhaps expressed through microtubule generation of dendritic force fields (Hamerof, Davies), to account for consciousness. Proponents of quantum approaches to consciousness have held their own (Tuscon-derived) conferences (1999, 2003, 2007) and have an online journal, *NeuroQuantology* (2003). So that Einsteinian relativity not be left out, Burr suggests saccades cause relativistic misperception of time and space, with perceived order consistently reversed; and Nijhawan suggests that visual–tactile–motor neurons in premotor cortex subserve relativity. Notwithstanding the interest in these positions, most consciousness researchers assume that neither relativity, which operates on macro-scales, nor quantum mechanics, which operates on micro-scales, has any discernible impact on those brain processes that generate or underpin consciousness.

The philosophical study of consciousness. The *philosophical study of consciousness has had a complex, and at times difficult, relationship to the scientific study of consciousness. Much of the philosophical discussion has focused on the question of whether there *can* be a comprehensive scientific account of consciousness. Many would grant that science can make some progress in understanding consciousness, but there continues to be much debate about whether consciousness is a straightforwardly biological phenomenon that can be expected to succumb to the methods of science in the way that (say) life and reproduction have, or whether consciousness will resist such explanatory forays. The sticking point has been the phenomenal character of consciousness—what, following Nagel, is often referred to as its '*what it's likeness'. There seems to be an *explanatory gap (Levine) between the physical or functional properties associated with conscious states and their phenomenal character, and it is not clear how this gap might be bridged. Some hold that it has already been bridged, others hold that the gap will—or at least can—be bridged by the advance of science and the construction of new concepts, and still others hold that that the gap cannot be bridged, no matter how hard we work at bridge building.

Philosophers have not restricted their attention to the question of whether a fully reductive account of consciousness is attainable, but have also attempted to contribute to the science of consciousness itself. Some philosophers have focused on characterizing in precise detail the exact phenomenon that a science of consciousness is attempting to explain. What kinds of mental states can be conscious? What, in general terms, are the properties of consciousness? In what way is consciousness unified? What is its temporal structure? Other philosophers have concerned themselves with analysing the concepts and methodology of consciousness science. Just what is a neural *correlate of consciousness? How should we go about the search for the neural correlates of consciousness? What criteria ought we use for the ascription of consciousness? There is now a nascent literature applying the tools and techniques of the philosophy of science to issues raised by the study of consciousness.

3. Neuroscience

Much of the contemporary enthusiasm within consciousness studies is due to the dramatic development of neuroscience, particularly in terms of the widespread availability of powerful functional brain imaging methods that make it possible to see the brain in action. We are now able to use positron emission tomography (PET), single photon emission computed tomography (SPECT), functional magnetic resonance imaging (fMRI), *electroencephalography of event-related potentials (ERP-EEG), *magnetoencephalography (MEG), and *single-cell recordings, not to mention more exotic methods such as optical imaging, to identify the neural correlates of conscious states and processes. The techniques have well-known various limitations and advantages, with fMRI, particularly its more powerful variants (i.e. 7 T imaging), leading the way in terms of spatial resolution, and EEG offering the best temporal resolution. MEG, with its excellent temporal resolution and increasingly sophisticated source localization algorithms, makes it possible to appreciate the dynamics of information processing in unprecedented ways. The method is very recent, however, and awaits further development insofar as the required data analysis methods are concerned. Some relatively deprecated methods such as PET continue to have great potential in specific applications, such as *sleep research; for in contrast to fMRI, PET operation is almost silent. Single-cell recording offers the best possible insights into neural activity, but is limited to very small populations of neurons and may only be deployed in very specific settings because of its invasive nature. Finally, methods such as *transcranial magnetic stimulation (TMS) open up the possibility of inducing 'virtual lesions', thus making it possible to explore specific causal hypotheses about the involvement of certain cerebral regions in the tasks of interest.

Is there a general picture of the neural correlates of consciousness that emerges from this work? Perhaps. It is clear that many perceptual features are processed in localized regions. For example, with respect to visual experience, MT specializes in motion, V3 specializes in shape, V4/V8 specializes in colour; and the fusiform face area specializes in faces. It seems likely that in general the contents of consciousness are localized to a few fairly specific regions. But what is needed in order for the areas in question to generate (say) visual experiences of motion, colour, or faces? Local accounts hold that activation in that particular neural region is sufficient for generating the conscious states in question, as long as it is (say) sufficiently strong or sustained. Global accounts hold that local activation of content-specific regions is not sufficient to generate a conscious percept. Instead, the content needs to be either bound with other content so as to generate a unified conscious state (a gestalt of some kind), or it needs to enter a *neuronal global workspace, from which it can be accessed by various executive systems.

Despite a general wave of enthusiasm for the search for the neural correlates of consciousness, there are sceptics. Some doubt that we will be able to identify robust neural correlates of consciousness, perhaps on the grounds that consciousness ought to be understood on (say) the quantum level rather than the neuronal level. Others hold that although we will be able to identify correlates, it is unlikely that we will be able to proceed from correlation to causation or explanation, and that we will be left with brute and rather unsatisfactory correlations between physical states and conscious states. Our ability to identify the neural correlates of consciousness improves with each passing year, but there seems to be no concomitant development in our understanding of the conceptual issues surrounding this research.

4. Conclusion

In 1860 Fechner complained that the psycho-physical relationship 'has up to now remained merely a field for philosophical argument without solid foundation and without sure principles and methods for the progress of inquiry'. Although many lament the continued lack of agreement concerning methods and techniques in consciousness science, it is clear that we have come a long way in the last 150 years. Not only is there a concerted research effort within many branches of science to understand consciousness, these branches are in active dialogue with each other. The Tucson and ASSC conferences, together with their affiliated journals, present researchers working in different fields with opportunities to learn from each other. Methodological debates are becoming more sophisticated, and tools for identifying the neural basis of consciousness are improving year on year. This generation's students of consciousness have a bright future ahead of them.

BILL FAW

conscious resting state Historically, *functional brain imaging work with positron emission tomography (PET) and functional magnetic resonance imaging (fMRI) has emphasized task-induced increases in regional activity associated with the execution of a wide variety of tasks. More recently, however, researchers have become aware of the presence of task-induced decreases in regional brain activity in their data. These deactivations in response to goal-directed tasks are commonly found in a set of areas encompassing posterior cingulate cortex/precuneus, bilateral temporoparietal junctions, and medial frontal cortices (Raichle and Mintun 2006). These areas are found to be among the most active in FDG (fluorodeoxyglucose)-PET measurements of conscious resting human brain metabolism. These areas also show among the most important decreases of activity in various states of transient or permanent unawareness such as vegetative state, slow wave *sleep, general *anaesthesia, or absence seizures (Laureys 2005).

In the average adult brain, the brain accounts for 20% of the oxygen consumption of the body, despite the fact that it represents only 2% of body weight. Relative to this high rate of ongoing or *basal* metabolism, the amount of dedicated task-related activity is relatively small. These findings led to the concept of a 'default mode' of brain function or *conscious resting state*. The functions of this baseline brain activity are spontaneous and virtually continuous, being attenuated only when we engage in goal-directed actions. This is consistent with the continuity of a stable, unified perspective of the organism relative to its environment (a 'self'). The areas the most activated in baseline brain activity have also been involved in processes such as self-referential processes, episodic memory retrieval, mental *imagery, and *inner speech. This may reflect the recall and maintenance of multimodal thoughts through free association which characterize this mental state (Mazoyer et al. 2001).

Recent fMRI studies have observed low-frequency spontaneous blood oxygen level dependent (BOLD) fluctuations within specific neuroanatomical systems (e.g. visual, motor, auditory networks) in the resting human brain (Raichle and Mintun 2006). Coherent spontaneous fluctuations in human brain activity seem to account for part of the variability in event-related BOLD responses. Preliminary EEG and fMRI studies show that resting state activity influence subsequent task performance and perception. These results extend the concept of a default mode or resting-state functionality of the brain by showing a dynamic interplay within and between large, spatially distributed neural networks. They offer a new approach to understand brain function as an intrinsically organized oscillating system, with sensory information modulating rather than determining the operation of the system.

MÉLANIE BOLY AND STEVEN LAUREYS

Boly, M., Phillips, C., Balteau, E., et al. (2008). 'Consciousness and cerebral baseline activity fluctuations'. *Human Brain Mapping*, 29.

Laureys, S. (2005). 'The neural correlate of (un)awareness: lessons from the vegetative state'. *Trends in Cognitive Science*, 9.

Mazoyer, B., Zago, L., Mellet, E. et al. (2001). 'Cortical networks for working memory and executive functions sustain the conscious resting state in man'. *Brain Research Bulletin*, 54.

Raichle, M. E. and Mintun, M. A. (2006). 'Brain work and brain imaging'. *Annual Review of Neuroscience*, 29.

contents of consciousness Of all the mental states that humans have, only some of them are conscious states. Of all the information processed by humans can have, only some of it is processed consciously. What are the contents of consciousness? This entry provides an overview of two approaches to this question. The first approach asks what kinds of states can be conscious. The second approach asks what information conscious mental states convey to the subject who has them. Both questions are central to the philosophical and scientific study of consciousness.

1. Kinds of conscious mental states
2. Kinds of information conveyed by conscious states

1. Kinds of conscious mental states

When there is something it is like to be in a mental state, that mental state has a **phenomenal aspect* or *phenomenal character* to it (see 'WHAT IT'S LIKE'). *Pain, for instance, has a distinctive phenomenal aspect or character: it is painful. For the purposes of this entry, conscious states will be those states with phenomenal character.

For each of kind of conscious state, it is an open question whether it is essentially conscious, or whether it can exist without phenomenal character. For instance, one might think that while there could be an unfelt fear, there could be no such thing as an unfelt pain. Yet some people who have taken anaesthetics report having pains that do not hurt, which suggests that at least some conscious aspects of pain are not essential to a state's being a state of pain.

What kinds of mental states can be conscious? Some clear cases of conscious mental states include (1) perceptual experiences in the modalities of vision, audition, gustation, olfaction and tactile perception; and (2) bodily sensations, including pain, nausea, and awareness of one's own body's position and movement. There are plenty of other examples of conscious states, but the ones listed above share the feature of each having a *distinctive* phenomenal character—one that is not derivative from any other kind of mental state. Consider seeing. There is something it is like to see things, as opposed to hearing them or feeling them. Visual experience seems to have its own distinctively visual phenomenal character, which does not derive from, say, bodily sensations, or moods, or mental imagery.

Which other conscious mental states are like visual experience in having distinctive phenomenal character, and which of them have a merely derivative phenomenal character? This is a matter of controversy. The 18th century empiricist philosopher David Hume held a systematic composition thesis: he thought that all mental states, conscious and otherwise, were ultimately built up out of primitive sensory ingredients, which he called *impressions*. This view denies that the fundamental contents of consciousness include emotions, imagery (see IMAGERY, PHILOSOPHICAL PERSPECTIVES), and cognitive states such as beliefs, decisions, and intentions.

Even if Hume's systematic view turns out to be false, there might be more local cases of composition. Are any or all of the emotions just bodily sensations? Are any or all emotions partly composed of beliefs? For example, one might fear going to see the dentist only if one believes that something bad will or might happen. One position says that there is nothing to emotion besides its perceptual or bodily aspects (Prinz 2004). A more liberal position allows non-bodily, non-perceptual emotional phenomenology.

In the case of visual imagery, it is controversial whether imagistic phenomenology is parasitic on the phenomenology of seeing (analogous controversies apply to the other sensory modalities). In the case of conscious thoughts, it is controversial whether their phenomenal character is distinctive, as opposed to parasitic on the phenomenal character of other states. Suppose you suddenly think to yourself, 'Oh no! I've left my keys in the cinema!' According to one position, the phenomenal character of this thought is parasitic on acoustic or visual imagery (for example, you picture your keys on a seat in the cinema, or you hear yourself saying the sentence 'Oh no! . . . etc.'), or of emotion (for example, you may feel a pang of panic), or some combination. More generally, this position says that the phenomenal character of conscious thought is always exhausted by other kinds of phenomenal character (see Robinson 2005). The opposed position says that the kind of phenomenal character had by conscious states is its own kind. Analogous positions could be formulated for conscious desires.

A related controversy about conscious thought concerns the relation between their phenomenal character (or equivalently, how it feels from the inside to have a conscious thought), and the conscious thought itself. Return to the case where you suddenly think to yourself, 'Oh no! I've left my keys in the cinema!' Would anyone who felt from the inside exactly like you do when you think this thought likewise be thinking that very thought—as opposed to thinking some other thought, or thinking nothing at all? Conversely, if someone were thinking that exact thought, would there have to be anything in common between the way that they feel and the way that you feel? One position on these questions is that conscious thoughts covary with their phenomenal character, so that someone is consciously thinking that *p* just in case they have that phenomenal character. An opposed position allows that when you consciously think a thought, your thought has a phenomenal character that could in principle be had by a mental state that was not a thought. This latter position goes naturally with the view that the phenomenal character of this conscious thought is parasitic on panic, since panic is a feeling you can have even without thinking that specific thought (for further discussion, see Strawson 1996, Siewert 1998, Horgan and Tienson 2002, Robinson 2005).

So far, we have been focusing on mental states that clearly can be conscious, and asking which of those have a distinctive phenomenal character. We can also step back and ask which mental states can be conscious in the first place. Consider *background states*, such as moods (e.g. depression), alertness, intoxication, or hypnotic state. Moods, such as depression, seem to remain in the background of attention, unless you attend to them. It is not obvious whether background states are distinctive sorts of conscious states. We associate alertness, for example, with a disposition to acquire information from the environment. Depression—a mood—is associated with a disposition to expect the worst, and to feel sad. But should alertness or depression be identified with their associated dispositions? If so, then perhaps they are not themselves conscious states after all: perhaps the phenomenal character in the vicinity just attaches to specific instances of fulfilling the disposition, e.g. to specific occurrences of pessimism or sadness in the case of depression, or to specific acquisitions of information in the case of alertness. Or perhaps the dispositions are implemented by imagery or other phenomenal mechanisms, without being identical with them. One could ask the same questions about intoxication and the disposition to act more boldly than usual.

The state of being hypnotized raises a slightly different controversy. Does *hypnosis consist in the operation of regular psychological processes? If so, then it can be wholly accounted for by a theory of how those processes interact with the hypnotized subject's expectations. Alternatively, hypnosis involves the operation of non-standard psychological processes, leading to a truly *altered state of consciousness. If hypnosis involves an altered state of consciousness, then it would be something over and above the mental states that are uncontroversially conscious.

How are simultaneous contents of consciousness related to one another? For instance, you might hear the sounds of a truck groaning by, at the same time as you feel the rain coming down on your umbrella. These auditory and tactile sensations can both be within the same focus of attention. But are all conscious states that a subject has at a time necessarily unified? It might seem impossible to enjoy two conscious states at the same time, without experiencing them together, but people with split brains challenge this assumption (see COMMISSUROTOMY AND CONSCIOUSNESS).

A potentially different sort of unity is *temporal unity* among experiences. The early 20th century philosopher Edmund Husserl discussed the way that the sounds of a series of musical notes could be heard as unified into a single melody, as opposed to a series of motley sounds is heard simply as a succession. His notion of *retention* was meant to capture a special way a succession of inputs may nonetheless seem to be present all at once, as a whole (see TEMPORALITY, PHILOSOPHICAL PERSPECTIVES). The same phenomenon might apply to a succession of experiences, such as the different parts of a conversation, which may feel as if it is a single experience, present all at once.

2. Kinds of information conveyed by conscious states

One idea guiding investigations into the nature of consciousness is that the contents of consciousness are analogous to the contents of a newspaper story. Perhaps the most influential version of this idea is that the contents of an experience are given by the conditions under which it is accurate. What an experience conveys to the subject, according to this conception, is that those conditions are satisfied (see Searle 1983, Peacocke 1992, Siegel 2010).

We can say that the accuracy conditions of experience are its *representational contents*. On this conception, there is a broad analogy between the contents of experience and the representational contents of thoughts and utterances: both contents are assessable for accuracy. Suppose I utter the sentence 'Fish can swim' and thereby express my belief that fish can swim. The representational content of my utterance is what I assert, and the representational content of my belief is what I believe—in both cases, that fish can swim.

The conception of the contents of experience as given by its accuracy condition is motivated by the idea that it often makes sense to ask, 'How would things have to be, in order for what my experience is conveying to me to be accurate?' The conditions under which the experience would be accurate determine the contents of the experience. This conception can easily account for how experiences may mislead. Suppose you see a fish while unwittingly looking in a mirror. It may look as if there is a red fish in front of you, when in fact the red fish you see is behind you. Similarly, in auditory or olfactory *hallucinations, one may seem to hear voices when in fact no one is speaking, or to smell an odour when in fact nothing is emitting that smell. In *phantom limb pain, one feels pain as located where one's limb used to be but is no longer. These are cases of being misled by one's senses, and it is natural to say that in these cases things are not as they appear to be. Given an experience—either one we actually have, or a hypothetical one—we sometimes have intuitions about whether the experience is accurate (*veridical*) or inaccurate (*falsidical*). To this extent, we seem to be able to assess experiences for accuracy. Experiences that have contents represent the world as being a certain way, so they are said to have *representational contents*.

If experiences have representational contents, which properties do experiences portray things as having? Suppose you see a bowl of wax peaches. Does your visual experience represent that there is fruit in the bowl, or, more minimally, that there are variously coloured roundish volumes in the bowl (or perhaps, yet more minimally, that there are items with pastel orange coloured convex surfaces in the bowl)? On the first option, the experience will be inaccurate, since the bowl contains wax fruit, not peaches. In contrast, since the other options convey less committal information, the experience will be accurate, since there really are roundish volumes with pastel orange coloured convex surfaces in the bowl. This dispute about visual experiences concerns whether they represent only colours and shapes and illumination properties, or higher-level properties such as a being a piece of fruit (Siegel 2006).

Which experiences, if any, have representational contents? It is natural to think of standard cases of visual consciousness, such as seeing a fish tank, as presenting the environment as being a certain way, e.g. containing a fish tank full of fish. It might appear to be in a location slightly different from the location it is actually in, due to the distortion of seeing things in water. For the experience to be accurate, the fish would have to be floating exactly where it appears to be—which is different from the place where it is. It is also possible, however, for experiences to represent occurrences inside the body. For instance, pains may represent that there is damage in the part of the body that hurts, so that if the painful experience is accurate then there really is damage in that part of the body.

While it may seem natural to hold that standard visual experiences of seeing have representational contents, for other kinds of conscious experience it is harder to say what the contents would be. If you gently press your eyeball with your finger, you will seem to see a *phosphene*, a coloured patch of light. Perhaps rather than conveying that there is a luminous occurrence behind the eyelid, the phosphene experience is not conveying anything at all, either about the space outside the body or the space inside the body. Switching modalities, when you hear the notes of a melody, what would have to happen in the world for the experience to be accurate, besides the sounds succeeding one another? It is difficult to say. Does the experience of smelling odours convey to you any way the world has to be in order to be accurate, or is olfactory experience nothing more than a sensory affliction? Some philosophers have argued that conscious experiences in the modalities of taste and smell do not convey anything to the subject (Smith 2002). Other philosophers deny that even standard visual experiences are assessable for accuracy (Travis 2004).

We have been discussing conscious experiences in the sensory modalities. When we consider such experiences to be accurate or inaccurate, we are taking them to have something in common with belief: just as the belief that fish swim is true in virtue of the truth of its content *fish swim*, so too sensory experiences are accurate when their contents are true and inaccurate when they are false. Other kinds of conscious states, such as some emotions, might not themselves be assessable for accuracy. For example, fear is not by itself correct or incorrect, but it might nonetheless have parts that are so assessable. A fear that your dentist will hurt you could have as a component the belief that dentists are apt to cause harm. Relatedly, the relational component of your fear might have the structure of a belief: when you fear that your dentist will hurt you, this might (unfortunately) be true, or it might be false. Either way, your fear will have a content that is assessable for truth, even though the fear itself is not assessable for truth. Alternatively, fear might be a mere sensation that is not in any way directed at the environment. Finally, there might be two kinds of fear, or more generally two kinds of emotion—the kind that is directed at the world, and the kind that is merely a bodily sensation (see EMOTION, PHILOSOPHICAL PERSPECTIVES].

One of the central debates concerning the representational contents of experience is whether they determine its phenomenal character. *Representationalists* say that the phenomenal character of experiences derives wholly from their representational content. The most far-reaching version of *representationalism applies across the board to all conscious states, whereas more modest versions are directed at specific kinds of experiences, such as visual experiences, or pain.

Whereas representationalists say that representational contents determine phenomenal character, others say that phenomenal features of conscious states determine representational features. If two experiences are phenomenally the same, will there necessarily be some contents that they share? Or, more strongly, will the experiences share all their contents? Some philosophers hold both representationalism and the latter (and stronger) claim, on the grounds that phenomenal properties are identical to representational properties (see Dretske 1995, Carruthers 2000). Other philosophers embrace the former (and weaker) claim by holding that there is a kind of content that experiences have in virtue of their phenomenology, so that their phenomenology has explanatory priority over the content itself (Siewert 1998, Horgan and Tienson 2002).

The contents of experience raise methodological questions for the scientific study of consciousness, particularly with the search for neural *correlates of conscious experiences. According to a standard definition (Chalmers 1998), a neural representational system counts as a correlate of an experience, just in case the neural correlate's having content *C* suffices for the experience to have content *C*. If there are neural representational systems whose contents match the contents of experience in this way, then knowing what the contents of an experience are help us identify its neural correlate. Conversely, if one already knew what the neural correlate of an experience was, its role in information processing could tell us what contents the experience has. It is controversial, however, whether there are any such neural representational systems. Some philosophers think that neural systems cannot by themselves encode the kind of information that is present in the content of conscious experience: rather, aspects of the body and the environment are also required (Noë and Thompson 2004). If so, then there will be no purely neural correlates of experiences of the sort defined above: either experience has no neural correlates at all, or else neural correlates will not be defined in terms of matching contents.

There are many other debates in philosophy about the representational contents of consciousness. Do they always or ever involve concepts? What sorts of differences in contents do we find between humans, infants, and animals? Do different sensory modalities, such as vision and touch, share the same sorts of contents? Is the content of experiences determined wholly by what is in the subject's head, or is it also determined by the subject's environment? These issues are discussed in other entries (see ANIMAL METACOGNITION AND CONSCIOUSNESS; NON-CONCEPTUAL CONTENT).

SUSANNA SIEGEL

Carruthers, P. (2000). *Phenomenal Consciousness: a Naturalistic Theory.*

Chalmers, D. (1998). 'On the search for neural correlates of consciousness'. In Hameroff, S. R. et al. (eds) *Toward a Science of Consciousness II.*

Dretske, F. (1995). *Naturalizing the Mind.*

Horgan, T. and Tienson, J. (2002). 'The intentionality of phenomenology and the phenomenology of intentionality'. In Chalmers, D. (ed.) *Philosophy of Mind.*

Noë, A. and Thompson, E. (2004). 'Are there neural correlates of consciousness?' *Journal of Consciousness Studies*, 11.

Peacocke, C. (1992). *A Study of Concepts.*

Prinz, J. (2004). *Gut Reactions.*

Robinson, W. (2005). 'Thoughts without distinctive non-imagistic phenomenology'. *Philosophy and Phenomenological Research*, 70.

Searle, J. (1983). *Intentionality.*

Siegel, S. (2005). 'The contents of perception'. In Zalta, E. N. (ed.) *Stanford Encyclopedia of Philosophy (Spring 2006 Edition)*, http://plato.stanford.edu/archives/spr2006/entries/perception-contents/.

Siegel, S. (2006). 'Which properties are represented in perception?' In Szabo, T. G. and Hawthorne, J. (eds) *Perceptual Experience.*

Siewert, C. (1998). *The Significance of Consciousness.*

Smith, A. D. (2002). *The Problem of Perception.*

Strawson, G. (1996). *Mental Reality.*

Travis, C. (2004). 'The silence of the senses'. *Mind*, 113.

contextual cueing Contextual cueing refers to how observers use predictive contextual information to facilitate the detection and identification of visual objects in complex scenes. As a real-world example, consider how generally effortless it is to find one's home on a street or the fuel gauge on one's car dashboard. Contextual information of surrounding homes and landmarks provide cues for one's home, while the stable layout of other instrumentation helps one locate the car's fuel gauge with ease. Without visual memory, we would struggle to search for our home or the fuel gauge every time we needed to find it. However, biological vision possesses powerful learning mechanisms that encode regularities in the visual input. Interestingly, such rich, complex information from the environment can be encoded without conscious effort or intention. Related examples of such implicit learning include *artificial grammar learning of word strings, *sequence learning of motor responses, and statistical learning of phonemes or novel shapes (see LEARNING, EXPLICIT VS IMPLICIT). All of these examples show how observers are sensitive to structure in the input, conferring performance benefits when responses are predictable from structure (e.g. sequence learning).

The contextual cueing paradigm reveals how sensitivity to visual structure can facilitate the deployment of attention. In a prototypical search task, observers are

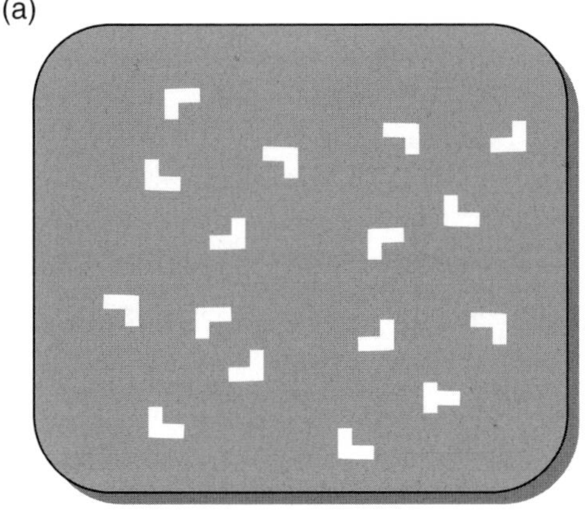

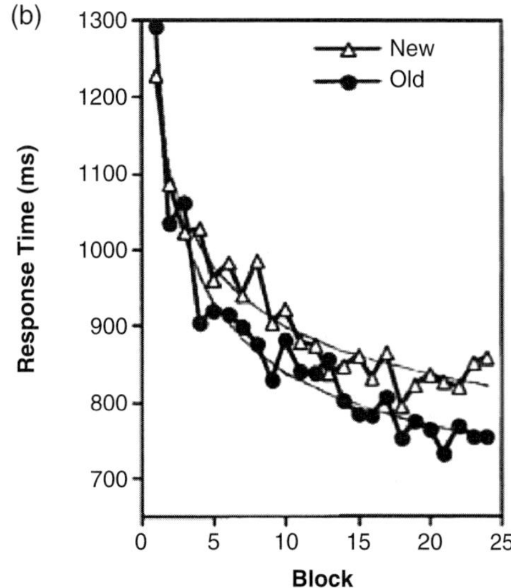

Fig. C7. (a) Sample usual search display. The task is to search for the rotated I and report its orientation. The distractors in the display form the context for the target. (b) Search response time for old, repeated and new, randomized, control displays, shown as a function of block. Search time is faster for old displays than for new displays. From Chun and Jiang 2003, with permission from the American Psychological Association.

asked to search for a target amongst distractors, for example, a T target rotated 90° to the left or right amongst rotated L distractors (Fig. C7a). This task is difficult, so it takes time to find the target. The question is how one can find the target faster. If memory serves vision, repeating the displays of items may be beneficial (Chun and Jiang 1998). In repeated displays, the target appears in a consistent location relative to its context, in this case, the positions of the distractors. If observers can learn the displays and their associations with embedded targets, they will perform search more quickly in these repeated (old) displays than in randomly generated (new) displays. Figure C7b shows the results from a prototypical contextual cueing study, plotting average response time to locate the T target as a function of block.

Two types of learning are revealed by this task. The first is general improvement in both old and new conditions; such commonly observed improvement simply represents practice effects with the stimuli and task. Contextual cueing is measured by the larger improvement in the old displays relative to the new displays as displays are repeated. This difference cannot be attributed to general practice, but instead it represents learning of the repeated contexts and the use of such predictive information to detect targets more quickly.

1. Contextual cueing is implicit
2. Contextual cueing is dependent on medial temporal lobe structures
3. Contextual cueing requires attention
4. Summary

1. Contextual cueing is implicit

When people think of learning and memory, they commonly think of their ability to remember someone's name or some facts for an exam. These abilities have been described as explicit, declarative, conscious memory because they refer to information that can be consciously recalled. However, a great deal of information is learned without such conscious effort or intention and even without one's awareness of having learned anything. Of great interest to consciousness research, the contextual cueing benefit is implicit. When asked to distinguish between old and new displays, observers performed at chance, even though this recognition test was presented immediately after observers had shown robust contextual cueing benefits in the search task (Chun and Jiang 1998). It is possible that such old/new familiarity recognition tasks are not sensitive, as the judgements differ from search. Thus, as a more sensitive measure, observers were presented with old displays in which the target was replaced by a distractor. They were asked to simply give their best guess as to which quadrant of the display was most likely to contain a target given the particular display before them. This memory test asks for the same kind of information that would be used to facilitate search, yet observers were at chance at this guessing task as well (Chun and Jiang 2003). Not only was memory for the displays and contextual associations implicit, but the learning itself was incidental. Observers were not informed of the repetitions, and they almost never reported having tried to encode the displays. Even when given explicit instruction to actively encode the displays and their embedded target locations, subjects were unable to perform above chance on the subsequent guessing task (Chun and Jiang 2003).

Of course, in the real world, observers can and usually do become aware of environmental regularities, such as the location of one's home. However, the laboratory version shows that learning can be implicit. The displays were highly similar, and there were hundreds of novel, random displays, causing robust interference in explicit memory. Indeed, it is remarkable to observe implicit memory amidst such noise, and the memory is so robust that it can even span a one-week interval (Chun and Jiang 2003). In fact, there has not yet been a published report challenging the characterization of contextual cueing as implicit. The implicit nature of the contextual cueing task makes it useful to study basic debates in implicit learning and memory. For example, does implicit memory depend on the same or different brain structures as explicit memory? Does implicit memory require *attention?

2. Contextual cueing is dependent on medial temporal lobe structures

An enduring debate in cognitive neuroscience concerns whether conscious (explicit) and unconscious (implicit) memory abilities map onto the same or independent neural systems. The hippocampus and neighbouring medial temporal lobe areas are key brain structures in this debate. Undoubtedly, the hippocampus is important for explicit, declarative, conscious memory. Damage to the hippocampus severely impairs such explicit memory, while leaving implicit memory preserved. For example, *amnesic patients show *priming effects from stimuli they cannot recognize as having been seen before. Beyond its role in conscious, explicit memory, the hippocampus also plays a more general role in configural, contextual learning. If so, this raises the theoretical possibility that some forms of implicit memory could show hippocampal dependence. The challenge is that explicit memory and configural processing are usually confounded. However, contextual cueing provides a unique test for theories of hippocampal function because it is both configural and implicit. If awareness is critical, then human patients with hippocampal damage should show robust contextual cueing. However, if the configural nature of the learned information is important, then the hippocampal patients should not show contextual cueing. A group of amnesic patients with hippocampal and extended medial temporal lobe damage did not show contextual cueing (Chun and Phelps 1999). Even in normal observers, contextual cueing can be eliminated by midazolam (Park et al. 2004), which induces temporary amnesia and is thought to impair medial temporal lobe function.

The specific anatomical substrate of implicit contextual learning remains controversial, however. In a separate study, patients with hippocampal and extended medial temporal lobe damage did not show contextual cueing, while patients with damage restricted to the hippocampus proper showed normal contextual cueing (Manns and Squire 2001). One complication is that their hippocampal patients only showed partial atrophy to the hippocampus, and a subsequent neuroimaging study reported significant hippocampal activation during contextual cueing (Greene et al. 2007). Thus, it seems likely that the hippocampus is engaged during implicit contextual learning.

3. Contextual cueing requires attention

It is commonly assumed that implicit learning can occur unaffected by a demanding task being performed at the same time, suggesting that attention is not required. However, such dual-task results are open to the criticism that the concurrent tasks were not taxing enough to impair the ongoing learning task. Another strategy to study the role of attention is to have the subject perform just one task, but vary which stimuli the subject must attend. Attention can be manipulated in the contextual cueing search paradigm by presenting displays that contain half red and half green items. The target for any given subject was always presented in one of the two colours. The distractors that shared the target colour could be denoted as the attended set because observers focus their attention on items that share the target colour. The remaining distractors of the non-target colour comprised the ignored set. With this manipulation, one can vary whether the attended context (distractors) was predictive of target location or whether the ignored context was predictive (Jiang and Chun 2001). Only attended, predictive contexts produced contextual cueing. Ignored contexts did not, even though these were intermingled amidst the attended contexts and were equally predictive of target location. Thus, although contextual cueing is implicit, it is dependent on selective attention. Subsequent work suggests that ignored contexts can be learned in some cases, but that attention is required for the expression of this learning (Jiang and Leung 2005). Although more work is needed to clarify the role of attention in implicit learning, it seems fair to assume that implicit memory is dependent on attention and impaired by dual task load (Mulligan 1998, Jiménez and Méndez 1999). This dependence on attention simply reflects the fact that cognitive systems are limited in *capacity. Although intentional, conscious effort may not be required for learning, some degree of selection prevents the wasteful encoding of task-irrelevant events.

4. Summary

In sum, contextual cueing is a useful laboratory task that reveals how powerful associative learning mechanisms enable observers to encode important, predictive regularities in the perceptual input. Encoding the regularities allows observers to deploy attention more effectively to complex scenes, improving search performance. This form of visual learning operates beneath awareness, but it does require attention and selection.

MARVIN M. CHUN

Chun, M. M. and Jiang, Y. (1998). 'Contextual cueing: implicit learning and memory of visual context guides spatial attention'. *Cognitive Psychology*, 36.

—— —— (2003). 'Implicit, long-term spatial contextual memory'. *Journal of Experimental Psychology: Learning, Memory, and Cognition*, 29.

—— and Phelps, E. A. (1999). 'Memory deficits for implicit contextual information in amnesic subjects with hippocampal damage'. *Nature Neuroscience*, 2.

Greene, A. J., Gross, W. L., Elsinger, C. L., and Rao, S. M. (2007). 'Hippocampal differentiation without recognition: an fMRI analysis of the contextual cueing task'. *Learning and Memory*, 14.

Jiang, Y. and Chun, M. M. (2001). 'Selective attention modulates implicit learning'. *Quarterly Journal of Experimental Psychology A*, 54A.

—— and Leung, A. W. (2005). 'Implicit learning of ignored visual context'. *Psychonomic Bulletin and Review*, 12.

Jiménez, L. and Méndez, C. (1999). 'Which attention is needed for implicit sequence learning?' *Journal of Experimental Psychology: Learning, Memory, and Cognition*, 25.

Manns, J. and Squire, L. R. (2001). 'Perceptual learning, awareness, and the hippocampus'. *Hippocampus*, 11.

Mulligan, N. W. (1998) 'The role of attention during encoding in implicit and explicit memory'. *Journal of Experimental Psychology: Learning, Memory, and Cognition*, 24.

Park, H., Quinlan, J., Thornton, E., and Reder, L. M. (2004). 'The effect of midazolam on visual search: implications for understanding amnesia'. *Proceedings of the National Academy of Sciences of the USA*, 101.

contrastive analysis There are two ways to study conscious experiences scientifically: one way is to compare them to closely matched *unconscious* experiences, a method that has been called *contrastive analysis* (Baars 1988).

Comparing conscious contents to each other is a method that has been long exploited in the study of perception and psychophysics. These *conscious-to-conscious* comparisons go back to Isaac Newton's prism experiments, which involve judgements of colour differences. Prism experiments first drew attention to the difference between perceived (conscious) categorical differences in the light wavelength continuum. Conscious-to-conscious comparisons have been enormously useful over the last four centuries, and still provide an indispensable source of evidence on the sensory systems.

In contrastive analysis, *conscious-to-unconscious contrasts* are experiments in which consciousness is treated as a variable, and all other factors are held as constant as possible. A great deal of modern research can be described in this way, using a variety of techniques that allow precise experimental control. They include *binocular rivalry, dual-task experiments, studies of *automaticity after practice, *attentional blink, *inattentional blindness, episodic vs implicit *memory, and much more. Many pathologies of consciousness, such as *blindsight, visual neglect, face blindness and *anosognosia also involve conscious-to-unconscious comparisons. And of course, comparisons between waking vs coma, deep *sleep, general *anaesthesia, sedation, and *epileptic loss of consciousness also involve such contrasts. Some brain structures, like the ventral *visual stream in cortex, appear to support conscious contents directly, while others, like the cerebellum, do not. Thus contrastive cases provide a very large and reliable set of constraints on any theory of consciousness.

Contrastive analysis is the experimental method applied to consciousness. But a key breakthrough was the ability to think of unconscious brain activity as comparable to conscious contents, i.e. as complex and 'intelligent'. This is a relatively new insight, although it was anticipated in the 19th century. The Western intellectual tradition fiercely resisted the notion of unconscious intelligence. In the 1860s Helmholtz was forced to withdraw the notion of 'unconscious inference' for perceptual *filling-in, because his contemporaries found logical inference without consciousness to be shocking. Conscious mental activity, from Aristotle onward, was seen as the rational and logical domain of the intellect. It was the marker of distinctively human, intellectual work. Even William James fiercely resisted the intelligent unconscious in his *Principles of Psychology* of 1890. When Freud's work became famous, beginning in 1900, it did not postulate an intelligent unconscious, but rather a chaotic 'cauldron of seething excitations', Freud's metaphor for the emotional unconscious. It was not until desktop computers became household items that scientists accepted the notion of intelligent unconscious processes. This did not become commonplace until the late 20th century.

Table 1. Some widely studied polarities between matched conscious and unconscious phenomena (from Baars 2003)

Conscious	Unconscious
Explicit cognition	Implicit cognition
Immediate memory	Longer-term memory
Novel, informative, and significant events	Routine, predictable, and non-significant events
Attended information	Unattended information
Focal contents	Fringe contents (e.g. familiarity)
Declarative memory (facts, etc.)	Procedural memory (skills, etc.)
Supraliminal stimulation	Subliminal stimulation
Effortful tasks	Spontaneous/automatic tasks
Remembering (recall)	Knowing (recognition)
Available memories	Unavailable memories
Strategic control	Automatic control
Grammatical strings	Implicit underlying grammars
Intact reticular formation and bilateral intralaminar thalamic nuclei	Lesioned reticular formation, or bilateral intralaminar nuclei
Rehearsed items in working memory	Unrehearsed items
Wakefulness and dreams (cortical arousal)	Deep sleep, coma, sedation (cortical slow-waves)
Explicit inferences	Automatic inferences
Episodic memory (autobiographical)	Semantic memory (conceptual knowledge)
Autonoetic memory	Noetic memory
Intentional learning	Incidental learning
Normal vision	Blindsight (cortical blindness)

Without an intelligent unconscious to compare with conscious events, it is impossible to treat conscious experience as one pole of an experimentally testable dimension. That leaves consciousness as the only scientific construct in history that is in principle not treatable as a variable. By itself, conscious experience provides no comparison conditions, because it is not possible to experience unconscious events from a conscious point of view. That would leave only comparisons between conscious events as a scientifically viable way to study experiential contents. As we have noted, conscious-to-conscious comparisons have a long and productive history in science. Conscious-to-unconscious comparisons are surprisingly recent as an accepted scientific method.

Some contrastive cases are listed in Table 1, showing how widespread such comparisons are today in domains like perception, immediate memory, long-term learning and retrieval, action control, emotion, and aspects of *brain anatomy and physiology. All the standard topics in the mind–brain sciences can be divided into conscious (operationalized as reportable) and unconscious (unreportable) events. However, so far only visual perception, memory, and certain brain events have been thoroughly studied with contrastive analyses.

A clear pattern of evidence has emerged (Table 2). Conscious events are strongly associated with the so-called *limited capacity system*, including immediate memory, voluntary control, novel rather than practised skills, mental effort, decision-making, conceptual thinking, and perception. This is not to say that those events are entirely conscious; all tasks are mixed. However, there is no doubt that by comparison to more conscious events, it is the large-capacity domains that are unconscious, particularly long-term memory storage, practised automatisms, the stored vocabulary of language, and the complex motivational systems involved in human personality and social interaction.

Conscious events appear to require internal consistency. The brain has tens of billions of neurons, hundreds of functional regions in cortex (the Brodmann areas), and even more massive white matter fibres, allowing for almost endless patterns of connectivity. Yet conscious con-

Table 2. Capabilities of comparable conscious and unconscious processes (modified from Baars 1988)

Conscious processes	Unconscious processes
Computationally inefficient (e.g. mental arithmetic: high errors, low speed, mutual interference)	Each process is highly efficient at its own tasks (e.g. syntax: low errors, high speed, little mutual interference)
Great range of different contents over time	Each process has a limited range of specialized contents, and is relatively isolated and autonomous
Great ability to relate different conscious contents to each other in novel ways.	Little or no ability to make novel connections between unconscious processes
Great ability to relate conscious events to their unconscious contexts	
Internal consistency, seriality, and limited capacity	Diverse, can operate in parallel, and together have great capacity

tents are both limited and internally consistent. That becomes particularly obvious when the brain is presented with mutually incompatible stimuli, as in binocular rivalry, mismatched stimuli to the two ears, and audiovisual integration tasks, as in watching a movie or listening to a teacher in a classroom. In all such cases, small mismatches between the two incoming streams cause competition for consciousness. Just a few tenths of a second difference between the audio and video track of a movie will separate those signal streams perceptually, and degrade comprehension. Thus the internal consistency of conscious contents at any single time seems mandatory.

Conscious experiences are classically described as a 'stream', in William James and other sources (see STREAM OF CONSCIOUSNESS), while each conscious content clearly activates widespread parallel regions in the brain. Many such activations are unconscious or *fringe conscious. Thus as a generalization, conscious contents appear to be more serial, while unconscious ones may function in parallel. The most obvious case is long-term memory storage of all types, which is both unconscious and highly distributed in the brain.

Long-term memory is believed to be encoded in cortical and subcortical synaptic connectivities. Conscious contents make use of these web-like altered connectivities, but play actively upon them by way of local and regional waveforms in the theta to *gamma range. The thalamocortical system is often viewed as the broad substrate of conscious experiences, modulated by brainstem nuclei that control major waking and sleep stages. However, not all parts of cortex directly support conscious contents. The ventral stream of visual cortex (*V1) appears to support conscious visual objects and scenes, while the dorsal stream provides unconscious spatial maps (Goodale and Milner 1992).

Several theories depart from some specific set of crucial contrasts between conscious and unconscious events. Thus Edelman and Tononi (2000) remark upon the difference between thalamocortical brain activities associated with conscious contents, and the cerebellum, which may have similar numbers of neurons, but which is generally believed not to support conscious events directly. The difference between slow, high-amplitude *electroencephalography (EEG) and fast, low-amplitude waveforms, also corresponds well to conscious and unconscious processes. Global workspace theory is largely shaped by the contrasts shown in Table 2. Dehaene's *neuronal global workspace models have been tested on a variety of precise experimental comparisons between conscious and unconscious conditions (Dehaene 2001). Tulving and coworkers routinely compare conscious (episodic) memories to unconscious (implicit) ones. Shiffrin and Schneider based their work on automatic vs effortful tasks, which often correspond to 'more unconscious' vs 'more conscious' events.

While debate continues about the exact relationship between these sets of contrasts, the fundamental idea of comparing similar events, some of which are reportable while others are not, seems both well established and scientifically productive.

BERNARD J. BAARS

Baars, B. J. (1988). *A Cognitive Theory of Consciousness.*
—— (2002). 'The conscious access hypothesis: origins and recent evidence'. *Trends in Cognitive Science,* 6.
—— (2003). 'Introduction: treating consciousness as a variable: the fading taboo'. In Baars, B. J. et al. (eds) *Essential Sources in the Scientific Study of Consciousness.*
Dehaene, S. (2001). *The Cognitive Neuroscience of Consciousness.*
Edelman, G. M. and Tononi, G. (2000). *A Universe of Consciousness: How Matter Becomes Imagination.*
Goodale, M. A. and Milner, A. D. (1992). 'Separate visual pathways for perception and action'. *Trends in Neuroscience,* 15.

core consciousness

Core consciousness is our *sense of ourselves* and *things happening around us*, but not a level of awareness. . . . Core consciousness is continuous from the time you wake up in the morning until you again go to sleep. Core consciousness is personal to you . . . confined to the here and now—there is no past or future. Extended consciousness has core consciousness as a base, but it provides us with 'awareness' of the fact that we are alive and acting on the stage of life; that we have had a past we can recall; and that we have a future we can contemplate. *http://www.architecture-mind.com/damasio.htm* (my italics)

How experienced life emerges from brain activities continues to be the premiere conceptual and empirical challenge for neuroscience. It is unlikely that we can achieve a scientifically satisfactory understanding of conscious *awareness*, a reflective higher brain function, until we clarify the most primitive forms of mentality—immediate subjective experience in the animal kingdom. Such primordial phenomenal experiences constitute *core consciousness* and appear to be integrally interrelated with a study of the *core self* (Panksepp 1998, 2005a, Damasio 1999), which may one day help illuminate the biological rudiments of the soul.

It is becoming axiomatic, at least in neuroscience, that consciousness is critically dependent on specific types of brain neurodynamics. We can coarsely divide the subjective world into here-and-now *primary process* core consciousness (raw bodily affective feelings and perceptions of the external world), *secondary consciousness* (having thoughts and other perspectives about our raw experiences), and *tertiary* varieties (having thoughts about thoughts, leading to self-awareness). These aspects of consciousness, each with variants and elaborations, are critically dependent on diverse brain systems, including deeply unconscious ones. However, they also share the primary process core faculties that generate immediate phenomenal experience, both perceptual (the movie in the head) and affective (the many nonpropositional ways we feel alive).

Since the nature of core consciousness can finally be studied neuroscientifically, I will not consider dualistic *panpsychic* alternatives—that consciousness is a property of the universe as opposed to physiologically grounded properties of living brains and bodies. Within such *panexperientialist* views, core consciousness would have to be envisioned rather differently, perhaps like the empirically inconsequential 'mind-dust' that William James entertained in his *Principles of Psychology*. In the current neuroscientific era, one is tempted, tongue in cheek, to relate such 'dust' to glutamatergic neurotransmission. Glutamate, the most prevalent excitatory synaptic transmitter, is essential for all mental activities. Without glutamate, consciousness fades.

For the foreseeable future, the fuzzy concept of **emergence* remains essential to conceptualize how raw phenomenal experience, namely core consciousness, arises from neurodynamics. Regardless, novel scientific predictions are essential to estimate how core consciousness *emerges* from brain activities. At present the best strategy is to specify the brain regions, chemistries, neurodynamics, and experiences that contribute critically to primary process consciousness. If we correctly decode those dispositional glimmers of mentality in evolution, we have a solid platform for dealing with subsequent complexities. The mind–brain strategy known as **dual aspect* monism—that mentality is an intrinsic property of complex brain network activities—allows investigators to pursue empirical inquiries into how experience emerges from neural activities. For instance, it is almost certain that various negative and positive emotional feelings (affects), those primal phenomenological aspects of core consciousness, arise from evolutionarily ancient recesses of the brain (Panksepp 1998, 2005a, Denton 2006, Merker 2007).

Raw affects may be primal brain–body representations (a primordial *sense of ourselves*), informing higher, more cognitive regions of the brain–mind, how organisms are faring in survival. But affects come in diverse flavours—sensory, emotional and bodily homeostatic—and we do not know which had primacy in the evolution of consciousness. Maybe it was some simple feeling of pleasure and pain—goodness and badness—arising from approach and avoidance systems of the brain. Maybe it was the perception of light and darkness. Several neuroscientists have cultivated the idea that core consciousness is fundamentally constituted of primary-process affective feelings, critically dependent on specific brain networks. Damasio (1999) proposed that core consciousness includes somatosensory neocortical functions, heavily dependent on the sensory-perceptual capacities of body and brain. In contrast, **emotional* affects, perhaps the aspects of core consciousness easiest to understand, are grounded in subneocortical instinctual emotional *action* systems readily elucidated with animal models, with a dose of critical anthropomorphism (Panksepp 1998, 2005a).

Existing data affirm the existence of various emotion-generating neural substrates (homologous across all mammalian species) concentrated deep in the brainstem, especially the hypothalamus and the periaqueductal grey (PAG) of the midbrain. These ancient medial brain regions are more important for sustaining consciousness than more lateral ones that harvest information from the external senses (Watt and Pincus 2004). Indeed, it is within the PAG that (1) the smallest amount of brain damage severely injures the capacity for consciousness; (2) electrical stimulation can provoke emotional experiences and behaviours with the lowest amount of current; (3) where one can find all neurochemistries known to instigate emotional behaviours; (4) one finds as much interaction with other brain regions as any area in the brain; (5) many basic emotional behaviours continue to be coordinated without any necessary input from higher brain regions. This speaks forcefully for the importance of such ancient brain regions—ones that many neuroscientists assume are deeply unconscious—in the control of emotional-instinctual competence and raw affective experience.

These core emotional capacities are closely associated with higher brain regions (cingulate, insular and frontal cortical areas) that allow organisms to process external information in self-referential ways (Northoff et al. 2006). These medially situated neural networks elaborate a primordial *homuncular representation of the body, especially visceral organs essential for life. The core self may have emerged early in vertebrate evolution (Panksepp 1998, Denton 2006). These self-representational substrates help elaborate raw affects such as hunger, thirst, pain, anger, fear, desire, and other primal homeostatic 'comfort zones' of body and brain. Emotional vocalizations, coordinated in the PAG and nearby limbic circuits, are excellent indicators of core emotional feelings.

We can also seek to discuss core consciousness in terms of perceptual abilities (the feeling of *things happening around us*). No one knows how raw perceptual phenomenology emerges from the neurodynamics of the external senses. How can mere sensory information become perceptual experience? Testable conjectures that might close the *explanatory gap are rare. Most rely on neural *correlates, such as cortical *gamma activities, even though critical analysis suggests subcortical systems suffice for raw perceptions (Merker 2007). Ever-present explanatory gaps are less intimidating for brain systems that mediate intrinsic values—the varieties of life-supporting 'goodness' and life-detracting 'badness'—that are affectively experienced by organisms. Affective neuroscience has demonstrated that all basic emotional feelings, for instance the pounding intensity of anger and the shivery withdrawal of fear, arise from neural systems that generate observable emotional–instinctual actions. Emotional feelings may have dynamics resembling those accompanying instinctual actions, and both may arise from the neurodynamics of a core-self that is laid out in primal instinctual action coordinates.

When one provokes such emotional actions with localized electrical stimulation of specific sub-neocortical circuits, animals are rarely neutral about the aroused states. They readily learn to turn them on (to self-stimulate) or off (to escape or avoid). Human report intense affective experiences from similar brain sites and report 'ownership' of those experiences. Since there is a self-similarity between emotional-instinctual behaviours and emotional feelings, a *dual aspect monism* strategy can situate physically expressive and mentally experienced aspects of raw emotions on the same explanatory plane. This can help counter 'radical behaviourism' and 'ruthless reductionism' in neuroscience by providing a novel vision of how the explanatory gap between neural and psychological dynamics can be narrowed. To the extent that basic psychological processes intrinsically reflect large-scale neural network dynamics, mental events can be envisioned to *causally* control behaviour. Thereby rewards and punishments—and hence 'reinforcement'—can be neuroscientifically linked to fluctuating affective experiences (Panksepp 2005b).

How might we resolve whether primary-process affective or perceptual experiences, or both, are foundational for core consciousness? Functional neuroanatomy can be a guide here. As noted already, PAG-mediated emotional responses arise from brain regions that are evolutionarily more ancient than surrounding tissues that integrate exteroceptive inputs to the organism. It is generally accepted that medial regions of the brain were constructed earlier in brain evolution than lateral ones, and clearly consciousness is more impaired by modest damage to the medial affective systems of the brainstem than the more lateral sensory-perceptual ones. Thus, core affective consciousness may have been a necessary pre-adaptation for the emergence of experienced perceptions, leading eventually to emotion–cognition co-evolution permitting higher kinds of mentality. This vision helps conceptualize free-floating emotional feelings seemingly unconnected to perceptions: most object-relations—namely, the linking of affects to world events—must be learned.

The possibility that emotional affects were among the earliest forms of experienced life raises some troublesome clinical issues. For instance, do individuals in persistent vegetative states (PVS)—people who clearly no longer perceive the world— completely lose their capacity to experience themselves as feeling creatures, without perceptual awareness (Schiff 2006)? When the legal system allowed Terry Schiavo to die from dehydration in the spring of 2005, did she, in the recess of her uncomprehending mind, experience excruciating thirst, the subjective concomitant of dehydration (Denton 2006)? This important question cannot yet be answered, but raw affective experience may survive the destruction of exteroceptive consciousness.

Those who do not believe in the foundational role of affect in mental life commonly subscribe to 'read-out' theories where higher brain processes (usually *re-entrant neural loops with emergent properties) are essential for consciousness, typically assumed to be synonymous with *awareness*. Such beliefs thrive among those who ignore vast amounts of evidence concerning the subcortical sources of raw emotional and perceptual life within animal brains (Panksepp 1998, 2005a, Merker 2007). Of course, doubt must outweigh certainty on such topics. The most critical scientific work remains to be done.

JAAK PANKSEPP

Damasio, A. (1999). *The Feeling of What Happens: Body, Emotion and the Making of Consciousness.*

Denton, D. (2006). *The Primordial Emotions: the Dawning of Consciousness.*

Merker, B. (2007). 'Consciousness without a cerebral cortex: a challenge for neuroscience and medicine'. *Behavioral and Brain Sciences*, 30.

Northoff, G., Henzel, A., de Greck, M., Bermpohl, F., Dobrowolny, H., and Panksepp, J. (2006). 'Self-referential processing in our brain—a meta-analysis of imaging studies of the self'. *Neuroimage*, 31.

Panksepp, J. (1998). *Affective Neuroscience. The Foundation of Human and Animal Emotions.*

—— (2005a). 'Affective consciousness: core emotional feelings in animals and humans'. *Consciousness and Cognition*, 14.

—— (2005b). 'On the embodied neural nature of core emotional affects'. *Journal of Consciousness Studies*, 5.

Schiff, N. D. (2006). 'Multimodal neuroimaging approaches to disorders of consciousness'. *Journal of Head Trauma Rehabilitation*, 21.

Watt, D. F. and Pincus, D. I. (2004). 'Neural substrates of consciousness: implications for clinical psychiatry'. In Panksepp, J. (ed.) *Textbook of Biological Psychiatry.*

correlates of consciousness, computational The expression 'computational correlate of consciousness' was first used by Mathis and Mozer (1995), who, taking a computational approach to the problem of consciousness, asked 'What conditions must a mental representation satisfy in order for it to reach consciousness? What are the computational consequences of a representation reaching consciousness? Does a conscious state affect processing differently than an unconscious state? What is the computational utility of consciousness?' (1995:11). In contrast to current efforts to identify the *neural correlates of consciousness*, this perspective on the problem of consciousness is thus focused more specifically on identifying the *computational principles* that differentiate between information processing with and without consciousness rather than on identifying and localizing their neural underpinnings. Of course, any putative computational principle that differentiates between information processing with and without consciousness will necessarily be implemented by specific neural mechanisms occurring in the brain. But the point is that by analysing the relationships between neural and mental states from a point of view that amounts neither to hardcore neuroscience nor to pure phenomenology, one may hope to identify *bridging* principles that better characterize how particular neural states are associated with conscious processing.

Such principles can take the form of abstract characterizations of types of information processing in our cognitive system (i.e. holistic vs analytical processing; controlled vs automatic processing, etc.), or be expressed in terms of high-level properties of neural processing (i.e. recurrent vs feedforward processing). Further, such characterizations can concern either processes or the representations that are manipulated by such processes.

1. Organization of computational theories
2. Stability
3. Strength and 'fame in the brain'
4. Re-entrant processing and adaptive resonance
5. Synchrony and gamma oscillations
6. Global availability
7. Information integration and differentiation
8. Meta-representation
9. Conclusion

1. Organization of computational theories

Computational theories of consciousnesscan be organized along two dimensions (see Atkinson et al. 2000): (1) A *process vs representation* dimension, which contrasts theories that characterize consciousness in terms of specific processes operating over representations with theories that characterize consciousness in terms of intrinsic properties of mental or neural representations, and (2) a *specialized vs non-specialized* dimension, which contrasts theories that posit the existence of specific information-processing systems dedicated to consciousness with theories for which consciousness can be associated with any information-processing system as long as this system has the relevant properties.

Thus, *specialized vehicle theories* assume that consciousness depends on the properties of representations occurring within a specialized system in the brain. An example of such an account is Atkinson and Shiffrin's model of short-term *memory (Atkinson and Shiffrin 1971), which specifically assumes that representations contained in the short-term memory store (a specialized system) only become conscious if they are sufficiently strong (a property of representations).

Specialized process theories assume that consciousness arises from specific computations that occur in a dedicated mechanism, as in Schacter's *conscious awareness system* (CAS) model (Schacter 1989). Shachter's model indeed assumes that the CAS's main function is to integrate inputs from various domain-specific modules and to make this information available to executive systems. It is therefore a specialized model in that it assumes that there exist specific regions of the brain whose function it is to make its contents available to conscious awareness. It is a process model to the extent that any representation that enters the CAS will be a conscious representation in virtue of the processes that manipulate these representations, and not in virtue of properties of those representations themselves. More recent computational models of consciousness also fall into this category, most notably Dehaene and colleagues's *neuronal global workspace model (Dehaene et al. 1998) and Crick and Koch (2003)'s framework, both of which assume, albeit somewhat differently, that the emergence of consciousness depends on the occurrence of specific processes in specialized systems (e.g. specific long-distance cortico-cortical connectivity).

Non-specialized vehicle theories include any model that posits that availability to consciousness only depends on properties of representations, regardless of where in the brain these representations exist. The *connectionist theory of phenomenal experience* of O'Brien and Opie (1999) is the prototypical example of this category, to the extent that it specifically assumes that any stable neural representation will both be causally efficacious and form part of the contents of phenomenal experience. Mathis and Mozer (1995) likewise propose to associate consciousness with stable states in neural networks (see CONNECTIONIST MODELS). Zeki and Bartels' (1998) notion of **microconsciousness* is also an example of this type of perspective.

Non-specialized process theories, finally, are theories in which it is assumed that representations become conscious whenever they are engaged by certain specific processes, regardless of where these representations exist in the brain. Many recent proposals fall into this category. Examples include Tononi and Edelman's (1998) 'dynamic core' model, Crick and Koch's (1990) idea that synchronous firing constitutes the primary mechanisms through which disparate representations become integrated as part of a unified conscious experience, or Grossberg's (1999) characterization of consciousness as involving processes of *adaptive resonance* through which representations that simultaneously receive bottom-up and top-down activation become conscious because of their stability and strength.

Cutting across this classification, several computational principles through which to distinguish between conscious and non-conscious processing have now been proposed.

2. Stability

Mathis and Mozer (1995), as well as O'Brien and Opie (1999), have proposed that stability of activation is a computational correlate of consciousness. The claim is thus that stable representations, i.e. representations that continue to exist beyond some temporal interval, form the *contents of consciousness, wherever they occur in the brain. According to this perspective, consciousness does not depend on specialized systems. Rather, any module that produces stable representations can contribute to the contents of consciousness. Representations acquire stability as a result of relaxation processes as they occur in dynamical systems. An interactive network, for instance, will tend to 'settle' in one of a limited number of stable, 'attractor' states (see ATTRACTOR NETWORKS). In O'Brien and Opie's theory, such states—stable activation patterns in a connectionist network—constitute explicit representations, the ensemble of which form the contents of phenomenal consciousness at any point in time. Further, stable representations, because they persist in time, will tend to exert more influence on other modules than shorter-lived representations. As O'Brien and Opie put it, 'Stability begets stability' (1999:48): stable states in one network will promote the emergence of stable states in other networks, hence allowing a 'winning coalition' of stable states to form.

3. Strength and 'fame in the brain'

Dennett (2001), along with others, has put forward the closely related proposal that consciousness amounts to 'fame in the brain', i.e. that the contents of phenomenal experience consist of just those states that have 'won the competition', and hence have achieved not only stability (as in Mathis and Mozer's proposal), but also strength. Strength, in this context, could refer to the number of neurons involved in the representation relative to the number of neurons involved in competing representations, or to the fact that a self-sustaining coalition of neurons has formed and inhibits other competing coalitions. Dennett's proposal, like O'Brien and Opie's, remains mute concerning the reason why such states are conscious states. Conscious experience, in this perspective, requires no further explanation; it merely consists of the fact that a particular representation has come to dominate processing at some point in time, so making its contents conscious.

4. Re-entrant processing and adaptive resonance
Several authors have independently proposed that *re-entrant* or *recurrent* processing constitutes a computational correlate of consciousness. Neural networks in the brain are massively recurrent, with downstream neurons connecting back to the upstream neurons from which they receive connections. Recurrent networks have very different computational properties from purely feedforward networks. In particular, recurrent networks have internal dynamics and can thus settle on to particular attractor states independently of the input, whereas feedforward networks only become active when their preferred inputs are present. Lamme (2006) has argued that it is only the processing that occurs in such re-entrant pathways that is associated with conscious experience. The representations that arise in purely feedforward pathways are thus never associated with conscious experience. It is easy to see how this principle is closely related to both stability and strength: recurrence is necessary to achieve either in a dynamical neural network. It is indeed in virtue of the existence of recurrent connectivity that neural patterns of activity can gain temporal stability, for in a purely feedforward pathway any pattern of activity will tend to fade away as soon as the input vanishes. Likewise, it is again in virtue of recurrent connectivity that an ensemble of interconnected neurons can 'settle' in a state that represents the most likely (the 'strongest') interpretation of the input. Grossberg (1999), in earlier work, had proposed similar ideas in the context of his *adaptive resonance theory* (ART).

5. Synchrony and gamma oscillations
Crick and Koch (1990) suggested that synchronized *gamma oscillations, i.e. the observation of fast, synchronized firing in neural assemblies in response to visual input, for instance, constitutes a neural correlate of consciousness. Computationally, synchronous firing constitutes one way of addressing the so-called **binding problem*, since such synchronous firing makes it possible to bind together the activity of distributed assemblies into functionally coherent sets (Engel and Singer 2001) through temporal correlation. Thus, the different features of a single object presented among many, for instance, can be selected out of multiple possible alternative bindings in virtue of the fact that the neurons that specifically represent the features of that object fire synchronously. Synchronous firing has further computational consequences, among which the fact that precisely timed firings have a larger impact on postsynaptic neurons, thus achieving greater effect. Such consequences—i.e. the fact that synchrony enables selection and amplification—constitute an alternative or complementary mechanism to strength and stability: all enable the emergence of specific global states in the vastly interconnected dynamical system that the brain is.

6. Global availability
It is commonly assumed that conscious representations are available globally in a manner that that unconscious representations are not. Bernard Baars (1988), and later Stanislas Dehaene, have proposed that conscious processing engages a network of interconnected high-level processors or modules dubbed the **global workspace* or the **neuronal workspace*, to which unconscious processors continuously compete for access. The core hypothesis of global workspace theory is that one is conscious of those representations that form the contents of the global workspace at some point in time. Activity in the global workspace thus 'ignites' a large network of cortical processors interconnected by long-range cortico-cortical connections. Patterns of activity in this large-scale flexible network can in turn temporarily amplify (a process dubbed *dynamic mobilization*) information represented in other cortical areas and subsequently broadcast these contents to yet further processors, thus making the information 'globally available' in a way that would be impossible without involvement of the workspace. Global workspace theory thus builds on all the computational principles identified so far: stability, strength, recurrent processing, and synchrony. The theory specifically focuses on the main computational consequence of the momentary existence of stable, strong representations made possible by recurrent connectivity, namely that such representations (and only such representations) can then bias and influence processing globally, thus implementing a form of global constraint satisfaction (Maia and Cleeremans 2005).

7. Information integration and differentiation
Tononi (see INFORMATION INTEGRATION THEORY) has proposed that conscious states, from a computational point of view, are characterized by the fact that they are both highly integrated and highly differentiated states. Integration refers to the fact that conscious states are states in which contents are fundamentally linked to each other and hence unified: one cannot perceive shape independently from colour, for instance. Differentiation refers to the fact that conscious states are one among many possible states; for each conscious state, there is almost an infinity of alternative possibilities that are

ruled out. Thus, only systems capable of both integrating and of representing a wide array of distinct states are capable of consciousness. Based on this hypothesis, one can thus analyse, from a computational point of view, what kinds of systems are capable of such integrated and differentiated representation. In this light, Tononi has proposed a measure called *phi* of such integrated information in neural networks.

8. Meta-representation

The different computational correlates described so far have all involved sub-personal properties of information processing systems. In contrast, David Rosenthal has offered a completely different view of the putative mechanisms associated with consciousness, one that is pitched at the personal level. According to Rosenthal's (2006) **higher-order thought* (HOT) theory, at any given time a representation is conscious to the extent that one has a thought that one is conscious of that representation. In other words, a representation is a conscious representation when there is a further higher-order representation that targets this representation. Mere 'fame in the brain' is therefore neither sufficient nor necessary to make a representation conscious in this perspective; what is needed instead is the occurrence of meta-representations that re-describe in specific ways lower-level representations.

9. Conclusion

Different computational correlates of consciousness have now been proposed. Most converge towards the key idea that conscious states instantiate a form of 'global constraint satisfaction' whereby widely distributed neuronal populations continuously compete to form stable coalitions that offer the best interpretation of the current state of affairs. Such competition requires mechanisms that make it possible for stable, strong states to emerge and to bias processing elsewhere by making their contents globally available. Such mechanisms may involve synchronous firing and re-entrant processing. The main competing proposal is that consciousness involves the unconscious occurrence of higher-order thoughts in virtue of which the target first-order representations become conscious. This mechanism has not so far received a computational implementation (but see Cleeremans et al. 2007 for a recent attempt).

In many cases, the proposed principles have been instantiated in the form of specific models of certain cognitive tasks that differentiate between information processing with or without consciousness (see Maia and Cleeremans 2005 for a review). Thinking about consciousness in terms of specific computational mechanisms is undoubtedly a useful strategy to further our understanding of its neural underpinnings and of its function.

AXEL CLEEREMANS

Atkinson, A. P., Thomas, M. S. C., and Cleeremans, A. (2000). 'Consciousness: mapping the theoretical landscape'. *Trends in Cognitive Sciences*, 4.

Atkinson, R. C. and Shiffrin, R. M. (1971). 'The control of short-term memory'. *Scientific American*, 225(2).

Baars, B. J. (1988). *A Cognitive Theory of Consciousness*.

Cleeremans, A., Timmermans, B., and Pasquali, A. (2007). 'Consciousness and metarepresentation: a computational sketch'. *Neural Networks*, 20.

Crick, F. H. C. and Koch, C. (1990). 'Towards a neurobiological theory of consciousness'. *Seminars in the Neurosciences*, 2.

—— —— (2003). 'A framework for consciousness'. *Nature Neuroscience*, 6.

Dehaene, S., Kerszberg, M., and Changeux, J.-P. (1998). 'A neuronal model of a global workspace in effortful cognitive tasks'. *Proceedings of the National Academy of Sciences of the USA*, 95.

Dennett, D. C. (2001). 'Are we explaining consciousness yet?' *Cognition*, 79.

Engel, A. K. and Singer, W. (2001). 'Temporal binding and the neural correlates of sensory awareness'. *Trends in Cognitive Science*, 5.

Grossberg, S. (1999). 'The link between brain learning, attention, and consciousness'. *Consciousness and Cognition*, 8.

Lamme, V. A. F. (2006). 'Toward a true neural stance on consciousness'. *Trends in Cognitive Sciences*, 10.

Maia, T. V. and Cleeremans, A. (2005). 'Consciousness: converging insights from connectionist modeling and neuroscience'. *Trends in Cognitive Sciences*, 9.

Mathis, W. D. and Mozer, M. C. (1995). 'On the computational utility of consciousness'. In Tesauro, G. and Touretzky, D. S. (eds) *Advances in Neural Information Processing Systems*, Vol. 7.

O'Brien, G. and Opie, J. (1999). 'A connectionist theory of phenomenal experience'. *Behavioral and Brain Sciences*, 22.

Rosenthal, D. (2006). *Consciousness and Mind*.

Schacter, D. L. (1989). 'On the relations between memory and consciousness: dissociable interactions and conscious experience'. In Craik, H. L. R. III and F. I. M. (eds) *Varieties of Memory and Consciousness: Essays in Honour of Endel Tulving*.

Tononi, G. and Edelman, G. M. (1998). 'Consciousness and complexity'. *Science*, 282.

Zeki, S. and Bartels, A. (1998). 'The asynchrony of consciousness'. *Proceedings of the Royal Society of London Series B: Biological Sciences*, 265.

correlates of consciousness, philosophical perspectives Most people in consciousness studies believe that we are extremely far from having a scientific explanation of how consciousness arises. Many harbour doubts that it is ever going possible to explain consciousness scientifically. In contrast, many people believe it is possible to identify the material correlates of various types of states of consciousness. It is most common to expect the correlate to be neural (whence *neural correlates of consciousness*, NCC). Even if brain states do not constitute conscious states, as for example dualists believe, brain states may still correlate systematically with conscious states. This entry deals with philosophical issues in the definition of the NCC, its methodology, its purpose, and current challenges to it (see also CORRELATES OF CONSCIOUSNESS, SCIENTIFIC PERSPECTIVES; and CORRELATES OF CONSCIOUSNESS, COMPUTATIONAL).

1. Definitions of the NCC
2. Methodological issues
3. Purposes of the NCC search: explanation, therapy, metaphysics
4. Challenges and alternatives

1. Definitions of the NCC

There is most interest in mapping the NCC for two broad types of states of consciousness. *Creature consciousness* concerns the contrast between being conscious and not being conscious at all (neuroscientists often refer to this as a creature's overall conscious 'state'). *Content consciousness* concerns the contrast between being consciously aware of one content (such as a face) rather than another (such as a house; see CONTENTS OF CONSCIOUSNESS). Corresponding to this, it is possible to search for either the creature NCC (where research points to various brainstem nuclei and subcortical structures) or the content NCC (where much research focus on parietal and prefrontal areas). (Other NCC searches focus on background consciousness, moods, or classes of conscious content.)

Most researchers focus on finding *content* NCCs. It is common to define this search in the following terms: to identify states of neural systems that correlate with subjects' content consciousness in such a way that it is reasonable to say those states of the neural system are *minimally sufficient*, given background conditions, for occurrence of those contents in consciousness (Chalmers 2000, Koch 2004).

The definition concerns *sufficient* but not *necessary* conditions because it remains a possibility that different neural systems are responsible for the same experiences in different creatures. The definition appeals to *minimal* sufficiency in order to exclude from the NCC states of systems that are theoretically redundant for the formation of conscious content. For example, certain states of the eye's retina are, together with states of the so-called fusiform face area in the temporal cortex, part of a sufficient neural substrate for face perception. But in certain conditions (e.g. *binocular rivalry, described below) there can be retinal activation in response to face stimuli without there being conscious perception of faces; and during *dreaming there can be experience of a face without retinal activation. Therefore this part of a sufficient condition can be left out of the minimal content NCC for face perception. The more of such redundant states that are left out the closer one gets to the minimal content NCC.

Strictly speaking, the minimally sufficient NCC does not amount to sufficiency. For example, to most people it seems obvious there would be no experience of faces if the minimal NCC of face experiences were scooped out of the brain, put in a jar, and activated in the required manner. Rather, the minimal NCC needs to be wired up in a certain way to other parts of the brain. Therefore it is natural to work with a distinction between the minimal or *core* NCC and the *total* NCC where the latter includes systems that serve as background conditions for the proper functioning of the core NCC (Chalmers 2000). (Note that the notion of minimal sufficiency is a pragmatic one; what counts as the minimally sufficient conditions for something depend on which aspect of a phenomenon one aims at exploring, as well as on one's assumed background conditions. Put differently, they are the conditions that will make a difference to the occurrence of the phenomenon one is investigating; as such it is a notion that it best understood in terms of causal analysis than of propositional logic.)

2. Methodological issues

An example of an experimental design in many studies of content NCC is use of *binocular rivalry* in which different stimuli (e.g. a picture of a face and picture of a house) are shown to each eye while subjective experience alternates between the two stimuli. In this way, the neural activity one records is not explained by changes in the stimulus since it is kept constant. Instead it should be explained by the mechanism that ensures the representation of one content rather than another in consciousness. In this way, the fusiform face area, for example, has become a candidate for the content NCC for face perception (Tong et al. 1998). Though a series of landmark (e.g. *single-cell recording and *functional brain imaging) studies have been done in monkeys and humans, it has nevertheless proved extremely hard to give the combined evidence concerning rivalry a univocal interpretation (Tong et al. 2006). Also, once studies with different types of experimental design are compared with each other, it appears that minimal sufficiency is hard to attain. In the condition known as unilateral *neglect*, patients with damage to the right parietal cortex are no longer consciously aware of what is presented in their left visual field (see BRAIN DAMAGE). However, in neglect patients, the fusiform face area can be active even when a face presented to the left is not consciously perceived (Rees 2000).

Stated in terms of mere correlation, the NCC will just match conscious states with whatever neural activity one can find in these studies. Nothing systematic is said about the nature of these neural states and what they may have in common. Without such systematicity it is hard to see how one can begin formulating theories on the basis of the NCC or use previous findings as reliable guidelines for further research. To address this, many go beyond mere correlation and try to find the minimal neural *representational* systems that suffice for conscious content (Chalmers 2000). On this definition of the content NCC one must, in addition to finding the neural activity minimally sufficient for perception of faces, ensure that this correlate is a neural representational system rather than a system devoted to other aspects of face processing. This requirement thus makes the study of content NCCs more demanding. The benefit should be more explanatory and predictive power. For example, we might be able to see how altering the properties of the neural representation could map invariantly onto changes in the conscious content. (Notice that this methodological desire for systematicity could be satisfied by other properties of neural systems than their receptive fields, such as patterns of re-entrant processing.)

This suggests that a central element, as one tries to go beyond the less demanding or 'raw' NCC, is systematicity, where this notion may usefully be understood in terms of how interventions on specific types of properties at the neural level are tied in an invariant manner with changes at the conscious level. On this somewhat broader definition, the NCC search would be in line with current thinking about causal inference (Woodward 2003).

3. Purposes of the NCC search: explanation, therapy, metaphysics

If the NCC can be discovered, then what? Many hope that it will be the first step towards a theory or explanation of consciousness. The question will then be: how can *that* neural system, which correlates with consciousness, explain it too? At the moment we cannot even ask that question, since we don't know what the NCC is. So the strategy is: first correlation, then explanation.

In practice, however, the progress of science is less clear cut. Some theorizing seems necessary to embark even on unsystematic NCC studies. For example, it is strictly speaking a theoretical hypothesis that it is the brain and not the foot that matters for consciousness. In general, explanation and discovery often evolve in tandem, and it may be that we only get to fully discover the NCC when we can begin explaining consciousness. This gives rise to the worry that if there is an unbridgeable *explanatory gap, then, if explanation and discovery evolve in tandem, discovery of the NCC will be jeopardized too.

Another worry is that it seems probable that other domains may have to be explained before we get to consciousness. At the moment it is not known how the brain arrives at explicit or full-blooded *representation of its environment and it is likely that the explanation of conscious experience will have to await explanatory progress in this area. How can we come to know how consciousness arises if we do not even know how the brain represents? Similarly, it is difficult to disentangle issues about *attention from consciousness. These issues probably underlie some of the mentioned difficulties with arriving at a univocal interpretation of binocular rivalry studies, so they probably also hold back the discovery of the NCC.

A not unreasonable answer to these worries is that, viewed as a working hypothesis, the NCC project is performing quite well: there are a number of reasonable experimental paradigms, there has been some progress in identifying the NCC, and there are a number of fledgling theories (even though they are tied closely to theories of representation or attention; Koch 2004).

In addition, even if the final theory will explain representation or attention but somehow fall short of making us understand how *qualia arise, this may still be a considerable step forward. *Schizophrenia and depression, for example, are mental disorders that are closely related to our conscious experience of the world, *self, and our *emotions, and they are tied to our *learning and inference on the basis of that experience. Discovery of the brain basis for these aspects of conscious experience may prove very useful for clinical purposes, even if we do not understand how the associated qualia arise.

These issues connect to somewhat more metaphysical issues about the NCC. Even though most researchers probably would agree that they are searching for the neural *constituent* of consciousness, one often finds the debate couched in terms of finding the neural *cause* of consciousness (e.g. Searle 2000, Koch 2004). If it was really a causal search then these researchers would seem to be subscribing to *dualism since, as many following Hume believe, cause and effect are distinct existences. This is not a charitable reading of the widespread causal language. A better reading may be that it marks a methodological concern about avoiding spurious correlations, rather than metaphysical doctrine. This would, again in line with the recent work on causation mentioned above, involve testing the supposed NCC for invariance under interventions (e.g. using *transcranial magnetic stimulation). The philosophical details of this approach as applied to matters of constitution rather than matters of causation still needs to be worked out, however (see e.g. Bechtel 2007).

4. Challenges and alternatives

In the standard approach to identifying the correlates of consciousness there is a focus on the *neural* correlates of *accessed* (that is, reported) *contents* of consciousness. Each of these three emphasized aspects has been criticized.

Too much focus on access consciousness, too little on phenomenal consciousness. In a series of influential papers, Ned Block has argued that the search for the NCC needs to recognize a distinction between *access consciousness and phenomenal consciousness (e.g. Block 2007). This distinction has methodological consequences because the access NCC may differ from the phenomenal NCC: it may be that once we have discovered the access NCC we still have made no inroads on the phenomenal NCC. Some people object that the idea of inaccessible yet phenomenally conscious content is impossible and perhaps does not even make sense. Some people stress that consciousness science must rely on subjective reports of conscious states and thus that for methodological reasons, unreportable phenomenal consciousness cannot be an object of scientific inquiry (on the other hand, many people strongly believe that the reliance on such subjective reports is unscientific and is therefore the Achilles heel of the NCC search; see OBJECTIVE VS SUBJECTIVE MEASURES OF CONSIOUSNESS; INTROSPECTION; HETEROPHENOMENOLOGY (for discussion, see Chalmers 1998, Jack and Roepstorff 2004)).

Perhaps the least controversial way of putting this debate is in terms of the admissible evidence in consciousness science. If one insists on allowing only the use of subjective reports as one's evidence of phenomenality, then one can recognize only access consciousness. The disadvantage of this policy is that the restriction will be based, not on empirical evidence, but on a contested methodological preference. The alternative is to admit more kinds of indirect evidence for phenomenality (of the type Block mentions, e.g. *signal detection theory for neural and psychophysical data) and then see what one can discover. On this more inclusive approach one will not have foreclosed the possibility that the neural properties crucial for phenomenality differ from those that ensure accessibility. The argument would then be that the more inclusive strategy is in line with the generally accepted scientific practice of using inference to the best explanation to discover unobservables. On this way of putting the issue about access vs phenomenality it is primarily an empirical and methodological issue, rather than a question of prior intuitions about the concept of consciousness.

Too much focus on contents of consciousness, too little on unified field of consciousness. It is not entirely clear how precisely to draw the distinction between content and creature NCC. In particular, in the search for the content NCC, it seems that it is presupposed that the creature is already conscious (e.g. in studies using binocular rivalry already conscious subjects are exposed to different stimuli). This means that the experimental variable that is being manipulated is not consciousness as such but merely the contents represented in consciousness. Then the worry arises whether the search for content NCCs is at all relevant for consciousness, given that it presupposes that the creature in question is already conscious. This in turn suggests that the NCC search should be focused on creature consciousness, i.e. the question of what is minimally sufficient for a creature having a 'unified conscious field' as such, never mind the contents that happen to be represented in this field (Searle 2000).

Perhaps it is reasonable to respond that when there is a unified conscious field (e.g. when one has just woken up) there is also always conscious content of some sort. It is very hard to conceive of an utterly empty 'conscious' field as being conscious in any clear sense. The content NCC approach could then adopt a 'building block' strategy where the unified field NCC is simply the sum of the occurring content NCCs. This, however, does not explain what it is that is in fact presupposed in content NCC studies, e.g. using binocular rivalry. Alternatively, it could adopt a more provisional strategy according to which revealing content NCCs is expected to simultaneously reveal the NCC for the unified field but subject to a subsequent disentangling of theoretically interesting core and total NCCs.

Too much focus on neural substrate, too little on phenomenology and embodiment. Naturally, systematicity (see above) in the NCC will not be in terms of the *vehicle of the conscious content having the properties of the experience (e.g. one does not expect the NCC of blue experiences to itself be blue). Instead, there could be a match of the *content* of the neural representational system with the content represented in consciousness. The question is how to interpret this notion of 'match'. If it is interpreted in terms of 'identity', then correlates of *all* the experiential properties must in principle be found in the neural representational system. Researchers inspired by *phenomenology (see also NEUROPHENOMENOLOGY) argue that this is not possible (Noë and Thompson 2004).

The argument is that phenomenological analysis shows that conscious experience has some representational properties that neural content does not, and cannot, have. One such property is the *perceptual coherence* of experience (e.g. in the sense of always experiencing things as in a figure–ground context), and it is argued that atomic or 'building block' content NCCs cannot encompass coherence.

Were it correct that the NCC approach is misguided because neural systems cannot have the requisite representational properties, then it would make sense to look for a correlate of consciousness that is not exclusively neural. Accordingly, advocates of the **sensorimotor* or *enactive* approach suggest looking at the subject as an essentially embodied agent. Proponents of this approach support their view by various experimental findings concerning interaction between embodiment and conscious content that, if interpreted correctly, would mandate extending the scope of the correlates of consciousness from neural systems to the subject's body and environment. (Some believe that neurophenomenology will change the NCC search yet more radically.)

The challenge concerning how *all* representational properties could have a neural correlate can possibly be met by arguing that 'match' should not be understood as identity but rather in terms of an invariant relation between the neural system and the conscious experience under interventions on the neural system. Then one could argue for a content NCC e.g. by giving evidence of how perceptual coherence is itself modulated by interventions on the neural systems that dynamically provide a context for the processing of the specific content under scrutiny. In this manner, one could still focus on the NCC of specific parts of conscious experience without having to hold that all of its representational properties are there in isolation from context parameters. Perhaps this area will see progress in tune with the increased focus on effective connectivity in *functional brain imaging; see Friston (2002).

The further challenge concerns how the experimental evidence cited in favour of the sensorimotor approach can be incorporated in the orthodox approach. It can possibly be met by noticing that there are two ways to deal with this evidence. Either one must say that factors in the body and environment *cause* conscious states and that the brain is just a causal intermediary. That would be subscribing to *dualism if, as many believe, cause and effect are distinct existences. Or, one must say that conscious states *supervene* on brain plus environment. As it stands, the second option seems compatible with a situation where a change in conscious state is underpinned by a change in the environment but with no neural change. Many find this hard to believe: even if we accept that sensorimotor embodiment is crucial to our interpretation of consciousness, we still think the brain must be involved somehow (in contrast, mental changes can happen without environmental change, as when *delusions* arise following brain lesions). This points to supervenience of consciousness on the brain, with the understanding that the sensorimotor evidence should be interpreted as factors that causally interact with the neural supervenience base for consciousness (see the Peer Commentary on Noë and Thompson 2004).

JAKOB HOHWY

Bechtel, W. (2007). *Mental Mechanisms.*

Block, N. (2007). 'Consciousness, accessibility and the mesh between psychology and neuroscience'. *Behavioral and Brain Sciences*, 30.

Chalmers, D. (1998). 'On the search for the neural correlate of consciousness'. In Hameroff, S. et al. (eds) *Toward a Science of Consciousness II: the Second Tucson Discussions and Debates.*

—— (2000). 'What is a neural correlate of consciousness?' In Metzinger, T. (ed.) *Neural Correlates of Consciousness: Empirical and Conceptual Issues.*

Friston, K. (2002). 'Functional integration and inference in the brain'. *Progress in Neurobiology*, 68.

Jack, A. I. and Roepstorff, A. (eds) (2004). *Trusting the Subject.*

Koch, C. (2004). *The Quest for Consciousness: a Neurobiological Approach.*

Noë, A. and Thompson, E. (2004). 'Are there neural correlates of consciousness?' *Journal of Consciousness Studies*, 11.

Rees, G. (2000). 'Unconscious activation of visual cortex in the damaged right hemisphere of a parietal patient with extinction'. *Brain*, 123.

Searle, J. R. (2000). 'Consciousness'. *Annual Review of Neuroscience*, 23.

Tong, F., Nakayama, K., Vaughan, J. T., and Kanwisher, N. (1998). 'Binocular rivalry and visual awareness in human extrastriate cortex'. *Neuron*, 21.

——, Meng, M., and Blake, R. (2006). 'Neural bases of binocular rivalry'. *Trends in Cognitive Sciences*, 10.

Woodward, J. (2003). *Making Things Happen.*

correlates of consciousness, scientific perspectives In general terms, a neural correlate of consciousness (NCC) is some aspect of brain activity that is correlated with states of conscious experience. Determining the NCCs could therefore potentially help understand the relationship between states of consciousness and neural activity, assuming that there is a systematic relationship between brain states and mental states. If this assumption is false (as held by some *Cartesian *dualists*, for example) then there may be no NCCs, as any given brain state might be instantiated without a corresponding state of consciousness. Dualist worries notwithstanding, the notion that the first step towards understanding consciousness is to discover NCCs has over the last decade become a central theme of most empirical work in this area and is held to be symbolic of a fundamentally scientific approach to consciousness research (Crick and Koch 1995).

To make empirical progress, such a general description of an NCC needs conceptual clarification. Clarity is required in terms of what is meant by the phrases 'state of consciousness' and 'neural state'.

1. States of consciousness
2. Neural states
3. Empirical research
4. Location-based and activity-based theories
5. Neural activity and consciousness

1. States of consciousness

Conscious states are generally held to refer to at least two, or perhaps three, aspects of phenomenal experience. First, a conscious state might refer to the overall level of consciousness of a person or creature: for example, being awake (conscious) compared to being asleep (unconscious), or compared to some other level of arousal such as *dreaming, coma, or *hypnosis. In such circumstances an NCC would be a neural state that individuated whether a person is conscious or not and their particular level of arousal. This is often referred to as *creature consciousness*. However, there is clearly more to consciousness than simply being awake. When awake, we have conscious experiences with specific subjective content that vary throughout the day. We can thus speak of conscious states being individuated by their specific phenomenal content, and in such circumstances an NCC would be some neural state that correlated with specific *contents of consciousness. Finally, some authors also like to draw a distinction between the contents of consciousness and the reflexive, self-referential aspects of consciousness. People normally not only individuate particular thoughts and perceptions by their content but also in self-referential terms; that is, as belonging to themselves. Such individuation may break down in psychiatric disorders such as *schizophrenia. Like other states of consciousness, self-awareness might also be correlated with particular types of brain activity. Thus, consideration of different phenomenal aspects of consciousness suggests that there may be more than one type of NCC. This provides a simple framework for understanding how different types of empirical study might relate to each other, as well as raising important conceptual questions.

The relationship between these different states of consciousness is complex and not completely determined. For example, both very low levels of arousal and very high levels of arousal are associated with relatively impoverished contents of consciousness. But this is not always the case; during dreaming, a relatively low level of arousal is nevertheless associated with vivid mental *imagery. Thus level of arousal is not simply a facilitating factor for contents of consciousness, but instead there is a more complex and at present poorly understood interaction between the two. It should therefore be expected that there might be similarly complex interactions between the underlying neural mechanisms. At present this is also not well understood, partly because of the practical difficulties associated with (e.g.) studying the contents of consciousness under different levels of arousal.

2. Neural states

Conceptual clarity is also required concerning what is meant by the 'neural states' that might show correlation with conscious states. It is often assumed that a complete theory of brain function would be specified at the level of single neurons, since they appear to reflect the basic element underlying the anatomical structure of brains. Indeed, it is striking that the firing rate of *single neurons can often show direct correlations with the contents of consciousness in both monkey (Leopold and Logothetis 1996) and human (Kreiman et al. 2000). However, it is an open empirical question whether NCCs must or should be specified exclusively at the level of single neurons. The brain is hierarchically organized at levels ranging from subcellular components such as synapses to single neurons to local circuits to larger networks of anatomically interconnected areas. For any given mental capacity, it is likely that there will be 'neural correlates' expressed at many different levels of such a system, with a complex mapping between mental states and brain states. The notion that one particular level is the most promising one at which to look for NCCs is an attractive one, but it should be borne in mind that it may not be correct. For example, in many cases cognitive functions might not necessarily best understood at the level of a single neuron but instead at the level of a network. If this is the case, then the neural states that individuate particular conscious states might be instantiated at different levels of neural organization.

3. Empirical research

A great deal of empirical work in the last decade has focused on determining NCCs for particular conscious contents. This work has sought to determine whether there are aspects of neural activity that are both necessary and minimally sufficient to evoke a particular content of consciousness (Chalmers 2000). It relies on non-invasive techniques in humans such as *electroencephalography (EEG), *magnetoencephalography (MEG), positron emission tomography (PET), or *functional brain imaging, supplemented by rare investigations of the function of single neurons in patients with *epilepsy, invasive experiments in animals, and neuropsychological inferences drawn from *brain-damaged patients. This permits the identification of situations where changes in particular aspects of neural activity (typically measured using brain imaging) predict changes in the contents of consciousness (determined by verbal reports or non-verbal behaviour such as pressing a button) or vice versa. However, it is necessary to show that any such relationship between neural activity and conscious state is not simply the concomitant consequence of changes in physical stimulation or changes in behaviour (Frith et al. 1999). For example, while it is easy to identify neural activity in the human visual system that represents particular features and objects in the visual environment, not all such activity will be associated with the contents of consciousness. Some will instead be associated with computations underlying fundamental aspects of perceptual processing that are inaccessible to consciousness. Similarly, while verbal or non-verbal (e.g. button press) reports are used to indicate changes in conscious experience, changes in behaviour can occur in the absence of awareness. For example, in *blindsight, individuals with damage to visual cortex (see V1) can nevertheless respond accurately to unseen stimuli presented in the blind portion of their visual field. This need to distinguish NCCs from neural activity associated with unconscious perception or behaviour has led to the use of experimental paradigms in which these unwanted effects are held constant.

A simple taxonomy identifies three broad classes of experimental paradigms relevant to determining NCCs. In the first class, perception changes while sensory stimulation and/or behaviour remains constant. Consequently changes in brain activity can be unambiguously associated with changes in the contents of consciousness. One example of such a situation arises during bistable perception, when a physical stimulus readily allows two different perceptual interpretations. For example, when dissimilar images are presented to the two eyes, they compete for perceptual dominance causing *binocular rivalry. Each monocular image is visible in turn for a few seconds while the other is suppressed. Because perceptual transitions occur spontaneously without any change in the physical stimulus, neural correlates of this change in the contents of consciousness may be distinguished from neural correlates attributable to stimulus characteristics. Brain activity time-locked to these perceptual transitions can be identified in prefrontal and parietal cortices, while fluctuations in brain activity specifically related to the content of perceptual experience can be identified in ventral visual cortex. This suggests that a network of brain areas comprising both cortical locations traditionally assumed to represent the content of the visual scene, plus *frontal and parietal cortex, might represent an NCC for visual content (Rees et al. 2002).

A second class of paradigms comprises situations where sensory stimulation changes while subjective experience remains constant. For example, changes in a visual stimulus that is masked and invisible can nevertheless influence brain activity. Such changes in activity are neural correlates of sensory stimulation that remains unconscious and so can potentially be dissociated from neural correlates of changes in the contents of consciousness.

Finally, a third class of paradigms where behaviour changes but subjective experience remains constant permit determination of neural correlates of unconscious motor behaviour. For example, the neural correlates of correct guessing in the absence of awareness (e.g. during blindsight) can be used to identify brain activity associated with such behaviour that does not alter consciousness. The goal is to identify the neural correlates of different behavioural responses to conscious states, so as to factor these out and reveal only the NCCs of conscious states rather than the NCCs of responses to the conscious states.

This taxonomy represents a loose framework in which different empirical studies can be linked to one another, and make explicit their potential significance for determining the neural correlates of conscious experience. The advent of non-invasive brain imaging technologies has led to a dramatic increase in the number of such empirical studies in the last two decades. Taken together, findings from such a variety of different physiological techniques used to measure brain activity during different experimental paradigms converge to suggest a large number of possible candidates for NCCs. However, no consensus has yet been reached on whether a single minimally sufficient correlate has been identified.

4. Location-based and activity-based theories

Proposals for the neural correlates of conscious content can be divided into two broad types: location-based theories that particularly implicate a particular region or regions of the brain, and activity-based theories that particularly implicate a particular type of neural activity.

Location-based proposals for the neural correlates of visual consciousness include neurons in the brainstem reticular–thalamic activation system; visual processing within the ventral visual pathway (e.g. Milner and Goodale 2006); neurons in extrastriate cortex projecting to frontal regions (e.g. Crick and Koch 2005); intralaminar nuclei in the thalamus; neuronal populations in parietal and prefrontal cortex (e.g. Rees et al. 2002); neurons in the claustrum (e.g. Crick and Koch 1995); and neurons in inferotemporal cortex (e.g. Leopold and Logothetis 1996).

Activity-based proposals for the neural correlates of visual consciousness include 40 Hz (*gamma) oscillations in the cerebral cortex (e.g. Crick and Koch 1990); 40 Hz oscillations in thalamocortical systems (e.g. Edelman 1989); *re-entrant processing in the cerebral cortex (e.g. Lamme and Roelfsema 2000); and threshold level of activity in ventral visual cortex.

These two broad types of proposal (or indeed, almost any suggested NCC candidate) are not necessarily mutually exclusive, and indeed it is apparent from the list above that many activity-based proposals also make reference to specific locations in the brain. It remains possible that neural correlates of phenomenal content will be individuated both anatomically (not all regions of the brain might be involved in conscious content) and functionally (not all types of neural activity within an area may be involved in conscious content). At present, there are few empirical studies that directly test competing accounts for NCCs and so it is difficult to reach any firm conclusions.

5. Neural activity and consciousness

The typical goal of empirical programmes seeking to determine NCCs is to establish what aspects of neural activity are both necessary and sufficient for the corresponding state of consciousness. Achieving this goal is both conceptually challenging (Chalmers 2000) and likely to require synthesis of much converging evidence from multiple methodologies. Techniques that measure brain activity such as single-unit recording, EEG/MEG, and functional MRI can establish correlations between brain activity and states of consciousness. However, such purely correlational techniques cannot establish whether changes in brain activity lead to changes in conscious state. To make such an inference requires manipulation of brain state in order to determine whether that leads to alteration in the state of consciousness. Both invasive techniques in experimental animals (such as electrical microstimulation) or non-invasive techniques in humans (such as *transcranial magnetic stimulation, TMS) can provide such information. For example, applying TMS to primary visual cortex (V1) and the visual motion area V5/MT can be used to show that both make critical contributions to the visual awareness of moving stimuli, but at different times after presentation of a stimulus (Silvanto et al. 2005). In addition to the use of experimental techniques that directly manipulate brain activity, studying behaviour and brain activity in patients who have suffered brain damage from stroke or other neurological disorders can provide additional evidence about the relationship between states of consciousness and brain states. For example, patients with visual neglect following parietal damage lack phenomenal experience of objects in one half of the visual field, suggesting that signals from parietal cortex may be necessary for visual experience. However, objects presented in their neglected hemifield that do not reach awareness nevertheless evoke activity in striate and extrastriate visual cortex. This suggests that the simple elicitation of activity in these areas is not sufficient for awareness (Rees et al. 2000).

Implicit in experimental programmes that attempt to determine the characteristic neural signatures of consciousness is the notion that such attempts will be helpful in addressing more difficult questions. Two such questions are the function of consciousness or the mechanisms by which conscious experience might arise from neural activity. However, it is important to recognize that even if the answers to such questions remain obscure, the fundamentally empirical nature of enquiries concerning NCCs ensures that such data retain the potential to provide fundamental insights into human brain function.

GERAINT REES

Chalmers, D. J. (2000). 'What is a neural correlate of consciousness?' In Metzinger, T. (ed.) *Neural Correlates of Consciousness—Empirical and Conceptual Questions.*

Crick, F. and Koch, C. (1990). 'Some reflections on visual awareness'. *Cold Spring Harbor Symposia on Quantitative Biology*, 55.

—— —— (1995). 'Are we aware of neural activity in primary visual cortex?' *Nature*, 375.

—— —— (2005). 'What is the function of the claustrum?' *Philosophical Transactions of the Royal Society of London Series B: Biological Sciences*, 360.

Dehaene, S., Naccache, L., Cohen, L. et al. (2001). 'Cerebral mechanisms of word masking and unconscious repetition priming'. *Nature Neuroscience*, 4.

Edelman, G. M. (1989). *The Remembered Present: a Biological Theory of Consciousness.*

Frith, C., Perry, R., and Lumer, E. (1999). 'The neural correlates of conscious experience: an experimental framework'. *Trends in Cognitive Science*, 3.

Kreiman, G., Koch, C., and Fried, I. (2000). 'Imagery neurons in the human brain'. *Nature*, 408.

Lamme, V. A. and Roelfsema, P. R. (2000). 'The distinct modes of vision offered by feedforward and recurrent processing'. *Trends in Neuroscience*, 23.

Leopold, D. A. and Logothetis, N. K. (1996). 'Activity changes in early visual cortex reflect monkeys' percepts during binocular rivalry'. *Nature*, 379.

Milner, A. D. and Goodale, M. (2006). *The Visual Brain in Action*, 2nd edn.

Rees, G., Wojciulik, E., Clarke, K., Husain, M., Frith., C, and Driver, J. (2000). 'Unconscious activation of visual cortex in the damaged right hemisphere of a parietal patient with extinction'. *Brain*, 123.

——, Kreiman, G., and Koch, C. (2002). 'Neural correlates of consciousness in humans'. *Nature Reviews Neuroscience*, 3.

Silvanto, J., Lavie, N., and Walsh, V. (2005). 'Double dissociation of V1 and V5/MT activity in visual awareness'. *Cerebral Cortex*, 15.

creature consciousness vs See AROUSAL VS AWARENESS; CONSCIOUSNESS, CONCEPTS OF

cross-modal sensory integration Most objects and events in the environment stimulate our nervous system through more than one sense. When we observe a person walking towards us, the electromagnetic energy (light) reflected by the individual produces visual stimulation, the sound waves produced by the footsteps result in auditory stimulation, and the increasing concentration of the molecules associated with the person's cologne provides olfactory stimulation. The visual processing starts at retina, proceeds to optic nerve, onward to lateral geniculate nucleus on to visual cortex, while the auditory processing starts at the ear, proceeds to brainstem, on to medial geniculate nucleus on to auditory cortex, and olfactory stimulation starts at olfactory epithelium in the nose, on to olfactory bulbs on to the piriform cortex. The various types of energy that provide stimulation to the different sensory modalities are processed in separate pathways in the nervous system, and yet, they are not experienced as a collection of separate sensations, but rather as a unified, coherent, and monolithic percept. The experiential unity of consciousness implicates that the convergence or *binding of cross-modal sensory signals occurs prior to conscious perception. This is consistent with within-modality binding where, for example, the redness, smoothness, and roundness of an apple are experienced in a unified monolithic fashion. Similar to the within-modality binding of features, which can break down under conditions of high attentional load leading to illusory conjunctions (a red square and blue triangle may be confused with a red triangle and blue square), the cross-modality binding can also break down under divided attention conditions, leading to illusory conjunctions (Cinel et al. 2002). For example, a touched texture can be reported as seen or vice versa; i.e. the modality of a stimulus can become inaccessible to conscious awareness.

But is multisensory processing in the nervous system limited to binding and/or convergence of information from multiple senses? The answer is no. The signals of the different sensory modalities corresponding to the same object may carry information about the same property of the object, each providing an estimate that is often noisy, and not entirely reliable. By combining multiple estimates from different sensory modalities the nervous system obtains a better overall estimate of the property of the object. For example, when holding an apple in our hands, both tactile and visual modalities provide information about shape, surface properties, and size of the apple. By combining the haptic and visual estimate of the size, surface smoothness, or roundness, the nervous system obtains a more accurate representation of the object. As in perception in general, multisensory integration is a process of inference, and this inference has been shown to be statistically optimal in many cross-modal integration tasks. External noise (e.g. occlusion, fog, dim lighting, background noise, dirty hands) as well as internal noise (e.g. noise in the firing pattern of the neurons) can lead to discrepancies among estimates that are provided by the different senses. The nervous system, therefore, has to resolve these discrepancies in order to arrive at a single estimate of the cause in the environment (Knill and Pouget 2004). In order to gain insight into this process, scientists have employed experimental paradigms in which a conflict is artificially imposed (by the experimenter) between the signals of the different modalities by manipulating the relationship between two sensory stimuli, and then test how such conflicting information is interpreted by human observers. Some well-known examples are the ventriloquist illusion, the McGurk illusion, the visual capture, and the sound-induced flash illusion. In the *ventriloquist* and *visual capture* illusions, a spatial conflict is imposed between modalities, and vision captures the location of the sound and touch, respectively. In the *McGurk effect*, a conflict is imposed between auditory and visual syllables, and the perceived syllable is something in between the two presented. In *sound-induced flash illusion*, there is a conflict between the number of pulsations in the visual and auditory modalities, and sound captures the visual pulsations. In none of these illusions is the observer aware of any conflict between the signals of the different modalities, again suggesting that integration precedes conscious awareness.

Is the preconscious integration limited to conditions in which the signals of different modalities are completely fused? It does not appear so. Even when observers do perceive a conflict between the sensory signals, and thus, do not fuse them, partial integration can occur. This phenomenon is also seemingly preconscious. When the discrepancy between the signals is too large, they do not get fused. For example, if the spatial discrepancy between visual and auditory stimuli is large, then vision no longer 'captures' the location of sound, i.e. the sound is no longer perceived to originate from the same location as the visual stimulus, and they are perceived as two independent events. Nevertheless, the perceived position of sound is shifted towards the location of the visual stimulus (and vice versa), although they do not converge. In other words, although the observer is consciously aware that the sound and visual stimulus do not correspond to the same object, the auditory and visual stimuli nonetheless interact and affect each other's percepts. While this phenomenon may appear to be non-adaptive or suboptimal, it has been shown that it is consistent with a statistically optimal strategy for combining cross-modal stimuli (Shams et al. 2005, Körding et al. 2007). Even when observers are aware of conflict between the senses, they are not aware of the interactions between the senses, and cross-modal interactions do occur even when the signals are perceived to correspond to independent objects. Therefore, multisensory integration seems to be an automatic, streamlined process that probably occurs at various levels of processing, but importantly, at early stages of sensory processing. Low-level cross-modal interactions among various sensory modalities have been recently demonstrated by a myriad of experimental techniques. One of the most surprising and recent findings is the following. Humans are considered visual animals; the human visual system is highly efficient and sophisticated; and it is believed that half of the brain is involved in processing visual information. Vision scientists have held the mammalian visual cortex to be strictly visual, dedicated to processing visual information, and functioning in isolation from other modalities. Interestingly, however, it has been recently shown that the human visual cortical activity, as early as in primary visual cortex (*V1), is modulated by auditory stimulation (Watkins et al. 2006). Other studies have shown similar cross-modal effects in auditory, and somatosensory cortices (Ghazanfar and Schroeder 2006, Newell and Shams 2007). In light of these findings, *synaesthesia, which is a condition in which stimulation in one modality invokes sensation in another modality, can be viewed as an accentuation or extension of cross-modal interactions as opposed to an anomaly.

Therefore, multisensory integration is ubiquitous in the human nervous system, and can occur at early sensory processing stages. Cross-modal sensory integration is also not unique to humans, primates, or mammals, and goes far back in evolution. Thus, it is not surprising that this process precedes, and does not require, conscious awareness.

LADAN SHAMS

Cinel, C., Humphreys, G. W., and Poli, R. (2002). 'Cross-modal illusory conjunctions between vision and touch'. *Journal of Experimental Psychology: Human Perception and Performance*, 28.

Ghazanfar, A. and Schroeder, C. E. (2006). 'Is neocortex essentially multisensory?' *Trends in Cognitive Science*, 10.

Knill, D. C. and Pouget, A. (2004). 'The Bayesian brain: the role of uncertainty in neural coding and computation'. *Trends in Neurosciences*, 27.

Körding, K., Beierholm, U., Ma, W. J., Tenebaum, J. M., Quartz, S., and Shams, L. (2007). 'Causal inference in multisensory perception'. *PLoS ONE*, 2.

Newell, F. and Shams, L. (eds) (2007). 'Special issue: multisensory perception'. *Perception*, 36.

Shams, L., Ma, W. J., and Beierholm, U. (2005). 'Sound-induced flash illusion as an optimal percept'. *NeuroReport*, 16.

Watkins, S., Shams, L., Tanaka, S., Haynes, J.-D., and Rees, G. (2006). 'Sound alters activity in human V1 in association with illusory visual perception'. *Neuroimage*, 31.

cultural differences The research on cultural differences in perception was stimulated by work on cognition showing that inferential processes are shaped by participation in cultural practices (Nisbett et al. 2001). For example, a number of cross-cultural studies have shown that when asked to attribute the causes of an event, Westerners tend to focus on causes internal to the object or person, whereas East Asians tend to focus on contextual or situational causes more than do Westerners. In addition, Westerners are more likely to rely on rules and analytic features to categorize objects, whereas East Asians are more likely to base their categorization on relationships and similarities. Such an accumulating body of evidence on cultural differences in cognition suggests that perceptual processes are also influenced by culture. That is, Westerners may tend to engage in context-independent and analytic perceptual processes by focusing on a salient object independently from the context in which it is located. On the other hand, East Asians may tend to engage in context-dependent and holistic perceptual processes by attending to the relationship between the object and the context in which the object is embedded.

Empirical research has provided support for such a speculation. When describing an animated video clip of an underwater scene containing both salient objects and contextual objects, Americans started their statements by referring to salient objects more frequently than did Japanese, whereas Japanese started their statements by referring to contextual information more frequently than did Americans. Such cultural differences in attentional pattern can be observed with a task as simple as adjusting a length of a line (i.e. a focal object) presented in a square frame (i.e. context), which is stripped of any cultural or social meanings.

Do such cultural differences in perceptual processes extend to relatively unconscious and uncontrollable processes? Recent research that employed methods from cognitive psychology has suggested that it is the case. Using the *change blindness paradigm, Masuda and Nisbett (2006) presented both Americans and Japanese with two animated video clips of scenes (e.g. an airport) which differed in several details. Some of the changes were made in the attributes of the focal objects and other changes were made in the field or context. They found that Americans detected a larger number of changes in the focal objects whereas Japanese detected a larger number of changes in the context. Such cultural differences in perceptual processes have also been located at the level of eye movements (Chua et al. 2005), which are relatively unconscious actions. Both European Americans and Chinese were presented with pictures of a focal object (e.g. a tiger) placed on a complex background (e.g. the jungle) and asked to rate how much they liked each picture while their eye movements were tracked. Americans looked at the focal object more quickly and fixated on it longer than did Chinese, whereas Chinese made more saccades (i.e. rapid eye movements from one fixation to another) to the background than did Americans. The converging evidence, thus, seems to suggest that Westerners are more likely to attend to the focal objects whereas East Asians are more inclined to attend to contexts and relationships, at conscious as well as unconscious levels.

What underlies such cultural differences in perception? Nisbett and his colleagues agree that social organization is the crucial factor. If one lives in a relatively complex social environment to which many roles are prescribed, one needs to attend to the social field and to the context, instead of attending to one's own goal. In contrast, if one lives in a relatively independent social environment with fewer role constraints, one can attend to the salient objects in the field without being overly constrained by the surrounding context. Because Asian societies have historically been more interdependent than Western counterparts, they may have been inclined to pay more attention to context.

According to this argument, one should find perceptual differences between two societies that are based on different social organization even if both of the societies are located within Western culture, such as eastern Europe and western Europe. Social structures and organizations in eastern Europe have historically been more close-knit and interdependent than in western Europe. Reflecting such differences in social environments, perception for eastern Europeans has found to be more context-dependent and holistic than that of western Europeans.

Furthermore, the processes through which social environments can influence perception have shown to be chronic as well as temporary. People may acquire a chronic pattern of attention through participation in socialization and parental practices. For example, whereas American mothers tend to guide their child's attention to salient objects by pointing out the name and properties of toys, Japanese mothers tend to direct a child's attention to relationship or context by using toys to engage their child in social practices. If cultural differences in attentional pattern partly stem from such divergent socialization processes, the more socialization children have gone through the larger the cultural differences would become. In fact, several developmental studies have shown that cultural differences in reasoning and perception become larger as children grow older (e.g. Miller 1986).

At the same time, social environments may exert temporary influence on perception. *Priming Hong Kong Chinese or Chinese American bicultural individuals with either Chinese or American cultural icons (or Chinese or American cultural identity) can shift their reasoning styles (e.g. Hong et al. 2000). Furthermore, activating particular social orientations, namely independent and interdependent notions of relationship, can shift cognitive and perceptual processes of those who do not necessarily have bicultural experience. Such priming procedures vary from asking participants to read either individualistic or collectivistic stories to as subtle as instructing participants to circle either singular first-person pronouns (i.e. I, my, me, or mine) or plural first-person pronouns (i.e. we, our, us, or ours) appearing in a short paragraph. Reading individualistic stories or circling singular first-person pronouns are shown to lead to more analytic and context-dependent performances in a subsequent cognitive or perceptual task than reading collectivistic stories or circling plural first-person pronouns (e.g. Kühnen and Oyserman 2002).

Once people acquire certain perceptual styles induced by social environments, they may construct the environment in a way that fit their perceptual styles. For example, portraits drawn by East Asian artists tend to have a smaller central figure and a larger background than those drawn by Western artists. In addition, Japanese perceptual environments contain a larger number of objects and look more ambiguous and complex than their American counterparts, which makes it more difficult to extract salient objects from Japanese backgrounds (Miyamoto et al. 2006). Participating in such environments may, in turn, afford certain patterns of attention. In fact, using an incidental priming procedure, Miyamoto et al. (2006) showed that when exposed to Japanese scenes, people attend more to contextual information in a subsequent ostensibly unrelated perceptual task. Such findings indicate the mutual support of the ways the perceptual environment is arranged in Western and Asian societies and the ways Westerners and East Asians attend to the world.

Growing evidence of cultural differences in perceptual processes suggests that culture influences perceptual processes at both conscious and unconscious levels as well as through both conscious and unconscious mechanisms. Future research needs to examine how deeply perceptual processes are shaped by culture and elucidate dynamic ways by which sociocultural context shapes and is shaped by perceptual processes.

YURI MIYAMOTO

Chua, H. F., Boland, J. E., and Nisbett, R. E. (2005). 'Cultural variation in eye movements during scene perception'. *Proceedings of the National Academy of Sciences of the USA*, 102.

Hong, Y. Y., Morris, M. W., Chiu, C. Y., and Benet-Martinez, V. (2000). 'Multicultural minds: a dynamic constructivist approach to culture and cognition'. *American Psychologist*, 55.

Kühnen, U. and Oyserman, D. (2002). 'Thinking about the self influences thinking in general: cognitive consequences of salient self-concept'. *Journal of Experimental Social Psychology*, 38.

Masuda, T. and Nisbett, R. E., (2006). 'Culture and change blindness'. *Cognitive Science*, 30.

Miller, J. G. (1986). 'Early cross-cultural commonalities in social explanation'. *Developmental Psychology*, 22.

Miyamoto, Y., Nisbett, R. E. and Masuda, T. (2006). 'Culture and the physical environment: holistic versus analytic perceptual affordances'. *Psychological Science*, 17.

Nisbett, R. E., Peng, K., Choi, I., and Norenzayan, A. (2001). 'Culture and systems of thought: holistic versus analytic cognition'. *Psychological Review*, 108.

D

deafferentation See PROPRIOCEPTION

déjà vu 'Déjà vu' means, literally, 'already seen'. In colloquial English it is often used indiscriminately to refer to familiar events and experiences. In its more precise or technical sense, it describes the disconcerting sense that our current experience echoes some ill-defined, elusive, past experience. It has been described repeatedly in literature, for example by Charles Dickens (1849–50/1985):

> We have all some experience of a feeling which comes over us occasionally, of what we are saying or doing having been said or done before, in a remote time—of our having been surrounded, dim ages ago, by the same faces, objects and circumstances—of our knowing perfectly what will be said next, as if we suddenly remembered it.

The experience often incorporates the further sense that the felt familiarity 'is fictitious and the state abnormal' (Hughlings-Jackson 1888). Neppe's widely cited definition summarizes its key features: déjà vu is a 'subjectively inappropriate impression of familiarity for a present experience [in relation to] an undefined past' (Neppe 1983). It contrasts with the less common phenomenon of *jamais vu*, the inappropriate impression of unfamiliarity with circumstances that are, in fact, familiar. The term *déjà vecu* has recently been used to pick out the mistaken conviction that one has lived through and can recollect a novel episode (Moulin et al. 2005).

The experience of déjà vu is common (Brown 2003). Around 70% of subjects have experienced it, usually repeatedly. It is reported more commonly by those with longer education and higher socioeconomic status; it has a peak incidence in the third decade of life with a declining frequency thereafter. It can be triggered by fatigue and emotional stress and typically lasts for a matter of seconds. It is usually a harmless anomaly of everyday experience, but sometimes it is symptomatic of neurological or psychiatric disorder. It occurs as an aura in temporal lobe *epilepsy, and as an accompaniment of neuroses and psychoses. The clue to diagnosis is given by the presence of associated features of the underlying disorder.

This arresting phenomenon has attracted numerous explanations, ranging from accounts in terms of psychological processes through attempts to localize its underlying neuroanatomy to supernatural theories appealing to reincarnation and prophetic dreams.

Psychological theories include (1) the suggestion that a system involved in the detection of familiarity is activated independently of a—normally closely coupled—system involved in recollection; (2) the related idea that some aspect or aspects of the current experience are indeed familiar but that their source is inaccessible; and (3) the theory that some disruption of attention or perception leads to anomalous 'dual' processing of sensory information (Brown 2003). This creates two representations of a single event, leading, in turn, to a false sense of familiarity.

Following Wilder Penfield's early work, the use of electrodes implanted in the brain to record the source of epileptic seizures and to stimulate the brain has provided opportunities to study the neural substrates of déjà vu. These studies have implicated a network of regions including the medial temporal lobe and superior temporal gyrus (Bancaud et al. 1994). Recent research has linked psychological and anatomical theories of déjà vu by suggesting that 'parahippocampal' areas, adjacent to the hippocampus, play a key role both in normal familiarity discrimination and in déjà vu (Spatt 2002, Bartolomei et al. 2004).

Déjà vu is a subtle but—to most of us—familiar and distinctive disturbance of awareness. Research on the neuropsychological basis of the experience over the past hundred years exemplifies the scope for the scientific study of such elusive subjective phenomena.

ADAM ZEMAN

Bancaud, J., Brunet-Bourgin, F., Chauvel, P., and Halgren, E. (1994). 'Anatomical origin of déjà vu and vivid 'memories' in human temporal lobe epilepsy'. *Brain*, 117.

Bartolomei, F., Barbeau, E., Gavaret, M. et al. (2004). 'Cortical stimulation study of the role of rhinal cortex in déjà vu and reminiscence of memories'. *Neurology*, 63.

Brown, A. S. (2003). 'A review of the déjà vu experience'. *Psychological Bulletin*, 129.

Dickens, C. (1849–50/1985). *The Personal History of David Copperfield*.

Hughlings-Jackson, J. (1888). 'On a particular variety of epilepsy ("intellectual aura"), one case with symptoms of organic brain disease'. *Brain*, 11.

Moulin, C. J., Conway, M. A., Thompson, R. G., James, N., and Jones, R. W. (2005). 'Disordered memory awareness: recollective confabulation in two cases of persistent déjà vecu'. *Neuropsychologia*, 43.

Neppe, V. M. (1983). *The Psychology of Deja Vu*.

Spatt, J. (2002). 'Déjà vu: possible parahippocampal mechanisms'. *Journal of Neuropsychiatry and Clinical Neuroscience*, 14.

delirium Delirium is a medical term used to describe a syndrome of acute (in the sense of sudden, or suddenly worsening) state of impaired consciousness (Lindesay et al. 2002). The term stems from the Latin *delirare, de* meaning away, and *lira*, the ridge between the furrows. Delirium is thus what happens when the plough jumps out of its straight course; the vernacular meaning is to be deranged, crazy, out of one's wits (Lipowski 1990:3). This term includes both the older meaning of delirium (as typified by *delirium tremens*) and acute confusional states (Lipowski 1990). Typically, delirium occurs in the very old, the very young, or anyone with an underlying brain disorder. It is most common among elderly people, in whom delirium can be viewed as the high-order failure of a complex system. It is not a disease state, but rather a syndrome that is usually the result of multiple interacting medical problems such as a drug reaction, or an infection, or a heart problem, or stroke, often predisposed by cognitive problems such as dementia or visual impairment. In younger people, delirium generally represents a specific brain disorder, intoxication or poisoning, or very severe illness. In elderly people, delirium is best studied in the hospital setting where 5–30% of those admitted to hospital may be diagnosed with delirium, depending on the population studied and the criteria employed (Lindesay et al. 2002). Although there are fewer studies in other settings, the rates appear higher in nursing homes or similar long-term care settings where they may range from 30% to 60% (Lindesay et al. 2002).

The symptoms of delirium and some of its causes have been recognized for many centuries:

> Delirium, trembling, tottering, falling down,
> a constant patter of incoherent babbling,
> these are the sure signs of foul fevers, life-threatening,
> and of drunkenness as well.
> From *The Pañcatantra, Pūrnabhadra recension AD 1199 (Visnu 1995)*

In the early 19th century Greiner (Lipowski 1990) characterized it as a disorder of consciousness, so one might expect that its systematic study might yield insights about this notoriously hard to define concept. Below, we will see what might be adduced about consciousness if one were to accept delirium as one of its disordered states, but first we will describe delirium, focusing on its most non-controversial aspects.

Delirium affects cognition and is commonly accompanied by an altered state of arousal as well as impairments in attention, orientation, and memory. The disordered arousal can manifest as either a hypoalert–hypoactive state, in which the patient appears to be sleepy, or a hyperalert–hyperactive state, in which the patient is highly aroused, easily distracted, and frequently agitated. The *delirium tremens* of acute alcohol withdrawal serves as a prototype of *delirium with psychomotor agitation*, whereas the patient on the verge of coma would represent *delirium with psychomotor retardation*. The disordered attention is often prominent, and a test of attention—such as the ability to list the months of the year backwards, or even accessibility to interview over a 2-minute period rated on a 10-point visual analogue scale—can be used to follow the fluctuation in the overall course of the delirium. Patients commonly are disoriented, have profound memory problems, and problems in most 'higher-order' cortical functions, such as judgement, language, calculation, and visuospatial tasks. The thinking of a person with delirium is typically effortful and disorganized: e.g. a sentence may be interrupted in the middle and another idea produced, or there may be sudden expression of emotion for no apparent reason (Chédru and Geschwind 1972). Fragmented delusions are quite common and some also experience visual *hallucinations, usually of objects, animals, and the dead. Psychotic symptoms are more common in those with hyperalert–hyperactive delirium. In addition to these cognitive and perceptual changes, impaired mobility and falls, as noted by the writers of the *Pañcatantra*, are generally observed in delirium, contributing to increased morbidity. Other than acuity of onset, another hallmark of delirium is that it fluctuates. A person might seem well in the morning, very confused at lunch, better in the afternoon, and more confused again in the evening.

Although people have profound memory problems during the episode of delirium, more than 50% of patients recall the delirium experience, spontaneously referring to it as a 'waking dream' or a 'living nightmare' (Breitbart et al. 2002). Most people feel trapped in incomprehensible experiences, in which the past is not readily distinguished from the present and the real from unreal, accompanied by a sense of loss of control (Andersson et al. 2002). For example 'I would constantly turn up, myself, in places that I really did not know what they were. . . . I was more or less in another world.' (Andersson et al. 2002:656). One of our own patients was quite preoccupied by the television remote control, saying 'if only I can find the right button then all of this would stop'. Queries about the capacity for self-reflection are typically met incredulously—'I couldn't have thought about anything like that! It was all

I could do to keep going!' The notion of being under threat with loss of self-control implies, however, that some sense of self is maintained.

Delirium is one of the commonest causes of psychotic symptoms in elderly people (Bhat 2005). Usually, it can be differentiated from other well-known causes of psychosis such as *schizophrenia and bipolar disorder (with episodes of mania and depression) which typically occur in younger people, but which do not have impairments in arousal or disorientation, and which are often insidious in onset. However, in the older literature 'delirious mania' has been described as the final stage of mania. More recently, there have been reports of co-occurrence of delirium and mania. With the former, mania rarely progresses to a delirious stage these days and manic symptoms are readily identified in its progression, and the latter is uncommon and usually caused by strokes. It is often more difficult to distinguish delirium from the psychosis sometimes seen in *dementia, especially the type known as Lewy body dementia. This is a form of dementia that in some patients bears many features of a persisting delirium, in that consciousness fluctuates (McKeith et al. 2005). Psychotic disorders in dementia share with delirium features such as visual hallucinations, fluctuating consciousness, and impaired mobility. In distinguishing between dementia with psychosis and delirium, it is often the acuity of onset and association with medical problems that come to the aid of the clinician.

Within this apparently straightforward description of delirium lurk a number of problems. For more than 50 years, it has been pointed out that delirium is often missed by physicians and health-care professionals, even though it is readily recognized by the family members of patients (Breitbart et al. 2002). This perhaps reflects that delirium results in a disorder of self, the recognition of which requires prior knowledge of the undisordered self for the new state to be seen as a problem. In turn, what does it mean to the conceptualization of delirium as a disorder of consciousness if we must also consider that it results in a disorder of self? The status of delirium as a disorder of consciousness has fluctuated. The difficulty has not been whether or not delirium is a disorder of consciousness—there is general agreement amongst researchers and expert clinicians that it is so—but how that disturbance is to be conceptualized. Delirium shows disturbance in most of the neuropsychological components of consciousness such as arousal, *attention, orientation, *memory, and awareness (Schiff and Plum 2000). To this, many scholars would add disturbances in mood and *emotion. Nevertheless, current classifications tend to be either unidimensional in their approach—defining delirium as impairment of global attention, while still failing to incorporate such important components of consciousness as impaired arousal and disorientation—or simply defining disturbance of consciousness loosely. This has led to considerable difficulties in operationalizing disturbance of consciousness in all its important domains. Although delirious patients commonly have disordered attention (i.e. impaired attention is a sensitive sign of delirium) many other brain disorders also result in inattention (i.e. impaired attention is not a specific sign of delirium).

As noted, the classical account of how delirium is conceptualized (as an acute confusional state, arising from a disorder of consciousness) must also be annotated to understand how it should be distinguished from dementia. In the classical formulation, dementia does not impair the level of consciousness. This is not true of some types of dementia, however. Lewy body dementia and rare disorders such as those associated with antibodies to voltage-gated potassium channels (Vincent et al. 2006) can each result in disordered levels of consciousness. The latter type of disorders—which would include encephalitides that have discernible causes and that are potentially amenable to treatment—also undermine another of the hallmarks of the delirium/dementia dichotomy, which is that the former has a short duration, and the latter a long one. Patients with so-called *limbic encephalitis* can show a delirium-like presentation for months. In DSM-IV (American Psychiatric Association 2000), the attempt to distinguish delirium from dementia has meant that some symptoms of delirium are no longer included in the definition because of their overlap with dementia.

These troubling conceptual and operational issues aside, what might be inferred about consciousness if delirium was the result of it being disordered? Several features of the deranged consciousness of delirium shed light. Consciousness especially allows experience to be understood as happening to ourselves, and we understand ourselves to have a certain unity even when we are unable to clearly articulate what constitutes that self. We also understand that experience happens to us in a serially time-organized way. That there is an us, and something happening to us, or which we are participating in some sequence, also means that the experience is susceptible to reflection and *introspection. Finally, the fluctuation seen in delirium admits to grades of experience. This account of consciousness harks back to William James, in a formulation by the physicians Schiff and Plum (2000): 'At its least, normal human consciousness consists of a serially time-ordered, organized, restricted and reflective awareness of self and the environment. Moreover, it is an experience of graded complexity and quantity.' For us, this implies that consciousness must include a sense of *self in time (and body), existing in a sufficient level of wakefulness/

arousal and with enough attention to allow environmental inputs to be ordered. Phenomenological studies of delirium, together with clinical studies and observations, highlight the delirium experience of great threat to self, with early disorientation and confusion of time, disturbed sense of reality, and loss of control. As Greiner has observed, for the delirious person the dead come back to life, or one is maybe a child once again in school facing a teacher but fails to recognize familiar people at the bedside (Lipowski 1990).

Despite this evidence and this formulation there has been curiously little discussion of delirium as a disorder of self. We think that delirium is a disorder of consciousness, which can be evaluated through changes in arousal, attention, and temporal orientation (Bhat and Rockwood 2007). This alteration in control and contents of consciousness on the background of a varying disturbance in the level of consciousness leading to a dislocation of self in time and space. Thus serial time-ordered, organized, restricted, and reflective awareness of both self and the environment is impaired. This conceptualization would appear to have greater specificity for delirium than impaired consciousness or inattention, despite disorders of self seen in schizophrenia and in the neglect syndromes of patients with non-dominant parietal lobe lesions, because in these latter conditions disorder of self rarely involves more than one aspect of consciousness. Delirium as a disorder of consciousness in these ways gives insight into consciousness itself.

KENNETH ROCKWOOD AND RAVI BHAT

American Psychiatric Association (2000). *Diagnostic and Statistical Manual*, 4th edn.

Andersson, E. M., Hallberg, I. R., Norberg, A., and Edberg, A. K. (2002). 'The meaning of acute confusional state from the perspective of elderly patients'. *International Journal of Geriatric Psychiatry*, 17.

Breitbart, W., Gibson, C., and Tremblay, A. (2002). 'The delirium experience: delirium recall and delirium-related distress in hospitalized patients with cancer, their spouses/caregivers, and their nurses'. *Psychosomatics*, 43.

Bhat, R. S. (2005). 'Psychotic symptoms in delirium'. In Hassett, A., Ames, A., and Chiu, E. (eds) *Psychosis in the Elderly*.

—— and Rockwood, K. (2007). 'Delirium as a disorder of consciousness'. *Journal of Neurology, Neurosurgery and Psychiatry*, 78.

Chédru, F. and Geschwind, N. (1972). 'Disorders of higher cortical functions in acute confusional states'. *Cortex*, 8.

Lindesay, J., Rockwood, K., and MacDonald, A. (eds) (2002). *Delirium in Old Age*.

Lipowski, Z. J. (1990). *Delirium: Acute Confusional States*.

McKeith, I., Dickson, D. W., Lowe, J. et al. (2005). 'Diagnosis and management of dementia with Lewy bodies: third report of the DLB Consortium'. *Neurology*, 65.

Schiff, N. D. and Plum, F. (2000). 'The role of arousal and 'gating' systems in the neurology of impaired consciousness'. *Journal of Clinical Neurophysiology*, 17.

Vincent, A., Lang, B., and Kleopa, K. A. (2006). 'Autoimmune channelopathies and related neurological disorders'. *Neuron*, 52.

Visnu, Sarma (1995). *The Pañcatantra*, transl. Chandra Rajan.

delusions According to the American Psychiatric Association (2000), a delusion is a 'false belief based on incorrect inference about external reality that is firmly sustained despite what everyone else believes and despite what constitutes incontrovertible or obvious proof or evidence to the contrary'. There is much that is problematic about this characterization—it is arguable that delusions need be neither false nor about external reality—but it is widely agreed that delusions are beliefs that are held with a degree of certainty that is not warranted by the evidence available to the patient. The delusional person either has no evidence for the belief in question, or has overwhelming evidence against the belief. Delusions can occur in a variety of contexts, including (but by no means limited to) paranoid *schizophrenia, Alzheimer's disease, Lewy body dementia, *epilepsy, *frontal lobe pathology, and head trauma (see BRAIN DAMAGE).

It is useful to distinguish between *monothematic* and *polythematic* delusions. Monothematic delusions concern a single topic, and tend to be relatively circumscribed. The topic of the delusion can be mundane, for example that one's spouse is being unfaithful (delusional jealousy) or that one is being persecuted by one's neighbours (persecutory delusions), but monothematic delusions can also have fantastical content. Individuals with the *Capgras delusion* believe that someone close to them has been replaced by an impostor (such as a robot or an alien); individuals with the *Cotard delusion* believe that parts of their bodies are rotting or that they have died; and individuals with delusions of *alien control* believe that their movements are directly controlled by other beings. Patients with polythematic delusions, by contrast, have unusual beliefs about a wide variety of subjects. A classic case is that of Schreiber, a former high court judge whose web of delusional beliefs included the conviction that God was transforming him into a woman, transmitting rays down to enact 'miracles' upon him, and sending little men to torture him (Sass 1994, Schreiber 1903/2000).

Broadly speaking, we can distinguish two ways in which abnormalities of consciousness can be invoked to account for delusions: via a coarse-grained delusional mood, and via fine-grained anomalous experiences. The delusional mood is distinctive of schizophrenic delusion (Anscombe 1987). The psychiatrist Karl Jaspers described what he called delusions proper (or *primary delusions*) as 'the vague crystallizations of blurred delusional experience and diffuse, perplexing self-references' (Jaspers

1963:107). In some manifestations of the delusional mood, the patient experiences stimuli—a table, a remark, the arrangement of flowers in a vase—as possessing a degree of personal significance that they do not have. Other patients may complain of an inability to grasp the significance of things. A patient might say that she feels alienated from the world, that she experiences her body as an object, or that she cannot understand the relationship between objects (Sass and Parnas 2003). These experiences—often difficult for the patient to articulate—can give rise to polythematic delusions as the patient attempt to find some meaning in the face of experiential chaos. Thus far, cognitive neuropsychiatry has made little progress in identifying the neurophysiological mechanisms that underpin these abnormalities in the experience of significance and meaning.

For the most part, cognitive neuropsychiatry has focused on the relatively fine-grained anomalous experiences hypothesized to account for certain monothematic delusions. The poster-child for this approach is Ellis and Young's (1990) account of the Capgras delusion. The Ellis and Young model builds on a two-route model of face-processing, according to which face-processing involves a visuo-semantic pathway that processes semantic information about facial features, and a visual-affective pathway that produces a specific affective response to familiar faces (the feeling of familiarity). Damage to the visuo-semantic pathway leaves the patient unable to recognize familiar faces (leading to prosopagnosia), whereas damage to the visual-affective pathway leaves the patient able to recognize familiar faces but deprives them of the normal and expected feeling of familiarity. This model has been confirmed by the finding that Capgras patients, unlike controls, show reduced autonomic arousal in response to familiar faces (Ellis et al. 1997). Ellis and Young suggest that the Capgras delusion results from the patient's attempt to reconcile the fact that the person in front of him looks like his wife with the loss of expected feelings of familiarity and associated emotions: 'It must be an impostor masquerading as my wife!' Following Campbell (2001), we might think of this as an empiricist account of the Capgras delusion, for it presents the Capgras delusion as arising out of an anomalous experience.

Another important example of the empiricist approach to monothematic delusions can be found in recent treatments of the delusion of alien control (Frith 1992, Spence 2001). There is good reason to think that delusions of alien control involve disruptions to the experience of initiation and control that normally accompanies voluntary or willed agency. Evidence that patients with delusions of alien control have disrupted agentive experiences is provided by experimental results showing that such patients have difficulty correcting for errors in movement in the absence of visual feedback, and that such patients—unlike controls—are able to *tickle themselves. It is very much a moot question whether the delusion of alien control might be fully explained by appeal to abnormal agentive experiences—as the *anarchic hand syndrome demonstrates, not all those who experience disruption of agentive experience become delusional—but there is good reason to think that an account of alien control delusions will have an experiential element.

It is very much an open question just how many delusions might be grounded in anomalous experiences. A plausible case can be made for thinking that delusions of thought-insertion, Cotard delusion, Frégoli delusion, the delusion of mirrored-self misidentification, reduplicative paramnesia, and certain forms of *anosognosia might be prompted by an experiential anomalies of some kind (see Davies et al. 2001). However, this is only a very partial list of monothematic delusions, and many monothematic delusions seem unlikely to succumb to an empiricist treatment. Patients with *erotomania* (de Clérambault syndrome) believe that someone of a higher social status is secretly in love with them. It seems implausible to suppose that one might explain the genesis of erotomania by appealing to the kind of focused experiential anomalies that underlie the Capgras delusion and delusions of alien control, although one might make some progress in explaining it by appealing to the relatively labile experiences of significance and self-references that occur in the context of the delusional mood.

How exactly are anomalous experiences and the delusions to which they give rise related? To answer this question it is instructive to return to the Capgras delusion. On one account, the patient's anomalous experience is simply that 'something is not quite right' when he looks at his wife. It is natural for those working with this thin conception of the anomalous experience to suppose that the patient adopts the belief that the person confronting him is not his wife in an attempt to *explain* why he has this feeling of something being 'not quite right'. Another account of the Capgras delusion construes the anomalous experience underlying the delusion as having much richer content—perhaps even the content 'this person is not my wife'. Proponents of this thick approach to the Capgras delusion are at liberty to hold that the patient adopts the delusional belief that his wife has been replaced by an impostor by believing what it is that he experiences. Whereas proponents of the thin account need to work hard to fill the gap between the anomalous experience and the delusional belief, proponents of the thick account need to work hard (that is, harder than proponents of the thin account must work) in order to account for the genesis of anomalous experience. There are important points of contact here between accounts of delusions and debates over the representational *content of consciousness.

Can delusions be fully accounted for in terms of anomalous experiences? The pure form of empiricism—associated most closely with the work of Maher (1988, 1999)—regards delusions as essentially normal responses to unusual experiences. Pure empiricist theories of delusions are also known as *one-factor accounts*, for they hold that one need advert only to experiential factors in explaining why someone has a particular delusion. Impure versions of the empiricist approach—known, unsurprisingly, as *two-factor accounts*—hold that delusions are caused by an anomalous experience together with a second (non-experiential) factor of some kind, such as a cognitive or motivational bias.

Versions of the two-factor account differ in their conception of what exactly it is that the second-factor is meant to explain. Some versions invoke a second factor to account for why the delusional belief acquires the precise content that it does, while others invoke a second factor to explain why the patient adheres to their delusional belief in the face of 'incontrovertible or obvious proof or evidence to the contrary'.

Stone and Young's (1997) model of the Capgras delusion provides us with an example of the former kind of two-factor theory. Noting the existence of patients who fluctuate between the Capgras delusion and the Cotard delusion (the belief that one is dead, or that parts of one's body are rotting), Stone and Young suggest that these two delusions involve a single experiential anomaly—a feeling of unfamiliarity or strangeness—that is elaborated in different ways depending on the patient's attributional bias. When the patients has an *externalizing* attributional bias he accounts for the feeling of strangeness by supposing that certain individuals near and dear to him have been replaced (the Capgras delusion), but when he has an *internalizing* attributional bias he responds to those same feelings by supposing that he is dead or unreal in some way (the Cotard delusion). Although ingenious, Stone and Young's proposal is problematized by evidence that the experiential states underlying the Capgras and Cotard delusions are different: whereas the Capgras delusion appears to involve a fairly focal impairment in face processing, the Cotard delusion seems to involve a global alteration in affective experience. Rather than experiencing only familiar faces as alien, the Cotard patient experiences *everything* as strange, devoid of meaning and lifeless (Gerrans 2000).

Coltheart's (2007) two-factor model of delusion invokes a second factor to explain why the delusional patient refuses to give up the delusional belief in the face of more plausible alternatives. There are two reasons for thinking that we need to invoke a second factor of this kind. Firstly, it seems a priori implausible to suppose that normal processes of belief-formation would take one from abnormal experiences of the sort posited by empiricist theorists all the way to delusional belief. If Capgras patients have intact belief-evaluation systems, why do they not accept the explanations of their unusual experiences provided by others—e.g. that they have suffered dorsal stream damage? If patients with delusions of alien control have intact belief-evaluation systems, why do they not accept the hypothesis that their action-monitoring system is damaged in favour of their own explanations—explanations that are not only outlandish but are sustained despite what everyone else believes? A second reason to deny that anomalous experiences are sufficient to account for delusions is that there appear to be patients who manifest the experiential anomaly without becoming delusional. For example, patients with bilateral frontal lobe damage show reduced affective responses to familiar faces, but they do not develop the belief that their relatives have been replaced by impostors.

What might explain why delusional patients cling to their outlandish beliefs rather than adopt one of the more plausible alternatives (or, indeed, settle for the belief that they do not know what has happened to them)? Whereas the one-factor theorist argues that the delusional patient clings to his belief because the anomalous experience underlying it is both intense and incessant, the two-factor theorist argues that we need to appeal to an impairment in belief-evaluation—perhaps involving right frontal damage (Coltheart 2007)—at this point. Whether or not (some) delusions can be fully accounted for in experiential terms, there is no doubt that students of consciousness and students of delusions have much to learn from each other.

TIM BAYNE

American Psychiatric Association (2000). DSM IV-TR.

Anscombe, R. (1987). 'The disorder of consciousness in schizophrenia'. *Schizophrenia Bulletin*, 13.

Campbell, J. (2001). 'Rationality, meaning, and the analysis of delusion'. *Philosophy, Psychiatry and Psychology*, 8.

Coltheart, M. (2007). 'Cognitive neuropsychiatry and delusional belief'. *Quarterly Journal of Experimental Psychology*, 60.

Davies, M., Coltheart, M., Langdon, R., and Breen, N. (2001). 'Monothematic delusions: towards a two-factor approach'. *Philosophy, Psychiatry and Psychology*, 8.

Ellis, H. D. and Young, A. (1990). 'Accounting for delusional misidentification'. *British Journal of Psychiatry*, 157.

——, Young, A. W., Quayle, A. H., and de Pauw, K. W. (1997). 'Reduced autonomic responses to faces in Capgras delusion'. *Proceedings of the Royal Society of London Series B: Biological Sciences*, 264.

Frith, C. (1992). *The Cognitive Neuropsychology of Schizophrenia.*
Gerrans, P. (2000). 'Refining the Explanation of Cotard's delusion'. *Mind and Language*, 15.
Jaspers, K. (1963). *General Psychopathology*, transl. J. Hoenig and M. W. Hamilton.
Maher, B. (1988). 'Anomalous experience and delusional thinking: the logic of explanations'. In Oltmanns, T. F. and Maher, B. A. (eds) *Delusional Beliefs.*
—— (1999). 'Anomalous experience in everyday life: its significance for psychopathology'. *Monist*, 82.
Sass, L. (1994). *The Paradoxes of Delusion: Wittgenstein, Schreber, and the Schizophrenic Mind.*
—— and Parnas, J. (2003). 'Schizophrenia, consciousness and the self'. *Schizophrenia Bulletin*, 29.
Schreber, D. (1903/2000). *Memoirs of My Nervous Illness.*
Spence, S. (2001). 'Alien control: from phenomenology to cognitive neurobiology'. *Philosophy, Psychiatry and Psychology*, 8.
Stone, T. and Young, A. (1997). 'Delusions and brain injury: the philosophy and psychology of belief'. *Mind and Language*, 12.

dementia Dementia is a clinical syndrome characterized by deterioration of cognitive or social abilities, sufficient to impair daily living activities. For a long time, a vascular aetiology was put forward and most patients were said to suffer from 'arteriosclerosis'. Subsequently, clinical and pathological series demonstrated that degenerative diseases, and principally Alzheimer-type dementia, were most frequently observed.

The pathological characteristics of degenerative dementias are loss of specifically distributed groups of neurons and deposits of abnormal (intra- or extracellular) proteins that disrupt functional brain networks. The aetiology of degenerative dementias is still unknown and many researches are devoted to the understanding of abnormal protein metabolism. However, the disruption of cerebral networks can be visualized in vivo using *functional brain imaging. Note that there is a great number of other (less frequent) non-degenerative types of dementia, with aetiologies as diverse as brain injury, thyroid pathology, or infection in prion diseases, for example. Dementia is very frequent, and in some studies it has been diagnosed in about 40% of subjects of more than 80 years of age.

Consciousness is profoundly altered in end stages of dementia, when patients are unaware of their environment and of their place in this environment, and react only to very few emotional stimuli. However, even in early (mild) stages of a progressive degenerative dementia, different patients are unaware of some of their symptoms. In this entry, various facets of impaired consciousness will be described in two main types of degenerative dementia: Alzheimer's disease, and frontotemporal lobe dementia. Moreover, we will describe our present understanding of the contribution of specific brain dysfunctions to impaired consciousness in demented patients.

1. Alzheimer's disease
2. Frontotemporal dementia
3. Conclusion

1. Alzheimer's disease

Alzheimer's disease (AD) is the most frequent type of dementia, clinically characterized by progressive deterioration of several cognitive functions. The pathological landmarks are extracellular brain deposits of amyloid and intraneuronal fibrillary tangles. Different stages are recognized in the illness, from mild dementia when patients remain relatively autonomous, to a severe stage of the disease when they are extremely dependent for most daily activities.

The most frequent and earliest cognitive deficit in AD is an episodic *memory impairment. This means that patients have difficulties in remembering events that they personally lived, and that they cannot recollect those episodes in a precise contextual format that makes them unique subjective experiences. Accordingly, AD patients progressively lose the autonoetic (self-knowing) consciousness of their autobiographical past (Tulving 2002). The neural correlates of episodic autobiographical impairment in AD (demonstrated by functional neuroimaging) correspond to a dysfunction in medial temporal structures, medial posterior cortices (posterior cingulate and precuneus), and associative lateral cortices.

Since AD patients do not remember precise contextual memories, they rely on familiarity and relatively preserved (or less impaired) semantic knowledge to accept or reject information on recent autobiographical events (for example: 'I probably paid my telephone bill already, since I do it systematically, and moreover the line was not cut off'). More generally, AD is characterized by an early loss of controlled (conscious) cognitive processes, with a relative preservation of *automatic behaviours. AD patients are able to maintain relatively complex routines, but they progressively encounter difficulties when they need to consciously adapt their behaviour to changing circumstances. The neural correlates of decreased controlled processes in AD probably correspond to disruption of frontal-posterior cortical associative networks that participate in an attentional workspace (Salmon et al. 2005).

A puzzling clinical feature in AD is a variable lack of awareness of the dementia syndrome. AD patients may recognize that they present slight memory impairment, but they frequently show *anosognosia for the daily consequences of their cognitive impairment. A psychological denial of an emerging disease may intervene in initial stages of AD, but a profound anosognosia for cognitive and behavioural changes may also occur early, and it is extremely disturbing for the relatives. In most studies, but not all, anosognosia has been related to the severity of dementia. More specifically, a relationship was sometimes established between the degree of anosognosia and a decrease in memory and executive abilities. Accordingly, impaired judgement on self-capacities in AD might depend on reduced availability of episodic and semantic autobiographical information and disturbed updating of autobiographical memories, and on decreased (executive) abilities for self reflection (Klein et al. 2002). There are few cognitive models of anosognosia, and they suggest a dysfunction of (or between) episodic memory, personal knowledge database, posterior cognitive modules (responsible for cognitive awareness), and anterior cognitive modules which monitor, compare, and update information (Agnew and Morris 1998). Lack of awareness into cognitive impairment may be measured by a decrease in meta-memory performances, when AD patients overestimate (i.e. erroneously monitor) their cognitive abilities in neuropsychological tasks. More frequently, anosognosia is measured by questionnaires providing judgements from a clinician, a patient, and/or a patient's relative. A patient's evaluation about his own cognitive abilities may reflect anosognosia if the judgement is in contradiction with actual daily performances. Anosognosia measured by a patient's self-assessment of cognitive functioning was related to dysfunction in a medial temporal and orbitofrontal network involved in monitoring current self performances (Salmon et al. 2006). Those patients are impaired in evaluating information for its current personal significance. However, the most frequent measurement of anosognosia consists in a discrepancy score between the judgement of the patient and that of a close relative. Comparisons between patients' and relatives' perspectives were used to assess decrease of knowledge concerning personality traits, daily functioning, cognitive abilities and behaviour in AD. A high discrepancy score (reflecting lack of awareness of patients' own cognitive abilities compared to relatives' evaluation) was related to decreased activity in temporoparietal junction in AD (Fig. D1). Lesions of this region were also related to mirrored self-misidentification in demented patients, i.e. an inability to see the self with a third-person perspective. More generally, the parietotemporal junction is part of a network activated when self and others' perspectives have to be distinguished. In summary, lack of awareness concerning dementia symptoms in AD is a type of impaired consciousness which may depend on dysfunction of different cognitive abilities. Different forms and degrees of unawareness are related to variable impairment of monitoring capacities in AD patients (related to anterior cerebral dysfunctions), to impaired mechanisms of perspective taking, to decreased availability of episodic and semantic memories (which are not updated), mainly related to lesions in

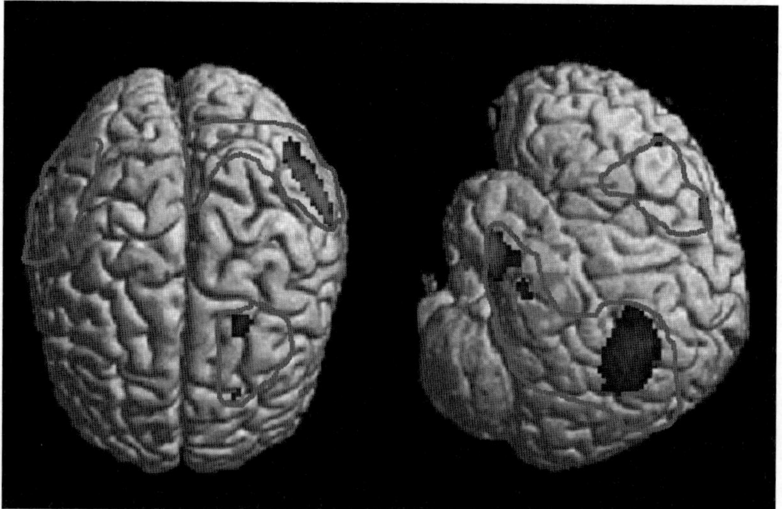

Fig. D1. A brain structural image is represented from a dorsal (left image) and lateral view (right image). The plain red lines indicate cerebral regions where the metabolism is significantly decreased in Alzheimer's disease compared to controls. The red 'blobs' illustrate regions where the cerebral activity is correlated to the degree of anosognosia for cognitive impairment (measured by a discrepancy score between patient and relative). (See Colour Plate 9.)

posterior associative cortices, and to dysfunction of an attentional frontoposterior cerebral workspace.

2. Frontotemporal dementia

The behavioural variant of the large group of frontotemporal lobe dementias (bvFTLD) is clinically characterized by a progressive change in personal, social, and emotional behaviour. Lack of awareness, or lack of insight into these dementia symptoms, is also a cardinal feature of the disease, causing major problems of legal and financial responsibility. Impaired cerebral activity in the medial prefrontal cortex is the essential neural *correlate of social disability in bvFTLD. Such a medial prefrontal dysfunction would also disturb self-referential processing, since the ventromedial prefrontal cortex is particularly involved in self-representation.

Patients with bvFTLD have a deficit in autobiographical memory and *autonoetic consciousness (Piolino et al. 2003). In end stages, there is a profound disconnection from the environment and a complete loss of self-consciousness. Discrepancy scores have also been calculated in FTD to measure the degree of anosognosia concerning personality traits and social reactions (Rankin et al. 2005). Anosognosia for social behaviour (measured by discrepancy between the patient's and a relative's assessment) was related to decreased activity in the left temporal pole, a cerebral structure important to provide access to episodic and semantic emotional and social memories used in perspective taking. In summary, lack of consciousness about behavioural changes in FTD would depend on impaired access to autobiographical social information and to decreased self-referential processing, related to dysfunction of different regions in the frontal and temporal lobes.

3. Conclusion

Patients with degenerative dementia present a progressive loss of consciousness, ranging from variable decrease of autonoetic memory to impaired consciousness about their place in an environment they are unaware of. Lack of consciousness about disability is also a characteristic early feature of dementia. However, different patients may be unaware of different symptoms. Moreover, anosognosia of a given symptom is variable in patients with a same diagnostic, because it may depend on dysfunction of different networks, related to monitoring abilities, personal memories and self, perspective taking, and controlled cognitive processes.

ERIC SALMON

Agnew, S. K. and Morris, R. G. (1998). 'The heterogeneity of anosognosia for memory impairment in Alzheimer's disease: a review of the literature and a proposed model'. *Aging and Mental Health*, 2.

Klein, S. B., Rozendal, K., and Cosmides, L. (2002). 'A social-cognitive neuroscience analysis of the self'. *Social Cognition*, 20.

Piolino, P., Desgranges, B., Belliard, S. et al. (2003). 'Autobiographical memory and autonoetic consciousness: triple dissociation in neurodegenerative diseases'. *Brain*, 126.

Rankin, K. P., Baldwin, E., Pace-Savitsky, C., Kramer, J. H., and Miller, B. L. (2005). 'Self awareness and personality change in dementia'. *Journal of Neurology, Neurosurgery and Psychiatry*, 76.

Salmon, E., Lespagnard, S., Marique, P. et al. (2005). 'Cerebral metabolic correlates of four dementia scales in Alzheimer's disease'. *Journal of Neurology*, 252.

——, Perani, D., Herholz, K. et al. (2006). 'Neural correlates of anosognosia for cognitive impairment in Alzheimer's disease'. *Human Brain Mapping*, 27.

Tulving, E. (2002). 'Episodic memory: from mind to brain'. *Annual Review of Psychology*, 53.

depersonalization The term 'depersonalization' refers to a disturbance of self-awareness characterized by a feeling of detachment or estrangement from one's *self. The following description by Schilder (1953) conveys well the experiential complexity of this phenomenon:

> [T]he person afflicted by depersonalization complains he is no longer the same, no longer himself. Indeed, in clear-cut cases the patients complain that they no longer have an ego, but are mechanisms, automatons, puppets; that what they do seems not done by them but happens mechanically; that they no longer feel joy or sorrow, hatred or love; that they are as though dead, not alive, not real; that they cannot imagine their body, it is feelingless, and they experience neither hunger, thirst, nor any other bodily needs; that they cannot image nor remember, or intuit how their relatives look. The world too appears to them changed, strange, unreal; to some objects look like those on another planet. In a word, the perceptual world is estranged.

In spite of the bizarreness of the experience, patients retain their critical faculties and reality testing remains intact (i.e. descriptions of the experience are usually accompanied by 'as if' qualifiers).

Although the condition was repeatedly described in the medical literature throughout the 19th century, it was not until 1898 that the term 'depersonalization' was coined by the French psychologist L. Dugas. To him, depersonalization resulted from a failure in a putative mental process, whose normal function would be that of 'personalizing' conscious experience. Thus, Dugas defined 'personalization' as 'act of psychical synthesis, of appropriation or attribution of states to the self'. In the same vein a disruption of this process was thought to result in a 'feeling or sensation that thoughts and acts elude the self and become strange' (Sierra and Berrios 1997).

Current definitions of depersonalization emphasize a 'feeling of unreality' as the distinctive element of depersonalization. Unfortunately, this introduces a negative definition which has poor explanatory value as it alludes to something missing from normal experience, without clarifying its nature. However, patients typically complain of a whole range of anomalous experiences, which seem distinct enough to suggest that depersonalization may be best conceptualized as a syndrome rather than a symptom (Shorvon 1946). It would seem that depersonalization is characterized by four main underlying experiential dimensions (Sierra et al. 2005):

1. *Anomalous body experience*. The most characteristic *body image abnormality in depersonalization is that of 'disembodiment'. This can take the form of lack of body ownership (e.g. 'my body does not seem to belong to me'); a feeling of not being inside the body (e.g. 'it feels as if I am not really here'); and the feeling that their actions happen automatically without the intervention of a willing self (e.g. 'I feel like a robot or an automaton'). Associated with this experience of disembodiment, patients often describe the experience of being detached onlookers to their own behaviour (e.g. 'although my legs moved as I walked, I had the feeling that my mind was elsewhere').
2. *Emotional numbing*. Most patients with depersonalization report attenuated or a complete absence of emotional feelings. However, unlike the flat affect commonly seen patients with *schizophrenia or depression, the behavioural expression of emotions seems normal in people affected with depersonalization, and to an external observer they would seem to be emotionally engaged.
3. *Anomalous subjective recall*. Patients with depersonalization often complain of a number of subjective experiences affecting recall and the subjective experience of time. Typically patients state that recalled personal events feel 'as if' they had not really happened to them, or have the feeling that recent personal events happened long ago. In severe cases patients complain of a complete loss of a subjective sense of time, and feel as if they exist in a timeless realm. Subjective *imagery complaints, such as an inability to evoke visual memories of people or places, are also frequent.
4. *Derealization*. Most patients with depersonalization describe a feeling of being cut off from the world around, and of things around seeming 'unreal'. Derealization is frequently described in terms of visual metaphors (e.g. looking through a camera, mist, veil, etc.), and indeed, many patients claim that it is in the visual modality where the experience is most noticeable. Interestingly, such experiences are not typically ascribed to perceptual distortions, but rather to an inability to 'colour' perception with concomitant emotional feelings (see above). As a result of this, things perceived seem to lack 'vividness', 'immediacy', or a sense of familiarity. It is likely that this 'qualitative change' in the experiencing of perception, and related cognition, is at the core of what subjects describe as 'unreality feelings'. Supporting this view, neurological patients with lesions disconnecting the visual cortex from emotion processing areas in the temporal lobe (i.e. visuo-limbic disconnection) have been known to complain of subjective visual experiences that show a striking resemblance to those of patients with derealization (Sierra et al. 2002a).

As a fleeting experience, depersonalization does not seem to be uncommon in the general population. Surveys amongst college students have revealed a prevalence of 30–60%. These transient episodes typically last from minutes to a few hours, and seem to be triggered by fatigue, stress, or sleep deprivation. Depersonalization has also been reported to occur in approximately 45–50% of people during life-threatening situations such as earthquakes or car accidents.

Prevalence studies have indicated that 40–80% of psychiatric inpatients suffer from depersonalization, mainly associated with anxiety disorders, depression, and schizophrenia (Hunter et al. 2004). In neurological contexts depersonalization seems to be most frequent in temporal lobe *epilepsy and migraine (Lambert et al. 2002). More rarely, depersonalization can also occur as a primary disorder, in which case it tends to be chronic and persistent (i.e. depersonalization disorder; Simeon et al. 2003). Although the prevalence of the latter in the general population has not been established with certainly, it seems to range from 0.8 to 2.4%.

Regardless of the clinical or situation context in which it occurs, depersonalization has been shown to correlate with anxiety measures. This, together with the high prevalence of depersonalization at times of life-threatening situations, has been interpreted as suggesting that depersonalization represents a hard-wired, anxiety-triggered *dissociative response, geared to preserving adaptative behaviour in the face of threatening situations, normally associated with overwhelming and otherwise potentially disorganizing anxiety (Sierra and Berrios 1998). It has been hypothesized that this dissociative response would result in the inhibition of nonfunctional emotional and autonomic responses, while enhancing vigilant attention. Recent *functional brain imaging and psychophysiological studies support this model and have indicated that, as compared with normal controls and patients with anxiety disorders, patients with depersonalization disorder show lack of activation in limbic areas (Phillips et al. 2001), and marked autonomic attenuation in response to distressing visual stimuli (Sierra et al. 2002b). It is still unclear what causes this normative dissociative response to become unstable and dysfunctional, as seems to be the case in patients with depersonalization disorder. What is clear, however, is that an understanding of the severe fragmentation of self-experience characteristic of depersonalization can provide important insights into the nature of self-consciousness.

MAURICIO SIERRA

Hunter, E. C., Sierra,M., and David, A. S. (2004). 'The epidemiology of depersonalisation and derealisation. A systematic review'. *Social Psychiatry and Psychiatric Epidemiology*, 39.

Lambert, M. V., Sierra, M., Phillips, M. L., and David, A. S. (2002). 'The spectrum of organic depersonalization: a review plus four new cases'. *Journal of Neuropsychiatry and Clinical Neuroscience*, 14.

Phillips, M. L., Medford, N., Senior, C. et al. (2001). 'Depersonalization disorder: thinking without feeling'. *Psychiatry Research*, 30.

Sierra, M. and Berrios, G. E. (1997). 'Depersonalization: a conceptual history'. *History of Psychiatry*, 8.

—— —— (1998). 'Depersonalization: neurobiological perspectives'. *Biological Psychiatry*, 44.

——, Lopera, F., Lambert, M. V., Phillips, M. L., and David A. S. (2002a). 'Separating depersonalisation and derealisation: the relevance of the "lesion method" '. *Journal of Neurology, Neurosurgery and Psychiatry*, 72.

——, Senior, C., Dalton, J. et al. (2002b). 'Autonomic response in depersonalization disorder'. *Archives of General Psychiatry*, 59.

——, Baker, D., Medford, N., and David, A. S. (2005). 'Unpacking the depersonalization syndrome: an exploratory factor analysis on the Cambridge Depersonalization Scale'. *Psychological Medicine*, 35.

Simeon, D., Knutelska, M., Nelson, D., and Guralnik, O. (2003). 'Feeling unreal: a depersonalization disorder update of 117 cases'. *Journal of Clinical Psychiatry*, 64.

Schilder, P. (1953). *Medical Psychology*.

Shorvon, H. J. (1946). 'The depersonalization syndrome'. *Proceedings of the Royal Society of Medicine*, 39.

descriptive experience sampling Descriptive experience sampling (DES) is a method of investigating human inner experience (thoughts, feelings, sensations, perceptions, etc.) by collecting beeper-cued random samples of lived experience in participants' natural environments. Created by Russell Hurlburt in the late 1970s, DES was developed in response to the ongoing tension between the need for a high-fidelity method of exploring inner experience and the valid criticisms levelled against prior attempts at *introspection (including mistakes due to retrospection, disagreements about what is introspected, and the prevalence of social desirability effects). DES seeks to discover the phenomena of inner experience as they are experienced by each participant with sufficiently detailed accuracy and fidelity to support a science of inner experience.

1. Methodology
2. Applications

1. Methodology

DES asks participants to wear a random beeper in their natural environments. The randomly occurring beep cues participants to pay attention to whatever experience (or experiences) happens to be ongoing at the moment of the beep and immediately to jot down in a notebook (or otherwise record) the features of that experience (or experiences). Within 24 hours after collecting a number (typically 6) of such samples, participants meet with the DES investigator for an 'expositional interview' designed to help the participants provide faithful descriptions of the sampled experiences. In essence, the expositional interviewer asks each participant one and only one question, albeit repeatedly and in many different forms: 'What was ongoing in your inner experience at the moment of the beep?' After the expositional interview, the investigator prepares a written description of the ongoing inner experience at each sampled moment. The sample/interview/describe procedure is repeated over a series of (typically 4–8) sampling days until a sufficient number (typically 25–50) of moments have been collected. The investigator then surveys all of that participant's moments and extracts their salient characteristics, producing an idiographic characterization of that particular participant's experiences.

Some DES studies investigate a collection of participants who have some external feature (e.g. psychiatric diagnosis) in common. In those studies, the investigator produces an idiographic characterization of each participant as described above and then examines all those characterizations to discover whatever salient characteristics might emerge across the particular collection of participants. This allows the investigator to discover any features of inner experience that members of that specific population might share and thus to produce an across-participant nomothetic characterization of their in-common inner experiences.

Thus the aim of DES is to produce high-fidelity descriptions of inner experience. DES investigations have found that most people have a somewhat mistaken, perhaps substantially mistaken, understanding of the characteristics of their own inner experiences. These mistakes can be the result of presuppositions, self-schemas, heuristics such as availability or representativeness, and so on. Overcoming those mistakes requires the bracketing of presuppositions about what will or will not be found in experience, both by the participant and by the investigator. This bracketing is facilitated by (1) selecting random moments to be examined (thus avoiding presuming to know what kinds of experience are or are not important); (2) focusing on specific occurrences (and actively discouraging general statements, inferences, and assumptions about causation that may reflect self-characterization); (3) minimizing retrospection (thus reducing self-concept-driven distortions of memory); (4) asking, during the expositional interview, open-beginninged questions (requesting the description of whatever happened to be ongoing at the moment of the beep, thus avoiding the presumption that some particular feature of experience is important); (5) iterating the method by sampling/interviewing/describing over several days (thus allowing successively improving approximations to the fidelity of the phenomena being apprehended); and (6) valuing a bottom-up way of building the understanding of experience, starting with carefully described naturally occurring moments of individual experience, and out of a mosaic of such experiences building a true generalization about experience.

DES is similar to *protocol analysis in that both aim to externalize aspects of inner experience. It differs from protocol analysis in that (1) protocol analysis is typically aimed at thoughts, whereas DES considers all forms of experience; (2) protocol analysis is typically aimed at understanding the cognitive processes involved in executing some particular task, whereas DES seeks to describe freely occurring experience; and (3) protocol analysis asks participants to think aloud while continuing to perform the task, whereas DES interrupts (beeps) whatever is ongoing and asks for a report of the inner experience that was ongoing just before the interruption. Protocol analysis assumes that thinking aloud reflects the important ongoing cognitive processes; by contrast, DES believes that experience is often substantially richer than can be captured by concurrent thinking aloud. For example, DES frequently discovers visual *imagery and also discovers multiple simultaneous processes, both of which are too complex to be adequately characterized by concurrent think-aloud methods.

DES is similar to other sampling methods such as the experience sampling method, ecological momentary assessment, and thought sampling in that all use some form of beeper or other signalling device to aim at ecological validity, sampling in the participant's own natural environments rather than in special (e.g. laboratory) situations. DES differs from the other sampling methods in that those methods are primarily quantitative, asking participants to respond to a series of predefined items usually presented as Likert scales, whereas DES is qualitative and descriptive.

DES is similar to classical introspection in that both aim at describing very brief moments of experience. However, classical introspection aimed at discovering basic elements of consciousness as revealed in the reports given by participants as they perform specific tasks set by the investigator, whereas DES aims at describing the salient features of experience as participants engage in their everyday activities.

The salient features that emerge from DES studies (both within-participant idiographic and across-participant nomothetic) are often features of the *form* or pattern of how experience occurs within individuals. For example, salient form characteristics frequently involve inner speech, visual images, unsymbolized (unworded, unimaged) thinking, sensory awareness, or feelings. *Content* features or the pattern of what is being experienced can also emerge as salient characteristics, but they are less common.

2. Applications

Hurlburt and his colleagues have used DES to characterize the inner experience of individuals with psychiatric diagnoses such as *schizophrenia (Hurlburt 1990), depression, anxiety, bulimia, and borderline personality disorder (Hurlburt 1993). For example, Hurlburt et al. (1994) found that patients with Asperger's syndrome (high-functioning *autism) had only visual images in their experience, if they had any inner experience at all. That offers a plausible explanation for the frequent observation that patients with Asperger's syndrome have a difficult time taking another person's point of view (it is extremely difficult, if not impossible, to represent another's point of view using only visual imagery) and suggests that the usual explanation for that deficit (that individuals with Asperger's syndrome have no *theory of mind) is incorrect.

Schwitzgebel (2007) used a variant of DES to explore the issue of whether consciousness is rich or thin. There are always many modalities available to experience (visual, auditory, tactile, olfactory, imagistic, proprioceptive, emotional). The rich view maintains that consciousness holds a wide variety of those modalities simultaneously in experience; the thin view maintains that only one or a few modalities are experienced simultaneously. Schwitzgebel used DES modified by including the additional instruction that participants were to note whether, at the moment of the beep, they were conscious of visual experience, of visual experience in the far right visual field, of tactile experience, and/or of tactile experience of the left foot. His tentative conclusion was that conscious experience is moderately rich: consciousness contains more than a few modalities but not all modalities. Hurlburt and Schwitzgebel (2007) discussed whether Schwitzgebel's variant of DES undermined essential features of DES.

RUSSELL T. HURLBURT

Ericsson, K. A. and Simon, H. A. (1993). *Protocol Analysis: Verbal Reports as Data.*
Hurlburt, R. T. (1990). *Sampling Normal and Schizophrenic Inner Experience.*
—— (1993). *Sampling Inner Experience in Disturbed Affect.*
—— (1997). 'Randomly sampling thinking in the natural environment'. *Journal of Consulting and Clinical Psychology*, 65.
—— and Heavey, C. L. (2006). *Exploring Inner Experience: the Descriptive Experience Sampling Method.*
—— and Schwitzgebel, E. (2007). *Exploring inner experience?*
——, Frappe, F., and Frith, U. (1994). 'Sampling the form of inner experience of three adults with Asperger's syndrome'. *Psychological Medicine*, 24.
Schwitzgebel, E. (2007). 'Do you have constant tactile experience of your feet in your shoes?' *Journal of Consciousness Studies*, 14.

detection See SIGNAL DETECTION THEORY

determinism See FREE WILL AND CONSCIOUSNESS

development and consciousness There is widespread agreement that the *contents of consciousness are continually in flux and likely to change in systematic ways over the course of human development. But questions about the development of consciousness itself remain controversial. At what age does a human being first become conscious? Are there different aspects, kinds, or levels of consciousness that emerge at different times? How is consciousness related to the acquisition of language? Does consciousness depend on conceptual understanding (e.g. an explicit concept of psychological states)?

In recent years, questions about the emergence of consciousness have become increasingly common, being raised in the context of debates about fetal pain and research on children's developing *theory of mind. Some scientists have suggested that the basic mechanisms for conscious *pain perception develop during the second trimester, but others have argued that fetuses are not conscious at all until the third trimester (at around 30 weeks' gestational age)—when there is clear evidence of functional neural pathways connecting the thalamus to sensory cortex. In contrast, work on children's theory of mind (i.e. their understanding of their own and others' mental states) has led to the suggestion, based on a version of *higher-order thought (HOT) theory, that most children are not conscious until at least the age of 4 years. According to HOT theory, consciousness consists in a belief about one's psychological states (i.e. a psychological state is conscious when one believes that one is in that state). A considerable body of research has shown that children do not reliably display an explicit understanding of the notion of psychological states (or subjective perspectives on an independent reality) until sometime during the fifth year of life, when they start passing standard measures of theory of mind such as the false belief task.

Obviously, views about when consciousness emerges depend on the criteria that one uses for inferring consciousness, and there are a variety of possible criteria. One way to address this problem has been to consider multiple criteria simultaneously and see whether, on balance, the evidence points to a particular age. Perner and Dienes (2003) argue that it does. These authors examined the development of three types of behaviour for which, they argued, consciousness is necessary in human adults: verbal communication (i.e. first words), executive function (e.g. planning, as indexed by combining two familiar actions into a novel sequence), and explicit memory (as indexed by delayed imitation). All three types of behaviour typically appear around the end of the first year of life, consistent with the suggestion that consciousness emerges at this age. But while many students of infant development agree that important changes occur around the first birthday, few will be comfortable (we suspect) concluding that younger infants are mere automata—capable of cognitive function but lacking sentience.

Apart from the question of when consciousness first emerges in ontogeny, the idea that consciousness itself undergoes developmental changes may be surprising. Many contemporary models characterize consciousness as an 'all-or-nothing' phenomenon (i.e. information is either available to consciousness or not). From this perspective, one might suppose that organisms are either conscious or not, and capable of consciousness or not. A more nuanced picture of the development of consciousness can be gleaned from research on children's developing self-awareness. In this context, researchers often distinguish between a first-order sensory consciousness of present sensations and an adult-like *self-consciousness, raising the possibility that sensory consciousness develops early (e.g. before birth) while self-consciousness develops later. Even so, there is disagreement about when self-consciousness emerges: although some researchers suggest that self-consciousness emerges relatively early in infancy (during the first few months), most researchers have focused on a set of behavioural changes occurring during the second half of the second year of life—when children begin to use personal pronouns, first appear to recognize themselves in *mirrors, and first display self-conscious emotions such as shame and embarrassment (see Kagan 1981 and Lewis and Ramsay 1999 for reviews).

One way to reconcile the discrepancies among accounts of the emergence of consciousness is to propose that consciousness develops gradually, in a graded fashion, as opposed to emerging full-blown in an all-or-nothing fashion. Different theorists may be focusing on the emergence of different aspects, degrees, or levels of consciousness. Indeed, there has been growing support in recent years for the suggestion that consciousness develops through a series of not just two but several dissociable levels of consciousness.

One kind of evidence for this suggestion is the existence of age-related dissociations between conscious knowledge and the ability to use that knowledge to control behaviour. Consider, for example, the performance of 3-year-olds on the Dimensional Change Card Sort. Children are shown two target cards (e.g. a blue rabbit and a red car) and asked to sort a series of bivalent test cards (e.g. red rabbits and blue cars) according to one dimension (e.g. colour). After sorting several cards, children are then told to stop playing the first game and switch to another (e.g. shape, 'Put the rabbits here; put the cars there.'). Regardless of which dimension is presented first, 3-year-olds typically continue to sort by that dimension despite being told the new rules on every trial. Moreover, they do this despite responding correctly to explicit questions about the post-switch rules. For example, children who should be sorting by shape (but persist in sorting by colour) may be asked, 'Where do the rabbits go in the shape game? And where do the cars go?' Children almost always answer these questions correctly. When they are then told to sort a test card ('Okay, good, now play the shape game: Where does this rabbit go?'), however, they persist in sorting by colour.

This type of dissociation raises the possibility that 3-year-olds consciously represent the post-switch rules at one level of consciousness (which allows them to provide verbal answers to the explicit knowledge questions), and consciously represent the pre-switch rules at that same level of consciousness (which allows them to keep the pre-switch rules in *working memory to guide their sorting). Because they fail to reflect on their representations of the two rule pairs from a higher level of consciousness, however, they cannot consider them in contradistinction and make a deliberate decision about which pair of rules to use.

By contrast, 4-year-olds, like adults, seem to recognize immediately that they know two ways of construing the stimuli. These children spontaneously reflect on their multiple perspectives on the situation, consider them from a higher level of consciousness, and integrate them into a relatively complex rule structure: 'If we're sorting by shape, then if it's a red rabbit, it goes here . . . ' The close connection between conscious reflection on rules and the use of those rules to control responding in the face of interference is underscored by the robust finding that children's performance on the Dimensional Change Card Sort is correlated with their ability to reflect on their own and others' mental states in tasks assessing theory of mind.

The discrete levels of consciousness revealed by developmental research may be useful for understanding the complex, graded structure of conscious experience in adults. What changes with age may be the highest, most developmentally sophisticated level of consciousness that one is able to muster. Within these age-related constraints, however, one may continue to operate at lower levels under some circumstances (e.g. when tired or distracted or performing routine, *automatic operations).

In an influential early proposal, Karmiloff-Smith (1992) described the way in which the level of explicitness of children's representations may vary as a function of experience in particular domains. More recently, models identifying different age-related levels of consciousness have been advanced in the context of work in several areas, including children's developing sense of themselves in time, and relatedly, children's developing capacity for autobiographical memory (see Nelson 2005). The most comphrehensive model of this type, however, is the *levels of consciousness* (LOC) model expounded by Zelazo and his colleagues (e.g. Zelazo 1999, 2004; Zelazo et al. 2007). According to the LOC model, there are at least four age-related increases in children's highest level of consciousness, and each level has distinct consequences for the quality of subjective experience, the potential for episodic recollection, the complexity of children's explicit knowledge structures, and the possibility of the conscious control of thought, emotion, and action.

Consciousness is hierarchical, according to this model. Higher levels of consciousness are brought about through the recursive reprocessing (see RE-ENTRANT PROCESSING) of the contents of consciousness via thalamocortical circuits involving regions of prefrontal cortex, which develops markedly over the course of childhood. Each degree of reprocessing recruits another region of prefrontal cortex and allows for the integration of more information into an experience of a stimulus before the experience is replaced by new intero- or exteroceptor stimulation. As a result, each additional level of consciousness results in a richer, more detailed subjective experience—one that is more likely to be remembered in the future, and more likely to figure in the conscious cognitive control of behaviour. The relation between levels of consciousness and the control of behaviour is mediated by rule use: higher levels of consciousness allow for the formulation (and maintenance in working memory) of more complex systems of if-then rules linking stimuli and responses.

The LOC model starts with the assumption that simple sentience is mediated by *minimal consciousness*, the first-order consciousness on the basis of which more complex hierarchical forms of consciousness are constructed (through degrees of reprocessing). Minimal consciousness is unreflective and present-oriented and makes no reference to an explicit sense of self; these features develop during the course of childhood. In adults, this level of consciousness corresponds to so-called *implicit information processing*, as when we drive a car without full awareness, perhaps because we are conducting a conversation at a higher level of consciousness.

According to the LOC model, minimal consciousness emerges during the third trimester of prenatal development—between about 24 and 30 weeks' gestational age—as a result of the functional development of fibres linking the thalamus to sensory cortex (and not prefrontal cortex). The onset of minimal consciousness is reflected in a variety of neural and behavioural changes occurring at this age, e.g. the first appearance of *electroencephalograph (EEG) patterns that distinguish between *sleep and wakefulness, and the first evidence of heart rate increases and habituation to vibroacoustic stimuli.

The attribution of minimal consciousness is intended to explain infant behaviour until the end of the first year, when numerous new abilities (e.g. first words and executive function) appear, as noted earlier. According to the LOC model, these new abilities are made possible changes by the emergence of a new level of consciousness—*recursive consciousness*.

In recursive consciousness, the contents of minimal consciousness at one moment are reprocessed via thalamocortical loops involving prefrontal cortex, allowing the toddler to *label* the initial contents of minimal consciousness. Because a label can be decoupled from the experience labelled, the label provides an enduring trace of that experience that can be deposited into both long-term *memory (allowing for recollection) and working memory. The contents of working memory (e.g. representations of hidden objects) can then serve as explicit goals to trigger action programmes indirectly so that the toddler is no longer restricted to responses triggered directly by minimal consciousness of an immediately present stimulus.

The emergence of subsequent levels of consciousness depends on the further growth of prefrontal cortex, allowing additional degrees of reprocessing and reflection. These levels include the emergence of *self-consciousness* during the second year of life, the emergence of *reflective consciousness 1* around age 3 years, and the emergence of *reflective consciousness 2* sometime between 4 and 5 years of age. This last transition allows children to reflect on two incompatible perspectives and integrate them into a single system of inferences—something hypothesized to underlie the important changes in children's rule use and theory of mind that occur in this age range.

Notice that language plays an important role in the development of consciousness, according to this model. Higher levels of consciousness allow for the more effective selection and manipulation of rules (i.e. they permit greater control of language in the service of thought), but they also allow children to respond more appropriately to linguistic meaning despite a potentially misleading context—increasing the extent to which language influences conscious thought. As Vygotsky (1934/1986) observed: with development, language and conscious thought become increasingly intertwined in a complex, reciprocal relation.

The LOC model is intended to provide a comprehensive account of the development of consciousness that addresses extant data, but it serves here to illustrate many of the questions that need to be asked about the way in which consciousness develops during childhood and, probably, beyond. Developmental data suggest that not only the contents of consciousness but consciousness itself may be in flux, undergoing transformations correlated with the marked changes seen in children's behaviour, on the one hand, and their brain function, on the other.

PHILIP DAVID ZELAZO AND HELENA HONG GAO

Kagan, J. (1981). *The Second Year: the Emergence of Self-Awareness.*

Karmiloff-Smith, A. (1992). *Beyond Modularity: a Developmental Perspective on Cognitive Science.*

Lewis, M. and Ramsay, D. (1999). 'Intentions, consciousness, and pretend play'. In Zelazo, P. D. et al. (eds) *Developing Theories of Intention: Social Understanding and Self-control.*

Nelson, K. (2005). 'Emerging levels of consciousness in early human development'. In Terrace, H. S. and Metcalfe, J. (eds) *The Missing Link in Cognition: Origins of Self-reflective Consciousness.*

Perner, J. and Dienes, Z. (2003). 'Developmental aspects of consciousness: how much of a theory of mind do you need to be consciously aware?' *Consciousness and Cognition*, 12.

Rochat, P. (2003). 'Five levels of self-awareness as they unfold early in life'. *Consciousness and Cognition*, 12.

Vygotsky, L. S. (1934/1986). *Thought and Language*, ed. A. Kozulin.

Zelazo, P. D. (1999). 'Language, levels of consciousness, and the development of intentional action'. In Zelazo, P. D. et al. (eds) *Developing Theories of Intention: Social Understanding and Self-control.*

—— (2004). 'The development of conscious control in childhood'. *Trends in Cognitive Sciences*, 8.

——, Gao, H. H., and Todd, R. (2007). 'The development of consciousness'. In Zelazo, P. D. et al. (eds) *Cambridge Handbook of Consciousness.*

diaphanousness See TRANSPARENCY

dissociation methods Perceptual and cognitive processes and associated mental representations cannot be directly observed or measured. Consequently, researchers attempt to infer their existence by measuring changes in brain and behaviour that are produced by variations between experimental conditions or groups. Typically, the term *dissociation* is used to denote a pattern of differential responding to experimental manipulations across several indicators of performance. Such a pattern is often considered to be evidence against theories or models which postulate that a single cognitive process or system underlies observed changes in brain and behaviour. Claimed demonstrations of unconscious influences on perception, learning, or memory are by definition set in opposition to a *single-process conscious performance model*. Indeed, findings of dissociations and related methodological paradigms constitute the cornerstone of the argument that both conscious and unconscious processes mediate observed behaviour.

During the past three decades, studies investigating dissociations between cognition and awareness have rejected the notion of a single-process conscious performance model and argued instead for models based on the distinction between explicit vs implicit processes. For example, Graf and Schacter (1985:501) stated that 'Implicit memory is revealed when performance on a task is facilitated in the absence of conscious recollection; explicit memory is revealed when performance on a task requires conscious recollection of previous experiences'. More recently, the distinction has been extended to the study of conscious vs unconscious perception, as exemplified in the following definition by Kihlstrom et al. (1992:22). 'Explicit perception refers to the person's conscious perception of some object or event in the current stimulus environment... By contrast, implicit perception is demonstrated by any change in experience, thought or action that is attributable to some event in the current stimulus field, even in the absence of conscious perception of that event'.

Similar definitions have also been proposed for implicit and explicit *knowledge. As described by Berry and Dienes (1993:2), 'explicit knowledge is said to be accessible to consciousness, and can be communicated or demonstrated on demand, whereas implicit knowledge is said to be less accessible to consciousness, and cannot be easily communicated or demonstrated on demand'. Finally, in reviewing the implicit learning literature, Shanks and St John (1994:368) pointed out that 'different authors have used a variety of definitions to capture the fine detail of the explicit/implicit learning distinction, but the key factor is the idea that implicit learning occurs without concurrent awareness of what is being learned, and represents a separate system from that which operates in more typical learning situations, where learning does proceed with concurrent awareness (i.e., explicitly)'. Thus, with respect to recollection, perception, knowledge, and learning, implicit processes are invariably defined by the absence of consciousness or awareness.

To illustrate the concept of a dissociation between cognition and awareness, consider the contrast between two phenomena: *cryptomnesia* (or unconscious plagiarism) and *confabulation* (a type of false memory). Cryptomnesia occurs when a person falsely believes they have generated a novel idea (i.e., an absence of an awareness of remembering), when in fact they are retrieving an idea that they were exposed to in the past (i.e., objective evidence of memory retrieval). Cryptomnesia occurs in a variety of fields, including music, literature, politics, and academia. For example, George Harrison was sued because his song 'My Sweet Lord' resembled a song from the 1960s, called 'He's so Fine', by the Chiffons. Although the lawsuit was successful, it was believed that Harrison's use of the song was not intentional and instead reflected an unconscious memory influence. In contrast, confabulation involves a situation in which an individual might recount a vivid, detailed, and coherent recollection (i.e., a subjective phenomenal experience of remembering), which objective evidence suggests is false (i.e., no objective recollection). Confabulations are not due to psychosis, delirium, or other mental disorders and confabulators are not lying or deliberately intending to mislead. In fact, some *brain injury patients who produced bizarre confabulations (e.g., claiming to have dated a famous movie star) strenuously insist their memories are true and accurate (e.g., Stuss et al. 1978). Taken together, cryptomnesia and confabulation constitute an impressive demonstration that objective evidence of memory retrieval and subjective awareness of remembering are distinct and dissociable.

Currently, implicit or unconscious memory research represents one of the dominant themes in the study of human memory. Underlying this surge in popularity was the development of numerous indirect or implicit memory tasks. In all of these tasks participants are not instructed to refer back to the original study phase. Instead, an effort is made to disguise the linkage between the study and test phases of the experiment.

A prototypic example of an implicit memory task is word-stem completion. In this task, participants are given word stems (e.g. DEF_ _ _) and are instructed to complete them with the first word that comes to mind. In an earlier study phase of the experiment participants are exposed to words that are potential completions for some of the stems (e.g., DEFEND). Typically, stem completion is presented as a new and unrelated task in order to disguise the link between this task and the earlier study phase of the experiment. Memory for words presented in the study phase is measured as an increase in the tendency to produce these words (as opposed to other possible completions such as DEFINE, DEFER, DEFACE, DEFRAY, etc.) as responses to the stems.

Perceptual identification is another common implicit task. Participants are presented with words during a study phase, and are then required to identify briefly flashed words at test. Perceptual identification is enhanced for recently presented study-phase words, even when participants are unaware of the link between the study and test phases. Such facilitation effects are referred to as *priming. Performance on implicit or indirect memory tasks is often compared to performance on traditional explicit memory tasks, such as recognition and recall. In explicit or direct memory tasks, participants are instructed to refer back to the study phase and to retrieve study items.

Numerous studies have compared the effects of independent variables on explicit vs implicit measures of memory in both *amnesic patients and normal subjects (for reviews see Moscovitch et al. 1993, Roediger and McDermott 1993). The basic aim of these studies was to demonstrate functional dissociations between explicit and implicit measures of memory. Briefly, a functional dissociation is observed if the nature of the effect of an experimental manipulation differs across the explicit and implicit tasks (see Dunn and Kirsner 1988 for a critique of the functional dissociation paradigm).

To illustrate this paradigm, consider a seminal early demonstration of a functional dissociation that was reported by Winnick and Daniel (1970). In this study, performance in an explicit recall task was contrasted with performance in an implicit perceptual identification task. During the study phase of the experiment participants either read words or generated words from pictures and definitions. Generated words were better recalled than read words. In marked contrast, read words were better identified than generated words. Such a pattern of results in which an experimental manipulation (e.g., generate vs read) produced opposite effects on an explicit vs an implicit task is referred to as a double dissociation and is considered by many investigators to be a conclusive demonstration of processing without conscious awareness (but see Dunn and Kirsner 1988 for a counter-argument).

In addition to the functional dissociation paradigm, several other methodologies were developed in order to document unconscious/implicit influences on cognition including the process dissociation procedure (see MEMORY, PROCESS-DISSOCIATION PROCEDURE), stochastic independence, reverse association, and the relative sensitivity paradigm (see Roediger and McDermott 1993 for a review). An examination of these paradigms is beyond the scope of this entry. Instead, we focus on the classic dissociation paradigm, as it constitutes the most influential methodological framework designed for investigating perception, learning, or memory without awareness. This paradigm establishes three prerequisites for demonstrating unconscious cognition: (1) a valid measure of cognitive information available to consciousness must be selected, and compared with another measure of cognitive processing; (2) the measure of conscious awareness indicates null sensitivity, or null awareness; and (3) the second measure of cognitive processing must be shown to have greater than zero sensitivity. Although the logic underlying the classic dissociation paradigm is relatively straightforward, research guided by this framework resulted in widespread controversy. Specifically, the same empirical findings that some researchers argue provide little or no evidence for unconscious processing are considered by others as conclusive and overwhelming proof of performance without conscious awareness. To better understand this puzzling state of affairs, some of the issues underlying the controversy are briefly outlined here (for a more thorough discussion see Reingold and Merikle 1990, Reingold and Toth 1996).

Much of the long-standing controversy surrounding the study of unconscious processing revolves around the lack of a general consensus as to what constitutes an adequate operational definition of conscious awareness. In the absence of an agreed-upon operational definition of consciousness, a variety of measures have been, often arbitrarily, used as indicators of conscious awareness. Two general approaches to the measurement of conscious awareness were used in the context of the classic dissociation paradigm: the subjective approach employing a subjective report or *claimed awareness* measure, and the objective approach that defines awareness in terms of performance on tasks that measure perceptual or cognitive discriminations.

The *subjective approach* is based on the idea that conscious content is accessible to *introspection and as such participants can meaningfully report on their subjective phenomenal awareness in general, and on their confidence that they possess task relevant information, in particular. For example, in the earliest studies of unconscious perception, the behavioural measure used to index conscious awareness was based simply on an individual's subjective confidence that they detected or could identify briefly presented or degraded stimulus information. The results of these studies, as well as subsequent investigations, provided ample evidence that observers can make above-chance perceptual discriminations even when they report that their perceptual experiences are inadequate to guide their choices and that they are simply guessing. In fact, perception in the absence of claimed awareness is a relatively easy phenomenon to demonstrate, and the phenomenon is so robust that Adams (1957), who reviewed many of the early studies in this area, suggested its use as a classroom demonstration (see PERCEPTION, UNCONSCIOUS).

Even more dramatic demonstrations of perception, learning, and memory without subjective confidence are based on observations of cortically blind and amnesic patients. Specifically, case studies of brain injury patients with lesions in their visual cortex that result in scotomas (blind regions) in their visual field demonstrate that such patients perform perceptual discriminations (e.g. detection, location, orientation) concerning stimuli presented in their blind field well above chance, while at the same time proclaiming to be purely guessing. This phenomenon has been termed *blindsight (see Weiskrantz 1986 for a review). Similarly, the amnesic syndrome constitutes a powerful demonstration of retention in the absence of reported subjective phenomenal awareness of remembering (see Moscovitch et al. 1993 for a review). Consider the famous case of H. M. who became amnesic after an operation was performed in order to alleviate his epilepsy attacks by bilaterally removing parts of his temporal lobes. As a result of his surgery, H. M. became severely amnesic and seemingly unable to commit new material to memory. For example, after his operation he was very poor at learning the names or recognizing the faces of people he met, or at remembering an article he read just hours before. However, upon closer examination, H. M. was found to have retained information for experiences that occurred following his surgery. This preserved learning capacity by H. M. included, for example, the ability to learn the mirror-drawing task. In this task the participants must carefully trace the outline of shapes (e.g. a star) while viewing their hands and the shapes through a mirror. H. M. performed this task on consecutive sessions. Although at the beginning of each session he strongly denied having performed this task before, his performance improved across sessions.

However, the measurement of conscious awareness solely in terms of subjective reports has been often criticized. This is because it is difficult to know what criteria individuals use to decide that they are guessing. Statements indicating an absence of subjective confidence may only reflect an individual's own theories of how their subjective experience guides their behaviour rather than a true absence of task relevant conscious information. For example, some participants who report null awareness may disregard having conscious access to partial or degraded information regarding a stimulus or an event, while other participants may use such information as the basis for reporting awareness of perceiving a stimulus or remembering an event. Another factor that may negatively impact the validity of subjective report is the tendency of participants to respond on the basis of what they perceive to be the goals or expectations of the experimenter. This tendency is referred to as *demand characteristics*. It is therefore likely that subjective report, at least on some occasions, may fail to reflect all of the relevant information that is accessible to consciousness. Thus, the validity of the subjective report approach to the measurement of awareness critically depends on distinguishing between the participants' response bias, affected by factors such as preconceived notions and demand characteristics, and their subjective phenomenal experience.

Given the problems associated with subjective confidence as a measure of awareness, many researchers instead measure conscious awareness by asking participants to make discriminative responses concerning relevant stimulus information. This approach is often referred to as the *objective approach* to the measurement of awareness to distinguish it from the subjective approach described above. For example, in recent investigations of unconscious perception, typical indices used to measure awareness are forced-choice discriminations among a small set of stimulus alternatives or present–absent decisions, which require participants to distinguish between the presence of a stimulus and a null stimulus. Methodologically, measures of discriminative responding have an important advantage over measures based on subjective reports. This is because measures of discriminative capacity allow the assessment of perceptual sensitivity with considerable precision, and independent of any possible influence of response bias.

Unfortunately, robust and replicable findings of unconscious processing under conditions of chance-level discriminative capacity have proved very difficult to obtain. For example, both Eriksen (1960) and Holender (1986) forcefully advocated for the use of the objective approach to the measurement of awareness and, after extensively reviewing the literature on unconscious perception, concluded that there was no convincing evidence for perception in the absence of discriminative responding. Consequently, these authors argued in favour of a single-process conscious perception model. A similar conclusion has been reached by Shanks and St John (1994) in their review of the literature on learning without awareness.

The most important problem with the objective approach to the measurement of awareness is that it involves a one-to-one mapping of tasks and processes. Specifically, above-chance discrimination performance is considered a necessary and sufficient condition for establishing conscious awareness. However, discriminative responding may constitute a valid measure of awareness if and only if it is influenced exclusively by conscious processing. If, on the other hand, a measure of discriminative responding is sensitive to both conscious and unconscious information, then equating awareness with discriminative responding may result in at best underestimating the magnitude unconscious processing, and at worst defining it out of existence.

Thus, neither the subjective and the objective approaches to the measurement of awareness can be justified on an a priori basis. Given that a valid measure of conscious awareness is a vital prerequisite for the use of the classic dissociation paradigm, employing this paradigm in the absence of such a measure is clearly problematic; hence the ensuing controversy. Specifically, whether strong evidence of processing without awareness is obtained crucially depends upon how awareness is operationally defined. While processing in the absence of subjective confidence is a very robust phenomenon, evidence of unconscious processing under conditions that establish chance discrimination has been elusive.

What appears on the surface to be a debate over empirical findings is more often a reflection of differences in implicit theoretical starting points or assumptions. To interpret any obtained dissociation as evidence for unconscious processing, such a measure must be assumed to be sensitive to all task-relevant conscious information. In addition, to interpret the absence of a dissociation as evidence against processing without awareness, the selected measure of conscious awareness must be assumed to be sensitive only to conscious, but not unconscious, task-relevant information. In their critique of the classic dissociation paradigm, Reingold and Merikle (1988, 1990) termed these assumptions the *exhaustiveness assumption* and the *exclusiveness assumption* respectively. The controversy and polarization concerning the validity of unconscious processing is a direct consequence of the relative emphasis assigned to the exhaustiveness and the exclusiveness assumptions by different investigators. The problematic aspect of the subjective approach to the measurement of conscious awareness is related primarily to a failure to satisfy the exhaustiveness assumption, while a failure to satisfy the exclusiveness assumption underlies the interpretive problems associated with the objective approach.

The idea that cognitive processes can be meaningfully classified as conscious or unconscious has a long history in philosophy and psychology. However, the empirical explorations of the conscious–unconscious distinction have been marred by a preoccupation with trying to prove or disprove the existence of the unconscious and by the quest for a theory-free methodological silver bullet. Progress in the study of the relation between consciousness and cognition will require going beyond existence proofs and towards the development of multiple conceptual and methodological frameworks in order to converge upon a satisfactory exploration of this complex and controversial topic. No amount of methodological rigour could replace the urgent need for the development of more comprehensive theoretical frameworks that would provide testable predictions and guide future research in a fruitful direction.

EYAL M. REINGOLD AND HEATHER SHERIDAN

Adams, J. K. (1957). 'Laboratory studies of behavior without awareness'. *Psychological Bulletin*, 54.

Berry, D. C. and Dienes, Z. (1993). *Implicit Learning: Theoretical and Empirical Issues*.

Dunn, J. D. and Kirsner, K. (1988). 'Discovering functionally independent mental processes: the principle of reversed association'. *Psychological Review*, 95.

Eriksen, C. (1960). 'Discrimination and learning without awareness: a methodological survey and evaluation'. *Journal of Psychological Review*, 67.

Graf, P. and Schacter, D. L. (1985). 'Implicit and explicit memory for new associations in normal and amnesic subjects'. *Journal of Experimental Psychology: Learning, Memory, and Cognition*, 11.

Holender, D. (1986). 'Semantic activation without conscious identification in dichotic listening, parafoveal vision, and visual masking: a survey and appraisal'. *Behavioral and Brain Sciences*, 9.

Kihlstrom, J. F., Barnhardt, T. M., and Tataryn, D. J. (1992). 'Implicit perception'. In Bornstein, R. F. and Pittman, T. S. (eds) *Perception Without Awareness: Cognitive, Clinical, and Social Perspectives*.

Moscovitch, M., Vriezen, E. R., and Goshen-Gottstein, J. (1993). 'Implicit tests of memory in patients with focal lesions or degenerative brain disorders'. In Spinnler, H. and Boller, F. (eds) *Handbook of Neuropsychology*, Vol. 8.

Reingold, E. and Merikle, P. (1988). 'Using direct and indirect measures to study perception without awareness'. *Perception and Psychophysics*, 44.

—— —— (1990). 'On the inter-relatedness of theory and measurement in the study of unconscious processes'. *Mind and Language*, 5.

—— and Toth, J. P. (1996). 'Process dissociations versus task dissociations: a controversy in progress'. In Underwood, G. (ed.) *Implicit Cognition*.

Roediger, H. L. and McDermott, K. B. (1993). 'Implicit memory in normal human subjects'. In Spinnler, H. and Boller, F. (eds) *Handbook of Neuropsychology*, Vol. 8.

Shanks, D. R. and St John, M. F. (1994). 'Characteristics of dissociable human learning systems'. *Behavioral and Brain Sciences*, 17.

Stuss, D. T., Alexander, M. P., Lieberman, A., and Levine, H. (1978). 'An extraordinary form of confabulation'. *Neurology*, 28.

Weiskrantz, L. (1986). *Blindsight*.

Winnick, W. A. and Daniel, S. A. (1970). 'Two kinds of response priming in tachistoscopic word recognition'. *Journal of Experimental Psychology*, 84.

dissociative identity disorder Formerly known as *multiple personality disorder*, dissociative identity disorder (DID) is a pathological disturbance in which individuals seem to split into two or more simultaneously existing, and relatively independent, centres of *self-consciousness. Among clinicians who accept the DID diagnosis as legitimate, the received view is that this disorder has two principal causes. The first is a capacity for profound dissociation; significantly, DID patients tend to be highly *hypnotizable. The second is a history of childhood trauma, often severe or chronic, and in many cases apparently connected with a combination of emotional, physical, or sexual abuse.

As virtuosic dissociators, DID patients seem to have a distinctive way of dealing with intolerable pain or trauma. To put it roughly, they create an alternate identity (or *alter*) to experience the pain or trauma in their place. When these alters assume executive control of the body, the previous host identity might experience periods of 'lost time', and in some cases the differences between alters can be extreme. They might differ in age, gender, and personality type, and as they spend more time in executive control of the body, the more complex and well-rounded they tend to become. Moreover, some DID patients, especially those subject to chronic trauma or abuse, learn to use dissociation as an habitual coping strategy. And when that happens, they might begin to create alters under less extreme provocation—e.g. to deal with relatively minor stress and annoyances. As a result, some alters of these patients seem only to be personality fragments created for very specific tasks, such as cleaning toilets or baking cookies. Trauma victims who lack this dissociative coping mechanism might instead develop different types of disorders, e.g. less dramatic forms of sexual dysfunction.

Some have argued that DID is a purely iatrogenic phenomenon, and that the formation of alters is simply a form of social compliance, possibly to conform with popular conceptions of psychopathology, but usually in response to naive therapists on the lookout for the disorder. No doubt this is true in some cases. However, DID has been documented in many patients who have never been in therapy, including children who do not know the relevant literature and who also have a documented history of trauma or abuse.

On the surface, of course, it appears that DID demonstrates a profound form of psychological disunity. A single patient may seem to contain several distinct identities, of different ages and genders, and with their own sets of agendas, interests, abilities, perceptions, and even physical characteristics. In fact, some but not all alters may require optical prescriptions, or be resistant to certain drugs, or have food allergies. And some but not all alters might be talented artistically, or mathematically, or have a gift for languages. Furthermore, some alters clearly try to kill off others in their alter system, apparently quite unaware that this 'internal homicide' would be lethal to them as well.

Moreover, while some alters seem to be unaware of other alters' perceptions or thoughts and feelings, certain alters seem to know what others are experiencing or doing. As a result, it is difficult to generalize about the structure of these alter-systems, except to say that in many cases that structure can be quite complex. In fact, DID patients occasionally appear to exhibit a form of *co-presence*, in which two alters seem simultaneously to exert some executive control. This could be manifest in dramatic actions in which patients appear to battle with themselves (à la Dr Strangelove), or perhaps in peculiar testimony regarding apparently partial integration (as when a patient once said to me, 'I'm mostly Jane right now'.)

Ever since multiple personality was first diagnosed in the late 19th century, some have thought that the disorder reveals a deep pre-existing disunity in the self, one whose nature somehow correlates with the divisions presented by the alter system. For example, Ribot remarked, 'Seeing how the Self is broken up, we can understand how it comes to be'. However, this position seems to commit what Braude has called the *Humpty Dumpty fallacy*. Certainly, it is not a general truth that things always split along some pre-existing grain, or that objects divide only into their historically original components. To put it another way, just because we find something now in pieces, it does not follow that those pieces correspond to pre-existing or natural elements of that thing. For example, I can break a table in half with an axe, but it would be a mistake to conclude that the table resulted initially from the uniting of those two pieces. Similarly, Humpty Dumpty's fall might have broken him into 40 pieces, but there is no reason to think that Humpty was originally assembled and united out of 40 parts, much less those particular 40 parts. In fact, some types of splitting are clearly evolutionary, such as cell division, which creates entities that did not exist before.

Thus it seems that, in order to argue for the pre-dissociative disunity or complexity of the self, one must show that it is required to explain *non-dissociative* phenomena. Otherwise, one can always contend, quite plausibly, that alter identities are products, and not prerequisites, of the extreme dissociation found in DID.

One familiar strategy is to use a type of argument, probably first employed by Plato and later used notoriously by Freud, which appeals to the law of non-contradiction to establish the existence of functionally distinct—and conscious—elements of the soul or mind. Roughly, the idea is that since a thing cannot have contradictory properties, a person's internal conflicts cannot be assigned to a single conscious subject. But this is a very contentious dialectical strategy, and it can be challenged on numerous grounds. These range from finding plausible ways to describe the conflicts so that they are not literally contradictory, to questioning the viability or applicability of the law of non-contradiction in these contexts.

It is certainly tempting to describe DID patients in terms of functionally distinct agents and subjects (as it were) inhabiting a single body. And to some extent, that is undoubtedly accurate. After all, different alters have different agendas and interests, they apparently exist at distinct developmental stages, and as they become more complex and well-rounded, it is clear that they have different personalities. These differences are so pronounced that people close to DID patients (such as family members) establish distinct relationships with different alters, just as they would with other people. For example, they might give them different gifts at Christmas, treat some like children and others as adults, trust some and distrust others, etc. Moreover, even when alters have introspective access to the mental states of other alters, their reports and behaviour indicate it is from a different subjective point of view. For example, alter *A* may think, 'I want to go shopping', and alter *B* may simultaneously be aware that *A* wants to go shopping. Even more dramatically, *A* might think 'I want to prevent *B* from controlling the body', and *B* might simultaneously be aware that *A* wants to prevent it from controlling the body. Understandably, then, many suppose that alters are best explained with respect to functionally distinct modules of the brain or mind.

Nevertheless, there are reasons for thinking that even the profound splitting of DID presupposes a deeper functional unity. And that unity can be of two sorts. The first is *diachronic* unity (i.e., continuity), linking one experience to subsequent experiences—e.g. connecting the parts of a sentence or melody. The second is *synchronic* unity, connecting simultaneous parts of experience—e.g. hearing a melody *while* driving a car.

DID patients seem to be fundamentally unified in both respects. There are many reasons for saying this, but perhaps the most important are (a) the overlapping and interlocking abilities of different alters, and (b) the adaptational nature of alter formation and maintenance.

In the first case, the issue is that an alter's capacities, abilities, traits, skills, etc. are not literally isolable features of a person, and as a result, an alter's characteristic functions inevitably overlap those of other alters in many respects. Thus it seems reasonable to regard an alter's idiosyncratic set of abilities, traits, etc. as drawn from a common pool of dispositions and capacities most plausibly attributed to the multiple as a whole. So although two alters might have distinctive sets of dispositions and capacities, it seems most plausible to suppose they share the numerically same capacity (say) to count, speak a language, understand jokes, feel compassion, drive a car, etc.

As far as (b) is concerned, once an alter identity is created, with its distinctive set of memories and other dispositions, those dispositions must be *maintained*. Moreover, they must be maintained in the face of situations that conflict with them. For example, suppose a patient dissociates the memory of sexual abuse by a parent and erects a sexually promiscuous alter identity to minimize the horror of sexual encounters generally. Now to keep the memory of abuse functionally isolated, the patient will need to reconstruct her past and creatively (and perhaps constantly) reinterpret present events in order to obscure the nature of that painful episode. For example, this might involve interpreting the parent's continued sexual advances or innuendos as non-sexual, or deflecting inquiries from those who suspect that abuse had occurred. But these strategies seem to make most sense when assigned to a *single* underlying subject who orchestrated the initial dissociative split, who experiences the relevant conflicts, and who takes steps to resolve them.

In fact, this is exactly how most would interpret the coping strategies of ordinary hypnotized subjects (e.g. experiencing negative *hallucinations) who contrive ways to preserve suggested *illusions in the face of events that tend to undermine them. This parallel between dissociation in DID and in less dramatic dissociative phenomena is reinforced by two considerations: first, that DID patients seem significantly hypnotizable compared to non-DID patients, and second, that DID is plausibly understood as lying at the far end of various continua of dissociative phenomena, ranked (say) in terms of severity of symptoms and degree of functional isolation, but all the others of which would be naturally interpreted as dispositions assigned to a single dissociative subject.

STEPHEN. E. BRAUDE

Braude, S. E. (1995). *First Person Plural: Multiple Personality and the Philosophy of Mind.*

Hacking, I. (1995). *Rewriting the Soul: Multiple Personality and the Sciences of Memory.*

Humphrey, N. and Dennett, D. C. (1989). 'Speaking for ourselves: an assessment of multiple personality disorder.' *Raritan: a Quarterly Review*, 9.

Radden, J. (1996). *Divided Minds and Successive Selves.*

Ribot, T. (1887). *Diseases of Personality.*

Wilkes, K. V. (1988). *Real People: Personal Identity Without Thought Experiments.*

divided attention See ATTENTION AND AWARENESS

dorsal stream See VISUAL STREAMS: WHAT VS HOW

dreaming, lucid Lucid dreams are dreams in which the dreamer is aware that she is having a dream. Lucidity, or awareness that one is dreaming, is somewhat unstable and easily lost and may wax and wane several times during a dream (Green 1968). Thus, rather than speaking of *lucid dreams* we should perhaps speak of *periods of lucidity within dreams*. Awareness often comes suddenly, as a revelation, in the midst of a conventional dream, often brought about by the recognition of some oddity in the dream. Flying in dreams is clearly one of the most radical violations of the physical laws of the waking world and it is tempting to imagine that it is such extreme deviations from the waking world that capture the attention of the dreamer. Flying episodes most often follow lucidity, however, rather than preceding it (Green 1968). Indeed, the subtlety of many of the anomalies that lead to lucidity is quite remarkable. One of the early lucid dreamers describes a dream of exquisite detail, in which he becomes lucid when he notices that the paving stones outside his home appear to have changed their orientation (Fox 1962). For many, the cue may not even be anything specifically odd, but simply some subtle implausibility. Van Eeden (1913), who coined the term lucid dreaming, was convinced that there was something 'wrong' with the pattern of a carpet. Although he admitted that it was impossible to define what was wrong with the carpet, he was none the less convinced beyond doubt by this that he was dreaming. Conversely, dreamers often notice quite bizarre features of dreams without becoming lucid (Green 1968, McCarley and Hoffman 1981).

Upon becoming aware, lucid dreamers typically attempt to direct their dreams, with varying success. So common is this that some have claimed that the definition of lucidity should include control over the dream (e.g. Tart 1988). Nonetheless, awareness that one is dreaming seems quite adequate for a definition and the issue of control exercised in the dream a matter for empirical investigation. One can certainly be very much aware without having very much control—dreaming or awake! In any case, attempts to control aspects of dreams are quite variable in their success and occasionally lead to quite surprising results (Green 1968). One might speak separately, however, of 'guided' dreams (Saint-Denys 1982). An interesting feature of control in lucid dreams is that of delayed control and causality. Van Eeden reports trying unsuccessfully to break a glass and notices, a few moments later, that the glass is broken. Perhaps the best-known anomaly of control is the *light switch phenomenon* in which the flipping of a light switch leads to delayed or attenuated light onset or, as has been experienced by the present author, results in the shower turning on!

Lucid dreaming has acquired something of a cult status as a royal road to creativity, spiritual enlightenment, and a portal to higher realities. Lucid dreams are sometimes claimed to achieve a remarkable degree of clarity exceeding anything experienced even in the wake world. Not surprisingly, lucid dreaming has been embraced by New Age mystics, astral travellers, and the like, and there is no shortage of techniques and technologies claiming to promote lucid dreaming. In contrast, the scholarly and scientific community has tended to view lucid dreams with considerable scepticism. Nevertheless, rather convincing experimental demonstrations of lucid dreaming do exist. In independent research programmes, expert lucid dreamers Keith Hearne and Steven LaBerge developed techniques enabling lucid dreamers to communicate with researchers while being electrophysiologically monitored during lucid dreaming. In numerous studies they convincingly demonstrated lucid dreamers' awareness both of dreams and of external signals delivered to them while dreaming. In addition, good evidence exists that lucid dreaming appears to be strongly associated with REM *sleep and that time duration estimates (in the order of seconds at least) in lucid dreams are very similar to those of waking (LaBerge 1985). Additional observations and claims have been made about enhanced ability to reason clearly, to formulate and act on plans, and to remember specifics of one's waking life during lucid dreaming (LaBerge 2000).

Frequent claims to the contrary notwithstanding, however, the quality of thinking in lucid dreams often seems every bit as bizarre as in non-lucid dreams. Worsley has puzzled over his ambiguous lucidity (Worsley 1988). In one study he was attempting to carry out experimental tasks while lucidly dreaming and being monitored in a sleep lab. In the lucid dream he was outside in the rain and worried about the equipment in the lab getting wet because of the rain. In another series, the equipment was set up to enable him to electrically stimulate his forearm by signalling eye movements. He was puzzled during the dream because, although the stimuli felt like electrical stimulation, he decided that this was not possible because, in the dream, he was walking down the street unattached to the machine. The appearance of his dream world appeared to override the distinct sensation of the electrical stimulations; stimulations that were, moreover, entirely consistent with his expectations. Thus, it turns out to be quite difficult to 'bracket' the dream experience, even when lucid. Arnold-Forster (1921) reports a dream of espionage in which she found herself in great danger. She was torn between using her lucid skills to terminate the dream to avoid the 'danger' and, even more oddly, her sense of duty to stay and expose some traitors. Green describes another lucid dreamer who spends much time, in a lucid dream, trying to convince his mother of the reality of lucid dreams. To prove his point, he informs her that this is a lucid dream! Such examples could be multiplied. It is also rather common for people to 'test' their dreams by rather dramatic, not to say bizarre, gestures such as jumping out of windows (e.g. Fox 1962) to see if one will simply float down to the ground. The present author, perhaps hedging his bets, attempted to throw his wife out a window in a test of what, fortunately, turned out to be indeed a lucid dream. Happily, no reports of disconfirmation in such experiments have been recorded. In must be admitted that many decades of research in cognitive psychology have revealed that even under optimal waking conditions humans are often irrational, careless, and muddled thinkers, as well as inattentive to significant environmental events. Such observations should not, however, be taken to blind us to the fact that such limitations are greatly exacerbated by altered states of intoxication, infection, and dreaming.

Though it seems doubtful that lucid dreaming represents a portal to a truer reality or a higher plane of thought, there do seem to be grounds for considering it a unique mode of consciousness: a mixed state straddling waking and dreaming. Consistent with this view, lucid dreams tend rapidly to devolve into, or emerge from, waking, non-lucid dreaming, false awakenings, and sleep paralysis (Green 1968, LaBerge 2000). This observation, in turn, is consistent with the association of lucid dreaming with very active (phasic) REM states. In such unstable states, slight increases in activation levels would rapidly lead to waking and slight decreases to non-lucid dreams. Nonetheless, LaBerge (2000) has argued vigorously that lucid dreaming represents a useful technique for hypothesis testing. One intriguing, and potentially critical, hypothesis about lucid dreaming itself to be tested is that the very high levels of REM activation during lucid dreaming might be associated with partial reactivation of the dorsolateral prefrontal cortex (Kahn and Hobson 2005), which is generally associated with executive functions and normally deactivated during REM (e.g. Maquet et al. 1996). Such partial activation would be consistent with the ambiguous and unstable awareness of lucid dreaming.

JAMES A. CHEYNE

Arnold-Forster, M. (1921). *Studies in Dreams.*

Green, C. E. (1968). *Lucid Dreams.*

Fox, O. (1962). *Astral Projection.*

Kahn, D. and Hobson, J. A. (2005). 'State-dependent thinking: a comparison of waking and dreaming thought'. *Consciousness and Cognition*, 14.

LaBerge, S. (1985). *Lucid Dreaming.*

—— (2000). 'Lucid dreaming: evidence and methodology'. *Behavioral and Brain Sciences*, 23.

Maquet, P., Péters, J.-M., Aerts, J., Delfiore, G., Degueldre, C., Luxen, A., and Franck, G. (1996). 'Functional neuroanatomy of human rapid-eye-movement sleep and dreaming'. *Nature*, 383.

McCarley, R. W. and Hoffman, E. (1981). 'REM sleep dreams and the activation-synthesis hypothesis'. *American Journal of Psychiatry*, 138.

Saint-Denys, H. de (1867/1982). *Dreams and How to Guide Them*, ed. M. Schatzman transl. N. Fry.

Tart, C. T. (1988). 'From spontaneous event to lucidity: A review of attempts to consciously control nocturnal dreaming'. In Wolman, B. (ed.) *Handbook of Dreams: Research, Theories and Applications.*

Van Eeden, F. (1913/1969). 'A study of dreams'. In Tart, C. T. (ed.) *Altered States of Consciousness.*

Worsley, A. (1988). 'Personal experiences in lucid dreaming'. In Gackenbach, J. and LaBerge, S. (eds) *Conscious Mind, Sleeping Brain: Perspectives On Lucid Dreaming.*

dreaming, philosophical perspectives Having fascinated some of the greatest philosophers from the earliest times, dreaming figures importantly in the history of philosophy, as in Plato's *Theaetetus*, Augustine's *Confessions*, and, perhaps most famously, Descartes's *Meditations*. By far the greatest philosophical focus on dreaming has been epistemic: Socrates suggests to Theaetetus that since he cannot tell whether he is dreaming, he cannot trust his senses to know contingent facts about the world around him. And a similar worry drives Descartes's radical doubt in the *First Meditation*. We might think that dream scepticism is, among the radical Cartesian sceptical scenarios, a particularly worrying one, since dreams, unlike evil demons, are a commonplace of everyday life.

In more recent years, philosophers have challenged some of the assumptions implicit in arguments for dream scepticism. A thorough evaluation of these challenges touches on many interesting and difficult philosophical questions; the survey we offer here will highlight connections between dreaming and contemporary philosophical questions about consciousness, imagination, and scepticism.

1. Do dreams involve experiences?
2. Dreaming and imagination
3. The imagination model and scepticism

1. Do dreams involve experiences?

The sceptical problem posed by dreaming threatens to impugn knowledge derived from sensory experience: you cannot know there is a book before you because the sensory experiences on which you would base a belief to that effect might be the result of a dream. An essential assumption, then, is that dreams sometimes do cause such experiences. This is certainly the received view; most philosophical and psychological discussion of dreams through history has found the idea that dreams involve experiences to be so obvious as to be barely worth mentioning. But this assumption did receive a philosophical challenge in the 20th century.

The earliest sustained challenge to the assumption that dreaming involved experience came in Norman Malcolm's book, *Dreaming* (Malcolm 1962). Malcolm, developing ideas from Wittgenstein, found the idea of dream experience to be paradoxical—dream experience is thought to occur during *sleep, but sleep is by definition an unconscious state. And to experience a dream while unconscious is, Malcolm thought, a contradiction. Malcolm's argument depends on Wittgensteinian ideas about criteria. To understand the sense of 'dreaming' language, we consider what sort of criterion there could be for sentences like 'Susan dreamt that she was inside a factory'. The only criterion, according to Malcolm, is Susan's waking report after the fact—'I was inside a factory'. But this is a waking criterion—it tells us only of a false memory she has upon waking; it does not entail anything about Susan's alleged experience during sleep. It is, Malcolm suggested, a mere grammatical accident that we describe Susan as having had an experience while asleep.

Few contemporary thinkers have been much impressed by Malcolm's argument. It strikes most as both illicitly verificationist and psychologically naive (Malcolm did not much appreciate incipient psychological data indicating that dreams are particularly associated with REM [rapid eye-movement] sleep, going some way to explain how dream experience arises.) Nevertheless, Malcolm can be seen at least to raise an epistemic question about the nature of dreams by suggesting a possible alternative explanation for dream experience—one that competes with the received one: perhaps sleeping really is an *unconscious*—in the strong sense—state, and dream reports are the results of new memories (false ones) that we acquire upon waking. It is not trivial to find reasons favouring one view over the other. Proponents of the received view may take some solace in the structural similarities between Malcolm's challenge and more radical sceptical questions about memory—we may ask quite generally how we know some past experience to have occurred, pressing the sceptical threat that we merely acquired some (false) memory to that effect. (Compare: perhaps no one ever experiences excruciating pain; instead, certain kinds of physical damage result in *false memories of having experienced* excruciating pain.) Presumably there is an answer to this general sceptical question; one may hope that it will generalize to the case of dreaming.

Dennett (1976) argued, on independent grounds, for something like Malcolm's approach to dreaming. Dennett was struck by dreams that seem to develop gradually and deliberately to a particular sort of ending, which then correlates with a real-world experience that awakens the dreamer. For example, a subject might dream about adventures on a pirate ship: he dreams that the crew turns against him, and forces him to walk the plank; just as he falls into the ocean in his dream, he wakes up as the result of a splash of cold water to his face. The striking thing about this sort of dream, to Dennett, is that the narrative of the dream seems too temporally extended to explain the connection between the real-life water and the extended water-themed story. Dennett suggests that this sort of dream is best explained by a denial of the received view that dreams involve experiences that occur over time during sleep; instead, dreams involve an unconscious 'memory-loading' that is activated upon waking. This memory-loading, Dennett, thinks, may occur extremely quickly, immediately prior to waking—this explains why the whole dream seems sensitive to the waking conditions.

However, Dennett admits that his evidence for the prevalence of such 'premeditated' dreams is anecdotal, and philosophical and psychological discussion of dreaming has, for the most part, retained the assumption that dreaming involves some sort of experience.

2. Dreaming and imagination

But the sceptical threat from dreams requires more than the assumption that dreaming involves some kind of experience—the assumption is that the dream can cause the same kind of experience that we have while waking; that this very experience I am having now might have been the result of a dream. This conception of dream experience has been the subject of contemporary attack, with the best-articulated critiques having come from Colin McGinn and Ernest Sosa, each of whom emphasizes similarities between dream experience and imaginative experience, suggesting that the former is more different from waking experience than has been historically appreciated.

McGinn emphasizes the distinction between the kind of sensory experience we undergo when perceiving or hallucinating—*percepts*—and **imagery*. Imagery is the product of an act of imagination, and does not purport to provide an imprint of the external world. With this distinction in mind, McGinn suggests, we will find reason to categorize the percept-like experience of dreams as imagery, and therefore a significantly different sort of conscious experience than we have while engaged in waking perception. He thinks, for instance, that the coherence of the dream narrative could only be explained by its genesis in an intelligent agency; and imagery, unlike percept, is the kind of thing that comes about as the product of agency. For more his several arguments, see McGinn (2004:Ch. 6).

It is tempting to think that the answer to this question about what sort of experience dreaming involves is to be found in neuroscience; this is right to an extent, but the role of conceptual investigation should not be underestimated. Even granted all the facts about brain activity during dreaming, there is still a place to question, for any given neural state, whether that state realizes percepts or imagery. Defenders of the orthodox view, on which dream experience is very much like waking experience, sometimes emphasize neural similarities between dream experience and perception. Thus, Hobson (2003:108) writes: '[Positron emission tomography studies]... show an *increase* in activation of just those multimodal regions of the brain that one would expect to be activated in hallucinatory perception.... In other words, in REM sleep—compared with waking—hallucination is enhanced.' But it is not clear that the body of data Hobson points to favours the claim that dream experience is percept over the competing hypothesis that it is imagery; after all, subjects who are simulating perceptual experience—who are engaging with visual imagery—may also exhibit similar neural patterns to those actually undergoing the corresponding perceptual stimuli.

If McGinn is right, and dream experience is imagistic, not perceptual, then it is natural to wonder why we seem so often to be deceived by our dreams; why do we believe the contents of our dreams, when they are presented to us so differently from the way in which our waking experience presents the world around us? McGinn's answer is that dreams cause a kind of systematic irrationality; our dream comprises a brief period of temporary insanity, during which we believe that which we imagine seeing.

But this is not the only option; we need not attribute such widespread, nightly irrationality. As Ernest Sosa has emphasized, there is room to question the assumption that we believe the contents of the dream at all. Just as, when a person dreams that he is being chased by a lion, it does not follow that it is true that he is being chased by a lion, so might we question whether one truly believes oneself to be chased, merely in virtue of dreaming that one is chased (or dreaming that one believes oneself to be chased). Perhaps our dreamer is not deceived at all.

At any given time, nearly all one's beliefs remain latent. A belief might be manifest when formed, or it might occasionally rise to consciousness from storage. To make one's belief explicit is to *judge* or *assent* or *avow*, at least to oneself. One does of course retain countless beliefs while asleep and dreaming. So, one knows as one dreams that one is in bed; one lay down in the knowledge that one would be there for hours, and this knowledge has not been lost. One retains, as one drifts off to sleep, beliefs about the layout of the room, e.g. the location of one's shoes, or the alarm clock, and so on. It is hard to see how one could then concurrently believe that one is being chased by a lion, rather than lying in bed, with the shoes a certain distance and direction from where one lies.

Is there something special about belief, such that dream beliefs are granted status as real beliefs, even though dream lions are not real lions? One might think that the deliberate, mental nature of dreaming might explain such a connection—perhaps anything as deliberate and internally grounded as a belief would have to really occur in order for it to occur in the dream. But a normative argument suggests otherwise; consider intentions. In a dream you covet your neighbour's wife, in the dream a sultry object of desire. Do you then violate the biblical injunction? If, in the dream, you go so far as to succumb, are you then subject to blame? Having sinned in your heart, not only in your dream, but in actuality, you could hardly escape discredit. Is one then blameworthy for choices made in a dream? Augustine (*Confessions X*) thought not; if he was right, then we must think carefully about whether dream intentions really imply actual intentions. And if they do not, it is not clear why beliefs should be importantly different in this respect.

A thorough investigation of the question of whether dreams involve beliefs would require as its starting point a theory of belief—something well beyond our present scope. However, it is worth noting that some plausible necessary conditions on belief-hood do not appear to be met by dreaming sleepers. Some philosophers have claimed that beliefs are, or entail, long-term dispositions; but the person dreaming himself chased by a lion has no long-term disposition to act as if he were being chased by a lion. Likewise, philosophers who emphasize behavioural or functional requirements of belief must confront a puzzle to explain what role our dreamer's representation of the lion state of affairs plays, in order to justify its belief status.

An attractive alternative proposal would have it that dreaming is an imaginative activity; when one dreams that he is being chased by a lion, one is *imagining* that one is being chased by a lion, while still tacitly believing oneself to be safe in bed. This view may or may not be combined with McGinn's view about imagery, according to which the subject does not really have perceptual sensory experience as of a lion, but rather imagery instead. If we do combine this view with the imagery view, then dreams become much like vivid daydreams: we imagine stories, and supplement them with imagery. If we deny McGinn's view about imagery in favour of a more orthodox approach on which dreams do involve perceptual sensory experience, dreaming becomes more like going to the cinema: we have real perceptual sensory experiences, and use them to guide our imaginings. Either way, we need not accept that we believe the contents of the dream.

It seems, then, that the assumption that we believe what we dream is at least open to question, and may ultimately prove unfounded. What epistemic consequences follow from adopting the imagination view instead?

3. The imagination model and scepticism

Have we here found a way to defend our perceptual knowledge from the sceptic's dream argument? We have denied a premise in the sceptical argument: that, if you were dreaming, you would be having the same beliefs and sensory experience you are having now. Even if we might just as easily be dreaming that we see a hand, this does not entail that we might now be astray in our perceptual beliefs; for, even if we might be dreaming, it does not follow that we might be believing we see a hand on this same experiential basis, without seeing any hand. After all, when we believe in the dream, we do not thereby really believe. So, even if I had now been dreaming, which might easily enough have happened, I would not thereby have been thinking that I see a hand, based on a corresponding experience.

That disposes of the threat posed by dreams for the safety of our perceptual beliefs—it is not the case that our perceptually beliefs could easily have been false beliefs, caused by a dream. Does it dispose of the problem of dream scepticism? It does so if dreams create such a problem only by threatening the safety of our perceptual beliefs. Is that the only threat posed by dreams? Perhaps not. Perhaps our new, imagination-based, conception of dreams gives rise to an even more radical form of scepticism.

If dreaming is just imagining, then traditional formulations of radical scepticism, Descartes's included, are not radical enough. The possibility that we dream now threatens not only our supposed perceptual knowledge but even our supposed introspective knowledge, our supposed takings of the given. It is now in doubt not only whether we see a fire, but even whether we think we see a fire, or experience as if we see it. Just as we might be dreaming we perceive a fire without really doing so, so in a dream we might affirm the cogito and have experience as of a fire, without in reality affirming or experiencing any such thing. If dreams pose a problem for our perception of our surroundings, then on the imagination model they equally pose a problem for our apprehension of the given (Sosa 2007).

JONATHAN ICHIKAWA AND ERNEST SOSA

Ayer, A. J. (1960). 'Professor Malcolm on dreams'. *Journal of Philosophy*, 57.

Dennett, D. C. (1976). 'Are dreams experiences?' *Philosophical Review*, 73.

Dreisbach, C. (2000). 'Dreams in the history of philosophy'. *Dreaming*, 10.

Flanagan, O. (2000). *Dreaming Souls: Sleep, Dreams, and the Evolution of the Conscious Mind.*

Hobson, J. A. (2003). *Dreaming: an Introduction to the Science of Sleep.*

Ichikawa, J. (2009). 'Dreaming and imagination'. *Mind and Language*, 24.

Malcolm, N. (1962). *Dreaming.*

Mann, W. E. (1983). 'Dreams and immorality'. *Philosophy*, 58.

Matthews, G. B. (1981). 'On being immoral in a dream'. *Philosophy*, 56.

McGinn, C. (2004). *Mindsight.*

Pears, D. (1960). 'Professor Norman Malcolm: dreaming'. *Mind*, 70.

Sartre, J.-P. (1991). *The Psychology of Imagination.*

Schwitzgebel, E. (2002). 'Why did we think we dreamed in black and white?' *Studies in History and Philosophy of Science*, 33.

Sosa, E. (2005). 'Dreams and philosophy'. *Proceedings and Addresses of the American Philosophical Association*, 79.

—— (2007). *A Virtue Epistemology: Apt Belief and Reflective Knowledge*, Vol. 1.

Stone, J. (1984). 'Dreaming and certainty'. *Philosophical Studies*, 45.

Williams, B. (1978). *Descartes: the Project of Pure Inquiry.*

dreaming, scientific perspectives Dreaming can be defined as the images and thoughts that are experienced during sleep. Approximately 14% of people report dreaming every night, 25% of people report dreaming frequently, and 6% never. This dream recall decreases with age. Specific emotions or moods occur in 75% of dreams, with positive and negative emotions occurring equally often across individuals, and joy being the most common single emotion, with anger and fear as next most common (Strauch and Meier 1996). The scientific study of dreaming relates dream content and measures of the form of dreams (such as bizarreness and vividness) to the physiology of the brain during sleep, and to the waking life events and personality of the dreamer (Hobson 2003, Barratt and McNamara 2007). There are two major aspects of brain physiology that relate to dreaming. Firstly, *sleep in humans is divided into light sleep (stages 1 and 2), deep sleep (stages 3 and 4), and rapid eye movement sleep (REM sleep). REM sleep occurs approximately every 90 min, each REM period becoming longer across the night; the last one can be as long as 40 min, the first as short as 5 min. These eye movements can also be visible to a person watching. Brainwaves during REM sleep have some similarity to waking brainwaves, and parts of the brain are very active, while muscle tone is very low; due to this conjunction of the brain being very active while the body is asleep, REM sleep has been termed *paradoxical sleep*. In 1953 Aserinsky and Kleitman found that dream recall was more likely if people were woken from REM sleep than from sleep stages 1–4 (non-REM sleep). In 1962 Foulkes showed that dreams can occur in non-REM sleep but that they were usually shorter and less dramatic and vivid than REM dreams. It is currently a matter of dispute whether differences between REM and non-REM dreams are just due to non-REM dreams being shorter on average than REM dreams, or due to non-REM dreams being forgotten more easily, or whether there are fundamental differences between them in how they are produced, such as REM dreams being more bizarre, with these differences possibly being physiologically based (Pace-Schott et al. 2003). On the latter, Hobson has proposed a cholinergic neurochemical difference between REM sleep and both being awake and non-REM sleep, to explain the amnesic and irrational nature of REM dreams.

The second relevant aspect of brain physiology is that whereas the brain becomes very much less active during non-REM sleep compared with being awake, during REM sleep the brain becomes very active, including activation of areas of the parietal lobe related to visual *imagery, and of the amgydala and paralimbic cortex which are related to emotional processing. From his own work, and from over a century of the neuropsychological literature, Solms (1997) shows that lesions to the ventralmesial quadrant of the frontal lobe (at the front of the brain, and involved with emotional motivation and wishes), or to the parietotemporo-occipital junction (the sensory areas of the brain nearer the back at the side), result in the loss of dream recall, but with REM sleep preserved. These brain areas thus seem to be important for creating dreams.

The relationship of REM dreaming to the limbic system provides a basis to findings that there are dream content changes following emotional waking experiences. However, although dream content can be related to waking life experiences, this seems to account for only a minority of the entire dream content, leading to the claim by Hobson (1999) that much of dream content is *delirium-like, rather than motivated or meaningful.

This leads to the empirical work on whether individual differences in dream content can be related to individual differences in waking life experiences or personality. Domhoff proposes a methodology for quantifying samples of dreams, taken either from one person over time, or from a group of people, who are then compared with another group, or with a population mean. Many variables can be derived, for example the percentage of characters who are aggressive, the percentage of negative emotions, the number of dreams that contain a misfortune, or the number that contain a success. Domhoff shows that these variables can be stable across time in people. The methodology of scientific studies on dream content, and their related statistics, is described on the website maintained by Schneider and Domhoff, and in Domhoff (2003).

Given that some of the dream content can be related to waking life cognition and emotions (Kramer 2007) the next question is whether dream content provides information about waking cognition and emotions that are not within conscious awareness, that is, whether studying dreams can provide therapeutic insight. Clara Hill (2003) has developed a cognitive method for obtaining insight from dreams and initiating altered cognition and action, and Hartmann (1998) provides evidence that dreams can provide a form of therapy without a therapist. There have been claims that dreams can provide the inspiration for inventions and discoveries, such as the structure of the benzene molecule by Kekulé, but some of these claims are disputed: accounts of the claims have been collated in works by Deirdre Barrett.

Freud (1900) claimed that dreams provide a 'royal road to the unconscious', because during sleep we censor thoughts less than when awake. His method of dream interpretation required the person undergoing analysis to free-associate to each component of the dream, the theory being that this would lead from the manifest dream content (the dream that was remembered) to the latent dream thoughts (the wishes and other factors, often unconscious, that were the source of the dream). Clearly this method can result in confabulation of links between the dream content and waking cognition and memories; however, a similar free-association method is now used by Cavallero and many others to distinguish whether items in dreams have as their source a waking episodic memory, a semantic memory, or abstract memory or knowledge about the self. The claim of Cavallero and colleagues has been that REM dreams have less reliance on episodic sources than do non-REM dreams or sleep-onset dreams, but as with most claimed differences between REM and non-REM dreams, the differences are small, especially when dreams of similar length are compared.

Although dreams can be very vivid and dramatic, they are easily forgotten if effort is not made to recall or write them down immediately upon waking. Whereas Freud claimed that dreams were easily forgotten because of repression, it is now thought that a lack of memory consolidation during sleep causes this forgetting, although the fact that delayed dream recall can suddenly occur hours after waking due to cues later in the day indicates that some memory consolidation of dreams does occur prior to waking. People who are more creative have been found to have more dreams, and dreams that are more bizarre, although it is not clear if their dreams are different from less creative people or if this is a reporting effect, in that they may have a greater interest in dreams than less creative people, or a more favourable attitude towards them (Blagrove 2007). In favour of it being a reporting effect, people who never recall dreams usually do recall some if woken in the sleep laboratory during REM sleep.

The widely held continuity theory of dreams holds that individual differences in waking cognition and personality correlate with formal and content characteristics of dreams; much evidence for this is provided by Schredl. Notwithstanding this continuity there is also another widely held view that highlights the deficiencies of cognition in dreams, such as of memory, rationality, and volition. This has led to Rechtschaffen's view of dreams being 'single-minded', i.e. it is rare to have critical thoughts during a dream about the events of the dream, such as noticing bizarre instances, or deliberating about what to do next in the dream, and especially realizing that it is a dream. It has been claimed that deficiencies in volition during dreams occur due to the lack of activity of the dorsolateral prefrontal cortex during sleep. However, there is evidence from Kahan and La Berge that volition, choice, and deliberation can be shown to occur in dreams if the dreamer is asked about it soon after waking, rather than the usual method of having an independent judge rating written dream reports for the presence of these characteristics. This then raises the issue of the rare occurrence of lucid dreams (see DREAMING, LUCID), defined as dreams in which one knows one is dreaming, and can decide to alter the plot of the dream (Gackenbach and LaBerge 1988). Their rarity—approximately just 20% of the population will have them at least once per month—reinforces the deficiency view of dreaming, but levels of self-awareness and lucidity in dreams can be increased by cognitive training methods, and Blagrove and Hartnell (2000) found lucid dreamers have a greater internal locus of control and need for cognition than non-lucid dreamers, which is evidence for the continuity hypothesis.

More common than lucid dreams but equally of theoretical importance are nightmares. Some studies have shown that people with frequent nightmares have lower well-being or greater anxiety in their waking lives (Hartmann 1998). However, many other studies have not found a relationship between nightmare frequency and current waking life psychopathology, leading to the possibilities that it is the degree of suffering from nightmares, rather than the number of them, that is related to psychopathology, or that nightmares and bad dreams are common in all people, or that nightmares are related to specific trauma. The last possibility is explored in Barrett (1996), but may only hold for some nightmares, especially those early in the night.

The work of David Foulkes (1999) shows that dreaming develops with age, from simple scenes with no plot and no participation by the dreamer in children aged 3–5, social interaction in dreams developing at ages 5–7, self-participation at ages 7–9, and diverse emotions and novel characters at ages 9–13. That dreaming is a complex symbolic activity that thus develops in parallel with cognitive development may mean that animals do not dream, or that, if they do, their dreams are simpler copies of the waking environment than are the dreams of humans.

Whether dreams have a function is disputed (Flanagan 2000). There is much evidence that REM sleep is needed for forming memories (Maquet et al. 2003), and so it may be that the dreams that occur during REM sleep are involved with this function of forming novel connections between memories. That dreams are themselves so easy to forget may count against this theory, or some say in its favour, and there are of course many dreams, called *impactful dreams*, that surprise and intrigue us and remain strong in our memory throughout life. Others claim that dreams help us adapt to stress, but disputed then is whether we need to be able to remember a dream for its function to occur, or whether the 2–3 hours of dreams that we may have each night have a function even if we do not wake during them and hence never remember them.

MARK BLAGROVE

Barrett, D. (ed.) (1996). *Trauma and Dreams*.
Barrett, D. and McNamara, P. (eds) (2007). *The New Science of Dreaming*, Vols 1–3.
Blagrove, M. (2007). 'Personality and dreaming'. In Barrett, D. and McNamara, P. (eds) *The New Science of Dreaming, Vol. 2: Content, Recall, and Personality Correlates*.
—— and Hartnell, S. J. (2000). 'Lucid dreaming: associations with internal locus of control, need for cognition and creativity'. *Personality and Individual Differences*, 28.
Domhoff, G. W. (2003). *The Scientific Study of Dreams: Neural Networks, Cognitive Development, and Content Analysis*.
Flanagan, O. (2000). *Dreaming Souls*.
Foulkes, D. (1999). *Children's Dreaming and the Development of Consciousness*.
Freud, S. (1900). *The Interpretation of Dreams*.
Gackenbach, J. and LaBerge, S. (eds) (1988). *Conscious Mind, Sleeping Brain: Perspectives on Lucid Dreaming*.
Hartmann, E. (1998). *Dreams and Nightmares: the Origin and Meaning of Dreams*.
Hill, C. B. (ed.) (2003). *Dream Work in Therapy: Facilitating Exploration, Insight, and Action*.
Hobson, J. A. (1999). *Dreaming as Delirium: How the Brain Goes Out of Its Mind*.
—— (2003). *Dreaming: an Introduction to the Science of Sleep*.

Kramer, M. (2007). *The Dream Experience.*
Maquet, P., Smith, C., and Stickgold, R. (2003). *Sleep and Brain Plasticity.*
Pace-Schott, E. F., Solms, M., Blagrove, M., and Harnad, S. (eds) (2003). *Sleep and Dreaming: Scientific Advances and Reconsiderations.*
Schneider, A. and Domhoff, G. W. (accessed 2009) 'The quantitative study of dreams', http://www.dreamresearch.net
Solms, M. (1997). *The Neuropsychology of Dreams.*
Strauch, I. and Meier, B. (1996). *In Search of Dreams: Results of Experimental Dream Research.*

dual aspect theories Dual aspect theories of mind are forms of *panpsychism which posit a substratum of reality that is neither wholly mental nor wholly physical but possesses both mentalistic and materialistic features (or aspects). The core principles of panpsychism are the ubiquity and fundamentality of mind. Within a dual aspect theory these principles imply that (1) nothing 'in' the substratum is left uncharacterized in the complete mentalistic characterization of it, although the mental aspect does not exhaust all there is to know about the substratum and (2) the mentalistic aspect cannot be explicated in terms of any other feature of the substratum, nor reduced to any such. The same can be said of the material aspect of the substratum—mind and matter can be regarded as co-fundamental and equally ubiquitous throughout nature.

The most famous example of a dual aspect theory is that of Spinoza. Following long-standing tradition, Spinoza accepted the definition of substance as that which can exist independently of everything else. It was thus evident to Spinoza that what Descartes had called substances—extension (or matter) and mind—were no such thing, since each required the creative activity of God to come into and persist in existence. Only God is self-subsistent and Spinoza regarded the ontological argument as sufficient to demonstrate His existence. It follows that God is a substance and Spinoza attempted to prove that in fact there could only be one substance (via an argument of 'plenitude' that there would be a substance with all possible attributes and there could not be two identical substances). It was Spinoza's view that both mind and matter were but merely two attributes of this underlying, infinite and infinitely complex substance. Every material thing has its mentalistic aspect, and vice versa. As he wrote:

> a circle existing in nature and the idea of the existing circle, which is also in God, are one and the same thing . . . therefore, whether we conceive nature under the attribute of Extension, or under the attribute of Thought . . . we shall find one and the same order, or one and the same connection of causes . . . (Spinoza 1677/1985:Prop. 7, scholium).

In terms of the core principles of panpsychism, Spinoza clearly holds that mind is fundamental, though not uniquely so, and ubiquitous—there is nothing that is not, when considered from the appropriate viewpoint, mentalistic in its nature. The distinctive characterization of the dual aspect theory is to posit the underlying substance as 'carrier' of both mental and physical attributes (in Spinoza's case, the theory is a multi-aspect view for there are an infinite number of ontologically distinct attributes, only two of which are humanly knowable).

Spinoza's apparent identification of God and nature, a serious heresy, made his views hard to endorse. Following Leibniz, continental philosophers turned decisively towards mental monisms, or idealism, of one sort or another. In the British Isles, empiricism reigned, and while Berkeley endorsed an idealist version, it is arguable that Hume favoured something like a dual aspect view. In general however, dual aspect metaphysics languished until in the 19th century views akin to dual aspect theory were revived, notably by William James, who then had a strong influence on Bertrand Russell, who might be counted as the principal exponent of a dual aspect theory in the 20th century (see Russell 1921, James 1971). More recently still, the quasi-physicalist panpsychism of Nagel (1979), the 'real physicalism' of Strawson (2006), the 'neo-Russellianism' of Lockwood (1991), the informational panpsychism bruited by Chalmers (1996), and the explicitly labelled dual aspect panpsychism of Rosenberg (2004) can all be regarded as forms of dual aspect theory.

But another theory with a rather uncertain relation to dual aspect theory intrudes here to complicate the story: *neutral monism*. Both James and Russell identified themselves as neutral monists. Seemingly in line with dual aspect views, neutral monism posits a single fundamental kind of stuff which is 'neutral' in nature—neither mental nor physical but upon which both the mental and physical depend. Although there are no definitive characterizations of neutral monism and it is frequently grouped with dual aspect theory, it is useful to distinguish the two views. I suggest, following Stubenberg (2005), we accept that neutral monism denies both the fundamentality and ubiquity of both the mental and physical features of the world. Instead, a neutral monist thinks that mental features can be reduced to structures within the neutral substrate. Certain neutral configurations appear as mental entities, others appear as physical entities.

This contrast between neutral monism and dual aspect theory can be expressed in terms of the property *dualism endorsed by dual aspect theory. Both the mental and physical are properties of the underlying substance. The fundamental and irreducible nature of these properties entails that dual aspect theory is a form of property dualism (or pluralism, depending on one's view on whether all other kinds of properties can be reduced to combinations of mental and physical properties). In contrast, neutral monism asserts that both mental and physical features are reducible to constellations of neutral structures.

There is a certain ontological elegance to the neutral monist scheme, but the cost is irredeemable ignorance about the nature of both the mental and the physical. The dual aspect theorist, on the other hand, can allow that insofar as the mental and physical are irreducible and fundamental they are perhaps knowable in themselves via our experience of them (although, of course, mind has traditionally been seen as epistemically favoured insofar as it is 'directly' knowable). It is also worth pointing out that the neutral monist must embrace a form of **mysterian* **emergence* in which the mental and physical emerge out of the operations of the entirely mysterious neutral 'stuff'. Given the complete ignorance we face with regard to the neutral, this emergence must be entirely inexplicable—a kind of brute intrusion which must be accepted with, at best, 'natural piety' (to use the phrase Samuel Alexander applied to his own theory of radical emergence).

It might be held that no account of the radical emergence of consciousness is possible—that only basic features which were, in some sense, already conscious could permit the development of richer structures of consciousness. This familiar argument threatens to deneutralize the basic stuff and replace it with some protomental feature. But this would be to replace neutral monism with a kind of panpsychism of a traditional sort. The apparent epistemic asymmetry in our access to the mental and physical realms further drives the tendency to 'mentalize' the neutral (both Russell and James give some indication of the strength of this tendency; recent followers of Russell, such as Lockwood 1991 and Strawson 2006, seem to almost give in to it). In this respect, the panpsychism of the dual aspect theory might be more attractive. The tendency is further enhanced by the argument, frequently deployed by panpsychists, that there must be some intrinsic properties of the fundamental stuff of the world and the only intrinsic property we seem to be acquainted with is consciousness.

As a form of panpsychism, dual aspect theory can avail itself of the arguments in support of the former position and it suffers from the difficulties which face panpsychism. It remains perhaps the most attractive version of panpsychism.

WILLIAM SEAGER

Chalmers, D. (1996). *The Conscious Mind.*

James, W. (1971). *Essays in Radical Empiricism and a Pluralistic Universe.*

Lockwood, M. (1991). *Mind, Brain and the Quantum: the Compound 'I'.*

Nagel, T. (1979). 'Panpsychism'. In Nagel, T. (ed.) *Mortal Questions.*

Rosenberg, G. (2004). *A Place for Consciousness: Probing the Deep Structure of the Natural World.*

Russell, B. (1921/1978). *The Analysis of Mind.*

Spinoza, B. (1677/1985). *Ethics.* In *The Collected Works of Spinoza*, ed. and transl. E. Curley.

Strawson, G. (2006). 'Realistic monism: why physicalism entails panpsychism'. *Journal of Consciousness Studies*, 13.

Stubenberg, L. (2005). 'Neutral monism'. In Zalta, E. N. (ed.) *The Stanford Encyclopedia of Philosophy*, http://plato.stanford.edu/

dualism Dualism in the philosophy of mind is customarily differentiated into two broad kinds: property dualism and substance dualism. *Property dualism* is the view that mental properties are distinct from and irreducible to physical properties, although it allows that properties of both kinds may, in suitable cases, be possessed by the very same thing, such as a human being, person, or brain. *Substance dualism* is the view that mental and physical properties are not only distinct and mutually irreducible but, in addition, that the things that possess mental properties are always distinct from and irreducible to the things that possess physical properties. For example, according to one version of substance dualism, the human mind or soul is distinct from and irreducible to the human body or any part of it, such as the brain, and possesses mental properties but no physical properties. Hence we see that substance dualism is a stronger view than property dualism, in the sense that the former entails the latter, but not vice versa.

1. Substance dualism
2. Property dualism

1. Substance dualism

Undoubtedly, the best known advocate of substance dualism in the history of philosophy was the French philosopher and scientist René Descartes (1591–1650). Descartes maintained that there is, as he puts it, a 'real distinction' between the human mind or soul and the human body (see Descartes 1984). According to Descartes, the mind and the body are distinct and separable substances. By a *substance* in this context, Descartes does not mean a kind of stuff, but just an individual thing or object which possesses properties and exists independently of other such things (except, of course, God, upon whom all things ultimately depend for their existence, in Descartes's view). Descartes maintained that the mind and the body each possess just one essential attribute—*thought* or *consciousness* in the case of the mind and *spatial extension* in the case of the body—and that all of the properties of each of these distinct substances are different modes of its one essential attribute. Thus he considered that the body possesses properties such as shape, size, motion, and spatial location but no mental properties, whereas the mind possesses properties such as belief, desire, and volition but no physical properties. In defence of this view, Descartes offered two chief arguments, which we can appropriately call the *argument from conceivability* and the *argument from divisibility*. Each deserves some further consideration here.

Here is one way to reconstruct Descartes's conceivability argument. First, (1) it is clearly and distinctly conceivable that I—that is, my mind or soul—should exist without a body. Next, (2) what is clearly and distinctly conceivable is therefore possible, because at least God could bring it about—for instance, He could bring it about that I continued to exist but without a body. Hence, (3) it is possible that I should exist without a body. But, (4) if it is possible that I should exist without a body, then I must be distinct and separable from my body. Therefore, (5), I am distinct and separable from my body.

However, there are many aspects of this argument that can be queried. The very first premise is debatable, as is the second: for, although I may be able to *imagine* existing without a body, it is not so evident that I can clearly and distinctly *conceive* of doing so, at least in a sense of 'conceive'—if indeed there really is such a sense—in which this would imply that it is genuinely possible for me to exist without a body. These doubts alone suffice to render the argument unpersuasive in the minds of many philosophers.

Descartes's divisibility argument is, if any thing, even less persuasive. It may be reconstructed as follows. First, (1) my mind or soul contains no parts into which it is divisible. However, (2) my body, being spatially extended, is necessarily divisible into parts. Hence, (3) my mind or soul must be distinct from my body and cannot be spatially extended, with the further consequence that it can possess no physical properties. Again, though, the crucial first premise of this argument has seemed unconvincing and indeed question-begging to many philosophers who do not already sympathize with substance dualism, for it seems to presume already that the mind or soul is *not* spatially extended like the body.

Even though Descartes's arguments have generally failed to prove persuasive to philosophers, his view of the mind–body relationship—*Cartesian dualism*—undoubtedly has a certain amount of intuitive appeal and is clearly in accord with the religious beliefs of many people. On the other hand, it is widely regarded in philosophical and scientific circles as being thoroughly incompatible with current scientific understanding of the workings of the human brain and nervous system. More specifically, it is considered that Cartesian dualism is confronted with an insuperable problem concerning *psychophysical causation*—that is, concerning the causal interaction between mind and brain. Descartes himself believed that this interaction was centred upon the *pineal gland, situated in the middle of the human brain. He considered that the human mind was capable of affecting and being affected by the flow of 'animal spirits' in this gland. These spirits he took to be highly volatile and rarefied fluids flowing through our nerve filaments, changes in whose motions could thus be communicated to other parts of the body, thereby ultimately altering the disposition of our limbs in accordance with our will, while nervous flows in the reverse direction could supply us with sensory information about the current state of our body. However, as some of Descartes's own near contemporaries (notably Leibniz) realized, this theory and anything remotely like it is apparently incompatible with well-confirmed physical conservation laws, such as the law of conservation of momentum (see Woolhouse 1985). As a consequence, *interactionist* substance dualism of the Cartesian kind rapidly fell out of favour amongst philosophers, to be replaced by *parallelist* and *epiphenomenalist* versions of the doctrine, according to which there is no real causal interaction of the mind upon the body (Leibniz himself favouring the former of these views). Unfortunately, these versions of substance dualism are highly counterintuitive, since we all have a strong conviction that our mental deliberations and decisions can indeed have a genuine effect upon our bodily behaviour. As a result, substance dualism rapidly fell out of favour altogether—and not only on account of the causal interaction problem, but also in virtue of a general sense that the positing of an immaterial soul was at odds with the world view and methodology of modern empirical science and an unacceptable retreat into mystery.

2. Property dualism

As was remarked earlier, substance dualism is a stronger view than property dualism, in the sense that the former entails, but is not entailed by, the latter. Property dualism too has a distinguished pedigree, however. It is a *monistic* theory with regard to the nature of the things or substances which possess mental and physical properties—holding that these are of just one basic kind—but *pluralistic* with regard to those properties, holding that they are of two distinct and mutually irreducible kinds. One of the earliest versions of this view was advanced by Descartes's contemporary, Baruch Spinoza (1632–77), at least according to some interpretations of his position. Spinoza firmly denied that the mind and the body are distinct substances. Indeed, he denied that they are substances at all. He held that *God or Nature*—in other words, the entire universe as a whole—is the only genuine substance, because it is the only fully independent thing. However, Spinoza agreed with Descartes in distinguishing between the attributes of thought and extension and in viewing mental and physical properties as being modes of these two attributes. In effect, he regarded the human mind and the human body as being, respectively, collections of these modes of the two attributes, rather than as being substances in their own right. Crucially, for our purposes, he held that the very same substance or thing can possess *both* physical *and* mental properties—and this is why he qualifies as a property dualist in our terms. At the same time, it should be acknowledged that Spinoza seems in places to endorse a version of the *identity* theory, holding that mental and physical modes are in fact the very *same* entities conceived of in two different ways—and this is why he is also often described as maintaining a '*dual aspect' view of the mind–body relationship. Be that as it may, most present-day versions of dualism are likewise versions of monistic property dualism (see e.g. Chalmers 1996, Robinson 2004), typically maintaining that the human brain possesses both mental and physical properties but that these properties are distinct and mutually irreducible.

It would seem that the most compelling case for monistic property dualism rests on appeal to the apparently irreducible character of the properties of phenomenal consciousness—**qualia*, as they are commonly now called. This is something that is supposed to be revealed by *introspection or reflection on the character of our sensory experiences. Thus, it may be said, it is hard to see how such allegedly mental qualities as the bitter taste of a lemon, the pungent smell of woodsmoke, or the vivid redness of a rose could simply be physical properties of our brain or nervous system, such as complex patterns of activity in our gustatory, olfactory, or visual neurons. There would seem to be an enormous and unbridgeable *explanatory gap (see Levine 2001) between such conscious sensory qualia on the one hand and the neurophysiological activity that is going on in our brains when we have those experiences—and this apparently rules out any attempt either to identify the qualia with the neural features in question or even to maintain that there is a necessary connection between them. At most we seem to be able to contend that there is a purely contingent causal correlation between items of the first sort and items of the second sort—a correlation which seems to defy any deeper explanation as to why it should obtain, since it seems so easy to imagine that it might not have obtained at all, or that a quite different correlation should have obtained (one in which, for instance, the bitter taste of lemon is correlated with another sort of neural activity, such as that which happens in fact to be correlated with the vivid redness of a rose).

Physicalist philosophers of mind object that monistic property dualism is beset by at least some of the problems that are faced by substance dualism, especially the problem of psychophysical causal interaction. These critics typically appeal to the principle of the *causal closure of the physical* in advancing their case (see, for example, Kim 1998). The latter principle has several variants, but one quite popular version runs something like this: however far we attempt to trace back in time the causes of any particular physical effect, we shall always find ourselves confined to causal chains of purely physical states and events. Thus, for example, if we try to trace back the causal antecedents of a certain human bodily movement, such as the movement of my finger as I depress a key on a computer keyboard, we shall only ever come across other purely physical events, such as certain neural events in my nervous system and brain. It seems most unlikely that we shall ever need to suppose that, at some point in tracing back such a causal chain, we shall come across a physical event which apparently has no other physical event as its immediate cause—that is to say, a point at which we might need to posit a purely mental event, such as an irreducible sensory quale, as an immediate cause of a certain physical event. As a result, these physicalists maintain, we are compelled to take one or other of two views regarding sensory qualia. Either we must regard them as being purely **epiphenomenal*—and this is what we must say if we deny that they are identical with or reducible to purely physical properties of any kind. Or else we must indeed maintain that they are identical with or reducible to such properties, even if we cannot presently see how this can be so. Of these two options, they would advise us to adopt the latter, because they will say that epiphenomenalism is faced with an insuperable mystery as to why mental properties should exist at all and, indeed, how we can even know of their existence, given their supposed causal insulation from the physical world. On the face of it, any sort of *evolutionary explanation for their existence and our knowledge of them is ruled out by this consideration. In reply, some epiphenomenalists may courageously defend a *panpsychist version of their theory, according to which it is just a very basic metaphysical fact about the constitution of our universe that every physical property is coinstantiated with a corresponding mental property. Indeed, Spinoza's own theory seems to be something like this. However, even its advocates would have to acknowledge that such a theory is speculative in the extreme and incapable, even in principle, of being confirmed by empirical means.

Unquestionably, *physicalism is currently the dominant position in the philosophy of mind. Dualists of all kinds constitute a small minority and interactive substance dualists (see e.g. Popper and Eccles 1977, Swinburne 1986) an especially small one. Even so, physicalism has difficulties of its own which are increasingly being recognized, with the consequence that dualism—especially property dualism—is presently undergoing something of a revival (see, for instance, Chalmers 1996). The chief difficulty for physicalism seems to be the explanatory gap described earlier. Dualists complain that we simply cannot see how mental properties—and especially sensory qualia—might turn out just to be, or to be entirely reducible to, physical properties of certain kinds, such as neurophysiological ones. Physicalists may urge, first, that this does not matter, since positing the identities in question provides the best theoretical explanation of the acknowledged correlations between mental and physical goings-on, and that fact should satisfy us. Secondly, they may contend that the fact that we find such putative identities puzzling has a purely psychological explanation, residing in the circumstance that our access to our own mental properties via introspection is very different in character from our access to the neurophysiological properties of other people, which is through observation, so that we conceive of these properties in very different ways (see PHENOMENAL CONCEPTS). For instance, when a neurosurgeon looks at another human being's visual cortex, his experience of what he is seeing will naturally be very different from his patient's experience of what he is seeing—a red rose, say. The patient's visual experience, as it appears to the patient through introspection, seems to have a vivid redness about it, but the neurosurgeon's experience of the relevant neurophysiological properties of the patient's visual cortex will not, of course, register any such feature: he may simply seem to be experiencing something—part of the patient's brain—that to him looks soggy and grey. But that, according to the physicalist, is just because the neurosurgeon is only observing the very same neurophysiological properties of the patient's brain that the patient is introspecting—whereas what introspection gives the neurosurgeon access to is only neurophysiological features of his own brain, not the patient's.

The idea that has just been mooted to help demystify the explanatory gap is that we can distinguish between how an experience appears to the subject of that experience and how it appears to an external observer. However, the very notion that any kind of distinction can be drawn between 'appearance' and 'reality' in the case of mental properties has been challenged in recent times, notably by Saul Kripke (1980), and this challenge has been deployed in support of property dualism. Kripke invites us to suppose, for the sake of argument, that the conscious feeling of pain, say, just is (i.e. is identical with) a certain kind of physical feature of our brains, such as the firing of C-fibres. The positing of such a theoretical identity is, we are invited to suppose, analogous to that of other identities successfully posited by empirical scientists, such as the identity between *heat* (in a gas) and the kinetic activity of molecules, or the identity between *visible light* and electromagnetic radiation of certain wavelengths. Kripke contends, on quite general grounds to do with the logic and semantics of so-called natural kinds terms (like 'pain', 'heat', and 'light'), that if such an identity obtains, then it obtains necessarily, not merely contingently. Thus, for example, according to Kripke, given that heat is in fact identical with the kinetic activity of molecules, it could not have been anything else. He would readily concede that we seem to be able to imagine that heat might have been something else. But this is explained by the fact that there could have been a different kind of physical activity which had the same appearance as heat—that is, that felt to us like heat, or, in other words, that gave rise to the same phenomenal experience that the kinetic activity of molecules actually gives rise to in us. But now we face an evident difficulty in applying this model to the putative case of pain's identity with the firing of C-fibres. For if pain just is the firing of C-fibres, then it will, once again, be necessarily identical with the firing of C-fibres, according to Kripke. By analogy with the case of heat, however, we ought then to be able at least to imagine that pain might have been some other kind of physiological activity. And, indeed, the correlation of pain with the firing of C-fibres seems contingent, just as the correlation of heat with the kinetic activity of molecules does. However, if this circumstance is to be explained in the case of pain in the same way as was adopted in the case of heat, then we shall have to say that there could have been a different kind of physiological activity which had the same appearance as pain, and yet was not pain. And yet this appears to be absurd: for whatever seems like pain surely is pain, even if not everything that seems like heat is heat. The analogy appears to break down, and therewith the attempt to represent the putative identity of pain with the firing of C-fibres as being an empirically discovered truth which is nevertheless metaphysically necessary.

This line of argument against physicalism has certainly proved appealing in some quarters, but its acceptability depends on many delicate matters in the semantics, epistemology, and metaphysics of modality. A key issue, as with Descartes, is the relationship between what is *imaginable*, what is *conceivable*, and what is *possible*. Some present-day philosophers are certainly prepared to urge that conceivability is a reliable guide to possibility and thence to argue in favour of property dualism, on the grounds that we can conceive of beings (*zombies) who are physically just like us but lack properties of phenomenal consciousness (see Chalmers 1996). Others, naturally, dispute this. What seems clear, however, is that the truth or falsehood of dualism in any of its forms is not, ultimately, a purely scientific matter, but one that depends crucially on the validity of various distinctively philosophical presuppositions.

E. JONATHAN LOWE

Chalmers, D. J. (1996). *The Conscious Mind.*

Descartes, R. (1984). 'Meditations on first philosophy'. In Cottingham, J. et al. (eds) *The Philosophical Writings of Descartes*, eds.

Foster, J. (1991). *The Immaterial Self: a Defense of the Cartesian Dualist Conception of the Mind.*

Kim, J. (1998). *Mind in a Physical World.*

Kripke, S. A. (1980). *Naming and Necessity.*

Levine, J. (2001). *Purple Haze: the Puzzle of Consciousness.*

Popper, K. R. and Eccles, J. C. (1977). *The Self and its Brain.*

Robinson, W. S. (2004). *Understanding Phenomenal Consciousness.*

Spinoza, B. (1994). *Ethics*, ed. E. Curley.

Swinburne, R. (1986). *The Evolution of the Soul.*

Woolhouse, R. S. (1985). 'Leibniz's reaction to Cartesian interactionism'. *Proceedings of the Aristotelian Society*, 86.

dual-task interference See ATTENTION AND AWARENESS

dynamic control task See LEARNING, EXPLICIT VS IMPLICIT

dynamic core See INFORMATION INTEGRATION THEORY

easy problems See HARD PROBLEM OF CONSCIOUSNESS

efference copy See ACTION, SCIENTIFIC PERSPECTIVES; SCHIZOPHRENIA

electroencephalography Synaptic currents in synchronously active neurons constitute the basis of the electroencephalogram (EEG). When a sufficiently large number of cells are active simultaneously, the weak currents generated by synaptic neural activity sum up and become large enough to be recorded from the scalp surface, using electrodes that are stuck to the scalp surface using a conductive paste. Importantly, EEG signals reflect changes in brain activity with a millisecond time resolution. EEG has fundamentally been used in two ways: as an index of a cascade of processing stages, using event-related potentials, and as a measure of mass dynamics.

1. Event-related potentials
2. Objective correlates of smart unconscious processing
3. Assessing the time course of conscious access
4. Mass dynamics
5. Oscillatory synchrony and perceptual awareness?
6. Ongoing activity

1. Event-related potentials

In awake adults, a sensory stimulus elicits a response that is so small that it cannot be readily be observed in the ongoing scalp EEG. The classical way to isolate the cerebral response to a stimulus from background activity is to present this stimulus many times (from 30 to hundreds) and average the EEG responses to this stimulus: electrical waves that occur at a fixed latency after stimulus onset sum up, while so-called 'noise' averages out (Fig. E1). Such averaged responses are called *evoked potentials* or *event-related potentials* (ERPs). They are influenced by physical properties of stimuli as well as higher cognitive processes such as attention (Luck 2005).

ERPs may be considered as 'reaction times of the 21st century' (Luck 2005). They give access to the intermediate processing stages preceding the final behavioural output, in an ordered sequence. They have been very useful in analysing perception, attentional capture, novelty detection, semantic processing, and motor preparation. Indeed, each of these processes is indexed by a well-defined electrophysiological marker. For instance, the violation of semantic expectation elicits a negative potential about 400 ms after a word that is not related to the semantic context, termed N400. This strategy has proved particularly useful in showing the depth of unconscious processing.

2. Objective correlates of smart unconscious processing

ERPs have been very successful in providing objective neural *correlates of sophisticated implicit processing. For instance, two studies of ERPs demonstrated that unseen words trigger a semantic analysis. The first study was based on the *attentional blink paradigm, using a stream of briefly presented words and digits. The trick in this study was to provide the subject with a 'context' word, to which blinked words could be semantically related or not (Luck et al. 1996). Because ERPs to semantically related words and semantically unrelated words are very different, it was possible to show that word meaning is accessed, although the word itself cannot be reported consciously. In the second study, epileptic patients with implanted depth electrodes, used to localize the epileptic focus before its resection, were presented with *masked words. Unseen words elicited long-latency ERPs in the amygdala that differed depending on the emotional valence of the unseen word (Naccache et al. 2005). Both these studies thus show that the meaning of words that cannot be consciously reported is accessed and analysed unconsciously.

Other studies have taken advantage of the ERP indexing motor preparation—a slow variation of voltage preceding a movement, which develops over the contralateral motor region. In pioneering studies, Libet used this so-called *motor readiness potential* to ask whether or not the subject's conscious decision to move is preceded by unconscious brain activity. By measuring the time-shift between the readiness potential onset latency and the time at which subjects were reporting to be willing to move, he found that the conscious decision lagged behind an unconscious motor preparation by about 300 ms (Libet et al. 1983). Although Libet's experiment has been criticized on methodological grounds, it opened a new field of research relating agency and consciousness.

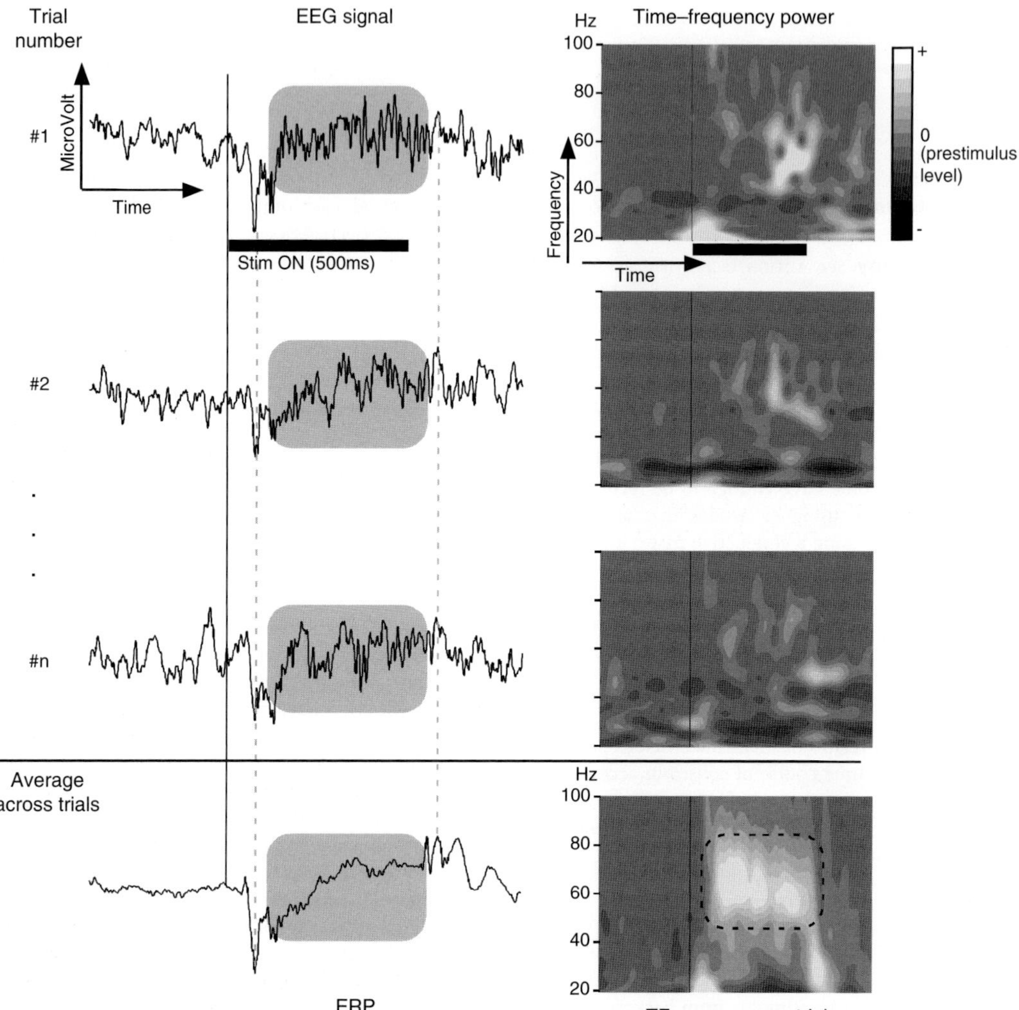

Fig. E1. Single-trial EEG traces from the cortical surface of area V1 in an anaesthetized monkey, in response to a 1° white square flashed for 500 ms. Because the electrode is lying directly on the cortical surface, the signal-to-noise ratio is high and single events can be observed directly. The signal-to-noise ratio of the scalp recordings in humans is much lower. Left column: EEG traces are shown for 400 ms before stimulus onset (black vertical line) and until 300 ms after stimulus offset. A deflection can be seen about 80 ms after stimulus onset in single trials, followed by high-frequency oscillations (grey rectangle). Because the initial deflection occurs at a fixed latency, it sums up in the signal averaged across trials (event-related potential, ERP). In the ERP, pre-stimulus fluctuations are cancelled out by the averaging process, as are the stimulus-related high-frequency oscillations. Right column: to quantify induced oscillations, power in each frequency band and time-point is estimated for each single trial. This power estimation is summarized in a time (abscissa) and frequency (ordinate axis) plot that is colour-coded: white indicates an increase in power at a given latency and frequency, compared to the pre-stimulus power at the same frequency; black a decrease. Time–frequency plots are then averaged across trials and reveal the presence of high-frequency oscillations, in this example centred around 60 Hz and lasting for the 500 ms of stimulus presentation (dashed rectangle).

3. Assessing the time course of conscious access
At what neural processing level does a consciously perceived stimulus differ from an unconsciously perceived one? Does consciousness depend on the strength of the initial perceptual activation, on attentional amplification, or on a transfer of sensory signals in short-term memory? EEG studies have not yet provided a definitive answer to that question: depending on the stimuli and task, the divergence between stimuli that are consciously or not consciously accessed has been reported to be as little as 100 ms to as much as 700 ms.

For instance, using a grating at threshold for visual consciousness, Pins and ffytche found that the P1 wave was reduced when the stimulus was not consciously perceived (Pins and ffytche 2003). The P1 wave is a positive deflection with onset typically around 80 ms after the stimulus, peaking between 100 and 120 ms and reflecting the activation of a number of extrastriate retinotopic areas. This result is consistent with the idea that to be consciously perceived, a stimulus must give rise to a sufficiently strong initial activation of sensory cortices. However, because the amplitude of the P1 wave is affected by the direction of spatial attention and the subject's state of arousal, P1 amplitude reduction for unperceived stimuli in this experiment may be due to fluctuations in the subject's attentional or arousal state. When attentional confounds were controlled for, the processing of consciously and unconsciously perceived stimuli was found to diverge much later, in the 300–700 ms range.

The time-course of conscious access seems to depend on the type of process probed: if the issue is whether the subject has consciously detected the presence of a sensory stimulus, then a neural correlate of awareness seems to appear rather early, before 250 ms. If the task is to consciously recognize or identify the stimulus, the critical point of divergence seems to occur later, after at least 300 ms of processing time.

4. Mass dynamics
The EEG captures a quality of brain processing that is probably fundamental, namely the dynamics of neural interactions. Indeed, scalp EEG is sensitive only to *coordinated* neural activity. This can be a drawback, but also an advantage. Imagine you want to analyse the functional relevance of the trajectory of a school of fish. What would be more relevant, a global measure or detailed information on each individual fish? This example is typical of non-linear systems in which 'the whole is larger than the sum of its parts'—in other words, a global measure captures an irreducible trait (be it the trajectory a school of fish, or consciousness) that cannot be derived from measures taken from each individual fish or neuron. In such systems, a global pattern can emerge from the interactions between low-level components. Interestingly, the rules specifying these interactions are local; they do not imply that each individual component 'knows' anything about the global pattern. Such properties are particularly relevant in the current view that consciousness is not a localized property, but rather an *emergent characteristic of a widely interconnected system.

What kind of methods are used to investigate these properties? All the methods devised by physicists to characterize non-linear systems could in principle be applied, and how to best use these methods is at the moment a flourishing domain of methodological research. In practice, the first step was to recognize the existence of cerebral responses that are not tightly locked in time to stimulus onset. So-called *induced oscillatory responses* appear after stimulus onset with a jitter in latency from one trial to the other (see Fig. E1). They could be a signature of non-linear interactions, either within a functional area or in a larger-scale network involving several distinct areas. Whether consciousness will ultimately be accounted for using tools developed to analyse inanimate complex systems remains an open issue.

5. Oscillatory synchrony and perceptual awareness?
Oscillatory synchrony could be a general and powerful mechanism for collaborative neural behaviour. Oscillations, particularly in the *gamma range (30–100 Hz), have been shown to be relevant whenever extensive neural communication is required to solve a task (Tallon-Baudry and Bertrand 1999). Because awareness could result from wide broadcasting of information within the brain, oscillatory synchrony has received particular attention in recent years. For instance, scalp-recorded gamma oscillations covary with awareness in hemianopic patient G. Y. (Schurger et al. 2006). On the other hand, robust gamma oscillations are observed in area *V1 of the anaesthetized monkey, as shown in Fig. E1. The reactions of the electrophysiology community to such findings is as diverse as the findings themselves. Aficionados of the oscillatory synchrony hypothesis will argue that scalp-recorded gamma oscillations reflect between-area interactions that are a necessary prerequisite for consciousness, and that although a single area may oscillate as in anaesthetized monkey, this phenomenon remains too local for perceptual awareness. Sceptics will simply note that whenever a system is interconnected, it generates oscillations—and this has nothing to do with consciousness.

6. Ongoing activity
A stimulus can be perceived because the neural activity it elicits is large. But large with respect to what? There are certainly some internal states of the subjects that are

more favourable to perceptual awareness than others. Ongoing EEG activity is a good marker of such internal states. Indeed, a routine clinical application of EEG is monitoring of *sleep stages, with deep sleep stages being characterized by a large and low-frequency EEG spontaneous activity. In awake adults, is it possible to determine which components of the EEG characterize a state fostering perceptual awareness? A recent study analysed the frequency content of ongoing EEG while a weak somatosensory stimulus was delivered (Linkenkaer-Hansen et al. 2004). The stimulus was always the same, but consciously perceived only about half of the time. The authors found that intermediate levels of 10, 20, and 40 Hz oscillations over sensorimotor regions were associated with the highest probability of conscious detection. Spontaneous EEG dynamics have received only little experimental attention so far, but this field will most certainly rapidly increase.

CATHERINE TALLON-BAUDRY

Libet, B., Gleason, C. A., Wright, E. W., and Pearl, D. K. (1983). 'Time of conscious intention to act in relation to onset of cerebral activity (readiness-potential). The unconscious initiation of a freely voluntary act'. *Brain*, 106.

Linkenkaer-Hansen, K., Nikulin, V. V., Palva, S., Ilmoniemi, R. J., and Palva, J. M. (2004). 'Prestimulus oscillations enhance psychophysical performance in humans'. *Journal of Neuroscience*, 24.

Luck, S. J. (2005). *An Introduction to the Event-related Potential Technique*.

——, Vogel E. K., and Shapiro, K. L. (1996). 'Word meanings can be accessed but not reported during the attentional blink'. *Nature*, 383.

Naccache, L., Gaillard, R., Adam, C. et al. (2005). 'A direct intracranial record of emotions evoked by subliminal words'. *Proceedings of the National Academy of Sciences of the USA*, 102.

Pins, D. and ffytche, D. (2003). 'The neural correlates of conscious vision'. *Cerebral Cortex*, 13.

Schurger, A., Cowey, A., and Tallon-Baudry, C. (2006). 'Induced gamma-band oscillations correlate with awareness in hemianopic patient GY'. *Neuropsychologia*, 44.

Tallon-Baudry, C. and Bertrand, O. (1999). 'Oscillatory gamma activity in humans and its role in object representation'. *Trends in Cognitive Science*, 3.

eliminitavism Eliminativism regarding consciousness is the view that consciousness does not exist: there is no such real phenomenon, just as there are no real phenomena of magic or sorcery. Most people—and many philosophers—find such a proposal too preposterous to be worth considering. However, even if it turns out to be false, like many philosophical views, it is worth taking seriously if only for the light that doing so sheds on the topic by saying precisely where it goes wrong. Moreover, as we shall see, some of its more qualified forms may also turn out actually to be plausible.

Note that *eliminativism* regarding a phenomenon is to be distinguished from **reductionism* about it: scientists who think that life can be wholly explained and so 'reduced' to some physical processes are not claiming that there is no real phenomenon of life, in the way that they might well claim that there is no phenomenon of sorcery. Sorcery cannot be *identified* with any physical processes, whereas life can. And so scientists tend to be eliminativists about sorcery, but reductionists about life.

Some philosophers are *total eliminativists* about mental phenomena, and some restrict their eliminativism only to consciousness and related phenomena, especially *qualia, or the apparent idiosyncratic contents of sensory experience, willing to be reductionists about, say, *non-conscious propositional attitudes*, such as beliefs, desires, and perceptions.

Ironically enough, total eliminativism is often motivated by precisely the same considerations that motivate *Cartesian *dualism* about the mind. Dualism, here, involves two claims: (1) the concept of mental phenomena is essentially of phenomena that are 'private', not located anywhere in objective space in the way that all physical phenomena are; and (2) that these non-physical phenomena exist. Total eliminativists are often those who concede the first claim, but, because they are **physicalists*, believing that everything real is objective and physical, deny the second.

There is this to be said for total eliminativism: every movement of every human being, from the gestures of one's limbs to the contractions of one's larynx, to electrical discharges in one's brain, seems to be explainable by current physics (including physiology). But if the processes described by current physics are adequate to explain all bodily activity, and if no mental phenomena can be identified with those processes, then it would seem we have no reason to believe that mental phenomena are responsible for any of that activity. Positing minds to explain the motions our limbs would seem as superfluous as positing special, non-physical 'life forces' to explain growth; and so, by Occam's razor, we should deny their existence (see Rorty 1979, Rey 1997:Ch. 3).

Of course, the dualist might reply that, although physics may very well explain the motions of our bodies, it does not explain our thoughts and feelings. But the total eliminativist can reasonably reply that appealing to thoughts and feelings only *begs the question*, since it is the very existence of such phenomena as thoughts and feelings that the 'no causal break' argument is providing a reason to doubt.

'But,' the dualist might well go on to insist, 'I'm more certain of the existence of at least my own thoughts and feelings than I ever could be of the existence of any physical phenomena.' Here the eliminativist might draw on any number of views in epistemology that question such first-person claims: doubts have been raised about 'the given', about the reliability of introspective reports (Wilson 2002), and about whether such reports should always outweigh the simplicity and coherence of one's system of beliefs on the whole (Quine 1960). 'Ah, but all these doubts take for granted there are beliefs!' Not necessarily. In one of the most influential defences of eliminativism, Quine (1960:Ch. 2) cast doubt on those notions as well, replacing them by mere dispositions to emit certain patterns of sound in reaction to certain patterns of stimuli. These are not *beliefs*, since, according to his notorious 'thesis of the indeterminacy of translation', they do not have determinate content. True, you might be disposed to emit the sentence, or *sequence of sounds*, 'I'm certain I'm a conscious, thinking thing', but this sequence of sounds is not *true*, which, by a redundancy account of truth, is merely a way of saying that you are not a conscious, thinking thing.

Total eliminativism, however, needs to account not only for specific bodily motions, but for the rational *patterns* of them. In resorting to dispositions to emit sequences of sounds, Quine relied on Skinner's 'radical behaviourism', which is to date the most sustained eliminativist effort to explain behaviour in terms of merely stimuli, responses, and reinforcements. However, the effort is now almost universally regarded as a failure (see, e.g., Gallistel 1990). In its stead, theories about at least *mental representation* are taken increasingly seriously throughout present psychology. But, partly to avoid the 'no causal break' argument, these theories also abandon the dualist assumption that at least concepts referring to propositional attitudes are referring to non-physical phenomena. That is, they will tend to embrace instead one or another kind of reductionism, allowing that these mental concepts can succeed in picking out physical phenomena. A salient recent example of this strategy is a *computational/representational theory of thought*, whereby thoughts are identified with states of the brain roughly in the way implementations of a program may be identified with states of a computer (see Fodor 1975).

Although still in its infancy, a computational theory promises to explain patterns in intelligent behaviour and so save at least our thoughts and desires from eliminativism. But many have worried that it won't be able to save our conscious sensations or qualia. Here, dualists again try to make their case (see Chalmers 1996), and eliminativists again cite the lack of a causal break (see Quine 1960:264). But this more restricted eliminativism is harder to refute. For the eliminativist now concedes that people have *beliefs* and *desires*, but sees no reason why one should further insist upon the existence of, say, pain over and above the belief that one is in pain and the strong desire not to be so. Developing suggestions of Ryle (1949) and Wittgenstein (1953/1967:§§271–308), Dennett (1988, 1991) argues that belief in qualia betrays an excessive commitment to a picture of one's inner mental life on the model of some sort of outer 'theatre', a commitment for which there is in the end no rational support. Rey (1997:Ch. 11) points also to our tendency to project special properties onto things that look and act like human beings, independently of whether any internal physical phenomenon supports this projection. Both in the first person and the third, we may simply be imposing a certain uncritical conception of ourselves upon what are really no more than computational/representational states of our brains. The imposition not only invites dualistic claims that seem incompatible with physics, but also risks a surprising first-person scepticism about one's own conscious states, since it raises the serious possibility of someone introspecting all the (computationally defined) *unconscious beliefs and desires* of someone suffering from conscious pains, but without actually being in genuine pain: she might, after all, fail to have the further special, dualistic property, and so be a *zombie. Reflections on the possibility of oneself turning out to be a zombie can make eliminativism about consciousness seem a less worrisome view than one might have initially supposed.

It should be borne in mind that eliminativist proposals are not proposals about how people should ordinarily talk. It is an issue about whether there really are mental phenomena. Most eliminativists are quite happy to use mental talk instrumentally, just as they might be happy to speak in geocentric terms when navigating at sea (Quine 1960:221, Dennett 1991).

Moreover, eliminativism is sometimes not regarded as an issue so much about the actual *existence* of mental phenomena, as about the role of talk of them in serious science, as in Chomsky (2000:22–3) and Collins (2007). In a way, for this weakest form of eliminativism, it is the mental terms that get 'eliminated', not the phenomena to which those terms might nevertheless refer. Talk of 'consciousness'—and maybe even of 'belief' and 'desire'—may simply go the way of talk of 'weeds' in biology, which, while not serious employing the category, need not deny the ordinary claim that there are weeds in many gardens.

GEORGES REY

Chalmers, D. (1996). *The Conscious Mind: In Search of a Fundamental Theory*.

Chomsky, N. (2000). *New Horizons in the Study of Language*.

Collins, J. (2007). 'Meta-scientific eliminativism: a reconsideration of Chomsky's review of Skinner's *Verbal Behavior*'. *British Journal for the Philosophy of Science*, 58.

Dennett, D. (1988). 'Quining qualia'. In Marcel, A. and Bisiach, E. (eds) *Consciousness in Contemporary Science*.

—— (1991). *Explaining Consciousness*.

Fodor, J. (1975). *The Language of Thought.*
Gallistel, C. (1990). *The Organization of Learning.*
Quine, W. (1960). *Word and Object.*
Rey, G. (1997). *Contemporary Philosophy of Mind.*
Rorty, R. (1979). *Philosophy and the Mirror of Nature.*
Ryle, G. (1949). *The Concept of Mind.*
Wilson, T. (2002). *Strangers to Ourselves.*
Wittgenstein, L. (1953/1967). *Philosophical Investigations*, 3rd edn, transl. G. E. M. Anscombe.

emergence Within philosophy and the sciences the term 'emergence' is used in such a variety of bewildering and heterogeneous ways that it seems the word itself is the only thing shared across these various usages. All emergentists agree that consciousness depends on the physical in some way and 'emerges' from it, but they differ widely in their conception of this dependence relation. Some emergentist theories of consciousness are designed to be consistent with *physicalism, but others are not. Perhaps the central motivation behind emergentism is the idea that although consciousness is not itself physical, it is not completely independent of the physical either. We might say that emergentists attempt to find a position between 'crass *reductionism' on the one hand and 'spooky *dualism' on the other.

Is consciousness emergent? In recent history perhaps the most famous person in the mind sciences to claim that consciousness is an emergent property/process was the neuroscientist Roger Sperry. At roughly the same time, the neuroscientist John Eccles and the philosopher Karl Popper also claimed that consciousness is emergent. What exactly did these theorists mean by the claim that consciousness is emergent? Did Eccles and Popper mean to be making the same claim as Sperry, or did they have something rather different in mind? To answer these questions we must have some idea of the different possible meanings of the term 'emergent'. The primary aim of this entry is to provide a taxonomy of emergentist theories of consciousness.

Broadly speaking, three categories of emergentism can be identified. From strongest to weakest, they are as follows. *Metaphysical emergentism* is the view that conscious properties are not strongly (metaphysically/logically) fixed by physical (or functional) properties. The metaphysical emergentist may hold that conscious properties depend on physical properties as a matter of law-like necessity, but denies that the relationship between physical and conscious properties is stronger than law-like determination. *Determination emergentism* is the view that consciousness has unique determinative capacities or powers of either a diachronic (generally causal) or synchronic (generally mereological) nature—e.g. by a process of so-called *downward causation*, it can exert an influence on neurophysiological processes. Finally, *explanatory emergentism* is the view that either (1) we cannot predict or explain consciousness from the basis of neuroscience even though the identity theory is true *or* (2) we cannot model consciousness in physical terms but must instead appeal to distinctively high-level explanatory frameworks, such as that provided by folk psychology, in order to do so.

Although there are deep connections between these various forms of emergentism, they are at least conceptually distinct; self-described emergentists might want to endorse some of these positions without endorsing all of them. The failure to recognize this fact is responsible for much of the confusion surrounding discussions of emergence. In all probability, Eccles and Popper held that consciousness is emergent in each of these three senses. However, Sperry's version of emergentism was more restrictive, for although he endorsed a form of determination and explanatory emergence for consciousness, he rejected metaphysical emergence, holding instead that consciousness is metaphysically fixed by physical properties.

1. Metaphysical emergentism
2. Determination emergentism
3. Explanatory emergentism

1. Metaphysical emergentism

Although the metaphysical emergentist might allow that there is some sense in which consciousness depends on—or is determined by—the physical world, he holds that there is a deeper sense in which the conscious facts are not determined by the physical facts. The metaphysical emergentist denies that the physical determination of consciousness is 'thorough-going'. This notion of thorough-going determination is often unpacked in terms of metaphysical supervenience, where a property P is metaphysically supervenient on Q if and only if there no way in which an object could have had Q but lacked P.

Debates about whether or not conscious facts metaphysically supervene on the physical facts are often approached via the question of whether the concept of consciousness admits of a full physical or functional analysis. Emergentists sometimes argue that since the facts about consciousness cannot, in principle, be derived from the physical facts, then the conscious facts do not metaphysically supervene on the physical facts. Chalmers (1996) is well known for taking this position; in fact, he argues that conscious properties are the only properties that fail to metaphysically supervene on fundamental physical properties.

The failure of metaphysical supervenience would not preclude conscious properties from supervening on the physical with nomological necessity—i.e. in virtue of the laws of nature—and emergentists typically hold that conscious facts are nomologically dependent on the physical facts. In taking this position, the emergentist posits brute psycho-physical bridge laws which determine the distribution of conscious properties given physical properties. According to many theorists, it is the need to posit such brute psycho-physical bridge laws which distinguishes consciousness from other 'high-level' properties, such as chemical or biological properties, for—according to many contemporary metaphysical emergentists—we have no need to posit brute bridge laws in order to account for the relationship between physical and chemical properties or between physical and biological properties. (Of course, these 'high-level' properties might be emergent in some other sense.) In taking this line contemporary metaphysical emergentists depart from their predecessors, such as C. D. Broad, who typically held that chemical and biological properties are also metaphysically emergent.

2. Determination emergentism

Metaphysical and nomological determination must be distinguished from both diachronic and synchronic forms of determination. *Diachronic* notions of emergence are generally causal. Causal emergentists generally hold that consciousness possesses its own distinctive *causal powers*. These causal powers might depend on the causal powers of the physical properties on which the conscious properties in question depend, but they will not simply be identical to them. Self-described dualists typically hold that consciousness is emergent in this sense, but many non-dualists also endorse some form of causal emergentism. On the *synchronic* side, *mereological emergentism* is the thesis that the properties of wholes are not fully determined by the properties and relations of their parts. That is, mereologically emergent properties of a whole are not 'realized' by the properties of their proper parts. A mereologically emergent property is a property of the whole that is not mereologically determined at a time *t* by the properties of its proper parts. I deal with mereological emergence before turning to causal emergence.

Mereological determination needs to be distinguished from both *smallism* and *localism*. Smallism is the claim that mental states and functions are determined by the smallest scale of physical reality (see Bickle 2007). Localism (or *vehicle internalism*) is the view that conscious states reside solely within the head or body. If you believe that mental states and functions supervene essentially on large-scale neural dynamics (Skarda and Freeman 1987) then you are a localist but not a smallist. If you believe that brain–body–world are truly dynamically (non-linearly) coupled—as some extended, embodied, and dynamical accounts of conscious experience and cognition maintain (Thompson 2007, Silberstein 2006, and Chemero forthcoming)—then you are neither a smallist nor a localist. The point is that the failure of smallism or localism does not *necessarily* imply a thoroughgoing mereological emergence but rather speaks to the scope or level of the supervenience base for conscious systems.

It is important to note that the proponent of mereological emergence need not deny that consciousness can be explained in terms of fundamental physical theory. Take the following analogy. On any interpretation of quantum mechanics, quantum entanglement implies mereological emergence: entangled states are neither formally (the non-factorizability of such states) nor empirically (experimentally confirmed distinct quantum probabilities for outcomes in EPR correlations) a function of the (intrinsic) properties of the particles that 'make them up' (Silberstein 2002). Obviously entangled states do not imply metaphysical or explanatory emergence since they are a logical consequence of the fundamental laws of quantum mechanics. (It must be stressed that this is only an analogy; no claim is being made that consciousness has anything to do with quantum mechanics or vice versa!) More generally, mereological emergence does not entail the failure of scientific explanation *as such*, it only entails the failure of a certain kind of 'atomistic' reductive explanation. Sometimes a more fundamental theory such as quantum mechanics can predict and explain the occurrence of a qualitatively new phenomenon that is 'more than the sum of its parts' or 'at a higher level' and the same thing could turn out to be true about the neuroscientific explanation of conscious experience (Silberstein 2001).

Let us turn now to causal emergence—the view that consciousness possesses its own causal powers. Causal emergentism is intuitively compelling, but it faces a notoriously difficult challenge in the form of Kim's causal exclusion problem (Kim 1993). If (1) all instances of conscious states are *synchronically* determined by underlying microphysical states (the realization thesis), and if (2) all microphysical states are completely *diachronically* necessitated by antecedent microphysical states (causal or dynamical closure of the physical), then (3) there is no casual work left for conscious states as such to do. What gaps in the causal nexus are there for consciousness to fill?

There are three main responses to Kim's challenge. Firstly, one can accept (1) and (2) and try to cook up some notion of conscious cause that does not violate them. In other words, one could accept that although, strictly speaking, consciousness has no autonomous causal powers or efficacy, it does play some sort of deflationary causal role. Some proponents of this approach hold that conscious states are *causally relevant* without being causes as such; others hold that conscious states are causes in a counterfactual sense of the notion, for they figure in robust counterfactual supporting higher-level explanations of behaviour.

A second response to the causal exclusion problem is to accept (2) but deny (1). In one way or another, all such responses give up the principle of downward causation which says that a mental property instance *m* can only cause another mental property instance m^* to come about by causing its physical realizer property p^* to come about. Examples of this strategy include the kind of mereological emergence discussed above (Silberstein 2001) and Humphreys' emergence as 'fusion' (1997), synchronically conceived, in which the original property instances at a time *t* no longer exist as separate contemporaneous entities and they no longer have all their *i*-level determinative powers available for use at the $i + 1$ level. Gillett (2002) defends a somewhat weaker and subtler version of this position, arguing that conscious states are truly determinative in that they synchronically (and therefore non-causally) determine the 'causal powers' provided by the fundamental microphysical properties that realize them. For example, a microphysical property *p* may contribute a certain causal power C^* only upon realizing the pain state. We might note that although Gillett's account is perhaps technically consistent with (2), it appears to violate the spirit of the realization doctrine or alternatively, it is in danger of being trivial.

A third way of responding to the causal exclusion problem is to reject both (1) and (2). O'Connor and Wong (2005) defend this position, arguing that given the instantiation of certain complex microstructural properties, basic mental properties will be caused (diachronically) to come into being. Such emergent mental properties will have 'causal powers' not had by any microphysical or microstructural properties and will in turn cause the instantiation of both other microphysical properties and other emergent mental properties. On this view, the causal arrow goes from physical states to conscious states *and* from conscious states to physical states. Of course, the O'Connor and Wong view is explicitly at odds with physicalism, and will thus be found wanting by many.

3. Explanatory emergentism

Metaphysical emergentism and determination emergentism are overtly ontological notions. As such, they can be contrasted with explanatory emergentism. According to many theorists, although conscious states are not themselves distinct from physical states, we cannot appeal fully to physical models or theories in order to understand them. Here are two such versions of emergentism, the first kind stronger than the second and probably entailing it.

Certain wholes (systems) appear to have features that cannot in practice be derived, explained, or predicted from the features of their parts, their mode of combination and the laws governing their behaviour, even though the features of the whole are logical consequences of the features of the parts. We can say that in such cases *X* bears predictive/explanatory emergence with respect to *Y*. McGinn and other so-called '*mysterians' famously hold that conscious experience is emergent in this sense with respect to neuroscience even though the identity theory may well be true. A notable form of predictive/explanatory emergence is what Mark Bedau (1997) calls *weak emergence*, according to which features of a macroscopic state can be derived from a knowledge of the system's microdynamics and external conditions, but only by simulating it—i.e. by modelling all the interactions of the realizing microstates leading up to it from its initial conditions.

A second form of explanatory emergence concerns the representational resources needed to represent consciousness. Certain wholes (systems) exhibit features, patterns, or regularities that cannot be fully represented and understood using the theoretical and representational resources adequate for describing and understanding the features and regularities of their parts and reducible relations. Even when the properties of the whole are metaphysically determined by the properties of the proper parts of the whole, we might not be able to model the properties of the whole in terms of the vocabulary that we use to model the properties of the parts. According to many, this is precisely the situation that confronts us in attempting to understand consciousness: conscious events themselves are 'nothing but' neurophysiological events, but we cannot accurately model them with the descriptive resources of neuroscience alone. Instead, many claim, we must appeal to folk psychology and phenomenology in order to understand consciousness. *X* bears representational/cognitive emergence with respect to *Y*, if *X* does *not* bear predictive/explanatory emergence with respect to *Y*, but nonetheless *X* represents higher-level patterns or regularities that cannot be fully, properly, or easily represented or understood from the perspective of *Y*. Many non-reductive physicalists take this view about both folk and scientific psychology. They hold that even if one could derive folk psychology from neuroscience one would still lack the powerful understanding of conscious processes and their relation to behaviour that the former provides.

Those who adopt either form of explanatory emergence are likely to argue that conscious states constitute a *distinct natural kind* (i.e. a qualitatively new type of property); this claim is on the border of *epistemology and metaphysics and can thus be spun either way. Kim (2006) arrives at natural kind of emergence by way of predictive/explanatory emergence. He holds that a property is reducible if and only if it is functionally reducible and conscious experience fails to be so. He argues that there is no a priori connection between the functional role of *pain and the qualitative or conscious experience of pain. So even though the physical realizer of pain fixes all its causal powers, one could not a priori predict the existence of the conscious experience of pain even given the relevant functional and physical background knowledge. In light of this, he holds that conscious properties constitute distinct natural kinds. Searle (2004) arrives at the same position by way of representational/cognitive emergence. Although he denies that consciousness is causally emergent, he holds that the phenomenological and perspectival features of consciousness are distinct from the objective third-person neurophysical aspects of brain states, and therefore that conscious properties qualify as distinct natural kinds.

M. SILBERSTEIN

Bedau, M. (1997). 'Weak emergence'. *Philosophical Perspectives*, 11.

Bickle, J. (2007). 'Who says you can't do a molecular biology of consciousness?' In Schouten, M. and Looren de Jong, H. (eds) *The Matter of the Mind: Philosophical Essays on Psychology, Neuroscience and Reduction*.

Chalmers, D. (1996). *The Conscious Mind*.

Gillett, C. (2002). 'The dimensions of realization: a critique of the standard view'. *Analysis*, 62.

Humphreys, P. (1997). 'How properties emerge'. *Philosophy of Science*, 64.

Kim, J. (1993). *Supervenience and Mind*.

—— (2006). 'Being realistic about emergence'. In Clayton, P. and Davies, P. (eds) *The Re-emergence of Emergence*.

O'Connor, T. and Wong, Hong Yu (2005). 'The metaphysics of emergence'. *Noûs*, 39.

Searle, J. (2004). *Mind: a Brief Introduction*.

Silberstein, M. (2001). 'Converging on emergence: consciousness, causation and explanation'. *Journal of Consciousness Studies*, 8.

—— (2002). 'Reduction, emergence, and explanation'. In Machamer, P. and Silberstein, M. (eds) *The Blackwell Guide to the Philosophy of Science*.

—— (2006). 'In defense of ontological emergence and mental causation'. In Clayton, P. and Davies, P. (eds) *The Re-emergence of Emergence*.

—— and Chemero, A. 'Extended phenomenological cognitive systems'. In van Orden, G. and Stephen, D. (eds) *Topics in Cognitive Science: Special Issue on the Role of Complex Systems in Cognitive Science*.

Skarda, C. and Freeman, W. (1987). 'How the brain makes chaos to make sense of the world'. *Behavioral and Brain Sciences*, 10.

Thompson, E. (2007). *Mind in Life: Biology, Phenomenology, and the Sciences of Mind*.

emotion, implicit Emotions are complex and often rapid responses of the nervous system that typically involve bodily changes. They generally arise from the continual evaluation of stimuli, often in relation to a particular context and particular goals. As such, and insofar as they are identified with feelings, they are often thought to be necessarily accessible to consciousness. There is considerable evidence that stimulus evaluation by specialized neuronal circuits can sometimes trigger automatic and rapid emotional responses in the absence of awareness of the stimuli that elicited them. More controversial are recent data suggesting that the emotional response itself can show hedonic influences on behaviour in the absence of conscious experience of the emotion.

It was long believed that awareness of the emotion is a necessary constituent of an emotional reaction. For instance, it seems commonsensical that preparing to flee a fear-inducing stimulus would not be possible without being aware both of the stimulus and of its threatening quality. Yet recent evidence suggests that in many cases emotional responses do not require awareness and that *feelings*, the conscious perception of emotions, and the emotional responses themselves, are distinct processes.

Emotions can be implicit in two ways: one can be unaware of the stimulus or of the emotional reaction itself. It has been demonstrated in recent experiments that neither the awareness of the stimulus itself, the emotional quality of the stimulus, nor the feeling of the emotional reaction are necessary for emotions to have an impact on behaviour. Emotions can, under some circumstances, be completely unconscious, or implicit.

The best understood and most publicized example of emotion without recognition of the stimulus comes from studies using Pavlovian fear *conditioning. Those studies have shown that fast emotional responses to conditioned stimuli can occur under conditions in which the stimulus is subliminal. The presumed neurological pathway mediating this effect involves subcortical structures such as the amygdala, and bypasses standard neocortical processing routes that are thought to be necessary for conscious detection, discrimination, and identification of the stimulus (LeDoux 1996). This is also the pathway that has been shown to be involved in humans with *blindsight: following abolition of conscious vision due to a lesion of visual cortex, such patients can nonetheless exhibit behaviour demonstrating they can categorize visual stimuli based on some aspect of their emotional meaning. The pathway in the case of vision is thought to proceed from retina to superior colliculus, to the pulvinar nucleus of the thalamus and hence to the amygdala (Morris et al. 2001).

Other studies have used a technique called *binocular rivalry to experimentally manipulate the awareness of visual stimuli. When the visual system is confronted with two different stimuli, one to the left eye and another to the right, only one will be consciously perceived and awareness will alternate between the two percepts. One study presented photographs of faces and houses to viewers, one to each eye, and measured brain responses in a magnetic resonance scanner (Williams et al. 2004; see FUNCTIONAL BRAIN IMAGING). The photographs showed images of faces with either a fearful, happy, or neutral expression. Brain activity in the fusiform gyrus, an area involved in conscious face processing, correlated with the perception of the face. However, parts of the amygdala reacted more strongly to fearful faces than to neutral or happy ones. Importantly, the amygdala's discrimination of the emotion in faces was seen regardless of whether the subjects were conscious of the face or of the house. Another study used a related technique, called *continuous flash suppression*, to arrive at similar conclusions with careful psychophysical demonstration of non-conscious perception (Jiang and He 2006). Interestingly, that study found that while the amygdala's response to neutral faces was decreased when the faces were not consciously perceived, its response to unseen fearful faces remained as strong as when they were processed consciously. These findings argue that specific brain areas process the emotional value of stimuli without the need for their conscious perception.

But can emotions themselves be non-conscious? Although this question may sound confused, some have argued it in the affirmative (Winkielman and Berridge 2004). In one experiment, subjects were shown subliminal happy or angry faces and then asked to drink a novel lemon–lime beverage. The faces were displayed for 16 ms, followed by a photograph with a neutral facial expression to mask the perception. Thirsty subjects who were shown the happy faces consumed twice as much beverage and rated its pleasantness higher than subjects who were shown neutral or angry faces. When asked to give an estimate of the monetary value of the beverage in a second experiment, they indicated that they were willing to pay about twice as much after having been exposed to the happy faces as compared to the angry faces. This experiment indicates that motivational aspects of emotional states, at least, can change without our awareness of the change.

A second demonstration that the influences of stimuli on motivated behaviour can be dissociated from their recognition comes from patient B., who has extensive bilateral lesions including gustatory cortex (Adolphs et al. 2005). As a consequence of the *brain damage he has lost taste perception and cannot identify different flavours or odours. When offered solutions of sugar, saline, or lime juice, he drank all of them with a pleased facial expression. Normal subjects could identify all solutions and found the saline and lime juice so aversive that they stopped drinking it after the first sip. Although B. thus showed no indication either that he was conscious of the sensory properties of the solutions, or that he was conscious of their hedonic properties, he nevertheless showed a strong preference when given a choice between contemporaneously presented beverages. After sampling from both, he reliably preferred to drink the sugar solution rather than the saline solution. Despite no conscious perception of the unpleasant salty taste, he vehemently refused to drink the salty solution when encouraged to do so in the comparison condition. Thus, he had strong motivational preferences based on emotional processing of which he was unaware: he knew he wanted one drink more than the other, but he did not know why. This study also hints at one of the possible functional roles for consciousness: it allows us to tag stimuli to the modality through which we perceived them (e.g. for the above experiment, we normally know our preference is based on taste).

Having implicit emotions makes good engineering sense for the same reason that it is advantageous, under some circumstances, to be unaware of what goes on in our minds more generally: were we aware of everything we process, we would be overwhelmed. Implicit emotions may thus bias our behaviour more efficiently, reserving explicit emotions for those occasions where we need to know about their source or be in a position to volitionally regulate their influence on our actions. There may be an interesting bias towards a greater contribution of explicit processing for those emotions that require more deliberate appraisal, such as the 'social' or 'moral' emotions (shame, guilt, embarrassment, etc.). The extent to which different emotions may differentially engage implicit versus explicit processing is an important topic for future research.

Where does this leave us with respect to the relationship between emotion and consciousness? We have argued here that consciousness may not be necessary for emotion, and we have argued elsewhere that emotion may instead be a necessary prerequisite for consciousness, if the two are construed sufficiently broadly (Tsuchiya and Adolphs 2007). In particular, the state of consciousness may depend on a particular content that all conscious states share—one's awareness that it is oneself that is having the conscious experience, a process thought to involve body-state representations that also underpin emotions (Damasio, 1999).

DIRK NEUMANN AND RALPH ADOLPHS

Adolphs, R., Tranel, D., Koenigs, M., and Damasio, A. (2005). 'Preferring one taste over another without recognizing either'. *Nature Neuroscience*, 8.

Damasio, A. R. (1999). *The Feeling of What Happens: Body and Emotion in the Making of Consciousness*.

Jiang, Y., and He, S. (2006). 'Cortical responses to invisible faces: dissociating subsystems for facial-information processing'. *Current Biology*, 16.

LeDoux, J. (1996). *The Emotional Brain.*
Morris, J. S., deGelder, B., Weiskrantz, L., and Dolan, R. J. (2001). 'Differential extrageniculostriate and amygdala responses to presentation of emotional faces in a cortically blind field'. *Brain*, 124.
Tsuchiya, N., and Adolphs, R. (2007). 'Emotion and consciousness'. *Trends in Cogntive Science*, 11.
Williams, M. A., Morris, A. P., McGlone, F., Abbott, D. F., and Mattingley, J. B. (2004). 'Amygdala responses to fearful and happy facial expressions under conditions of binocular suppression'. *Journal of Neuroscience*, 24.
Winkielman, P., and Berridge, K. C. (2004). 'Unconscious emotions'. *Current Directions in Psychological Science*, 13.

emotion, philosophical perspectives Contemporary philosophers differ widely on how they understand the nature of emotion. There is no consensus on what emotions are, nor any agreement on how to individuate emotions and distinguish them from other affective states such as moods, sentiments, and feelings. Even the idea that emotions form a distinct class, or natural kind, is suspect. To complicate things, there is no methodological agreement on how to address these issues. It is therefore not surprising to find there is no uniform position on the relation between consciousness and emotion in contemporary philosophy of emotion. Paradoxically, many philosophical discussions of emotion ignore consciousness entirely while others consider it their daily bread.

Some explanation for this general state of affairs can be gleamed from the history of the philosophy of emotion over the last century. There is a trend that leads away from analytical philosophical approaches that focus primarily on the logical and conceptual analysis of emotion terms and concepts, to discussions that build instead on experimental and theoretical developments in emotion science. This trend suggests a distinction between two methodological approaches to the philosophy of emotion. On the one hand, there is the *analytic* approach, which some scientific philosophical critics sardonically refer to as an 'odd backwater' (Griffiths 1997:172). According to this approach, conceptual and linguistic analysis is the final arbiter of truth in matters that concern emotion. The methodology is still widely popular today. Then there is scientific philosophy of emotion. According to that approach, the final arbiter of truth about emotion is emotion science. This methodology is becoming increasingly popular.

The new scientific philosophy of emotion is heavily invested in questions of consciousness. Some proof of this can be gleamed from the fact that there is a special journal and book series devoted to the topic, namely, *Consciousness and Emotion* (Ellis and Newton 2000). The situation is more complicated when we turn to analytic philosophy of emotion. Here we find *cognitive* theories of emotion, which tend to neglect the topic of consciousness entirely, and *perceptual* (or 'feeling') theories of emotion, which typically make strong assumptions about the relevance of consciousness to emotion. Despite challenges, this division of labour between cognitive and perceptual theories of emotion remains a hallmark of the philosophy of emotion. Accordingly it will play an important role in this discussion, which will focus on the subject of consciousness from the vantage point of analytic philosophy of emotion. The status of consciousness in scientific philosophy of emotion is considered elsewhere in this volume (see EMOTION, IMPLICIT; EMOTION, SCIENTIFIC PERSPECTIVES).

1. Cognitive theories
2. Perceptual theories
3. Emotionality
4. Valence
5. Permeability
6. Indeterminacy

1. Cognitive theories

The history of cognitive theories of emotion really starts with the ancient Stoics, many of whom considered emotions to be akin to judgements. Analytic philosophers of emotion often take this to mean that emotions take propositional objects as their intentional relata. Those intentional objects specify the content of each emotion; what it is about. On this view, the intentional object of an emotion is usually specified by citing a proposition. To be angry, is to be angry that *P*, where *P* is some proposition. Since propositions are cognitive posits *par excellence*, this makes emotions cognitive. The propositional content of emotion has led some analytic philosophers to treat them as a species of the propositional attitudes (Gordon 1987). It is also possible to speak of emotions as *thoughts* (Solomon 2004). Others emphasize the normative character of emotions and prefer to speak of them as *judgements of value* (Nussbaum 2001). Common to all these views is the thesis that emotions are fundamentally cognitive—even if they have other components, such as outer behavioural and internal physiological accompaniments.

Cognitive accounts of emotion build on the fact that emotions are about putative events or states of affairs in the world. The cognitive content of an emotion is usually said to be expressed by a proposition, which can either fail or succeed to correspond that putative event or state of affair. As a result, emotions are susceptible to rational assessment. I can be angry about the fact that Bob stole my car, even though, as a matter of fact, I am mistaken about that fact. In such a case, my anger is unreasonable, or irrational. Because of their propositional content, emotions also have logical structure; at minimum, a subject term and predicate clause. Consequently, emotions have internal logical structure and they can stand in logical relation to other emotions and cognitive mental states, like beliefs and desires. This illustrates another way in which emotions are subject to rational assessment. For example, it is logically inconsistent, and therefore irrational, for me to be overjoyed that it is Monday if I also believe that it is it is Tuesday. And I cannot logically both hope and not hope that you will win at the races.

Now what about consciousness? How does the subject figure in analytic cognitive philosophical theories of emotion? To start, there is an obvious sense in which cognitive theories of emotion are committed to the fact that emotions are conscious. Emotions are conscious for the same reasons, and to the same extent, that their underlying cognitive states are conscious. Generally, this fact is taken to be so obvious that it does not need to be mentioned. What is surprising is that most cognitive theories go no further than this. In fact, many key texts in the area do not even cite the term 'consciousness' in their index.

So, consciousness as such is rarely discussed in contemporary analytic philosophy of emotion. Admittedly, some cognitive theorists are interested in consciousness peripherally. For example, some wonder whether emotions can be unconscious (Wollheim 1999). Moreover, the attempt to determine the exact nature of cognition in emotion is sometimes thought to have implications for the contents of emotional consciousness (Salmela 2002). However, aside from exceptions such as these, the topic of consciousness is seldom explicitly discussed in analytical cognitive theories of emotion. The situation is very different with perceptual theories.

2. Perceptual theories

Perceptual theories of emotion burst and buzz with speculations about the nature and content of emotional consciousness. They usually tie emotional consciousness to the experience of subjective feelings, with which emotions are often identified. According to these theories, the subjective feelings we normally associate with emotions carry important information about the world. Emotional feelings are tantamount to a special form of perception, or feeling. Most importantly, they inform us about our internal physiological and psychological reactions to external events and situations. On some accounts, they also inform us about external events and situations themselves.

Sometimes, perceptual theories of emotion differ from their cognitive counterparts because of the kinds of intentional objects they take. Cognitive theories must take 'cognitive' items as their intentional objects in order to count as cognitive. However, perceptual theories are not restricted to that requirement. Indeed, perceptual theories are often said to take intentional items that are less than propositional as their intentional objects. These are variously called *quasi-intentional* or *sub-propositional*.

Partly, but not simply, because of their different intentional objects, cognitive and perceptual emotional states can also differ in the kinds of psychological attitudes they are. In some cases, perceptual theories relate a subject's feelings to intentional objects of various sorts, sometimes even propositional ones. This is different from the cognitive case, where it is a subject's cognitive-emotive mental states, but not feelings, that are related to an intentional object. Finally, there are cases where perceptual theorists allude to emotional feelings that are not intentional in any sense, but instead more like sensations (Be'en Ze'ev 2000). Note that, like their cognitive analytical counterparts, perceptual theories of emotion of the analytic variety do not usually raise or discuss the possibility of unconscious emotions.

3. Emotionality

We have seen that consciousness figures variably in analytic cognitive and perceptual philosophical theories of emotion. Supposing that there is such a thing as emotional consciousness according to the terms of either of these approaches, in what does the *emotionality* of emotional consciousness reside? This is a question on which perceptual theorists have more to say than their cognitive counterparts.

The cognitive answer to this question is limited and lies in the special nature of the so-called *formal objects* of the emotions. Consider John, who is angry that Bob stole his car. We have seen that John's anger has an intentional object, which in this case is expressed by the proposition 'Bob stole my car'. This propositional object specifies the content of John's anger; what it is *about*. Now, in addition to this kind of *epistemological* intentional object, emotions are also sometimes said to have an *affective* or *formal* object (de Sousa 1987:121–3).

Every emotion has its own formal object and 'there are as many formal objects as there are emotion types' (de Sousa 1987:123). It is helpful to define the formal object of an emotional state as 'the *standard of correctness* for that state' (de Sousa 1987:122). Thus John's anger is 'correct' or appropriate only if the event or situation that serves as the intentional epistemological object of his anger is the sort of situation that can be described as anger-provoking. In a similar manner, John's fear or hope that *P* is 'correct' or 'appropriate' only if its object can be described as fearsome or fear-provoking, or 'hopeful' and 'hope-provoking'. Otherwise, his fear and hope do not fit the situation they are about; they are not correct or appropriate.

We can now return to our question regarding emotionality. According to some cognitivist theorists, the emotionality of emotions is probably best explained by the special affective status of the formal objects of emotion, which define the conditions of emotional correctness or appropriateness for those emotional states. However, this answer simply shifts the explanatory burden to the formal objects of emotion. For now we must ask wherein lies the emotionality of those objects. Then, there is the additional matter of whether and in what sense the formal objects of emotion might be conscious. By this point, we have strayed rather far from the letter of cognitive theories themselves.

4. Valence

Aside from the formal objects of emotion, another clue to the emotionality of emotions in cognitive theories of emotion can be gleamed from the idea of *emotional tone*; this is the special *psychic quality*, or feeling, that accompanies many emotional states. But what exactly is this special kind of emotional tone, or feeling? And wherein does its emotionality reside? Ironically, this cognitive answer to our question regarding emotionality leads us directly to the perceptual camp in analytic philosophy of emotion.

From the vantage point of perceptual theories of emotion, one answer to our question about emotionality lies in the pleasant or unpleasant character of emotional feelings. In his seminal work on emotional feeling, William James alludes to his contemporary, Wundt, as a thinker who holds such a view. But it is certainly not an option for James himself, who treats the idea with derision and ridicule. It is, he says, 'one of the most artificial and scholastic of the untruths that disfigure our science' (James 1894/1994:208, note 11).

In stark contrast to James's attempt to distance emotionality from feelings of pleasure and pain, many analytically oriented philosophers endorse the view that pleasurable and painful feelings are central to emotion; or, at least, that emotions can be classified as *positive* or *negative*, which is a more neutral, non-hedonic, interpretation of the concept of *valence*. Historically, valence in both these senses can be seen in thinkers such as Aristotle, Descartes, Locke, Spinoza, and others.

The main idea behind the concept of valence is that emotions or their associated feelings can be classified as positive or negative (Solomon 2001). What is positive is often associated with pleasure in some way, while what is negative is associated with pain or some form of displeasure. Unfortunately, while interest in the topic of valence is growing in scientific philosophy of emotion, little is said about it in analytic philosophy of emotion. Admittedly, on the analytic side, many cognitive theorists of emotion regularly classify emotions as either positive or negative. This represents one interpretation of how valence relates to emotion. Again, however, the link to consciousness as such is left mostly unexplored.

In the case of perceptual analytic theories, the link between valence and emotional consciousness should be more obvious. This is because the idea that emotional feelings can be positive and pleasurable, or negative and painful, is so prevalent in historical philosophical work on emotion. However, unlike their scientific counterparts in the philosophy of emotion, contemporary analytic perceptual theorists seem reticent to discuss or adopt the idea of valence. This leaves most of them with no clear account of what exactly makes the consciousness of emotional feelings *emotional*. In scientific philosophical work on emotion, the concept of valence is a prominent candidate for the emotionality of experience (Prinz 2004, Charland 2005). But unfortunately there has little progress on this approach to the question in either cognitive or perceptual analytical philosophical theories.

5. Permeability

There is one last intriguing twist to the ambiguous status of consciousness in analytic philosophy of emotion. Cognitive states are sometimes said to be *cognitively penetrable*; that is, they are subject to rational alterability in light of changes in other cognitive states like beliefs and desires. In like manner, cognitive *emotional* states are sometimes said to be cognitively penetrable as well, although at times they are also held to be notorious for their impenetrability and unresponsiveness to reason. This opens one interesting line of inquiry into the dynamic, changing nature of conscious emotional life. Another dynamic feature of conscious emotional life is its permeability to other emotional states and their associated feelings. This permeability is expressed in a number of ways in recent philosophical writings on emotion. It has interesting implications for the relation between consciousness and emotion.

Amélie Rorty has argued that emotions such as love are permeable in a way that marks them off from traditional cognitive states like belief (Rorty 1986). According to her, the permeability of an emotional state involves a dynamic interactive causal interplay between the loving subject and the subject that is loved: 'the lover is affected, changed not only by loving but by the details of the character of the person loved' (Rorty 1986:401). The point here is that love 'is permeable in that the lover is changed by loving and changed by truthful perception of the friend' (Rorty 1986:402).

So, for Rorty, psychological attitudes such as love and other emotions are unlike mental states like beliefs. In particular, they 'are not states identified by a functional relation between the subject and some object:

a person, a state of affairs, a propositional content' (Rorty 1986:399). Instead, psychological attitudes like love 'arise from, are shaped by, dynamic interactions between a subject and an object' (Rorty 1986:399). What is special about such attitudes is their *historicity*: 'they are identified by a characteristic narrative history' (Rorty 1986:401).

Another account of the peculiar dynamic and interactive character of affective states can be found in the work of William Lyons. He argues that 'feelings do not come labelled as to what they are feelings of or as to what they are caused by' (Lyons 1980:130). Instead, 'one labels them as feelings *of* something only by working out a cause or content' (Lyons 1980:130; emphasis in original). According to this view, we do not simply introspect and report the content of emotional feelings. Meaning is attributed to emotional states based on social and other contextual determinants.

6. Indeterminacy

The interactive and dynamic character of emotions and their associated feelings points to an intriguing mystery in the study of consciousness. In many theories of emotional consciousness, the valence of emotional feelings is assumed to be an objective and determinate psychic phenomenon that can be objectively accessed and studied through verbal self-reports. In response to this, it can be argued that there is no objective scientific fact of the matter about what the valence of a particular feeling state is, apart from its being singled out and elaborated in consciousness through attention. In a manner that is reminiscent of some of the alleged indeterminacies of quantum mechanics, valence is probably mostly a product of 'measurement' and the reporting process (Charland 2005:87). This undercuts the widespread assumption that feelings simply have the valence they do, which is then read off by consciousness and made available for verbal report.

Emotional feelings, then, do not wear their valence on their sleeves. It appears there may be no objective scientific fact of the matter, and no determinate philosophical answer, to the question how emotional feelings acquire the personal meaning they have for us and what that meaning is. To attend to and describe a feeling is at the same time to change it forever. In this respect, the nature of emotional consciousness may ultimately turn out to be a mystery rather than a *hard problem that we might solve one day.

LOUIS C. CHARLAND

Be'en Ze'ev, A. (2000). *The Subtlety of Emotion.*

Charland, L. C. (2005). 'The heat of emotion: valence and the demarcation problem'. *Journal of Consciousness Studies*, 12.

De Sousa, R. (1987). *The Rationality of Emotion.*

Ellis, R. and Newton, N. (eds) (2000–). *Consciousness and Emotion.*

Gordon, R. M. (1987). *The Structure of Emotions: Investigations in Cognitive Philosophy.*

Griffiths, P. (1997). *What Emotions Really Are: the Problem of Psychological Categories.*

James, W. (1894/1994). 'The physical basis of emotion'. *Psychological Review*, 1. Reprinted in *Psychological Review*, 101.

Lyons, W. (1980). *Emotion.*

Nussbaum, M. (2001). *Upheavals of Thought.*

Prinz, J. (2004). *Gut Reactions: a Perceptual Theory of Emotion.*

Rorty, A. (1986). 'The historicity of the psychological attitudes: love is not love which alters not when it alteration finds'. *Midwest Studies in Philosophy: Studies in the Philosophy of Mind*, 10.

Salmela, M. (2002). 'The problem of affectivity in cognitive theories of emotion'. *Consciousness and Emotion*, 3.

Solomon, R. C. (2001). 'Against valence ('positive' and 'negative' emotions)'. In *Not Passion's Slave.*

—— (2004). 'Emotions, thoughts, and feelings: emotions as engagements with the world'. In Solomon, R. C. (ed.) *Thinking and Feeling.*

Wollheim, R. (1999). *On the Emotions.*

emotion, scientific perspectives Not so long ago, emotion was a topic that few brain scientists felt was worth pursuing. This was due in large part to the fact that emotions did not figure prominently in the cognitive approach to psychology, which strongly influenced the direction of research on the relation of brain and mind. And, besides, there seemed to be a perfectly good explanation of how the brain makes emotions—the limbic system. It is now widely recognized that a purely cognitive approach to mental function that ignores emotions is at best incomplete, and the limbic system theory of emotion no longer carries the explanatory weight it once did. With these hindrances now in the background, emotions are being avidly pursued across the spectrum of neuroscience, occupying the interests of researchers who study genes and molecules, cellular properties of neurons, behavioural processes, and imaging in normal and pathological brains.

1. Historical aspects of the emotional brain
2. Modern view of the emotional brain
3. Neural circuits of fear
4. Neural basis of other emotions
5. How do conscious feelings come about?
6. Conclusion

1. Historical aspects of the emotional brain

Early theories of the emotional brain by Cannon and Papez proposed that the hypothalamus was responsible for the expression of emotion in behavioural and visceral responses while the conscious experience of emotion depended on the cortical areas. Building on Cannon and Papez, Paul MacLean proposed the influential limbic system theory of emotion, arguing that emotional responses and feelings are both mediated by an evolutionarily old set of cortical structures located in the medial wall of the hemisphere and connected with the hypothalamus either directly or via several subcortical structures, such as the amygdala and other regions. Like his predecessors, MacLean proposed that the hypothalamus meditates the expression of emotion and the cortex, especially the hippocampal cortex, mediates the conscious experience of emotion.

The limbic system theory has been criticized on numerous grounds over the years. First, the evolutionary basis of the limbic system concept was weakened by the discovery of neocortical-like structures in reptiles and birds, thus challenging the crisp distinction between old and new cortex that MacLean proposed. Second, there are still no criteria that define what constitutes a limbic area. Third, the hippocampus, the centrepiece of the limbic system theory, turned out to be more involved in *memory and cognition than in emotion. In spite of these criticisms, the limbic system theory is still a powerful force in neuroscience.

Each of these historical models has thus sought to identify the neural basis of both emotional expression and experience, but much of the actual research on emotion has traditionally involved the expression of emotion in animals. This focus was necessitated by two facts. First, conscious emotional feelings are not easily studied in animals (this is not a statement about whether animals have feelings but a statement about methodology). Second, until recently, techniques for studying the brain were crude. In the absence of other clues, the mechanisms uncovered for emotional responses in animals were assumed also to mediate emotional feelings in humans.

2. Modern view of the emotional brain

The limbic system theory stimulated much research on 'emotion' in the general sense of the term. In recent years, though, research findings have allowed the development of an empirically based, bottom-up, understanding of the emotional brain. This goal of this new work is not so much to explain 'emotion' as to use specific emotion tasks that lead to quantifiable measures of emotional reactions to understand specific aspects of emotion. Since much of this work has focused on tasks that measure fear reactions, this work will be emphasized here. However, research on some other emotions will also be discussed. While much of the work on fear and other emotions in the brain has involved studies of experimental animals, in which the brain can be explored in detail, studies in humans have confirmed and extended the basic findings from animals.

3. Neural circuits of fear

Fear is a particularly useful emotion to focus on, for several reasons. First, it is a universal emotion related to survival. Second, there are good tasks to study it in animal models. Third, it is very closely tied to the psychopathology of anxiety disorders, one of the most prevalent psychiatric conditions that afflict humans today.

The neural circuitry of fear has been known to involve the amygdala for some time. In 1937, Klüver and Bucy discovered that damage to the temporal lobes led to alterations in emotional behaviour, such as the loss of fear responses in the face of threatening stimuli. This is one of the main findings that prompted MacLean to update the Cannon–Bard and Papez theories. Later, Weiskrantz showed that damage to the amygdala accounted for the emotional changes seen by Klüver and Bucy with large lesions of the temporal lobe. In the decades that followed, much research focused on the role of the amygdala in emotion. In fact, evidence that the amygdala contributed to emotion largely justified the limbic system theory since the amygdala was a component of the limbic system. However, the exact manner in which the amygdala participated was unclear.

Part of the difficulty was that the behavioural tasks used to study the role of the amygdala in fear involved complex avoidance conditioning procedures that were carried out in different ways by different labs, making difficult the build up of a systematic understanding of the underlying circuits. Starting in the late 1970s, researchers began to turn to a simpler task, *Pavlovian fear conditioning*.

In fear conditioning, the subject receives a neutral conditioned stimulus (CS), usually a tone, followed by an aversive unconditioned stimulus (US), typically footshock. After one or at most a few pairings, the CS comes to elicit emotional responses that naturally occur in the presence of threatening stimuli. It is important to note that avoidance conditioning involves a Pavlovian phase, and the emotional learning that occurs in avoidance conditioning occurs during this phase. Pavlovian conditioning is thus a more direct means of studying emotional processing.

The simpler approach allowed progress to be made in mapping the fear circuitry because it involves a specific stimulus that is under the complete control of the investigator, and the stimulus, when presented, leads to the expression of a coordinated reaction involving emotional behaviour (freezing) and corresponding changes in autonomic nervous system activity and endocrine responses.

Not surprisingly, research using fear conditioning implicated the amygdala in the acquisition and expression of fear reactions. In brief, CS and US convergence takes place in the lateral nucleus of the amygdala (LA). This convergence leads to synaptic plasticity and the formation of a CS–US association. When the CS later occurs, the associative memory formed by CS–US convergence in LA is retrieved and leads to activation in the central amygdala, which then connects to hypothalamic and brainstem areas that control behavioural, autonomic, and hormonal responses that help the organism cope with the threat. Thus, the lateral amygdala can be thought of as a threat detector or appraiser and the central amygdala as the reaction control region. (This simplified description of the fear conditioning circuitry omits many details.)

Research in humans has confirmed the essential role of the amygdala in fear conditioning. Thus, damage to the amygdala in humans prevents fear conditioning from occurring and *functional brain imaging (fMRI) studies show that activity increases in the amygdala during fear conditioning. Further, fear conditioning can occur in the absence of awareness of the CS and its relation to the US in humans. Other studies showed that emotional faces, unconditioned emotional stimuli, elicit activity in the amygdala, and that these responses occur in the absence of any conscious awareness of the stimulus. Thus, both conditioned and unconditioned emotional stimuli elicit activity in the amygdala and autonomic nervous system responses independent of conscious awareness of the stimulus.

Recent studies in humans have added additional dimensions to the amygdala's role in fear processing. For example, instructed fear conditioning involves telling subjects that a CS may be followed by a shock. Even if the shock is never delivered, the CS comes to elicit GSR responses. Functional imaging studies show that the amygdala is activated by such instructed stimuli. GSR responses can also be conditioned by watching others be conditioned and the amygdala is also involved in this social fear learning.

The amygdala does not function alone in fear. One important additional region is the medial prefrontal cortex (mPFC). Damage to this region interferes with the ability to regulate emotion, as assessed in extinction tests where the subject is exposed to the CS repeatedly until the fear reaction weakens. Connections between the mPFC and amygdala are believed to contribute to extinction. Recent fMRI studies in humans also implicate mPFC areas in extinction and other aspects of fear regulation.

Thus, emotional processes that control emotional responses involve the same basic circuits in humans as in other animals, and occurs unconsciously in humans. At the same time, under normal conditions people will often be consciously aware of the stimulus that is eliciting emotional arousal. As we see below, this involves additional circuits. First, though, we will consider the circuitry underlying some other emotions.

4. Neural basis of other emotions

Emotions besides fear that have also been studied include aggression, attachment and separation, pleasure and reward, and some social emotions. However, the neural mechanisms of these are understood in less detail than in the case of fear. For illustrative purposes we will consider some aspects of the neural basis of positive emotions, especially in the context of reward-based motivation and addiction.

Just as a CS paired with shock acquires aversive properties, a CS paired with tasty food or addictive drugs acquires appetitive properties. The appetitive properties of a CS are evident from the fact a rat will orient to and approach a stimulus that has been paired with a positive US. Further, just as rats will work to avoid a CS paired with shock, they will work to obtain a CS paired with a positive stimulus. Through this kind of learning, cues associated with drug use are believed to trigger relapse.

Much work on appetitive conditioning has examined the role of dopamine inputs to the nucleus accumbens. Release of dopamine in this region leads to the invigoration of behaviour, guiding behaviour towards goal objects. The amygdala also plays a key role in processing a CS during appetitive conditioning. In contrast to aversive conditioning, appetitive conditioning seems to involve the central amygdala. The basal and lateral amygdala seem to be especially important in the ability of a CS to function as a second-order or conditioned reinforcer that supports new learning. Another brain region involved is the orbitofrontal cortex, which contribute the evaluation of the incentive or motivating properties of a CS through interactions with the amygdala and nucleus accumbens.

5. How do conscious feelings come about?

There are three major hypotheses about how conscious feelings come about. Panksepp's theory emphasizes the similarity of a conscious emotional experience in humans and other animals. Damasio's somatic marker hypothesis highlights the importance of bodily feedback during emotion in defining conscious feelings. My *working memory theory of feelings accepts the basic premises of the other two theories but focuses on the unique aspects of human emotional experience made possible by unique evolutionary features of the human brain.

Panksepp's model seeks to explain what might be common in human and non-human emotional experience. For him, similar behavioural expression of emotion in two species is evidence for similar conscious experience. While I accept that there may be core mechanisms of consciousness that are common in humans and other animals that give rise to coarse feeling states, I think that a theory of human feelings needs to account for unique features of human consciousness made possible by, in fact defined by, the unique features of the brain the emerged with human evolution. More about this below.

Damasio has proposed that a feeling involves the awareness of bodily responses. This is an update of an earlier theory by William James. Damasio's somatic maker hypothesis assumes that conscious feelings are based on emotional responses initiated by the unconscious processing of emotional stimuli. Damasio has amassed evidence for his theory showing that so-called body-sensing areas of the cortex (somatosensory and insular areas) are active when people consciously feel emotions. However, these findings are largely correlational rather than causal. It remains to be determined that information about the bodily response (either in the form of actual feedback or in the form of memory) determines what one feels.

Even if information about the bodily expression of emotions turns out to be necessary in some situations for feelings, the question would arise as to the sufficiency of such information. In particular, feelings are associated not only with the activation of body sensing areas, but also of working memory circuits. I will therefore argue that the conscious experience of a feeling occurs in the same way as the any other conscious experience—by the representation of the relevant information in working memory. This is most easily understood by considering how we become aware of an external stimulus.

Much research suggests that the conscious awareness of external stimuli involve the representation of the stimulus in a multipurpose workspace (working memory) that (1) is regulated by attention, (2) holds onto attended stimuli temporarily, (3) integrates information from multiple sensory modalities, (4) integrates currently processed events with long-term memories, and (5) uses these temporary multisensory, memory-integrated representations in the control of thought (decision-making, planning, imagining, monitoring) and action. Further, it is well established from studies in humans and monkeys that areas in the prefrontal cortex play a key role in working memory. This is especially important in light of the fact that certain areas of the prefrontal cortex involved in working memory are more elaborate in humans than in other primates, and non-existent in other mammals. Human working memory is indeed likely to be unique. Further, the capacity of the human brain for natural language allows working memory to have unique qualities in humans.

Functional imaging studies show that, when subjects are consciously aware of external stimuli, posterior cortical areas that process sensory modality-specific information and prefrontal areas are active, whereas when awareness is prevented by *masking or other techniques posterior sensory but not prefrontal activation occurs. These studies used non-emotional stimuli, but a similar pattern of results occur when emotional stimuli are used. Sensory processing regions in the cortex and/or thalamus and the amygdala are active when emotional stimuli are prevented from entering awareness, but when subjects are consciously aware of emotional stimuli prefrontal activation also occurs.

The working memory hypothesis of feelings proposes that a feeling occurs when several kinds of information are simultaneously processed in working memory: information about the stimulus and the context (social and physical) in which it is occurring; long-term memories (semantic and episodic memories) that provide meaning to the stimulus and its physical and social context); and information about emotional arousal. There are several sources of emotional information that can influence working memory. First, connections from emotional processing regions such as the amygdala to cortical areas provide a means by which emotional processing can directly affect cortical processing. Second, there are connections from the amygdala to brainstem arousal systems that release neuromodulators throughout the brain. These change signal to noise processing, emphasizing the salience of stimuli being processed and memories being activated during the aroused state. Third, connections from the amygdala to brainstem areas that control emotional responses allow such responses to be expressed and their effects to feedback to the brain. The extent to which all of these must be present is not known, but is testable.

6. Conclusion

After a long hiatus, research on emotion has flourished in the past few decades. Much progress has been made in understanding how the brain processes stimuli with emotional significance and controls emotional reactions to such stimuli. While aversive emotions such as fear have been most thoroughly studied, progress has also been made in understanding positive emotional processing as well. Most research on the brain mechanisms of emotion has traditionally involved animal studies. Functional imaging has allowed the confirmation of many of the basic findings in humans, and also new discoveries. Although it is hard to study consciousness, including conscious emotional feelings, recent theories have proposed testable hypotheses that should shed light on how feelings are processed and represented in the brain.

JOSEPH LEDOUX

Buchel, C. and Dolan, R. J. (2000). 'Classical fear conditioning in functional neuroimaging'. *Current Opinion in Neurobiology*, 10.

Cardinal, R. N. and Everitt, B. J. (2004). 'Neural and psychological mechanisms underlying appetitive learning: links to drug addiction'. *Current Opinion in Neurobiology*, 14.
Charney, D. (2003). 'Neuroanatomical circuits modulating fear and anxiety behaviors'. *Acta Psychiatrica Scandinavica Supplement*, 417.
Dolan, R. J. and Vuilleumier, P. (2003). 'Amygdala automaticity in emotional processing'. *Annals of the New York Academy of Science*, 985.
Damasio, A. (1994). *Descartes' Error.*
Davidson, R. and Erwin, W. (1999). 'The functional neuroanatomy of emotion and affective style'. *Trends in Cognitive Science*, 3.
Fellous, J.-M. and Arbib, M.A. (eds) (2005). *Who Needs Emotion?*
Holland, P. C. and Gallagher, M. (2004). 'Amygdala–prefrontal interactions in reward expectancy.' *Current Opinion in Neurobiology*, 14.
Lang, P. J., Davis, M., and Ohman, A. (2000). 'Fear and anxiety: animal models and human cognitive psychophysiology'. *Journal of Affect Disorders*, 61.
LeDoux, J. E. (1996). *The Emotional Brain.*
—— (2002). *Synaptic Self.*
Ohman, A. and Mineka, S. (2001). 'Fears, phobias, and preparedness: toward an evolved module of fear and fear learning'. *Psychological Review*, 108.
Panksеep, J. (1998). *Affective Neuroscience.*
Phelps, E. A. and LeDoux, J. E. (2005). 'Contributions of the amygdala to emotion processing: from animal models to human behavior'. *Neuron*, 48.
Rolls, E. (2005). *Emotion Explained.*

empathy The construct of empathy denotes, at a phenomenological level of description, a sense of similarity between the feelings one experiences and those expressed by others. It can be conceived of as an interaction between any two individuals, with one experiencing and sharing the feeling of the other. Yet, empathic concern is not a clear-cut expression. First, empathy poses a paradox, as sharing of feelings does not necessarily imply that one will act or even feel impelled to act in a supportive or sympathetic way. Second, the social and emotional situations eliciting empathy can become quite complex depending on the feelings experienced by the observed and the relationship of the target to the observer (Feshbach 1997). The caveats demonstrate that understanding others and experiencing their feelings manifests in relation to oneself, illustrating the social nature of the *self, its inherent intersubjectivity. Among the various forms of emotional connections with others, empathy has received much attention from philosophers and psychologists, and more recently from social neuroscientists.

The complexity of human social interaction is among the most pertinent aspects differentiating us from our non-human counterparts. Among our advanced social skills is empathy, the ability to experience and share the feeling of another. Interestingly, comparative psychologists and ethologists suggest that some behaviours homologous to empathy can be found in non-human primates. Preston and de Waal (2002) argue that empathy is not an all-or-nothing phenomenon, and many forms of empathy exist intermediate between the extremes of mere agitation at the distress of another and full understanding of their predicament. Many other comparative psychologists view empathy as a kind of induction process by which emotions, both positive and negative, are shared, and by which the probabilities of similar behaviour are increased in the participants. Though certain non-human primates may share feelings between individuals and respond appropriately, humans may be uniquely able to intentionally 'feel for' and act on behalf of other people whose experiences may differ greatly from their own (Batson 1991). Such a capacity may help explain why empathic concern is often associated with prosocial behaviours such as helping a kin, and has been considered as a chief enabling process to altruism. Evolutionary biologists suggested that empathic helping behaviour has evolved because of its contribution to genetic fitness (kin selection). In humans and other mammals, an impulse to care for offspring is almost certainly genetically hard-wired. Less clear, however, is whether an impulse to care for more remote kin, and similar non-kin, is genetically hard-wired (Batson 2009). The emergence of altruism, of empathizing with and caring for those who are not kin, is thus not fully explained within the framework of neo-Darwinian theories of natural selection. Social learning explanations of kinship patterns in human helping behaviour are thus highly plausible. Indeed, one of the most striking aspects of human empathy is that it can be felt for virtually any target, even a target of a different species.

The debate surrounding empathy among psychologists and philosophers tends to revolve around the meaning of the term. For many psychologists, empathy implies at least three different processes: feeling what another person is feeling; knowing what another person is feeling; and having the intention to respond compassionately to another person's distress (Thompson 2001). Regardless of the particular terminology used, scholars broadly agree on three primary aspects: (1) an affective response to another person, which often, but not always, entails sharing that person emotional state; (2) a cognitive capacity to take the perspective of the other person; and (3) some self-regulatory and monitoring mechanisms that modulate inner states and keep a minimal separation between self and other. This latter aspect is critical because a complete blurring of self and other would be detrimental and is not the purpose of empathy.

Cognitive neuroscience may help reveal the processing components that contribute to empathy. The initial component in the overall processing leading to empathy draws on the somatic mimicry also known as *emotion contagion*, i.e. the tendency to automatically mimic and synchronize facial expressions, vocalizations, postures, and movements with those of another person and, consequently, converge emotionally (Hatfield et al. 1993). The mechanism behind emotional contagion and motor mimicry, which was already posited by Lipps a century ago, relies on the automatic coupling between perception and action. There is now considerable evidence that when we perceive emotions and actions of others, we use the same neural circuits as when we produce the same emotions and actions ourselves (e.g. watching another individual being disgusted and experiencing disgust in oneself activates similar neural substrates). For instance, viewing facial expressions triggers expressions on one's own face, even in the absence of conscious recognition of the stimulus.

Emotional expression is not the only behaviour that leads to an empathic response. Often, humans respond empathetically to threatening situations such as painful events. The existence of the action–perception coupling mechanism apparent in emotional contagion also seems to account for our ability to perceive and understand the pain of others. Recently, a handful of *functional brain imaging studies performed with healthy volunteers revealed that brain areas implicated in processing the affective and motivational aspects of pain mediate the observation of pain in others. In one study, participants in the scanner either received painful stimuli in some trials or, in other trials, observed a signal that their partner, who was present in the same room, would receive the same stimuli (Singer et al. 2004). Interestingly, first-hand experience of pain resulted in the activation of the somatosensory cortex, which encodes the sensory-discriminative dimension of a noxious stimulus such as its bodily location and intensity. Furthermore, the anterior medial cingulate cortex (ACC), the anterior insula, and the cerebellum were activated during both conditions. These regions contribute to the affective and motivational processing of noxious stimuli, i.e. aspects of pain that pertain to desires, urges, or impulses to avoid or terminate a painful experience. Thus merely observing another individual in a painful situation yields pain-related responses in the neural network associated with the coding of the motivational-affective dimension of pain in oneself.

It is worth noting that the mimicry component of empathy is already in place during the first days of life and plays a fundamental role in the development of empathy. Such a perception–action coupling mechanism offers an interesting foundation for intersubjectivity because it provides a functional bridge between first-person information and third-person information, grounded on self–other equivalence, and offers a possible route to understanding others.

Of course, human empathic abilities are more sophisticated than simply yoking of perceptions of the self and other. In the 18th century, the Scottish philosopher and economist Adam Smith proposed that through imagination, 'we place ourselves in his situation . . . enter as it were into his body, and become in some measure the same person with'. By means of imagination we come to experience sensations, which are generally similar to, although typically weaker than, those of the other person. This capacity to engage in role-taking has been theoretically linked to the development of empathy, moral reasoning, and more generally prosocial behaviour. Unlike the motor mimicry and emotional contagion aspect of empathy, perspective-taking develops later, possibly because it draws heavily on the maturation of executive resources (i.e. the processes that serve to monitor and control thought and actions, including self-regulation, planning, cognitive flexibility, response inhibition, and resistance to interference) of the prefrontal cortex, which continues to mature from birth to adolescence. Importantly, research in social psychology has documented a distinction between 'imagine other' and 'imagine self' by showing that the former may evoke empathic concern (defined as an other-oriented response congruent with the perceived distress of the person in need) while the latter induces both empathic concern and personal distress (i.e. a self-oriented aversive emotional response such as anxiety or discomfort). Findings from cognitive neuroscience demonstrate that when individuals are asked to imagine how they would feel in reaction to emotion-laden familiar situations and to imagine how one known person would feel if she was experiencing the same situations, common neural circuits are activated both for the self and the other. However, imagining the other results in specific activation of parts of the *frontal cortex that are implicated in executive control. It has been hypothesized that the role of the frontal lobes could be in holding separate perspectives or in resisting interference from one's own perspective (Decety and Jackson 2004). In a recent fMRI study, participants were shown pictures of people with their hands or feet in painful or non-painful situations with the instruction to imagine themselves or to imagine another individual experiencing these situations (Jackson et al. 2006). Both the self-perspective and the other-perspective were associated with activation in the neural network involved in pain processing, including the parietal operculum, ACC, and anterior insula. These results reveal the similarities in neural networks representing first- and third-person information, which is consistent with the shared representations account of social interaction (Decety and

Sommerville 2003). In addition, the self-perspective yielded higher pain ratings and involved the pain matrix more extensively in the secondary somatosensory cortex, posterior part of the ACC, and middle insula. These results also highlight important differences between the self- and other-perspectives. For instance, while the anterior insula and the ACC are activated both when participants imagine their own pain and when they imagine another's pain, self-perspective is specifically associated with non-overlapping clusters within the middle insula, another aspect of the ACC and the right parietal cortex.

Altogether, these empirical findings demonstrate the similarities between self and other affective representations stemming from shared neural circuits that can be emulated either automatically or intentionally by the act of perspective taking. Importantly, they also point to some distinctiveness between these two representations. This may be what allows us to distinguish empathic responses to others versus our own personal distress.

JEAN DECETY

Batson, C. D. (1991). 'Empathic joy and the empathy-altruism hypothesis'. *Journal of Personality and Social Psychology*, 61.

—— (2009). 'These things called empathy: eight related but distinct phenomena'. In Decety, J. and Ickes, W. (eds) *The Social Neuroscience of Empathy.*

Decety, J. and Jackson, P. L. (2004). 'The functional architecture of human empathy'. *Behavioral and Cognitive Neuroscience Reviews*, 3.

—— and Sommerville, J. A. (2003). 'Shared representations between self and others: a social cognitive neuroscience view'. *Trends in Cognitive Sciences*, 7.

Feshbach, N. D. (1997). 'Empathy: the formative years implications for clinical practice'. In Bohart, A. C. and Greenberg, L. S. (eds) *Empathy Reconsidered.*

Hatfield, E., Cacioppo, J. T., and Rapson, R. L. (1993). 'Emotional contagion'. *Current Directions in Psychological Science*, 2.

Jackson, P. L., Brunet, E., Meltzoff, A. N., and Decety, J. (2006). 'Empathy examined through the neural mechanisms involved in imagining how I feel versus how you feel pain'. *Neuropsychologia*, 44.

Preston, S. D. and de Waal, F. B. M. (2002). 'Empathy: its ultimate and proximate bases'. *Behavioral and Brain Sciences*, 25.

Singer, T., Seymour, B., O'Doherty, J., Kaube, H., Dolan, R. J., and Frith, C. D. (2004). 'Empathy for pain involves the affective but not the sensory components of pain'. *Science*, 303.

Thompson, E. (2001). 'Empathy and consciousness'. *Journal of Consciousness Studies*, 8.

enactive approach See SENSORIMOTOR APPROACH TO (PHENOMENAL) CONSCIOUSNESS

epilepsy Epilepsy, Hippocrates' 'sacred disease', is characterized by recurrent episodes of neurological dysfunction—epileptic seizures—capable of affecting both behaviour and experience, due to the abnormally synchronized electrical discharges of large groups of neurons. There are many different kinds of epilepsy: both the clinical features of seizures and their underlying causes are protean (Duncan et al. 1995).

The most fundamental distinction in seizure classification lies between focal and generalized seizures. *Focal seizures* result from epileptic activity occurring in a circumscribed region of brain tissue—usually, though not always, a region of the cerebral cortex. The resulting clinical features involve alterations of behaviour, experience, cognition, or autonomic function. They are determined by the normal function of the affected brain region. Thus epileptic activity involving the motor cortex may give rise to jerking in the opposite limbs, typically spreading between the parts of the limb over seconds, a *Jacksonian seizure*. This sometimes leaves *postictal* (literally 'after the seizure') weakness in its wake for minutes or hours, a *Todd's paresis*. Seizures arising in the occipital lobe give rise to paroxysmal visual experiences, ranging from coloured patterns to *hallucinatory images. Parietal lobe seizures give rise to paroxysmal disturbance of bodily sensation, including *out-of-body experiences. Temporal lobe seizures, the most common type of focal seizures, are associated with a rising sensation spreading rapidly from the stomach to the head, the *epigastric aura*, olfactory hallucinations, and more complex alterations of experience and cognition including *déjà vu, 'dreamy states', intense emotions, and transient *amnesia. These phenomena provide particularly striking demonstrations of the dependence of the *contents of consciousness on the activity of the brain, and contributed to the evidence for localization of brain function in the early years of clinical neurology (Hughlings-Jackson 1888, 1898). *Reflex epilepsies*, in which a seizure can be triggered by a particular stimulus or activity, including mental acts such as recollection, illustrate the converse relationship: the contents of consciousness can powerfully affect the activity of the brain (Martinez et al. 2001).

In *generalized seizures*, by contrast, the epileptic activity invades the entire cerebral cortex, usually extinguishing awareness. The public stereotype of epilepsy, the *tonic-clonic seizure* or *grand mal*, involves loss of consciousness and tonic stiffening of the body followed by vigorous 'clonic' jerking of all four limbs, lasting a minute or so, often accompanied by tongue-biting and incontinence. *Absence seizures*, which cause transient loss of awareness with little else to see, and *myoclonic seizures*, involving sudden, short-lived muscle jerks, also reflect generalized epileptic activity in the brain.

Some complexities relating to the distinction between focal and generalized seizures should be noted here. Focal epileptic activity can spread gradually through

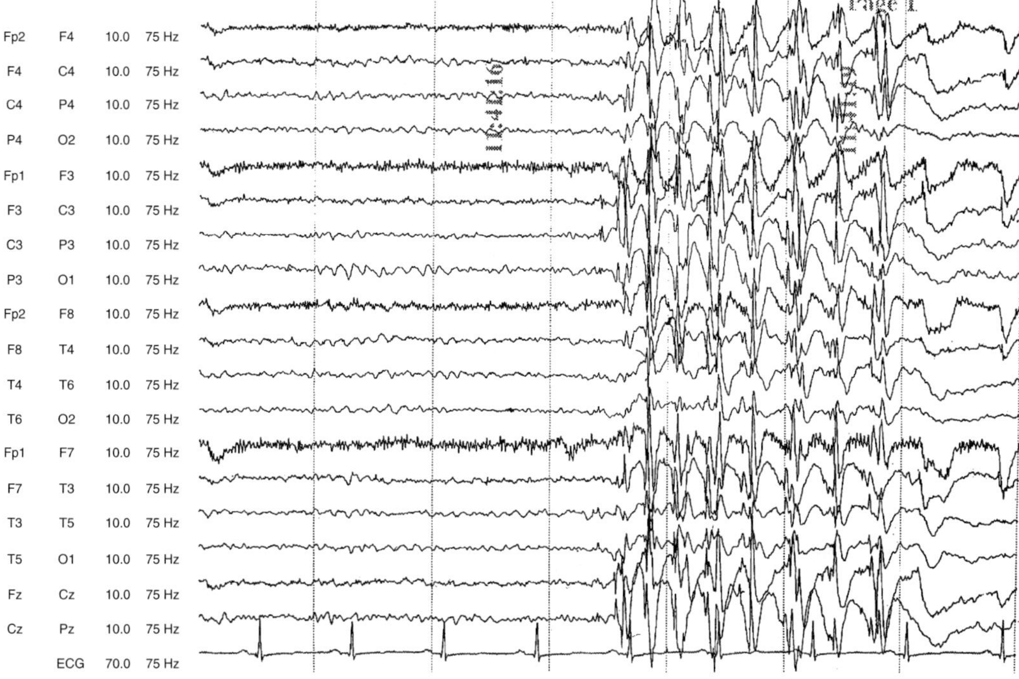

Fig. E2. EEG showing 3 cycles/second 'spike and wave' activity across the entire scalp from a patient with primary generalized (absence) epilepsy.

the brain, giving rise, for example, to a seizure that starts with an experience of déjà vu, progresses to loss of awareness as the sufferer looks blankly ahead, and culminates in a 'secondarily generalized' tonic-clonic seizure. On the other hand, true absence seizures and some tonic-clonic seizures reflect 'primary generalized' activity that appears simultaneously throughout the cortex (Fig. E2), although recent work suggests that cortical involvement may not be absolutely uniform. Identification of seizure type is the first step in classifying epilepsy, but it is often possible to provide a more informative classification into *epilepsy syndrome* by taking into account additional information, such as age, family history, and the results of tests including *electroencephalography (EEG) and brain imaging.

Epilepsy is extremely common, and is presumably a price the brain pays for its massively interconnected organization. Around 10% of us will have an epileptic seizure at some time (half of these are febrile seizures of childhood). At any one time, the prevalence of epilepsy in the developed world approaches 1%. Epilepsy often starts in childhood and old age, less often in early/mid-adulthood. The prognosis of epilepsy depends upon its cause, but about two-thirds of people who develop epilepsy stop having seizures either spontaneously or on treatment. The causes of epilepsy include genetic predisposition (some single gene mutations with epilepsy as their chief manifestation have recently been defined), abnormalities of brain development including subtle disturbances of cortical migration, brain infections (meningitis and encephalitis), head trauma, stroke, and *dementia.

The detailed pathophysiology of epilepsy is understood only in part. Discharges seen between attacks in the EEG of patients with epilepsy are associated with abrupt depolarization shifts in the majority of neurons in the seizure focus, causing them to fire rapid bursts of action potentials (a depolarization shift is an increase in the electrical charge within the neuron that tends to increase its activity). The likelihood of these events is increased by factors that increase neuronal excitability and the strength of excitatory neurotransmission, reduce the strength of inhibitory neurotransmission, and allow the formation of tightly coupled networks of neurons. The physiological processes that allow subclinical events to develop into seizures are complex and controversial. Primary generalized epilepsies are thought to arise from abnormal interaction between cortex and thalamus, but the details here also remain a focus of current research.

The diagnosis of epilepsy can be difficult. It rests above all on a clear description of the events occurring in seizures, both from the sufferer's perspective and by an eye witness. Competing possibilities often include syncope, due to temporary loss of the blood supply to the brain, as in a faint, and non-epileptic attack disorder, an umbrella term for a variety of 'psychological' causes of paroxysmal symptoms, e.g. panic attacks. Several tests can be helpful, but the diagnosis may nevertheless remain unclear. Standard investigations include the EEG (see Fig. E2); brain imaging, ideally with magnetic resonance imaging (MRI; Fig. E3); an electrocardiogram (ECG), to help exclude cardiac causes; and blood tests (e.g. blood glucose and calcium concentrations). A single EEG will detect clear epileptiform abnormalities in about a third of people with epilepsy; repeated recordings, particularly after sleep deprivation, can raise this figure to around three-quarters.

Although epilepsy remains a worrying and sometimes stigmatizing disorder, effective treatments are available. Anticonvulsant drugs are the mainstay of treatment. These work principally by reducing the tendency of neurons to fire spontaneously and/or by increasing inhibition through an action on synaptic receptors. Modern anticonvulsants often control seizures with little sedation or other side effects, though these sometimes occur. In highly selected cases, surgical removal of the brain tissue that is responsible for generating seizures, most often in the temporal lobes, can be curative. Other, broadly 'psychological' approaches to treatment are being explored.

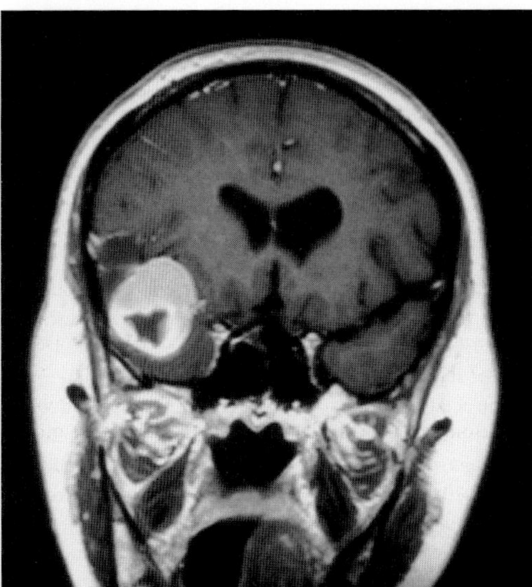

Fig. E3. MRI scan of the brain showing a large benign tumour (meningioma) in the right temporal lobe of a patient who presented with symptoms of panic associated with visual hallucinations that proved to be due to epilepsy. The tumour was successfully removed.

Epilepsy is a 'natural laboratory' for students of the neurology of consciousness. In focal seizures experience can be modified subtly by the epileptic activity, as for example in the experience of epileptic déjà vu. Hughlings Jackson, the 19th-century 'father of neurology' in Britain, coined the term *double consciousness* to describe the experience of patients with temporal lobe epilepsy associated with the 'dreamy state' or 'intellectual aura': sufferers remain aware of their surroundings but are simultaneously aware of an intrusive and pervasive sense of recollection.

The tendency for awareness to be impaired as focal seizures spread through the brain has given rise to a distinction between simple and complex focal seizures: consciousness is preserved in the former, impaired in the latter. Gloor drew attention to the difficulty of drawing this distinction in practice (Gloor 1986, Lux et al. 2002). The impression of 'impaired awareness' may result from amnesia, preoccupation with hallucinatory experiences, altered mood, or language impairment as well as from the complete extinction of consciousness. It is clinically and scientifically unhelpful to lump together these very different explanations for 'unawareness'. The most recent International League Against Epilepsy classification of seizures (ILAE 1989) has taken up Gloor's suggestion that the simple/complex distinction should be abandoned.

There is, however, undoubtedly an important, if sometimes ambiguous, distinction between seizures that do and do not impair consciousness, i.e. between those that do and those that do not, partially or completely, extinguish mental activity. New techniques of *functional brain imaging, in particular the combined, simultaneous, use of functional MRI and the EEG to identify the regional brain activity that correlates with epileptic discharges, are helping to elucidate the neurobiological explanation for the loss of awareness during some seizures, Results to date suggest that the activation of deep structures, especially the thalamus, may be a common factor in seizures that impair awareness, with correlated hyper- or hypoactivation of frontal, parietal, and temporal association cortices (Blumenfeld and Taylor 2003, Blumenfeld 2005).

ADAM ZEMAN

Blumenfeld, H. (2005). 'Consciousness and epilepsy: why are patients with absence seizures absent?' In Laureys, S. (ed.) *The Boundaries of Consciousness*.

—— and Taylor, J. (2003). 'Why do seizures cause loss of consciousness?' *Neuroscientist*, 9.

Duncan, J., Shorvon, S., and Fish, D. R. (1995). *Clinical Epilepsy*.

Gloor, P. (1986). 'Consciousness as a neurological concept in epileptology'. *Epilepsia*, 27.

Hughlings-Jackson, J. (1888). 'On a particular variety of epilepsy ("intellectual aura"), one case with symptoms of organic brain disease'. *Brain*, 11.

Hughlings-Jackson J. (1898). 'Case of epilepsy with tasting movements and "dreamy state"—very small patch of softening in the left uncinate gyrus'. *Brain*, 21.

ILAE (1989). 'Commission on Classification and Terminology of the International League Against Epilepsy. Proposal for revised classification of epilepsies and epileptic syndromes'. *Epilepsia*, 30.

Lux, S., Kurthen, M., Helmstaedter, C., Hartje, W., Reuber, M., and Elger, C. E. (2002). 'The localising value of ictal consciousness and its constituent functions: a video-EEG study in patients with focal epilepsy'. *Brain*, 125.

Martinez, O., Reisin, R., Andermann, F., Zifkin, B. G., and Sevlever, G. (2001). 'Evidence for reflex activation of experiential component of complex partial seizures'. *Neurology*, 56.

epiphenomenalism Epiphenomenalism is the view that conscious events—perceptual experiences, mental images, subvocal speech, bodily sensations, emotional feelings, and so on—do not themselves have effects. Instead, our behaviour (including reports about the items just listed) causally depends on neural events, and some of these neural events are also causes of our conscious events. Tasks that can be done only when we use conscious processing are not, according to epiphenomenalism, tasks whose outcomes are caused by consciousness, but rather tasks that can be done only through activation of brain processes that also cause conscious events (often in the form of subvocal speech).

1. Reasons for epiphenomenalism
2. Objections and replies

1. Reasons for epiphenomenalism

Contemporary epiphenomenalism is motivated by (1) the view, based on neuroscience, that every step in the causation of our behaviour, from sensory neuron activations to central neuron activations and *re-entrant processes, to motor neuron activations and contractions of muscle cells, can be accounted for by physical principles applied to parts of the physical body. (Quantum mechanical indeterminacy requires that we allow the possibility of irreducibly statistical dependencies. Epiphenomenalists, along with many others, deny that such indeterminacy provides an opening for influence of consciousness on neural activation.)

A further motivation is (2) rejection of the view that all properties are physical properties. (a) Some anti-epiphenomenalists hold that qualities in conscious events, e.g. painfulness, are literally identical with the neural properties of certain brain events. Epiphenomenalists can allow that painfulness could be regarded as a (non-physical) property of a neural event, and that this non-physical property can be caused by an activation property (e.g. firing rates, ratios of firing rates, and so on) of neural events, but they balk at the claim that painfulness itself—the felt quality that one has after an injury—is the very same property as an activation property of a group of neurons. (b) Some anti-epiphenomenalists hold that conscious events *represent* properties, e.g. red, that are properties of physical things—e.g. the property of reflecting various wavelengths of light with various efficiencies. In this view, redness does not occur in experiences at all: it occurs in objects such as Gala apples, and experiences merely represent those physical properties. Epiphenomenalists, in contrast, allow that perceptual experiences represent a world of objects to us, but they hold that an experience of a red thing differs from the experience of a blue thing in respect of an intrinsic experiential property. It is the difference among intrinsic experiential properties that constitutes the conscious difference between representing things of one kind and representing things of another kind; and these properties are neither properties of things nor neural activation properties.

To reach an epiphenomenalist conclusion, one must also (3) reject systematic overdetermination. This rejection denies that behaviour has both a sufficient physical cause and also a cause that is a non-physical, conscious event. If (1) above is accepted, conscious events can never be supposed to produce a behavioural effect 'on their own'. Epiphenomenalists take this fact to undercut the view that conscious events could make a genuinely causal contribution to behaviour.

If there are conscious events that have non-physical properties, and behaviour is caused by the physical properties of neural events, and overdetermination is rejected, then our behaviour has only physical causes and the non-physical properties of conscious events are inefficacious in our behaviour. Strictly, one might consistently hold out for a purely mental efficacy of conscious events, but it would seem difficult to motivate such a view and the standard objections to epiphenomenalism turn on their inefficacy in our behaviour.

2. Objections and replies

A frequent objection to epiphenomenalism is that *introspection delivers certain knowledge that the qualities in our experiences cause appropriate behaviour. (For simplicity, it will be useful to take reports of those qualities as key examples of appropriate behaviour, but the point is a general one, applying, for example, to the selection of Gala apples rather than

Granny Smiths when asked to buy some red apples.) Epiphenomenalists reply that introspection delivers no such thing. It does not even deliver the existence of neurons, let alone the complexity of the neural transactions in our brains. Claims of introspective knowledge of causation run against Humean inclinations that many contemporary philosophers have quite independently of views about epiphenomenalism. Researchers in several fields routinely teach their students to avoid our natural propensity to attribute causation between events even when our evidence does not rule out their being co-effects of an underlying cause. Epiphenomenalists allow that something in this area is very intuitive, and correct—namely, counterfactuals, e.g. that one would not be reporting having a pain, or smelling oregano, or seeing red, unless one were actually having these experiences. But, they point out, it is a confusion to move from the truth of such counterfactuals to the claim that the experiences are causing the reports; for the counterfactuals are equally compatible with the experiences and the reports being co-effects of neural events, provided that the following *uniqueness condition* is met: in normal conditions there is no neural cause of (sincere) reports that bypasses the neural events that also cause the experiences that are reported. And they can take the uniqueness condition to be ensured by our history of learning (in particular, our learning of language, in the case of reports).

An important objection to epiphenomenalism is the charge that it is a self-stultifying view. The argument behind the charge is this. (SS1) If a report expresses knowledge that *x* is *F*, then the report must be caused by *x* in virtue of its being *F*. (SS2) Epiphenomenalism implies that a report about a present *F* experience is not caused by that experience in virtue of its being *F* (e.g. not in virtue of its being a pain, or an itch, or a red afterimage). Therefore, (C1) If epiphenomenalism is true, reports about our experiences do not express knowledge of those experiences. (SS3) Philosophers should not make claims that their own view implies are unknowable. (SS4) Epiphenomenalism claims that there are experiences of various kinds. Therefore, (C2) Epiphenomenalism makes a claim that it implies cannot be known (by SS1 and SS2). Therefore, (C3) Philosophers should not claim that epiphenomenalism is true (by C2 and SS3). What epiphenomenalism says might, as far as this argument goes, be true, but no one could be in a position to responsibly affirm its truth.

Epiphenomenalists can reply to this argument by rejecting (SS1). It is true that knowledge by perception requires causation of beliefs by the objects perceived, but knowledge of one's own conscious events is not knowledge by perception. In this latter case, the reliability of one's reports is not due to causation by the objects reported; it may be due, instead, to causation by the causes of the objects reported, together with satisfaction of the uniqueness condition. Alternatively, epiphenomenalists may hold that there can be genuine beliefs about one's own conscious events only if those conscious events are present; in this case, again, the ground of knowledge of one's own conscious events is not causation by those events (but rather, inclusion of those events as a necessary condition of genuinely having the belief).

The first of these alternatives allows for the possibility of a breakdown of normal conditions, which in turn would allow for a sincere but erroneous belief about one's own conscious events. This consequence may be thought to imply that this version of epiphenomenalism cannot underwrite the primordial certainty we are often thought to have regarding our own conscious events. But if it can be successfully argued that no belief can include its truth as a necessary condition of having the belief, then the first alternative demands no more than any coherent theory of knowledge of one's own conscious events must allow; and if this proposition about belief cannot be established, then the second alternative is available in reply to the self-stultification argument.

A third popular objection to epiphenomenalism arises from evolution. It is held that consciousness could not have *evolved under pressures of natural selection unless it causally contributed to behaviour. Epiphenomenalists can reply that natural selection works on the physical body, and that what was selected for were the neural causes of conscious events, not the conscious events or their properties themselves. They may point out that biology seeks, at least in principle, a complete, neuromuscular set of causes that are sufficient triggering causes for behaviour. It would be odd to premise an evolutionary critique of epiphenomenalism on the assumption that this biological project must fail. But, if its success is assumed, then there cannot be such a critique, because if natural selection has produced a sufficient neuromuscular causal background for behaviour, its force is exhausted, i.e. it cannot produce a second, redundant set of causes.

WILLIAM S. ROBINSON

Chalmers, D. J. (1996). *The Conscious Mind: In Search of a Fundamental Theory.*

Horowitz, A. (1999). 'Is there a problem in physicalist epiphenomenalism?' *Philosophy and Phenomenological Research*, 59.

Hyslop, A. (1998). 'Methodological epiphenomenalism'. *Australasian Journal of Philosophy*, 76.

Jackson, F. (1982). 'Epiphenomenal qualia'. *Philosophical Quarterly*, 32.

Kim, J. (1993). *Supervenience and Mind: Selected Philosophical Essays.*

Libet, B. (1985). 'Unconscious cerebral initiative and the role of conscious will in voluntary action'. *Behavioral and Brain Sciences*, 8.

Popper, K. R. and Eccles, J. C. (1977). *The Self and its Brain*.

Robinson, D. (1993). 'Epiphenomenalism, laws and properties'. *Philosophical Studies*, 69.

Robinson, W. S. (1982). 'Causation, sensations and knowledge'. *Mind*, 91.

—— (2004). *Understanding Phenomenal Consciousness*.

Van Rooijen, J. (1987). 'Interactionism and evolution: a critique of Popper'. *British Journal for the Philosophy of Science*, 38.

Wegner, D. M. (2002). *The Illusion of Conscious Will*.

epistemology of consciousness Epistemology studies the questions of whether and how people can have knowledge, evidence, and warrant for their beliefs, either their beliefs in general or selected categories of belief. The epistemology of consciousness asks whether and how we can have knowledge or warrant about our own conscious states and those of others. Two grades of warrant may be distinguished: common sense and scientific. Common sense credits people with knowledge of conscious states, but its epistemic standards may not be very demanding. Science imposes higher standards for knowledge, evidence, and warrant, so additional questions may arise about the status of scientific evidence for consciousness. Perhaps common sense licences *introspection as a way of gaining knowledge about conscious states, but psychology is leery of such a method. Science allegedly restricts itself to *public* methods, so introspection, being a private method, should be avoided. Subjects' verbal reports are not merely behavioural expressions of conscious states. They are intended to be expressions of knowledge, or warranted belief, about those states. However, if those beliefs are based on introspection, and introspection is not scientifically legitimate, how can scientists rely on these reports as scientific evidence?

1. Introspection and reliability
2. Introspection and publicity
3. Confabulation
4. Interpreting verbal reports
5. Error versus ignorance
6. Self-awareness as displaced perception
7. Introspection and the nature of consciousness
8. Alien and robot consciousness

1. Introspection and reliability

Many epistemologists hold that people have *privileged access* to their own conscious states. A person can seemingly know her current intention to order an espresso from the waiter without inferring this intention from her behaviour. There seems to be a 'direct' way of forming beliefs about current conscious states, using introspection, inner sense, or self-monitoring. If use of this direct method of belief formation makes the resulting beliefs warranted or justified (for the user), which properties of this method confer such epistemic status? On one line of thinking (refinements omitted), a belief is justified if it is produced by a *reliable* process or method, i.e. a method with belief-outputs that are mostly true. Beliefs based on sight or hearing are justified (in normal conditions) because their methods of production are reliable. Similarly, beliefs based on self-monitoring might be warranted because self-monitoring is a reliable belief-forming method.

Is de facto reliability sufficient for warrant? Some would answer in the negative, arguing that reliability per se does not confer warrant unless the user believes—indeed, *justifiably* believes—that the method used is reliable. If one insists on justified belief in reliability, above and beyond reliability itself, another requirement may also seem imperative. Must not the justification come from an *independent* source? If a source were invoked to validate its own reliability, would this not constitute objectionable circularity?

On the other hand, insisting on an independent source to establish reliability may be too restrictive. It threatens *global scepticism*, the impossibility of having warrant for any belief at all (Goldman 2004). Consider memory. If the reliability of memory must be established without appealing to memory, it is doubtful that this demand can be met, because we have no access to the past that does not ultimately rest, directly or indirectly, on memory. The unfeasibility of non-circular validation is characteristic of 'basic' epistemic sources such as memory, perception, and inductive reasoning. So independent validation seems to be an excessive requirement on legitimate sources of warrant.

2. Introspection and publicity

What about publicity, an oft-proposed requirement for a method's scientific legitimacy? The acceptability of this restriction partly depends on how publicity is defined. One possible definition is this: 'Method *M* is public if and only if *M* can be used by two or more inquirers.' This criterion is too weak, however, because it is fulfilled even by introspection, the paradigm case of a non-public method. Multiple individuals can apply introspection, each to their own conscious states. A revised definition captures a stronger sense of publicity: 'Method *M* is public if and only if *M* can be applied by two or more inquirers *to the very same questions*' (not merely analogous questions). Introspection fails this test of publicity (as it should) because a user of introspection can apply it only to questions about the user's own conscious states, not to questions about anybody else's conscious states.

Is publicity, so defined, a suitable constraint on scientific legitimacy? This is dubious. Imagine a universe with only a handful of spatiotemporally isolated inquirers, each living outside the space-time cone of every other inquirer. A certain reliable observational technique can be used by each of these inquirers to answer a certain class of questions, but only questions concerning their own local environment. Such a method would not be public, but this should not disbar it from being a legitimate scientific method (Goldman 1997). At any rate, scientists should not be disbarred from relying on their subjects' introspection-based reports, even if those reports make use of a non-public method. In fact, scientists of consciousness regularly rely on their subjects' introspective reports. For example, a subject is deemed to suffer from *blindsight when she makes visual discriminations in the absence of visual consciousness. How does a vision scientist know that visual consciousness is absent in a portion of the subject's visual field? Because the subject reports not seeing the stimuli—that is, not consciously seeing them—and the scientist relies on these introspective reports.

3. Confabulation

Despite the prevalence of this kind of methodological procedure, some cognitive scientists regard the very existence of introspection as a myth. In issuing verbal reports of their mental states, people are said to use inference, even confabulation, to arrive at these reports. Gazzaniga et al. (1977) studied a *commissurotomy (split-brain) patient by flashing different visual stimuli to his two hemispheres. The left brain saw a chicken claw and the right brain a snow scene, and the patient was asked to choose an associated item from an array of pictures shown to both hemispheres. The right brain chose a shovel and the left brain a chicken. When the patient was asked why he chose these items, the talking left hemisphere replied, 'The chicken goes with the chicken claw and you need a shovel to clean out the chicken shed.' Evidently, the left hemisphere was simply *confabulating; it had no inkling, really, why the shovel had been selected. Gazzaniga postulated an 'Interpreter', whose job is to create plausible theories of the agent's mental states to explain its behaviour. This is nothing like a special 'channel' to one's mental states that figures in the introspection story.

How plausible is confabulation as a general account of reading one's own mind? There are ways to check up on a person's report of his current states. His behaviour can be observed to see if it conforms to his self-ascription. If someone reports an intention to curl his left index finger in the next five seconds, then, barring reasons to change his mind, one can verify whether he had this intention by seeing whether he curls the finger. If stories about conscious states were regularly confabulated, they would not generally be accurate, and there would be a dramatic disconnect between reported states and associated behaviour. Such a dramatic disconnect is not generally observed, so the confabulation story seems far-fetched. Confabulation (or explanatory inference) might well be a backup method, but it is doubtful that it is the default method. All this lends plausibility to a *dual-method* approach to verbal reports (Goldman 2006:Ch. 9), which holds that two different methods are used to arrive at verbal reports about conscious states. It is plausible that the default method is introspection, but when introspection is unavailing, the system resorts to inference or confabulation as a fallback.

Explanatory inference may well be used to arrive at verbal reports in response to certain questions, e.g. questions about the causes of one's own behaviour. Nisbett and Wilson (1977) found a *position effect* in their subjects' choice behaviour. The subjects themselves denied that their choices were influenced by the test objects' position, and offered alternative explanations. Thus, according to Nisbett and Wilson, the real causes of their choices went undetected while the subjects confabulated different explanations. In this type of case, however, it is doubtful that the real causes of the behaviour figured in conscious thought, so they were unavailable to introspection. If the subjects felt pressured to answer the interrogator's questions, confabulation was their only recourse. This does not show that confabulation is used even when relevant information is present in consciousness.

4. Interpreting verbal reports

Assuming there is such a process as introspection, how can its reliability be assessed? Care must be taken in interpreting verbal reports that issue from it. Dennett (2003) discusses Shepard and Metzler's work on mental *imagery and writes that subjects reported rotating their mental images. (Actually, this is incorrect. Subjects answered questions about the congruence or non-congruence of pairs of figures, and it was psychologists who offered 'mental rotation' hypotheses. Suppose, however, that subjects *had* reported rotating their mental images.) How should cognitive scientists interpret such reports? Distinguish between *architecturally loaded* and *architecturally neutral* interpretations of subjective reports (Goldman 2004). On an architecturally loaded interpretation, 'I mentally rotated my visual image' makes a claim about the cognitive architecture of visualization, e.g. that it involves analogue transformations in the brain. On a neutral interpretation, by contrast, the statement is equivalent to 'I visualized the figure being rotated', which lacks any such architectural commitment. Dennett interprets verbal reports in a loaded way, and so interpreted they are probably unreliable. Interpreted neutrally, however, they are much less suspect. There is no reason to think that introspection intends to make claims about microstructural features of consciousness. Rather, it classifies states in gross folk-psychological terms, and on these matters its prospects for reliability are substantially brighter.

5. Error versus ignorance

In assessing reliability, it is essential to distinguish *error* and *ignorance*. A reliable method is one that avoids a high proportion of errors, but error avoidance does not imply knowledge of most facts in the target domain. Introspection may leave us ignorant of many properties of our conscious states and yet be reliable with respect to those on which it does yield an opinion. Schwitzgebel (2002) asks people to form a visual image of a familiar object and then answer questions about the image. Does it have a focal part, and if so how much detail does it have? How stable is it? Does it gradually fade toward the periphery, or does it fade abruptly? Do the peripheral elements of the image have colour at all before you think to assign a colour to them? And so forth. He reports that most people who are asked such questions find them extremely hard; they feel uncertain how to answer them. He takes this reaction to cast doubt on the reliability and accuracy of our introspective abilities. On the contrary, it only points to our extensive ignorance about certain features of our conscious states, not to introspective error or inaccuracy. People generally refrain from forming introspective beliefs about the questions Schwitzgebel surveys. But if introspection generates few if any beliefs on these matters, it does not generate (many) false beliefs. This is compatible with high reliability. Of course, Schwitzgebel adduces other arguments for introspection's unreliability, e.g. that people are systematically mistaken about their dream experiences. This problem, however, may be the product of special characteristics of *dreaming. Perhaps introspection is partly disabled or attenuated during dream states.

6. Self-awareness as displaced perception

Introspection is usually portrayed as becoming aware of one's own conscious states by 'looking inward' and detecting some of their properties. But certain recent accounts of self-awareness offer a dramatically different picture. Dretske (1995, 1999) and Tye (2000) offer a *displaced-perception* account, according to which one learns facts about one's own conscious states by observing objects and properties external to the mind. This is similar to discovering how much one weighs not by looking at oneself but by looking at the bathroom scales. A putative advantage of this approach is that it dispenses with the vexing mental properties that traditional theories invoke. Traditional *qualia and sense-data are eschewed. The properties of which one is aware in conscious visual experience are simply properties of ordinary physical objects, the objects of vision. The entire idea of knowledge by inward-oriented property detection is rejected. Whether this can work, however, is highly debatable. Are we not often aware of such conscious states as urges and repulsions? Setting aside the contents of these feelings, do we not also detect their respective types? How do we do this without being aware of the properties of the conscious states, not (merely) the properties of any external objects that attract or repel us? Similarly, when I declare myself 'agnostic' about the hypothesis of extraterrestrial intelligence, how do I detect that my attitude is one of agnosticism rather than conviction? Do I find agnosticism in the external world? (Where in the external world?)

7. Introspection and the nature of consciousness

Let us return, then, to the idea of introspection or inner sense. What can cognitive science do to assess the existence and reliability of inner sense? An obvious project is to see whether science can construct an account of how an inner sense system could work, how it might interact with the objects—i.e. conscious states—that comprise its targets. Cognitive science tries to do this for vision. It tries to show how the visual system responds to external stimuli by producing generally accurate representations of the three-dimensional objects it tracks. Such a story must show how light transmission can convey suitable information about distal objects to the retina and how the visual system can extract this information to create generally accurate representations of those objects. Although vision science has not completed this task, it is presumably on the road towards doing so.

Can a similar story be told for inner sense? The first part of such a story should say what states of consciousness are, in virtue of which their identities or properties can be communicated to the introspecting 'organ'. One widely respected theory, the **global workspace theory*, tries to do this job. It says that conscious states are active areas of the brain that 'broadcast' their messages—hence aspects of their identity—to a widely distributed neural system or workspace. This workspace provides a common 'communication protocol' between multiple sites (Baars 1989, Dehaene et al. 1998). This is analogous to the light-reflecting properties of three-dimensional objects, which enable information about them to be communicated to the eyes.

8. Alien and robot consciousness

Our main topic has been the common-sense or scientific basis of attributing specific states of consciousness to self or other. Now we turn to the epistemological basis of attributing consciousness to non-human objects. Are mice conscious? Are robots? How could we tell whether a highly complex robot is conscious? A vivid case from fiction, discussed by Block (2002), is Commander Data of *Star Trek* fame (see SPOCK). If Commander Data existed, how could we decide whether he is conscious? Block narrows his discussion to a certain pair of popular philosophical positions in the mind/brain area: phenomenal realism and naturalism. *Phenomenal realism* is the view that people are phenomenally conscious (their mental states have qualitative feels). *Naturalism* is the view that it is a default that consciousness has a scientific, *physicalist nature. Block then claims that there is an epistemic tension between phenomenal realism and naturalism. He calls this the 'harder problem of consciousness.'

Commander Data is a superficial functional isomorph of human beings. Characterized in purely functional terms, his behaviour and mental life instantiate the same common-sense folk psychology as human behaviour and mental life. The physical basis of Commander's Data's mental life, however, is entirely different from ours. We are different physical 'realizations' of the same functional organization. The science of (qualitative) consciousness is inevitably based on humans, and perhaps non-humans neurologically similar to humans. But how can science based on us generalize to creatures that do not share our physical properties? Block argues that we cannot have a ground of rational belief strong enough for knowledge in this area. Commander Data's consciousness, he says, is 'meta-inaccessible', in the sense that we not only lack a ground for belief, but we lack a conception of any ground for belief. This is the kind of conundrum about consciousness and the natural world that keeps philosophers—and scientists—buzzing around this blossom.

See also SELF-CONSCIOUSNESS.

ALVIN I. GOLDMAN

Baars, B. (1989). *A Cognitive Theory of Consciousness*.

Block, N. (2002). 'The harder problem of consciousness'. *Journal of Philosophy*, 99.

Dehaene, S., Kerszberg, M. and Changeux, J. P. (1998). 'A neuronal model of a global workspace in effortful cognitive tasks'. *Proceedings of the National Academy of Sciences of the USA*, 95.

Dennett, D. C. (2003). 'Who's on first? Heterophenomenology explained'. *Journal of Consciousness Studies*, 10.

Dretske, F. (1995). *Naturalizing the Mind*.

—— (1999). 'The mind's awareness of itself'. *Philosophical Studies*, 95.

Gazzaniga, M., LeDoux, J. E. and Wilson, D. H. (1977). 'Language, praxis, and the right hemisphere: clues to some mechanisms of consciousness'. *Neurology*, 27.

Goldman, A. I. (1997). 'Science, publicity, and consciousness'. *Philosophy of Science*, 64.

—— (2004). 'Epistemology and the evidential status of introspective reports'. *Journal of Consciousness Studies*, 11.

—— (2006). *Simulating Minds: The philosophy, Psychology, and Neuroscience of Mindreading*.

McLaughlin, B. (2003). 'A naturalist-phenomenal realist response to Block's harder problem'. *Philosophical Issues*, 13.

Nisbett, R. E. and Wilson, T. D. (1977). 'Telling more than we can know: Verbal reports on mental processes'. *Psychological Review*, 84.

Schwitzgebel, E. (2002). 'How well do we know our own conscious experience?' *Journal of Consciousness Studies*, 9.

Tye, M. (2000). *Consciousness, Color and Content*.

event-related potential (ERP) See ELECTROENCEPHALOGRAPHY

evolution of consciousness The evolution of consciousness remains, alas, a mystery on which very little light has been thrown; but the reasons for the intractability of the problem provide much food for thought.

Conscious human beings evolved from organisms at least some of which (it is generally supposed) were not conscious. Three related questions face the investigator seeking to establish how consciousness evolved. First, in which organisms did consciousness first appear? Second, what selective advantage was gained by those organisms that gained consciousness over those that did not? Third, what heritable physical change was responsible for the transition to consciousness?

As is the case for all cognitive traits, a major difficulty in establishing when consciousness evolved is that there is no direct fossil evidence for its presence or absence in any extinct species. One way to obviate this problem is to investigate consciousness in living organisms, to establish in which groups it is found, and perhaps to trace its evolution by considering the phylogenetic relationships between groups of conscious animals. The immediate difficulty facing this course is that there is no universally accepted criterion for consciousness in (non-human) animals. Most Westerners would probably agree that consciousness of some form is to be found in mammals, in birds, and, with less certainty, in reptiles, amphibians—possibly in fish. There is likely to be much less confidence about the existence of consciousness in invertebrates, and very few would support the idea of any form of consciousness in organisms that do not belong to the animal kingdom, e.g. protozoa or plants.

Two forms of consciousness that are commonly recognized are **self-consciousness*—the awareness that we humans have of ourselves as independent entities with memories of episodes in our lives—and what might be called *feeling-consciousness*—basic 'raw' experience, perhaps best exemplified by the experiences of pleasure and *pain. There may or may not be a link between these two forms, but it seems plausible that if one form can exist without the other, it would be feeling-consciousness and it makes sense to concentrate initially on this form. The arguments concerning the evolution of pleasure are closely analogous to those concerning pain (and, indeed, any other aspect of feeling, such as emotion), and as the experience of pain may seem the most critical of all feelings, a focus on pain will serve well to illustrate the difficulties in making sense of the evolution of feeling-consciousness.

A sensible way in which to test for the existence of feelings in other animals is to see whether their behaviour parallels human behaviour when we experience feelings. Darwin, for example, used similarities in the expression of emotions in animals and humans to support the case for continuity of mental evolution between non-human animals and humans. The clear parallels between our response to painful stimulation (e.g. rapid withdrawal, vocalization) and the pattern of response of non-human mammals to similar stimuli provides, of course, strong support for the idea that their experience parallels ours. But when we extend this approach to non-mammals, and, in particular, to invertebrates, uncertainties arise. Invertebrates may not vocalize when noxious stimuli are administered, but they may nevertheless show vigorous withdrawal. Is this a pattern that either implies or denies consciousness?

Vocalization is clearly not a safe criterion of painful experience—in humans, vocalization is neither sufficient to demonstrate pain, nor a necessary accompaniment. But withdrawal is also insufficient as a criterion, because we know of preparations in which withdrawal occurs but in which we do not suppose that consciousness is to be found. If an earthworm is severed in two and a hook inserted in each part, the hindpart 'struggles' more violently than the anterior segment—but the anterior segment possesses that concentration of ganglia that constitutes what 'brain' the worm possesses. In case it might be supposed that both the anterior and the posterior nervous structures were sufficient to support conscious experience, it is worth noting that in humans whose spinal cord is severed from the brain, noxious stimulation of regions served by the spinal nerves may elicit vigorous withdrawal in the absence, inevitably, of any conscious experience. Thus although there are indeed clear parallels between the expression of feelings (including emotions), there is no guarantee of similarities in the feelings concomitant with emotional behaviour.

As analogous difficulties clearly emerge with proposals to use any of the standard behavioural accompaniments of painful experience as a criterion for comparable experience in non-humans, it may be profitable to turn now to the second of the major questions—what advantage is gained by organisms that experience feelings? The common-sense response to this question is, of course, that our experiences of pleasure and pain serve to make us approach 'good' objects and to avoid 'bad'. The notion is that our neural apparatus has evolved to classify external stimuli as potentially advantageous (e.g. the taste of a source of food), as potentially noxious (e.g. a hot surface), or as neutral. So, a noxious stimulus causes pain, which engages systems that result in such behavioural phenomena as withdrawal, vocalization, and learning to avoid previously 'neutral' stimuli that are associated with the noxious stimulus. There are two difficulties with this common-sense view.

The first difficulty is that of making sense of the role of the experience of pain in the sequence of events outlined. It is not controversial that the sensory apparatus has evolved to enable organisms to distinguish between dangerous and desirable stimuli, nor that motor systems have evolved that respond appropriately according to the classification made by the senses. But what is the adaptive value of having an intervening state of feeling between the sensory apparatus and the response? All that seems necessary is that the senses, should, in response to biologically significant stimuli, generate a high-priority signal that would obtain the appropriate response—withdrawal, in the case of potentially dangerous stimuli.

The second difficulty, related to the first, is as follows: if there is no necessary functional role for the feeling of pain, it seems inevitable that at least some organisms will have evolved to escape and avoid noxious stimuli without developing feelings associated with those responses. Many might suppose that this is a plausible interpretation of the behaviour of some invertebrates, for example (consider again the worm on the hook). And this raises the question: how could we distinguish between organisms that show appropriate approach and avoidance without experiencing pleasure or pain from those that do have such experience?

These difficulties lead naturally into the third major question, one that lies at the heart of the problem of consciousness: suppose there did evolve a species of organism that successfully sustained itself without feelings, how could it evolve into one that does have experience? What heritable physical change could transform a non-feeling organism into a feeling one? This latter question presupposes that the change must be physical. But, of course, there is a long tradition that supposes that consciousness is an attribute, not of a physical body, but of a mind or soul that is not a physical substance. The *dualistic view meets serious challenges over questions concerned with the interaction of mind and body (or with their miraculous parallel existence) but what is most pertinent here is that it has little to say about the evolution of consciousness: there is no general agreement amongst dualists over which (if any) non-human organisms are conscious, and which are not.

Given that we conscious humans have brains that are anatomically larger and more complex than those of most non-humans, one possibility is that a change in *brain anatomy is responsible for the emergence of consciousness. It does not seem likely that an increase in size alone could be sufficient to obtain consciousness: the human spinal cord is very much larger than the nervous system of many mammals, but does not support conscious experience. The most plausible candidate must be a change in brain complexity, one that would be reflected in changes in behavioural function, changes that would, of course, include the emergence of consciousness.

We should, then, explore between-species differences in behaviour to see whether any known difference could plausibly account for the emergence of consciousness. Two domains in which it seems possible that functional change could bring about consciousness are perception and cognition. Could an advance in sensory processing give rise to what might be called *perceptual consciousness*, and could that be a forerunner of our human consciousness?

There is, of course, an enormous range of variation in sensory capacities across species, but it is not obvious that specialized developments within or between modalities could provide a clear step-like advance that could plausibly bring about a form of consciousness: does the primate specialization in vision make primates more likely to be conscious than animals, such as hedgehogs, with relatively poor vision, or than dogs, with a highly developed olfactory sense? It could be argued that a species with restricted sensory input could not construct for itself a 'perceptual world' in which relatively complex internal representations of external objects would develop. Such a perceptual world would allow conceptual discrimination between a self and the outside world, and so, would be a prerequisite of self-consciousness. But this possibility cannot be explored by looking at sensory capacities: it requires analysis of such central processes as the formation of internal representations—in other words, an analysis of cognitive processes.

A second approach to the idea that perceptual consciousness might be the primary form of consciousness is related to the traditional distinction between sensation and perception in humans. Put simply, sensation is the set of mechanical processes that act directly upon external physical stimuli, conveying information about them to a variety of more central locations; perception is the interpretation put upon sensory input by central processes (the decision that one is, for example, seeing a dog running). A reflex may occur before the stimulus, although (necessarily) sensed, is perceived: perception is, then, the entry into consciousness of some external event. Once perception occurs, we know what caused the reflex. Could it be that animals with sensory processes but without perception evolved into (non-human) animals with a conscious process of perception? This in effect asks whether we can discriminate between animals that (unconsciously) respond appropriately to stimuli and animals that both respond appropriately and know what they are responding to. To answer that question requires that we delve into higher-level central processes to seek a difference in cognitive processes that could allow such knowledge to occur. This second approach to perceptual consciousness leads us on, then, like the first, to our other domain of interest, cognition.

Unfortunately there are very few (if any) generally accepted species differences in cognition. Around the end of the 19th century, it was supposed that the ability to learn might be restricted to 'higher' animals, and this belief led to the suggestion that the ability to learn might coexist with consciousness: but we now know that learning is found across virtually all groups of animals, vertebrate and invertebrate (as well as in the non-conscious isolated spinal cord). We also know not only that a process of association-formation is ubiquitous in those animals whose learning processes have been investigated, but also that numerous details of the way in which associations are formed are found in all those animals. Although it is generally believed that some animals are, in some sense, more 'intelligent' than others, there is no generally accepted specific qualitative difference in learning between groups of non-human animals. Correspondingly, there have been numerous specific suggestions of cognitive processes that could provide an index of consciousness, and none of those has met with widespread acceptance. This entry will end with an outline of just one of those proposals.

Recent decades have seen a number of experimental investigations, using apes and other vertebrates, of the possibility that some animal species might be capable of language acquisition. Interpretation of this work has been controversial, particularly with regard to the question whether animals can use syntax. At present, in fact, the only proposal for a qualitative difference in cognition that has gained widespread (though far from universal) support is the claim that the capacity to acquire language is unique to humans. Could the acquisition of language, then, be responsible for the emergence of consciousness? Descartes' claim that thought is the essence of consciousness has, of course, much in common with the idea that language is critical to consciousness. A more recent suggestion (Macphail 1998) has been that language may be necessary for the development of a concept of self, and that the self-concept in turn may be necessary for conscious experience. There have been a number of studies of the existence of the self-concept in non-humans, many of which have focused on the question whether they can recognize themselves in mirrors (see MIRROR TEST). However, like language acquisition, this is a controversial issue for which experiments have not yet provided a decisive answer.

Until we can uncover some cognitive process other than language that plausibly discriminates some species from others, it seems that we have advanced little from Descartes and that, like Descartes, we may have to embrace the generally implausible notion that non-human animals are unconscious machines. Those who, not unreasonably, find this a reductio ad absurdum can find alternative accounts of the evolution of consciousness in the suggestions below for further reading.

See also ANIMAL CONSCIOUSNESS: DOLPHINS; ANIMAL CONSCIOUSNESS: GREAT APES; ANIMAL CONSCIOUSNESS: RAVEN

E. M. MACPHAIL

Dawkins, M. S. (1993). *Through Our Eyes Only? The Search for Animal Consciousness.*
Dennett, D. C. (1996). *Kinds of Minds: Towards an Understanding of Consciousness.*
Eccles, J. C. (1992). 'Evolution of consciousness'. *Proceedings of the National Academy of Sciences Of the USA*, 89.
Griffin, D. R. (2001). *Animal Minds: Beyond Cognition to Consciousness.*
Heyes, C. and Dickinson, A. (1990). 'The intentionality of animal action'. *Mind and Language*, 5.
Humphrey, N. (1992). *A History of the Mind.*
Jaynes, J. (1976). *The Origin of Consciousness in the Breakdown of the Bicameral Mind.*
Macphail, E. M. (1998). *The Evolution of Consciousness.*

exclusion task See MEMORY, PROCESS-DISSOCIATION PROCEDURE.

explanatory gap The term relates to the gap between conscious experience and the physical events underlying it.

The principal aim of a scientific theory is to explain the phenomena within its domain. To explain a phenomenon is to provide a sufficiently rich description of that domain so that one understands why it happened, or happens. So, for instance, Newtonian theory explains the trajectories of the planets and missiles by appeal to the basic force laws of mechanics. Given these laws, it is clear that physical objects must move as they do, which explains why they do.

A science of consciousness, then, should explain why conscious experience is as it is, in the circumstances in which it occurs. I am currently sitting at my desk writing this piece at my computer, having a host of visual, auditory, tactile, and other conscious experiences. These experiences clearly depend in a systematic way on the physical stimuli impinging on my body and on the neurological states subsequent to that stimulation. A science of consciousness should show why just these experiences had to happen in these circumstances; otherwise, I do not know why they happened, and they are not fully explained.

Of course not every phenomenon can be explained by appeal to some more fundamental phenomenon. In Newtonian mechanics, if one asks why force equals mass times acceleration, the answer is that this is just the way the world is. This law is fundamental, or basic. Similarly, one does not explain why oppositely charged particles attract, as this too is a basic law. This reflects the generally acknowledged fact that explanations must come to an end somewhere. So some scientific theories articulate fundamental or basic laws that do not get explained; they are left as brute facts.

One way of describing the difference between *dualism and materialism, then, concerns the explanatory status of conscious experience. The dualist maintains that the connection between the neurological events occurring within the body and the conscious experiences correlated with them reflects a basic law of nature, not subject to further explanation. The materialist, on the other hand, believes that conscious experiences can be explained by appeal to these internal physical events. The principal reason behind the materialist's confidence here is the success heretofore in showing most phenomena that have physical causes and physical effects to be ultimately explicable in terms of basic physical elements and forces. To admit conscious experience as an exception would constitute a major deviation from the naturalist framework that embraces current scientific investigation and theorizing.

But can we explain conscious experience by appeal to its neurological correlates? Prima facie, the prospects are not good. The basic problem is this. If we consider the sequence of events that begin, say, with light reflected off a ripe tomato and ending with a visual experience of a red shape, the role of the intervening physical events, from detection of the light by retinal receptors to activity in the visual cortex, seems to be solely a matter of implementing certain causal-informational roles. That is, so long as we are looking for an information-processing story, we have an idea how appeal to the neurological events in the visual system could explain its implementation. But when we reflect on what we want explained when considering the nature of conscious visual experience, we see that it is not exhausted by the information concerning the external world it undoubtedly contains. We want to know, as well, why it is like *what it is like for us to have this experience

(Nagel 1974). Why do red things look just that way and green things differently, and why is there not a 'way it's like' for cameras connected to computers to detect the very same information?

That there is indeed an 'explanatory gap' (a term introduced in Levine 1983) between the physical events underlying conscious experience and the experience itself can be made evident by three related arguments. First, there is the conceivability of *zombies. A zombie is a creature that is physically identical to a normal human being, but lacking in conscious experience altogether. There is nothing it is like to be a zombie, just as, presumably, there is nothing it is like to be my laptop computer. Now whether zombies are even metaphysically possible is a matter of considerable controversy, but many would agree that the very idea of a zombie is internally consistent and coherent. However, if appeal to one's physical states really did explain why one had the conscious experience one has, then zombies should not be even conceivable. It should be clear why a creature with our kind of physiology would have to have conscious experience, and of the kind we have. The very fact that zombies are even conceivable is thus a symptom of the explanatory gap between our physical structure and consciousness.

The second argument is the one made famous by Frank Jackson (1982) concerning the 'super-scientist' Mary, who knows all the physical facts about colour vision but until a certain point never sees or experiences colour (see KNOWLEDGE ARGUMENT). Jackson argues that when Mary sees colour for the first time she will learn something new, what it's like to see colour. Assuming one accepts this judgement about what would happen to Mary in these circumstances, the question arises as to why she would learn anything by the experience. After all, if the physical facts, which she already knew, truly explained the qualitative character of the relevant visual experience, why would she not already know what it is like to see colour? She should have been able to predict what it would be like. Thus the fact that she would not be able to predict this is again a sign of the explanatory gap. (It should be noted here that Chalmers [1996] and Jackson [1982] use the zombie and Mary arguments, respectively, to argue directly for dualism, not merely for the explanatory gap. Levine [1983, 2001] adapts these arguments for the purpose of establishing the explanatory gap.)

Finally, there is a kind of 'other minds' argument. While zombies may be conceivable, it is clear that we in fact have no doubts that any creature physically just like us is a subject of conscious experience. However, suppose we discover alien life forms, or develop advanced robots like C3PO of *Star Wars* fame. Let us imagine that at a sufficiently abstract level of description they are functionally and computationally similar to us, though their underlying structure is different. The question is: just how similar to us does a creature have to be in order to have conscious experience, and, in particular, experiences qualitatively just like ours? While in principle it is clear we could determine what their information-processing capabilities were from a thorough knowledge of their physical structure, how would we ever really know what their experience was like, or whether they had any at all? Again, if we knew just what it was about our own physical structure that explained our conscious experience, we would be in a position to determine whether just those features were present in the alien and the robot. The fact that we do not know how we would answer such a question points again to the existence of the explanatory gap.

There are two basic kinds of materialist response to the explanatory gap argument. The first is to deny that there really is such a gap (Dennett 1991). The fact that there seems to be a gap stems from an insufficiently clear conception of conscious experience. When properly educated by philosophical reflection, one comes to see that information processing really is all there is to conscious experience, and therefore appeal to one's underlying neurological structure is adequate to explain it.

The other strategy (Loar 1997) is to admit (in a way) the existence of the gap but argue that it is not really a threat to materialism in the end. There are two steps in the argument. First, one emphasizes the distinction between properties and concepts, maintaining that concepts stand to properties in a many–one relation. Thus the very same property can be represented both by a neurological concept and by the kind of concept that is employed in first-person reflection on one's conscious experience—currently called a **phenomenal concept*. Since the relevant neurological properties are actually identical to the relevant experiential properties, there really is no point to trying to explain the one in terms of the other. One does not explain an identity, since things just are what they are.

Still, that is not the end of the matter, since one has to now explain why it seems to make so much sense to ask why we have an experience of this type when in this type of neurological state. This is the second step in the argument. In order to now explain the appearance of an explanatory gap, and to explain its persistence despite our ability to account for all the information-processing details, one appeals to the special nature of phenomenal concepts. The idea is that our cognitive access to our own experience is such as to cordon it off from integration with our 'third-person' concepts in such a way that we are cognitively barred from seeing how the two kinds of concept really are about the same phenomenon. Thus it is due to our cognitive architecture that we cannot appreciate how our physical structure explains our experience. (For objections to this argument see Chalmers 2006 and Levine 2006.)

JOSEPH LEVINE

Chalmers, D. (1996). *The Conscious Mind.*
—— (2006). 'Phenomenal concepts and the explanatory gap'. In Alter, T. and Walter, S. (eds) *Phenomenal Concepts and Phenomenal Knowledge.*
Dennett, D.C. (1991). *Consciousness Explained.*
Jackson, F. (1982). 'Epiphenomenal qualia'. *Philosophical Quarterly*, 32.
Levine, J. (1983). 'Materialism and qualia: the explanatory gap'. *Pacific Philosophical Quarterly*, 64.
—— (2001). *Purple Haze: The Puzzle of Consciousness.*
—— (2006). 'Phenomenal concepts and the materialist constraint'. In Alter, T. and Walter, S. (eds) *Phenomenal Concepts and Phenomenal Knowledge.*
Loar, B. (1997). 'Phenomenal states'. In Block, N. et al. (eds) *The Nature of Consciousness.*
Nagel, T. (1974). 'What is it like to be a bat?' *Philosophical Review*, 83.

extended consciousness See CORE CONSCIOUSNESS

extended reticular thalamic activating system See GLOBAL WORKSPACE THEORY; NEURONAL GLOBAL WORKSPACE

externalism and consciousness The term *externalism* denotes a confederation of views, united by the general, if difficult to pin down, idea that the contents of the mind are not exhaustively determined by the contents of the head (or indeed the body). The relevant notion of determination, here, is a *synchronic* one (such as supervenience), rather than a diachronic one (such as causation). Two broad genera can be distinguished (each in turn divisible into a variety of species): (1) *content externalism*: the content of (some) mental items is not determined exhaustively by what is going on inside the body of their subject; (2) *vehicle externalism*: the vehicles of (some) mental items are not restricted to a subject's neural or bodily occurrences but extend out, in various ways, into the subject's environment.

The notion of a vehicle, in this context, is not an unambiguous one, but corresponds roughly to the notion of cognitive *architecture*—the neural nuts and bolts of cognition. Vehicle externalism currently goes by a variety of names, including *active externalism*, the *extended mind*, and *environmentalism*.

The application of externalist principles to consciousness varies, depending on the form of externalism in question. Content externalism has been defended in classic thought experiments developed first by Putnam, then Burge, and also by certain work on indexicals associated with Kaplan and Perry. Putnam (1975) asks us to imagine a near duplicate of Earth—Twin-Earth. The only difference between Earth and Twin-Earth is that the latter contains no water. Instead, there is a substance that is indistinguishable from water except by chemical test; but is not water since it is not made up of hydrogen and oxygen. Putnam argues that when you—a resident of Earth—utter the sentence-form 'water is wet', then the meaning of this utterance is quite different from the identical form uttered by your counterpart on Twin-Earth. Your utterance is about water, but your twin's utterance is about another substance altogether. The truth-conditions of your utterances differ, and so, therefore, do their meanings. Nevertheless, your counterpart is, ex hypothesi, a molecule-for-molecule duplicate of you, and so what is going in his/her head is precisely the same as what is going on in yours. So, the meaning of your utterances differs despite there being no differences in the contents of your heads.

However, this difference in meaning in turn affects the contents of one's propositional attitudes—beliefs, desires, hopes, fears, etc. Not only do you and your twin not mean the same thing when you say 'water is wet'; you do not even think the same thing when you think, as you would both put it, that water is wet. Your thought is about water; your twin's thought is about a quite distinct substance. A propositional attitude is individuated by its content, and this content is identical with the meaning of the sentence used to ascribe this attitude to a subject. So, if Putnam's externalist argument applies to the meaning of sentences, it must also, it is argued, apply to the content of propositional attitudes.

Despite appearing outlandish, Putnam's thought experiment, in fact, makes a simple point. If you fix what is going on inside the head of a subject, and vary their environment, then (certain of) the subject's mental states will vary with the variations in the environment, even though everything that is going on inside the head remains fixed. The mental states possessed by a subject, therefore, are not exhaustively determined by what is going on inside that subject's head.

Content externalism is externalism about the **intentional* or **representational* content of mental states: it applies only to mental states that have such content, and when it applies, it applies in virtue of this content. Its mooted application to phenomenal consciousness, then, is typically based on the idea that the phenomenal properties that constitute such consciousness are inextricably connected with, intentional properties. The reasons for this vary significantly. Some (Searle 1992, Strawson 1994) argue that intentional properties presuppose phenomenal properties in the sense that there can be no intentionality in the absence of *phenomenology. Others (Tye 1995, Dretske 1995) argue for a converse dependence:

phenomenology is a specific form of intentionality. And yet others (Horgan and Tienson 2002) advance a two-way inseparability thesis: intentional content is inseparable from phenomenal character, and phenomenal character is inseparable from intentional content.

Proponents of these views are also divided on the implications of these claims for externalism. Dretske (1995), for example, defends a form of *global externalism* based on the ideas that (1) all experiential states are intentional, and (2) phenomenal properties reduce to representational ones. Externalism with respect to the latter, therefore, entails externalism with respect to the former. Others, however, see the inseparability of the phenomenal and the intentional as a reason for rejecting externalism about consciousness. Searle (1992) and Horgan and Tienson (2002) take this line. These issues are still the subject of vigorous debate.

The basic contours of vehicle externalism can be captured in terms of the following claims: (1) The world is an external store of information relevant to processes such as perceiving, remembering, reasoning, ..., experiencing. (2) Mental processes are hybrid—they straddle both internal and external operations. (3) The external operations take the form of *action*: manipulation, exploitation and transformation of environmental structures—ones that carry information relevant to the accomplishing of a given task. (4) At least some of the internal processes are ones concerned with supplying the subject with the ability to appropriately use relevant structures in its environment.

The application of this general framework to phenomenal consciousness has been attempted, in somewhat different ways, by O'Regan and Noë (2001), Hurley (1998), and Rowlands (2001). According to O'Regan and Noë's **sensorimotor* model of perception, seeing is fundamentally an act that involves an organism exploring its environment. They argue that visual perception, a process that is traditionally thought to require the construction and deployment of internal visual representations, can be explained in terms of an organism's ability to manipulate and exploit structures in its environment. To see is to have mastery of the sensorimotor contingencies that specify the way in one's activity is systematically related to changes in the perceived environment. Roughly: to see is to have the ability to anticipate how what one does will change the character of one's sensory experience.

Hurley's vehicle externalism about consciousness is based on her attack on the input/output model of perception and action (Hurley 1998). The traditional view of the mind, Hurley claims, regards the mind as akin to a sandwich in which cognition is the filling. On the traditional model, perception is regarded as input, and the relation between perception, cognition and action is conceptualized in terms of *vertical modules*. Each vertical module performs its own allotted function, and then passes the results of this functioning to the next module. In place of this, Hurley introduces the idea of *horizontal modules*, content-specific layers that loop dynamically not only through internal sensory and motor processes but also through the environment. These processes are dynamic in that they involve continuous feedback between perception and action, and they are not bounded, in any salient way, by the skin of the cognizing organism.

Rowlands (2001) argues for vehicle externalism about consciousness by way of an attack on the idea of consciousness as an object of inner awareness. What it is like to have an experience is not something of which we are aware in the having of that experience, but something in virtue of which we experience non-phenomenal, typically environmental, items. What it is like to have an experience is not an object of experience but attaches only to experience as act. This is true not only of standard cases of outer-directed experience but also of introspective experience. On the basis of this, Rowlands argues for an expanded model of phenomenal consciousness based on an expanded account of the experiential act.

Vehicle externalist accounts of phenomenal consciousness can be *modest* or *ambitious*. Modest versions see themselves as trying to demonstrate that the phenomenal character of experience is not exhaustively determined by what is going on inside the heads or bodies of subjects. Ambitious versions think that vehicle externalism can shed at least some light on the *hard problem of consciousness: the problem of understanding how consciousness can be produced or constituted by physical activity. O'Regan and Noë (2001) have argued that their sensorimotor account of visual experience provides a solution to (or perhaps dissolution of) the hard problem—at least for visual experience. This claim has been contested by Rowlands (2001), who argues that O'Regan and Noë (2001) have merely *externalized* the hard problem rather than solved it.

MARK ROWLANDS

Dretske, F. (1995). *Naturalizing the Mind*.

Horgan, T. and Tienson, J. (2002). 'The intentionality of phenomenology and the phenomenology of intentionality'. In Chalmers, D. (ed.) *Philosophy of Mind: Classical and Contemporary Readings*.

Hurley, S. (1998). *Consciousness in Action*.

O'Regan, K. and Noë, A. (2001). 'A sensorimotor account of vision and visual consciousness'. *Behavioral and Brain Sciences*, 24.

Putnam, H. (1975). 'The meaning of "meaning"'. In Gunderson, K. (ed.) *Language, Mind and Knowledge*.

Rowlands, M. (2001). *The Nature of Consciousness*.

Searle, J. (1992). *The Rediscovery of the Mind*.
Strawson, G. (1994). *Mental Reality*.
Tye, M. (1995). *Ten Problems of Consciousness*.

extinction See CONDITIONING

extrasensory perception Extrasensory perception (ESP) is the apparent ability to acquire information by paranormal means, without the use of known physical senses. Parapsychologists distinguish three types: *telepathy* (when the information comes from another person), *clairvoyance* (when the information comes from a distant object or event), and *precognition* (when the information is about the future). Together with *psychokinesis* (PK), or mind over matter, these four are all types of *psi*, the supposed mechanism or force underlying paranormal or psychic phenomena.

ESP is often assumed to be associated with consciousness. For example, there are claims that certain *altered states are conducive to ESP, including *out-of-body and near-death experiences, deep *meditation, and mystical states. In many cultures drug-induced or trance states are believed to lead to true visions of distant or future events. In New Age theories ESP is sometimes described as a power of higher states or part of the untapped potential of human consciousness.

After more than a century of scientific research, there is very little reliable evidence that ESP exists, and there is almost no research that reveals a direct connection with consciousness. Nevertheless, reports of ESP are common and levels of belief are high. Surveys in developed countries typically show that over 50% of the population believes in the paranormal, especially in telepathy. Believers are more often female, score higher on tests of temporal lobe epileptic signs, have poorer reasoning skills, and show more cognitive biases than non-believers.

Scientific investigation of ESP began when the spiritualist mediums of the mid 19th century claimed to be able to communicate with the dead, read hidden messages, and perform other paranormal feats. Scientists, including Michael Faraday and William Crooks, tried to design controlled tests but results were mixed and several mediums were caught cheating. In 1882 the Society for Psychical Research (SPR) was founded and its members carried out research on *hallucinations, visions of the dying, premonitions, and psychic communications. In experiments on 'thought transference' (later renamed telepathy) one person drew a picture and another tried to reproduce it. Although impressive results were obtained, the experiments were badly flawed by modern standards. For example, the first person was allowed to choose the target, which means that if the two were friends or relatives, or had spent time together just before the test, they might easily draw similar things.

In the 1930s, in an attempt to avoid psychical research's association with the largely discredited claims of spiritualism, J. B. and Louisa Rhine gave the name *parapsychology* to the scientific study of paranormal phenomena. At their laboratory at Duke University in North Carolina, Louisa concentrated on collecting accounts of spontaneous cases, while J. B. carried out laboratory experiments. He developed a simple set of 25 cards (originally called Zener cards after their designer), bearing the symbols circle, square, wavy lines, cross, and star. In a typical telepathy experiment the sender looked at a series of cards while the receiver guessed the symbols. For clairvoyance the pack of cards was hidden from everyone while the receiver guessed. For precognition, the order of the cards was determined only after the guesses were made. Rhine used ordinary people as subjects and claimed that, on average, they did significantly better than chance expectation.

Rhine's 1934 book, *Extrasensory Perception* (in which the term was coined), was highly controversial and prompted others to try to replicate the experiments. Most failed, including the London mathematician Samuel Soal, who worked for five years before apparently finding a star subject who gave astronomically significant results under tightly controlled conditions. Soal's results convinced many scientists of the existence of ESP until 1978 when SPR member Betty Markwick finally showed how Soal had cheated by manipulating the pre-prepared target sequences.

Modern experiments on ESP rarely use these tedious card-guessing methods. Instead they use various free response techniques in which the receiver can respond with descriptions or drawings. These free responses are then matched up with one of a small set of possible targets. This method was effectively used in the 1960s to test one of the most commonly reported forms of spontaneous ESP—precognitive or telepathic dreams—but early successes were not repeated.

Later the popular *ganzfeld* method was developed, in which the receiver relaxes, hearing white noise through headphones, and with halved ping pong balls over their eyes to provide a uniform visual field (the ganzfeld). Meanwhile a sender looks at one of four pictures or videos in a distant room. After emerging from the ganzfeld the receiver is shown the four possible targets and asked which one most closely matches their experiences. In the mid 1980s the authors of competing meta-analyses claimed either that ESP in the ganzfeld had been conclusively demonstrated or that the results were all due to error and deception. Subsequently automated ganzfeld experiments were carried out, and the disputes continued. Psychologist Daryl Bem was among those convinced of the reality of ESP, yet his meta-analysis relied on experiments that had already been shown to be deeply flawed or even fraudulent.

In remote viewing, one person travels to a randomly selected location while the other tries to visualize the location from the laboratory. As with ganzfeld, there were initial successes followed by much controversy. In 1995 a CIA report, covering more than 20 years of government research, concluded that although a small effect had been demonstrated in the laboratory it was not useful for intelligence purposes.

Other ESP research includes telepathy in twins, ESP in young children, the use of hypnosis, relaxation, dreams and meditation to improve ESP, the claimed ability of people to detect when they are being stared at (remote staring), and tests of psychic claimants. After more than a century of research there is no agreement on the best methods for inducing ESP; no consistent evidence that ESP correlates with age, sex, imagery ability, fantasy proneness, or any other variables; no evidence of a specific link with consciousness; and no plausible theory to explain how it works—that is, if it does.

SUSAN BLACKMORE

Bem, D. J. and Honorton, C. (1994). 'Does psi exist? Replicable evidence for an anomalous process of information transfer'. *Psychological Bulletin*, 115.

Blackmore, S.J. (2001). 'What can the paranormal teach us about consciousness'. *Skeptical Inquirer*, 25.

Irwin, H. J. (1999). *An Introduction to Parapsychology*, 3rd edn.

Marks, D. (2000). *The Psychology of the Psychic*, 2nd edn.

Stein, G. (ed.) (1996). *The Encyclopedia of the Paranormal.*

eye of origin Neural signals travel independently from the retina of each eye and remain independent until they reach the visual cortex. Thus one might expect that humans would be conscious of which eye receives a signal (the eye of origin). It is relatively easy to set up viewing conditions using either mirrors or eyeglasses with shutters so that visual stimulus come into a single eye. Experiments have shown that under a broad range of viewing conditions observers are unable to discriminate eye of origin. This phenomenon is called *utrocular viewing*. The lack of eye of origin discrimination is one of the most powerful items narrowing the locus of the neural correlates of consciousness since the first cortical visual area, *V1, has dramatically distinct eye of origin anatomical structures called *ocular dominance columns*. These structures consist of 1 mm wide strips of cortex that predominantly consist of bands of neurons sensitive to signals from the right eye, interleaved with 1 mm bands of neurons responding to signals from the left eye. Later visual areas and the V1 output neurons do not have this distinctive alternation of ocular dominance bands. Since conscious awareness does not have access to this dramatic eye of origin, one can immediately place constraints on the locus of the neural *correlates of awareness.

This argument is strengthened by the even more dramatic finding that eye of origin confusions have also been found in stereo-deficient and amblyopic observers (Barbeito et al. 1985) after care is taken to remove visual cues such as the blurring associated with stimuli coming into the amblyopic eye. It has been shown that neurons in the amblyopic brain are almost exclusively monocular (driven by one eye), so eye of origin confusions in these individuals provides further constraints on the locus of the neural correlates of awareness.

Even though there is no conscious awareness, there is an eye of origin cue that closely resembles *blindsight. It has been found that subjects cannot report the direction of vertical disparity (which eye has the higher image) but vertical vergence (eye movement) responses are robust. We assume that these eye movements are based on cortical disparity processing. Subjects may see diplopia (double images), but cannot identify the eye of origin for each of the diplopic images, nor can they identify which image is higher. This finding is similar to blindsight in that the motor system knows what conscious awareness does not. Interestingly, horizontal disparity information are readily available to both perception (apparent depth) and motor response.

STANLEY KLEIN

Barbeito, R., Levi, D. L., Klein, S. A., Loshin, D., and Ono, H. (1985). 'Stereo-deficients and stereoblinds cannot make utrocular discriminations'. *Vision Research*, 25.

Cormack, L. K., Landers, D. D., and Stevenson, S. B. (1996). 'Correlation detection and utrocular discrimination in displays with unequal monocular contrasts'. ARVO abstract.

false belief task See THEORY OF MIND AND CONSCIOUSNESS

feature inheritance In backward *masking, a target stimulus is followed by a masking stimulus which renders the target barely visible. Surprisingly, in some cases, features of such an invisible target can still be perceived as features of the mask.

1. The feature inheritance phenomenon
2. Feature integration and attention
3. Feature inheritance, grouping, and consciousness
4. Relations to other phenomena

1. The feature inheritance phenomenon

A single line presented at four consecutive locations is invisible when followed by a grating made up of eight lines (Fig. F1a; Herzog and Koch 2001). Still, although the whole grating is presented simultaneously, it appears to be in motion with one line drawn after the other. A vertical line vernier (e.g. two vertical line segments that are slightly displaced in the horizontal direction either to the left or right) is followed by a grating comprising five aligned verniers. Whereas the first vernier is largely invisible, its offset is perceived at an edge element of the grating. *Feature mislocalization* has occurred because the vernier was presented at the central location (Fig. F1b; Herzog and Koch 2001). Similarly, a vernier followed by two streams of lines is rendered unconscious. Still, the vernier offset is perceived in the motion streams (Fig. F1c; Otto et al. 2006).

When observers are asked to prepare a line drawing of the stimulus, they often draw a grating with all lines offset (Fig. F1b) or two streams of offset lines (Fig. F1c). For this reason, the effect is called *feature inheritance* because a 'parental' element can bequeath its features to a number of 'filial' elements.

2. Feature integration and attention

In the case of Fig. F1b, observers usually report perceiving the entire grating as offset. If observers are asked on which elements they have based their decision, they report having attended to one of the edges of the grating. Indeed, if the attended edge element is offset itself, this offset is integrated with the mislocalized vernier offset (Fig. F1b, middle). Offsets of grating elements outside the focus of *attention, e.g. the non-attended edge, do not influence performance (Herzog and Koch 2001, Sharikadze et al. 2005). Analogous results were found with the motion streams (Fig. F1c; Otto et al. 2006). For this reason, attention seems to play an important role in feature inheritance. However, this does not imply that attention is the 'glue' that *binds or integrates features, as proposed by *feature integration theory*. It might be that features are integrated pre-attentively and only the result of this integration is read out by selective attention.

Feature inheritance can be considered a double *illusion. First, a *perceptual illusion* occurs in the focus of attention; i.e. offsets of the vernier and the attended edge element are integrated and the percept depends on the respective offset sizes. Second, an *inference illusion* occurs because the whole grating is perceived as offset depending on the illusory offset of the attended edge but not on the physical parameters of the non-attended grating elements (Herzog and Koch 2001). Thus, the offsets in the line drawings of observers seem to be cognitively inferred. Possibly feature inheritance is a toy version of *inattentional blindsight and *change blindness, because only attended features are consciously perceived.

3. Feature inheritance, grouping, and consciousness

It seems that feature inheritance occurs when single elements are grouped together, e.g. when single lines are grouped into a grating or into a motion stream. It has recently been shown that motion grouping is more important for feature inheritance than masking (Breitmeyer et al. 2008).

Feature inheritance is a *metameric* percept; that is, observers cannot distinguish whether a grating is offset itself or the offset is inherited by the preceding vernier (Fig. F1b, bottom; Herzog and Koch 2001). Feature inheritance poses a theoretical problem: although the vernier is rendered invisible, its offset can still be perceived. Thus, is the vernier *conscious or unconscious?

4. Relations to other phenomena

The feature inheritance effect bears similarity to other feature mislocalization effects such as illusory conjunctions, feature migration, and feature pooling. Usually, these effects are interpreted to reflect limitations or errors of the visual system, such as a lack of attention or a limited spatial resolution of the visual system.

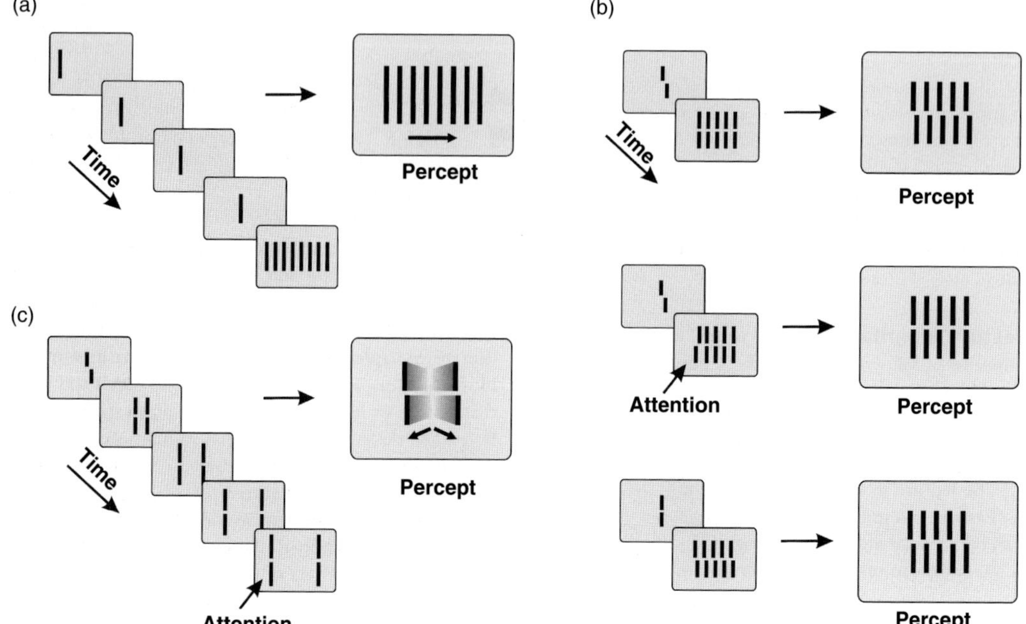

Fig. F1. Three examples of feature inheritance. (a) A single line is flashed consecutively at four locations (here from left to right) and is followed by a grating comprising eight lines displayed simultaneously. Observers perceive only the grating whose lines appear to be drawn one after the other in the direction of the single 'moving' line (for an animation see http://lpsy.epfl.ch/animation/motion-fi.htm). (b) *Top:* A vernier (i.e. two line segments slightly offset to each other) is followed by a grating comprising five aligned verniers. Although the vernier is invisible because of masking, its offset is perceived in the mask. *Middle:* Observers usually attend to one of the edge elements of the grating. If this attended edge is offset in the opposite direction to the offset of the vernier, both offsets are integrated and cancel out each other. *Bottom:* Metamerism. Observers cannot discriminate between a real (i.e. vernier aligned, grating offset) and an inherited grating offset (i.e. vernier offset, grating aligned); that is, *top* and *bottom* conditions yield comparable percepts. (c) A vernier is followed by a sequence of straight flanking lines. A percept of two streams of lines is elicited, with the vernier being invisible. The offset of the vernier can still be perceived in the stream of lines.

However, the feature inheritance effect occurs in the focus of attention and feature integration follows precisely the grouping of single elements into motion streams (Otto et al. 2006). Hence, feature inheritance seems not to reflect an error of the visual system but rather a computational strategy of feature attribution when single elements are grouped into wholes.

MICHAEL H. HERZOG AND THOMAS U. OTTO

Breitmeyer, B. G., Herzog, M. H., and Öğmen, H. (2008). 'Motion, not masking, provides the medium for feature attribution'. *Psychological Science*, 19.

Herzog, M. H. and Koch, C. (2001). 'Seeing properties of an invisible object: feature inheritance and shine-through'. *Proceedings of the National Academy of Sciences of the USA*, 98.

Otto, T. U., Öğmen, H., and Herzog, M. H. (2006). 'The flight path of the phoenix—the visible trace of invisible elements in human vision'. *Journal of Vision*, 6.

Sharikadze, M., Fahle, M., and Herzog, M. H. (2005). 'Attention and feature integration in the feature inheritance effect'. *Vision Research*, 45.

feedback, neural See RE-ENTRANT PROCESSING

feeling of knowing A feeling of knowing is a feeling that certain sought-for information is present in one's *memory even though one cannot currently access it. A familiar example of a phenomenon involving a strong feeling of knowing is a *tip-of-the-tongue* state, in which people sense imminent retrieval of sought-for information from memory. A feeling of knowing is a form of *metacognition—that is, cognition about cognition, knowing about knowing—in that the judgement requires an assessment of the contents and processes comprising one's own memory, in particular comparing current and predicted memory performance.

In a typical experiment examining this phenomenon, participants are asked to make an explicit prediction of the likelihood they will be able to access currently inaccessible information on a future memory test. Data show that people are fairly accurate in making these explicit feeling-of-knowing judgements. The correlation between such explicit judgements and subsequent performance is typically in the moderately positive range, around 0.50 or so. How is it that people are able to say accurately that they will know something later that they obviously do not know now? Different theories emphasize different processes assumed to underlie such judgements, and these theories differ as to the degree to which these processes occur consciously vs unconsciously.

The earliest theory of feelings of knowing (Hart 1965) claimed that people know the information they are seeking and are simply unable to access it fully; their feeling-of-knowing judgements are based on direct and privileged access to correct information in their memory concerning the inaccessible target. The *direct access hypothesis* readily explains the accuracy of feeling-of-knowing judgements, in that it assumes that people are accessing correct information about the target. It also explains the typical ability to output partial target information, such as the first letter or the length of a target word when in a tip-of-the-tongue state. However, subsequent theorists have largely rejected the direct access hypothesis (but see Metcalfe 2000). They point to the frequent accessing of incorrect partial information (e.g. the wrong first letter of the target word) and to the outputting of incorrect responses as evidence that people do not base their judgements solely on direct access to correct information (see e.g. Koriat 2000).

There is also evidence challenging whether the direct access hypothesis adequately explains accurate feeling-of-knowing judgements. In a key study, Nelson et al. (1986) compared the extent to which each of three measures correlated with an individual's subsequent memory performance. Two of these measures were *subjective in nature: each participant's own idiosyncratic feeling-of-knowing judgement for a particular item; and a normative feeling-of-knowing judgement, which is the average of the idiosyncratic judgements for a particular item among all participants. The third measure was *objective in nature: the *normative item difficulty*, which is the average proportion of participants that answer a particular item correctly on the subsequent memory test. Nelson et al. reported that, across all items, the idiosyncratic judgements were better correlated with the participants' own memory performance than were normative judgements, but neither of those subjective measures correlated with such memory performance as well as the objective measure, normative item difficulty. This suggests that a participant who is currently unable to answer a question correctly will be less accurate in predicting her own subsequent memory performance than would an observer who bases a prediction solely on objective knowledge about how many people are able to answer the question. Thus, it seems that the accuracy of feeling-of-knowing judgements may not be based on any special insight into one's own memory contents and processes, but instead could be attributed to the influence of objective item difficulty on such judgements.

Two more recent theories claim that people base their feelings of knowing not on direct access to correct target information, but rather on inferences they make using the information they are able to access. The two main hypotheses in this vein are the accessibility hypothesis and the cue familiarity hypothesis.

The *accessibility hypothesis* (Koriat 1995) assumes that people base their feeling-of-knowing judgements on the information that is retrieved from memory, regardless of the source of that information and in particular regardless of whether the information pertains to the correct target or not. Thus, such judgements are sensitive to the total amount of information that is accessed—both correct and incorrect—and the speed with which it is accessed. Unlike the direct access hypothesis, the accessibility hypothesis can explain the inaccuracy as well as the accuracy of such judgements: If the information retrieved from memory is incorrect, the feeling-of-knowing judgements can be inaccurate. However, in most cases the information retrieved from memory tends to be correct, and this explains the moderately positive correlation between feeling-of-knowing judgements and eventual retrieval (Koriat 2000). Evidence supporting this hypothesis includes the finding that people have stronger feelings of knowing as the amount of accessed information increases, regardless of the correctness of the accessed information (Koriat 1995).

The *cue familiarity hypothesis* claims that people base their feeling-of-knowing judgements initially on a rapid assessment of the familiarity of the cue that is being used to search memory (Reder 1987). For example, one might be asked a question such as 'What is the proper name for a badminton birdie?' If one knows a good deal about badminton and birdies, perhaps because of frequent or recent encounters, and those things are therefore familiar, one can make a quick feeling of knowing judgement even before attempting to retrieve the target information (shuttlecock—but note that this example does not work for British badminton players, who do not call it a birdie). Such a judgement based on cue familiarity can be used to determine whether the target information is likely to be found in memory, and this determination can in turn be used to determine whether to engage in a more effortful search of memory in an attempt to retrieve the target information. Evidence supporting this hypothesis includes the finding that people have stronger feelings of knowing after steps are taken to make the cue more familiar (e.g. by repeated pre-judgement exposures to the cue), notwithstanding a lack of improvement in final memory for the target (e.g. Reder 1987).

There is disagreement regarding the degree to which the processes underlying feeling-of-knowing judgements are conscious vs unconscious. Koriat (2000) asserts that the feeling of knowing is a conscious judgement that arises from an unconscious application of non-analytic, heuristic inferences about the probability that the target information is present in memory, based on such things as the amount of information accessed and the speed of access. The goal of this judgement, according to Koriat, is to increase conscious control over subsequent behaviour, such as determining whether to continue retrieval efforts. Thus, according to Koriat, metacognitive monitoring and control are both conscious processes.

In contrast, Reder (1987; Spehn and Reder, 2000) asserts that cue familiarity judgements and consequent determinations to search or not to search memory typically occur unconsciously, rising to the level of consciousness only on those relatively rare occasions, such as tip-of-the-tongue states, when strong feelings of knowing accompany continuing retrieval failure. Reder points to evidence showing that, in a mathematical problem-solving task that includes repetitions of problems, participants were unaware of their own shift in strategy between a direct retrieval strategy and a strategy of solving problems anew. According to this perspective, then, metacognitive monitoring and control are both implicit, unconscious processes.

It should be noted that these two perspectives are not mutually exclusive. People may make both implicit and explicit feeling-of-knowing judgements, and based on those judgements, may make unconscious and conscious determinations that control subsequent behaviour. These perspectives could thus be viewed as emphasizing different aspects of feeling-of-knowing judgements, with key differences between the perspectives being claims regarding the relative frequency and theoretical importance of the conscious vs unconscious processes related to such judgements.

DANIEL KIMBALL

Hart, J. T. (1965). 'Memory and the feeling-of-knowing experience'. *Journal of Experimental Psychology*, 56.

Koriat, A. (1995). 'Dissociating knowing and the feeling of knowing: further evidence for the accessibility model'. *Journal of Experimental Psychology: General*, 124.

—— (2000). 'The feeling of knowing: Some metatheoretical implications for consciousness and control'. *Consciousness and Cognition*, 9.

Metcalfe, J. (2000). 'Feelings and judgments of knowing: is there a special noetic state?' *Consciousness and Cognition*, 9.

Nelson, T. O., Leonesio, R. J., Landwehr, R. S., and Narens, L. (1986). 'A comparison of three predictors of an individual's memory performance: the individual's feeling of knowing versus the normative feeling of knowing versus base-rate item difficulty'. *Journal of Experimental Psychology: Learning, Memory, and Cognition*, 12.

Reder, L. M. (1987). 'Selection strategies in question answering'. *Cognitive Psychology*, 19.

Spehn, M. K. and Reder, L. M. (2000). 'The unconscious feeling of knowing: A comment on Koriat's paper'. *Consciousness and Cognition*, 9.

filling-in Among vision scientists, filling-in is defined in terms of the experience of a certain visual aspect where there is no stimulus in the corresponding region, only in the surrounds.

Our visual experience has boundaries, however hard they are to pin down exactly, but within these it seems to be smooth and continuous and certainly lacking any major gaps. From an anatomical point of view this gaplessness of the visual field is remarkable because of the presence of the *blind spot* in the retina: at the place where the optic nerve leaves the eye, there are no receptors at all. Yet instead of experiencing a glaring hole at the corresponding locus of the visual field, our perception is such that what surrounds that locus is also present inside it. If the area is surrounded by a colour, the colour flows in, if it is a texture, the texture spreads in. It seems as if the visual gap has been filled in by the brain, resulting in an experiential completion.

Many other perceptual phenomena not involving the blind spot are covered by this definition, some relatively common, such as filling-in of areas which correspond to parts of the retina which have been injured, others only known to vision scientists, such as *neon colour spreading*, in which colours present only in the lines of a grating spread over the total area covered by the grating. Filling-in of surface features such as colour, brightness, texture, or motion is sometimes distinguished from completion of incomplete contours. Filling-in is also distinguished from amodal completion, which occurs in the perception of a partially occluded object. Though the unseen part is present in perception in some sense, it does not have genuine modal visual features as filled-in parts do (Fig. F2).

1. Filling-in and the relation between the experiential and the neural
2. Filling-in as a neuroscientific issue

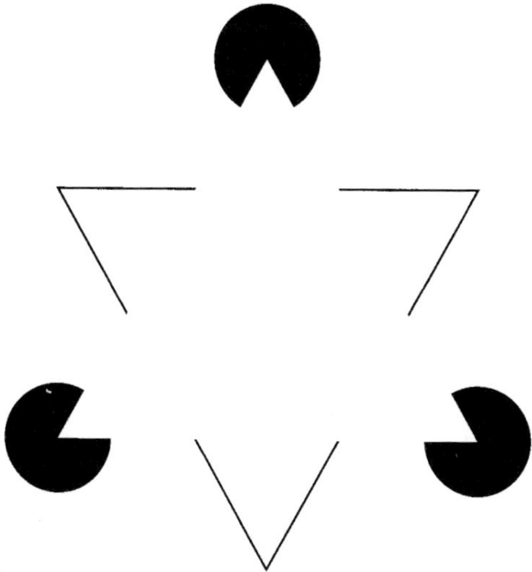

Fig. F2. The Kanisza triangle illustrates modal filling-in of the surface of a brighter triangle in the foreground, as well as completion of illusory contours, both modal (foreground figure) and amodal (occluded triangle). Amodal surface feature completion also occurs for the black circles.

1. Filling-in and the relation between the experiential and the neural

Filling-in raises questions about the relation between perceptual experience and underlying neural representations and mechanisms. There is common agreement that there is experiential filling-in, in the sense that it does seem to subjects that they have visual experience at the blind spot. Yet there is a debate about what form a neural explanation of this experiential filling-in should take.

The most straightforward possibility seems to explain *experiential filling-in* through a process of *neural filling-in*: subjects see something where the blind spot is, because the brain itself provides a stand-in for the missing stimulus. An initially incomplete neural representation is filled-in through an active neural process, which provides, at some stage of visual processing, the effects actual stimulation would have had. As a result, subjects have the experience of seeing a complete, gapless image.

Dennett (1991) ignited a theoretical debate about filling-in by raising concerns regarding two additional properties this straightforward model of filling-in might have. First, such a model might be *isomorphist*, in that it would be assumed that there is a direct point-to-point correspondence between experience and some *neural map*. An explicit representation in some 'pictorial' neural map would correspond to every detail that is experienced as 'seen', or every detail in 'visual experience'. Secondly, Dennett warns against thinking that such an explicit neural, map-like representation might be found at a single place in the brain: a specific *bridge locus* (Teller 1984, Pessoa et al. 1998) where neural activity becomes conscious.

Dennett posits that there is no need for the machinery underlying visual awareness either to be isomorphic or to occur at a single locus. To think so would be to fall prey to the lures of a *picture theory* of vision, according to which seeing a scene is accounted for by positing the existence of a mental picture of the scene in one's head. Many philosophers and theorists have argued that such a conception of vision is deeply unsatisfactory, as it only replaces the original explanandum (how the scene is seen) with something standing in need of exactly the same explanation (how the picture is seen).

Dennett argues—contrary to this assumption of a bridge locus—that the substrate of visual consciousness must be spatially and temporally distributed in the brain: consciousness cannot be something that instantaneously happens at some designated area in the brain and thus can be sustained by neural processes differing from occasion to occasion (Pessoa et al. 1998 provide some experimental evidence to back this claim). Applying this line of thinking to filling-in phenomena, Dennett has argued that the task for vision is to find out about the environment in order to produce suitable behaviour. This requires interpretative processes in the brain, but these might operate in a variety of ways, and occur at a variety of stages in the brain. As such, experience need not be related to the construction of a detailed isomorphic representation. In the case of the blind spot, all that matters is that the blind region in the scene is functionally treated as its surrounding regions. The brain may achieve this end, as well as by actually filling-in a spatially isomorphic representation, by using a symbolic—and thus non-picturesque—*labelling technique* to categorize the different parts of the percept, or by simply ignoring an absence of information—thus never noticing the blind spot.

2. Filling-in as a neuroscientific issue

Recently, neuroscientists have been acquiring a rich collection of evidence about neural activity associated with filling-in. This evidence is generally taken by neuroscientists to refute the theory that filling-in is merely a matter of ignoring an absence and to confirm an isomorphic empirical theory, at least for some types of filling-in, for some kinds of visual features (Pessoa et al. 1998 and Komatsu 2006 provide references to more individual studies than we can explicitly refer to here).

The occurrence of such phenomena as motion *after-effect—an illusory motion in the opposite direction of previously observed motion— and negative after-images in filled-in areas is, together with other evidence, taken as indicating that filling-in involves some kind of active construction, rather than just ignoring a lack of information.

According to what has become more or less standard isomorphic theory, filling-in involves spreading neural activation in low-level retinotopic maps—representations in the brain that share the spatial structure of the retina—of visual surface features such as brightness, colour, orientation or texture. This theory seems supported by *single-cell recording studies that have shown that cells in the zone corresponding to the blind spot in visual area *V1 respond as if an unbroken bar stimulus was registered in a regular way by the retina if the bar crosses over the blind spot (Fiorani et al. 1992), and cells in V2 have been designated as the neural *correlates of brightness filling-in (Roe et al. 2005). Moreover, both for brightness (Rossi and Paradiso 2003) and textural filling-in (Spillman and De Weerd 2003), psychophysical investigations have unveiled a temporal dynamics as of a gradual filling-in process, and, in the case of brightness, this has been measured as having a roughly constant speed of 0.15–0.4 m/s (Rossi and Paradiso 2003).

The discovery of empirical evidence for neural filling-in mechanisms isomorphic to experiential effects has been taken by some as a case where armchair philosophy, incarnated by Dennett, has been proved wrong by empirical science (Ramachandran and Churchland 1993). There are, however, various provisos to be made before one can consider these data as convincingly establishing the kind of full-blown isomorphic theory attacked by Dennett. Different types of filling-in seem to have correlating neurons in different areas of the visual brain (Komatsu 2006). Moreover, the neurons active during filling-in are not always the neurons that would be active if the filled-in stimulus were actually present (Komatsu 2006) and neurons apparently involved in filling-in also carry information about visual aspects other than the filled-in features (Rossi and Paradiso 2003). Also, psychophysically observed spreading of brightness has not been directly related to a neural process of propagation of signals (Rossi and Paradiso 2003).

While certainly not rendering an isomorphist theory impossible, these data indicate that the isomorphic areas may be distributed over the brain. Moreover, they suggest that a similar experience, depending on whether or not it involves filling-in, may correlate with neural activation in different parts of the brain, considerably complicating the notion of a bridge locus. In addition, some theorists (von der Heydt et al. 2003) have taken the evidence available as indicating that for colour filling-in, a *symbolic theory*—according to which colours are processed only in terms of colour transients or discontinuities, without any isomorphic spreading taking place—is correct. Moreover, most theorists emphasize that as yet uncharted higher-level processes play a role in filling-in, further convoluting the issues of isomorphism and the bridge locus. Many also point out that filling-in is probably due to very general visual mechanisms operative in the perception of boundaries and surfaces and their three-dimensional layout (Pessoa and De Weerd 2003, Komatsu 2006).

Despite the technical sophistication of the recent wave of neuroscientific research, the fundamental issue underlying Dennett's worries has hardly been addressed: Whether and how an isomorphic, and thus roughly pictorial, representation provides an acceptable explanation of visual awareness. Indeed, dissatisfaction with any broadly pictorial approach, has led some thinkers to try to account for filling-in in terms of expectations of what one would see if one moved one's eyes rather than in terms of operations on some internal rendering of the scene one is faced with (O'Regan 1992, Noë 2004).

ERIK MYIN AND LARS DE NUL

Churchland, P. S. and Ramachandran, V. S. (1993). 'Filling in: Why Dennett is wrong'. In Dahlbom, B. (ed.) *Dennett and his Critics*.

Dennett, D. (1991). *Consciousness Explained*.

Fiorani, M., Rosa, M. G. P., Gattas, R., and Rocha-Miranda, C. E. (1992). 'Dynamic surrounds of receptive fields in primate striate cortex: a physiological basis for perceptual completion?' *Proceedings of the National Academy of Sciences of the USA*, 89.

Komatsu, H. (2006). 'The neural mechanisms of perceptual filling-in'. *Nature Reviews Neuroscience*, 7.

Noë, A. (2004). *Action in Perception*.

O'Regan, J. K. (1992). 'Solving the 'real' mysteries of visual perception: The world as an outside memory'. *Canadian Journal of Psychology*, 46.

Pessoa, L. and De Weerd, P. (eds) (2003). *Filling-In: From Perceptual Completion to Cortical Reorganization*.

——, Thompson, E., and Noë, A. (1998). 'Finding out about filling-in: A guide to perceptual completion for visual science and the philosophy of perception'. *Behavioural and Brain Sciences*, 21.

Roe, A. W., Lu, H. D., and Hung, C. P. (2005). 'Cortical processing of a brightness illusion'. *Proceedings of the National Academy Sciences of the USA*, 102.

Rossi, A. F. and Paradiso, M. A. (2003). 'Surface completion: psychophysical and neurophysiological studies of brightness'. In Pessoa, L. and De Weerd, P. (eds) *Filling-In: From Perceptual Completion to Cortical Reorganization*.

Spillman, L. and De Weerd, P. (2003). 'Mechanisms of surface completion: perceptual filling-in of texture'. In Pessoa, L. and De Weerd, P. (eds) *Filling-In: From Perceptual Completion to Cortical Reorganization*.

Teller, D.Y. (1984). 'Linking propositions'. *Vision Research*, 24.
von der Heydt, R., Friedman, H. S., and Zhou, H. (2003). 'Searching for the neural mechanisms for color filling-in'. In Pessoa, L. and De Weerd, P. (eds) *Filling-In: From Perceptual Completion to Cortical Reorganization*.

first person/third person The distinction between the first-person and third-person perspectives is intended to capture an asymmetry in our access to certain features of the world. Take the fact that my legs are currently crossed. This feature is accessible to the third-person point of view, for by looking at me you can know that my legs are crossed just as well as I can. But contrast the fact that my legs are crossed with the fact that I am currently thinking about *All Quiet on the Western Front*. I can know that I am thinking about *All Quiet on the Western Front* in a way that you cannot. My knowledge that I am thinking about *All Quiet on the Western Front* is direct and immediate, whereas your knowledge is indirect and mediated. Even when conscious states can be detected from the third-person perspective, the subject of the states in question has a certain kind of epistemic authority over them. (This is not to say that one cannot be wrong about what conscious state one is currently in '—', for example, those who are subject to the *refrigerator light illusion may think that the contents of their stream of consciousness are richer than they in fact are.)

The asymmetry between the first-person and third-person perspectives is basic to many discussions of consciousness. Conscious states, and perhaps only conscious states, enjoy some kind of first-person privilege. The *knowledge argument, the *explanatory gap, and the problem of other minds all turn on the fact that certain kinds of knowledge about consciousness seem unobtainable from the third-person perspective alone. (not everyone grants that the facts in question *are* unobtainable from the third-person perspective alone, but it is widely granted that this appears to be the case.) Exactly what implications these epistemological concerns have for the ontology or nature of consciousness is a further question.

See also EPISTEMOLOGY OF CONSCIOUSNESS; SELF-CONSCIOUSNESS; SUBJECTIVITY

TIM BAYNE

flash-lag effect In the standard flash-lag experiment observers are presented with a moving object and a flashed object such that at the instant of the flash the moving object is aligned (or co-localized) with the flashed object. Observers report the flashed object as trailing behind the moving object.

Traditionally, the most influential analyses concerning the topics of space and time have emerged from the field of physics. Ernst Mach, an eminent physicist, neurophysiologist, and psychologist recognized that these topics belonged as much (if not more) to the study of sensory neurophysiology and psychology. This recognition led to his relativistic view of space and time, which culminated in Einstein's theory of relativity (Ratliff 1965:29). Recently, there has been growing interest in the neurophysiological and psychological bases of time and space, in particular from the point of view of the observer's perceptions and actions (Müsseler et al. 2004, Nijhawan and Khurana in press). Several paradigms, including the flash-lag effect, have emerged as promising psychophysical methods for empirical investigation of time and space. The flash-lag effect involves movement, either of objects in the world or of observer's limbs (and other end-effectors such eyes) during behaviour. There are a number of variations of the flash-lag experiment. Several of the variations involve observer's eye movements (Brenner et al. 2001, Nijhawan 2001, Schlag and Schlag-Rey 2002) or limb movements (Nijhawan and Kirschfeld 2003). Figure F3 shows the ring-disk version of this effect.

The flash-lag effect is a spatial phenomenon. However, as movement is involved issues concerning time immediately come to the fore. Among the temporal issues arising are time delays in neural processing, the impact of sensory delays on visual awareness, and more generally the relationship between mental (mind) and neural (brain) processes.

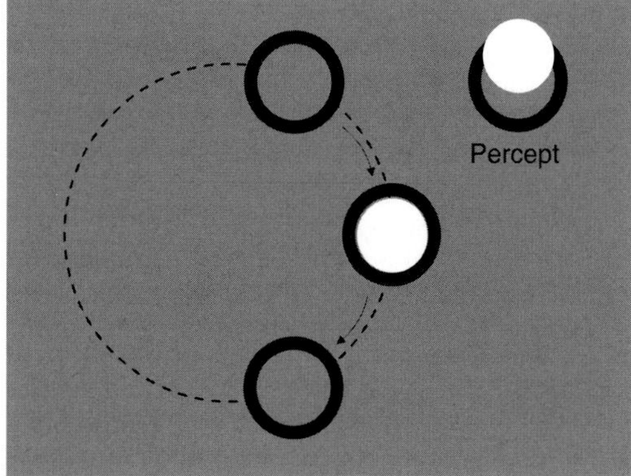

Fig. F3. In this version of the flash-lag display an observer holds their eyes still and views a black ring moving on a circular path. The figure shows three discrete positions of the ring moving in the direction of the arrow. A white disc is flashed in the centre of the ring at the 3 o'clock position when the ring arrives at the 3 o'clock position. The observers perceive the white disc in a lagging position, as depicted by the *percept* (see inset). The percept shows some additional details of what the observers see: a grey crescent-shaped space (called the *perceived void*), and illusory white/grey and black/grey edges that are not present in the world (or on the retinal image).

Helmholtz, another well-known physicist, neurophysiologist, and psychologist, made a remarkable discovery in 1850 when he measured the speed with which neural signals propagate in a frog nerve–muscle preparation. His calculations yielded a speed of 30 m/s, which is 10 times slower than the speed of sound in air! Neural delays imply that the response of the various components of the nervous system of an animal will be delayed relative to the stimulating physical event(s). For example, when a human observer attempts to catch a moving ball the neural information from the eye (the ball's retinal image) must travel to and activate the arm muscles. Here various time-consuming processes are involved: (1) processing of the light reflected from the ball by the photoreceptors and other retinal neurons, (2) transmission of retinal output signals via the thalamus to the primary visual cortex, (3) communication of visual information to the motor cortex, and from there to the spinal cord, and (4) finally the 'sluggish' response of the muscles to neural stimulation. There is one significant aspect of neural processing that is not captured by the ball interception example, and this is related to visual awareness. What about the delay in the visual perception of the ball? Can the delay in visual perception be measured? As the interception task involves mechanical, motor, and other non-visual delays (in addition to visual delays), a ball-catching task cannot be used to address this question. The flash-lag effect suggests a possibility.

Understanding of the flash-lag effect is as yet not complete, but the results so far have led to some provocative ideas. The output cells of the retina (ganglion cells) make topographic connections with neurons in the primary visual cortex leading to a precise map of the retina in the cortex (Fig. F4a). Moving objects stimulating the retina give rise to a travelling wave of neural activity in the cortical map. The transmission of information from the retina to the cortex can take up to a tenth of a second. As everything we know about the neural basis of visual awareness suggests that spatial perceptions are based in part on what goes on in the primary visual cortex and numerous other maps (see V1), at the most simplistic level one might say that when we look at a moving object the position where we see it is where it was a tenth of a second ago. This expected spatial lag in perception (Fig. F4b), known as *ds-error*, is analogous to the way the Sun appears to us in a lagging position, as the light from the Sun takes about 8 minutes to arrive on Earth. When in 'reality' the Sun is directly overhead, for example, its apparent position lags (appears to be shifted eastward) by 2°. In terms of neural pathway length, the farther a visual centre is from the photoreceptors, the longer the delay generally is, and the larger the spatial lag. Numerous findings since the time of Helmholtz suggest that delays in vision are particularly large because of the time-consuming phototransduction process and the relatively large number of steps separated by synapses in visual processing (there are three within the retina alone). This means that human observers should see a moving object where it was in the recent past, and that there should be a lag (= object velocity × time delay) between the object's 'real' position and its visible position.

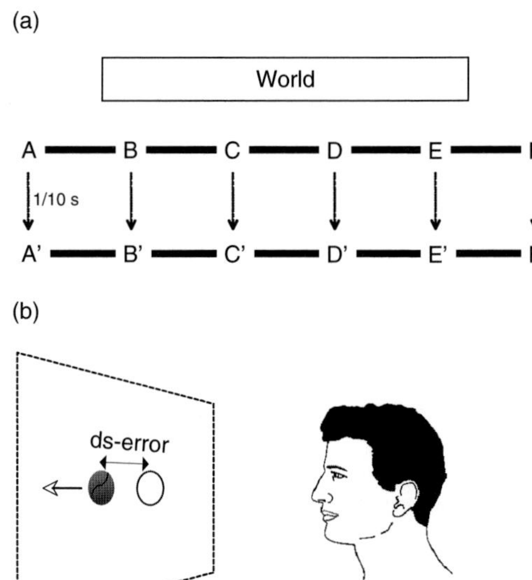

Fig. F4. (a) The retinal ganglion cells A, B, C,... are connected with cortical cells A′, B′, C′, ..., respectively. The horizontal lines between the ganglion cells (A, B, C, ...) and the cortical cells (A′, B′, C′, ...) depict lateral (horizontal) connections between neurons. The downward arrows depict transmission of signals from the retinal ganglion cells to cortex with a delay of 0.1 s. (b) An observer viewing a moving tennis ball (motion in the direction of arrow) should perceive the ball as occupying the position it actually occupied up to 0.1 s ago. Outline circle depicts perceived position of the tennis ball. For a tennis ball travelling at 30 mph (50 km/h), the lag, known as the ds-error, should be more than 4 feet (1.2 m).

The frequently quoted value of the flash-lag effect in time units is 80 ms (Nijhawan 1994); the moving object appears ahead of the flashed object by the distance it travels in 80 ms. One natural explanation of this effect is that the neural processing speed of moving objects is 80 ms faster than that for the flashed objects. This explanation is analogous to the frequently observed phenomenon, due to the large difference in speed between light and sound, in which the visible position of an aeroplane in flight is in advance of the position from which the sound of the jet engines appears to emanate.

Why might moving objects be processed faster than flashes? One possible basis for faster processing of moving objects could be *priming. When a given neuron is stimulated there is *spread of activation* via lateral connections (shown by horizontal lines in Fig. F4a) to neighbouring neurons. New incoming retinal signals could then more quickly trigger these primed cortical neurons in the path of motion, thus effectively reducing the latency with which these neurons respond to external input.

The main problem with this account, known as the *differential latency account* (Purushothaman et al. 1998, Whitney and Murakami, 1998), is that the latency difference of about 80 ms is necessary to explain the flash-lag effect. As flashes are extremely effective in stimulating the retina, it is difficult to imagine that flashes would take more than a few milliseconds longer to process than moving objects. Furthermore, 80 ms is a large time difference that would be relatively easy to measure neurophysiologically. Yet, most neurophysiological studies do not show more than a few millisecond latency difference between moving and flashed objects. So we must look for another explanation.

The alternative possibility is that the activated neurons in the path of motion are not just primed to process external input from the world more quickly, but rather the activity of these neurons *represents* the predicted position of the moving object. Just as the ball player must predict the position of the ball in order catch it, the *visual prediction account* (Nijhawan 2008) suggests that the visual system is predictive, and the perceived position of the moving object incorporates prediction by visual neurons. The flash-lag effect occurs because no prediction is possible for the flash.

An analogy helps to clarify the difference between the differential latency and the visual prediction models. Imagine a row of ball players named A, B, C, . . . , F standing across from another row we can call A′, B′, C′, . . . , F′ (Fig. F5a). Once players receive a signal from the world (a stimulus), their task is to send information (in the form of throwing a ball) to their counterpart in the other row. Thus, A throws to A′, B throws to B′, and so on. A′, B′ etc., in turn, catch the ball. In addition A′ can communicate with B′, B′ can communicate with C′, and so on. As an object, in the present example a car, moves in the world it causes A, B, and C to make throws to A′, B′, and C′ in succession. Suppose a moving car arrives at C and then D. Once the ball thrown by C has arrived at C′, C′ tells D′ to be ready for an incoming throw. Thus D′ has been primed to receive an incoming ball from D. So when D makes the throw D′ indeed makes the catch more quickly. In our example the

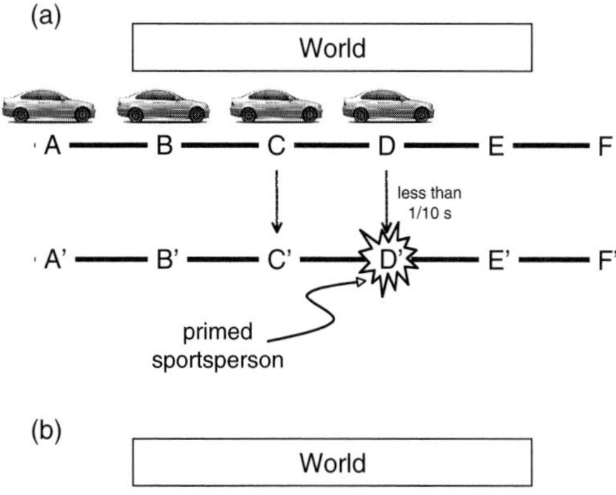

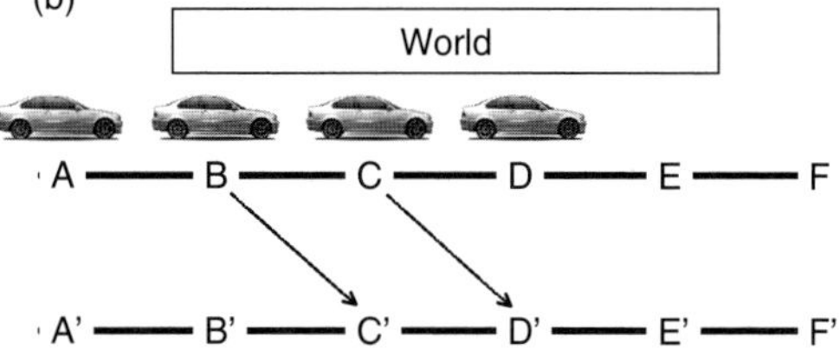

Fig. F5. An analogy to explain the difference between the differential latency and the visual prediction accounts. Ball players in two rows, separated by some distance, stand facing each other. A′, B′, C′, . . . , F′ (the cortical row) are ready to catch the ball thrown (retinal signal) by the A, B, C, . . . , F (the retinal row). An object moving in the world (a car) arrives in position D at the instant depicted. (a) Differential latency model. Due to the communication between C′ and D′ via lateral interaction, D′ is primed to efficiently and quickly receive the ball throw from D. (b) Visual prediction model. Due to communication between B and C, C throws the ball to D′, who in turn is ready to receive a diagonal throw as a result of communication via the lateral interaction between C′ and D′.

arrival of the ball at D′ constitutes perception of the moving car at D. This example shows how primed cortical cells might be able to process moving objects more quickly. Clearly this type of priming is possible only for moving objects and not for flashed objects.

The prediction model is quite different. Consider the analogy of the ball players again. The crucial difference between the two models can be appreciated by considering what happens when the moving car arrives at position C. One effective way to compensate for neural processing delays for moving objects would be for C *not* to throw the ball to C′ but to throw it diagonally to D′ (Fig. F5b). Compensation would occur when the ball arrives at D′ precisely when the moving car arrives at D. But our analogy is overly simplistic. In a more realistic model there would be many rows consisting of many neurons with many connections between neurons. However, the only requirements for the visual prediction model are that there should be diagonal pathways, and the neural signal speed along the horizontal component of the diagonal is high compared to speed of object motion. Both these requirements are easily fulfilled. Segments of horizontal and vertical pathways, well known to exist in the visual system, form the diagonal pathways, and speed requirement for moving objects is easily fulfilled in most flash-lag experiments.

The notion of visual prediction raises some basic philosophical and neurophysiological issues. It has been argued that we have no direct immediate access to the world (Neisser 1976), and that visual perception is a generative process that 'creates' the visual image on the basis of a multiplicity of information (Kandel and Wurtz 2000). Why do influential scientists frequently find it necessary to remind the scientific community of this peculiarity of visual perception? It is because in the absence of such reminders we acquiesce in believing that our visual percepts directly inform us of what is present in the world. It has been suggested that visual perception is like a hypothesis about what is present in the world (Gregory 1980). The visual prediction model reinforces and extends these ideas by suggesting that the perceived position of a moving object is a type of guess regarding the object's true position.

ROMI NIJHAWAN

Brenner, E., Smeets, J. B. J., and van den Berg, A. V. (2001). 'Smooth eye movements and spatial localization'. *Vision Research*, 41.

Gregory, R. L. (1980). 'Perceptions as hypotheses'. *Philosophical Transactions of the Royal Society London Series B: Biological Sciences*, 290.

Kandel, E. R. and Wurtz, R. H. (2000). 'Constructing the visual image'. In Kandel, E. R. et al. (eds) *Principles of Neural Science*.

Müsseler, J., Van der Heijden, A. H. C., and Kerzel, D. (2004). *Special Issue of Visual Cognition: Visual Space Perception and Action*.

Neisser, U. (1976). *Cognition and Reality: Principles and Implications of Cognitive Psychology*.

Nijhawan, R. (1994). 'Motion extrapolation in catching'. *Nature*, 370.

—— (2001). 'The flash-lag phenomenon: object-motion and eye-movements'. *Perception*, 30.

—— (2008). 'Visual prediction: psychophysics and neurophysiology of compensation for time delays'. *Behavioral and Brain Sciences*, 31.

—— and Khurana, B. (in press). *Space and Time in Perception and Action*.

—— and Kirschfeld, K. (2003). 'Analogous mechanisms compensate for neural delays in the sensory and the motor pathways: evidence from motor flash-lag'. *Current Biology*, 13.

Purushothaman, G., Patel, S. S., Bedell, H. E., and Ogmen, H. (1998). 'Moving ahead through differential visual latency'. *Nature*, 396.

Ratliff, F. (1965). *Mach Bands: Quantitative Studies on Neural Networks in the Retina*.

Schlag, J. and Schlag-Rey, M. (2002). 'Through the eye slowly: delays and localization errors in the visual system'. *Nature Reviews Neuroscience*, 3.

Whitney, D. and Murakami, I. (1998). 'Latency difference, not spatial extrapolation'. *Nature Neuroscience*, 1.

forward models A forward model is one that describes the causal relationship between actions and their consequences. The ability to predict the consequences of our actions is fundamental for action and also for many cognitive functions. In this brief review we discuss the role of forward models underlying *prediction* in sensorimotor control and in higher cognitive functions, including *agency*, which is integral to *conscious experience.

Prediction refers to the estimation of future states of a particular system. In sensorimotor control, we are primarily interested in predictive processes in systems that are directly and immediately influenced by our motor commands; for example, predicting how our arm moves in response to a motor command. Skilled action relies on accurate predictions of both our own body and objects with which we interact (such as a tool) because sensorimotor feedback loops are simply too slow because of the significant delays that arise in receptor transduction, neural conduction, and central processing. An influential idea in sensorimotor control is that the brain predicts the consequences of action by simulating the dynamic response of our body and environment to the outgoing motor command. Such as system is termed an *internal forward model* as it is internal to the central nervous system, models the behaviour of the body, and captures the forward or causal relationship between actions and their consequences.

A fundamental role of forward models in motor control is to monitor performance by comparing predicted sensory outcomes to actual outcomes. For example, when I lift an object my brain predicts the timing of lift-off as signalled by mechanoreceptors in the skin and reacts rapidly if these signals occur either earlier (if the object is lighter than expected) or fail to occur (if the object is heavier than expected; for a review see Flanagan and Johansson 2002). Moreover, these prediction errors can be used to update forward models themselves with a view to improving future predictions. Thus forward models are not fixed entities but are updated through experience. Well-established computational learning rules can be used to translate the prediction error into changes in synaptic weights which will improve future predictions.

Another important function of forward models is state estimation. Knowing our body's state, e.g. the positions and velocities of our body segments, is fundamental for accurate motor control. However, sensory signals that convey information about state are subject to significant delays and provide information which is corrupted by random processes, known as *noise*. An approach that deals with these obstacles is to estimate state using prediction based on motor commands. Here the estimate is made ahead of the movement and therefore is better in terms of time delays, but the estimate will drift over time if the forward model is not perfectly accurate. The drawbacks of both these mechanisms can be ameliorated by combining sensory feedback and motor prediction to estimate the current state. Such an approach is used in engineering and the system which produces the estimate is known as an *observer*, an example of which is the Kalman filter. The major objectives of the observer are to compensate for the delays in the sensorimotor system and to reduce the uncertainty in the state estimate which arises due to noise inherent in both the sensory and motor signals. An example of such state prediction is seen in object manipulation. When moving grasped objects, people modulate grip force in precise anticipation of the changes in load caused by acceleration of the object (Flanagan and Wing 1997). Sensory detection of the load is too slow to account for this increased grip force which instead relies on predictive processes.

In addition to state estimation, prediction allows us to filter sensory information, attenuating unwanted information or highlighting information critical for control. Sensory prediction can be derived from the state prediction and used to cancel the sensory effects of movement, which is known as *reafference*. By using such prediction, it is possible to cancel out the effects of sensory changes induced by self-motion, thereby enhancing more relevant sensory information. For example, predictive mechanisms underlie the observation that the same tactile stimulus, such as a *tickle, is felt less intensely when it is self-applied (Blakemore et al. 1999). This mechanism has been supported by studies in which a time delay is introduced between the motor command and the resulting tickle. The greater the time delay the more ticklish the percept, presumably due to a reduction in the ability to cancel the sensory feedback based on the motor command.

Similarly, sensory predictions provide a mechanism to determine agency—whether motion of our bodies has been generated by us or by an external agent. For example, when I move my arm, my predicted sensory feedback and the actual feedback match and I therefore attribute the motion as being generated by me. However, if someone else moves my arm, my sensory predictions are discordant with the actual feedback and I attribute the movement as not being generated by me. Therefore, in general, movements predicted on the basis of my motor command are labelled as self-generated and those that are unpredictable are labelled as not produced by me. Frith has proposed that a failure in this mechanism may underlie delusions of control in *schizophrenia, in which it appears to the patient that their body is being moved by forces other than their own (Frith et al. 2000).

Forward models, used to predict the consequences of motor commands, may be distinguished from *inverse models* that are used to estimate in advance the motor commands required to achieve desired consequences. A study of grip force control has shown that when learning to manipulate an object with novel properties the brain learns to predict the consequences, as measured by grip force, before learning how to control the object so as to achieve a desired trajectory (Flanagan et al. 2003). This suggests that the brain maintains distinct forward and inverse models for prediction and control. Whereas in delusion of control normal movements are made but are perceived as coming from an external source, in *anarchic hand abnormal movements are made and are attributed by the patient as self-generated. This suggests that in delusions of control the inverse model functions normally and the forward model is faulty, whereas in anarchic hand syndrome the inverse model is impaired and produces an non-desired movement, but the normal forward model correctly predicts the consequences and thereby attributes the movements as self-generated (Frith et al. 2000).

Not only is prediction essential for motor control, it may also be fundamental for high-level cognitive functions including action observation and understanding, mental practice, imitation, and social cognition. The forward model may provide a general framework for prediction in all of these domains. For example, forward models can be used in mental practice to predict the sensory outcome of an action without actually performing the action. In this way mental practice could improve performance by tuning controllers or selecting between possible mentally rehearsed actions. *Functional brain imaging and behavioural studies have shown that brain areas active during mental rehearsal of an action are strikingly similar to those used in performing the action. Similarly, in social interaction, a forward social model could be used to predict the reactions of others to our actions (Wolpert et al. 2003). It may be that the same computational mechanisms that developed for sensorimotor prediction, which largely lie outside the conscious domain, may have been adapted for other cognitive functions, some of which are integral to conscious experience.

DANIEL M. WOLPERT AND J. RANDALL FLANAGAN

Blakemore, S. J., Frith, C. D., and Wolpert, D. M. (1999). 'Perceptual modulation of self-produced stimuli: the role of spatio-temporal prediction'. *Journal of Cognitive Neuroscience*, 11.

Flanagan, J. R. and Johansson, R. S. (2002). 'Hand movements'. In: Ramachandran, V. S. (ed.), *Encyclopedia of the Human Brain*, Vol. 2.

—— and Wing, A. M. (1997). 'The role of internal models in motor planning and control: evidence from grip force adjustments during movements of hand-held loads'. *Journal of Neuroscience*, 17.

——, Vetter, P., Johansson, R. S., and Wolpert, D. M. (2003). 'Prediction precedes control in motor learning'. *Current Biology*, 13.

Frith, C. D., Blakemore, S. J., and Wolpert, D. M. (2000). 'Abnormalities in the awareness and control of action'. *Philosophical Transactions of the Royal Society of London Series B: Biological Sciences*, 355.

Wolpert, D. M., Doya, K., and Kawato, M. (2003). 'A unifying computational framework for motor control and social interaction'. *Philosophical Transactions of the Royal Society of London Series B: Biological Sciences*, 358.

four-item limit See CAPACITY LIMITS AND CONSCIOUSNESS

free will and consciousness The reality of free will has sometimes been argued for by appeal to a consciousness we are supposed to have of our own freedom. But equally there are modern writers who claim that a proper understanding of consciousness will show free will to be wholly or partly an illusion. And finally many philosophers, especially in the English-language tradition, have taken the view that the question of free will has nothing to do with consciousness. For them the free will problem is about the correct semantic analysis of the expression 'could have done otherwise'; and such an analysis is to be provided simply by considering concepts or sentence meanings, without any reference to consciousness or experience. So, given this wide variety in approach, what might the real connection be between free will and consciousness?

1. What is free will?
2. Experience, causal power, and freedom
3. Freedom and experience
4. Does consciousness or experience show free will to be an illusion?

1. What is free will?

Each of us has a sense that, within limits set by our intelligence, physical capacities and resources, what we do is up to us or within our control. This up-to-usness is what philosophers have long termed *freedom*. It applies to our intentional agency—to things we can intentionally do or refrain from doing, such as walking or standing still or concentrating our thought on a particular problem, and taking decisions to do any of these things; and it consists in alternatives by way of action being open to us.

The central question in dispute about free will is the compatibility of this freedom with causal determinism. If our actions are causally predetermined by prior occurrences not of our own doing and outside our control, can we still be free to act otherwise? *Compatibilism*, the doctrine that free will is compatible with causal determinism, maintains that we can be; while *incompatibilism*, the doctrine that causal determinism would rule out any free will, denies this.

Freedom seems to be a kind of power that we possess over our action. For freedom is a capacity to determine for ourselves how we act. And that is exactly what a power is—a capacity to determine or at least influence what happens. Causation too seems to involve a power. For causes have the capacity to determine or at least influence the occurrence of their effects; which is why we naturally think of causation as involving a power exercised by causes over effects. The free will problem, then, is about the compatibility of one kind of power, that of prior causes over how we act, with that other power which is our own control over our action.

The free will problem may even be about the compatibility between two kinds of causal power. For perhaps freedom is itself a form of causal power, so that free action occurs as a kind of effect. But of what? For compatibilists it can occur as an effect of prior events not of the agent's own doing: the cause involved in the exercise of freedom and which produces the free action is not the agent himself but a passive motivation within the agent. Indeed, since Thomas Hobbes (1588–1679) many compatibilists have seen freedom as consisting simply in this—a causal power of prior passive motivations, among which, following Hobbes, they often include our decisions and intentions, to determine that we act as motivated. Freedom is just the capacity to act however we desire or decide. But for incompatibilists, if free actions are effects, they must ultimately be determined not by passive happenings but by the agent. The free agent must himself be a free cause of his decisions and the further actions which execute them.

2. Experience, causal power, and freedom

One connection between freedom and consciousness might simply be this: that our knowledge of our freedom is derived from some experiential representation of it, albeit a representation that is fallible and subject to correction. So many scholastic philosophers such as Suarez (1548–1617) thought (see Suarez 1994, especially Disputation 19 'On Necessary and Free Causes', section 2 para. 13). If we have reason to believe in our freedom, that is because this freedom is something we experience ourselves to possess. Experience reveals that we are indeed a free cause, which by its very nature as free operates undetermined by prior events to cause any one of a number of possible effects—which effect this is being up to us to determine. So if as free agents we have control over whether we raise our hand or lower it, this comes to our being causes with the power to produce either one of the following effects—that our hand goes up or that it goes down; and it is up to us which we cause. Whereas ordinary, unfree causes are necessary in that they generally produce but one effect and are not able to determine for themselves which effect this will be. Thus a solid brick hitting a thin pane of glass will just cause the glass to break, and it will not be up to the brick whether it produces this effect or some other.

Now we rely on experience to inform us of what causal powers exist within the world, and which causal powers defeat or preclude the operation of which other causal powers. So if freedom were this special kind of causal power, would we not expect experience to reveal its existence, and to confirm that its operation does indeed preclude its own causal determination by prior events?

Later philosophical doctrines about causal power and its relation to experience made this scholastic view of freedom and our knowledge of it very problematic. Hume (1711–76) famously and influentially denied that causal power can itself be represented in experience (Hume 1748). At best, only the regularities which that power explains and gives rise to can be represented. Thus suppose that hitting a thin pane of glass with a solid brick will cause the glass to break. Then all experience will ever represent is this regular succession of events: that whenever such a brick hits such a pain of glass, the glass breaks. Experience will never represent anything beyond this regularity that explains this succession of events, such as a power or force applied on impact by the brick which causes the glass to break. Causal power is itself invisible to and unrepresented in experience. (Perhaps, as subsequent followers of Hume have often supposed, though it is not clear that Hume himself went so far, causal power does not exist at all, even unobserved, so that there really is nothing more to causation than mere regularities in nature.)

This Humean claim about what experience represents is far from obviously true. When, for example, bricks hit us, or people or objects knock us down, do we not feel that a force is being exerted on us? And is this feeling of force, this feeling of being pushed or thrown down, not a clear case of experience representing causal power to us? Nor is Hume obviously right even about the observation of motion or impact from a distance, where we are not ourselves the object moved or impacted. There is important work within recent psychology that suggests that Hume might well be wrong even about what it is to observe one object causing another to move. Even in these cases there may be an experiential representation not just of a sequence of motions, but of causal force or connection (Leslie 1984, Leslie and Keeble 1987). Nevertheless the Humean doctrine that experience does not directly represent causal power itself but only regularities has come to constitute near orthodoxy with modern philosophy. And the doctrine has important implications for free will.

For regularities will arise only in relation to the powers of what the scholastics had termed *necessary causes*—causes that produce the same specific kind of effect whenever they operate. By its very nature, 'free' causal power does not involve a regular correlation between a given cause and a given effect, but leaves it open to the cause which effect it produces. Since free causal power is not revealed to us through regularities, Humeanism leaves it invisible to experience. And this banishment from experience of freedom understood as a causally undetermined power over alternatives was reinforced by Kant (1724–1804) who similarly taught that freedom so understood is not a phenomenon that is revealed by experience and so not something of which we can have theoretical knowledge. For Kant the world of phenomena, of things as we experience them, is a sequence of causally predetermined events from which freedom is absent. If we do believe in freedom as an undetermined power which we possess over alternatives, this belief is a kind of practical commitment that comes with our identity as agents, not a theoretical conclusion.

The 20th century analytic tradition inherited a broadly Humean view of experience—one which ruled out any experiential representation of power. It added a view of philosophy as consisting in some form of conceptual or semantic analysis, to be carried out by reflection on sentence meanings. So what freedom involves and, in particular, its relation to causal determinism, must be a conceptual question, to be resolved by appeal to some form of semantic analysis of the assertion that someone 'can act otherwise'. On this view, whether compatibilism or incompatibilism is true has nothing to do with experience but is determined just by concepts and their contents. If freedom is incompatible with prior causal determination, this must be something which follows, by logic, from platitudes about freedom or the capacity to act otherwise common to all competent users of the concept. Thus van Inwagen (1983) has devised a *consequence argument* to show that incompatibilism is conceptually true in just this way—though unfortunately without managing to convince many compatibilists that incompatibilism is indeed a conceptual truth (for an argument that van Inwagen's argument is inconclusive see Lewis 1986).

But perhaps experience is not irrelevant. For why need compatibilities or incompatibilities between powers be conceptually determined? The question becomes especially pressing if freedom is indeed a causal power, as the reality of various causal powers and the relations between them is usually supposed to be an empirical question, not a conceptual one. Whether one causal power permits or precludes the operation of another—that is something we may have to find out by observation. We do not normally discover truths about what causes what and when by reflecting on sentence meanings. So perhaps we really do need to attend to experience to determine both whether the power of freedom does exist, and also whether its operation can be causally predetermined.

3. Freedom and experience

Whatever its ultimate nature, the power of freedom does seem to be represented to us in experience—whether this representation be veridical or not. For example, we can and do have experience as of change in the degree of our freedom. Arguing over the telephone with a selfish and deeply exasperating colleague, I raise my voice, deliberately speak ever more woundingly—and then, as my temper mounts, finish by quite intentionally delivering a gross insult and smashing down the phone. I feel myself doing all this—and I feel my control over what I do lessening progressively as I do it. As I experience my action, I feel it is increasingly my growing anger which is determining how I am acting, not I, so that it is decreasingly open to me to act otherwise. Who is to say that my experience of my agency is not representing all this to me? My experience is just the kind that leads those having it to believe that they are losing control. It is just the kind of experience that we would report as the 'feeling that one was *losing it*'. And the feeling really is a feeling and not a belief. For I may feel that I am losing control but at the same time be wondering whether I really am.

Through vivid representation of the change in power we are reminded that experience does represent the power, though we could equally have considered a case where power is represented as increasing rather than decreasing. The emotion, whether it be anger or terror, that overcame us earlier lessens and we feel ourselves regaining our control. What is the nature of this power that experience represents; and, in particular, is its operation represented by experience as compatible or incompatible with prior causal determination?

Some recent discussion in the philosophy of *psychology and consciousness has begun to take this possible experiential dimension to the free will problem seriously. And it has been suggested that people's experience of their own freedom may support compatibilism. For people appear to report that they feel less effectively in control of decisions that are finely balanced, where the decision is least likely to be causally predetermined, than they do of those decisions where one option in particular is already clearly favoured in their judgements or desires. So control may not only be consistent with, but even require, prior causal determination. (I take the argument from Nahmias et al. 2004.)

But to assume that these reports show experiential support for compatibilism is to ignore an important distinction—between the possession of control, and its ease of exercise. For we may possess control over two options, but have difficulty in exercising it effectively to attain a certain end—such as the end of doing the right thing. In which case we may control the means, but not whether we attain the end. Thus in the case of a finely balanced decision about whether to accept or refuse an important job offer, we may have perfect control just over whether we say the words 'yes' or 'no'. But we may still feel it difficult to exercise this control in the right way simply because it is unclear to us which the right choice is. What we lack control over is not so much what we do, but whether in doing it we do the right thing. It is not that control is consistent with or even requires prior determination. It is simply that its possession in relation to an end may require knowledge of how to attain that end.

In fact it is striking that incompatibilist intuitions are very widely held by students coming to philosophy for the first time. And they seem to have some basis, not in conceptual argument, to which the students have not yet been exposed, but in experience. For as the example of a felt loss of control above suggested, to feel our own action to be causally determined by something prior to our own decision, such as by anger or by terror or by exhaustion, just is to feel ourselves to be losing control. The loss of control is represented to us precisely through a feeling of being determined to act by something, such as an emotion, that exists outside our will—in other words, by just the kind of prior cause that incompatibilism predicts would be freedom-threatening.

Clearly, the relevance of experience both to our ordinary intuitions about free will and to the solution to the free will problem deserves further investigation. At the heart of the problem lies a topic that the legacy of Humeanism has led us to neglect too long and which is as yet insufficiently understood. How does experience represent power, including causal power; and in particular, how does it represent the relation of one power to another?

4. Does consciousness or experience show free will to be an illusion?

Libet (2002) has argued that a correct understanding of consciousness casts doubt on the reality of some or all of our freedom. He argues that our voluntary actions are effects of initiating neural events that slightly precede our awareness of any free decision so to act. Now in Libet's view the exercise of freedom is inherently conscious: to exercise freedom is to do so in awareness of its exercise. So as preceding awareness such initiating events must precede any exercise of our control. At least on an incompatibilist understanding of freedom, Libet concludes, our actions are free only to the degree that we can intervene and block their final causation once we begin to be aware of their likely production.

But why should we not be aware of exercising freedom because and as an effect of our exercising it, so that our exercise of freedom narrowly precedes, as cause, our awareness of its exercise? If there is an intuitive link between our freedom and our having a fairly immediate awareness of its exercise, perhaps this can be explained—but in a way consistent with that awareness being strictly a distinct and subsequent effect. The link may be something to do with the nature not of freedom itself but of the intentional agency through which it is exercised. For, arguably, action only counts as properly deliberate or intentional if it takes a form that sufficiently allows for reason to be applied in its performance. And central to practical reason is a capacity readily to coordinate each thing that we decide to do with the other things we are also intent on doing. The mechanism of this awareness might be an ability to become aware of our actions as a direct and fairly immediate effect of deciding to perform them. Where that is lacking, so that we have to look to see what we ourselves are doing—as when we 'find ourselves' absent-mindedly scratching or doodling—we may be acting, but we are not doing so intentionally. And if our action is in no way intentional, it cannot involve any exercise by us of control.

Of course, even if we do experience some or much of our action as occurring through the exercise of a power of freedom then still, as Wegner (2002) has argued, this experience may sometimes be deceptive; and it may fail to inform us about much of the precise mechanism through which action occurs. Certainly Wegner has devised carefully constructed experiments which contain what he calls *illusions of control*. In these cases people are misled into thinking that they are exercising control to produce outcomes that are in fact the doing of others. But the mere possibility of such carefully constructed cases of illusion does not itself argue against our ordinarily trusting our experience of our own freedom. Nor, contrary to what Dennett (2003) claims, does Wegner's work show that experience fails to contain any representation of freedom at all.

In his discussion of Wegner cases, Dennett infers from the possibility that experience sometimes misleads us about a phenomenon such as freedom to its failing to represent that phenomenon at all. In fact Dennett concludes that Wegner cases show that Hume must be right, and that 'you can't *perceive* causation' or the exercise of power, such as a power of freedom (Dennet 2003:243). But this is clearly a mistaken inference. At best, all Wegner's cases show is that if there is an experience of control, it is fallible; i.e. there are some cases at least where such experience can misrepresent what is really going on. But that does not show that the experience of freedom is never veridical, still less that such experience never occurs at all. After all, most forms of experience are fallible; there can always be some cases at least where they misrepresent. It would clearly be rash to infer that, therefore, experience always misleads, and still more absurd to infer that experience fails to represent anything at all, veridically or otherwise. And the Humean doctrine of the invisibility of causation is, as we have seen, anyway controversial amongst empirical psychologists themselves.

Clearly, if it is to guide rational belief, experience need not be infallible; nor need its representation of what is going on be comprehensive. There may be many processes underlying what is represented that experience is not displaying to us. What is important is that, under normal conditions, the experience be reliable at least in respect of what it does represent. Devising unusual cases where experience is or seems to be deceptive, as Wegner does, does nothing of itself to undermine the authority of experience in the ordinary case—unless we have some independent argument to suggest that experience must be deceptive in those ordinary cases too. But as yet we lack such argument, for two very simple reasons. First, we still lack any detailed and agreed theory of what kind of power freedom might be were it present, and of its relations to other forms of power. And related to this, as the last section showed, there is no settled and agreed understanding of whether and how experience might represent that or other forms of power to us. How can we determine whether experience deceives us in relation to our own agency and freedom when it is still so disputed what precisely experience represents?

One reason for this continuing unclarity about the content of experience is a persisting allegiance, unreflective and not obviously warranted, to Humeanism, especially among philosophers. Thus in his discussion of determinism, Dennett (2003) simply assumes that there can be nothing more in nature to causation or to power in general than regularities; and that if any conception of freedom demands something more, then it must be illegitimate. He does not seriously explore the idea of power as something beyond and distinct from any mere regularity in relation to either freedom or causation. But it is very plausible that we do have such an idea of power, and that we deploy it not only in thinking about our own freedom but also in thinking about causation; that this idea of power is central to our thinking, not only about ourselves, but about nature generally. A solution to the free will problem will then require a developed theory of power. We need a better understanding of what power in general must involve; of what differing forms of power are possible; and which of these various forms of power might be represented in experience and how. It is on the nature of power and its relation to experience that future research into free will must therefore concentrate.

THOMAS PINK

Bayne, T. (2006). 'Phenomenology and the feeling of doing: Wegner on the conscious will'. In Pockett, S. et al. (eds) *Does Consciousness Cause Behavior? An Investigation of the Nature of Volition.*
Dennett, D. (2003). *Freedom Evolves.*
Hume, D. (1748). *An Enquiry Concerning Human Understanding*, section 7 'Of the idea of necessary connexion'.
Inwagen, P. van (1983). *An Essay on Free Will.*
Leslie, A. (1984). 'Spatiotemporal continuity and the perception of causality in infants'. *Perception*, 13.
—— and Keeble, S. (1987). 'Do six-month-old infants perceive causality?' *Cognition*, 25
Lewis, D. (1986). 'Are we free to break the laws?' In *Philosophical Papers*, Vol. 2.
Libet, B. (2002). 'Do we have free will?' In *The Oxford Companion to Free Will.*
Nahmias, E., Morris, S., Nadelhofer, T., and Turner, J. (2004). 'The phenomenology of free will'. *Journal of Consciousness Studies*, 11.
Pink, T. (2004). *Free Will: A Very Short Introduction.*
Pink, T. (forthcoming). *The Ethics of Action: Self-Determination.*
Suarez, F. (1994). *On Efficient Causality: Metaphysical Disputations 17, 18 and 19*, transl. A. J. Freddoso (see especially Disputation 19 'On Necessary and Free Causes', section 2 para 13).
Wegner, D. (2002). *The Illusion of Conscious Will.*

fringe The metaphoric use of 'fringe' denotes components of conscious experience occurring outside a *core* of focal, attentive, detailed, sensed, and/or articulated conscious content. The fringe is by nature somewhat paradoxical. On the one hand, as an aspect of conscious awareness the fringe is neither tacit nor implicit, and distinct from pre-, sub-, or unconscious states, processes, or other background conditions. On the other hand, *fringe states* seem to be essentially elusive. To scrutinize the fringe seems to require moving it into focal awareness or elaborating its vagueness, thus obliterating the very 'fringiness' one seeks to understand. For this and historical reasons the contemporary literature on the fringe per se focuses primarily on its *phenomenology, which remains controversial. Nonetheless, separate aspects of fringe cognition, some at the fringes of the core concept of the fringe itself, have become targets for empirical study, including 'cognitive feelings' of familiarity, rightness, fluency, 'tip of the tongue', and others (see FEELING OF KNOWING). While these excursions can potentially illuminate the fringe as an element of consciousness, only when fringe phenomenology is understood will there be an unambiguous target for cognitive and neural explanation.

1. Fringe phenomenology
2. Fringe cognition and its neural substrates
3. The significance of the fringe

1. Fringe phenomenology

The classic exposition of the fringe is found in William James's *Principles of Psychology* (1890). Two famous metaphors characterize James's psychology overall and provide the setting for his account of the fringe. First, to emphasize the continuous and seamless flow of consciousness, he coined the 'stream of thought' (see STREAM OF CONSCIOUSNESS). The rate of flow of this stream varies, at some times settling in relatively stable 'resting-places', and at others fleeting through transitions between one thought and the next. This inspired a second metaphor:

> Like a bird's life, [the stream of consciousness] seems to be made of an alternation of flights and perchings.... Let us call the resting-places the 'substantive parts,' and the places of flight the 'transitive parts,' of the stream of thought. (1890:243)

Within this framework of substantive and transitive parts of the stream, James situated the idea of the fringe. Examples of fringe thinking abound in the *Principles*, but general statements about it are few. The examples shuffle two aspects of fringe experience: its structural relationship to the substantive parts of the stream of consciousness; and its characteristic content.

Structurally, the fringe might fit among the succession of substantive 'perchings' in three ways:

(1) As arpeggio, denoting the fleeting states at the points of transition between substantive thoughts. Its contents are the relations that link thoughts, and its function is to lead from one thought to the next. James writes:

We ought to say a feeling of *and*, a feeling of *if*, a feeling of *but*, and a feeling of *by*, quite as readily as we say a feeling of *blue* or a feeling of *cold*. (245)

(2) As overtone, denoting the awareness of potential relations between the current thought and other thoughts in the stream. This fringe is continuous and synchronous with the substantive thoughts, accompanying them as a *penumbra* or *halo* (James's metaphors). The fringe communicates context for a thought. This serves to distinguish knowledge about a subject from mere acquaintance, or to signal its entailments, or to convey a feeling of overall form (e.g. of an opera). Several examples relate thoughts to their temporal context:

If I recite *a, b, c, d, e, f, g*, at the moment of uttering *d*, neither *a, b, c*, nor *e, f, g* are out of my consciousness altogether, but both, after their respective fashions, 'mix their dim lights' with the stronger one of the *d* . . . (257)

(3) As independent harmonic theme, denoting specific states of awareness that lack substantive content. These fringes tend not to shadow explicit thoughts, but rather point to gaps where a thought is wanting. James's examples include feelings of knowing like the 'tip of the tongue' phenomena, feelings of familiarity, feelings of 'rightness' (being on the right track), feelings of intentions to act, and feelings of expectancy.

Cutting across these structural possibilities are differing ideas about the content of fringe states: (a) Fringe content and nuclear content are of the same types, but fringe content is degraded, vague, or inarticulate. (b) Fringe content is restricted to relations (among thoughts or among things). (c) Fringe content is restricted to metacognitive content, i.e. the fringe is the awareness of success or failure in recall, problem-solving, or action.

Which combination of fringe structure and content is James's target poses an interesting interpretive question, but for present purposes we may note that all are variations of plausible aspects of phenomenology. Experience flows among states with differing but compatible fringes. Arpeggios and harmonic themes, for example, may be differing examples of overtones in the absence of substantive melody. Similarly, consciousness certainly includes the kinds of contents above, frequently in combination. The multiplicitous and ubiquitous fringe, then, seems to be the symphonic setting of conscious life, from which substantive thoughts periodically emerge.

Common to the many fringes is a distinctive motif in James's psychology, namely his emphasis on non-sensory 'feelings', including feelings directed at absent, abstract, or not-yet-existent objects. In this James anticipates themes emergent at the same time and later in continental phenomenology. For example, in lectures and writings from around the turn of the century, Edmund Husserl construed *appearance* as a compound including sensation and non-sensory *apprehension*, where the apprehended content is characterized as the *horizon* of perception/sensation. (In *The Crisis of the European Sciences* [1954], Husserl explicitly related his concept of the horizon to the Jamesian fringe.) A central function for apprehension in the phenomenological tradition is as the vehicle of temporality, just as in James. The metaphors 'halo' and 'fringe' both appear in Husserl's characterization of the horizons of temporality in his lectures on the phenomenology of internal time consciousness (Husserl 1928/1964). Like James, Husserl richly observed the many aspects of consciousness that go beyond the sensory manifold of the present moment, and developed technical phenomenological terms for many details not distinguished in James. One notable Husserlian innovation is his realization that much of apprehension includes sensory qualities that are currently present but nonetheless not sensed. For example, in perceiving objects we presume that they have back sides with specific colouring and shape, albeit we may or may not have definite knowledge of these sensory properties, a theme developed at length in *Thing and Space* (1907/1997).

Non-sensory *contents of consciousness also dominate the existential phenomenology of Heidegger (1927/1962) and Sartre (1943/1966). These authors and their followers emphasize the manifold influences of instrumentality and social setting in shaping conscious experience. Like James, authors in the phenomenological tradition attacked empiricist attempts to build consciousness out of atomic sensations, and the resultant clamping of conscious experience to the immediate sensory environment.

Notwithstanding the abstruseness of continental phenomenology, the import of non-sensory content is readily demonstrated. Consider this figure: ■.

What is it? Fans of cognitive science will recognize a schematic diagram of the legendary black box of functionalism. This is readily distinguished from this ■, the proposed design for a novel keyboard button, the new short-cut for 'Delete Everything.' And this in turn is readily distinguished from ■, a thumbnail image of the Eiffel Tower, downloaded from a digital camera, although the hapless photographer evidently left the lens cap on. This ■ is a printer's error, and the last in the series is nothing but a black square in an encyclopedia entry introduced to make a point about non-sensory consciousness: ■. These variations of 'seeing as' are readily manipulated by descriptive context; despite a duplication of the literal stimulus, what is experienced ranges wildly. Yet the varying content is fully conscious and explicit.

Similar considerations inform John Searle's hypothesis of the *Background*, a cloud of competencies that scaffold intentional states (Searle 1994). (For Searle, intentional and [potentially] conscious states are equivalent.) For Searle, 'each intentional state requires for its functioning a set of Background capacities', consisting of 'mental capacities, dispositions, stances, ways of behaving, know-how, savoir faire, etc.' (1994:190, 196). The Background is necessary for intentional states to be 'satisfied,' i.e. to identify their referents or truth conditions. It need not be conscious. The phenomenological idea of non-sensory content comprises a different kind of background, an *experiential* background that will include some but not necessarily all of Searle's Background. The phenomenological background constitutes a fringe that modifies the meaning of the core or focal contents of consciousness, the overtones of experience.

2. Fringe cognition and its neural substrates

For most of the 20th century, the fringe was neglected in psychology, more so even than the study of consciousness in general. In the 1990s, however, the Jamesian fringe reappeared in cognitive science, owing to papers by Bruce Mangan and others (see Mangan 2001 and appended commentaries); scientific approaches to phenomenology in the tradition of Husserl emerged as well, although to a lesser extent (e.g. Petitot et al. 1999). Contemporary fringe studies are largely devoted to mapping the concept(s) of the fringe onto other cognitive processes, thereby establishing a function for fringe cognition and its concomitant neural implementation. The setting for fringe theorizing has shifted since the time of James and Husserl, however. Now the cognitive primacy of consciousness has been eclipsed by the intricate machinations of the cognitive unconscious (a general picture of mind scorned by James and Husserl). Consciousness is seen as a faculty of comparatively limited capacity, saddled with the tasks of monitoring, directing, and selecting information and behaviour grounded in a larger unconscious domain. Fringe experience may arise at the interface of consciousness and the unconscious processes. In this framework, the fringe is less a connector among conscious states (an arpeggio or overtone) but rather the harmonic clue to unconscious processes.

Just as there are several concepts of the fringe, there have been multiple proposals for its cognitive function; these correspond to the options for fringe content. For example, fringe cognition has been likened to dim or vague awareness at the periphery of the 'spotlight' of *attention. Mangan hypothesizes that fringe phenomena may be pointers to stored *memories, affording direction to deliberate recall. Or perhaps the fringe should be recast as the study of *metacognition overall (see Nelson 1996). Finally, several authors have stressed the affective and motivational properties of fringe states. As with fringe phenomenology, these hypotheses are not necessarily incompatible. But most contemporary commentators argue that there is no single process or state equivalent to the fringe overall. Instead, fringiness is a loose metaphorical adjective shared by several processes with little else in common (see COGNITIVE FEELINGS).

At the neural level, the resurgence of parallel distributed processing suggests general models for the implementation of fringe cognition. *Connectionist networks mimic the flights and perchings of the stream of consciousness, as networks settle into temporarily stable states in a dynamic 'flow.' (In the *Principles*, James presciently described the cognitive manifestations of parallel distributed processing.) Distributed representations also allow for content that encodes both a 'nucleus' and its context, supporting the fringe-as-overtone. Specific architectures can model other aspects of fringe dynamics. Temporal context, for example, emerges from recurrent architectures that permit short-term storage and feedback of internal states (Elman 1990).

Considering the diversity of fringe phenomenology and function, it seems unlikely that a dedicated brain region or network will support all of fringe cognition. Nonetheless, specific fringe functions may have regional affiliations in the brain. Epstein (2000), for example, likens the path of thinking to a spatial path, and accordingly assigns the 'feeling of rightness' to medial temporal areas, including the hippocampus. Other metacognitive control functions, then, may be concentrated in the frontal lobes. Various lesions and disorders also seem to entail dissociations of nucleus and fringe. Obsessive-compulsive disorder (OCD), for example, seems to express a deficit in a fringe 'feeling of knowing', as a person with OCD refuses to acknowledge the veracity of something which is abundantly confirmed in his or her experience. Another striking fringe disorder is Capgras syndrome (see BRAIN DAMAGE), which seems to impair a feeling of familiarity. Patients fully recognize spouses and other family members, but the absence of some additional phenomenal aspect of their experience leads them to conclude that the familiar person is an imposter. *Delusional symptoms seem to reflect the opposite, namely, an exaggerated feeling of knowing accompanying the delusional thought process. There is no consensus, however, about the underlying neural dysfunctions responsible for the symptoms of these disorders.

3. The significance of the fringe

Cognitive science is centrally concerned with the mind's construction of an effective representation of an external world. Stability, regularity, and predictability are the anchors of useful mental models. Consciousness studies, accordingly, often take as their paradigm case the achievement of anchored percepts of steady objects, and address themselves to problematic aspects of these perceptual states (e.g. their qualitative 'feels'). But experience as it is lived includes more than the steady presentations of a sturdy world. That vague 'more' can be collected under the metaphor of the fringe.

One might conclude from the contemporary discussions that the fringe continues to lurk at the fringes of understanding. In the *Principles*, James wrote that 'it is, in short, the re-instatement of the vague to its proper place in our mental life which I am so anxious to press on the attention' (p. 254). The vague, largely non-sensory experiences of the fringe are nonetheless common and essential to perception and cognition, and a science of consciousness will be seriously incomplete until it addresses this second '*hard problem', the mystery of the fringe.

DAN LLOYD

Elman, J. (1990). 'Finding structure in time'. *Cognitive Science*, 14.
Epstein, R. (2000). 'The neural-cognitive basis of the Jamesian stream of thought'. *Consciousness and Cognition*, 9(4).
Heidegger, M. (1927/1962). *Being and Time*, transl. J. Macquarrie and E. Robinson.
Husserl, E. (1928/1964). *The Phenomenology of Internal Time-consciousness*, transl. J. Churchill.
—— (1954/1970). *Crisis of European Sciences and Transcendental Phenomenology*, transl. D. Carr.
—— (1907/1997). *Thing and Space*, transl. R. Rojcewicz.
James, W. (1890). *The Principles of Psychology*.
Mangan, B. (2001). 'Sensation's ghost: the non-sensory 'fringe' of consciousness'. *Psyche*, 7.
Nelson, T. O. (1996). 'Consciousness and metacognition'. *American Psychologist*, 51.
Petitot, J., Varela, F., Pachoud, B., and Roy, J. (eds) (1999). *Naturalizing Phenomenology: Issues in Contemporary Phenomenology and Cognitive Science*.
Sartre, J.-P. (1943/1966). *Being and Nothingness*, transl. H. Barnes.

frontal cortex The frontal cortex is the part of the cerebral cortex that lies forward of the central sulcus, which separates the frontal lobe from the parietal lobe, and above the Sylvian fissure, which separates the frontal lobe from the temporal lobe.

1. Basic anatomy of the frontal cortex
2. Theories of frontal function and dysfunction
3. Prefrontal cortex and consciousness

1. Basic anatomy of the frontal cortex

Anatomically the frontal cortex itself consists of the motor cortices (the primary motor cortex and the supplementary motor cortex), which occupy the rear of the frontal cortex adjacent to the central sulcus, and the *prefrontal cortex* (PFC), which is relatively larger in humans and higher primates than in other mammalian species (Fig. F6).

Interest in the PFC stems in part from its relative size in humans—over 30% of the cortex. The PFC is also connected via projections of axons to virtually all other cortical areas and to most subcortical structures, implying that the frontal cortex can affect or be affected by most other brain regions and structures. This connectivity is consistent with the hypothesized functions of the PFC, which relate to control and monitoring of global aspects of behaviour.

Various anatomical subdivisions of the PFC are frequently made. Thus, it is common to distinguish between dorsal (upper) and ventral (lower) portions of the PFC, between lateral (side) and medial (middle) portions, and between rostral (front) and caudal (rear) portions. These coarse distinctions allow contact to be made between neuroanatomy and the growing body of evidence which suggests that there is some degree of functional specialization within the PFC. For example, dorsolateral PFC (DLPFC) has frequently been associated with *working memory functions, while ventromedial PFC (VMPFC) has been associated with the management of social behaviour. In addition to the above, the anterior portion of the cingulate cortex (the ACC) is also normally considered to be part of the PFC. (The cingulate cortex lies on the inner surface of the cortex, curving around the corpus collosum.)

2. Theories of frontal function and dysfunction

It was common in early 20th century theorizing of brain function to regard the frontal lobes as essentially devoid of cognitive function. This view, which was supported by the apparent lack of impact of neurological lesions of the frontal cortex on mental functioning as measured by standard tests of intelligence, coexisted with a diametrically opposite view: that the frontal lobes were the seat of higher-level cognitive functions involved in coordinating intentional action. A substantial body of evidence now supports the latter view, and it is now generally agreed that the frontal lobes serve a variety of functions critical

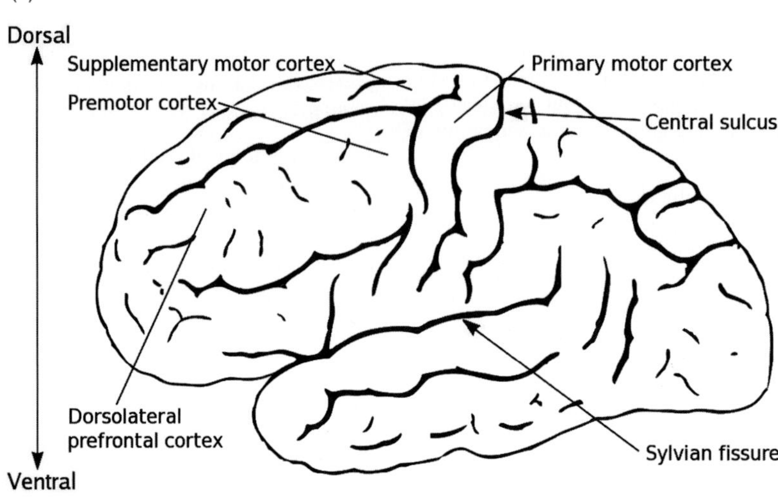

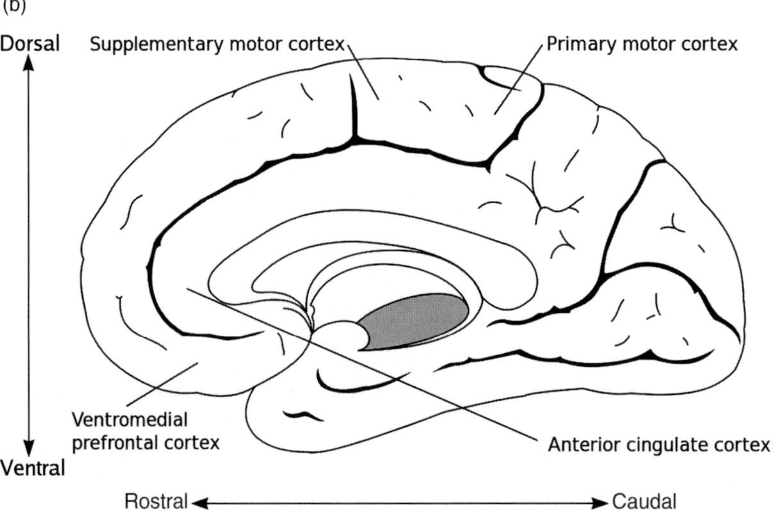

Fig. F6. (a) Lateral and (b) medial views of the human brain.

to the control of intentional behaviour and the normal operation of the cognitive system as a whole. At the same time, there are several distinct theories of precisely how the frontal lobes fulfil their critical functions, and many areas of controversy remain.

One theory of frontal function is that the frontal lobes are specialized for the task-directed storage and use of information, with different regions of PFC being dedicated to different types of information (Goldman-Rakic 1996). This view was developed from *single-cell recording of primates performing a variety of tasks with differing requirements for temporary information storage and use. For example, rhesus monkeys were trained to perform two tasks, a delayed oculomotor response task and a delayed anti-saccade task. In the former a mark is presented at a central fixation point and a cue flashes at some peripheral point. After a delay the fixation mark disappears and the monkey is required to make a saccade towards the cue position. In the latter, a different coloured fixation mark is used, signalling that the monkey is required to make a saccade away from the cue position. In this situation, it has been shown through single-cell recording that, within a single area of PFC and during the delay period, some neurons code for the direction of the response while others code for the location of the cue. Furthermore, these neurons encode this information for the duration of the delay period. In particular, it is not the case that neurons in one area code direction of the response while those in another code location of the cue. This suggests that a single area of PFC codes sensory, memory, and response information. Furthermore, different areas within the monkey frontal cortex have been implicated in the processing of different types of information (spatial, olfactory, colour). On the basis of this and related evidence it has been suggested that different regions of human frontal cortex are specialized for different working memory 'domains'.

A second approach to understanding PFC function emphasizes the role of PFC in guiding deliberate, intentional or endogenously generated behaviour. The key theoretical claim here is that PFC serves to guide behaviour when immediate stimulus-response associations must be over-ridden. Thus, in both the anti-saccade task and the delayed oculomotor response task PFC would be required to override the immediate response of making a saccade to the cue's position when the cue first appears. PFC would then also be involved in generating the correct response (a saccade either towards or away from the cue's position) when the fixation mark disappears. In particular, PFC must select different rules for generating the response depending on the colour of the fixation mark. Theories of this form tend to characterize the role of PFC as providing bias signals to other neural systems. Miller and Cohen (2001), for example, argue that these bias signals 'guide the flow of neural activity along pathways that establish the proper mappings between inputs, internal states, and outputs needed to perform a given task' (Miller and Cohen 2001:171). The feasibility of such an approach has been demonstrated by numerous computational studies (e.g. Rougier et al. 2005).

Related theories maintain the operation of PFC as biasing other neural systems but emphasize hierarchical aspects of both neural physiology and cognitive control. The former is exemplified by Fuster (2002), who argues on physiological grounds for a pyramid-type structure to behavioural control, with primary sensory and motor cortices lying at the base of the pyramid and PFC lying at its apex. The latter is exemplified by Koechlin et al.'s (2003) cascade model of cognitive control, in which it is postulated that different levels of control functions are localized within different regions of the lateral surfaces of the PFC. The cascade model of cognitive control identifies three different types of response: those that depend only on the immediate stimulus, those that depend on the stimulus and its immediate context, and those that depend on the stimulus in the context of some previous episode. It is argued that the first of these requires only premotor control, while the second requires control exerted by the caudal parts of lateral PFC, and the third requires control exerted by the rostral parts of lateral PFC. Numerous *functional imaging studies are consistent with this claim. It should also be stressed that the approach does not deny that PFC also serves a role in the active maintenance of information. Indeed, contextual and episodic control require that the representations which guide contextual and episodic behaviour be maintained for the duration of that behaviour.

An alternative conception of the functions of PFC derives from a top-down analysis of cognitive function. Thus, it has been argued that complex behaviour requires the coordination of special-purpose subsystems, and that this coordination is performed by an executive system located primarily within the PFC (see, for example, Shallice 2004). Candidate functions for such a system include prioritization, selection and maintenance of goals, selective inhibition of environmentally appropriate actions and habits in the light of current goals, online maintenance and manipulation of information during reasoning and problem solving (i.e. working memory), and monitoring or checking of other cognitive subsystems and of behaviour in general. Neuropsychological evidence suggests that each of these functions may be selectively impaired following brain lesions. The neuropsychological evidence also implies that the different functions are performed by different regions of the PFC (Shallice 2004, Stuss and Alexander 2007). Both the existence of separable executive functions and their localization are further supported by brain imaging evidence from neurologically healthy volunteers, although localization of function currently remains coarse.

Consider first the prioritization, selection, and maintenance of goals. Neurological patients with damage to the PFC have frequently been reported to show deficits in situations that require the coordination of multiple tasks (see BRAIN DAMAGE). Such patients may perform at normal or better levels on single tasks such as mental arithmetic or verbal fluency, but perform poorly when required to complete a number of such tasks in a fixed time and subject to clearly specified constraints. It is as if these patients are able to select one goal from many, but are not then able to spontaneously suppress the selected goal in favour of an alternative. The available evidence suggests that these kind of multitasking deficits arise most often following lesions to rostral or ventromedial PFC.

That the PFC plays a role in the selective inhibition of actions and habits can be seen in the performance of patients with frontal lesions on the Wisconsin Card Sorting Task. In this task subjects are required to sort a series of cards into four categories. Cards show, for example, one red square or four blue triangles, and may be sorted according to the colour, shape, or number of figures on the card. Subjects are not told how to sort the cards, but are given feedback after they have sorted each card so that they may induce the sorting rule that the experimenter has in mind. Once subjects have identified the rule (as evidenced by a sequence of correctly sorted cards) the experimenter switches to a different sorting rule. In some versions of the task subjects are warned when the sorting rule is changed. Patients with PFC lesions are, like neurological controls with lesions involving other cortices, able to use feedback to determine the first sorting rule correctly. However, once a rule has been established some patients (particularly those with DLPFC lesions) have specific difficulties in switching away from that rule: their responses tend to be perseverative, with continued use of the now incorrect rule in spite of continued negative feedback. This and related behaviour is commonly interpreted as demonstrating that DLPFC plays a critical role in inhibiting established response schemas.

A substantial body of imaging evidence supports the assertion that DLPFC is involved in what is generally referred to as the *active maintenance* of information during the performance of temporally extended tasks. For example, in one imaging study a condition in which subjects counted from 1 to 10 was contrasted with conditions in which subjects generated all integers from 1 to 10 (without repetition) in a random order and a condition in which subjects heard all but one of the first 10 integers and were required to respond with the missing integer. Increased activation of DLPFC was found in both experimental conditions in comparison with the control condition. It was argued that the two experimental conditions tapped verbal working memory maintenance and manipulation, and on these grounds that this was a function of DLPFC (Petrides et al. 1993). Preferential DLPFC activation has also been observed during a spatial version of the same memory task, though the precise region of DLPFC active in each case was slightly different. Thus, this work is also consistent with the working memory domains account of PFC function.

The experiments of Petrides et al. (1993) require not just the maintenance of information in DLPFC, but also the manipulation of that information. Other work also supports the view that the working memory functions of DLPFC have a manipulative component. For example, in another imaging study subjects were required to memorize a list of 16 words while performing a distracting motor task. The word lists consisted of four words from each of four categories. In one condition the words were presented in category order, while in another they were randomly organized, so that in this latter condition subjects needed to organize the words (manipulating them in working memory) in order to optimize their recall performance. Significantly greater activation of the left DLPFC was found in this condition, suggesting that the left DLPFC is specifically implicated in the manipulation and structuring of information during encoding (Fletcher et al. 1998). In a related study, right DLPFC was implicated in monitoring of recall.

Monitoring functions have also been attributed to the anterior cingulate cortex (ACC). Thus, ACC has been shown to be preferentially activate in tasks that involve response conflict, such as the *Stroop task (where subjects must identify either a word or the colour of ink in which the word is printed, and where words that are also colour-names pose particular difficulties) and the Eriksen flankers task (where subjects must respond to a stimulus that appears between two distracting items that may be associated with an alternative response). It has been suggested that the function of the ACC is to monitor for conflict within cognitive and response subsystems and configure the cognitive system as a whole to minimize such conflict (Carter et al. 1998). Other work has suggested that the ACC has a more general evaluative function, providing feedback on errors to other cognitive subsystems and for subsequent use in guiding action selection (Rushworth et al. 2004).

Two further accounts of frontal function deserve mention. First, selective damage to VMPFC has been associated with difficulties in social decision-making. Thus, a patient with VMPFC damage may be impaired at using social cues to select between alternatives. This, and the widespread difficulties that VMPFC patients have across a range of everyday tasks, has led to the suggestions that *somatic markers* act as critical cues in a range of decision-making situations and that VMPFC is responsible for associating somatic markers with situational features (Damasio 1996). This is consistent with the fact that VMPFC patients may show reduced galvanic skin responses (in comparison to control patients with neurological damage elsewhere) to highly affective stimuli such as pictures of dismembered corpses.

Second, it has been argued that, whereas the temporal lobes store semantic or conceptual knowledge, the frontal lobes store schematic knowledge of tasks and situations arranged at different levels of abstraction (so-called *Managerial Knowledge Units*: Grafman 1995). This view is supported by the fact that patients with frontal lobe damage can show impairments in the performance of everyday routines. These impairments have been attributed to the lose of schematic knowledge of everyday tasks, and the subsequent use of more abstract situational knowledge, which by hypothesis is more resilient to neural damage. According to this hypothesis, different regions of PFC may be specialized for different types of knowledge, so the behavioural deficits of VMPFC patients may be attributed to lose of schemas relating to social cognition, which are held to normally be represented within VMPFC.

There is therefore good evidence of localization of PFC function, but this apparent localization must be tempered by the fact that few studies have shown unequivocal dissociations between regions, while others have shown that some regions (such as parts of lateral PFC and dorsal ACC) are responsive to a variety of experimental manipulations that may loosely be characterized as increases in cognitive load. This has led some theorists (e.g. Duncan and Owen 2000) to argue that significant portions of PFC have an adaptive function, being recruited by different goal-directed tasks in different ways. On this account, the degree of adaptivity of lateral PFC reflects general intelligence, and the characteristic behaviour following lesions to PFC (including perseveration and loss of set) arises from decay or neglect of goal representations.

3. Prefrontal cortex and consciousness

One consequence of the range and nature of functions that appear to be performed by the anterior portion of frontal cortex is that this region plays a central role in many theories of consciousness.

At the social level, PFC lesions frequently lead to alterations in aspects of personality and (particularly in the case of VMPFC lesions) impairments in social decision-making. There is therefore a role for PFC in social theories of consciousness.

At the cognitive level, the apparent role of PFC in high-level behavioural control implicates the PFC in *functionalist theories in which consciousness serves to monitor and set the inputs of other processing systems. For example, the roles of DLPFC in inhibiting prepotent responses and rostral PFC in goal selection and prioritization imply that, at least within such theories, PFC is crucial for these aspects of conscious functioning. In a similar vein, the relation between DLPFC and working memory ensures that PFC is implicated in theories of consciousness in which the contents of consciousness are equated with the contents of working memory. Furthermore, several studies have shown that various areas of PFC are more active during early stages of *sequence learning, when attention to action is required, than at later stages, when a sequence of responses has been routinized. These studies imply that PFC plays a role in the phenomenology of attention to action.

At the neuronal level, the extensive connectivity between PFC and other cortical and subcortical areas ensures that PFC is well placed to form temporary associations between other brain systems (as required by *global workspace theory: Dehaene et al. 2003). Consistent with this, imaging studies have shown greater activation of portions of the frontal cortex (specifically DLPFC and ACC) during tasks that involve conscious processing, intentional control, or awareness than during otherwise equivalent tasks that do not involve conscious processing, intentional control, or awareness (e.g. contrasting implicit and explicit *learning, or contrasting early stages of learning a motor task with later over-learned performance of the same task).

Given the roles ascribed to PFC by many scientific approaches to consciousness, it is noteworthy that neurological disturbances of consciousness such as *blindsight and neglect occur in the absence of lesions to the frontal cortex. It is possible that this is because such disturbances affect early stages of processing, resulting in areas of frontal cortex receiving degraded input and hence being unable to integrate that input into conscious experience.

RICHARD P. COOPER

Carter, C. S., Braver, T. S., Barch, D. M., Botvinick, M. M., Noll, D. and Cohen, J. D. (1998). 'Anterior cingulate cortex, error detection, and the online monitoring of performance'. *Science*, 280.

Damasio, A. R. (1996). 'The somatic marker hypothesis and the possible functions of the prefrontal cortex'. *Philosophical Transactions of the Royal Society of London Series B: Biological Sciences*, 351.

Dehaene, S., Sergent, C., and Changeux, J-P. (2003). 'A neuronal network model linking subjective reports and objective physiological data during conscious perception'. *Proceedings of the National Academy of Sciences of the USA*, 100.

Duncan, J. and Owen, A. M. (2000). 'Dissociative methods in the study of frontal lobe function'. In Monsell, S. and Driver, J. (eds) *Control of Cognitive Processes. Attention and Performance, XVIII.*

Fletcher, P. C., Shallice, T. and Dolan, R. J. (1998). 'The functional roles of prefrontal cortex in episodic memory. I. Encoding'. *Brain*, 121.

Fuster, J. M. (2002). 'Physiology of executive functions: the perception-action cycle'. In Stuss, D. T. and Knight, R. T. (eds) *Principles of Frontal Lobe Function.*

Goldman-Rakic, P. S. (1996). 'The prefrontal landscape: implications of functional architecture for understanding human mentation and the central executive'. *Philosophical*

Transactions of the Royal Society of London Series B: Biological Sciences, 351.
Grafman, J. (1995). 'Similarities and distinctions among current models of prefrontal cortical functions'. *Annals of the New York Academy of Sciences*, 769.
Koechlin, E., Ody, C., and Kouneiher, F. (2003). 'The architecture of cognitive control in the human prefrontal cortex'. *Science*, 302.
Miller, E. K. and Cohen, J. D. (2001). 'An integrative theory of prefrontal cortex function'. *Annual Review of Neuroscience*, 24.
Petrides, M. Alisivatos, B., Meyer, E., and Evans, A. C. (1993). 'Functional activation of the human frontal cortex during the performance of human verbal working memory tasks'. *Proceedings of the National Academy of Sciences of the USA*, 90.
Rougier, N. P., Noelle, D. C., Braver, T. S., Cohen, J. D., and O'Reilly, R. C. (2005). 'Prefrontal cortex and flexible cognitive control: Rules without symbols'. *Proceedings of the National Academy of Sciences of the USA*, 102.
Rushworth, M. F. S., Walton, M. E., Kennerley, S. W., and Bannerman, D. M. (2004). 'Action sets and decisions in the medial frontal cortex'. *Trends in Cognitive Sciences*, 8.
Shallice, T. (2004). 'The fractionation of supervisory control'. In Gazzaniga, M. S. (ed.) *The Cognitive Neurosciences III*.
Stuss, D. T. and Alexander, M. P. (2007). 'Is there a dysexecutive syndrome?' *Philosophical Transactions of the Royal Society of London Series B: Biological Sciences*, 362.

functional brain imaging Functional brain imaging refers to a group of technologies developed in the last quarter of the 20th century that allow the non-invasive measurement of human brain activity. These technologies have revolutionized the study of human consciousness. Before these developments, knowledge was derived indirectly, through inference from behavioural experiments, invasive recording in animals, or the study of patients who had sustained *brain damage.

The first step in the development of functional imaging came with the development of methods for the non-invasive measurement of structural images of the human *brain. Computed tomography (CT) scanners first came into use in 1972, with magnetic resonance imaging (MRI) following in 1977. Both techniques are now widely used in hospitals around the world. CT uses X-rays projected through the skull to create an image of brain anatomy. MRI scanners use a powerful static magnetic field that causes the spin of protons (the nuclei of hydrogen atoms, found in molecules throughout the brain) to align with it. The application of a radio-frequency pulse (radio wave) perpendicular to this field causes the spins to be perturbed. As they relax back to their original alignment the protons give off signals which subtly vary in strength depending on the density of brain tissue that they come from. These signals can be detected by a receiver coil and analysed by a computer to produce an image of the brain. This procedure is non-invasive and has no known adverse effects, yet can produce highly detailed structural images that are now widely used in medical practice. However, the real breakthrough of significance for consciousness research arose with the development of functional brain imaging.

The average adult human brain represents about 2% of the body weight. Despite its relatively small size, the brain accounts for about 20% of the oxygen, and hence of the energy, consumed by the body. This energy is supplied through the bloodstream, with oxygen bound to haemoglobin in red blood cells. It has been known for over 100 years that an increase in neural activity in the brain causes a corresponding change in blood flow locally (Roy and Sherrington 1890). In addition to increased blood flow, there are also subtle changes in blood volume and the overall ratio of oxygenated and deoxygenated haemoglobin. These changes are collectively known as the *haemodynamic response* and bring increased supplies of oxygen and glucose to neurons (and their supporting glial cells) that are metabolically active. Functional brain imaging technologies typically measure one or more aspects of the haemodynamic response, so provide an indirect measure of neural activity. Their precision is limited by the precise details of how the neurovascular coupling works (which remain incompletely understood), and by the spatial precision with which changes in neural activity are reflected in changes in blood flow (a few millimetres at best).

The first functional brain imaging technique to be widely used was *positron emission tomography* (PET; Ingvar 1975). This relies on injection into the bloodstream of a radioisotope, such as $H_2{}^{15}O$, which has a short half-life. The radioisotope circulates in the bloodstream to the brain and undergoes rapid radioactive decay, emitting a positron in the process. The positron travels only a very short distance in brain tissue before meeting an electron and thus creating two gamma rays, which can be detected and then used to build up a picture of the distribution of $H_2{}^{15}O$, and thus the blood flow, within the brain. By comparing blood flow images obtained under different psychological conditions, the neural processes underlying consciousness can thus be studied. PET scanning requires an invasive procedure (venous cannulation) and carries a small but finite risk associated with injection of the very small doses of radioisotope (as does CT scanning, from X-rays). For these reasons, PET scanning is no longer widely used to measure brain activation. However, PET is very versatile because radiochemistry procedures can be used to label more complex substances located in other places in the brain, and thus measure things other than cerebral blood flow. For example, PET can be used with radiolabelled compounds that bind to postsynaptic receptors to study the distribution and function of neurotransmitter systems in the brain. This is useful both in medical practice and as a research tool.

More recently it has proved possible to use MRI scanning for the non-invasive detection of changes in neural activity (Kwong et al. 1992). This has come about because oxygenated and deoxygenated haemoglobin behave differently in a magnetic field and so changes in the ratio of the two can be detected using an appropriate MRI sequence. As neurons become active, the first change in the brain vasculature appears to be an increase in deoxyhaemoglobin concentration, due to the increased metabolic demand of neural activity consuming oxygen. This then causes a compensatory increase in local cerebral blood flow (as can be detected using PET) that brings an oversupply of oxygenated haemoglobin. It is this strong but transient increase in oxygenated haemoglobin that can be detected as the *blood oxygenation level dependent* (BOLD) signal using MRI. After a brief burst of neural activity, the BOLD signal rises to a peak in 4–6 s before decaying back to baseline. This delayed haemodynamic response is the basis of *functional MRI* (fMRI). To track its relatively rapid rise and fall requires the use of *echo-planar imaging* (EPI; Mansfield 1977). This is a way of collecting whole-brain MR images very rapidly over a few seconds (instead of the few minutes more commonly found when MRI is used in medical practice). The combination of EPI and BOLD makes it possible to track dynamic changes in the pattern of neural activity in the human brain through this indirect signal.

Not only is fMRI non-invasive; because it does not depend on administration of radioactivity, it can be used repeatedly. Moreover, while PET has a spatial resolution of 1–2 cm, the resolution of fMRI is typically a few millimetres. It also provides reasonable temporal resolution, though because it measures the haemodynamic response it cannot directly resolve the fast temporal dynamics of neural activity. The haemodynamic response is a delayed and temporally blurred version of neural activity. To track neural activity with greater temporal resolution, a technique that measures the electrical or magnetic activity associated with neural firing such as *electroencephalography (EEG) or *magnetoencephalography (MEG) is required. Although these techniques have excellent temporal resolution, they have relatively poor spatial resolution and it can be very difficult to determine which particular brain locations give rise to the signals measured at the scalp. fMRI offers a compromise, with good spatial resolution but only moderate temporal resolution (because of the delayed haemodynamic response), and has become a particularly popular and informative technique in consciousness research.

All brain imaging techniques in humans measure the activity associated with relatively large populations of neurons extending over a few millimetres of brain tissue. In order to understand how the results of functional brain imaging experiments relate to those obtained by invasive technologies such as *single-neuron recording in the monkey, it is necessary to understand the relationship between the BOLD signal and single-neuron activity. Recently, it has become possible to perform fMRI scans on experimental animals such as monkeys while simultaneously recording from single neurons in the brain using an implanted microelectrode (Logothetis et al. 2001). This extremely difficult technique permits simultaneous measurement of BOLD (using fMRI), single-neuron firing, and local field potentials (using the microelectrode) from the same brain area. *Local field potentials* (LFP) are an aggregate measure of all local electrical activity in the brain (not just neuronal firing) and tend to reflect the overall synaptic activity (both inputs and outputs) in a local region. Both single-neuron firing and LFPs correlate well with the BOLD signal, but LFPs correlate slightly better overall. This indicates that the BOLD signal does not always reflect the activity of single cells. Instead, it more reliably reflects the aggregate synaptic activity within an area of cortex. As most studies of monkey neuronal activity measure single-neuron activity rather than LFPs, the interpretation of the relationship between results from single-unit studies in monkey and BOLD experiments in humans is made more complicated. Nevertheless, for most situations there has been very good agreement, further validating the use of fMRI.

BOLD contrast fMRI is not the only functional brain imaging technique possible using MRI. *Perfusion imaging* MRI sequences can non-invasively measure blood flow changes in the brain directly (rather than indirectly through changes in deoxyhaemoglobin concentration). However, this type of blood flow signal is typically weaker than the BOLD signal and so the latter is most commonly used for studies of human cognition. *Magnetic resonance spectroscopy* can measure signals associated with particular neuronal metabolites in the brain, and is often used to study how these signals change in neurological and psychiatric disease. New and emerging approaches to functional brain imaging are seeking to develop new compounds that can be detected by MRI and used to label particular cellular or molecular processes such as calcium influx or gene expression. At present such new approaches are highly experimental, invasive, and only implemented in animals.

BOLD contrast fMRI is typically used as a research tool to measure local changes in brain activity associated with changes in cognitive or perceptual state. Visual, auditory, or somatosensory stimuli are typically presented to experimental subjects, who can make responses using a keypad or joystick while their brain activity is measured. In an *event-related design*, the brain responses evoked on a single trial are measured repeatedly. In a *blocked design*, the mean responses evoked during a block of trials lasting 20–30 s are measured. Each BOLD image consists of many thousands of measured locations or *voxels* and in a typical experiment several hundred such images are obtained. The blocked or event-related BOLD response is then compared at each and every voxel in the brain under two or different experimental conditions using standard statistical tests. This results in a *statistical parametric map* that, when overlaid on an anatomical MRI image of the brain, indicates the location of regions that showed statistically significant activation when comparing the two conditions.

If the two conditions where brain activity was measured differed only in the involvement of a particular psychological state or mental process, then it can be concluded that the brain regions identified represent a neural *correlate of that state. In consciousness research, it is common to compare two conditions that reflect identical physical input, but evoke different phenomenal states (Frith et al. 1999). For example, during *binocular rivalry, constant but conflicting retinal input to the two eyes gives rise to conscious perception that alternates between each monocular view every few seconds. As the *contents of consciousness change without any change in the retinal input, the resulting changes in brain activity measured using fMRI have been interpreted as neural correlates of consciousness. One limitation of fMRI (in common with all physiological techniques) is that demonstrating that a particular area shows activity correlated with a particular cognitive process does not mean that it necessarily plays a causal role. Correlation does not imply causation. In order to conclude whether particular brain areas are either necessary or sufficient for a specific cognitive process, converging evidence from experiments using multiple methodologies are required. In particular, fMRI observations are often combined with evidence from *transcranial magnetic stimulation or *neuropsychology where causality can be inferred from disruption or damage to a particular brain area. Taken together, such integrated study of human cognition using multiple converging methodologies has become known as *cognitive neuroscience*.

Functional brain imaging has therefore become a flexible and versatile tool that has greatly facilitated the study of the neural basis of human cognition. It offers a non-invasive technique that can indirectly measure activity throughout the brain with reasonable temporal and spatial resolution. The technology continues to evolve, with new and different aspects of neuronal and network activity likely to come under study in the future.

RICHARD SYLVESTER AND GERAINT REES

Frith, C., Perry, R., and Lumer, E. (1999). 'The neural correlates of conscious experience: an experimental framework'. *Trends in Cognitive Science*, 3.

Ingvar, D. H. (1975). 'Patterns of brain activity revealed by measurements of regional cerebral blood flow'. In Ingvar, D. H. and Lassen, N. A. (eds) *Brain Work: The Coupling of Function, Metabolism and Blood Flow in the Brain*.

Kwong, K. K., Belliveau, J. W., Chesler, D. A. et al. (1992). 'Dynamic magnetic resonance imaging of human brain activity during primary sensory stimulation'. *Proceedings of the National Academy of Sciences of the USA*, 89.

Logothetis, N. K., Pauls, J., Augath, M. et al. (2001). 'Neurophysiological investigation of the basis of the fMRI signal'. *Nature*, 412.

Mansfield, P. (1977). 'Multiplanar image formation using NMR spin echoes'. *Journal of Physics C*, 10.

Roy, C. S. and Sherrington, C. S. (1890). 'On the regulation of the blood supply to the brain'. *Journal of Physiology*, 11.

functionalist theories of consciousness The term 'functionalism' occurs with distinct meanings in several disciplines; this article concerns functionalism as a philosophical theory, or better a family of theories, about the nature of mental states. At the core of functionalism is a metaphysics of mental types (see section 1, below). Perspectival and phenomenal aspects of consciousness pose vivid challenges for this account, but some broad functionalist strategies may be deployed in response (section 2). Recently prominent functionalist theories of consciousness may be seen as implementations of these strategies (section 3). Functionalism persists as a controversial backdrop for current themes in *philosophy of consciousness (section 4).

1. Functionalism as a metaphysics of mental types
2. Functionalist strategies in response to the challenge of consciousness
3. Implementing the strategies: theories and variations
4. Further problems and prospects

1. Functionalism as a metaphysics of mental types

Since the 1960s functionalism has been the most prominent of a set of *isms* (*dualism, behaviourism, *physicalism, . . .) that address the mind–body problem. Consider the 'metaphysical' question: in virtue of what are distinct particular mental states or events grouped together as instances of the same mental type? Functionalism denies that a given type of mental state is to be characterized in terms of its *intrinsic* properties, its constitution or ontology. Instead, mental types are fundamentally *relational*, where the relevant relata include input stimuli, output behaviours, and other mental states. The core idea is that a type of mental state is a type of causal role in a larger network linking inputs, outputs, and other internal states.

Computing theory supplied an early model for functionalist ideas in philosophy of mind. The internal states of a *Turing machine are defined by their role in the machine table, which defines all relevant internal states simultaneously, without vicious circularity, and in abstraction from their material realization. By analogy, *pain can be characterized simultaneously with other internal states (e.g. pain-typical desires, emotional responses such as anxiety) in a causal network linking internal states to each other and to typical inputs (e.g. tissue damage) and outputs (e.g. avoidance behaviours), in abstraction from its material realization.

Contrast functionalism with two other broadly materialist programmes: behaviourism, and a physicalism that identifies mental types with neurological types. Functionalism corrects behaviourism's reluctance to postulate 'inner' states, yet it articulates a level of description at which mental types and neurological types cross-classify. A human being, a non-human animal, a futuristic automaton, and an extraterrestrial organism might all be in the inner mental state-type *pain* even if they share no relevant neurological state-type. In brief, mental state-types are *multiply realizable*. It is compatible with this, and many functionalists went on to assert, that each particular instance of pain—each pain *token*—is strictly identical with some neurological (or silicon, etc.) state or event token in the relevant human being, non-human animal, automaton, or extraterrestrial. In that case we would have identity between mental tokens and neurological (or silicon, etc.) tokens, but no identity, or even universal correspondence, between mental types and neurological types.

The functional role that defines a mental type must be articulated by way of a prerequisite larger theory of the causal relations into which that mental type enters. One sort of functionalist theory—*psychofunctionalism*—sees the prerequisite causal theory as given by empirical cognitive science. Think of empirical sciences as revealing the hidden natures of the kinds they treat; e.g. the nature of water is empirically revealed to be H_2O. Mental kinds are empirically revealed by cognitive science to be functional in nature, according to psychofunctionalism.

Another sort of functionalist theory sees the required theory of causal relations as given by folk psychology, that network of causal relations our knowledge of which constitutes shared common-sense understanding of the mental, and which we presuppose in our practical explanations of human action. Or the causal theory may be restricted to just those causal relations entailed by the very meanings of the relevant mentalistic terms; these causal principles will be analytic—truths of meaning. *Folk-psychological functionalism* and *analytic functionalism*, as these latter two variants are termed, are best understood as aiming to directly explicate our mentalistic concepts, rather than the natures of mental kinds as such.

2. Functionalist strategies in response to the challenge of consciousness

Functionalism has always been motivated primarily by third-person, public aspects of mentality, but it has faced a series of vivid challenges keyed to first-person, perspectival or phenomenal aspects of consciousness. In Jackson's thought experiment, for example, Mary is brought up in a controlled environment in which she can have no chromatic colour experience (see KNOWLEDGE ARGUMENT). Black and white visual experiences are adequate, however, for her training as a vision scientist, and indeed Mary learns all of the physical and functional facts about colour experience. One day she escapes her controlled environment, looks at a ripe tomato, and learns what it is like to see red. Since she learns a new fact about colour vision, after already knowing all the physical and functional facts, it seems to follow that some facts about colour vision—*what-it-is-like facts—are neither physical nor functional.

Chalmers (1996), building on ideas from S. Kripke, argues that we can coherently conceive of a philosophical *zombie—a creature molecule-for-molecule identical to an ordinary human being, but in which there is no phenomenal consciousness. Your zombie twin would perfectly replicate your physical and functional organization, down to the minutest details of input stimulation, output behaviour, and neurofunctional intermediaries, but there is nothing that it would be like to be your zombie twin. Zombies are metaphysically possible—they might have existed, had the natural order been different. Chalmers concludes that no physical or functional organization can be metaphysically sufficient for phenomenal consciousness.

From the conceivability of zombies, J. Levine draws an epistemic rather than a metaphysical conclusion: we cannot explain, on the basis of the underlying physical or functional facts, the fact of a conscious state having a particular phenomenal character, rather than having a different phenomenal character or none at all. This *explanatory gap is a permanent feature of our epistemic condition. The gap persists even if we postulate metaphysically necessary connections between the underlying functional facts and the facts of phenomenal consciousness, for we cannot explain why those connections hold and not others.

These thought experiments—and others, such as the *inverted spectrum, and J. Searle's *Chinese room—put pressure on functionalists to attend to the phenomenal and first-person perspectival aspects of consciousness. In this effort the distinction between *phenomenal properties* and *phenomenal concepts* has come to loom large. Concepts are ways of thinking about entities or properties; the distinct concepts 'water' and 'H_2O', for example, pick out the same entity or property in the world. Jackson's protagonist Mary has first, we may suppose, a functional concept of what it is like to see red; on exiting the controlled environment she gains a phenomenal concept of, a new way of thinking about, what it is like to see red. But these two concepts pick out the same phenomenal property. Mary's visual experience of the ripe tomato enters into her phenomenal concept of what it is like to see red; she thus acquires fresh and vivid knowledge of what it is like. But the phenomenal fact that she thereby knows is the very fact that she previously knew via functional concepts. By insisting on a dualism of concepts rather than a dualism of properties or facts, a functionalist can interpret the case of Mary as consistent with the thesis that all properties and facts of consciousness are functional in nature.

Similarly, many functionalists have responded to the zombie thought experiment by arguing that the scenario is not conceivable in any sense strong enough to entail metaphysical possibility. Zombies are conceivable in a weaker sense that does not entail metaphysical possibility because we can refer to a single phenomenal property via distinct concepts. Imagining a zombie, we use functional concepts when specifying its construction, then use phenomenal concepts when denying it consciousness. Thus the dualism of concepts makes zombies weakly conceivable. But if a third-person functional concept and a corresponding first-person phenomenal concept pick out the same property of consciousness with respect to every possible world, then zombies are metaphysically impossible. The distinction between *first person (subjective)* and *third person (objective)* in philosophy of consciousness is fundamentally a distinction between kinds of concepts, not kinds of properties or facts, according to functionalism.

If some discomfort or sense of mystery still attaches to the idea that a phenomenal/perspectival fact could simply be a functional fact, it may be dispelled by conceptual or empirical progress in articulating the two sides of the identity. Two broad theoretical strategies dominate recent functionalist accounts of consciousness; these strategies are often deployed in tandem, with details varying from one philosopher to another. The first strategy, focused mainly on the phenomenal/perspectival side of the equation, is to 'divide and conquer'; that is, to make appropriate distinctions between kinds of consciousness, or aspects of consciousness, and then to attack them piecemeal. Perhaps functionalism is true for some aspects of consciousness but not others.

The second strategy, focused mainly on the functional side of the equation, is to take **intentionality* as more basic than consciousness, and to explain consciousness in terms of intentionality. Intentionality is the 'aboutness' of mental states, their property of referring to some thing, or representing some state of affairs. The thing referred to may or may not actually exist, and the state of affairs represented may or may not actually obtain. Hence intentional mental states may be accurate or illusory, true or false, satisfied or unsatisfied. Suppose that intentionality can be explained functionally; causal theories of reference, or functional role theories of intentional content, may be recruited toward this end. Suppose further that consciousness can be explained in terms of intentionality. Conjoining these two suppositions yields a functionalist explanation of consciousness.

3. Implementing the strategies: theories and variations

As an example of the first strategy, consider Block's notorious distinction between phenomenal consciousness (P-consciousness) and *access consciousness (A-consciousness; see Block 2007). A mental state is P-conscious in virtue of its experiential properties, broadly construed to include not only properties of sensations, feelings, and perceptions, but also those of thoughts, wants, and emotions. A mental state is A-conscious in virtue of being poised for direct control of reasoning and for rational control of action or speech. P-conscious states give rise to the so-called **hard problem* of consciousness, but are candidates for neurophysiological reduction. A-conscious states, by contrast, essentially make representations accessible to a larger system, and so may be understood in terms of functional role.

Block takes the P-vs-A distinction to pick out not two aspects but rather two kinds of consciousness, or two senses of the word 'conscious'. (Chalmers draws a similar distinction.) It is conceptually possible, given Block's account, for a creature to have A-conscious states without ever having any P-conscious states. Yet it has seemed to many philosophers that, given Block's broad construal of the phrase *experiential property*, a creature with no P-consciousness during its entire career would not be conscious in any reasonable sense. This suggests that the P-vs-A distinction is badly drawn. As a divide-and-conquer strategy, the P-vs-A distinction meets further resistance from functionalist programmes that aim to explain the phenomenal in terms of the intentional.

Dennett (2005) favours broadly functionalist metaphors for consciousness such as *cerebral celebrity*, *fame in the brain*, or *competition for clout*. Mental contents instantiated in the brain form coalitions and compete for control of action and verbal report. Coalitions that succeed in this competition count as having conscious contents. Those contents need not be transmitted to any part of the brain that implements consciousness; they need only be organized into successful coalitions. Such a functional process may be realized in humans by a kind of reverberation or amplification loop. Efficacy in feedback and control of action is key. As S. Hurley and A. Noë have argued, there need be no discrete input and output layers, and the reverberation or loop may be conceived as extending out into the world.

Dennett's account is more than usually metaphorical. Yet it is functionalist in spirit, for it characterizes consciousness in terms of a *causal role*, hence at a more abstract level than that of a physiological *role-player*, and the possibility of physiologically diverse realizers is left open. By contrast, an account that simply identified consciousness with, say, synchrony of neural oscillation plus ventral stream activation (for visual contents), or *re-entrant neural circuits, would not be functionalist. On the other hand, **global workspace* or *global broadcast* theories in psychology, and Schacter's Conscious Awareness System, are functionalist in spirit, in the manner of cerebral celebrity.

Philosophical critics worry that a zombie, lacking consciousness, could nevertheless instantiate such functional patterns. It is therefore unclear how cerebral celebrity or its ilk could simply be consciousness, as opposed to something normally accompanying consciousness though in principle separable. Moreover, examples of habituated stimuli, and perhaps also subliminal stimuli, suggest the possibility of phenomenality—the most philosophically puzzling aspect of consciousness—without cerebral celebrity. Dennett's discussions of phenomenal and perspectival aspects of consciousness are multifaceted and pose interpretive difficulties. In some respects Dennett's account is neo-behaviourist and appears to treat phenomenal and perspectival aspects as less than robustly real.

One striking way to develop the second strategy mentioned above, that of explaining consciousness in terms of intentionality, takes phenomenal properties to be represented properties of ordinary external, nonmental things. Many contemporary philosophers, including Harman (1990), Dretske, and Tye (2000), accept some form of the *transparency thesis*, which insists that conscious experience never has any directly *introspectible phenomenal properties of its own. What are often taken to be phenomenal properties of conscious experience are actually properties that experience represents external non-mental things as having. A conscious visual experience of a ripe tomato has no introspectible property of phenomenal redness; it merely represents, accurately or inaccurately, the tomato as red. Further, the represented property of redness may be identical to a complex physical property of external surfaces, a matter of reflectance frequencies. In the modern tradition we inherited from Descartes, phenomenal properties were 'kicked upstairs' into the mind to make the nonmental world safe for mechanistic physics. The transparency thesis kicks represented phenomenal properties back out into the non-mental world, and lets them be identical to mechanistic physical properties.

The transparency thesis is a natural ally of *first-order *representationism*, the doctrine that the phenomenal character of consciousness is exhausted by—supervenes on and depends on—certain of its first-order representational properties. A *first-order* representational property is one that purports to represent external, nonmental objects or states. (A representational property that purported to represent a mental state or event would be termed *higher-order*.) But not all first-order representational properties contribute to phenomenal character. Which do, and which do not? According to Tye's first-order representationist theory of consciousness, phenomenal character is *poised, abstract, non-conceptual intentional content* (PANIC). Of these functional conditions, two are most relevant here: *poised* content stands ready to directly impact general cognition and action, assuming attention is properly focused and certain concepts are possessed; *non-conceptual* content has features for which the subject need not possess matching concepts. Thus on Tye's account the phenomenal character of consciousness is entirely a matter of properties of external, non-mental objects or states as represented in a certain functionally specific way.

Critics of Tye's theory cite the **inverted spectrum*, which seems to show the possibility of two subjects who are representationally exactly alike but who differ phenomenally. In a variant, *Inverted Earth*, the environment is imagined to vary so as to suggest that a subject on Earth and her twin on Inverted Earth may be phenomenally exactly alike but representationally dissimilar. Both inversion arguments exploit the alleged dependence of the purely phenomenal on the subject's central nervous system, and the dependence of representation on the history of the subject's environment. Discussion has also focused on whether the phenomenal character of sensations such as headaches and *orgasms are truly representational, given that a conscious state's having a biological function does not yet amount to its being representational. Similar doubts arise with respect to the phenomenal character of emotions and moods.

Higher-order representationism also aims to explain consciousness in terms of intentionality, but unlike its first-order counterpart it takes mental states to be conscious in virtue of their being the intentional objects of other mental states. Armstrong (1980) and Lycan (1996) argue that a mental state *M* is conscious in virtue of *M*'s being the object of an inner perception or scanning process—a *higher-order perception* (HOP). Precursors of this idea can be found in the history of philosophy, most notably in Locke. Non-conscious perceptual representation, e.g. in *blindsight, is taken to be more fundamental than consciousness, and amenable to a functionalist treatment. Often perceptual representation is directed upon mundane external things, but there is no reason why it cannot also be directed instead upon other mental states, in which case the represented mental states are conscious.

A variant of this idea is Rosenthal's **higher-order thought* (HOT) theory (Rosenthal 2005), which takes the relevant higher-order state to be an occurrent thought rather than a perception. A first-order mental state *M* is 'like something' for the subject when *M* is the intentional object of a second-order thought. A second-order state may, in some cases, be the intentional object of a third-order state, but this occurs when the subject engages in conscious introspection, as a philosopher, psychologist, or poet might do, and not in everyday consciousness. Introspective consciousness reveals that the second-order state introduces no distinctive phenomenal quality of its own, not already present in the first-order state. Hence the need, according to Rosenthal, to make the higher-order states thoughts rather than perceptions.

Recall that according to functionalism, a mental token belongs to its mental type in virtue of the token's relational properties. In HOP and HOT theories the relevant type is simply that of a state's being conscious, which is not any intrinsic property but a matter of its being an intentional object of a distinct higher-order state. Note that the higher-order state itself need not be conscious, so there is no need for an infinite hierarchy of representations.

HOP and HOT theories both distinguish a state's having *phenomenal quality* from its being *phenomenally conscious*. The latter is explained in terms of higher-order representation, while the former is explained in some other physicalist or functionalist manner. The distinction entails the intelligibility of *unconscious phenomenal quality*, a striking and theoretically fruitful result, according to the theory's proponents, but a conceptual vulnerability according to some critics. Critics also argue that higher-order representationism, especially the HOT theory, is caught on the horns of a dilemma: either it over-intellectualizes consciousness in babies and lower animals such as mice or fish, or it implausibly denies them consciousness. Finally, a hallmark of intentionality is the possibility of error and illusion, so erroneous or illusory HOPs or HOTs must be intelligible and presumably actual. Again, proponents find this a striking and theoretically fruitful result, to be interpreted in light of cognitive science. Critics, however, charge confusion—an erroneous or illusory HOP or HOT would determine what it is like for the subject, but it is the first-order state, not the HOP or HOT, that is supposed to be conscious.

In response to these and other alleged difficulties, a variety of *self-representationist* or *same-order representationist* approaches are also being explored. R. Van Gulick's *higher-order global states* (HOGS) model (Van Gulick 2006), for example, may perhaps be classified as self-representationist. The central idea is that a mental state *M* becomes conscious in virtue of *M*'s being subject to a rich set of implicit sub-personal processes that (a) recruit *M* into a globally integrated complex, and (b) amount to reflexive awareness of *M* itself. Condition (a) is a form of cerebral celebrity, condition (b) a form of representationism.

4. Further problems and prospects

The ferment over representationism shows the resilience of functionalist ideas in the face of prima facie damning thought experiments. One of the above theories may well emerge as rendering it plausible that certain kinds of phenomenal or perspectival facts simply are causal-role facts. Moreover, as of this writing (2007), functionalism persists as a backdrop to a range of current questions and obsessions in the philosophy of consciousness. Three categories may be briefly noted.

First, can the functionalist metaphysics be modified to accommodate a recognition that conscious worldly agency is typically temporally extended and involves dynamic sensory feedback? The 'vehicles' of such conscious events are naturally seen as looping out into the world; the inputs and outputs of the functionalist metaphysics seem implausibly discrete buffers.

Second, can functionalism be coherently articulated with respect to the *first-person phenomenologies* of attention, of mental agency, of immediate self-knowledge, or of the (apparent, alleged) attribution in conscious colour perception of 'revealed', primitive, Edenic qualities to external things?

Third, richer integration with neuroscience is both desirable and inevitable. Functionalists distinguish between *core* and *total realizations* of conscious state *M*: the core is a physical state *N* that plays the distinctive causal role, and the total is a wider state within which *N* plays that role, sufficient for N to constitute an M token. What in the neurobiology of consciousness answers to such a distinction? And—Block's 'harder problem' of consciousness—what basis could we ever have for attributing phenomenality to, or withholding it from, conceivable creatures that are functionally *isomorphic* to us but that have nothing like our nervous systems?

BERNARD W. KOBES

Armstrong, D. M. (1980). 'What is consciousness?' In *The Nature of Mind*.
Block, N. (2007). *Consciousness, Function, and Representation: Collected Papers*, Vol. 1.
Burge, T. (1997). 'Two kinds of consciousness'. In Block, N. et al. (eds) *The Nature of Consciousness: Philosophical Debates*.
Chalmers, D. J. (1996). *The Conscious Mind: In Search of a Fundamental Theory*.
Dennett, D. C. (2005). *Sweet Dreams: Philosophical Obstacles to a Science of Consciousness*.
Gennaro, R. J. (ed.) (2004). *Higher-order Theories of Consciousness: An Anthology*.
Harman, G. (1990). 'The intrinsic quality of experience'. In Tomberlin, J. E. (ed.) *Philosophical Perspectives 4*.
Kriegel, U. and Williford, K. (eds) (2006). *Self-representational Approaches to Consciousness*.
Lycan, W. G. (1996). *Consciousness and Experience*.
Papineau, D. (2002). *Thinking About Consciousness*.
Rosenthal, D. M. (2005). *Consciousness and Mind*.
Shoemaker, S. (2003). 'Content, character and color'. In Sosa, E. and Villanueva, E. (eds) *Philosophical Issues, 13, Philosophy of Mind*.
Tye, M. (2000). *Consciousness, Color, and Content*.
Van Gulick, R. (2006). 'Mirror, mirror—is that all?' In Kriegel, U. and Williford, K. (eds) *Self-representational Approaches to Consciousness*.

functional magnetic imaging (fMRI) See FUNCTIONAL BRAIN IMAGING

functions of consciousness An account of the functions of consciousness would be a very nice thing to have. Unfortunately, there is little agreement about what the function(s) of consciousness are, or even about how we might go about finding them. Why would it be good to have an account of the functions of consciousness? Because we could use such an account to constrain accounts of how and why consciousness. We might even be able to use it to constrain accounts of what consciousness *is*.

1. General issues
2. Some proposed functions of consciousness

1. General issues

A full account of the function(s) of consciousness needs to address each of the various manifestations of consciousness. At the most coarse-grained level there is the property of being conscious. Some creatures are conscious; other creatures are not. We might call this *creature consciousness*. At the most fine-grained level there are particular conscious states, such as the states distinctive of hearing a trumpet, having a pain in one's elbow, and smelling lilies. We might call this *state consciousness*. In addition to creature and state consciousness lie *background (or global) states of consciousness*, such as normal wakefulness, REM *dreaming, the minimally conscious state, and so on. A comprehensive treatment of the functions of consciousness needs to address itself to creature consciousness, state consciousness, and background state consciousness. For the most part, theorists have focused on the functions of fine-grained (as opposed to background) conscious states, and I will follow suit here.

A wide variety of mental states can be conscious. There are perceptual experiences (seeing traffic, tasting cherries, feeling sandpaper), affective experiences (feeling depressed, jealous, elated), bodily sensations (pains, tickles, orgasm), and the conscious states associated with memory, imagination, and central cognition (judgement, intention, decision, and so on). It is a matter of some controversy whether all of these states are conscious in the same sense. Some theorists hold that there is a single property of consciousness—*phenomenal consciousness*—that each of these states can enjoy, others deny that this is the case, holding (for example) that cognitive states are not phenomenally conscious. This issue is of some significance, for if there are multiple types of state consciousness then it may well be the case that there is no single function associated with all conscious states. I will assume here that there is a single form of state consciousness—phenomenal consciousness—but the reader should note that this assumption is controversial.

The notion of function is no less problematic than that of consciousness. The term is used in a wide variety of ways, and much discussion of the functions of consciousness is impaired by a failure to be precise about what exactly is meant by 'function'. Two notions are central: *causal role function* and *teleological function*. The causal role function of a state (or property) is simply the causal role that it plays—the array of effects that it has. Some of these effects will be internal to the cognitive system in which the state is embedded, but others will extend out beyond the boundaries of that system and into its environment. Some of the state's effects may be of benefit to the system, but others could impair its overall operation.

The teleological function of a state (or property) is the causal role that it *ought* to play—the role that it has been designed to play. Only certain components of a state's overall causal profile are relevant to its teleological function. It is part of the causal role of noses that they support spectacles, but this is not part of their teleological function; my heart produces sounds of a certain pitch, but that it does so is no part of its teleological function. It is a matter of much debate just what determines the teleological function of a state and how such functions are to be identified. These are troubled waters, and despite the fact that the teleological function of consciousness is important I will leave it to one side here (Polger and Flanagan 2002). Instead, I will focus on the causal role function of consciousness. What does consciousness do?

Before we turn to some candidate answers to that question, further discussion of the relationship between consciousness and its causal role is useful. Here, we can contrast two basic approaches. According to one approach, consciousness is distinct from any causal role that it plays. What makes a state conscious is one thing; what it does is another thing entirely. In principle, so this account runs, conscious states might have played causal roles other than those which they actually play. According to another approach—which is held by certain brands of *functionalists—consciousness cannot be pulled apart from some elements of its causal role: it is essential to conscious states that they play a certain causal role. But note that even functionalists need not hold that all of the functions that are associated with consciousness are essentially related to consciousness. In other words, functionalists can (indeed, should) hold that conscious states have effects over and above those that are essential to their status as conscious states. A functionalist might conceive of the search for the functions of consciousness as a search for that causal role which is essential to consciousness as such, but there is no reason for them to restrict the search for the functions of consciousness in this way.

How might we identify the causal role of consciousness? One view, more often assumed than defended, is that an account of the functions of consciousness can be read off from the concept of consciousness. This *aprioristic* approach is implicit in the thought that *zombies—unconscious creatures that are functionally identical to normal human beings—are conceptually impossible. This position is controversial, and many theorists deny that there is any conceptual connection between conscious states and functional states. This is not to deny that one can 'work up' a functional concept of consciousness—Ned Block (1995) has done precisely this with his notion of *access consciousness—but it is arguable that the concept of phenomenal consciousness contains little to no functional content.

A second method for identifying the function(s) of consciousness looks to theories of consciousness (Kriegel 2004). Here, one moves from an account of what consciousness is to an account of what it does. For example, *higher-order representation theories—according to which a state is conscious in virtue of being the intentional object of a suitable mental state—suggest that the function of consciousness is largely *metacognitive. But other theories of consciousness suggest that consciousness has a very different function. For instance, first-order theories of consciousness typically hold that what it is for a mental state to be conscious is for its content to be poised to make a direct impact on the subject's cognitive states. Accordingly, proponents of such accounts see consciousness as having first-order rather than higher-order functions. We can see here the dialectical weakness in attempting to identify the functions of consciousness by appealing to theories of consciousness: where one ends up depends rather too heavily on where one begins, and different theorists begin in rather different places.

Arguably, the central method employed by consciousness studies for identifying the functions of consciousness is contrastive. By contrasting conscious states with their unconscious counterparts one might hope to screen off the causal influence of the content of the mental states in question and isolate the difference that consciousness itself makes. One problem with the contrastive approach is that one might not always be able to find states with unconscious analogues. It is at least arguable that there are certain types of mental states that cannot—or at least do not—take an unconscious form. For example, many will argue that there is no such thing as unconscious decision-making, judgement, or desire. If such claims are correct, then applying the contrastive methodology to such states will be problematic.

A second problem with the contrastive approach is that the specification of causal roles is highly idealized. Although accounts of the function of consciousness have the form, 'Conscious states of kind *A* have the function of facilitating *F*-ing', this should not be taken to imply that any creature in conscious state *A* will be able to *F*. Functions talk is invariably hedged with *ceteris paribus* clauses—clauses that are designed to protect the proposal from conditions in which various background conditions are not met. Faced with a case in which a creature is in conscious state *A* but cannot *F*, one could reject the proposal in question, but one could also hold that the relevant background conditions are not satisfied. (The fact that hearts can fail to pump blood around the body does not falsify that hypothesis that the function of the heart is to pump blood around the body, for sometimes the background conditions that are needed in order for hearts to pump blood do not obtain.) Particular care must be taken when applying the contrastive approach to data derived from pathological syndromes, for in such cases we might have good reason to doubt whether the relevant background conditions are met.

A third challenge for the contrastive approach is that it requires determining whether or not the subject is in a certain conscious state. This is often problematic, for not only are there few uncontroversial markers of consciousness, in defending such markers as there are it is often tempting to appeal to accounts of the function of consciousness. As an example of this problem, consider the proposal that consciousness facilitates goal-directed behaviour. Some theorists argue against this proposal on the grounds that individuals in a state of *automatism are capable of carrying out goal-directed behaviour. This argument clearly presupposes that such individuals are not conscious, a claim that is likely to be rejected by someone who thinks that facilitating goal-directed behaviour is a function of consciousness. In short, evaluating accounts of the function of consciousness appears to demand that we either appeal to an account of the function of consciousness (and thus reason in a circle), or use as our markers of consciousness behavioural measures that have not been confirmed. One potential solution to this problem is to validate measures of consciousness of which we are unsure against measures of which we are highly confident. Whether or not this approach escapes the circularity that we are seeking to avoid is an open question.

2. Some proposed functions of consciousness

Let us turn now from the general issues regarding the relationship between consciousness and its function to some concrete proposals for what the functions of consciousness might be.

It is widely held that consciousness has something to do with facilitating action. Common sense holds that we withdraw our hand from the hot stove because we experience pain, and that in reaching for the coffee cup we are guided by our visual experience of its handle. Such claims are also encountered in discussions of consciousness, with more than one theorist claiming that long-distance truck drivers must be conscious of the road even when not attending to it, for how else would they be able to avoid misadventure?

Despite such claims, there is reason to think that consciousness plays relatively little role in the online guidance of action (Clark 2001, Gray 2004). One line of evidence for this thesis derives from the study of D. F., a woman with visual form *agnosia. D. F. suffers from severe deficits in visual experience, and can no longer recognize everyday objects. However, she is able to pick up the very objects that she cannot identify, and when reaching for objects her grip is proportioned to the size of the target. These findings, together with other research on normal visual perception, suggests that there are two *visual systems, a ventral stream for object identification and a dorsal stream for online motor control, with the contents of the latter stream largely falling outside consciousness. Converging evidence for the claim that unconscious representations play a role in behavioural guidance comes from the finding that *masked stimuli are able to activate motor programmes (Dehaene et al. 1998).

Of course, these findings leave open the possibility that both unconscious and conscious states play a role in online motor control. However, there is direct evidence against this proposal: patients with optic ataxia are unable to use their visual awareness of stimuli in the service of motor control. The temporal structure of consciousness also suggests that it might play only a limited role in online motor control. It may seem as though the sensation of pain causes one to withdraw one's hand from the hot stove, but given the time it takes for conscious states to arise it seems likely that the action was initiated independently of the experience of pain.

Even if online motor control is largely in the hands of so-called zombie systems, consciousness may facilitate other forms of agency (van Gulick 1994, Dretske 2006). Morsella (2005) suggests that phenomenal states are necessary for the production of actions that require interaction between different responses systems. More generally, it is often suggested that one of the functions of consciousness is to instigate and guide willed, voluntary, and executive agency. One might be able to perform routine or over-learned actions unconsciously, but—so the claim goes—in order to carry out complex, novel, or willed actions one must be conscious of what one is doing. This view is of a piece with the thought that unconscious representations are not available to personal-level control: they can influence cognitive processing—for example, by priming the subject to make one judgement rather than another, or to perform one kind of action rather than another—but they cannot be employed by the subject in the service of the rational control of agency. Consciousness might have little role in the implementation of executive actions, but it does seem to be necessary for the selection of targets and action types (Clark 2001).

Arguably the most influential account of the function of consciousness holds that consciousness is in the business of making information *globally available* for behavioural and cognitive control. Unconscious information might be available to a restricted range of systems, but—so this account goes—only conscious information is available to a wide range of consuming systems. As a rough approximation we might say that the effects of unconscious states on cognition are rigid (or 'implicit') whereas those of conscious states are flexible (or 'explicit'). The contrast between implicit and explicit influence is seen in a wide variety of clinical conditions, including (but not limited to) unilateral neglect, *agnosia, *blindsight, *amnesia, and alexithymia (Weiskrantz 1997).

Although the global availability approach is popular, it is often unclear what the evidence for it is supposed to be. Global availability theorists often seem to argue that mental states whose contents are not globally available cannot be conscious on the grounds that consciousness just is (or is at least correlated with) global availability. But this is to argue in a circle: it is no surprise to 'discover' that consciousness is correlated with global availability if that is how consciousness is measured!

A further challenge involves clarifying just what global availability amounts to (see *access consciousness). In studies of brief-visual displays, partial-report conditions suggest that subjects are aware of much more than they can report at any one point in time (see MEMORY, ICONIC). In such cases, it is plausible to suppose that the *contents of consciousness 'outrun' or 'overflow' those of reportability, memory consolidation, and other forms of cognitive access. Whether or not this literature really puts pressure on the claim that consciousness facilitates global availability depends in no small measure on just how the notion of global availability is unpacked.

In whatever way the notion of global availability is unpacked, there appear to be conditions—such as dreaming, *delirium, and psychosis—in which consciousness is retained but rationality and executive control are severely impaired. These conditions indicate that the contents of consciousness need not be globally available for cognitive and behavioural control, and hence put pressure on the proposal that it is consciousness itself that facilitates global availability. In response to this challenge, proponents of the global availability account might argue that these conditions involve some kind of malfunction in the mechanisms of consciousness, and hence they have no bearing on the question of consciousness's teleological function. This response has some merit in the case of delirium and psychosis, but it seems unlikely that dreaming consciousness involves a malfunction of the mechanisms of consciousness. However, one might argue that in dreaming the subject's conscious states are globally available to those systems that remain *online; alternatively, one could argue that the global availability account is intended only as an account of the function of consciousness in the normal waking state. But even in normal wakefulness consciousness can frustrate rather than facilitate performance. As has often been noted, expert performance in the dance studio, on the sports field, and at the jazz club is typically hampered by conscious attention to the fine-grained detail of what one is doing. Even certain types of thought might be impeded by consciousness. We are all familiar with instances in which the solution to a difficult problem emerges only after conscious reflection on it has ceased. In a similar vein, there is evidence that conscious deliberation can impair rather than improve the quality of decision-making (Dijksterhuis 2004).

Another account of the function of consciousness looks not to the dissemination of information but to its integration. Perhaps consciousness—at least, *sensory consciousness*—is the glue that puts (and keeps) perceptual features together as the features of individual perceptual objects. This proposal derives intuitive support from the correlation between consciousness and feature *binding: for the most part, conscious representations are bound. However, it is possible that the mechanisms of consciousness are not themselves responsible for feature binding and that the correlation between consciousness and binding holds only because the architecture of consciousness prevents unbound representations from entering consciousness.

Thus far I have left to one side the question of how consciousness might facilitate (bring about, execute, generate) its functions. The reason for my reticence here is simple: we have no conception of how consciousness carries out its functions. Our best model of cognition—the computational theory of the mind—makes no reference to consciousness, and despite the intuitive appeal of the thought that consciousness must make some contribution to cognitive function we are hard-pressed to give a model of how it might make such a contribution. Here we confront the *hard problem and *explanatory gap. Optimists might be tempted to think that we need not solve the hard problem or close the explanatory gap in order to identify the function(s) of consciousness—indeed, they might suggest that identifying the function of consciousness will enable us to solve the hard problem and close the explanatory gap. Pessimists, however, might suppose that we cannot identify the function(s) of consciousness without having an account of *how* consciousness might subserve its function(s), and we will not be able to work out how consciousness subserves its functions without solving the hard problem and closing the explanatory gap. Perhaps giving an account of the function (s) of consciousness is so difficult precisely because the hard problem is so hard and the explanatory gap so wide.

See also EVOLUTION OF CONSCIOUSNESS; FUNCTIONALIST THEORIES OF CONSCIOUSNESS; METACOGNITION; OBJECTIVE VS SUBJECTIVE MEASURES OF CONSCIOUSNESS; VISUAL STREAMS: WHAT VS HOW

TIM BAYNE

Block, N. (1995). 'On a confusion about a function of consciousness'. *Behavioural and Brain Sciences*, 18.

Clark, A. (2001). 'Visual experience and motor action: are the bonds too tight?' *Philosophical Review*, 110.

Dehaene, S., Naccache, L., Le Clerc'H, G. et al. (1998). 'Imaging unconscious semantic priming'. *Nature*, 395.

Dijksterhuis, A. (2004). 'Think different: the merits of unconscious thought in preference development and decision making'. *Journal of Personality and Social Psychology*, 87.

Dretske, F. (1997). 'What good is consciousness?' *Canadian Journal of Philosophy*, 27.

—— (2006). 'Perception without awareness'. In Gendler, T. S. and Hawthorne, J. (eds) *Perceptual Experience*.

Flanagan, O. (1992). *Consciousness Reconsidered*.

Gray, J. (2004). *Consciousness: Creeping up on the Hard Problem*.

Kriegel, U. (2004). 'The functional role of consciousness: a phenomenological approach'. *Phenomenology and the Cognitive Sciences*, 3.

Morsella, E. (2005). 'The function of phenomenal states: supramodular interaction theory'. *Psychological Review*, 112.

Polger, T. and Flanagan, O. (2002). 'Consciousness, adaptation, and epiphenomenalism'. In Fetzer, J. (ed.) *Evolving Consciousness*.

Rosenthal, D. (2007). 'Consciousness and its function'. *Neuropsychologia*, 46.

Shallice, T. (1972). 'Dual functions of consciousness'. *Psychological Review*, 72.

Tye, M. (1996). 'The function of consciousness'. *Noûs*, 30.

van Gulick, R. (1994). 'Deficit studies and the function of phenomenal consciousness'. In Graham, G. and Stephens, G. L. (eds) *Philosophical Psychopathology*.

Weiskrantz, L. (1997). *Consciousness Lost and Found*.

G

gamma oscillations Neural signals in the gamma frequency range (≥30 Hz) have recently received considerable attention in neuroscience. Although the phenomenon of fast neuronal oscillations had been described already 50 years earlier, it started to attract major interest only in the late 1980s when it was shown to correlate with perceptual *binding (Gray et al. 1989). These so-called gamma oscillations can be observed with a variety of different methods. One approach is to use microelectrodes to record activity from nerve cells located in the brain of an experimental animal (Fig. G1). In humans, such oscillations can be studied using non-invasive methods such as *electroencephalography (EEG) or *magnetoencephalography (MEG).

Using these approaches, fast oscillations in the gamma frequency range have been found in a large number of different neural systems and across a wide range of species (for review, see Engel and Singer 2001, Engel et al. 2001). It has been observed in all sensory systems, in the motor system, and in memory/association structures. Importantly, gamma-band activity occurs not only in cortex, but also in subcortical structures such as brainstem, thalamus, and the basal ganglia. The species where gamma oscillations have been studied include primates, carnivores, lagomorphs, rodents, birds, reptiles, amphibia, and insects. In humans, gamma-band activity was demonstrated first in the auditory cortex. Subsequently, gamma-frequency oscillations have been studied in visual and tactile processing and during language processing, as well as in *memory systems and the motor system.

This striking ubiquity strongly suggests that gamma oscillations have a functional role for processing in the respective systems. What the available studies demonstrate is the relation of gamma activity to a wide variety of cognitive processes including feature

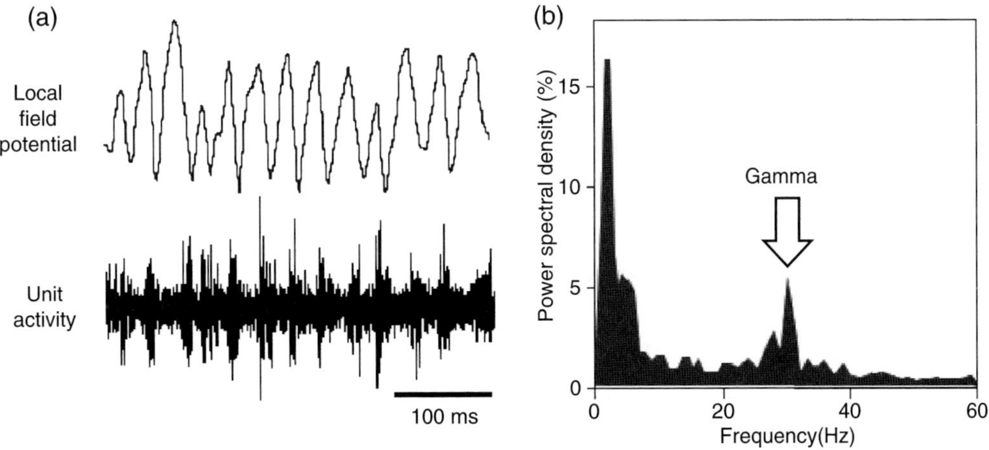

Fig. G1. Gamma oscillations in mouse visual cortex. (a) Using microelectrodes, action potentials (unit activity) can be recorded from small clusters of nerve cells. When activated by an appropriate sensory stimulus, the cells engage in coherent bursts of spikes (black 'needles' in the bottom trace). These bursts occur at rather regular intervals, reflecting an oscillatory process in the local network. Frequently, the temporal interval between the bursts is of the order of 10–30 ms, yielding an oscillation frequency around 30–100 Hz. The oscillatory fluctuations can also be observed in a simultaneously recorded local field potential (top trace). (b) Spectral analysis of the recorded signals often reveals a distinct peak in the gamma frequency range.

integration, object recognition, focused attention, *working memory, long-term memory, sensorimotor integration, and language processing. Typically, the observed amount of gamma is positively correlated with increased 'processing load' and, thus, with the level of *attention, as well as with the difficulty or integrative nature of the processing (Herrmann et al. 2004).

Crick and Koch (1990) were the first to suggest a relation between the occurrence of synchronized gamma oscillations and consciousness. Inspired by the finding that visual stimuli can elicit synchronized oscillatory activity in the visual cortex (Gray et al. 1989), they proposed that an attentional mechanism induces synchronous oscillations in selected neuronal populations, and that this temporal structure would facilitate transfer of the encoded information to working memory. In their proposal, Crick and Koch elaborated upon the earlier hypothesis that temporal correlations might play a fundamental role in neural processing, since they could serve to bind distributed signals into functionally coherent cell assemblies (von der Malsburg 1981). According to their view, only appropriately bound neuronal activity could enter short-term memory and, hence, become available for access to phenomenal awareness.

1. Dynamic binding by neural coherence
2. Experimental support for TCH
3. Relation of fast oscillations to consciousness
4. Coherence and consciousness

1. Dynamic binding by neural coherence

Originally, the notion that temporal correlations might be important for dynamic integration of neural signals had been proposed in the context of perceptual processing and scene segmentation (von der Malsburg 1981, Engel et al. 1992, Singer and Gray 1995). This *temporal correlation hypothesis* (TCH) has been strongly motivated by the insight that perception, like most other cognitive functions, is based on highly parallel information processing involving large neural assemblies spread across numerous brain areas. One of the key predictions of the TCH is that neurons which support perception of a sensory object might fire their action potentials in temporal synchrony (with a precision in the millisecond range). However, no such synchronization should occur between cells which are activated by different objects appearing in sensory space (Fig. G2). According to the TCH, synchronization of spatially separate neurons is a key principle of brain function since it allows the

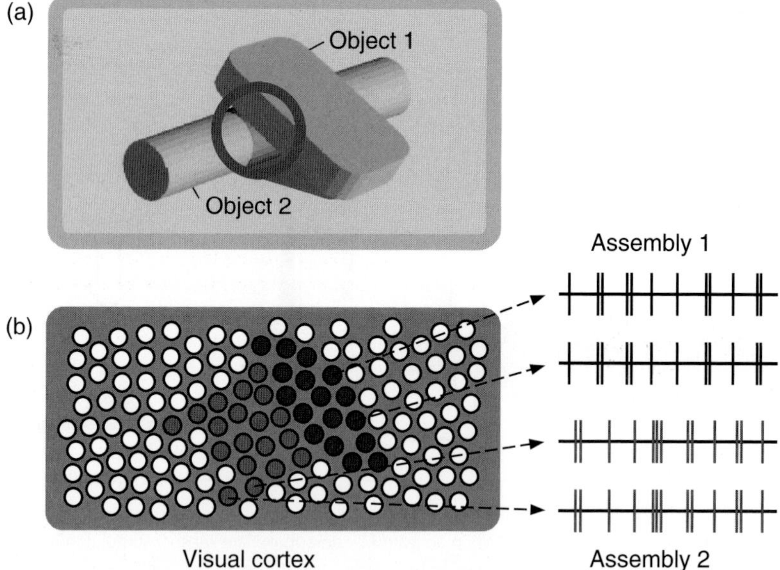

Fig. G2. Establishment of coherent neural assemblies by temporal correlations. (a) Visual scene containing two objects. The circle demarcates a region of the scene where segmentation is particularly demanding. (b) The TCH posits that segmentation is achieved by selective correlation between cells that support the percept of one object, i.e. cells that make up one coherent assembly. The signals of cells that are part of different assemblies are not correlated in time (right).

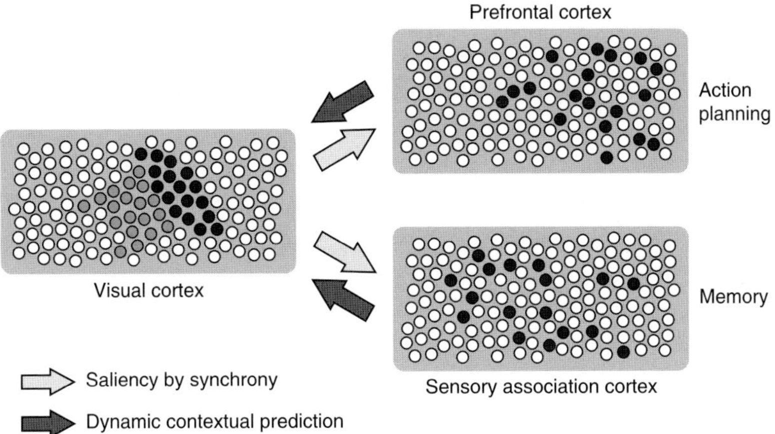

Fig. G3. Role of neural synchrony in bottom-up and top-down processing. The TCH assumes that correlated neural activity (in particular, synchronized oscillations) can have a dual role for transmitting information in thalamocortical and cortico-cortical networks: one the one hand, synchronized signals are much more 'salient' from the viewpoint of other receiving regions (*saliency by synchrony*); on the other hand, intrinsically activated assemblies in other regions can generate contextual constraints for processing in sensory areas through top-down modulation (*dynamic contextual prediction*).

formation of functionally coherent activity patterns supporting particular cognitive functions. In the example illustrated in Fig. G2, synchrony would support the construction of perceptual coherence, or *gestalt quality*, of objects.

A critical assumption of the TCH is that synchrony in a distributed network of neurons is subject to both bottom-up and top-down influences (Engel et al. 2001). As illustrated schematically in Fig. G3, temporal correlations might subserve a dual function in such networks. On the one hand, synchrony could permit the rapid and reliable selection of perceptually or behaviourally relevant information (*saliency by synchrony*). Because precisely synchronized discharges have a high impact on the respective postsynaptic cells, the information tagged by such a temporal label could be rapidly and preferentially relayed to other processing centres (Fries 2005). On the other hand, formation of assemblies is not only constrained by stimulus-related information, but presumably much more strongly by the intrinsic dynamics of the system. In the case of perceptual integration, factors like expectation, attention or previous knowledge about the objects encountered are often crucial for the outcome of the segmentation process. The TCH accounts for this by assuming that temporally coordinated signals from other regions of the network can have a strong impact on assembly formation in sensory regions by modulating the local neural dynamics in a top-down manner (Fig. G3, *dynamic contextual prediction*). Such modulatory top-down signals could arise, for instance, from regions involved in memory and action planning. In both cases, bottom-up routing of signals, and top-down modulation of processing, neuronal communication is thought to be rendered highly selective by correlated oscillatory fluctuation of the cell populations involved (Fries 2005).

These mechanisms postulated by the TCH might be relevant for understanding the emergence of conscious mental states in several respects (Engel and Singer 2001). Obviously, generating sensory awareness seems to require some mechanism that selects relevant information and enhances its impact on subsequent processing stages. Moreover, awareness seems to presuppose the capacity for structuring sensory contents, which in turn rests on the ability to establish specific relationships between sensory signals. Furthermore, consciousness very likely requires large-scale integration across different brain regions which contribute different aspects to phenomenal experience. Finally, it has been postulated that conscious states are associated with the build-up of a **global workspace*, i.e. a fleeting memory capacity whose contents are widely distributed to specialized networks. In recent years, empirical evidence is emerging which indeed suggests that coherent oscillatory activity may relate to these different prerequisites for awareness and, thus, be critical to understanding the neural basis of consciousness.

2. Experimental support for TCH

As mentioned already, the basic phenomenon of correlated neural activity is well documented for a wide range of neural systems and species. It is well established that neurons in both cortical and subcortical centres can synchronize their discharges with a precision in the millisecond range (for reviews, see Engel et al. 1992, Singer and Gray 1995, Engel et al. 2001). As observed in many animal studies and confirmed in human EEG and MEG experiments, synchrony is often associated with oscillatory activity, and it has been argued that, at least over larger distances, oscillations may be critical in setting up neuronal communication (Engel et al. 1992, Fries 2005).

Direct support for the TCH comes from studies showing that neuronal synchronization in the cortex depends on the stimulus configuration. In the visual systems of cats and monkeys, it could be demonstrated that spatially separate cells show strong synchronization only if they respond to the same visual object. However, if responding to two independent stimuli, the cells fire in a less correlated manner or even without any fixed temporal relationship (Gray et al. 1989). The experiments demonstrate that gestalt criteria such as continuity or coherent motion, which have psychophysically been shown to support perceptual grouping, are important for the establishment of synchrony among neurons in the visual cortex. In humans, coherent visual stimuli have been shown to lead to augmentation of gamma-band power, reflecting enhanced neural interactions in this frequency range (Siegel et al. 2007).

As stated above, other critical predictions of the TCH concern the role of correlated activity in selection of signals and in top-down modulation of local processing. Both aspects are addressed by studies on attentional selection. Strong evidence for an attentional modulation of neural synchrony is provided by experiments in awake-behaving macaque monkeys. Steinmetz et al. (2000) have investigated cross-modal attentional shifts in awake monkeys that had to direct attention to either visual or tactile stimuli that were presented simultaneously. Neuronal activity was recorded in the secondary somatosensory cortex. For a significant fraction of the neuronal pairs in this area, synchrony depended strongly on the monkey's attention. If the monkey shifted attention to the visual task, temporal correlations typically decreased among somatosensory cells, as compared to task epochs where attention was not distracted from the somatosensory stimuli. In the visual system, strong attentional effects on temporal response patterning have also been observed in monkey V4 (Fries et al. 2001). In this study, two stimuli were presented simultaneously on a screen, one inside the receptive fields of the recorded neurons and the other nearby. The animals had to detect subtle changes in one or the other stimulus. If attention was shifted towards the stimulus

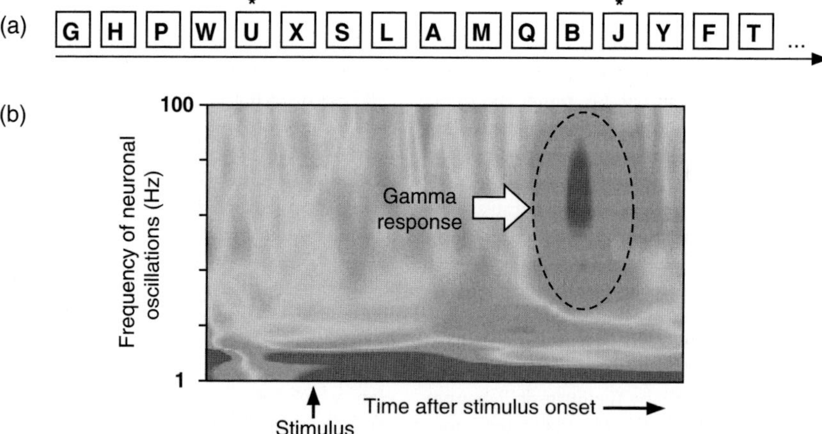

Fig. G4. Gamma-band oscillations and attention. The EEG reflects coherent potential changes in populations of cortical neurons. These signals are recorded non-invasively by electrodes placed on the scalp. Modern techniques allow us to analyse how the frequency spectrum changes over time in response to stimulus presentation. (a) In this example, subjects had to detect and silently count target letters that deviate in colour (marked by asterisks) from unattended black letters. (b) An increase of spectral power occurs in the gamma band (30–100 Hz) several hundred milliseconds after a target stimulus has appeared. This gamma-band activity occurs selectively for the attended stimuli.

processed by the recorded cells, there was a marked increase in local synchronization. More recently, this finding has been confirmed by Taylor et al. (2005) using a demanding visual task where monkeys had to track changes in an object's shape over time. In both the latter studies, the attentional effects were observed specifically in the gamma-frequency band.

In humans, several EEG and MEG studies also suggest a clear relation between attention and modulation of synchronized oscillations. Thus, it has been shown that gamma-band activity is enhanced by attention in the human auditory system (e.g. Debener et al. 2003). Similar evidence is available for the visual system (e.g. Kranczioch et al. 2006) and the tactile system (e.g. Bauer et al. 2006). In all these cases, attention specifically enhances gamma-band activity. Figure G4 illustrates an example for this attentional effect observed using rapid serial visual presentation, a paradigm where stimuli were presented at 10 Hz, and subjects had to silently count target items embedded in the stimulus stream. Processing of the targets is associated with a gamma-band response which is missing for the ignored stimuli (Kranczioch et al. 2006). Additional evidence shows that other top-down factors such as long-term memory, expectation, or action planning can also influence the timing of neural signals (for reviews, see Engel et al. 2001, Herrmann et al. 2004).

3. Relation of fast oscillations to consciousness

In line with hypotheses that can be derived from the TCH, evidence from both animal and human experiments suggests that neural synchrony may be of critical relevance for the emergence of consciousness in at least two respects (for review, see Engel and Singer 2001). First, high-frequency oscillations relate to the build-up of conscious states and, thus, to changes in the *level* of consciousness; second, gamma-oscillations seem to facilitate the selection of sensory information for access to awareness and, thus, have an impact on the **contents* of consciousness. Regarding the former, evidence from animal and human studies shows that neuronal synchronization in the gamma-band covaries with arousal and is particularly prominent during epochs of higher vigilance. Moreover, gamma components of sensory evoked potentials, which indicate precise neuronal synchronization when recorded in the awake state, have been shown to disappear under deep *anaesthesia (reviewed in Engel and Singer 2001).

A relation of gamma-band activity to changes in contents of conscious states is suggested by experiments in which activity was recorded from the visual cortex of awake cats under conditions of *binocular rivalry (Fries et al. 1997, 2002). Binocular rivalry is a particularly interesting case of dynamic response selection which occurs when the images in the two eyes are incongruent and cannot be fused into a coherent percept. In this case, only signals from one of the two eyes are selected and perceived, whereas those from the other eye are suppressed. In normal subjects, perception alternates between the stimuli presented to the left and right eye. This shift in perceptual dominance can occur without any change of the physical stimulus. Obviously, this experimental situation is particularly suited for studying the basis of consciousness, because neuronal responses to a given stimulus can be studied either with or without being accompanied by awareness (Crick and Koch 1990) and, thus, there is a chance of revealing the mechanisms leading to the selection of perceptual information.

Fries et al. (1997, 2002) tested the hypothesis that response selection in early visual areas might be achieved by modulation of neural coherence rather than of the rate of discharges. These measurements were performed in awake cats with electrodes chronically implanted in primary and secondary visual cortex. The animals were subjected to dichoptic visual stimulation, i.e. patterns moving in different directions were simultaneously presented to the left and the right eye respectively (Fig. Ga). The results obtained with this experimental approach show that visual cortical neurons driven by the dominant and the suppressed eye, respectively, differ in neither the strength nor the synchronicity of their response to monocular visual stimulation. They do, however, show striking differences with respect to their synchronization behaviour when exposed to the rivalry condition (Fig. G5b). Neurons supporting the dominant percept increase their synchrony, whereas cells processing the suppressed visual pattern decrease their temporal correlation. This effect occurs specifically in the gamma-frequency band, but not in other frequency ranges (Fries et al. 1997, 2002).

A paradigm that has been used to study neural correlates of awareness in humans is the so-called **attentional blink*. This paradigm involves the rapid serial visual presentation of stimuli such as digits, letters, words, or pictures, typically at a fixed location with presentation frequencies ranging from 3 to 20 items per second (cf. Fig. G4). The notion of 'attentional blink' refers to a behaviourally well-described transient reduction of attention, which can occur if more than one target has to be processed in such a series of stimuli. In this dual-task situation, a second target stimulus often goes unnoticed if it appears in close temporal succession after the first target. Using this paradigm, a straightforward approach is to compare the neural activity occurring during trials with 'hits' and 'misses': since the physical stimulus has been identical in the two cases, the intrinsic dynamics of thalamocortical circuits must be critical for the difference in awareness about the stimulus. In a recent EEG study,

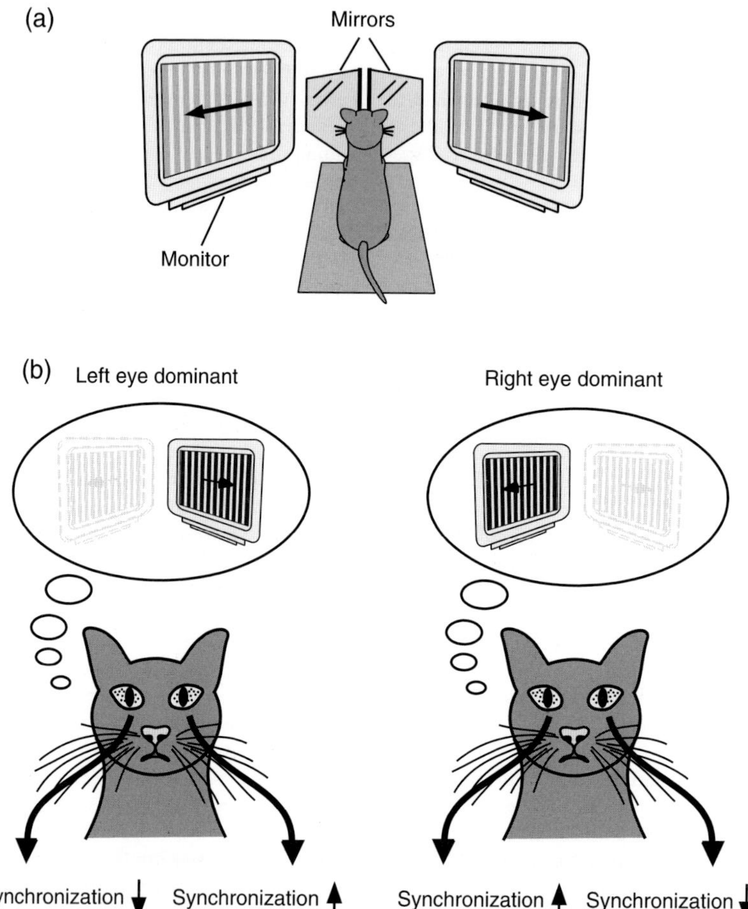

Fig. G5. Neuronal synchronization under binocular rivalry in awake cats. (a) To induce binocular rivalry, two mirrors are mounted in front of the animal's head such that the eyes are viewing different stimuli. If drifting gratings are used as stimuli, perceptual dominance for a given set of stimuli can be inferred from the direction of eye movements induced by the gratings (the so-called optokinetic nystagmus). (b) In certain episodes, the pattern presented to the left eye will dominate perception, while the information conveyed by the right eye is suppressed and excluded from perception (left). In other instances, perceptual dominance of the pattern presented to the right eye is observed (right). As indicated in the bottom panel, synchrony will increase between neurons processing the perceived stimulus, while it decreases between cells responding to the suppressed pattern. Thus, for instance, during dominance of the left eye, neurons driven by this eye will increase their temporal correlation, but correlation becomes weaker for cells driven by the right eye.

a complex pattern of changes in the alpha-, beta-, and gamma-frequency ranges was observed. A significant enhancement of oscillatory activity in the gamma band was observed late after appearance of the second target (Kranczioch et al. 2007). This late condition-specific increase may reflect active retrieval and utilization of target-related information (Herrmann et al. 2004).

Taken together, both the data on binocular rivalry and those obtained with the attentional blink support the proposal by Crick and Koch (1990) that coherence in neuronal activity may be a necessary condition for the occurrence of awareness. In both cases, the outcome of perceptual selection is not determined by bottom-up factors, but very likely by intrinsically generated large-scale dynamic patterns, which result from *re-entrant interactions of action planning, memory and limbic regions with sensory brain areas. As suggested by Tononi and Edelman (1998), large-scale assemblies activated by such interactions may constitute a 'dynamic core' that could control the access of signals to awareness and provide the substrate for a global workspace.

4. Coherence and consciousness

The studies reviewed above strongly suggest that phenomena predicted by the TCH, i.e. the temporal patterning in neuronal activity and, in particular, coherent oscillations in the gamma frequency range, may be critical for the emergence of conscious states. The available data show that coherent high-frequency oscillations relate to a whole set of processes indispensable for consciousness. These can be summarized as follows (Engel and Singer 2001): (1) Central activating systems may act to modify the efficacy of temporal binding mechanisms, in a task- and context-dependent manner. This may change both the spatial range and the specificity of neuronal interactions. (2) Segmentation may be implemented in the temporal domain. Synchrony allows to establish functional relations among neurons and, thus, the structuring of conscious mental contents. (3) Selection can be mediated by neural synchronization, because coincident signals are particularly efficient in driving other neural assemblies. (4) Reverberation in selected assemblies may underlie working memory; such assemblies provide the contents for conscious mental states. (5) Synchrony can mediate specific cross-system interactions that bind subsets of signals in different areas; this may set up a global workspace for consciousness.

While some of these issues certainly require further clarification and experimental study, this may ultimately lead to a new framework for studies of consciousness which puts neural dynamics into the very core of mechanisms underlying this mental capacity.

ANDREAS K. ENGEL

Bauer, M., Oostenveld, R., Peeters, M., and Fries, P. (2006). 'Tactile spatial attention enhances gamma-band activity in somatosensory cortex and reduces low-frequency activity in parieto-occipital areas'. *Journal of Neuroscience*, 26.

Crick, F. and Koch, C. (1990). 'Towards a neurobiological theory of consciousness'. *Seminars in Neuroscience*, 2.

Debener, S., Herrmann, C. S., Kranczioch, C., Gembris, D., and Engel, A. K. (2003). 'Top-down attentional processing enhances auditory evoked gamma band activity'. *NeuroReport*, 14.

Engel, A. K. and Singer, W. (2001). 'Temporal binding and the neural correlates of sensory awareness'. *Trends in Cognitive Sciences*, 5.

——, König, P., Kreiter, A. K., Schillen, T. B., and Singer, W. (1992). 'Temporal coding in the visual cortex: new vistas on integration in the nervous system'. *Trends in Neurosciences*, 15.

——, Fries, P., and Singer, W. (2001). 'Dynamic predictions: oscillations and synchrony in top-down processing'. *Nature Reviews Neuroscience*, 2.

Fries, P. (2005). 'A mechanism for cognitive dynamics: neuronal communication through neuronal coherence'. *Trends in Cognitive Sciences*, 9.

——, Roelfsema, P. R., Engel, A. K., König, P., and Singer, W. (1997). 'Synchronization of oscillatory responses in visual cortex correlates with perception in interocular rivalry'. *Proceedings of the National Academy of Sciences of the USA*, 94.

——, Reynolds, J. H., Rorie, A. E., and Desimone, R. (2001). 'Modulation of oscillatory neuronal synchronization by selective visual attention'. *Science*, 291.

——, Schröder, J.-H., Roelfsema, P. R., Singer, W., and Engel, A. K. (2002). 'Oscillatory neuronal synchronization in primary visual cortex as a correlate of stimulus selection'. *Journal of Neuroscience* 22/9.

Gray, C. M., König, P., Engel, A. K., and Singer, W. (1989). 'Oscillatory responses in cat visual cortex exhibit inter-columnar synchronization which reflects global stimulus properties'. *Nature* 338/6213.

Herrmann, C. S., Munk, M. H. J., and Engel, A. K. (2004). 'Cognitive functions of gamma-band activity: memory match and utilization'. *Trends in Cognitive Sciences*, 8.

Kranczioch, C., Debener, S., Herrmann, C. S., and Engel, A. K. (2006). 'EEG gamma-band activity in rapid serial visual presentation'. *Experimental Brain Research*, 169.

——, Debener, S., Maye, A., and Engel, A. K. (2007). 'Temporal dynamics of access to consciousness in the attentional blink'. *Neuroimage*, 37.

Siegel, M., Donner, T. H., Oostenveld, R., Fries, P., and Engel, A. K. (2007). 'High-frequency activity in human visual cortex is modulated by visual motion strength'. *Cerebral Cortex*, 17.

Singer, W. and Gray, C. M. (1995). 'Visual feature integration and the temporal correlation hypothesis'. *Annual Review of Neuroscience*, 18.

Steinmetz, P. N., Roy, A., Fitzgerald, J., Hsiao, S. S., Johnson, K. O., and Niebur, E. (2000). 'Attention modulates synchronized neuronal firing in primate somatosensory cortex'. *Nature*, 404.

Taylor, K., Mandon, S., Freiwald, W. A., and Kreiter, A. K. (2005). 'Coherent oscillatory activity in monkey V4 predicts successful allocation of attention'. *Cerebral Cortex*, 15.

Tononi, G., and Edelman, G. M. (1998). 'Consciousness and complexity'. *Science*, 282.

von der Malsburg, C. (1981). *The Correlation Theory of Brain Function*. Reprinted (1994) in Domany, E. et al. (eds) *Models of Neural Networks*, Vol. II.

gestalt theory The Gestalt School of psychological thought originated in Germany early in the 20th century (for a comprehensive review, see Koffka 1935). It is best known for its theoretical and empirical contributions to understanding the organization of perceptual experience, including the nature of perceived groups, objects, parts, properties, and the relations among them, but was extended to address issues concerning problem solving (e.g. Köhler 1925) and social psychology (e.g. Lewin

1951). Before the advent of gestalt theory, ideas about perceptual organization were dominated by the structuralist proposal, derived primarily from British empiricist philosophy, that complex perceptions were constructed from atoms of elementary sensation and unified by associations due to spatiotemporal contiguity. Gestalt theorists rejected both atomism and associationism, arguing forcefully that perceptual experience was intrinsically holistic and organized. In addition to the theoretical ideas outlined below, gestalt psychologists made many important empirical contributions to understanding the structure of perceptual experience, including seminal studies of perceptual grouping, figure–ground organization, frames of reference, apparent motion, induced motion, perceived transparency, and illusory contours, all of which highlight the crucial role played by global structure in determining perceptual experience.

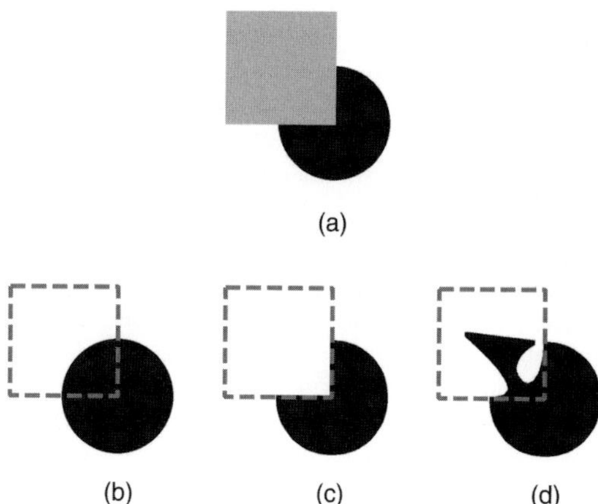

Fig. G6. Square partly occluding a circle.

At its broadest level, gestalt theory can be understood as a comprehensive attempt to account for the interlocking relations among phenomena in three domains: stimulus structure, brain mechanisms, and conscious experience (e.g. Wertheimer 1924/1938, Koffka 1935, Köhler 1940). The theory rests largely on three foundational ideas—the principle of *Prägnanz* (or minimum principle), the concept of a physical gestalt, and the doctrine of psychophysiological isomorphism—that together support the unique gestalt view of perception.

1. The principle of Prägnanz
2. Physical gestalts
3. Psychophysiological isomorphism

1. The principle of Prägnanz

Perception is generally regarded as inherently ambiguous in the sense that any given stimulus is logically compatible with many different interpretations. In vision, for example, much of this ambiguity arises from the optical projection of three-dimensional structure in the external world to two-dimensional structure on the retina, a transformation that necessarily loses not only information about an object's distance from the viewer, but about what is hidden behind it. In Fig. G6a, for example, people spontaneously see a grey square partly occluding a black circle that is amodally completed behind it, as indicated in Fig. G6b. There are many other logically possible completions, however, two of which are illustrated in Fig. G6c, d. How does the visual system manage to arrive at the 'correct' interpretation of a square partly occluding a circle?

Helmholtz's (1867) classic answer was that perception involved unconscious inferences based on the likelihood principle: choosing the most likely environmental situation that could have produced the stimulus. Thus, we see a dark circle behind a light square in Fig. G6A because that is statistically more likely than any other alternative. This answer, which is consistent with a modern Bayesian approach to perceptual inference, provides the observer with maximally accurate knowledge about the environment, but it is not entirely clear how the brain can determine the actual likelihoods of alternative external situations. The problem is that the brain ultimately does not have access to the actual state of the world, but only to indirect, imperfect, and inherently ambiguous sensory information.

Gestalt theorists proposed a radically different answer in their principle of Prägnanz: perception will be as 'good' as the prevailing conditions allow. The 'prevailing conditions' refer to the structure of the stimulus event that constrains the set of logically possible interpretations, and 'goodness' is an internal quantity that the perceptual system maximizes. The key assumptions here are that each possible interpretation includes an aspect that reflects its perceptual 'goodness' (in the sense of simplicity/regularity) and that the process of perception arrives at the interpretation that maximizes this quantity. (Equivalently, one can assume that perception minimizes complexity/irregularity, leading to an alternative formulation in terms of the *minimum principle.*) Perceived 'goodness' is, at least in part, available to conscious experience, because people provide systematic responses when they are asked to rate the 'goodness' of figures that vary in complexity and/or symmetry (e.g. Leeuwenberg 1971). The gestalt principle of Prägnanz is preferable to Helmholtz's likelihood principle in the sense that it is clear that the brain could maximize an internally defined measure of 'goodness' or informational simplicity, whereas it is unclear that it can maximize an externally defined measurement of likelihood. Gestalt theorists linked Prägnanz with innate brain processes, but it could also arise from learning environmental regularities.

The principle of Prägnanz can be illustrated in Fig. G6, where the alternative black figures that might be perceived behind the closer gray square can be characterized by varying degrees of symmetry and complexity: Fig. G6b contains a single curved contour and is symmetric over all central reflections and rotations, Fig. G6c contains a curved contour plus two straight contours and is symmetric over only one diagonal reflection, and Fig. G6d contains at least four distinct contours and has no symmetries at all. Thus, the gestalt principle of Prägnanz specifies that we perceive the circle behind the square because it is 'better' in the sense of having fewer components and being more symmetric. Unfortunately, gestalt theorists never provided a formal definition of 'goodness' that would allow the principle of Prägnanz to be tested empirically. Later theorists in the gestalt tradition did so, however, with noteworthy success (e.g., Leeuwenberg 1971, Leeuwenberg and Buffart 1984). Even with a quantitative theory to hand, however, it is often difficult to distinguish between the principles of likelihood and Prägnanz, because the simplest interpretation is also usually the most likely.

2. Physical gestalts

Gestalt theorists did not develop their ideas about Prägnanz in the direction of abstract formal theories, but they did try to explain it via hypotheses about the operation of brain processes. Central to this view was their notion of a *physical gestalt*: a dynamical physical system that naturally converges on a state of minimum energy (Wertheimer 1924/1938). The physical gestalt to which they most often appealed in explaining this idea was a soap bubble, whose shape has the interesting property that, no matter what its initial shape, it evolves over time into a perfect sphere.

The fact that a perfect sphere is, in the gestalt view, the 'best' of all three-dimensional shapes was not entirely coincidental, because 'goodness' forms a bridge between their ideas about physical gestalts and their principle of Prägnanz. In particular, gestalt theory hypothesized that the brain was a massively complex physical gestalt that worked by converging on a minimum energy state after being perturbed by stimulus energy. The structure of the external event determined the nature of these perturbations, which began a chain of neural events that caused the brain to settle dynamically into a state that reflected the 'best' interpretation of the stimulus. Thus, gestalt theory implied that 'good' alternatives (in the sense of simplicity/regularity) corresponded to low energy neural states and that the brain's operation as a physical gestalt thus implemented the principle of Prägnanz.

These ideas eventually led Köhler (1940) to propose a new theory of brain function based on electromagnetic fields, which had many of the properties that gestalt theorists believed were important. Subsequent experiments failed to support his conjecture, however, because when electrical conductors and/or insulators were placed in cortex to disrupt such fields, the predicted massive decrements in perceptual performance were not observed. Although these findings were taken to refute Köhler's specific hypothesis and gestalt theory more generally, recent work with computational simulations of neural networks may provide a better alternative: neural circuits with recurrent feedback mechanisms may dynamically converge on brain states that are formally equivalent to minimum energy solutions, without appealing to electromagnetic field in the brain (see CONNECTIONIST MODELS).

3. Psychophysiological isomorphism

The third foundational assumption of gestalt theory was the doctrine of psychophysiological isomorphism: the claim that the structure of conscious experiences is the same as the structure of the corresponding neural events. (This proposal is a historical antecedent to recent discussions about the conditions for identifying the neural correlates of consciousness.) One of the best examples of psychophysiological isomorphism arises in *colour perception. Based on a brilliant analysis of the structure of human colour experience, Hering (1878/1964) proposed an opponent-process theory of colour in which all colour experiences arise from the pattern of responses in three independent, bipolar, colour systems: red/green, blue/yellow, and black/white. Many years later, *single-cell recording techniques enabled researchers to discover cells in the early visual system that fire to coloured light in ways that are largely compatible with Hering's theory (De Valois et al. 1966). Some cells are excited by red and inhibited by green, whereas others are excited by green and inhibited by red; some cells are excited by blue and inhibited by yellow, whereas others are excited by yellow and inhibited by blue; and some cells are excited by white and inhibited by black, whereas others are excited by black and inhibited by white. These underlying neural events are thus largely isomorphic to (i.e. have the same structure as) the conscious colour experiences people have when viewing light with different physical spectra.

Gestalt theorists proposed the idea of psychophysiological isomorphism long before any such examples had been discovered, of course. For them, it was an inevitable consequence of their unique view of how stimulus energy interacted with underlying brain processes to produce conscious experiences. Their distinctive theoretical approach focused on the concept of structure: The structure of stimulus events interacts with the complex of possible structures of neural events, which, in turn, produce conscious experiences that are simultaneously isomorphic to the internal neural events that underlie them and informative about the nature of the environmental events that cause them.

STEPHEN E. PALMER

De Valois, R. L., Abramov, I., and Jacobs, G. H. (1966). 'Analysis of response patterns in LGN cells'. *Journal of the Optical Society of America*, 56.

Ellis, W. D. (1938). *A Sourcebook of Gestalt Psychology*.

Helmholtz, H. von (1867/1925). *Treatise on Physiological Optics*, Volume III (transl. of 3rd German edn).

Hering, E. (1878/1964). *Outlines of a Theory of the Light Sense*, transl. L. M. Hurvich and D. J. Jameson.

Koffka, K. (1935). *Principles of Gestalt Psychology*.

Köhler, W. (1925). *The Mentality of Apes*.

—— (1940). *Dynamics in Psychology*.

Lewin, K. (1951). *Field Theory in Social Science; Selected Theoretical Papers*, ed. D. Cartwright.

Leeuwenberg, E. L. J. (1971). 'A perceptual coding language for visual and auditory patterns'. *American Journal of Psychology*, 84.

—— and Buffart, H. (1984). 'The perception of foreground and background as derived from structural information theory'. *Acta Psychologica*, 55.

Wertheimer, M. (1923/1938). 'Untersuchungen zur Lehre von der Gestalt, II'. *Psychologische Forschung*, 4. (Condensed translation published as: 'Laws of organization in perceptual forms' in Ellis 1938.)

—— (1924/1938). 'Gestalt theory'. In Ellis 1938.

global neuronal workspace SEE NEURONAL GLOBAL WORKSPACE

global workspace theory Global workspace theory (GWT) is a theoretical framework for conscious and unconscious brain events. GWT has only three basic constructs (Fig. G7). The first is a *global workspace* (GW), defined as a momentary memory that can be accessed by numerous *input assemblies*, such as the active cell assemblies involved in visual experiences and motor control. The most obvious example is a sensory input process. Input assemblies provide the seeds of specific contents of consciousness. The second construct is a very large set of *receiving assemblies*, both cortical and subcortical. Third are *contexts*, defined as coalitions of neuronal assemblies, which can select, evoke, and shape the contents of the global workspace, without themselves becoming conscious. These three constructs can be shown to account qualitatively for standard cognitive ideas like working memory, selective attention, and voluntary control. They reintroduce conscious experience as a central determinant of cognition.

A stable coalition of such contexts, which routinely controls access to the global workspace in the waking state, is called a *dominant context*. Such a dominant context is taken to be equivalent to the subjective self of common-sense psychology, an 'executive interpreter' in the brain (Baars 1988, 1997, 2002). It is also taken to control voluntary selective attention, where attention is defined as the ability to select conscious contents. Note that the subjective self is taken to be unconscious; it is not the self-concept, which is a type of conscious **content* (James 1890).

Conscious experiences are proposed to arise in the interaction between GW contents, the subjective self, and receiving assemblies. All interactions are potentially two-way. GWT converges well with approaches like neural Darwinism (Edelman and Tononi 2001).

GWT can be thought of in terms of a theatre metaphor, with conscious contents corresponding to information presented in a brightly lit spot on a dark theatre stage, communicating with a dark unconscious audience, and scripted in turn by a behind-the-scenes stage crew, director, and scriptwriter. Only the content in the bright spot is conscious in this metaphor. But GWT is not a metaphor but a theory, i.e. a consistent set of testable hypotheses about the human mind–brain. Figure 1 shows how this framework may be applied to visual consciousness. Several novel predictions from GWT have received empirical support, including the crucial finding of widespread brain coherence associated with conscious stimulation, but not matched unconscious input (reviewed in Baars 2002, Baars and Franklin 2007).

1. Evidence
2. Experimental tests
3. Functional tests

1. Evidence

Given that the brain is massive and parallel, why is the conscious component so limited and serial? It seems that humans cannot perform two conscious tasks at the same time, such as conversing intently while driving in traffic. Competition between such tasks depends upon the extent to which they are conscious: The more they become habitual and unconscious, the less they compete. This suggests that consciousness as such may be responsible for capacity limits. Why are conscious functions so limited in a brain that is so large?

One possibility is that consciousness, though limited in capacity at any one moment, nevertheless offers a gateway to much more extensive unconscious knowledge sources in the brain. Consciousness seems to be needed to access at least four great bodies of unconscious knowledge: the lexicon of natural language, autobiographical memory, the automatic routines that

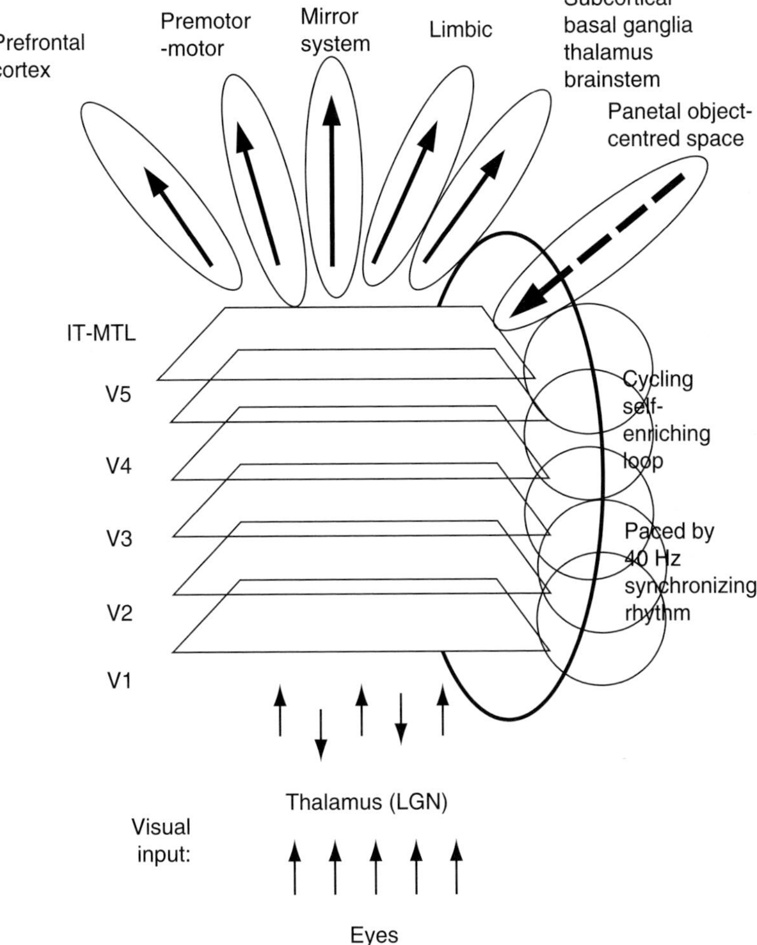

Fig. G7. A GWT model of visual consciousness. Resonances between maps generate brain rhythms, paced by distributed pacemaker cell clusters. Rhythms range from <2 Hz (unconscious) to theta, alpha, beta, and low and high gamma. Theta coordinates hippocampal–neocortical interaction during retrieval of conscious episodes. Broadcasting is marked by N2–P3 evoked waveforms.

control actions, and even the detailed firing of neurons and neuronal populations, as shown in biofeedback effects. Consciousness appears to create access to vast unconscious domains of expert knowledge and skill.

A persuasive case can be made that we can create access to any part of the brain by way of conscious input. Consciousness of the feedback appears to be a necessary condition to establish control, though the neural activities themselves remain entirely unconscious. It is as if mere consciousness of results creates access to unconscious neuronal systems that are normally quite autonomous.

The recognition vocabulary of educated speakers of English contains about 100 000 words. Yet all we do as humans to access these complex unconscious bodies of knowledge is to become conscious of a target word. It seems that understanding language demands the gateway of consciousness.

The size of long-term episodic *memory is unknown, but we do know that simply by paying attention to as many as 10 000 distinct pictures over several days, without attempting to memorize them, we can spontaneously recognize more than 90% a week later. Mere consciousness of some event helps to store a recognizable memory of it, and when we re-experience it again, we can distinguish it accurately from millions of other experiences.

The ability to access unconscious processes via consciousness applies also to the vast number of unconscious *automatisms that can be triggered by conscious events, including eye movements evoked by visual motion, the automatic *inner speech that often accompanies reading, the hundreds of muscle groups that control the vocal tract, and those that coordinate and control other skeletal muscles. None of these automatic neuronal mechanisms is conscious in any detail under normal circumstances. Yet they are triggered by conscious events. This triggering function is hampered when the conscious input is degraded by distraction, fatigue, somnolence, sedation, or low signal fidelity.

The major predictions include: (1) The *global access hypothesis*: conscious contents enable widespread, coordinated brain interaction between specialized neuronal assemblies. (2) The **working memory hypothesis*: conscious contents recruit unconscious working memory functions needed for verbal rehearsal,visual semantics, metacognition, and executive functions. (3) Among these working memory capacities are the ability to accurately report on very recent conscious contents; *accurate report* is of course the most commonly used operational index of human conscious experience. Thus GWT is able to explain the most widely used empirical index of consciousness, a classical need for any scientific theory. (4) The *conscious learning hypothesis*. All significant learning is evoked by conscious contents, but the learning process itself may be unconscious.

2. Experimental tests

Dehaene and co-workers have performed experimental tests of *neuronal global workspace models (e.g. Dehaene and Naccache 2001). Because close comparisons between conscious and unconscious conditions are critical for such tests, they have used several methods designed to make such comparisons. The include the *attentional blink, visual backward *masking, *inattentional blindness, and subliminal vision. As dependent measures they have used visual event-related potentials (VERPs) and *functional brain imaging (fMRI), particularly in visual face and word perception regions. In general, they support a neuronal global workspace framework. Particularly striking is the repeated finding that conscious contents evoked widespread brain activity when compared to closely matched unconscious events (Dehaene 2001, Dehaene et al. 2006).

Recent studies of brain rhythms suggest that a similar pattern of findings obtains for endogenous oscillations in the waking state. Melloni et al. (2007) show, for example, that 'synchronization of neural activity across cortical areas correlates with conscious perception'. Similar findings have been reported for at least a decade, both in animals and humans.

Studies of conscious (and unconscious) states show comparable results. Loss of consciousness occurs not just in deep (slow-wave) *sleep, but also in general *anaesthesia, vegetative states due to *brain damage, *epileptic absence seizures, and fainting. While such states are less uniform than they were once thought to be, a number of findings show that the conscious state enables long-range interactivity within the brain, which is generally blocked in unconscious states. In GWT terms, it seems that conscious conditions enable global distribution of information.

3. Functional tests

A crucial question is whether a conception of consciousness is actually able to carry out biological or psychological functions. GWT was derived from applications in *artificial intelligence, as a computational tool to enable multiple specialized processors to cooperatively solve problems that they could not solve individually. GWT has also been built into Franklin's LIDA model, which simulates human expert performance in a complex job-assignment task. Franklin has argued that 'autonomous agents', like living animals and survivable robots, must be equipped with some such capacity. Finally, Shanahan (2006) has proposed that a GW architecture can also resolve the 'frame' problem that is encountered in robotics: as environmental conditions change, how does an autonomous agent know which contextual frame to apply to novel problems? It appears that a GW architecture can serve functions similar to those resolved by conscious processes in the mammalian brain.

Regular updates on GWT and related work can be found at *www.bernardbaars.pbwiki.com* and *http://ccrg.cs.memphis.edu/*

BERNARD J. BAARS

Baars, B. J. (1988). *A Cognitive Theory of Consciousness*.

—— (1997). *In the Theater of Consciousness*.

—— (2002). 'The conscious access hypothesis: origins and recent evidence'. *Trends in Cognitive Science*, 6.

—— and Franklin, S. (2003). 'How conscious experience and working memory interact'. *Trends in Cognitive Science*, 7.

—— —— (2007). 'An architectural model of conscious and unconscious brain functions: global workspace theory and IDA'. *Neural Networks*, 20.

Dehaene, S. and Naccache, L. (2001). 'Towards a cognitive neuroscience of consciousness: basic evidence and a workspace framework'. *Cognition*, 79.

——, Changeux, J. P., Naccache, L., Sackur, J., Sergent, C. (2006). 'Conscious, preconscious, and subliminal processing: a testable taxonomy'. *Trends in Cognitive Science*, 10.

Edelman, G. M. and Tononi, G. (2001). *Consciousness: How Matter Becomes Imagination.*
James, W. (1890). *The Principles of Psychology.*
Melloni, L., Molina, C., Pena, M., Torres, D., Singer, W., and Rodriguez, E. (2007). 'Synchronization of neural activity across cortical areas correlates with conscious perception'. *Journal of Neuroscience*, 27.
Shanahan, M. P. (2006). 'A cognitive architecture that combines internal simulation with a global workspace'. *Consciousness and Cognition*, 15.

grand illusion The phrase 'grand illusion' was first used by Noë et al. (2000) in a critique of work on *change blindness, although it had probably been in informal use before then. The term stuck and has subsequently been used more widely to apply to *inattentional blindness, to other senses, and even to consciousness in general.

The term **illusion* is frequently applied to consciousness, self, and free will—with much consequent confusion. By definition an illusion is something that is not what it seems to be; whether that means an erroneous perception of reality such as a visual illusion, or an erroneous concept or belief about the world. Confusingly, the term is often misinterpreted to mean that something is non-existent. So, for example, when Wegner (2002) claims that conscious will is an illusion he means that we have a false idea about how it works: if someone believes that their conscious thoughts cause their actions they may be wrong, and in this sense conscious will is an illusion. Similarly, when Dennett (1991) describes self as a user illusion he does not mean that there is no self at all, but that it is not the kind of persisting subject of experiences that it seems to be. One problem here is that whether something counts as an illusion depends on what people believe to start with, and in the case of consciousness this is far from clear. Another point to note is that if we say that consciousness is an illusion we must give up the idea that people are infallible about their own experiences.

Change blindness is a curious inability to detect changes in an image when they occur during a saccade or blink, or when the two images are separated by a brief flash or distraction. Under these conditions subjects are very unlikely to notice even large changes, even though they expect to be able to, and are surprised when they cannot. In some of the earliest experiments on change blindness, Blackmore et al. (1995) demonstrated the effect by changing images at the same time as moving them slightly, to simulate an eye movement. They argued that the effect is surprising because people imagine that their visual experience is rich, stable, and detailed and they therefore assume that they would notice if something changes. In fact the visual experience may consist of fleeting retinal images and very sketchy, higher-level representations, along with 'pop-out' mechanisms to redirect attention when required. They concluded that the richness of our visual world is an illusion.

It is important to note that this is not a claim about a reality/appearance distinction or about the veridicality of perception (as it would be for visual illusions or perceptual errors); it is a claim about the nature of vision itself—that people believe that their visual experience is richer and more stable than it is.

Such errors had been noted before. For example, when we look around the world it appears to be stable, even though our head moves around, and our eyes make saccades several times a second. What we see may seem to be something like a large picture that is coloured and detailed all over, when in fact we have blind spots where nothing can be seen, resolution drops rapidly from the centre of the field of view to the periphery, and only the central area, or fovea, responds well to colour. As Dennett (1991) pointed out, many people are surprised to discover these facts, implying that they held false views to begin with. In fact, he argued, much less information is available in vision than our subjective impression leads us to believe.

The change blindness research also seemed to challenge another common assumption about the nature of vision. That is, that the brain takes in information from the eyes and processes it in order to construct a rich and detailed internal representation of the external world that then becomes conscious experience. On this assumption the contents of visual awareness are an internal model of the world. Change blindness seemed to challenge this because if we have detailed representations in our head then we ought to be able to compare them with the visual input and easily detect changes.

In fact there are many possible interpretations here, and the subsequent theories of change blindness cover a wide range of ideas. Many argue that we use the world as an external memory rather than constructing detailed internal models but they then differ over just what kind of *representations vision uses, and how detailed and long-lasting they are (Simons 2000, Noë 2002). Perhaps the most extreme are the enactive or *sensorimotor theories of perception. For example O'Regan and Noë (2001) argue that our visual experience consists in our practical knowledge of the way that our own actions and sensory stimulation depend on each other. In other words, seeing is action, not representation.

According to all these theories vision is an illusion in the following sense—to the extent that people believe that seeing means absorbing lots of information and building up a picture inside their heads that they then consciously experience they are wrong. So vision is not the way it seems to be.

Finally, the term 'grand illusion' is sometimes extended to the idea that we are similarly deluded about consciousness in general. As with vision, this has to start with what people generally believe about their own consciousness. One traditional and very popular assumption is that consciousness is something like a theatre in which a conscious observer experiences the stream of conscious contents appearing as though in the spotlight on a stage. Most versions of this entail what Dennett (1991) refers to as the 'Cartesian theatre' which, he argues, cannot exist because it would involve a time or place where previously unconscious brain processes come together, or a finishing line that brain processes have to cross to mark the order in which they enter the stage and are shown to a conscious observer. But neither the show nor the observer can be found in the brain; it simply is not organized that way, and has no need of them.

Another related assumption is that the brain contains both conscious and unconscious processes and that detecting these might uncover the neural *correlates of consciousness. Another is that waking life consists of a unified stream of conscious experiences perceived by a conscious self. Although James (1890) coined the term '*stream of consciousness' he expressed doubts about our ability to introspect on its nature. He said the attempt is like 'trying to turn up the gas quickly enough to see how the darkness looks' (i, 244). Similarly, Jaynes (1976) compares it with shining a flashlight around looking for a place where the light is not shining. Blackmore (2004) likens this flashlight to asking ourselves such questions as 'Am I conscious now?'. Whenever we ask ourselves this question the answer is always yes, and whenever we ask 'What am I conscious of?' we can always find something that we take to be the contents of consciousness. We then leap to the erroneous conclusion that this is always the case. Instead, she suggests that when we are not asking such questions (i.e. most of the time), there are no *contents of consciousness and no one to experience them. Instead the brain carries out multiple tasks in parallel, attributing consciousness to them only after the fact. In this way an illusion of continuity and of a self experiencing a stream of experiences is created.

This is similar to Dennett's (1991) *multiple drafts theory, which suggests that there are no fixed facts about the stream of consciousness independent of particular probes. That is, we may think that there must always be a fact of the matter about what a given person is conscious of at a given time, because whenever we probe them appropriately there seems to be, but in fact there is not.

These are just some of the way in which common assumptions about the nature of consciousness may be completely wrong. In this sense consciousness, as well as vision, may be a grand illusion.

SUSAN BLACKMORE

Blackmore, S. (2004). *A Very Short Introduction to Consciousness.*

——, Brelstaff, G., Nelson, K., and Troscianko, T. (1995). 'Is the richness of our visual world an illusion? Transsaccadic memory for complex scenes'. *Perception*, 24.

Dennett, D. C. (1991). *Consciousness Explained.*

James, W. (1890). *The Principles of Psychology.*

Jaynes, J. (1976). *The Origins of Consciousness in the Breakdown of the Bicameral Mind.*

Noë, A. (2002). *Is the Visual World a Grand Illusion?*

——, Pessoa, L. and Thompson, E. (2000). 'Beyond the grand illusion: what change blindness really teaches us about vision'. *Visual Cognition*, 7.

O'Regan, J. K. and Noë, A. (2001). 'A sensorimotor account of vision and visual consciousness'. *Behavioral and Brain Sciences*, 24.

Simons, D. J. (2000). 'Current approaches to change blindness'. *Visual Cognition*, 7.

Wegner, D. (2002). *The Illusion of Conscious Will.*

grandmother neuron See SINGLE-CELL STUDIES

habituation See CONDITIONING; INFANT CONSCIOUSNESS

hallucination Derived from Greek (*aluô*) through Latin (*alucino/halucino*), to wander in mind, talk idly/unreasonably, the term hallucination has held many different meanings over the centuries, linked as much to the spirit world and demonic possession as to mental illness. Its current usage can be traced to the birth of psychiatry as a discipline and the definition of a class of conscious experiences by one of psychiatry's founding fathers, Jean-Etienne Esquirol (1772–1840):

> A person is said to labor under a hallucination, or to be a visionary, who has a thorough conviction of the perception of a sensation, when no external object, suited to excite this sensation, has impressed the senses.

The rationale for separating hallucinations from other conscious experiences was that they might provide a marker for mental pathology. Yet in this hope psychiatry was confronted with a problem. Central to the definition was the absence of an external object, a criterion met by a large part of our waking and sleeping consciousness in experiences such as *imagery, afterimages (see AFTER-EFFECTS, PERCEPTUAL), and *dreams. Furthermore, an early achievement of experimental psychology was the recognition that normal perception was far from being a faithful representation of the world around us. Lack of a suitable external object was clearly not in itself sufficient to mark an experience as pathological. Today we recognize a family of perceptual experiences related in varying degree to external objects, some with links to pathological states of the brain and mind, others not. At one end of the spectrum lie normal percepts—mental constructions constrained by objects in the world around us. At the other end lie hallucinations, imagery, and dreams—mental constructions without the constraint of an external object. Illusions, afterimages, eidetic images (the positive afterimages of photographic memory), and *synaesthetic experience lie somewhere between these two extremes.

Hallucinations are indistinguishable from normal, externally driven percepts, their true nature only becoming apparent through rational appraisal. For example, a bizarre feature or anomaly such as inappropriate size or incongruous location may be observed in an experience that indicates it to be false. Alternatively, the experience may be put to the test, e.g. by reaching out to touch it or questioning a second observer as to its presence. Recurrent hallucinations may be recognized through remembering previous encounters. The term *pseudohallucination* is sometimes used to refer to a specific subtype of hallucination that is recognized as false, contrasting with true hallucinations that are accepted as reality, the two being otherwise indistinguishable in terms of their *phenomenology. Confusingly, the same term is also sometimes used to refer to vivid imagery experiences. While normal percepts are phenomenologically identical to hallucinations, imagery is not. The perceptual locus of imagery and hallucinations differs, with hallucinations typically projecting externally to the world and imagery located internally in the mind's eye, ear, or *body schema. Hallucinations are more vivid than imagery, and imagery is under volitional control whereas hallucinations are not. Hallucinations are broadly classified by the sensory modality they involve (i.e. visual, auditory, tactile, olfactory, or gustatory), although many cross modality boundaries and may be simultaneously seen, heard, and felt.

What causes hallucinations? The question may not have a single answer, as many differing normal and pathological states give rise to the same class of phenomena. Hallucinations are perhaps most commonly experienced in the healthy population at the margins of sleep, termed **hypnagogic* at sleep onset and *hypnopompic* at sleep's end. They are experienced in the context of the use of psychedelic drugs, particularly LSD, mescaline, psilocybin, cocaine, and MDMA (ecstasy; see HALLUCINOGENIC DRUGS). Some subjects experience the phenomena when deprived of sensory stimulation, for example in caves. Repetitive stimulation by light at certain frequencies induces visual hallucinations in some subjects.

In the clinical realm, hallucinations are found in a range of psychotic disorders where they are typically accepted as reality by the patients experiencing them. These disorders include *schizophrenia, where hallucinations tend to be of voices talking about the patient, and manic-depressive psychosis, where the hallucinations fit with the patient's mood—bleak when depressed, exuberant when elated. In *delirium, particularly if related to alcohol withdrawal, hallucinations are visual and frightening, e.g. swarms of small animals. Both visual and auditory hallucinations occur in Alzheimer's disease and other *dementias such as Lewy body dementia where the presence of visual hallucinations helps diagnose the condition. In Parkinson's disease, patients experience both visual and auditory hallucinations but may also sense a presence without the involvement of a specific sensory modality (*extracampine hallucinations*). Epileptic seizures involving sensory cortex are associated with hallucinations (*sensory auras*), the modality of the hallucination defined by the location of the seizure, e.g. the smell of burning rubber if in the temporal lobe, pinpricks of light and fireworks if in visual cortex, and sounds if in auditory cortex. The same is true of migraine, the location of the underlying pathophysiology defining the modality of the aura hallucination, typically a zigzag pattern in association with pathophysiological change in the visual cortex. Patients undergoing surgery to treat *epilepsy may have hallucinations induced during the operation by direct stimulation of the cortex. In narcolepsy, a disorder of sleep regulation, patients experience terrifying visual hallucinations at the margins of sleep, sometimes while simultaneously paralysed by a sleep-related loss of muscle tone. Eye disease and lesions of the visual pathways (see BRAIN DAMAGE) are associated with visual hallucinations, typically geometrical patterns, disembodied faces and figures in elaborate costume often sporting flamboyant hats or wigs. Auditory pathway lesions are associated with the sound of heavenly choirs.

Although the different circumstances and clinical states in which hallucinations occur appear to have little in common, from one perspective they are all the same. In each, a conscious experience has arisen without a change in sensory input. In terms of the underlying neurobiology, the neural *correlate of a conscious percept has occurred without being triggered by sensory input from an external object. This property of hallucinations provides an opportunity to study the neural mechanisms of conscious perception in isolation. Under normal perceptual circumstances, a change in an external object results in a change in afferent input and a mixture of brain activities, some related to conscious perception, others to the unconscious processing of the input, but all 'correlating' with the conscious experience of a perceptual change. To characterize the neural substrate of perceptual consciousness, *functional brain imaging studies must devise ways to dissociate the different types of activity—the solution provided by hallucinations being that sensory input remains constant while conscious perception changes (ffytche 2000). Imaging studies of brain activity during a hallucination thus provide a guide to the correlate of consciousness for the type of percept hallucinated. This approach has been used to identify correlates of visual consciousness through imaging studies of visual hallucinations. Such studies have found that individual visual hallucination episodes are linked to spontaneous increases in activity within specialized regions of the visual system, with the content of a given hallucination defined by where the increase in activity is located. For example, if located in cortex specialized for faces, the associated hallucination will be of a face. If located in cortex specialized for colour, the associated hallucination will be of a colour, and so forth (ffytche et al. 1998). For auditory hallucinations, spontaneous increases in activity are found within motor and sensory components of language circuitry (Lennox et al. 2000). The neural correlate of consciousness for specific visual experiences revealed by studies of hallucinations thus appears to be localized within individual, specialized cortical areas. The hallucination evidence lends support to the theory of *microconsciousness (Zeki 2001) and the view that the difference between consciously perceiving or unconsciously processing a sensory attribute is the addition of an extra level of neural processing or representation within the relevant specialized cortical region (Zeki and ffytche 1998, ffytche 2002, Moutoussis and Zeki 2002, Pins and ffytche 2003). A hallucination is the perceptual manifestation of this extra level of processing when triggered without appropriate sensory input.

The use of hallucinations to explore consciousness is not new. Scientists, clinicians, and philosophers alike have long used them to gain insights into the workings of the mind and consciousness. Such studies began in the 18th century when Charles Bonnet used hallucinations to develop a theory of how brain and mind are related (see CHARLES BONNET SYNDROME). In the clinical realm, the psychoanalytical tradition has used hallucinations as a window in consciousness through which to examine the unconscious. Drug-induced hallucinations and allied phenomena, as well as hallucinations induced by sensory deprivation and photic stimulation, were used throughout the 20th century to study issues as diverse as creativity, schizophrenia, the neurobiology of vision, and the boundaries of human consciousness. The use of hallucinations to study the neural correlates of consciousness continues these long-standing traditions and provides a unique perspective into their neurobiology.

DOMINIC H. FFYTCHE

ffytche, D. H. (2000). 'Imaging conscious vision'. In Metzinger, T. (ed.) *Neural Correlates of Consciousness: Empirical and Conceptual Questions*.

—— (2002). 'Neural codes for conscious vision'. *Trends in Cognitive Sciences*, 6.

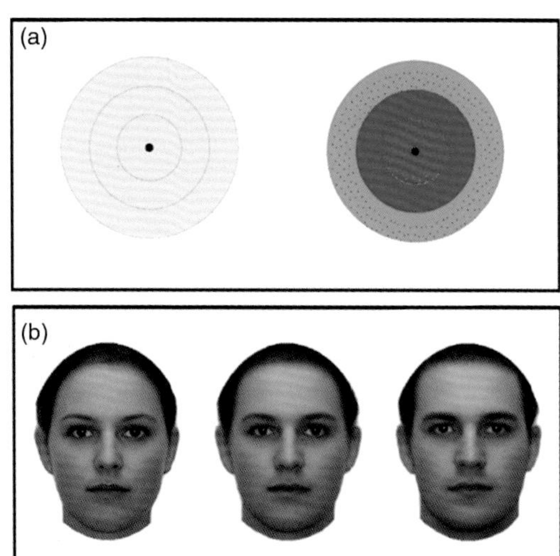

Colour Plate 1. Opponent visual after-effects. (a) Colour afterimages. The three concentric circles on the left are identical in colour. To colour these circles, stare for 20 s at the small black dot in the middle of the three coloured circles on the right, holding your fixation as steady as possible. At the end of this adaptation period, shift your gaze to the black dot in the centre of the uncoloured figure on the left. The illusory colours you experience should be the complements to the real colours in the adaptation figure. (b) Face adaptation. The middle photograph constitutes a gender-neutral face, and the two photographs on either side of the neutral face are versions biased toward female (left) and toward male (right). Maintain fixation on the right-hand photograph for 20 s or so and then look at the middle photograph—for the first few seconds, it should look more 'female'. Next, adapt for 20 s to the left-hand photograph and notice how the appearance of the gender-neutral face now looks more 'male'. Photographs courtesy of Tamara Watson and Colin Clifford, University of Sydney.

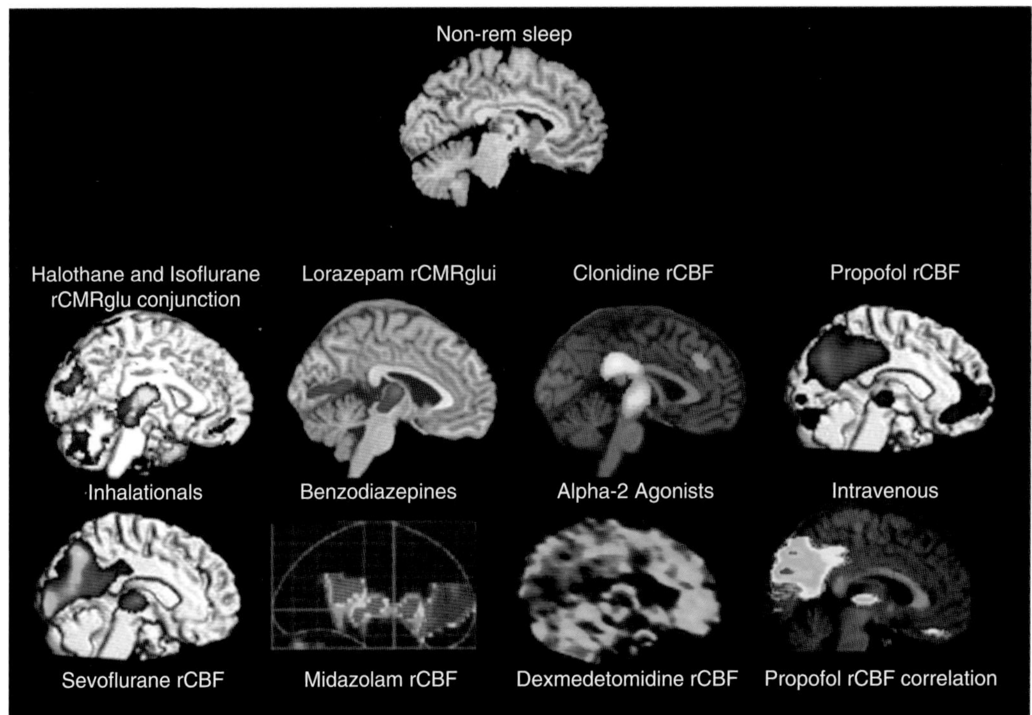

Colour Plate 2. The regional effects of anaesthetics on brain function are shown in humans who were given various anaesthetic agents at doses that caused, or nearly caused, a loss of consciousness. The data are from eight different groups of investigators and encompass the study of eight different agents and normal non-REM sleep (as detailed in Alkire and Miller 2005). The agents studied were halothane and isoflurane, lorazepam, clonidine, propofol, sevoflurane, midazolam, dexmedetomidine, and sleep. The regional effects were measured using techniques based on either blood flow or glucose metabolism. The images were reoriented, and resized to allow for easy comparisons between studies. The original colour scales were used. Nevertheless, all images show regional decreases of activity caused by anaesthesia (or sleep) compared to the awake state, except the propofol correlation image, which shows where increasing anaesthetic dose correlates with decreasing blood flow. The figure identifies that the regional suppressive effects of anaesthetics on the thalamus is a common finding associated with anaesthetic-induced unconsciousness and sleep.

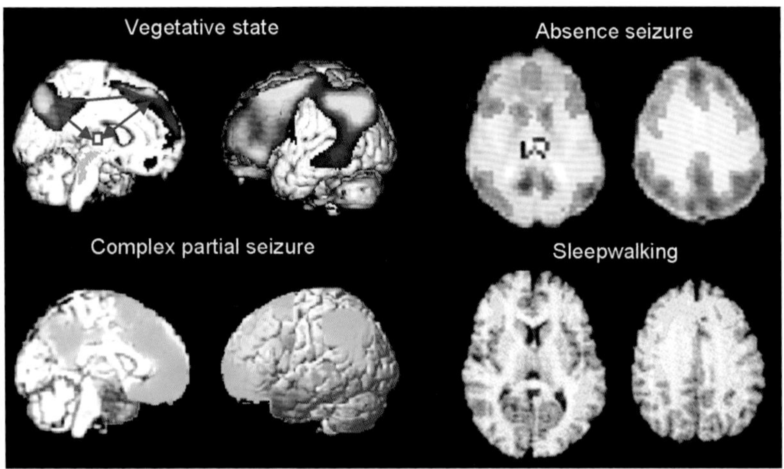

Colour Plate 3. The neuronal global workspace underlying awareness in pathological dissociations of awareness and arousal. The common hallmark of the vegetative state is a metabolic dysfunctioning of a widespread cortical network encompassing medial and lateral prefrontal and parietal multimodal associative areas. This is due to either direct cortical damage or to cortico-cortical or cortico-thalamocortical disconnections (shown by blue arrows). The arousal systems in the brainstem and mesencephalon remain intact (green). Recent functional imaging studies in similar, albeit much more transient, dissociations between wakefulness and awareness resulting in 'automatic' unwilled action have shown decreased blood flow in this frontoparietal network when patients suffer from complex partial seizures (in green), absence seizures (in blue), and sleepwalking (in yellow).

Colour Plate 4. Technique devised by Volkmann et al. (1980). Light is passed into the mouth via a fibre-optic cable and transilluminates the retina via the palatine bone.

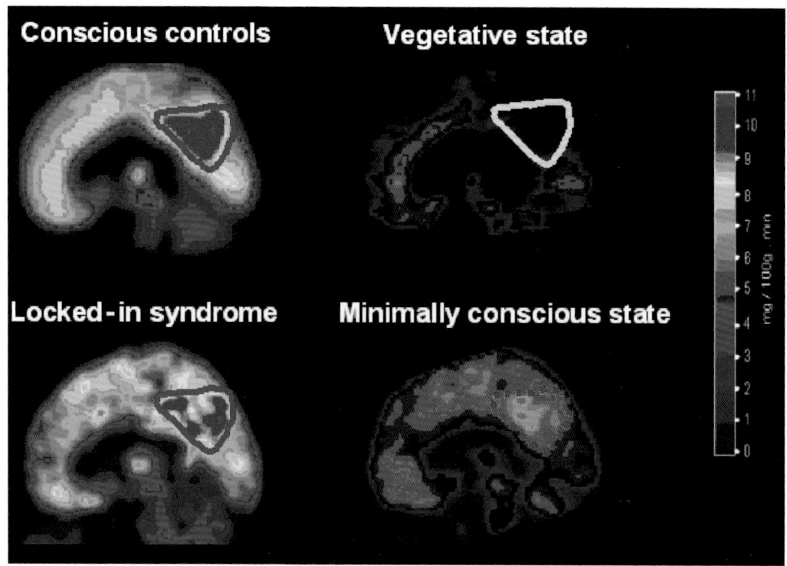

Colour Plate 5. In normal conscious waking, the medial posterior cortex (encompassing the precuneus and adjacent posterior cingulate cortex, delineated by a red line) is the metabolically most active region of the brain; in waking vegetative patients, this same area (delineated by a blue line) is the metabolically least active region. In the locked-in syndrome, no supratentorial brain region shows significant decreases in metabolism. In the minimally conscious state, the precuneus and posterior cingulate cortex shows an intermediate metabolism, higher than in vegetative patients, but lower than in conscious controls. We hypothesize that this region represents part of the neural network subserving (human) consciousness. Reproduced from Laureys et al. (2004).

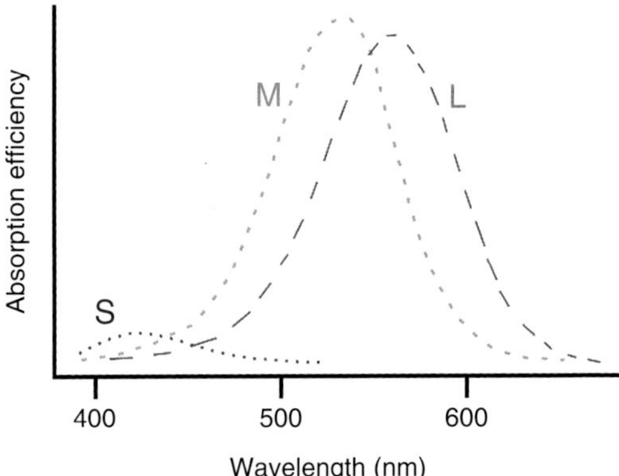

Colour Plate 6. The retina contains three types of daylight photoreceptors called *cones*. Each type contains a different light-sensitive pigment which absorbs light and produces neural signals in response. The three pigments are sensitive to short- (blueish), medium- (greenish), or long- (reddish) wavelength lights as shown above, and are hence referred to as S, M, and L cones.

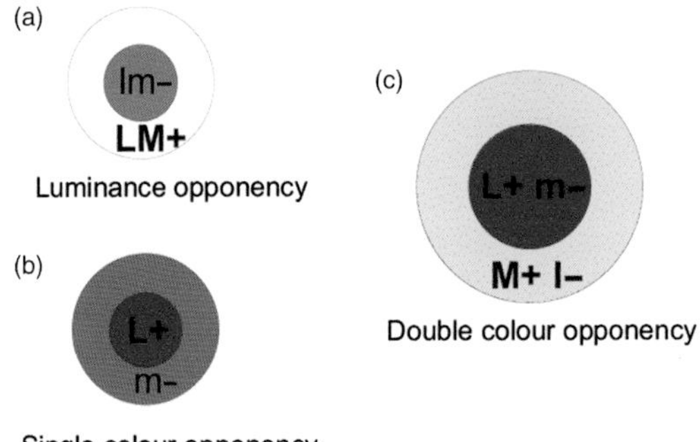

Colour Plate 7. Outputs from cones feed into cells further into the visual system with a 'centre–surround' spatial organization. (a) At the start of the M-channel combined L and M cone signals in one part of visual space inhibit a cell while the same combination in the surrounding part of space excite it (inhibition and excitation switch roles in other cells). The result is a cell which is sensitive to luminance contrast (edges). (b) At the start of the P-channel L and M cone signals are not combined but are themselves put into opposition. For example, L signals in one part of visual space excite a cell while the M signals in the surrounding part of space inhibit it (inhibition and excitation switch roles in other cells; there are also cells which have inputs from S cones). The result is a cell which is sensitive to variation in the wavelength of light but whose response does not change as luminance varies. (c) In primary visual cortex, combinations of cone signal with excitatory and inhibitory action are put into spatial opposition. Unlike the cells in (b) these 'double-opponent' cells are sensitive to chromatic contrast.

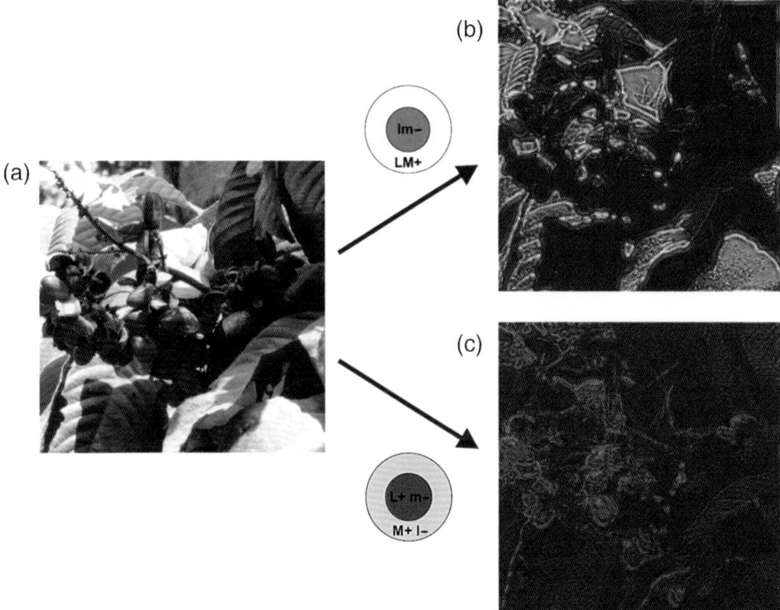

Colour Plate 8. Chromatic contrast can be more useful in detecting the edges of objects than brightness contrast, which is often due to lighting effects such as shadows. The cone activations elicited by the image (a) were used to compute areas of high brightness contrast (b) and high colour contrast (from L and M cone signals). Brightness contrast is detected by luminance opponent cells in the retina and LGN. Colour contrast is detected only by double opponent cells in striate cortex. The photograph and cone activation data were kindly supplied by Professor T. Troscianko and Dr P. G. Lovell, from Lovell et al. (2005). The image processing is by the author (RWK).

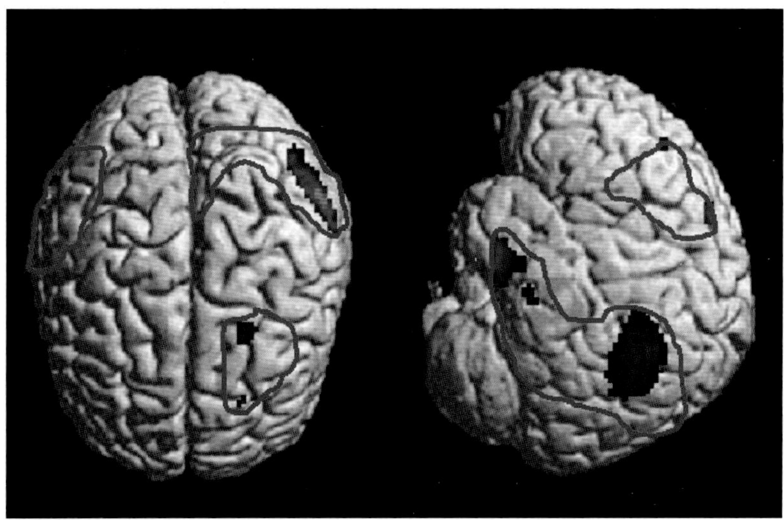

Colour Plate 9. A brain structural image is represented from a dorsal (left image) and lateral view (right image). The plain red lines indicate cerebral regions where the metabolism is significantly decreased in Alzheimer's disease compared to controls. The red 'blobs' illustrate regions where the cerebral activity is correlated to the degree of anosognosia for cognitive impairment (measured by a discrepancy score between patient and relative).

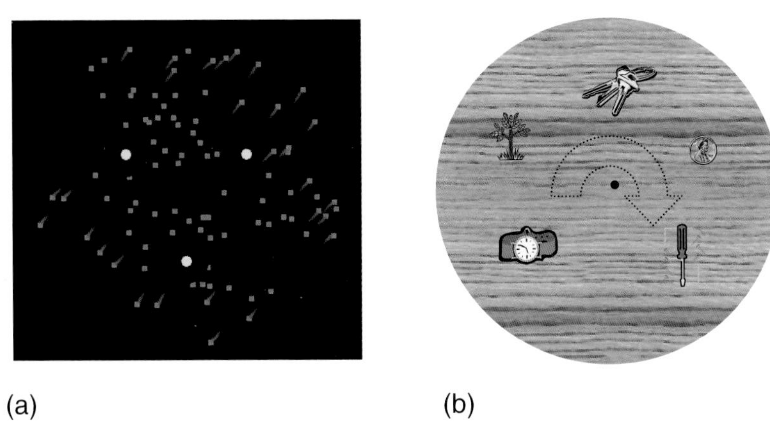

Colour Plate 10. Typical stimuli that produce motion-induced blindness. (a) A snapshot of a dynamic computer display in which the blue dots produce a three-dimensional sphere that rotates around, while the yellow dots are static. With steady fixation, observers report the disappearance of one or more yellow dots for periods of a few seconds at a time. (b) Illustration of a physical set-up that produces MIB. Several salient objects are placed on a static transparent glass surface, under which a textured plate can be rotated. When the textured surface is set in motion while observers fixate in the centre, the objects often disappear.

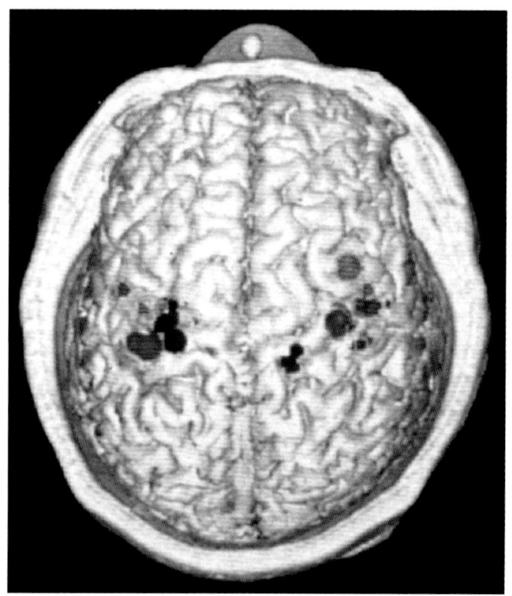

Colour Plate 11. Magnetoencephalogram confirming the remapping hypothesis.

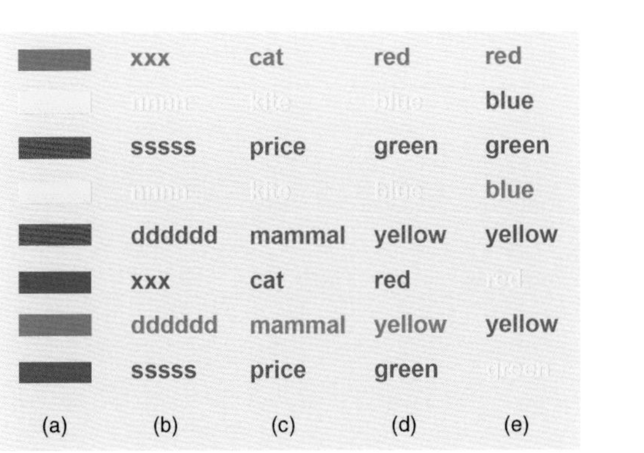

Colour Plate 12. Stroop task and its experimental conditions. The effect is quite readily experienced: for each column, name aloud the eight colours as rapidly as possible, ignoring the printed characters. To measure performance, start a stopwatch, then name aloud the eight colours in a column, then stop the stopwatch. Record the time and do the same for the remaining columns. The conditions are (a) colour patch neutral, (b) non-word neutral, (c) word-neutral, (d) incongruent, and (e) 'super' incongruent. Stroop himself used the colour patch neutral condition; most researchers today use either the non-word or the word-neutral condition. Stroop interference is the time difference between the incongruent condition and any of the neutral conditions, a cost due to the word's incompatibility with the colour to be named. The three neutral conditions will not differ much from each other in response time (although the word-neutral usually will be a little slower) but the incongruent condition will be substantially slower. Condition (e) is a special case of the incongruent condition in which each successive colour names the word that had to be ignored in the preceding stimulus. This version of the incongruent condition ordinarily produces the most interference, combining standard Stroop interference with *negative priming*, the incremental cost in responding with a colour name that has just been ignored (permitting colour naming to be accomplished on the preceding trial).

—— et al. (1998). 'The anatomy of conscious vision: an fMRI study of visual hallucinations'. *Nature Neuroscience*, 1.

Lennox, B. R. et al. (2000). 'The functional anatomy of auditory hallucinations in schizophrenia'. *Psychiatry Research: Neuroimaging*, 100.

Moutoussis, K. and Zeki, S. (2002). 'The relationship between cortical activation and perception investigated with invisible stimuli'. *Proceedings of the National Academy of Sciences of the USA*, 99.

Pins, D. and ffytche, D. H. (2003). 'The neural correlates of conscious vision'. *Cerebral Cortex*, 13.

Zeki, S. (2001). 'Localization and globalization in conscious vision'. *Annual Review of Neuroscience*, 24.

—— and ffytche, D. H. (1998). 'The Riddoch syndrome: insights into the neurobiology of conscious vision'. *Brain*, 121.

hallucinogenic drugs It makes perfect sense that this volume would contain an entry on hallucinogens, as these drugs produce more profound effects on human consciousness than nearly any other class of psychoactive substance. These materials, also referred to in the past as *psychotomimetics*, and in the popular culture as *psychedelics* (and more recently as *entheogens*), have been with us for millennia, although our modern awareness of them dates mostly from the 1960s and early 1970s when their use was associated with the so-called 'hippy' culture. Because of the unusual psychopharmacology of these substances, even the name for this class has been controversial. The name hallucinogen suggests that they produce hallucinations, but they do not, except perhaps at very high doses. 'Psychotomimetic' connotes the possibility that their effects produce a model psychosis, an early idea that was disproved. 'Psychedelic' is a popular term that has been interpreted to mean that these substances manifest some beneficial qualities of the mind. This name has never been widely embraced in formal scientific circles, although it is the most popular name in the popular culture and in the media. 'Entheogen' is a term that recently has been gaining in popularity, particularly on the Internet, and reflects a belief that these drugs can manifest or reveal 'the god within'.

Agreement on a name for the class has been difficult because there is no complete consensus as to what these substances do. A good general description of the class is that they are drugs that produce changes in consciousness that do not otherwise occur except during dreaming or at times of religious exaltation (see ALTERED STATE OF CONSCIOUSNESS). This characterization is most relevant at higher dosages, because at lower or modest doses these drugs primarily distort and alter sensory perceptions. The visual field may seem to wave and undulate, and kaleidoscopic colours may be seen with the eyes closed. Music may be perceived as brilliant colours and shapes, in a *synaesthesia, or merging of the senses; the sense of time may be altered in that intervals of a few minutes may be perceived as lasting for hours. The senses of *touch, smell, and taste may be amplified or exaggerated, and colours may be perceived as brighter and more radiant.

Physiological functions such as body temperature, heart rate, or blood pressure are generally unaffected by any direct action of the drug. Drugs in this class are not addictive, and no overdose deaths have been described, although a few fatalities occurred when individuals had access to bulk amounts of pure LSD. Death and serious injury also have occurred when individuals were impaired by the effect of the drug and engaged in activities such as swimming, mountain climbing, etc.

The most serious consequences of use are psychological; these drugs may precipitate psychosis or other psychiatric disorders in susceptible individuals, or may exacerbate pre-existing illnesses. Although rare, suicide following use of psychedelics is not unknown. There is no evidence, however, that serious psychiatric illness is caused in healthy, well-adjusted individuals.

The historical use of these materials extends back many millennia. In ancient India a substance known as *Soma* was revered for its ability to provide visions of paradise—its power celebrated by many hymns of praise in the Rig Vedas. Persuasive arguments have been made that *Soma* may have been a mushroom, *Amanita muscaria*, but the evidence is far from conclusive and today we simply do not know the identity of *Soma*.

In the village of Eleusis, in ancient Greece, for nearly 2000 years, a yearly ritual each autumn involved a ceremony centred on the use of a beverage known as *kykeon*. Although we know very little about this ceremony, because to speak of it was punishable by death, the little that has survived suggests that *kykeon* may have had hallucinogenic properties. A central component of *kykeon* was barley, and it has been speculated that barley contaminated with a species of the ergot fungus may have been a key ingredient. Ergot is the source of ergot alkaloids, many of which are potent psychoactive agents, and which also serve as the source of lysergic acid, the chemical scaffold for lysergic acid diethylamide (LSD), the most potent hallucinogenic agent known.

In South America and Mexico, the Aztecs used several substances dating to pre-Columbian times, the most well known being *teonanacatl*, *peyotl*, and *ololuiqui*. All of these had uses in social and religious rituals. We know today that they all have similar effects, and their active components have similar pharmacological properties. *Teonanacatl* ('god's flesh') were species of psilocybin mushrooms such as *Psilocybe mexicana*. They grow widely throughout the world, and in addition to their traditional sacred uses in Mexico, are used recreationally today. Their active component is a tryptamine derivative known as psilocybin. *Peyotl* was the peyote cactus,

Lophophora williamsii, used at the present time as a sacrament by the Native American Church. The dried tops, or 'buttons', of the cactus are ingested during an all-night religious ceremony. The active component in peyote is mescaline, a simple phenethylamine. *Olouiqui* are the seeds of species of morning glories, which have been shown to contain lysergamide, or ergine, a chemical structure closely related to that of LSD.

One of the most remarkable studies to have come out of the 1960s has been called the 'Good Friday Experiment'. Dr Walter Pahnke gave either psilocybin or placebo to 20 theology students during a 1962 Good Friday service in a Boston chapel. In this setting, a high percentage of subjects given psilocybin experienced effects that were indistinguishable from spontaneous mystical experiences. This report occurred during a period when there was considerable debate as to whether psychedelic drugs could produce 'authentic' *religious experiences. From an objective and scientific view, there was no evidence that psychedelic drug-induced transcendent experiences differed in any fundamental way from spontaneous ones. More recently, Griffiths and colleagues at Johns Hopkins University (Griffiths et al. 2006) have extended this finding, showing that when administered under supportive conditions, psilocybin occasioned experiences similar to spontaneously occurring mystical states, producing sustained positive changes in attitudes and behaviour consistent with changes rated by community observers.

In addition to these molecules, there are others that occur in nature with a history of use by indigenous peoples. For example, *N,N*-dimethyltryptamine (DMT) occurs naturally in many plant species, and indeed has been detected as a trace component of human cerebrospinal fluid. This finding led to research aimed at identifying whether or not DMT might be an endogenous material that produced psychosis or *schizophrenia, but no positive correlations were ever found. A similar compound, 5-methoxy-*N,N*-dimethyltryptamine, is also found in nature and has been used by natives in the Amazon basin in the form of snuffs. This substance is extremely potent, and can cause a rapid loss of contact from reality.

Except for mescaline, all of the naturally-occurring hallucinogens of this type contain a tryptamine molecular framework within their structures (see Fig. H1), which is also the basic scaffold for the natural neurotransmitter molecule serotonin (5-HT). Although mescaline (and chemically related synthetic molecules) does not resemble serotonin in structure, it nevertheless also produces its effects through a mechanism that involves brain serotonin circuitry.

Our modern awareness of hallucinogens occurred subsequent to the accidental discovery of the profound effects of LSD (LSD-25). LSD was first synthesized in 1938 by Dr Albert Hofmann, a natural products chemist at the Sandoz Pharmaceutical Laboratories in Basel, Switzerland. During the resynthesis of a sample in 1943, he accidentally ingested an unknown amount, which led to an unusual intoxication. Three days later, to confirm that the effects were due to the LSD, he ingested a solution containing 0.25 mg of LSD tartrate. This dose was sufficient to produce a profound effect, and in fact later clinical research typically employed only 0.1 mg as a standard dose (Hofmann 1979a, 1979b).

It was only six years later, in 1949, that the molecular structure of serotonin was reported. The obvious relationship between the chemical structure of serotonin and LSD provoked intense research interest in the role of serotonin in the brain. The basis for mental illness was not understood in that era, and it was not widely appreciated that disturbances in brain chemistry could produce changes in behaviour. Thus, these two events, occurring so close in time, strengthened ideas that mental illness was a result of brain neurochemistry, and catalysed research into the neuroscience of brain serotonin systems that continues to the present day.

The principal target for LSD and other hallucinogenic drugs is a type of brain serotonin receptor known as the 5-HT_{2A} receptor. Evidence so far indicates that hallucinogens activate this receptor, leading to the production of at least four biochemical second messengers known as inositol phosphates, diacylglycerol, arachidonic acid, and 2-arachidonyl glycerol. In humans, ketanserin, a drug that prevents hallucinogens from binding to the 5-HT_{2A} receptor, blocks their effects.

This type of serotonin receptor is heavily expressed on neurons known as pyramidal cells, in the *frontal cortex of the brain. These cells are the major functional units in the cortex, and are involved in processes of higher cognition and integration of sensory information. Serotonin 5-HT_{2A} receptors are also located in the thalamus, a sort of gateway for the transmission of sensory data to the cortex, and in the reticular nucleus of the thalamus, a sheath of cells wrapped around the thalamus that strongly modulates the thalamic gating process. Current theories of consciousness posit that corticothalamic loops are an essential functional component of consciousness, and that idea is compatible with the localization of 5-HT_{2A} receptors in cortex and thalamus, where it might be speculated that activation of these receptors would have a profound disrupting effect on consciousness.

Hallucinogens also affect function in other brain areas, either by direct action on 5-HT_{2A} receptors, or indirectly, through effects at other sites for the neurotransmitters serotonin and dopamine. The most important of these are evolutionarily old areas in the midbrain known as the

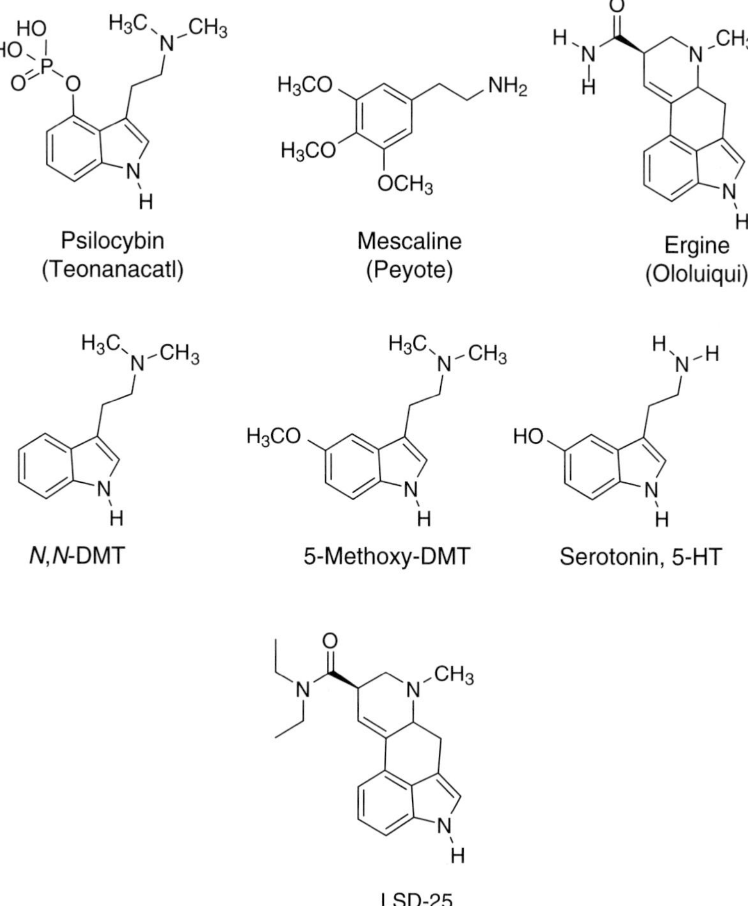

Fig. H1. Molecular structures of hallucinogenic drugs.

raphe nuclei, and locus coeruleus. They represent the source of brain serotonin and norepinephrine (noradrenaline), respectively, with their axons widely and diffusely innervating vast areas of the brain, including the cortex. A third region, the ventral tegmental area (VTA), is the origin of dopamine axons that also project to the cortex as well as limbic areas of the brain. These brain areas send projections not only to the cortex, but to a number of areas essential for various aspects of cognition, memory, and emotion. Serotonin, norepinephrine, and dopamine are all known to modulate cortical cell activity, and hallucinogens disrupt normal function in these systems.

There had been no clinical research on hallucinogens in the United States since they were placed in the most restrictive drug category, Schedule I of the Controlled Substances Act. In the mid 1990s Dr Rick Strassman, at the University of New Mexico, initiated the first human studies with DMT in the 'modern era' (Strassman and Qualls 1994, Strassman et al. 1994, Strassman 1996) Since then a number of other research projects have been reported. Europe has been particularly active in that regard, with several studies from Germany, and the most extensive clinical research being reported by Dr Franz Vollenweider in Zurich (e.g. see Hasler et al. 2004).

Currently, there appears to be a resurgence of interest in these substances, and within the past few years a small pilot study has been completed at the University of Arizona examining the efficacy of psilocybin in treating obsessive-compulsive disorder (OCD). As of this writing, another study is under way at UCLA to examine the effects of psilocybin in dying patients, to determine whether it can reduce anxiety and improve mood. Most recently, workers at Johns Hopkins University (Griffiths et al. 2006) have completed a remarkable study of psilocybin in drug-naive subjects. Essentially an extension of the original Good Friday experiment, but with better experimental design, controls, and data analysis, and volunteers who were not theology students, a high percentage of subjects experienced effects resembling mystical/religious states, which they reported to be some of the most profound experiences in their entire lives.

For a comprehensive recent treatise that expands on this discussion, primarily from a scientific perspective, but which also includes some historical information see the review by Nichols (2004).

DAVID E. NICHOLS

Griffiths, R., Richards, W., McCann, U. and Jesse, R. (2006). 'Psilocybin can occasion mystical-type experiences having substantial and sustained personal meaning and spiritual significance'. *Psychopharmacology*, 187.

Hasler, F., Grimberg, U., Benz, M. A., Huber, T., and Vollenweider, F. X. (2004). 'Acute psychological and physiological effects of psilocybin in healthy humans: a double-blind, placebo-controlled dose-effect study'. *Psychopharmacology (Berlin)*, 172.

Hofmann, A. (1979a). 'How LSD originated'. *Journal of Psychedelic Drugs*, 11.

—— (1979b). *LSD: My Problem Child.*

Nichols, D. E. (2004). 'Hallucinogens'. *Pharmacology and Therapeutics*, 101.

Strassman, R. J. (1996). 'Human psychopharmacology of *N,N*-dimethyltryptamine'. *Behavioral and Brain Research*, 73.

—— and Qualls, C. R. (1994). 'Dose-response study of *N,N*-dimethyltryptamine in humans. I. Neuroendocrine, autonomic, and cardiovascular effects'. *Archives of General Psychiatry*, 51.

——, Qualls, C. R., Uhlenhuth, E. H. and Kellner, R. (1994). 'Dose-response study of *N,N*-dimethyltryptamine in humans. II. Subjective effects and preliminary results of a new rating scale'. *Archives of General Psychiatry*, 51.

hard problem of consciousness As I type these words, cognitive systems in my brain engage in visual and auditory information processing. This processing is accompanied by states of phenomenal consciousness, such as the auditory experience of hearing the tap-tap-tap of the keyboard and the visual experience of seeing the letters appear on the screen. How does my brain's activity generate those experiences? Why those and not others? Indeed, why is any physical event accompanied by conscious experience? The set of such problems is known as the hard problem of consciousness.

1. The problem
2. History
3. Deflationist approaches
4. Non-deflationist physicalism
5. Fundamental theories

1. The problem

The hard problem was distinguished from various 'easy' problems of consciousness by David Chalmers (1995); others, such as Galen Strawson (1994: Ch. 4.4), had drawn similar contrasts before then. Examples of the easy problems include explaining the reportability of one's own states of consciousness, the integration of information, the discrimination and categorization of environmental stimuli, the focus of attention, and the deliberate control of behaviour. For all such phenomena, the challenge is to explain how some function is performed. By contrast, the hard problem does not appear to be a problem of explaining the performance of functions. For every function associated with consciousness, the question remains: why is the performance of that function accompanied by experience?

Compare explaining consciousness with explaining reportability. *Reportability* may be defined roughly as the ability to accurately describe one's experiences. To explain it, one specifies a neurophysiological or cognitive mechanism that performs it. If the mechanism explains the ability, then nothing about reportability remains to be explained. By contrast, *experience* does not seem to be functionally definable. Even after all the associated functions and abilities are explained, one might reasonably wonder why there is something it is like to see letters appear on a computer screen (see WHAT IT-IS LIKE).

Neurobiological and cognitive theories of *consciousness do not seem to solve the hard problem. Consider Francis Crick and Christof Koch's (1990) theory that 35–75 Hz oscillations in the cerebral cortex form the neural basis of consciousness (see GAMMA OSCILLATIONS). This theory has implications for how the brain binds together separate pieces of information, such as information about the shape and colour of a perceived object. *Binding is said to occur when neural groups that encode the information oscillate with the same frequency and phase. But even if this hypothesis is correct, this just raises the question of why binding is accompanied by experience.

Four points of clarification are in order. First, 'consciousness' is ambiguous. In this article, I use this and related terms exclusively for experience, i.e. phenomenal consciousness, unless otherwise specified. But researchers tend to use them for a diverse variety of phenomena, including not only experience but also reportability, integration, etc. Insofar as the latter are functionally definable, no hard problem arises for them. The ambiguous use of terminology tends to encourage the view that the standard methods of cognitive science, which were developed to explain the performance of cognitive functions, apply unproblematically to the hard problem. This view is less readily embraced when it is made clear that the explanandum is experience.

Second, the so-called easy problems are not so easy. When Chalmers introduced the hard/easy distinction, he wrote, 'Of course, "easy" is a relative term. Getting the details right will probably take a century or two of difficult empirical work' (1995:10). But unlike the hard problem, the easy problems present no obvious difficulty for the application of standard cognitive science methodology.

Third, the hard/easy distinction must be drawn with care. Patricia Churchland (1996) construes the distinction as that between problems of (a) explaining consciousness and (b) explaining *memory, *attention, *learning, and various other mental phenomena. But 'memory', 'attention', etc., pick out phenomena that have both functional and phenomenal aspects. Therefore, there are hard and easy problems of memory, attention, etc. It is better to conceive of the distinction as that between problems of (c) explaining how consciousness arises from physical processes and (d) explaining functions associated with consciousness, in the various senses of 'consciousness'.

Fourth, while it is important to distinguish the hard problem from others in the vicinity, one should not lose sight of connections to those problems. Progress on the easy problems may lead indirectly to progress on the hard problem. Also, some see ties between the hard problem and other enduring philosophical problems, such as that of explaining mental representation.

2. History

The hard problem has long been appreciated in some form or other. Locke found the emergence of consciousness from 'Matter... and Motion' (*Essay*, Bk. IV) so extraordinary that he proposed a supernatural (theistic) explanation. Leibniz's appreciation of the problem emerged in a thought experiment. He imagined one entering a huge machine that 'produces thinking, feeling, and perceiving... as if it were a mill', and opined that one would observe 'nothing that could explain perception' (*Monadology*, section 17). And T. H. Huxley formulates the problem memorably:

> how it is that anything so remarkable as a state of consciousness comes about as a result of irritating nerve tissue, is just as unaccountable as the appearance of the Djin when Aladdin rubbed his lamp in the story, or as any other ultimate fact of nature (1866:193)

Locke, Leibniz, and Huxley are by no means alone in recognizing the hard problem long before Chalmers coined the phrase: an appreciation for the problem informs virtually every philosophical position on mental–physical relations. Even those philosophers who dismiss the hard problem as confused typically recognize the substantial burden of explaining it away.

Historically, there has been a tendency to run the hard problem together with other issues. Locke and other modern philosophers rarely distinguished it from the more general problem of how to explain mental–physical causal interaction. Descartes tended to focus more on thought than experience, placing special emphasis on human linguistic abilities. These abilities are remarkable, but today they are not generally thought to give rise to a hard problem. Descartes also regarded all mental states as conscious and transparent to the thinker. Such doctrines, which have been widely repudiated since Freud's day, served to muddy the waters even further.

More recent writings have brought the hard problem into sharper relief. Consider three examples. Thomas Nagel's (1974) 'What is it Like to be a Bat?' helped clarify the limitations of objective physical explanations of experience. He argued that no such explanation could reveal to us what it is like, from the bat's viewpoint, to echolocate. Colin McGinn's provocative argument that we are constitutionally incapable of understanding how 'technicolour phenomenology [can] arise from soggy grey matter' (1989:1) led to a greater appreciation of the problem's depth. And Chalmers (1995, 1996) reinvigorated interest in the problem by drawing the hard/easy distinction, developing a taxonomy of different approaches to the problem, criticizing certain approaches, and defending others. Since then, ideas on the topic have continued to multiply.

The hard problem is often discussed in connection to arguments against *physicalism (also known as materialism), the view that the world is entirely physical. These include both historical arguments, such as Descartes' argument from the possibility of his mind and body existing without each other; and contemporary arguments, such as the conceivability argument. One version of the latter runs roughly as follows. *Zombies are defined as creatures that lack consciousness but are physically and functionally identical to ordinary conscious human beings. A zombie world, in which consciousness does not exist and yet the physical facts are just as they actually are, is a priori conceivable; even upon ideal reflection one cannot find any incoherence in the supposition that such a world should exist. If so, then a zombie world is metaphysically possible; the physical truth does not metaphysically necessitate the existence of consciousness. Physicalism's falsity follows.

That argument's first, epistemic premise relates closely to the hard problem. If zombies are conceivable, then this is because the existence of consciousness cannot be fully explained in physical terms. In other words, the conceivability of zombies rests on the existence of an *explanatory gap (Levine 1983) between the physical and the phenomenal. Philosophical approaches to the hard problem may be divided into *deflationist* approaches, which reject the existence of such a gap, and *non-deflationist* approaches, which accept it. But many are agnostic about the hard problem. Indeed, agnosticism may be the most common attitude, especially among scientists.

3. Deflationist approaches

Deflationists believe that the hard problem reduces to a combination of easy problems or derives from misconceptions about the nature of consciousness. For example, Daniel Dennett (1991) holds that once one has solved the easy problems, one has explained everything. Deflationists thus reject the first, epistemic premise of antiphysicalist arguments such as the conceivability argument. They often support their view with analogies from the history of science, comparing those who take the hard problem at face value to 17th century vitalists worrying about a hard problem of life or to the scientifically ignorant worrying about hard problems of heat or light (Churchland 1996). Science has shown that such worries are misguided: life, heat, and light can be physically explained. Likewise, deflationists say, for consciousness.

Such analogies are disputed. Consider the analogy to life. Granted, the vitalists doubted that how organisms reproduce, move, self-organize, etc., could be explained in purely physical terms. But notice that what they sought to explain was how certain functions are performed. By contrast, consciousness does not present itself as consisting in the performance of functions. The analogies to light and heat raise similar concerns. To be sure, there is a hard problem of how those features generate experience; how does (decoherent) molecular motion cause the sensation of heat? But that is just an instance of the problem that the analogies are supposed to deflate.

Deflationism is entailed by important theories in the philosophy of mind, including philosophical behaviourism, analytic functionalism, and *eliminative materialism. Some philosophers take the merits of those positions, such as their relative parsimony, to provide grounds for a deflationist approach to the hard problem. Other philosophers accept the explanatory gap and thus regard the hard problem as evidence against those theories.

4. Non-deflationist physicalism

All non-deflationists accept the explanatory gap. Some are also physicalists (Loar 1990/97). Non-deflationist physicalists claim that, despite the existence of an explanatory gap, there is no corresponding metaphysical gap: the physical truth metaphysically necessitates the truth about consciousness. For example, the zombie world is conceivable but not metaphysically possible.

Why is the zombie world metaphysically impossible? Deflationists have a straightforward answer: consciousness is a functional concept; therefore, there is no conceptual room for duplicating a conscious person's functional features without duplicating her phenomenal features. Non-deflationists, however, deny that consciousness is a functional concept. How, then, can they defend their claim that zombies are impossible? Here some emphasize that conceivability does not in general entail metaphysical possibility. But many accept that more is required by way of defence.

Here analogies to Kripkean (1972) a posteriori necessities are sometimes invoked. According to Kripke, the fact that heat is molecular motion is metaphysically necessary—there is no possible situation in which there is one without the other—even though it was discovered empirically. How can this be? Cannot we imagine a situation in which there is heat but, as scientists discover, no molecular motion? Kripke thinks not. On his view, heat itself just is molecular motion and thus cannot exist without it. What we can imagine existing without molecular motion, and wrongly describe as heat, is the *sensation* of heat—an experience typically caused in us by molecular motion.

Non-deflationist physicalists sometimes suggest that similar reasoning could be used to explain the necessities entailed by non-deflationist physicalism. But this is unclear. As Kripke himself emphasizes, in the case of consciousness there does not appear to be a distinction corresponding to that between heat and the sensation of heat. For example, anything that feels like pain is ipso facto pain. So, Kripke's reasoning does not straightforwardly extend to the a posteriori necessities to which non-deflationist physicalists are committed.

In response to such difficulties, some non-deflationists attempt to provide alternative grounds for such a posteriori necessities. Other non-deflationists reject physicalism. On most non-physicalist views, consciousness is regarded as an irreducible component of nature. These views tend to differ primarily on how they characterize the relationship between consciousness and the physical world. For example, on interactionist *dualism consciousness has both physical causes and physical effects; on *epiphenomenalism consciousness has physical causes but no physical effects; and on some versions of neutral monism phenomenal properties are the categorical bases of physical properties, which are dispositional (neutral monism might or might not count as a version of physicalism, depending on whether the categorical bases physical properties are considered physical).

5. Fundamental theories

For deflationists, solutions to the easy problems of consciousness will yield a solution to the hard problem. For non-deflationists, the hard problem presents a special challenge. Some non-deflationist physicalists suggest that the challenge consists in the concern noted above, about explaining the necessary truths that physicalism entails. Other non-deflationists suggest that solving the hard problem requires positing a psychophysical theory that includes fundamental laws: laws that are explanatory but not derived from more fundamental principles.

Few such theories have been developed in detail, but some proposals have been advanced. Certain interactionist dualists (e.g. Eccles 1986) argue that phenomenal properties affect brain processes by filling in gaps resulting from quantum indeterminacy. The quantum physics-based theories of consciousness emerging from that sort of argument may involve positing psychophysical laws.

Chalmers tentatively advances a different proposal, on which the basic link between the phenomenal and the physical exists at the level of information. He formulates a *double aspect* principle, on which phenomenal states realize informational states that are also realized in physical, cognitive systems such as the brain (Chalmers 1996:Ch. 8). He formulates other psychophysical principles as well. One connects experience with *awareness*, which is 'roughly explicable as a state wherein some information is directly accessible and available for the deliberate control of behavior and for verbal report' (1996:220). The principle is that where there is experience, there is awareness, and vice versa. Unlike the double aspect principle, this one is not a candidate for a fundamental law, since it mentions the high-level concept of awareness. But it might form part of a psychophysical theory that takes phenomenal (or *proto*-phenomenal) properties as irreducible components of nature, alongside properties postulated by fundamental physics. Such a psychophysical theory would provide a kind of solution to the hard problem: the laws would enable deductions of specific instances of experience from underlying physical structures.

Such proposals need not presuppose that physicalism is false. Indeed, physicalists might regard them as grounds for psychophysical identities. More generally, although one's view on the metaphysics of consciousness can affect how one conceives of the hard problem, many avenues of investigation are largely independent of metaphysical views.

Perception, memory, and other cognitive capacities may be exercised both consciously and unconsciously. Deflationists and non-deflationists alike could agree that increased understanding of this contrast and its neural basis, along with other research into the neural correlates of consciousness, might lead to progress on the hard problem, if only because such knowledge may help refine our understanding of consciousness.

Similarly, deflationists and non-deflationists can agree that psychological research concerning the contents of consciousness might help. Examples of such research include psychophysics, which investigates such things as how the intensity of the subjective brightness associated with a visual experience relates to the intensity of corresponding physical stimuli; recent work on perceptual *illusions and attention; and recent research on *synaesthesia and other abnormal experiential phenomena. More direct progress may result from combining psychological research, including first-person data, with research in neuroscience.

TORIN ALTER

Chalmers, D. J. (1995). 'Facing up to the problem of consciousness'. *Journal of Consciousness Studies*, 2.

—— (1996). *The Conscious Mind: In Search of a Fundamental Theory*.

Churchland, P. S. (1996). 'The hornswoggle problem'. *Journal of Consciousness Studies*, 3.

Crick, F. and Koch, C. (1990). 'Towards a neurobiological theory of consciousness'. *Seminars in the Neurosciences*, 2.

Dennett, D. C. (1991). *Consciousness Explained*.

Eccles, J. C. (1986). 'Do mental events cause neural events analogously to the probability fields of quantum mechanics?' *Proceedings of the Royal Society of London Series B: Biological Sciences*, 227.

Huxley, T. H. (1866). *Lessons in Elementary Physiology*.

Kripke, S. (1972). 'Naming and necessity'. In Harman, G. and Davidson, D. (eds) *The Semantics of Natural Language*.

Levine, J. (1983). 'Materialism and qualia: the explanatory gap'. *Pacific Philosophical Quarterly*, 64.

Loar, B. (1990/97). 'Phenomenal states'. In Tomberlin, J. (ed.) *Philosophical Perspectives 4: Action Theory and Philosophy of Mind*. Revised version in Block, N. et al. (eds) *The Nature of Consciousness*.

Locke, J. (1690). *An Essay Concerning Human Understanding*.

Leibniz, G. (1714/1991). *Monadology*, transl. N. Rescher.

McGinn, C. (1989). 'Can we solve the mind-body problem?' *Mind*, 98.

Nagel, T. (1974). 'What is it like to be a bat?' *Philosophical Review*, 83.

Strawson, G. (1994). *Mental Reality*.

Helen, 'a blind monkey who saw everything'

In my supervisor Larry Weiskrantz's laboratory at Cambridge in 1967, there was a monkey named Helen. She had undergone a surgical operation to remove the primary visual cortex, *V1, at the back of her brain, with the purpose of discovering more about the role this area of cortex plays in normal vision. The operation had been done in 1965, and during the two years that followed the monkey had seemed to be almost completely blind, capable of discriminating little more than light from dark.

However, I had reasons for thinking this might not be the whole story. As part of my own PhD research I had been studying the visual responses of *single cells in the superior colliculus of monkeys, and had found evidence that this 'primitive' subcortical visual system, which remains intact after removal of the visual cortex, might be capable on its own of supporting quite finely tuned visually guided behaviour (Humphrey 1968). I wondered now whether in Helen's case this secondary visual system could somehow be brought into action. Thus, one week when I had time on my hands and the monkey was not involved in Weiskrantz's research, I decided to find out more.

Over several days I sat by Helen's cage and played with her. To my delight it soon became clear that this blind monkey was sometimes *watching* what I did. For example, I would hold up a piece of apple and wave it in front of her, and she would clearly *look*, before reaching out to try to get it from me. As the game continued, she soon changed from being a monkey who sat around listlessly, gazing blankly into the distance, to one who had become interested and involved in vision again.

I persuaded Weiskrantz to let me go on working with Helen. Over the next seven years I took her with me to Oxford, and then back to Cambridge, to the Department of Animal Behaviour at Madingley. I became her tutor on a daily basis. I took her out on a leash in the fields and woods at Madingley. I encouraged her and coaxed her, trying in every way to help her realize what she might be capable of. And slowly but surely her sight got better. Eventually she could, for example, run around a room full of obstacles picking up crumbs off the floor. Anyone who was unaware that she had no visual cortex, could well have assumed she had completely normal vision.

Yet I was pretty sure her vision was not normal. I knew her too well. We had spent so many hours together, while I continually wondered *what it was like to be her. And, although I found it hard to put my finger on what was wrong, my sense was that she still did not *really believe* that she could see. There were telling hints in her behaviour. For example, if she was upset or frightened, she would stumble about as if she was in the dark again. It was as if she could only see provided she did not try too hard.

In 1972 I wrote an article for the *New Scientist*, and on the front cover of the magazine they put the headline, under Helen's portrait, 'a blind monkey that sees everything'. But this headline surely was not right. Not *everything*. My own title for the paper inside the magazine was 'Seeing and nothingness', and I went on to argue that this was a kind of seeing of which we had never before had any inkling (Humphrey 1972).

With a monkey who could not describe her inner world there seemed no way of knowing what her experience was really like. To find out we would need evidence from human beings, and at that time there were no human cases comparable. Indeed what evidence there was suggested that people with similar brain damage would *not* recover vision. I wrote:

> When people suffer extensive damage to the visual cortex it is said that their blindness is total and permanent. Perhaps with a more flexible definition of vision, it will yet be discovered that there is more to seeing than has so far met either the clinician's or the patient's eye.

Then, within a couple of years, Weiskrantz, spurred on by what we had found with Helen, moved the research to a new level by showing that a human patient with extensive damage to the visual cortex could be coaxed, like the monkey, into demonstrating a significant degree of vision in the blind part of his visual field. But now, with this human patient, it was possible to have him tell the researchers what it was like for him. And, to everyone's astonishment it turned out that, yes, this was indeed a kind of *unconscious vision*. The patient believed he was blind, and reported that he was having no visual sensation, and yet he could still guess the position and shape of objects (Weiskrantz 1986).

No human patient with primary visual cortex damage has yet reached the same level of skill as Helen when using the blind part of their field; nor apparently do human patients find their capacity of practical value in their lives, as Helen clearly did (she could climb trees, catch cockroaches, feed herself , etc. under visual control). Compared to human cases, Helen had 'super-blindsight'. Perhaps the difference can be explained by the fact in all known human cases the damage to the visual cortex is incomplete, leaving the patient with normal vision in part of the field—and hence with less incentive to rely on blindsight in daily life. No case of a clean total lesion of V1 is likely to occur in humans, so we may never know.

Helen was killed in 1974 so that her brain could be examined and the extent of the lesion confirmed. To be sentimental about her would be inappropriate. Nonetheless, I think we should acknowledge our debt as scientists and philosophers to a creature who, through a human experiment that deprived her of visual consciousness, has taught us so much about what consciousness is all about.

The research with Helen is described in a series of papers, beginning with Humphrey and Weiskrantz (1967) and ending with Humphrey (1974). For further reading, see Humphrey (2006), from which this account is partly taken.

See ALSO BLINDSIGHT

NICHOLAS K. HUMPHREY

Humphrey, N. K. (1968). 'Responses to visual stimuli of single units in the superior colliculus of rats and monkeys'. *Experimental Neurology*, 20.
—— (1972). 'Seeing and nothingness'. *New Scientist*, 53.
—— (1974). 'Vision in a monkey without striate cortex: a case study'. *Perception*, 3.
—— (2006). *Seeing Red: a Study in Consciousness.*
—— and Weiskrantz, L. (1967). 'Vision in monkeys after removal of the striate cortex'. *Nature*, 215.
Weiskrantz, L. (1986). *Blindsight.*

Web source

http://tinyurl.com/dbfj7y A short film clip of Helen

heterophenomenology Heterophenomenology is a scientific methodology for gathering and interpreting data on human consciousness, described by Dennett (1982, 1991, 2003, 2005). Human consciousness involves phenomena that at first glance seem to occur in something rather like another dimension: the private, subjective, first-person dimension that each of us occupies with regard to our own consciousness, and to which nobody else can gain direct access. What, then, is the relation between the standard third-person objective methodologies for studying meteors or magnets (or human metabolism or bone density), and the methodologies for studying human consciousness? Can the standard methods be extended in such a way as to do justice to the phenomena of human consciousness? Or do we have to create some radical or revolutionary alternative science? Dennett defends the hypothesis that there is a straightforward, conservative extension of objective science that handsomely covers all the ground of human consciousness, doing justice to all the data without ever having to abandon the rules and constraints of the methods that have worked so well in the rest of science. This third-person methodology, heterophenomenology (phenomenology of an other not oneself), is, he claims, the sound way to take the first-person point of view as seriously as it can legitimately be taken.

The term 'heterophenomenology' was coined to emphasize a contrast with autophenomenology: the exploration of one's own consciousness 'from the first-person point of view' without due attention to how the deliverances of such a subjective inquiry were to be put into registration with the objective data-gathering of the physical sciences. It has often been maintained that, for one reason or another, the subjective and objective realms are incommensurable, or that the subjective realm lies outside science altogether, a prior and fundamentally incommunicable sort of knowledge inaccessible to scientific confirmation or disconfirmation. These claims are denied by Dennett.

Obviously the key difference between experiments with rocks, roses, and rats on the one hand, and experiments with awake, cooperative human subjects on the other is that the latter can communicate in language, and hence can collaborate with experimenters, making suggestions, interacting verbally, telling them *what it is like under various controlled conditions. That is the core of heterophenomenology: it exploits our capacity to perform and interpret speech acts, yielding a catalogue of what the subject believes to be true about his or her conscious experience. This catalogue of beliefs fleshes out the subject's *heterophenomenological world*, the world according to S, the subjective world of one subject. The total set of details of heterophenomenology, plus all the data we can gather about concurrent events in the brains of subjects and in the surrounding environment, comprise the total data set a theory of human consciousness must explain. Dennett claims that it leaves out no objective phenomena and no subjective phenomena of consciousness.

The interpretation required to turn data about speech sounds and button pressings into reports and expressions of beliefs involves adopting what Dennett calls the *intentional stance (Dennett 1987): adopting the working hypothesis that the subject is an agent whose actions are rationally guided by beliefs and desires that are themselves rational, given the subject's perceptual history and needs. (For instance, the constraints of the intentional stance can be clearly discerned in the standard precautions taken in such experiments to prevent subjects from having experiences that might give them either beliefs or desires that would tend to bias their responses in ways that would distort our interpretation of their actions: we keep them in the dark about what we hope they will say, for instance, while at the same time taking steps to assure ourselves that they understand the tasks we set them.) This adoption of the intentional stance is not, Dennett argues, an irreparably subjective and relativistic affair. Rules of interpretation can be articulated, standards of intersubjective agreement on interpretation can be set and met; deviations can be identified; the unavoidable assumption of rationality can be cautiously couched, and treated as a defeasible, adjustable, defensible, and evolutionarily explicable assumption.

Dennett claims that he is not proposing a new methodology for studying consciousness but just explaining and defending the standard methods already adopted by researchers in psychophysics, cognitive psychology, and neuroscience, for instance. These methods, correctly understood and followed, obviate the need for any radical or revolutionary first-person science of consciousness, and leave no residual phenomena of consciousness inaccessible to controlled scientific study.

What kinds of things does this methodology commit us to? Beyond the unproblematic things all of science is committed to (neurons and electrons, clocks and microscopes, ...), just to beliefs—the beliefs expressed by subjects and deemed constitutive of their subjectivity. And what kind of things are beliefs? We may stay maximally non-committal about this—pending the confirmation of theory—by treating beliefs and their contents or objects as *theories*, *fictions*, or *abstractions* similar to centres of mass, the Equator, and parallelograms of forces. (This systematically non-committal stance is similar to, and inspired by, Husserl's concept of *epoché* or bracketing, the key methodological move in *phenomenology, the philosophical/psychological school of inquiry of which heterophenomenology is a descendant.)

Mermaid-sightings are real events, however misdescribed, whereas mermaids do not exist. Similarly, a catalogue of beliefs about experience is not the same as a catalogue of experiences themselves, and it has been objected (Levine 1994) that conscious experiences themselves, not merely our verbal judgements about them, are the primary data to which a theory must answer. But how, in advance of theory, could we catalogue the experiences themselves? In the quest for primary data, Levine wants to go all the way to (a) conscious experiences themselves, instead of stopping with (b) subjects' beliefs about their experiences, but this, Dennett argues, is not a good idea, for two reasons. First, if (a) outruns (b)—if you have conscious experiences you do not believe you have—those extra-conscious experiences are just as inaccessible to you as to the external observers. So Levine's proposed alternative garners no more usable data than heterophenomenology does. Second, if (b) outruns (a)—if you believe you have conscious experiences that you do not in fact have—then it is your beliefs that we need to explain, not the non-existent experiences. Sticking to the heterophenomenological standard, then, and treating (b) as the maximal set of primary data, is the way to avoid any commitment to spurious data, while ensuring that all phenomena accessible to anybody get included.

What if some of your beliefs are inexpressible in verbal judgements? There is nothing to prevent heterophenomenologists and subjects from collaborating on devising analogue or other non-linguistic modes of belief expression (such as bisecting a line segment between two poles or pressing a sensitive button harder or less hard to indicate intensity). And if you believe that there are still ineffable residues unconveyed after exhausting such methods, you can tell this to the heterophenomenologists, who can add that belief to the list of beliefs in your primary data:

S claims that he has ineffable beliefs about X.

If this belief is true, then science has the obligation to explain what such beliefs are and why they are ineffable. If this belief is false, science still has to explain why S believes (falsely) that there are these particular ineffable beliefs.

The defence of heterophenomenology as the methodology of choice for the scientific study of consciousness has occasioned substantial controversy. In addition to the objections sketched and rebutted above, it has been argued that heterophenomenology underestimates or ignores aspects of consciousness that Husserlian phenomenology gets right (see e.g. Marbach 2007) and that its metaphysical assumptions are inconsistent (see Schwitzgebel 2007.) Dennett (2007) provides a detailed reply to his critics.

DANIEL C. DENNETT

Dennett, D. C. (1982). 'How to study consciousness empirically, or nothing comes to mind',. *Synthese*, 59.

—— (1987). *The Intentional Stance*.

—— (1991). *Consciousness Explained*.

—— (2003). 'Who's on first? heterophenomenology explained'. *Journal of Consciousness Studies, Special Issue: Trusting the Subject? (Part 1)*, 10.

—— (2005). *Sweet Dreams: Philosophical Obstacles to a Science of Consciousness*.

—— (2007). 'Heterophenomenology reconsidered'. *Phenomenology and the Cognitive Sciences*, 6.

Jack, A. and Roepstorff, A. (eds) (2003). *Trusting the Subject?* Volume 1.

Levine, J. (1994). 'Out of the closet: a qualophile confronts qualophobia'. *Philosophical Topics*, 22.

Marbach, E. (2007). 'No heterophenomenology without autophenomenology: variations on a theme of mine'. *Phenomenology and the Cognitive Sciences*, 6.

Schwitzgebel, E. (2007). 'No unchallengeable epistemic authority of any sort, regarding our own conscious experience—contra Dennett'. *Phenomenology and the Cognitive Sciences*, 6.

higher-order representation theories of consciousness According to higher-order representation (HOR) theories, a mental state or event is a *conscious* state or event just in case it, itself, is the intentional object of one of the subject's mental representations. But to which of the 'c'-word's many senses are such theories directed? What exactly is the explanandum?

1. The theories
2. Objections to HOR
3. HOP vs HOT
4. Dispositionalist HOT
5. Intrinsicality and HOGS

1. The theories

First and foremost, HOR theories have been directed toward 'conscious states' in a very particular sense of that term: M defined as a conscious state if it is *a mental state whose subject is (directly or at least non-evidentially) aware of being in it*. This definition is stipulative, but not brutely so; cf. 'conscious memory', 'conscious decision'. (Note that the phrase has been used in several quite disparate senses, e.g. by Fred Dretske and differently by Ned Block; failure to keep these senses separate has led to much confusion.)

Thus, occurrent mental or psychological states fall roughly into three categories: those whose subjects are aware of being in them; those whose subjects are not aware of being in them, but could have been had they taken notice; and those, such as language-processing states, which are entirely subterranean and inaccessible to introspection. Any HOR theory easily explains these differences: a state is, or is not, or could not be a conscious state accordingly as it itself is, or is not, or psychofunctionally could not be the object of a higher-order representation. It is assumed that the higher-order representation in question is person-level, since it is the whole person that is aware (or not) of her/his first-order state.

Other, more sophisticated explananda in which HOR has figured include: the correlation between states we intuitively classify as conscious and states we can report (David Rosenthal, Robert Lurz); 'knowing what it's like' (Lycan 1996, Rosenthal 1997); and 'phenomenal consciousness' in one or another sense of that feloniously ill-defined term (e.g. Carruthers 2000). In particular, if knowing *what it is like to undergo such-and-such an experience is genuinely factual knowledge, we must suppose that someone who has such knowledge internally represents the experience in question, and HOR theories provide precisely for that.

But HOR is not, and has never been, a theory of sensory qualities such as colours or smells or tastes. Obviously, if a mental state does not already present a sensory quality, the mere HOR of the state would not produce one. (As noted, HOR has figured in explanations of 'what it's like' to experience a sensory quality, but that too presupposes the relevant sensory quality.) It is no objection to HOR theories to point out that they do not explain sensory qualities.

HOR theories are not always held on merely explanatory grounds. Lycan (2004) offered a deductive argument in favour of HOR, roughly: If I am aware of being in mental state M, then tautologically, my awareness itself is an awareness *of*, and that 'of' is the 'of' of *intentionality; my state of awareness has M as its intentional object or representatum. Therefore, for M to be a conscious state is at least for M to be represented by one of my mental states, QED.

2. Objections to HOR

Here are five objections that have been urged against HOR theories per se.

Regress. If the second-order representation is to confer consciousness on the first-order state, it must itself be a conscious state; so there must be a third-order representation of it, and so on for ever. But HOR theorists reject the opening conditional premise. The second-order representation need not itself be a conscious state. (Of course, it *may* be a conscious state, if there happens to be a higher-order representation of it in turn.)

Fallibility. Some philosophers have complained that representational theories leave *introspective beliefs too fallible and underrate the privileged access we have to our own mental states. An internal monitor, or whatever device produces a higher-order thought, is a mechanism, and every mechanism is fallible and works only contingently; it might produce a false representation. But the objectors contend that our awareness of our own mental states is either infallible or, if not flatly infallible, non-contingently constrained against unreliability. Sydney Shoemaker, for example, grants that pain can 'occasionally' escape awareness, but he insists that that could not happen 'as a matter of course; it may be true in Lake Wobegon that all of the children are above average, but it can't be true everywhere'. Lycan (1996) replied to Shoemaker that introspection is certainly fallible to some degree; e.g. having been elaborately *primed to expect being branded, the freshman undergoing a fraternity initiation ceremony mistakes the cold sensation produced on his bare skin by an ice cube for burning heat. There is no obvious reason why such mistakes should be *necessarily* rare.

Karen Neander (1998) has prosecuted an especially incisive version of the fallibility objection: Since the relevant representation could be a false positive, it could seem to me introspectively that I was in agonizing, unbearable pain, when I was, in fact, in no pain whatever. Does that even make sense? Against Neander, Lycan argues not very convincingly that there are reasons why the egregious sorts of false positive she cites would not happen. There being no actual pain, neither would there be the standard first-order behavioural and mental effects; so the false-positive 'pain' experience would feel different, probably very strange. Though its strict sensory quality might be the same as that of a real pain, it would be a weird dissociative state that would not have the same overall feel as pain.

Function. Fred Dretske and Droege (2003) have complained that HOR theories make it mysterious what the point or use or function of consciousness could be. The relevant first-order states are themselves sufficient for navigation and interacting with the world; what further benefit is conferred by their subjects' representing them? HOR theorists have gestured in the direction of integration, coordination, feedback, planning, deliberation, and the like. But these gestures are vague, and Droege also rightly asks why such good things should not more straightforwardly be achieved by causal relations among the first-order states themselves. It would be more to the point for the HOR theorist to suggest that the problem is created by the datum, not by the theory: what is the benefit, in the first place, of being aware of one's own mental state?

Ubiquity. Georges Rey (1983) objects that if all it takes to make a first-order state a conscious state is that the state be the object of a HOR, then consciousness is a lot more prevalent than we think. Any laptop computer, for example, has monitoring devices that keep track of its 'psychological' states. Perhaps no existing computer has genuinely psychological states, but Rey argues that once we had done whatever needs to be done in order to fashion a being that did have non-conscious first-order intentional and sensory states, the addition of an internal monitor or two would be a trifling afterthought, hardly the sort of thing that could turn a simply non-conscious being into a conscious being. This objection clearly calls for a thoughtful response. Stephen White and Lycan (1996) have tried to rebut it. Lycan appeals to the fact that consciousness is the present sense comes in degrees, descending from 'intensely conscious' through 'vividly,' 'modestly', and 'dimly' to 'just barely conscious'; assuming that a creature has genuine mental states in the first place, there is little reason to doubt that adding an internal monitor or two would produce a very low degree of consciousness.

Computational/cognitive overload. Carruthers (2000) points out that, given the richness of a person's conscious experience at a time, the alleged higher-order representing devices would be kept very busy. The HORs would have to keep pace with every nuance of the total experience. The complexity of the experience would have to be matched in every detail by a higher-order perception or thought. It is hard to imagine that a human being would have so great a capacity for complex HOR, much less that a small child or a non-human animal would have it. Carruthers concludes that if a HOR theory is true, then to say the least, few if any creatures besides human adults have conscious experiences.

Perhaps HOR theorists can live with that apparent consequence; perhaps not. Some are willing to maintain that very few of our first-order mental states are conscious states in the sense defined above; it is comparatively rare that we are aware of our own mental states.

3. HOP vs HOT

HOR theories divide into two main sub-varieties: the Lockean *inner sense* or *higher-order perception* (HOP) view offered by Armstrong (1981; see also Lycan 1996), and the *higher-order thought* (HOT) theory defended by Rosenthal (1997; see also Gennaro 1996 and Carruthers 2000). HOP has it that the higher-order representing is done quasi-perceptually, by a set of functionally specified internal attention mechanisms of some kind, that scan or monitor first-order mental/brain states. HOT theorists say that merely having a thought about the first-order state will suffice, provided that the thought arose from the state itself without benefit of (person-level) inference.

HOT has two obvious advantages over HOP: it does not require the higher-order representations to be in any way perception-like, and in particular it posits no special scanning or monitoring mechanism. Rosenthal (1997) adds the objection that since standard perceiving always involves some sensory quality, HOP would itself have to involve some distinctive sensory quality. But attention to one's own sensory state does not present any such quality over and above that of the first-order sensory state itself.

HOP theorists grant the latter disanalogy; obviously they do not contend that 'inner sense' is like external-world perception in every single respect. In particular, we should not expect inner sense to involve some distinctive sensory quality at its own level of operation, because unlike 'outer' sense organs, it does not have the function of environmental feature detection. Moreover, HOP is held to have some compensating attractions of its own (Van Gulick 2001, Lycan 2004), though these are disputed by Rosenthal (2004).

Phenomenology and voluntary control. Though Wittgenstein and Ryle pooh-poohed the etymology of 'introspection,' it is at least a good metaphor. When we attend to our own mental states, it feels like that is just what we are doing: focusing our internal attention on something that is there for us to discern. Moreover, that focusing is under voluntary control; at will, we can shift our attention around our phenomenal field. When we do so, our first-order states are phenomenologically *present to* our minds and not (or not just) represented by them, much as in external vision, physical objects are present to us without seeming to be represented by us.

Rosenthal (2004) replies: '[W]e attend to objects of thought no less than those of perception. . . . We can also direct and focus our thought processes, perhaps even more readily than we can our perceiving.'

Degrees of awareness. Awareness of our own mental states comes in degrees. Given a bodily sensation that I have, I may be only very dimly and peripherally aware of it (assuming I am aware of it at all); or I may be more than dimly aware of it though still only mutedly; or I may be well aware of it; or I may be excruciatingly aware of it. This range of possibilities is of course characteristic of external-world perception as well. It is not characteristic of mere thought. Rosenthal (2004) replies: '[T]houghts vary in how focused and attentive they are no less than perceptions.'

**Epistemology.* Our awareness of our own mental states justifies our beliefs about them. Indeed, my only justification for believing that I now have a certain bodily sensation and that I am hearing the faint whirr of my computer's fan is that I am aware of both states. This is just what we should expect if awareness is a perception-like affair. By contrast, merely having a thought to the effect that one is in state M by itself does nothing to justify the belief that one is in M. We think of our perceptual capacities as reliable channels of information, and for the most part they are. We do not think of the having of thoughts, per se, as reliable information channels. Rosenthal responds: 'That holds at least as well for the thoughts we have about small numbers, simple shapes, logical connections, and the everyday behaviour of common-sense objects.'

Grain. Thoughts differ from perceptual states in being more thoroughly and more discretely conceptual. Their contents are reported in indirect discourse using complement clauses made of natural-language words. But words are fairly coarse-grained representations. A phenomenal region such as a sub-area of your visual field will often be rich in irregular outlines, textures, gradations of shading and the like; its phenomenal contents would be at best very difficult to describe in words at all. According to Rosenthal: 'Thinking distinguishes among properties in at least as fine grained a way as does perceiving. . . . We can readily capture [the fine-grained qualitative variations] using comparative concepts.'

Purely recognitional concepts .We seem to have 'purely recognitional' concepts that classify sensations without inference or criteria. Peter Carruthers notes that HOP can explain how it is possible for us to acquire such phenomenal concepts. 'For if we possess higher-order perceptual contents, then it should be possible for us to learn to recognize the occurrence of our own perceptual states immediately—or 'straight off'—grounded in those higher-order analog contents.' HOT can make no parallel claim about the acquisition of recognitional concepts, at least not straight away. For one thing, how could we have a higher-order thought about a sensory state without already having the pertinent concept? Rosenthal's responds: '[I]t's unlikely that any concepts for qualitative states are purely recognitional in this way. Rather, our concepts for mental qualities connect in crucial ways with our concepts for the physical properties that those mental qualities enable us to perceive; indeed, our concepts for mental qualities very likely derive from our concepts for perceptible properties.'

4. Dispositionalist HOT

HOP and HOT theorists have assumed that the relevant higher-order representation is an actual, occurrent psychological state. That assumption is challenged by Carruthers (2000), who proposes that a first-order state may be conscious in virtue merely of being disposed to give rise (non-inferentially) to a HOT. As a categorical basis for the disposition, Carruthers suggests that the target state is held in short-term *memory, and is thereby available to thought.

The dispositional theory inherits the advantages of HOT noted above. It also avoids the *computational/cognitive overload* objection to HOP and *actualist* HOT theories. But, accordingly, it incurs an aggravated version of the *ubiquity* objection: the dispositional requirement is of course much weaker than that of an actual HOR. So, many more first-order states will be counted as conscious states in our sense. Also, intuitively (cf. the deductive argument sketched in section 1 above), I am intentionally aware of being in a first-order state only if I do represent that state, not merely by dint of being disposed to do so.

Carruthers puts an additional spin on his theory in order to account for elements of *phenomenal consciousness*, the *subjective feels* of the target states. He appeals to *consumer semantics* in the sense of Ruth Garrett Millikan, and argues that the target states themselves are endowed by Millikan's psychosemantics with dual content, their own original content and a second that involves seeming or appearing.

5. Intrinsicality and HOGS

It is usually thought by HOR theorists that for M to be a conscious state is for M to be represented by another of my mental states. But Franz Brentano wrote:

> [Every conscious act] includes within it a consciousness of itself. Therefore, every [conscious] act, no matter how simple, has a double object, a primary and a secondary object. The simplest act, for example the act of hearing, has as its primary object

the sound, and for its secondary object, itself, the mental phenomenon in which the sound is heard.

This idea has been pursued by Gennaro (1996), Natsoulas (1996), Kriegel (2003), and Van Gulick (2004), who maintain that the 'higher-order' content in virtue of which a conscious state is conscious is not that of a separate and distinct state, but is intrinsic to the original state itself. Van Gulick offers a 'higher-order global state' (HOGS) theory designed to capture that idea; on his view, the first-order state is 'recruited' into a complex global state that constitutes the subject's 'conscious self-awareness' at a time; indeed, it is incorporated into that higher-order global state as a component. Van Gulick argues that this view has several advantages over both HOP and HOT. (see *free will and consciousness; *readiness potentials and human volition).

The intrinsicality view is usually presented as a rival of HOR theories, but the degree of opposition is unclear. Is the question of separateness not simply a matter of individuation? Why not merely take the first-order state and the higher-order representation together and call them a single state? That is Gennaro's (1996) move. But Joseph Levine and Uriah Kriegel object: (1) The re-individuation ploy does not capture Brentano's duality; after all, there are still two mutually independent parts to the resulting 'state,' each of which could have occurred without the other. (2) In any case we cannot thus just legislate individuation. The single conscious state must be genuinely single even though it has two contents.

We may agree that separatist HOR cannot deliver Brentano's duality. But the alleged duality is a little elusive. It is over and above the mereological sum of the first-order state and the HOR, and Kriegel says there must be a 'real relation' that the genuinely single state bears to itself. Perhaps the best model of the dual content is that of a conjunctive sentence: 'I am in state M and I am aware of that in virtue of being in M itself.' (Even so, the whole state remains numerically distinct from its first-order component.)

There are more arguments for the intrinsicality view; see SELF-REPRESENTATIONAL THEORIES OF CONSCIOUSNESS.

WILLIAM G. LYCAN

Armstrong, D. M. (1981). 'What is consciousness?' In *The Nature of Mind and Other Essays*.

Carruthers, P. (2000). *Phenomenal Consciousness*.

Droege, P. (2003). *Caging the Beast: A Theory of Sensory Consciousness*.

Gennaro, R. (1996). *Consciousness and Self-consciousness*.

Kriegel, U. (2003). 'Consciousness, higher-order content, and the individuation of vehicles'. *Synthese*, 134.

Lycan, W. G. (1996). *Consciousness and experience*.

—— (2004). 'The superiority of HOP to HOT'. In Gennaro, R. (ed.) *Higher-order Theories of Consciousness*.

Natsoulas, T. (1996). 'The case for intrinsic theory: II. An examination of a conception of consciousness$_4$ as intrinsic, necessary, and concomitant'. *Journal of Mind and Behavior*, 17.

Neander, K. (1998). The division of phenomenal labor: a problem for representational theories of consciousness. In Tomberlin, J. E. (ed.), *Language, Mind, and Ontology* (*Philosophical Perspectives*), vol. 12).

Rey, G. (1983). 'A reason for doubting the existence of consciousness'. In Davidson, R. et al. (eds) *Consciousness and Self-regulation*, Vol. 3.

Rosenthal, D. (1997). 'A theory of consciousness'. In Block, N. et al. (eds) *The Nature of Consciousness*.

—— (2004). 'Varieties of higher-order theory'. In Gennaro, R. (ed.) *Higher-order Theories of Consciousness*.

Van Gulick, R. (2001). 'Inward and upward: reflection, introspection, and self-awareness'. *Philosophical Topics*, 28.

—— (2004). 'Higher-order global states (HOGS): an alternative higher-order model of consciousness'. In Gennaro, R. (ed.) *Higher-order Theories of Consciousness*.

homunculus The homunculus—literally, 'little man'—owes much of its fame to the fallacy to which it lends its name. You have committed the *homuncular fallacy* if you have attempted to explain the abilities of a person by positing something in their head that is as smart as they are. Barely a week goes by without someone somewhere being accused of committing the homuncular fallacy. Notorious examples of the fallacy at work include (but are not limited to): wondering how we see the world the right way up given that the retinae inverts the optic image (see INVERTED VISION); worrying about how a brain with two halves could produce a single stream of experience (see COMMISSUROTOMY AND CONSCIOUSNESS); and thinking that the notion of autonomous agency must be in trouble because the readiness potential begins to ramp up before one is aware of having decided to lift a finger.

Of course, the brain does contain little people of a kind: representational systems that are somatotopically organized. Representation in the somatosensory cortex roughly follows the spatial structure of the body itself, although some body parts are given more prominence than others (the lips commandeer as much somatosensory space as the entire trunk of one's body), and some body parts are not where they ought to be were sensory representation perfectly homuncular (e.g. the area subserving the face is not next to that which represents the neck but lies below that which represents the hand; see PHANTOM LIMBS, Fig. P2). The sensory homunculus has a twin—the motor homunculus—which can be found in the motor cortex.

The sensory and motor homunculi are not to be confused with the homunculi invoked by *homuncular functionalism*, an approach to the mind that recommends explaining the activities of smart people by referring to the activities of their slightly-less-smart modules—activities which are to be explained in turn by reference to the activities of even-less-smart modules out of which they are composed, and so on all the way down to the level of light switches. Its advocates insist that homuncular functionalism is the working philosophy of cognitive science and the only real hope that we have for understanding cognition, but the approach struggles to do justice to the *unity of consciousness. We each have a single experience of the world. Various 'homunculi' are involved in generating this experience, but none of them is itself a subject of experience. One can see—in outline at least—how *intelligence* could be explained by positing nested coalitions of increasingly smarter homunculi, but how could *consciousness* be explained by positing nested coalitions of increasingly conscious homunculi? Consciousness occurs only at the personal (or animal) level, and it is unclear how we can account for its emergence by appealing to the operation of unconscious modules.

Notwithstanding their differences, proponents and detractors of homuncular functionalism alike agree that being called a homunculus has never been a sign of endearment.

TIM BAYNE

hypnagogic and hypnopompic experiences Hypnagogic and hypnopompic experiences (HHEs) refer to *hallucinatory experiences immediately prior to falling asleep (*hypnagogic*) or upon waking (*hypnopompic*), most often when the individual is lying in a supine position. HHEs sometimes consist of relatively simple visual imagery during a drowsy waking state: bursts of light, geometrical forms, human faces, or common objects. These are often referred to as *entoptic images*, arising from activity within the visual system, essentially as electrochemical noise normally suppressed by sensory input. More elaborate HHEs, which are the subject of the remainder of this entry, consist of multimodal hallucinations of threat and assault, as well as intense bodily vestibulomotor sensations. In addition, and in contrast to the first set of experiences, these multimodal experiences have intense emotional content, most often of overwhelming fear. Despite a temporary but profound paralysis that prevents movement of major muscles the person is lucid, awake, and aware of the immediate surroundings. In addition, individuals are often able to open their eyes and scan the surrounding area. Finally, although the experiences are quite bizarre and often frankly impossible, they have a quality of compelling reality (Hishikawa and Shimizu 1995, Cheyne 2001).

HHEs have been reported in a wide variety of traditional cultures and probably play a (possibly universal) role in cultural myths and legends concerning nocturnal spirits and demons (Hufford 1982). In modern industrialized societies, HHEs have been proposed as a likely source of alien abduction, spirit possession, and astral travel. Treatises on the nightmare in the 18th and 19th centuries clearly describe HHEs with sleep paralysis as the prototypical nightmare (Liddon 1967). Until recently, HHEs have been more likely to attract the attention of mystics, theosophists, and students of the paranormal than of mainstream scholars and neuroscientists.

In recent decades, however, HHEs have been reported during polysomnographic recording in sleep laboratories and have been associated with sleep-onset REM or mixed REM and waking patterns (Takeuchi et al. 1992; see SLEEP). Consistent with the notion that HHEs are REM phenomena is the almost universally reported paralysis, a defining feature of REM, as a component of HHEs. Thus, the most obvious explanation for HHEs is that they constitute REM-related dream imagery intruding into waking consciousness and superimposed on the waking environment. HHEs thus appear to represent a blend of waking and *dreaming consciousness, a feature shared with lucid dreaming and false awakenings.

HHEs have been classified into three conceptual and empirically corroborated clusters labelled intruder, incubus, and vestibulomotor experiences (Cheyne et al. 1999). The core of *intruder experiences* is a sensed presence, a compelling feeling, independent of sensory corroboration, of someone or something present watching or approaching, usually with malevolent intentions. Thus, the sensed presence shares with a number of phenomena, such as *déjà vu, Capgras and Fregoli syndromes (see BRAIN DAMAGE), and tip-of-the-tongue experiences (see FEELING OF KNOWING), a compelling sense of knowing in the absence of any evidence of what is taken to be known. The sensed presence is technically a *delusion, usually with paranoid content, rather than a hallucination inasmuch as it has no sensory content. It is, however, often associated with, or followed by, auditory, visual, and tactile hallucinations. Auditory experiences range from random sounds to voices and approaching footsteps. Visual hallucinations range from vague silhouettes to highly detailed apparitions of humans (often old or disfigured), animals, and demonic creatures. Tactile hallucinations are often of being grabbed and held. Sometimes, but not always, these separate sensations are roughly integrated into a vivid impression of a threatening intruder entering the room.

The *incubus* factor includes experiences consistent with traditional cross-cultural accounts of the old hag experience, spirit possession, or incubus attack, in which a creature is perceived to sit on the chest suffocating the experient (Hufford 1982). A major factor in such experiences is likely the REM-induced motor paralysis producing a feeling of restraint. Additional relevant features of REM include shallow rapid breathing, hypoxia, hypercapnia, and partial occlusion of airways. Such physiological events are consistent with classic incubus experiences of thoracic pressure, suffocation, pain, and physical assault by a mysterious assailant. These experiences share with intruder experiences a plausible relation to the actions of an external agent.

All the foregoing experiences are consistent with known REM neurophysiology and neuropsychology, particularly activation of limbic and paralimbic regions, including the amygdala, a likely source for both REM sleep organization and the predominately negative affective qualities of dreams (Schwartz and Maquet 2002). The amygdala is also the core of a threat-activated vigilance system, the function of which is to disambiguate incipient signs of danger by lowering sensory thresholds and biasing perceptions to corroborate the sense of threat (Whalen 1998). Such hypervigilant states may also bias interpretation of perceived events as agentic, experienced as a sense of a threatening presence. Such a bias during REM would also likely affect the generation of associated dream imagery. During sleep paralysis, the fact that one is awake, in the dark, aware of the fact that one is paralysed, and typically in a vulnerable supine position, likely increases fear and hence the threat bias during sleep paralysis relative to normal dreams. More generally, recent cognitive research and arguments have posited that belief in supernatural agents is a default of a general bias to see invisible, intelligent agents as responsible for natural events and that this bias is enhanced by hypervigilant states (Atrans 2002).

Such strong negative biases are, however, not inevitable. In some cases, fear is somewhat attenuated and a very different complex of experiences is reported. *Vestibulomotor experiences* include sensations of floating, falling, and flying, as well as *out-of-body experiences and autoscopy, during which experiences individuals report sensations of leaving their bodies and viewing themselves lying in bed. Thus, in contrast to the other-oriented nature intruder and incubus experiences, vestibulomotor experiences are very much focused on one's own body, suggesting involvement of vestibular functions as well as motor programmes and their associated corollary discharge similar to that which produces movement *imagery during REM dreams (Hobson et al. 1998). Moreover, direct stimulation of parietal sites in the human cortex produces a virtually identical set of phenomenological reports of vestibular sensations including out-of-body experiences with autoscopy (Blanke et al. 2002).

It is worth noting that, despite their apparently bizarre and outlandish properties, HHEs correspond to two fundamental domains of consciousness. One of these involves the essential task of becoming aware of the presence and disposition of animate objects (agents) in the immediate environment. An equally basic task is that of knowing the position, orientation, and movement of the bodily self in surrounding space. These domains are rather clearly implicated in the intruder and incubus experiences, on the one hand, and in the vestibulomotor experiences, on the other, consistent with the hypothesis that REM state activates neural circuitry embodying fundamental genetic programming (Jouvet 1998).

JAMES A. CHEYNE

Atrans, S. (2002). *In Gods We Trust: The Evolutionary Landscape of Religion*.

Blanke, O., Ortigue, S., Landis, T., and Seeck, M. (2002). 'Stimulating illusory own-body perceptions'. *Nature*, 419.

Cheyne, J. A. (2001). 'The ominous numinous'. *Journal of Consciousness Studies*, 8.

—— (2003). 'Sleep paralysis and the structure of waking-nightmare hallucinations'. *Dreaming*, 13.

——, Rueffer, S. D., and Newby-Clark, I. R. (1999). 'Hypnagogic and hypnopompic hallucinations during sleep paralysis: neurological and cultural construction of the night-mare'. *Consciousness and Cognition*, 8.

Hishikawa, Y., and Shimizu, T. (1995). 'Physiology of REM sleep, cataplexy, and sleep paralysis'. *Advances in Neurology*, 67.

Hobson, J. A., Stickgold, R., Pace-Schott, E. F., and Leslie, K. R. (1998). 'Sleep and vestibular adaptation: implications for function in microgravity'. *Journal of Vestibular Research*, 8, 81–94.

Hufford, D. J. (1982). *The Terror That Comes in the Night: An Experience-Centered Study of Supernatural Assault Traditions*.

Jouvet, M. (1998). 'Paradoxical sleep as a programming system'. *Journal of Sleep Research*, 7.

Liddon, S. C. (1967). 'Sleep paralysis and hypnagogic hallucination: their relationship to the nightmare'. *Archives of General Psychiatry*, 17.

Schwartz, S. and Maquet, P. (2002). 'Sleep imaging and neuropsychological assessment of dreams'. *Trends in Cognitive Science*, 6.

Takeuchi, T., Miyasita, A., Sasaki, Y., Inugami, M., and Fukuda, K. (1992). 'Isolated sleep paralysis elicited by sleep interruptions'. *Sleep*, 15.

Whalen, P. J. (1998). 'Fear, vigilance, and ambiguity: initial neuroimaging studies of the human amygdala'. *Current Directions in Psychological Science*, 7.

hypnosis Practices similar to hypnosis can be found in the historical and cultural records of virtually every human community where such records are available. Individuals utilize a diverse range of culturally defined rituals to induce dramatic and abrupt alterations in their own or another's conscious experience in ways that defy the framework of everyday reality (see ALTERED STATE OF CONSCIOUSNESS). This can include (without the ingestion of drugs); vivid *hallucinatory experiences, *deluded beliefs, behavioural compulsions, transformations in the sense of self-identity, *body image or time sense, apparent failures of volitional control of mind and body, and insensibility to pain or numerous other sensory experiences. In all cultures these rituals and their associated experiences are closely tied to religion, healing, and to the social power of (either dominant or marginalized) individuals in the key roles they offer.

The modern practice of hypnosis has its roots in the efforts of the 18th century German physician Franz Anton Mesmer to seek a naturalistic understanding of the apparently miraculous public cures of physical and mental suffering brought about by the religious exorcisms of his famous contemporary, the Roman Catholic priest Father Johann Gassner. Mesmer applied the leading scientific ideas of his day (based around physical fluids and magnetic forces) to develop the theory and practice of 'animal magnetism' as a system of inexpensive, effective public health interventions widely available to the general community. The French royal commission of 1784, led by Benjamin Franklin, effectively discredited Mesmer's theory of animal magnetism. However, the Franklin commission conspicuously failed to discredit the practical efficacy of Mesmerism's psychological healing techniques. The medical practice of what came to be known as hypnosis continued to grow throughout Europe, Britain, and later the United States in the 19th century while academic theories came and went as to its true nature. At the same time hypnosis fascinated the general public and rapidly became a popular pastime. Today stage hypnosis has become a multimillion pound industry which aggressively defends its financial interests against any perceived threats from the practitioners of medical and scientific hypnosis.

Since the 19th century theories of hypnosis can be divided into two broad categories; those that invoke explanatory mechanisms which in some important way lie outside the domain of the processes that are believed to explain ordinary behaviour and experience, and those that explain hypnosis in terms of essentially the same mechanisms that are believed to account for ordinary behaviour and experience. At various time this divide has been framed as a distinction between psychological or neurophysiological explanations. Since the 1960s it has most typically been cast as a debate between *state theorists*, those who believe that hypnosis requires the induction of an altered state of consciousness, and *non-state theorists*, who believe that the experiences and behaviours found in hypnosis can be wholly accounted for by mundane psychological processes. These distinctions belie the fact that theories on either side have changed beyond recognition from one historical era to another and that the differences between contemporary state accounts are at least as great as their differences with leading non-state theories. The same can be said for the differences between non-state theorists who have proposed a multitude of differing mundane processes (e.g. goal-directed fantasy, strategic enactment, response expectancy) to account for hypnosis. Then there are many theorists who simply do not fit comfortably into the state or non-state categorization. Though readers need not accept this traditional division, they must at least be aware of it in order to make sense of much of the existing literature and perhaps to avoid being caught in the academic cross-fire which it continues to generate.

The hypnotic induction ritual (itself a suggestion to respond hypnotically) is typically followed by a series of suggestions to experience the fictitious situations and events described to the subject as if they were actually real; suggestions are then given for these experiences, and later for all responses to hypnotic suggestion to terminate. Robert W. White, the seminal mid 20th century figure, from whom both later state and non-state theorists diverged, observed that hypnotic suggestions implicitly contain within themselves a profound contradiction between the demand on one hand to experience the suggestion as if real, and on the other hand to be aware of and continue to respond to the changing communications of the hypnotist, i.e. the actual situational reality (White 1941). For example, a subject age-regressed to age 5, when they could only speak and understand French, may answer in French to a hypnotist's question posed in English. Alternatively, a hypnotically deaf subject will regain their hearing when the hypnotist tells them that they are again able to hear. Hypnotic responding therefore requires an experience that is both at odds with reality and in tune with reality. As such, it is neither straightforward hallucination nor simple compliance. Contemporary phenomenological studies of hypnosis confirm a richly varied and fluidly shifting mix of illusion and reality (unapparent to simple behavioural observation) at the heart of hypnotic experience. At its most extreme this may take the form of *duality*, the spontaneous report of an actual and suggested self, in some sense, coexisting in the same experience.

Hypnotized individuals are profoundly sensitive to the literal wording of suggestions, their idiosyncratic meaning, and the person's prior beliefs and expectations about hypnosis (which seem to act as additional suggestions). Martin Orne famously demonstrated that highly susceptible individuals with a (false) expectation that hypnosis results in an inability to move their dominant hand will spontaneously demonstrate this 'phenomenon' in hypnosis while naive subjects will not (Orne 1959, 1972). The profound influence of expectations, implicit (contextual), and explicit communications of the hypnotist on the detail and content of unfolding hypnotic responses has led many (non-state theorists) to believe that hypnosis is best explained primarily as a social psychological phenomenon. Other (state theorists) have sought in various ways to separate the 'artefact' of social psychological influences from the 'essence' of hypnosis, which is what is believed to be left when such influences have been subtracted. Still others (state theorists) have identified hyper (rather than normal) suggestibility to expectation and contextual influences as a core phenomenon (part of the essence), which must be explained by a successful theory of hypnosis.

The sense of involuntariness accompanying the response to hypnotic suggestions is widely considered to be one of the core characteristics of hypnosis. Weitzenhoffer (1953) called this 'the classic suggestion effect'. In response to *challenge* suggestions hypnotized individuals readily experience themselves as unable to make simple movements, while in response to *ideomotor* suggestions they experience themselves as making movements that they have not willed. They may experience themselves as unable to (volitionally) retrieve memories for recent events or to consciously access specific semantic information (e.g. about the number 3) in simple mental operations (such as arithmetic). All these effects are readily reversible with the termination of suggestion. A self-consciously volitional response in these circumstances would not be considered as a genuine hypnotic response. This may be considered either as one of the social demand characteristics of the hypnotic context and hypnotic communication or as a key component of the regulation of cognitive control that is altered when a person becomes hypnotized (of course these are not mutually exclusive alternatives).

From the beginning it was apparent to hypnosis practitioners that some individuals appear to be unresponsive to hypnosis, and only a minority are able to experience the most dramatic and profound suggested alterations in experience. One of the most important contributions of mid 20th century hypnosis research was the development of reliable and valid instruments for the measurement of hypnotic susceptibility. This research has confirmed that individual differences in hypnotic susceptibility are a remarkably stable feature of adults even when tracked across decades of life experience. Despite an intensive investigation over many decades, hypnotizability has not been found to reliably correlate with any of the standard psychological dimensions of personality or of intellectual or mental abilities. It appears to be a fundamental human attribute (like musical, artistic, or athletic abilities), which exists alongside other fundamental attributes such as verbal and visuospatial problem solving, *working memory capacity, sociability, anxiety, or other major dimensions of human personality. This begs the questions both of its biological bases and its evolutionary development (see Heap et al. 2004).

Reliable correlates of hypnotic susceptibility have been found in numerous studies which sought to measure the occurrence of 'trance-like' experiences in everyday life. Josephine Hilgard (1979) reported that high susceptibility was associated with deep biographical involvements in reading fiction, drama, religion, aesthetic experiences, and imagination (including imaginary childhood companions). Tellegen and Atkinson (1974) developed the 'Absorption' questionnaire with questions about imagination, involvement in nature, mystical experiences, ESP, and *synaesthesia-like experiences which correlated modestly but reliably with hypnotic susceptibility. Wilson and Barber (1983) confirmed that vivid and frequent experiences of magic, fantasy, and make-believe in childhood and adulthood were positively related to hypnotic susceptibility. Despite these convergent findings, later studies demonstrated that such measures account for only a small proportion of the variability in hypnotic responsiveness and that high scores on such measures are neither necessary nor sufficient for high hypnotic susceptibility (though low scores may preclude high hypnotic susceptibility). Nonetheless they offer an important clue to the ecological role of the human abilities which underlie hypnotic-like responsiveness outside its otherwise recent Western context.

The clinical applications of hypnosis also provide valuable clues to its underlying nature. The major application of hypnosis has been in the control of *pain. Despite the availability of chemical *anaesthetics there continue to be many circumstances in which they are either unavailable or unsuitable. Though hypnotic susceptibility is related to the degree of analgesia experienced, most people derive significant pain relief from hypnotic suggestion, especially in emergency situations. Research confirms that hypnotic analgesia is not blocked by the opioid antagonist naloxone. Hypnotic analgesia suggests the existence of additional central nociceptive mechanisms or perhaps the additional role of opioid receptor sub-types not targeted by naloxone. An earlier *functional brain imaging study of hypnotic analgesia has identified the role of the anterior cingulate cortex (ACC) in the representation of the affective (as distinct from the sensory) components of pain experience (see e.g. Rainville et al. 2002). The effectiveness of hypnotic analgesia has subsequently been linked to the engagement of this dorsal region of the ACC in modulating activity in a wide network of pain-related regions within the brain (Faymonville et al. 2003). In addition to pain control, studies of medical and dental procedures that employ hypnotic analgesia have widely reported reduced bleeding during the procedures, lower complication rates, and improved outcomes.

A common denominator in many medical conditions in which there is consistent evidence for the effectiveness of hypnosis (e.g. hypertension, the treatment of burns patients, various dermatological disorders) is the role of vascular reactivity and local blood supply. There is strong evidence for a deep link between hypnotic susceptibility, hypnosis, and the regulation of medically important peripheral vascular functions. For example, hypnotic susceptibility has been repeatedly found to buffer the negative effects of pain and stress on arterial blood flow (Jambrik et al. 2005) and self-reported hypnotic depth has been found to be closely related to measures of parasympathetic nervous system involvement in the regulation of heart rate variability (Diamond et al. 2008). The major effects of hypnosis are therefore not limited to alterations in conscious experience but must also include alterations in integrated central and peripheral nervous system networks which mediate key aspects of somatic self-regulation. As such, hypnosis provides both a major challenge and an important opportunity for cognitive and affective neuroscience research to extend our understanding of the links between the neural mechanisms which regulate our conscious states and those which regulate our somatic states.

Hypnotic interventions have been successfully incorporated in many forms of psychotherapy, and this remains the other major area of clinical application. Hypnosis is not a magic cure-all, however, and careful investigation must continue to delineate the areas in which it is effective and those in which it is not. When used in conjunction with cognitive behavioural approaches, hypnosis adds to the effectiveness and maintenance of therapeutic outcomes for the self-management of many important behavioural problems. Important areas of current research include the role of hypnosis and hypnotic susceptibility in the modulation of aspects of immunological functioning and the role of hypnosis-related processes in the aetiology and maintenance of 'dissociative' symptoms in psychiatric disorders such as conversion disorder (see DISSOCIATIVE IDENTITY DISORDER).

One popular area in which the use of hypnosis is fraught with danger is in the recovery of *memories not previously accessible to non-hypnotic recall. Hypnotically recovered memories may be profoundly influenced, wittingly or unwittingly, by both the explicit and implicit suggestions of the hypnotist and by the expectations of the subject. It is unsafe to accept the content of such memories at face value without independent corroboration by objective evidence.

Both positive and negative perceptual hallucinations in response to hypnotic suggestions have led some researchers to propose that hypnosis should be understood as an expression of the capacity for top-down control and/or attentional regulation within the brain. However, many of the changes in experience reported in hypnosis appear to indicate disruptions in the executive control of behaviour and cognitive processes. This has led still other researchers to propose that hypnosis is instead the outcome of a breakdown in the hierarchical organization of cognitive control processes within the *brain. Recently *electroencephalographic (EEG) and fMRI findings have converged to show a breakdown in the flow of information (functional connectivity) amongst anterior cortical regions which implement monitoring and control functions as well as between anterior and central or posterior cortical regions. These findings support a breakdown in at least some aspects of executive control as a core feature of hypnosis; however, it is also possible that this very breakdown of higher-level controls may allow attentional mechanisms to operate unhindered in generating responses to some hypnotic suggestions (Egner and Raz 2007).

In addition, there is also clear evidence for differing functional roles between left and right anterior cortical regions in the generation of hypnotic experience (Szechtman et al. 1998, Miltner and Weiss 2007). Characteristic alterations in aspects of experience during hypnosis such as relaxation and absorption have been shown to be mediated by alterations in activity in posterior, mid, and rostral cingulate cortex constituting a series of central midline structures integrating the regulation of bodily self-representations, pain, motor, and cognitive control as well as affective and somatic states (Rainville et al. 2002). Rainville et al. (2002) have also demonstrated that these alterations in hypnotic experience are closely tied to alterations in activity in brainstem and midbrain nuclei previously known to play a critical role in the regulation of consciousness. In the last decade, then, hypnosis has been shown to produce an organized set of changes in the activity and functional integration of regions within the brainstem, midbrain, and cortex (including posterior, midline and left/right anterior cortex) which are systematically linked to specific alterations in conscious functioning reported during hypnosis. Suggestive though this is, such work does not unambiguously establish hypnosis as the product of a unique altered-state-like process. For example, (non-state) socio-cognitive influences on experience during hypnosis may also be expected to have their characteristic patterns of neurophysiological implementation. Much more remains to be understood about the functional significance of dynamic patterns of spatial and temporal interaction within the brain, how they are driven and organized and how they may change across hypnotic and non-hypnotic contexts in individuals with high and low susceptibility before this controversy can finally be laid to rest.

Hypnosis presents an intriguing set of phenomena where the everyday experience of self and reality seems dramatically turned on its head. Hypnosis occurs against a backdrop of social rituals, roles, expectations, and relationships which play an essential role in structuring hypnotic responses. Not everyone is able to experience hypnosis, and only some are able to undergo the most profound transformations of experience. Hypnosis is closely related to a species-wide capacity for the temporary restructuring of basic elements of the human experience. The capacity to experience hypnosis is likely to have deep roots in human evolution and biology. It is intimately linked to basic human capacities for the self-regulation of experience, behaviour, and clinically significant aspects of somatic (as well as central nervous system) physiology. For consciousness researchers in particular hypnosis provides a tool through which many of the core experiences of the self, volition, and reality may be teased apart and reconstructed, thereby allowing unique experimental tests of the underlying processes that govern their ordinary construction.

GRAHAM A. JAMIESON

Diamond, S. G., Davis, O. C., and Howe, R. D. (2008). 'Heart-rate variability as a quantitative measure of hypnotic depth'. *International Journal of Clinical and Experimental Hypnosis*, 56.

Egner, T. and Raz, A. (2007). 'Cognitive control processes and hypnosis'. In Jamieson, G. A. (ed.) *Hypnosis and Conscious States: The Cognitive Neuroscience Perspective.*

Faymonville, M. E., Roediger, L., Del Fiore, G. et al. (2003). 'Increased cerebral functional connectivity underlying the antinociceptive effects of hypnosis'. *Brain Research Cognitive Brain Research*, 17.

Heap, M., Brown, R. J. and Oakley, D. A. (eds) (2004). *The Highly Hypnotizable Person: Theoretical Experimental and Clinical Issues.*

Hilgard, J. R. (1979). 'Imaginative and sensory-affective involvements in everyday life and in hypnosis'. In Fromm, E. and Shor, R. E. (eds) *Developments in Research and New Perspectives.*

Jambrik, Z., Santarcangelo, E. L., Rudisch, T. et al. (2005). 'Modulation of pain-induced endothelial dysfunction by hypnotisability'. *Pain*, 116.

Miltner, W. H. F. and Weiss, T. (2007). 'Cortical mechanisms of hypnotic pain control'. In Jamieson, G. A. (ed.) *Hypnosis and Conscious States: the Cognitive Neuroscience Perspective.*

Orne, M. T. (1959). 'The nature of hypnosis: artifact and essence'. *Journal of Abnormal and Social Psychology*, 58.

—— (1972). 'On the simulating subject as a quasi-control group in hypnosis research: what, why, and how'. In Fromm, E. and Shor, R. E. (eds) *Developments in Research and New Perspectives.*

Rainville, P., Hofbauer, R. K., Bushnell, M. C., Duncan, G. H., and Price, D. D. (2002). 'Hypnosis modulates activity in bran structures involved in the regulation of consciousness'. *Journal of Cognitive Neuroscience*, 14.

Szechtman, H., Woody, E., Bowers, K. S., and Nahmias, C. (1998). 'Where the imaginal appears real: a positron emission tomography study of auditory hallucinations'. *Proceedings of the National Academy of Sciences of the USA*, 95.

Tellegen, A. and Atkinson, G. (1974). 'Openness to absorbing and self-altering experiences ("absorption"), a trait related to hypnotic susceptibility'. *Journal of Abnormal Psychology*, 83.

Weitzenhoffer, A. M. (1953). *Hypnotism: an Objective Study in Suggestibility.*

White, R. W. (1941) 'An analysis of motivation in hypnosis'. *Journal of General Psychology*, 24.

Wilson, S. C. and Barber, T. X. (1983). 'The fantasy-prone personality: implications for understanding imagery, hypnosis, and parapsychological phenomena'. In Sheikh, A. A. (ed.) *Imagery: Current Theory, Research, and Application.*

I

idealism Philosophical idealism holds a prominent place in Eastern and Western thought and comes in many, importantly distinct, varieties. There is no unique doctrine to which all idealists would subscribe, but any philosophy worthy of the name denies that reality (either as intelligible to us or in some more ultimate sense) can be adequately characterized in purely mind-independent ways—i.e. in ways that do not recognize the fundamental and constitutive contributions of the mental or spiritual. As such, idealists reject any philosophy that is founded on the hope or assumption that reality can be adequately and exhaustively understood in entirely disenchanted, impersonal terms. This opposition is evident in all of its major variants which include subjective–ontological, transcendental, and absolute idealism.

1. Subjective–ontological idealism
2. Transcendental idealism
3. Absolute idealism
4. Idealism in Eastern thought
5. The importance of idealism

1. Subjective–ontological idealism

Berkeley's writings constitute the *locus classicus* of subjective–ontological idealism. He held that all thought and conception was ultimately grounded in 'ideas' of a perceptual nature and experiential origin. This empiricism was based on the view, prevalent in the 17th and 18th centuries, that *representation is a kind of resemblance. From it Berkeley argued for an ontological thesis, insisting that the only existents are minds, human or divine, and their contents. He challenged the realism promoted by others such as Locke, who posited the existence of primary qualities which were distinct from and causally responsible for sensations. According to Berkeley, such mind-independent things, e.g. 'matter', were literally beyond our comprehension; the idea of such things was not given to us in direct sensory encounters nor could it be constructed from such.

An obvious worry is that in denying the intelligibility of a super-sensible world, Berkeleyian idealism would be unable to provide a satisfactory explanation of the causes of our reliable and systematic experience of the world. Berkeley's answer was to allow that there exists a world beyond our senses while maintaining that anything which exists unperceived by human minds must be an idea perceived in the mind of some other spirit—e.g. the mind of God. Hence the famous motto *esse est percipi*—to be is to be perceived.

2. Transcendental idealism

Idealism of an entirely different kind originates from Kant, whose self-styled Copernican Revolution turned the tables on prior thinking by arguing that representations make their objects possible rather than objects making representations possible. Accordingly, the sum total of what exists, empirically, is limited to what can be grasped by human objective thought. No aspect of the world is forever beyond human conceivability since empirical reality is always in principle knowable. In Kantian thinking this idea is combined with another: it is not possible to explain or understand the basis of 'our view of things' by appeal to any of the objective categories that apply in our everyday worldly encounters—including those of our best sciences. In seeking to explicate the necessary conditions, both formal and material, that make objective representation of the world possible, Kant also observed that as our categories of experience only apply to empirical reality they cannot shed light on anything that might be imagined to transcend such a reality—i.e. the world as-it-is-in-itself. The result is transcendental idealism. Its central insight is preserved in contemporary versions of linguistic idealism, which regards concepts as dependent upon our evolving linguistic practices rather than as fixed and universal inheritances (see LINGUISTICS AND THE STUDY OF CONSCIOUSNESS).

3. Absolute idealism

More radically, emphasizing the unity and connectedness of all things, absolute idealists deny that there is any contrast between our ways of representing the world and the way the world is in-itself at all; there is no genuine division between mind and reality (or being). This idea, which dominated much 19th century philosophy, was developed in Germany in quite distinct ways by such diverse thinkers as Hegel, Fichte, and Schelling. It appeared in revised form and remained influential in Anglo-American thinking until the turn of the 20th century through the efforts of Bradley, Green, McTaggart, and Royce.

Hegel's version emerged as a direct response to what he saw as unacceptable *dualisms residual in Kant's philosophy—dualisms that prevented the realization of important religious and political ideals. Taking critical philosophy to its extremes, he found fault with Kant's method of deducing the categories, arguing that their validity could only be legitimately demonstrated if what is inherent in thinking was made manifest. For Hegel this could only be achieved by means of a historical, dialectical process in which antecedent assumptions about the nature of the categories or judgement forms had no place. Familiar distinctions between, say, thought and reality or self and other could neither be the basis nor the end product of philosophical endeavour. For Hegel, conceptual explication and expression turn out to be a kind of rational, spiritual development; the fundamental self-determination of the idea through dialectical activity. Over time, spirit develops by itself and for itself.

Not every form of absolute idealism acknowledges such progressive development. For Bradley, the absolute was not something to be concretely realized: rather, its ever-present unity underlies all appearance but resists intellectual characterization in terms of our partial concepts. Our best available analogy of it is as a kind of non-conceptual experience that admits of no distinctions of thought. At the core of absolute idealism is the thought that ultimately all familiar things and everyday relations—including those distinguishing mind and reality—are merely apparent, they are manifestations of a deeper underlying unity.

4. Idealism in Eastern thought

Idealism also figures centrally in much Eastern thought. Philosophical reflection on the Vedas and the Upanishads, which treat consciousness as epistemically and metaphysically fundamental, inspired a rich variety of Indian schools. Although these resist easy classification, some are decidedly idealist in character. For example, the Advaita Vedānta conceives of consciousness as the eternal, undifferentiated, self-luminous ground of all being. In contrast, all that we seemingly encounter as distinct forms in the empirical world is regarded as illusory. In a way reminiscent of the absolute idealism, its proponents make no distinction between the subjective and the objective. Like Hegel, in their view, consciousness is universal and public, not individual and private.

Yogācarā Buddhism—also called the 'mind-only' or 'consciousness-only' school—can look, prima facie, similar to Berkeleyian idealism. Its adherents argue that consciousness and its objects are identical because it is not possible to separate one's phenomenal awareness from that which one is aware of—e.g. one cannot prise apart blueness from the awareness of blueness. They also maintain that all conceptions must be finally grounded in experience. For example, they try to show that our understanding of materiality is ultimately not theoretically based but always based in what is felt and perceived.

Such arguments and reminders, however, are not offered in order to sponsor a positive metaphysics. They are designed to encourage us to relinquish all objective modes of thought so as to enable us to surrender attachment to the idea of an enduring self or ego. In seeking to overcome unenlightened forms of consciousness, they are sceptical and therapeutic in character, having an ethical as opposed to ontological import.

5. The importance of idealism

Idealistic philosophies matter because they offer alternative ways of understanding consciousness and its place in nature. To accept idealism is to abandon the aspirations of realistic metaphysicians who promote scientific naturalism of the sort that generates the so-called problem of consciousness (see HARD PROBLEM OF CONSCIOUSNESS). The latter arises because of our apparent inability to successfully explain how or why consciousness fits into the natural order of things. Straight solutions to such problems require the development of a theory that shows how consciousness coheres in a satisfactory way with entities postulated by our best sciences (or those that they will postulate when they have finished their work). Attempts to address this family of problems have led to the development of theories seeking to account for the most intractable features of consciousness in purely functional, physical and other categories that already feature in (or can be accommodated without difficulty by) our scientific world view.

Starting in a different place, idealists do not recognize the same set of problems (or at least they do not see them as problems in the same way). In denying the very idea of a genuinely mind-independent reality and taking the presence of mind (or minds) to be in some sense fundamental, idealists upset the sort of thinking that makes consciousness appear problematic. In contrast, their greatest challenge—at least for those who wish to make their position credible to modern eyes, avoiding the charge of romantic sentimentalism—is to provide an adequate non-realist account of the status of scientific practice and its theoretical constructs.

If anything, idealists could be said to have a problem with reality, or at least certain philosophical conceptions of it. They face the challenge of making sense of the status of the theoretical posits of modern science and of accounting for its successes. The ambitions and agenda of logical positivism, one of the most recent and influential forms of subjective–ontological idealism, clearly acknowledges this. As latter-day empiricists, the members of the Vienna Circle and others such as A. J. Ayer engaged in sophisticated and impressive attempts to show that all meaningful claims, including those of the most abstract theoretical sciences, must ultimately be analysable as verifiable sensory or observational statements. Concomitantly, they held that any apparent substantial claims that resist such analysis—including those purporting to be about an external, mind-independent reality—were to be understood, not as false but as nonsense.

Positivism has been pretty thoroughly rejected, chiefly because of intractable problems in justifying its restrictive theory of meaning. Interestingly, early versions of *physicalism inherited their general structure and methodological goal of reductionism directly from positivism, but importantly they traded the epistemic bedrock of sense-data for an ontological ground floor of theoretical entities, events, and their relations. Notably, therefore the fall of positivism not only constitutes the collapse of an interesting version of idealism, it also marks the inauguration of the now dominant form of scientific naturalism which sponsors contemporary problems of consciousness.

Since realists and idealists disagree about such fundamental matters as the nature of reality, their debates are not always straightforward. Historically, idealism has been motivated by appeal to transcendental arguments and attempts at philosophical therapy. Using similarly indirect methods, many contemporary idealists seek to demonstrate that we are logically compelled to endorse some version of it due to the explanatory failures of realism in various domains.

Revealing the inadequacies of direct realist and representational theories of *perception, Foster (2000) argues for idealism on the grounds that any physically relevant ultimate reality—one that causally sustains our sensory organization—cannot be truly logically independent of the human mind because its laws must be partially concerned with human mentality.

Hutto (1998, 2000) and D'Oro (2005) have argued that explanatory versions of physicalism, reductive or non-reductive, are condemned to fail because our concepts of the 'mental' and 'physical' belong to incompatible domains to the extent that they are meaningfully well defined. If so, it is impossible to render the relation between the mental and the physical intelligible. Although this would rule out the prospects for satisfactory conceptual reductions or explanations, some version of a psychophysical identity theory might still be true. Considerations about mental causation and metaphysical unity supply independent grounds for believing in such a truth and there are other familiar reasons for rejecting metaphysical dualism (or pluralism) in favour of monism of some kind. But in their pure forms, these are not arguments for physicalism per se. Monism –the view that reality is not ultimately divided into distinct ontological kinds—does not entail physicalism. This fact gains importance if we doubt that a privileged but impersonal specification of ultimate reality is so much as possible—not even as the outcome of a future, completed ideal physics. These concerns provide excellent reasons to take some form of idealism seriously, even today.

DANIEL D. HUTTO

D'Oro, G. (2005). 'Idealism and the philosophy of mind'. *Inquiry*, 48.

Foster, J. (1982). *The Case for Idealism*.

—— (2000). *The Nature of Perception*.

Garfield, J. (2002). *Empty Words: Buddhist Philosophy and Cross-Cultural Interpretation*.

Gupta, B. (2003). *CIT Consciousness*.

Hutto, D. D. (1998). 'An ideal solution to the problem of consciousness'. *Journal of Consciousness Studies*, 5.

—— (2000). *Beyond Physicalism*.

identity theory The doctrine that mental states are identical with physical states was defended in antiquity by Lucretius and in the early modern era by Hobbes. It achieved considerable prominence in the 1950s as a result of the writings of Herbert Feigl, U. T. Place, and J. J. C. Smart (see e.g. Smart 1959). These authors developed reasonably precise formulations of the doctrine, clarified the grounds for embracing it, and responded persuasively to a range of objections. More recently it has been defended systematically by Hill (1991) and Papineau (2002). Other contemporary advocates include Loar (1990), McLaughlin (2003), and Polger (2004). The doctrine also figures explicitly or implicitly in the writings of dualists, who are of course concerned to oppose it. Thus, for example, it plays an important role in Kripke's influential defence of *dualism (Kripke 1980).

1. Token identity and type identity
2. Qualia
3. Type materialism and property dualism
4. Supervenience
5. Representationalism
6. Objections to type materialism

1. Token identity and type identity

It is necessary to distinguish between theories of mental states that make claims of *token* identity and theories that make claims of *type* identity. Theories of the first sort maintain that concrete mental events, such as the *pain I experienced at 3 p.m. today, are identical with particular physical events, such as the processing of information from peripheral nociceptors that took place in my brain at 3 p.m. Theories of the second sort assert that mental properties are identical with physical properties. A view of this sort might claim, for example, that the property *being a pain* is identical with the property *being a burst of activity in regions* $R_1, R_2, \ldots, R_n$ *of the cerebral cortex*. Now the proposition that a mental property φ is identical with a physical property ψ entails that all concrete tokens of φ are identical with tokens of ψ, but there is no entailment running in the other direction. In view of these facts about entailment, it is clear that claims of type identity are logically stronger than claims of token identity, and have correspondingly greater power to unify and simplify our theories of human nature and the universe. In part because of this greater power, and in part also because claims of type identity are thought to be much more problematic than claims of token identity, the former claims have received much more attention than the latter. Indeed, the contemporary literature focuses almost exclusively on type identity.

2. Qualia

Discussions of type identity generally presuppose the notion of *qualitative characteristics* or **qualia*. There is no universally accepted definition of this notion, but there is wide agreement that qualia include the intrinsic, introspectible characteristics of bodily sensations, such as *being a pain*, the intrinsic, introspectible characteristics of emotions, such as the feeling of awe, and the characteristics of perceptual experiences that we keep track of by expressions like 'looks yellow,' 'tastes sweet,' or 'smells sulphurous.' It is often said that a mental state counts as qualitative if there is something it is like to be in that state (see 'WHAT IT'S LIKE').

Contemporary advocates of type identity generally restrict their claims to qualia. Thus, the most common version of the type identity thesis is the claim that qualia are identical with certain properties that fall within the domain of neuroscience. There are several reasons for this restriction. Perhaps the most important of these is that much of the motivation for the doctrine of type identity, and also much of the justification, comes from correlation laws linking qualia to neural properties. There is considerable evidence, for example, that conscious pain is correlated with a complex pattern of neural firing that includes activity in certain frontal regions of the cortex and also activity in certain somatosensory regions. It seems quite unlikely that there are similar correlation laws linking such representational states as beliefs and desires to specific forms of brain activity (see CORRELATES OF CONSCIOUSNESS). This is because representational states presumably owe their representational contents to informational relations linking agents to phenomena in the external environment. In order to believe that Bill Clinton is tall, for example, it seems that an agent must possess a concept that he uses to encode information about Bill Clinton.

3. Type materialism and property dualism

There are three principal reasons for accepting the view that qualitative properties are identical with neural properties (hereafter *type materialism*). The first reason, which played a large role in the early discussions by Smart, is that type materialism provides us with a simpler and more coherent picture of the world than some alternative views. In particular, the picture of the world that it presents is much simpler, and much more coherent, than the picture that is presented by *property dualism*, which maintains that qualia are sui generic, playing no role in physics, biology, or any other natural science. Where type materialism sees only a single characteristic, a quale that is also a neural property, property dualism recognizes two. But it appears to be a counsel of reason that all other things being equal, we should prefer simpler theories to complex ones. Second, type materialism is the only theory that fully honours our intuitions about the causal powers of qualia. We attribute important causal powers to pain, but neuroscience shows that these causal powers also reside in the neural property that is correlated with pain. Accordingly, if pain is distinct from that property, we will be obliged to conclude either that pain has turned out to be epiphenomenal, possessing no causal powers in its own right, but merely seeming to possess them because of its association with the neural property, or that there is a weird duplication of causal powers, with an attendant overdetermination of the concrete events that are caused by pains. Neither of these options is appealing. Third, as is emphasized in Hill (1991), type materialism is supported by a best explanation argument. The thesis that qualia are identical with neural properties provides an explanation of why there are correlation laws linking the former properties to the latter. Moreover, the explanation is significantly better than the explanations that other theories afford. Now it is a generally accepted principle of inductive reasoning that, all other things being equal, it is appropriate to give preference to theories that provide the best explanations of phenomena in their domains. In combination with the foregoing observations, this principle provides us with a strong prima facie reason to embrace type materialism.

The views competing with type materialism are principally property dualism, **functionalism*, and **representationalism*.

4. Supervenience

In addition to denying that qualia are identical with physical properties, property dualism denies that the former properties *supervene* on the latter. A set of properties S_1 is said to supervene on another set S_2 if there are no possible worlds that are exactly alike with respect to the members of S_2 but different with respect to S_1. Since property dualism denies supervenience, it allows that there are worlds that coincide with the actual world with respect to all physical phenomena, but diverge from it with respect to qualitative phenomena. From the perspective of property dualism, it is a kind of accident that qualitative phenomena are arranged the way they are in relation to physical phenomena. Indeed, it is an accident that there are any qualitative phenomena at all.

Functionalism and representationalism agree with type materialism in asserting that the qualitative supervenes on the physical, but they deny the much stronger thesis that qualitative properties are identical with neural properties. Where type materialism entails that qualitative properties are individuated in the same way as neural properties, in terms of the organization of neural tissue and its material composition, functionalism asserts that the individuation is causal. Thus, for example, it entails that the essential nature of pain consists of causal properties like *being a state that causes withdrawal from damaging or potentially damaging stimuli*. Because of this, it allows that qualitative states can be realized by a wide variety of physical systems, including the *Star Wars* robot C3PO and other creatures with artificial brains. After all, it is clear that C3PO has a state that causes it to withdraw from potentially damaging stimuli.

5. Representationalism

The third alternative, representationalism, has several forms. In one version it claims that qualitative states are identical with certain representational states. On this view, pain is a kind of perceptual or quasi-perceptual representation, though one that is in the service of an internal, introspective perceptual modality. It represents actual or potential bodily damage. According to another version, qualia are the properties that are represented by certain perceptual or quasi-perceptual representations. Pain, for instance, is said to be bodily damage *as represented by* an introspective perceptual representation. Most versions of representationalism diverge from functionalism in their positive claims about the individuation of qualia. This is because it is generally thought that the representational content of a state depends on factors other than its causal powers. Thus, for example, it is often claimed that whether a representational state has the property φ as its content depends on whether the state has the *function* of encoding information about φ. It seems unlikely that the notion of a function can be explained exhaustively in causal terms.

6. Objections to type materialism

There are several impressive objections to type materialism. First, there is the *multiple realization argument*, which was originally propounded in a series of papers that Hilary Putnam published in the 1960s (see e.g. Putnam 1973). It is inituitively plausible, Putnam claimed, that the members of many different species have mental lives that are qualitatively similar, at least in part, to those of human beings. It is natural to suppose, for example, that rodents and octopuses can experience pain, and also that certain birds and fish share some of our colour qualia. Now the brains of these creatures are structurally quite different from human brains, and also quite different from each other. Because of these structural differences, it seems unlikely that the correlation laws that link pain and colour qualia to neural properties in human brains prevail throughout the animal kingdom. That is to say, it seems unlikely that there are any universal correlation laws. But multiple realization of this sort precludes identity: unless a qualitative property is universally correlated with a neural property, it cannot possibly be identical with a neural property. It follows that type materialism is wrong. In addition to refuting type materialism, Putnam maintained, the multiple realization argument establishes the correctness of functionalism.

Another objection derives from the fact that we do not normally distinguish between its appearing to one that one is in a qualitative state and its being the case that one is in that state. Thus, for example, when it seems to an agent that he is introspectively aware of a pain, we conclude that he is aware of a pain. Because of this, it is natural to suppose that that when an agent is *introspectively aware of a pain, he must be aware of its essential nature. After all, if there is no distinction between the appearance of pain and the underlying reality, the agent is in direct epistemic contact with the pain itself. Having made these initial points, the objection goes on to point out that one is not aware of any of the structural characteristics that are definitive of neural states in being introspectively aware of a pain: one could contemplate a pain for an eternity without getting any inkling of the fact that it is accompanied by such things as the firing of action potentials and the release of neurotransmitters. Now clearly, when we combine the initial points with this additional one, we arrive at the conclusion that the essential nature of pain does not include the structural features that are definitive of neural states. But of course this implies that pain is not identical with a neural state. (This line of thought is a version of the so-called *grain argument* that was originally devised by Wilfrid Sellars.)

The *knowledge argument* is a third important objection to type materialism. This argument can be summarized as follows:

First premise: It is possible to have detailed theoretical knowledge of the physics and neuroscience of colour vision without thereby knowing anything at all about what it is like to experience colour—i.e. about colour qualia. A vision scientist who had been colour blind from birth would be in exactly this situation (see KNOWLEDGE ARGUMENT).

Second premise: If it is possible to know all of the physical facts about colour vision without knowing any of the qualitative facts, then the qualitative facts cannot be identical with physical facts.

Conclusion: Facts involving colour qualia are not identical with any facts involving physical properties. (Other objections include the *Cartesian modal argument* and the **explanatory gap argument*.)

Many philosophers have been persuaded by these objections, but advocates of type materialism have developed replies that appear to have considerable dialectical force. To begin with the multiple realization argument, they have maintained with some plausibility that our intuitions do not mandate the view that members of remote species share highly determinate qualitative properties with human beings. Rather, our intuitions indicate only that they share highly determinable or generic properties. But this means that the shared properties may after all be universally correlated with neural properties, for in addition to sharing our determinable qualitative properties, members of remote species also share many of our determinable neural properties. Another consideration is that Putnam presupposes the view that if the members of a species exhibit the behaviour that accompanies a qualitative state in human beings, then there is good reason to think they share the given qualitative state. In combination with clinical studies of phenomena like *blindsight, advances in comparative neuroanatomy have recently brought this view into question. This research appears to show that many of the complex behaviours that are normally guided by conscious, qualitatively individuated states in human beings may be produced in members of various other species by unconscious states that lack qualitative character. Human beings are equipped with powerful 'internal *zombies,' and it may be that it is our 'zombie minds' that are widely shared by other creatures.

Type materialists have also evolved a strategy for neutralizing the grain argument. If we fail to apprehend the organizational complexity of neural states in attending introspectively to pains, it is urged, this is because (a) introspection involves conceptualization, and (b) the concepts we deploy in introspection fail to register the complexity of these states, much as our commonsense concepts of plants fail to register facts about their cellular organization or DNA. In other words, type materialists maintain that it is after all possible to draw an appearance/reality distinction in connection with pains, though it is one that must be explained in terms of the distinction between conceptualized reality and reality as it is in itself, rather than, as is usual, in terms the distinction between perceptually represented reality and reality as it is in itself.

A concern about this reply is that conceptualization may not be essential to introspective awareness of pain. Perhaps such awareness is, or can be, purely experiential in character.

Type materialists also appeal to conceptualization in responding to the knowledge argument. More specifically, they appeal to the doctrine of *conceptual dualism*—the doctrine that the concepts we use to represent pain and other qualia have special features that distinguish them from the concepts that we use for physical properties. Conceptual dualism is developed in different ways in Hill (1991), Hill (1997), Loar (1990), and Papineau (2002). On all of these interpretations, it implies that the use of our qualitative concepts is epistemically autonomous: it is not in any way responsible to the factors that govern the use of physical concepts. Accordingly, on all of the interpretations, conceptual dualism predicts and fully explains the fact that it is possible to conceive of phenomena in terms of physical concepts without deploying, or being in any way committed to deploying, any qualitative concepts. Now knowledge requires conceptualization. Because of this, conceptual dualism is able to predict and fully explain the fact that it is possible to know all of the physical aspects of colour vision without knowing any of the qualitative aspects. Since conceptual dualism predicts and explains the fact in question, and conceptual dualism is compatible with type materialism, advocates of type materialism conclude that their view can accommodate the fact. Moreover, since their view has the epistemological and metaphysical advantages we noticed earlier, they conclude that it provides the *best* way of accommodating it. This conclusion calls the knowledge argument into question. (Specifically, it undercuts the intuitive motivation for the second premise of the argument.)

Type materialists tend to hold that it is possible to use similar lines of thought to neutralize the remaining objections to their view. They maintain that conceptual dualism can account fully for all of the phenomena involving qualia to which the objections appeal. To account for these phenomena, they maintain, it is enough to distinguish between neural properties as conceptualized in terms of physical concepts and neural properties as conceptualized in terms of qualitative concepts. It is not necessary to countenance a dualism of properties.

Although the strategy of using conceptual dualism to counter objections is appealing, it remains to be seen whether it is applicable in all cases. In applying the strategy, it is generally necessary to assume that one or another of our various forms of cognitive access to qualia (introspective awareness, imagination, expectation, etc.) involves conceptualization. As we saw in connection with the reply to the grain argument, it is not always clear that assumptions of this sort are correct.

CHRISTOPHER S. HILL

Hill, C. S. (1991). *Sensations: A Defense of Type Materialism.*
—— (1997). 'Imaginability, conceivability, possibility, and the mind-body problem'. *Philosophical Studies*, 87.
Kripke, S. (1980). *Meaning and Necessity.*
Loar, B. (1990). 'Phenomenal states'. *Philosophical Perspectives*, 4.
McLaughlin, B. (2003). 'Color, consciousness, and color consciousness.' In Smith, Q. and Jokic, A. (eds) *Consciousness.*
Papineau, D. (2002). *Thinking about Consciousness.*
Polger, T. (2004). *Natural Minds.*
Putnam, H. (1973). 'Psychological predicates'. In Capitan, W. H. and Merrill, D. D. (eds) *Art, Mind, and Religion.*
Smart, J. J. C. (1959). 'Sensations and brain processes'. *Philosophical Review*, 68.

illusions Illusions confuse and bias the machinery in the brain that constructs our representations of the world, because they reveal a discrepancy between what we perceive and what is objectively out there in the world. But both illusions and accurate perceptions are governed by the same lawful perceptual processes. Despite the deceptive simplicity of illusions, there are no fully agreed theories about their causes.

Illusions include geometrical illusions, in which angles, lengths, or shapes are misperceived; illusions of lightness, in which the context distorts the perceived lightness of objects; and illusions of representation, including puzzle pictures, ambiguous pictures, and impossible figures.

1. Geometrical illusions
2. Illusions of lightness
3. Illusions of representation

1. Geometrical illusions

Figure I1 shows some illusory distortions in perceived *angles*, named after their discoverers; the Zollner, Hering and Poggendorff illusions, and Fraser's LIFE figure. *Length* illusions include the Müller–Lyer, the vertical–horizontal, and the Ponzo illusion. *Shape* illusions include Roger Shepard's tables and Kitaoka's bulge illusion.

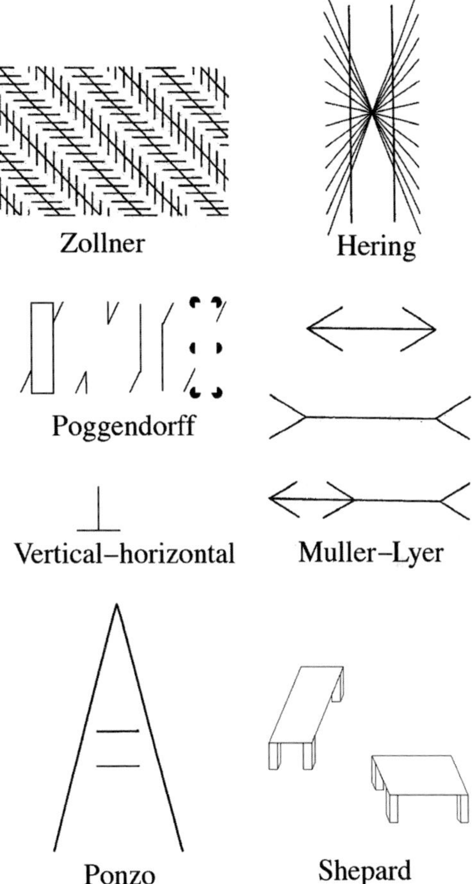

Fig. I1. Some well-known illusions.

In the Zollner illusion, the long oblique lines are parallel, but they appear to be tilted away from the small fins that cross them. In the Hering illusion the verticals are parallel but appear to be bowed outward, again in a direction away from the inducing lines. In the Poggendorff illusion, the right-hand oblique line looks as though it would pass above the left-hand oblique if extended, although both are really exactly aligned.

Geometrical illusions are not retinal, since they can be seen in random-dot stereograms, in which the patterns exist not on the retina but only as a correlation between the eyes, which is present only after the point of binocular fusion. And they are not caused by eye movements, since they can still be seen during a brief flash, and also in the (retinally stable) afterimage resulting from such a flash (see AFTER-EFFECTS, PERCEPTUAL).

There is no single accepted theory of the geometrical visual illusions. We shall consider four: (1) low-level interactions between neural detectors of length, angle, or spatial frequency; (2) depth processing theory; (3) contrast theory; and (4) statistical probability theory. The first is based upon properties of single neural cells, the second and third on more general mechanisms, and the fourth on the statistics of natural stimuli.

1. *Neural interactions*. Neurons in the primary visual area (*V1) of the cortex are tuned to lines of different orientations. If neurons tuned to similar orientations (say, 1 o'clock and 2 o'clock) inhibit each other, this will make acute angles look bigger than they really are. This would explain the Zollner illusion. In the same way, V1 neurons are tuned to different sizes, and inhibition between these might perhaps explain the Ponzo illusion.

The Poggendorff is an illusion of angle, not length. The two oblique lines are aligned but appear to be misaligned. The angular overestimation theory proposes that acute angles are overestimated, because each line comprising the angles is sensed by a population of orientation-tuned neurons, probably in brain area V1, and these two populations tend to inhibit each other, shifting the excitation peaks of the populations further apart. However, this theory cannot be quite right because the Poggendorff illusion disappears if only the acute angle are shown, though it survives if only the obtuse angles are shown. The angle theory does provide a good fit to other illusions such as the Zollner and Hering illusions, in which the test lines appear to bend away from the inducing lines that cross them. The angle theory has trouble with a Poggendorf illusion produced by an illusory vertical contour. The brain supplies the missing contour to give the overall illusion, but it cannot supply acute angles for the supposed orientation detectors to distort. Although this does not disprove a theory of misperceived angles, it goes against the idea of lateral inhibition between orientation detectors. In Kitaoka's bulge illusion, the tiny black and white squares give rise to perceived obliques, probably owing to low-level neural interactions, and the apparent obliques in turn generate an illusory three-dimensional bulge.

2. One of the most successful theories relates the illusions to *depth processing* (Thiery 1910 cited in Purves and Lotto 2003, Gregory 1966/1997). For example, the Müller–Lyer illusion is the best-known illusion of length. The line with the outgoing arrowheads looks up to 25% longer than an equal line with ingoing arrowheads. Gregory has argued that the two arrowed lines look different lengths because the arrows act as depth cues, triggering an impression that the line with the outward arrows represents a concave corner, like the corner of a room, while the line with the inward arrows triggers the perception of a three-dimensional box seen from the outside. Therefore the room corner looks further away than the box corner, and since the two vertical lines in the figure cast the same size retinal image, the brain concludes that the apparently further away line must be a physically larger object. Similarly, the horizontal lines in the Ponzo illusion look like two railway ties or sleepers, and the oblique lines are interpreted as a perspective picture of two rails receding into the distance. The upper line looks further away, so it is interpreted as a more distant, hence larger object. According to this depth processing theory, the oblique lines look like the flat projection of a three-dimensional scene of lines receding into the distance like a railway line. So we see the figure as if it had depth, and because the upper line looks further away it must be longer, because *size constancy* perceptually expands more distant objects to compensate for their smaller retinal size. Gregory (1966/1997) has argued that depth need not be consciously perceived; the presence of depth cues, such as angles, can trigger a primitive *primary size constancy*, whether or not the usual *secondary size constancy* driven by conscious depth perception, is occurring. But this theory is rather hard to test.

There is also an aptly named *confusion theory*, to the effect that one is unable to isolate the shafts from the arrow heads perceptually, so the line lengths assimilate perceptually to the full length of the outward arrows.

In Roger Shepard's table illusion, the left-hand tabletop looks long and narrow, while the right-hand table looks more nearly square. Yet the two tabletops are geometrically identical, and give identical retinal images. The illusion occurs because the vertical dimension lies in depth and is foreshortened by perspective. According to the depth processing model, the brain compensates for this by perceptually expanding the vertical (near–far) dimension.

3. Against the depth processing theory, it is not clear why the concave corner in the Müller–Lyer diagram should appear to lie at an absolutely greater distance from the observer than the convex corner. Also, the Müller–Lyer still works when the arrowheads are replaced by squares or circles, which give no particular depth cues. This has led Irvin Rock (1995) to propose a *contrast* theory of this and other illusions. He suggests that observers judge the length and angle of an object by comparing it with other objects in the field, and by exaggerating the differences. Thus the upper line in the Ponzo illusion fills most of the space between the obliques, whereas the lower line looks smaller in contrast to the large empty spaces on either side of it.

Brightness contrast is already well known—a grey spot looks darker when on a white background than on a black background. *Assimilation* is the opposite process to contrast; a grey field looks lighter when criss-crossed with white lines rather than with black lines. Rock suggests that analogous processes happen in the size domain. Contrast is the tendency to compare an object with the properties of its surround and to exaggerate the differences. In the Ponzo illusion, the lower line looks short in contrast with the large empty space at either end of it. Size assimilation illusions exist, for instance in the Delboeuf illusion the outer circle in the upper half looks apparently smaller than the inner circle in the lower half; each circle assimilates to its companion.

4. Purves and Lotto (2003) propose an extreme empiricist theory, in which the lines in the illusion figures (and indeed in all other stimuli) are interpreted according to the *statistical probability* of the objects that they might represent, based upon the observer's life-long perceptual diet. They examined the statistical relationship between the retinal image and the probability distribution of its possible real-world causes. For instance, vertical-line images tend to come from long objects because ground planes are statistically so common, leading to retinal foreshortening, so the observer overestimates vertical lines.

2. Illusions of lightness

Perceived brightness is strongly affected by contrast. When two identical grey patches are exposed side by side, a patch on a white surround looks darker than a identical patch on a dark surround. This phenomenon is called *simultaneous brightness contrast*, or *brightness induction*, and it is usually attributed to lateral inhibition within, or between, nearby retinal ganglion cells. (Retinal, not cortical, because backgrounds viewed by one eye have no effect on test patches viewed by the other eye.) The receptive field of a retinal ganglion cell comprises an excitatory ON-centre with an inhibitory OFF-surround, or vice versa. So if the grey test patch just fills the ON-centre on a dark surround the ganglion cell will fire, but if a white surround is added that activates the OFF-surround, this will reduce the firing rate and hence the perceived brightness. A similar lateral inhibition within separate colour-cone channels explains why a grey patch looks greenish when it lies on a red surround.

This story fails for White's effect (1979, 1981), in which the right-hand grey bars look lighter than the identical left-hand bars, even though the right-hand bars are surrounded by a larger area of white and therefore ought to look darker than the left-hand bars. This puzzling illusion is still not really understood. Some attribute it to banks of low-level oriented filters with elongated receptive fields. Others believe that the visual system parses the stimulus into three-dimensional layers, with the grey areas parsed as transparent greys in front of the stripes. Probably the right-hand gray bars are judged in comparison to the black embedding bars, to which they are interpreted as 'belonging', so the grey bars look light. Similarly, the left-hand bars are compared with the white embedding bars to which they perceptually 'belong', so they look dark.

In addition, many higher-level processes may be involved in brightness induction. In Adelson's figure, the square marked A is printed with the same grey ink as the square marked B. This illusion, which is far stronger than the conventional simultaneous contrast, is based upon lightness constancy that splits up the retinal luminance, assigning it partly to the illumination and partly to the reflectance of the surface. Thus, cues that increase the perceived illumination can hugely darken the perceived reflectance of a surface.

The diamonds in Cavanagh's figure are all identical, but each row looks lighter than the one above because the sharp dark–light edges are more salient that the gradual light–dark gradient within each diamond, and these edge effects accumulate. Probably, low-level processes account for simultaneous contrast and the edges of the diamonds, whilst the Adelson phenomenon also involves higher-level interpretive processes.

3. Illusions of representation

Pictures are like a language whose syntax consists of the internal picture geometry and whose semantic content, or meaning of the picture, lies in the objects represented. Thus low-level theories of the geometric illusions refer to the picture syntax, and depth processing theories refer to the semantics. Other illusions are more openly and specifically semantic; *puzzle pictures* at first have zero meanings but then settle on one meaning after the brain solves the puzzle. *Ambiguous* pictures, such as two faces/one vase, alternate between two (or more) meanings. Finally, *impossible* pictures at first seem to have one three-dimensional meaning but then settle on zero meanings.

Most pictures represent an easily recognized scene, but in *puzzle pictures* the meaning is hard to grasp, until an 'aha!' experience reveals the object represented, which once seen is never forgotten and is immediately recognized on a subsequent viewing, even years later. An example is the famous Dalmatian dog (see MULTISTABLE PERCEPTION, Fig. M6a). Here, 'bottom-up' scattered spots provide an input that is matched to a 'top-down' model or theory of what object is out there. On the other hand, *ambiguous pictures*

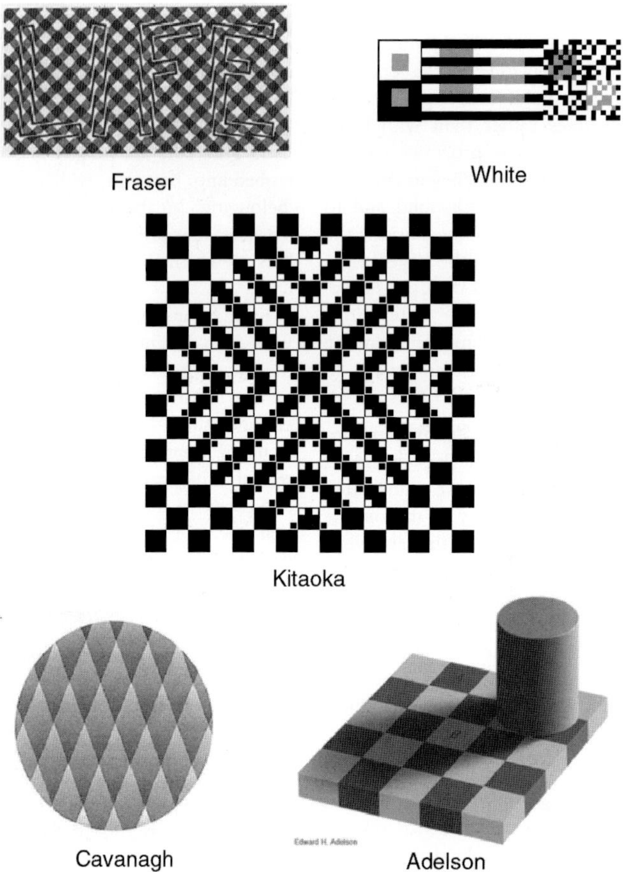

Fig. 12.

have more than one possible meaning, and the percept often flips between these different meanings. The perceptual process of settling upon a meaning is related to the figure–ground process. *Priming can affect ambiguous percepts; before viewing an ambiguous duck–rabbit figure, persons pre-exposed to a picture of a real duck tend to see it as a duck, whilst those pre-exposed to a picture of a real rabbit tend to see it as a rabbit.

An *impossible* figure is a two-dimensional flat representation of what at first looks like a three-dimensional object, but in fact there is no possible object that it can represent. Examples are the impossible triangle, the impossible staircase of Penrose (père et fils), and Shepard's many-legged elephant. The object cannot be globally separated from the non-object or background, and a flat impossible picture cannot be consistently coloured with paints. The local features at each corner of an impossible triangle are fully consistent with a three-dimensional object, and are perceptually accepted. It is only the long-range relationships between corners that are inconsistent. This shows that perception operates here, as in the Fraser 'LIFE' figure, upon local votes and not on a long-range scale. In the same way, try slowly uncovering the elephant from the top, or from the bottom. The Dutch engraver Maurits Escher (1898–1972) has made much use of ambiguous and impossible figures.

STUART ANSTIS

Gilchrist, A. (2006). *Seeing Black and White.*

Gregory, R. L. (1966/1997). *Eye and Brain.*

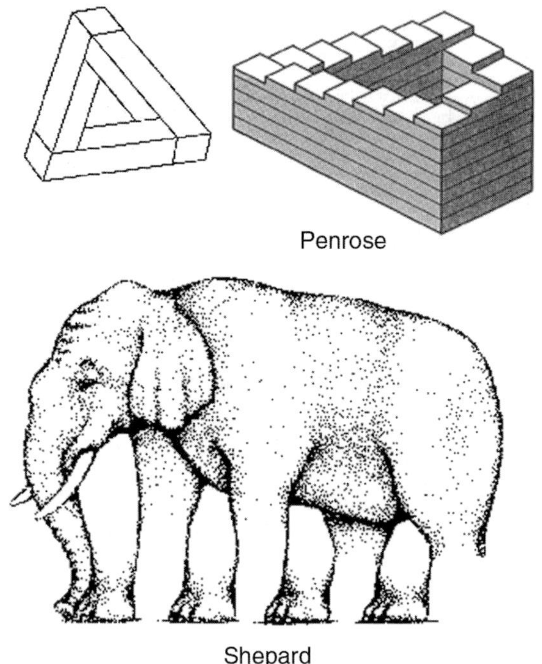

Fig. 13.

Luckeish, M. (1915/1965). *Visual Illusions*.
Ninio, J. (2001). *The Science of Illusions*, transl. F. Philip.
Purves, D. and Lotto, R. B. (2003). *Why We See What We Do: An Empirical Theory of Vision*.
Robinson, J. O. (1972/1998). *The Psychology of Visual Illusion*.
Rock, I. (1995). *Perception*.
Seckel, A. (2004). *Masters of Deception: Escher, Dali & the Artists of Optical Illusions*. Has a fine collection of illusions as used and glorified by some accomplished artists.
White, M. (1979). 'A new effect on perceived lightness'. *Perception*, 8.
—— (1981). 'The effect of the nature of the surround on the perceived lightness of gray bars within square-wave test gratings'. *Perception*, 10.

Web sources

http://lite.bu.edu/vision/applets/lite/lite/lite.html
http://www.cut-the-knot.org/Curriculum/Geometry/Shepard.shtml
http://www.eyetricks.com/
http://www.lottolab.org/
http://www.michaelbach.de/ot/index.html Michael Bach has assembled an excellent collection of illusions, many of them involving motion.
http://www.purveslab.net/
http://www.ritsumei.ac.jp/~akitaoka/index-e.html Akiyoshi Kitaoka's web page has an array of dazzling illusions. Many of these new illusions are not well understood.
http://www.skytopia.com/project/illusion/illusion.html

imagery, philosophical perspectives Mental imagery plays a crucial role in our mental life. Whether you are trying to remember your grandmother's smiling face, to imagine a dream vacation on a tropical beach, or to determine whether the television you are about to purchase will fit in the boot of your car, the task almost certainly involves mental imagery. These three examples suggest visual mental imagery, but there are analogues for the other senses as well. You might try to remember the sound of your grandmother's voice instead of the sight of her face, just as you might try to imagine the smell of the ocean rather than the sight of the sand. We are also able to produce images associated with affective states such as pleasure and pain. For example, you might imagine the pain you would feel if you were to drop the television on your toe as you were trying to load it into your car.

However familiar the phenomenon of mental imagery may seem to be, some philosophers, most notably those in the behaviourist tradition, have questioned the very existence of mental images. Gilbert Ryle, for example, argues that it is a mistake to posit the existence of mental images that are seen with 'the mind's eye' (Ryle 1949). When a murder is staged as part of a play, this does not imply that there exists someone who was murdered. Likewise, argues Ryle, when we engage in acts of visualizing, this does not imply there exists something (i.e. a mental image) that was visualized.

Even among philosophers who accept the existence of mental images, they have been the subject of considerable debate. One significant locus of discussion, often referred to as the *imagery debate*, concerns the representational nature of mental images. On one side of the imagery debate are the pictorialists who take mental images to be mental pictures—or at least, quasi-pictures (see e.g. Fodor 1975, Kosslyn 1980). This view coincides with our intuitive view of mental images; we are naturally inclined to think of them by analogy to non-mental images like drawings or photographs. My mental image of George W. Bush seems to be the same sort of representation as a photograph of him, only one is in my head and one is on the front page of today's newspaper.

Pictorialism derives support from various empirical experiments concerning mental image rotation and scanning (see e.g. Shepard and Metzler 1971, Shepard and Cooper 1982). In one experiment, subjects were presented with a pair of figures, such as letters, digits, or block formations, and asked to determine whether they were identical. The second figure in each pair had been rotated to an orientation different from the first. The fact that subjects' response times varied directly with the degree of rotation between the figures has been taken to suggest that the subjects came up with their answers by mentally rotating images of the objects presented.

One of the biggest problems facing pictorialism, however, is to account for the mental pictures that it posits. For the theory to be compatible with a scientific conception of mind, these pictures must in some way be located in the *brain. The challenge for the pictorialist is thus to locate neural structures that can be plausibly identified as mental pictures, or at the very least, to provide a plausible explanation of how this identification might work.

In the absence of such explanation, many philosophers and other researchers in contemporary cognitive science support an alternative view called *descriptionalism* (see e.g. Dennett 1969, Pylyshyn 1973, Dennett 1979). A newspaper photograph of George W. Bush and a sentence in the accompanying front-page story might both convey what he was wearing during the State of the Union address. But while pictorialists take the photograph to be the appropriate model for the way mental images represent, the descriptionalists claim that the sentence provides us with a better model for the representational nature of mental images.

This does not mean, however, that the imagery debate between the descriptionalist and the pictorialist is a debate over whether we 'think in words' or 'think in images'. Both pictorialists and descriptionalists generally accept that we sometimes think in images. In other words, pictorialists and descriptionalists typically agree that we have certain imagistic *experiences*, that we experience what we would call 'imaging'. When we *introspect, it seems to us as if we are experiencing mental pictures. But the experience is one thing, the *representation that accounts for this experience another. The pictorialists think that the introspective data should be interpreted just as it seems—our mind manipulates representations that are pictorial in nature. The pictorialist view thus offers us a unified conception of our experiences and the representations that underlie them. In contrast, the descriptionalists think that the introspective data is misleading in a certain sense; our experiences are not quite as they seem. According to the descriptionalists, the representations at the neural level that account for our imagistic experiences are not pictorial representations.

As indicated above, descriptionalists claim that the representational nature of mental images is best understood in terms of description, not depiction. Unlike depictive representations, descriptions do not look like what they represent. Representations need not be literally descriptive of the states of affairs represented, however, in order to count as descriptional representations; the binary language of a computer, for example, is a paradigmatic case of descriptional representation, though the 1s and 0s do not describe anything. In rejecting pictorialism, then, the descriptionalist suggests that the way that the phenomenon of mental imagery gets encoded in the brain will not be by way of mental pictures but by way of descriptional representations.

Such descriptional representations are characterized primarily negatively, i.e. for the purposes of the imagery debate, a representation counts as descriptional as long as it is not pictorial. This assumes, however, that we have a clear understanding of what makes a representation pictorial. Unfortunately, spelling out exactly what makes a representation a pictorial one—or, to put it another way, spelling out the nature of depiction—turns out to be rather difficult.

As a starting point, we might note that what sets depictive representations apart from other representations is that they represent in virtue of having at least one feature in common with what they represent. This is far too broad, however. The fact that every inscription shares a feature with every physical object (namely, being physical) does not mean that every inscription depicts every physical object. In the case of visual depictions, we might try to limit ourselves to visual features, but this requires that we can specify the notion of 'visual feature' without begging any questions. Perhaps we might simply identify some uncontroversial examples of visual features, such as form, colour, and shape, even if we cannot give a precise specification of what makes something a visual feature. Nonetheless, it soon becomes apparent that merely sharing the visual feature of colour with the thing represented is insufficient to make a representation pictorial. To take an obvious example, writing the noun 'apple' in red ink does not make it a pictorial representation of an apple.

In the absence of a clear characterization of pictorial representation, some recent accounts of mental images are difficult to classify as either pictorialist or descriptionalist. For example, Michael Tye claims that his own view of mental imagery—which treats images as interpreted, symbol-filled arrays—is a 'hybrid' one (Tye 1991). Since these arrays are in some respects like pictures but in other respects like linguistic representations, Tye claims that his view cannot be easily classified as either pictorialist or descriptionalist.

Above I noted that imagery seems to play a central role in imagination, memory, and spatial reasoning. Settling the imagery debate—and, more generally, developing an understanding of the nature of mental images—would thus be necessary for a full understanding of these mental processes. The imagery debate, however, has critical significance for many other deep philosophical issues about both perception and thought. First, introspective evidence suggests that imagery is like *perception. People typically report that imagistic experience is like perceptual experience—only fainter, perhaps. There is also empirical evidence to suggest that the mechanisms underlying imagery are similar to those underlying perception. (For an overview of some of the empirical evidence, see Finke and Shepard 1986.) Thus, understanding the nature of mental images will likely be necessary for us to understand the nature of perception. Second, certain theories of concepts propose that we should understand concepts imagistically. If such theories are right, then settling the question of the nature of mental images would also be necessary for us to achieve a full understanding of the nature of thought itself.

AMY KIND

Dennett, D. (1969). *Content and Consciousness*.

Dennett, D. (1979). 'Two approaches to mental images'. In Dennett, D. (ed.) *Brainstorms: Philosophical Essays on Mind and Psychology*.

Finke, R. A. and Shepard, R. N. (1986). 'Visual function of mental imagery'. In Boff, K. R. (eds) *Handbook of Perception and Human Performance*.

Fodor, J. (1975). *The Language of Thought*.

Kosslyn, S. M. (1980). *Image and Mind*.

Pylyshyn, Z. (1973). 'What the mind's eye tells the mind's brain—a critique of mental imagery'. *Psychological Bulletin*, 80.

Ryle, G. (1949). *The Concept of Mind*.

Shepard, R. N. and Cooper, L. (1982). *Mental Images and Their Transformations*.

—— and Metzler, J. (1971). 'Mental rotation of three-dimensional objects'. *Science*, 171.

Tye, M. (1991). *The Imagery Debate*.

imagery, scientific perspectives When we perceive the external world, we become aware of complex objects, sounds, and so on. This is possible because, although we have no direct contact with these external entities, our brains construct internal *representations based on the pattern of stimulation of our peripheral sensory organs (such as our eyes). Mental imagery occurs when internal representations are reactivated from long-term *memory and held in *working memory (in the absence of the appropriate stimulus), which produces the experience of 'seeing with the mind's eye', or 'hearing with the mind's ear'. We will focus on the visual modality because this has been the most studied, but many of the same arguments and considerations apply also to other modalities.

The concept of mental imagery has been important in theories of mental life at least since Plato. However, the scientific study of mental imagery is extraordinarily difficult, in part because mental images are private affairs. Because of the difficulties of studying imagery, some researchers came to doubt that mental images actually exist. John B. Watson, the founder of behaviourism, with its exclusive focus on observable behaviour as the only valid object of study in psychology, went so far as to assert that reports of mental images were 'sheer bunk', and that all thought consisted of subtle movements of the throat and larynx.

The modern study of imagery began in the 1960s, with studies of the effects of mental imagery on memory. With the advent of cognitive psychology, which studies internal representations, a debate arose about the nature of visual mental images. *Depictive* (also sometimes called *pictorial*) accounts postulated that such images are representations that depict objects or scenes as they would be perceived visually. According to such accounts, points on the represented object or scene correspond to points in the visual mental image such that distances among points on the represented object correspond to distances among points in the internal representation. Conversely, *propositional* (also sometimes called *descriptive*) accounts argued that underlying representations of images describe objects or scenes, rather than depicting them; this type of representation is no different from that of *linguistic representations. This view is usually associated with the additional assumption that a single *language of thought* supports all cognitive processes. After researchers had conducted numerous behavioural studies to try to distinguish between these accounts, it became clear in the 1980s that behavioural data alone cannot resolve this issue, because each behavioural result was ultimately consistent with both accounts.

In recent decades, knowledge accumulated about the neural basis of vision has led to major insights into the nature of visual mental imagery. In particular, research has shown that the primate visual system is composed of a hierarchy of cortical areas (Sereno and Tootell 2005). At the lowest level of this hierarchy, in the occipital lobe, are multiple *topographically organized areas* (TOAs), beginning with primary visual cortex (*V1 or area 17), which receives input from the eyes via the lateral geniculate nucleus. Crucially, topographically organized areas depict information; they use space on the cortex to represent space in the world. This matches the type of organization predicted by depictive accounts of imagery: locations of points in visual space are represented by activation at corresponding points on the cortex, and distances among points in visual space are represented by distances among the corresponding points on the cortical surface.

Moreover, evidence shows that the topographic organization of these areas is not simply structural, but also functional. For example, focal damage to cortical sites in these areas disrupts visual processing of the corresponding locations in space. Similarly, electrical stimulation of nearby cortical points can produce focal visual sensations in nearby locations in visual space. Although the representation of visual space in TOAs is not linear (e.g. the amount of cortex devoted to the representation of the central parts of the visual field is greater than that of more peripheral parts), this does not undermine depictive accounts: TOAs function within a neural system in which the pattern of connections with higher-level areas compensates for these distortions.

Numerous lines of neurobiological evidence support the idea that at least some types of visual mental imagery rely on the same depictive representations in TOAs used during vision. Consider four sorts of evidence:

1. **Functional brain imaging studies* have shown that TOAs are activated during some visual mental imagery tasks (Kosslyn et al. 2006). For instance, tasks in which participants are asked to 'mentally rotate' patterns (i.e. are asked to incrementally change their orientation in a mental image) usually recruit parietal cortex, which is involved in spatial tasks, but not necessarily TOAs. In contrast, tasks that require participants to evaluate subtle shape differences in an image activate TOAs, but not parietal cortex. Crucially, with these latter types of tasks, the precise pattern of activation in TOAs is consistent with their known topographical organization. For example, visualizing small objects, which would cover only the central parts of the visual field, activates more posterior parts of V1 (where central regions of the visual field are represented) than does visualizing larger objects.
2. Temporary disruption of neural processing in posterior parts of V1 by **transcranial magnetic stimulation (TMS)* slows down not only visual perception, but also imagery tasks that rely on posterior V1.
3. *V1 activation is highly correlated with performance* on visual imagery tasks across individuals, even after the contribution from other areas is statistically removed.
4. **Single-cell recordings in monkeys* have provided fine-grained evidence that TOAs depict visual information used during vision and certain visual imagery-like tasks. For instance, in one study monkeys were trained to mentally trace one of two lines, without moving their eyes, while firing rates were recorded from neurons in V1 with receptive fields covering the part of space covered by those lines. On each trial, neurons that had receptive fields closer to where the mental tracing began were engaged earlier than neurons that had receptive fields farther away on the line, which follows the temporal sequence of the mental tracing operation. Furthermore, when the monkey mistakenly traced the wrong line, neurons that represented such a line had increased firing rates. These types of findings strongly support the notion that TOAs represent visual information in a depictive manner, and that such representations are used in visual tasks.

How are TOAs recruited during visual mental imagery? During vision, representations in TOAs and then higher-level areas are activated by signals that originate from our eyes. In contrast, during imagery, there are no signals from the eyes. Rather, memories stored in higher-level visual areas in the temporal lobes trigger the representations that give rise to the experience of seeing (now without any stimulus input from the eyes). However, these visual memories cannot support detailed visual imagery by themselves because—at least in the monkey brain—they are stored in a compressed manner that does not make depictive information explicit (Tanaka 1996). Borrowing a computer graphics analogy, it is very difficult to compute spatial attributes of an image directly from its JPEG-compressed version: the image needs to be uncompressed first. Similarly, during imagery, the visual memories in the temporal lobes need to be 'uncompressed', and this apparently is achieved by means of feedback connections that run backwards from the anterior temporal lobes to TOAs in the occipital lobe; this process allows the reconstruction of the original two-dimensional geometrical properties, which correspond to the visual images in TOAs.

Furthermore, during visual mental imagery, representations in TOAs also function as information hubs because they are cross-linked with information stored in other visual areas, for instance colour information (posterior temporal lobes) and spatial information (parietal lobes). Finally, visual imagery usually involves more than the simple re-instantiation of stored information because images can be inspected, transformed, and combined in novel ways. In fact, research has shown that novel information can be extracted from visual mental images, within the *capacity limits of *attention and working memory (Finke et al. 1989). This is probably why visual mental imagery is essential for many cognitive skills (such as reasoning), and plays a role in many domains (such as mathematics and engineering).

Although TOAs play a crucial role in images of shapes, there is considerable evidence that both vision and visual mental imagery depend on the integrity of extended sets of brain areas. Neurological damage to these areas can produce deficits in some visual imagery tasks (e.g. mental rotation), but not others (e.g. face imagery; see BRAIN DAMAGE). Such findings underscore the fact that visual mental imagery is not an undifferentiated ability, but rather depends on numerous dissociable components. Brain damage often affects vision and visual mental imagery similarly. For instance, some patients with damage in the posterior temporal lobe who are selectively unable to recognize faces also show similar deficits during imagery of faces. This is consistent with neuroimaging studies showing that the sets of brain areas activated during vision and visual mental imagery are largely overlapping (Ganis et al. 2004). These sets of areas, however, are not identical. Damage to the non-overlapping areas can explain the few cases of patients exhibiting dissociations between vision and visual mental imagery. Nevertheless, so similar are the neurological representations of visual mental images and visual perception that we are well-justified in speaking of visual imagery as 'seeing with the mind's eye'.

GIORGIO GANIS, STEPHEN M. KOSSLYN, AND WILLIAM L. THOMPSON

Finke, R. A., Pinker, S., and Farah, M. J. (1989). 'Reinterpreting visual patterns in mental imagery'. *Cognitive Science*, 13.

Ganis, G., Thompson, W. L., and Kosslyn, S. M. (2004). 'Brain areas underlying visual mental imagery and visual perception: an fMRI study'. *Brain Research: Cognitive Brain Research*, 20.

Kosslyn, S. M., Thompson, W. L., and Ganis, G. (2006). *The Case for Mental Imagery*.

Sereno, M. I. and Tootell, R. B. (2005). 'From monkeys to humans: what do we now know about brain homologies?' *Current Opinion in Neurobiology*, 15.

Tanaka, K. (1996). 'Inferotemporal cortex and object vision'. *Annual Review of Neuroscience*, 19.

implicit attitude See ATTITUDE, IMPLICIT

inattentional blindness The term inattentional blindness was coined by Arian Mack and Irvin Rock (1998), referring to a tendency for people to be unaware of stimuli that are currently unattended. Bright and salient objects with well-defined contours can be presented directly where one is fixating, and yet if attention is engaged elsewhere, they can go entirely unnoticed by most viewers. Even large and significant objects, like a person in a gorilla suit, can go unnoticed when an observer's attention is engaged by some other aspect of the scene (Neisser and Becklan 1975, Simons and Chabris 1999). Moreover, the stimuli do not have to be brief. Inattentional blindness can occur to stimuli that are present for many seconds (Most et al. 2001). Importantly, objects that go unnoticed in the face of inattention are often overwhelmingly easy to see when they are attended.

Laboratory demonstrations of inattentional blindness are reminiscent of the common experience of having arrived at work or school after driving for some time and having no recollection of having experienced any of the sights along the way. In the same way that this experience arouses one's curiosity about what it means to 'see' and to wonder how we can have no memory of seeing things along the way and yet have arrived safely, inattentional blindness highlights a number of important questions about perception, attention, and awareness.

Like *change blindness, which is the failure to detect large and otherwise salient changes in a visual scene, e.g. across film cuts, eye movements, or other points of view (see Simons and Rensink 2005 for a review), inattentional blindness has been taken as evidence that our representation of the world is fairly sparse. Given that we can only attend to a small subset of the information that is available in a scene, and given that we only perceive that which we attend, it follows that we must not be representing very much of our world. Insights along these lines have been taken as indicating that our conscious sense of perceiving the world in rich detail is illusory (see Cohen 2002 for a review and critique).

One of the most frequently asked questions about inattentional blindness, and one that is directly relevant to whether inattentional blindness does in fact reflect a so-called '*grand illusion' of rich visual representation, is whether people really fail to perceive unattended information or whether they simply fail to remember it (Moore and Egeth 1997, Wolfe 1999). In other words, do people experience inattentional blindness or do they experience 'inattentional *amnesia'? The general point is that demonstrations of inattentional blindness almost always require observers to reflect upon the recent past and report something about it. As recollections, these reports can offer only limited insight into what was perceived at the time that the information was unattended. A failure to remember seeing things on your recent drive, for example, does not necessarily imply that you failed to see them at the time. In order for perceptual experience to be reportable after the fact, that experience has to have been encoded in a retrievable format. It is possible, perhaps even likely, that a great deal of perceptual processing unfolds without attention, but that the outcome of that processing requires attention to be reliably encoded in memory.

There is substantial evidence supporting the view that despite being unable to report much about unattended information, a large amount of perceptual processing unfolds without attention. For example, personally important stimuli such as one's own name or emotionally laden pictures can capture attention and cause people to become aware of stimuli of which they had been previously unaware (Mack et al. 2002; see also Moray 1959). People can be *primed to respond in particular ways on the basis of unattended, and presumably not experienced, stimuli. For example, when asked to complete a string of letters with additional letters that form a word, observers are more likely to complete the string as a word that had been presented to them earlier than with any other equally appropriate word. Relevant to inattentional blindness, this is true even if the word was unattended, un-experienced, and un-remembered (Mack and Rock 1998). Finally, unattended information can influence conscious perception even at the time it is unattended. In one study, observers were asked to report which of two lines was longer (Moore and Egeth 1997). Without the knowledge of the observers, patterns of dots in the background formed the inducing regions of standard geometric illusions, such as the converging lines of the Ponzo (railroad track) *illusion or the arrow heads of the Müller–Lyer (arrow) illusion. Despite being unaware of these patterns, and unable to report anything about them when directly queried about them, the patterns nonetheless caused observers to misperceive one line as longer than the other when they were actually identical in length. Thus, online visual perception was influenced by perceptual information of which observers were apparently unaware (see also Moore et al. 2003, Russell and Driver 2005). All of these findings suggest that we are consciously aware of a relatively small proportion of the amount of information that we process, but that this does not necessarily reflect an impoverished representation of the world.

Yet another alternative characterization of our apparent blindness under conditions of inattention, is that we suffer from 'inattentional agnosia' rather than inattentional blindness (Simons 2000). *Agnosia is a disorder, occurring with selective *brain damage, that renders patients unable to make sense out of a visual stimulus as any particular object even though they are still able to 'see' and report basic visual properties such as colour, orientation, and size. It is as though these patients see 'visual stuff' that fails to form a coherent picture of anything in particular. The idea of inattentional agnosia is that information in unattended parts of one's visual field is similarly perceived as 'visual stuff'. Until and unless it is attended, then, it will not be perceived as anything meaningful, and therefore will not be memorable.

Finally, a frequently asked question about inattentional blindness is what are the things that make us not blind, that 'capture' our attention and cause us to both process and be aware of those things. Most of the evidence on this question points the conclusion that what we become aware of depends on what we are looking for, or in the terms of the literature, what we are 'set' for (Most et al. 2005). These things may include information that is fundamentally important to us, and for which we are arguably always set, such as our names (Mack et al. 2002). Alternatively, this may be determined by the particular task that we are engaged in at the time, such as moving objects in the path of our car when driving.

In summary, there is little disagreement surrounding the fact that unattended stimuli are processed differently than attended stimuli or that, in particular, we can experience striking failures to notice unattended aspects of our visual world. However, the fact that researchers and theorists continue to struggle with how to characterize these failures—is it inattentional blindness, inattentional amnesia, or inattentional agnosia?—highlights the burning question of what constitutes phenomenal awareness and how one can get a handle on it empirically. An intriguing implication of inattentional blindness, regardless of one's preference for labelling the nature of the failures of perception, is that the visual world that we experience consciously is to a great extent determined by what it is that we expect to see and therefore how we allocate our attention. In this context, it is perhaps no wonder that experiences that alter one's expectations or attentional states, through the administration of drugs, meditation, distraction, or otherwise, also tend to alter one's conscious experience.

CATHLEEN M. MOORE

Cohen, J. (2002). 'The grand grand illusion'. *Journal of Consciousness Studies*, 9.
Kovisto, M. and Revonsuo, A. (2007). 'How meaning shapes seeing'. *Psychological Science*, 18.
Mack, A. and Rock, I. (1998). *Inattentional Blindness*.
——, Pappas, Z., Silverman, M., and Gay, R. (2002). 'What we see: inattention and the capture of attention by meaning'. *Consciousness and Cognition*, 11.
Moore, C. M. and Egeth, H. (1997). 'Perception without attention: evidence of grouping under conditions of inattention'. *Journal of Experimental Psychology: Human Perception and Performance*, 23.
——, Grosjean, M., and Lleras, A. (2003). 'Using inattentional blindness as an operational definition of unattended: the case of perceptual completion'. *Visual Cognition, 10*.
Moray, N. (1959) 'Attention in dichotic listening: affective cues and the influence of instructions'. *Quarterly Journal of Experimental Psychology*, 11.
Most, S. B., Simons, D. J., Scholl, B. J., Jimenez, R., Clifford, E., and Chabris, C. F. (2001). 'How not to be seen: the contributions of similarity and selective ignoring to sustained inattentional blindness'. *Psychological Science*, 12.
——, Scholl, B. J., Clifford, E. R., and Simons, D. J. (2005). 'What you see is what you set: sustained inattentional blindness and the capture of awareness'. *Psychological Review*, 112.
Neisser, U. and Becklan, R. (1975). 'Selective looking: attending to visually specified events'. *Cognitive Psychology*, 7.
Russell, C. and Driver, J. (2005). 'New indirect measures of 'inattentive' visual grouping in a change-detection task'. *Perception and Psychophysics*, 67.
Simons, D. J. (2000). 'Attentional capture and inattentional blindness'. *Trends in Cognitive Sciences*, 4.
—— and Chabris, C. F. (1999). 'Gorillas in our midst: sustained inattentional blindness for dynamic events'. *Perception*, 28.
—— and Rensink, R. A. (2005). 'Change blindness: past, present, and future'. *Trends in Cognitive Sciences*, 9.
Wolfe, J. M. (1999). 'Inattentional amnesia'. In Coltheart, V. (ed.) *Fleeting Memories: Cognition of Brief Visual Stimuli*.

infant consciousness Infants have little knowledge, but they show intentions to gain experience with the aid of sympathetic company. Is this consciousness?

1. Intentions and personal consciousness before language
2. Foundations in animal awareness
3. The special consciousness of being human
4. Age-related development of meaning in cultural consciousness
5. Brain mediation of infant consciousness
6. Developmental disorders of infant consciousness, and effects of neglect or abuse

1. Intentions and personal consciousness before language

Rational philosophy and cognitive psychology attempt to explain consciousness as made up of perceptions, which are conditioned by cultural interpretations of language and learned executive strategies. They focus on how language and reason categorize and parse an educated experience (manipulating what Alfred North Whitehead calls the 'products of logical discernment'), and they conceive movements, motives, and feelings of bodies as effects or symptoms of thoughts and articulate reasons. The active 'taking on' the world of the intentional self, with the compelling emotional forces of sympathy between human selves and other persons, is deemed less conscious. How we create meaning as *persons in relation* remains mysterious.

But the motives of the human condition have a long evolutionary history. If it turns away from the origins of all intelligent awareness, the being in movement that is shared through feelings in social communities, a cognitive mind science cannot explain what imaginative knowing gives to the ecology of animal life or what personal relating gives to being a person. It offers no theory of how human consciousness and co-consciousness begins and grows.

Research on how infants act and communicate challenges this scholastic and materialistic attitude which separates mind from body. Infants show states of intention and emotion, and they engage with expressions of mind in other persons. They have an innate self-and-other 'spirit' or impulse that appears to be essential to the learning of all forms of cultural ritual and historically created sense of shared reality, including meanings coded in language. By sharing narratives of experience with others, the infant is led to take on an individual personality or unique manner of being. A child is a person with self-consciousness, both by virtue of emotional *attachments* to those who share their feelings, and by *companionships* that grow with all who participate in intimate, playful, and affectionate purposes in a common world. Months before first words are uttered, the infant acts with subtle feeling for many forms of social gesture, for simple rituals of artistic performance (song and dance, for instance), sensing known others' individual personalities, judging the moral qualities of their actions.

2. Foundations in animal awareness

Consciousness, I propose, is not just awareness of things sensed, but an essential function of all animal agency—the being in movement that 'motivates' a lifetime experience, assessing within the organism's motive system the perceived and remembered effects of actions in the world. Even single-celled animalcules act with *prospective perception*, testing engagements with the environment with innate preferences, showing a *self-feeling* and *time sense* that monitors the 'rhythm' and 'flow' of action, and that employs *'emotional' evaluation* to estimate the power, risks, and benefits of each action with respect to vital needs. Animals as agents have this elementary *subjective consciousness and feelings*. And, as we shall see, these functions may be performed to serve more than the needs of the individual alone. Organization of conscious life also flourishes in communities.

More complex animal life, more versatile in the ways a multiplicity of senses pick-up environmental affordances, entails what Bjørn Merker (2005) calls 'liabilities of mobility'. The integrated actions of the self as agent required increasingly complex **proprioception*—a foreknowledge of forces felt throughout the body caused by moving in intricate ways—and an ability to discriminate *exteroceptive* sensory effects and qualities that are provoked in them by things outside the body. These may be called, respectively, *body self-consciousness*, and *object consciousness*. As Merker explains, every circumstance perceived in the animal's phenomenal awareness or felt being generates the question, 'Did I do it, or did something else happen?' Bodies have self-consciousness of action built in their brains as maps that match the bodies' axes, symmetry, and segmentation. Brains grow body-mapping (somatotopic) circuitry under homeotic (*Hox*) gene regulation, representing body form as a field of behaviours in which directions of action may be defined and their objects perceived and categorized, exteroceptively. These nerve-net maps hold self-awareness intact and coherent, synchronizing actions in a time-generating and time-keeping rhythmic process regulated by emotions, generating projects and recollections, and relating them to vital needs.

For a community, self-awareness is not enough. Social animals detect motives and feelings in other animals from signals passed between them, including secretions and the shape and timing of perceived movements, especially the self-regulating rhythmic movements that endlessly adjust feelings of being. These 'expressions' excite sympathetic response and transfer the sense of being. By this means *intersubjective, self–other*, or *synrhythmic consciousness* comes about, which, for mobile creatures, depends on the generation of *sympathetic synchronization* with separately generated but corresponding and rhythms of action in social members.

3. The special consciousness of being human

The organs of human consciousness have animal foundations, and they are active from birth. Newly born animals are both conscious of themselves in their bodies and ready for some sociable awareness. Human infants, with exceptionally complex bodies, are richly equipped with senses and motor abilities for an intense intersubjectivity that, even at this earliest stage, moments after birth may seek to imitate *arbitrary forms of expressive moving*, showing uniquely human inventiveness and affective appreciation.

All these manifestations of *meaning in the consciousness of actions with other persons* grow and become more elaborate by learning. Driven by an epigenetic process, they take up representations of both proprioceptive and exteroceptive affordances, guiding or *conditioning* the experience of moving. The peculiar intensity of human innate intersubjectivity activates organs 'made' for social signalling: movements of the eyes, intonations of voice, turns of the head, expressions of the face, and gestures of the hands. By active attention to demonstrations of feelings in another person, and especially by efforts made to engage in a reciprocal exchange of experimental 'playful' expressions, a newborn infant shows the rudiments of *cultural consciousness* by which creative forms of action become meaningful narratives and propositions about shared life. Infant consciousness is motivated for intent participation in a humanly 'made up' world.

4. Age-related development of meaning in cultural consciousness

Through age-related steps in the development of human awareness before language, the anatomical and functional systems in the child's body and brain change. They actively engage with the mother's body from early in gestation, and after birth their elaboration requires sharing of intentions and emotions with a caring companion. As actions become more powerful, varied, and effective, new goals for action demand exploration, new possibilities occur for communicating intentions, interests and feelings, new risks and anxieties as well, as new benefits and joys arise. Other people respond to these transitions in the spirit of the child, changing the human environment in various degrees of harmony or disharmony with the developing motives of the child.

Embryology of equipment for consciousness and feelings—consciousness 'in formation'. Moving comes before knowing. Fetuses move with rhythmic whole-body coordination of parts before sensory inputs from receptors to the CNS are established. Among the first integrative structures of the embryo brain is the *core affective neural system*, the neurochemical excitations and inhibitions of which will determine ways the body will protect and use its vital resources. They begin as morphogenetic regulators shaping growth of neural networks for eventual conscious perception of situations outside the body to which movements will be directed. The fetal brain develops 'neural clocks' that coordinate synchrony and rhythmic succession of activity throughout the central nervous system and for all parts of the body.

The fetal and neonatal mind in engagement with experience of action—'latent' and 'nascent' consciousness. In the last trimester before a human birth, there is intimate chemical engagement with the mother's body, and the proprioceptive body-feeling senses of the fetus regulate posture changes with movements of the limbs, turning of the head, and 'seeking' movements of hands and eyes in an aquatic environment. The fetus can turn the two eyes as if 'looking', and can find, place, and suck its thumb. Hearing is active by 27 weeks and can mediate auditory learning to identify the mother's voice sounds transmitted through her body. An infant born prematurely, 2 months before term, can engage in a well-timed vocal dialogue with an adult who is holding it close against the body, infant and adult demonstrating a matching sense of the pulse and phrasing of the voice in an exchange of simple 'coo' sounds. Both vocal and gestural displays of the hands, as well as eye saccades, show a time sense for moving the same as that by which adults regulate the slower components of their actions of reaching and manipulation, and the measured syllables and phrases of their speech. In this period human consciousness, anatomically defined though not yet functioning, can be said to be 'grown for experience', or *latent*.

In the first minutes after a full-term birth a calm and comfortable infant will explore the novelty of body sense in air with the aid of self-touching movements of the hands, and make conjugate orientations of the eyes coordinated with head rotations aimed with reaching and pointing movements of arms and hands, which may be guided to feel the mother's body. The infant can also focus attention on the sight of a nearby object and modify body movements to track it. Hand movements guided by touch make grasping or stroking movements. Sounds of the mother's voice speaking affectionately leads looking to her face, which is fixated with attention to her eyes, mouth, and hands. Rapid learning of her appearance is facilitated by recognition of her voice. When an adult offers isolated and emphasized expressive gestures of eyes, voice, mouth, or hands in sensitive engagement with the attentive newborn, this can elicit imitation, and, if the adult acts 'politely'—leaving the baby a chance to repeat an imitated gesture as a 'provocation' to 'invite' a reply—a rhythmic interchange or dialogue can be established. The infant's heartbeat accelerates with excitement before an 'imitation' and decelerates with attention to the effect of a 'provocation'. This is important evidence of innate intersubjective emotions adapted to acquire new skills by what the educational psychologist Barbara Rogoff (2003) calls 'intent participation learning' with other persons, of *nascent* interpersonal awareness sensitive to the mutual contingency of experience.

Crucial developments in this intersubjectivity occur before language and before any acquired 'theory' of mindfulness can be articulated to modify intuitive sympathy for the mental processes implicit in other persons' movements. Fully human consciousness is *emergent* in the first two years, through the following four phases.

The narrative 'musicality' of first conversations. Two-month-olds participate with skill in rhythmic exchanges of expressions with a sympathetic partner. 'Proto-conversations' of voice sounds are composed with a 'communicative musicality' comprising precisely regulated timing or 'pulse', sensitive melodic emotional 'quality', measured phrases, and 'narrative' patterns lasting tens of seconds. The infant is immediately sensitive to the timing in the other's behaviour and becomes disturbed and avoidant if their behaviour is 'non-contingent'. The infant begins to adapt to the expressive style of the companion, and learns some culture-specific features of expression in body movements and vocalizations.

Action games and shared ritual performances. From the third month the stronger and more alert baby turns away from gentle proto-conversation, drawn to explore surroundings more thoroughly, and to seize and manipulate available objects. However, a communicative sense remains strong. Parents discover the infant has a developing sense of fun and a fascination with rituals of song and body play that can be repeated to attract eager participation. Action songs and games in different cultures show similar 'musicality', and there are universal forms of rhythmic emotional modulation or 'attunement' in close engagement with the mood of the infant's responses. Research on the communicative play of this period is revealing the foundations of language.

New self-consciousness within growing friendships. As infants grow in independent curiosity and enjoyment of play, they show a more 'tricky' sense of humour and self-consciousness response to the coaxing or teasing of others. Increasingly, it matters who the other person is. Communication with familiar friends is playful, with 'showing off', but strangers are regarded with caution and if they act inappropriately according to the infant's expectations, this may provoke expressions of shame or dislike. It is clear that a 6-month-old has a performer's sense of social identity and expectations about how engagements with others should go. More and more, too, objects that interest the child and provoke exploration become 'toys' for games with parents and siblings.

Shared intentions and joint tasks—motives for cultural learning in companionship. Changes about 9 months cause the infant to show a greater 'cooperative awareness' with companions, and both a willingness and cleverness that leads to 'sharing tasks'. By paying deliberate attention to the intention and feeling in another's moves, the infant is beginning to be deliberately 'helpful', or 'obstructive', in insightful ways. This new level of 'person–person–object awareness' or *secondary intersubjectivity* is now recognized as the 'beginning' of cultural learning, identified as a shared sense of how to act and how to use situations and objects to learn arbitrary expressions to identify and describe things by various mimetic forms of behaviour.

Thus the way is opened for the making of symbols and the learning of language, with which infancy ends. The child's mind attains a new complexity, able to explore a rapidly growing range of experience in imagination and memory, finding sense in the talk and reading of a community of words. Donaldson (1993) describes the consciousness of the speaking child as 'reflective and transcendent'.

5. Brain mediation of infant consciousness

The above account of infant consciousness and its innate motives is supported by brain science. For more than a century, neuropsychologists and developmental brain scientists have had evidence that animal and human awareness is motivated by systems that coordinate and regulate movement before they are capable of processing environmental input. In the 1980s physiologists recording activity of cells in the frontal cortex of monkeys discovered motivating neural systems active in hand to mouth coordination. The same neurons are active when intentions are communicated between individuals, and when imitation occurs. They were called **mirror neurons*, though they are manifestly involved in making reciprocal and complementary social activities that transmit intentions in cooperative, co-conscious ways, as no mirror can do.

With *functional brain imaging, it is now possible to observe pro-conscious attentional events in the brains of humans of any age without invading the body, though usually in circumstances where action is restricted. It is found that brain activity of intentions and emotions can be immediately communicated by the forms and sequences of body movement with or without the coded signals of language. The brain of a 2-month-old infant responds in communicative sympathy with the experience of another person, even to a photograph of a woman's face. Symbolic communication, and all reasoning that it mediates, depends on the initiatives of body movement and conscious regulation, and on sympathetic transmission of these to other individuals. The consciousness of infants demonstrates the foundations for this convivial vitality in human form.

6. Developmental disorders of infant consciousness, and effects of neglect or abuse

A psychology that accepts that infants innately share consciousness with other persons puts developmental disorders of childhood, such as *autism, and the effects of emotional stress and abuse, in a different light. Attention is directed to the immediate and early effects of different conditions on the young child's motives for engaging intentions and feelings with the human world. Developmental disorders can be recognized earlier, and it is easier to predict where severe stress will damage the brain. This knowledge requires qualification and revision of the criteria used to make a diagnosis, and calls for a new approach to therapy: one that gives support to weakened intersubjective systems, rather than to training intended to reshape intelligence or skills.

COLWYN TREVARTHEN

Bråten, S. and Trevarthen, C. (2007). 'Prologue: from infant intersubjectivity and participant movements to simulations and conversations in cultural common sense'. In Bråten, S. (ed.) *On Being Moved: From Mirror Neurons to Empathy.*

Donaldson, M. (1993) *Human Minds: An Exploration.*

Malloch, S. and Trevarthen, C. (eds) (2008). *Communicative Musicality: Narratives of Expressive Gesture and Being Human.*

Merker, B. (2005). 'The liabilities of mobility: A selection pressure for the transition to consciousness in animal evolution'. *Consciousness and Cognition*, 14.

Nagy, E. (2008). 'Innate intersubjectivity: newborns' sensitivity to communication disturbance'. *Developmental Psychology*, 44.

Reddy, V. (2008). *How Infants Know Minds.*

Rogoff, B., Paradise, R., Mejía Arauz, R., Correa-Chávez, M., and Angelillo, C. (2003). 'Firsthand learning by intent participation'. *Annual Review of Psychology*, 54.

Thomson, E. (2008). *Mind in Life: Biology, Phenomenology, and the Sciences of Mind.*

Trevarthen, C. (1979). 'The tasks of consciousness: how could the brain do them?' *Brain and Mind, CIBA Foundation Symposium 69 (New Series).*

—— (2004). 'Infancy, mind in'. In Gregory, R. L. (ed.) *Oxford Companion to the Mind*, 2nd edn.

—— and Reddy, V. (2007). 'Consciousness in infants'. In Velman, M. and Schneider, S. (eds) *A Companion to Consciousness.*

——, Aitken, K. J., Vandekerckhove, M., Delafield-Butt, J., and Nagy, E. (2006). 'Collaborative regulations of vitality in early childhood: stress in intimate relationships and postnatal psychopathology'. In Cicchetti, D. and Cohen, D. J. (eds) *Developmental Psychopathology, Volume 2. Developmental Neuroscience*, 2nd edn.

information integration theory The integrated information theory of consciousness claims that consciousness is a function of the quantity of information generated by an integrated system (first problem), and that its quality is specified by the informational relationships within the system (second problem; Tononi 2004). Only the first problem will be addressed here. The theory begins by identifying the essential phenomenological properties of consciousness, develops a theoretical framework for those properties, provides a parsimonious account of key facts about the relationship between consciousness and the brain, and makes several predictions.

Experience can be very simple: think of a blue sky. And seeing a blue sky is all one needs to face the two main problems posed by consciousness: First, under what conditions is there any kind of experience, as opposed to nothing at all? Second, what conditions determine the particular quality of that kind of experience—in this case visual, homogeneous, coloured, and blue?

1. Phenomenology: consciousness as integrated information
2. Measuring integrated information
3. Accounting for neurobiological facts
4. Some corollaries

1. Phenomenology: consciousness as integrated information

That consciousness is integrated information may not seem self-evident, perhaps because, being endowed with consciousness for most of our existence, we take its gifts for granted. So it is worth illustrating its two key properties—information and integration—by resorting to thought experiments: one involving a photodiode and the other a digital camera.

Information. Consider the following: you are facing a blank screen that is alternately on and off, and you have been instructed to say 'light' when the screen turns on and 'dark' when it turns off. A photodiode (a very simple light-sensitive device) has also been placed in front of the screen, and is set up to beep when the screen emits light and to stay silent when it does not. The first problem of consciousness reduces to this: when you distinguish between the screen being on or off, you have the subjective experience of seeing light or dark. The photodiode can also distinguish between the screen being on or off, but presumably it does not have a subjective experience of light and dark. What is the key difference between you and the photodiode?

According to the theory, the difference has to do with how much information is generated when that distinction is made. Information is classically defined as reduction of uncertainty when a particular outcome occurs out of a repertoire of alternative outcomes: the more numerous the outcomes, the greater the reduction of uncertainty, and thus the information. Information can be measured using the *entropy function*, which is the logarithm of the number of alternatives (assuming they are equally likely). For example, tossing a fair coin and obtaining heads corresponds to $\log_2(2) = 1$ bit of information, because there are just two alternatives; throwing a fair die yields $\log_2(6) = 2.59$ bits of information, because there are six possibilities. When the blank screen turns on, the photodiode enters one of its two possible states and beeps. As with the coin, this corresponds to one bit of information. However, when you see the blank screen turn on, the state you enter rules out a very large number of alternative states. Imagine that, instead of turning homogeneously on, the screen were to display at random every frame from every movie that was ever produced. Without any effort, each of these frames would cause you to enter a different state and see a different image. This means that when you enter the particular state ('seeing light') you rule out not just 'seeing dark', but an extraordinarily large number of alternative possibilities. Whether or not you think of the bewildering number of alternatives (you won't and you can't), this corresponds to an extraordinary amount of information. Importantly, this information has nothing to do with how complicated the scene is—a simple blue sky or a busy city street—but only with the number of alternative outcomes. This point is so simple that its importance has been overlooked.

Integration. Although the ability to distinguish among a large number of states is a fundamental difference between you and the photodiode, by itself it is not enough to account for the presence of consciousness. To see why, consider an idealized megapixel digital camera, whose sensor chip is essentially a collection of a million photodiodes. Even if each photodiode in the sensor chip were just binary, the camera could distinguish among $2^{1\,000\,000}$ states, an immense number, corresponding to 1 000 000 bits of information. Indeed, the camera would enter a different state for every frame from every movie that was ever produced. Yet few would argue that the camera is conscious. What is the key difference between you and the camera?

According to the theory, the difference has to do with integrated information. An external observer may consider the camera chip as a single system with a repertoire of $2^{1\,000\,000}$ states. In reality, however, the chip is not an integrated entity: since its 1 000 000 million photodiodes have no way to interact, the state of each photodiode is causally independent of that of the others: in reality, the chip is a collection of 1 000 000 independent photodiodes, each with a repertoire of 2 states. This is easy to prove: if the sensor chip were cut down into its individual photodiodes, the performance of the camera would not change at all.

By contrast, your vast repertoire of conscious states truly belongs to an integrated system, since it cannot be subdivided into repertoires of states available to independent components. Thus, a conscious image is always experienced as an integrated whole: no matter how hard you try, you cannot experience colours independent of shapes, or the left half of the visual field of view independently of the right half. Underlying this unity of experience are causal interactions within your brain, which make the state of each element causally dependent on that of other elements. Indeed, unlike the camera, your brain's performance breaks down if its elements are disconnected. And so does consciousness: for example, splitting the brain in two along the corpus callosum prevents causal interactions between the two hemispheres and splits experience in two—the right half of the visual field is experienced independently of the left.

2. Measuring integrated information

This phenomenological analysis suggests that, to generate consciousness, a physical system must have a large repertoire of states (information) *and* it must be unified, i.e. it should not be decomposable into a collection of causally independent parts (integration). But how can one measure integrated information?

First, we need to evaluate how much information is generated by the system when it enters a particular state. Consider a simplified network isolated from the environment—like the brain when it is dreaming—constituted of neural elements that can be either on or off. At a given time the system enters a particular state—a particular combination of elements that are on and off. The information generated by the system depends on how many states from its repertoire of possible states are ruled out when, through interactions among its elements, the system enters its current state. To measure exactly how much information is generated, we perturb the system with all possible initial states, and find out which of these lead to the current state. The information generated is plentiful if the system's repertoire of states is large and only one initial state leads to the current outcome, since a large number of initial states are ruled out (in fact, all but one). By contrast, the information generated is little if the system's repertoire is small, or many initial states lead to the current outcome, since few initial states are ruled out. For instance, in a neural system where all elements end up firing no matter how it is perturbed—say, an epileptic brain with hyperexcitable neurons—no information is generated by entering the state 'all elements firing', because no alternatives are ruled out—the system could have started from any possible state of its repertoire and would have ended up the same way. Similarly for a system dominated by noise: whichever state the system enters, it does not rule out any alternatives from the repertoire of initial states. Technically, the information generated when the system enters a particular state can be measured by the relative entropy between the repertoire of possible states and that of the states that could have caused the current one.

Second, we need to find out how much of the information thus generated is integrated information. The key idea here is to consider the parts of the system independently, ask how much information they generate by themselves, and compare it with the information generated by the system as a whole (again, the comparison can be made using relative entropy). Integrated information, then, is the information generated by the system as a whole over and above that generated by its parts taken independently. Integrated information is indicated by the symbol Φ, where the vertical bar 'I' stands for information and the circle 'O' for integration (Tononi and Sporns 2003, Tononi 2004).

To see how this works, consider again the sensor of a digital camera with a million photodiodes (each containing an input element connected to an output element through a resistance that determines whether it will turn on or off). By turning on or off depending on its input, each photodiode generates 1 bit of information. Considered independently, then, 1 million photodiodes will generate 1 million bits of information (since the photodiodes are not connected and are therefore causally independent). Of course, the sensor as a whole also generates 1 million bits. Just as clearly, however, the sensor does not generate any information above and beyond what is generated by its parts: integrated information is zero. Clearly, for integrated information to be high, a system must be connected in such a way that a lot of information is generated by causal interactions *among* its elements, rather than *within* its parts. Thus, a system can generated integrated information only to the extent that it cannot be decomposed into informationally independent parts (in general, the parts have to be chosen so as to maximize what they can do independently).

Finally, it may not always be obvious which sets of elements constitute a unified system, so one should consider many candidate sets of elements, and measure Φ for each of them. We would then discount all sets of elements with $\Phi = 0$, or sets that are included in sets having higher Φ (being merely parts of a larger whole). What we are left with are *complexes*—entities that can generate integrated information. For a complex, and only for a complex, it is appropriate to say that, when it enters a particular state out of its repertoire, it generates an amount of information corresponding to its Φ value.

3. Accounting for neurobiological facts

The integrated information theory thus claims that the substrate of consciousness must be a complex of high Φ. But does the theory account for key empirical observations, some of them paradoxical, about the relationship between *brain and *consciousness? It is worth considering a few examples.

It is well established that consciousness depends on the functioning of certain portions of the thalamocortical system, but not on other parts of the brain. Thus, massive lesions of the thalamocortical system abolish consciousness, leading to coma and vegetative states, whereas lesions of the cerebellum, a similarly complicated neural system with even more neurons, leave consciousness essentially intact (see BRAIN DAMAGE). Why is it so? Computer simulations show that integrated information is optimized (Φ is highest) if the elements of a complex are connected in such a way that they are both functionally specialized (connection patterns are different for different elements) and functionally integrated (all elements can be reached from all other elements of the network (Tononi 2004). Thus it seems fitting that the thalamocortical system is organized in a way that appears well suited to the integration of information: it comprises a large number of elements that are functionally specialized; at the same time these specialized elements are integrated through an extended network of connections that permit rapid and effective interactions within and between areas.

On the other hand, further simulations show that if the elements of a system are organized in a strongly modular manner, with little interactions among modules, the system breaks down into many small complexes each with a low value of Φ. According to both anatomical and physiological studies, the cerebellum appears to be just such a highly modular structure. Which would make it unfit to generate high levels of consciousness.

Here is another puzzling observation: what we see usually depends on the neural signals conveyed to the brain by the retina, yet those signals do not seem to contribute directly to visual experience: there are no retinal fibres in the blind spot, yet we do not perceive a hole there; the retinal periphery is colour blind, but we do not notice; retinal firing patterns shift rapidly, but visual experience appears stable; and certainly, blind people without retinas can still imagine or dream visually. In this case, computer simulations show that afferent pathways can influence the activity states of a 'thalamocortical' complex of high Φ without partaking in it. Instead, together they form a larger complex of low Φ. Similar considerations apply to efferent pathways.

Or consider the large amount of neural activity in cortico-subcortical loops, and even in local loops within the cortex, which are involved in object recognition, depth perception, language parsing, and in the sequencing of action, thought, and speech. This activity clearly influences what we become conscious of, but it remains unconscious. For instance, think of the name of a famous philosopher who claimed that to be is to be experienced: after a few instants, 'Berkeley' surfaces to consciousness, but one is completely unaware of the neural search that found his name. As with afferent and efferent pathways, simulations show that separate processing loops can be attached to a 'thalamocortical' complex of high Φ without becoming part of it: these loops effectively constitute fast, specialized subnetworks that remain informationally insulated.

The effects on consciousness of anatomical or functional disconnections are accounted naturally in terms of integrated information. For example, it can be shown that cutting through the corpus callosum produces two separate complexes out of a large complex corresponding to the connected hemispheres (see COMMISSUROTOMY AND CONSCIOUSNESS). However, because of redundancy between the two sides, their Φ value is not greatly reduced compared to when they formed a single complex, consistent with observations in split-brain patients. Functional disconnections between certain parts of the brain may also underlie the restriction of consciousness in neurological neglect syndromes and in psychiatric conversion and *dissociative disorders, may occur during *dreaming and *hypnosis, and may even underlie certain *attentional phenomena.

We are all familiar with the dramatic change in the level of consciousness that occurs between wakefulness and *sleep: indeed, during slow-wave sleep early in the night, consciousness fades to the point that, upon awakening, we often have nothing to report. Yet the anatomy of the brain is unchanged, and neural activity levels are similar to wakefulness. The theory predicts that the fading of consciousness must be due to a collapse of either integration or of information. Recent experiments employing *transcranial magnetic stimulation in conjunction with *electroencephalography have confirmed these predictions. During wakefulness, stimulating a cortical area leads to the sequential activation of a specific set of connected areas. By contrast, during early slow-wave sleep, stimulation dies off locally, revealing a breakdown of cortico-cortical interactions and thereby a loss of integration (Massimini et al. 2005); alternatively, local stimulation leads to a global, stereotypic responses, where all cortical areas turn on and off together, revealing a loss of repertoire and therefore of information (Massimini et al. 2007).

Finally, consider the characteristic speed of consciousness. It takes up to 100–200 ms to develop a specific, fully formed sensory experience. Why is this so? According to the theory, because this is precisely the time it takes to build up effective interactions among the elements of the thalamocortical complex.

4. Some corollaries

As briefly discussed, the theory seems to provide a principled explanation for why consciousness is associated with certain structures and much less with others, or of why it fades during certain stages of sleep, though it must be said that attributing higher or lower Φ to realistic systems is a matter of supposition rather than of actual measurement. The theory also makes several counterintuitive predictions. For example, consider again seeing a perfect blue sky, with nothing else occupying your mind. Presumably, in such a state cortical neurons selective for the colour blue are intensely active, while the rest of the cortex is not. Now imagine that, for a few seconds, the connections among all cortical neurons are blocked; the blue neurons, however, go on firing just as before. Most people guess that, since neural activity has not changed at all, the conscious experience of blue should not be affected. According to the integrated information theory, however, we should become completely unconscious since, with connections blocked, the system has lost its potential repertoire of integrated states.

An important feature of the integrated information approach is that, if properly validated, it would allow us to infer the extent of consciousness in the absence of verbal report, as with infants or animals, or with neurological conditions such as akinetic mutism, psychomotor seizures, and sleepwalking. In practice, of course, measuring Φ accurately in such systems will not be easy, but approximations and informed guesses are at least conceivable.

The integrated information theory implies that consciousness is not an all-or-none property, but increases in proportion to a system's repertoire of integrated states. In fact, any physical system capable of integrated states would have some degree of experience, irrespective of the stuff of which it is made. While this means that conscious artefacts are a definite possibility, one should not conclude that any system composed of many connected elements—say the Internet—would qualify for high Φ: simulations show that it is easy to build many small interconnected complexes forming a large number of complexes of low Φ, but it is hard to build a large complex with a large integrated repertoire. Moreover, while Φ is a graded quantity, common-sense distinctions between being 'conscious' and 'unconscious' are certainly justifiable in practice: anything having a Φ value much lower than a human being in dreamless sleep or deep anaesthesia should not raise excessive concerns: as far as we can say, there would not be much it is like to be that thing.

In summary, the integrated information theory argues that a system is conscious to the extent that it is unified (a complex) *and* it has a large repertoire of possible states (high Φ): whenever such a system enters a particular state, a large amount of integrated information is generated. In this view, consciousness, i.e. integrated information, is a fundamental quantity, just like mass or energy. Also, the most 'actual' thing in the world—our private, subjective experience, would depend on a 'potential'—the repertoire of states discriminable by a certain part of our brain.

GIULIO TONONI

Massimini, M., Ferrarelli, F., Huber, R., Esser, S. K., Singh, H. and Tononi, G. (2005), 'Breakdown of cortical effective connectivity during sleep'. *Science*, 309.

——, ——, Esser, S. K. et al. (2007). 'Triggering sleep slow waves by transcranial magnetic stimulation'. *Proceedings of the National Academy of Sciences of the USA*, 104.

Tononi, G. (2004). 'An information integration theory of consciousness'. *BMC Neuroscience*, 5.

—— and Sporns, O. (2003). 'Measuring information integration'. *BMC Neuroscience*, 4.

inner speech 'I must not forget to buy bread on my way home tonight'; 'I look great in these jeans'; 'What's John's phone number again?' These are simple examples of inner speech, the activity of talking to oneself in silence. Related terms can be found in the literature: self-talk, subvocal/covert speech, *working memory, verbal rehearsal, internal dialogue/monologue, subvocalization, utterance, self-verbalization, auditory imagery, and self-statement. The expression *private speech* designates self-talk emitted out loud by adults when alone, whereas *egocentric speech* refers to young children's outer speech produced in social situations without preoccupation of being understood by others. It is assumed that inner speech is universal, but important individual differences exist in terms of its frequency, content, and sophistication. People talk to themselves more or less often, use varied proportions of positive and negative self-statements, and articulate more or less complex sentences with important discrepancies in vocabulary richness.

The origin of inner speech is social in nature: it represents the gradual internalization of adults' speech that comes to be self-directed. Inner speech differs from social speech in that it is abbreviated and predicative (i.e. the context of speech is implicit to the talking agent). Philosophers such as Plato, Porphyre, and Ryle have examined the phenomenon of inner speech and its relation to thought. The Wurzburg school's view (late 1800s) was that pure thought can exist without language, and thus inner speech; the behaviourist's view instead emphasized that thought should be equated with silent speech. Darwin, in *The Descent of Man* (1871: Ch. 3), clearly embraced the later when he wrote that 'A long and complex train of thought can not be carried on without the aid of words, whether spoken or silent, than a long calculation without the use of figures or algebra.' Blachowicz (1999) has recently contrasted two conceptions of inner speech. According to the dialogical/social view there are two distinct internal cognitive interests in internal *dialogue*, the articulating and listening 'partners', each alternatively changing role as one corrects proposals made by the other. The foundationalist/reflection view rather proposes that the conversational duality of inner speech is more apparent than real. It is only the reflecting self that does the talking; inner speech is *monologue*, not dialogue.

The scientific study of inner speech is relatively recent. The most popular tool is questionnaires consisting of self-statements along various possible dimensions—e.g. anxious vs non-anxious, positive vs negative, functional vs dysfunctional; participants indicate their frequency of self-talk use on a Likert scale. Spontaneous outward manifestations of inner speech (egocentric speech in children and private speech in adults) can be recorded while participants engage in some activity or problem-solving task; verbalizations are coded and classified into different categories that are then correlated with behaviour or performance. A variation of this technique is the *'think out loud' method*, where adult participants are explicitly instructed to vocalize their thoughts. In the videotape reconstruction procedure, subjects are shown video recordings of their behaviour in specific situations and are asked to report ('reconstruct') inner speech activity. The *thought listing method* consists in asking participants to catalogue their verbal mental activity after completion of a task, whereas the thought sampling technique aims to obtain a representative sample of people's inner speech in natural settings (see DESCRIPTIVE EXPERIENCE SAMPLING). Electromyographic recordings of movements of the tongue have also been employed to assess inner speech frequency during problem-solving activities.

These assessment techniques have assisted researchers in identifying the main functions of inner speech. Verbal self-guidance (i.e. self-regulation) has been extensively studied by Vygotsky (1934/1962) and Luria (1978). Their work indicates that children first learn to respond to adult verbal commands to orient and control their behaviour, and that this regulatory function of language gradually gets internalized and becomes increasingly self-generated. Self-regulation includes setting immediate and distant goals, planning, problem-solving, and decision-making. Tasks that require the elaboration of complex behavioural sequences and the simultaneous appreciation of multiple behavioural options are usually better performed with the aid of self-talk. Research conducted by Kendall and Hollon (1981) identifies four effective categories of problem-solving self-verbalizations: (1) a precise definition of the problem; (2) an effective approach to the problem; (3) a sustained focus on the problem; (4) a progress evaluation that includes praise or strategy readjustment. A vast array of studies have examined the use of inner speech in athletes for instructional (skill and strategy) or motivational (arousal, mastery, and drive) purposes in competitive and practice settings. Inner speech has also been shown to play a key-role in mnemonic functions, especially in rehearsal of material in short-term working memory.

Despite the overall adaptive quality of self-directed talk, distorted use of inner speech may lead to—or maintain—psychological disorders. Research suggests that conditions such as bulimia and anorexia, insomnia, social anxiety, agoraphobia, compulsive gambling, male sexual dysfunction, and depression involve maladaptive self-talk. More benign transitory negative states such as worry, guilt, and shame are most likely mediated by inner speech. The intriguing phenomenon of auditory verbal *hallucinations in *schizophrenic patients is now explained in terms of deficient monitoring of their own self-generated subvocal activity (see McGuire et al. 1996). A lack of inner speech in hyperactive children can partially account for inadequate self-control, and behavioural cognitive therapy developed by Meichenbaum (1977) teaches agitated children to talk to themselves in order to effectively engage in verbal self-guidance. Therapy involves five gradual steps leading to the internalization of self-regulatory speech: (1) modelling, (2) overt external guidance, (3) overt self-guidance, (4) faded overt self-guidance, and (5) covert self-guidance.

Research on inner speech does not limit itself to its functions. A representative example in developmental psychology is the study of the gradual transformation of egocentric/private speech into inner speech in children. Work conducted by Kohlberg et al. (1968) shows that external speech for self has a curvilinear course of development inflecting at ages 6–7 and disappearing at age 10. Other studies have determined that children become aware of engaging in private speech at around age 4. Vygotsky (1934/1962) originally postulated that once self-talk has been fully internalized as inner speech, it does not resurface as external speech for self. However, work by Duncan and Cheyne (1999) demonstrates that healthy adults do use private speech when alone for self-regulatory purposes, as well as for spatial navigation/search, concentration, and affective discharge/control. Current non-developmental research focuses on measurement issues, inner speech in bilinguals, and neuroanatomy. One precise brain area has been shown to be more active during inner speech production: the left inferior frontal gyrus.

Inner speech is related to *consciousness in at least two ways. First, self-talk can be conceived of as a running verbal commentary on one's current subjective experience—what one is presently perceiving, thinking about, doing, feeling, and so forth. Seen as such, inner speech represents an inherent part of being conscious. Second, some past and current theories of consciousness and self-awareness explicitly implicate inner speech. Mead's thesis (1912/1964) suggests that egocentric speech in early childhood makes young speakers aware of their actions and separate existence. Dennett (1991) sees the self as a centre of narrative gravity—a verbal autobiography—and Carruthers (2002) proposes that one becomes aware of a mental state when one verbally generates a higher-order thought about that state. Burns and Engdahl (1998) add that through the process of labelling, categorizing, and engaging in language-based modes of representation, one not only represents internal states and experiences—one reflects on them. And Steels (2003) notes that inner speech leads to the construction of a self-model (see BICAMERAL MIND). Morin (2005) further indicates that self-talk can reproduce social mechanisms leading to self-awareness—i.e. with inner speech one can engage in verbal conversations with oneself and replicate comments emitted by others or internalize others' perspective. Inner speech can also create a psychological distance between the self and mental events it experiences, thus facilitating self-observation. It can act as a problem-solving mechanism where the self represents the problem and self-information the solution, and can label aspects of one's inner life that would otherwise be difficult to objectively capture.

Perhaps it is no accident that most Eastern religions encourage followers to 'quiet' the self by inhibiting self-talk through *meditation. The self engaged in subjective experience can better perceive the various elements that constitute this experience by verbally identifying them; the same self can also become more explicitly cognizant that it is the subject of this experience by stepping back and saying 'I'm the one going through this'.

ALAIN MORIN

Blachowicz, J. (1999). 'The dialogue of the soul with itself'. In Gallagher, S. and Shear, J. (eds) *Models of the Self.*

Burns, T. and Engdahl, E. (1998). 'The social construction of consciousness. Part 1: Collective consciousness and its socio-cultural foundations'. *Journal of Consciousness Studies*, 5.

Carruthers, P. (2002). 'The cognitive functions of language'. *Behavioral and Brain Sciences*, 25.

Darwin, C. R. (1871). *The Descent of Man, and Selection in Relation to Sex.*

Dennett, D. C. (1991). *Consciousness Explained.*

Duncan, R. M. and Cheyne, J. A. (1999). 'Incidence and functions of self-reported private speech in young adults: a self-verbalization questionnaire'. *Canadian Journal of Behavioural Science*, 31.

Kendall, P. C. and Hollon, S. D. (1981). 'Assessing self-referent speech: methods of measurement of self-statements'. In Kendall, P. C. and Hollon, S. D. (eds) *Assessment Strategies for Cognitive-Behavioral Interventions.*

Kohlberg, L., Yaeger, J. and Hjertholm, E. (1968). 'Private speech: four studies and a review of theories'. *Child Development*, 39.

Luria, A. R. (1978). *Les fonctions corticales supérieures de l'homme* [Superior cortical functions in man].

McGuire, P. K., Silbersweig, D. A., Wright, I., Murray, R. M., Frackowiak, R. S. J., and Frith, C. D. (1996). 'The neural correlates of inner speech and auditory verbal imagery in schizophrenia: relationship to auditory verbal hallucinations'. *British Journal of Psychiatry*, 169.

Mead, G. H. (1912/1964). 'The mechanism of social consciousness'. In *Selected writings: George Herbert Mead*, ed. A.J. Reck.

Meichenbaum, D. (1977). *Cognitive-Behavior Modification: An Integrative Approach.*

Morin, A. (2005). 'Possible links between self-awareness and inner speech: theoretical background, underlying mechanisms, and empirical evidence'. *Journal of Consciousness Studies*, 12.

Steels, L. (2003). 'Language re-entrance and the "inner voice" '. *Journal of Consciousness Studies*, 10.

Vygotsky, L. S. (1934/1962). *Thought and Language.*

intentionality The notion of intentionality is arguably the single most important in the philosophy of mind, and its relation to the notion of consciousness has seen many a turnaround over the past few of centuries.

1. The nature of intentionality
2. Intentionality as the essence of mind
3. The relationship between intentionality and consciousness

1. The nature of intentionality

Many thoughts and experiences are 'about' or 'of' something. My current thought is about a chocolate sundae and my current visual experience is of the laptop in front of me. In this way, both my thought and my experience are directed at something other than themselves. They are both *contentful*, in that it makes sense to ask what I am thinking or experiencing. This contentfulness is what the philosophical term 'intentionality' is supposed to capture. The term derives from the Latin *intentio*, which means roughly 'to be directed at'.

It has sometimes been claimed that it is of the essence of thought and experience—and perhaps all other modes of mentation—that they are contentful in this way. Suppose I tell you I'm thinking. You ask: 'what are you thinking?' I answer: 'I'm not thinking anything, I'm just thinking.' You would be justified in concluding that I either do not understand the English word 'thinking' or am deliberately trying to annoy you. Where there is thinking, something is being thought. This is the contentfulness of thought.

A more precise characterization of intentionality, which has subsequently become all but definitive, was offered by the philosopher Roderick Chisholm (1957). On this characterization, a certain type of activity is intentional if it is denoted by an intensional verb; and a verb is intensional if it exhibits certain logical features. Two of these stand out. They derive from the facts that (1) we can think about things that do not exist, such as dragons and witches, and (2) we can think of the same thing in such different ways that we are unaware of its sameness.

The first logical feature of intensional verbs is failure to support so-called *existential generalization*. This feature derives from our ability to think about things that do not exist. Consider the sentence 'Jim is sitting in his jacuzzi.' It entails the following sentence: 'There is an *x*, such that Jim is sitting in *x*.' (The first entails the second in the sense that it is impossible for the first to be true while the second is false.) This sort of entailment is called existential generalization by logicians. For most sentences, existential generalization is a valid inference. But not for all. Consider 'Jim is thinking of his jacuzzi'. This sentence does not entail 'There is an *x*, such that Jim is thinking of *x*.' For it may be that Jim is thinking of his jacuzzi during his lunch break, but the jacuzzi was already burned to the ground just after breakfast. In that case, the first sentence would be true and the second false—which shows that the first does not entail the second. The verb 'thinking', then, fails to support existential generalization in a way the verb 'sitting' does not. It thus exhibits the first logical feature definitive of intensionality.

The second logical feature is failure to support truth-preserving substitution of co-referential terms. This feature derives from the fact that we can think about the same thing in very different ways. Suppose that, unbeknownst to Jim, his jacuzzi is his most envied possession. The sentences 'Jim is sitting in his jacuzzi' and 'Jim's jacuzzi is his most envied possession' together entail the sentence 'Jim is sitting in his most envied possession.' But 'Jim is thinking of his jacuzzi' and 'Jim's jacuzzi is his most envied possession' do not together entail 'Jim is thinking of his most envied possession.' So substitution of terms that refer to the same entity (*co-referential terms*) preserves the truth of the original sentence when 'sitting' is used, but not when 'thinking' is used. Thus the verb 'thinking' exhibits the second logical feature definitive of intensionality.

If this is right, we can conclude that the verb 'to think' is intensional, and therefore that the activity it denotes, namely thinking, is intentional. It has intentionality (content, aboutness). On the same grounds, sitting does not have intentionality (content, aboutness).

2. Intentionality as the essence of mind

There is a tradition, going back at least to the 19th century Austrian philosopher Franz Brentano, of taking intentionality to capture the essence of mind. Brentano (1874) put it by saying that 'intentionality is the mark of the mental'. Brentano's claim can be formulated as the thesis that all and only mental phenomena are intentional. This thesis has two parts, then: (a) all mental phenomena are intentional; (b) only mental phenomena are intentional.

How plausible are these claims? The first has struck many as very plausible. As we noted, experiences and thoughts are always contentful. The same can be said of emotions, decisions, and other kinds of mental state. Thus, when one is disappointed that one has not won the lottery, the fact that one has not won the lottery is the content of one's feeling of disappointment; when one decides to join the army, the act of joining the army is the content of one's decision.

It has sometimes been claimed, however, that some kinds of mental state are not intentional. The examples usually cited are somatic experiences, such as pain and pleasure, and moods, such as depression and elation. On the face of it, a toothache is not about anything, and nor is an *orgasm. Likewise, depression, anxiety, and elation do not appear to be about anything in particular. Yet all these are clearly mental phenomena.

Both kinds of counter-example have been contested, however. Some philosophers (e.g. Tye 1990) have argued that somatic experiences are about something, after all: they are about physiological events in one's body. Thus, the content of a toothache is tissue damage in one's tooth, and the content of an orgasm is an altogether different event in an altogether different place. As for moods, a natural idea is that although they are not about *anything in particular*, they are about *everything in general*. Thus, when one is depressed, everything seems dull and unexciting to one; when one is anxious, everything seems worrisome; and so on.

The second claim associated with Brentano's mark thesis—that *only* mental phenomena are intentional—is the one most often contested. Many non-mental phenomena, such as linguistic expressions and traffic signs, are about something. The word 'cat' is about cats, for example, and a 'children crossing' traffic sign is about children crossing the road. These are contentful yet non-mental entities.

In response, however, it might be claimed that linguistic expressions and traffic signs have a content only because we *interpret* them. Moreover, they have the contents they do, rather than other contents, only because we interpret them the way we do, rather than another way. There is nothing intrinsic to the concatenation of symbols c^a^t that makes it about cats rather than dogs or nothing at all. The only thing that makes it about what it is about is our decision to use it in the way we do. The same is true for traffic signs and other forms of non-mental intentionality. They all derive from the intentionality of mental states (especially such states as interpreting, deciding, intending to communicate, etc.). Mental states, in contrast, do not derive their intentionality from any external source. They have it in and of themselves. These considerations suggest that while (b) above may be inaccurate, a modified version of it would be highly plausible. This modified version might be formulated as follows: (b′) only mental phenomena are *non-derivatively* intentional.

When we couple (a) and (b′), we obtain the thesis that non-derivative intentionality is the mark of the mental: all and only mental phenomena are non-derivatively intentional. To be sure, both parts of this claim are contentious. Contrary to (a), some (e.g. Searle 1983, 1991) hold that moods are after all non-intentional; contrary to (b), some (e.g. Millikan 1984) hold that *linguistic expressions are just as non-derivatively intentional as mental phenomena, and some (e.g. Dennett 1987) that mental phenomena are just as derivatively intentional as linguistic expressions. Nonetheless, the thesis that non-derivative intentionality is the mark of the mental is quite plausible on the face of it.

This is significant because, historically, it has often been taken for granted that consciousness captures the essence of mind. Two main 20th century developments have colluded to erode this notion. The first is Freud's claim to account for much of human behaviour in terms of personality traits and dispositional states that are subconscious. The second was cognitive science's claim to account for much of our cognitive functioning in terms of sub-personal events and processes. Given that the subconscious and the sub-personal are by and large (perhaps universally) unconscious, the emerging picture gave a very limited place to consciousness in our mental life. Indeed, it is now customary to think of consciousness as just the tip of the mental iceberg, as it were. The contemporary outlook is that most of what takes place in the mind occurs below the threshold of conscious awareness, and therefore consciousness is not as crucial to the mind as was historically thought. Consciousness has been usurped by intentionality as the mark of the mental.

3. The relationship between intentionality and consciousness

This contemporary outlook depends on a view of intentionality and consciousness as two separate aspects of mental life, a view sometimes referred to as *separatism* (a term introduced by Horgan and Tienson 2002). This separatist assumption has come under critical scrutiny, however, in the more recent philosophical literature. It has been undermined from two different angles. On the one hand, some philosophers have attempted to explain consciousness in terms of intentionality. On the other, some have argued that intentionality cannot be understood independently of consciousness.

The view that consciousness can be reductively explained in terms of intentionality (defended most thoroughly by Dretske 1995 and Tye 1990) is sometimes referred to as 'intentionalism'. (More often, it is referred to as **representationalism*, on the assumption that intentionality is best understood in terms of mental representation.) According to intentionalism, every conscious experience or thought has an intentional content, and moreover, the experience or thought's specific *phenomenology is in fact nothing but its intentional content. Thus, the phenomenal feel of a visual experience of purple is just the experience's intentional directedness at a purple surface or volume. The experience's purple content constitutes its purplish character.

The main motivation for intentionalism is the so-called *transparency of experience*, a consideration popularized among philosophers by Harman (1990). When we turn our attention inward and introspectively examine our ongoing conscious experiences, the only thing we become aware of are what these experiences are experiences of—what their content is. Thus, when I examine my current experience of the white wall before me, I am aware only of the fact that the experience is of a white wall. Importantly, I do not become aware of any secondary whiteness in addition to the wall's. This consideration supports intentionalism in two ways. First, the fact that the phenomenology of consciousness seems intentional suggests that it probably is intentional. Second, on the assumption that phenomenology is necessarily introspectible, the fact that the only introspectible aspect of consciousness is its intentionality suggests that there is nothing more to phenomenology than intentionality.

There are several arguments by counter-example against intentionalism (a good number of which are due to Ned Block, e.g. Block 1990) that are routinely debated in the literature. But the view also faces a more principled problem. On the face of it, it would seem that any feature of the world that could be the content of a conscious mental state could also be the content of an unconscious mental state. My laptop is the content of my visual experience of it, but conceivably it could also be the content of a visual state of induced *blindsight and surely is the content of some of my tacit beliefs (e.g. my belief that whenever I fall asleep my laptop does not transform into a pecan pie for the duration of my sleep). More generally, for every conscious intentional state directed at some object or feature of the world, there could easily be an unconscious intentional state directed at the same object or feature. If so, it cannot be that the essence of consciousness is intentionality. Intentionality is not the mark of the conscious.

One response to this challenge is to claim that what distinguishes conscious intentional states from unconscious intentional states is their functional or cognitive role, that is, the kinds of causes and effects they typically have. This view may be plausible, but it is not genuinely intentionalist. The idea behind intentionalism was that there is nothing more to a conscious state's being conscious than its intentionality. If we adopt the response under consideration, there actually is more to a conscious state's being conscious than its intentionality, namely, its cognitive role.

A different response to our challenge is to claim that there is a distinctive kind of intentionality that is present only in conscious intentional states. Conscious intentional states, on this view, have a special intentionality that unconscious intentional states do not have. Conscious states may be intentionally directed at the same things as unconscious states, but they are not directed at these things in the same way as those unconscious states. For example, my visual experience of my laptop is directed at the same object (the laptop) as my tacit beliefs about my laptop, but it is directed at it in a very different and distinctive way. It is directed at it, we might say, in an *experiential* way. *Experiential intentionality*, or *felt aboutness*, may thus be a suitable candidate for the status of 'the mark of the conscious'. The problem with this response is that, although it saves intentionalism, it undercuts its original reductive aspirations, that is, its attempt to reductively explain consciousness in terms of intentionality. The result is a sort of *non-reductive intentionalism* (defended by Chalmers 2004 among others). According to non-reductive intentionalism, there is a kind of intentionality that is common and peculiar to conscious experiences and thoughts, but it is impossible to understand this form of intentionality without first understanding the nature of consciousness. Intentionality therefore cannot be used to explain consciousness.

Indeed, the existence of a special experiential intentionality—or *phenomenal intentionality*, as it is sometimes called—has been claimed by some (e.g. McGinn 1988) to show that our understanding of intentionality is actually incomplete, and is bound to remain so at least until we have a full theory of consciousness. For until we reach a full understanding of consciousness, there will be an important kind of intentionality that we do not understand.

Some philosophers (most notably Searle 1991) have taken this line of thought a step further, claiming that phenomenal or conscious intentionality is in fact the only kind of non-derivative intentionality. On this view, the intentionality of unconscious mental states is on a par with that of linguistic expressions and traffic signs. Only conscious experiences and thoughts are intentional in and of themselves. If this is right, then the theory of consciousness is not only indispensable for the theory of intentionality, it is in some sense its cornerstone. Phenomenal intentionality becomes the basis, and source, of all intentionality.

The original idea behind intentionalism was that intentionality is the key to understanding consciousness. That order of explanation is reversed if we take phenomenal intentionality to be the basis of all intentionality: consciousness becomes the key to understanding intentionality, rather than the other way round. What these two approaches—intentionalism and the notion that phenomenal intentionality is basic—share is the thought that consciousness and intentionality are not two separate phenomena that must be tackled separately and understood in separation from one another. On both views, that kind of separatism is unwarranted.

The debate on the relationship between consciousness and intentionality is nowise settled, however. All three positions—separatism, intentionalism, and the basicness of phenomenal intentionality—have something to recommend them. The debate can thus be expected to intensify over the next decade or two.

URIAH KRIEGEL

Block, N. J. (1990). 'Inverted Earth'. *Philosophical Perspective*, 4.

Brentano, F. (1874). *Psychology from Empirical Standpoint*, ed. O. Kraus, transl. A. C. Rancurello et al.

Chalmers, D. J. (2004). 'The representational character of experience'. In Leiter, B. (ed.) *The Future of Philosophy*.

Chisholm, R. (1957). *Perceiving: A Philosophical Study*.

Dennett, D. C. (1987). *The Intentional Stance*.

Dretske, F. I. (1995). *Naturalizing the Mind*.

Harman, G. (1990). 'The intrinsic quality of experience'. *Philosophical Perspectives*, 4.

Horgan, T. and Tienson, J. (2002). 'The intentionality of phenomenology and the phenomenology of intentionality'. In Chalmers, D. J. (ed.) *Philosophy of Mind: Classical and Contemporary Readings*.

McGinn, C. (1988). 'Consciousness and content'. *Proceedings of the British Academy*, 76.

Millikan, R. G. (1984). *Language, Thought, and Other Biological Categories*.

Searle, J. R. (1983). *Intentionality: an Essay in the Philosophy of Mind*.

—— (1991). 'Consciousness, unconsciousness, and intentionality'. *Philosophical Issues*, 1.

Tye, M. (1990). 'A representational theory of pains and their phenomenal character'. *Philosophical Perspectives*, 9.

intentional vs incidental learning See LEARNING, EXPLICIT VS IMPLICIT

internalism See EXTERNALISM AND CONSCIOUSNESS

intersensory integration See CROSS-MODAL SENSORY INTEGRATION

intransitive consciousness See CONSCIOUSNESS, CONCEPTS OF

introspection 'The word introspection need hardly be defined—it means, of course, the looking into our own minds and reporting what we there discover' (James 1890/1981:85). Alas, things are not quite so simple. As James implies, the term 'introspection' literally means 'looking within', but of course we do not visually inspect the interiors of our crania. What unites proponents of introspection is the claim that we can recognize our own mental states through some sort of *attention—a non-visual 'looking'—whose immediate objects are thoughts or sensations within oneself, in a non-spatial sense of 'within'. (The term 'introspection' is occasionally given an ecumenical gloss, to refer to any method of knowing one's own mental states, and not just self-directed attention. But the more restrictive use is standard, and provides the topic of the current entry.) As we will see, some contemporary philosophers and psychologists doubt that any such introspective process underlies self-knowledge.

Even those who believe that we do engage in introspection generally acknowledge that some types of mental states cannot be introspected. The first section of this entry outlines widely accepted restrictions on the range of introspectible states. The next section surveys the leading philosophical accounts of introspection. These accounts differ as to how introspection proceeds and how it contrasts with other methods of knowledge. I then examine key objections to the claim that self-knowledge is introspective, and sketch some replies to these objections. The final section briefly discusses the controversy over the role of introspective data in scientific research about the mind.

1. Restrictions on introspection
2. Philosophical accounts of introspection
3. Objections to introspection
4. The use of introspection in scientific study of the mind
5. Conclusion

1. Restrictions on introspection

Early psychologists such as Wilhelm Wundt and Edward Titchener championed the judicious use of introspection, training their subjects to exercise scrupulous attention, and to report their introspective discoveries in meticulous detail. They hoped to generate pure introspective data, unaffected by the subjects' background assumptions about their own thoughts and experiences. While introspection is no longer the primary focus of psychological research, most psychologists and philosophers allow that introspection is ubiquitous in human lives.

But even advocates of introspection usually deny that introspection directly reveals the motivational sources of actions, or that one can introspectively identify standing (dispositional) beliefs or desires. There are several reasons for this denial. First, influential psychological studies (such as Nisbett and Wilson 1977) have shown that subjects are often mistaken about their own motivations in acting, and about the sources of their own preferences and biases (see ATTITUDE, IMPLICIT). This suggests that we lack introspective access to the fact that one particular desire, rather than another, prompted an action. Second, there is evidence that these errors are systematic: for introspection seems to identify the conscious rationale for a choice, but this rationale is often constructed after the choice is made, and so is not the actual cause of the choice. In that case, what is introspected is only one's current thoughts about the likely cause, which may be affected by one's assumptions about what sort of reasons would justify the choice. Third, epistemological considerations cast doubt on the claim that we have direct introspective access to states individuated by their characteristic causes and effects. And standing beliefs and desires—such as the belief that one must drive on the left in Britain, and the desire to advance in one's career, when these are not being actively entertained—seem at least partly defined by their causal roles.

From an evolutionary perspective, the unrestricted use of introspection would not be beneficial. Adaptive fitness would apparently be compromised if crucial mental processes, including some inferences and emotional responses, were open to introspection. Consider the cognitive processes responsible for detecting danger and initiating an appropriate response: if these were easily introspectible, then higher-level cognitive systems could interfere in their operation, thus delaying the response and putting the organism in jeopardy. This suggests that processes that result in—or, perhaps, even constitute—propositional attitudes (such as the belief that one is in danger) and emotions (such as the fear of a predator) are sometimes unconscious, and thus inaccessible to introspection.

For these reasons, most contemporary philosophers and psychologists claim that we introspect only short-lived states such as occurrent thoughts and sensations.

This restriction has done little to diminish the importance of introspection in philosophy, where introspection remains both an important topic and a common (if controversial) method. For instance, the claim that introspective knowledge is epistemically special shapes some theories of knowledge; and some philosophers believe that introspective reflection yields evidence for mind–body *dualism. I now turn to consider the leading philosophical accounts of introspection.

2. Philosophical accounts of introspection

There are several prominent accounts of introspection in the contemporary philosophical literature. These accounts naturally fall into two types, according to how they construe the relationship between the introspective state and its target, the thought or sensation that is introspected. The first type glosses this relationship as merely causal, while the second envisions a more intimate relationship.

Causal accounts. An ordinary perceptual process exemplifies a causal relationship between a state of awareness and its object: I am visually aware of the chair in the corner by virtue of an appropriate causal relationship between that chair and my current visual state. According to causal accounts of introspection, introspection is structurally similar to perception: I am introspectively aware of a thought or sensation by virtue of an appropriate causal relationship between that thought or sensation and my current introspective state. This similarity may pave the way for a naturalistic explanation of introspection (see REDUCTIONISM) Just as we can explain how vision occurs by identifying the relevant causal relations between visual objects (such as the chair) and states of the visual system, we can, perhaps, explain introspection by identifying the relevant causal relations between introspective objects (a thought or sensation) and introspective states.

For some philosophers, the idea that both introspection and perception involve a causal process of awareness exhausts the analogy between these processes. But others see the analogy as more comprehensive, and argue that introspection is the product of a specialized, perception-like faculty. This is the *inner sense* view of introspection (Armstrong 1968, Lycan 1997). It is inspired by John Locke's description of an introspective faculty:

> And though it be not Sense, as having nothing to do with external Objects; yet it is very like it, and might properly enough be call'd internal Sense. (Locke 1690/1975, II.i.iv.)

The inner sense view holds that introspection is the operation of an internal scanning mechanism, which has the function of monitoring (some of) our thoughts and sensations. The view is often combined with a theory of consciousness. For instance, Lycan argues that conscious states—which, in his terminology, are 'states one is conscious of being in'—are simply those mental states that one is aware of, through the operation of inner sense.

But is introspection really so similar to perception? Some philosophers worry that perceptual accounts neglect what is special or distinctive about introspection, relative to perceptual processes. For instance, Sydney Shoemaker (1994) argues that the capacity for introspection plays a distinctive role in one's status as a rational agent, and that this role requires introspection to be more reliable, and more tightly tied to its objects, than perception.

A more obvious difference between introspection and perception is that introspection is necessarily first-personal: it is inconceivable that I could have introspective access, or even access that is relevantly introspection-like, to someone else's states. It is a matter of controversy whether any sort of causal account can accommodate the first-personal nature of introspection. The worry is that, if the relation between my introspective states and my thoughts is merely causal, then another person could, in principle, have the same sort of access to my thoughts as I do. Suppose that, in the science fiction future, we identify the neurophysiological (or computational) state that perfectly correlates with my 'ice cream' thoughts. An agent of Big Brother could then set up a monitor that caused him to think 'BG is now thinking about ice cream' when, and only when, I was in the relevant state. This process would be very similar to introspection, as construed by the causal model: it would be causal and non-inferential, and it could conceivably be as reliable as ordinary introspection.

There are, of course, differences between the agent's awareness of my 'ice cream' thoughts, and my own introspective awareness of them. For instance, only the former depends on an artificial device. But these differences seem too insubstantial to undergird the seemingly profound difference between introspective knowledge and other-knowledge. Arguably, this difference is tied to the distinction between self and other: for even if I cannot introspect all of my thoughts, still it seems indisputable that I can introspect only my own thoughts. If it is a conceptual truth that one can introspect only one's own thoughts, then as we blur the distinction between introspective and non-introspective access, we obscure the line between self and other. (see SELF-CONSCIOUSNESS; SELF, PHILOSOPHICAL PERSPECTIVES).

The benefit of causal accounts is that they brighten the prospects for a naturalistic explanation of introspection, by assimilating introspection to more familiar, perceptual processes. The current objection claims that this assimilation bears costs as well, for it prevents causal accounts from capturing what is special about introspection. Defenders of causal accounts could respond that introspective-like access to others' thoughts is conceivable, after all; they might attribute its apparent inconceivability to the fact that we do not live in the science fiction future.

But most defenders of causal accounts agree that others could not, even in principle, introspect one's states. Some claim that the first-personal nature of introspection derives from the presence of indexicals in introspective reference. In ordinary use, indexicals such as 'I' and 'here' refer to oneself and one's location; without further qualification, they cannot refer to another person or place. The idea, then, is that introspection involves a type of indexical reference that is similarly tied to oneself (or one's mental state). The naturalistic benefits of causal accounts will be preserved if this simple semantic feature can fully explain why one can introspect only one's own states. Whether it can do so is, of course, open to debate.

Non-causal accounts. The rivals to causal accounts of introspection have their historical antecedents in Descartes (1641/1984). Descartes argued, in the *Cogito*, that while a supremely powerful 'evil genius' could deceive me about the objects of perception, even an evil genius could not deceive me in the belief that I am thinking. It seems plausible that this difference derived, for Descartes, from the comparative directness of introspective awareness. When it comes to any causal process, the logical distance between cause and effect allows for things to go awry. Light can be unknowingly filtered, so that a white chair appears red; visual spectra can be limited, so that a green light appears grey. But if no causal process mediates between introspective awareness and its objects, then there seems to be no logical room for that introspective awareness to mislead about the thoughts or sensations it is fixed upon. This idea of non-mediated awareness is also at work in Russell's claim that we are directly acquainted with our own occurrent mental states, but not with others' mental states or external physical objects (see ACQUAINTANCE).

There are two leading types of account that envision introspective awareness as logically tied to its objects. (Call these *logical* accounts of introspection.) These are not competing accounts, but rather focus on different types of state.

The first type focuses on thoughts, and has been advanced by Tyler Burge. Burge claims that, when one is introspectively aware that one is thinking that *p* (that it is raining, say), the introspective awareness incorporates the thought that *p*.

> One is thinking that *p* in the very event of thinking knowledgeably that one is thinking it. It is thought and thought about in the same mental act. (Burge 1988:116)

According to Burge, then, the introspected state (a thought) is incorporated into the subject's introspective awareness. While Burge's account is specifically intended to show how a particular view about content—namely, externalism—can accommodate first-person privilege, the logical account of introspecting thoughts is not wedded to any specific theory of content.

The relation of *incorporation* also appears in the second type of logical account, which applies to sensations. Proponents of this account argue that, in introspection, a sensation is incorporated into a larger state, which constitutes introspective awareness of that sensation (Gertler 2001, Chalmers 2002) This account is intended to capture the ordinary experience of introspection and to fit with the epistemic and conceptual features of introspection described above.

To understand this second type of logical account, focus for a moment on a current sensation: pinch your thumb and focus on the feeling of the pinch. Even if you are mistaken about the causal source of that feeling, it is hard to conceive that you are wrong in thinking that you are now feeling a 'pinched thumb' sensation. This suggests that your awareness of the sensation is direct, and not an awareness of something (like the chair you see) that you are merely causally related to. Finally, the idea that it is someone else's sensation that you are aware of, and not your own, seems incoherent—though of course the causal source of the sensation may lie outside yourself.

Just as a significant benefit of causal accounts is that they are well suited to naturalism, a significant worry about logical accounts, of either variety, is that they sit uneasily with naturalistic explanations of mental processes. There is no simple way to translate the logical model into an empirically testable hypothesis: the claim that introspective states incorporate their objects does not imply that one brain state is a proper part of another. In response to this worry, proponents of logical accounts can argue that the special epistemic features of introspective knowledge are a kind of data, and hence any adequate theory of mental processes must explain them.

Logical accounts face other objections as well. Chief among these is the worry that they reduce introspection to a simple event of awareness, and thus cannot explain how introspection could yield substantive knowledge of a mental state. Genuine knowledge requires that we somehow conceptualize the object known, but logical accounts claim only that there is a brute (incorporation) relation between the introspective and the introspected states. Wittgenstein seems to have had this sort of problem in mind when he wrote, 'Imagine someone saying: "But I know how tall I am!" and laying his hand on top of his head to prove it' (1953:279).

The best reply on behalf of logical accounts is to acknowledge that the incorporation relation does not, on its own, provide for self-knowledge. The account must be supplemented by an account of how sensations and thoughts are conceptualized, within the introspective state. But some philosophers doubt that a single, introspective state can simultaneously incorporate its object and constitute an epistemically substantial conceptualization of that object.

3. Objections to introspection

Not all philosophers accept that self-knowledge is achieved via introspection. Some claim that we determine our own mental states in the same way that we determine others', namely, from observations of our own behaviour. Gilbert Ryle defended the most extreme view of this type, arguing that the appearance of special first-person access derives from the simple fact that we are always present to observe ourselves (Ryle 1949).

While Ryle's position is extreme, it still construes self--knowledge as an *epistemic* phenomenon. Other philosophers make the more radical claim that self-knowledge is non-epistemic; so introspection, an epistemic process, cannot be the source of self-knowledge. These philosophers allege that introspective models of self-knowledge rest on an implausible conception of mental states, namely, as static objects that await introspective attention. The worry is not just the familiar point that observational processes sometimes alter their targets. It is instead a conceptual worry: the idea that I know my own thoughts by introspective attention overlooks the kind of commitment that is involved in acknowledging a thought as mine. As G. E. Moore (1942) noted, it is pragmatically incoherent to assert, 'It is raining but I don't believe that it is'. Sartre (1956) made a related point when he argued that a rational agent cannot coherently express an intention to quit gambling while predicting that he will fail. In both cases, the incoherence stems from the fact that the mental state (the belief or intention) is simply *reported*, but not *owned* or *avowed*.

Gareth Evans makes a somewhat similar objection to introspection in claiming that, to determine one's own beliefs, attention must be directed outward rather than inward. 'I get myself in a position to answer the question whether I believe that *p* by putting into operation whatever procedure I have for answering the question whether *p*' (Evans 1982:225). By using a single method to simultaneously determine whether it's raining, and whether I believe it's raining, one avoids the sort of pragmatic incoherence just described. This method is decidedly non-introspective, and seems less a method of knowing one's own beliefs than of formulating them.

Defenders of introspection can respond by pointing out that these conceptual worries concern *attitudes modes* like belief, desire, and intention—aspects of mental states that lie outside introspection's narrow purview. Even if one cannot simply introspect that one intends to quit gambling (or believes that one will quit, or doubts that one will quit), one may be able to introspect the *occurrent thought* 'I will quit gambling', where the fact that one is entertaining this thought content is neutral as to whether it is the content of a belief, a doubt, or an intention. But those who doubt that self-knowledge occurs through a fundamentally epistemic process will question whether we can conceive our own thought contents in this neutral way. And even if we can, it is not clear that recognition of such fleeting thoughts, unconnected to an attitude mode, qualifies as genuine self-knowledge.

4. The use of introspection in scientific study of the mind

Must we take introspective data into account when we engage in scientific theorizing about the mind? Daniel Dennett is a prominent opponent of using introspective data. He claims that if a scientist asks subjects to introspect their experiences, the data generated are beliefs about experiences, not the (purportedly introspected) experiences themselves (Dennett 2003). Nor, he thinks, is it possible to sidestep this problem by using one's own introspective data. For a study limited to one's own case violates familiar strictures of scientific methodology, which require that evidence be available to other observers, and that experimental results be duplicated in multiple subjects.

Dennett's argument raises many questions. But perhaps the most interesting issue concerns the contrast between introspective data and perceptual data. Because introspective evidence is accessible only to the subject herself, introspection cannot meet some requirements of scientific methodology relevant to perceptual data, including the requirement that data be public. To deem introspective evidence non-scientific on that basis, however, is to adopt a very narrow notion of 'scientific'. This will have some worrisome consequences: it seems to imply that a scientific theory of mind need not accommodate the presence of *sensations*. After all, we never see, hear, or otherwise perceive sensations; our only evidence for the existence of sensations depends on introspection. We can, of course, perceive neural states that are correlated with sensations. But it is only through introspection that we can establish such correlations in the first place.

A more nuanced view treats introspective reports of experiences as evidence, not only of beliefs about experiences, but also of the experiences themselves. The use of introspective data does not require that such data is sacrosanct. As with perceptual data, researchers may justifiably discount a single introspective datum that is unrepeatable, violates well-established generalizations (based on other introspective reports), etc. For instance, if we had established that C-fibre firing perfectly correlated with pain, and only one subject had ever reported feeling pain in the absence of C-fibre firing, we may have reason to disregard that report. Some contemporary neuroscientists advise that experimenters develop categories of experience, using experiences that bear a relatively straightforward relationship to external stimuli, and train subjects in their use (Jack and Shallice 2001). The subjects can then apply these established categories to more inchoate experiences. Like Wundt and Titchener's work, this contemporary approach recognizes that obtaining accurate introspective evidence is both vitally important and exceedingly difficult.

5. Conclusion

Subjects are often mistaken about their own motives and emotions. But we have seen no reason to deny that introspection is a reliable guide to one's occurrent thoughts and sensations. And since introspection arguably provides the only evidence that there are sensations, its judicious use may be not only legitimate but also necessary to a comprehensive theory of the mind.

BRIE GERTLER

Armstrong, D. M. (1968). *A Materialist Theory of the Mind*.

Burge, T. (1988). 'Individualism and self-knowledge'. *Journal of Philosophy*, 85.

Chalmers, D. (2002). 'The content and epistemology of phenomenal belief'. In Smith, Q. and Jokic, A. (eds) *Consciousness: New Philosophical Essays*.

Dennett, D. (2003). 'Who's on first? Heterophenomenology explained'. *Journal of Consciousness Studies*, 10.

Descartes, R. (1641/1984). 'Meditations on first philosophy'. In *The Philosophical Writings of Descartes, Volume II*, transl. J. Cottingham et al.

Evans, G. (1982). *The Varieties of Reference*.

Gertler, B. (2001). 'Introspecting phenomenal states'. *Philosophy and Phenomenological Research*, 63.

Jack, A. and Shallice, T. (2001). 'Introspective physicalism as an approach to the science of consciousness'. *Cognition*, 79.

James, W. (1890/1981). *Principles of Psychology*.

Locke, J. (1690/1975). *An Essay Concerning Human Understanding*, ed. P. H. Nidditch.

Lycan, W. G. (1997). 'Consciousness as internal monitoring'. In Block, N. et al. (eds) *The Nature of Consciousness: Philosophical Debates*.

Moore, G. E. (1942). 'Reply to critics'. In Schilpp, P. A. (ed.) *The Philosophy of G. E. Moore*.

Nisbett, R. and Wilson, T. (1977). 'Telling more than we can know: verbal reports on mental processes'. *Psychological Review*, 84.

Ryle, G. (1949). *The Concept of Mind*.

Sartre, J. P. (1956). *Being and Nothingness: an Essay on Phenomenological Ontology*, transl. H. Barnes.

Shoemaker, S. (1994). 'Self-knowledge and "inner sense" '. *Philosophy and Phenomenological Research*, 54.

Wittgenstein, L. (1953). *Philosophical Investigations*, transl. G. E. M. Anscombe.

inverted Earth See INVERTED SPECTRUM; FUNCTIONALIST THEORIES OF CONSCIOUSNESS

inverted spectrum In an inverted spectrum scenario, a person has *colour experiences that are systematically inverted with respect to the experiences of another subject when looking at objects of the same colour. For instance, if Jack is spectrum inverted relative to Jill, then the colour experience had by Jack while looking at a red thing, such as a ripe tomato, is phenomenally like the experience had by Jill while looking at a green thing, and vice versa. The inverted spectrum hypothesis often involves the further assumption that the inversion is behaviourally undetectable. We might imagine that Jack's colour vision has been inverted (relative to Jill's) since birth, such that his inversion is not reflected in his use of colour vocabulary. Both Jack and Jill learned to apply the word 'red' to the same sorts of objects, although those objects cause experiences in them that are different in their phenomenal character. It might be said that Jack and Jill associate particular colour terms with different colour *qualia, but with the very same external properties of objects. If Jack and Jill's spectrum inversion is to be behaviourally undetectable, it must also be the case that they can make the same colour discriminations and comparisons.

The idea of the inverted spectrum appears to have first entered philosophical discussion in John Locke's *Essay Concerning Human Understanding* (1689/1975). Whether or not various sorts of spectrum inversion scenarios are conceivable and/or possible has implications for philosophical theories about the relationship between the mental and the physical, as well as theories of colour. In contemporary philosophy of mind, inverted spectrum scenarios have most often been considered in arguments against functionalism and in arguments concerning the intentional content of colour experiences. The inverted spectrum hypothesis has also been presented as a challenge to behaviourism, *physicalism, and our knowledge of other minds.

1. Against functionalism
2. Against representationalism

1. Against functionalism

According to functionalism, mental states are individuated by their functional roles within the cognitive system of which they are a part. With regard to colour experiences, functionalism entails that what makes something a 'red experience' (an expression that we can stipulate as denoting the type of experience Jill has while viewing a red object and that Jack has while viewing a green object) is determined by its causal relations to sensory inputs, other mental states, and behavioural outputs. *Analytic functionalism* holds that it is analytic or a matter of meaning that mental states are functional states. *Psychofunctionalism* instead holds that the identification of types of mental states with particular functional roles is only discoverable empirically. Inverted spectrum arguments have been employed against both forms of functionalism.

The argument against analytic functionalism runs as follows (Block and Fodor 1972, Shoemaker 1975). It is conceivable that two subjects that are functional duplicates could nonetheless be spectrum-inverted relative to one another. But if, as analytic functionalism holds, it is a matter of meaning alone that experiences of a certain phenomenal type occupy a particular functional role, then this inverted spectrum scenario should not even be conceivable. It would be a priori that, in virtue of being in functionally identical states, functional duplicates will have phenomenally identical colour experiences.

It is at least in principle possible for psychofunctionalism to allow for the conceivability of spectrum inversion between functional duplicates, since according to psychofunctionalism, the identification of a mental state type with its functional role is not a priori. If the psychofunctionalist were to further claim that it is a posteriori that mental states *in general* are identical to functional roles, such that the truth of psychofunctionalism itself is an empirical matter, then she might allow that it is in some sense conceivable for there to be an inverted spectrum between functional duplicates. But psychofunctionalism is incompatible with the possibility of spectrum inversion between functional duplicates. Discussion of the possibility of functionally undetectable spectrum inversion has centred on the empirical question of whether or not the colour space is symmetrical along some dimension. Some have objected, however, that even if the actual human visual system is asymmetrical, the mere possibility of a creature with a symmetrical colour space is sufficient for the inverted spectrum argument to threaten functionalism (Shoemaker 1982).

There are many transformations of the human colour space that would be detectable. For example, some hues are binary (appearing to be composed of two other hues) and others are unique. The four unique hues also come in opponent pairs. There can be neither a hue that is a mixture of red and green nor a hue that is a mixture of blue and yellow. It follows that a mapping of a unique hue onto a binary hue, or a mapping of a unique hue onto another unique hue from a different opponent pair, would be behaviourally and functionally detectable.

Hue is not the only dimension along which colour experiences vary. Colours also differ with respect to saturation and lightness. Here there are further asymmetries. For example, yellows at maximum saturation appear lighter than maximally saturated blues. This asymmetry would show up in any blue–yellow inversion (Hardin 1988). It has also been argued that asymmetries in colour categories pose a problem for behaviourally undetectable spectrum inversion (Harrison 1973). Palmer (1999) argues that there are nonetheless three inversion scenarios that remain functionally undetectable: red–green inversion, blue–yellow and black–white inversion together, and the conjunction of these two sets of inversions.

2. Against representationalism

The inverted spectrum hypothesis has been employed against certain forms of *representationalist theories of consciousness (Block 1990, Shoemaker 1994), according to which the contents of consciousness are exclusively representational. These arguments typically do not rely on the assumption that a spectrum inversion would be behaviourally undetectable. Instead, they depend on the idea that it is possible for inverted subjects to each be veridical perceivers of colour. One way of motivating this possibility is to consider a scenario in which spectrum inversion is widespread within the population, such that half see colour the way that Jack does and half see colour the way that Jill does. Advocates of this form of argument contend that there would be no grounds for claiming that only one half of the population, and not the other, sees colours veridically (Shoemaker 1994; Tye 2000 responds to this sort of argument).

Block (1990) supports the possibility of spectrum inversion without misrepresentation by having us consider a case of constant phenomenal character and inverted intentional contents, rather than a case of inverted phenomenal character. In the *Inverted Earth* scenario, a subject (unknowingly) has colour-inverting lenses placed in his eyes and is transported to Inverted Earth. Inverted Earth is identical to Earth except that everything on Inverted Earth has the complementary colour of its counterpart on Earth, and the colour vocabulary of the residents of Inverted Earth is also inverted. Due to the colour-inverting lenses, however, the subject's experiences are phenomenally the same as they would have been if he had remained on Earth. This suggests that the subject initially has systematically illusory colour experiences. But Block argues that after some amount of time has passed, the representational content of the subject's colour experiences will become inverted and will veridically represent the colours on Inverted Earth.

Representationalism requires that phenomenally identical experiences have the same intentional content. Many representationalists also hold that the intentional content of a colour experience consists solely in the representation of physical colours (Dretske 1995, Tye 1995). On this view, if Jack and Jill are viewing the same object and having inverted experiences relative to each other, their experiences will also attribute different physical colours to the object. It follows that they cannot both be veridical perceivers of colour. Philosophers who are compelled by the idea that there is no principled basis for saying that either Jack or Jill is the only veridical perceiver of colour have found this consequence of standard formulations of representationalism as a reason to either reject representationalism altogether (Block 1990) or to develop a different form of representationalism that accommodates the possibility of spectrum inversion without misrepresentation (Shoemaker 1994, Chalmers 2004, Thompson 2009).

BRAD THOMPSON

Block, N. (1990). 'Inverted Earth'. *Philosophical Perspectives*, 4.
Block, N. and Fodor, J. (1972). 'What psychological states are not'. *Philosophical Review*, 83.
Chalmers, D. (2004). 'The representational character of experience'. In Leiter, B. (ed.) *The Future of Philosophy*.
Dretske, F. (1995). *Naturalizing the Mind*.
Hardin, C. L. (1988). *Color for Philosophers*.
Harrison, B. (1973). *Form and Content*.
Locke, J. (1689/1975). *Essay Concerning Human Understanding*, ed. P. H. Nidditch.
Palmer, S. (1999). 'Color, consciousness, and the isomorphism constraint'. *Behavioral and Brain Science*, 22.
Shoemaker, S. (1975). Functionalism and qualia. *Philosophical Studies*, 27.
—— (1982). 'The inverted spectrum'. *Journal of Philosophy*, 79.
—— (1994). Phenomenal character. *Noûs*, 28.
Thompson, B. (2009). 'Senses for senses'. *Australasian Journal of Philosophy*, 87.
Tye, M. (1995). *Ten Problems of Consciousness*.
—— (2000). *Consciousness, Color, and Content*.

inverted vision The return of upright vision during adaptation to inverting spectacles has been of great interest to the psychology of perception and the philosophy of consciousness. If the world was perceived in its canonical orientation although the retinal image is inverted (or rather not inverted with respect to the external world, as it normally would be) this would suggest a very high degree of plasticity in sensory cortex and its afferent connections and cast doubt on the stability of any perceptual experience. However, more recent experiments have shown that this radical claim of full perceptual adaptation to inverting spectacles cannot be maintained (Linden et al. 1999, Klein and Love 2006).

Stratton (1897) was the first to describe canonical perception through inverting prisms. Kohler's Innsbruck experiments in the 1950s with upside-down reversing mirrors also resulted in reports of upright vision after one week, which occurred in parallel with considerable improvement of visuomotor coordination (Kohler 1964). However, the participants in the Innsbruck experiments mainly reported ambiguities of the visual image of particular objects that they handled. Moreover, more recent studies of adaptation to visual inversion (180° rotation) and reversal have found that the awareness of visual transposition remained stronger than the sense of reality of the new vision. Participant's introspective reports were supplemented with an objective test of the perception of shade from shading where subjects had to judge the orientation of a hemisphere based on the direction from which it is lit. While wearing the goggles, participants (with the exception of one who showed ambiguous results) judged the shapes in the 'wrong' (opposite to pre-experimental baseline) way, because the prisms inverted the direction of the light. Furthermore, *functional magnetic resonance imaging documented stable retinotopic maps of primary visual cortex (*V1) throughout the experiment. These results were confirmed in two additional participants who each wore the goggles for three weeks.

Sekiyama et al. (2000) studied four participants with left–right reversing goggles over an adaptation period of five weeks. They focused on the perception of hands. Participants at first failed to identify right or left hands correctly but were able to switch back and forth between the 'old' (pre-adaptation) and 'new' (mirror reverted) hand image by the 25th day of adaptation. They became capable of dissociating perception of their own hand from somatic cues and visualizing them in harmony with the new visual image. A shortcoming of such findings is that cognitive restructuring that leads to a change in the internal set of instructions (e.g. introducing the step of mentally reversing the hand) can never be excluded (and is actually supported by the higher reaction times for the 'new' compared to the 'old' representation).

Most recent evidence thus converges to describe a dissociation of often impressive motor adaptation to visual inversion or reversal and partial perceptual ambiguities of objects that are actively interacted with on the one hand, and absence of global perceptual switches on the other.

DAVID E. J. LINDEN

Klein, C. and Love, G. (2006) 'Kicking the Kohler habit'. In *10th Annual Meeting of the Association for the Scientific Study of Consciousness*.
Kohler, I. (1964). *The Formation and Transformation of the Perceptual World*.
Linden, D. E., Kallenbach, U., Heinecke, A., Singer, W., and Goebel, R. (1999). 'The myth of upright vision. A psychophysical and functional imaging study of adaptation to inverting spectacles'. *Perception*, 28.
Sekiyama, K., Miyauchi, S., Imaruoka, T., Egusa, H., and Tashiro, T. (2000). 'Body image as a visuomotor device revealed in adaptation to reversed vision'. *Nature*, 407.
Stratton, G. M. (1897). 'Vision without inversion of the retinal image'. *Psychological Review*, 4.

J

jamais vu See DÉJÀ VU

knowledge argument The knowledge argument is an argument against *physicalism that was first formulated by Frank Jackson in 1982. Although Jackson no longer endorses it, it is still regarded as one of the most important arguments in the philosophy of mind.

Physicalism is the metaphysical thesis that, roughly speaking, everything in this world—including tables, galaxies, cheese cakes, cars, atoms, and even our sensations—are ultimately physical. The knowledge argument attempts to undermine this thesis by appealing to the following simple imaginary scenario:

> Mary is confined to a black-and-white room, is educated through black-and-white books and through lectures relayed on black-and white television. In this way she learns everything there is to know about the physical nature of the world. She knows all the physical facts about us and our environment, in a wide sense of 'physical' which includes everything in *completed* physics, chemistry, and neurophysiology, and all there is to know about the causal and relational facts consequent upon all this, including of course functional roles. (Jackson 1986:291)

The knowledge argument says that if physicalism is true, Mary knows everything in this world. However, it seems obvious that her knowledge is not yet complete. Suppose that Mary leaves her black-and-white environment for the first time in her life. She will then apparently learn something; namely, *what it is like to see colour. Given that she knows everything physical in her black-and-white environment and that she still learns something upon her release, it seems reasonable to conclude that physicalism is false.

Jackson presents the knowledge argument schematically as follows: (1) Mary (before her release) knows everything physical there is to know about other people. (2) Mary (before her release) does not know everything there is to know about other people (because she learns something about them on her release). Therefore, (3) there are truths about other people (and herself) that escape the physicalist story (Jackson 1986:293). Jackson formulates premises (1) and (2) in terms of truths about other people in order to emphasize that Mary certainly learns some truths about the external world.

Given the simplicity of the Mary scenario, it is not surprising to find that similar scenarios had already been envisaged by many other philosophers. For instance, the 17th century philosopher John Locke writes as follows:

> I think it will be granted easily that if a child were kept in a place where he never saw any other than black and white till he were a man, he would have no more ideas of scarlet or green, than he that from his childhood never tasted an oyster, or a pine-apple, would have of those relishes. (Locke 1689:Bk II, Ch.1, Sect 6.)

Or, to take another example, Meehl (1966) discusses a scenario in which two people, *K1* and *K2*, share 'knowledge of the Utopian scientific network'. The knowledge of *K1* and *K2* includes 'the psychophysiology of vision and the psycholinguistics of color language', but *K2* is congenitally blind. Meehl points out that many people would think intuitively that in this case *K1* knows something that *K2* does not.

Jackson's knowledge argument is impressive, not because of the intuition about Mary's knowledge upon which it is based, but because of its dialectic structure. First, Jackson formulates the argument for the specific purpose of refuting physicalism. Locke does not derive any claim about physicalism from his thought experiment; he merely uses it to illustrate his empiricism. While Meehl does consider whether his example undermines physicalism, he concludes that it does not. The second distinctive characteristic of the knowledge argument is that it is designed in such a way that while its premises seem to be ontologically neutral, it derives a significant ontological conclusion. Both premises (1) and (2) of the argument are apparently innocuous claims about Mary's knowledge, which do not, if taken individually, force one to endorse any specific ontological view. However, once one accepts these premises at the same time one cannot but reject physicalism, which is certainly a significant ontological commitment.

While most philosophers affirm the validity of the knowledge argument, they are divided as to its soundness. Some philosophers accept it and endorse *dualism. However, many others reject it. Moreover, even among those who reject it, there is no consensus at all as to exactly what is wrong with it. During the course of the dispute, a number of distinct objections to the argument have been proposed.

As noted earlier, the knowledge argument is based on the intuition that even Mary's complete physical knowledge does not subsume everything in this world. The most straightforward reaction to the argument is to reject this intuition. According to such philosophers as Jeff Foss (1989) and Daniel C. Dennett (1991), it is a mistake to think that Mary learns something upon her release. If we take physicalism seriously, they claim, we can safely conclude that she will not learn anything when she leaves her black-and-white environment.

However, most philosophers share the intuition that upon her release, Mary does learn something, or at least something epistemologically significant happens to her. Yet it is contentious whether that entails the falsity of physicalism. Laurence Nemirow (1990) and David Lewis (1988), for instance, defend physicalism from the knowledge argument by appealing to the distinction between *knowledge-that* and *knowledge-how*. According to their *ability hypothesis*, what Mary acquires upon her release is not new knowledge-that, i.e. propositional knowledge, but knowledge-how, i.e. a set of abilities. When she looks at a red tomato, for instance, Mary will acquire various abilities, such as how to identify red objects as red, imagine and remember a red experience, and so on. If Mary did acquire knowledge-that upon her release, then it would seem that physicalism is false. However, according to proponents of the ability hypothesis, the mere fact that she acquires new abilities does not prove the falsity of physicalism. Defenders of the knowledge argument, by contrast, are dissatisfied with the ability hypothesis because even if Nemirow and Lewis are right in saying that Mary does gain new abilities upon her release, it still seems implausible that they are all she acquires.

Bigelow and Pargetter (1990) and Conee (1994) defend the *acquaintance hypothesis*, which is comparable to the ability hypothesis. This hypothesis relies on the distinction between knowledge by description and knowledge by acquaintance. According to the proponents of the hypothesis, when Mary has a colour experience she gains only knowledge by acquaintance, i.e. she only becomes acquainted with the experience. Given that Mary does not gain any new knowledge by description, i.e. propositional knowledge, they claim, the knowledge argument fails to refute physicalism. The acquaintance hypothesis seems to have the same difficulty that the ability hypothesis has; while Mary does seem to gain knowledge by acquaintance upon her release, it is not clear that that is all she gains.

Unlike proponents of the ability and acquaintance hypotheses, some critics accept that Mary does acquire propositional knowledge upon her release. Nevertheless, they think that physicalism can still be defended. For, according to them, what Mary acquires upon her release is not new propositional knowledge but old propositional knowledge in a new mode of presentation. She merely regains, they claim, knowledge that she has already acquired in her black-and-white environment in a different mode of presentation. In order to illustrate this point, consider the following two sentences:

(1) Superman can fly.
(2) Clark Kent can fly.

While (1) and (2) attribute the same property to the same individual, Lois Lane knows only what is expressed as (1), but not (2). This is because in order to know what is expressed as (2) she needs to be in a new mode of presentation, which is distinct from the one that corresponds to the knowledge of (1) (Horgan 1984). Some philosophers elaborate upon this response further and defend *a posteriori physicalism*. According to this, while phenomenal truths are entailed by physical truths, the entailment is not a priori but a posteriori. It appears that Mary can know what it is like to see colour without having a colour experience if (1) phenomenal truths are entailed by physical truths and (2) the entailment is a priori. A posteriori physicalism accepts (1) but rejects (2). A posteriori physicalists think, in other words, that if the knowledge argument undermines anything, it undermines only *a priori physicalism*, which holds both (1) and (2). This is the most common objection to the knowledge argument. Defenders of the knowledge argument try to undermine this objection by arguing either (a) that if physicalism true, then a priori physicalism must be true or (b) that the knowledge argument can be reformulated so that it is directed against a posteriori physicalism as well.

All of the objections to the knowledge argument discussed so far assume that Mary does have complete physical knowledge before her release. However, some critics are sceptical about this assumption. Alter (1998), for instance, says that this assumption is tenable only if all physical truths can be learned discursively. That is, the Mary scenario makes sense only if all physical truths can be learned by reading black-and-white books and watching black-and-white television; but it is not obvious that they can be learned in such a limited way. To take another example, Stoljar (2006) argues as follows. It is reasonable to believe that we are ignorant of some type of physical truths relevant to phenomenal experiences. If we assume that these truths are covered by the quantifier 'all physical truths' that occurs in the description of the Mary scenario, we have no reason to think that she learns something upon her release at the same time as knowing everything physical. On the other hand, if we assume that these truths are not covered by the quantifier, then the knowledge that Mary acquires prior to her release is not complete physical knowledge.

In his 1982 paper, Jackson endorses *epiphenomenalism. Given that the knowledge argument seems to refute physicalism and that interactionism is implausible, the only reasonable option left for him seems to be epiphenomenalism. However, some philosophers hold that the knowledge argument is not consistent with epiphenomenalism. Epiphenomenalism claims that *qualia are causally inefficacious in the physical world. Ironically, this claim appears to contradict the Mary scenario, for if qualia really are causally inefficacious in the physical world, then surely she does not come to know anything by having colour qualia upon her release. Therefore, according to this objection, one cannot consistently accept both the knowledge argument and epiphenomenalism at the same time. This objection does not show exactly which premise of the knowledge argument is false, but it does show—if it shows anything—that there must be something wrong with the argument. This objection is obviously based on a version of the causal theory of knowledge, which itself is a matter of controversy.

Churchland (1989) provides an objection to the knowledge argument in the same vein. According to him, there must be something wrong with the knowledge argument because if the argument successfully refuted physicalism it would equally successfully refute some versions of dualism as well. Suppose, for example, that substance dualism is true and that in her black-and-white environment Mary learns not only all truths about the physical entities, but also all truths about mental substance. That is, she learns everything about the causal, relational, and functional roles of physical entities as well as of mental substance. However, it still seems obvious that she learns something when she has a colour experience for the first time. Therefore, Churchland concludes, the knowledge argument is unreasonably strong.

As I noted earlier, Jackson no longer endorses the knowledge argument. In his second postscript published in 1998, he declared that he had come to think the knowledge argument failed to refute physicalism. Moreover, in his 2003 paper, he introduced and explained in detail his own objection to the knowledge argument. In constructing his objection he appeals to *representationalism, according to which phenomenal states are representational states. He says that what happens to Mary upon her release is not to learn new non-physical truths, but merely to be in a new kind of representational state. While this position might appear similar to the new mode of presentation response mentioned above, Jackson characterizes it as a version of the ability hypothesis. For, unlike many proponents of the new mode of presentation response, he rejects the idea that Mary acquires any propositional knowledge, whether it is old or new, upon her release. Mary merely comes to be in a new representational state without acquiring or reacquiring any knowledge. Mary acquires instead, according to Jackson, abilities to recognize, imagine, and remember the new representational state.

Along with the conceivability argument and the *explanatory gap argument, the knowledge argument is regarded as one of the greatest objections to physicalism. While there are a number of strong arguments for physicalism, any version of physicalism that is vulnerable to the knowledge argument is inadequate.

Many of the papers referred to in this entry are reprinted in Ludlow et al. (2006).

YUJIN NAGASAWA

Alter, T. (1998). 'A limited defence of the knowledge argument'. *Philosophical Studies*, 90.

Bigelow, J. and Pargetter, R. (1990). 'Acquaintance with qualia'. *Theoria*, 61.

Churchland, P. (1989). 'Knowing qualia: a reply to Jackson'. In *A Neurocomputational Perspective*.

Conee, E. (1994). 'Phenomenal knowledge'. *Australasian Journal of Philosophy*, 72.

Dennett, D. C. (1991). *Consciousness Explained*.

Foss, J. (1989). 'On the logic of what it is like to be a conscious subject'. *Australasian Journal of Philosophy*, 67.

Horgan, T. (1984). 'Jackson on physical information and qualia'. *Philosophical Quarterly*, 34.

Jackson, F. (1982). 'Epiphenomenal qualia'. *Philosophical Quarterly*, 32

—— (1986). 'What Mary didn't know', *Journal of Philosophy*, 83.

—— (2003). 'Mind and illusion'. In O'Hear, A. (ed.) *Minds and Persons*.

Lewis, D. (1988). 'What experience teaches'. *Proceedings of the Russellian Society (University of Sydney)*, 13.

Locke, J. (1689). *An Essay on Human Understanding*.

Ludlow, P., Nagasawa, Y. and Stoljar D. (eds) (2000). *There's Something About Mary: Essays on Phenomenal Consciousness and Frank Jackson's Knowledge Argument*.

Meehl, P. E. (1966). 'The complete autocerebroscopist'. In Feyerabend, P. and Maxwell, G. (eds) *Mind, Matter, and Method: Essays in Philosophy and Science in Honor of Herbert Feigl*.

Nemirow, L. (1990). 'Physicalism and the cognitive role of acquaintance'. In Lycan, W. G. (ed.) *Mind and Cognition: A Reader*.

Stoljar, D. (2006). *Ignorance and Imagination: The Epistemic Origin of the Problem of Consciousness*.

knowledge, explicit vs implicit In the scientific study of mind a distinction is drawn between *explicit knowledge*— knowledge that can be elicited from a subject by suitable inquiry or prompting, can be brought to consciousness, and externally expressed in words—and *implicit knowledge*—knowledge that cannot be elicited, cannot be made directly conscious, and cannot be articulated. Michael Polanyi (1967) argued that we usually 'know more than we can say'. The part we can articulate is explicitly known; the part we cannot is implicit.

Three things are worth noting about the prevailing distinction. First, as studied today in cognitive psychology, it rests on the ability of a subject to present information in linguistic form, to verbally report the thing known. Since there is nothing intrinsic in the idea of externalization and expression that need restrict it to language, this is needlessly confining. When someone has explicit *memory of an event or process, the thing remembered might be a visual scene, a body movement, a taste, smell, or sound. To communicate body-based or sensory recollections it may be necessary to use non-verbal forms of expression, such as illustrations, musical or vocal expression, dance, gesture, and so on. 'I remember: you perform the step like *this*.' The bodily movement is necessary for the subject herself to both know and communicate the details of the step.

Second, to successfully prompt or elicit information, it may be necessary to give subjects tools or artefacts they normally use when in their normal context. Some people can remember telephone numbers only if they have their phone in hand, or remember the combination to a lock if they turn the dial. Other people need a pen in their hand to recall what they wrote earlier, or need shoes to show how to tie shoelaces. There is nothing intrinsic to the idea of prompting or eliciting knowledge that restricts it to verbal requests in a sterile laboratory environment, or prohibits using tools to express the content of a behaviour-governing rule. Subjects often need artefacts to enact their knowledge.

Third, the range of things licensed as implicitly knowable under the prevailing definition is enormous. Things like implicit grammars, implicit rules of inference, implicit memories, implicit knowledge of physical principles such as the speed of sound or the rigidity of objects, implicit knowledge of environmental regularities, even implicit knowledge of the distance between one's ears, are all, in principle, objects of knowledge because each might be implicit or built into a process model. This would not be so problematic if there were a settled theory explaining how knowledge may be 'in' a system. (Kirsh 2006). But there is not. This is a concern because knowledge attributions in science are meant to designate causal states. So a deeper theory of how implicit knowledge is represented or incorporated in a system is required to fully justify claims that a subject 'really' has implicit knowledge. (cf. Dienes and Perner 1999).

1. The basic idea of implicit knowledge

Before cognitive psychologists and neuroscientists developed special methods for studying implicit knowledge, theorists like Polanyi (1967) and Noam Chomsky (1965) had already discussed the importance of *tacit knowledge*. When Polanyi spoke of knowing 'more than we can tell' he was talking about how practical know-how, or procedural knowledge, is tied to our context of work, and resists articulation and *codification*. Our practical knowledge is often highly *situated*, to use a more recent term, and so it is something we frequently are not aware that we know, and cannot tell anyone about.

For instance, the visuo-motor-tactile programs that control how we flip an egg 'over easy' are causal programs; they are procedures that rely on registering subtle details of a situation that we are often not explicitly aware of and usually cannot describe. We can show someone how to flip an egg, possibly tell them about certain explicit factors to watch out for; but there are other, more tactile features relating to the feel of the spatula and egg that practice has taught us to monitor *automatically and unconsciously. We cannot describe them because we are unaware of the highly contextualized 'micro-features' we are attending to. Even if we explicitly know what those contextualized features are we cannot codify them in rules, or even point them out to others because the things to be shown may be tactile, which are not readily communicable, or they are features that only someone simultaneously flipping an egg can identify, and only then if the listener has the prior skills to register those micro-features. For example, a wine expert may prefer one wine to another for reasons he cannot explain. He does not know all the gustatory and olfactory features that go into his classification. Explanations he does give invariably contain words, such as 'round tannins', that non-experts lack the training to understand. Even for experts, the shared vocabulary falls far short of the features that causally affect judgement. Polanyi believed that many of the component elements of expertise are unconscious, non-communicable, and tacit.

Chomsky (1965) also argued for tacit or implicit knowledge, this time for implicit knowledge of linguistic structure and generative grammar. On his view, anyone who knows her mother tongue must, in a sense, know the syntax of her language. If she were unschooled in grammar, or her culture never defined a grammar for her language, she has none of the technical concepts such as noun, subject, verb, and adjectival phrase that figure in the rules of generative grammar. So she cannot state those rules or recognize them if stated by someone else. Hence, she does not explicitly know her grammar.

Nor can she be conscious of those rules when they are operative since she does not have the conceptual repertoire to form thoughts about them. Chomsky thought they were in a modular subsystem inaccessible to conscious probing. Consequently, if she knows her grammar at all she knows it implicitly.

Despite differences in the types of knowledge that Chomsky and Polanyi considered, both maintained that tacit or implicit knowledge is real: it is causally active, it drives behaviour, it is learned, and it is encoded somewhere in the mind–brain in informational states, structures, or processes. Those informational states figure in mechanistic explanations of language production and recognition, or of skilled workplace performance, regardless of what the underlying mechanism is: rule-based system, symbolic constraint system, neural network, or something else. Neither Chomsky nor Polanyi, however, thought it their job to say how tacit knowledge is actually realized in cognitive systems.

We expect cognitive psychologists to provide theories explaining how different types of implicit knowledge are embodied in cognitive or neural systems. What are the mechanisms by which this or that type of implicit knowledge is able to unconsciously influence thought or behaviour? What is the route by which it enters the cognitive system? To probe for such states experimentalists have developed methods for detecting the effect of knowledge without informing a subject that they are interested in that knowledge.

For instance, to test *implicit memory* a subject may be given a list of words and asked to alphabetize them. The experimenter gives no hint that she is interested in the subject's memory for the words on the list, so the subject has no reason to form the intention to memorize the words. Later, the subject is shown a new list consisting of three kinds of words: those drawn from the original list, words not on the list, and pseudo-words—letter sequences that could be words but are not (e.g. bluck). Each word or pseudo-word is shown for 50 ms or a bit less, the normative time subjects take to recognize a word correctly 50% of the time. The subject's task is to state whether the stimulus word is a real word or non-word. It has been found that words on the original list are correctly recognized as words more often than non-list words and both are recognized as words more often than pseudo-words are recognized as non-words. This shows that subjects have some sort of memory for the words on the original list, despite their not trying to remember the list words, and despite not realizing that list words are being tested for. The list words are said to be **primed* because they seem ready to surface faster. Importantly, if the test stimuli are different in appearance to the list stimuli (in font, size, or colour) the effect of priming greatly decreases. Some psychologists see this as evidence that there are two kinds of memory system based on different brain systems (Squire 1992). Others see this as showing that priming is an early stage of processing, and that explicit tasks require stimuli to be more deeply processed (Craik and Lockhart 1972).

Other examples of implicit knowledge discussed in the psychological and neuropsychological literature include, among many others, *blindsight and implicit *learning. In blindsight, patients who have lost part or all of their visual field as a result of a stroke or injury to their visual cortex can often tell whether a visual stimulus is present (though not with great reliability) despite reporting, quite convincingly, that they can see nothing. (Weiskrantz 1986). Blindsight is a form of perception where the subject has no explicit awareness of the visual stimulus but can show by other means that they know something about the stimulus. Whereas normal perception yields explicit knowledge, blindsight yields implicit knowledge, or something close to it, since probing regularly elicits correct answers without the awareness or confidence that comes with normal perception: 'How can I tell you if I don't see it?' The presence of blindsight shows that something is getting in somewhere in those subjects' visual system, but not in a form, or to a processing location, where it can have its full range of normal effects. It is not brought to conscious mind.

In implicit learning experiments subjects are trained to classify items as either in or out of a category. In a famous set of experiments Reber (1989) showed subjects sequences of letters like *aaba*, *abaa*, *bba* that were either generated by an *artificial grammar (a Reber grammar), or randomly. After being trained on a set of exemplars, subjects were shown additional sequences and told whether their own classifications were correct or incorrect. They then had to predict whether new sequences were in or out of the language. If subjects reported trying to conjecture the rule governing legal sequences, and they used that rule successfully in their answers, then they had explicit knowledge of the grammar. If they could not report the rule, either because they did not use one, or were unaware they used one, or their answers were inconsistent with their stated rule, then the basis for their category judgement could not have been explicit knowledge of a rule. They were assumed to have implicit knowledge of a categorizing principle, however, because they categorized in a self-consistent manner.

The final type of implicit knowledge to be mentioned is one that further extends the range of implicit knowledge. David Marr (1983) in his influential account of visual processing discussed the importance of posing visual information processing problems as computational problems: a level of analysis where theorists study the assumptions about the visual world that must be built into human or animal visual systems. He asked: What must particular modules of the visual system implicitly know about the visual world if they are to work correctly? For example, to extract three-dimensional shape from the sequence of two-dimensional retinal images made by a moving object, Marr suggested that the system must assume that objects are rigid and piecewise smooth. He then went on to suggest various algorithms and representations that might operate in a visual subsystem based on those assumptions.

Because Marr did not suppose that these assumptions are explicitly represented anywhere in the creature, it is hard to understand in what sense the creature (or visual subsystem) has knowledge, albeit implicit. Is it causal? One might argue that these assumptions are better understood as *success conditions*: if a moving object meets these conditions then algorithms that presuppose their truth will generate the right shape. If the object does not meet the conditions then algorithms presupposing it will not terminate, or the subject will see an *illusion.

Rigidity and continuity are presumably not learned by the visual system; they are the outcome of natural selection sifting through algorithms for the ones that work best. The same might be said for Chomsky's universal grammar. They set constraints on all viable generative grammars. Yet Chomsky maintained that universal grammar as well as particular grammars are causal. They shape language learning. Why not assume a similar causal role for rigidity? This makes it more important than ever to explain how implicit knowledge might be represented, instantiated, or embodied in cognitive systems.

Given the variety of implicit knowledge, it is likely there are major differences in the way such information states are encoded or embodied in cognitive systems. By definition, all implicit forms resist linguistic processing, but there are many possible reasons for this. It has been speculated that knowledge is implicit because it is stored in parts of the cognitive or neural system that do not directly communicate with linguistic parts, hence the thing known is not articulable (the modularity of cognitive sub-systems). Alternatively, some contentful states might require too much processing to be converted into words in reasonable time (computationally too distant), or because content is encoded initially in too shallow a manner and hence overly dependent on interaction with other (currently inaccessible) representations of knowledge to become explicit. These are just a few of the process model explanations that would show how knowledge that cannot be made conscious can nonetheless causally affect thought and behaviour.

Despite recent empirical advances, we are still in the early days of understanding the causal pathways leading to consciousness and behaviour. We can be certain that our conception of implicit and explicit knowledge will change as new process models and theories are proposed, and scientists shift their understanding of what it means to say that someone knows something implicitly. For instance, it is a significant defect of current process models that they do not fully accommodate the importance of non-verbal awareness and expression. That means that the concept of explicit knowledge in use today is so narrow that it forces us to call some knowledge states implicit when a more multimodal notion of consciousness, one that admits non-verbal imagery and artefact use, would warrant calling them explicit.

Similarly, the concept of implicit knowledge is today so broad that it is unclear whether we could ever have process models that reveal how all the different types of implicit knowledge play a causal role in affecting thought, talk, and action. For instance, we assume that a person will come to know the implications of their beliefs, if given time to reflect on them. Are those implications therefore implicitly known before reflection but explicitly known after reflection? That would be odd, because other types of implicit knowledge are never explicitly knowable, regardless of reflection. Similarly, humans are assumed to share a vast realm of implicit common knowledge with their cultural peers. Yet it is doubtful whether all members of a culture share this common ground equally. At the cultural level we say they know it implicitly, at a more process level they do not. That means that the concept of implicit knowledge in use today is so broad and heterogeneous that the term will be negotiated and renegotiated as new process theories re-characterize how implicit knowledge can be causally active.

2. The connection to representation

One promising way of lending rigour to the distinction, even before future negotiations, is to tie it with the notion of explicit and implicit *representation. On virtually every account, explicit knowledge is connected with thought. Although knowledge and thought are different in kind—knowledge is a dispositional state and thought an occurrent process—thought is the way that explicit knowledge typically manifests itself. This means that if someone explicitly knows something then she *can* bring the thing known 'before' mind. She can 'grasp' the content of the known thing. This raises the provocative idea that something is known explicitly by an agent, only if she can represent it, and in a form that is 'immediately' graspable, presumably by the conscious mind. To represent something in a form that is immediately graspable is to *represent* it explicitly (Kirsh 1990).

Viewing things in this light partially resolves several issues. First, it explains the historical bias for verbalizing knowledge and lets us get beyond it. The classical justification, were it ever to be given, would go like this: knowledge is explicit for someone if she can bring it to mind as a thought—she can think it; if she can think it she can speak it—assumed because language is the most structured account of content available (see Fodor 1975), and a public language, like English, is universally expressive (see Searle 1970). Sentences in English are, accordingly, explicit representations of what is known. Hence anything known explicitly should be articulable.

This vaguely behaviourist move saves having to identify explicit knowledge with what can be brought to consciousness per se because it associates bringing to mind with being verbalizable. But it is imperfect for reasons that reveal there is a more fundamental notion of explicit representation.

First, language is not perfectly expressive. How can a squiggly curve, for instance, be expressed accurately without gesturing or making a drawing? Demonstratives such as 'this' often take non-linguistic things as completions. For example, when a person hears a sound the only adequate way of identifying where it comes from is usually by pointing. Would anyone doubt the person had explicit knowledge of where the sound was? Their explicit knowledge consists in having an 'active' set of orienting responses, the most easily shared being to point. The same applies to dance movements, sounds, and sights. Words are useless, or of limited use, in trying to expose, even to oneself, what is explicitly known. Some things must be shown, not told. This calls into doubt the *necessity* of encoding explicit knowledge in language, and identifying the content of knowledge with linguistically expressed propositions.

Second, many things presented in language are not immediately graspable, so linguistic expression may not be *sufficient* for explicit knowledge. For example, the sentence, 'Police police police police police' is grammatical and means police who are policed by police themselves police police. Considerable processing must occur before this sentence can be grasped. Indeed, most people cannot readily extract its meaning any more than they can extract the meaning of a complex mathematical formula. This suggests that being encodable in a natural language is not a sufficient condition of being explicit. To be explicitly known the content of thought must be encoded in a form that is immediately graspable according to some prior measure of immediacy.

Kirsh suggested that the degree to which a given representation R explicitly encodes information I, for a given creature C, should be measured by the amount of computation C must perform to extract I. For instance 'fifth root of 3125' is a less explicit encoding of 5 than the numeral '5'. The creature must compute the fifth root before it can grasp the referent. Hence the information is not on the surface in '3125' but is on '5'. It is implicit, but less so than $\sqrt[17]{762\,939\,453\,125}$.

The value of such an approach is that it ties explicitness to computation in a manner that is not parochially bound up with language. But it also leaves open the need to tie explicitness to the computational resources a creature has. Thus if one creature has memorized exponents of 5 up to 5^{17}, the computation of $\sqrt[17]{762\,939\,453\,125}$ may be a simple retrieval process. Similarly, a creature with a highly parallel computational system, such as human vision or motor control, may be able to process complex structures rapidly when they are visually or motor encoded, but more slowly when linguistically encoded. So content shown visually might be explicit while being more implicit when given linguistically. It also gives a place for learning, since highly practised agents can immediately grasp contents, such as wine tastes, musical structures, concepts and so forth, that would be difficult for the unpractised. They have automatized or parallelized them.

The upshot is that when explicit knowledge is tied to explicit representation it makes the notion less behavioural and more closely tied to discovering the processing pathways by which information stored or built into a system makes its way to an explicit representation. If no such pathway exists, or if the result of further processing falls short of complete explicitness, the system's knowledge is to some specifiable degree implicit. This rightly emphasizes that knowledge lies on a continuum with fully explicit at one end.

DAVID KIRSH

Chomsky, N. (1965). *Aspects of the Theory of Syntax*.

Craik, F. I. M. and Lockhart, R. S. (1972). *Levels of Processing: A Framework for Memory Research*.

Davies, M. (2001). 'Knowledge (explicit and implicit): philosophical aspects.' In Smelser, N. J. and Baltes, P. B. (eds) *International Encyclopedia of the Social and Behavioral Sciences*.

Dienes, Z. and Perner, J. (1999). 'A theory of implicit and explicit knowledge'. *Behavioral and Brain Sciences*, 22.

Fodor, J. (1975) *The Language of Thought*.

Kirsh, D. (1990). 'When is information explicitly represented?' In Hanson, P. (ed.) *Information, Language, and Cognition*.

—— (2006) 'Implicit and explicit representation'. In Nadel, L. (ed.) *Encyclopedia of Cognitive Science*.

knowledge, explicit vs implicit

Marr, D. (1983) *Vision: A Computational Investigation into the Human Representation and Processing of Visual Information.*

Polanyi, M. (1967). *The Tacit Dimension.*

Reber, A. S. (1989). 'Implicit learning and tacit knowledge'. *Journal of Experimental Psychology: General*, 118.

Searle, J. (1970). *Speech Acts.*

Squire, L. R. (1992). 'Declarative and nondeclarative memory: multiple brain systems supporting learning and memory'. *Journal of Cognitive Neuroscience*, 99.

Weiskrantz, L. (1986). *Blindsight: a Case Study and its Implications.*

L

learning, explicit vs implicit Skills and knowledge can be acquired either implicitly, where the learning takes place without the learner being aware of it, or explicitly, where the individual is conscious of what is being learned and how it is being acquired. Since this distinction became important in cognitive psychology, a variety of criteria have been proposed for distinguishing implicit from explicit learning and not all of them sit gently with each other. We will take a common-sense approach and assume that *explicit learning* represents the acquisition of knowledge modulated by the use of consciously controlled mental operations while *implicit learning* is characterized by learning that takes place largely independently of awareness both of the process and of the products of acquisition.

We can get a better feeling for this distinction if we look at one of the classic studies and see how explicit, top-down processes can be distinguished from bottom-up, implicit ones. The experimental platform here is the **artificial grammar learning* (AGL) procedure first introduced some 40 years ago (Reber 1967).

Suppose you are presented with an extended series of letter strings such as TXTP, TVXTVSP, KVTPP, KVKVP. If we tell you these were created using a complex set of rules that determine letter order, you will engage in a distinctly top-down, consciously controlled process whereby you attempt to figure out what these rules could be. You would likely create various hypotheses about which letters can start a string, which can end one, which can be repeated, which can follow others, etc. Later, we present you with a new set of letter strings, some of which follow the rules and some of which do not and ask you to categorize them as 'grammatical' (i.e. they follow the rules) or 'non-grammatical' (i.e. they violate the rules).

The data from such studies show that you will learn some of the rules, be able to apply them in the test phase, and, when asked, be able to provide a reasonably coherent statement about which rules you know and how you went about learning them. This, of course, is an example of explicit learning. It is characterized by a top-down decoding process that is under conscious control. It is marked by an ability to articulate a good deal about what is known and how it was acquired and often erroneous notions about this highly complex stimulus domain.

On the other hand, suppose we present you with the same set of letter strings but do not mention anything about rules. Instead, we tell you that you are in a memory experiment and ask you to reproduce each string as quickly and accurately as possible. Then we give you the same 'grammaticality' test. This, of course, is the first time you have heard anything about rules and you might find such a statement a bit disconcerting. Nevertheless, the data show that you will be able to make grammaticality judgements about as well as in the first condition. In fact, you might be better at it in some ways, e.g. less prone to inventing inappropriate rules.

However, the phenomenal experience of being in the latter study is very different from the former. You will have little communicable knowledge of the rules, be largely unaware of having learned anything during the memorization phase, and will often think that you are just guessing about the grammatical status of each test string. This demonstration that abstract knowledge about highly complex, rule-governed domains could be acquired automatically, relatively quickly, with little conscious effort and little or no awareness of what was being learned attracted a good deal of attention and a host of other experimental protocols were developed to examine the generality of the initial findings.

1. Methods of study
2. Evolutionary considerations
3. Lingering controversies
4. Summary

1. Methods of study

In addition to the AGL protocol, other procedures have been introduced to explore implicit learning, such as the *sequential reaction time* (SRT) task where lights flash at different locations on a computer screen and subjects react to each by pressing a positionally appropriate button; an *auditory sequence task* where various sounds are played according to set rules; *dot pattern classification*, where the learner views a series of apparently random dot patterns that are, in fact, spatial distortions of an underlying prototype; and several others where subjects learn to control some laboratory analogue of a real-world system such as the weather, an agricultural system, or factory production.

There are several important features in these experiments. First, all use a structured stimulus domain that is sufficiently complex so that it is not easily apprehended consciously. Second, subjects acquire sufficient knowledge about these domains to be able to function effectively when presented with physically novel stimuli that share underlying structural features. They are able to make decisions about whether novel items follow rules (as in the AGL studies); they learn to anticipate events (SRT task), to classify novel patterns (dot pattern task), and to control complex systems (e.g., manufacturing plants). Third, learning occurs when subjects are not attempting to uncover structural features of the displays. Rather, their attention is focused upon the stimulus domain while being asked to memorize letter-strings, press buttons as rapidly as possible, try to guess which dot pattern just flashed, estimate the likelihood of rain, or increase productivity. Fourth, despite using materials from several stimulus domains (visual, auditory), a variety of processing modalities (sensorimotor reactions, visual scanning) and several different tasks (memorize, predict, categorize, control) the empirical findings have been remarkably consistent (see Reber 1993 for a review).

At the core of all of this research, of course, is the issue of consciousness and the role that it plays in human cognitive activity. Largely because of the manner in which the implicit/explicit distinction connects to this issue, it has been enthusiastically pursued. The literature on it is enormous, a number of controversies have emerged, a variety of critical questions still remain unanswered, and a framework based on principles of evolutionary biology for examining the distinction has been proposed.

2. Evolutionary considerations

The neurological structures that handle implicit learning are almost certainly evolutionarily older than those that modulate explicit functions, having developed to enable less complex organisms to form associations, detect and represent the statistical nature of their environments, and to anticipate events. Mechanisms that handle explicit learning confer an advantage in exploitation of environmental structures once they are learned; however, their cognitive costs and later development make them unlikely to be universal functions.

The temporal priority of the implicit system leads to a number of interesting predictions (Reber 1993). Relative to explicit cognitive functions, the implicit system should: (1) show consistency across the lifespan, (2) display robustness in the face of neurological injury and psychological trauma, (3) show less inter-individual variation, and (4) be neurologically and behaviourally distinct.

Learning across the lifespan. Early-emerging adaptations and structures should show lack of variation in comparison to later-emerging functions. A corollary of this principle is age-independence; implicit learning should show less change over the lifespan than explicit learning. Although *infants are unable to report on their conscious awareness, it seems reasonable to assume that at the earliest stages of development, knowledge acquisition is implicit. The learning about language and socialization that takes place during infancy and early childhood occurs largely, if not completely, independent of top-down, conscious control.

The studies carried out on this population show that infants pick up the statistical structure of auditory and visual sequences, learn to anticipate patterned events and can even transfer knowledge to novel stimulus domains. In one study (Saffran et al. 1996), 8-month-old infants picked up on the stochastic patterns in an ongoing auditory stream as quickly and accurately as adults. Although functional verbal skills and representations do not emerge until later in infancy, it appears that implicit learning is present from the earliest days. Explicit learning post-infancy has been well studied, and forms the bulk of the cognitive development literature from the 1970s to the 1990s, as well as the work of Jean Piaget. The general picture is one of inexorable emergence of explicit functions, accompanied by debates focusing on exactly what develops, how it develops, and whether it develops gradually or in a saltatory fashion.

At the other end of the lifespan, age-related declines in explicit functions are the norm and most research focuses on examining the nature, correlates, and reversibility of decline. Implicit cognitive functions, on the other hand, are expected to show far less in the way of systematic decline. This prediction has been supported to the degree that implicit learning of simple serial patterns does not decline among normally ageing adults. However, there is evidence that older adults do not learn very complex or hierarchical serial patterns as well as younger adults (e.g. Howard and Howard 2001). Age-related impairments have been found for both implicit and explicit serial pattern learning, particularly when the stimulus domain is very complex. It is not clear whether this observed diminished capacity is truly a decline in implicit learning or whether age-related declines in *working memory capacity or motivation are responsible.

Robustness of underlying mechanisms. Early-evolving systems tend to be more robust than late-evolving systems, and so implicit functions should be more resilient to neurological and other traumas than explicit. Research on patient populations with various neurological impairments reveals a consistent pattern in the lost and retained functions of various patient populations (see BRAIN DAMAGE). *Amnesic patients manifest virtually normal AGL even when they cannot consciously recall items from the learning set. Psychotic patients with severe cognitive deficits in explicit problem solving also show normal learning in an AGL setting. Early Alzheimer's patients retain implicit learning and recall functions (see DEMENTIA). Individuals with traumatic brain injuries that broadly compromise explicit processing manifest intact implicit learning in an SRT task. A similar mosaic of lost and retained functions has been observed in individual with *autism, children with Williams syndrome, highly anxious individuals, and those of varying intellectual level. The robustness of implicit learning in the face of most neurological and emotional assaults is well established (see Litman and Reber 2005 for a review).

Individual variation. The prediction of more restricted individual variation in implicit than in explicit learning is difficult to evaluate. Individual differences in explicit learning are well documented and form the basis of intelligence and aptitude testing. However, relatively little attention has been paid to individual differences in implicit learning, at least to those not attributable to the types of factors outlined above. The research that has been carried out points toward a few tentative conclusions: (1) individual-to-individual differences in implicit learning exist, (2) they seem to be unrelated to individual variation in explicit cognitive functions and intelligence, (3) the variation seems to be related to a few non-cognitive functions such as internal locus of control and focusing style, and (4) they are sometimes less than, often equal to, but never greater than the variation found in explicit learning of comparable material (see Reber and Allen 2000 for a review).

Neurological and behavioural distinctiveness. Recent work using cortical scanning techniques (see FUNCTIONAL BRAIN IMAGING) suggest the existence of two neurologically distinct systems. Lieberman et al. (2004) used the AGL procedure with its standard protocol; however, the test phase was run in a scanner. The variable of interest was the statistical nature of the letter strings used during testing. Some of these items had high 'chunk strength;' that is, they were physically quite close to items used during learning in terms of the commonly occurring two- and three-letter groupings or 'chunks'. The others had low chunk strength. When subjects classified items with high chunk strength they showed strong hippocampal activity; items with low chunk strength were processed primarily in the basal ganglia, specifically the caudate nucleus. The implication is that when items are presented that are reminiscent of learning strings, the medial temporal lobes, known to be fundamental for conscious memorial processing, go online. However, when decisions are being made about items that can be classified best by logging deeper structural features of the underlying grammar, other areas are operative.

A similar pattern was found using the dot-pattern task (Reber et al. 2003). In this study half the participants were informed before the learning phase about the existence of the underlying prototype, half were not. Functional MRI scans showed that participants who learned implicitly used different cortical structures in categorizing novel dot patterns than those who learned explicitly.

3. Lingering controversies

Despite the consistency of the evidence, a number of controversies have surfaced and a variety of unanswered questions remain. Briefly, they include:

The nature of the learning mechanism. There is a consensus that implicit learning operates by the detection of patterns of covariation among elements in the environment. The working hypothesis is that neural nets throughout the brain function to capture and represent the statistical nature of events that are detected. However, questions are unanswered. Are these nets dedicated to implicit mechanisms or do they share operating characteristics with those that feed into consciousness? How flexible are these structures? How powerful? Are they limited in terms of the kinds of displays they can process?

The nature of implicit representations. While there is little doubt that consciously represented knowledge is abstract and flexible, there is less of a consensus with implicitly acquired knowledge. Some maintain that abstract rules are learned implicitly; others argue that representations consist primarily of stored instances that have been observed; still others maintain that the memorial residue of learning is no more than sets of associations among elements. The jury is still out on this issue, although we suspect that there is no simple answer. In all likelihood the system will turn out to be rather adaptive and establish representations that reflect the demands on particular settings and requirements for use of knowledge.

Probing consciousness. Determining what an individual consciously knows at any given moment is a methodologically complex problem. Knowledge that some researchers conclude is implicit may, in fact, be partly or even wholly conscious but the 'right' questions simply have not been asked. It is possible that subjects are consciously aware of things early in an experiment but have forgotten them when asked at the end. It is also possible that participants realize after they have left the lab that they did know things they denied knowing earlier. The issue, at this juncture, is largely one of methodology. Some researchers feel that assessment of consciousness should be 'natural'. That is, subjects should simply be asked what they knew and what they thought they were doing. Others maintain that more penetrating probes should be used to extract as much metacognitive information as possible.

Perhaps even more troubling is the lack of consensus on the criteria for determining whether knowledge is held implicitly or explicitly. One method used in AGL experiments is to have subjects give a confidence rating to their decisions about the structural integrity of letter strings. If confidence ratings correlate with correctness, does this imply that knowledge is held explicitly? Some argue that it does, on the grounds that metaknowledge is ipso facto consciously held knowledge. Other, however, note that we can discern the grammaticality of sentences we read without consciously knowing the specific syntactic rules violated and, hence, that that one can be confident of judgements made without awareness of the basis of the judgement. Another method used in both AGL and SRT tasks is to present subjects with a partial sequence and ask them to complete it. If they succeed at rates better than chance, does this mean that the knowledge held was conscious? Some claim it does. Others demur, noting that in standard *priming experiments, subjects routinely carry out stem-completion tasks using implicit knowledge that they were unaware of engaging. The situation is a difficult one, because the methodology in use may be unhappily linked with particular outcomes. Again, there are no clear answers.

The role of attention and working memory. There is good evidence to suggest that implicit learning is dependent upon both *attention and working memory, although probably to a lesser extent than explicit learning. It appears that attention needs to be paid to the displays for learning to occur. Working memory is critical in that stimulus elements need to be held in some form so that associations with later-appearing elements can be formed—and this applies to both implicit and explicit learning. Indeed, cases where implicit learning functions seem to have been compromised are likely cases where either attentional resources were diverted elsewhere or working memory functions were compromised. Again, these issues need to be worked out.

How smart is the implicit system? In one sense, the implicit system would seem to be rather stupid. Since it appears to function primarily by capturing statistical features that are present in the environment, its underlying cognitive functions would be little more than those that could be accomplished by a primitive *connectionist system. But connectionist systems have hidden complexities and establish representations that appear to be abstract and function like complex rule-governed domains.

One way to think about this issue is to see an implicit representational system not so much as encoding the connections between specific stimuli, but as capturing the privileges of occurrence between them. That is, squirrels do not necessarily learn the statistical connections between specific nuts and particular trees; they learn the links between categories of objects (e.g. small round things that are nutritious) and clusters of other objects (e.g. large wooded poles that co-occur with the former with fairly high probability). You can dramatically change the nature of the elements in the displays and the squirrel will respond flexibly. Similarly, in the AGL studies, you can change the letters used to instantiate the items during learning and participants can still reliably make grammaticality decisions. The key seems to be that each new letter shares the same privileges of occurrence as a particular old one did during learning, and subjects pick this up.

How does implicit knowledge become explicit? As noted earlier, questions like this are encumbered by methodological difficulties. However, there are least two possible mechanisms operating here. First, consciousness may be capable of slowly, perhaps laboriously penetrating implicitly acquired and held knowledge and bringing it into the full light of awareness. This assumption has been the operative one in current research. However, there is a second possibility, to the effect that implicitly acquired knowledge is totally encapsulated and impenetrable. When knowledge that was acquired implicitly becomes open to consciousness it is because other environmental circumstances occurred, additional learning took place, or separate priming episodes were presented making the knowledge available to consciousness through standard top-down executive functions. (Thanks to P. J. Reber for suggesting this possibility.)

These two conceptualizations are different in interesting ways. They suggest very different kinds of neurocognitive architectures. There are, to date, no data that we are aware of to distinguish between them.

4. Summary

Implicit learning is a bottom-up acquisitional system that is sensitive to patterns of covariation of stimuli in the environment. Compared with explicit learning, it operates rapidly and efficiently, without benefit of conscious control, shows little in the way of change over the lifespan, is robust in the face of injury and trauma and is likely modulated by distinct brain areas with different evolutionary histories.

ARTHUR S. REBER AND RHIANNON ALLEN

Howard, D. V. and Howard, J. H. (2001). 'When it *does* hurt to try: adult age differences in the effects of instructions on implicit pattern learning'. *Psychonomic Bulletin and Review*, 8.

Lieberman, M. D., Chang, G. Y., Chiao, J., Bookheimer, S. Y., and Knowlton, B. J. (2004). 'An event-related fMRI study of artificial grammar learning in a balanced chunk strength design'. *Journal of Cognitive Neuroscience*, 16.

Litman, L. and Reber, A. S. (2005). 'Implicit and explicit thought'. In Holyoak, K. J. and Morrison, R. G. (eds) *Cambridge Handbook of Thinking and Reasoning*.

Reber, A. S. (1967). 'Implicit learning of artificial grammars'. *Journal of Verbal Learning and Verbal Behavior*, 5.

—— (1993). *Implicit Learning and Tacit Knowledge*.

—— and Allen, R. (2000) 'Individual differences in implicit learning'. In Kunzendorf, R. G. and Wallace, B. (eds), *Individual Differences in Conscious Experience*.

Reber, P. J., Gitelman, D. R., Parrish, T. B., and Mesulam, M.-M. (2003). 'Dissociating explicit and implicit category knowledge with fMRI'. *Journal of Cognitive Neuroscience*, 15.

Saffran, J. R., Aslin, R. N., and Newport, E. L. (1996). 'Statistical learning by 8-month old infants'. *Science*, 274.

learning, perceptual Perceptual learning is the relatively permanent improvement in detecting, discriminating, or categorizing sensory stimuli through experience (e.g. Fahle and Poggio 2002). Thus, perceptual learning is a type of task learning that improves the representation of the outer world in the brains of animals including humans, starting at birth. It adjusts and normalizes different types of sensory stimuli, as in so-called *prism adaptation*, to optimize behavioural responses. Most often, it requires attention or a conscious effort, while some learning may also occur subconsciously. Typical examples of perceptual learning are improvement in the discrimination of different line-orientations of different bars, or of different types of wine.

Perceptual learning does not lead to *knowing-that*, i.e. to explicit forms of memory that can be true or false (such as one's mother's birthplace), but to implicit memory (such as in *priming). It is of the procedural type, hence cannot be easily communicated to others. Perceptual learning appears to directly modify the neuronal mechanisms underlying the processing of the task required (e.g. visual and auditory cortices), while declarative forms of learning lead to some form of memory trace, stored in structures such as the hippocampus that are separated from those analysing the stimuli. Unlike associative learning, perceptual learning does not usually bind together separate entities (such as food and the sound of a bell in classical *conditioning based on Hebbian mechanisms), but improves detection and discrimination of stimuli that were not discriminable before the training. Perceptual learning moreover transforms some serial search tasks requiring sequential processing through (conscious) selective attention (such as searching for the enemy in a video game) to 'automatic' parallel processing. In certain instances such as *blindsight, a special form of perceptual learning even seems to transform 'unconscious knowledge' to conscious knowledge (see below).

Well-studied examples of perceptual learning include the discrimination of very simple stimuli, such as the ability to discriminate between different speeds of motion. But perceptual learning also involves learning to discriminate between quite complex classes of stimuli, such as between different butterflies. In many of these tasks, training leads to improvements up to 30% within an hour of training, but there are large inter-individual differences between subjects even in quite homogeneous groups such as students. The causes for these differences in the ability to improve perception through training are so far very poorly understood.

At least two processes or neuronal mechanisms seem to be involved in perceptual learning: a fast, somewhat unspecific and general mechanism (possibly related to the *connectionist's *activation-based learning* and modifying the strength of existing synapses) and a much slower and highly specific one, which may be realized in different parts of the brain and maybe related to the connectionist's *weight-based learning*, possibly relying on the formation of new synapses. The fast and general mechanism may be located in more central or 'late' parts of sensory cortices, such as the parietal and temporal lobes, while the slow and specific mechanism seems to involve early cortical areas including the primary sensory cortices.

While the fast form of learning is usually transferred to other, similar tasks, the improvement obtained through the slow mechanism cannot be generalized to even very similar stimuli or tasks. Subjects may have to relearn the task of discriminating between different curvatures in a line if this line is rotated by just 5°, let alone by 90°. This specificity for stimulus features such as the exact stimulus orientation and position, and even for the eye trained under monocular conditions, suggests an involvement of 'early' stages of cortical information processing, where neurons are specific for visual field position and are activated monocularly. This view is supported by the results of both sum-potential recordings in humans and *single-cell recordings in animals that describe long-lasting changes in the activation patterns of neurons as a result of training and experience—even in primary sensory cortices and not only in 'higher' cortices. Somewhat preliminary evidence from *functional brain imaging (fMRI) studies is also compatible with the hypothesis of 'early' modification of sensory processing.

In one respect, such a fine tuning of information processing on as early a level as possible seems reasonable, removing irrelevant noise as early as possible during cortical processing. In another respect, however, the fine-tuning of peripheral levels of processing is unacceptable for a mature nervous system, since learning of a new task would modify the neuronal front end used to process *all* stimuli. Hence learning on an early level would interfere with performance in other tasks. For example, shallow luminance gradients are best detected by large receptive fields, which in turn are unable to detect fine gratings. Training to detect fine gratings could therefore improve their detection by decreasing receptive field size, but the detection of shallow gradients would deteriorate. A solution of this apparent paradox would be a task-dependent switching of early cortical signal processing under top-down influence (see Li et al. 2004, Fahle 2005). According to this view, filtering and processing on early cortical stages would be chosen from a repertoire of previously learned alternatives under the influence of top-down control. While this hypothesis is still open to debate, it is in accordance with electrophysiological results mentioned above demonstrating modifications of neuronal activity patterns as a result of training already on the level of the primary somatosensory and visual cortex (e.g. Recanzone et al. 1992, Li et al. 2004). The hypothesis also solves the apparent paradox, outlined above, of interference with other tasks and stresses the importance of top-down influences such as error feedback and directed attention. Learning indeed strongly depends on top-down influences and is generally faster under the influence of error feedback, while it can be completely eliminated by randomized feedback that is unrelated to the subject's performance—possibly by preventing the development of a successful strategy to fine-tune the relevant neurons.

*Attention is another type of top-down influence exerted by more central, conscious cortical levels on the probably unconscious primary sensory levels. Attention certainly plays an important role in perceptual learning. A number of studies have demonstrated that a stimulus feature usually has to be attended for learning to proceed—mere presentation of a feature most often does not improve its perception over time. However, when a feature is always coupled in time with the attended stimulus (Watanabe et al. 2001), its detection improves, indicating that attention may improve perception for all features presented at a critical point in time, through some form of general 'arousal'. In these (rare) instances, perceptual learning occurs subconsciously, without subjects attending to a specific stimulus feature.

As mentioned above, perceptual learning can achieve a transformation highly relevant to the study of consciousness. After specific lesions of the visual system, typically disrupting the optic radiation, patients are blind in the contra-lesional visual field. However, many of them, if pressed, are still able to guess the location and colour of stimuli presented in the blind field with probabilities far above chance level. Hence, they are able to guess and correctly indicate stimulus qualities they are not aware of: a phenomenon called *blindsight*. Over time, in this case over several years of experiments in several laboratories, such patients may gradually become aware of the stimuli, as a result of perceptual training implicitly provided through the perceptual experiments (Sahraie et al. 1998). In these patients, the unconscious reaction to the stimuli (blindsight) becomes conscious through perceptual learning. Similar processes may occur with subliminal priming: perceptual learning may move these subliminal stimuli closer to threshold and/or closer to conscious perception.

A somewhat related phenomenon is also present in normal observers. Subjects in typical psychophysical experiments undergo a so-called forced-choice procedure: after each stimulus presentation they have to choose one of several (often two) possible responses to the stimulus, e.g. 'horizontal' versus 'vertical'. This is to ensure that they have to guess after each stimulus presentation and cannot abstain from responding when they feel unsure about a relevant stimulus feature. This procedure separates the 'objective' ability to discriminate between two stimuli (present in blindsight) from subjective confidence about this discrimination (absent in blindsight). While the subjective aspect is not usually tested in experiments on perceptual learning, it may be well worth testing whether confidence improves slower or faster than objective performance, or at the same speed. In any case, inexperienced observers in particular are often surprised when they learn that they responded correctly in more than, say, 80% of presentations while subjectively they felt as if they were 'just guessing'.

In summary, perceptual learning can greatly improve the sensitivity of perception with thresholds decreasing by a factor of two or more within a rather short period of training. This represents one aspect of 'sensory plasticity' that allows primates to adapt fast to changing environments, variable sensory signals (such as when wearing prism goggles), and changing tasks (walking with or without a load such as a rucksack). It seems to rely on more than one neuronal process, with the different processes probably located on different cortical levels of signal processing and proceeding at different speeds. Improvement through modifications on an early cortical level such as the primary sensory cortices tends to be quite specific for the exact stimulus dimensions such as stimulus orientation, because of the high specificity of neurons there. On the other hand, mechanisms relying on more 'cognitive' processes that are achieved at higher, multimodal cortical levels yield improvements that generalize to similar tasks. Perceptual learning usually requires some form of attention (hence, no learning without attending to a stimulus) and it may even, over time, transform 'subconscious percepts' into conscious ones.

MANFRED FAHLE

Fahle, M. (2005). 'Perceptual learning: specificity versus generalization'. *Current Opinion in Neurobiology*, 15.

—— and Poggio, T. (eds) (2002). *Perceptual Learning*.

Li, W., Piech, V., and Gilbert, G. D. (2004). 'Perceptual learning and top-down influences in primary visual cortex'. *Nature Neuroscience*, 7.

Recanzone, G. H., Merzenich, M. M., and Dinse, H. R. (1992). 'Expansion of the cortical representation of a specific skin field in primary soma-sensory cortex by intra-cortical micro stimulation'. *Cerebral Cortex*, 2.

Sahraie, A., Weiskrantz, L., and Barbur, J. L. (1998). 'Awareness and confidence ratings in motion perception without geniculo-striate projection'. *Behavioral Brain Research*, 96.

Watanabe, T., Nanez, J. E., and Sasaki, Y. (2001). 'Perceptual learning without perception'. *Nature*, 413.

linguistics and the study of consciousness There are reasons to believe that the study of language can shed useful light on the nature of consciousness and that, conversely, knowing more about consciousness can contribute to a better understanding of language. Nevertheless, during most of the 20th century linguists virtually ignored these possibilities. To quote Stamenov (1997): 'there is at present little research in linguistics, psycholinguistics, neurolinguistics and the adjacent disciplines which explicitly addresses the problem of the relationships between language and consciousness.'

In the early 20th century, linguistics in America was dominated by Leonard Bloomfield and his followers, who were heavily influenced by behaviourism and logical positivism. They associated consciousness with 'mentalism', a supposedly unscientific approach to language which they forcefully rejected. Later in the century Noam Chomsky's influence eclipsed Bloomfield's, but research in that tradition was largely restricted to an abstract variety of syntax whose nature precluded a significant role for consciousness. Stamenov described his volume as 'the first one dedicated to a discussion of some of the aspects of this topic'. Its authors, nevertheless, tended to focus on the fact that there are aspects of language which lie outside consciousness. Ronald Langacker, for example, concluded his chapter in that volume by writing that 'it should be evident that grammar is shaped as much by what we are not consciously aware of as by what we are'. We are left, however, with the question of whether there are, in addition to these unconscious influences, important ways in which language and consciousness do interact.

Any serious exploration of this question necessarily relates consciousness to *thought* and *imagery*, other mental phenomena that have also been largely ignored by linguists. Consciousness, thought, and imagery all refer to private experiences that are inaccessible to direct public observation. Although *introspection may suggest that such experiences are pervasive ingredients of people's mental lives, it can be frustratingly difficult to achieve agreement on what they include or even what they are.

One linguist who has been actively concerned with these issues is Ray Jackendoff (1987, 1997), who identifies three basic levels of information processing in the *brain. Closest to 'the outside world' are processes of which we are not conscious, e.g. the fusing of two retinal images into a perception of depth. We are conscious of the results of these processes—say, of depth—but not of how they happen. We may also be conscious of speech sounds such as vowels, consonants, syllables, and pitch contours, but not of how raw sound comes to be interpreted in those ways. What happens in this outer layer of perception lies outside consciousness.

What we are conscious of are such phenomena as the speech sounds that belong to what Jackendoff calls the intermediate level of information processing—intermediate between unconscious perceptual processes and a deeper level that constitutes thought, of which we are also not conscious. We are conscious of imagery that is associated with the various sense modalities, but that is all. Although we have thoughts, it is only through their manifestations in imagery, both verbal and non-verbal, that we can be conscious of what they are. 'We become aware of thought taking place—we catch ourselves in the act of thinking—only when it manifests itself in linguistic form, in fact phonetic form' (Jackendoff 1997). Non-verbal imagery provides other conscious manifestations of thought, but it too is distinct from thought itself.

Jackendoff emphasizes the importance of separating thought from language. A major ingredient of consciousness is *inner speech, and for that reason we may be tempted to equate inner speech with thought. He believes, however, that 'thinking is largely independent of what language one happens to think in', and that the form of a particular language is irrelevant to the thoughts it conveys. We can even be conscious of language that is dissociated from any thought at all, as with the rote learning of a poem, ritual, or song in an unfamiliar language. He cites various other kinds of evidence that thought is unconscious, and that all we are conscious of is the phonetic imagery that expresses it. He concludes 'that although language *expresses* thought, thought itself is a separate brain phenomenon'.

Jackendoff sees reasoning as fundamental to thought. He suggests that if he were to say to you 'Bill killed Harry', you would infer from that statement that Harry died. You might at first think you knew that because you had an image of Bill stabbing Harry and Harry falling dead, but that image would be too specific, because 'the thoughts expressed by the words *kill* and *die*, not to mention the connections between them, are too general, too abstract to be conveyed by a visual image.' Thus, the knowledge that killing entails dying must belong to unconscious thought. Furthermore, there are many concepts like 'virtue' or 'social justice' for which no useful images may be available at all. Such words express elements of thought of which it is impossible to be directly conscious.

A different view is represented by Chafe (1994), who suggests that in addition to the imagery recognized by Jackendoff as the sole ingredient of consciousness we are also conscious of what he calls *ideas*, which constitute fundamental ingredients of thought. The person who said 'Bill killed Harry' was conscious of the idea of this particular event, aside from whatever imagery might have been associated with it. Because it is obviously impossible for a language to relate every particular idea to a particular sound, language requires that ideas be interpreted as instances of *categories*. Assigning an idea to a category accomplishes two things. First, the category enables a speaker to express the idea with a sound, such as the sound *kill*. Second, the category creates expectations that apply generally to instances of it, in this case the expectation that killing entails the death of its victim. The knowledge that Harry died is derived from entailments established by the *kill* category. Both particular ideas and generally applicable categories are fundamental to thought. Chafe believes that we are conscious of ideas, and that we are conscious of categories indirectly through their entailments as well as through the sounds they assign to their instances.

According to Chafe, language gives evidence that consciousness of thoughts has priority over consciousness of sounds in ordinary mental life. It is instructive, for example, to compare the experience of listening to one's own language with that of listening to a language that is unfamiliar. In the latter case it is only the sounds of which one *can* be conscious. Listening to one's own language is very different, and normally one is primarily consciousness of the ideas the language conveys. Those ideas may be accompanied by conscious imagery, but they need not be.

As mentioned above, Jackendoff notes that one may have learned 'by heart' the sounds of a poem, ritual, or song with little or no consciousness of the thoughts that were originally associated with those sounds. A basic element of linguistic processing is missing, and one recognizes that it is unusual to produce linguistic sounds that are divorced from conscious thoughts. The fact that we sometimes have such experiences is evidence that under normal circumstances we are conscious of thoughts. We find it unusual when they are absent.

In the tip-of-the-tongue phenomenon (Brown and McNeill 1966) there is consciousness of an idea, perhaps associated imagery, and whatever expectations are created by the way the idea is categorized, but there is difficulty in becoming conscious of the phonetic realization the category provides (see FEELING OF KNOWING). There is consciousness of thought, but without the normally associated sound. This experience, when imagery is lacking, can be the purest kind of evidence for 'imageless thought', a major issue for the Würzburg school a century ago (Humphrey 1951).

Chafe's observations of language in ordinary use suggest that thoughts are organized from moment to moment into a focus and a periphery, with a limited area of fully active consciousness surrounded by a penumbra of ideas in a semi-active state. Each focus is expressed in language with a brief *prosodic phrase*, typically occupying only one or two seconds, which is characterized by coherent patterns of pitch, volume, tempo, and voice quality. Prosodic phrases are a ubiquitous feature of natural speech, and it is helpful to view them as expressions of constantly changing *foci of consciousness* in the ongoing flow of thought—segments of thought whose capacity is highly limited. Each focus usually includes no more than one 'new' idea, an idea the speaker assumes was previously inactive in the consciousness of the listener. The status of ideas as new or already given in consciousness affects the shape of language in both the arrangement of words and the prosody assigned to them.

Ordinary speech also suggests that thoughts are organized within larger *topics*, conceptual elements too large to be accommodated within the limited capacity of fully active consciousness. An entire topic can be present in consciousness in no more than a semi-active state. Once a topic has been introduced, the more limited focus of active consciousness, expressed linguistically in a succession of prosodic phrases, navigates through it, activating first one included idea and then another until the speaker judges the topic to have been adequately covered. This process is likely to be guided by a *schema*, a familiar pattern that provides a path for speakers to follow (Bartlett 1932), its progression often modified by ongoing interaction among the participants in the conversation.

Observations of people talking are not the only linguistic evidence for the relation of consciousness to language. Writers of fiction have discovered various ways to involve their readers in an imagined consciousness, and the study of such devices can promote understandings of consciousness that might otherwise be difficult to achieve (Cohn 1978).

Literary language, for example, may illuminate a distinction between *immediate consciousness*, focused on the here and now, and *displaced consciousness*, focused on experiences that are either recalled from an earlier time or imagined. These two modes of consciousness are qualitatively different, and fictional literature sometimes exploits that difference. An immediate consciousness has access to a richness of detail that is attenuated in a displaced consciousness. When something is available to direct perception, a wealth of information is potentially available. When a displaced consciousness is engaged in remembering or imagining, detail is necessarily impoverished. Writing gives writers the freedom to include the amount of detail appropriate to an immediate consciousness, even when that consciousness is displaced from the consciousness of the narrator. Language like the following allows readers to experience vicariously the consciousness of a protagonist:

> He started a fire with some chunks of pine he got with the ax from a stump. Over the fire he stuck a wire grill, pushing the four legs down into the ground with his boot. Nick put the frying pan on the grill over the flames. He was hungrier. The beans and spaghetti warmed. Nick stirred them and mixed them together. They began to bubble, making little bubbles that rose with difficulty to the surface (Hemingway 1987, cf. Chafe 1994).

The impression conveyed by such language is that these experiences were immediately experienced, rather than being reported from the perspective of a separate consciousness with relation to which they would be displaced. They were, nevertheless, verbalized in the past tense, which in ordinary speech signals a displaced consciousness recalled from an earlier time. The past tense as well as third person references to 'Nick' and 'he' show the perspective of a separate narrating consciousness. Chafe terms this artifice *displaced immediacy*. The experiences of the protagonist, although displaced in tense and person, achieve immediacy through the richness of detail. This immediacy may be reinforced with temporal adverbs like 'now' or 'today', which locate a time that coincides with that of the displaced consciousness rather than the consciousness of the narrator:

> Nick did not want to go in there now.... He did not want to go down the stream any further today.

Recognizing the two separate consciousnesses that are involved in language of this type highlights a contrast between adverbs, centred in the protagonist's consciousness, and tense and person, centred in the narrator's consciousness, thus providing an excellent example of how investigations of consciousness can further an understanding of language.

In summary, linguists have tended to emphasize the extent to which language is shaped by unconscious forces. If we assume that language provides a way of associating thoughts with sounds, Jackendoff takes the extreme position that the thoughts themselves lie entirely outside consciousness and that we are conscious only of the sounds. Chafe, in contrast, believes that consciousness influences the shape of language in a variety of ways. Observing the prosodic phrases of ordinary speech, he views them as the expression of foci of consciousness, which are organized within larger, semi-active topics along paths established by familiar schemas. He also finds useful clues to the relation between consciousness and language in written fiction, where displaced immediacy involves the reader in the consciousness of a protagonist. It remains true, however, that few contemporary linguists take consciousness seriously, most preferring to avoid the subject. More evidence may need to be accumulated and disseminated before its potentially important contributions to linguistic studies can be more widely recognized.

WALLACE CHAFE

Bartlett, F. C. (1932). *Remembering: a Study in Experimental and Social Psychology.*

Brown, R. and McNeill, D. (1966). 'The 'tip of the tongue' phenomenon'. *Journal of Verbal Learning and Verbal Behavior*, 5.

Chafe, W. (1994). *Discourse, Consciousness, and Time: the Flow and Displacement of Conscious Experience in Speaking and Writing.*

Cohn, D. (1978). *Transparent Minds: Narrative Modes for Presenting Consciousness in Fiction.*

Hemingway, E. (1987). 'Big two-hearted river'. In *The Complete Short Stories of Ernest Hemingway: the Finca Vigía Edition.*

Humphrey, G. (1951). *Thinking.*

Jackendoff, R. (1987). *Consciousness and the Computational Mind.*

—— (1997). *The Architecture of the Language Faculty.*

Stamenov, M. I. (ed.) (1997). *Language Structure, Discourse and the Access to Consciousness.*

literature and consciousness Literature can help us understand consciousness by providing detailed information about human behaviour, ideas, feelings, and experience. Works of literature may be seen as the fieldwork of consciousness studies, in contrast to the benchwork of psychologists, biologists, and neuroscientists. As such, the human experience represented in literature may be placed beside neurological studies and first-person reports by subjects about their experience and subjective states that allow researchers to investigate the brain and conscious experience. Steven Rose does so in ending *The Making of Memory* with a nod to the 'hard work' of creative writers:

But psychobiology and neuroscience are never going to replace the equally hard work of the novelist or poet in exploring [. . .] subjectivity, in re-membering and re-creating the foreign country which is the past (Rose 1992:328).

In this formulation, writers are heroic forgers into unknown territory, bringing back information about a strange land usually inaccessible to others. In referring to works distinguishing among 'sex, attachment, and romantic love,' Antonio Damasio directs readers '[f]or the classical view' to Flaubert, Stendhal, Joyce, and Proust in contrast to 'modern and science-inspired' writers (2003:308–9).

The area where literature and the study of consciousness intersect perhaps most interestingly is that of narrative. Stories exist outside literature, of course, when we tell others what happened to us when they were not present to observe the events themselves. This capacity surely pre-existed writing and may have first been non-verbal, as cave paintings may suggest. The ability to produce narrative in some form seems to many researchers fundamental to the idea of being conscious. Damasio (1999), for instance, sees non-verbal storytelling about one's own states of being as the basis of consciousness. He writes:

Consciousness begins when brains acquire the power . . . of telling a story without words, the story that there is life ticking away in an organism, and that the states of the living organism, within body bounds, are continuously being altered by encounters with objects or events in its environment, or, for that matter, by thoughts and by internal adjustments of the life process. Consciousness emerges when this primordial story . . . can be told using the universal nonverbal vocabulary of body signals. The apparent self emerges as the feeling of a feeling. When the story is first told, spontaneously . . . and forevermore after that when the story is repeated, knowledge about what the organism is living through automatically emerges as the answer to a question never asked. From that moment on, we begin to know (1999:30–31).

Mark Turner (1996) goes further, to argue that the use of parable—the projection of one story on another—underlies all cognition and preceded the development of language in human evolution. Writing stories down, however, fixes and formalizes them, makes them available for wide distribution, and thus creates a common fund of narratives on which readers of all sorts, including children, parents, and researchers into consciousness, draw. Our terms for understanding narrative of any sort are those usually applied to the study of written stories, so a literary understanding of narrative will, at least in part, inform models of consciousness involving any narrative—non-verbal, oral, or written.

Repeated features of written narrative, not to mention specific stories, become useful markers for consciousness and investigations into it. For example, the narrative styles of novels by the 20th-century writers James Joyce, Virginia Woolf, and William Faulkner—loosely labelled with William James's term **stream of consciousness* (1907:239)—have encouraged the widespread understanding of consciousness as free-flowing, ungovernable, and arbitrary since composed of often random internal and external perceptions. James's description of consciousness as a 'blooming, buzzing confusion' may have influenced these writers' ideas of it. James certainly influenced his former Harvard student Gertrude Stein, whose experimental writing renders thought as repetitive, sometimes apparently mindlessly so, and as wandering, subtle variations on simple perceptions or ideas.

Empirical and theoretical studies by psychologists Jerome Bruner (1990), Katherine Nelson (2003), and many others have established the centrality of telling stories in the formation of children's sense of self. For these psychologists, there is no self without an ability to tell a coherent narrative of one's own past activities, so that one's self is a function of one's narrative ability. Philosopher Owen Flanagan states the case succinctly: 'Evidence strongly suggests that humans in all cultures come to cast their own identity in some sort of narrative form' (1992:198). Basing their conclusions on studies of *brain-damaged patients, literary scholar Kay Young and neurologist Jeffrey L. Saver (2001) maintain that

Individuals who have lost the ability to construct narrative . . . have lost their selves. . . . Consciousness needs a narrative structure to create a sense of self based on the features of storytelling, like coherence, consequence, consecution (Young and Saver 2001:78–79).

For Young and Saver, consciousness is anchored in a self that, if not itself a story, is structured very like a story—with a beginning, middle, and end; with events that lead one to another in explainable ways; and with a sense of something at stake in the unfolding of events. Understanding self as structured like a narrative accords with the arguments of literary scholar Paul John Eakin, for whom written autobiographies are larger, more complicated, externalized versions of the ongoing internal narrative activity about themselves that humans engage in continuously from a very early age (Eakin 1999:99–141).

A more straightforward use of literature to elucidate consciousness is as a source of illustrations and explanations of human thought and behaviour. Damasio (2003) uses a speech in Shakespeare's play *Richard II* to introduce his distinction between emotions and feelings (2003:27–30) and Wordsworth's 'Tintern Abbey' to describe how physical contentment leads to 'pleasurable feelings' and happy thoughts (2003:84). He also likens G. K. Chesterton's story of an invisible murderer—a postman literally not seen by those guarding the house because they do not imagine him as a possible suspect—to the current state of the mind–body problem. Damasio (2003) believes that a change in perspective such as would have helped Chesterton's guards is needed in order to recognize that the human mind arises out of the brain, which is ineluctably connected to the body (2003:190–91). Turner (2004) finds support in children's stories about talking animals for a theory of conceptual blending as a basic human mental operation that he developed with Gilles Fauconnier. For Turner, children's literature offers a handy repository of images and thought patterns that reproduce folk beliefs, both of which reveal largely unconscious patterns of thought that undergird conscious thought. Among many other works, Fauconnier and Turner (2002) use material from an elegy by Catullus, Dante's *Divine Comedy*, Milton's *Paradise Lost*, and Yeats's poem 'Fergus and the druid' to elaborate aspects of their theory. They treat literature as they do folklore, myths, and advertisements—as windows into human phenomena that may be analysed and explained in terms of their theory.

The professional study of literature occasionally offers general insights into consciousness. Analysing narrative techniques in the modernist fiction of Joseph Conrad, literary critic Ian Watt has identified *delayed decoding*—the presentation of a 'sense impression' but 'withhold[ing] naming it or explaining its meaning until later' (1979:175). The faithfulness of this literary technique to experience is confirmed by neuroscientists' discovery of the short delay between sensory stimuli and full cognition of them.

In his 2001 novel *Thinks*..., David Lodge dramatizes the parallels and oppositions between scientific and literary exploration of subjective experience. One of his main characters, Ralph Messenger, a professor of cognitive science, believes in *artificial intelligence (AI), the theory that the mind is nothing more than a vast computing device. Against that hard-line position on the nature of the mind, Lodge situates the belief in an essential self or soul in a visiting teacher of creative writing, Helen Reed, with whom Messenger has an affair. The professor succinctly poses his field's central problem to her: 'How to give an objective, third-person account of a subjective, first-person experience.' Reed retorts, 'Oh, but novelists have been doing that for the last two hundred years' (Lodge 2001:42). Discussions of *qualia in the novel lead to reports of experiments in sensory deprivation from birth to determine the nature of a person's first experience of colour (see KNOWLEDGE ARGUMENT). At the novel's close, Messenger asks his lover to make the final presentation at a scientific conference on consciousness studies. Using Marvell's 'The Garden' to develop her points, Reed offers a strong defence of the existence of an ineffable self and of the power of literature to evoke sensation as well as the private, feeling-laden nature of consciousness. Lodge cedes nothing to science in asserting literature's usefulness in expressing the textures of consciousness. But he also recognizes the importance and fascination of the questions science is raising about it. Lodge sees science and literature as providing parallel, and perhaps complementary, means of representing the phenomenon of consciousness. He also addresses these issues and others at length in a 2002 essay, 'Consciousness and the novel.'

Literature as well as film, television, cartoons, and graphic novels will continue to provide illustrations of aspects of consciousness that often go unremarked in ordinary life. Representations of experience in writing and visual media offer a wealth of detail about human consciousness that can augment and clarify clinical observations, first-person reports, and neurological studies. Long before the scientific study of consciousness began in the 20th century, oral storytellers and then writers were representing consciousness in their creations. In addition to providing a cultural legacy, they have created—and will continue to create—a storehouse of data potentially useful in understanding consciousness.

THOMAS R. SMITH

Bruner, J. (1990). *Acts of Meaning.*

Damasio, A. (1999). *The Feeling of What Happens: Body and Emotion in the Making of Consciousness.*

—— (2003). *Looking for Spinoza: Joy, Sorrow, and the Feeling Brain.*

Eakin, P. J. (1999). *How Our Lives Become Stories: Making Selves.*

Fauconnier, G. and Turner, M. (2002). *The Way We Think: Conceptual Blending and the Mind's Hidden Complexities.*

Flanagan, O. (1992). *Consciousness Reconsidered.*

James, W. (1907). *The Principles of Psychology*, Vol. 1.

Lodge, D. (2001). *Thinks*...

—— (2002). 'Consciousness and the novel.' In *Consciousness and the Novel: Connected Essays*.

Nelson, K. (2003). 'Narrative and the emergence of a consciousness of self'. In Fireman, G. et al. (eds) *Narrative and Consciousness: Literature, Psychology, and the Brain*.

Rose, S. (1992). *The Making of Memory*.

Turner, M. (1996). *The Literary Mind*.

—— (2004). 'The origin of selkies'. *Journal of Consciousness Studies*, 11.

Watt, I. (1979). *Conrad in the Nineteenth Century*.

Young, K. and Saver, J. L. (2001). 'The neurology of narrative'. *SubStance*, 30.

locked-in syndrome See BRAIN DAMAGE

M

machine consciousness Machine consciousness (or artificial consciousness) is an emerging discipline which is aimed at the creation of conscious artefacts. Although practical engagement with the topic has only occurred in the last decade or so, the issue of whether and how a machine could be conscious, and in what sense, has been familiar for a much longer period. The invention of the digital computer gave rise to a debate on the extent to which computers and other symbol manipulators could possess the properties of minds—originally intelligence, but more recently *consciousness. This discussion began more than 50 years ago with what is now called the *Turing test, expanded 30 years later with Searle's *Chinese room, and developed still further with Penrose's reprise of Lucas's argument based on Gödel's theorem, and his suggestion that quantum physics may be relevant. It still shows no signs of reaching a consensus, although non-symbolic methods of computation, such as neural networks (see CONNECTIONIST MODELS), have been claimed by some to solve or avoid the problems associated with purely symbolic systems. A related theoretical issue, that of whether and how it could be verified that a machine was conscious, has also accumulated a substantial literature, broadly negative in tone (and reminiscent of the *zombie argument) where phenomenal consciousness is the target, and almost uniformly positive where the focus is on the more cognitive aspects, such as *access consciousness. Clarity is not helped by the fact that those working within machine consciousness, who may have a background in engineering or *artificial intelligence (AI), do not always trouble to define what they mean by consciousness, nor to relate their position to the established theoretical bases within consciousness studies.

We can distinguish several different technical approaches to machine consciousness. The *speculative* approach stops short of any actual implementation, being essentially a statement of the form: 'If you built a machine like this, or that did this, then it would be conscious'. Provided that the proposed scheme is well grounded, and sufficiently detailed to be implementable, as some are, this is potentially useful. Of course, many proposed theories of biological consciousness also have a core mechanism that is potentially implementable—for example, Damasio's (2000): 'The neural patterns and images necessary for consciousness to occur are those which constitute proxies for the organism, for the object, and for the relationship between the two.' However, unless such theories go on to consider their implementation in an artefact, they remain strictly outside machine consciousness.

The *unembodied* approach uses a set of mechanisms embedded in an architecture, but with no analogue of a body, sensors, actuators, or any spatial location. Perhaps the best example of this is Franklin's (2003) 'conscious software', IDA, which uses a variety of AI technologies to implement all the constituent mechanisms of Baars' (1988) *global workspace theory of consciousness, but deals only with the limited and non-spatial world of email processing. Franklin considers that the system demonstrates a form of functional consciousness, but not phenomenal consciousness. Regardless of the type or level of consciousness it may be thought to have achieved, IDA still makes a valuable contribution to consciousness studies, in that it is a successful test of the complex cognitive architecture proposed by Baars; most rival theories have not yet passed such a test.

In recent years, many theorists have emphasized the importance of embodiment to consciousness, as well as to cognition, and this is reflected in many efforts in machine consciousness. In most cases, the candidate for consciousness is *virtually embodied*: a simulated agent is embedded within a simulated world, so that the actions of the agent, by changing the world or (more usually) by changing the agent's position in the world, change the simulated sensory input. Where the intended focus is on the operation of processes internal to the agent rather than on performance in the world, this approach is extremely attractive, offering speed, tractability, and flexibility while suffering from none of the problems associated with the engineering of real complex robots. Shanahan (2006) shows the potential of this approach, using a commercially available robot simulator to support a sophisticated neural implementation of a Baars-like global workspace, and identifying both behavioural and process-based analogues of phenomena related to consciousness.

It is certain that complex *physically embodied* agents, especially those capable of mimicking humans' physical abilities, will constitute the acme of any technology of machine consciousness, but it is also clear that they currently require resources unlikely to be available to many working in consciousness studies. Robotics is in itself one of the most complex branches of engineering, combining sensing, motor control, mechanical engineering, and computing in very challenging ways. Purpose-built robots are invariably expensive and require constant skilled attention. Relatively simple wheeled robots are of course available, but most are so limited in performance that they offer no real advantages over the corresponding robot simulators. Many of the good reasons for using a humanoid robot, along with some of the associated difficulties, were set out by Dennett (1994) in the early stages of MIT's COG project in what is still a useful introductory paper.

As noted above, any potentially implementable theory of consciousness provides an opportunity for creating a conscious machine, but much of the work reported to date has a rather narrow span. There are some outliers concentrating on cognitive processing or on brain-inspired visual processing, but most work is concerned with the investigation of mechanisms of internal simulation or modelling, often as a vehicle for a form of imagination. There is no unanimity about what has to be simulated, or exactly how this relates to consciousness; some focus on simulating the world, some on simulating the agent itself, and some on simulating the interaction between them. This emphasis is not found elsewhere in consciousness studies, and may have been influenced by similar work in robotics and embodied cognition.

The complex issues associated with the identification of consciousness in an artefact have been sidestepped by some within the machine consciousness community through the use of a set of axioms proposed by Aleksander and Dunmall (2003) as 'a formal statement of the mechanisms that are thought minimally necessary to underpin consciousness'. The axioms, which are essentially postulates rather than self-evident truths, can be summarized rather informally as follows:

Axiom 1: a sense of place. We feel that we are at the centre of an 'out there' world, and we have the ability to place ourselves in the world around us.

Axiom 2: imagination. We can 'see' things that we have experienced in the past, and we can also conjure up things we have never seen. Reading a novel can conjure up mental images of different worlds, for example.

Axiom 3: directed attention. Our thoughts are not just passive reflections of what is happening in the world—we are able to focus our attention, and we are conscious only of that to which we attend.

Axiom 4: planning We have the ability to carry out 'what if?' exercises. Scenarios of future events and actions can be mapped out in our minds even if we are just sitting still.

Axiom 5: decision/emotion Emotions guide us into recognizing what is good for us and what is bad for us, and into acting accordingly.

The axioms are intended to be used to generate 'tests for the presence of minimal consciousness in agents', and serve both as a target and a touchstone; a system's performance in relation to each is easily assessed, and no physically embodied system has yet satisfied all five.

What are the long-term prospects for machine consciousness? If it is possible at all, and if in addition it is possible to devise some means of demonstrating success, then the remaining obstacles must be of two kinds: technical, and conceptual. Unless, as some have claimed, some non-computational property of brain tissue is essential to support consciousness, adequate computational resources for almost any conceivable scheme are available now at relatively low cost, and it has been claimed that a detailed and fine-grained simulation of the human brain (as envisaged within the Blue Brain project) may be possible within a decade. If real embodiment is crucial, then current work in robotics offers bodies with numbers of degrees of freedom comparable to those of a human, and visual sensors at least comparable to the human eye. In other words, the available technology is probably up to the job. As far as conceptual limitations are concerned, at the present pace of work it will be several years before even the major theories of consciousness have been embedded in artefacts, and so we cannot yet say whether our existing conceptual resources are inadequate.

It should also be noted that the pursuit of machine consciousness has already given rise to ethical concerns. Having identified one particular potentially implementable structure (the phenomenal self model, or PSM) as being capable of supporting suffering, Metzinger (2003) urges: 'Therefore, we should ban all attempts to create (or even risk the creation of) artificial and postbiotic PSMs from serious academic research.' However, if his voice is not heard, and conscious machines do make an appearance, then the issue of their ethical status may arise; a recent UK government document predicted that such robots would have to be given legal and other rights.

OWEN HOLLAND

Aleksander, I. and Dunmall, B. (2003). Axioms and tests for the presence of minimal consciousness in agents. *Journal of Consciousness Studies*, 10.

Baars, B. J. (1988). *A Cognitive Theory of Consciousness*.

Damasio, A. R. (2000). *The Feeling of What Happens: Body, Emotion and the Making of Consciousness*.

Dennett, D. C. (1994). 'The practical requirements for making a conscious robot. *Philosophical Transactions of the Royal Society* Series A: *Physical Sciences*, 349.

Franklin, S. (2003). 'IDA: a conscious artifact?' *Journal of Consciousness Studies*, 10.

Metzinger, T. (2003). *Being No One. The Self-model Theory of Subjectivity*.

Shanahan, M. P. (2006). 'A cognitive architecture that combines internal simulation with a global workspace'. *Consciousness and Cognition*, 15.

magical number seven See CAPACITY LIMITS AND CONSCIOUSNESS

magnetoencephalography Alongside *electroencephalography (EEG), magnetoencephalography (MEG) completes the electromagnetic signature of electric neural activity recorded from the scalp. Biomagnetic fields produced by the brain's ongoing activity are minute, typically ranging from 10 to 100 fT (1 fT = 10^{-15} of a tesla); about 1 billion times smaller than the Earth's static magnetic field that makes the needle of a compass point north. Such a tiny scale of measurement obviously makes substantial technological demands (Hämäläinen et al. 1993).

1. Instrumentation
2. Neural genesis of MEG
3. From scalp measurements to brain activity
4. Electromagnetic source imaging in the study of consciousness

1. Instrumentation

Heart biomagnetism was the first to be evidenced experimentally, by Baule and McFee (1963) and Russian groups, followed in Chicago and then in Boston by David Cohen who introduced significant technological improvements (e.g. the magnetically shielded room) in the late 1960s. The first MEG recording followed in 1971 when Cohen reported on spontaneous oscillatory brain activity (the alpha rhythm).The technique had been revolutionized by the introduction of extremely sensitive magnetometers, developed in collaboration with James Zimmerman at the Massachusetts Institute of Technology (MIT). These were—and still are—built from superconducting quantum interference devices (SQUIDs) which are able to detect exquisitely small current levels induced by a tiny magnetic flux passing through a coil.

The MEG gantry itself consists of a rigid helmet containing the sensors and liquid helium to cool the superconducting equipment down to about −269° C. Environmental electromagnetic interference (from any number of sources such as motor traffic, elevators, and the omnipresent power line contamination) is extremely unfavourable to MEG. The systems are therefore still confined to magnetically shielded rooms and usually coupled to hardware and software noise-cancellation systems which all work on the same principle: subtracting or blocking out interfering magnetic fields from the MEG recordings. With these precautions, the instrumental MEG signal-to-noise (SNR) ratio is typically limited to a few fT/Hz.

The major technological innovation in recent years has been the integration of an increasing number of sensors into the MEG helmet. Today, systems include up to 300 MEG channels with optional simultaneous EEG recordings from dense electrode nets. Higher-temperature sensor techniques with satisfactory SNR are currently being investigated for forthcoming generations of MEG equipment. These technological precautions make MEG significantly more expensive than EEG, but it has substantial benefits. For example, while EEG is strongly degraded by the heterogeneity in conductivity within head tissues (e.g. insulating skull vs conducting scalp), in MEG this effect is extremely limited, resulting in greater spatial discrimination of neural contributions. Installation of new MEG systems is presently steadily increasing within research and clinical centres.

2. Neural genesis of MEG

Neural currents produce magnetic fields, according to Maxwell's laws of electrodynamics. In the specific case of MEG, the distance from neural sources to sensors and the rapidly decreasing power spectrum of neural signals with frequency—reaching the instrumental noise level at a few kHz—make propagation time delays negligible, and the magnetostatics assumption is therefore considered as valid. Since the early work of Lorente de Nó in the late 1940s, the physics of neural sources of MEG and EEG have been studied using the concept of the equivalent current dipole (ECD), denoted by Q. The ECD is a model for a current flowing for a certain distance in a certain direction, an amplitude which is expressed in ampere metres (A·m). The architecture of the neural cell conditions the paths taken by its tiny intracellular currents, which all sum up vectorially to the net current dipole of the neuron. This summation at the cellular level is particularly efficient when the dendrites are organized along a single preferential direction rather than radially. It is complemented by a group effect at the cell assembly level, when multiple adjacent neurons are synchronously active. For these reasons, assemblies of pyramidal cells in neocortical layers II/III and V are considered to be the main sources of MEG (and EEG) signals. Recent quantitative investigations using realistically shaped computer models of neurons with voltage-sensitive channels suggest that neocortical columns made up of as few as 50 000 pyramidal cells—each with an individual Q of about 0.2 pA m, resulting in a net Q of

10 nA m, a typical source level for MEG/EEG signals—could be detectable on the scalp. These models also suggest that the contribution of fast spiking activity of intracellular currents might well be greater than formerly expected, which supports the experimental evidence of high-frequency brain oscillations (>100 Hz) recorded with MEG (Murakami and Okada 2006).

3. From scalp measurements to brain activity
The physicists engaged in early MEG research suggested investigating the localization of MEG sources, beyond the traditional analysis of scalp traces. Unfortunately, finding the current sources responsible for the magnetic fields measured outside a closed volume conductor (like the head) is an ill-posed 'inverse problem'—the 'forward problem' referring to the basic modelling of neural currents and measurement principles—with no unique solution if no additional a priori information is considered, as demonstrated by von Helmholtz in the late 19th century. Depending on the nature of the priors, the estimation of MEG sources can be approached from either a localization or an imaging perspective (Baillet et al. 2001). The localization approach explicitly considers that only a limited number of brain areas might be active at a single time instant. Each active brain region is therefore modelled using e.g. an ECD, the parameters of which (location, orientation, and amplitude) need to be estimated from the data. The alternative imaging approach derives from image reconstruction techniques where the number of sources of a signal is unknown but restricted to a circumscribed spatial domain; in the case of MEG, a three-dimensional grid of elementary sources that samples the brain volume or even the individual cortical anatomy obtained from co-registration with magnetic resonance imaging (MRI) sequences. The spatial resolution of MEG source estimation principally depends on the SNR in the data, which is contingent in part on the brain systems at stake during the experiment: deeper brain structures produce smaller magnetic fields. Quantitative evaluations from physical head phantoms have reported an average localization error of about 3 mm for MEG (vs 7 mm for EEG), which should be considered as a minimum. The methodology for MEG source estimation is now coming to a satisfactory degree of maturity to complement with other *functional brain mapping approaches. The time-resolved images of mass neural activity at the sub-millisecond range produced by MEG are very attractive for the study of dynamical aspects of brain activation at the system level.

4. Electromagnetic source imaging in the study of consciousness
Emerging measures of neural dynamics both at the local scale (e.g. task-related modulations of oscillatory activity in selective frequency bands) and at larger scales (e.g. evaluation of task-related *connectivity models between neural source activations with high temporal resolution) are of particular interest to cognitive neuroscience. A growing number of investigations are benefiting from the unique temporal resolution of this imaging approach. For example, in the context of conscious vs unconscious visual perception, recent studies have revealed that the conscious perception of visual objects might be revealed by phase shifts of oscillatory neural activity in the midline *frontal lobe (Srinivasan and Petrovic 2006). Distributed brain synchronous activity was also found to correlate with the spontaneous flow of perceptual dominance during binocular rivalry (Cosmelli et al. 2004). Such studies illustrate two of the many ways in which MEG may contribute to the elucidation both of the spatial substrates and of the dynamic processes encountered in the study of consciousness.

SYLVAIN BAILLET

Baillet, S., Mosher, J. C., and Leahy, R. M. (2001). 'Electromagnetic brain mapping'. *IEEE Signal Processing Magazine*, 18.

Baule, G. M. and McFee, R. (1963). 'Detection of the magnetic field of the heart'. *American Heart Journal*, 66.

Cosmelli, D., David, O., Lachaux, J.-P., Martinerie, J., Garnero, L., Renault, B., and Varela, F. (2004).'Waves of consciousness: ongoing cortical patterns during binocular rivalry'. *Neuroimage*, 23.

Hämäläinen, M., Hari, R., Ilmoniemi, R., Knuutila, J., and Lounasmaa, O. (1993). 'Magnetoencephalography: theory, instrumentation and applications to the noninvasive study of human brain function'. *Revue of Modern Physics*, 65.

Murakami, S. and Okada, Y. (2006). 'Contributions of principal neocortical neurons to magnetoencephalography and electroencephalography signals'. *Journal of Physiology*, 575.

Srinivasan, R. and Petrovic, S. (2006). 'MEG phase follows conscious perception during binocular rivalry induced by visual stream segregation'. *Cerebral Cortex*, 16.

Mary See KNOWLEDGE ARGUMENT

masking, visual Visual masking occurs when the visibility of one brief (≤50 ms) stimulus, the *target*, is reduced or eliminated by the presentation of a second brief stimulus, the *mask* (Breitmeyer and Öğmen 2006). Refined over the last 100 years, masking is useful for investigating the microgenesis of (processing dynamics leading up to) conscious perception. The rationale for dynamic masking rests on the following: (1) an interval, up to tens or a few hundreds of milliseconds, is required from onset of a stimulus to its measurable effects on behaviour or its conscious registration; (2) active processing of stimulus features occurs during this interval; (3) this processing occurs in several pathways, each with several levels; and (4) the response to a mask, interacting with that to the target at specifiable levels of processing, affects the visibility of the target.

To study centrally located processes of object perception, the mask and target typically consist of spatial patterns whose contours are defined by luminance or wavelength differences (Breitmeyer and Öğmen 2006: Chs 1 and 2). The outcomes of pattern masking studies depend on the choice of display, stimulus, timing, and task parameters. Display parameters include the luminance and wavelength of the background on which target and mask are presented. Stimulus parameters include the shape, size, luminance, wavelength, retinal eccentricity, number, and degree of spatial overlap of the target and mask. Timing parameters include the durations of the target and mask and the stimulus onset asynchrony (SOA) separating the onsets of the target and mask. Task parameters depend on the viewing condition (i.e. monocular, binocular, or dichoptic), and the response criterion (e.g. visibility rating, luminance matching, forced-choice pattern discrimination, detection) used in the masking study. By varying SOA and the other parameters, one can infer from the results how, at what stages, and in which information-processing pathways the responses to the target and mask interact.

Figure M1 shows several variants of pattern masking depending on the shape of the stimuli and the time interval separating their onsets. Forward and backward masking occur when the mask onset respectively precedes and follows that of the target. Although some forward masking effects are of theoretical interest, backward pattern masking is especially useful in studying the microgenesis of conscious perception.

The left panel of Fig. M1a illustrates target and mask used in a masking procedure termed *masking by noise* as well as the associated percept when the they are presented simultaneously or very close in time. Here the elements that comprise the mask and spatially overlap the target are designed to bear little, if any, structural relationship to the target. The target, here an **X**, is partially visible and may be confused with another target, e.g. a **Y**, thus masking its true identity. As shown in the right panel of Fig. M1a, when the overlapping mask elements structurally resemble those of the target, *masking by structure* prevails. The associated target–mask percept at and near target–mask synchrony totally obscures the target, here a **K**. The middle panel of Fig. M1b shows a typical non-overlapping target and mask stimuli used in *metacontrast* masking. Since the target and mask share contour contiguity and similarity, metacontrast is a special case of structure masking. The associated percepts depend on the figural aspects of the target and mask and on SOA. For example, when the target is a disk and the mask a surrounding ring, the target is totally visible at very small and large SOAs (e.g. 0 ms and >150 ms). At an intermediate SOA of, say, 90 ms a partial masking of the target results; and at an optimal SOA of, say, 50 ms, its visibility is totally suppressed. Under favourable conditions, the area occupied by the target is actually perceived in opposite contrast (*phenomenal contrast reversal*). On the other hand, despite the complete masking of contour and contrast features, an observer can often detect the mere presence of the target via an explosive objectless motion or by a transient 'blip'. Masks that partially surround the target yield correspondingly partial suppression of target features. Moreover, when a target such as an outline square bears a feature such as a gap, the target's visibility as such can be totally suppressed at optimal SOAs; yet an observer can infer where the its gap was located, since it appears transposed to, or inherited by, the adjacent mask contour.

The phenomenology implies that these masking methods yield distinctive functions relating target visibility to the SOA separating the target and mask. Fig. M1c shows typical backward masking functions. In the monotonic case target visibility is lowest when the target and mask are presented simultaneously and increases as their SOA increases. In the U-shaped case, visibility is high at target-mask simultaneity, lowest at intermediate SOAs (30–80 ms) and high again at large SOAs (>150 ms). Monotonic functions can be obtained with noise or structure masks when the stimuli are presented to one or both eyes. However, structure masking is monotonic only when the ratio of mask to target energy (duration × luminance) is larger than 1 (e.g. 2.5), but tends to be U-shaped when the ratio is less than 1 (e.g. 0.4). This indicates that the process underlying the U-shaped function can itself be 'masked' by the monotonic process when target energy is large. In fact, the underlying U-shaped process can be revealed, regardless of target-to-mask energy ratios, when the target and mask are presented to separate eyes (dichoptic viewing).

These findings are significant in three ways. (1) Dichoptic interactions occur at cortical levels of processing, levels on which object perception (while initiated by activity at retinal and other precortical levels of processing) ultimately also depends. Consequently, since monotonic masking effects with overlapping masks are significantly attenuated or eliminated with dichoptic viewing, (2) the process responsible for monotonic backward masking, called *masking by integration*, occurs primarily at precortical levels whereas (3) the process responsible for maximally suppressing the visibility of the target at an intermediate SOA (e.g. 50 ms), called *masking by interruption*, occurs at cortical levels.

Backward pattern masking is informative for several reasons. (1) It is interesting in its own right because of

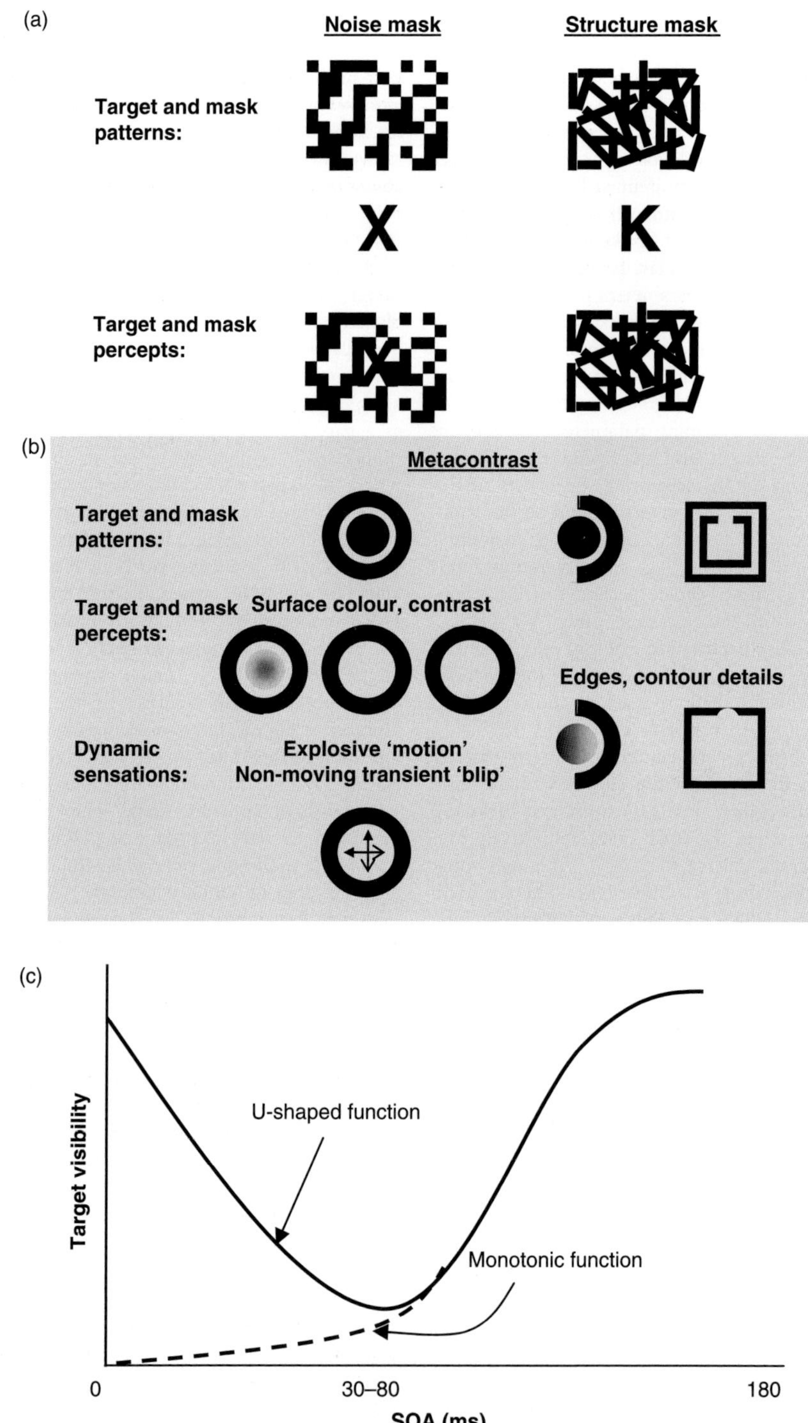

Fig. M1. (a) Target and mask stimuli used in pattern masking by noise (left) and by structure (right) with associated target and mask percepts. (b) Examples of typical target and mask stimuli used in metacontrast masking and their associated percepts. (c) Schematic representation of typical monotonic and nonmonotonic (U-shaped) backward masking functions relating target visibility to target-mask SOA.

the counter-intuitive finding that the mask can suppress the target's visibility even though it follows the target. Several models of backward masking have been proposed (Breitmeyer and Öğmen 2006:Chs 4 and 5), and testing them requires the study of pattern masking. (2) Visual processing is a dynamic, evolving phenomenon (VanRullen and Thorpe 2001), and masking is useful for investigating the sequences and levels of feedforward and *re-entrant information processing that are deemed important to the emergence of visual consciousness (Di Lollo et al. 2000, Lamme et al. 2002). (3) Higher-level visuo-cognitive processes such as perceptual grouping, figure–ground segmentation, *attention, and visual imagery can modulate visual masking. The role of *gestalt grouping and attention in backward masking is currently of particular theoretical interest (Breitmeyer and Öğmen 2006:Ch. 7). Conversely, masking plays a role in the temporal dynamics of the attentional blink and transient and sustained types of attention. (4) The relation of backward masking to suppression by *binocular rivalry and by *transcranial magnetic stimulation (TMS) has recently been explored (Breitmeyer and Öğmen 2006:Ch. 8, Breitmeyer et al. 2004). This is important, since (5) all three methods of suppressing stimulus visibility are currently used to explore visual awareness and the controversial field of 'subliminal perception'. With each of these methods, a variety of implicit or unconscious motor, cognitive and emotional processes have been reported in recent years (Breitmeyer and Öğmen 2006:Ch. 8).

BRUNO G. BREITMEYER

Breitmeyer, B. G. and Öğmen, H. (2006). *Visual Masking: Time Slices Through Conscious and Unconscious Vision.*

——, Ro, T., and Öğmen, H. (2004). 'A comparison of masking by visual and transcranial magnetic stimulation: implications for the study of conscious and unconscious visual processing'. *Consciousness and Cognition*, 13.

Di Lollo, V., Enns, J. T., and Rensink, R. A. (2000). 'Competition for consciousness among visual events: the psychophysics of reentrant visual processes'. *Journal of Experimental Psychology: General*, 129.

Lamme, V. A. F., Zipser, K., and Spekreijse, H. (2002). Masking interrupts figure–ground signals in V1. *Journal of Cognitive Neuroscience*, 14.

VanRullen, R. and Thorpe, S. J. (2001). The time course of visual processing: from early perception to decision making. *Journal of Cognitive Neuroscience*, 13.

materialism See PHYSICALISM

meditation, neurocognitive approaches It is not easy to define meditation, or demonstrate how meditative states contribute to the study of consciousness, in part because the term 'meditation' encompasses many activities and in part because of the paucity of empirical data currently available in this field. Thus, this entry remains largely programmatic (for details see Lutz et al. 2006).

In order to narrow the explanandum to a more tractable scope, this article uses Buddhist contemplative traditions as a framework. The reason, in brief, is that unlike many contemplative traditions, Buddhist traditions tend to offer extensive, precisely descriptive, and highly detailed theories about their practices in a manner that lends itself readily to appropriation into a neuroscientific context.

1. Meditation in the Buddhist tradition
2. Transforming the mind and neuroplasticity
3. Interaction between mind and body
4. Neural counterpart of subjectivity

1. Meditation in the Buddhist tradition

Despite the variety of contemplative practices encompassed by the term meditation within Buddhism, most Buddhist traditions use a term for meditation that correlates with the Sanskrit term *bhāvanā*, literally, 'causing to become'. In Tibetan traditions, the usual translation for *bhāvanā* is *gôm (sgom)*, which roughly means 'to become habituated to' or 'to become familiar with'. These Buddhist traditions share two axioms articulated in highly detailed scholastic texts such as the *Abhidharma*: (1) that a central goal of Buddhist practice is the elimination of suffering, where 'suffering' coarsely refers to the negative affects associated with physical pain, ageing, neurosis, or social stress; and (2) that any effective method to eliminate suffering must involve changes in one's cognitive and emotional states, in particular one's self-centred habits (Gethin 1998). *Focused attention meditation* (FA), the most commonly practised style of meditation, consists of focusing or stabilizing concentration on an object such as the breath, so as to develops skills regulative of attention: FA meditation aims at calming the mind, reducing distractions and developing a monitoring state, attentive moment by moment to anything that occurs in experience. As FA advances, the well-developed monitoring skill becomes the main point of transition into *open monitoring* (OM) practice, often called *Vipaśyanā* or mindfulness meditation. OM practice consists of remaining only in the monitoring state without focusing on any explicit object. This practice aims to gain greater access to the rich features of each experience, such as the degree of phenomenal intensity, the emotional tone, and the active cognitive schema, like one's autobiographical self. FA and OM practices are traditionally paired with practices such as compassion and loving-kindness meditations, whose purpose is to cultivate altruistic behaviours and positive affect and to counteract self-centered tendencies. The Buddhist project to eliminate suffering is thus intrinsically embodied in an explicit effort to directly examine, understand, and transform one's mind through meditative training.

The neuroscientific study of advanced practitioners of the aforementioned styles of meditation may contribute to the study of consciousness through, among others, three methodological hypotheses: (1) Advanced practitioners can generate new data that would not exist without sustained mental training. These data encompass either meditative states or traits induced by meditation that might enlighten us about some characteristics of consciousness. (2) Advanced practitioners can robustly reproduce specific features in experience as cultivated in a given meditative practice. This reproducibility makes those features scientifically tractable. (3) Advanced practitioners provide more refined first-person descriptions of their experiences than naive subjects. Thus, the neurophysiological counterpart of these first-person accounts can be defined, identified, and interpreted more easily by the experimentalist. These hypotheses appear particularly relevant in relation to three neuroscientific agendas: neuroplasticity, the interaction of mind and body, and the possibility of neural counterparts to subjective experience.

2. Transforming the mind and neuroplasticity

In the Buddhist tradition, emotions, attention, and introspection are viewed as ongoing and labile processes to be understood and studied as skills that can be trained, similar to other human domains like music, mathematics, or sports. As a result, the methods employed by Buddhist contemplative practices resonate with widely accepted developmental models of basic cognitive processes. This basic stance also reflects another well-documented theory: namely, that experience changes the brain, a process known as neuroplasticity. The current findings on neuroplasticity raise the possibility that training that is specifically designed to cultivate specific mental traits such as compassion will produce specific alterations in brain function and structure. In one study (Lutz et al. 2004), we showed that, in comparison to controls, the ratio of fast-frequency *electroencephalogram (EEG) activity (25–42 Hz) to slow oscillatory activity (4–13 Hz) is initially higher on average across electrodes in the resting baseline before meditation for advanced practitioners. During objectless compassion meditation, this difference increases sharply over medial frontoparietal electrodes and remains higher than the initial baseline in the post-meditative baseline. In another study, we showed using performance in an *attentional blink task and scalp-recorded brain potentials, that three months of intensive training in FA and OP practices enhanced the efficient deployment of limited attentional brain resources (Slagter et al. 2007). Finally, Brefczynski-Lewis et al. and Lazar et al. respectively assessed meditation-related functional and structural changes using magnetic resonance imaging (MRI). The functional difference found during FA practice between expert and novice meditators supports the idea that, after FA meditation training, minimal effort is necessary to sustain attentional focus (Brefczynski-Lewis et al. 2007). Cortical brain regions associated with attention, interoceptive, and sensory processing were found to be thicker for a group of mid-range practitioners than for matched controls (Lazar et al. 2006). These changes across group and time support the view that meditative practice induces short-term and possibly long-term functional and structural changes in brain processes, in particular attention processes.

3. Interaction between mind and body

Although there are many popular claims about the health benefits of meditation and contemplative practice, relatively little is reliably known about this potentially crucial issue. It is established that there is bidirectional communication between the brain and peripheral biological systems, and that this communication proceeds along three basic routes: the autonomic nervous system, the endocrine system, and the immune system. Some conditions of the peripheral biological systems may be potentially affected by meditative practices because those conditions—such as an illness—are susceptible to modulation by the autonomic, endocrine, and/or immune pathways involved in brain–periphery communication. Davidson et al. examined this possibility on individuals randomly assigned to a secularized, 8-week course in meditation called the Mindfulness Based Stress Reduction programme (Kabat-Zinn et al. 1985) or a waiting-list control group. This programme is routinely used in a clinical environment as a complementary treatment to a variety of illnesses such as depression, chronic pain, or anxiety (Kabat-Zinn et al. 1985). After this training, meditators exhibited a significantly greater antibody response to the influenza vaccine than controls. The individual differences in patterns of prefrontal brain activity, previously found to be associated with affective style and well-being, were also positively associated with differences in antibody response to the influenza vaccine (Davidson et al. 2003).

4. Neural counterpart of subjectivity

As stated above, meditation training may develop *introspective skill. Thus, the neurophysiological counterpart of the first-person accounts from advanced practitioners may be identified more easily by the experimentalist. Furthermore, various meditative practices induce a wide variety of *altered states of consciousness. Some forms of Buddhist objectless meditation, for example, attempt to de-emphasize the explicit sense of narrative or autobiographical self, that encompasses categorical or moral judgement, emotions, anticipation of the future, and recollections of the past, so as to further enhance access to a minimal subjective sense of 'I-ness' in experience, or ipseity (for details see Lutz et al. 2006). The collaboration with long-term Buddhist practitioners is thus of great potential interest in the study of the physical correlates of subjectivity or the self.

Finally, while this discussion has focused largely on long-term Buddhist practitioners, it is crucial to note the importance of future research on novices or on practices from other contemplative traditions. Overall the neuroscientific study of contemplative practices is still in its infancy, but the early findings promise both to reveal the mechanisms by which such training may exert its beneficial effects on physical health and underscore the plasticity of the brain circuits that underlie complex mental functions and consciousness.

ANTOINE LUTZ

Brefczynski-Lewis J. A., Lutz, A., Schaefer, H. S., Levinson, D. B., and Davidson, R. J. (2007). Neural correlates of attentional expertise in long-term meditation practitioners. *Proceedings of the National Academy of Sciences of the USA*, 104.

Davidson, R. J., Kabat-Zinn, J., Schumacher, J. et al. (2003). Alterations in brain and immune function produced by mindfulness meditation. *Psychosomatic Medicine*, 65.

Gethin, R. (1998). *The Foundations of Buddhism*.

Kabat-Zinn, J., Lipworth, L., and Burney, R. (1985). 'The clinical use of mindfulness meditation for the self-regulation of chronic pain'. *Journal of Behavioural Medicine*, 8.

Lazar, S. W., Kerr, C. E., Wasserman, R. H., Gray, J. R. et al. (2005). 'Meditation experience is associated with increased cortical thickness'. *NeuroReport*, 16.

Lutz, A., Greischar, L. L., Rawlings, N. B., Ricard, M., and Davidson, R. J. (2004). 'Long-term meditators self-induce high-amplitude gamma synchrony during mental practice'. *Proceedings of the National Academy of Sciences of the USA*, 101.

——, Dunne, J. D., and Davidson, R. J. (2006). 'Meditation and the neuroscience of consciousness: an introduction'. In Zelazo, P. et al. (ed.) *Cambridge Handbook of Consciousness*.

Slagter, H. A., Lutz, A., Greischar, L. L. et al. (2007). 'Mental training affects use of limited brain resources'. *PLoS Biology*, 5

memory, consciousness and The phenomenon of *consciousness is often intertwined with the capacity for memory. With the exception of the split instant of the present and occasional contemplation of the future, consciousness is filled with memory. And even awareness of the present and consideration of the future is coloured by memory. We parse the external world with knowledge structures formed in the past and imagine the future in part based on previous episodes. Thus, a consideration of how consciousness is supported by the brain should include a consideration of how memory is supported by the brain. Yet the mammalian *brain contains several different *memory systems and supports many different examples of memory. This article provides an overview of memory and the brain and considers its relationship to consciousness.

1. Memory and the brain
2. The hippocampal memory system
3. Hippocampus-dependent memory and conscious recollection
4. Work with experimental animals
5. Insights for the study of consciousness

1. Memory and the brain

A general distinction can be made between short-term memory that relies on sustained neural activity and long-term memory that depends on structural changes in the brain. Within short-term memory, a further distinction can be made between an active maintenance of neural activity and a passive persistence of activity. The passive and fleeting visual and auditory after-images of the present, usually referred to as sensory memory, are likely supported by the same sensory cortices that initially participated in the perception of the stimuli (see MEMORY, VISUAL SHORT TERM). Working memory, the ability to actively maintain information in consciousness through rehearsal or elaboration, depends heavily on the prefrontal cortex and on other, posterior cortical areas (see FRONTAL CORTEX and WORKING MEMORY; Muller and Knight 2006). Both working memory and sensory memory are thought to be available to consciousness.

Long-term memory, memory that outlasts the capacity of either sensory memory or working memory and depends on structural changes relating to synaptic plasticity and membrane excitability, can be divided into a number of brain systems (see MEMORY SYSTEMS, NEURAL BASIS OF). Most memory systems of the brain support examples of memory that occur outside the scope of consciousness, such as classical conditioning of reflexive motor responses (see CONDITIONING), cognitive skill learning (see ARTIFICIAL GRAMMAR LEARNING), perceptual *learning, motor skill learning, habit learning, and *priming. The capacity for conscious recollection is supported by a network of structures that includes the hippocampus and adjacent cortical areas. This network of structures (referred to here as the hippocampal memory system) is the only memory system in which stored information can be subsequently brought back to mind. In other systems, memory is expressed through a variety of behaviours other than explicit report (see KNOWLEDGE, EXPLICIT VS IMPLICIT; LEARNING, EXPLICIT VS IMPLICIT).

2. The hippocampal memory system

The hippocampus is a three-layered cortical structure that includes areas CA1, CA3, the subiculum, and the dentate gyrus (see Amaral and Witter 2004 for a detailed review). The hippocampus receives most of its cortical input from, and sends most of its cortical output to, the adjacent parahippocampal region, which is composed of the entorhinal, perirhinal, and parahippocampal cortices. The parahippocampal region receives inputs from, and sends outputs to, widespread unimodal and polymodal cortical areas. Thus, the anatomy of the hippocampal memory system can be thought of as a confluence of high-level information in which cortical information is funnelled to the hippocampus via the parahippocampal region. Further, the output of hippocampal processing is directed back to widespread areas of the cerebral cortex. It is presumably due to its bidirectional interactions with so many cortical areas that the hippocampus draws its influence over conscious recollection.

In humans, damage to the hippocampus and parahippocampal region produces *amnesia, a neurological disorder characterized by profound forgetfulness. Amnesia typically involves an impaired or absent ability to acquire new memory such as information about facts and events (anterograde amnesia) and a partial loss of information learned prior to the onset of amnesia (retrograde amnesia). In particular, memories acquired immediately prior to onset are most likely to be lost whereas memories acquired long before the onset of amnesia are likely to be spared. Thus, there is a time-limited aspect to retrograde amnesia, such that personal memories and world knowledge acquired in childhood are typically intact. In cases in which damage is restricted to the hippocampus and parahippocampal region, amnesic patients typically show normal performance on a broad range of non-conscious memory tasks and perform normally on tests of non-memory abilities. In addition, amnesic patients are typically normal in their capacities for short-term and working memory. That is, outside their impairment in recollection of newly acquired memories and memories obtained shortly before becoming amnesic, these patients do not have any obvious abnormality in their experience of consciousness. Thus, the brain system crucial for conscious recollection appears to be unnecessary for consciousness itself.

3. Hippocampus-dependent memory and conscious recollection

Although there is general agreement that the hippocampal memory system supports conscious recollection of facts and events, the exact nature of the relationship between hippocampus-dependent memory and awareness of the retrieved information is unclear. One question concerns the correspondence between a memory's dependence on the hippocampus and its availability to awareness. That is, are all hippocampus-dependent memories available to awareness? One possibility is that the experience of conscious recollection is an obligatory feature of memories that are stored and retrieved via the hippocampal system. That is, the brain networks involved in successful conscious recollection may be identical to the brain networks involved in successful hippocampus-dependent memory, and conscious recollection may be a defining feature of hippocampus-dependent memory. Another possibility is that awareness of retrieved information is simply a frequent correlate of hippocampus-dependent memory. By this view, the networks involved in conscious recollection may overlap with the networks involved in retrieving hippocampus-dependent memory but may not be identical. If so, it would be possible for hippocampus-dependent memories to be retrieved but not enter consciousness. This possibility is difficult to test for several reasons. It is sometimes difficult to distinguish between weak conscious memory and non-conscious memory. In addition, the memory would have to be assessed in some way other than by verbal report (or other explicit means). Also, one would need to know that the retrieved information was supported by the hippocampal memory system and not by the many other brain systems that ordinarily support non-conscious memory (see CONTEXTUAL CUEING and Manns and Squire 2001 for further discussion).

A second question concerns how to best understand the phenomenon of conscious recollection in those memories that are available to awareness. There are at least two general ways to understand the relationship. Awareness of the retrieved information may be part and parcel of the memory. Recollection is the memory and vice versa. This strongest version of the relationship would parallel the argument that awareness is a defining feature of hippocampus-dependent memory. Alternatively, the experience of conscious recollection may be an *emergent property of the successful retrieval of hippocampus-dependent memory. That is, the experience of conscious recollection may be a product of hippocampal activity and may reflect post-retrieval processing rather than retrieval itself.

Regardless of whether conscious recollection is a defining feature or a frequent correlate of hippocampus-dependent memory, there is a strong connection between the workings of the hippocampal memory system and the capacity to bring retrieved information into consciousness. Thus, understanding the operating characteristics and functional circuitry of the hippocampal memory system may help in understanding the neurobiology of consciousness. Several ideas have been put forward regarding the characterization of hippocampus-dependent memory in addition to its availability to awareness. For example, memories dependent on the hippocampus have been characterized by rapid formation, complex associative properties, and flexible expression (Eichenbaum and Cohen 2001).

4. Work with experimental animals

Effort in this direction has been provided with much of its momentum by research with experimental animals. The difficulty of assessing consciousness in experimental animals (see entries under ANIMAL CONSCIOUSNESS) has necessitated that researchers look to other memory functions supported by the hippocampal memory system that are common to animals and humans. This approach has had several benefits for the understanding of conscious recollection in humans. First, much greater neurobiological detail and experimental control is available in work with experimental animals. Second, the findings with experimental animals are very much relevant to human memory due to the strong evolutionary conservation of the hippocampal memory system (Manns and Eichenbaum 2006). Third, the push to identify the conserved and fundamental operating characteristics of hippocampus-dependent memory has offered insights towards a deconstruction of the phenomenon of conscious recollection. These studies have shown that memories that are subject to conscious recollection in humans, and are dependent on the hippocampus in animals and humans, have three fundamental features (Eichenbaum 2004). They involve memory for items in the context they were experienced, the ability to recall the flow of events in experiences, and the capacity to link memories that share common events. It is reasonable to think of these abilities as the basic primitive elements of conscious recollection.

Work in both humans and experimental animals has led to the view that the hippocampus accomplishes these aspects of memory processing as a central node in a distributed and hierarchical cortical network (McClelland et al. 1995). Information from many cortical areas converges on the hippocampus, allowing a small number of rapid cellular changes in the hippocampus to create complex memories containing disparate types of information. Subsequent cues trigger reactivation of memory by bringing back to mind these disparate pieces of information via their common connections with the hippocampal memory system. Either through rehearsal or spontaneous reactivation, the separate cortical areas eventually become interconnected in a way that does not depend on the hippocampus. This process is termed *consolidation* and is thought to explain the time-limited aspect of retrograde amnesia (Squire et al. 2001). The idea that rapid nodal changes in the hippocampus temporarily bind high-level cortical areas is consistent with the description of hippocampus-dependent memory as being rapid, associative, and flexibly expressed.

5. Insights for the study of consciousness

The study of conscious recollection and the hippocampal memory system offers several insights into the study of consciousness. Several issues have been considered in the study of memory that might be relevant to the study of consciousness.

A first point is that the primitive elements of conscious recollection outlined above are all present in experimental animals. The anatomy of the hippocampal memory system is relatively conserved across the mammalian taxon, and a good deal of correspondence has been observed between the operating characteristics of hippocampus-dependent memory in humans and experimental animals (Squire 1992). Thus, even if experimental animals do not experience a 'true' conscious recollection, it is likely that they experience an evolutionary precursor in the form of the same basic information-processing mechanisms that underlie conscious recollection in humans. By extension, animals may experience a precursor to consciousness even if they do not experience the same phenomenon as human consciousness.

A second point is that conscious recollection is thought to be supported by a reactivation of distributed cortical regions enabled by their common connection with the hippocampal memory system. It is likely that consciousness also involves widely distributed cortical networks, but it is unclear whether the dependence of conscious recollection on a central node necessarily means that consciousness would also depend on a central node to bind these distributed cortical areas. Indeed, memories learned long ago often no longer depend on the hippocampus, and thus consciousness may result from activation of a more interconnected cortical network. Thus, it is possible that the network important for consciousness could be either hierarchical with at least one central node or more uniformly interconnected. Several structures that enjoy widespread cortical connections, such as the thalamus and claustrum, have been suggested to play a central role in the network supporting consciousness (Crick and Koch 2005), but this work is in its infancy.

A third point is that memory is usually considered to involve encoding, storage, and retrieval. Encoding is the process by which neural activity leads to structural changes in the hippocampal memory system. Storage is often thought of as the maintenance of these structural changes, and retrieval is the activation of the circuit created by these structural changes. It is generally the case that only attended information (information brought into consciousness) holds the possibility for being encoded (but see SUBLIMINAL TAPES), and that the retrieval of hippocampus-dependent memory is usually available to conscious recollection. Although one is generally unaware of the structural changes that bridge encoding and retrieval, conscious recollection would not be possible without these changes. Thus, although a memory depends on both structural changes and activation of the new circuitry created by these changes, we are aware of only the activation. The extension of this idea to consciousness in general suggests that consciousness may be experienced only during activation of cortical networks but that the physical structure of these networks must be considered an essential mechanism of consciousness as well.

JOSEPH R. MANNS AND HOWARD EICHENBAUM

Amaral, D. G. and Witter, M. P. (2004). 'Hippocampal formation'. In Paxinos, G. (ed.) *The Rat Nervous System*, 3rd edn.

Crick, F. C. and Koch, C. (2005). 'What is the function of the claustrum?' *Philosophical Transactions of the Royal Society of London Series B: Biological Sciences*, 360.

Eichenbaum, H. (2004). 'Hippocampus: cognitive processes and neural representations that underlie declarative memory'. *Neuron*, 44.

—— and Cohen, N. J. (2001). *From Conditioning to Conscious Recollection: Memory Systems of the Brain.*

Manns, J. R. and Eichenbaum, H. (2006). 'Evolution of the hippocampus'. In Krubitzer, L. and Kaas, J. (eds) *Evolution of Nervous Systems: The Evolution of Nervous Systems in Mammals*, Vol. 3.

—— and Squire, L. R. (2001). 'Perceptual learning, awareness, and the hippocampus'. *Hippocampus*, 11.

McClelland, J. L., McNaughton, B. L., and O'Reilly, R. C. (1995). 'Why there are complementary learning systems in the hippocampus and neocortex: insights from the successes and failures of connectionist models of learning and memory'. *Psychological Reviews*, 102.

Muller, N. G. and Knight, R. T. (2006). 'The functional neuroanatomy of working memory: contributions of human brain lesion studies'. *Neuroscience*, 139.

Squire, L. R. (1992). 'Memory and the hippocampus: a synthesis from findings with rats, monkeys, and humans'. *Psychological Reviews*, 99.

——, Clark, R. E., and Knowlton, B. J. (2001). 'Retrograde amnesia'. *Hippocampus*, 11.

memory, distortions of Human memory is amazing in its ability to capture important elements of the world. It can hold people, places, events, facts, and emotions, often for decades. And yet, it is far from indelible. The same processing short cuts that allow memory to work efficiently without constantly taking over consciousness sometimes lead to memory errors and distortions (see Schacter 2001). Because attention is a limited resource, many details of the events we experience and of our surroundings are never fully encoded—that is, they never make it into memory at all. This leaves gaps in our memory that we are largely unaware of, and these gaps make us susceptible to various types of memory errors.

No matter how appealing the metaphors, remembering is not like finding a book in a library, opening it, and reading the correct passage, or like putting in a DVD and selecting the right chapter. Instead, remembering is a reconstructive process (Loftus 1979/1996). Each time we remember a complex event, we reconstruct the event from various partial traces. Some traces include unique details of the event. Others include existing memory schemas and assumptions and perhaps details from other similar events.

Reliance on existing memory schemas can lead to intrusions of other similar ('schema consistent') events or ideas. One way that researchers study this phenomenon is by exposing subjects to lists of words that tap into a particular schema, but do not include the most obvious schema-relevant word (Roediger and McDermott 1996). For example, a list might include the words 'bed', 'nap', 'pillow', and 'tired', but not the word 'sleep'. This missing word is called the *critical lure* because subjects are lured, through the content of the list, into believing that this word was part of the list. When later presented with a memory task, subjects in these studies are often as likely to remember the critical lure ('sleep') as they are to remember many of the words that were actually part of the original list. That is, they reliably, but falsely, remember that the critical lure was part of the original list. This presumably happens because subjects are relying on the schema rather than just their specific memories at retrieval.

Another way that memory distortion is studied is through the use of *post-event information*, or information that is supplied to a person after some critical event is over. Post-event information, including leading questions and memories shared by co-witnesses, can serve to fill in gaps at memory retrieval. In laboratory studies of these phenomena, subjects witness a complex, sometimes even violent, simulated event like a car accident or robbery (usually via staged slide-show or video). Then a subset of subjects receives misleading information about the event in the form of leading questions (in which details as small as the article preceding a key word are potentially important), information from co-witnesses, or other post-event information. Additional subjects receive accurate information about the original event, and control subjects receive no additional information. Then, after a delay, the memories of misled, non-misled, and control subjects are tested for the details of the original witnessed event. The extent to which misled subjects' memories are changed in light of the misleading information is assessed. These studies have shown that memory alterations after misleading information, called the *misinformation effect*, can be substantial. In various studies, stop signs have been remembered as give-way signs and screwdrivers as hammers, and broken glass, tape recorders, and even barns have been remembered as parts of events in which they did not exist at all (Loftus 2004).

It is important to note that these alterations of memory occur in the absence of any awareness on the part of the subjects. In fact, they occur because the subjects are unaware that they have been exposed to contradictory information. These memory distortions are called *source-monitoring errors*, because subjects misjudge the source of the critical information at test, attributing it to the original event rather than to the misleading post-event information. Source-monitoring errors also occur when people confuse imagined events or intentions with experienced events. For example, an individual might have the intention to run a number of errands on her way home and imagine completing each errand in turn. She might stop at the grocery store and the drug store but completely forget the dry cleaner. When she arrives at home, she may well confuse her imagined trip to the dry cleaner with reality and think that she has completed her errands (until she needs that missing jacket).

In addition to altering existing memories, researchers have been able to implant wholly false memories into people's minds (e.g. Loftus and Pickrell 1995). In these studies, subjects are told that a particular event happened to them, usually as children. This information is said to have come from an authoritative source—the subjects' parents, a powerful computer program, or even photographic evidence—but in fact the information has been invented by the researchers. In response to these memory suggestions, some subjects produce false beliefs and memories. The false memories that have been produced in these studies include amusing but implausible events like riding in a hot air balloon as a child, bizarre events like spilling punch on the bride's parents at a family wedding, potentially traumatic events like getting lost in a shopping mall, and painful events like getting one's finger caught in a mousetrap.

In the case of the misinformation effect, subjects appear to be completely unaware that they have been affected by the misinformation. There is likewise evidence that many subjects in false memory studies are unaware of the effect of the false memory manipulations on their memories, because they are unaware any manipulation has occurred. We know this, in part, because when subjects are asked about the study when it is over, they often report that they believed that the information really did come from their parents or the powerful computer. And sometimes they don't even remember what the false information was.

Once existing memories are altered or new false memories are formed, they are difficult, if not impossible, to distinguish from accurate memories. Distorted and false memories can be detailed, complex, confidently held, and even emotional for those who have them. Recent studies have shown that false memories can also have genuine consequences for subjects. For example, subjects in one study who came to believe that they got sick as children after eating strawberry ice cream reported liking strawberry ice cream less and wanting to eat strawberry ice cream less than those without this false memory (Bernstein et al. 2005).

Some populations have been shown to be more vulnerable to memory distortion than others. In particular, young children may be particularly susceptible to suggestive techniques (Bruck and Ceci 2004). Among adults, individuals who have more active imaginations or who are more prone to lapses in attention may be more susceptible. But lacking these characteristics does not, unfortunately, guarantee memory accuracy. In fact, no known characteristic provides complete immunity to memory distortion, or even to wholly false memories. In fact, some memory distortion is almost certainly present in all human minds.

CARA LANEY AND ELIZABETH F. LOFTUS

Bernstein, D. M., Laney, C., Morris, E. K. and Loftus, E. F. (2005). 'False beliefs about fattening foods can have healthy consequences.' *Proceedings of the National Academy of Sciences of the USA*, 102.

Bruck, M. and Ceci, S. J. (2004). 'Forensic developmental psychology: unveiling four common misconceptions.' *Current Directions in Psychological Science*, 13.

Loftus, E. F. (1979/1996). *Eyewitness Testimony*.

—— (2004). 'Memories of things unseen'. *Current Directions in Psychological Science*, 13.

—— and Pickrell, J. E. (1995). 'The formation of false memories.' *Psychiatric Annals*, 25.

Roediger, H. L., III, and McDermott, K. B. (1996). 'Creating false memories: Remembering words not presented in lists.' *Journal of Experimental Psychology: Learning, Memory, and Cognition*, 21.

Schacter, D. L. (2001). *The Seven Sins of Memory: How the Mind Forgets and Remembers*.

memory, iconic The term 'iconic memory' was introduced by Neisser (1967) and the concept was widely accepted in the 1960s and 1970s. It is closely related to *persistence*.

1. Persistence and iconic memory
2. The specious present
3. Access consciousness
4. The capacity of phenomenal consciousness

1. Persistence and iconic memory

It was a dark and stormy night. As I gazed from my window at an invisible countryside, it was suddenly lit up by a bolt of lightning, and I could briefly see every hill, even every tree. A bolt of lightning lasts for only 50 microseconds, but the visual experiences it evokes last much longer than that. So my visual experience of the countryside around my house continued for some time after the physical offset of the visual stimulus which generated that experience; there was a persistence of vision.

Here is a different scenario: you are looking at a computer screen. I present you with a row of eight letters on that screen for a brief time—say, 50 ms—and then very soon after those letters vanish you see a small arrow on the screen pointing to one of the locations that had contained a letter. Your task is to report just the letter that had been presented in that location (hence this is known as a *partial-report task*). You can do this easily. So information about the location and the identity of each of the eight letters you had seen continues to be available to you for some time after the physical offset of the visual stimulus that was the letter row—again, a persistence of vision.

In both examples, the persistence of vision is short-lived. A second or so after the lightning bolt, I no longer had any phenomenal experience of the landscape—the view through my window had faded to black. And if the arrow specifying the desired letter location is not presented until a second or more after the row of letters has been turned off, you will no longer be able to reliably report what letter had occupied that position in the display.

These examples are similar enough for it to be an attractive idea that it is the same phenomenon that is occurring in the two situations, and indeed precisely that view was uniformly held at one time: the phenomenon was called *iconic memory* (by Neisser 1967). After the offset of the lightning, there exists for some time a fading iconic memory of the countryside; after the offset of the computer display, there exists for some time a fading iconic memory of the letters it had contained. That was the idea, widely accepted in the 1960s and 1970s.

And yet there is a very clear distinction between these two kinds of persistence. In the first situation, what briefly persists is a conscious visual experience. In the second situation, what briefly persists is information about some visual property of the items in the display—in the example I give, information about where each item was located in the display. So we might want to distinguish at least in principle between the two situations by giving different terms to the two persistences, calling the first one *visible persistence* and the second one *informational persistence* (Coltheart 1980). Is this in-principle distinction of any significance? Or are these two terms just both synonymous with the term 'iconic memory'?

There are various task which allow one to transfer the lightning experience to the laboratory (see Coltheart 1980 for a list of these).One is the temporal integration task, as illustrated in Fig. M2. Frame 1 is briefly presented to the subject (for, say, 20 ms), there is then a blank screen for some period controlled by the experimenter (the inter-stimulus interval, ISI), and then frame 2 is briefly presented in the same position as was occupied by frame 1. The observer's task is to report at which of the 25 possible positions no dot had been presented. This task is very easy if the frames are presented simultaneously (i.e. superimposed)—the location of the one missing dot is glaringly obvious. But it is just as easy if the frames are presented sequentially, provided that the ISI is small—say 50 ms—because with a small ISI the frames are not experienced as having occurred sequentially. Instead, they are experienced as a single display, containing 24 dots plus a glaringly obvious gap. The reason that they are seen as a single display is, of course, because frame 1 has remained visible after its offset, and the visible persistence of frame 1 has been phenomenally integrated with the visual presentation of frame 2. If the ISI is longer, though still short—say 200 ms—the task is completely impossible; this is because the visible persistence of frame 1 has ended before frame 2 is presented.

At much longer ISIs something very interesting happens (Brockmole et al. 2002): performance *improves* as ISI increases from 500 ms to 1500 ms where it stabilizes at a level (68% correct) that is not much different from the performance when ISI is zero (79%). Level of performance remains around 68% as ISI is increased across the range 1500 ms to 5000 ms. The subjects in this study were instructed that a good strategy for them to use would be to imagine the frame 1 dots still being present after they disappeared. This they could do, but the generation of the visual image is clearly a very slow and effortful process taking as long as 1500 ms to complete. However, if a visual image of frame 1 is available when frame 2 is presented, an integration of this image with the percept of frame 2 produces a representation that allows the missing-dot task to be performed well. These effortfully generated visual images (though they are visible) are not visible persistence as defined here, and they are not visual after-images.

So one can measure the duration of visible persistence simply by determining the minimum ISI at which the subject can no longer perform the temporal integration task at an above-chance level; just as one can measure the duration of informational persistence by determining the minimum delay of the arrow cue at which the subject can no longer report the cued letter at an above-chance level.

If these two tasks really are measuring the same phenomenon, iconic memory, then the tasks will yield compatible results when any particular stimulus parameter is varied. One such parameter is stimulus duration. What effect, if any, does varying stimulus duration have on the duration of the visual persistence in these two tasks? Intuition suggests that the longer a stimulus lasts, the more powerful its effects should be, and so the longer-lasting its persistence should be. But just the opposite is true with respect to visible persistence: studies measuring the duration of visible persistence with the temporal integration task (and other tasks) have repeatedly found that the longer the duration of a visual stimulus is, the shorter-lasting is the visible persistence it generates, measured from the offset of the stimulus. Critically, this is not so for informational persistence: studies measuring the duration of informational persistence with the partial report task have generally found that this duration is independent of stimulus duration. This dissociation of effects is clear evidence that visible persistence and informational persistence are different phenomena.

A dissociation is also observed when one varies stimulus brightness rather than stimulus duration: the brighter the stimulus, the *shorter* its visible persistence after stimulus offset (again, the counter-intuitive result) whereas the duration of the informational persistence generated by a visual stimulus is independent of how bright the stimulus was (again, a dissociation).

It is important, by the way, to appreciate that neither of these persistences has anything to do with positive or negative retinal after-images. The stimuli used in these kinds of experiments are not bright enough to generate such after-images, and there are other major differences between after-images and these two kinds of persistence (di Lollo and Hogben 1988)

So the idea that visible persistence and informational persistence are two sides of the same coin—two manifestations of a single entity, iconic memory—must be abandoned. Visible persistence and informational persistence are distinct cognitive entities with different properties. One critical difference is that observers are consciously aware of visible persistence when it is present, but are not consciously aware of informational persistence when it is present. Visible persistence (as measured in the temporal integration task) has a phenomenology; informational persistence (as measured in the partial-report task) does not.

As mentioned above, in the early days of the concept of iconic memory, it was not appreciated that one must distinguish between visible persistence and informational persistence; so both were called 'iconic memory'. This led to much confusion. For example, suppose one asked the question: 'Is iconic memory conscious, i.e. are people aware of its contents?' If one treats both visible persistence and informational persistence as iconic memory, the answer to this question is yes and no, because visible persistence is a conscious phenomenon—it is what you are aware of still seeing after a visual display is turned off—whereas informational persistence is not.

This confusion is not confined solely to the early days of the concept of iconic memory. It can still be found in much current work. For example, Koch (2004:202) treats visible persistence and informational persistence as the same thing, calling both 'iconic memory', and makes the following statement: 'The duration of iconic memory depends not so much on the time of image *offset* as on the time of image *onset*.' This statement is true for visible persistence, but false for informational persistence. The longer the duration of a stimulus, the shorter the duration of the visible persistence after its offset (see Coltheart 1980 for examples of such studies). But the duration of the informational persistence present after a stimulus goes off is independent of the duration of the stimulus (Yeomans and Irwin 1985). This conflation of visible persistence with informational persistence vitiates Koch's discussion of the relationship of iconic memory to consciousness.

2. The specious present

The reason that long stimuli have no visible persistence if this is measured from stimulus offset is that visible persistence is triggered by the onset of a visual stimulus; its lifetime begins then, and since that lifetime is fixed—it is the duration of the 'specious present' of a visual stimulus—if stimulus duration exceeds that lifetime, visible persistence will terminate earlier than does the stimulus. With very brief stimuli the specious present of the stimulus lasts much longer than its physical presence. One can only perform the temporal integration task when the two sets of dots occupy the same 'instant' of the specious present (unless one uses visual image generation as described above; only possible at relatively long ISIs).

3. Access consciousness

To say that the contents of the form of memory we use to perform the cued-letter task—that is, the contents of informational persistence—are not available to consciousness is to ignore the distinction proposed by Block (1995) between phenomenal consciousness and *access consciousness. Visual information is available to access consciousness if it is available to mental processes that guide the organism's behaviour, and that is clearly so for the information in informational persistence: the organism can apply spatial cues to such information, can translate such information from its visual form to its name, and can then utter that name. Thus the contents of informational persistence are not phenomenally conscious but are access conscious. The contents of visible persistence are conscious in both senses.

4. The capacity of phenomenal consciousness

If the contents of visible persistence are available to phenomenal consciousness, then studies of visible persistence are relevant to questions about the capacity of such consciousness. One has the impression that the lightning bolt has illuminated the entire countryside, suggesting that the capacity of phenomenal consciousness is very large; but this impression may be illusory. It might, for example, be created by some kind of constructive process using part of the scene to create a complete scene in consciousness. How could this be investigated? Suppose the observer were quizzed about some region of the countryside immediately after the bolt of lightning; would less than perfect performance here indicate limitations on the capacity of phenomenal consciousness? Not at all; because the processes of understanding the words expressing the quiz, and then applying these instructions to the relevant part of the scene, would take some hundreds of milliseconds, during which the contents of visible persistence will be decaying. Such considerations have led to the experimental technique called *change detection* (Simons and Rensink 2005): subjects see a brief presentation of a complex scene, then a brief blank display, then another brief presentation of the complex scene in which just one detail has changed (e.g. a person has been deleted from the scene). The task is very simple: did anything change? Observers are very poor at detecting such changes (see CHANGE BLINDNESS). Does that mean that many details are absent from the stored conscious representation of the first scene, and thus that the capacity of phenomenal consciousness is limited? Unfortunately not, because detection failures might occur not because of limitations in the representation of the first scene but limitations of the obviously quite complex process by which the two scenes are compared to detect differences between them. The change detection technique is a powerful addition to the armoury of methods for studying visible persistence and phenomenal consciousness but we don't know yet what it will tell us about the *capacity-of-consciousness issue.

Here again the distinction between visible persistence and informational persistence is important, because questions about the capacity of informational persistence (which is normally argued to be very high) are not relevant to questions about the capacity of phenomenal consciousness (since we are not phenomenally conscious of informational persistence).

And, finally: given that this distinction is now generally accepted in vision science, where does that leave the term 'iconic memory'? It is incoherent to use this term to refer both to visible persistence and to informational persistence, as was done by the originator of the term (Neisser 1967) and by others since. That seems a very good reason for abandoning the term altogether.

MAX COLTHEART

Averbach, E. and Coriell, H. S. (1961). 'Short-term memory in vision'. *Bell Systems Technical Journal*, 40.

Block, N. (1995). 'On a confusion about the function of consciousness'. *Behavioral and Brain Sciences*, 18.

Brockmole, J. R., Wang, F. and Irwin, D. E. (2002). 'Temporal integration between visual images and visual percepts'. *Journal of Experimental Psychology: Human Perception and Performance*, 28.

Coltheart, M. (1972). 'Visual information-processing'. In Dodwell, P. C. (ed.) *New Horizons in Psychology*, II.

—— (1978). 'Contemporary models of the cognitive processes, I: iconic storage and visual masking'. In Hamilton, V. and Vernon, M. D. (eds) *The Development of Cognitive Processes*.

—— (1980). 'Iconic memory and visible persistence'. *Perception and Psychophysics*, 27.

—— (1980). 'Persistences of vision'. *Philosophical Transactions of the Royal Society, Series B: Biological Sciences*, 290.

—— (1983). 'Iconic memory'. *Philosophical Transactions of the Royal Society Series B: Biological Sciences*, 302.

Di Lollo, V. and Dixon, P. (1988). 'Two forms of persistence in visual information processing'. *Journal of Experimental Psychology: Human Perception and Performance*, 14.

—— and Hogben, J. (1988). 'Separating visible persistence from retinal afterimages'. *Perception and Psychophysics*, 44.

Irwin, D. E. and Thomas, L. E. (2008). Visual sensory memory. In Luck, S. J. and Hollingsworth, A. (eds) *Visual Memory*.

Koch, C. (2004). *The Quest for Consciousness*.

Neisser, U. (1967). *Cognitive Psychology*.

Simons, D. J. and Rensink, R. A. (2005) 'Change blindness: past, present, and future'. *Trends in Cognitive Sciences*, 9.

Sperling, G. (1960). 'The information available in brief visual presentations'. *Psychological Monographs*, 74.

Yeomans, J. M. and Irwin, D. E. (1985). 'Stimulus duration and partial report performance'. *Perception and Performance*, 37.

memory, process-dissociation procedure The process-dissociation procedure (PDP) takes it as a starting point that all tasks necessarily involve both conscious and unconscious components. For memory research, PDP tasks are devised to separate consciously controlled from automatic (unconscious) influences of memory by assuming that consciousness equals the ability to control one's use of memory. The PDP approach contrasts with the treatment of performance on an indirect test of memory as being a process-pure measure of unconscious influences of memory. For an indirect test, people are not directly asked to report on memory, as is done for direct tests of memory (e.g., recognition or recall tests), but, rather, to engage in a task such as word-fragment completion that can reveal unconscious influences of memory.

Identifying consciousness with control allows consciousness to be measured by combining results from inclusion and exclusion tasks. To illustrate how this is done, consider the task of intentionally responding on the basis of memory for an earlier event (an *inclusion task*) as compared to withholding responses that are based on memory for the earlier event (an *exclusion task*). As commonplace examples, delivering a message constitutes an inclusion task whereas keeping a secret constitutes an exclusion task. One means of implementing such tasks in the laboratory is to first ask people to study a list of words and then ask them to complete word fragments, some of which can be completed with earlier-studied words (e.g. study *motel*; test *mot__*). For an inclusion task, participants are instructed to complete the fragment with an earlier-studied word or, if unable to remember an appropriate earlier-studied word, to complete the fragment with the first word that comes to mind (*motel* would be the correct response). For an exclusion task, participants are instructed to complete fragments with words that were *not* studied earlier (producing *motel* as a response would be an exclusion error whereas *motor* would be among the possible correct responses).

A message can be successfully delivered either because of recollection, a consciously controlled use of memory, or, when recollection fails, because the message comes to mind as a result of unconscious influences. Similarly, for the laboratory inclusion task, an earlier-studied word could be used to complete a test fragment either because of recollection (R) or because of automatic influences of memory (A) when recollection fails ($1 - R$). If one assumes that the two bases for responding are independent, the equation for the probability of a correct response on the inclusion task is $P(R) + P(A)\,(1-R)$. To keep a secret, consciously controlled memory must be used to withhold a secret that comes to mind as a result of unconscious influences of memory—consciously controlled memory acts in opposition to automatic influences of memory. Similarly, for the fragment-completion task, participants in an exclusion condition will mistakenly produce an earlier-studied word only if the word automatically comes to mind (A) and they do not recollect its earlier study. If independence is assumed, the probability of an error on the exclusion task is: $P(A)\,(1-R)$. The difference between the probability of a correct response in an inclusion condition and the probability of an error in an exclusion condition serves as a measure of recollection. If a person is as likely to produce an earlier-studied word in the exclusion condition as in the inclusion condition, recollection is zero. At this extreme, an *amnesiac might be as likely to disclose information that was meant to be kept secret as to intentionally deliver a message, showing automatic influence of memory in the complete absence of consciously controlled memory. Given a measure of consciously controlled memory, the probability of unconscious use of memory can be computed.

Older adults are typically far from amnesic, but there are age-related declines in the ability to consciously recollect prior events. PDP tasks have been used to show an age-related decline in ability to recollect along with preserved unconscious use of memory. The tendency of older adults to tell a story repeatedly to the same audience can be explained as due to such differential effects on conscious recollection and unconscious use of memory. Telling a story increases a habit-like, unconscious form of memory and so increases the likelihood of the story later coming to mind. Recollection of the earlier telling of a story is required to successfully oppose this unconscious influence so as to avoid unwanted retelling. The combination of a deficit in conscious memory along with preserved unconscious memory results in older adults producing unwanted repetitions, and also makes them more vulnerable to memory scams. Jacoby and Rhodes (2006) describe means of computing estimates of consciously controlled and automatic influences of memory, and review evidence of age-related decline in conscious memory.

Use of PDP tasks has revealed a large number of dissociations between consciously controlled and automatic influences of memory. As described above, age-related differences in memory typically have their influence on recollection while leaving unconscious influences of memory unchanged. Similarly, requiring fast responding can reduce recollection while leaving unconscious influences intact and thereby produce results for young adults that are similar to those found for older adults (Jacoby 1999). Varying the baseline probability of a particular response can produce an opposite dissociation, by influencing unconscious use of memory while leaving the ability to recollect a particular response unchanged. Jacoby et al. (2007) used PDP tasks to show that effects of proactive and retroactive interference are sometimes fully because of an influence on unconscious use of memory. PDP tasks have also been used to separate the contributions of conscious and unconscious perception (e.g. Debner and Jacoby, 1994). Payne and colleagues have used PDP tasks to measure the contribution of unconscious stereotyping to racial biases of a sort that can lead to disastrous consequences (for a review, see Payne 2007).

Procedures for separating the contributions of conscious and unconscious influences within tasks necessarily rest on assumptions about the relation between the two types of processes. Curran and Hintzman (1997) as well as others have been critical of the independence assumption that underlies the PDP. Against that assumption, they argue that consciously controlled and automatic influences of memory are correlated. Jacoby et al. (2007) discuss possible alternative assumptions regarding the relation between conscious and unconscious influences, and provide strong evidence for their independence assumption. They argue that separating the contributions of different forms or uses of memory is important for applied purposes as well as for theory. As an example, distinguishing between consciously-controlled and automatic influences of memory is important for both diagnosis and treatment of memory disorders.

LARRY L. JACOBY

Curran, T. and Hintzman, D. L. (1997). 'Consequences and causes of correlations in process dissociation'. *Journal of Experimental Psychology: Learning, Memory, and Cognition*, 23.

Debner, J. A. and Jacoby, L. L. (1994). 'Unconscious perception: attention, awareness, and control'. *Journal of Experimental Psychology: Learning, Memory and Cognition*, 20.

Jacoby, L. L. (1999). 'Ironic effects of repetition: measuring age-related differences in memory'. *Journal of Experimental Psychology: Learning, Memory, and Cognition*, 25.

—— and Rhodes, M. G. (2006). 'False remembering in the aged'. *Current Directions in Psychological Science*, 15.

——, Bishara, A. J., Hessels, S., and Hughes, A. (2007). 'Probabilistic retroactive interference: the role of accessibility bias in interference effects'. *Journal of Experimental Psychology: General*, 136.

Payne, B. K. (2007) 'Weapon bias: split-second decisions and unintended stereotyping'. *Current Directions in Psychological Science*, 15.

memory systems, neural basis of The analysis of consciousness is closely linked with the analysis of memory. On the one hand, memory depends critically on consciousness: the contents of memory reflect, with varying degrees of accuracy, aspects of previous conscious experiences. On the other hand, the nature and content of conscious experience depend on, and are shaped by, knowledge and experience that is stored in memory. It therefore seems safe to conclude that progress in understanding consciousness will likely depend on progress in understanding memory.

Achieving that goal, however, is complicated by the fact that during the past few decades, there has been a growing consensus among researchers that memory is not a unitary entity, but instead consists of different processes, forms, and systems. This basic insight has had numerous and important consequences for our understanding of memory (Schacter and Tulving 1994). At the same time, a non-unitary view of memory has implications for the analysis of consciousness, because different types of memory may be associated with distinct forms of consciousness. Yet the general consensus favouring a non-unitary view of memory is not matched by a corresponding consensus concerning the nature and identity of the different systems of memory. Many different kinds of memory have been proposed, and there is—at best—modest agreement among extant proposals. Indeed, it is sometimes difficult for researchers even to agree on how they define a 'memory system' or a 'form of memory.'

1. Historical development of ideas concerning memory systems: a brief synopsis
2. Memory systems: definitions and criteria
3. The major memory systems: some proposals

1. Historical development of ideas concerning memory systems: a brief synopsis

The idea that memory consists of multiple forms or systems is not new: it has been advanced by a variety of philosophers, psychologists, and neuroscientists during the past 200 years (for a detailed historical summary, see Schacter and Tulving 1994). This section summarizes some key developments during the past few decades concerning the notion of multiple memory systems.

Beginning in the 1960s and 1970s, there have been two distinct lines of research relevant to the issue of memory systems, one concerned with distinguishing between short-term and long-term memory, the other focusing on distinctions among types of long-term memory. Interestingly, research in both areas was sparked, at least in part, by observations concerning an interesting group of neurological patients who suffer from a condition known as the **amnesic syndrome*. Amnesic patients exhibit severe difficulties remembering their recent experiences and acquiring new information, despite relatively intact perception, language, and other cognitive abilities that do not depend on remembering recent experiences. The amnesic syndrome typically results from damage to the hippocampus and related structures in the medial temporal lobe (Squire et al. 2004), which can occur following a variety of neurological insults, including encephalitis, anoxia (loss of oxygen to the brain), and head injury.

Early studies of the famous amnesic patient H. M., who became severely amnesic in 1953 after bilateral removal of the medial temporal lobe to relieve intractable epilepsy, revealed that he could remember small amounts of new information normally when tested immediately after studying the information (see Corkin 2002 for a summary of research with H. M.). This observation provided an important basis for drawing a distinction between short-term memory, which could hold a limited amount of information for a brief period of time, and long-term memory, which holds much larger amount of information across much longer time periods. A debate raged during the 1960s and 1970s concerning whether it was necessary to distinguish between short- and long-term memory, or whether experimental results could be understood by postulating a single memory system. In the early 1970s, Baddeley and Hitch (1974) helped to settle the debate by re-conceptualizing short-term memory as **working memory*: a separate system from long-term memory whose main function is to hold information in mind while an individual works on other cognitive tasks.

At around the same time, a number of researchers were beginning to draw distinctions between different kinds of long-term memory. For example, Tulving (1972) put forward the influential distinction between *episodic memory*, which is involved in recollecting personal experiences that occurred in a particular time and place, and *semantic memory*, which handles general knowledge of the world, including facts and concepts. Researchers began to pay increasing attention to this distinction (and related ideas) in part because it was becoming clear that amnesic patients—who exhibited profoundly impaired long-term episodic memory—could nonetheless exhibit some forms of intact long-term retention. For example, research initially conducted during the 1960s with patient H. M., and pursued intensively during the 1970s and 1980s with many other amnesic patients, revealed that such patients can learn new perceptual and motor skills, and also that they can show normal *priming effects, where presentation of an item influences subsequent identification or production of that item on a test that does not require subjects to think back to the prior episode in which the item was presented. Such observations stimulated cognitive studies of healthy, non-amnesic individuals that began to document and characterize such phenomena as priming effects, and show that these effects could be dissociated experimentally from traditional measures of recall and recognition (for review of this early work, see Schacter 1987). Taken together, these studies of amnesic and healthy individuals led to spirited discussions and debates concerning what form or forms of long-term memory might underlie amnesic patients' preserved abilities for long-term retention, and also account for dissociations between forms of memory observed in healthy, non-amnesic individuals.

2. Memory systems: definitions and criteria

The scientific literature is replete with distinctions among forms of memory, which are often couched in terms of dichotomies. Visual vs auditory, short term vs long term, explicit vs implicit, associative vs item, recall vs recognition, and episodic vs semantic are just a few of the better-known distinctions. But do all of these distinctions reflect the operation of different memory systems? If not, how can we tell whether a proposed distinction among forms of memory reflects the existence of distinct memory systems?

To address this question, it is necessary to define what we mean by a 'memory system'. The general idea of a 'system' implies the operation of an ensemble or network of processes that function in conjunction with one another. More specifically, a memory system includes encoding, storage, and retrieval processes that operate together. By contrast, a form or type of memory need not involve a network of correlated processes; individual processes such as recall or recognition are often referred to loosely as different 'forms of memory'. Three criteria can be used to distinguish a 'memory system' from the weaker notion of a 'form of memory': class inclusion operations, properties and relation, and convergent dissociations (Schacter and Tulving 1994).

Class inclusion operations refers to the notion that a memory system allows one to carry out various tasks or functions within a class or domain. A memory system should not be identified with performance on only a single task, but instead operates across a range of tasks. Damage to the system, in turn, will affect performance to some degree on all tasks that tap that system. For this reason, the study of patient populations with *brain damage that selectively affects neural structures associated with particular systems can be a highly productive research strategy: such patients should have difficulty performing various tasks subserved by a damaged system while performing well on tasks that depend on systems that are spared by brain damage.

Properties and relations refers to the idea that a memory system should be described by a list of properties that specifies features of the system and how they are related to those of other systems. Properties and relations include the types of information that the system handles, the neural networks that underlie the system, the rules according which the system operates, and functions that the system serves. Of course, developing an understanding of properties and relations constitutes a major goal of the research enterprise, so it is hardly surprising that, at the present time, hypotheses regarding properties and relations of memory systems are at a relatively early stage of development.

Convergent dissociations refers to evidence that reveals differences between classes of tasks that tap postulated memory systems. Convergent dissociations can take different forms: dissociations produced by manipulating cognitive features of behavioural tasks (e.g. manipulating how information is encoded affects tasks that tap system A but not system B), neuropsychological dissociations from brain-damaged patients (e.g. a particular patient population performs poorly on tasks that tap system B while performing normally on tasks that tap system A), or demonstrating different neural characteristics (e.g. a region of the prefrontal cortex is more active on tasks that tap system A than system B). Without convergent dissociations, there would be no reason in the first place to postulate multiple memory systems. However, different systems should not be proposed based merely on dissociations between a particular pair of tasks, because such dissociations are easy to produce even within a particular system (Roediger et al. 1990).

As suggested earlier, the criteria of class inclusion operations, properties and relations, and convergent dissociations distinguish a 'memory system' from the less constrained construct of a 'form of memory' or 'type of memory'. Because the notion of 'form' or 'type' of memory is less constrained than that of a memory system, forms of memory need not and often do not satisfy all of the criteria. For example, one commonly used distinction between forms of memory is that between explicit memory, which involves conscious recollection of previous experiences, and implicit memory, which involves non-conscious influences of past experiences on current performance and behaviour (Schacter 1987). Explicit and implicit memory were proposed as descriptive terms to characterize an important difference in the way that memory can be expressed at the time of retrieval—not as different memory systems. While there are convergent dissociations to support the implicit/explicit distinction, it is more difficult to satisfy the criteria of class inclusion operations or properties and relations.

3. The major memory systems: some proposals

Numerous forms and systems of memory have been proposed—more than can be reviewed in this brief entry (for a comprehensive survey of memory systems, see Schacter and Tulving 1994, Eichenbaum and Cohen 2001). Schacter and Tulving (1994) distinguished among five major memory systems: (1) *working memory*, a short-term or transient form of retention that supports the online maintenance of internal representations for use in ongoing cognitive tasks, and also supports the controlled manipulation of these representations; (2) *episodic memory*, which supports the encoding and retrieval of personal experiences that occur in a particular time and place; (3) *semantic memory*, which refers to a person's general knowledge about the world, containing a complex web of associated information, such as facts, concepts, and vocabulary; (4) the *perceptual representation system*, a collection of domain-specific subsystems that operate on perceptual information about the form and structure of words and objects; and (5) *procedural memory*, which supports the acquisition and retention of perceptual, motor, and cognitive skills, and is involved in everyday tasks such as learning to ride a bicycle or becoming skilled in cognitive domains such as reading or motor domains such as athletics.

Much research has been done to elucidate the cognitive and neural properties of these (and other) memory systems. Working memory, episodic memory, and semantic memory are all thought to operate primarily in the domain of conscious awareness, whereas the perceptual representation system and procedural memory are thought to rely on largely non-conscious processes. For example, amnesic patients can show intact procedural memory even though they lack any conscious recollection of having engaged in procedural learning. Similarly, amnesic patients can also show intact priming effects that are thought to reflect modification of the perceptual representation system, despite lacking conscious memory for the stimuli that produced priming. Given that amnesia is associated with damage to the medial temporal lobe, including the hippocampus, it is thought that the neural basis of the perceptual representation system and procedural memory lie outside the medial temporal region. Posterior cortical regions involved in visual and auditory processing have been linked with the perceptual representation system (Schacter et al. 2004), and subcortical structures such as the basal ganglia have been linked with procedural memory (Poldrack and Rodriguez 2004). The relationship between semantic memory and the medial temporal lobe has been the subject of debate: amnesic patients are capable of adding new knowledge to semantic memory, but they typically do not show normal semantic learning (Squire et al. 2004). Semantic memory is thought to depend importantly on widely distributed networks, involving regions with the lateral *frontal and temporal cortices (for review, see Schacter et al. 2000).

Because issues related to consciousness have been most closely linked to working memory, episodic memory, and the perceptual representation system, let us consider some of the basic properties of these systems in a bit more detail. As mentioned earlier, working memory was initially advanced as an extension of the concept of short-term memory. Much of the pioneering research on working memory was carried out by Alan Baddeley and colleagues (for a recent review, see Baddeley 2002). According to the model initially proposed by Baddeley's group, working memory can be fractionated into three subsystems: a limited-capacity central executive involved in controlling ongoing cognitive processes, and two domain-specific 'slave subsystems' that assist the central executive: a phonological loop involved in temporary storage of speech-based information, and a visuospatial sketch pad dedicated to the temporary storage of information about objects and their spatial locations. Information held in each subsystem is available online to conscious awareness.

Evidence supporting the fractionation of working memory into subsystems has come from multiple sources, including cognitive studies concerned with functional capacity of the subsystems and the types of informational codes they rely, studies of brain-damaged patients that reveal how selective damage to particular regions can disrupt each of the subsystems, and brain imaging studies that have delineated distinct neural correlates associated with each subsystem. For example, *functional brain imaging studies suggest that regions within the lower left frontal lobe (i.e. Broca's area) and parts of the left parietal lobe are associated with the phonological loop, whereas other parietal and prefrontal regions are associated with the visuospatial sketch pad.

Much research on working memory has examined the two 'slave subsystems', but more recently increasing attention has been paid to the central executive. In fact, Baddeley (2002) argues that it is necessary to propose a fourth subsystem of working memory that he has called the *episodic buffer*: a limited-capacity system that provides temporary storage of information held in a general, multimodal code (as opposed to the unimodal codes relied on by the phonological loop and visuospatial sketch pad). According to Baddeley, the episodic buffer binds or links together information from the slave systems (and from long-term memory) into a unified, conscious representation of a current episode. There is as yet relatively little direct evidence concerning the cognitive and neural properties of the episodic buffer but in Baddeley's view it plays a key role in linking working memory with long-term memory, specifically the form of long-term memory referred to earlier as *episodic memory*.

Many of our ideas about the nature of the episodic memory system come from Tulving (1972, 2002), who has emphasized its role in providing us with the ability to store information about our personal pasts and to consciously re-experience aspects of what had happened to us. Indeed, Tulving views episodic memory more generally as allowing us to engage in 'mental time travel', entailing both re-experiencing of the past and projecting ourselves into the future (see AUTONOETIC CONSCIOUSNESS). When episodic memory is destroyed or seriously damaged, as in some cases of amnesia, the ability to engage in mental time travel is absent and patients' consciousness is temporally restricted to the present. Much psychological and neuroscientific research has attempted to delineate the cognitive and neural properties of episodic memory by analysing episode encoding and retrieval process. Cognitive psychologists have established that episodic memory is enhanced by deep or elaborative encoding processes that link incoming information to pre-existing knowledge structures. Episodic memory also depends heavily on encoding of contextual information that links an event to a particular time and place. Episodic retrieval, in turn, relies on retrieval cues that help to re-instate or re-activate aspects of episodic encoding.

Evidence from the analysis of both brain-damaged patients and neuroimaging studies indicates that both the medial temporal role and regions with the frontal lobe play an important role in episodic memory. When the hippocampus and related medial temporal lobe structures are damaged, episodic memory is severely impaired. When the frontal lobes are damaged, more subtle episodic memory problems are often observed: patients have difficulty recalling source or contextual information concerning when and where an episode occurred, and are sometimes prone to memory distortions (Schacter et al. 1998). In healthy adults, specific regions within the medial temporal and frontal lobes often show increased activity during episodic encoding and/or retrieval. Indeed, there is some evidence that hippocampal activity is sometimes related to the conscious re-experiencing of the details of a prior episode (Eldridge et al. 2000).

In contrast to the experience of conscious recollection that is a hallmark of episodic memory, research concerned with the perceptual representation system has focused on the phenomenon of priming, which is thought to reflect non-conscious changes in the perceptual representation system as a result of exposure to a stimulus. Neuroimaging studies suggest that such priming effects are associated with decreased activity in occipital, temporal, and frontal regions, perhaps reflecting sharpening of perceptual representations as a result of stimulus exposure (Schacter et al. 2004). One recent neuroimaging study has provided compelling evidence for a neural distinction between priming in the perceptual representation system and episodic memory by examining how brain activity during encoding is related to subsequent episodic memory or priming (Schott et al. 2006). Increased activity in the bilateral medial temporal lobe and left prefrontal cortex at the time of encoding predicted subsequent episodic remembering (i.e. greater activity at encoding for subsequently remembered than forgotten items). By contrast, decreased activity at the time of encoding in a variety of posterior regions thought to be involved in perceptual processing (i.e. extrastriate cortex, fusiform gyrus) predicted subsequent priming. These findings clearly point to distinct neural bases for episodic memory and the perceptual representation system that supports priming.

As these latter results suggest, current research on memory systems is providing an ever more refined analysis of the cognitive and neural constituents of each of the major systems considered here. Moreover, recent research has begun to attack the important issue of how memory systems interact with each other (Poldrack and Rodriguez 2004). It is now clear that memory systems do not operate independently of one other, so understanding the neural basis for their interactions constitutes a critical task for researchers. Studies concerning the nature of and interactions between memory systems will no doubt go a long way toward furthering our understanding of the nature of consciousness itself.

DANIEL L. SCHACTER

Baddeley, A. D. (2002). 'Is working memory still working?' *European Psychologist*, 7.

—— and Hitch, G. J. (1974). 'Working memory'. In Bower, G. H. (ed.) *The Psychology of Learning and Motivation: Advances in Research and Theory*.

Corkin, S. (2002). 'What's new with the amnesic patient H.M?' *Nature Reviews Neuroscience*, 3.

Eichenbaum, H. and Cohen, N. J. (2001). *From Conditioning to Conscious Recollection: Memory Systems of the Brain*.

Eldridge, L. L., Knowlton, B. J., Furmanski, C. S., Bookheimer, S. Y., and Engel, S. E. (2000). 'Remembering episodes: a selective role for the hippocampus during retrieval'. *Nature Neuroscience*, 3.

Poldrack, R. A. and Rodriguez, P. (2004). 'How do memory systems interact? Evidence from human classification learning'. *Neurobiology of Learning and Memory*, 82.

Roediger III, H. L., Rajaram, S. and Srinivas, K. (1990). 'Specifying criteria for postulating memory systems'. In Diamond, A. (ed.) *The Development and Neural Bases of Higher Cognitive Functions*.

Schacter, D. L. (1987). 'Implicit memory: history and current status'. *Journal of Experimental Psychology: Learning, Memory, and Cognition*, 13.

—— and Tulving, E. (1994). 'What are the memory systems of 1994?' In Schacter, D. L. and Tulving, E. (eds) *Memory Systems 1994*.

——, Norman, K. A., and Koutstaal, W. (1998). 'The cognitive neuroscience of constructive memory'. *Annual Review of Psychology*, 49.

——, Wagner, A. D., and Buckner, R. L. (2000). 'Memory systems of 1999'. In Tulving, E. and Craik, F. I. M. (eds) *The Oxford Handbook of Memory*.

——, Dobbins, I. G., and Schnyer, D. M. (2004). 'Specificity of priming: a cognitive neuroscience perspective'. *Nature Reviews Neuroscience*, 5.

Schott, B. H., Richardson-Klavehn, A., Henson, R. N. A., Becker, C., Heinze, H. J., and Duzel, E. (2006). 'Neuroanatomical dissociation of encoding processes related to priming and explicit memory'. *Journal of Neuroscience*, 26.

Squire, L. R., Stark, C. E., and Clark, R. E. (2004). 'The medial temporal lobe'. *Annual Review of Neuroscience*, 27.

Tulving, E. (1972). 'Episodic and semantic memory'. In Tulving, E. and Donaldson, W. (eds), *Organization of Memory*.

—— (2002). 'Episodic memory: from mind to brain'. *Annual Review of Psychology*, 53.

memory, visual short term When we have just looked away from a scene we can still see it in our mind's eye, but how much do we actually remember? Visual short-term memory (VSTM) is defined as short-lasting memory for visual properties of just-viewed objects or scenes. Whereas iconic memory lasts for less than 0.5 s under most conditions, is eliminated by new visual stimulation, is precategorical, and is highly detailed, VSTM lasts for several seconds, is more resistant to interference from new stimulation, is postcategorical, and is limited in how much information can be represented (Phillips 1983). Although VSTM is more abstract than perception in that the viewer does not mistake it for concurrent perception, it maintains information about many characteristics of visual perception, including spatial layout, shape, colour, and size.

By definition, contents in VSTM are currently available to conscious awareness. Just as selective attention ensures conscious access, the contents in VSTM are also gated by attention. A standard test of VSTM for an array or picture is to show a second array that may have a change, requiring the viewer to detect the change. Visual input that is not selectively attended is poorly remembered in VSTM. Once information is encoded in VSTM, continued attention is required for memory maintenance and consolidation. Dividing attention between a VSTM task and other cognitive tasks, including auditory choice reaction time (RT) tasks, impairs VSTM maintenance. During the retention interval, spatial attention tags the location of encoded items, and the distribution of spatial attention affects the durability of VSTM. Distributing attention to multiple items in VSTM leaves them vulnerable to new visual input, whereas orienting attention to one of these makes memory robust. On the other hand, contents in VSTM can also influence attentional allocation. Perceptual input that matches VSTM contents tends to receive attentional priority compared with other input.

The close link between VSTM and consciousness is also reflected in their shared neural substrates. In the primate brain, maintaining objects or locations in VSTM activates lateral prefrontal cortex, posterior parietal cortex, thalamus, and other dorsal brain areas. These areas are also considered the neural network for voluntary attention and consciousness.

Much research in VSTM has been devoted to characterizing its *capacity limits (Jiang et al. 2007). This capacity is often considered to be no more than three or four units, with the units being individual visual objects rather than visual features (Luck and Vogel 1997). There is apparently no limit to the number of visual features one can remember as long as they belong to a single object: a compound object of four features including colour, size, orientation, and the presence of a gap is easily remembered and we can retain about four of such objects in VSTM. Object-based chunking is not always efficient, however. Chunking features of the same kind together, such as juxtaposing two colours to form a single object, does not make these features easier to remember than separating them into two objects.

The capacity limit in VSTM is not a magical number; its exact value varies widely as a function of the similarity between the memorized items and the test stimuli. The more similar the memorized items are to each other and to test items, the more difficult it is to detect a change across a delay interval, and the lower the estimated VSTM capacity. Some researchers describe this variability in capacity in terms of the visual complexity of each object, proposing that complex objects such as random polygons fill up VSTM capacity more quickly than simple objects such as colours (Alvarez and Cavanagh 2004). However, complex objects tend to be visually similar to other complex objects used as testing stimuli, and simple objects tend to be visually distinctive from testing stimuli. The exact capacity of VSTM for object features, therefore, cannot be universally quantified without specifying how it is measured.

Even in optimized situations involving simple and distinctive visual features, the measured capacity is still small, suggesting that the capacity of momentary consciousness is also small. This limit is partly imposed by failure in attentional selection, as individuals who are poor at filtering out irrelevant input from memory also have low VSTM capacity. Additionally, the limit may reflect the amount of information that can be stored in VSTM. The storage limit is often conceptualized as a fixed number of slots, where extra objects overflow existing slots and get left out of VSTM. In reality, all attended objects may be partially registered in VSTM, but the fidelity of the registration declines with increasing number of objects.

Attempts to increase VSTM capacity by training subjects with particular shapes have met with limited success. VSTM for the identity and arrangement of a set of items is no better for upright letters than inverted letters even though viewers are more familiar with upright letters (Pashler 1988). Similarly, a new arrangement of familiar objects and faces is no better remembered than arrangements of novel objects and faces, although highly familiar faces such as those of friends or celebrities are remembered better than unfamiliar ones. With highly familiar materials, contributions to performance from naming cannot be ruled out. Prolonged training on unnamable dot patterns sometimes enhances performance, although the improvement may reflect improved chunking efficiency rather than enlarged VSTM capacity.

Although VSTM has historically been considered a separate memory store from visual long-term memory, recent studies have failed to support this distinction. Both memories allow the detection of changes to visual details and semantic gist and both rely on similar brain regions. Patients with medial temporal lobe damage (see BRAIN DAMAGE), with impaired ability to consolidate information in long-term memory, who have traditionally been considered to have normal short-term memory, have difficulty with visual STM tasks. Nonetheless, a distinction between VSTM and long-term visual memory is useful, as memory for a newly viewed array is lost rapidly; further consolidation is required for retention in visual long-term memory.

A significant function of VSTM is that it allows us to maintain a sense of temporal continuity across brief temporal interruptions due to occlusion or observer motion. VSTM is also thought to play a role in integrating information across eye movements, which typically generate three or four new fixations a second. Meaningful pictured scenes in a rapid serial visual presentation (RSVP) mimic successive fixations in an idealized situation in which there is no overlap in content from one 'fixation' to the next. At durations of 120–333 ms (in the range of most fixations), RSVP pictures can be momentarily understood, but most are quickly forgotten within a few seconds (Potter et al. 2004). Most RSVP pictures can be remembered when tested for recognition within a second of the end of the sequence, indicating retention that persists over a sequence as long as 20 pictures at 6/s. Presumably viewers do not remain simultaneously conscious of all the pictures in the sequence; instead, conscious awareness of having seen the picture before arises when the test picture is presented. As the test continues over 8 s, more than half the pictures are forgotten, indicating that there was a transient VSTM or CSTM (conceptual short term memory) trace that was lost.

Are viewers conscious of the pictures as they are presented? Viewers report that they seem to see and understand all the pictures during presentation. The ability to respond to a conceptually defined target (e.g. 'a picnic') that has never been seen before suggests momentary consciousness of each of the pictures, although the possibility remains that the search definition allowed the target to reach consciousness while other pictures did not.

For simple VSTM arrays of coloured geometric shapes as well as meaningful pictures, momentary consciousness of both appearance and meaning is followed by rapid forgetting of much of the information. This pattern is seen in a number of related visual phenomena using RSVP. In the *attentional blink*, when a viewer searches an RSVP stream for targets such as letters, the second of two targets is missed when it arrives 200–600 ms after the onset of the first target. In *repetition blindness*, when the task is to view and then recall all the items in RSVP, the second of two identical items often fails to be recalled (e.g. in the sentence 'When Nancy spilled the *ink* there was *ink* all over.'). In RSVP word lists, sentences, and paragraphs there is evidence for comprehension, followed quickly by forgetting. Thus, we comprehend the meaning or meanings of a stimulus early in processing (possibly before conscious awareness), which allows us to take immediate action if necessary, but we then rapidly forget unless conditions are favourable for retention. The two kinds of favourable conditions are deliberate target selection and the availability of associations or meaningful relations between momentarily active items. For example, in a VSTM study an array of letters is easy to retain if the letters form a meaningful word. The power of these two factors—selective attention that is defined by visual or conceptual properties of the target, and the presence of potential visual or conceptual structure—is felt early in processing, determining whether conscious memory will be transient (as in VSTM and CSTM) or longer-lasting.

MARY C. POTTER AND YUHONG JIANG

Alvarez, G. A., and Cavanagh, P. (2004). The capacity of visual short-term memory is set both by total information load and by number of objects. *Psychological Science*, 15.

Jiang, Y. V., Makovski, T., and Shim, W. M. (2009). 'Visual memory for features, conjunctions, objects, and locations'. In Brockmole, J. R. (ed.) *The Visual World in Memory*, http://jianglab.psych.umn.edu/webpagefiles/publications/JiangMakovskiShimChapter09.pdf

Luck, S. J., and Vogel, E. K. (1997). 'The capacity of visual working memory for features and conjunctions'. *Nature*, 390 (6657).

Pashler, H. (1988). 'Familiarity and visual change detection'. *Perception and Psychophysics*, 44.

Phillips, W. A. (1983). 'Short-term visual memory'. *Philosophical Transactions of the Royal Society of London Series B: Biological Sciences*, 302.

Potter, M. C., Staub, A., and O'Connor, D. H. (2004). 'Pictorial and conceptual representation of glimpsed pictures'. *Journal of Experimental Psychology: Human Perception and Performance*, 30.

mental causation See EPIPHENOMENALISM

mental time travel See AUTONOETIC CONSCIOUSNESS

metacognition Of all human capacities, surely one of the most important is the ability to turn thought upon itself. Thinking about thinking (i.e. metacognition) enables individuals to refine their cognitive strategies, regulate current mental states, anticipate future mental events, and ultimately provides the foundation for self- insight. Despite its centrality, the field of metacognition is still in its youth. While there have been important advances in all three of its major components (knowledge about cognition, monitoring cognition, controlling cognition) this work has been carried out by a relatively small cadre of researchers. Moreover, and of particular pertinence to the present volume, the relationship between metacognition and consciousness remains somewhat elusive, as researchers have only recently begun to attend to the possibilities that (1) metacognition can happen outside awareness; (2) conscious processes can occur in the absence of explicit meta-awareness of their occurrence; (3) consideration of the relationship between metacognition and consciousness may help to overcome the paradox of introspection.

1. A brief history of metacognition
2. Metacognition and consciousness
3. Metacognition is a double-edged sword

1. A brief history of metacognition

Although important insights about metacognition peppered the literature throughout the history of psychology, the field was brought into focus with Flavell's (1979) discussion of children's capacities for monitoring their cognitions. Flavell distinguished two general classes of metacognitive phenomena: (1) *metacognitive knowledge*—world knowledge about how cognition operates, for example believing that rehearsal will improve memory; and (2) *metacognitive experience*—an affective or cognitive experience associated with an intellectual enterprise, for example sensing that a currently unavailable word is on the tip of one's tongue (see FEELING OF KNOWING).

In the cognitive domain, a watershed moment was Nelson and Narens' (1990) rudimentary model of the application of metacognition to the regulation and control of cognition. Nelson and Narens introduced two levels of cognition: the *object level* and the *meta-level*. The object level involves cognitions concerning external objects, whereas the meta-level involves cognitions about object-level cognitions. Critical to this model is the flow of information between the two levels. Accordingly, monitoring occurs when information reaches the object level from the meta-level, and control occurs when information from the meta-level modifies the object level. Following the seminal work of Flavell and Nelson and Narens, numerous studies have explored the three aspects of metacognition: knowledge, monitoring, and control.

Metacognitive knowledge develops over the lifespan. As children age, they gain an increasingly sophisticated *theory of mind of others which is accompanied by a growing understanding of their own mental states. With age, people develop beliefs about the emergence of forgetting and strategies to manage them as well as more general beliefs about how the mind operates. In addition, metacognitive beliefs have been shown to contribute to various mental pathologies. For example, generalized anxiety disorder is associated with the belief that worrying will help to prevent the undesired event.

Metacognitive monitoring. Considerable research has focused on individuals' awareness of their own knowledge state. In the domain of problem-solving, differences in metacognitive monitoring have been shown to distinguish insight from analytical problem solving. Specifically, individuals tend to be relatively accurate in anticipating when they are approaching a successful solution to an analytic logical problem, whereas a sense that a solution is imminent is actually predictive of a failure to solve insight (aha!-type) problems.

Although metacognitive monitoring has been explored in a variety of domains, its application to memory has probably been the most extensive. One intriguing finding is introducing a very brief delay between the *encoding* of an association and the judgement of whether it has been learned markedly improves individuals' *calibration*, i.e. the degree to which prediction corresponds to performance. The role of metacognitive monitoring in *retrieval* is perhaps most familiar in the 'feeling of knowing' where one senses that a memory is accessible even thought it cannot currently be retrieved.

Two general classes of theories have been offered to account for feeling-of-knowing judgements. According to the direct-access account (Hart 1965), the feeling of knowing is the consequence of sub-threshold levels of activation associated with the target. According to inference-based accounts (Koriat 2000) the likelihood of retrieving the target is a result of inferences drawn from either the familiarity of the cue or the amount and quality of what is retrieved. Numerous empirical studies favour inference-based accounts by demonstrating that manipulations that have no effect on the availability of the target, nevertheless influence the feeling of knowing.

Metacognitive control. As illustrated by Nelson and Narens' model, cognitive control emerges when metaknowledge about cognitive operations is used to modulate performance. Typically individuals allocate greater study effort to the items they perceive as harder to learn, although sometimes (e.g. when study time is limited or the difficult items appear particularly hard) individuals will allocate effort to the easier items. The use of metacognitive monitoring in the service of metacognitive control also applies to a variety of other domains including emotional regulation, juror decision-making, and modulating mental health difficulties such as depression and anxiety. In general, the more sensitive individuals are to fluctuations in their mental states, the better they are at regulating those states effectively.

2. Metacognition and consciousness

Implicit metacognition. It is often assumed that metacognition is an inherently conscious process. Nevertheless there are good reasons to suspect that metacognition sometimes operates in the absence of explicit awareness. A number of studies have found evidence of implicit strategy selection. For example, Lemaire and Reder (1999) gave participants an equation verification task in which they had to determine whether simple equations (e.g. $6 \times 32 = 192$) were correct. Lemaire and Reder found that participants were faster at rejecting problems when odd/even status of the proposed and actual solutions differed, and this advantage was especially pronounced when there was a high proportion of parity mismatch problems. Nevertheless, participants were unaware either of using this strategy or of the proportion of problems for which this strategy could be applied. Such findings suggest that the metacognitive processes necessary to select strategies and regulate their effectiveness can occur without explicit awareness.

Although not typically characterized in the context of metacognition, various social psychology findings also suggest that metacognitive regulation occurs without awareness. For example, the finding that cognitive load increases the frequency of unwanted thoughts (Wegner and Schneider 2003) suggests an implicit monitoring process that unconsciously searches for unwanted thoughts. The finding that goals can be activated and implemented without awareness (Bargh and Chartrand 1999) similarly implicates sophisticated implicit metacognitive processes in the control of behaviour.

Meta-consciousness. The claim that the monitoring of cognition can occur either with or without explicit awareness suggests the utility of explicitly distinguishing between these two types of monitoring processes. Schooler (2002) proposed the terms 'meta-consciousness' or 'meta-awareness' (used interchangeably) to refer to the metacognitive process of consciously appraising and thereby explicitly re-representing the current contents of thought. According to this view, meta-consciousness simply reflects situations in which consciousness is turned on to itself such that the current contents of consciousness become the focus of attention. This view does not assume that meta-consciousness necessarily entails a qualitatively different type of representation, process, or brain region and it is agnostic regarding claims that implicit meta-representations are required for consciousness itself (e.g. Rosenthal 2004).

Two types of dissociations follow from the claim that meta-awareness involves the intermittent re-representation of the contents of consciousness. *Temporal dissociations* occur when one temporarily fails to attend to the contents of consciousness. Once the focus of conscious turns on to itself, *translation dissociations* may occur if the re-representation process misrepresents the original experience.

Temporal dissociations between experience and meta-awareness are indicated in cases in which the induction of meta-awareness causes one to assess aspects of experience that had previously eluded explicit appraisal. A variety of psychological phenomena can be thought of in this manner.

*****

Mind-wandering. Everyone has had the experience of suddenly noticing that although we have been superficially attentive to the external environment, our mind has been entirely elsewhere. The occurrence of mind-wandering during attentionally demanding tasks such as reading is particularly informative because mind-wandering is incompatible with the successful creation of a narrative. Evidence that mind-wandering during reading is associated with an absence of meta-awareness comes from studies in which individuals report every time they notice their minds wandering during reading, while also being probed periodically and asked to indicate whether they were mind-wandering at that particular moment. These studies demonstrate that individuals frequently lack meta-awareness of the fact that they are mind-wandering, even when they are in a study where they are specifically instructed to be vigilant for such lapses.

Automaticity. Automatic behaviours are often assumed to be non-conscious. However, there is a peculiarity to this designation because it is difficult to imagine that such behaviours never form the contents of consciousness. Consider a person driving automatically while engaging in some secondary task (e.g. talking on a mobile phone). Although such driving is compromised, one still experiences the curves of the road, the changing of the gears, but just not the fact that these experiences are currently part of what one is doing. Similarly, when one engages in habitual consumptive behaviours, e.g. smoking or eating, one presumably experiences the consumption without taking explicit stock of the significance of the action. This example suggests that temporal dissociations of meta-awareness may help to explain why people often unwittingly relapse in habits they are trying to quit. In short, it seems that rather than being unconscious, many automatic activities may be experienced but are lacking in meta-awareness.

If meta-awareness requires re-representing the contents of consciousness, then it follows that some information may become lost or distorted in the translation. Examples of translation dissociations include the following.

Verbal reflection. There are some experiences that are challenging to put into words: the appearance of a face, the taste of a wine, the intuitions leading to insights. If individuals attempt to translate these inherently non-verbal experiences into words, then the resulting re-representations may fail to do justice to the original experience (Schooler and Fiore 1997). Consistent with this view, studies have demonstrated that when people try to describe their non-verbal experiences performance disruptions can ensue (Chin and Schooler 2008). Importantly, verbal reflection does not hamper performance when individuals describe experiences that are more verbalizable.

Motivation. Sometimes individuals may be explicitly motivated to misrepresent experiences to themselves. For example, individuals labelled as 'repressors' can show substantial physiological (galvanic skin response) markers of experiencing stress when shown stressful videos but nevertheless report experiencing no stress (Lambie and Marcel 2002). Because they are highly motivated to deny their stress, they simply do not allow themselves to acknowledge it.

Faulty theories. If individuals have a particularly strong theory about what they should be experiencing, this may colour their appraisal of their actual experience. For example, most people believe that when they catch a ball their eyes first rise and then go down following the trajectory of the ball. Nevertheless, when asked what they experienced, people who just caught a ball reported their theory of what they thought should have happened rather than what they actually experienced.

One area of interest for future research is the impact of faulty theories of affective regulation on people's appraisal of their happiness (Wilson and Gilbert 2005). Faulty beliefs about emotional regulation processes are a primary source of errors in predicting how one will feel in the future. For example, following a negative event (e.g. learning that they did badly on a test), people typically overestimate how upset they will feel. The disparity between people's affective theories and their self-reports raises the intriguing possibility that even *online assessment may be biased by erroneous theories. Accordingly, erroneous theories about how people believe they should be feeling may cause them to report that they are unhappy longer then they really are. Examination of disparities between individuals' self-reports and covert measures of experience (e.g. psychophysiological measures, implicit affect measures) may help to reveal the potentially widespread situations in which people misconstrue their own affective state.

*Metacognition and *introspection.* The distinction between consciousness and meta-awareness also helps to resolve a fundamental paradox of introspection (Nelson 1990, Schooler and Schreiber 2004) namely that introspection is simultaneously unassailable and suspect. On the one hand, there is no single source of knowledge that is more important than introspection. One's experience simply is what it is. If one perceives a white elephant hovering above one's bed, we can reasonably question the existence of the elephant, but can we really question the existence of the experience? While unassailable at one level, introspection is also suspect as it is difficult to appraise an experience at the same time that one is having it. As Comte put it 'The thinker cannot divide himself into two, of whom one reasons whilst the other observes his reason' (p. 188, cited in James). James similarly noted, 'The attempt at introspective analysis in these cases is in fact like seizing a spinning top to catch its motion, or trying to turn up the gas quickly enough to see how the darkness looks.' (1893:244). Indeed, the history of introspection has been plagued by the challenge of reliably characterizing the nature of first-person experience (Nisbett and Wilson 1977).

Although the paradox of introspection may be inevitable, it is not insurmountable. Two insights from the distinction between consciousness and meta-awareness offer hope in circumventing the paradox of introspection. First, as Nelson (1990) observed, the concern that we cannot simultaneously be the observer and the observed can be addressed by recognizing that consciousness involves an alternation between the basic and metacognitive levels. We can experience something at the basic level, and then introspect on that experience at the metacognitive level. While introspection will necessarily suffer from the fact that the metacognitive level must re-represent the basic level, it nevertheless affords a way for us to observe (albeit imperfectly) our own experience. Second, using multiple sources it is possible to assess the veracity of introspections as our explicit characterizations of our experience should correspond in systematic ways with the environmental factors that invoke it, the physiological states that underlie it, and the behavioural responses that it induces. Thus by examining the correspondence between individuals' appraisals of their experience and environmental, physiological, and behavioural measures it is possible to determine when introspective reports of experience are likely to reflect underlying experience, and when they may be suspect (Schooler and Schreiber 2004).

3. Metacognition is a double-edged sword

The unique capacity of thought to be turned in on itself affords some of the greatest capacities but also some of the peculiar costs associated with human consciousness. On the positive side, metacognition enables the monitoring, regulation, and implementation of complex goal-driven behaviour. However, the price for this remarkable capacity is the myriad of situations in which self-analysis undermines the very goal one is attempting to implement. As anyone who has ever scrutinized *automatized motor performance knows, sometimes watching oneself can lead to 'paralysis through analysis'. Moreover, metacognitions can be a significant source of angst, as in the case of worrying about the fact that one is worrying or ruminating on why one is sad. Although the two-edged sword of metacognition may never be completely avoidable, some forms of metacognition may be more benign then others. For example, explicit analytic reflection may be more disruptive then the more intuitive mindful awareness that develops through contemplative practices such as *meditation. Whereas analytically decomposing a motor skill may disrupt it, and verbally ruminating about an emotional state may exacerbate it, being quietly mindful of what one is doing may afford many of the benefits of metacognition with fewer of the costs. While the cultivation of an intuitive manner of watching consciousness has a venerable history, modern psychology is only beginning to seriously address the nature and value of such practices. In the future, exploring the differences between analytic and non-analytic modes of metacognition may offer insight for honing our capacity to watch ourselves without stepping on our own toes.

JONATHAN W. SCHOOLER AND JONATHAN SMALLWOOD

Bargh, J. A. and Chartrand, T. L. (1999). 'The unbearable automaticity of being'. *American Psychologist*, 54.

Chin, J. M. and Schooler, J. W. (2008). 'Why do words hurt? Content, process, and criterion shift accounts of verbal overshadowing'. *European Journal of Cognitive Psychology*, 20.

Flavell, J. H. (1979). 'Metacognition and cognitive monitoring: A new area of cognitive-developmental inquiry'. *American Psychologist*, 34.

Hart, J. T. (1965). 'Memory and the feeling-of-knowing experience'. *Journal of Educational Psychology*, 56.

James, W. (1893). *The Principles of Psychology*, Vol. 1.

Koriat, A. (2000). 'The feeling of knowing: some metatheoretical implications for consciousness and control'. *Consciousness and Cognition*, 9.

Lambie, J. A. and Marcel, A. J. (2002). 'Consciousness and the varieties of emotion experience: a theoretical framework'. *Psychological Review*, 109.

Lemaire, P. and Reder, L. M. (1999). 'What affects strategy selection in arithmetic? An examination of parity and five effects on product verification'. *Memory and Cognition*, 27.

Nelson, T. O. (1990). 'Consciousness and metacognition'. *American Psychologist*, 97.

—— and Narens, L. (1990). 'Metamemory: a theoretical framework and new findings'. In Bower, G. H. (ed.) *The Psychology of Learning and Motivation*, Vol. 26.

Nisbett, R. and Wilson, T. (1977). 'Telling more than we can know: verbal reports on mental processes'. *Psychological Review*, 84.

Rosenthal, D. M. (2004). 'Varieties of higher-order theory'. In Gennaro, R. (ed.) *Higher-order Theories of Consciousness*.

Schooler, J. W. (2002). 'Re-representing consciousness: dissociations between consciousness and meta-consciousness'. *Trends in Cognitive Science*, 6.

—— and Fiore, S. M. (1997). 'Consciousness and the limits of language: You can't always say what you think or think what you say'. In *Scientific Approaches to Consciousness*.

—— and Schreiber, C. A. (2004). 'Experience, meta-consciousness, and the paradox of introspection'. *Journal of Consciousness Studies*, 11.

Wegner, D. M., and Schneider, D. J. (2003). 'The white bear story'. *Psychological Inquiry*, 14.

Wilson, T. D. and Gilbert, D. T. (2005). 'Affective forecasting: knowing what to want'. *Current Directions in Psychological Science*, 14.

microconsciousness The theory of microconsciousness states that instead of a single, unified, visual consciousness, there are many different visual consciousnesses that are distributed in time and space. The following facts about the visual *brain lead ineluctably to this conclusion.

(a) The visual brain consists of many different areas which are specialized to process and perceive different attributes of the visual scene (Zeki et al. 1991). There are many such specializations, but the theory is derived principally from the observation that *colour and visual motion are processed in two anatomically and functionally distinct visual areas, the former centred on V4 and the latter on V5. In humans, damage to V4 leads to the syndrome of cerebral achromatopsia (colour imperception) without affecting motion vision, while damage to V5 leads to cerebral akinetopsia (motion imperception) without affecting colour perception. The specialized areas of the visual brain are not only processing centres but also perceptual ones (ffytche and Zeki 1998, Moutoussis and Zeki 2002). In other words, activity in them can generate a phenomenal experience without the mandatory involvement of higher cognitive centres, such as the *frontal or parietal cortex. Activity in a given specialized area acquires a conscious correlate when it becomes intense enough but it is still not clear whether this heightened activity is due to the recruitment of previously unresponsive cells or an increased firing of previously responsive ones. The conscious correlate caused by the activity of an area is itself modular in the sense that it can occur independently of other conscious correlates.

(b) We perceive colour before we perceive motion, by about 80–100 ms (Moutoussis and Zeki 1997). Since perceiving something is tantamount to becoming aware of it, it follows that we become aware of colour some 80–100 ms before we become aware of motion. The theory supposes that the differences in time taken to perceive two (or more) visual attributes are due to differences in the time that it takes to process them and endow them with conscious correlates. There is some evidence for this, since manipulating the colour or motion stimuli can modify significantly (though not reverse) the advantage in time that the perception of one attribute has over the other. Since awareness of colour is due to activity in V4 and that of motion due to activity in V5, it follows that visual consciousness is distributed in space. Since we become aware of colour some 80–100 ms before we become aware of motion, it follows that visual consciousness is distributed in time. It follows therefore that there is not a single visual consciousness but that there are many visual microconsciousnesses that are distributed in time and space. Visual consciousness is therefore modular. This statement would be correct even if colour and motion were the only two specializations in the visual brain, which of course they are not.

(c) Over very brief time windows, the brain *binds the colour presented at time t to the direction of motion presented at time $t - \Delta t$. It follows that the brain *mis-binds* in terms of veridical reality (Moutoussis and Zeki 1997). This implies that the brain does not have an area or system that waits for all the processing systems to terminate their tasks. Since the mis-binding is a mis-binding of what we have already become conscious of, it follows that *binding is post-conscious* (Zeki and Bartels 1999).

(d) It takes longer to bind two stimuli belonging to the same attribute (e.g. colour to colour) than two stimuli belonging to different attributes (e.g. colour to motion; Bartels and Zeki 2006). Such inter-attribute binding leads to what may be called *macroconsciousness*.

It thus becomes possible to distinguish at least two hierarchically related levels of consciousness, microconsciousness and macroconsciousness. A hierarchically more complex level is the unified consciousness—that is the experience of myself as the source of the perception. The latter depends on language and communication and comes under the general rubric of reportable consciousness (*access consciousness), to distinguish it from phenomenal consciousness (Block 1990). The theory of microconsciousness—in addition to stressing that consciousness has many constituents—draws a sharp distinction between phenomenal consciousness and access consciousness.

The evidence given above shows that the visual areas (or processing–perceptual centres) are reasonably autonomous of one another, but the extent of their dependence on other cortical areas, whether visual or not, is not clear. They do not appear to be dependent upon activity in the frontal cortex or the 'frontoparietal network of areas' if reportability is not involved. As well, activity in V5, without a forward input from *V1 or a return input to it, appears to be sufficient to generate a crude but conscious experience of vision. The latter is especially well demonstrated in *Riddoch syndrome*, a condition in which a patient blinded by damage to V1 is nevertheless capable of experiencing visual stimuli in motion crudely but consciously. It follows that V1 is not necessary for the generation of conscious experience, which is not to say that involvement of V1 does not enhance the conscious experience considerably.

It is of course very unlikely that the processing–perceptual centres of the visual brain can act with complete autonomy, but what other brain areas they are dependent on remains unknown. It has been conjectured that the healthy activity of the reticular–pontine system is critical and that the latter acts in the capacity of an enabling system, although this is conjectural.

SEMIR ZEKI

Bartels, A. and Zeki, S. (2006). 'The temporal order of binding visual attributes'. *Vision Research*, 46.

Block, N. (1990). 'Consciousness and accessibility'. *Behavioral and Brain Sciences*, 13.

ffytche, D. H. and Zeki, S. (1998). 'The Riddoch syndrome: insights into the neurobiology of conscious vision'. *Brain*, 121.

Moutoussis, K. and Zeki, S. (1997). 'A direct demonstration of perceptual asynchrony in vision'. *Proceedings of the Royal Society of London Series B: Biological Sciences*, 265.

—— —— (2002). 'The relationship between cortical activation and perception investigated with invisible stimuli'. *Proceedings of the National Academy of Sciences of the USA*, 99.

Zeki, S. and Bartels, A. (1999). 'Toward a theory of visual consciousness'. *Consciousness and Cognition*, 8.

——, Watson, J. D. G., Lueck, C. J., Friston, K. J., Kennard C., and Frackowiak, R. S. J. (1991). 'A direct demonstration of functional specialization in human visual cortex'. *Journal of Neuroscience*, 11.

mind–body problem See HARD PROBLEM OF CONSCIOUSNESS

mind-wandering The mind never stays still. Without constant vigilance our minds can, and often do, wander from the constraints of our current task to our own private thoughts and feelings. The experience of mind-wandering is one of the most *introspectively accessible examples of the challenges of mental control. For example, everyone is familiar with the experience of suddenly realizing, while reading, that although one's eyes have continued to move across the page, one's mind has been fundamentally elsewhere. The example of mindless reading strikingly illustrates two fundamental aspects of mind-wandering (also known as daydreaming, stimulus-independent thought, or task-unrelated thought). First, the frequent disparity between what one is doing and what one is thinking about illustrates the process of *decoupling* (Smallwood and Schooler 2006) whereby attentional resources cease to be constrained by external sources, and instead become focused on information of an internal origin. This reduced dedication of resources to the ongoing task compromises task performance.

A second striking aspect of mind-wandering is illustrated by the surprise we feel when we recognize that our mind has wandered. In contrast to other less demanding tasks such as driving or listening to music, in which we may knowingly allow our mind to wander, we know that when we read it is not possible to follow the narrative while at the same time maintaining an unrelated train of thought. When our mind wanders during reading, our comprehension of the narrative is clearly compromised. Since mind-wandering unrelated to the narrative is unlikely to be deliberate (at least when one is sufficiently motivated) its common occurrence in tasks like reading demonstrates that we often temporarily lack awareness that our mind has wandered. As such, mind-wandering can be seen as common everyday example of a failure to take stock of the current contents of consciousness. The ability to reflect on the contents of consciousness is referred to as *meta-awareness*.

1. Measuring mind-wandering
2. Situational constraints on mind-wandering
3. The neurophysiology of mind-wandering

1. Measuring mind-wandering

Under laboratory conditions two different approaches have been used to sample mind-wandering. The first approach, the *probe-caught* method, samples the experience of the individual at varying time intervals as they perform a cognitive task. The second approach, the *self-caught* method, requires that the individual responds with a button push whenever they catch their own mind-wandering.

Probe- and self-caught measures of mind-wandering yield different information on the occurrence and awareness of mind-wandering because they systematically sample the different aspects involved in off-task experiences. The probe-caught technique provides evidence of how readily the mind turns inward, and can be used to study the onset of *decoupling*, or the likelihood that attention has drifted from the task in hand. On the other hand, the self-caught method requires the individual to recognize that their mind is wandering, and so illustrates the engagement of *meta-awareness* of their own mind-wandering. Evidence of the value of distinguishing between probe-caught and self-caught mind-wandering comes from the findings that the two measures are differentially associated with task performance. Interestingly, it is the probe-caught mind-wandering episodes that tend to be maximally associated with detriments in performance. The more modest consequences of self-caught mind-wandering episodes suggest that when individuals become aware of mind-wandering, they are able to circumvent its costs either by more effectively dividing attention or terminating the episode and returning attention to the task.

2. Situational constraints on mind-wandering

Generally, if the primary task occupies *working memory resources then attention stays coupled to the task more effectively and for longer periods; as a result, mind-wandering is infrequent. For example, Antrobus et al. (1966) observed that mind-wandering was more frequent in a simple *signal detection task with a slow stimulus presentation rate than in one with a faster rate of presentation. More recently, the suppression of mind-wandering was shown to depend on whether the task involves rehearsal within working memory (Teasdale et al. 1993). Interestingly, the working memory of the individual seems to moderate the extent to which mind-wandering is experienced (Kane et al. 2007).

The simple involvement of working memory, however, is not the whole story with respect to mind-wandering. Attention is often drawn to objects that are interesting rather than complex. Moreover, according to ironic processing theory (Wegner 1994) in certain circumstances a working memory load can, in fact, be detrimental to our attempts to remain on task. In the context of tasks with a narrative, such as reading, it appears that our experience is held by features of the task which interest us rather than those which are simply difficult to complete. Grodsky and Giambra (1989) demonstrated that mind-wandering during reading was predicted by interest in text rather than difficulty in following. Presumably, participants find it a more absorbing experience to read an interesting story and as a result their minds wander less. Difficult expository texts, while requiring effort, do not lead to absorption and so attention is maintained on the task through our own vigilance.

When tasks are simple, the extent to which they occupy working memory resources determines whether mind-wandering occurs. As task complexity increases, however, mind-wandering is suppressed not simply by working memory involvement, because a task such as reading a dry expository text requires more resources than does reading an intriguing fiction story. Instead, mind-wandering is suppressed when we engage in a task which absorbs us in the experience of task-completion. We have suggested that the influences of factors like absorption or structure on mind-wandering, provides evidence that certain situations provide a cognitive *affordance* which help to anchor attention in the current context (Smallwood and Schooler 2006). The notion of an affordance emphasizes that certain situations provide the individual with the opportunity to focus on the here and now and that, if motivated to do so, can be used to temporarily escape from our own private thoughts and experiences. Considering our last visit to the cinema, for instance, it is obvious that the skill of the director and the effectiveness of the actors, rather than the amount of working memory load, determined whether the film afforded absorption or encouraged mind-wandering.

3. The neurophysiology of mind-wandering

The relative dearth of research on mind-wandering means that few studies have directly examined the neuropsychological concomitants of mind-wandering. Studies have documented that physiological activity (such as heart rate and skin conductance) is elevated during periods of mind-wandering. This physiological activity reflects the fact that during mind-wandering our attention is often drawn to our own current concerns—topics which are more emotionally arousing than the dry and relatively uninteresting cognitive situations in which these studies take place (see Smallwood and Schooler 2006).

One important implication of understanding the neuropsychological substrates of mind-wandering is that it provides a novel method for understanding brain activity that is unconstrained by the external environment. Research has documented that when deprived of external stimulation the brain recruits a network of discrete areas which are commonly referred to as the *default network* (Raichle et al. 2001). One plausible reason why this phenomenon occurs is because when resting participants can indulge in private thought, an activity which shares the same lack of environmental constraint as is involved in mind-wandering. Researchers have recently documented that situations that lead to task-induced deactivations in the default network correspond to the same situations in which mind-wandering is reduced. Indeed, a recent *functional brain imaging study using fMRI (Mason et al. 2007) found that under circumstances when practice on a task had reduced the need for attentional supervision there was enhanced default network activation.

In the future, it may be possible to use changes in the activity of the default network, or other indirect measures of mind-wandering including response time, physiological activation, or evoked response to task stimuli (Smallwood et al. 2008), to reveal mind-wandering unfolding in real time. Methodologically, this would revolutionize the study of mind-wandering by enabling the empirical examination of these private experiences without bringing them to the attention of the participant, and thereby prematurely terminating the episode.

JONATHAN SMALLWOOD AND JONATHAN W. SCHOOLER

Antrobus, J. S., Singer, J. L., and Greenberg, S. (1966). 'Studies in the stream of consciousness: experimental suppression of spontaneous cognitive processes'. *Perceptual and Motor Skills*, 23.

Grodsky, A. and Giambra, L. (1989). 'Task unrelated images and thoughts whilst reading'. In Shorr, J. et al. (eds) *Imagery: Current Perspectives*.

Kane, M. J., Brown, L. H., McVay, J. C., Silvia, P. J., Myin-Germeys, I., and Kwapil, T. R. (2007). 'For whom the mind wanders, and when: an experience-sampling study of working memory and executive control in daily life'. *Psychological Science*, 18.

Mason, M., Norton, M., Van Horn, J. D., Wegner, D. W., Grafton, S. T., and Macrae, C. N. (2007) 'Wandering minds: the default network and stimulus-independent thought'. *Science*, 315.

Raichle, M. E., MacLeod, A. M., Snyder, A. Z., Powers, W. J., Gusnard, D. A., and Shulman, G. L. (2001). 'A default mode of brain function'. *Proceedings of the National Academy of Sciences of the USA*, 98.

Smallwood, J., and Schooler, J. W. (2006). 'The restless mind'. *Psychological Bulletin*, 132.

——, Beach, E., Schooler, J. W., and Handy, T. C. (2008). 'Going AWOL in the brain: mind-wandering reduces cortical analysis of external events'. *Journal of Cognitive Neuroscience*, 20.

Teasdale, J. D., Lloyd, C. A., Proctor, L., and Baddeley, A. (1993). 'Working memory and stimulus-independent-thought: effects of memory load and presentation rate'. *European Journal of Psychology*, 5.

Wegner, D. M. (1994). 'Ironic processes of mental control'. *Psychological Review*, 101.

minimally conscious state See BRAIN DAMAGE

mirror neurons In the mid 1990s a new class of premotor neurons was discovered in the rostral sector of the macaque monkey's ventral premotor cortex, known as area F5. These neurons discharge not only when the monkey executes goal-related hand actions like grasping objects, but also when observing other individuals (monkeys or humans) executing similar actions. These neurons were called *mirror neurons* (Gallese et al. 1996). Neurons with similar properties were later discovered in a sector of the posterior parietal cortex reciprocally connected with area F5.

Action observation causes in the observer the automatic activation of the same neural mechanism triggered by action execution. The novelty of these findings is the fact that, for the first time, a neural mechanism that allows a direct matching between the visual description of an action and its execution has been identified. Such a matching system constitutes a parsimonious solution to the problem of translating the results of the visual analysis of an observed action—devoid of meaning for the observer—into an account that the individual is able to understand. It was proposed that this mechanism could be at the basis of a direct form of action understanding. If mirror neurons really mediate action understanding, their activity should reflect the meaning of the observed action, not its visual features.

1. Mirror neurons in monkeys
2. Mirror neuron systems in humans

1. Mirror neurons in monkeys

Typically, mirror neurons in monkeys do not respond to the sight of a hand mimicking an action in the absence of the target. Similarly, they do not respond to the observation of an object alone, even when it is of interest to the monkey (see Rizzolatti and Craighero 2004).

Prompted by these considerations, two series of experiments were carried out in which the monkey had no access to the visual features that normally activate mirror neurons. The first experiments tested whether the mental representation of an action triggers F5 mirror neurons, the second whether the monkeys are able to recognize actions from their sound. The results of these experiments provided positive answers to both questions, by showing that what drives the discharge of mirror neuron is not the pictorial description of an action, but rather the goal of the action, or to use a more mentalistic term, the motor idea of that action (see Rizzolatti and Craighero 2004).

In the most lateral part of area F5 a population of mirror neurons related to the execution/observation of mouth actions was described (see Rizzolatti and Craighero 2004). Most of these neurons discharge when the monkey executes and observes transitive, object-related ingestive actions, such as grasping, biting, or licking. However, a small percentage of mouth-related mirror neurons discharge during the observation of intransitive, communicative facial actions performed by the experimenter in front of the monkey (*communicative mirror neurons*). Macaque monkeys seem to have an initial capacity to control and emit 'voluntarily' social signals mediated by the frontal lobe. Most interestingly, this capacity develops in a cortical area—area F5—that in humans became Brodmann's area 44, a key area for verbal communication.

More recently the role of parietal mirror neurons in intention understanding has been unveiled. Fogassi et al. (2005) described a class of parietal mirror neurons whose discharge during the observation of an act (e.g. grasping an object), is conditioned by the type of not yet observed subsequent act (e.g. bringing the object to the mouth) specifying the overall action intention. This study shows that parietal mirror neurons, in addition to recognizing the goal of the observed motor act, allow the observing monkey to predict the agent's next action, henceforth its overall intention. This neural mechanism could scaffold more sophisticated mind reading abilities, as those characterizing our species (Gallese 2006, 2007).

2. Mirror neuron systems in humans

Several studies using different experimental methodologies and techniques have demonstrated that a mirror neuron system matching action perception and execution also exists in the human brain (for reviews see Gallese et al. 2004, Rizzolatti and Craighero 2004). During action observation there is a strong activation of premotor and posterior parietal areas, the likely human homologue of the monkey areas in which mirror neurons were originally described. The mirror neuron system for actions in humans is somatotopically organized, with distinct cortical regions within the premotor and posterior parietal cortices being activated by the observation/execution of mouth-, hand-, and foot-related actions.

The mirror neuron system for actions in humans is directly involved in imitation, in the perception of communicative actions, and in the detection of action intentions (see Gallese 2006). Furthermore, the premotor cortex containing the mirror system for action is involved in processing action-related sentences (see Gallese 2007), suggesting that mirror neurons together with other parts of the sensorimotor system could play a relevant role in language semantics (Gallese and Lakoff 2005, Gallese 2007).

Mirror neuron systems also underpin our capacity to *empathize. When we perceive others expressing a given emotion such as disgust, the same brain areas are activated as when we subjectively experience the same emotion. Similar direct matching mechanisms have been described for the perception of pain and touch (see Gallese et al. 2004, Gallese 2006). These results taken together suggest that our capacity to empathize with others is mediated by embodied simulation mechanisms; that is, by the activation of the same neural circuits underpinning our own emotional and sensory experiences (see Gallese et al. 2004, Gallese 2006). Recent studies suggest that these mechanisms could be deficient in individuals affected by *autistic spectrum disorders (see Gallese 2006).

The discovery of mirror neurons opens new exciting perspectives in a variety of different fields in social cognitive neuroscience, like our understanding of language, ethics and aesthetics (see Freedberg and Gallese 2007).

VITTORIO GALLESE

Fogassi, L., Ferrari, P. F., Gesierich, B., Rozzi, S., Chersi, F., and Rizzolatti, G. (2005). 'Parietal lobe: from action organization to intention understanding'. *Science*, 302.

Freedberg D. and Gallese V. (2007). 'Motion, emotion and empathy in esthetic experience'. *Trends in Cognitive Sciences*, 11.

Gallese, V. (2006). 'Intentional attunement: a neurophysiological perspective on social cognition and its disruption in autism'. *Brain Research: Cognitive Brain Research*, 1079.

—— (2007). 'Before and below "theory of mind": embodied simulation and the neural correlates of social cognition'. *Philosophical Transaction of the Royal Society of London Series B: Biological Sciences*, 362.

—— and Lakoff, G. (2005). 'The brain's concepts: the role of the sensory-motor system in reason and language'. *Cognitive Neuropsychology*, 22.

——, Fadiga, L., Fogassi, L., and Rizzolatti, G. (1996). 'Action recognition in the premotor cortex'. *Brain*, 119.

——, Keysers, C., and Rizzolatti, G. (2004). 'A unifying view of the basis of social cognition'. *Trends in Cognitive Sciences*, 8.

Rizzolatti, G. and Craighero, L. (2004). 'The mirror neuron system'. *Annual Review of Neuroscience*, 27.

mirror test The mirror test is employed to examine an individual's ability to recognize itself in a mirror. It has been used as a test for self-recognition in primates and other non-human species, developmentally in humans and primates, and in clinical populations. Though proponents of this test argue that positive self-recognition indicates the presence of self-awareness, this idea is still debated.

Testing for self-recognition using a mirror has a long and rich history. The earliest published report was in 1828, when J. Grant presented a looking glass to orangutans and monkeys. Grant noted that neither species appeared to self-recognize; the monkeys appeared surprised and the orangutans did not express any noticeable emotional reaction. Charles Darwin also tested nonhuman primates in 1872 when he too examined the reaction of orangutans. They also failed to exhibit self-recognition. Darwin is also thought to be the first researcher to formally employ a mirror to determine when human children develop self-recognition and self-awareness. Though his studies of children (he tested his own) originated in 1839, he did not publish his findings until 1877. A number of other prominent researchers employed mirrors to test for self-recognition including Wilhelm Preyer in the 1880s and Wolfgang Kohler in the 1920s (see Keenan et al. 2003).

However, the first formalized experimental tests of mirror recognition did not occur until the late 1960s when the *mirror-mark test* was introduced by Gordon G. Gallup, Jr. (Gallup 1970). The mirror-mark test (typically referred to as the mirror test) introduced sterner controls and a true dependent variable in testing for self-recognition. The test involves four distinct phases. First, the individual is exposed to a mirror to establish baseline recognition and familiarity. Second, the individual is placed under anaesthesia and a mark is placed on the body in an area only observable via the mirror (e.g. the individual's forehead). The anaesthesia is used in order to eliminate all other cues that would alert the individual to the presence of the mark and therefore influence the direction of attention once in front of the mirror. The mark is meant to be viewed as a novel stimulus discriminated on the basis of prior knowledge. The last phase of the testing involves re-introducing the animal to the mirror and observing mark-directed responses. If the individual touches the mark while in front of the mirror, it is considered to have self-recognition. A number of controls are normally put in place, such as replications of the procedure and only counting movements to the mark while in front of the mirror. Gallup's initial examinations involved the testing of monkeys and chimpanzees. To most people's surprise, it was found that chimpanzees actually 'passed' the test while monkeys did not. His data provided the first solid evidence that humans are not the only species to self-recognize.

Through extensive testing, it has been found that chimpanzees do possess self-recognition abilities; on average about 50% pass the mirror test. Orangutans, contrary to the earlier historical accounts, also pass the test. Monkeys, regardless of species or length of exposure, do not demonstrate self-recognition (one report of tamarins passing has failed to replicate). These data suggest a clean phylogenic trend such that the closest relatives to humans (the apes) self-recognize, while our more distant relatives the monkeys do not. Unfortunately, the results for gorillas, who are genetically more related to humans than orangutans, are puzzling. Gorillas do not pass the mirror-test on a consistent basis, and only anecdotal reports exist of them passing (for review, see Parker et al. 1994).

In addition to the apes, there is now evidence that other animals may pass. A recent report demonstrated that at least one elephant made mark-directed responses in front of a mirror using its trunk, which ran contrary to earlier negative reports in elephants. Further, dolphins appear capable of passing the mirror test, though it is difficult to replicate the original experiment in these animals as they are unable to make a clear mark-directed response. Although B. F Skinner reported that pigeons could pass, the evidence is now clear that they were trained to do so and there is no evidence of spontaneous mark-responding.

The mirror test has also been used in children to determine the timeline of self-recognition (Amsterdam 1972). It has been found that in normally developing children, a positive mark-directed response is observed around 18 months. Although there is a high degree of variability, it is rare to see a child pass the test before the age of 14 months. Personality may play a role, as might individuation and separation, with children who are more independent recognizing their image earlier than those who are more dependent. Clinically, the mirror test has been used to test for self-recognition in a number of populations including *schizophrenics (who have a variable response) and Alzheimer's patients (who lose self-recognition in the later phases of *dementia). Of particular interest are individuals with *autism and Aspergers syndrome, who appear to have a deficit in mirror-recognition. Both published and unpublished data suggest that these populations fail to self-recognize on a consistent basis, though here too there is heterogeneity of response. These findings are of significant interest because both autism and Asperger's patients suffer from deficits in other self-related abilities. Because populations that have self-awareness deficits fail the mirror test, some have speculated that the mirror test be an indicator of general self-awareness abilities rather than self-recognition per se.

Perhaps the main question in terms of the mirror test involves the implication of passing. As has been suggested, passing the mirror test may indicate the possession of self-awareness, or the ability to take a third-person perspective in regards to oneself. Evidence for this comes from a number of sources. First, children who pass the mirror test exhibit self-conscious emotions (such as pride and embarrassment), while those that fail the test do not exhibit such emotions (Lewis et al. 1989). Clinical populations that perform poorly on the mirror test, such as individuals with autism or schizophrenia, often show deficits in other self-related abilities. On a species level, it has been found that the animals that pass the test excel in terms of other self-related tasks. Finally, brain regions that are activated during self-recognition are similar to brain areas activated for other self-related processes such as autobiographical and introspective processing. Unfortunately, most of these data are correlational and it is difficult to know if the mirror test is truly tapping into self-awareness.

It has also been speculated that there is a relationship between self-recognition and recognition of others. True self-recognition, as implied by passing the mirror test, appears to be related to both physical recognition of others, and more importantly the ability to recognize mental states as well. That is, there appears to be a relationship between self-recognition and the ability to infer mental states, or theory of mind. For example, soon after passing the mirror test, children begin to employ theory of mind in tasks such as the intentional deception of others. Further, there is a relationship between self-recognition performance and theory of mind such that increased self-recognition and self-awareness results in improved deception and deception detection. Both theory of mind and self-recognition appear to be subserved via similar brain regions, providing at least correlative evidence that the two are related (Platek et al. 2004). That there is a correlation between self-recognition and theory of mind provides further evidence that self-face recognition may in fact be measuring self-awareness.

While many support the idea that self-recognition indicates higher-order self-reflective abilities, it is argued that visuo-kinaesthetic matching may account for self-recognition in a mirror. According to this theory, animals (or individuals) that fail are simply unable to match the reflection in a mirror with their own activity (Mitchell 1997). This theory is appealing as it avoids the phylogenetic difficulties posed by the fact that divergent species appear to pass the test. The theory runs into difficulty in a number of ways, however, including the fact that animals that fail to pass the mirror test can identify others in a mirror and successfully use the mirror to retrieve food.

The mirror test has garnered popularity, as it is language-free, relatively easy to employ, and flexible in design. However, it is not without issues. The test requires memory (an individual must contrast the pre-test image with the post-test image), visual abilities, and face recognition as the mark is normally placed on an individual's forehead or eyebrow ridge. Finally, motivation is clearly an issue, as an individual must have impetus to actually make a response to the mark.

JULIAN PAUL KEENAN AND MONISHA ANAND KUMAR

Amsterdam, B. (1972). 'Mirror self-image reactions before age two'. *Developmental Psychobiology*, 5.

Darwin, C. (1877). 'A biographical sketch of an infant'. *Mind*, 2.

Gallup, G. G. (1970). 'Chimpanzees: self-recognition'. *Science*, 86.

Keenan, J. P., Gallup, G. G., and Falk, D. (2003). *The Face in the Mirror: The Search for the Origins of Consciousness.*

Lewis, M., Sullivan, M. W., Stanger, C., and Weiss, M. (1989). 'Self development and self-conscious emotions'. *Child Development*, 60.

Mitchell, R. W. (1997). 'Kinesthetic-visual matching and the self-concept as explanations of mirror-self-recognition'. *Journal for the Theory of Social Behaviour*, 27.

Parker, S., Mitchell, R., and Boccia, M. (eds) (1994). *Self-Awareness in Animals and Humans: Developmental Perspectives.*

Platek, S., Keenan, J. P., Gallup, G. G., and Mohamed, F. B. (2004). 'Where am I? The neurological correlates of self and other'. *Cognitive Brain Research*, 19.

Molyneux's question William Molyneux, a Dublin lawyer, posed his problem in a letter to John Locke in 1688, and sparked several centuries of discussion (see BLINDNESS, RECOVERY FROM). The scientific and philosophical questions are still not well understood. Locke's formulation of Molyneux's question in the second edition of the *Essay* is:

> Suppose a Man born blind, and now adult, and taught by his touch to distinguish between a Cube, and Sphere of the same metal, and nighly of the same bigness, so as to tell, when he felt one and t'other, which is the Cube, and which the Sphere. Suppose then the Cube and the Sphere placed on a Table, and the Blind Man to be made to see. Quaere, Whether by his sight, before he touch'd them, he could now distinguish, and tell, which is the Globe, which the Cube. (*Essay* II ix 8)

Locke's own answer was negative. The proper object of vision is 'light and colours'; there is no perception of shape in vision itself. It is only vision as instructed by *touch that can be said to involve perception of shape (Bolton 1994). But the whole point about the newly sighted man is that his vision has not yet been instructed by touch. So seeing the Cube and the Globe will merely present him with an array of light and colours.

Locke's claims about the calibration of vision by touch are open to challenge. Habituation to the three-dimensional shapes of seen objects is observed in neonates, who have not had the opportunity to investigate visual–tactile correlations. Moreover, neonates who have been visually habituated to a particular shape seem to prefer tactile investigation of the visually presented shape, suggesting recognition of the sameness of the visually and tactilely presented shapes (Meltzoff 1993). And in adults, vision seems to calibrate touch rather than touch calibrating vision. For example, when someone wears a rectangular prism over a period of days, so that vision and touch initially conflict, it is vision that instructs touch, so that things start to feel the way they look; there is 'visual capture' of tactual perception (Rock 1983).

What about Locke's idea that shape is not among the proper objects of vision? Is there not an ordinary sense in which we see the shapes of things? Evans (1985) proposed that in vision there is a spatial content we conceptualize in terms of shape; similarly, in touch there is a spatial content we conceptualize in terms of shape. Molyneux's question can then be reformulated as a problem about conceptualization: Are the shape concepts we exercise on the basis of vision the same as those that we exercise on the basis of touch? If the visual and tactile concepts are the same, there is no need for an innate structure to establish the connection between them; there are not distinct types of concept to be linked.

In what sense are the concepts of shape exercised on the basis of sight and touch the same? You might argue that grasp of shape concepts is achieved as grasp of an intuitive physics, a rudimentary theory about the behaviours of objects. And, you might argue, it is the same physical theory that penetrates vision as penetrates touch. Whether perceived through vision or touch, round things roll, square things stack together without leaving gaps, and so on. We take the regularities governing the behaviours of objects of particular shapes to be the same, whatever the modality through which they are perceived. You might argue that this sameness of intuitive theory penetrating the sensory modality is all it takes for it to be the same shape concepts we exercise on the basis of sight and touch (Thompson 1974).

Evans (1985) took a different tack, arguing that sameness of concept follows from the sameness in sight and touch of the sensory basis on which shape concepts are applied. This sensory basis was supplied by non-conceptual content identifying the locations of things in an egocentric space. Perceptions were said to have their egocentric spatial content in virtue of their systematic relations to behaviour; and 'there is only one egocentric space, because there is only one behavioral space' (Evans 1985). All perceptual spatial content feeds into a single repertoire of behaviours. This approach faces a number of problems. It seems unlikely that visual shape perception extracts shape information from information about egocentric locations. Shape perception is possible in the absence of egocentric spatial information. Models of the processing pathways in vision generally distinguish between the pathways involved in finding shapes and those involved in finding egocentric locations (Goodale and Milner 1995). It is in any case not obvious that egocentric spatial content can be analysed in terms of its connections with behaviour.

We might look again at the idea that shape concepts are embedded in an intuitive physics. To know the causal significance of shape properties is to know something about what difference they make to the behaviour of an object. An ordinary person knows something about the differences manipulating the shape of an object will make to the behaviour of that object. We all manipulate the shapes of objects a hundred times a day, folding and bending and stacking and so on. Whether we have a single repertoire of shape concepts may depend on whether there is a single repertoire of manipulative behaviour for shapes based in just the same way on sight as on touch.

Of course there are differences between vision and touch, in virtue of which we typically know which modality we are using. But consider the position of someone who holds that the content of perception is conceptual and that the same shape concepts figure in both vision and touch. She will hold that the phenomenological difference between sight and touch is consistent with everything specific to the experience of shape being the same in sight as in touch.

Philosophers who think that the phenomenology of perception is more primitive than any conceptual content will feel that the basic question has still to be addressed: Is conscious experience specifically of shape the same in vision and touch? Moore's (1903) discussion of phenomenology provides an approach that does not appeal to conceptualization. According to Moore, conscious experience is a generic relation between the perceiver and a property; the specific qualitative character of the experience depends entirely on what property is being experienced. A conscious experience of blue and a conscious experience of green are differentiated only by their objects, not by any difference in the relation of experiencing, which is generic. If this is correct, then experiences of shape in sight and touch are bound to be qualitatively identical, since they have the same external objects.

Moore seems to have been thinking of consciousness of the property as a two-place relation between subject and property. But there can be awareness of the same external property from different standpoints. Do we not then have to have a three-place relation: the subject is conscious of the property from a particular standpoint (van Cleve in press)? All the substantive work is then in characterizing the notion of the standpoint from which a property is experienced, and the relation between this notion of a standpoint and the sensory mo-

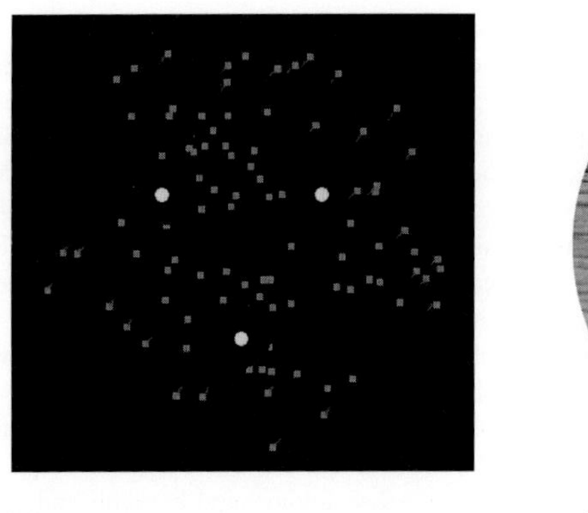

(a)

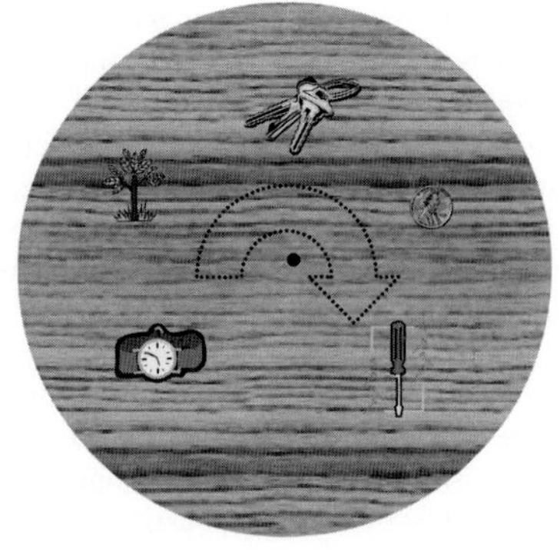

(b)

Fig. M2. Typical stimuli that produce motion-induced blindness. (a) A snapshot of a dynamic computer display in which the blue dots produce a three-dimensional sphere that rotates around, while the yellow dots are static. With steady fixation, observers report the disappearance of one or more yellow dots for periods of a few seconds at a time. (b) Illustration of a physical set-up that produces MIB. Several salient objects are placed on a static transparent glass surface, under which a textured plate can be rotated. When the textured surface is set in motion while observers fixate in the centre, the objects often disappear (see Colour Plate 10).

dalities. Molyneux's question is stated quite simply, but comprehensive resolution of the philosophical issues requires resolution of far-reaching problems about the characterization of perceptual consciousness.

JOHN CAMPBELL

Bolton, M. B. (1994). 'The real Molyneux question and the basis of Locke's answer'. In Rogers, G. A. J. (ed.), *Locke's Philosophy: Content and Context*.

Evans, G. (1985). 'Molyneux's question' In his *Collected Papers*.

Goodale, M. A. and Milner, A. D. (1995). *The Visual Brain in Action*.

Meltzoff, A. N. (1993). 'Molyneux's babies: cross-modal perception, imitation, and the mind of the preverbal infant'. In Eilan, N. et al. (ed.) *Spatial Representation: Problems in Philosophy and Psychology*.

Moore, G. E. (1903). 'The refutation of idealism'. *Mind*, 12.

Rock, I. (1983). *The Logic of Perception*.

Thompson, J. J. (1974). 'Molyneux's problem'. *Journal of Philosophy*, 71.

Van Cleve, J. (in press). 'Troubles for radical transparency'. In Greco, J. et al. (eds) *Festschrift for Robert Audi*. Forthcoming

monism See DUAL ASPECT THEORIES

motion-induced blindness Motion-induced blindness (MIB) refers to a phenomenon of 'visual disappearance' in which a relatively small but salient object disappears from awareness for several seconds at a time when embedded within a global moving pattern. In a typical example (see Fig. M3), a swirling cloud of blue dots is superimposed on three highly salient but stationary yellow spots. When one fixates anywhere on the display, after a while, one, two, or even all three spots simply disappear. The swirling cloud appears to wipe the yellow spots from sight, even though the spots continue to stimulate the retina. The properties of this phenomenon can best be appreciated by a dynamic demonstration (see e.g. Bonneh et al. 2000, Bach 2002). Although some observers fail to see the effect at the beginning, most observers tend to improve with practice and some are even able to get small patterns to disappear almost indefinitely. Overall, the MIB phenomenon is quite robust. The size of the disappearing pattern (the *target*) should generally be small, but patterns as large as a thumb at arm's length distance can also disappear. The disappearing pattern need not be very peripheral and can disappear even when as close as 1° off fixation, whereas fixated patterns rarely or never disappear. Eye movements such as abrupt saccades typically terminate the disappearance, although it can often survive small eye movements around fixation. The type of moving pattern (the *mask*) affects the disappearance but many types of motion can induce some disappearance even for very sparse masks of only a few dots, as long as the mask surrounds the target.

The MIB phenomenon can occur under more natural conditions than those described above, and perhaps even in everyday life situations. Richard Brown, from the Exploratorium science museum in San Francisco, created a version of the phenomenon, which is illustrated in Fig. M3b. Objects as salient as a silver watch or keys, which are placed on a round transparent table, can disappear when a textured plate underneath the table is rotated. Interestingly, a strong disappearance effect occurs immediately after the onset of the rotation movement, thus demonstrating that a transient stimulus is especially effective in inducing disappearance. Professor Shinsuke Shimojo, from Caltech, used a mirror ball (as found in discotheques) to create an optical flow field on the walls of a large, dark room. Watching a standing figure from a distance of a few metres in this setting creates the illusion of a floating figure, followed by the complete disappearance of this figure. Interestingly, this demonstration may suggest a possible link between the loss of 'whereness' (the floating position of the figure) and the loss of awareness (its disappearance). A third example of MIB is night driving, where the driver is often exposed to an optical flow field from the road lights while fixating on the relatively static back lights of the car in front of him. These lights could possibly disappear, especially when the driver is tired and does not move his eyes or blink much.

Motion-induced blindness can be considered in relation to other conditions in which salient visual stimuli are blocked from conscious perception. For example, we often fail to notice stimuli that appear too briefly or stimuli that are of a very low contrast or are masked by some noise or a cluttered environment or when our attention is distracted. Such phenomena are studied as masking, *change blindness, *inattentional blindness, and the *attentional blink. Among the cases in which visual stimuli do not register consciously, there is a class of phenomena in which the lack of perception has an explicit nature of 'visual disappearance', as if stimuli are erased in front of the observer's eyes. The most prominent among these phenomena are *binocular rivalry, in which dissimilar patterns presented to different eyes disappear in alternation, and Troxler fading, in which low-contrast peripheral stimuli disappear under strict fixation. Other phenomena include images stabilized on the retina (e.g. drawn on a contact lens) that fade away, meta-contrast masking (see MASKING, VISUAL), after-images (e.g. that occur following exposure to a flash) that similarly disappear and reappear (see AFTER-EFFECTS, PERCEPTUAL), perceptual *filling-in of artificial scotoma, transient-induced fading (Kanai and Kamitani 2003) and its earlier version, which resembles MIB (Grindley and Townsend 1967). MIB belongs to this class of phenomena and is similar to some of them; however, its stochastic nature makes it related to *multistable phenomena in general. Among these, the most interesting comparison is with binocular rivalry. Although both are bistable and have a similar time-course, MIB does not require an unnatural dissociation between the eyes, but on the other hand, the disappearing pattern must be relatively small with more local and independent disappearance at different locations.

What can MIB reveal to us about consciousness? Consider what happens when a bright and salient spot suddenly disappears, having been wiped out by a moving pattern for several seconds. Perceptually, this is identical to erasing the spot from the screen and in fact, observers cannot tell the difference and are often convinced that the spot was erased. However, the bright spot reaches the eyes continuously and from there arrives to the brain, and apparently, it is represented there without being visible. This allows us to compare the neural responses under two physically identical conditions: one visible or conscious, and the other invisible or subconscious. Thus, we can ask: what is the neural representation that underlies visibility, or more generally, what is the neural *correlate of conscious perception? For example, is consciousness confined to specific brain regions, perhaps excluding some low-level processing stages, or alternatively, is it spread in many regions, perhaps dynamically? Is it related to neural firing rates, or alternatively, to specific temporal patterns of firing or synchrony? Is the representation of the invisible accessible to interaction with visible stimuli and does it retain all properties compared to the representation of the visible? This approach of investigating the neural correlates of consciousness (NCC) through the study of visual perception has been advocated and pursued by Christof Koch and Francis Crick (Crick and Koch 2003).

MIB has been studied for only a few years. Its study focuses on understanding the underlying neural mechanism, with the aim of discovering some general mechanisms and principles that underlie visual awareness. Currently, the underlying mechanisms are largely unknown, but there are several pieces of evidence that provide possible explanations. The first intuitive idea of early suppression by peripheral sensory mechanisms, perhaps even at the retina, seems unlikely for several reasons. First, retinal adaptation, owing, for example, to reduced eye movements or any local adaptation, can be rejected because a slowly moving pattern can disappear at one position and reappear after a few seconds on the other side of the screen. Second, the moving mask can be quite far from the disappearing pattern as long as it surrounds it, thus ruling out any local masking mechanism. Third, at least under certain conditions, the brighter the pattern is, the more it disappears, thus ruling out a simple 'gain-control' mechanism that discards low-contrast stimuli in a cluttered environment.

Another line of evidence focuses on the fate of the invisible stimuli, and the type of their residual subconscious processing. According to this viewpoint, if a visual object is completely erased at a certain level of a hierarchical process, then it will not affect higher-level processing and its disappearance properties will not be affected by these higher levels, at least not the invisible periods. Importantly, it was shown that stimuli rendered invisible by MIB retain their capacity to produce orientation-selective adaptation (Montaser-Kouhsari et al. 2004) and to induce negative afterimages (Hofstoetter et al. 2004), suggesting a cortical representation of the invisible at these levels of processing. Moreover, stimuli that group perceptually into objects or *gestalts, such as collinear line segments or proximal dots tend to disappear and reappear in synchrony and less frequently, rather than disappear and reappear independently (Bonneh et al. 2001). When the configuration is changed during the invisible stage, its reappearance depends on the new configuration, with good gestalts reappearing in unity and bad gestalts in parts (Mitroff and Scholl 2005). This suggests that a representation of the invisible objects is available at the level of gestalt grouping. Finally, the three-dimensional segmentation of the mask relative to the target has a significant effect on disappearance. Specifically, more disappearance occurs when the mask is presented in front of the target, e.g. via binocular stereo disparity; thus, it is interpreted that the mask occludes the target.

Even though accumulating evidence does not enable us to explain the MIB phenomenon and its underlying mechanisms, we can still speculate. A useful first step is to view the visual system not as a device for representing external images, but instead as an interpretation system that may discard part of the input and complete missing input in order to arrive at a coherent and useful interpretation of the visual scene (see PERCEPTION, PHILOSOPHICAL PERSPECTIVES and ILLUSIONS for a discussion of related ideas). Accordingly, visual stimuli could be discarded if they are inconsistent with the selected interpretation. Indeed, a possible interpretation of a typical MIB stimulus is that the yellow spots are occluded by the mask. But why should the system make such an interpretation even when this appears least likely? One answer assumes that different levels of processing are involved. At the sensory level, the lack of transient stimulation of the targets may cause a decay of the response owing to adaptation mechanisms. This occurs all the time, even without the surrounding motion, but the system normally knows not to interpret this decay as a physical disappearance and to fill in the missing representation across time. However, when there is a perceptual hint that suggests otherwise, then the system may interpret the sensory decay as a real disappearance. Thus, MIB results from a sensory level process, an interpretation or decision level process and their interaction.

Conscious perception, as reflected in MIB and other multistable phenomena is fragile and unreliable, since under certain conditions salient objects may suddenly disappear or change their appearance dramatically. MIB, like other phenomena of this kind, is subject to experimental investigation, and may be used to study the neural correlates of consciousness.

YORAM S. BONNEH

Bach, M. (2002). 'Motion-induced blindness'. In *80 Optical Illusions and Visual Phenomena*. www.michaelbach.de/ot/mot_mib/

Bonneh, Y., Cooperman, A., and Sagi, D. (2000) 'Motion induced blindness'. www.weizmann.ac.il/home/bnbobbeh/MIB/mib.html

—— —— —— (2001). 'Motion-induced blindness in normal observers'. *Nature*, 411.

Crick, F. and Koch, C. (2003). 'A framework for consciousness'. *Nature Neuroscience*, 6.

Grindley, G. C. and Townsend, V. (1967). 'Further experiments on movement masking'. *Quarterly Journal of Experimental Psychology*, 18.

Hofstoetter, C., Koch, C., and Kiper, D. C. (2004). 'Motion-induced blindness does not affect the formation of negative afterimages'. *Consciousness and Cognition*, 13.

Kanai, R. and Kamitani, Y. (2003). 'Time-locked perceptual fading induced by visual transients'. *Journal of Cognitive Neuroscience*, 15.

Mitroff, S. R. and Scholl, B. J. (2005). 'Forming and updating object representations without awareness: evidence from motion-induced blindness'. *Vision Research*, 45.

Montaser-Kouhsari, L., Moradi, F., Zandvakili, A., and Esteky, H. (2004). 'Orientation-selective adaptation during motion-induced blindness'. *Perception*, 33.

motor representation See ACTION SCIENTIFIC PERSPECTIVES

multiple drafts model The multiple drafts model of consciousness (Dennett 1991, 1996, 1998, Dennett and Kinsbourne 1992) was developed as an alternative to the perennially attractive, but incoherent, model of conscious experience that Dennett calls Cartesian materialism. According to Cartesian materialism, after unconscious processing occurs in various relatively peripheral brain structures, 'everything comes together' in some privileged and central place in the brain—which Dennett dubs the Cartesian Theatre—for 'presentation' to the inner self or *homunculus. (The homunculus is not literally a little man—with arms and legs and eyes, for instance—but just a whole self, capable of enjoying, suffering, deciding, and so forth.) Consciousness of an item occurs, according to this model, at the moment the homunculus witnesses the presentation of that item. There is no such place in the brain, but many theories seem to presuppose that there is. For instance:

(1) They provide analyses of the 'early, unconscious' processing in perception, but postpone indefinitely the task of saying where and when the results of all the transformations and discriminations are 'made available to conscious awareness'. Or (2) They argue that a decision 'by the brain' to act (e.g. to move a limb) takes several hundred milliseconds to 'rise' to consciousness, creating an ominous picture of human agents as sequestered in outposts in their own brains and deluded about their ability to make a conscious decision (e.g. Libet 1985, Wegner 2002). Or (3) They suppose that the initial transduction by sense organs of light and sound and odour and so forth into an unconscious neural code must be followed (somewhere in the brain) by a second transduction into some other medium, the 'medium of consciousness' (e.g. Mangan 1993).

It seems obvious that there has to be a time before which we are not conscious of some item and after which we are conscious of it. In some sense, then, we *become* conscious of various features of our experience, so there must be some kind of transition, if not arrival at a place or crossing of a boundary, then a change of functional state of one sort or another. Consider the simple case of consciously seeing a flash of light and thereupon pressing a button. Neither arrival of the flash at the retina, nor the subsequent triggering of a signal in the optic nerve is sufficient for consciousness, obviously. If there is no second transduction, occurring at a particular time and place in the brain, then how can we understand the difference between those brain processes that somehow subserve conscious experience and those that are entirely unconscious but nevertheless involve, or are responsive to, perceptual or other contents? The multiple drafts model is an attempt to improve on this question and then answer it with a deliberately non-committal sketch—not tied to specifics of neuroanatomy—that avoids the seductive trap of positing a (functionally defined) place in the brain arrival at which is sufficient for consciousness. A wide variety of quite different specific models of brain activity could thus qualify as multiple drafts models of consciousness if they honoured its key propositions:

(a) The work done by the imaginary homunculus in the Cartesian Theatre must be broken up and distributed *in time and space* to specialized lesser agencies in the brain.
(b) Once a specialist has done its work, *that work does not have to be done again* in a central re-presentation process. That means that the content involved does not have to be perceived again, discriminated again, enjoyed again, abhorred again (if it is, for instance, a pain) nor does it have to be moved somewhere and presented again in order to be stored in memory.
(c) There is a massively parallel process in the brain—in the cortices and subcortical structures they interact with—in which *multiple* (and often incompatible) streams of content fixation, transformation, influence, suppression, enhancement, 'binding', memory-loading, etc., take place simultaneously (and asynchronously). These are the *multiple drafts* out of which the appearance of a 'final draft'—the imagined draft of consciousness enacted on the imagined stage of the Cartesian Theatre—is created by the occurrence of 'probes' that retrospectively elevate some drafts at the expense of others. In the absence of such probes, the question of whether or not a content was conscious is ill-posed. (This will be explained below.)
(d) 'Since *you* are nothing beyond the various subagencies and processes in your nervous system that compose you, the following question is always a trap: 'Exactly when did *I* (as opposed to various parts of my brain) become informed, aware, conscious, of some event?' (Dennett 1998:105)

Dennett replaced the metaphor of multiple drafts with the metaphor of *fame in the brain*. Just as *becoming famous* is not a precisely datable event like being transduced into a medium (such as television), so achieving fame (or 'clout') in the brain is not a precisely datable transition in the brain. It is a competitive phenomenon—not all can be famous. Even more important, consciousness is only retrospectively determinable. Since it is *constituted* by its sequelae, one must always ask the hard question: 'And then what happens?' (Dennett 1991:255) One cannot—logically cannot—be famous for just 15 minutes; that would not be fame. And a content cannot be conscious for 15 ms and utterly forgotten afterwards; that would not be consciousness.

The perplexing questions about the timing of conscious experiences, to which the multiple drafts model is particularly addressed, can be further clarified by yet another analogy, where the same curious status can be transparently observed: speciation events in evolution. What animal was the last common ancestor of all the chimpanzees, bonobos, and human beings? We know the split occurred roughly 6 million years ago, and that some one animal in fact must be the most recent ancestor of them all. Every birth in every lineage is a potential speciation event but not one in a million turns out, in the fullness of time, to have been a speciation event. It is logically impossible to discern which births are speciation events at the moment they occur, because nothing about them at the time distinguishes them; that status depends on whether or not they lead to further births and still further births, and the eventual triumph of that lineage of births over others. Speciation events are discriminable only by 'retrospective coronations'.

Similarly, those content-fixations in the brain that turn out to be have been conscious are those that happen to have the sequelae that ensure their fame—and this depends not just on their temporally and spatially local properties, but on the subsequent competition for fame with their rivals. (This means that there cannot be, except in some arbitrary way, any temporally local neural *correlates of consciousness, any more than there are temporally local biological correlates of speciation.) Contents begin to have influencing effects on other contents and other processes as soon as they are locally discriminated, and not only do these effects not have to be postponed until after some special state of consciousness is somehow achieved; their cumulative occurrence composes, over time, the very 'fame' that we retrospectively acknowledge as presence to consciousness. We can call the space in which all this competition and elaboration occurs the *global workspace and then note that arrival in the global workspace (however we draw its boundaries) is necessary but not sufficient for consciousness of some content, since not all contents vying in the global workspace achieve fame. Precisely when do these winning contents become conscious? That is an ill-posed question, for exactly the same reason that the parallel question is ill-posed in biology. All the specific events that go to compose the eventual 'fame' can be located in both space and time with considerable accuracy, but the onset of fame itself is clockable with precision only in those unusual cases in which all the relevant events are squeezed into a narrow time window.

A familiar version of the same problem arising for the timing of consciousness can be observed in the phenomenon of coming to notice the chiming of a clock. Only on the fourth peal, perhaps, did you become aware of the clock chiming, but you discover you can retrospectively count the chimes in conscious memory. But when were you first conscious of the first chime? When it happened, five seconds ago, or just now, when you experienced it in recollection just as the fifth chime pealed? If the clock had chimed just three times, would you ever have been conscious of those chimes? We could no doubt discover a host of processes initiated in your brain by the discrimination of those three chimes at the time they occurred, but would those processes have been 'enough for consciousness' (of a sort)? How much is enough? How much influence is enough for fame? How many descendants are enough for a species?

When these analogies are set aside, the literal claims of the multiple drafts model are so bland as to seem to be a denial of the very existence of consciousness—nothing dramatic happens:

> Contents arise, get revised, contribute to the interpretation of other contents or to the modulation of behavior (verbal or otherwise), and in the process leave their traces in memory, which then eventually decay or get incorporated into or overwritten by later contents, wholly or in part. This skein of contents is only rather like a narrative because of its multiplicity; at any point in time there are multiple drafts of narrative fragments at various stages of editing in various places in the brain.... Probing this stream at various intervals produces different effects, precipitating different narratives—and these *are* narratives: single versions of a portion of 'the stream of consciousness.' If one delays the probe too long, the result is apt to be no narrative left at all. If one probes 'too early' one may gather data on how early a particular discrimination is achieved in the stream, but at the cost of disrupting the normal progression of the stream. (Dennett 1991:135–6)

This is not a denial of the existence of consciousness; it is the claim—hard for some people to credit—that consciousness is not what it seems to be (a magic show illuminating an inner stage). It is, instead, the relatively greater influence of various contents on the processes that control the body of an agent composed of those processes and capable of telling us (and reminding itself) about some of them. According to the multiple drafts model, any agent with such a phenomenon installed in it is conscious in just the way we are.

DANIEL C. DENNETT

Dennett, D. C. (1991). *Consciousness Explained.*

—— (1996). 'Consciousness: more like fame than television' (in German translation) 'Bewusstsein hat mehr mit Ruhm als mit Fernsehen zu tun'. In Maar, C. et al. (eds) *Die Technik auf dem Weg zur Seele.*

—— (1998). 'The myth of double transduction'. In Hameroff, S. et al. (eds) *International Consciousness Conference, Toward a Science of Consciousness II. The Second Tucson Discussions and Debates.*

—— (2001). 'Are we explaining consciousness yet?' *Cognition*, 79.

—— (2005). *Sweet Dreams: Philosophical Obstacles to a Theory of Consciousness.*

—— and Kinsbourne, M. (1992). 'Time and the observer: the where and when of consciousness in the brain'. *Behavioral and Brain Sciences*, 15.

Libet, B. (1985). 'Unconscious cerebral initiative and the role of conscious will in voluntary action'. *Behavioral and Brain Sciences*, 8.

Mangan, B. (1993). 'Taking phenomenology seriously: the fringe and it implications for cognitive research'. *Consciousness and Cognition*, 2.

Wegner, D. (2002). *The Illusion of Conscious Will.*

multiple personality disorder See DISSOCIATIVE IDENTITY DISORDER

multiple realizability See FUNCTIONALIST THEORIES OF CONSCIOUSNESS; REDUCTIONISM

multistable perception For some objects or events, perception can fluctuate over time, with alternative perceptual interpretations replacing one another even though the physical conditions of stimulation remain unchanged; this is known as multistable perception. These beguiling phenomena fascinate psychologists and philosophers because multistable perception reveals a patent dissociation of physical reality and mental experience. In recent years, brain scientists have been keenly interested in multistable perception: identification of the changing patterns of neural activity coincident with fluctuations between perceptual states could shed light on the neural *correlates of consciousness (Koch 2005).

Most instances of multistable perception arise in vision, and they can take a number of different forms. Some figures produce fluctuations in visual perception because they portray alternative, contradictory figure/ground interpretations—in Fig. M3a, for example, you can see black arrows against a white background or white arrows against a black background. Another classic example of figure/ground multistability is the vase/face illusion often pictured in textbooks. Other multistable figures portray ambiguous depth relations among constituent features, leading to spontaneous perspective reversals over time. Thus, for example, in Fig. M3b you may see the front surface of the outline cube facing in either of two directions, down and to the right or up and to the left. Still other figures connote alternative object interpretations—thus, for example, Fig. M3c can be seen as a duck or as a rabbit. Artists sometimes incorporate bistable figures into their paintings, a notable example being Savador Dali's *The Slave Market with Disappearing Bust of Voltaire*. The beguiling, ephemeral smile of Leonardo da Vinci's *Mona Lisa* also represents a form of perceptual ambiguity.

Perceptual multistability can also occur when viewing visual animations in which the directions of motion of the moving objects are ambiguous. Thus, for example, perception of motion experienced when viewing the animation sequence shown in Fig. M4 is bistable: the two objects can appear to move in either of two directions, and with repeated exposures to the sequence both possible visual interpretations will be experienced. There exists an auditory analog to bistable motion: when listening to an unchanging, rhythmic sequence comprised of two sounds (e.g. 'tick' and 'tock'), an individual tends to hear one of the two as the 'leading' sound, but over time the particular sound heard as the 'lead' will fluctuate. In all of these instances, the perceptual ambiguity is resolved by a time-sharing compromise: an observer experiences first one interpretation and then the other, with switches in perception typically occurring irregularly over time. Most examples of multistable perception entail two alternative interpretations, but in some instances three or more interpretations can be supported by the same physical stimulus (Suzuki and Grabowecky 2002).

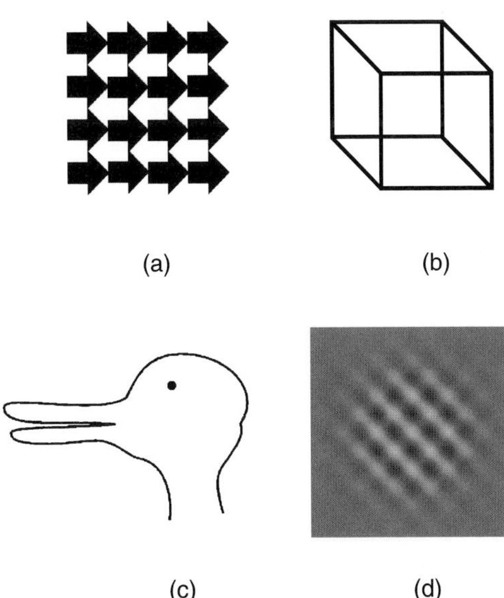

Fig. M3. Examples of bistable figures. (a) Figure/ground reversal, wherein one sees either an array of white objects (arrows) against a black background or an array of black objects (arrows) against a white background. (b) Example of the Necker cube, an implied three-dimensional object whose perspective is ambiguous (named after the 19th century Swiss crystallographer L. Necker who apparently first described the phenomenon). (c) An ambiguous figure that can be seen as a duck or as a rabbit (the original version was first commented on by American psychologist Joseph Jastrow in 1899). (d) Superimposed red and green diagonally oriented contours that, over time, wax and wane in visibility, a phenomenon sometimes called pattern rivalry or monocular rivalry.

In the examples just described, a given stimulus leads to one of several alternative perceptual interpretations: the stimulus itself remains present continuously within one's conscious awareness, with the perceptual interpretation of the stimulus fluctuating over time. Another striking category of multistable perception comprises the various forms of perceptual rivalry in which a stimulus itself disappears from conscious awareness (Kim and

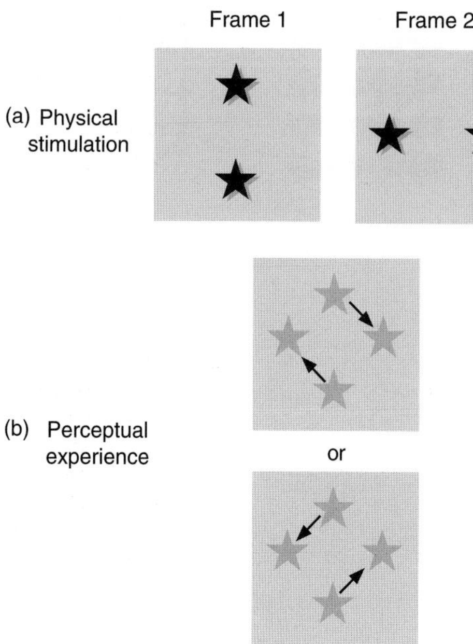

Fig. M4. Bistable visual motion. (a) When these two pictures are shown in rapid succession at the same location, one sees the two stars move from the top and bottom positions of the frame to the left and right positions in the frame. (b) The perceived directions of motion can switch upon repeated exposure to this simple animation, because the two alternatives are equally likely.

Blake 2005). Included in this category are *binocular rivalry, monocular rivalry (Fig. M3d), and *motion-induced blindness. Unlike bistable figures, these various forms of rivalry are characterized by the complete perceptual disappearance of a visual figure for several seconds at a time. Rivalry is caused by conflict that is resolved by the intermittent dominance of one stimulus and the simultaneous suppression of another, competing stimulus. As with bistable figures, individual periods of dominance during perceptual rivalry are unpredictable in duration. Perceptual rivalry also exists in hearing, in the situation called dichotic stimulation wherein different auditory messages are presented separately to the two ears. A listener confronted with these conflicting messages tends to perceive just one and can, with effort, hold one of the messages dominant in perception indefinitely.

For almost all forms of perceptual multistability, *attention plays a modest but limited role in the resolution of the perceptual conflict. Thus actively attending to a given perceptual interpretation can prolong awareness of that interpretation, but attention cannot prevent the alternative from eventually achieving dominance. Some theorists believe these involuntary switches in perceptual state result from selective adaptation, or neural fatigue. According to this idea, the neural representation of the currently dominant perceptual interpretation wanes over time, eventually weakening to the point where the alternative neural representation is stronger and thereby achieves dominance (e.g. Wilson 2003). Other theorists construe alternations in perception as a by-product of the *brain's propensity to plan and generate exploratory behaviour; according to this view, the mind is constantly monitoring the environment for new, alternative perceptual events (Leopold and Logothetis 1999). Still others think bistable perception is driven by an internal neural oscillator whose intrinsic frequency varies among individuals (Pettigrew 2001).

It is also possible to create visual figures in which the 'correct' perceptual interpretation emerges only after careful scrutiny, because the figure is concealed by its context or obscured by its highly schematized format. Once discovered, however, the concealed figure remains perceptually conspicuous and, moreover, it is immediately recognized when encountered subsequently. Figure M5a shows one well-known example of irreversible perceptual bistability: when first experienced, this figure looks like a meaningless array of black and white splotches, but with effort and, perhaps, some subtle hints, one can organize the black and white splotches into a meaningful object or scene. Cognitive psychologist Craig Mooney created sets of these kinds of visually concealed figures (Fig. M5b), which he and others used to study *gestalt organization and its development in children.

An analogue to visually concealed figures exists in the case of hearing: a familiar tune whose notes are distrib-

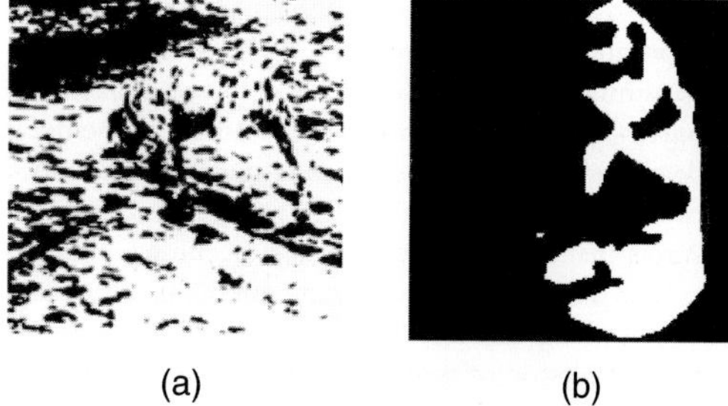

Fig. M5. Concealed figures. (a) Reproduction of photograph by R. C. James. When viewing this for the first time, one sees an irregular scattering of black shapes on a white background, but with time the mind organizes the shapes into a meaningful scene (a Dalmatian dog sniffing the ground). (b) An upside-down picture of a normally recognizable object that has been stylized to disclose only high-contrast borders.

uted randomly over three adjacent octaves is unrecognizable until listeners are *primed about the tune, after which they readily recognize it (Deutsch 1972; see MUSICAL EXPERIENCE, SCIENTIFIC PERSPECTIVE). Patterns of activity within the human brain presumably change significantly when a person recognizes what is portrayed in a previously unrecognizable, concealed figure (Murray et al. 2002). These dynamic patterns of neural activity distributed across the brain may form the neural substrate of conscious awareness.

RANDOLPH BLAKE

Deutsch, D. (1972). 'Octave generalization and tune recognition'. *Perception and Psychophysics*, 11.

Kim, C. Y. and Blake, R. (2005). 'Psychophysical magic: rendering the visible "invisible" '. *Trends in Cognitive Sciences*, 9.

Koch, C. (2005). *The Quest for Consciousness: A Neurobiological Approach*.

Leopold, D. A. and Logothetis, N. K. (1999). 'Multistable phenomena: changing views of perception'. *Trends in Cognitive Sciences*, 3.

Murray, S. O., Kersten, D., Olshausen, B. A., Schrater, P., and Woods, D. L. (2002). 'Shape perception reduces activity in human primary visual cortex'. *Proceedings of the National Academy of Sciences of the USA*, 99.

Pettigrew, J. D. (2001). 'Searching for the switch: neural bases for perceptual rivalry alternations'. *Brain and Mind*, 2.

Suzuki, S. and Grabowecky, M. (2002). 'Evidence for perceptual 'trapping' and adaptation in multistable binocular rivalry'. *Neuron*, 36.

Wilson, H. R. (2003). 'Computational evidence for a rivalry hierarchy in vision'. *Proceedings of the National Academy of Sciences of the USA*, 100.

musical experience, philosophical perspectives

Musical experience is built upon the perceptual quality of organized sounds. Timbre, pitch, rhythm, melody, and harmony are music's basic elements. These already involve structure; composers create more. Musicians interpret; listeners explore. The intermingling of these factors results in additional musical experiential phenomena, for example, the feeling or quality of the tonic's tonal stability, the feeling of melodic expectation, the feelings of tension or resolution emerging at various junctures in a sequence of chords, the feeling of stress in the downbeat, and the leaning quality of a groove.

By examining a piece of music's structure, its form—a representation of which we find in musical notation—we can progress toward discovering why it sounds the way it does, i.e. why certain musical qualities or feelings arise where they do. Musical analysis, the work of music theorists, takes this examination a step further by offering *interpretations* of music's structure. We can witness the relationship between form and experience being leveraged in musical analysis, and we can discern the relevance to the investigation of consciousness, by considering a specific case of musical experience that has been influential in the philosophy of mind's intentionalism–*qualia debate.

One view held by philosophers is that a perceptual experience's phenomenal character is *determined* by its representational content; another is that some *phenomenal character floats free of content. The free-floating phenomenal character is known as (non-intentional) qualia, or *sensational properties* (Peacocke 1983). Now, consider one sound-event that can result in different musical feelings or qualities: we can hear the pairing of middle C and the F sharp above it as two different intervals, an augmented fourth or a diminished fifth. At first blush, there seems to be no difference in representational content between these two experiences; after all, the same two notes are represented in each case. If this were correct, the difference between the two ways of hearing would be due to sensational properties (this was Peacocke's view in 1983). Contrariwise, DeBellis (1991) demonstrated that the difference between these two experiences can be captured in terms of content by characterizing two different ways one can hear the notes to be related. When the notes are heard in a G major context, we perceive an augmented fourth; when they are heard in a D flat major context, we perceive a diminished fifth (in the latter case, the F sharp is heard as a G flat). What is more, DeBellis points out that even when a given contextual background is neither sounding nor imagined we can still hear the notes in relation to one context or another, and even in this case, the *phenomenology involves a difference in content. DeBellis's key move is in viewing a certain kind of musical analysis (*Schenkerian analysis*) as descriptive phenomenology of musical experiences, where the descriptions of musical works given in these analyses 'coincide with the content of musical perception' (DeBellis 1991:310). In the relevant cases of analysis, one unsounded background context or another is hypothesized, which specifies different ways of hearing the sounded musical foreground. Both DeBellis and Peacocke have gone on to posit a distinct level of content to deal with the structural dimension of perceptual content that shows up in such examples (Peacocke 1992, DeBellis 1995).

Hearing an interval in two different ways does not depend upon its being played differently. But musicians, of course, do perform 'expressive variations' of what is represented on a score, and some of these variations are fine-grained. A cellist may play a high A natural that is not quite an A sharp, and this may affect the way we hear the music's structure, or it may add a certain 'colour' to the tone. Just as we are able to perceive more shades of red than can be captured by means of our observational concepts, so too, we are able to perceive, in a performance, fine-grained differences that fall within the music-theoretical categories represented on a score. Raffman (1993) claims that such 'musical nuances' are ineffable in the sense that limitations of perceptual memory prevent them from being re-identified, categorized, and thus reported. There is an interesting line of thought to pursue here regarding the role of such nuances in rock music (and other genres of contemporary popular music as well, such as hip-hop): arguably, musical structure is less prominent in rock music than in classical. Gracyk (1996) has claimed that the musical work in rock, the 'primary text', is not identified in terms of musical structure; rather, the musical work is the nuance-rich recording itself. If this view (or something like it) is right, then nuances are not merely features of performances but essential properties of the work itself.

We have been considering perceptual quality—what about emotions? One tenacious view of the relationship between music and emotions is that music *arouses* emotions. Eduard Hanslick, in his enduringly influential *On the Musically Beautiful*, claimed that emotional reactions to music are merely 'secondary effects'; attempting to understand the aesthetic principles of music through emotional reactions is, he thought, akin to attempting to understand the nature of wine by getting drunk (Hanslick 1854/1986:6). He also criticized the view that instrumental music can represent emotional states. He observed—in 1854—that emotions necessarily involve a cognitive component; he then argued that instrumental music cannot represent emotions, because it does not possess the apparatus with which to convey concepts, judgements, etc. Hanslick did grant, however, that music bears certain 'dynamic analogies' to emotions (to take a modern example, a punk rock rhythm may have an abrupt dynamic quality that is similar to the abruptness of, say, angst). He cautiously concluded, however, that such analogies cannot provide a basis for asserting that a particular piece of music represents a particular emotion, because dynamic analogies are too vague to individuate emotions (two different emotions may share the same dynamic quality). (Hanslick's positive view is based on a formalist approach to music.) Many writers have espoused views on the nature of music's relation to emotions. One view is that music expresses the emotions of the composer/musician. Another view is that a piece of music is, itself, 'expressive of' one emotion or another (in the way that a willow tree seems to be expressive of sadness). Many of the problems that arise for such views—and there are many—also arise with respect to other arts. (For a survey of the issues see Davies 1994.)

Lurking in the background of the issues above is the fact that the perception of music is not passive, not merely receptive. Collingwood (1938/1958:141) drew an analogy between listening to music and listening to a lecture: understanding a lecture requires more than merely hearing the noises emerging from a speaker's mouth in a lecture hall, just as understanding music requires more than merely hearing the noises emerging from the musicians' instruments in a concert hall. 'In each case, what we get out of it is something which we have to reconstruct in our own minds, and by our own efforts'. Similarly, Dewey's view (1934/1958) is grounded on the notion that art experiences involve both a passive and active component ('doing and undergoing').

An influential example of an attempt to account for the *unconscious* variety of active musical perception is the Chomsky-like 'generative theory of tonal music', proffered by Lerdahl and Jackendoff (1983). Their theory posits an underlying competence, largely unconscious knowledge, which listeners have gleaned from previous exposure to the musical idiom (classical Western tonal music). This knowledge is embodied in a set of analytical rules that a listener unconsciously applies to pitch–time events in order to 'infer' a musical structure. The theory's explananda are the musical intuitions or 'understanding' enjoyed by a listener familiar with the idiom; it is thanks to our ability to apply such rules, to assign such a structural analysis, that we experience music as we do.

Musical experience is also a conscious, active exploration of perceptual qualities, musical feelings, structure, nuance, etc. Through probing attention, contemplation, and imagination, the perception of music comes to be less like a photographic snapshot and more like *touch—akin to the spatial perception a blind person achieves through her cane (cf. Merleau-Ponty 1945/1996:143–153). The fact that music is perceived through time makes such an active model of perception particularly apt. Is musical experience active in the sense that it is dependent upon the body? Consider rhythm; body movement may not be merely a by-product of hearing a rhythm; body movement may have an effect upon the *way* we hear a rhythm. If so, is the role of the body in these experiences merely causal (instrumental), or is it constitutive? That is, does the supervenience base of these experiences extend beyond the skull? At the very least, there is evidence that the perception of rhythm depends upon neural systems associated with motor activity (see Carroll-Phelan and Hampson 1996).

TIGER C. ROHOLT

Carroll-Phelan, B. and Hampson, P. J. (1996). 'Multiple components of the perception of musical sequences: a cognitive neuroscience analysis and some implications for auditory imagery.' *Music Perception*, 13.

Collingwood, R. G. (1938/1958). *The Principles of Art*.

Davies, S. (1994). *Musical Meaning and Expression*.

DeBellis, M. (1991). 'The representational content of musical experience'. *Philosophy and Phenomenological Research*, LI.

—— (1995). *Music and Conceptualization.*
Dewey, J. (1934/1958). *Art as Experience.*
Gracyk, T. (1996). *Rhythm and Noise; an Aesthetics of Rock.*
Hanslick, E. (1854/1986). *On the Musically Beautiful.* Translated by Geoffrey Payzant. Hacket.
Lerdahl, F. and Jackendoff, R. (1983). *A Generative Theory of Tonal Music.*
Merleau-Ponty, M. (1945/1996). *Phenomenology of Perception*, transl. C. Smith.
Peacocke, C. (1983). *Sense and Content.*
—— (1992). *A Study of Concepts.*
Raffman, D. (1993). *Language, Music, and Mind.*
Scruton, R. (1997). *The Aesthetics of Music.*

musical experience, scientific perspectives Music is a culturally based, complex, acoustical and temporal structure that induces refined emotions in listeners. In recent years, an increasing number of studies have demonstrated the consistency of emotional responses to music, as well as the richness and the strength of these responses. Music modifies the psychological states of listeners, provokes measurable physiological changes, reduces pain, and activates brain areas that are known to respond to biologically-relevant stimuli (see Juslin and Sloboda 2001 for a review). Music is thus a challenging medium by which to investigate the links between cognition, emotion, and consciousness. Psychoanalysts were probably the first to address this issue by suggesting that the structure of musical time reflects the unconscious of composers. A psychoanalytic approach is beyond the scope of this paper, but some bridges could easily be made to the cognitive perspective. According to Cleerermans and Jimenez (2002), the *cognitive approach to consciousness tends to oscillate between two extreme positions, referred to as the 'Commander Data' (see SPOCK) and '*zombie' theories of cognition. The former theories postulate that knowledge and cognitive processes are fully accessible to consciousness, explicit thinking, and reasoning. By contrast, the latter theory stipulates that human cognition is perfectly opaque and rests entirely on implicit knowledge and processes: consciousness then becomes an *epiphenomenon that has no functional role. Translated to the domain of music, these two approaches to consciousness would lead to the following question: would Commander Data or the zombie be more likely to be emotionally engaged with music? In other words, is consciousness of any importance for musical experience?

If we were asking this question of a large audience, we would probably find two very contrasting responses. The first type of answer would emphasize the fact that music is a sophisticated cultural product that depends on very refined rules. These rules are too subtle for access by listeners who have not learned them in an explicit and intensive way. Using the terminology of Francès (1958/1988), 'musically analphabetic' listeners are able to perceive basic musical structures but not elaborate ones.

There are two main arguments for this conception. First, music is a sound structure that does not refer to the external world. Some authors even claim that it refers to nothing other than itself. As a consequence, it is extremely difficult to describe the content of the musical experience explicitly without a technical vocabulary. Second, musical structure is rather difficult to apprehend explicitly, because its rests on a complex set of relationships between several parameters. These parameters deal with the pitch structures (tone, chords, keys), the time organization (duration, metre), local acoustical features such as timbre, loudness variations, as well as a more global organization such as melodic contour. A peculiar characteristic of music is that very small changes in one of these parameters can have considerable influence on the perceptual experience of listeners. For example, a given chord (say a C major chord) that functions as a strong cognitive reference point in a given key context (e.g. a tonic chord C in the C major key context) acts as a less important reference point in F major (dominant chord), or as an even less important subdominant chord in the key of G major. The same C major chord will not have structural importance in many other keys such as F sharp major (see Krumnahsl 1990).

The musical function of an event also depends on its rhythmical position. Modifying the temporal structure of a melody suffices to alter the musical function of its notes, and this results in a radically new percept. For example, the pitches B C D E F G imply a major key, with the B as a unstable leading note and the C as the most referential tonic. Played in reverse order, G F E D C B, these pitches imply the key of B major, with the C being perceived as an unstable tone anchored in the referential tonic of B.

In a related vein, very subtle changes in one acoustical parameter may modify the syntactic function of musical events. In the key of C major, a succession of G and C chords acts as a syntactic marker, referred to in music theory as a perfect cadence, indicating the end of a section. If a change in timbre, loudness, or tempo occurs between them, the two chords would no longer be perceived as belonging to the same group and this change would modify their syntactic function: the G chord would now mark a temporary ending (referred to as a half-close), and the C chord a structural beginning (see Lerdahl and Jackendoff 1983). Performers could thus modulate the musical expression of a given score in a considerable way merely by manipulating subtle acoustical parameters. Processing the musical functions of events is the most fundamental aspect of music cognition and it has a deep impact on the emotional experience of listeners. These musical functions are so context-dependent that it seems difficult to imagine that a listener could understand them without having been trained to identify them explicitly.

This 'Commander Data' theory of music cognition predominates in the large audience of musically untrained listeners. They acknowledge enjoying music, but they are convinced that an explicit understanding of musical structures is necessary for a full musical experience. This conception is shared by several music professors and psychologists (see Francès 1958/1988). Recent research showing anatomical and functional differences between the brains of musicians and non-musicians might even reinforce it.

By contrast, the second type of answer, using a zombie theory of music cognition, might claim that music rests on implicit knowledge and processes that do not greatly differ between musically trained and untrained listeners. As suggested by Lerdahl and Jackendoff (1983:3), listeners without musical training but with sufficient exposure to a given idiom can be viewed as 'experienced listeners', who use the same principles as musically trained ones in organizing the hearing of music, 'but in a more limited way'. Musical processing does not occur at an explicitly conscious level, and consciousness is not indispensable for full emotional experience of music (Levinson 1997). A primary argument in support of this approach is that most of the complexity of Western pitch structure can be internalized through passive exposure. The compositional rules of Western music instil strong regularities between pitches, chords, and keys that are learned implicitly and represented in a non-conscious way. A neural net model manages to simulate such learning and then to reproduce the context-dependency of the musical functions of tones and chords (Tillmann et al. 2000). Several sets of experimental data provide converging evidence that refined musical structures are processed implicitly by musically untrained listeners (see Bigand and Poulin-Charronnat 2006 for a review).

A second argument is that musical structures are not supposed to be perceived explicitly. Most composers (if not all) would claim that musical structures should influence the perceptual and emotional experiences of listeners without being understood explicitly. If the musical structure of a piece were easy to discover explicitly, none of the anticipatory processes that influence the emotional experience would be at work. A zombie theory of music would thus emphasize the functional importance of unawareness, and would deny a possible role for consciousness. Moreover, because music does not have any direct or immediate implication for survival, there is no evolutionary advantage in developing explicit representations of musical structure. The fact that in most cultures musical activities rest on abilities that are not explicitly described or transmitted reinforces the slight importance of consciousness. Other arguments come from the cases of very famous self-taught musicians (such as Charlie Parker or Django Reinhardt), who were able to perform extremely inventive music without having a sophisticated explicit knowledge. At the very least, musical awareness may be functional in only the restricted professional activities of some Western musicians.

Needless to say, neither of these perspectives is compelling. It is difficult to agree with the zombie perspective that all the skills that have been explicitly trained and learned over a period of years, from early childhood to adulthood, and that have imprinted musicians' brains, do not influence their perceptual and emotional experience of music. On the other hand, there is now enough evidence, in both experimental psychology and neurosciences, to conclude that consciousness may have a limited influence. For example, it was shown than listeners respond to refined musical manipulations in stimuli, even when they are required to pay attention to movies, or to process linguistic information (Bigand and Poulin-Charronnat 2006). Peretz (2006) also reported a case study of a patient who was unable to report obvious changes in musical structures explicitly, though she continued to respond as normal listeners do when an emotional task was required with the same stimuli.

In a related vein, we presented participants with very short excerpts of music, the duration of which was progressively increased by blocks from 250 ms up to 20 s. Participants were asked to evaluate the strength of the emotion experienced with these stimuli. On the basis of the responses given for the longest duration, the musical stimuli were sorted into two categories: 'moving' versus 'not moving'. The goal of the study was to analyse the minimum duration required to differentiate the categories. Not surprisingly, all participants were disappointed by the shortest excerpts of 250 ms, and complained that emotion could not be experienced in this case. Nevertheless, we found that the two groups of excerpts were significantly discriminated at this shortest duration. A supplementary argument comes from the comparison of musically trained and untrained listeners (see Bigand and Poulin-Charronnat 2006 for a review). The fact that musically trained and untrained participants behave in a very similar way in several experiments using different stimuli and tasks suggests that explicit knowledge of music may be of weak influence. *Functional brain imaging studies also suggest that the neural pathways involved in music processing are very similar in both groups, with the main exception that brain asymmetry generally tends to be more pronounced in musically trained listeners, who have more activation in the left hemisphere. All these findings indicate that consciousness in music may be the tip of the iceberg: the most important computations for both cognitive and emotional responses occur in the submerged part.

EMMANUEL BIGAND

Bigand, E. and Poulin-Charronnat, B. (2006). 'Are we all "experienced listeners"? A review of the musical capacities that do not depend on musical training'. *Cognition*, 100.

Cleeremans, A. and Jiménez, L. (2002). 'Implicit learning and consciousness: A graded dynamic perspective'. In French, R. and Cleerremans, A. (eds) *Implicit Learning and Consciousness*.

Francès, R. (1958/1988). *The Perception of Music*, transl. J. W. Dolwing.

Juslin, P. and Sloboda, J. (2001). *Music and Emotion: Theory and Research*.

Krumnahsl, C. (1990). *Cognitive Foundations of Musical Pitch*.

Lerdahl, F. and Jackendoff, R. (1983). *A Generative Theory of Tonal Music*.

Levinson, J. (1997). *Music in the Moment*.

Peretz, I. (2006) 'The nature of music from a biological perspective'. *Cognition*, 100.

Tillmann, B., Bharucha, J., and Bigand, E. (2000). 'Implicit learning of tonality: a self-organizing approach'. *Psychological Review*, 107.

mysterianism It has often been felt, mostly by philosophers but also by scientists, that explanatory theories of consciousness have been unsatisfactory, in a rather principled and systemic way. This sentiment has led some philosophers (notably Colin McGinn) and scientists (notably Noam Chomsky) to the view that there are principled and systemic reasons why the achievement of a satisfactory explanation of consciousness is not humanly possible. Perhaps we can expect a satisfactory explanation of the *mechanics* of consciousness—how conscious episodes interact among themselves and with non-conscious events—but not of the *experiential* aspect of consciousness, the fact that there is something it is like for us, from the inside, to *be* conscious. This is sometimes known as mysterianism about consciousness, or 'mysterianism' for short. A pessimistic outlook with venerable history, mysterianism goes back at least to the 1860s, when it was clearly articulated by T. H. Huxley, John Tyndall, and Emil du Bois-Raymond.

Conceptually, it is worth distinguishing two versions of mysterianism, one ontological and one epistemological. The former would hold that consciousness is mysterious in and of itself. The latter is the more modest claim that the mystery does not lie in consciousness itself, but rather flows from certain constitutional limitations of the human intellect. McGinn and Chomsky are epistemological mysterianists. They hold that there is nothing deeply mysterious about consciousness itself, which is as natural a phenomenon as any; it is just that we humans are incapable of understanding it. They thus combine ontological naturalism with epistemological mysterianism.

Central to their view of consciousness is the thesis of *cognitive closure*. According to this thesis, some aspects of the world are cognitively closed to some kinds of cognitive system. Just as a colour-blind dog is *perceptually* closed to colour, so it is *cognitively* closed to some phenomena and features of the world: it cannot understand algebra, for example, or market economics. These failures are, moreover, chronic and incontrovertible. They are part of the canine condition.

Mysterianists maintain that it is prejudicial hubris to suppose that humans are somehow spared this predicament and are cognitively closed to nothing. As a natural, evolved system, the human cognitive system must have its own constitutional limitations. Thus the initially reasonable position is that some phenomena and features of the world are bound to elude human comprehension. Just as a lack of understanding of algebra is part of the canine condition, so a lack of understanding of some other phenomena is part of the human condition.

Consciousness is a prime candidate for being such a phenomenon. There is a feeling that what stands between us and a naturalistic understanding of consciousness is not some further empirical discovery. The notion that someone might scurry out of a laboratory one afternoon and declare they have solved the problem of consciousness seems silly. The sense is that no amount of empirical information would demystify consciousness for us, and an insight of an altogether different order would be needed if we are to come to terms with the challenge posed by consciousness. Mysterianism offers the epistemology of cognitive closure as that insight.

Mysterianism represents an unusual approach to the intellectual problem raised by consciousness. Rather than offering an explanation of consciousness, it attempts to quell our intellectual discomfort by offering an explanation of why we cannot obtain such an explanation. It thus combines first-order pessimism with second-order optimism: although we have no clue about consciousness, we have a clue about why we have no clue about consciousness! And this may suffice to neutralize our sense of intellectual embarrassment in the face of this recalcitrant phenomenon.

The primary motivation for mysterianism may be captured by an inductive inference from the evident and flagrant inadequacy of all known theories of consciousness, coupled with the aforementioned sentiment that the inadequacy is unusually profound. But McGinn also adduces a deductive argument in favour of mysterianism. McGinn's argument is basically this. *Introspection is our only channel to the properties of consciousness, but it does not afford us any access to the properties of the brain. Sensory perception is our only channel to the properties of the brain, but it does not afford us any access to the properties of consciousness. There is no third channel that affords us access to both consciousness and the brain. Therefore, our concept-producing mechanisms cannot in principle produce a concept for the connection between consciousness and the brain. Consequently, our knowledge of consciousness and our knowledge of the brain are doomed to be insulated from one another. More specifically, we can have no knowledge of the manner by which the brain produces or yields consciousness. The connection between the two is necessarily opaque to us. Therefore, we cannot possibly grasp the solution to the problem of consciousness.

The literature on mysterianism has so far been somewhat dogmatically dismissive. Critical discussions of the merits and demerits of the view are few and far between. In particular, McGinn's argument is rarely if ever engaged. This is unfortunate, although perhaps understandable from a heuristic viewpoint. Nonetheless, some problems with, and suspicions about, the view have emerged in the literature.

Perhaps the main suspicion (aired by Daniel Dennett among others) is that the view is based on a mistaken conception of the relationship between an intellectual problem and its corresponding solution. We may well understand a problem but not know its solution, or be unable to understand a solution to a problem we do not fully grasp. But it is incoherent to suppose that we cannot in principle understand the solution to a problem we can and do understand and fully grasp. Plausibly, understanding what a problem is involves understanding what would count as an appropriate solution to it (if not necessarily a correct one). It is true that dogs cannot in principle understand algebra; but that is precisely why algebraic problems do not pose themselves to dogs.

As experimental and theoretical work on consciousness advances over the next few decades and becomes methodologically and conceptually more sophisticated, the sense of mystery surrounding consciousness may gradually dissipate. But it may also turn out that the ever-growing abundance of empirical findings about consciousness will only serve to further the spectre of mysterianism, as the sense of empirical impenetrability becomes more pronounced and acute. Trivially perhaps, time will tell if our inability to understand consciousness is chronic and principled or provisional and contingent.

URIAH KRIEGEL

Dennett, D. C. (1995). *Darwin's Dangerous Idea*.

McGinn, C. (1989). 'Can we solve the mind-body problem?' *Mind*, 98.

—— (1999). *The Mysterious Flame*.

N

naturalism See PHYSICALISM

Necker cube See MULTISTABLE PERCEPTION

neural coding See CORRELATES OF CONSCIOUSNESS; SINGLE-CELL STUDIES: HUMAN; SINGLE-CELL STUDIES: MONKEY

neural correlates of consciousness See CORRELATES OF CONSCIOUSNESS, SCIENTIFIC PERSPECTIVES

neural stimulation An important focus in the study of conscious perception has been the search for the *neural* **correlates of consciousness* (Koch 2005). In many typical approaches, investigators seek to find whether or not consciousness is correlated with activation in a given brain area (or a specific neuronal ensemble within an area). While these studies have provided many important insights, activation observed in electrophysiological, imaging,or other studies does not constitute proof that a given neuronal process is necessary, let alone sufficient, for conscious perception. The study of different types of lesions in humans and animal models has provided some clues about the necessity of certain areas for conscious activity. Establishing sufficiency may require showing that stimulation of a particular brain area (or specific neurons within an area) leads to conscious sensations.

One of the techniques used to stimulate the human brain is *transcranial magnetic stimulation (TMS). The non-invasive nature of this technique makes it a valuable research and clinical tool in spite of its low spatial resolution. In animals, investigators can inject current into smaller clusters of neurons in different areas of the brain using the same type of thin microwires employed to monitor *single-neuron spiking activity in electrophysiological experiments. In a paradigmatic study, it was shown that electrical microstimulation can bias perceptual decisions based on sensory information in macaque monkeys (Salzman et al. 1990). The investigators studied an area of dorsal visual cortex involved in motion discrimination (visual area V5). The monkeys were shown an image containing multiple dots moving in random directions. A fraction of those dots were moving coherently in a particular direction and, after training, the animals became quite proficient at indicating this overall direction of motion. During this motion discrimination task, the investigators used microwires to monitor the neuronal activity in area V5 and to perform electrical microstimulation. Current injection led to an enhanced behaviorual response in the direction corresponding to the preferred direction of the neuron recorded from the same microwire (Salzman et al. 1990). Similar observations were obtained in completely different tasks and brain areas, including shape discrimination in inferior temporal cortex (Afraz et al. 2006) and tactile discrimination in somatosensory cortex (Romo et al. 1998). Interestingly, in the latter case, the investigators even managed to induce a tactile sensation in the absence of any concomitant tactile input.

In general, these elegant and rigorous studies in monkeys show that, upon activating neurons selective to particular features through electrical stimulation, the animal's behaviour can be biased to favour those features. These observations suggest that current injection into potentially small neuronal clusters could induce specific percepts depending on the exact stimulation areas and conditions. Yet, the implications derived from these observations remain unclear. First, it is not yet known how many neurons or what types of neurons and circuits are activated through this technique (see, however, Brecht et al. 2004). Secondly, the behavioural effects are not necessarily a *direct* consequence of the stimulation protocol (particularly with high simulation currents). For example, it is conceivable that the activation of visual area V5 leads to enhancement in its target areas, that the activity in those target areas leads to conscious perceptions and that these conscious percepts are ultimately the ones responsible for the observed behavioural effects. Perhaps even more importantly, given that the animals need to be highly overtrained in order to report their percepts, the brain circuits activated after these extensive training periods might bypass the normal conscious processing of information (e.g. although learning how to drive a car may require conscious efforts, by and large driving proceeds without much awareness after learning, particularly for a well-known route).

In order to address some of these difficulties, it would be interesting to use similar experimental protocols in human subjects. Unfortunately, extending these studies to the human brain is very challenging, given the invasive nature of the recording and stimulation procedures. However, under some particular circumstances, it is possible to directly stimulate the human brain. Electrical stimulation of the human brain is usually performed in the clinical context of Parkinson's disease, intractable pain relief, or while mapping seizures in epileptic patients. When subjects with intractable *epilepsy are candidates for potential surgical resection of the epileptogenic tissue, they may be implanted with deep electrodes in order to more precisely map the seizure areas and minimize excision of other important brain tissue. In these studies, it has been possible to monitor human single-neuron activity (Engel et al. 2005) and also to electrically stimulate the human brain (see e.g. Penfield and Perot 1963, Libet 1982).

Electrical stimulation in human epileptic patients through intracranial electrodes has produced rather remarkable observations including motor and speech output, olfactory, tactile, visual and/or auditory sensations, fear or anxiety, feelings of familiarity, and many others (Penfield and Perot 1963). In fact, many of these stimulation studies helped shape the current dominant paradigm of functional specialization in the cerebral cortex whereby distinct brain areas are involved in specialized mental processes (Penfield and Perot 1963). In general, stimulation of sensory or motor cortex leads to the corresponding sensory feelings or behavioural output (although much remains to be understood about the map from stimulation parameters to sensation or behaviour). For example, electrical stimulation in primary visual cortex may lead to a visual sensation topographically matching the one obtained by natural stimulation in the corresponding area of the retina (Brindley and Lewin 1968). The arguments discussed above about direct vs indirect effects of stimulation still hold; this visual sensation does not necessarily imply that primary visual cortex is the locus of the conscious percept for vision. Electrical stimulation of association areas including the hippocampus, amygdala, perirhinal, and entorhinal cortex usually leads to much more complex and variable outputs (Penfield and Perot 1963, Halgren et al. 1978). Interestingly, the sensations evoked by electrical stimulation of temporal lobe targets have been likened to the type of *hallucinatory effects that may take place during epileptic seizures and some psychotic states, or also to *dreams. These observations may suggest the existence of a common substrate in the temporal lobe for the kind of sensory experience that occurs in the absence of concomitant external input during dreams, hallucinations, seizures, and electrical stimulation.

Libet and colleagues showed that electrical stimulation in the primary somatosensory cortex area can lead to subjective experience in human subjects. A further characterization of the stimulation train duration and intensity conditions that can give rise to conscious sensations leads to the notion that a certain activation threshold needs to be reached for electrical activity to activate consciousness (Libet 1982; see also Ray et al. 1999). This notion of a threshold requirement to elicit conscious activity has played an important role in the development of a theoretical framework to understand consciousness (Koch 2005).

There are still many open questions to further our understanding of how electrical stimulation in the brain leads to conscious percepts, including (1) the biophysics and mechanisms of activation through electrical stimulation and (2) how to dissociate direct from indirect effects of stimulation. Conceivably, techniques could be developed in the future to stimulate only specific neurons or neuronal circuits without affecting other circuits; this may therefore allow investigators to measure the direct and specific effects of the stimulation procedure. In spite of the multiple unknowns, electrical stimulation offers the promise of eventually being able to causally link physiologically observed correlates of consciousness with the actual conscious percepts.

GABRIEL KREIMAN

Afraz, S. R., Kiani, R., and Esteky, H. (2006). 'Microstimulation of inferotemporal cortex influences face categorization'. *Nature*, 442.

Brecht, M., Schneider, M., Sakmann, B., and Margrie, T. (2004). 'Whisker movements evokes by stimulation of single pyramidal cells in rat motor cortex'. *Nature*, 427.

Brindley, G. S. and Lewin, W. S. (1968). 'The sensations produced by electrical stimulation of the visual cortex'. *Journal of Physiology*, 196.

Engel, A. K., Moll, C. K., Fried, I., and Ojemann, G. A. (2005). 'Invasive recordings from the human brain: clinical insights and beyond'. *Nature Reviews Neuroscience*, 6.

Halgren, E., Walter, R. D., Cherlow, D. G., and Crandall, P. H. (1978). 'Mental phenomena evoked by electrical stimulation of the human hippocampal formation and amygdala'. *Brain*, 101.

Koch, C. (2005). *The Quest for Consciousness*.

Libet, B. (1982). 'Brain stimulation in the study of neuronal functions for conscious sensory experiences'. *Human Neurobiology*, 1.

Penfield, W. and Perot, P. (1963). 'The brain's record of auditory and visual experience. A final summary and discussion'. *Brain*, 86.

Ray, P. G., Meador, K. J., Smith, J. R., Wheless, J. W., Sittenfeld, M., and Clifton, G. L. (1999). 'Physiology of perception. Cortical stimulation and recording in humans'. *Neurology*, 52.

Romo, R., Hernandez, A., Zainos, A., and Salinas, E. (1998). 'Somatosensory discrimination based on cortical microstimulation'. *Nature*, 392.

Salzman, C., Britten, K., and Newsome, W. (1990). 'Cortical microstimulation influences perceptual judgments of motion direction'. *Nature*, 346.

neuroethics Neuroethics is a relatively new field that addresses the ethical, legal, and social issues raised by progress in neuroscience.

1. Brain, mind, and ethics
2. Ethical importance of consciousness
3. Neurological disorders of consciousness
4. Behaviour and brain activity as indices of mental processing

1. Brain, mind, and ethics

What makes neuroethics distinctive from bioethics more generally is that the brain is the organ of the mind. Most neuroethical issues derive a special level of interest and importance from this fact. For example, bioethicists have long grappled with the ethics of enhancing healthy human beings, e.g. administering human growth hormone to short but otherwise normal children. Issues that arise in this context include safety and fairness. These same issues arise for brain enhancements, but in addition we confront new issues because brain enhancements have the unique potential to change our cognitive abilities, emotional responses, and personalities. Issues such as personal identity—am I the same person on drugs such as fluoxetine (Prozac) or amphetamines as off?—and mental autonomy—am I entitled to determine my own psychological experience pharmacologically?—do not arise with biological enhancements of organs other than the brain (Farah 2005).

2. Ethical importance of consciousness

Consciousness is arguably the aspect of mental activity that has the greatest ethical importance. Without the ability to enjoy life or suffer, both of which involve conscious experience, it is hard to see how a being could have morally relevant interests. With these abilities a being clearly has moral status: e.g. we should avoid causing suffering to that being, assuming that all other things are equal. A being that is conscious of its own existence, and wants that existence to continue, should be accorded an even higher moral status: e.g. killing it would be wrong, even if the killing could be accomplished without causing suffering.

Consciousness figures more or less centrally in most neuroethical issues. It lies at the heart of one neuroethical issue in particular. This issue concerns severely *brain-damaged patients who have lost the ability to communicate through normal behavioural and linguistic channels. The result is a painfully immediate version of the classic philosophical 'problem of other minds' (Farah 2008). In particular, the profound epistemological problem of how we can know who or what has a conscious mind, and what the conscious experience of another is like, becomes a practical problem in the case of such patients.

Absence of verbal or non-verbal communication does not necessarily imply absence of a conscious mind. The detection of consciousness in those with whom we cannot communicate—including not only severely brain-damaged humans, but also immature humans and non-human animals—is therefore an important ethical goal, and has recently become the subject of study in cognitive neuroscience and neuroethics.

3. Neurological disorders of consciousness

Several categories of neurological condition are relevant to discussions of consciousness after severe brain damage (see Laureys et al. 2004 for a review). The concept of *brain death* refers to a state in which the whole brain or the brain stem has essentially ceased to function. Brain-dead patients may be sustained on life support for short periods, but medically and legally they are considered dead.

The category of *vegetative state* encompasses patients with preserved vegetative brain functions, including sleep–wake cycles, respiration, cardiac function, and maintenance of blood pressure, without any evidence of accompanying cognitive functions. Vegetative patients may vocalize and move spontaneously and may even orient to sounds and briefly fixate objects with their eyes, but they neither speak nor obey commands and are therefore assumed to lack conscious awareness (Multi-Society Task Force on PVS, 1994).

The diagnostic category of *minimally conscious state* (MCS) is distinguished from the vegetative state by the presence, possibly intermittent, of a limited form of responsiveness or communication. Indicative behaviours include the ability to follow simple commands (e.g. 'blink your eyes'), to respond to yes/no questions verbally or by gesture, any form of intelligible verbalization, or any purposeful behaviours that are contingent upon and relevant to the external environment (Giacino et al. 2002).

Finally, in the *locked-in state* patients are fully aware but paralysed as a result of the selective interruption of outgoing (efferent) motor connections. In its most classic form, a degree of preserved voluntary eye movement allows communication, e.g. answering questions with an upward gaze for 'yes' or spelling words by selecting one letter at a time with eye movements. For other patients, the de-efferentation is more complete and no voluntary behaviour is possible (Bauer et al. 1979).

4. Behaviour and brain activity as indices of mental processing

How do we know whether a patient is aware? We reason by analogy, much as J. S. Mill did in response to the problem of other minds. If a patient can display behaviours that, in us, are associated with cognition and awareness, then we attribute cognition and awareness to the patient. Unfortunately, the argument from analogy falls short of solving the problem. It simply begs the question of whether an incommunicative individual is conscious, and seems to lead us to the wrong answer in the case of locked-in patients.

*Functional neuroimaging has recently been used to measure the brain response to meaningful stimuli in severely brain-damaged patients, including patients classified as being in minimally conscious states and vegetative states. In some cases the brain activity recorded in response to stimuli indicates surprisingly preserved cortical information processing. For example, in one vegetative patient, visually presented photographs of faces activated face-specific processing areas of the brain (Menon et al. 1998). More recently, two MCS patients were played tapes of speech either forwards (meaningful) or backwards (meaningless). As with neurologically intact people, the brains of these patients distinguished the two types of speech (Schiff et al. 2005). Perhaps the most startling discovery so far was the apparently voluntary execution of a mental imagery task by a vegetative patient (who later recovered). When Owen and colleagues (2006) instructed the patient to imagine playing tennis she activated parts of the motor system, and when they asked her to imagine visiting each of the rooms of her home she activated parts of the brain's spatial navigation system. Furthermore, her patterns of brain activation were indistinguishable from those of normal subjects.

Is the brain imaging approach to the problem of other minds just a high-tech version of the same unworkable argument from analogy? I would argue that brain imaging in principle delivers more relevant information about mental states than behaviour. The gist of this argument is that, whereas behaviour is *caused by* mental states, and thus may serve as an (imperfect) *indicator* of patients' mental status, brain states are not caused by mental states or vice versa. Rather, according to most contemporary views of the mind–body relation, mental states *are* brain states or, at a minimum 'supervene on' brain states (e.g. Davidson 1970, Clark 2001). Either way, mental states are non-contingently related to brain states; assuming a sufficiently advanced cognitive neuroscience, one could not know a brain state without also knowing the mental state.

In closing, it is worth noting that some of the same scientific, epistemological, and ethical issues arise in the case of two other groups of non-communicative or minimally communicative individuals: immature humans and non-human animals. If fetuses, babies, or animals consciously suffer, they cannot tell us in the same ways that a normal mature human would, but we would nevertheless want to avoid causing such suffering. It is possible that we could obtain relevant evidence concerning the capacity for consciousness in such cases through empirical investigations of neural correlates of consciousness in such individuals.

MARTHA J. FARAH

Bauer, G., Gerstenbrand, F., and Rumpl, E. (1979). 'Varieties of the locked-in syndrome'. *Journal of Neurology*, 221.

Clark, A. (2001). *Mindware: An Introduction to the Philosophy of Cognitive Science*.

Davidson, D. (1970). 'Mental events'. In *Essays on Actions and Events*.

Farah, M. J. (2005). 'Neuroethics: The practical and the philosophical'. *Trends in Cognitive Sciences*, 9.

Farah, M. J. (2008). 'Neuroethics and the problem of other minds: Implications of neuroscience for the moral status of brain-damaged patients and nonhuman animals'. *Neuroethics*, 1.

Giacino, J. T. et al. (2002). 'The minimally conscious state: definition and diagnostic criteria'. *Neurology*, 58.

Laureys, S., Owen, A. M., and Schiff, N. D. (2004). 'Brain function in coma, vegetative state, and related disorders'. *Lancet Neurology*, 3.

Menon, D. K. et al. (1998) 'Cortical processing in the persistent vegetative state'. *Lancet*, 352.

Mill, J. S. (1979). *The Collected Works of John Stuart Mill, Volume IX—An Examination of William Hamilton's Philosophy and of The Principal Philosophical Questions Discussed in his Writings*, ed. J. M. Robson.

Multi-Society Task Force on PVS (1994). 'Medical aspects of the persistent vegetative state (1)'. *New England Journal of Medicine*, 330.

Owen, A. M., Coleman, M. R., Boly, M., Davis, M. H., Laureys, S., and Pickard, J. D. (2006). 'Detecting awareness in the vegetative state'. *Science*, 313.

Schiff, N. D. et al. (2005). 'fMRI reveals large-scale network activation in minimally conscious patients'. *Neurology*, 64.

neuronal global workspace The cognitive theory of a *global workspace was developed by Baars (1989). Here we describe a cognitive neuroscientific hypothesis, partially derived from Baars' architecture, and termed the 'global neuronal workspace' (GNW; Dehaene et al. 1998, 2003, 2006, Dehaene and Naccache 2001).

1. Neuronal basis of the global workspace
2. Simulations and predictions
3. Empirical evidence
4. Conclusion

1. Neuronal basis of the global workspace

Baars (1989), extending earlier proposals by Shallice and Posner, proposed a cognitive architecture in which a collection of specialized non-conscious processors,

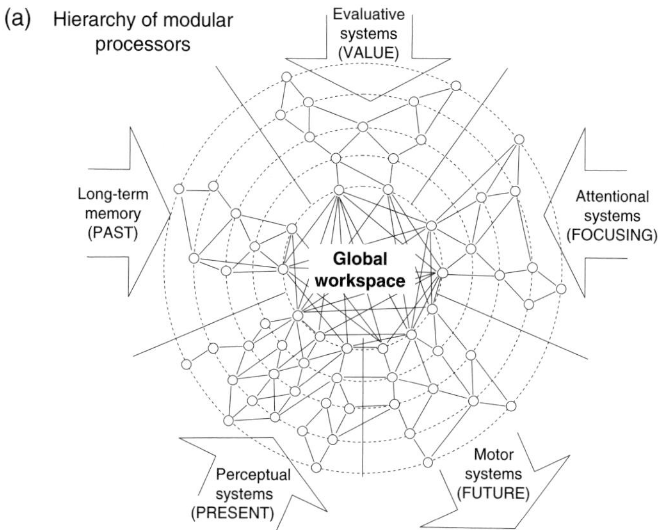
(a) Hierarchy of modular processors
Evaluative systems (VALUE)
Long-term memory (PAST)
Attentional systems (FOCUSING)
Global workspace
Perceptual systems (PRESENT)
Motor systems (FUTURE)

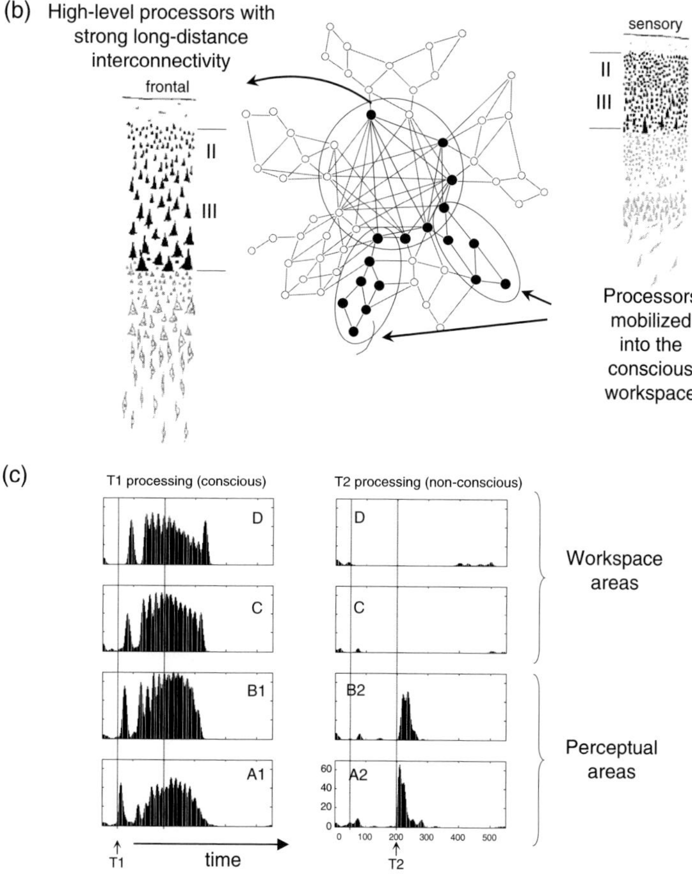
(b) High-level processors with strong long-distance interconnectivity
frontal
II
III
sensory
II
III
Processors mobilized into the conscious workspace
(c)
T1 processing (conscious)
T2 processing (non-conscious)
D
C
B1
A1
D
C
B2
A2
60
40
20
0
0
100
200
300
400
500
Workspace areas
Perceptual areas
T1
time
T2

Fig. N1

all operating in parallel, compete for access to the *global workspace* (GW), a capacity-limited system which allows the processors to flexibly exchange information. At any given time, the current content of this workspace is thought to correspond to the *contents of consciousness.

Baars (1989) initially proposed that the GW related to the reticular formation of the brainstem and to non-specific thalamic nuclei. Dehaene and collaborators (Dehaene et al. 1998, 2003, 2006, Dehaene and Naccache 2001), however, argued that to allow for the sharing of detailed, highly differentiated information, a larger-capacity system was needed and had to rely on *cortical* pyramidal neurons with long-distance cortico-cortical connections. Thus, the neuronal basis of the GW was proposed to consist of a highly distributed set of large pyramidal neurons which interconnect distant specialized cortical and subcortical processors and can broadcast signals at the brain scale. Those neurons break the modularity of the nervous system, not only because they link high-level cortical areas, but also because they can convey top-down, NMDA-receptor mediated amplification signals to almost all cortical regions. Thanks to this top-down mobilization mechanism, information represented within essentially any cortical area can be temporarily amplified, gain access to the workspace, and be broadcasted back to multiple regions beyond those initially activated. This brain-scale broadcasting creates a global availability that results in the possibility of verbal or non-verbal report and is experienced as a conscious state.

It is important to understand that the GW is not uniquely localized to a single cortical area, but is highly distributed. Nevertheless, pyramidal neurons with large cell bodies, broad dendritic trees, and very long axons are denser in some areas than in others. In all primates, prefrontal, cingulate, and parietal cortices, together with the superior temporal sulcus, are closely interlinked by a dense network of long-distance connections. At the beginning of the 20th century, Von Economo already noted that these regions are characterized by a thick layer of large pyramidal cells, particularly in cortical layers II and III, that send and receive long-distance projections, including through the corpus callosum. From these observations, Dehaene et al. (1998) predicted that these areas would be systematically activated in brain-imaging studies of conscious-level processing, but that finer intracranial *electroencephalography (EEG) or *single-cell recordings would ultimately identify a broadcasting of conscious contents to many other sites—a recently upheld prediction (see section 3 below).

The nature of the association areas that contribute most directly to the workspace can explain which operations are typically associated with conscious-level processing. These areas included five sets of brain systems (Dehaene et al. 1998): high-level perceptual processors (e.g. inferotemporal cortex), evaluation circuits (e.g. amygdala, cingulate, and orbitofrontal regions), planning and motor intention systems (e.g. prefrontal and premotor areas), long-term memory circuits (e.g. hippocampus and parahippocampal regions), and attention-orienting circuits (e.g. posterior parietal cortices). Thanks to the tight interconnections of these five systems, perceptual information which is consciously accessed can be laid down in episodic memory, be evaluated, and lead to attention reorienting and the formation of novel behavioural plans (including verbal reports).

2. Simulations and predictions

Parts of the GW architecture have been simulated, based either on networks of formal neurons (Dehaene et al. 1998), or on more realistic thalamocortical columns of integrate-and-fire units (Dehaene et al. 2003, Dehaene and Changeux 2005). These simulations have identified a set of essential properties of the GNW architecture.

Feedforward excitation followed by ignition. During processing of a brief external stimulus, two stages can be distinguished: perceptual activation first propagates in an ascending feedforward manner, then this bottom-up activity is amplified by top-down connections, thus leading to a sustained global reverberating 'ignition'.

Central competition. Each ignited state is characterized by the distributed but synchronous activation of a subset of thalamocortical columns, whose topology defines the contents of consciousness, the rest of the workspace neurons being inhibited. This inhibition temporarily prevents other stimuli from entering the GNW, thus creating a serial bottleneck and phenomena similar to the *attentional blink and *inattentional blindness.

All-or-none ignition. Ignition corresponds to a sharp dynamic phase transition and is therefore all-or-none: a stimulus either fully ignites the GNW, or its activation quickly dies out. This all-or-none property defines a sharp threshold for access to consciousness by external stimuli.

Oscillations and synchrony. Ignition is accompanied by an increase in membrane voltage oscillations, particularly in the high-frequency *gamma band (40 Hz and above), as well as by increased synchrony between distant cortical sites.

Stochasticity. Conscious access is stochastic: due to fluctuations in spontaneous activity, identical stimuli may or may not pass the ignition threshold.

Subliminal versus preconscious states. Two major factors may prevent ignition and therefore conscious access. First, the stimulus strength may be too weak, in which case its bottom-up activation progressively dies out as it climbs through the perceptual hierarchy (subliminal stimulus). Second, even with sufficient strength, the stimulus may be blocked because the GNW is already occupied by another competing conscious representation (preconscious stimulus).

Graded levels of vigilance. The ignition threshold is affected by ascending neuromodulatory vigilance signals. A minimal level of ascending neuromodulation exist, below which ignited states cease to be stable. This transition from and to a 'vigil' state corresponds to a Hopf bifurcation in dynamic systems theory, which can mimic a gradation of states of consciousness, from high attention to drowsiness or coma (Dehaene and Changeux 2005).

Spontaneous activity. The GNW is the seat of permanent spontaneous activity. Thus, global ignited states can also occur in the absence of external stimulation, due to spontaneous activity alone, in which case activation tends to start in high-level areas and to propagate top-down to lower areas. Even in the absence of external stimulation, the GNW ceaselessly passes through a series of metastable states, each consisting in a global brain-scale with a subset of active processors. Although stochastic, these states are constantly sculpted and selected by vigilance signals and reward systems (mediated by cholinergic, dopaminergic, and other neuromodulatory pathways).

3. Empirical evidence

Many predictions of the GNW model have been supported. In otherwise very different paradigms, neurophysiological and *functional brain imaging experiments have systematically related the conscious reportability of perceptual stimuli to both an amplification of activation in the brain areas coding the relevant content (e.g. area V5 for motion) and the additional activation of a prefrontoparietal network (Haynes et al. 2005). Temporally resolved studies of identical stimuli that did or did not lead to a subjective conscious experience revealed an early non-conscious feedforward activation, followed by a late anterior and global activation only on conscious trials. This conscious activation is late, durable, all-or-none, exhibits a non-linear stochastic threshold, and involves a distributed set of areas including prefrontal cortex (Sergent et al. 2005, Del Cul et al. 2007). When a stimulus crosses the threshold for consciousness, gamma-band oscillations are enhanced (Melloni et al. 2007), and long-distance synchrony selectively appears, particularly in the beta band (13–30 Hz; Gross et al. 2004), with a primary origin in prefrontal cortex accompanied by a global broadcasting to 70% of randomly selected cortical sites (Gaillard et al. 2009). Attended but masked stimuli evoke a detectable but weak propagation of activation (subliminal state), while non-atttended stimuli evoke an initial strong activation followed by sudden blocking occurring largely at the prefrontal level (preconscious state; Sigman and Dehaene 2008). Finally, even in the absence of stimulation, prefrontoparietal networks are spontaneously active in vigil subjects and their metabolism tracks states of vigilance, shows a disproportionate decrease during *sleep, vegetative state, or coma (see BRAIN DAMAGE).

4. Conclusion

The GNW theory is a precise and testable proposal backed up by considerable evidence. One challenge for this theory will be to account, not only for conscious access during specific processing tasks, but also for conscious experience in the absence of a task. Ned Block, amongst others, while not denying the idea of a global access, doubt that it can account for 'phenomenal awareness'. Naccache and I (2001) have argued that the illusion of a rich phenomenal world rests upon the variety of preconscious representations that can, at any moment, become brought in the GNW and therefore into consciousness. According the GNW, consciousness is both tightly limited (a single representation is accessed at one time) and yet enormously broad in its potential scope.

STANISLAS DEHAENE

Baars, B. J. (1989). *A Cognitive Theory of Consciousness*.
Dehaene, S. and Changeux, J. P. (2005). 'Ongoing spontaneous activity controls access to consciousness: a neuronal model for inattentional blindness'. *PLoS Biology*, 3.
—— and Naccache, L. (2001). 'Towards a cognitive neuroscience of consciousness: basic evidence and a workspace framework'. *Cognition*, 79.
——, Kerszberg, M., and Changeux, J. P. (1998). 'A neuronal model of a global workspace in effortful cognitive tasks'. *Proceedings of the National Academy of Sciences of the USA*, 95.
——, Sergent, C., and Changeux, J. P. (2003). 'A neuronal network model linking subjective reports and objective physiological data during conscious perception'. *Proceedings of the National Academy of Sciences of the USA*, 100.
——, Changeux, J. P., Naccache, L., Sackur, J., and Sergent, C. (2006). 'Conscious, preconscious, and subliminal processing: a testable taxonomy'. *Trends in Cognitive Science*, 10.
Del Cul, A., Baillet, S., and Dehaene, S. (2007). 'Brain dynamics underlying the nonlinear threshold for access to consciousness'. *PLoS Biology*, 5.
Gaillard, R., Dehaene, S., Adam, C. et al. (2009). 'Converging intra-cranial markers of conscious access'. *PLoS Biology*, 7.
Gross, J., Schmitz, F., Schnitzler, I. et al. (2004). 'Modulation of long-range neural synchrony reflects temporal limitations

of visual attention in humans'. *Proceedings of the National Academy of Sciences of the USA*, 101.

Haynes, J. D., Driver, J., and Rees, G. (2005). 'Visibility reflects dynamic changes of effective connectivity between V1 and fusiform cortex'. *Neuron*, 46.

Melloni, L., Molina, C., Pena, M., Torres, D., Singer, W., and Rodriguez, E. (2007). 'Synchronization of neural activity across cortical areas correlates with conscious perception'. *Journal of Neuroscience*, 27.

Sergent, C., Baillet, S., and Dehaene, S. (2005). 'Timing of the brain events underlying access to consciousness during the attentional blink'. *Nature Neuroscience*, 8.

Sigman, M. and Dehaene, S. (2008). 'Brain mechanisms of serial and parallel processing during dual-task performance'. *Journal of Neuroscience*, 28.

neurophenomenology Neurophenomenology was originally proposed by Francisco Varela (1996) as a response to the *hard problem of consciousness as defined by Chalmers. It is intended not as a theory of consciousness that would constitute a solution to the hard problem, but as a methodological response that maps out a non-reductionistic approach to discovering a solution. Neurophenomenology works on both sides of the problem by incorporating phenomenological method into experimental cognitive neuroscience. **Phenomenology* is an important part of this approach because it anchors both theoretical and empirical investigations of consciousness in embodied and situated experience as it is lived through, and as it is expressed as verbally articulated descriptions in the first person, in contrast to third-person correlates of experience or abstract representations (Varela and Thompson 2003). Neurophenomenology thus attempts to naturalize phenomenology, in the sense of providing an explicitly naturalized account of consciousness, specifically integrating first-person data into an explanatory framework where experiential properties and processes are made continuous with the properties and processes accepted by the natural sciences (see Roy et al. 1999).

Neurophenomenology follows Edmund Husserl in understanding phenomenology to be a methodologically guided reflective examination of experience. Some authors also adopt Buddhist traditions and contemplative techniques for this purpose (Varela et al. 1991). In neurophenomenological experiments both the experimenter(s) and experimental subjects receive some level of training in phenomenological method. This training, as Varela proposed it, includes the practice of phenomenological *bracketing*—the setting aside of opinions or theories about one's own experience or about consciousness in general. Subjects bracket their ordinary attitudes in order to shift attention from what they experience, or what they think they experience, to how they experience it. Varela identified three steps in phenomenological method:

1 Suspending beliefs or theories about experience and what is experienced (phenomenologists call this the *epoche*)
2 Gaining intimacy with the domain of investigation (this involves a *focused description* of experience and of how things appear in our experience)
3 Sharing descriptions and seeking *intersubjective verification*.

The phenomenological method can be either self-induced by subjects familiar with it, or guided by the experimenter through a set of open questions—questions not directed at opinions or theories, or by the experimenter's expectations, but at the subject's current experience. Using this method subjects provide focused descriptions that form the basis of specific, stable, and intersubjectively verifiable experiential categories that can guide the scientist in the analysis and interpretation of neurophysiological data. The goal, in the service of a science of consciousness, is to make the explanandum, in this case some relevant aspect of consciousness, more precise by providing an accurate description of it.

Several studies have shown the practicality of integrating this method with neuroscientific experiments. Varela and colleagues (Rodriguez et al. 1999), studying correlations between subjective experience and brain synchronization showed a relation between conscious perceptive moments and large-scale neural synchrony in the *gamma band. Lutz et al. (2002) build on this research and introduce more specific phenomenological methods. They study the variability in *electroencephalographic (EEG) measures of brain activity that appears in many experimental situations, presumed to be caused by the fact that experimental subjects sometimes get distracted from experimental tasks. The variability may be caused by fluctuations in the subject's attentive state, their spontaneous thought-processes, strategy decisions for carrying out experimental tasks, etc. The significance of these fluctuations is usually missed because experimenters tend to average results across a series of trials and across subjects, thereby washing out any interference caused by these subjective parameters. Lutz and his colleagues decided to ask whether the effect of these subjective parameters could be measured. Their neurophenomenological approach combined first-person data (reports guided by phenomenological method), EEG, and the dynamical analysis of neural processes to study subjects exposed to a three-dimensional perceptual *illusion.

Subjects were first trained to use phenomenological method, as outlined above. They developed descriptions (refined verbal reports) of their experience through a series of preliminary or practice trials on a well-known depth perception task. Through this training subjects became knowledgeable about their own experience, defined their own categories descriptive of the subjective parameters, and were able to report on the presence or absence or degree of distractions, inattentive moments, cognitive strategies, etc. when performing the task. Specifically, subjects were able to indicate whether their attention was steady, fragmented or disrupted, and based on these descriptions, descriptive categories were defined a posteriori and used to classify the trials into phenomenologically based clusters. Subjects were then able to use these categories as a reporting shorthand during the main trials when the experimenters measured reaction times, recorded electrical brain activity, and correlated the subject's own report of each trial. This process revealed subtle changes in the subject's experience which were correlated with both reaction times and dynamic measurements of the transient patterns of local and long-distance synchrony occurring between oscillating neural populations, specified as a dynamic neural signature (DNS). For example, characteristic patterns of phase synchrony recorded in the frontal electrodes prior to the stimulus correlated to the degree of preparation as reported by subjects. Lutz et al. showed that DNSs differentially condition the behavioural and neural response to the stimulus.

Neurophenomenological methods have also been used to study the pre-seizure experience of *epileptic patients. Experiences that occur at the beginning of a seizure often involve the visual and auditory modalities in the form of illusions or *hallucinations. The patient may see a scene, a face, or hear a voice or music or experience **déjà vu*. The patient is often aware of the illusionary nature of his experience. Penfield (1938) showed that these experiences can be reproduced by electrical stimulation of the temporal lobe in epileptic patients during surgical procedures. More controversially, it may be possible for a subject to voluntarily affect a neuronal epileptic activity. Penfield and Jasper (1954), for example, described the blocking of a parietal seizure by the initiation of a complex mathematical calculation. Subjects have also been trained in biofeedback techniques to reduce seizure frequency (Fenwick 1981). In studies of a patient with an unusually focal and stable occipitotemporal epileptic discharge, Le Van Quyen et al. (1997a, 1997b) discovered various clusters of unstable rhythms in the finer dynamic patterns of brain activity in the structure of the epileptic spike patterns. In subsequent studies of 47 patients the researchers used neurophenomenological methods to correlate changes in these patterns with pre-ictal (pre-seizure) experiences (Le Van Quyen et al. 1999, 2001; see Le Van Quyen and Petitmengin 2002).

The experimental protocol used in these experiments conducted by the Varela group shows that it is possible to integrate phenomenology and experimental procedures, and so allow for the mutual illumination of first-person accounts and third-person data. Phenomenology contributes to the analytic framework insofar as the categories that are generated in phenomenological description are used to interpret EEG data. Although neurophenomenologists emphasize long-range dynamic neural synchronization, they frame the problem of consciousness in terms that are not reducible to brain processes alone. They view consciousness as radically embodied, and they appeal to enactive models for understanding the embodied and environmentally embedded nature of the brain dynamics that underlie consciousness (Thompson and Varela 2001, Varela and Thompson 2003, see SENSORIMOTOR APPROACH TO (PHENOMENAL) CONSCIOUSNESS). In this regard they exploit phenomenological concepts of situated and enactive agency as found in writers such as Heidegger and Merleau-Ponty.

In a less strict sense the term 'neurophenomenology' has been used to signify any attempt to employ introspective data or phenomenal reports in neuroscientific experiments. Many scientific experiments use phenomenal reports. Whether such experiments count as neurophenomenological in the strict sense, however, depends on the amount and nature of training the subjects receive, and the focus of their reports. For example, if the subjects in a fMRI *masking experiment are simply asked if they see a target, the variable phenomenal reports may be a critical measure used to assess the neural activity being measured, but it is not clear to what extent these reports are reports about the target or reports about the subject's experience of the target (Gallagher and Overgaard 2005).

SHAUN GALLAGHER

Fenwick, P. (1981). 'Precipitation and inhibition of seizures'. In Reynolds, E. and Trimble, M. (eds) *Epilepsy and Psychiatry*.

Gallagher, S. and Overgaard, M. (2005). 'Introspections without introspeculations'. In Aydede, M. (ed.) *Pain: New Essays on the Nature of Pain and the Methodology of its Study*.

Le Van Quyen, M. and Petitmengin, C. (2002) 'Neuronal dynamics and conscious experience: an example of reciprocal causation before epileptic seizures'. *Phenomenology and the Cognitive Sciences*, 1.

——, Adam, C., Lachaux, J. P. et al. (1997a). 'Temporal patterns in human epileptic activity are modulated by perceptual discriminations'. *Neuroreport*, 8.

——, Martinerie, J., Adam, C., and Varela, F. J. (1997b). 'Unstable periodic orbits in a human epileptic activity'. *Physical Review E*, 56.

——, Martinerie, J., Baulac, M., and Varela, F. J. (1999). 'Anticipating epileptic seizure in real time by a nonlinear analysis of similarity between EEG recordings'. *NeuroReport*, 10.

——, Martinerie, J., Navarro, V. et al. (2001). 'Anticipation of epileptic seizures from standard EEG recordings'. *Lancet*, 357.

Lutz, A. et al. (2002) 'Guiding the study of brain dynamics by using first-person data: synchrony patterns correlate with ongoing conscious states during a simple visual task'. *Proceedings of the National Academy of Sciences of the USA*, 99.

Penfield, W. (1938). 'The cerebral cortex in man. I. The cerebral cortex and consciousness'. *Archives of Neurology and Psychiatry*, 40.

Penfield, W. and Jasper, H. (1954). *Epilepsy and the Functional Anatomy of the Human Brain*.

Rodriguez, E., George, N., Lachaux J. P., Martinerie J., Renault B., and Varela F. J. (1999). 'Perception's shadow: long-distance synchronization in the human brain'. *Nature*, 397.

Roy, J-M., Petitot, J., Pachoud, B. and Varela, F. J. (1999). 'Beyond the gap: an introduction to naturalizing phenomenology'. In Petitot, J. et al. (eds) *Naturalizing Phenomenology: Issues in Contemporary Phenomenology and Cognitive Science*.

Thompson, E. and Varela, F. (2001). 'Radical embodiment: neural dynamics and consciousness'. *Trends in Cognitive Sciences*, 5.

Varela, F. J. (1996). 'Neurophenomenology: a methodological remedy to the hard problem'. *Journal of Consciousness Studies*, 3.

—— and Thompson, E. (2003). 'Neural synchrony and consciousness: a neurophenomenological perspective'. In Cleeremans, A. (ed.) *The Unity of Consciousness: Binding, Integration, and Dissociation*.

——, ——, and Rosch, E. (1991). *The Embodied Mind*.

neuropsychology and states of disconnected consciousness Brain-damaged patients can be a source of highly privileged knowledge. Not only can they tell us what capacities can be disturbed in relative isolation from others, which anatomical systems of the brain are important for their processing, but they also offer a special route to the study of consciousness—because it turns out, surprisingly, that in virtually all of the major cognitive categories that are seriously disturbed by *brain damage, there can be remarkably preserved functioning without the patients themselves being aware of the residual function. Detailed evidence regarding all the syndromes reviewed here and some theoretical considerations can be found in Weiskrantz (1997). In this entry only highlights and more recent evidence are cited.

1. Residual function following brain damage
2. Blindsight and related phenomena
3. Commentary and capacity
4. Summing up

1. Residual function following brain damage

The best and most thoroughly studied example of this 'performance without awareness' is the *amnesic syndrome, a severe memory disorder. Amnesic syndrome patients are grossly impaired in remembering recent experiences, even after an interval as short as a minute. The patients need have no impairment of short-term memory, e.g. in reciting back strings of digits, nor need they have any perceptual or intellectual impairments, but they have grave difficulty in acquiring and holding new information (anterograde amnesia). Memory for events from before the onset of the injury or brain disease is also typically affected (retrograde amnesia), especially for those events that occurred a few years before the brain damage. Older knowledge can be retained—the patients retain their vocabulary and acquired language skills, they know who they are, they may know where they went to school, although they may be vague even about such early knowledge. The disorder is severely crippling, and yet there is evidence of good storage of new experiences.

Experimentally robust evidence was reported in the 1950s of the famous patient, H. M., who became severely amnesic after bilateral surgery to structures in the medial portions of his temporal lobes for the relief of intractable *epilepsy. It soon became apparent in studies by Brenda Milner and colleagues that H. M. was able to learn various perceptual and motor skills, such as mastering the path of a pursuit rotor in which one must learn to keep a stylus on a narrow track on a moving drum. He was also able to learn mirror drawing. He was retained such skills excellently from session to session, but he demonstrated no awareness of having remembered the experimental situations, nor could he recognize them.

The examples of perceptual-motor skill learning and possibly even of classical conditioning did not stretch credulity unduly, because such skills themselves can become more or less automatic, devoid of cognition. But counter-intuitive results were much more pressing when it was shown that amnesic subjects could also retain information about verbal material, but again without recognition or acknowledgement. The novel demonstration depended on showing lists of pictures or words and, after an interval of some minutes, testing for recognition for each item in a standard yes/no test. Not surprisingly, the patients performed at the level of chance. But when asked to 'guess' the identity of pictures or words from difficult fragmented drawings, however, they were much better able to do so for those items to which they had been exposed (Warrington and Weiskrantz 1968).

Another way of demonstrating this phenomenon was to present just some of the letters of the previously exposed word, e.g. the initial pair or triplet of letters The patients showed enhanced ability for finding the correct words to which they had been exposed earlier compared to control items to which they had not been exposed, a phenomenon called *priming—the facilitation of retention induced by previous exposure. The demonstration of retention by amnesic patients has been repeatedly confirmed, and retention intervals can be as long as several months: Successful retention for H. M. was reported over an interval of four months by Milner and colleagues. Such patients, in fact, can learn a variety of novel types of tasks and information, such as new words, new meanings, new rules. Learning of novel pictures and diagrams has also been demonstrated.

An early response by some memory researchers was that the positive evidence might be just be normal but 'weak' memory. But when dissociations started to appear for other specific forms of memory disorders that were different from the amnesic syndrome, it gradually became clear that there are a number of different *memory systems in the brain operating in parallel, although of course normally in interaction with each other. For example, other subjects had brain damage elsewhere that caused them to lose the meanings of words, but without behaving like amnesic subjects; that is, they could remember having been shown a word before, and remember that on that occasion they also did not know its meaning. Other brain-damaged subjects could have very impoverished short-term memory—being able to repeat back only one or two digits from a list—and yet were otherwise normal for remembering events and recognizing facts. They could remember that they could only repeat back two digits when tested the day before!

Another example of residual function following brain damage is that of unilateral *neglect*, associated with lesions of the right parietal lobe in humans. The patients behave as though the left half of their visual (and sometimes also their tactile) world is missing. Even though the subjects neglect the left half their visual world, it can be shown that 'missing' information is being processed by the brain. A report was made by Bisiach and Rusconi (1990) of unilateral neglect patients who were shown drawings of intact or wine glasses that were broken on the left, neglected side. In that study some patients actually followed the contour of the drawing with their hands but failed to report the details on its left side, and when questioned said they would prefer the unbroken wine glass. Other studies have asked whether an 'unseen' stimulus in the neglected left field can 'prime' a response by the subject to a stimulus in the right half-field. Thus, Ladavas et al. (1993) have shown that a word presented in the right visual field was processed faster when the word was preceded by a brief presentation of an associated word in the 'neglected' left field. When the subject was actually forced to respond directly to the word on the left, e.g. by reading it aloud, he was not able to do so—it was genuinely 'neglected'. A similar demonstration by others used pictures of animals and fruit in the left neglected field as primes for pictures in the right which their patients had to classify as quickly as possible, either as animals or fruit, by pressing the appropriate key. The unseen picture shown on the left generated faster reaction times when it matched the category of the picture on the right. And so material, both pictorial and verbal, of which the subject has no awareness in the left visual field, and to which he or she cannot respond explicitly, nevertheless gets processed. The subject may not 'know' it, but some part of the brain does.

There is a type of memory disorder that is socially very awkward for the patient. *Prosopagnosia* (see AGNOSIA) is an impairment in the ability to recognize and identify familiar faces. The problem is not one of knowing that a face is a face—it is not a perceptual difficulty, but one of facial memory. The condition is associated with damage to the inferior posterior temporal lobe, especially in the right hemisphere. The condition can be so severe that patients do not recognize the faces of members of their own family. But it has been demonstrated clearly that the autonomic nervous system can 'tell' the difference between familiar and unfamiliar faces. Tranel and Damasio (1985) carried out a study in which patients were required to pick out familiar from unfamiliar faces. They scored at chance, but notwithstanding their skin conductance responses were reliably larger for the familiar faces than for the unfamiliar faces. And so the patients do not 'know' the faces, but some part of their autonomic nervous system obviously does.

Even for that uniquely human cognitive achievement, the skilled use of language, when severely disturbed by brain damage, evidence exists of residual processing of which subjects remain unaware. One example comes from patients who cannot read whole words, although they can painfully extract the word by reading it 'letter by letter'. This form of *acquired dyslexia* is associated with damage to the left occipital lobe. In a study by Shallice and Saffran (1986), one such patient was tested with written words that he could not identify—he could neither read them aloud nor report their meanings. Nevertheless he performed reliably above chance on a lexical decision task, when asked to guess the difference between real words and nonsense words. Moreover, he could correctly categorize words at above chance levels according to their meanings, using forced-choice responding to one of two alternatives. He could say e.g. whether the written name of a country belonged inside or outside Europe, despite his not being able to read or identify the word aloud or explicitly give its meaning.

An even more striking outcome emerges from studies of patients with severe loss of linguistic comprehension and production, *aphasia*. An informative study that tackled both grammatical and semantic aspects of comprehension in a severely impaired patient is that by Tyler (1988), who presented the subject with sentences that were degraded either semantically or syntactically. The subject succeeded in being able to follow the instruction to respond as quickly as possible whenever a particular target word was uttered. It is known that normal subjects are slower to respond to the target word when it is in a degraded context than in a normal sentence. Even though Tyler's aphasic patient was severely impaired in his ability to judge whether a sentence was highly anomalous or normal, his pattern of reaction times to target words in a degraded context showed the same pattern of slowing characteristic of normal control subjects. By this means it was demonstrated that the patient retained an intact capacity to respond both to the semantic and grammatical structure of the sentences. But he could not use such a capacity, either in his comprehension or his use of speech. Tyler distinguishes between the *online use of linguistic information, which was preserved in her patient, and its exploitation offline.

Perhaps the most celebrated and earliest evidence of function without awareness has come from the study of **commissurotimized* patients, colloquially known as 'split-brain' patients (see Sperry 1974). This well-known work, the subject of much theoretical discussion, clearly demonstrated instances in which information directed to the right (silent) hemisphere could not be named or 'seen', but could nevertheless be demonstrated to have been processed through categorization, pointing, and other responses.

2. Blindsight and related phenomena

Thus, neuropsychology has exposed a large variety of examples in which, in some sense, awareness is 'disconnected' from a capacity to discriminate or to remember or to attend or to read or to speak. Of course, there is nothing surprising in our performing without awareness—it could even be said that most of our bodily activity is unconscious, and that many of our interactions with the outside world are carried on 'automatically' and, in a sense, thoughtlessly. What is surprising about these examples from neuropsychology is that in all these cases the patients are unaware in precisely the situations in which we would normally expect someone to be very much aware.

Perhaps the most dramatic and most counter-intuitive of all such examples is blindsight, the residual visual function that can be demonstrated after damage to the visual cortex. The story actually starts with animal research, some of it more than a century old, and the underlying neuroanatomy of the visual system. The major target of the eye lies in the occipital lobe (after a relay via the thalamus), in the striate cortex (V1). While this so-called geniculostriate pathway is the largest one from the eye destined for targets in the brain, it is not the only one. There are at least nine other pathways from the retina to targets in the brain that remain open after blockade or damage to the primary visual cortex.

From the end of the 19th century (e.g. as summarized in William James) until quite recently the standard view was that lesions of the visual cortex cause blindness. The change in outlook almost 100 years later arose when patients were tested in the way that one is forced to test animals, i.e. without depending on a verbal response, showing that human subjects can discriminate stimuli in the blind fields even though they were not aware of them (Weiskrantz et al. 1974, Weiskrantz 1986). There are conditions under which subjects do have some kind of awareness, and this has turned out to be of interest in its own right. That is, with some stimuli, especially those with very rapid movement or sudden onset, a subject 'knows' that something had moved in the blind field, even though he/she did not 'see' it as such. This has been dubbed blindsight type 2. With other stimuli the subject could discriminate by forced-choice guessing without any awareness of them (blindsight type 1). The distinction has allowed one to carry out functional imaging of the contrast between 'aware' and 'unaware' in blindsight (Sahraie et al. 1997) in the oft-studied subject, G. Y., showing differential foci for the two states.

It is not only in the visual mode that examples of 'unaware' discrimination capacity have been reported. There are reports of 'blind touch' and also a report of 'deaf hearing'. Cases of blind touch, following parietal lobe damage, are closely similar to the early accounts of blindsight. A similar recent case has been described more recently by Rossetti et al. (1995), who have invented the splendid oxymoron, 'numbsense'.

Because many subjects resist answering questions about stimuli they cannot 'see', indirect methods of testing for residual visual processing have been developed that allow firm inferences to be drawn about its characteristics without forcing an instrumental response to an unseen stimulus (Marzi et al. 1986). For example, responses to stimuli in the intact hemifield can be shown to be influenced by 'unseen' stimuli in the blind hemifield, as with visual completion or by visual summation between the two hemifields. Of the various indirect methods, pupillometry offers a special opportunity because the pupil is surprisingly sensitive to spatial and temporal parameters of visual stimuli in a quantitatively precise way. Barbur and his colleagues have shown that the pupil constricts sensitively, among other properties, to movement, to colour, to contrast and spatial frequency of a grating, and that the acuity estimated by pupillometry correlates closely with that determined by conventional psychophysical methods in normal subjects (Barbur and Forsyth 1986). The method is available not only for testing normal visual fields, but for the blind fields of patients, for animals, for human infants—indeed for any situation where verbal interchange is impossible or is to be avoided. There is good correspondence between the results of pupillometry and stimulus detection found with forced-choice guessing in a human blindsight subject and also from pupillometry in hemianopic monkeys.

The impetus for blindsight research actually started with results from monkeys with striate cortex lesions, and it is now seems that it may be possible to complete the circle. From the novel experiments of Cowey and Stoerig (1995) it has been found that the monkey with a unilateral lesion of striate cortex also has blindsight in the sense that it apparently treats visual stimuli in the affected half-field as non-visual events, i.e. 'blanks' (see BLINDSIGHT). A recent critique of the animal work has been offered by Mole and Kelly (2006) who argue that the animal (but not the human) results could reflect an attentional bias towards stimuli in the intact hemifield rather than a genuine judgemental decision. The similarity of human and monkey results looks encouraging and persuasive but perhaps the human–animal door awaits firm and final closure.

3. Commentary and capacity

What all of the neuropsychological examples cited here—from amnesia, neglect, agnosia, aphasia, blindsight, etc.—have in common is that the subject fails to make a commentary (a genuine voluntary commentary, not just a reflexive or automatic response) that parallels the actual capacity: there is good performance in the absence of acknowledged awareness. One theoretical possibility (among many) discussed in detail elsewhere (Weiskrantz 1997) is that the awareness may not be the instigator that enables a report to be made of an event or a capacity, but that it is the commentary system itself that actually endows awareness—in the medium lies the message. The commentary, of course, need not be verbal; the tail-wag of a dog often can be remarkably communicative and informative in this very context. Nor need a commentary be physically issued; the important step is in the specific and episodic activation of the commentary system. It may be of non-trivial significance that the locus of areas of fMRI activity in the aware state, at least for blindsight for both patients and normal subjects (in whom simulated blindsight was induced by backward masking), lie well forward of the sensory processing areas.

4. Summing up

First, across the whole spectrum of cognitive neuropsychology there are residual functions of good capacity that continue in the absence of the subject's awareness. Second, by comparing aware with unaware modes, with matched performance levels, there is a route to brain imaging of these two modes by comparing brain states when a subject is aware or when he or she is unaware but performing well. Third, in order to determine whether the subject is aware or not aware, it cannot be done by studying the discriminative capacity alone—it can be good in the absence of awareness. To go back to an earlier distinction, we have to go offline to do this. In operational terms, within the blindsight mode, but in similar terms for all of the syndromes, we have to use something like the 'commentary key' in parallel with the ongoing discrimination, or (as in the animal experiments, in the absence of a commentary key) to try to obtain an independent classification of the events being discriminated. The commentary key is the output of a commentary system of the brain that offers a possible theoretical inroad into concepts of conscious awareness. Fourth, wherever the brain capacity for making the commentary exists, it is certainly outside the specialized visual processing areas, which may be necessary but not sufficient for the task.

LARRY WEISKRANTZ

Barbur, J. L. and Forsyth, P. M. (1986). 'Can the pupil response be used as a measure of the visual input associated with the geniculo-striate pathway?' *Clinical Visual Science*, 1.

Bisiach, E. and Rusconi, M. L. (1990). 'Break-down of perceptual awareness in unilateral neglect'. *Cortex*, 26.

Cowey, A. and Stoerig, P. (1995). 'Blindsight in monkeys'. *Nature*, 373.

Lavadas, E., Paladini, R., and Cubelli, R. (1993). 'Implicit associative priming in a patient with left visual neglect'. *Neuropsychologia*, 31.

Marzi, C. A., Tassinari, G., Aglioti, S., and Lutzemberger, L. (1986). 'Spatial summation across the vertical meridian in hemianopics: a test of blindsight'. *Neuropsychologia*, 30.

Mole, C. and Kelly, S. (2006). 'On the demonstration of blindsight in monkeys'. *Mind and Language*, 21.

Rossetti, Y., Rode, G., and Boisson, D. (1995). 'Implicit processing of somaesthetic information: a dissociation between where and how?' *NeuroReport*, 6.

Sahraie, A., Weiskrantz, L., Barbur, J. L., Simmons, A., Williams, S. C. R., and Brammer, M. L. (1997). 'Pattern of neuronal activity associated with conscious and unconscious processing of visual signals'. *Proceedings of the National Academy of Sciences of the USA*, 94.

Shallice, T. and Saffran, E. (1986). 'Lexical processing in the absence of explicit word identification: evidence from a letter-by-letter reader'. *Cognitive Neuropsychology*, 3.

Sperry, R. W. (1974). 'Lateral specialization in the surgically separated hemispheres'. In Schmitt, F. O. and Worden, F. G. (eds) *The Neurosciences: Third Study Program.*

Tranel, D. and Damasio, A. R. (1985). 'Knowledge without awareness: an autonomic index of facial recognition by prosopagnosics'. *Science*, 228.

Tyler, L. K. (1988). 'Spoken language comprehension in a fluent aphasic patient'. *Cognitive Neuropsychology*, 5.

Warrington, E. K. and Weiskrantz, L. (1968). 'New method of testing long-term retention with special reference to amnesic patients'. *Nature*, 217.

Weiskrantz, L. (1986). *Blindsight.*

—— (1997). *Consciousness Lost and Found. A Neuropsychological Exploration.*

——, Warrington, E. K., Sanders, M. D., and Marshall, J. (1974). 'Visual capacity in the hemianopic field following a restricted occipital ablation'. *Brain*, 97.

non-conceptual content Typically, for a large variety of psychological states such as beliefs, thoughts, desires, hopes, perceptual experiences, sensations, emotions, etc., to be in such a state is to be conscious or aware of something: thus, to think about Dallas is to be conscious of that city; to see a kangaroo is to be visually aware of that particular marsupial. And, it is traditionally assumed, this sort of consciousness essentially consists in the fact that such mental states represent the objects, properties, relations, states-of-affairs, etc., that they are of or about—in other words, they have a representational content. For instance, that 'Dallas is a big city' may be the content of one's thought about Dallas; that 'there is a kangaroo in front of me', the content of one's visual experience.

One important issue about the nature of such content is whether the representational content of all conscious psychological states is *conceptual*, or whether there are in fact two different kinds of content such that, if thoughts like beliefs and judgements do indeed represent the world in a conceptualized manner, perceptual experiences, sensations, and perhaps even some emotions, have an entirely different kind of content—a *non-conceptual* one.

Thus, proponents of conceptualism about mental content have it that all conscious psychological states whose function is to represent parts of the subject's environment have a conceptual content, in the sense that what they represent—and more importantly, how they represent it—is fully determined by the conceptual capacities the subject brings to bear in such a state. One's awareness of the world, on this view, is entirely constrained by one's concepts. In contrast, their critics—*non-conceptualists*—argue that at least some psychological states (including, in particular, those representational mental states whose consciousness uncontroversially involves a distinctive phenomenology, or phenomenal character, like perceptual experiences and sensations) have a content that is not conceptual. On that view, one's consciousness of one's environment need not be mediated by one's concepts.

One of the central questions about this dispute concerns the distinction between two kinds of content—conceptual and non-conceptual—and what it really amounts to. Another concerns the link between these distinct kinds of content and consciousness: in particular, why is it that those psychological states whose consciousness is phenomenal are supposed to represent the world in a non-conceptualized manner?

1. Conceptual content?
2. Arguments for conceptualism—and against
3. Non-conceptual content and phenomenal consciousness

1. Conceptual content?

So what does the difference between conceptual and non-conceptual content consist in? Essentially the following: if one is in a conscious psychological state the content of which is conceptual, one must possess and deploy certain relevant concepts. In contrast, conscious psychological states with non-conceptual content do not require concepts: one can be in such a state without possessing or deploying concepts for the things thus represented (or any other concept, for that matter).

But what does it mean to 'deploy' a concept *in* a psychological state (and what does it mean to 'possess' a concept)? Here is a brief sketch of an answer. Whatever concepts are (and here we face a profusion of theories, with little consensus in sight), the possession of a concept is usually accompanied by certain psychological capacities: the sorts of capacities which play an essential role in thinking and reasoning. For instance, possession of the concept 'kangaroo' usually comes with such capacities as the ability to (1) think about kangaroos, to (2) recognize kangaroos and to (3) discriminate them from koalas and other non-kangaroos, to (4) draw inferences about kangaroos, etc. (Note that possession of distinct kinds of concepts may come with different kinds of capacities.) One might then say that to deploy the concept 'kangaroo' in a thought about kangaroos is simply to exercise some such capacities while thinking that thought—to use the concept in that thought.

Thus, the representational content p of a conscious psychological state is conceptual if, in order to be in that state with that content, one must exercise the sorts of conceptual capacities typically associated with concepts for the things p represents. In other words, to say of a psychological state that it has a conceptual content is to say that it has the particular content that it does 'by virtue of the conceptual capacities [. . .] operative in [it]' (McDowell 1994:66). For instance, the representational content of the thought that 'there is a friendly kangaroo living nearby' is determined by the conceptual capacities the thinker exercises when consciously thinking that thought—capacities associated with the use of concepts like 'kangaroo', 'friendly', 'living nearby', etc. Had the subject exercised capacities associated with distinct concepts (such as the concept 'koala', say) the content of her thought would have been different—i.e. about koalas, not kangaroos. (Note the term 'operative' above: it is the actual deployment of certain conceptual capacities associated with particular concepts that is supposed to determine the representational content of a conscious psychological state, on this view—not just the possession of such concepts, or the ability to use them: after all, we possess many concepts for many different things, and the mere fact that one possesses such concepts underdetermines the conceptual content of one's given conscious psychological state, since it is insufficient to specify which concepts are actually used in that occurrent mental state).

Finally, the relation of determination between concepts (or the deployment of associated conceptual capacities) and the representational content of conscious psychological states can be captured in terms of the following supervenience thesis—(CT): no representational difference (difference in content) without a conceptual difference. That is, according to (CT), any difference in *what* conscious psychological states represent—or *how* they represent it—comes with a difference in the concepts deployed by the subjects in such states. The representational content of a conscious psychological state is non-conceptual, on the other hand, if it is not so determined.

2. Arguments for conceptualism—and against

The distinction between conceptual and non-conceptual content is particularly significant when it comes to understanding the nature of the sort of consciousness constitutive of perceptual experiences. Conceptualists (Brewer 1999, McDowell 1994) take it that perceptual experiences are very much like thoughts—or, indeed, are a kind of thought—in the way they represent the environment: the deployment of concepts is necessary for perceptual representation. Non-conceptualists (Evans 1982, Heck 2000, Peacocke 1992, 2001, Tye, 1995), on the other hand, suspect that conceptualists over-intellectualize experiences: there can be perceptual representation without any conceptual meddling.

Why accept conceptualism, then? The following considerations have been advanced in its support:

(1) *The argument from understanding*: in order to be in any conscious psychological state with a representational content *p*, one must be able to understand *p*. But understanding is a conceptual matter: it requires concepts. Therefore, since perceptual experiences are conscious psychological states with content, being in such a state requires the possession of concepts (Peacocke 1983).

(2) *Conceptual influence*: thesis (CT) predicts that the deployment of different concepts can give rise to states with different content. Such variability seems to apply to perceptual experiences. For instance, once you realize that what you first took for the sound of applause on the stereo is in fact the sound of rain on the roof, your auditory experience of that sound—in particular, the way in which the sound is represented—changes (Peacocke 1983). Similarly, sentences uttered by French speakers are experienced differently depending on whether you understand French or not. This variability, according to conceptualists, shows that thesis (CT) is true of the representational content of experience.

(3) *The epistemic argument*: perceptual experiences serve an epistemic function: they can justify or provide reasons for some of our beliefs about the external world. Seeing a kangaroo in front of you provides you with a reason to believe that there is a kangaroo in front of you. But according to conceptualists, something is a reason for a belief only if there is a rational and inferential connection between such a reason and the content of your belief. And inferential connections, the argument continues, only hold between states with conceptual content. Hence, if perceptual experiences provide reasons for beliefs, they must have a conceptual content (McDowell 1994, Brewer 1999; and for critical discussion, Heck 2000, Peacocke 2001, Byrne 2005).

Critics of conceptualism have not only offered various diagnoses for the failure of the above arguments, they have advanced considerations against conceptualism. For instance:

(4) *Fineness of grain*: the representational content of perceptual experiences can be very fine-grained: visual experiences, for instance, can represent highly specific shades of colour and the differences between them, thus allowing us to discriminate many such shades. It seems plausible, however, that normal subjects do not possess concepts for all these specific colours. Hence, it seems, the content of fine-grained experiences is not conceptual (Evans 1982, Peacocke 1992).

(5) *Informational richness*: perceptual experiences are not just fine-grained, they can also be replete with

information. For instance, a visual experience can convey a lot of information about a busy street scene and the many objects in it (Dretske 1981)—information which need not be fine-grained or specific, note. The whole scene can be simultaneously represented in your experience, even if you only notice some of the elements in that scene. But then, it seems unlikely that you can simultaneously deploy concepts for everything in front of you. For if the way in which we usually deploy concepts in thoughts and beliefs is anything to go by, it seems as though it takes time for a normal subject to consciously think about all the objects present in a visual scene. Hence, perceptual experiences with an informationally rich content must have a non-conceptual content.

(6) *Concept acquisition*: Empiricism about concept acquisition seems true, at least for some concepts: we learn certain concepts, such as the concept 'red', on the basis of experience—experiences of red, in this case. But if conceptualism is true, one must already possess a concept for redness in order to be visually presented with instances of red. Hence, if the representational content of experience is conceptual, it is hard to see how one could acquire a concept like 'red' on the basis of experiences of red (Peacocke 1992, 2001).

(7) *Animal/infant perception*: intuitively, it seems as though young infants and many animals can have perceptual experiences which represent the environment in much the same way as ours. Yet it also seems plausible that animals and young infants do not possess concepts—or, at least, not as many concepts as adult subjects do. Hence, the representational content of the perceptual experiences of animals and young infants must be non-conceptual. But then, so must those of adult subjects, given the similarity between our experiences and theirs (Dretske 1993).

Of course, just as non-conceptualists resist arguments for conceptualism, there is a variety of responses available to conceptualists (see, in particular, Brewer 1999).

3. Non-conceptual content and phenomenal consciousness

Finally, there is the question of the relationship between these distinct kinds of representational content and consciousness—and in particular, between non-conceptual content and phenomenal consciousness. For conceptualists, we have seen, to be conscious of something is to be in a psychological state with a conceptual content. But many psychological states also have a distinctive **phenomenal character* or phenomenology: there is something distinctive it is like to be in such a state. For instance, there is something it is like to taste a lemon tart, quite distinct from what it is like to taste a meat pie, and even more distinct from what it is like to see the sun rise on Sydney harbour (see 'WHAT IT'S LIKE'). States with a distinctive phenomenal character are *phenomenally conscious*.

Not all conscious mental states have phenomenal consciousness, however (at least not uncontroversially): for instance, there does not seem to be any distinctive way it is like to think that the Democrats will lose the next election, or so it is often pointed out. Of course, the conscious entertaining of such a thought may be accompanied by various emotions or moods (joy, despair, frustration), which can be phenomenally conscious. But this should not be taken to show that the thought itself has a distinctive phenomenology (indeed, the fact that distinct phenomenal characters may be associated with that particular thought, as well as with many other thoughts, suggests that such a thought does not have a distinctive phenomenal character of its own).

Furthermore, most psychological states which, according to this common assumption, lack a distinctive phenomenal character, turn out to be states with conceptual content: thoughts, beliefs, presuppositions, judgements, and the like. Indeed, such types of psychological states are paradigmatic instances of states with conceptual content, as both conceptualists and non-conceptualists grant.

But then, the question for conceptualists becomes: if paradigmatic states with conceptual content lack phenomenal consciousness, how to account for the phenomenal consciousness of perceptual experiences and sensations, which, by the conceptualists' lights, also have a conceptual content? This question is problematic for conceptualists, because the phenomenal character of phenomenally conscious psychological states seems to have something to do with their content. For instance, the phenomenal differences between gustatory experiences of a lemon tart and of a meat pie, or between those and a visual experience of the sun rising on Sydney harbour, appear to map the differences in content between such experiences—differences in what they represent and how they represent it. Thus, according to intentionalists (e.g. Tye 1995), phenomenal character is determined by—supervenes upon—content, so that any difference in phenomenal character between any conscious psychological states entails a difference in their representational content.

If we accept this *intentionalist conception of phenomenal consciousness—and conceptualists like Brewer (1999) seem to accept it—conceptualists have a problem. When combined with (CT), this intentionalist supervenience thesis entails that, ultimately, phenomenal character (and differences therein) is determined by conceptual content (and differences therein). The problem is: the fact that perceptual experiences are phenomenally conscious cannot just be a matter of their having a conceptual content, since other types of psychological states with exactly the same kind of conceptual content, like thoughts, apparently lack phenomenal consciousness. It thus becomes mysterious how the conceptual content of experiences could ground their phenomenal character, whilst the same content in thoughts fails to generate any phenomenal consciousness. Conceptualists, it seems, owe us an account of this discrepancy.

This question—and the difficulties encountered answering it—has naturally led some to think that the distinction between conscious psychological states with non-conceptual content and states with conceptual content nicely maps onto the distinction between phenomenally conscious states and those without a distinct phenomenal character. In other words, intentionalism leads to the rejection of conceptualism. Alternatively, of course, conceptualists could always reject intentionalism. Either way, a rather plausible thesis about phenomenal consciousness—intentionalism—turns out to be incompatible with conceptualism.

PHILIPPE CHUARD

Brewer, B. (1999). *Perception and Reason.*

Byrne, A. (2005). 'Perception and conceptual content'. In Sosa, E.and Steup, M. (eds) *Contemporary Debates in Epistemology.*

Dretske, F. (1981). *Knowledge and the Flow of Information.*

—— (1993). 'Conscious experience'. *Mind*, 102.

Evans, G. (1982). *The Varieties of Reference.*

Heck, R. (2000). 'Non-conceptual content and the 'space of reasons'. *Philosophical Review*, 109.

McDowell, J. (1994). *Mind and World.*

Peacocke, C. (1983). *Sense and Content.*

—— (1992). *A Study of Concepts.*

—— (2001). 'Does perception have a nonconceptual content?' *Journal of Philosophy*, 1.

Tye, M. (1995). *Ten Problems of Consciousness.*

non-sensory experience See FRINGE; INTENTIONALITY

objective vs subjective measures of consciousness Research on consciousness gives rise to two kinds of data: subjective and objective. *Objective data* are quantitative measurements such as reaction times to specified targets, percentages of correct responses in a recognition task, brain activation measured in specific areas of the brain, or any other physiological measurement of neural activity. *Subjective data*, by contrast, are the verbal reports provided by a subject in reference to a given stimulation. Take, for example, the case of a visual task in which participants are presented with patches of different colours while lying on the bed of a magnetic resonance scanner. Their task instruction is to press a button when presented with a patch of red colour. In this situation, the objective measures of colour perception are the recorded reaction time and the brain activity measured in V4 (the brain area specializing in colour perception) at the onset of the red stimulus, while the subjective measure of consciousness is the subject reporting: 'I see the colour red' at the same time.

1. Verbal reports
2. Dissociation methods
3. Association methods

1. Verbal reports

Unlike objective measures, subjective measures of consciousness allow the subject to define when he is or is not conscious of a given stimulus. As these measures aim to assess an essentially private phenomenon, their application poses specific and challenging methodological and conceptual problems to science. When can one undoubtedly be considered as conscious of something and what is the best and most sensitive way to assess it? Free verbal reports constitute of course the most natural and straightforward way to know whether one is conscious or not of a stimulus, but they are also very open to various concerns of response bias and inter-individual differences that may influence confidence thresholds. For example, in an experiment in which visual stimuli are displayed only for a few milliseconds or in degraded presentation condition, conscious knowledge might be held with a very low confidence level. In other words, subjects might not be sure of what was presented to them. They might then refrain from reporting this knowledge when asked to in a verbal report task and would therefore mistakenly be considered as 'unconscious' of a given stimulus while they were in fact merely lacking confidence. Nisbett and Wilson (1977) indeed noted that, when asked retrospectively to verbalize about the motives for their behaviour, participants apparently changed their attitudes in the absence of any subjective experience of change and that this observation was a significant argument against the reliability of *introspection. Moreover, in their critical review of the use of verbal reports as behavioural data, Ericsson and Simon (1980) noted that participants had to speculate and theorize when asked to reflect on their own cognitive operations, with the consequence that verbal reports are difficult to accept as a reliable description of one's conscious content during a past experiment.

2. Dissociation methods

As subjective measures might not be sensitive enough to detect all conscious knowledge, many studies have used objective measures of consciousness. Most of these studies have taken the form of **dissociation* studies in which performance on some task is used as an objective measure to infer a lack of consciousness of a given stimulus while performance on some other task indicates sensitivity to the presentation of the stimulus. *Priming studies, for example, have suggested that briefly flashed prime words associated with chance level in a presence/absence discrimination task (i.e. 'not conscious' according to this objective measure) are nevertheless able to improve processing of a semantically related target word.

The dissociation paradigm in consciousness research has largely been used to study various phenomenon such as *subliminal perception, implicit *learning, and *memory. Dissociation studies are generally concerned with demonstrating that perception, learning, or memory might take place unconsciously, or with the comparison of what happens when processing takes place with or without consciousness. This dissociation framework has also been applied in *functional brain imaging studies in order to identify which regions of the brain are specifically involved in conscious processing by contrasting brain activity between 'conscious' and 'unconscious' conditions.

An unfortunate side effect of this approach, however, is that our conception of the difference between conscious and unconscious cognition has become oversimplified. Firstly, because tasks or training conditions are considered as 'process-pure', i.e. as involving exclusively conscious or unconscious processes—an assumption that seems very implausible. Secondly, because consciousness in this framework is viewed as a binary dimension: conscious access is essentially based on the ability to report on the presence or absence of a stimulus in a forced-choice task for instance, but there is no way to deal with potentially interesting intermediate states of consciousness.

Moreover, the use of objective measures can cause interpretation problems and endless methodological controversies. For some authors dissociation findings between the consciousness index and performance in a related task should be interpreted as reflecting the influence of unconscious knowledge, but opponents of unconscious cognition claim that they merely reflects the fact that the objective measure of consciousness is flawed or insensitive.

Because of these limitations, several researchers have advocated the need for the conjoint use of subjective and objective measures of consciousness, based on the notion that these two forms of results respectively provide an index of first- and third-person knowledge about awareness states (Overgaard 2001). Indeed, while objective measures reflect one's ability to discriminate between features in the outside world that could also be considered by an external observer, subjective measures require subjects to discriminate between their inner attitudes towards their own knowledge and behaviour. This is the case, for instance, when subjects are asked to indicate the level of confidence with which they hold some knowledge, or whether or not they were guessing in a forced-choice discrimination task (Dienes and Perner 1999). Such a confidence measure can further be categorized in terms of *signal detection theory in order to obtain a better characterization of the conscious or unconscious nature of a given piece of knowledge. In this framework, a 'hit' corresponds to a correct discrimination made with high confidence while an erroneous response given with high confidence is categorized as a 'false alarm' (Tunney and Shanks 2003).

3. Association methods

The comparison between first- and third-person data obtained through subjective and objective measures of consciousness is at the core of correlation studies that aim to elucidate the brain regions and neural mechanisms that subtend specific conscious experiences. While this framework seems to be the best way to learn about consciousness and its neural *correlates, many problems arise in actual experiments. Subjective measurement of conscious knowledge should indeed be interpreted with caution, given that it crucially depends on the way subjects understand task instructions. For instance, when asked to indicate whether their response was based on conscious knowledge or whether they were guessing in a discrimination task, conservative subjects might give a broader interpretation to the term 'guess' than the experimenter. In the same way, subjects might underestimate their level of confidence if they attribute a high level of expectancy to the experimenter.

In other words, subjects' self-reports seem able to give an intuitive notion of their subjective experiences but, so far at least, these data only reflect gross and simple features of conscious experience, which it may be hazardous to correlate with third-person data without further methodological constraints (Chalmers 1999). Taking first-person data into account requires us to devise a specific terminology on which subjects and researchers agree in order to precisely describe subjective experiences. This strategy is not without problems either, as subjects might try to adapt their reports to what they believed to be the experimenter's expectations, or also because one cannot be certain that a given mental state is not modified at the time of introspection (Overgaard 2001). Moreover, opponents of this method could still argue that consciousness cannot be assessed through self-reports because 'they measure what is reported, not what is reportable' (Hannula et al. 2005:249).

As consciousness differs from reportability, self-reports should not be used as the only measurement tool but in conjunction with different subjective measures, such as confidence ratings, and other tasks providing an objective measurement of awareness. However, it seems difficult to imagine how to address the issue of consciousness without taking into account subjects' reports about their subjective experience. One of the main challenges for the future science of consciousness will be to define and systematize our assessment of subjective experience in order to close the gap between first- and third-person data.

ARNAUD DESTREBECQZ

Chalmers, D. J. (1999). 'First-person methods in the science of consciousness'. *Consciousness Bulletin*.

Dienes, Z. and Perner, J. (1999). 'A theory of implicit and explicit knowledge'. *Behavioral and Brain Sciences*, 22.

Ericsson, K. A. and Simon, H. A. (1980). 'Verbal reports as data'. *Psychological Review*, 87.

Hannula, D. E., Simons, D. J., and Cohen, N. J. (2005). 'Opinion—imaging implicit perception: promise and pitfalls'. *Nature Reviews Neuroscience*, 6.

Nisbett, R. E., and Wilson, T. D. (1977). 'Telling more than we can do: verbal reports on mental processes'. *Psychological Review*, 84.

Overgaard, M. (2001). 'The role of phenomenological reports in experiments on consciousness'. *Psycoloquy*, 12.

Tunney, R. J. and Shanks, D. (2003). 'Subjective measures of awareness and implicit cognition'. *Memory and Cognition*, 31.

object substitution masking See BRAIN DAMAGE

olfaction The sense of smell is widely believed to be of relatively minor importance in humans. Most theories of mind and consciousness therefore build on other senses, especially visual perception. However, a growing body of research across many fields is documenting the crucial roles, most of them hidden from our conscious perception, that the sense of smell plays in human behaviour. Here we summarize briefly some of those roles that are most relevant to human cognition. It will be shown that, especially through its unconscious role in the human brain flavour system, smell is a hidden sense that is a powerful factor in shaping human lives.

The sense of smell arises from stimulation by odour molecules of olfactory receptor molecules in the nasal cavity. There are hundreds of different molecules, embedded in the membranes of tiny hairs extending from the olfactory receptor cells. Each cell expresses one type of receptor, which responds differentially to different odours. Thousand of these cells send their long fibres (*axons*) to two modules (*glomeruli*) within the brain, in a structure called the *olfactory bulb* that rests just below the frontal lobe of the brain. Here the activated glomeruli form a complex spatial pattern, referred to as an *odour image*, representing the stimulating molecules. Different molecules are represented by different patterns, and different odour objects, such as perfumes or foods, are represented by different combined patterns, and are therefore believed to be the basis for detecting and discriminating different odours, analogous to images in the visual system. The odour images are subjected to successive processing by neural microcircuits in the olfactory bulb, then the olfactory cortex, and finally the primary olfactory receiving area in the orbitofrontal cortex, where conscious perception arises. Thus, the sensory stimulus that is processed is in the form of an image, and not conscious, as in the case of the retinal image, but the conscious sensation does not retain the quality of a spatial image, as in the case of vision. How the initial spatial pattern in the glomeruli is changed into the quality of a smell is one of the greatest challenges in studies of human perception.

This is the *common olfactory pathway*, but its activation actually involves two distinct routes which, as noted by the psychologist Paul Rozin (1982), makes smell for most practical purposes not one sense, but two. One is called *orthonasal smell*, which is the sense we use when we sniff in the odours of our environment. These span a vast range, from floral scents, including perfumes and incense; alarm signals such as smoke; food aromas; and social odours such as prey/predator smells, pheromones and molecules from the major histocompatibility complex (MHC) that controls the immune response. Humans generally are aware only of the floral scents as found in our daily experience of perfumes and deodorants, unpleasant body odours, and the aromas of food. By contrast, the behaviour of most mammals is dominated by the social odours. Since the work of Martha McClintock in the 1970s, showing that there is synchronization of menstrual cycling among women living together in dormitory environments, there has been interest in revealing social odours in humans. There is evidence, for example, that sex pheromones can affect mate preferences in humans, and stimulation with these compounds can activate wide areas of the human brain as shown by *functional brain imaging. The roles of these and other social odours in humans are under active investigation. The fact that human social interactions depend on so many variables makes these investigations quite difficult.

The other olfactory sense is *retrograde smell*, which occurs when the receptors in the nasal cavity are activated by the molecules released from food and drink within our mouths. This occurs when we breath outward while masticating the food, releasing volatiles that pass from the back of the mouth through the nasopharynx and outward through the nasal cavity. This activation of the smell pathway is almost entirely unconscious, as evidenced by the fact that humans refer to the 'taste' of a food or drink, reflecting the fact that the perception appears to come from our mouths. However, many studies have shown that most of what we call *taste* is actually due to smell. You can show this yourself by the jelly bean test: chew on a jelly bean while holding your nose and you will sense practically no 'taste'; open your nose and the taste floods your perception. A better term is *flavour*. Taste and smell are often believed to be the basis of flavour, but in fact flavour is a multisensory perception. It includes the five traditional tastes (sweet, salt, sour, bitter, and umami), a wide range of texture (somatosensory) submodalities, such as temperature, astringency, deep pressure, light touch, creaminess, pain, etc.; vision (shape, colour), and even hearing, as we grind our teeth (reviewed in Shepherd 2006).

This multimodal character of flavour means that retronasal smell always occurs in conjunction with all these other senses. This is confirmed by brain imaging, showing the extensive brain areas that are activated during food tasting. In addition to these areas involved in flavour perception, food volatiles also activate many areas that subserve memory, motivation, and emotion. These latter areas involve the amygdala, a key area of the brain integrating and controlling different states of emotion. There is evidence that these areas are activated when subjects are presented with foods that they crave, or even when they just think about them. Marci Pelchat, of the Monell Chemical Senses Center, has called these patterns of activation 'images of desire' (Pelchat et al. 2004). A key point is that these areas of desire and craving for foods overlap with those that have been shown to be involved in the addictive states related to nicotine, alcohol, and other drugs of abuse. A better understanding of how these areas are engaged during eating behaviour may thus help us to understand better how flavour is related to the abnormal feeding behaviours that underlie excessive desire and craving and that lead to obesity and other feeding disorders.

The hidden role of smell in flavour is no better demonstrated than in Proust's iconic tale of the madeleine. Proust's hero Marcel is despondent, and is given tea and a cookie to cheer him up. At the first 'taste' of the tea-soaked madeleine, Marcel is immediately (according to the myth) transported back to scenes of his childhood in Combray, thus demonstrating the power of smell in evoking 'pure' memories. Closer examination, however (Shepherd-Barr and Shepherd 1998), reveals that Marcel's experience was much like our own: it involved stimulating his olfactory pathway by the retronasal route, and rather than coming back instantly, it took great mental effort over many minutes (some one and a half pages in the book) to recover the memory, and the emotional experience must have involved the areas mentioned above that are indicated by current brain scans.

The intensity of an olfactory memory may reflect two factors. First, the olfactory pathway feeds directly into the limbic system forebrain areas for memory, including the hippocampus, amygdala, and frontal lobe. Second, smell is distinguished from the other senses by having its primary neocortical receiving area, the orbitofrontal cortex, within the prefrontal cortex of the *frontal lobe, well known for containing the highest brain centres for cognition. This may give a higher potential intensity to the perception, emotional quality, and memory of smell than the other senses, which would be of adaptive value because of the dominant role of smell in mammalian behaviour.

Thus, the location of the smell area within the prefrontal cortex has many consequences. Within the orbitofrontal cortex, multimodal integration of all of the senses involved in flavour takes place (see Ongur et al. 2003). It means on the one hand that smell has direct access to these highest centres, so that it can strongly affect not only abstract thought and planning, but also the control by these centres of the limbic system centres for motivation and emotion. One the other hand, these higher centres can in their turn affect the primary smell perceptions, exerting a kind of top-down control or modulation of the perception of a smell. This makes smell highly contingent on its behavioural state and sensory modulation (Rolls 2006). As an example, in double-blind testing it has been shown that if a white wine is coloured red, it will be judged to have qualities of a red wine.

Another common belief about the olfactory system is that it is poorly connected to our language centres, as evidenced by our difficulty in describing a smell perception in words. However, the situation is more complicated than this. There is evidence that naming different smells is difficult because smell perception and language processing use the same neural substrates. It can also be shown that verbal cues can change odour perception; the same odour molecule was shown to be attractive or repulsive depending on whether the word 'cheese' or 'body' was flashed on a monitor half a second before the stimulus was presented.

Insight into our difficulty in using words to describe smells may be gained by recognizing that the stimulus being described is a neural representation that starts in the olfactory glomerular layer in the form of a complex spatial image (see Shepherd 2006). The nearest analogy in other sensory systems may be pattern recognition in vision, as exemplified by the complex pattern of a human face. Humans are extremely proficient in recognizing a human face, even though we have great difficulty in describing it in words. The same must apply to the odour images. With training and experience we become good at it, as any perfumer, wine taster, or chef can testify. Understanding smell identification as an example of pattern recognition may suggest strategies for further analysis.

In daily life, language is particularly important in characterizing the patterns elicited by retronasal smell as components of food flavours. Flavours produced by cooking played a central role in human evolution. Social anthropologists regard the shared common meal as the defining social activity of early humans. This required the emergence of language as the means to organize the activities of hunting and gathering, and also as the necessary means to communicate about the preparation of the meal and its communal assessment in terms of desirable flavours. The advantage of language enabled humans to put verbal labels on the novel flavours produced by cooking. Language is therefore an integral part of the human brain flavour system, making verbally specific the conscious appreciation of the perception of flavour.

This leads to the final point, that the sense of smell is interesting from the point of view of the neural mechanisms underlying consciousness. Most of the interest in this problem has been focused on the visual system, for example, at what stage in the successive stages of visual processing, from thalamus to the primary and secondary cortical areas and beyond, does conscious perception of a visual stimulus arise.

The interesting aspect of the sense of smell is that the pathway goes first to a three-layer cortical region, the olfactory cortex, and then projects to neocortex through two routes. The main route is direct to the orbitofrontal cortex, as described earlier. It is therefore an exception to the rule that conscious perception in sensory systems requires a relay through the thalamus to the cortex. It is not even known yet whether conscious perception of smell can arise at the level of three-layer olfactory cortex, independently of both the thalamus and the neocortex. However, there is also in most mammals a smaller pathway from the endopiriform nucleus just deep to the olfactory cortex to mediodorsal thalamus and on to orbitofrontal cortex. Joseph Price (personal communication) has suggested that the endopiriform nucleus collects inputs from broad areas of olfactory cortex, and thus may be involved more as a general arousal mechanism, leaving the specific identification and discrimination of odours to the direct pathway. It is a hypothesis worth testing, and worth including in theories of the neural basis of consciousness.

The sense of smell thus adds some novel puzzles to the *consciousness problem. All olfactory input, in the form of images, passes through olfactory cortex, yet some of these patterns due to ordinary odours are relayed on to the neocortex for conscious perception, as we have described, whereas others due to pheromones are directed to subcortical limbic regions for unconscious control of feeding, sexual maturation, and mating. It has been suggested that an intermediate level of consciousness may arise in relation to these subneocortical activations, called *vasana* (see McClintock et al. 2001). Recent studies make clear that many of these functions traditionally ascribed to the vomeronasal, accessory olfactory, pathway are in fact mediated by the main olfactory pathway, and this must be the case for any pheromones acting in humans. In addition, the olfactory cortex also contains a mechanism for sensing the absence of essential amino acids in the diet. The olfactory cortex is thus an extraordinary clearing house for different types of input patterns destined for conscious, intermediate conscious, and subconscious roles in behaviour. How it accomplishes this is a challenge for future study.

GORDON M. SHEPHERD

McClintock, M. K., Jacob, S., Zelano, B., and Hayreh, D. J. (2001). 'Pheromones and vasanas: the functions of social chemosignals'. *Nebraska Symposium on Motivation*, 47.
Ongur, D., Ferry, A. T., and Price, J. L. (2003). 'Architectonic subdivision of the human orbital and medial prefrontal cortex'. *Journal of Comparative Neurology*, 460.
Pelchat, M. L., Johnson, A., Chan, R., Valdez, J., and Ragland, J. D. (2004). 'Images of desire: food-craving activation during fMRI'. *Neuroimage*, 23.
Rolls, E. T. (2006). 'Brain mechanisms underlying flavour and appetite'. *Philosophical Transactions of the Royal Society of London Series B: Biological Sciences*, 361.
Rozin, P. (1982). 'Taste-smell confusions' and the duality of the olfactory sense'. *Perception and Psychophysics*, 31.
Shepherd, G. M. (2006). 'Smell images and the flavour system in the human brain'. *Nature*, 444.
Shepherd-Barr, K. and Shepherd, G. M. (1998). 'Madeleines and neuromodernism: reassessing mechanisms of autobiographical memory in Proust'. *Auto/Biography Studies*, 13.

online measures of non-conscious processing

An online measurement is one that is obtained in real time while the subject is engaged in a behaviour. The defining feature of an online measure is that the data must be collected in real time and not retrospectively. Viewed in this light, an online measure can provide an index of the processes underlying the behaviours of interest.

In recent years, the tools available for measuring processes underlying human cognition and behaviour—even unconscious ones—have improved dramatically. A range of *functional imaging techniques have allowed investigators, for the first time in history, to peer inside the living and working brain. With the advent of the computer, large quantities of data could be seamlessly collected and stored with a temporal precision at the order of milliseconds. These advances in methodology, data collection, and data storage have been paralleled by the development of more sophisticated online measures.

Often, a research participant can report verbally on aspects of the behaviour of interest. A special challenge arises when the behaviour is outside the realm of awareness and therefore cannot be probed by measures of simple self-report. It is in these latter situations that online measures can be especially informative. One of Sigmund Freud's central tenets was that the vast majority of mental life is unconscious, i.e. 'below' the level of conscious awareness. For many years, science could offer little empirical support for this postulate. Many researchers claimed that it was simply impossible to measure the unconscious. However, these claims have since been proved wrong, as a number of online measures have revealed unequivocal evidence of non-conscious processing. Broadly defined, 'non-conscious' refers to all aspects of information processing that take place outside the realm of awareness. In this context, non-conscious can connote other terms with similar meanings, including unconscious, automatic, covert, and implicit. The key point is that non-conscious processing is completely inaccessible to awareness.

There are a large number of online measures capable of detecting non-conscious processing. For example, reaction time data can be a sensitive online measure for a range of variables capable of operating in a non-conscious manner. Longer reaction times generally indicate higher levels of response conflict or uncertainty. Shorter reaction times across trials can be an indicator of learning and skill acquisition. Various neuroimaging techniques can provide online measurements of neural processing under non-conscious conditions. These techniques include functional magnetic resonance imaging (fMRI), positron emission tomography (PET), *electroencephalography (EEG), and *magnetoencephalography (MEG).

Psychophysiological techniques, such as the skin conductance response (SCR), can also be utilized to examine non-conscious processes. The SCR is measured by placing electrodes on the palm of the hand. Minuscule changes in sweat gland activity can be detected by computing the electrical resistance between the electrodes, and then greatly amplifying the resultant signal with a polygraph. The SCR provides an online psychophysiological measurement of the sympathetic nervous system and is exquisitely sensitive to a host of stimulus and processing features, such as novelty, familiarity, and salience—features that can be grouped under the broad concept of *signal value*. A number of instances of non-conscious processing indexed by the SCR have been used scientifically, and a brief summary of some of these is presented below. It is important to note that all of these online measures are also capable of detecting conscious processing. The critical factor determining whether the online measure is detecting non-conscious processes is either the paradigm (e.g. presenting sensory stimuli below the threshold of awareness) or the subject population (e.g. studying brain-damaged subjects who have selective deficits in awareness).

In healthy participants, it is challenging to rig an experimental paradigm in such a way that one can be certain that conscious processing was blocked and did not contribute to behavioural performance, but there are a few compelling examples. In one such example, fear-relevant stimuli (such as pictures of snakes, spiders, or angry and fearful faces) can be hidden from awareness by presenting the stimulus for a limited time (usually <50 ms) and then masking the stimulus from awareness by very quickly presenting a neutral stimulus. In this scenario, participants report seeing the neutral stimulus but do not consciously perceive the fear-relevant stimulus. Nevertheless, a significant SCR is still elicited by the unconscious fear-relevant stimulus. These experiments have been replicated using fMRI and the results indicate that the amygdala shows significant increases in activation when fear-relevant stimuli are unconsciously presented. This finding suggests that emotion plays a particularly important role in non-conscious processes. In addition, neuroimaging techniques have shown that stimuli which do not reach awareness still generate considerable activation in their corresponding sensory cortex. For example, a sound presented below the threshold of awareness may still elicit activity of the primary auditory cortex. Likewise, when a word is visually presented outside of one's awareness, the brain still elicits widespread activation in areas involved in visual and semantic processing. Thus, brain activation detected by neuroimaging can be a potent indicator of non-conscious processing.

Neurological patients with circumscribed *brain damage have afforded scientists a unique opportunity to explore potential preserved operations that may be unfolding beneath the level of conscious awareness. For example, damage to visually related brain areas, including the posterior lower sectors of the brain, can produce a condition known as prosopagnosia (see AGNOSIA). The affected patient has intact vision, but is incapable of recognizing familiar faces, including those of close family members (e.g. their son or daughter), famous people (e.g. the president or prime minister), or even their own face (e.g. when looking in a mirror). Researchers have shown that even though the patients are completely unaware of facial identity at a conscious level, there are processes operating below the level of conscious awareness that show that the brain can still 'recognize' familiar faces at a non-conscious level. For example, when prosopagnosic patients were shown pictures of complete strangers, they (appropriately) did not recognize them and also did not generate an SCR. However, when the patients were shown familiar faces, they verbally report not recognizing the faces, but nevertheless, show a robust SCR—an online non-conscious recognition response.

These important findings with prosopagnosic patients suggest that the SCR is a reliable indicator of non-conscious recognition of stimuli with signal value. This finding has been replicated using modalities other than vision and in a variety of different paradigms. For example, a patient with severe *amnesia due to circumscribed bilateral damage of the hippocampus showed large SCRs to a neutral stimulus that had previously been paired with a loud aversive tone during a fear-conditioning paradigm. The SCRs elicited by the neutral stimulus persevered despite the fact that the amnesic patient could not consciously recall the contingency between the neutral stimulus and the aversive tone. Amnesic patients have also shown new procedural *learning without any conscious knowledge of having learned how to do the task. In this situation, the amnesic patient practices the task multiple times over the course of a few months. Each time the amnesic patient is shown the task, they claim to have never performed it before. Yet, even without the conscious memory for having trained on the task, the amnesic patient performs the task quicker and with fewer errors each time they practice. Thus, a reduction in reaction time and number of errors is an online indicator of non-conscious learning. Another experiment, known as the 'good-guy/bad-guy experiment,' tested a patient with one of the most severe amnesias ever recorded. Over the course of a week, the patient was repeatedly exposed to a 'good guy' (who would always praise him and offer him rewards) and to a 'bad guy' (who would remain emotionally flat and engage the patient in hours of tedious neuropsychological tests). After the week was over, the patient had no conscious recollection of any of the week's events. Moreover, the patient did not remember meeting or interacting with either the good guy or the bad guy. Nevertheless, when asked to choose which person he would go to for a reward, the patient reliably selected the good guy and would consistently avoid the bad guy. In this scenario, the online measure is of the amnesic patient's preference for an individual who he claims to have never met before. The main finding is that reliable non-conscious preferences can still be acquired without any conscious knowledge of the acquisition process. Similar findings have been obtained using a gambling task composed of four packs of cards, where each pack contains cards with different levels of reward and punishment. In this experiment, healthy participants learn to avoid bad packs (which lead to an overall loss in money) and approach good packs (which lead to an overall gain in money). The interesting finding is that an SCR was elicited before selecting from a bad pack and before the participant could verbalize which packs were good and which were bad. Thus, the SCR provides an online anticipatory signal for disadvantageous decisions even before subjects are consciously aware that the decision is disadvantageous.

Science is only beginning to fully grasp the depth and complexity of the unconscious mind. Online measures offer a powerful way to study non-conscious processes underlying practically all forms of cognition and behaviour including perception, attention, emotion, language, memory, movement, sensation, and decision-making. Future advances in brain-imaging technology promise to be an integral step toward the creation of novel online measures of non-conscious processing.

JUSTIN S. FEINSTEIN AND DANIEL TRANEL

Bechara, A., Damasio, H., Tranel, D., and Damasio, A. R. (1997). 'Deciding advantageously before knowing the advantageous strategy'. *Science*, 275.

Feinstein, J. S., Stein, M. B., Castillo, G. N., and Paulus, M. P. (2004). 'From sensory processes to conscious perception'. *Consciousness and Cognition*, 13.

Ohman, A., Flykt, A., and Lundqvist, D. (2000). 'Unconscious emotion: evolutionary perspectives, psychophysiological data and neuropsychological mechanisms'. In Lane, R. D. and Nadel, L. (eds) *Cognitive Neuroscience of Emotion*.

Tranel, D. (2000). 'Nonconscious brain processing indexed by psychophysiological measures'. *Progress in Brain Research*, 122.

Westen, D. (1998). 'The scientific legacy of Sigmund Freud: Toward a psychodynamically informed psychological science'. *Psychological Bulletin*, 124.

orgasm, philosophical prespectives Philosophical interest in orgasms has centred on the question of whether orgasmic experience is at odds with the *representationalist account of phenomenal character. Representationalists argue that phenomenal character is fixed by a certain type of representational content. Although they differ amongst themselves on precisely how representational content fixes phenomenal character, they are united in the claim that *what it is like to have a particular phenomenal state involves nothing over and above what that state represents.

Orgasms appear to present a counter-example to representationalism, for it is far from clear that one can give a full account of what it is like to have an orgasm merely by invoking the properties and objects represented by orgasmic experience. Indeed, some have even suggested that orgasmic experience is not in any way representational: it does not 'say' anything about what is the case. In response, representationalists have pointed out that orgasms are experienced as taking place in certain regions of one's body, as having a characteristic temporal profile, and so on. These points can be buttressed by noting that phantom orgasms seem to be conceptually—if not empirically—possible: just as amputees can experience a missing limb as intact (see PHANTOM LIMBS), so too it seems possible that one might (falsidically) experience oneself as having an orgasm.

But it is one thing to acknowledge that orgasmic experiences have representational content, it is quite another to allow that their phenomenal character is exhausted by their representational content. And here matters are rather more delicate. It is not implausible to suppose that what it is like to have an orgasm outruns the representation of various bodily changes in the genital region, even if—as representationalists are at pains to emphasize—such changes are *non-conceptually represented. Consider just one aspect of the phenomenal character of orgasmic experience: its hedonic quality. What might this feature represent? It clearly does not represent the fact that the orgasm is met with pleasure, for unwelcome orgasms do not lose their hedonic character. And even when one is pleased to learn that certain changes have occurred in one's genital region, this pleasure seems not to underwrite the hedonic quality of orgasms, for the latter has a very specific phenomenal character. All sorts of states of affairs can generate representations of pleasure—meeting a publisher's deadline; soaking in a hot tub; the contemplation of a life well lived—yet the hedonic qualities accompanying these states are unmistakably different from those that accompany orgasm. Representationalists have yet to give a plausible account of the properties (events, relations) represented in orgasmic experience.

Even if a satisfactory representationalist treatment can be given of the phenomenal character of orgasm, it is far from clear that this would amount to the 'full account' of the phenomenal character of these states that we might be looking for. Would knowing just what is represented by one's lover's orgasmic experiences reveal what orgasm is like for them? Could one learn what it is like to have an orgasm without having had an orgasm? Could I, as a man, learn what it is like to experience the female orgasm without becoming a woman? Arguably not. Here, as elsewhere in the sexual realm, book learning is a poor substitute for experience.

Certain theorists might find this an unwelcome result, but there is no reason for dismay. Part of the wonder of sexual experience derives from the epistemic distance between oneself and one's lover. One has direct access to the phenomenal character of one's own sexual experiences, but the attempt to grasp the experiential perspective of one's lover is often futile. Paradoxically, one of the most potent manifestations of the gulf between one mind and another occurs in the most intimate of encounters.

TIM BAYNE

orgasm, scientific perspectives Orgasm is generally characterized as a peak in intensity of sexual pleasure, accompanied by reflexive phenomena such as contractions of the genitopelvic and anal muscles, whole-body rigidity and myotonia, cardiovascular changes, hyperventilation, and release of 'sexual tension' (Mah and Binik 2001, Meston et al. 2004). Most studies have focused on the genitopelvic changes associated with orgasm. Neurological studies have examined peripheral and central nervous system involvement. However, how these neurophysiological mechanisms not only control the orgasm response but also generate the subjective qualities of the orgasm experience remains a mystery.

The physiological events of orgasm and the neurophysiological systems that direct these events have received much research attention. The most overt indicator of male orgasm is ejaculation, though orgasm and ejaculation are considered separate phenomena. Masters and Johnson (1966) identified two phases of ejaculation: *emission*, during which sperm and seminal fluid collect in the bulbar urethra; and *ejaculation*, when the semen is ejected via contractions of the bulbar urethra and the surrounding bulbocavernosus, ischiocavernosus, and pelvic floor muscles. Female orgasm has been more difficult to investigate reliably, as there are no obvious external indicators like ejaculation. Studies also suggest that it is not as easily attainable as male orgasm. At orgasm, involuntary contractions of outer third of the vagina (the orgasmic platform) occur that are caused by contractions of the pelvic circumvaginal muscles (ischiocavernosus, bulbocavernosus, and levator ani muscles). Uterine contractions are also reported. Masters and Johnson (1966) linked the subjective experience of both male and female orgasm directly to these physiological events. In male orgasm, emission produces a feeling of ejaculatory inevitability, whereas ejaculation and seminal volume contribute to contractile sensations and pleasure. In female orgasm, there is a sensation of stoppage, followed by a suffusion of warmth radiating from the pelvis to the body and pelvic throbbing.

While it is generally agreed that direct or indirect clitoral stimulation may be necessary to trigger female orgasm, models of the orgasm response have nonetheless proposed various 'types' of female orgasm based on additional anatomical 'triggers' (see Mah and Binik 2001 and Meston et al. 2004 for review). One well-known model, for example, distinguishes between orgasm attained through clitoral vs vaginal stimulation. Another model distinguishes between vulval (induced by coital or non-coital stimulation), uterine (induced by cervical jostling from deep coital thrust), and blended orgasm (includes elements of vulval and uterine orgasm). These models have suggested that different 'types' of female orgasm have distinctive subjective characteristics. For example, orgasm attained through clitoral stimulation reportedly feels more localized and intense, sharper, and more physically satisfying, whereas orgasm achieved through vaginal stimulation feels more diffuse or 'deeper' and more psychologically satisfying (see Mah and Binik 2001). However, these models remain controversial, and research findings have not found consistent differences in subjective orgasm experiences based on anatomical triggers.

Other theoretical models have focused on the neurophysiological mechanisms controlling the orgasm response (see Mah and Binik 2001 for review). One model of male orgasm by Tuckwell describes a neurochemical feedback mechanism within the spinal cord, in which neurotransmitters build up in the lateral spinal centres until an 'ejaculatory threshold' is reached. Spinal motor neurons then trigger genitopelvic muscle contractions and ejaculation. Another model of female orgasm by Mould also describes a similar feedback system. Genitopelvic vasocongestion from clitoral stimulation produces increasing pelvic-muscle stretch, until a threshold is reached. Efferent signals then initiate pelvic-muscle contractions. Finally, Davidson's *bipolar hypothesis* model incorporates a psychological component to the orgasm experience, conceptualizing it as an *altered state of consciousness (ASC). In addition, a neurological component of the model distinguishes between emission and ejaculation. The model states that it is during ejaculation that neural substrates send impulses downward to initiate pelvic-muscle contractions and upwards to induce the ASC characterizing orgasm. This model thus cites the brain as central to the orgasm experience, though it does not indicate the brain structures involved. No research efforts have been made to evaluate these models.

The spinal centres and peripheral nervous system pathways that mediate the orgasm response have been described. The peripheral nervous pathways that innervate the genitopelvic structures involved in orgasm appear similar in males and females. The two phases of male orgasm are controlled by separate reflexive systems (see Motofei and Rowland 2005). Emission is thought to be under the control of the sympathetic nervous system. The genitopelvic structures involved in emission (vas deferens, prostate, and seminal vesicles) are stimulated via the hypogastric nerves, which originate from the T10–L3 spinal centre. Ejaculation appears to be controlled through the somatic nervous system. The S2–S4 spinal centre innervates the bulbocavernosus, ischiocavernosus, and pelvic floor muscles via the somatic pudendal nerves. Efferent impulses travelling through the pudendal nerves induce these muscles to contract, thereby expelling the collected semen. A reflex-control centre at T12–L2 that communicates with the S2–S4 centre to regulate timing of emission and ejaculation has been theorized. The same nerve pathways have been implicated in female orgasm (see Meston et al. 2004). Recent studies of sexual functioning in spinal-injured women have further suggested that sensory information from vaginal–cervical stimulation travels to the brain via the vagus nerve to generate the orgasm experience (Komisaruk et al. 2004).

Little is definitively known about the central nervous system structures involved in the orgasm experience. Early *electroencephalography studies produced inconsistent findings. Later *functional imaging studies showed activation in various brain structures during orgasm. One fMRI study investigated self-induced orgasm in women with spinal injuries (Komisaruk et al. 2004). Brain areas activated during orgasm included the hypothalamic paraventricular nucleus; medial amygdala; anterior cingulate; hippocampus; basal ganglia; frontal, parietal, and insular cortices; and the cerebellum. The investigators speculated on the role of some of these areas in orgasmic pleasure—e.g. cerebellar control of muscle tension during orgasm contributing to the pleasure of orgasm. Positron emission tomography (PET) studies have examined the brain regions involved in male ejaculation (Georgiadis et al. 2007) and female orgasm (Georgiadis et al. 2006) induced by genital stimulation by the participant's partner. Deactivation throughout the prefrontal cortex and activation of the deep cerebellar nuclei, the left lateral rostral midbrain, the globus pallidus, and lateral ventral thalamus were observed with male ejaculation (Georgiadis et al. 2007). Deactivation in the left orbitofrontal cortical, temporal lobe, insular cortical, and prefrontal cortical regions and activation in the deep cerebellar nuclei were noted during female orgasm (Georgiadis et al. 2006). In both men and women, the investigators theorized that deactivation of the prefrontal cortex was associated with behavioural disinhibition during orgasm, while cerebellar activation was linked to the genitopelvic muscle contractions of orgasm. Overall, though, it is unclear whether some or all of these areas directly contribute to the orgasm experience. How the peripheral neurophysiological events of orgasm contribute to brain events and, in turn, the psychological experience of orgasm also remains uncertain.

Characterizing the subjective characteristics of the orgasm experience itself has not been addressed systematically. The few psychological models that exist generally emphasize a two-dimensional nature to the orgasm experience: the perception of physiological events (e.g. contractile sensations), and cognitive-affective changes (e.g. pleasure, altered states of consciousness; see Mah and Binik 2001 for review). Since their development, these models have not been systematically investigated. Consequently, there has been a lack of a universally employed, validated self-report instrument and a corresponding standardized vocabulary with which to describe the psychological qualities of orgasm. Mah and Binik (2002, 2005) have begun to address this issue. They developed and assessed the Orgasm Rating Scale (ORS), a 28-item adjective-ratings scale that measures six sensory and four cognitive-affective components of the subjective orgasm experience. Applying the ORS in initial self-report studies, the investigators observed the following: (1) other than on the sensory component of 'shooting sensations', hypothesized to describe ejaculatory sensations, men and women did not differ substantively in scores on the remaining components; (2) orgasm attained through sex with a partner was rated as greater in pleasurable satisfaction and emotional intimacy than orgasm attained through masturbation; and (3) orgasmic pleasure and satisfaction were significantly associated with (a) the cognitive-affective components more than the sensory components, (b) the overall physical and psychological intensity of orgasm more than anatomical location of orgasmic sensations, and (c) relationship satisfaction (Mah and Binik 2002, 2005).

Overall, the neurocognitive mechanisms of the orgasm response require much more systematic exploration. The interrelationships between the peripheral neurophysiological events, the central brain regions, and, in turn, the subjective qualities of the orgasm experience warrant further investigation. To this end, integrating biological measures (e.g. imaging technology) with valid self-report questionnaires assessing the phenomenology of orgasm (see OBJECTIVE VS SUBJECTIVE MEASURES OF CONSCIOUSNESS) is the next direction in orgasm research.

KENNETH MAH AND YITZCHAK M. BINIK

Georgiadis, J. R., Kortekaas, R., Kuipers, R. et al. (2006). 'Regional cerebral blood flow changes associated with clitorally induced orgasm in healthy women'. *European Journal of Neuroscience*, 24.

—— Reinders, A. A., van der Graaf, F. H., Paans, A. M., and Kortekaas, R. (2007). 'Brain activation during human male ejaculation revisited'. *NeuroReport*, 18.

Komisaruk, B. R., Whipple, B., Crawford, A., Liu, W. C., Kalnin, A., and Mosier, K. (2004). 'Brain activation during vaginocervical self-stimulation and orgasm in women with complete spinal cord injury: fMRI evidence of mediation by the vagus nerves'. *Brain Research*, 1024.

Mah, K. and Binik, Y. M. (2001). 'The nature of human orgasm: A critical review of major trends'. *Clinical Psychology Review*, 21.

—— —— (2002). 'Are all orgasms alike? Evaluating a two-dimensional model of the orgasm experience across sex and sexual context'. *Journal of Sex Research*.

—— —— (2005). 'Are orgasms in the mind or the body? Psychosocial versus physiological correlates of orgasmic pleasure and satisfaction'. *Journal of Sex and Marital Therapy*, 31.

Masters, W. H. and Johnson, V. E. (1966), *Human Sexual Response*.

Meston, C. M., Levin, R. J., Sipski, M. L., Hull, E. M., and Heiman, J. R. (2004). 'Women's orgasm', *Annual Review of Sex Research*, 15.

Motofei, I. G. and Rowland, D. L. (2005). 'Neurophysiology of the ejaculatory process: developing perspectives'. *BJU International*, 96.

other minds Discussion of other minds is typically encountered in the context of the phrase 'the problem of other minds'. The phrase is something of a misnomer, for there are in fact multiple, albeit related, problems of other minds. Some of these problems are of interest only to philosophers; others are—or at least should be—of interest to consciousness scientists. All of them are difficult.

Two distinctions are needed in order to chart the conceptual space in which these problems lie. Firstly, we must distinguish two kinds of mental states (or properties): intentional states and phenomenal states. An *intentional* state is a state in which the subject represents (thinks about, perceives) its environment or itself. For example, we might say of a mouse that it perceives a predator. A *phenomenal* state is a state that there is something it is like for the subject in question to enjoy. For example, it may be the case that there is something that it is like for the mouse to perceive the predator in question. These two kinds of mental states bring with them two notions of mentality and thus two kinds of 'other minds' problem: a problem of other intentional minds, and a problem of other phenomenal minds. Although many discussions of the problem of other minds fail to distinguish intentionality from phenomenality, the distinction is an important one, for solutions to the one problem may not transfer to the other version of the problem. Of course, one might hold an account of the relationship between intentionality and phenomenality according to which it is not possible for a creature to have phenomenal states without having intentional states. Proponents of such views will expect there to be a unified account of the problem of other minds, but such views of the relationship between phenomenality and intentionality are contested, and many theorists will be sympathetic to the thought these two problems should be distinguished. As befits a volume on consciousness, we will focus here on the problem of other phenomenal minds.

A second important distinction is that between the *philosophical* problem of other minds and the *scientific* problem of other minds. (These terms should be taken with a grain of salt, for arguably each problem contains both scientific and philosophical aspects.) The philosophical problem of other minds is the problem of justifying the common-sense belief that other human beings have minds (and, indeed, have minds that are in their core features similar to one's own mind). You *do* know that those with whom you share your life are subjects of experience rather than mere *zombies, but *how* do you know this? The scientific problem of other minds is that of determining what sorts of creatures—other than adult, awake human beings—have minds. Do human neonates or very young infants have minds? Might some patients in a vegetative state retain mental states of some kind? Which, if any, non-human animals have minds? What would it take to build a robot with mental states? And how might we tell whether any Martians that we might happen to come across have minds? These questions are all versions of the scientific problem of other minds. We will examine both the philosophical and scientific problems of other (phenomenal) minds.

Before turning to the various responses to the philosophical version of the problem, it is useful to draw attention to some of the background assumptions that have framed the discussion. Firstly, philosophers have typically have taken it for granted that we *do* know that our near and dear are conscious; the problem is one of identifying the basis of that knowledge. (Those who doubt that others really do have minds are known as *solipsists, and are a rare breed indeed.) Secondly, philosophical discussion of other minds has generally shown little interest in the question of what mechanisms underwrite our assumption that our conspecifics have phenomenal lives. For the most part, philosophers have left such issues to the psychologists, and have assumed that account of the psychological principles operative in generating our belief in other minds will have little bearing on the question of how that common-sense belief might be epistemically justified. The merits of this assumption are far from unproblematic, but that issue must be left to one side here.

Two supposed solutions to the philosophical problem of other minds have dominated the literature: one based on an argument from analogy, and another based on inference to the best explanation (IBE). According to the former, my knowledge of other minds can be justified by noting analogies between my behaviour and that of others. Roughly speaking, the fact that my pain behaviour (e.g. saying 'ouch' and removing my body from the source of pain) is accompanied by an experience of pain, entitles me to infer that other examples of pain behaviour are also accompanied by experiences of pain. According to the IBE account, the attribution of conscious states to other creatures can be justified on the theoretical grounds that it provides the best explanation of the available data (such as pain behaviour).

Neither of these two accounts is free from objection. Critics complain that analogical arguments are really just inductive arguments from one case, and as such provide little epistemic justification for the conclusion, and certainly not enough justification to underwrite the common-sense assumption that we know that our friends and family are conscious. The IBE proposal comes up against the problem that it is not at all clear that ascribing conscious states to others *does* provide the best explanation of their behaviour—indeed, it is far from clear that it provides *any* kind of explanation of behaviour. It is one thing to claim that behaviour complexity justifies ascribing consciousness to a creature, but it is quite another thing to claim that this ascription is underwritten by the explanatory role that it provides.

Drawing on themes to be found in the philosophy of the later Wittgenstein (1953), a number of philosophers have argued that the problem of other minds is fundamentally ill-posed and should be dissolved rather than solved. Wittgensteinian challenges to the problem of other minds can be developed in a number of ways, but at their core is the thought that the subject's access to her own conscious states—in particular, her ability to refer to her own conscious states—is parasitic on the fact that she knows that other people have conscious states. Proponents of this line of thought sometimes suggest that the links between one's grasp of what it is to have a conscious state and one's recognition that those around one have conscious states is *criterial*—it is constitutive rather than evidential. Many philosophers reject this response as unsatisfactory. The issues here resist easy summary, for they turn on complex debates concerning the nature of reference and concept-possession (see Avramides 2001, Hyslop 1995).

The philosophical problem of other minds is of concern to few outside the ranks of professional philosophers. By contrast, the scientific problem of other minds is of interest far beyond the confines of academic philosophy. Not only does it have important implications for the science of consciousness, but it also has implications for debates within ethical and political theory, for on many accounts the community of moral significance is co-extensive with the community of the conscious.

Is the scientific problem of other minds particularly problematic? One might have thought not. One might have thought that in order to determine the distribution of consciousness within the natural order one need only develop a theory of consciousness. One could simply consult one's theory to determine whether (say) mice are conscious. But this view is overly optimistic. The problem is this: The task of building and evaluating a model of consciousness requires that one make assumptions about the distribution of consciousness. Unless one has already taken up a stance on the question of whether (say) mice are conscious, one cannot use data derived from mouse experiments as a constraint on one's theory of consciousness.

One might be tempted to respond to this worry by suggesting that theories of consciousness should draw only on data derived from normal, awake human beings, for it is only with respect to such creatures that we can be sure consciousness is present. Endorsing this suggestion would result in various practical difficulties for the science of consciousness, but it would also lead to a deeper problem (Block 2002). It is one thing to have an account of consciousness as it occurs in normal, awake adult human beings, but it is quite another thing to have an account of consciousness as it might occur in (say) dreaming human beings, the human fetus, dolphins, or E. T. Any science of consciousness that limited itself to normal, human subjects would face the problem of justifying the claim that it was a general theory of consciousness and not merely a theory of (normal, adult) human consciousness. An example might illustrate the point. Suppose that consciousness in adult, awake humans correlated mostly closely with 40 Hz activation in parietal cortex. (It doesn't, of course, but just suppose that it did.) Should we then infer that any creature lacking 40 Hz activation in parietal cortex is unconscious (on the grounds that such activation is responsible for consciousness as such), or should we instead infer only that (adult, awake, etc) human consciousness involves 40 Hz activation, and leave it as an entirely open question whether consciousness might involve some other mechanism in other organisms? Arguably, the second option is more reasonable, but adopting it is also to give up on the scientific problem of other minds.

The task of developing a non-question-begging theory of consciousness that can guide us in determining the distribution of consciousness is one of the central challenges for the science of consciousness. Judging by the current literature, this task is likely to be with us for some time.

See also BRAIN DAMAGE; FUNCTIONS OF CONSCIOUSNESS; TURING TEST

TIM BAYNE

Avramides, A. (2001). *Other Minds*.

Block, N. (2002). 'The harder problem of consciousness'. *Journal of Philosophy*, XCIX.

Hyslop, A. (1995). *Other Minds*.

McGinn, C. (1984). 'What is the problem of other minds?' *Proceedings of the Aristotelian Society*, supplementary vol. 58.

Melnyk, A. (1994). 'Inference to the best explanation and other minds'. *Australasian Journal of Philosophy*, 72.

Pargetter, R. (1984). 'The scientific inference to other minds', *Australasian Journal of Philosophy*, 62.

Sober, E. (2000). 'Evolution and the problem of other minds'. *Journal of Philosophy*, 97.

Tye, M. (1997). 'The problem of simple minds: is there anything it is like to be a honey bee?' *Philosophical Studies*, 88.

Wittgenstein, L. (1953). *Philosophical Investigations*.

out-of-body experience Have you ever had the experience of lying in bed, about to fall asleep, when you have the distinct impression of being up at ceiling level looking down at your body in the bed? This experience may be startling and frightening. Afterwards, you may briefly feel conscious of being back in the (body on the) bed again. What you experienced was an out-of-body experience (OBE). Although most readers probably have never had any trouble localizing themselves within their own bodily boundaries, research on OBEs suggests that this sense of self-location or embodiment requires specific brain mechanisms. OBEs are characterized by three phenomenological elements: (1) the impression that the self is localized outside one's body (disembodiment), (2) the impression of seeing the world from an extracorporeal elevated perspective, and (3) of seeing one's own body from this perspective (Irwin 1985, Blanke et al. 2004). OBEs are striking phenomena because they challenge our everyday experience of spatial unity of self and body and the experience of a 'real me' that resides in one's body and is the subject of experience and action (Blackmore 1982).

OBEs have been reported from time immemorial as occurring in about 5–10% of the general population in the Western world, including students as well as older people (Blackmore 1982, Irwin 1985). OBEs also occur in various medical conditions (Blanke et al. 2004), and several precipitating factors have been determined including neurological and psychiatric disease, *hypnagogic and hypnopompic hallucinations, awareness during general *anaesthesia, sensory deprivation, marijuana use, rapid body position changes (as during falls or car accidents), fear, and mental own-body imagery. To date few scientific investigations have been carried out on OBEs, probably because they generally occur spontaneously, are of short duration, and happen only once or twice in a lifetime (Irwin 1985). Investigations of neurological patients with OBEs are also rare (Blanke et al. 2004), but have several advantages. OBEs in these patients might occur repeatedly, sometimes in quick succession, and can in rare instances be induced by electrical stimulation of the human brain.

OBEs have been classified and compared with other autoscopic phenomena. *Autoscopic phenomena* are illusory own-body perceptions that affect the entire body and lead to striking abnormalities in localizing one's own body and self as well as self-identification. Three main types have been described: *autoscopic hallucination, heautoscopy*, and OBEs. In both autoscopic hallucinations and heautoscopy the subject experiences seeing a second own (illusory) body in extrapersonal space, but these phenomena differ with respect to self-identification and self-location with respect to the illusory body. In autoscopic hallucinations subjects do not self-identify and localize themselves at the position of the illusory body, but during heautoscopy subjects self-attribute the illusory body and may even experience themselves to be localized at the position of the illusory body (although they do not experience disembodiment as subjects with OBEs do; Blanke et al. 2004; Blanke and Metzinger 2009).

Neurological studies have permitted more detailed questioning about the OBE and associated sensations shortly after they occur. Moreover, in these cases researchers were able to analyse the associated neurological, causal, and anatomical findings. Clinicians have observed OBEs in association with various neurological conditions, but mainly in epileptic seizures and migraine (Brugger et al. 1997, Blanke et al. 2004). These data also showed that spontaneously occurring OBEs in healthy subjects (as in the above example) are in phenomenological terms the same as OBEs reported by neurological patients, even if induced artificially by electrical stimulation of human cortex:

> The patient lay in bed and awakened from sleep and the first thing she remembered was 'the feeling of being at the ceiling of the room' She '[...] had the impression that I was dreaming that I would float above [under the ceiling] of the room [...].' The patient saw herself in bed ('I was also lying in bed dressed in a red-green pyjama'), in front-view. She described that 'the bed was seen from above' and that 'there was a man with a beard, who was standing next to me, surveying me. I was very frightened.' (Blanke et al. 2004).

The neurological analyses by Blanke et al. (2004) and Blanke and Mohr (2005) suggest that autoscopic phenomena result from a failure to integrate multisensory bodily information. These authors proposed that autoscopic phenomena result from a disintegration of signals from the body and personal space (due to conflicting tactile, proprioceptive, kinesthetic, and visual information) and a second disintegration between signals from personal and extrapersonal space (due to conflicting visual and vestibular information). The importance of vestibular and multisensory mechanisms in OBEs was underlined by the occurrence of vestibular illusions (such as elevation, rotation, flying, lightness, vertigo) and multisensory bodily illusions (such as visual limb shortening and movement). In addition, vestibular and multisensory illusions could be evoked by electrical stimulation of the same cortical area where higher stimulation currents induced OBEs (Blanke et al. 2004). While disintegration in personal space was present in all three forms of autoscopic phenomena, differences between the different forms of autoscopic phenomena were mainly due to differences in strength and type of the vestibular dysfunction. Out-of-body experiences were associated with a strong vestibular disturbance, whereas heautoscopy was associated with a moderate and more variable vestibular disturbance, and autoscopic hallucinations without any vestibular disturbance. Moreover, the high frequency of visual *hallucinations and hemianopia in patients with autoscopic hallucinations suggested that deficient visual processing is the main causing factor for disintegration in personal space in autoscopic hallucinations. These clinical data suggest that heautoscopy is primarily due to abnormal somatosensory or *sensorimotor information processing, whereas OBEs are due to abnormal vestibular information processing (for further details see Blanke and Mohr 2005).

Several neurological patients with OBEs caused by circumscribed *brain damage to the temporal lobe have been described. More recent lesion analysis found that especially the posterior aspects of the superior and middle temporal gyri at the junction with the inferior parietal lobe of the right hemisphere are affected (Blanke et al. 2004), whereas brain damage in patients with autoscopic hallucinations and heautoscopy is anatomically distinct.

The right temporoparietal junction (TPJ) is part of a larger network of brain areas involved in the representation of body and self such as the multisensory coding of the human body, agency, ownership, self-other distinction, and visuospatial perspective taking (Blanke et al. 2005). Experimental clues that mentally imagining an extracorporeal position and perspective relies, at least partly, on similar brain mechanisms to those that are disturbed in OBEs come from neuroimaging studies. Using a mental imagery task in healthy subjects that mimics the disembodiment and visuospatial perspective that is generally reported by subjects with OBEs, these studies revealed an activation of the right TPJ (especially for the imagined position and visuospatial perspective mimicking OBEs). Moreover, *transcranial magnetic stimulation (TMS) of this area while subjects perform this mental imagery task impairs their ability to imagine themselves in a disembodied extracorporeal position (Blanke et al. 2005). These experimental neuroimaging data show that the functional and neural mechanisms of OBEs can be investigated by experimental neuroscience, just like other *illusions and hallucinations. These findings have recently been extended by the experimental induction of a bodily illusion that shares some aspects of OBEs and heautoscopy using virtual reality (Ehrsson 2007, Lenggenhager et al. 2007).

In science the most challenging phenomena are often the ones we take for granted in our everyday lives. Excellent examples are the self, the experienced spatial unity between self and body, and the fact that consciousness seems bound to a body-centred perspective. These phenomena are challenged by OBEs pointing to specialized brain mechanisms in embodiment, self-location, and related aspects of bodily *self-consciousness. In conclusion, the empirical data about OBEs from neurology and neuroscience suggest that the scientific investigation of OBEs (and other autoscopic phenomena; Brugger et al. 1997, Blanke et al. 2004) might allow the understanding of the following key aspects of consciousness: (1) What are the functional and neural mechanisms of embodiment and self-location? (2) How do these mechanisms relate to the subjectivity of consciousness, i.e. the fact that consciousness is bound to an individual first-person perspective? (3) How do these mechanisms relate to higher levels of self-consciousness such as explicit self-recognition, autobiographical memory, and self-concept? It is hoped that these findings will also advance our understanding of pathologies concerning the self and self consciousness in neurology and psychiatry.

See also ALTERED STATE OF CONSCIOUSNESS; ANAESTHESIA, AWARENESS UNDER; BODY IMAGE AND BODY SCHEMA; HALLUCINATION; ILLUSIONS; SELF-CONSCIOUSNESS; SELF, PHILOSOPHICAL PERSPECTIVES; SELF SCIENTIFIC PERSPECTIVES; SUBJECTIVITY

OLAF BLANKE

Blackmore, S. J. (1982). *Beyond The Body. An Investigation of Out-of-Body Experiences.*

Blanke, O. and Metzinger, T. (2009). 'Full-body illusions and minimal phenomenal selfhood'. *Trends in Cognitive Science*, 13.

—— and Mohr, C. (2005). 'Autoscopic phenomena of neurological origin. Implications for corporal awareness and self consciousness' *Brain Research Reviews*, 50.

—— Landis, T., Spinelli, L., and Seeck, M. (2004). 'Out-of-body experience and autoscopy of neurological origin'. *Brain*, 127.

—— Mohr, C., Michel, C. M. et al. (2007). 'Linking out-of body experience to self processing at the temporo-parietal junction'. *Journal of Neuroscience*, 25.

Brugger, P., Regard, M., and Landis, T. (1997). 'Illusory reduplication of one's own body : phenomenology and classification of autoscopic phenomena'. *Cognitive Neuropsychiatry*, 2.

Ehrsson, H. (2007). 'The experimental induction of out-of-body experiences'. *Science*, 317.

Irwin, H. J. (1985). *Flight of Mind: a Psychological Study of the Out-of-body Experience.*

Lenggenhager, B., Tadi, T, Metzinger, T., and Blanke, O. (2007). 'Video ergo sum. Manipulating bodily self-consciousness'. *Science*, 317.

P

pain, philosophical perspectives The ordinary conception of pain has two major threads that are in tension with each other. It is this tension that generates various puzzles in our philosophical understanding of pain. According to one thread, pain is something that we locate in body parts using sentences such as

(1) I *feel* a sharp pain in my knee.

We also use expressions such as 'I *have* a burning pain in my thigh' or 'I *experienced* a jabbing pain in my wrist when I served the ball', etc. According to this understanding, we not only routinely attribute pains to body parts but also *feel* them in those parts. Pains therefore seem to be a kind of objects or conditions of body parts that we stand in perceptual relation to, just as we can perceive trees, cars, apples, etc.

According to this thread, then, pains are spatio-temporally locatable objects of our perceptions, so that it becomes legitimate to ask about the nature of these objects. The most natural thing to say here is that in feeling pain in a body part we are perceiving (feeling) some physical condition of that part, some sort of tissue damage or a condition that would cause tissue damage if sustained. Let's use 'tissue damage' for whatever physical condition we may be said to be perceiving in those body parts we attribute pain.

Clearly, however, our ordinary conception does not equate pain with tissue damage, according to the common-sense understanding of pain. We can see that by conducting a little thought experiment. Suppose that pain = tissue damage, so that we do in fact attribute a physical condition, tissue damage (TD), when we attribute pain to body parts, and that the tissue damage is the object of perceptual experience. So, for instance, John's current excruciating experience (call this E) is caused by and represents a physical condition in his leg (e.g. a tear in his tendon), and our ordinary concept of pain applies in the first instance to this condition in his leg. From this it would follow that

(2) John would not have any pain if he had E, but no TD in his leg.

(as in the case of e.g. *phantom limb pains and centrally generated chronic pains), and, conversely,

(3) John would have pain if he had TD but no E.

(as would be the case e.g. if he had taken absolutely effective painkillers or his leg had been locally anaesthetized).

But these statements are intuitively incorrect. They clearly clash with our ordinary or dominant concept of pain, which seems to track the experience rather than the physical condition. But if we do not attribute a physical condition when we attribute pain to bodily locations, what else could we be attributing? There does not seem to be any other plausible candidate. This is, then, one of the puzzles about pain.

This brings us to the second major thread involved in our ordinary conception of pain: pain as *subjective experience. The thought experiment above shows that our concept of pain tracks experiences and not what these experiences may be said to naturally signal or represent, namely, tissue damage. This seems to be the more dominant thread, according to which pains are not any sort of extra-mental objects of our experiences but they are experiences or acts of experiences that are subjective and private. (Indeed, not only common sense but also the definition offered by the International Association for the Study of Pain picks up on this thread: 'an unpleasant sensory and emotional experience associated with actual or potential tissue damage, or described in terms of such damage'.) Thus it can be said that our ordinary conception of pain inherently exhibits some sort of *act–object* duality or ambiguity.

But this deepens the puzzle: how can these two threads even coexist? If pains are subjective experiences, they are *mental* states or events, and so, as such, they are not, prima facie, the kind of things that can be located in one's knee or toe or thigh (I can experience something in my knee but not locate subjective experiences in my knee!). This is the tension between the two threads in our ordinary understanding of pain. Still, observing that pains are subjective experiences does not prevent one from *correctly* using sentences like (1) above to attribute pains to bodily parts. And this is one of the major puzzles that have occupied philosophers: how could we correctly attribute pain to, say, one's left arm (even when the physical cause is in, say, one's heart), while simultaneously insisting that pain is primarily an experience?

Philosophical responses to this puzzle have tended to fall into either one of two categories, depending on what part of the act–object pair philosophers have tended to embrace. One category may be called *objectualist*. What unites this group is the agreement that sentences such as (1)—we can call these 'locating sentences'—should be taken more or less literally on the pattern of standard perceptual reports such as:

(4) I see an apple on the table.
(5) I feel the smooth texture of the surface, etc.

These report that I stand in a perceptual relation to a spatio-temporally locatable object, hence are true only if there is indeed an object that I see or feel. Similarly the objectualist says (1) is true only if there is an object that I feel. At this point, the objectualists may be split into two further groups.

One group says that this object should be identified with tissue damage, or more accurately, with a pathological physical condition of the body part to which pain is attributed (e.g. Newton 1989, Hill 2006). This group may be called *external objectualists*. The typical way in which external objectualists respond to the thought experiment above is to admit that their position clashes with the common-sense conception of pain, but to insist that that our ordinary understanding of pain is confused and the best way to remedy it is to revise it by adopting or stipulating that locating sentences are best understood as reports of perception of tissue damage, i.e. as a form of *exteroceptual* report where pains are identified with tissue damage. The basic motivation behind this revisionist position is to maintain naturalism or physicalism in the philosophy of perception by unifying all experience as exteroceptual.

The other objectualist group may be called *internal objectualist*. What unites this group is that feeling pain in a body part is to perceive or be aware of a non-physical object or property that either is literally located in that body part (e.g. Jackson 1977), or is internal to one's experience but is somehow projected to that part (e.g. Perkins 1983). Traditional sense-datum theories are internal objectualists (e.g. Broad 1959). According to these theories, the objects of one's direct and immediate awareness in perception are always sense-data usually understood as non-physical particulars. It is by directly and immediately perceiving sense-data that we indirectly come to perceive the extra-mental world that is the cause of these sense-data. On this view, perceptual experiences always involve an act–object duality internal to one's consciousness. The immediate awareness of this internal object constitutes one's indirect perception of a physical object if it is regularly caused by this object. Of course, this indirection is not ordinarily revealed in daily life, so one is normally under the impression that in perception we come into direct and immediate contact with the physical world. Sense-datum theories have been controversial, and these days very few people seem to hold these theories. But one need not be a sense-datum theorist to be an internal objectualist. In general anyone who claims that in feeling pain one is directly and immediately aware of some non-physical *quality* or *condition* (as opposed to *objects*) either literally located in or projected onto a bodily region is an internal objectualist in our classificatory scheme. What unites the internal and external objectualists is that both insist on a (more or less) literal interpretation of locating sentences. Sentences like (1) ought to be taken, on these views, on their face value and interpreted as reporting a perceptual relation to an object/quality located in a body part.

There is, however, a fundamental difference between the external and internal objectualists. The object of perception located in a body part is physical (tissue damage) according to the former, but non-physical (e.g. sense-data) according to the latter. The *internalist* is in a better position to explain why pains are subjective (they exists only insofar as they are being sensed/perceived), private (only the owner can access her pain in the direct and immediate manner in which she does), and the source of a kind of infallible knowledge (the owner cannot be mistaken about her pain). Mental objects/qualities internal to one's consciousness are considered paradigm examples exhibiting these features. But the internalist pays a price for that. Insofar as genuine perception requires the possibility of mistakes, i.e. possible mismatches between one's experience and its objects, feeling a pain in a bodily location cannot be a form of genuine perception, i.e. *exteroception*. The only sense, then, in which 'perception' may be used in relation to feeling pain is *introspection*, a form of perception-like inspection of the contents (mental objects/qualities) of onc's consciousness.

On the other hand, the externalist objectualist, by identifying pain with tissue damage, has no difficulty in taking feeling pain as genuine perception, as exteroception. Indeed, this is the primary motivation for this view. But then she goes against the common-sense view of pain by making them objective and public objects about which we may be, and often are, quite mistaken.

Neither form of objectualism, then, is free of difficulties. So let us take up the other group of philosophical responses to the puzzle generated by the act–object duality of pain, which we may call, in contrasting to objectualist, 'experientialist'. Experientialists respond to the puzzle by proposing that locating sentences should not be taken at face value and thus should not be interpreted on the model of standard exteroceptual reports such as (4) and (5). Rather, the proper model for locating sentences is 'appearance' sentences such as:

(4*) It visually appears to me that there is an apple on the table.
(5*) It feels as if the texture of the surface is smooth.

These sentences, unlike (4) and (5), are not falsified if it turns out that there is no apple on the table (*hallucination) or the texture is not in fact smooth (*illusion). They report 'appearances'. And many would agree that in some sense we may be infallible about perceptual appearances if we are careful about how to report them. Furthermore, my access to how things appear to me is radically different from your access to it, so appearances are private in this sense. Also, an appearance, in some sense, is always an appearance to someone, to a subject; so they are, intuitively, subjective. All this suggests that appearance sentences could be (or perhaps, should be) analysed as reporting perceptual experiences themselves, in the first place, without any conceptual commitment to whether these experiences are veridical or not. The suggestion, then, locating sentences likewise report 'appearances', i.e. experiences with a certain representational/perceptual content (Armstrong 1968, Pitcher 1970).

According to Armstrong, for instance, when we report pain in our hand, we say something like this: 'It feels to me that a certain sort of disturbance is occurring in my hand, a perception that evokes in me the peremptory desire that the perception should cease' (1968: 314). This explains why we can correctly use a locating sentence 'attributing pain' to a hand even if there is nothing physically wrong with it, even when no tissue damage is occurring there. The pain location is therefore an intentional location, a location that our pain experience represents as damaged. But whether or not this representation is veridical, it is still correct that I feel/experience it as damaged—it experientially appears to me that way. Experientialists tend to be representationalist about the content of pain experiences: they believe that pain experiences represent tissue damage in body parts. Therefore they think that ordinary talk, the practice of using locating sentences, is confused and thus prone to mislead. When I use a sentence like (1) to attribute a pain to my knee, I do not attribute a ghostly object there, nor do I directly attribute tissue damage there. Rather what I actually do is attribute a feeling state, an experience, to myself, which experience then attributes a damaged condition to my knee (i.e. represents my knee as damaged). Whether or not I come to believe what my experience tells me about the condition of my knee is a further matter, not immediately relevant to evaluating the truth-value of (1). Sentence (1) is true or false depending on whether or not I have the experience, not whether or not the experience is veridical. The colloquial ways of speaking just jumble the pain (experience) with the disturbance and thus mislead us. The experientialist view then proposes that we do not take locating sentences at face value but reinterpret them as attributing an experience with a content.

As mentioned before, the experientialists tend to be representationalist about the content of pain experiences and take them to represent a physical condition (damage) of the body part 'pain' is attributed to (Tye 1997, Dretske 1999). (But it is, of course, theoretically open to experientialists to hold that pain experiences represent something else—although it is difficult to fathom what that could be if they want to remain naturalist or physicalist.) Because of this, experientialists tend to also subscribe to a *perceptualist* view of pain. The core of this view is that feeling pain in a bodily location L is perceiving something extramental in L, typically some sort of tissue damage.

The difference between this experientialist version of the view and the external objectualist version we discussed above lies in how they propose to analyse locating sentences, our routine practice of talking of pains located in body parts. The experientialist says we report primarily experiences in reporting pains but insists that these experiences are perceptual in that they represent tissue damage. The external objectualist says we report tissue damage in those places we attribute 'pain' to. As we have seen, in this, objectualists come into conflict with how we ordinarily conceptualize and talk about pains in body parts, but they are closer to the core of a perceptualist view of pain.

The experientialists, on the other hand, although they seem capable to align themselves with common sense in regard to evaluating locating sentences, have the problem of explaining why we are focused on the experience itself rather than its object if feeling pain is a genuine case of perceiving some objective condition of bodily regions. Compare (4) and (5) to (4*) or (5*) respectively; the first pair are perceptual reports, and they are true or false partly depending on the existence or condition of the extramental object of perception. (4*) and (5*), on the other hand, seem more like *introspective* rather than perceptual reports. If talking about pains, reflecting as it does our ordinary understanding of them, is more like the latter pair, a natural worry arises as to whether why we should regard feeling pain as a genuine case of perception. This worry is intensified if we add the observation that we almost never ordinarily countenance the truth or falsity of pain talk to turn on whether or not there is a tissue damage in the locations to which we attribute pain. This is quite unlike the contrast between the two pairs above: both kinds have their place in ordinary speech. The problem of focus, as we may call it, needs therefore addressing by the experientialists who want to insist that feeling pain is perceiving something extra-mental.

A natural response (Armstrong 1968, Pitcher 1970) to the problem of focus is that feeling pain, unlike the experiences involved in most other forms of exteroception, has a distinctive affective/emotional phenomenology (in addition to having a sensory-discriminative dimension): pain experiences, whether or not they are veridical, hurt. They are almost always unpleasant and unwanted. This unpleasant/hurtful quality of pain experiences may be the reason why we conceptually focus on experiences rather than on their objects when we talk of pains. Pain experiences are phenomenologically and biologically complex events, consisting of (at least) affective–motivational and sensory–discriminative components, because of their vital importance. So, it might be said, it is not surprising to find our linguistic and conceptual responses aligning themselves differently with pain experiences—differently than with standard exteroceptual experiences. It is not clear, however, whether this response to the problem of focus is a vindication of a perceptual view of pain or a concession that feeling pain is not really perceptual. And so the philosophical debate goes on. . . .

MURAT AYDEDE

Armstrong, D. M. (1968). *A Materialist Theory of the Mind.*
Broad, C. D. (1959). *Scientific Thought.*
Dretske, F. (1999). 'The mind's awareness of itself'. *Philosophical Studies*, 95.
Hill, C. (2006). 'Ow! The paradox of pain'. In Aydede, M. (ed.) *Pain: New Essays on Its Nature and the Methodology of Its Study.*
Jackson, F. (1977). *Perception: a Representative Theory.*
Newton, N. (1989). 'On viewing pain as a secondary quality'. *Nous*, 23.
Perkins, M. (1983). *Sensing the World.*
Pitcher, G. (1970). 'Pain perception'. *Philosophical Review*, 79.
Tye, M. (1997). 'A representational theory of pains and their phenomenal character'. In Block, N. et al. (eds) *The Nature of Consciousness: Philosophical Debates.*

pain, scientific perspectives Pain is an unpleasant experience familiar to every normal human being. The International Association for the Study of Pain defines it as 'an unpleasant sensory and emotional experience associated with actual or potential tissue damage, or described in terms of such damage' (Chapman and Nakamura 1999). The word 'experience' acknowledges that pain is a first-person phenomenon, and the definition notes that it has emotional as well as sensory features.

The emotional features of pain are related to the defence response that an injury evokes: an adaptive reaction characterized by physiological arousal, hypervigilance, and a sense of threat. Although physicians focus on the sensory features of pain for diagnostic purposes, the emotional aspect is more important to the injured person, and this aspect is always intertwined with cognition. Research on emotional mechanisms reveals the second-person aspect of pain. Certain brain structures activated during pain actuate in an empathic observer (Loggia et al. 2007).

People differ widely as to how much pain they experience when injured. Because of genetic differences, some tend to experience intense pain while others are comparatively insensitive. In addition, the emotional, cognitive, and motivational features of an injurious event vary widely across people and consequently individuals experiencing a common injury construct dissimilar pain. Past experiences and contextual factors exert a great influence. For example, two patients presenting in an emergency department with identical hand injuries may experience pain differently. One, a professional musician, may fear that the injury is career-ending and suffer severe pain with strong emotion. The other, a manual worker with an industrial injury, may look forward to time off with pay or benefits from unfulfilling labour and experience much less pain. Cognitive processes such as the meaning of the injury, social context, memory, expectation, attention, and intention modify the brain's construction of pain.

Acute pain is an experience triggered by the onset of tissue trauma, for example postoperative pain. In general, acute pain has a clear somatic reference and its intensity dissipates with tissue healing. Its evolutionary purpose is to minimize activity, further injury, and risk of infection while healing is under way. Chronic pain, in contrast, serves no evolutionary purpose and is a major cause of suffering. It typically has little or no relationship to tissue injury. Some disorders, like fibromyalgia, involve generalized pain throughout the body. People living with severe chronic pain typically experience and suffer from physical deconditioning, fatigue, sleep disturbance, irritability, and depression (Loeser et al. 2001).

In the 19th century Claude Bernard distinguished between the *milieu intérieur* and the *milieu extérieur*. Pain is an aspect of the *milieu intérieur*, and its sensory feature normally fits into the brain's *body schema (Ramachandran 1998, Chapman and Nakamura 1999). The body schema derives principally from cortical topography. Although brain remapping occurs following limb amputation, the body schema resists alteration and chronic pain can persist indefinitely in a *phantom body part. In some cases, repeating or chronic pain states can alter the brain's representation of the body. Migraine headache patients, for example, tend to develop thicker than normal somatosensory cortices. In contrast, in some chronic pain conditions, the brain suppresses representation of the painful area. This is the case for many patients with complex regional pain syndrome, an abnormal and painful condition of a limb. A neglect-like syndrome occurs in which patients experience the limb as not belonging to the body, or they may have to muster extra attention in order to move it. They have delayed reaction times for the affected side when asked to view photos of limbs and identify right or left, and have trouble knowing the position of the limb (Moseley 2004). Brain imaging reveals reduced cortical representation of the affected area. Thus, at least some chronic pain states involve alteration of the body schema.

The most basic mechanism of pain is the nociceptor, which is a free nerve ending that detects injury on a C or A-delta fibre (Loeser et al. 2001). Nociceptors respond primarily to chemical changes in their surroundings, but they also fire in response to crushing mechanical, thermal, or electrical stimulation. Nociceptors in visceral tissues are insensitive to crushing mechanical and thermal stimulation and respond instead to tissue stretch.

There is rarely a tight fit between extent of tissue injury and human pain severity because several processes modulate the transmission of injury information to the brain. Several processes enhance pain, and these begin with the nociceptor itself. C fibre nociceptors are more than passive sensory end organs. When tissue injury occurs, they interact with the wound by releasing peptides that contribute to inflammation, and the chemical soup of inflammation, in turn, sensitizes the nociceptor so that its threshold for firing reduces. Sustained nociceptive signalling results in wind-up, or further sensitization at the level of the dorsal horn of the spinal cord. Here glutamatergic mechanisms extend hypersensitivity into adjacent, uninjured tissue. The term *hyperalgesia* refers to increased tissue sensitivity to normally painful stimuli; *allodynia* refers to the experience of pain in response to non-injurious stimuli that normally do not provide pain. Allodynia is 'touch-induced' pain (Loeser et al. 2000).

Descending inhibitory processes also exist. In a crisis calling for fight or flight, incapacitating pain from a wound is maladaptive. Several structures in the mesencephalic brain, including the periaqueductal gray and the nucleus raphe magnus, can control signals of tissue injury by gating nociceptive input at the dorsal horn of the spinal cord. During combat and other traumatic events, these processes can render a person or animal temporarily analgesic.

Extensive research with *functional brain imaging during naturally occurring and laboratory-induced pain states has revealed massively parallel, distributed processing within the brain (Apkarian et al. 2005). Areas typically active during pain include thalamus, primary and secondary somatosensory cortices, anterior cingulate, insula, cerebellum, and prefrontal cortices. Activity in these structures indicates that the construction of pain involves emotional and cognitive processing as well as sensory processing. This body of literature has demonstrated definitively that the notion of pain as a primitive sensation is scientifically incorrect. Pain is the emergent product of simultaneous interacting patterns of brain activity associated with sensation, emotion, and cognition.

In a healthy nervous system, pain represents in consciousness tissue damage or physical conditions associated with injury or disease such as inflammation. Sometimes pain is the product of an unhealthy nervous system; i.e. damage to nervous structures, or peripheral deafferentation, can cause abnormal firing patterns that lead the brain to create a pain state. This condition, called *neuropathic pain*, can result from some peripheral neuropathies including diabetic neuropathy. It can also occur in nervous structures damaged by viral infection, e.g. postherpetic neuralgia, and in nerves injured by physical trauma. Deafferentation associated with the loss of a limb or other body part can lead to a painful phantom. Spinal cord injury and stroke can cause chronic central pain states that are multifaceted, horrible, and all but indescribable.

The problem of measuring pain is a continuing barrier to progress in pain research. Because pain is subjective and first-person, the only avenue open for quantification and third-person rendering of pain is *introspection (Nakamura and Chapman 2002). This typically involves a mental appraisal and number assignment. It is difficult for some people to assign numbers to pain according to rules. Studies show that pain reports rarely correspond closely to measurable features of wounds. Moreover, patients rating pain severity tend report the emotional rather than the sensory dimension of pain. Measures of autonomic arousal and central nervous system activation during pain are useful physiological correlates, but they are not surrogates for first-person experience. Pain assessment in infants and cognitively compromised patients poses a challenge. Facial expression, which is also important in *empathy or second-person awareness, offers an approach to pain quantification in such patient populations (Williams 2002).

Although a substantial body of research addresses pain mechanisms and treatment, effective pain prevention and control still elude medical science. Consequently, pain is one of the major reasons why patients visit physicians, and chronic pain is a major cause of partial or complete disability throughout the industrialized world.

Chronic pain states rarely yield to surgical intervention, neural blockade, or medications.

Although medical schools have traditionally taught that pain is a sensory modality that basically functions in the same way across individuals, the confluence of several lines of research including functional brain imaging reveals unequivocally that pain is the integrated product of sensory, emotional, and cognitive processes. Because of this, clinical interventions for pain have highly varied effects across individual patients. Most interventions exert a cognitive and emotional as well as a sensory impact. Patient expectations, product advertising, the health-care professionals' behaviour, and family attitude can sometimes influence pain more than a new medication. Moreover, pain complaint and pain behaviour have an effect on the immediate social context, the patient's family, and often the patient's vocational setting. Pain, as an aspect of bodily awareness, is a feature of the whole person. Scientific inquiry must engage it at multiple levels ranging from basic neuroscience to epidemiology in order to characterize and understand it properly.

C. RICHARD CHAPMAN AND YOSHIO NAKAMURA

Apkarian, A. V. et al. (2005). 'Human brain mechanisms of pain perception and regulation in health and disease'. *European Journal of Pain*, 9.

Chapman, C. R. and Nakamura, Y. (1999). 'A passion of the soul: an introduction to pain for consciousness researchers'. *Consciousness and Cognition*, 8.

Loeser, J. D. et al. (eds) (2001). *Bonica's Management of Pain*, 3rd edn.

Loggia, M. L., Mogil, J. S., and Bushnell, M. C. (2007). 'Empathy hurts: compassion for another increases both sensory and affective components of pain perception'. *Pain.*

Moseley, G. L. (2004). 'Why do people with complex regional pain syndrome take longer to recognize their affected hand?' *Neurology*, 62.

Nakamura, Y. and Chapman, C. R. (2002). 'Measuring pain: an introspective look at introspection'. *Consciousness and Cognition*, 11.

Ramachandran, V. S. (1998). 'Consciousness and body image: lessons from phantom limbs, Capgras syndrome and pain asymbolia'. *Philosophical Transactions of the Royal Society of London, Series B: Biological Sciences*, 353.

Williams, A. C. (2002). 'Facial expression of pain: an evolutionary account'. *Behavioral and Brain Sciences*, 25 (4).

panpsychism Panpsychism is a family of views whose basic principles are that the mental is both fundamental and ubiquitous. The principle of the ubiquity of the mental is the claim that everything has a mental aspect. Panpsychists hold that mentality is fundamental in the sense that it cannot be reduced to or explained in terms of anything else. Depending upon how these principles are more exactly specified, many different forms of panpsychism can be developed. For example, if the fundamentality of the mental is taken to be absolute, so that no other feature of reality is similarly ontologically basic, then panpsychism appears as *idealism or *phenomenalism. However, panpsychists generally avoid setting up the mental as the sole fundamental feature of the world, frequently preferring to allow that matter and mind are co-fundamental in the sense that there are both mentalistic and materialistic attributes of things, neither explicable in terms of or reducible to the other.

Panpsychism can be usefully contrasted with the opposing doctrine of *emergentism: the view that certain attributes apply to complex systems which do not apply to the systems' constituents. Any view that sees the mental as arising from, or reducible to, completely non-mental features is a form of emergentism (although there are many forms of the doctrine with widely varying commitments). All the popular forms of modern physicalism, such as the neural identity theory and functionalism, are emergentist theories fundamentally opposed to panpsychism.

Thus one important form of argument used to support panpsychism proceeds by undercutting the concept of emergence. Thomas Nagel (1979) presented a version of the argument which can be expressed as follows: (1) Emergence is either 'ontologically radical' or merely 'epistemic'. (2) The idea of radical ontological emergence is incoherent. (3) Therefore, all emergence is merely epistemic. (4) Mind cannot be merely epistemically emergent. (5) Therefore mind cannot be emergent and hence must be fundamental.

Once mind is recognized as fundamental, only the claim of ubiquity is required to establish panpsychism. The crucial distinction between ontological and epistemological emergence depends on the idea that emergence entails a weak kind of reducibility and hence can represent no more than our ignorance of all the implications of immense complexity. Nagel put it thus: 'there are no truly emergent properties of complex systems. All properties of complex systems that are not relations between it and something else derive from the properties of its constituents and their effects on each other when so combined' (1979:182). While it is arguably true that what modern scientists in the field of complexity studies call emergence falls under Nagel's critique and thereby can be no more than epistemological emergence, it is not clear why Nagel thinks there can be no radical emergence. Such a form of emergence was developed and defended by the so-called British Emergentists, (see Mclaughlin 1992) and it is far from obvious that this doctrine in incoherent.

However, a radical emergence of mind makes mentality fundamental, in the sense that although it depends upon an underlying material constitution, there is no way to explain its emergence in terms of the physical properties of the constituents. If the emergentist wants to claim that it is the complexity of interaction of the material constituents which accounts for the emergence of the mind, then this form of emergence obviously threatens to collapse into mere epistemological emergence (see Strawson 2006). So the fundamental difference between radical emergence and panpsychism seems to come down only to the claim of ubiquity.

To see this more clearly, we can imagine a very strange form of the doctrine of radical emergence, in which it is claimed that all physical entities are by themselves enough to ground the radical emergence of mental features. Since radical emergentists regard emergence as lawful but such that the laws of emergence have to be 'super-added' to the world in addition to the laws governing the basic interactions of the fundamental physical features of the world, there would seem to be nothing incoherent about laws of emergence operating at the level of the fundamental physical entities. But such a doctrine would be nothing more than a different way of expressing panpsychism itself. The core difference, then, between radical emergence and panpsychism amounts to a dispute over the ubiquity of the mental.

Nagel's argument can also be attacked by denying the fourth premise. It can be asserted that the emergence of mind is no different from the emergence of any other complex feature of the world, such as chemical or biological properties of systems. Although this is the normal strategy of defenders of modern materialist theories of mind there is considerable doubt about its feasibility, since the former sorts of features all seem to be explicable in terms of the functional structure of systems, whereas mental features—most especially consciousness—appear to go beyond the functional to embody an occurrent qualitative aspect which resists explanation in functional terms. This is what has become known as the **hard problem* (Chalmers 1996) or the **explanatory gap* (Levine 2001). Appeal to these issues can bolster the claim that the mental is ontologically fundamental.

Are there arguments in favor of the ubiquity of the mental? Panpsychists typically appeal to three sorts of considerations: genetic arguments, arguments from analogy, and arguments from 'intrinsic nature'.

Analogical arguments are the most venerable and versions can be traced back to the Presocratic philosophers (for the history of panpsychism see Skrbina 2005). They operate by attempting to find universal aspects of the material world which are reminiscent of clearly mentalistic features. The ancient philosopher Thales argued that matter could exhibit self-motion (via magnetism and effects of static electricity) and hence shared with persons a fundamental animation. Our understanding of the operation of such phenomena has completely robbed Thales' argument of any force, but echoes of it can still be found. Whitehead (1929) discerned a kind of freedom of will in the fundamental indeterminacy entailed by quantum mechanics. More recently, the possibility that information plays a foundational role in the quantum world has suggested to some an analogy between mentality and the quantum phenomenon of entanglement (Chalmers 1996:Ch. 8, Seager 1999:Ch. 9). The measurement problem in quantum mechanics has also been taken to hint at some deep and pervasive role for 'observation' that might be linked to consciousness in some way. I think it must be said that none of these analogies are anything more than merely suggestive at this time.

Genetic arguments, of which Nagel's is an example, are perhaps more promising. While Nagel's argument is abstractly metaphysical, there are more empirical versions. The rise of Darwinism encouraged the idea that mind is an evolved feature. Clifford presents the evolution-based genetic argument for panpsychism very clearly: '... we cannot suppose that so enormous a jump from one creature to another should have occurred at any point in the process of evolution as the introduction of a fact entirely different and absolutely separate from the physical fact.' (1874/1886:266). Although Clifford's argument appears to apply only to living creatures subject to evolution, it is evident that the 'jump' from non-conscious to conscious would be just as momentous, if not more so, in the inorganic realm no less than the organic. Therefore, consciousness must have been implicated at the most fundamental physical level. Notice that this does not quite yield the ubiquity of the mental, since it remains possible to divide the basic physical constituents of the world into those that enjoy some mental aspect and those that do not. But there seems no reason to so limit mentality once it has secured a foothold at the physical foundation of the world.

A final line of argument in favour of panpsychism stems from the observation that our knowledge of the physical world is confined to the dispositional properties of matter, with no insight into its intrinsic nature. Presumably, there must be an intrinsic nature which grounds the dispositional and causal properties of material entities. Panpsychists suggest that a mentalistic aspect provides the intrinsic nature of matter. One reason for at least considering that mind provides this intrinsic nature is that consciousness is the only example of an intrinsic nature we possess. Maybe what we call subjectivity simply is what 'intrinsicness' amounts to. Another consideration is that, given that the brain is the physical ground of consciousness, we might regard experience as a kind of window into the intrinsic nature of at least this one, very complex, physical entity which we thus find to be mentalistic in nature (see Lockwood 1991). It is then perhaps a natural inference to the ubiquity of the mental, although the sort of experience that characterizes the physically fundamental entities in the world is presumably altogether different and radically simpler than our own complex mental lives, reflecting the differences in complexity between brains and electrons (see Rosenberg 2004, Strawson 2006).

Against these points stands the flat intuitive implausibility of the hypothesis that everything has a mental dimension. But in addition there are some counter-arguments. One is that the physical nature of reality seems to be entirely sufficient to account for everything that happens (this is often called the 'causal closure' of the physical world). If the mental is not itself a physical feature at bottom (via some sort of reductive relation or some other acceptable dependence upon the physical) then it threatens to become *epiphenomenal. A panpsychist might reply that at the fundamental level, the mental features are essential to the causal powers of things (see Rosenberg 2004).

Another objection holds that panpsychism has its own emergence problem (see James 1890/1950:Ch. 6, Seager 1999:Ch. 9). Somehow there is a transition from the 'elemental' mental features of the physical constituents of things to the complex minds possessed by composite entities such as ourselves. If the panpsychist is willing to admit this kind of emergence why not simply opt for an emergentist solution to the whole problem of mind, and avoid the basic implausibility of panpsychism? In reply, it might be noted that emergence of complexes of a given set of features is generally much easier to understand than the apparently radical emergent transformation of matter into consciousness.

Finally, there is a methodological objection to panpsychism. One of our chief metaphysical goals is to understand everything in terms of the best accounts of the world which we currently possess. The physical sciences provide these accounts and they do not avail themselves of the panpsychist option. One might argue that it is thus incumbent upon metaphysicians to exert every effort to understand mind from within the structure provided by the physical sciences. There is a kind of cogency to such an objection, if it is taken to encourage efforts at a naturalistic metaphysics. But such a metaphysics might fail, and it is good to explore options which might come in handy, even if they stretch imagination beyond its usual bounds.

WILLIAM SEAGER

Chalmers, D. (1996). *The Conscious Mind.*
Clifford, W. (1874/1886). 'Body and mind'. In *Fortnightly Review*, December. (Page references are to the 1886 reprint.)
James, W. (1890/1950). *The Principles of Psychology*, Vol. 1.
Levine, J. (2001). *Purple Haze.*
Lockwood, M. (1991). *Mind, Brain and the Quantum: The Compound 'I'.*
McLaughlin, B.(1992). 'The rise and fall of British emergentism'. In Beckermann, A. et al. (eds) *Emergence or Reduction.*
Nagel, T. (1979). 'Panpsychism'. In *Mortal Questions.*
Rosenberg, G. (2004). *A Place for Consciousness: Probing the Deep Structure of the Natural World.*
Seager, W. (1999). *Theories of Consciousness.*
Skrbina, D. (2005). *Panpsychism in the West.*
Strawson, G. (2006). 'Realistic monism: why physicalism entails panpsychism'. *Journal of Consciousness Studies*, 13.
Whitehead, A. N. (1929) *Process and Reality: An Essay in Cosmology.*

perception, philosophical perspectives Perception is a way of acquiring information, beliefs, or knowledge about the world by means of the senses. In philosophy, 'perceive' and its derivatives 'see', 'hear', and the like, are usually taken to be success verbs. Thus, when Macbeth claimed to see a dagger before him when there was no such dagger, he was mistaken; he merely seemed to see a dagger. In fact, he *hallucinated a dagger. A major goal of philosophical theories of perception is to provide an account of perception that differentiates it from hallucination and from other mental occurrences. Section 2 below looks at approaches to the latter, while sections 3 and 4 outline approaches to the former. Another goal is to address the question of how perception can yield and justify belief, thus making it a source of knowledge. In answering this second question philosophy of perception overlaps with epistemology.

Some terminological preliminaries need to be noted. First, when we consciously perceive the world we have 'perceptual experiences'. It is usually taken to be the case that we can also have perceptual experiences when we are hallucinating (and hence not perceiving). Whether the perceptual experiences involved in perception and hallucination are the very same kinds of states is an important question in recent philosophy of perception and supporters of common-kind and disjunctive theories of perception, discussed in sections 3 and 4 below, endorse very different answers.

Secondly, most philosophers hold that perceptual experiences are by definition conscious states. A great deal of philosophy of perception is concerned with the nature of these states. The *sense-datum theory* holds that such states involve perceiving non-physical mind-dependent objects. *Adverbialism* conceives of such states as states in which one is sensing in a certainly way.

Representationalism argues that such states represent the world to be a certain way. A great deal of modern philosophy of perception has been concerned with the precise nature of perceptual representation. Sense-datum theory, adverbialism and representationalism are discussed in sections 6–8 below.

Finally, perceptual experiences are said to have **phenomenal character*. This means that there is 'something that it is like' to undergo those experiences. Philosophy of perception comes closest to philosophy of mind when it discusses the nature of perceptual phenomenal character and consciousness and whether a physical account of it can be given. Recently, many philosophers have sought an answer by enquiring about the precise relationship between phenomenal character and representation and whether the former can be explained solely in terms of the latter. Section 8 elaborates on this issue.

1. Perception, sensation, and belief
2. Unconscious perception
3. The common-kind view and the causal theory of perception
4. Disjunctivism
5. Empirically informed direct realist views
6. Sense-datum theory
7. Adverbialism
8. Representational theories

1. Perception, sensation, and belief

Traditionally, philosophers have contrasted perception with sensation. Perception was taken to be a process that involved states that represented—or that were about—something. For example, typical visual experiences had at a beach might represent sand, crabs, or the blueness of the sea. These experiences might accurately represent the beach or misrepresent it, if undergoing an illusion or hallucination. Sensations like pains, itches, and tickles were not taken to be representational. For example, the feeling of pain was not taken to be 'about' anything—it was a mere feeling. At the same time, philosophers have traditionally recognized that sensations and perceptual experiences are alike in some respects. Both types of state have phenomenal character, and which phenomenal character they have determines or partly determines, which particular kind of sensation or experience they are.

Perceptual experiences have also usually been contrasted with beliefs. Although, like perceptual experiences, beliefs have been thought of as representing the world to be a certain way (in the case of belief, the way the subject of the belief takes the world to be) they are dissimilar in other respects. Beliefs need have no phenomenal character (for example, they can be unconscious) whereas perceptual experiences necessarily have phenomenal character. Moreover, as stated above, perceptual experiences have their phenomenal character essentially, but beliefs, qua beliefs, do not. Which particular belief a belief is, say the belief that crabs pinch hard, is a matter solely of which content it has, and any phenomenal character that a particular instance of a belief may have is irrelevant to its being that belief. (Note that many people think beliefs themselves have no phenomenal character—they are simply usually accompanied by states that do.)

However, the traditional view that perceptual experiences are different from sensations and beliefs has been challenged. On the one hand, arguing that sensations and perceptual experiences are not dissimilar, some representational views take sensations to be perceptions of one's own body. For example, pains might be thought of as states that represent damage or disorder at a location in one's body. On the other hand, arguing that perceptual experiences are more akin to beliefs than the traditional view, some doxastic views of experience hold that to have a perceptual experience is simply to believe, or to be inclined to acquire a belief, that we are immediately perceiving some physical object or state of affairs by means of the senses. However, this view is not widely endorsed for, plausibly, unlike belief-like states, experiences are necessarily conscious and occurrent and relatively unaffected by one's other beliefs. Furthermore, the content of perceptual experience is sometimes held to be different from that of belief in various ways, notably by being non-conceptual.

2. Unconscious perception

Can perception occur without a perceptual experience and without any conscious state? Recent empirical findings have led some to answer positively (see UNCONSCIOUS PERCEPTION). Consider the phenomenon of *blindsight, in which people claim to be blind. Nonetheless, when asked to guess what is in front of them in a forced-choice paradigm, they select the right answer more frequently than chance. Is this evidence of unconscious perception? It depends, first, on whether the subject really lacks a perceptual experience. This issue in turn depends on a commonly encountered question in consciousness studies: to what extent can belief or *introspection about experience be inaccurate? Secondly, it depends on whether the accurate guessing behaviour of the subject warrants our claiming that perception is occurring. This question arises because not any state of a subject that reliably indicates a stimulus is a perceptual state. For example, to have a verruca is to be in state that reliably indicates the presence of the human papilloma virus, but it seems incorrect to think that having a verruca amounts to perceiving the virus.

3. The common-kind view and the causal theory of perception

It is widely agreed that, when you perceive, things seem a certain way to you—but that things could seem just that way when you were hallucinating. In other words, for each case of perception there is a possible case of subjectively indistinguishable hallucination. The 'common-kind' view claims that perceptual experiences and their indistinguishable hallucinatory counterparts are fundamentally the same kind of state. The experiences will both have the same phenomenal character, will represent the same thing, and be similar in their intrinsic mental properties. The experiences will only differ in factors extrinsic to the experience such as their causal origin, and whether they represent accurately. This reflects a common thought: the major purpose of ascribing experiences to subjects is to try to capture how things seem to them.

The paradigmatic form of the common-kind view is the causal theory of perception. On this theory, one perceives an object or property if and only if one has an experience that to some degree represents that object or property, and that experience is caused in an appropriate way by that object or property. How accurate the representation needs to be is a tricky issue. We want to allow that perceptual *illusions (where one perceives, but inaccurately) are possible. For example, in the Müller–Lyer illusion two lines that are the same length look unequal in length but we do not want to say that this prevents us from perceiving the lines.

The causal condition is required in order to account for *veridical hallucinations*—hallucinations that nonetheless accurately represent the world. For example, imagine that an evil scientist gives you a hallucinogenic drug that makes you have a visual experience of a starfish. At the same time, by chance, there just happens to be a starfish in front of you. The causal theory holds that such cases are not perception, as an appropriate causal connection between what is perceived and the perceptual experience is missing. Spelling out the nature of the connection is difficult because of 'deviant causal chains'. The difficulty is that, intuitively, not every causal connection suffices for perception even when the experience accurately represents that which causes the experience. Imagine that Macbeth's brain is connected to a machine, which has a touch-sensitive pad that turns it on. The machine produces in Macbeth an experience as of a dagger when it is activated. If such a dagger came to rest on the sensitive pad and activated the machine, Macbeth would not see it, despite it causing his experience. David Lewis imaginatively addresses this problem, claiming that what is required for perception is a suitable pattern of counterfactual dependence of visual experience on the scene before the eyes. Thus, Lewis would claim that because Macbeth would have continued to have the visual experience of a dagger even if it had been a claymore that had activated the machine; his experience fails to be suitably dependent on the presence of a dagger, and this explains why he does not see it. The merits of this and other responses have been widely debated.

4. Disjunctivism

Common-kind theories of perception stand in contrast to metaphysical *disjunctivism*. The main claim of metaphysical disjunctivism has sometimes been articulated as being that there is nothing in common between the experience involved in perception and that involved in an indistinguishable hallucination. That claim is too hasty when one considers that both states will seem to a subject to be indistinguishable from the experience involved in perception and both will be mental states. A more accurate articulation is that metaphysical disjunctivism claims that a state indistinguishable from perception is either a state that constitutes perception (in the 'good case') or a state involved in hallucination (in the 'bad case'), and that these states exhibit further differences which amount to the states being different 'fundamental kinds' (to use M. G. F. Martin's terminology). What are these further differences?

Some metaphysical disjunctivists claim that, in the good case, the objects and properties that one perceives partly constitute one's experience. This is not true in the bad case where nothing is perceived. Such disjunctivists not only deny the common-kind view but also deny that in perception the relevant experience is caused by the objects and properties perceived. This is because causes and effects must be distinct states and this theory denies that the experience and what is perceived are distinct.

Some metaphysical disjunctivists think that experiences involved in perception represent, but others claim that such experiences consist of a direct relation or openness to the objects and properties perceived and therefore that representation is not required. This latter view is called a *no-content view*. One can see that some rationale for it would come from holding that the perceived objects and properties partially constitute the experiences and thus that representation is otiose.

One motivation for metaphysical disjunctivism is the desire to maintain a naive or direct realism about perception. This is the view that we are directly or immediately aware of objects in perception. Another motivation is an unwillingness to assert a certain form of infallibility concerning our own minds: this view denies that if two mental states seem the same to a subject then they must be the same. A third motivation is a desire to explain how perception can ground our knowledge of the world. If hallucination and perception involve the same fundamental kind of state, but hallucination does not yield knowledge, then how can perception do so? If the experiences involved in perception and hallucination are importantly different, as the metaphysical disjunctivist would have it, then this problem might be overcome. (Epistemological disjunctivism is the view that the experiences in the good and bad cases have a different epistemic status. Although metaphysical and epistemological disjunctivism have a clear affinity, the positions are distinct and neither entails the other.)

One concern for metaphysical disjunctivism is how to account for illusion (where one sees, but inaccurately). If illusory experiences are treated like veridical perceptual experiences then the illusory aspect is unaccounted for. If they are treated like hallucinatory experiences the illusory aspect is explained but at the expense of the perceptual aspect. Disjunctivists themselves disagree about how to treat illusion.

Another concern is that metaphysical disjunctivism typically has little to say about the mental states involved in hallucination apart from the fact that they are indistinguishable from experiences involved in perception (and indeed some varieties hold that there is nothing further that can be said). This lacuna provides future work for disjunctivists.

A third concern is whether metaphysical disjunctivism can provide a better epistemology of perception than common-kind views, as some of its proponents have claimed. The view certainly does not rule out the possibility that we are hallucinating all the time. Does it show how we could come to know about the world if we do perceive? Opponents complain that it does not as, if we are perceiving, we do not know that we are (due to the indistinguishability from hallucination). The disjunctivist is liable to claim that one can know something without knowing that one knows it. In the end, the debate seems to come down to whether one thinks that in the case of perception there is something that is *available to the subject* that grounds knowledge that is not present in the hallucinatory case. The disjunctivist will affirm this, as they will say that the world is directly *available to the perceiving subject*. The opponent will deny it because the subject cannot tell by reflection alone whether the world is so available.

5. Empirically informed direct realist views

There is a view in the philosophy of perception that shares certain features with some kinds of disjunctivism: the endorsement of direct realism and the eschewing, at least to some degree, of the role of representational states. This type of view often draws heavily on empirical work in psychology and neuroscience. An early version of the view is J. J. Gibson's ecological approach. According to Gibson, there is enough information in the 'ambient optic array'—the pattern of light in space and time that directly stimulates an observer—such that the visual system of an observer need not process the direct stimulus to produce representations of the world. Perception consists, not in the forming of mental representations, but in a direct response to invariances in the optic array. These invariances include surfaces and edges in the environment and 'affordances'. Affordances are what the environment provides or invites, such as somewhere to shelter or something to eat. Gibson also stresses that how you can act—what movements you can make—will affect what affordances there are for you and therefore what you can perceive. This type of view has recently been elaborated upon with the development of dynamic or sensorimotor theories of perception. (Some *sensorimotor theories invoke mental representations but insist that having such representations requires an ability to interact knowingly with one's environment.)

The assumptions that underlie these theories are highly controversial. Both thought experiments and empirical work question whether action is necessary for perception and whether Gibson's assumptions about the ambient optic array and the working of the brain are correct. The extent to which mental representations are required in perception, and how to account for illusion and hallucination if they are not, is the subject of much contemporary debate.

6. Sense-datum theory

Returning to common-kind theories now, and to the question of how such theories characterize perceptual experience, we find that there are three main views: sense-datum, adverbial, and representational theories. These, in turn, form the subject matter of the next three sections.

Sense-datum theory was popular in the first half of the 20th century and is often attributed to earlier empiricist thinkers, such as Locke. This view endorses the following: (1) in hallucination there are no worldly objects that answer to what one seems to be aware of; (2) if it appears to one as if one is perceptually aware of an object with a certain property then there must be something that one is aware of that has that property; and (3) the common-kind view. Point (2) is supported by the phenomenal character of experience: it at least seems as if we are aware of something when we are experiencing. Sense-datum theorists conclude that, in cases of hallucination, we are aware of mental or mind-dependent objects and, due to (3), that this is true when we perceive the world too. These special objects are termed *sense-data*. They do not exist in public space and they possess any property that they appear to have.

(Note that when the term 'sense-data' was first introduced it was used to refer to the direct objects of perception, whatever they were. At that time, the discussion in the literature about perception was whether sense-data were mental objects or public objects. Many people at that time concluded that sense-data were mental objects, and so the term came to be associated with only such objects.)

Realist versions of sense-datum theory hold that we indirectly perceive the mind-independent world in virtue of directly perceiving sense-data. We can do this because sense-data resemble or represent the mind-independent world. Irrealist sense-datum theorists are either idealists, who hold that what we normally take to be physical objects are simply collections of actual sense-data, or phenomenalists, who hold that they are collections of actual and possible sense-data.

Sense-datum theories have been heavily criticized. One criticism is that there is no good reason to believe (2); hence the motivation for the view is undermined. The issue turns on whether the phenomenology of experience provides a good reason. Another criticism is that sense-data are ontologically queer mind-dependent objects—for example, they do not exist in public space but seem to have some spatial characteristics—thus they should not be countenanced. A third is that not all aspects of phenomenal character seem to be explained by positing objects and their properties. For example, what would be the nature of sense-data corresponding to experiences as of impossible figures or experiences that seem to represent something indeterminate? A fourth is that realist versions of the theory provide a circular account of perception: perception of the mind-independent world is explained in terms of perception of sense-data, which is not itself explained. A fifth is that realist sense-datum theories make a plausible account of our knowledge of the mind-independent world impossible. It is said that such views impose a Lockean 'veil of perception' between us and the mind-independent world. A sense-datum theorist might attempt to answer this charge by saying that a mind-independent world that causes us to have sense-data can be inferred as it is the best explanation of our experience, and such inference is considered to be a source of knowledge in other fields of enquiry, particularly science. Another attempt would be to hold that so long as having a perceptual experience is a reliable way of forming true beliefs about the world then it is a way of gaining knowledge.

7. Adverbialism

The sense-datum theory claims every experience involves a subject's act of awareness of some object. A number of philosophers, starting around the middle of the 20th century, wished to reject such an 'act–object' theory but, nonetheless, wished to remain common-kind theorists. Rather than holding that a subject's seeing or hallucinating redness was to be explained by a subject bearing some relation to a red sense-datum, the subject was held to be experiencing in a certain manner: in this example, redly. This view is adverbialism.

One challenge facing adverbialism is explaining complex experiences. Consider two experiences: (a) an experience as of a red circle to the left of a blue triangle and (b) one as of a red triangle to the left of a blue square. A description like 'experiencing redly and circularly and bluely and triangularly and to the leftly' does not pick out (a) rather than (b). Adverbialists have offered solutions to these problems but some have argued that any plausible solution forces the adverbialists to elaborate their theory in a way that attributes experiences with representational content and thus this shows that a plausible adverbialism is just a species of the representational view. To see this, note that one way the adverbialist could answer the challenge is to say that when one has experience (a) one experiences in a certain manner, the manner is one in which one seems to be presented with a red circle to the left of a blue triangle. This seems to be equivalent to saying that one is having an experience that represents this. (The alternative would be to think of the manner of experiencing as not essentially representational, and thus as more like sensations as construed by the traditional view and outlined in section 1.)

Adverbial views, like sense-datum views, face worries about how experiences can give rise to knowledge of the external world. The debate on this matter follows a pattern similar to that outlined above for sense-datum theories, with the exception that adverbialists sometimes claim that they are not committed to the problematic indirect view of perception that the sense-datum theorist is, as they are not committed to mental intermediaries. Whether this is any advantage is disputable.

8. Representational theories

The representational or intentional theory of perceptual experiences holds that perceptual experiences represent the world. Reasons to think that they do include: (1) experiences seem to present the world to us, (2) ascribing perceptual experiences that represent is often the best way to explain and predict the behaviour of people and animals, (3) experiences seem to have correctness conditions, that is, there is a way the world could be that would make what is represented true and a way that would make it false, and (4) experiences are similar in some respect to beliefs, which are the paradigm of representational states. If one believes that the sun is shining then the 'that' clause specifies what is represented (equivalently, specifies the content) to which we take the attitude of belief. Similarly, if one seemed to see that the sun is shining then the 'that' clause would specify the content of the perceptual experience. Of course while the subject of a belief, by definition, takes the content to be true, the subject of a perceptual experience need not do so, if, for example, they have reason to think that their senses are deceiving them.

The most common form of representational theory is that which adheres to the common-kind commitment and the causal theory of perception. On such a view, when perceiving in a non-illusory manner the experience with content will accurately represent the world and be caused in the right way by it. Unlike the sense-datum view, this view of perception of the mind-independent world holds that it is direct and occurs partly in virtue of being in a state with content. However, other versions of the representational view are possible, in particular one might think of experiences as representational states but nonetheless reject the common-kind view.

There are very many debates concerning the nature of the content of perceptual experiences. (See, CONTENTS OF CONSCIOUSNESS; EXTERNALISM; INTENTIONALITY; NON-CONCEPTUAL CONTENT; REPRESENTATIONALISM.)

Representation and phenomenal character. Representational views differ on the relationship that they believe holds between representational content and phenomenal character. Some views hold that there are some phenomenal aspects of experience that are not representational at all. Such views therefore are faced with supplementing their account of experience to explain these aspects. Some theorists become physicalist about such aspects, usually identifying them with states of the brain (see PHYSICALISM). Other theorists could treat such aspects as mental primitives that cannot be given further explanation.

Other representational theorists maintain that phenomenal character either supervenes on or is identical to the representational content of experience. This view is often called *representationalism*. (Unhelpfully, this term is sometimes used to refer more broadly to what I have been calling 'representational theories'.) It is often held not only about perceptual experiences but also about all states with phenomenal character, such as sensations and emotions. Representationalists are often motivated by their belief that experience is transparent, that is to say their belief that when we introspect we find that we are only paying attention to the seemingly mind-independent objects and properties that we are perceiving, rather than attending to other distinctive mental features of experience or any apparent non-representational properties of experience. If such a view were true, then perhaps what it is like to have an experience is exhausted by the experience's contents. It might be tempting to think that an exhaustive description of what it was like to have an experience would be an exhaustive account of the apparent worldly scene before us. However, whether any version of the *transparency claim is true and, if it is, what it shows about the mind is a topic of much recent debate. Further, there are a battery of examples in the recent literature in which, it is claimed, there are experiences that have differing phenomenal character yet the same representational content and vice versa. Examples of this kind would provide counter-examples to the representationalist's identity or supervenience claim. Whether any of these constitute successful counter-examples to representationalism is an open question.

Representationalism is often conjoined with a naturalistic theory of representation and it is hoped that a naturalistic theory of phenomenal character or consciousness will be the result. This view is hotly disputed in the current literature, with many people claiming that no naturalistic theory of representation can account for the phenomenal character of certain unusual experiences known to exist, or our intuitions about the phenomenal character of experience in various hypothetical cases.

Objections to representational theories. Returning now to consider representational views more generally, it was stated above that representational views can be conjoined with either a common-kind and causal view or a disjunctivist view. Some objections to these views are therefore simply versions of objections to common-kind and causal views or disjunctivst views, some of which have been mentioned above.

More particular objections to representational views of perception focus on what account can be given of hallucinatory states. Consider the content of a perceptual experience involved in an accurate perception of a starfish (the good case) and one involved in an indistinguishable non-veridical hallucination (the bad case). Both states would seem to represent the same thing: a starfish, or a starfish-shaped thing. Thus, it is tempting to think that the content is the very same. However, in the good case if the content is the object perceived—the starfish—then it is not obvious that that starfish is the content in the bad case, for that starfish might not exist in the bad case. Two consequences follow. First, we seem now to be denying that the content is really the same, certainly the same in all respects, in both cases. Second, we still need to say what the content is in the bad case. Some representationalists have adverted to holding that the contents of hallucinatory experiences are intentional inexistents. That is to say, the contents are objects that do not exist. However, now an account of intentional inexistents is required. If they are to be treated really as 'things' then there is the worry that the view seems to collapse into a view with as unpalatable ontological commitments as the sense-datum view. If such a view does not treat intentional inexistents in this way then the worry is that such talk is just a way of labelling the problem that in hallucination subjects appear to be confronted by objects when none are there. In this case, the problem of accounting for the *phenomenology of hallucinatory experience, in which one appears to have contact with objects, remains.

One way to get round this problem is to deny that in the good case the content is the object perceived—the starfish. Instead, one might hold that the content is an abstract object—say the proposition that a starfish is before one—and that this is the content in the bad case too. This solution is tempting, but it is resisted by some representationalists who want to give a naturalistic theory of content and who think that giving a naturalistic explanation of how the mind grasps, or stands in relation to, such an entity is problematic. Other representationalists believe that existing naturalistic theories of content can meet this challenge. Of course, if one is not motivated by naturalism, then one might happily hold that it is simply a primitive fact that experiences seem to present objects to their subjects and thus that the notions of content and of representation are not to be given further explanation.

FIONA MACPHERSON

Armstrong, D. M. (1961). *Perception and the Physical World.*
Chisholm, R. (1957). *Perceiving: A Philosophical Study.*
Crane, T. (1992). *The Contents of Experience: Essays on Perception.*
Gendler, T. S. and Hawthorne, J. (2006). *Perceptual Experience.*
Gibson, J. (1979). *The Ecological Approach to Visual Perception.*
Grice, H. P. (1965). 'The causal theory of perception'. In *Proceedings of the Aristotelian Society, Supplementary Volume*, 35.
Jackson, F. (1977). *Perception: A Representative Theory.*
Haddock, A. and Macpherson, F. (2008). *Disjunctivism: Perception, Action, Knowledge.*
Hamlyn, D. W. (1961). *Sensation and Perception: A History of the Philosophy of Perception.*
Maund, B. (2003). *Perception.*
Noë, A. (2004). *Action in Perception.*
—— and Thompson, E. (2002). *Vision and Mind: Selected Readings in the Philosophy of Perception.*
Robinson, H. (1994). *Perception.*
Smith, A. D. (2002). *The Problem of Perception.*
Tye, M. (1995). *Ten Problems of Consciousness.*

perception, unconscious Unconscious perception paradigms seek to examine the effects of sensory stimuli (typically visual) that are rendered too weak to achieve conscious representation. The idea is to eliminate possibly confounding conscious perceptual influences entirely, thereby enabling strong conclusions that obtained effects, if any, reflect purely unconscious perceptual processes. Usually, one task is used to index conscious perception (e.g. identification, which assesses the direct, intentional use of stimulus information), while another task (often *priming, wherein the unintended, indirect influence of an initial stimulus on the processing of a later stimulus is examined) is used to index unconscious perceptual effects. If successful, such paradigms could potentially reveal much about not only unconscious mental processes, but even fundamental aspects of consciousness itself. Many believe, for example, that consciousness somehow enables more complex and flexible mental processes than are possible purely unconsciously. By varying whether stimuli are unconsciously vs consciously perceived, we can empirically test such hypotheses.

For unconscious perception paradigms to serve this role, however, requires solving a deceptively simple but surprisingly tenacious methodological problem: How can we really be sure that putatively unconscious effects are not, instead, actually weakly conscious after all? Given that unconscious perception currently enjoys relatively broad acceptance, one might think that some definitive methodological breakthrough had been achieved. Unfortunately, however, this is not the case. Consequently, until these core issues are satisfactorily addressed, the currently positive consensus runs the risk of simply perpetuating the boom and bust cycle of critical acceptability that has plagued unconscious perception throughout its controversial history. Moreover, and just as importantly, careful consideration of these issues is substantively informative in its own right—raising, for example, fundamental questions about how consciousness should be indexed, how conscious and unconscious processes interact, and the role of volition. Indeed, vigorous debate on these issues continues even among unconscious perception proponents, yielding sharp disagreement on which data are valid and their appropriate interpretation.

1. How should consciousness be indexed?
2. Modern unconscious perception models
3. Concluding remarks

1. How should consciousness be indexed?

Almost everyone agrees that conscious perception covaries with stimulus intensity, typically manipulated by varying stimulus duration, masking intensity, or both. Whereas strong stimuli are plainly visible, conscious perception diminishes as stimulus strength is reduced—finally disappearing altogether when stimuli are weak enough. But exactly how should this threshold be defined? It turns out that there are two basic alternatives.

The oldest and perhaps most intuitively appealing approach, taken from classical psychophysics, is to simply ask people when stimuli can no longer be seen. Because such methods focus on self-reports of phenomenal states, they are now often called *subjective threshold* approaches (Cheesman and Merikle 1984). Strikingly, when consciousness thresholds are defined in this way, performance on direct forced-choice discrimination tasks (e.g. 'Is this stimulus A or B?'), although reduced, nonetheless remains above chance. This robust phenomenon is the canonical subjective threshold effect, and is how such effects were originally discovered.

After flourishing in the 1940s and 1950s, however, unconscious perception research came to a virtual halt with the advent of modern psychophysics and *signal detection theory (SDT). The great insight of SDT is that discrimination reports are not simply unmediated readouts of perceptual states, as it might intuitively seem, but rather the joint product of independent, separable perceptual and decision processes. With this in mind, subjective thresholds might not actually delineate the conscious/unconscious boundary, but instead reflect confidence criteria applied to a single conscious perceptual process. After all, sufficiently weak stimuli produce very faint, ephemeral, and vague conscious perceptual experiences that observers are understandably quite uncertain about. Accordingly, denying awareness could simply indicate very low confidence rather than no awareness at all, and hence subjective threshold phenomena could plausibly be (very) weakly conscious after all.

In contrast, later-emerging *objective threshold* approaches (cf. Marcel 1983), influenced by the SDT critique, sought to avoid this difficulty by arranging stimulus conditions such that observers not only deny awareness but are moreover unable to discriminate stimuli above chance on the direct task (obviously, such performance is behaviourally observable; hence 'objective' threshold)—but yet nonetheless still show evidence of stimulus processing on other tasks such as priming. To accomplish this requires reducing stimulus intensities even further; hence, objective thresholds are below subjective thresholds. Unfortunately, this greater stringency seemed to produce more mixed results than subjective threshold methods, leading some (e.g. Holender 1986) to conclude that reliable objective threshold effects did not exist.

Moreover, reliability issues aside, even objective threshold approaches are not beyond methodological dispute. For example, intrinsic measurement error entails that true discrimination ability might actually exceed zero even when observed performance is at chance (cf. Reingold and Merikle's 1990 *null sensitivity problem*). Moreover, one must be certain that the particular conscious perception index utilized indeed assesses the relevant kinds of conscious perception that could conceivably drive putatively unconscious effects (Reingold and Merikle's *exhaustiveness problem*). Unless both conditions are met, sceptical weak conscious perception explanations again remain possible. At the same time, however, subjective threshold methods are at least as vulnerable to these difficulties as well. After all, relevantly exhaustive conscious perception indexes must be utilized regardless of the method used; moreover, subjective methods have their own, often-ignored version of the null sensitivity problem (i.e. demonstrating truly zero subjective confidence).

So which methods, if any, are valid? On the one hand, subjective methods may be too lax; on the other, objective methods too stringent. Moreover, methodological concerns aside, subjective and objective methods apparently entail fundamentally different models of unconscious influences. On the one hand, recalling the canonical subjective threshold effect (i.e. direct discrimination remains above chance even when awareness is denied), subjective models must postulate, obviously, that this elevated direct performance indeed reflects unconscious influences. If so, utilizing objective methods, which require chance direct performance, should seriously reduce or outright eliminate not only conscious but unconscious influences as well. With this in mind, objective methods must apparently assume that direct discrimination tasks somehow tap only conscious perceptual influences (cf. Reingold and Merikle's *exclusiveness problem*). On the other hand, if reliable objective threshold effects are obtainable (e.g. on indirect tasks such as priming), this would apparently confirm that direct tasks are indeed insensitive to unconscious influences. If so, this would in turn imply that subjective threshold effects on direct tasks are actually due to conscious influences, and hence that subjective methods are invalid. In short, it seems that subjective and objective methods are not just more or less stringent, but actually imply mutually incompatible models—and hence cannot both be valid.

2. Modern unconscious perception models

With all this in mind, any adequate unconscious perception model must deal both methodologically and theoretically with these issues. To date, three attempts have been made (see Snodgrass et al. 2004a, 2004b for a review):

Merikle and associates' subjective threshold model (e.g. Merikle et al. 2001) argues that subjective threshold effects are indeed unconscious and that genuine objective threshold effects do not exist. This model's primary challenge, then, is to refute the SDT criterion artefact critique and hence rule out alternative weak conscious explanations—a considerable hurdle for subjective models. To accomplish this goal, they influentially argued that subjective (and objective) models must demonstrate *qualitative differences* between conscious and putatively unconscious effects in order to be truly convincing. Perhaps most convincingly, Merikle and associates have shown that subjective threshold stimuli produce *exclusion failure* (i.e. responding with just-presented stimuli even when expressly instructed not to; cf. Jacoby 1991), whereas consciously perceived stimuli are instead successfully excluded. This qualitative difference is especially compelling because it conforms to the very widely held notion that conscious control over responding can only be exerted when stimuli are consciously, but not unconsciously, perceived.

Despite its intuitive appeal, however, even exclusion failure can be modelled as a criterion artefact (cf. Snodgrass 2002). From this perspective, exclusion is a decision process; if so, exclusion failure could reflect low confidence rather than unconscious perception. Accordingly, these impressive qualitative differences may simply imply two conscious processes (i.e. conscious perception itself and metacognitive decision processes), suggesting that demonstrating such differences alone is likely insufficient. Rather, independent demonstration that the relevant stimuli are unconsciously perceived seems necessary (cf. Holender 1986) in order for qualitative differences to carry probative force. Nonetheless, emphasizing obtaining qualitative differences has proved to be an important and generative approach and is now near-ubiquitous.

Greenwald and associates' objective threshold/rapid decay model (e.g. Draine and Greenwald 1998 and associated commentaries). Apparently persuaded by criterion artefact concerns, Greenwald and associates assume that subjective threshold effects are indeed weakly conscious. In contrast, they argue that objective threshold effects are intrinsically very short-lived, thereby accounting for heretofore mixed results. If so, paradigms requiring very rapid responses (e.g. their *response window* procedure) are necessary to reliably capture such phenomena. Using this technique in conjunction with response conflict priming paradigms (typically valence classification, in which pleasant and unpleasant words are the primes and targets, yielding either evaluatively congruent or incongruent pairs), Greenwald and associates have indeed produced large and apparently reliable objective threshold effects. Notably, these effects appear largely driven by part-word analysis, suggesting that unconscious perception is relatively primitive and unsophisticated (i.e. non-semantic). On the other hand, this result may be due to the severely limited processing time engendered by the response window procedure rather than intrinsic to unconscious perceptual properties. It is also possible that valence classification tasks, the usual conscious perception index in this paradigm, may not be exhaustively sensitive (e.g. to conscious partial identification); if so, these priming effects may be weakly conscious.

Greenwald and associates' most significant methodological contribution is the influential *regression approach* to the null sensitivity problem, in which regression analysis techniques are utilized to model the unconscious perception index effect (e.g. priming, on the *y*-axis) as a function of the conscious perception index effect (e.g. valence classification performance, on the *x*-axis). Given appropriate scaling, the *y*-intercept is the point estimate of the putatively unconscious effect when the conscious perception index is zero. If only conscious perception exists, *y*-intercepts should equal zero; in contrast, positive *y*-intercepts apparently implicate unconscious perception.

The regression approach appears to avoid the null sensitivity problem because *y*-intercepts can be obtained even when overall direct discrimination performance does not equal zero. Unfortunately, however, the direct measure still contains measurement error—the source of the null sensitivity problem to begin with. In various common situations, this can artefactually flatten regression slopes, yielding inflated (and hence invalid) *y*-intercepts. Although Greenwald and associates have proposed corrective procedures, it is not yet clear that these are sufficient. Further, in response window and other paradigms which produce very fast responding, there is typically no relationship between the direct and indirect measures. In this situation, it is unclear whether using the regression equation to predict the *y*-intercept is meaningful. Even so, the regression approach retains considerable promise, and in any event draws valuable attention to the relationship between conscious and unconscious influences. Indeed, much research now routinely presents regression analyses.

Finally, although they initially appeared dissimilar, it has recently become evident that various other increasingly popular objective threshold priming paradigms such as number classification (e.g. Naccache and Dehaene 2001) and motor activation (e.g. Eimer and Schlaghecken 1998) are, like Greenwald and associates' valence classification priming, response conflict paradigms as well. Strengthening this suspicion, they yield highly similar priming phenomena, including the flat regression slopes indicating no relationship between conscious and unconscious perception indexes. Further, these other priming paradigms, like valence classification, have importantly shown that consciously applied response strategies (e.g. to classify targets in one way or another) additionally affect unconscious prime processing, falsifying formerly widely held beliefs that unconscious processes were immune to influence by conscious intentions.

Snodgrass and associates' objective threshold/strategic (non-monotonic) model (Snodgrass et al. 2004a, 2004b, and associated commentaries). Methodologically, Snodgrass and associates stress specifying core features of the conscious-perception-only model, because demonstrating unconscious perception requires that this model be falsified (i.e. that an additional, unconscious perceptual process must be posited to account for findings). With this in mind, various considerations, including SDT and standard word recognition models, suggest that conscious perception functions on a hierarchical strength/complexity continuum, such that greater stimulus intensity is required in order for more complex and/or stronger effects to occur. Accordingly, if putatively unconscious effects are instead consciously driven, they should become stronger as conscious perception index performance increases. With this in mind, the conscious-perception-only model typically predicts positive relationships between conscious and (putatively) unconscious index effects.

This framework can aid in evaluating the inferential force of various qualitative differences. For example, if putatively unconscious effects are weaker, less complex, or less controlled than conscious effects, such qualitative differences are questionable (despite their plausibility) because this pattern would also be expected with weak vs strong conscious perception. Unfortunately, many qualitative differences are vulnerable to this criticism (e.g. the findings of Greenwald and associates; see above). Conversely, findings that violate the strength/complexity continuum—e.g. negative relationships between conscious and unconscious perception indexes—provide stronger qualitative evidence for unconscious perception. For example, Groeger (1988) found more complex (semantic) effects under objective conditions, but only less complex (structural) effects under subjective conditions, despite the latter's stronger stimuli—a pattern much more difficult to reconcile with weak conscious interpretations. Finally, because the exhaustiveness, null sensitivity, and exclusiveness problems all predict positive relationships, negative relationships help rebut these difficulties.

Snodgrass and associates further suggest that objective threshold results are not simply inconsistent, but rather strongly moderated by stimulus intensity: under objective detection threshold conditions, unconscious effects are both large and reliable (see the meta-analysis of Snodgrass et al. 2004b); conversely, under objective identification threshold conditions, such effects are largely absent. Because the former conditions require weaker stimuli than the latter, this pattern constitutes a methodologically powerful negative relationship, rendering alternative weak conscious explanations unlikely. Further, negative relationships allow valid use of regression techniques because they underestimate rather than overestimate *y*-intercepts; moreover, the presence (vs absence) of a relationship allows legitimate *y*-intercept derivation.

On the other hand, as stimulus intensities increase still further (e.g. into subjective threshold regions), the relationship becomes positive (see Cheesman and Merikle 1984). Overall, this non-monotonic relationship suggests that conscious and unconscious perceptual influences may be *functionally exclusive* (in contrast to the subjective and objective/rapid decay models, which implicitly assume that such influences are positively related or unrelated, respectively), such that conscious perception, when present, usually overrides unconscious perceptual influences. Initially, weak conscious detection is useless and hence only interferes with (e.g.) unconscious semantic effects, producing the negative relationship region. After the objective identification threshold is exceeded, however, conscious perceptual processes become able to drive semantic effects and the relationship becomes positive. Further, because subjective threshold effects are positively related to conscious perception index performance whereas the reverse often holds for objective threshold effects, they may reflect separate, qualitatively distinct processes, rather than the latter simply being weaker versions of the former, as often assumed.

Crucially, however, the non-monotonic relationship, including the vital negative portion, requires that objective detection thresholds indeed be below objective identification thresholds (see Holender and Duscherer 2004). If the reverse is true, or even if these thresholds turn out to be identical, this model would lose considerable inferential force. Although extant evidence is supportive, further tests are clearly necessary. Further, besides this particular issue, relatively few objective detection threshold studies in general have been conducted in recent years, likely because objective detection thresholds are difficult to attain using typical computer monitors. Consequently, at present the objective threshold/non-monotonic model's empirical base is considerably less extensive than that of the subjective and objective threshold/rapid decay models.

3. Concluding remarks

Despite various periods where it has seemed that the methodological obstacles were intractable, important ideas—including, qualitative differences, the regression approach, and the potential utility of negative relationships—have recently emerged which may allow definitive progress in this intensely controversial area. At the same time, sufficient unclarity remains that some distinguished researchers (e.g. Dulany 1997, Holender and Duscherer 2004) are as yet unconvinced that truly unconscious perception exists at all, especially any involving semantic processing. Accordingly, further work is clearly necessary to finally settle these crucial issues. Along the way, subjective and objective methods should be distinguished, not conflated, because they may index fundamentally distinct processes. More than merely methodological squabbles are at stake; the very nature of the mind remains at issue.

MICHAEL SNODGRASS AND E. SAMUEL WINER

Cheesman, J. and Merikle, P. M. (1984). 'Priming with and without awareness'. *Perception and Psychophysics*, 36.

Draine, S. and Greenwald, A. (1998). 'Replicable unconscious semantic priming'. *Journal of Experimental Psychology: General*, 127.

Dulany, D. E. (1997) 'Consciousness in the explicit (deliberative) and implicit (evocative)'. In Cohen, J. and Schooler, J. (eds) *Scientific Approaches to Consciousness*.

Eimer, M. and Schlaghecken, F. (1998). 'Effects of masked stimuli on motor activation: Behavioral and electrophysiological evidence'. *Journal of Experimental Psychology: Human Perception and Performance*, 24.

Groeger, J. (1988). Qualitatively different effects of undetected and unidentified auditory primes. *Quarterly Journal of Experimental Psychology*, 40A.

Holender, D. (1986). 'Semantic activation without conscious identification in dichotic listening, parafoveal vision, and visual masking: a survey and appraisal'. *Behavioral and Brain Sciences*, 9.

—— and Duscherer, K. (2004). 'Unconscious perception: The need for a paradigm shift'. *Perception and Psychophysics*, 66.

Jacoby, L. (1991). 'A process dissociation framework: Separating automatic from intentional uses of memory'. *Journal of Memory and Language*, 30.

Marcel, A. (1983). 'Conscious and unconscious perception: Experiments in visual masking and word recognition'. *Cognitive Psychology*, 15.

Merikle, P., Smilek, D., and Eastwood, J. (2001). 'Perception without awareness: perspectives from cognitive psychology'. *Cognition*, 79.

Naccache, L. and Dehaene, S. (2001). 'Unconscious semantic priming extends to novel unseen stimuli'. *Cognition*, 80.

Reingold, E. and Merikle, P. (1990). 'On the inter-relatedness of theory and measurement in the study of unconscious processes'. *Mind and Language*, 5.

Snodgrass, M. (2002). 'Disambiguating conscious and unconscious influences: Do exclusion paradigms demonstrate unconscious perception'? *American Journal of Psychology*, 115.

——, Bernat, E., and Shevrin, H. (2004a). 'Unconscious perception: A model-based approach to method and evidence'. *Perception and Psychophysics*, 66.

—— —— —— (2004b). 'Unconscious perception at the objective detection threshold exists'. *Perception and Psychophysics*, 66.

persistent vegetative state See BRAIN DAMAGE

phantom limbs When an arm or leg is amputated, patients continue to vividly feel the presence of the missing limb; this is referred to as a phantom limb. About 95% of amputees experience phantoms which often emerge immediately after amputation, but sometimes after weeks or months. More than two-thirds of the time the phantom is extremely painful. Phantoms are most commonly seen after limb amputation but can occur also occur for other body parts (e.g. phantom breasts, phantom penis, phantom uterus, phantom appendix.)

The term 'phantom limb' was coined by the Philadelphia physician Silas Weir-Mitchell (1872) who first described the syndrome. Since then hundreds of case studies have been reported in the medical literature (Riddoch 1941, Sunderland 1972, Melzack 1992) but there have been no systematic experiments. The current era of experimental work on human patients was inspired, in part, by animal experiments (Jenkins et al. 1990, Kaas and Florence 1996). The combined use of systematic psychophysics and *functional brain imaging has allowed researchers to link neurophysiological experiments in animals with perceptual *phenomenology in humans (Ramachandran et al. 1992, Ramachandran and Hirstein 1998).

1. Remapping
2. Mirror neurons
3. Phantoms, body image, and mirrors

1. Remapping

After amputation of an arm, sensory stimuli applied to the ipsilateral face are experienced by the patient as arising from the missing (phantom) arm. There is often a highly specific topographically organized map of the hand on the face (Fig. P1) with clearly delineated digits.

This referral of sensations is probably caused by reorganization of somatosensory maps in the brain (Fig. P2). The entire right side of the body is mapped on to the postcentral gyrus of the left hemisphere. The map is systematic except for the face being directly below the hand rather than near the neck. After arm amputation the sensory input from the face which normally projects only to the face area now 'invades' the vacated territory corresponding to the denervated hand territory. As a result, stimuli applied to the face now activate the hand region of the brain and are therefore interpreted by higher brain centres as arising from the missing phantom hand (the *remapping* hypothesis). A second map of referred sensations is often seen on the arm proximal to the amputation. This is probably caused by cross-activation of the hand area of cortex by afferents from the upper arm which normally project only to the upper arm region of cortex (Ramachandran and Hirstein 1998). These conjectures were confirmed by using *magnetoencephalography (MEG), a non-invasive brain imaging technique (Fig. P3).

The map of referred sensations is modality specific. Warmth on the face elicits warmth in the phantom thumb; cold and vibration elicit cold and vibration. This shows that the remapping is modality specific, with touch, warmth, cold, and vibration being separately remapped in separate brain regions. Some of this could be going on in the thalamus rather than cortex. However,when a stroke causes damage to the touch fibres going from thalamic hand representation to the cortical hand map, sensations are sometimes referred from face to hand, suggesting that cortical remapping is sufficient to cause the phenomenon.

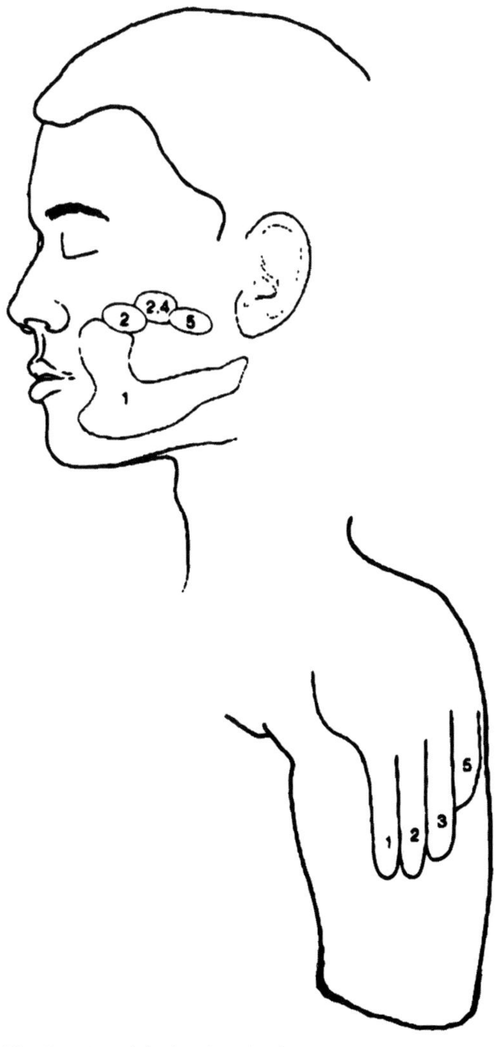

Fig. P1. Map of the hand on the face.

Other predictions from the hypothesis were also confirmed. If the trigeminal nerve innervating the face was cut, touching the hand evoked referred sensations in the face in a topographically organized manner (Clarke et al. 1996). Amputation of a finger results in referral of sensations from adjacent fingers (Ramachandran and Hirstein 1998) and sometimes a representation of a single finger is seen on the face (Aglioti et al. 1997).

The magnitude of phantom pain correlates well with the degree of remapping as explored with brain imaging, suggesting that the remapping is one of the main causes of phantom pain (Flor et al. 1995).

2. Mirror neurons

In a recent study a normal volunteer placed her intact arm near the patient's phantom limb (but not overlapping the phantom). If the patient watched the volunteer's hand being stroked or rubbed vigorously, he felt the sensations in his own hand (Ramachandran and Rogers-Ramachandran 2008). This curious observation can be explained in terms of the activity of *mirror neurons (Rizzolati et al. 2006). When you are touched, sensory neurons are activated in your brain's somatosensory cortex. It has been discovered that a subset of these neurons known as mirror neurons will fire even if you watch someone else being touched—as if the neuron was ' putting you in the other person's shoes' or 'empathizing' with the touch delivered to the other person.

But if your sensory/mirror neurons fire when you watch someone else being touched, why don't you literally feel her touch? This is presumably because the absence of touch signals from your skin sends a null signal that vetoes the output of the mirror neurons. If the arm were to be amputated then you would indeed quite literally feel the other person's sensations in your phantom. This hypothesis would explain why touching another person elicits phantom sensations in the patient.

One of the patients also reported relief of pain in his phantom when watching the other volunteer being rubbed; an observation that might have therapeutic implications and give new meaning to the word *empathy.

3. Phantoms, body image, and mirrors

Some subjects report a phantom arm even if their arm has been missing from birth, suggesting that in spite of its extreme malleability there must also be a genetic scaffolding for *body image (La Croix et al. 1992). The same might be true for transgender female to male subjects; they often report having had a phantom penis from early childhood (Ramachandran and McGeoch 2008).

After amputation, patients usually report feeling movements in the phantom ('it's waving goodbye',

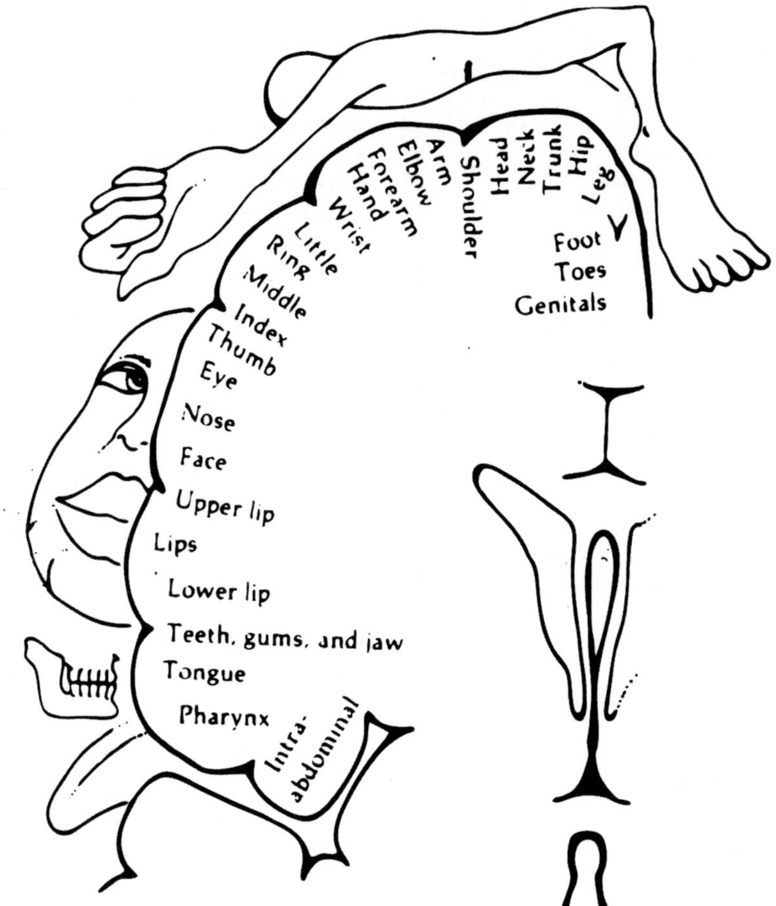

Fig. P2. Homunculus showing somatosensory mapping in the brain.

etc.) When you send a command to move your arm, a copy of the command originating in the motor and premotor cortex is sent to the parietal cortex where you monitor these commands, combining them with visual and proprioceptive feedback to construct your body image. The monitoring of commands continues to occur even after amputation, 'fooling' the brain into thinking that the phantom is moving.

Sometimes the arm had been paralysed and painful for a few months due to peripheral nerve injury. If the arm is then amputated, the paralysis is 'carried over' into the phantom. Perhaps the continued absence of visual feedback signals that the motor commands are being obeyed causes the brain to learn that the arm is paralysed and this 'learned paralysis' persists in the phantom.

The phantom is often fixed in a very painful position. You can prop up a mirror vertically (parasagittally) in front of the patient, and have him look into the mirror so that the reflection of his normal hand is superimposed optically on the felt position of the phantom. This creates the illusion that the phantom arm has been resurrected and if the patient sends motor commands to make bilaterally symmetrical hand movements, the phantom appears to obey the commands. This restores the visuo-motor loop and alleviates pain (Ramachandran and Hirstein 1998, Chan et al. 2007) by eliminating the discrepancy that is thought to cause phantom pain (Harris 1999). In some cases the entire phantom limb itself disappears, along with the pain (Ramachandran and Hirstein 1998).

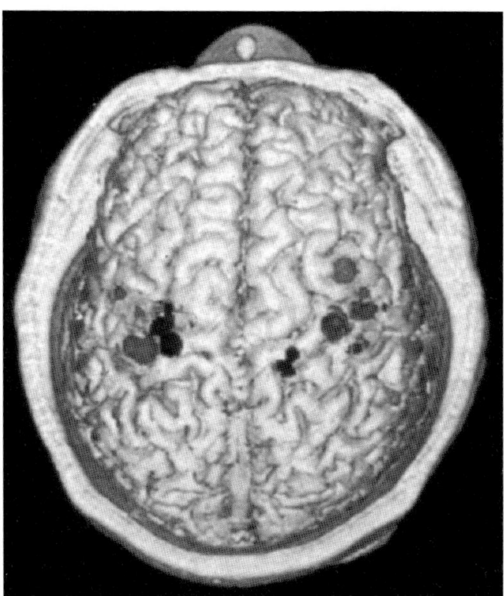

Fig. P3. (see Colour Plate 11).

It has been suggested that there may also be a 'learned paralysis' component to the paralysis (in addition to permanent damage to motor pathways) following stroke and that this could be overcome with visual feedback provided by mirrors or virtual reality (Ramachandran et al. 1992). There is considerable clinical evidence that this is the case (Altschuler et al. 1999, Yavuzer et al. 2008) Other neurological disorders such as complex regional pain syndrome (RSD) have also been treated successfully using this procedure (McCabe et al. 2003).

Ordinarily our sense of having an arm arises from at least four sources: (1) monitoring of feedforward or corollary discharge of commands sent from motor centres to the arm, (2) proprioceptive feedback arising from muscles and joint, (3) visual feedback, and (4) a genetic scaffolding of one's body image. An interplay of the same sources of signals (or lack thereof) must be involved in the genesis of phantom limbs and phantom pain. In addition to pain signals arising from stump neuromas, the discrepancy between these various sources of information may itself be contributing to phantom pain and removing the discrepancies (as with the mirror) seems to relieve the pain.

In the last decade the study of phantom limbs has moved from the dark ages of clinical phenomenology to the era of experimental science. In addition to providing insights into how the brain constructs body image, the study of phantom limbs has broader theoretical and clinical implications The idea that the adult brain consists of independent modules that are largely autonomous and fixed by genes has been replaced by the idea that the so-called modules are in a state of constant dynamic equilibrium with each other and with the sensory input. Neurological dysfunction is caused just as often by shifts in these equilibria as by permanent anatomical damage and if so adjusting the input can reset the equilibrium; a radical concept in rehabilitation neurology.

V. S. RAMACHANDRAN

Aglioti, S., Smania, A., Arzei, A., and Berlucchi, G. (1997). 'Spatiotemporal properties of the pattern of evoked sensations in a left index finger amputee patient'. *Behavioral Neurology*, 111.

Altschuler, E., Wisdom, S., Stone, L., Foster, C. and Ramachandran, V. S. (1999). 'Rehabilitation of hemiparesis after stroke with a mirror'. *Lancet*, 353.

Chan, B. L., Witt, R., Charrow, A. P. et al. (2007). 'Mirror therapy for phantom limb pain'. *New England Journal of Medicine*, 357.

Clarke, S., Regali, L., Janser, R. C., Assal, G., and De Tribolet, N. (1996). 'Phantom face'. *NeuroReport*, 7.

Flor, H., Elbert, T., Muhlnickel, W., Pantev, C., Weinbruch, C., and Taub, E. (1998). 'Cortical reorganization and phantom phenomena in congenital and traumatic upper-extremity amputees'. *Experimental Brain Research*, 119.

Harris, A. J. (1999). 'Cortical origin of pathological pain'. *Lancet*, 354.

Jenkins, W. M., Merzenich, M, Och, M. T., Allard, T., and Guic-Robles, E. (1990). 'Functional reorganization of primary somatosensory cortex in adult owl monkeys after behaviorally controlled tactile stimulation'. *Journal of Neurophysiology*, 63.

Kaas, J. and Florence, S. L. (1996). 'Brain reorganization and experience'. *Peabody Journal of Education*, 71.

La Croix, R., Melack, D., and Mitchell, N. (1992). 'Multiple phantom limbs in a child'. *Cortex*, 28.

McCabe, C. S., Haigh, R. C., Ring, E. F., Halligan, P., Wall, P. D., and Blake, D. R. (2003). 'A controlled pilot study of the utility of mirror visual feedback in the treatment of complex regional pain syndrome (type 1)'. *Rheumatology*, 42.

Melzack, R. (1992). 'Phantom limbs'. *Scientific American*, 266(4).

Merzenich, M. and Kaas, J. (1980). 'Reorganization of mammalian somatosensory cortex following peripheral nerve Injury'. *Trends in Neuroscience*, 5.

Pons, T. P., Garraghty, P. E.,Ommaya, A. K., Kaas, J., Taub, E., and Mischkin, M. (1991). 'Massive cortical reorganization after sensory deafferentation in adult macaques'. *Science*, 252.

Ramachandran, V. S. (1994). 'Phantom limbs, neglect syndromes, repressed memories, and Freudian psychology'. *International Review of Neurobiology*, 37.

—— and Hirstein, W. (1998) 'Perception of phantom limbs'. *Brain*, 121

—— and McGeoch, P. (2008). 'Phantom penises in female to male transsexuals'. *Journal of Consciousness Studies*, 15.

—— and Rogers-Ramachandran, D. (2008). 'Sensations referred to a patient's phantom arm from another subjects intact arm: perceptual correlates of mirror neurons'. *Medical Hypotheses*, 70.
——, ——, and Stewart, M. (1992). 'Perceptual correlates of massive cortical reorganization'. *Science*, 258.
Rizzolatti, G., Fogassi, L., and Gallese, V. (2006). 'Mirrors in the mind'. *Scientific American* 295(5).
Riddoch, G. (1941). 'Phantom limbs and body shape.' *Brain*, 64.
Sunderland, S. (1972). *Nerves and Nerve Injury*.
Yavuzer, G., Selles, R., Sezer, N. et al. (2008). 'Mirror therapy improves hand function in subacute stroke: a randomized clinical trial'. *Archives of Physical Medicine and Rehabilitation*, 89.

phenomenal concepts A concept that characterizes consciousness in terms of phenomenal character is a phenomenal concept.

1. What phenomenal concepts are
2. What phenomenal concepts are not
3. Accounts of phenomenal concepts
4. Phenomenal concepts and physicalism
5. Phenomenal concepts and other issues

1. What phenomenal concepts are

There is something it is like to be conscious and to have particular experiences. This phenomenal feature of experience can be conceptualized in different ways. For example, one can conceive of pain as *my least favourite sensation* or *the sensation that aspirin helps alleviate*. One can also conceive of pain in terms of its phenomenal character—how it feels or *what it is like to have it.

Phenomenal concepts figure essentially in phenomenal knowledge and phenomenal judgements. Consider Frank Jackson's (1982) famous case of Mary (see KNOWLEDGE ARGUMENT). Mary is a future super-scientist who is raised in a black-and-white room and learns the complete physical truth by watching science lectures on black-and-white television. She then leaves the room and sees colours for the first time. Many agree that when she leaves the room, she learns what it is like to see in colour. In other words, she gains phenomenal knowledge of colour experiences. The content of her new phenomenal knowledge is partly constituted by phenomenal colour concepts. She learns, for example, that seeing red has such-and-such phenomenal quality. Her *such-and-such phenomenal quality* concept is a phenomenal concept.

2. What phenomenal concepts are not

Phenomenal concepts differ from ordinary perceptual concepts. The latter are concepts of perceived properties, such as redness or roundness—properties of entities that are typically external to the perceiver's mind. By contrast, phenomenal concepts are concepts of mental properties. Thus we should distinguish the perceptual concept of redness from Mary's *such-and-such phenomenal quality* concept, that is, from her *phenomenal redness* concept. To be sure, these perceptual and phenomenal concepts are related, especially on views on which colour is defined partly in terms of dispositions to cause certain experiences. Also, some construe phenomenal concepts as special sorts of perceptual concepts (Papineau 2007). But identifying the two sorts of concept can create confusion. Mary does not learn only about colours when she leaves the room: she learns about colour experience. The concepts deployed in her new knowledge about what it is like to see in colour are concepts of colour experience, not of colour.

It is sometimes claimed that phenomenal concepts bear an especially intimate relation to their referents, namely, phenomenal properties and phenomenal states. But explicating this claim requires care. For example, one should not suppose that possessing a phenomenal concept requires having an experience with the corresponding phenomenal quality (Alter 2008). To see why, suppose scientists create Replica Mary: a molecule-for-molecule duplicate of Mary in the state she is in shortly after returning to the black-and-white room. Replica Mary has never seen colours. Nevertheless, she knows what it is like to do so. She possesses this knowledge no less than Mary does after Mary returns to the black-and-white room. And if Replica Mary knows what it is like to see in colour, then she must have phenomenal colour concepts. Therefore, it is possible to possess phenomenal knowledge without ever having an experience with the corresponding phenomenal quality.

It is occasionally denied that phenomenal concepts exist. But such denials almost always stem from dubious assumptions, such as the assumption that possessing a phenomenal concept requires having an experience with the corresponding phenomenal quality. Once such assumptions are cast aside, few will doubt that phenomenal concepts exist. However, how they should be understood raises issues, to which we now turn.

3. Accounts of phenomenal concepts

Phenomenal concepts as functional concepts. Some contend that phenomenal concepts should be explicated in terms of the causal roles typically played by the corresponding experiences. For example, the phenomenal pain concept should be explicated in terms of pain's characteristic causes and effects, including such things as 'being caused by bodily damage' and 'causing avoidance behaviour'. Which states play these roles may differ from population to population. Whereas in humans the pain role may be played by certain brain states (say, C-fibre stimulation or a certain sort of corticothalamic oscillation), in Martians the pain role may be played by the inflation of tiny cavities in their feet.

Phenomenal concepts as recognitional concepts. Brian Loar (1990/1997) construes phenomenal concepts as recognitional concepts. One deploys a recognitional concept when one recognizes something as one of *those*, without relying on theoretical knowledge. For example one might have both a recognitional concept of a certain sort of spider and a theoretical concept of that same spider. Here the two concepts will be associated with distinct properties as modes of presentation. For example, one's recognitional concept may be associated with the property of typically causing a certain sort of experience, whereas one's theoretical concept may be associated with a certain biological/taxonomic property. But Loar suggests that phenomenal concepts are unique in that the property to which they refer also serves as a mode of presentation.

Phenomenal concepts as quotational concepts/the constitution view. Some propose that phenomenal concepts are distinctive in that their referents—phenomenal states—are constituents of those very concepts. For example, David Papineau (2002) argues that phenomenal concepts have the form *that state:*—, where the blank is filled in by an embedded phenomenal state, in roughly the way a word may be embedded within quotation marks. This view requires a distinction between direct phenomenal concepts, which last only last as long as the embedded phenomenal states, and standing phenomenal concepts, which persist longer. Without such a distinction, the view would fail to accommodate the fact that one can know what it is like to see red even while one is not experiencing red (which follows from the point made in section 2 above, that one can have phenomenal knowledge without ever having relevant experiences). But proposals for drawing such a distinction have been developed (Chalmers 2003).

Other accounts have been proposed. To mention two: Perry (2001) argues that phenomenal concepts have an indexical structure, analogous to *here* and *now*; and Murat Aydede and Guven Güzeldere (2005) develop an information-theoretic analysis of phenomenal concepts, emphasizing their close connection to perceptual concepts. Some of the various accounts that have been proposed are mutually compatible. For example, both the recognitional and quotational accounts are compatible with (and may even entail) the view that phenomenal concepts have an indexical component.

4. Phenomenal concepts and physicalism

Accounts of phenomenal concepts are often developed with an eye towards defending *physicalism, the view that everything (including consciousness) is physical, from influential attacks, such as Jackson's (1982) knowledge argument. The knowledge argument begins with a non-deducibility claim: there are phenomenal truths that are not a priori deducible from the complete physical truth (more precisely: from a conjunction of complete physical truth, the complete indexical truth, and a second-order 'that's all' claim stating that there are no further truths than those). Jackson supports that claim with his Mary case, reasoning as follows. If the phenomenal truths were a priori deducible from the physical truth, then Mary would know what it is like to see red while in the room. But intuitively, she does not; when she leaves the room and sees a red rose she learns new truths about seeing red. That part of the argument establishes an *epistemic gap*: a gap between physical and phenomenal knowledge/concepts. Jackson then goes on to defend a corresponding *metaphysical gap*, between the physical and phenomenal themselves and not just our epistemic relation to them. He infers that there are phenomenal truths, such as those Mary learns upon leaving the room, that the physical truths do not metaphysically necessitate. Physicalism's falsity follows.

Physicalists sometimes argue that a proper understanding of phenomenal concepts helps answer the knowledge argument and related attacks on physicalism. Some argue that mistakes involving these concepts underlie the intuitions used to establish an epistemic gap. Others accept the existence of an epistemic gap but argue that it can be explained in terms of certain distinctive features of phenomenal concepts, in ways that do not support a metaphysical gap. Let us consider some examples.

Some physicalists contend that though there are truths that Mary cannot deduce from what she learns while in the room, this is not because they are not deducible from the physical truth, but rather because doing the deduction requires possessing phenomenal colour concepts—concepts that she does not acquire until she leaves the room. Therefore, the reasoning runs, Jackson's claim that she gains knowledge upon release fails to support the non-deducibility claim (Tye 2000). However, proponents of the knowledge argument might defend the non-deducibility claim in other ways. For example, they could appeal to the conceivability of *zombies—creatures that lack (phenomenal) consciousness but are physically and functionally indistinguishable from ordinary human beings. One may still find zombies conceivable even though one possesses all relevant concepts.

Another way to challenge the non-deducibility claim is to appeal to a *functionalist account of phenomenal concepts. If such an account is correct, then not only does the non-deducibility claim fail: there is no epistemic gap of any form. However, the intuitions driving the anti-physicalist arguments are sometimes held against functional analyses of phenomenal concepts. For example, some argue, if Mary gains phenomenal knowledge when she leaves the room, then she acquires new phenomenal concepts too. It is hard to see why this would be if phenomenal concepts could be analysed functionally. After all, she has access to the complete functional truth while still in the room.

Many physicalists reject the second step of the anti-physicalist arguments: the inference to the metaphysical gap. Some of these philosophers suggest that there are analogous cases in which distinct concepts refer to the same property; *heat* and *molecular motion*, for example. But such analogies are notoriously problematic. In particular, some argue, arguments for a posteriori necessities in the standard cases, such as the heat/molecular motion case, do not extend to the phenomenal/physical case (Kripke 1972). Some physicalists therefore reject such analogies and accept the existence of a distinctive epistemic gap in the phenomenal/physical case. These philosophers argue that this distinctive epistemic gap can be explained in terms of special features of phenomenal concepts in ways that do not support a metaphysical gap.

This tack has been developed in various ways. Let us consider two. Christopher Hill (1997) argues that phenomenal and physical concepts play different roles in the relevant cognitive systems. He also argues that this explains the distinctive epistemic gap in the phenomenal/physical case: the distinct roles are mistaken for distinct properties playing those roles. Others base their argument on specific accounts of phenomenal concepts, such as the quotational view. For example, Papineau (2002) argues that the quotational structure of phenomenal concepts will produce a distinctive phenomenal/physical epistemic gap even if the embedded state is physical. However, such strategies depend on the existence of an account of phenomenal concepts that (1) renders such concepts physically explicable and (2) explains our epistemic situation with regard to consciousness—and whether any account can meet both conditions is debatable (Chalmers 2007).

5. Phenomenal concepts and other issues

Phenomenal concepts figure in discussions of various issues besides physicalism. These include, among others, whether phenomenal beliefs are fallible (Chalmers 2003, Horgan and Kriegel 2007), whether such beliefs have a special epistemic status such as being foundational or 'given' (Chalmers 2003), whether *consciousness requires *self-consciousness (Horgan and Kriegel 2007), whether phenomenal content is wide or narrow (Ellis 2007), and whether colour anti-realism is defensible (Ellis 2005). That phenomenal concepts should be relevant to a host of epistemic, semantic, and metaphysical issues should come as no surprise. Such concepts constitute an intriguing point at which consciousness and representation—arguably the two most distinctive aspects of the mental—intersect.

TORIN ALTER

Alter, T. (2008). 'Phenomenal knowledge without experience'. In Wright, E. (ed.) *The Case for Qualia*.

Aydede, M. and Güzeldere, G. (2005). 'Cognitive architecture, concepts, and introspection: an information-theoretic solution to the problem of phenomenal consciousness'. *Noûs*, 39.

Chalmers, D. J. (2003). 'The content and epistemology of phenomenal belief'. In Smith, Q. and Jokic, A. (eds) *Consciousness: New Philosophical Essays*.

—— (2007). 'Phenomenal concepts and the explanatory gap'. In Alter, T. and Walter, S. (eds) *Phenomenal Knowledge and Phenomenal Concepts: New Essays on Consciousness and Physicalism*.

Ellis, J. (2005). 'Colour irrealism and the formation of colour concepts.' *Australasian Journal of Philosophy*, 83.

—— (2007). 'Content externalism and phenomenal character: a new worry about privileged access.' *Synthese*, 159.

Hill, C. S. (1997). 'Imaginability, conceivability, possibility, and the mind-body problem'. *Philosophical Studies*, 87.

Horgan, T. and Kriegel, U. (2007). 'Phenomenal epistemology: what is consciousness that we may know it so well?' *Philosophical Issues*, 17.

Jackson, F. (1982). 'Epiphenomenal qualia.' *Philosophical Quarterly*, 32.

Kripke, S. (1972). 'Naming and necessity'. In Harman, G. and Davidson, D. (eds) *The Semantics of Natural Language*.

Loar, B. (1990/1997). 'Phenomenal states'. In Tomberlin, J. (ed.) *Philosophical Perspectives 4: Action Theory and Philosophy of Mind*.

Papineau, D. (2002). *Thinking About Consciousness*.

—— (2007). 'Phenomenal and perceptual concepts'. In Alter, T. and Walter, S. (eds) *Phenomenal Concepts and Phenomenal Knowledge: New Essays on Consciousness and Physicalism*.

Perry, J. (2001). *Knowledge, Possibility, and Consciousness*.

Tye, M. (2000). *Consciousness, Color, and Content*.

phenomenology Phenomenology may be defined broadly as the study of consciousness from the first-person perspective—addressing experiences of perception, imagination, desire, thought, volitional bodily action, etc., just as we experience these phenomena in our everyday lives.

1. Phenomenology as a discipline
2. History
3. Methodology: naturalistic psychology, phenomenological psychology, transcendental phenomenology
4. Results of phenomenology: basic structures of consciousness
5. Conclusion

1. Phenomenology as a discipline

Phenomenology proceeds by the description, analysis, and interpretation of basic forms of conscious mental (and bodily) activity as experienced from the first-person perspective, that is, the perspective of the subject experiencing such states or acts of consciousness. In that sense phenomenology is a *subjective study of consciousness, unlike the study of the neural *correlates of consciousness or computational brain processes underlying consciousness. However, the results of phenomenological analysis are objective in the sense that phenomenology is a well-disciplined science whose results are conceptualizable, repeatable, and confirmable by others. So phenomenology is an objective science of subjective experiences.

In a more specific sense, phenomenology proper was launched by Husserl in the early 20th century, conceived as a 'strict science' of 'pure consciousness' practised by a method called 'bracketing' (Husserl 1900–01/2001, 1913/1983, Smith and McIntyre 1982, Bernet et al. 1989/1993, Moran 2006, Smith 2007).

2. History

The term 'phenomenology' was coined in the 17th century for the study of phenomena in the sense of the appearances of things, as opposed to their ultimate nature (perhaps known only to God).

In the late 19th century Franz Brentano (1874/1995) distinguished descriptive psychology, or phenomenology, from genetic psychology. Where the former characterizes the basic types and properties of mental states, such as visual experience, the latter studies their causal genesis, for example, in interaction with light impinging on the retinas. Having studied with Brentano, Edmund Husserl (1859–1938) extended this basic conception of phenomenology, developing specific methodological principles and mapping many detailed structures of consciousness (Husserl 1900–01/2001, 1913/1983).

Husserl distinguished pure or transcendental phenomenology from empirical or naturalistic psychology. Empirical psychology studies the way perception, thought, emotion, etc., happen to arise in people and animals in the natural world. By contrast, pure phenomenology studies the character of our 'pure' experience as lived, characterized in abstraction from its embedding in the surrounding natural world. Accordingly, phenomenology is practised by 'bracketing' considerations of the relation between consciousness and the natural (and cultural) world in which it arises. (Husserl 1913/1983.)

In recent philosophy of mind, some authors use the term 'phenomenology' in a very narrow sense, concerning only sensory qualities or *qualia experienced in perception, as distinct from the unconscious information processing posited in models of mind promulgated in cognitive science. A wider contemporary use of 'phenomenology' applies to the subjective character of any experience, or '*what it is like' to be in a given state of consciousness (not necessarily a sensory perception). Accordingly, a broad and neutral sense of 'phenomenology' covers any study of mind that gives credence to consciousness and its subjective character. Pure or transcendental phenomenology, however, focuses specifically on the 'pure' character of lived experience as such: in thought, perception, emotion, and action as experienced from the first-person perspective.

3. Methodology: naturalistic psychology, phenomenological psychology, transcendental phenomenology

For two decades now, philosophers of many persuasions have argued that consciousness is not adequately explained on the dominant functionalist or naturalist models of mind. Even theorists committed to naturalism have found consciousness the most difficult aspect of mind to explain in terms of physical activity or information-processing in the brain. The problem is precisely the character of lived conscious experience that phenomenology describes and analyses. At least three aspects of consciousness, it is argued, have eluded reduction to physical or functional properties of a human organism: (1) intentionality, or consciousness *of* something; (2) subjectivity, or what it is like to experience such-and-such; (3) awareness, or the self-consciousness that makes a mental state conscious. These aspects of consciousness have been explored in great detail in the practice of phenomenology from Husserl's time to the present day. (The problems of capturing these phenomenological aspects of consciousness are explored in many writings, including Petitot et al. 1999 and Kriegel and Williford 2006.)

In articulating the discipline of phenomenology, Husserl opposed reductive naturalism, long before our contemporary debates. Husserl placed psychology within the wide theory of nature, assuming that human beings and other animals are naturalistic organisms that have minds (they are 'animated' by minds). Consciousness is thus tied into nature. However, we can study consciousness in importantly different ways, Husserl held: in physiology, looking to the physical brain processes that underlie conscious experience; in phenomenological psychology, looking to the structure of conscious experience, assuming it occurs in the surrounding natural world; or in pure phenomenology, looking to conscious experienced without regard to its embedment in nature.

Natural science traditionally follows the so-called scientific method, where theories of natural phenomena are based on third-person observations. A naturalist theory of mind thus begins with third-person observations of people's behaviours and of their physiology:

notably, in today's neuroscience, the neural activities monitored in *functional brain imaging studies. Phenomenology departs from this third-person perspective.

Phenomenological psychology, for Husserl, studies conscious experience as experienced from the subject's *first-person* perspective, but assumes that acts of consciousness occur in human or animal organisms in nature (treating consciousness as 'mundane'). We might say William James practised phenomenological psychology. What has recently been called *neurophenomenology*, studying the neural correlates of consciousness as experienced, would fall under Husserl's conception of phenomenological psychology, amplified with modern neuroscience (cf. Petitot et al. 1999).

By contrast, Husserl proposed, *pure* or *transcendental phenomenology* studies conscious experience as experienced from the subject's first-person perspective, *without regard* to the ways in which consciousness arises from further activities in the surrounding world—from brain process, from causal interactions with the environment, or for that matter from the influences of culture in the 'life-world'. To practise pure phenomenology, Husserl proposed a specific *method*: we are to 'bracket' all consideration of the existence of the surrounding world of nature (and culture), and under this 'phenomenological [not ontological] reduction' we are to describe and analyse our familiar forms of consciousness just as we experience them—in perception, imagination, thought, volitional movement, etc. Practising this 'epoché', or abstaining from positing the surrounding world, we focus our regard on pure conscious experience. We thus describe, say, what we see just as we see it, regardless of its ultimate reality in nature.

Pure phenomenology, then, describes 'pure' consciousness: that is, conscious experience in its own right, just as it is experienced, in abstraction from any embedment in nature or even in human culture. Pure phenomenology is called 'transcendental' (as Husserl appropriated Kant's use of the term) because it analyses structures of consciousness—intentionality, subjectivity, self-consciousness, etc.—which are necessary or essential conditions of the possibility of conscious experience as we live it. In a sense, phenomenology is a *logic* of consciousness, as opposed to a physiology of consciousness. For, technically, the phenomenological theory of intentionality studies among other things the 'meanings' things have as experienced, the meanings that represent objects ('logically') in our consciousness (see Smith and McIntyre 1982, Smith and Thomasson 2005, Smith 2007.)

The method of bracketing has seemed puzzling to many, but Husserl offered a rather simple explication. Bracketing is a form of *quotation* (Husserl 1913/1983:§89). When I say 'that dog is sleeping', I talk about the animal itself. But when I say, 'Joe said, "That dog is sleeping" ', I talk about the sentence Joe uttered, and, knowing the language, the *proposition* he asserted in uttering the sentence. Similarly, when I see that that dog is sleeping, my visual experience is directed at the animal itself and its soporific state. When I bracket the question of the dog's existence and its actual properties, however, I can turn my attention from the dog to my visual *experience* of the dog. Thus, in phenomenological description I say, 'I see that that dog is sleeping'. The quotation marks indicate my shift in attention: from the dog to my experience *as if* of the dog. On Husserl's account of intentionality, the meaning of that description is (or approximates) the content of my visual experience, the content that presents the dog in a certain way. That content or meaning Husserl called the *noema* of the act of consciousness. Bracketing is thus a technique for turning from our surrounding world to our consciousness as if *of* things in the surrounding world. And thereby we analyse not the things themselves, but our typical forms of experience, or ideal meanings, that represent or 'intend' things. This technique, as Husserl stressed, is a form of *logical* analysis of the contents of consciousness, and that logical character sets phenomenological analysis apart from purely naturalistic analysis of, e.g., the physiology of consciousness. (On bracketing as quotation, akin to conceptual or semantic analysis, compare essays in Smith and Thomasson 2005, also Smith 2007:244 ff.)

In the practice of phenomenology, Husserl stressed, we find that consciousness is typically **intentional*, that is, a consciousness of something. Thus, I see some object, I think of someone, I judge some state of affairs, I desire something, etc. Indeed, the method of bracketing is precisely a technique for withdrawing from the object of consciousness to the consciousness of that object—and therewith to the *content of consciousness, through which the object is intended.

4. Results of phenomenology: basic structures of consciousness

Classical phenomenology, in continuing development today, has analysed a number of basic structures of conscious experience. Here is a brief summary of some of the chief results, cast in the form of a first-person narrative characterizing experiences from the subject's perspective 'as lived'.

As I look around me, I see that tree, that bird, that man talking with a woman across the street. I hear the song of the bird in the tree, as I feel the gentle rush of the morning breeze, carrying the scent of jasmine. I think about the essay I have been writing on consciousness. I walk on, lost in thought, until I step on rock that commands my attention. I pick up my telephone and call the office. My colleague and I go on to discuss ideas for a seminar in the fall. I feel enthusiastic about developing a new idea, and annoyed about what Nietzsche said on the topic. I decide to take a bicycle ride, and away I pedal. . . .

Upon analysis, such a stream of consciousness reveals a variety of noteworthy structures, which we may gloss as follows.

Perception and action. Our most basic forms of experience seem to be perception and action, which are typically coordinated. I see, hear, touch, smell, as I move about in my surroundings. In order to see, I turn my head and eyes toward an object I see. I listen with my ears (much as a dog pricks up its ears). I touch things with my hands, as I grasp an object with my right hand, moving around bodily to do so. Notice that what I perceive is not normally a sensory pattern of colour or sound or scent, a sense-datum, but rather a perceivable object with perceived shapes, colours, etc.

Temporality. My experiences flow off in time, ordered in my stream of consciousness. The objects of my experience occur or flow off in time: the flight of the bird I am watching, the melody of the bird's song I am hearing. My own action rolls along in time as I consciously pedal my bicycle down the lane, pressing down with my right foot, then my left, in a rhythmic circular motion.

Spatiality. The objects of my perception are presented in space as well as time. As I move about volitionally, I experience my body as spatial, with a familiar configuration of my hands, arms, torso, legs, feet, head, eyes, etc. And the world around me I experience as a spatial and temporal complex of things in my environs, but a complex centred on my bodily self, in which I perceive and act with regard to various objects around me in space and time.

Embodiment. As I perceive and act in everyday life, I am a living, embodied subject conscious of my environs, walking around, dealing with things at hand. In such activity, I am aware of my own body both kinaesthetically and perceptually. If, however, I regard my body as a mere physical object, then I experience it in an altogether different way—for example, when I examine my injured knee after a fall and look for torn blood vessels. Accordingly, pure phenomenology does not address the way my bodily action is realized in my physical organism, for instance, through the transmission and consumption of oxygen in various systems of cells in my body. Husserl distinguished the body as lived or living (*Leib*) from the body as physical organism (*Körper*), and in the 1940s the French phenomenologist Maurice Merleau-Ponty (1908–1961) detailed the structure of embodied consciousness in perception and action. This aspect of the phenomenology of perception has come to the fore once again in recent philosophy of mind, as contemporary phenomenology interacts with naturalistic theories of mind (see Merleau-Ponty 1945/2003, Petitot et al. 1999, and essays in Smith and Thomasson 2005.)

Thought, imagination, emotion, volition, etc. In my everyday life, I not only see and act. I also think about things, I feel emotions about things, and in response to what I perceive and think and feel (emotionally) I form desires to do various things. And accordingly I will to act, for example, to ride my bicycle down the lane and into town to buy something.

Intentionality. The overarching form of all these types of experience is the character of intentionality. That is, each experience or act of consciousness is a consciousness of something: the experience presents or represents or is directed toward—it 'intends'—some object. On Husserl's analysis, an object is always intended in a particular way, 'as' such-and-such. This mode of presentation is reflected in the content or 'meaning' of the experience: in the present experience I see 'that Douglas fir tree', not 'that Porsche roaring around the curve ahead'. Thus, every act of consciousness presents an object as thus-and-so, through a particular concept or percept or image, through a certain meaning.

Subjectivity. Every experience is experienced by a subject, from his or her point of view. That is, each act of consciousness is not only directed toward some object, but also directed from a subject, from 'I', so that 'I see that tree', etc.

Awareness of experience. When I have a conscious experience of seeing or thinking or acting, part of what makes the experience conscious is my *awareness* of my so seeing or thinking or acting. Conscious activity thus differs from *blindsight, subliminal reasoning, or involuntary motor activity, all of which lack any such awareness. However, as phenomenologists have argued ever since Brentano, this form of awareness of experience does not take the form of some further activity of monitoring the act of consciousness, but is rather an intrinsic part of the act (see the various positions argued in Kriegel and Williford 2006).

**Empathy.* I encounter other people, and I experience them as fellow subjects, other 'I's, who also experience perceptions, actions, thoughts, emotions, etc., albeit from their own perspective. It is through empathy, a basic understanding of the other's perspective, that I am able to experience that object before me as another 'I'. As I approach a woman on the stair at the museum to ask a question, I approach her empathically as another 'I'; but when I suddenly realize 'she' is a wax figure, I no longer experience 'her' as another 'I', but only as a figure made of wax.

Intersubjectivity. I live in a world with others, wherein I experience objects around me as there for others as well as for me. When I see that tree on which a vulture has landed, part of my sense of the tree as meant in this experience is its being there for others to see as well. I can walk closer to the tree, I can walk around it for a better view of the vulture, and I implicitly understand that another person, another subject, could see the tree and approach it from different sides for a better view, just as I can. In that sense the world around me, including trees and birds and other human beings, is an intersubjective world. My cultural circumstances, too, living in today's zeitgeist, are part of the intersubjective world around me.

Horizon of experience. When I see a tree, the tree is presented or intended in my experience as transcendent of my current visual experience, so that in seeing it I expect the tree to have further possible properties (e.g. regarding its back side), features beyond those I explicitly see or intend in this passing experience. This 'horizon' of possibilities for further experience of the same object is an implicit part of the content or meaning of my current experience. Indeed, this horizon structure frames all the above structures of consciousness, as experienced from the first-person perspective. Thus, an horizon of implicit significance frames my experience of sensible objects, temporality, spatiality, the flow of my experience, the varied objects I encounter in nature and in culture, other people I meet and interact with, the intersubjectivity of our common world, even my own awareness of my passing act of consciousness (on horizon see Smith and McIntyre 1982, Smith 2007).

5. Conclusion

There is of course much more to phenomenology than can be indicated in this brief introduction. Importantly, the practices of science, philosophy, and art all address in various ways the structures of consciousness whose appraisal is by definition the business of phenomenology. Phenomenology by any other name remains phenomenology—with or without adopting the language of pure phenomenology, bracketing, etc.

DAVID WOODRUFF-SMITH

Bernet, R., Kern, I., and Marbach, E. (eds) (1989/1993). *An Introduction to Husserlian Phenomenology*.

Brentano, F. (1874/1995). *Psychology from an Empirical Standpoint*, transl. A. C. Rancurello et al.

Husserl, E. (1900–01/2001). *Logical Investigations*, Vols 1 and 2, transl. J. N. Findlay, ed. and rev. D. Moran.

—— (1913/1983). *Ideas pertaining to a Pure Phenomenology and a Phenomenological Philosophy, First Book: General Introduction to Pure Phenomenology*, transl. F. Kersten.

Kriegel, U. and Williford, K. (eds). (2006). *Self-representational Approaches to Consciousness*.

Merleau-Ponty, M. (1945/2003). *Phenomenology of Perception*, transl. C. Smith.

Moran, D. (2006). *Edmund Husserl: Founder of Phenomenology*.

Petitot, J., Varela, F. J., Pachoud, B., and Roy, J. M. (eds) (1999). *Naturalizing Phenomenology: Issues in Contemporary Phenomenology and Cognitive Science*.

Searle, J. R. (1992). *The Rediscovery of the Mind*.

Smith, D. W. (2007). *Husserl*.

—— and McIntyre, R. (1982). *Husserl and Intentionality: a Study of Mind, Meaning, and Language*.

—— and Thomasson, A. L. (eds) (2005). *Phenomenology and Philosophy of Mind*.

philosophy and the study of consciousness Consciousness has always figured in philosophical discussions of the mind, but it is only relatively recently that philosophical writers have developed detailed theories about the nature of consciousness.

The development of such theories has arguably depended on an important advance in thinking about consciousness. In everyday life we typically restrict attention to thoughts, desires, perceptions, and feelings that are conscious. Indeed, most traditional philosophical writers, from Aristotle through René Descartes to Franz Brentano, have assumed without argument that such states do not occur without being conscious.

In the late 19th century, however, theorists came to recognize what novelists and playwrights have always known, that thoughts, desires, and emotions sometimes occur unconsciously. Individuals sometimes have thoughts, desires, and emotions without being in any way aware of them. Even sensations and perceptions occur subliminally, i.e. without being conscious. The recognition that all these states sometimes fail to be conscious has led to a fruitful focus on what distinguishes states that are conscious from states that are not, a question that would not arise if one denied that mental states ever occur without being conscious.

Focusing on this question has led to a second advance in thinking about consciousness. We use the term 'conscious' to apply to three distinct, independent phenomena. We call a person or other creature conscious when it is awake and responsive to sensory stimulation. But we also speak of people and other creatures as conscious of something when the person or creature senses or perceives that thing or has a thought about it as being present. And we refer, finally, to some mental states as conscious, in contrast with those mental states of which an individual is wholly unaware.

The view that mental states are invariably conscious encourages assimilating these three phenomena. On that view, the states in virtue of which one is conscious of something are all themselves conscious states. And it is then natural to think of conscious states as simply mental states that a conscious creature is in.

But mental states do sometimes occur without being conscious; so we cannot assimilate these three phenomena in this way. Many mental states that occur in conscious, waking life are not conscious states. And sensing something subliminally is a way of being aware of that thing, though not, as we might say, consciously aware of it. Only if we are conscious of the things we sense subliminally can we explain why we respond psychologically to those things, and why they sometimes affect our behaviour.

Distinguishing these three phenomena has been crucial to coming to have a satisfactory theoretical understanding of each. Our understanding of what it is for a creature to be conscious (e.g. Tononi and Cirelli 2003, Hill and Tononi 2005) does not appeal to mental states' being conscious or to creatures' being conscious of things. And our understanding of perceiving and thinking, in virtue of which one is conscious of things, has progressed largely independently of whether the perceiving or thinking is conscious. The following discussion will address only that third question, about what it is for a mental state to be conscious.

Findings in experimental psychology and cognitive neuropsychology have over the last few decades greatly expanded and deepened our understanding of the consciousness of mental states. Experimental work on *blindsight, masked *priming, *change blindness, and confabulation, all discussed below, have revealed much about the way mental states occur both consciously and non-consciously, and about the difference between the two kinds of occurrence.

Still, work in philosophy has much to contribute as well. For one thing, such work often gives detailed and penetrating descriptions of the common-sense psychological phenomena that scientific research must address and explain. Also, work in philosophy characteristically proceeds at a relatively abstract level, drawing connections with theories of related phenomena, so that work is often useful in discussing competing theories of consciousness both in abstraction from specific empirical findings and in relation to other relevant theories.

Work in philosophy is thus often continuous with that in the relevant sciences, differing largely in focus and emphasis. These continuities enhance the contributions each makes to the other, as well as their joint contributions to our overall understanding of consciousness.

1. Traditional theories
2. First-order theories
3. Global workspace and the function of consciousness
4. Inner sense
5. Other higher-order theories
6. Qualitative consciousness
7. Consciousness, timing, and speech

1. Traditional theories

René Descartes (1596–1650) regarded all mental phenomena as special cases of thinking, and claimed that 'no thought can exist in us of which we are not conscious at the very moment it exists in us' (Descartes 1964–75:VII, 246). We are conscious, he insisted, of all our mental states.

Descartes had little to say, however, about exactly how it is that we are conscious of our concurrent thoughts. John Locke (1632–1704) agreed with Descartes that no mental state occurs without one's being conscious of it, and indeed maintained that it is unintelligible to think otherwise. But Locke pressed further than Descartes in trying to explain the exact way we are conscious of our mental states, urging that '[c]onsciousness is the perception of what passes in a Man's own mind' (Locke 1690/1975:115 [II, i, 19]). Locke thereby echoed Aristotle's idea that 'if we perceive, we perceive that we perceive, and if we think, that we think' (Aristotle 1984:II, 1849 [1170a32]). Locke called such perceiving of our mental states *internal sense* (1690/1975:05 [II, i, 4]), but most today use Immanuel Kant's term *inner sense* (Kant 1787/1998:174 [A22/B37]).

Franz Brentano (1838–1917), also heavily influenced by Aristotle, advanced a different view about the way we are conscious of our mental states. He held that not only is each mental state about its ostensible object; it is also literally about itself. Each mental state is in that way a consciousness of itself. Brentano (1874/1973) held that the aspect of each mental state that is about itself is purely intentional; one is conscious of all one's mental states because internal to each state is a thought about that state itself.

Brentano also followed Descartes and Locke in thinking that mental states are all conscious. But where Locke insisted that it is unintelligible to suppose that a mental state could occur of which one is unaware, Brentano held that this is intelligible, but simply never happens. Still, both strove to do justice to Descartes's idea that consciousness is essential to mentality, Locke by insisting on the unintelligibility of non-conscious mental states, and Brentano by urging that the consciousness of each mental state is internal to that state itself.

Common to all these thinkers is the view that one is conscious of all one's mental states. This occurs by perceiving each state according to Locke, by having a thought about each state according to Brentano, and according to Aristotle by perceiving in the case of conscious perception and by having a thought in the case of conscious thinking. Among these theorists, only Brentano describes mental states as 'being conscious', as against states one is conscious of. But they all plainly have the same phenomenon in mind. And on all their views, a state's being conscious in effect consists in having a higher-order awareness of that state.

2. First-order theories

It is convenient to call being conscious of something *transitive consciousness*, because of the grammatical object. We can then describe the claim that a state's being conscious consists in one's being in some way conscious of that state as the *transitivity principle* (henceforth TP).

TP has strong common-sense appeal. If somebody has a thought, perception, or feeling but is wholly unaware of having it, we do not regard that state as conscious. And that is logically equivalent to TP: a state is conscious only if one is in some suitable way conscious of it. If TP is correct, a satisfactory theory must specify in what way we are conscious of those of our mental states that are conscious states.

Most contemporary theorists follow philosophical tradition in adopting TP, differing mainly about how it is that we are conscious of our conscious states, that is, about how TP is implemented. But some have contested TP, arguing that a state's being conscious does not consist in being conscious of that state. Such views are often called *first-order theories*.

Despite TP's common-sense appeal, there are also compelling common-sense reasons to challenge it. For one thing, it does not seem subjectively that we are generally aware of our conscious states, as against being conscious of the things those states represent. In particular, as John R. Searle has argued (Searle 1992:95–6), it does not seem that we ever observe our conscious states, contrary to what the inner-sense theory maintains. Searle concludes that TP is incorrect.

Advocates of TP, however, have answers to these challenges. Doubtless we never do literally observe our mental states, but observation is not the only way to be conscious of things. So TP might well be true because we are aware in some other way of our conscious states. Indeed, TP might be true even though it seldom seems subjectively that we are aware of our conscious states. We are sometimes conscious of things even when the states in virtue of which we are conscious of them are not conscious states. This happens with subliminal perception; we are aware of the things we perceive subliminally, but not consciously aware of them. So it is possible that conscious states are states we are aware of, but we are not typically conscious of that higher-order awareness of our conscious states.

Fred Dretske has advanced an elaborate argument that conscious states are not states that one is conscious of. One sometimes sees two scenes that differ in some slight way, but without being conscious of their differing in that way. The two scenes might be alike except that one scene has ten trees and another only nine. Dretske (1993) urges that in such a case one has a conscious visual experience of the tenth tree even though one is unaware of that conscious experience. The experience of the tenth tree would then be a conscious experience even though one is not conscious of it.

Scenes that differ in some unnoticed way are common in everyday experience, and are the focus of experimental work on change blindness, in which subjects fail to see consciously salient changes in scenes (Grimes 1996, Dretske 2004, Simons and Rensink 2005). Still, it is arguable that Dretske's argument does not undermine TP. One can be conscious of something in one respect and not another. So it might well be in Dretske's case that one is conscious of the experience of the tenth tree only as a part of the overall experience of the scene, but not conscious of it as a way in which the two overall experiences differ. If so, it would not be a counter-example to TP.

Daniel C. Dennett has argued that TP presupposes an unrealistic hierarchy of psychological states (Dennett 1991:Ch. 10). Being in a mental state results in things seeming a certain way to one. But because there is no difference, Dennett maintains, between how things seem to one and how they seem to seem, we cannot make clear sense of the idea that our mental states themselves appear to us in particular ways (1991:132). But subliminal perceiving does result in things seeming to us in particular ways even though we are unaware of that seeming. So a second level of awareness does arguably occur when such perceiving is conscious.

3. Global workspace and the function of consciousness

Conscious states typically seem to interact in a relatively global way with one another, and to have a widespread effect on our mental lives and on behaviour. And some theorists hold that these widespread interactions serve to distinguish conscious states from mental states that are not conscious.

Thus Ned Block distinguishes a class of states he calls **access conscious* as those whose content is 'poised to be used as a premise in reasoning, ... [and] for [the] *rational* control of action and ... speech' (Block 1995:231; cf. 2005,

2007). Dennett has epitomized this idea with his remark that '[c]onsciousness is cerebral celebrity' (1993:93); conscious states are those which have a global effect on memory, behavior, and other psychological functioning. These ideas echo the *global workspace theory of Baars (1988), which has been developed in neuropsychological terms by Dehaene and Naccache (2001) and Tononi (2004).

The idea that conscious states differ from mental states that are not conscious in being connected to a high degree with various psychological functions fits well with a particular view about why mental states are sometimes conscious and the function that their being conscious may have. It is tempting to hold that conscious states enhance our rationality in thought and practical planning, and that they would do this by having global connections with other mental states. And, if the consciousness of states does enhance rational thought and planning, that function might help explain how the consciousness of mental states could have been selected for evolutionarily.

Such theories in effect reject TP, since a state could have global connections without one's being in any way conscious of that state, and conversely. Robert Van Gulick has developed a version of global workspace theory on which the global connections make one conscious of oneself (Van Gulick 2004). But it is unclear even that his view implements TP, since being conscious of oneself need not result in one's being conscious of any particular mental state one is in.

TP aside, it is in any case arguable that global workspace theories fail. Many states that we do not count as conscious have global connections to many other mental states and to behaviour, e.g. many non-conscious desires and beliefs. And many indisputably conscious states, such as conscious peripheral perceptions, have at most minimal connections with other mental states and with behaviour. Global connectedness may be typical of many conscious states, but it is not a distinguishing mark of a state's being conscious.

It is also unclear that we can explain the function of consciousness by appeal to its ability to enhance rational thought and planning. The intentional content of beliefs and desires by itself arguably suffices for those states to have many causal ties with other mental states, causal ties that subserve most rational thought processes. And because these causal ties depend solely on intentional content, they occur whether or not the states are conscious.

Edmund T. Rolls has argued that correcting multi-step inferences requires higher-order mental monitoring that would result in the steps' being conscious (Rolls 2004). But it is unclear that the causal ties intentional states have to one another would not suffice, or that consciousness significantly enhances the causal connections that subserve rational thinking.

It is tempting to assume that consciousness enhances rationality because it seems that being conscious of one's mental states would enable one to rearrange those states rationally, much as one can rearrange objects when one is perceptually conscious of them. But it is unlikely that this metaphor can be sustained. So rational connections may well be largely independent of consciousness.

4. Inner sense

It is widely agreed that a satisfactory theory of consciousness must somehow do justice to TP. The inner-sense theory, on which a mental state is conscious in virtue of one's having a higher-order perception of that state, is the most commonly adopted way of implementing TP. It has been forcefully defended by D. M. Armstrong (1980) and William G. Lycan (1996).

Sensing and perceiving is very likely the first thing to come to mind when one thinks of being conscious of things. So it is natural to understand TP in terms of sensing or perceiving one's conscious states. The idea that we perceive our conscious states, moreover, may seem tempting as a way to explain the conscious qualitative character of many states. Also, it is inviting to hold that our awareness of our conscious states serve to monitor our mental states, much as ordinary perceiving monitors external and bodily conditions. This monitoring analogy between mental states' being conscious and perception is often held to constitute another advantage for the inner-sense theory.

But there is room for doubt about the inner-sense theory. Sensing and perceiving always involve mental qualities, but no mental qualities figure in higher-order states in virtue of which we are conscious of our conscious states. The mental qualities essential to ordinary perceiving enable us to perceive physical objects, not mental states, and no other mental qualities are available for perceiving mental states. The mental qualities that occur in qualitative consciousness are qualities of the states we are conscious of, not the states in virtue of which we are conscious of them.

The difficulty about mental qualities is underscored by noting that we are typically conscious of experiences in a way that groups together perceptions from several sensory modalities. But since every mental quality is special to a single perceptual modality, it is unclear how one could perceive an experience as involving several different modalities. Nor is it obvious how one could perceive purely intentional states, such as thoughts, which altogether lack qualitative character.

Armstrong and Lycan both advance representationalist views of perceiving, on which perceiving involves no mental qualities. Instead, perceiving has only intentional content that pertains to the perceptible properties of physical objects and events. This theory of perceiving obviates the need for mental qualities to figure when we perceive our conscious states. But *representationalism about perceiving is at best controversial. And even if it is correct and perceiving does involve no mental qualities, the advocate of inner sense must still show that we are conscious of our conscious states in a way that is significantly more like perceiving than like having thoughts about the relevant states. Lycan (2004) has argued that this is so, mainly by appeal to volitional and attentional factors, but many thoughts also exhibit the features he cites as special to perceiving (Rosenthal 2004:§III).

There is also some question about whether the appeal to monitoring does show that our awareness of our conscious states is more like perceiving those states than like having thoughts about them. For one thing, inner sense is not the only way we might monitor those states; since any way of being conscious of those states suffices for monitoring, thoughts about those states would do as well.

In addition, there are cases in which our awareness of our conscious states seems to play no monitoring play. As Richard E. Nisbett and Timothy DeCamp Wilson (1977) have shown, we are sometimes conscious of ourselves as being in particular mental states even when there is compelling evidence that we are not. Since monitoring is evidently not operative in these cases, the best explanation of them is that such confabulatory consciousness serves to construct a picture of our mental lives that makes sense to ourselves or to others, or that justifies our behaviour. The inner-sense model of consciousness thus remains controversial.

5. Other higher-order theories

An alternative way to implement TP can be found in the view that we are aware of our conscious states by having thoughts about them. Having a thought about something as being present to one does make one conscious of that thing. So having a *higher-order thought (HOT) that one is in a particular state will result in one's being conscious of that state.

Brentano held that view, adding that the thought one has about each conscious state is a part of that state itself. This intrinsicalist version of the HOT theory squares with the intuition that underlies first-order theories, that a state's being conscious involves nothing beyond that state itself. The intrinsicalist HOT theory has received contemporary support from Rocco Gennaro (2004) and Uriah Kriegel (2006; see also other essays in Kriegel and Williford 2006).

One reason advanced for this intrinsicalist view is that, if we are conscious of our mental states by way of distinct higher-order states, those higher-order states might represent the first-order states inaccurately. Indeed, the higher-order states might even occur without any relevant first-order state at all. And it is tempting to think that intrinsicalism precludes these awkward possibilities. But even if higher-order content is intrinsic to a state, it could misrepresent that state's other mental properties, and such higher-order content might even occur in a state that has no other mental properties. So intrinsicalism does not by itself rule these things out.

Intrinsicalism holds that the higher-order intentional content in virtue of which one is conscious of a conscious state belongs the state itself, rather than to a distinct state. Whether that is so depends on how we individuate intentional states. We do not do so by the content of the states, since a single state may have compound content that conjoins several simpler contents. Rather, we individuate intentional states by appeal to their mental attitude, such as believing, wondering, desiring, and the like; no single state has two distinct mental attitudes.

But an assertoric mental attitude is needed for one to be conscious of something; doubting or wondering about something does not make one conscious of that thing. So a conscious doubt must involve two mental attitudes, the doubting itself and the assertoric attitude in virtue of which one is conscious of the doubt. Higher-order content must accordingly belong to a distinct HOT.

Closely related to intrinsicalism is a dispositionalist version of the HOT theory advanced by Peter Carruthers (2000), on which a state is conscious if one is disposed to have a HOT about it. Like intrinsicalism, this dispositionalist theory avoids commitment to distinct, occurrent higher-order states. Carruthers argues that actual HOTs would in effect replicate the first-order states, and would strain our cognitive capacities. But it is unlikely that actual HOTs would come close to exhausting the relevant cortical capacity. Nor in any case do HOTs replicate the first-order content, since the content of HOTs would be about the first-order states, not whatever those states are themselves about.

There is also an issue about whether a dispositionalist theory can actually implement TP at all, since simply being disposed to have a thought about something does not result in one's being conscious of that thing. Carruthers seeks to meet this difficulty by appeal to a theory on a which state's intentional content depends in part on what other mental states the state is disposed to cause. If a state is disposed to cause an actual HOT, it has HOT content itself. But on this theory, no state that is even disposed to cause an actual HOT could fail to be conscious.

If the difficulties with inner sense and with the intrinsicalist and dispositional versions of the HOT theory cannot be met, the most credible alternative for implementing TP is a theory that posits distinct, occurrent HOTs, a view advanced by David Rosenthal (2005).

Consciousness represents our mental states in more or less fine-grained ways. Distinct HOTs permit such flexibility in the ways we are conscious of our mental states. Such HOTs also may explain the sense we have that our conscious states are unified in a single center of consciousness. Each HOT would have the content, 'I am in such-and-such a state'. And it is natural, absent countervailing factors such as those in *dissociative identity disorder, to take the 'I' in all one's HOTs to refer to a single individual (Rosenthal 2005:Ch. 13).

6. Qualitative consciousness

The most serious challenge any theory of consciousness faces has to do with conscious qualitative states. When a state with qualitative character, such as a bodily sensation or a perception, is conscious, there is 'something it is like' for one to be in that state (Nagel 1974). Giving an informative explanation of such conscious qualitative character seems to encounter difficulties.

One apparent difficulty, noted by Locke (1690/1975:389 [II, xxxii, 15]), is that it may seem that when we sense the same stimulus, the conscious mental qualities that occur in each of us may differ in ways that defy detection. One person's spectrum of conscious mental colour qualities, for example, might be inverted in undetectable ways relative to that of another person. Our access to conscious mental qualities would then be restricted to the way we are conscious of them, and it would then be unclear how conscious qualitative character could be informatively explained.

Indeed, if conscious qualitative character is thus independent of physical constitution and functioning, individuals identical to us in those ways might have no conscious mental qualities at all. This apparent possibility has been stressed by David J. Chalmers and others, and seems to raise difficulties for explaining conscious qualitative character by appeal to anything physical. Chalmers (1996) calls this the *hard problem of consciousness.

A third difficulty is that it is tempting to suppose that somebody who has never seen chromatic colour but knows everything physical there is to about such colours would nonetheless learn something new upon first seeing red, namely, that this is what it is like to see red (Jackson 1986; see KNOWLEDGE ARGUMENT). These and other related difficulties have suggested to some that no informative explanation of conscious qualitative character is possible, that an *explanatory gap separates conscious mental qualities from everything else (Levine 2001).

As noted in section 4, representationalist theories avoid these difficulties, since they deny that mental states have mental qualities. Perceiving, on this view, simply represents the presence of the perceptible properties of various objects (Harman 1990). But the way perceiving represents perceptible properties plainly differs from, and goes beyond, the way in which thinking represents those properties, and it is unclear why the additional factor in perceiving does not count as mental qualitative character.

It is arguable that the difficulties just rehearsed all result from assuming, as these authors do, that qualitative character cannot occur without being conscious. But there is compelling reason to hold that non-conscious states do sometimes have mental qualities. In subliminal perceiving, blindsight (Weiskrantz 1997) and masked-priming experiments (Marcel 1983), subjects respond psychologically to stimuli in ways that reflect their perceptible properties. Conscious perceptions, moreover, register these perceptible differences by corresponding differences among their mental qualities. So it is natural to suppose that non-conscious perceptions also have the very same mental qualities, even though we are not aware of them.

It may well be that higher-order theories of consciousness are better suited to give an informative explanation of conscious qualitative character than first-order theories, since higher-order theories posit two levels of awareness. On those theories, qualitative states unaccompanied by a suitable higher-order state will not be conscious; there is nothing it is like for one to be in such a state. It is being conscious of the state in a suitable way that results in there being something it's like for one to be in it.

This receives support from noting that the way one is conscious of perceptual states does make a difference to what it is like for one to be in those states. For example, learning new words for olfactory or auditory experiences that are new to one can result in one's being conscious of those experiences in new, more fine-grained ways; what it is like for one actually comes to be different. So it is not implausible that being conscious of a qualitative state is responsible for there being anything at all that it is like for one to be in a state.

Some theorists have argues that higher-order theories encounter a particular difficulty in the case of conscious qualitative states. As Levine (2001:§4.4) notes, a higher-order awareness may sometimes misrepresent one's mental states; one will be conscious of oneself as being in a state that one is not actually in. And Levine argues that this is problematic for cases in which the higher-order state misrepresents a qualitative state, say, by representing a sensation of a red as a sensation of green. Would the result be subjectively like consciously seeing red? Or subjectively seeing green? But this objection arguably overlooks the way TP functions. Since a state's being conscious is a matter of one's being conscious of that state, what it's like for one will be a matter simply of how one is conscious of the state. What it is like for one is a matter of what state the higher-order awareness makes one conscious of oneself as being in.

Ned Block has distinguished the *access consciousness* in virtue of which states figure in rational thought, action, and speech (see section 3) from what he calls *phenomenal consciousness*, which is distinctive of states that have some mental quality (Block 1995, 2005, 2007). Block's distinction has been influential in both philosophical and scientific discussions, since qualitative consciousness is plainly a special phenomenon. Still, there are issues about exactly what phenomenal consciousness consists of. In particular, it may be that phenomenal consciousness as Block conceives of it may occur in subliminal perception, which is not conscious in any common-sense, intuitive way. If so, phenomenal consciousness is simply a state's having mental qualities, which evidently need not occur consciously.

7. Consciousness, timing, and speech

Dennett (1991) has forcefully argued that our subjective impressions are the last word about the nature of conscious states, and that when those impressions conflict, there is in that respect no fact of the matter about the nature of the relevant conscious states. He advances strikingly vivid arguments for this conclusion in connection with the timing of conscious states (Dennett 1991:Ch. 5).

Higher-order theories again offer a salutary flexibility. Since we can distinguish the time one becomes conscious of a state from the time that state occurs, these questions may get distinct, but equally determinate answers (Rosenthal 2005:Ch. 12).

Indeed, work by Benjamin Libet (1985) and Patrick Haggard (1999) has shown that when we consciously decide to do something, the neural event that initiates the action occurs prior to that conscious volition. Libet has also shown that even though subjects' conscious experiences of somatosensory stimulation can occur as much as 500 ms later than the actual stimulation, subjects experience them as occurring earlier, within 10–20 ms of the actual stimulus. The best explanation of these striking results is that volitions and bodily sensations are distinct from, and may occur at a different time from, the events of being conscious of those volitions and sensations.

Our common-sense test for somebody's being in a conscious mental state is that the person can report being in that state in a way that seems non-inferential, a test that also underlies much work in experimental psychology. When a subject reports not sensing a stimulus but can guess with high accuracy about it, investigators conclude that the subject does sense the thing, but does not do so consciously. This happens, for example, in blindsight (Weiskrantz 1997) and in masked-priming experiments (Marcel 1983).

Not all conscious states are reported, and presumably many creatures with conscious states lack any capacity to report them. What explains, then, the connection between consciousness and reportability? The best explanation is that reports of mental states, when they do occur, express a creature's thoughts about those states. We regard reportability as a sound test for a state's being conscious because a creature can non-inferentially report a state only if that creature is aware of the state by being in a non-inferential higher-order state that a report would express.

Non-inferential reportability and consciousness coincide in creatures, like ourselves, that can talk non-inferentially about their own mental states. So it is inviting to ask whether non-inferential reportability might constitute not merely a reliable test for mental states' being conscious, but also a way in which their being conscious has a distinctive function (see section 3). Reportability might then explain why a creature's being in mental states some of which are conscious could confer an adaptive advantage on that creature.

But it is doubtful that reportability does provide any significant function for mental states' being conscious, compared with those states' simply occurring but without being conscious. There is little if any added usefulness in reporting what state one is in, compared with simply conveying the representational content of that state. If one has a sensation of red or of pain, one could say simply that something is red or that there is damage to one's body in a particular place; one need not report the sensations themselves. And if one thinks that the moon is round, one can just say that it is, rather than reporting the thought itself. Little if any significant additional function is served by also reporting these states.

Theorists have long noted a tight connection between consciousness and speech. Thus Descartes contended that only creatures with language have thoughts (1964–75:VI 58–59, AT VII 204–205, IV 573–576, V 275–279), since any creature that did have conscious thoughts would, he held, express them in speech. But he gave no argument for this connection, and as already noted he fails in any case to countenance thoughts that are not conscious.

Distinguishing conscious from non-conscious thoughts lends itself to a more nuanced picture. Verbally expressed thoughts are always conscious, at least in the human case. This contrasts with thoughts we express non-verbally, which often fail to be conscious; our behaviour often reveals thoughts we are unaware of. This more subtle correlation also allows for a convincing explanation. Any time one says something, it is equally natural to say that one thinks that thing. So saying something, thereby expressing one's corresponding thought, actually disposes one to be aware that one has that thought (Rosenthal 2005:Ch. 10). On this explanation, the tie between language and consciousness is due not to the nature of those phenomena themselves, but to a special feature of human speech, that expressing a thought and reporting it are for us readily interchangeable in practice.

DAVID M. ROSENTHAL

Aristotle (1984). *The Complete Works of Aristotle*, ed. J. Barnes.

Armstrong, D. M. (1980), 'What is consciousness?' In *The Nature of Mind*.

Baars, B. J. (1988). *A Cognitive Theory of Consciousness*.

Block, N. (1995). 'On a confusion about a function of consciousness'. *Behavioral and Brain Sciences*, 18.

—— (2005). 'Two neural correlates of consciousness'. *Trends in Cognitive Sciences*, 9.

——(2007). 'Consciousness, accessibility, and the mesh between psychology and neuroscience'. *Behavioral and Brain Sciences*, 30.

Brentano, F. (1874/1973). *Psychology from an Empirical Standpoint*, ed. O. Kraus; English edition ed. L. L. McAlister, transl. A. C. Rancurello et al.

Carruthers, P. (2000). *Phenomenal Consciousness: A Naturalistic Theory*.

Chalmers, D. J. (1996). *The Conscious Mind: In Search of a Fundamental Theory*.

Dehaene, S. and Naccache, L. (2001), 'Towards a cognitive neuroscience of consciousness: basic evidence and a workshop framework'. *Cognition*, 79.

Dennett, D. C. (1991). *Consciousness Explained*.

—— (1993). 'The message is: there is no medium,' *Philosophy and Phenomenological Research*, LIII.

Descartes, R. (1964–75). *Oeuvres de Descartes*, ed. C. Adam and P. Tannery.

Dretske, F. (1993). 'Conscious Experience'. *Mind*, 102.

—— (2004). 'Change Blindness,' *Philosophical Studies*, 120.

Gennaro, R. J. (1996). *Consciousness and Self-Consciousness*.

—— (ed.) (2004). *Higher-Order Theories of Consciousness*.

Grimes, J. (1996) 'On the failure to detect changes in scenes across saccades'. In Akins, K. (ed.) *Perception*.

Haggard, P. (1999). 'Perceived timing of self-initiated actions'. In Aschersleben, G. et al. (eds) *Cognitive Contributions to the Perception of Spatial and Temporal Events*.

Harman, G. (1990). 'The intrinsic quality of experience'. *Philosophical Perspectives*, IV.

Hill, S. and Tononi, G. (2005). 'Modeling sleep and wakefulness in the thalamocortical system'. *Journal of Neurophysiology*, 93.

Jackson, F. (1986). 'What Mary didn't know,' *Journal of Philosophy*, LXXXIII.

Kant, I. (1787/1998). *Critique of pure reason*, ed. and transl. Paul Guyer and Allen W. Wood.

Kriegel, U. (2006). 'The same-order monitoring theory of consciousness'. In Kriegel, U. and Williford, K. (eds) *Self-representational Approaches to Consciousness*.

Kriegel, U. and Williford, K. (eds) (2006). *Self-representational Approaches to Consciousness*.

Levine, J. (2001). *Purple Haze: The Puzzle of Consciousness*.

Libet, B. (1985). 'Unconscious cerebral initiative and the role of conscious will in voluntary action', *Behavioral and Brain Sciences*, 8.

Locke, J. (1690/1975). *An Essay Concerning Human Understanding*, ed. P. H. Nidditch.

Lycan, W. G. (1996). *Consciousness and Experience*.

—— (2004). 'The superiority of HOP to HOT'. In Gennaro, R. J. (ed.) *Higher-Order Theories of Consciousness*.

Marcel, A. J. (1983). 'Conscious and unconscious perception: an approach to the relations between phenomenal experience and perceptual processes'. *Cognitive Psychology*, 15.

Nagel, T. (1974). 'What is it like to be a bat?' *Philosophical Review*, LXXXIII.

Nisbett, R. E. and DeCamp Wilson, T. (1977). 'Telling more than we can know: verbal reports on mental processes'. *Psychological Review*, LXXXIV.

Rolls, E. T. (2004). 'A higher order syntactic thought (HOST) theory of consciousness'. In Gennaro, R. J. (ed.) *Higher-Order Theories of Consciousness*.

Rosenthal, D. M. (2004). 'Varieties of higher-order theory'. In Gennaro, R. J. (ed.) *Higher-Order Theories of Consciousness*.

—— (2005). *Consciousness and Mind*.

Searle, J. R. (1992). *The Rediscovery of the Mind*.

Simons, D. J. and Rensink, R. A. (2005). 'Change blindness: past, present, and future'. *Trends in Cognitive Sciences*, 9.

Tononi, G. (2004). 'An information integration theory of consciousness'. *BMC Neuroscience*, 5.

—— and Cirelli, C.(2003). 'Sleep and synaptic homeostasis: a hypothesis'. *Brain Research Bulletin*, 62.

Van Gulick, R. (2004). 'Higher-order global states (HOGS): an alternative higher-order model of consciousness'. in Gennaro, R. J. (ed.) *Higher-Order Theories of Consciousness*.

Weiskrantz, L. (1997). *Consciousness Lost and Found: A Neuropsychological Exploration*.

physicalism Physicalism is the thesis that everything is physical, or at any rate, that everything is necessitated by or supervenes on the physical. The claim is not that there are no biological or psychological or social properties or things; it is rather that, if there are such properties or things, they are either physical or supervene on the physical. Physicalism is intended to be a contingent but very abstract thesis about the actual world. It is rather like the claim attributed to the ancient philosopher Thales, that everything is water. Thales did not (or so we may suppose) think that everything is water necessarily, in every possible world; he thought that everything is water in this world, as a matter of fact.

Similarly, physicalists hold, not that everything is physical in every possible world, but rather than everything is physical in this world, as a matter of fact.

Physicalism is often known as 'materialism', and for most purposes these two words may be thought of as interchangeable in current usage. This was not always so. The word 'physicalism' was introduced into philosophy in the 1930s by Otto Neurath (1931/1983) and Rudolf Carnap (1932/1959), both of whom were key members of the Vienna Circle, a group of philosophers, scientists, and mathematicians active in Vienna before World War II. It is not at all clear that Neurath and Carnap conceived of physicalism in the same way, but one thesis that is often attributed to them is the linguistic thesis that every statement is synonymous with (i.e. is equivalent in meaning with) some physical statement. But materialism as traditionally construed is not a linguistic thesis but a metaphysical one, in that it tells us about the nature of the world as such. Hence we have a reason for distinguishing physicalism (a linguistic thesis) from materialism (a metaphysical thesis), a reason compounded by the fact that, according to official positivist doctrine, metaphysics is nonsense. Since the 1930s, however, the background assumptions that distinguished 'materialism' from 'physicalism' have for the most part been rejected, and this one reason why the two words are now interchangeable.

Some philosophers suggest that 'physicalism' is distinct from 'materialism' for a reason quite unrelated to the one emphasized by Neurath and Carnap: namely, that 'physicalism' has a certain generality that 'materialism' does not. The root notion of materialism is 'matter' and historically the notion of matter is quite constrained: matter is the stuff that fills up space, is inert, senseless, hard, impenetrable and so on; a materialist is someone who holds that everything is fundamentally material in this sense of 'matter'. The problem with this version of materialism is that physical science has itself shown that it is untrue; modern physics postulates events and properties that are non-material in this sense. Because of this, many contemporary philosophers prefer to speak of 'physicalism' on the grounds, first, that the root notion of physicalism is 'physical' and, second, that 'physical' includes more than simply 'matter'. Actually, the second of these grounds is somewhat implausible, since 'physical' might well be thought of having its primary occurrence in expressions such as 'physical object' and in turn that expression is synonymous with 'material object'. In any case, whatever the merits of this reason for adopting 'physicalism', it evidently has nothing to do with the historical (i.e. Viennese) origins of the word.

Physicalism (or materialism—we will follow recent practice in using them interchangeably)—is been a doctrine that has been prominent in various points in the history of philosophy. To begin with, there is the famous idea associated with the Greeks that nature consists of atoms and the void, an idea partially revived by early (pre-Newtonian) members of the scientific revolution in the 17th century. Perhaps because of the difference between Newtonian physics and classical atomism, in the 18th century, materialism evolved beyond mere atomism to be essentially the denial of the existence of a soul, and because of the soul's connections with a religious world view, to atheism. In the 20th century analytic philosophy the idea achieved considerable prominence again, finding support in such figures as Quine (1960) and Lewis (1994). Indeed, it not unreasonable to say that, just as idealism was the metaphysics *du jour* for the philosophers of the late 19th century, so physicalism has become the metaphysics *du jour* for the 20th. It may also be that physicalism (or something like it) is implicitly a common part of 20th and 21st century intellectual culture, though this is somewhat speculative.

Even if physicalism is a very common view among contemporary philosophers, it is surprisingly difficult to state in any clear way what it is. As we have noted, in the 1930s physicalism was often interpreted as a linguistic thesis entailing the synonymy of any statement with a physical statement. Understood this way, it is a remarkably strong claim. It apparently entails, for example, that the statement 'Otto is anxious' is synonymous with some statement formulated in the technical vocabulary of physics or perhaps neuroscience. But this is highly unlikely for various reasons, not least that the first statement has a linguistic environment completely distinct from that of the second.

In the immediate aftermath of positivism (roughly, the 1950s), the claim of synonymy was given up for a claim of (numerical) identity, particularly by Smart (1959) and others. On this version of the view, the facts reported by psychological statements are (numerically) identical to the facts reported by a physical statement. Since it does not follow from this that psychological sentences and physical sentences have the same meaning, identity versions of physicalism avoid objections having to do with synonymy. Still, they face other objections. Chief among these was the objection from multiple realization, posed first by Putnam (1975). This objection points out that if the fact reported by the sentence 'there is pain' is identical to a fact reported by a sentence in the physical sciences, say 'there are C-fibres firing', then pain could not occur in the absence of C-fibres firing. But there are many reasons to suppose that pain *can* occur in the absence of C-fibres firing. Creatures as different as yaks, robots, angels might feel pain just as much as we humans can—but since all of these creatures are physically different, pains cannot be identical to C-fibres firing. In short, pain is—as it came to be known—multiply realized, and if this is so no identity version of physicalism can be true.

In response to the multiple realization objection, many philosophers (e.g. Lewis 1994) modified physicalism again so that it entailed, not that the facts reported by psychological sentences are *identical* to those reported by physical sentences, but rather that the facts reported by psychological sentences *supervene* on those reported by physical sentences. The background idea of supervenience is usually introduced by considering examples such as the following. Suppose a particular sculpture is elegant. The elegance of the sculpture seems to be a function in a straightforward sense of the way in which its physical parts are arranged, and the properties of those parts, and the psychological reactions of various people to those parts—in short, the elegance of the sculpture seems to be a function of its natural properties. This relation may be captured in the language of supervenience, by saying that the aesthetic properties of the sculpture supervene on the natural properties. A different sculpture constructed so that it duplicated every natural property of the original; such a duplicate sculpture would be likewise elegant. So too, on the supervience formulation of physicalism, physicalism says that the psychological properties of a thing—say a person—supervene on its physical properties.

The shift from identity to supervenience permits a formulation of physicalism which allows multiple realization: just as elegance might supervene on a number of different natural features, so pain might supervene on a number of different physical features (or even non-physical features, in theory). But the supervenience formulation of physicalism has itself recently come under attack. The main problem this time is that supervenience formulations seem incapable of differentiating physicalism from a closely related view championed in the 1920s by the English philosopher C. D. Broad (1925), called *emergentism, and thought of, perhaps unfairly, as a *bête noire* by many philosophers in the 1950s and 1960s. The emergentist holds a view that is in some ways like that of a traditional *dualist. For example, Broad supported his position with a version of the famous *knowledge argument against physicalism rather like that advanced by Jackson (1982). But the emergentist *also* holds that psychological facts supervene on physical facts. How then can one distinguish emergentism and physicalism? This is a controversial question in philosophy of mind. Some philosophers, such as Kim (1998), suggest that there is no way to distinguish them, and recommend a move back to an identity version of physicalism. Others point out that emergentism involves some quite distinctive and potentially unclear metaphysical claims, e.g. that traditional dualism can be combined with a supervenience thesis. But if that is so, one might say that the difference is between emergentism and physicalism is that the first is of questionable clarity, while the second, regardless of whether it is true, is not.

The questions about the formulation of physicalism that we have just considered concern the relation asserted by physicalism between physical and other facts. Another set of questions concerns the notion of the physical itself—indeed, this problem afflicts every version of physicalism whether it is formulated in terms of synonymy, identity, or supervenience. What is a physical property or fact? It proves very difficult to answer this question in a satisfactory way (cf. Hempel 1969). As we have noted, for empirical reasons a physicalist cannot be a traditional materialist atomist in the sense associated with Greek atomism, for physics itself has shown that that view is false. But in seeking to produce a version of physicalism that avoids this problem, physicalists seems to fall into the trap of having a view that is by their own lights either too liberal or else too restrictive. On the one hand, if one liberalizes the notion of the physical to include properties or events postulated by both Greek atomism and contemporary physics, the resultant notion threatens to be consistent with many positions that are not normally thought of as physicalist. On the other hand, if one restricts the notion, as indeed many contemporaries do, so that the idea of a physical property is simply a property expressed in the language of contemporary or near contemporary physics, the resultant version is too restrictive: the view that the world is nothing but atoms and the void is a paradigmatic version of physicalism, and yet would not obviously count as a world in which physicalism is true on this reading.

In spite of these difficulties, many contemporary philosophers assume that they understand physicalism somehow, and concentrate instead on arguments for and against it. What are these arguments? It is sometimes suggested that one should believe that physicalism is true because it is part of the scientific world view. But this idea is objectionably vague: what is the scientific world view, and which of the many (non-equivalent) versions of physicalism are part of it? Perhaps because of this, in recent times, a very different argument for physicalism has emerged—the so-called *causal argument* for physicalism, which has been formulated and discussed in considerable detail (see Papineau 2002). The causal argument for physicalism seeks to infer the truth of physicalism from three premises: that every event has a physical cause (the closure thesis); that some event have mental causes (the efficacy of the mental); and that no event is overdetermined, i.e. that at least in general it is not the case that two distinct events cause a single third event (the exclusion thesis). These theses together tell us that mental events are identical to physical events. One problem with this argument is that the closure thesis inherits the problems of interpretation of the notion of the physical that we have just been discussing. In what sense of 'physical' is it being asserted that every event has a physical cause? Another problem is that the conclusion of the argument involves the identity of the mental and the physical and so the argument itself is an argument for the *identity* version of physicalism. But leaves us without an argument for the *supervenience* version of physicalism, which as we have noted in some respects more plausible than the identity version. Moreover, it is difficult to adjust the argument so that it does result in a supervenience version of physicalism, for it is hard to see how any resulting argument would establish physicalism as opposed to emergentism.

The causal argument is the most prominent argument for physicalism in contemporary philosophy—what of the arguments against? Here the main source of worry has to do with various features of psychological states, in particularly their *consciousness or *intentionality, which for various reasons seem inconsistent with the truth of physicalism. One major argument here is Quine's (1960) indeterminacy argument which seeks to show that the totality of physical facts leave it open which of different hypotheses about the meaning of words is true. For example, it seems that no matter how much physical information you have a about a person, you could still not tell whether their word 'gavagai' meant what 'rabbit' means or what 'undetached rabbit part' means. This argument is usually seen, not as an argument against physicalism so much as an argument about what the nature of meaning must be like if physicalism is true. Nevertheless, its starting point is the observation that the place of meaning in a physical world is somewhat insecure. Arguments similar to Quine's have been developed in different ways by different writers, some of whom (e.g. Kripke 1982) emphasize the normative nature of intentionality, while others (e.g. Fodor 1987) emphasize that a world in which physicalism is true seems to be a world in which intentional properties have no place. A different argument against physicalism concerns consciousness in at least one the sense of that complex notion: phenomenal or sensory consciousness. This argument, which was stated initially in modern modal terminology by Kripke (1980, but already available in 1972), and then improved on in many ways by Nagel (1974), Jackson (1982), and Chalmers (1996), goes roughly as follows. Physicalism says that the mental facts, and so the facts about consciousness supervene on the physical facts. This entails that the physical facts necessitated facts about consciousness. But it seems imaginable, and so possible, that the physical facts might be as they are and yet the facts about consciousness be different. But if that is so, physicalism is false. The question of how to respond to this argument (and similar arguments) is one of the main topics of philosophy of mind today, particularly in the areas of philosophy of mind that border on consciousness studies more broadly. The issues are very much open, not least because of their connection with the thesis of physicalism, and the unclarities of that thesis.

DANIEL STOLJAR

Broad, C. D. (1925). *The Mind and Its Place in Nature.*
Carnap, R. (1932/1959). 'Psychology in physical language.' In Ayer, A. J. (ed.) *Logical Postivism.*
Chalmers, D. (1996). *The Conscious Mind.*
Fodor, J. A. (1987). *Psychosemanitics.*
Hempel, C. (1969). 'Reduction: ontological and linguistic facets'. In Morgenbesser, S. et al. (eds) *Philosophy, Science and Method: Essays in Honour of Ernest Nagel.*
Jackson, F. (1982). 'Epiphenomenal qualia'. *Philosophical Quarterly*, 32.
Kim, J. (1998). *Mind in a Physical World.*
Kripke, S. (1980). *Naming and Necessity.*
—— (1982). *Wittgenstein on Rules and Private Language: an Elementary Exposition.*
Lewis, D. (1994). 'Reduction of mind'. In Guttenplan, S. (ed.) *A Companion to the Philosophy of Mind.*
Nagel, T. (1974). 'What is it like to be a bat'. *Philosophical Review*, 4.
Neurath, O. (1931/1983). 'Physicalism: the philosophy of the Vienna Circle'. In Cohen, R. S. and Neurath, M. (eds), *Philosophical Papers 1913–1946.*
Papineau, D. (2002). 'The rise of physicalism'. In Gillet, G. and Loewer, B. (eds) *Physicalism and Its Discontents.*
Putnam, H. (1975). 'Philosophy and our mental life'. In Putnam, H. *Mind, Language and Reality: Philosophical Papers*, Vol. 2.
Quine, W. V. (1960). *Word and Object.*
Smart, J. J. C. (1959). 'Sensations and brain processes'. *Philosophical Review*, 68.

pineal gland The pineal gland—so named on account of its pinecone shape—was known to the physicians of antiquity, but it became famous beyond medicine only with Descartes's claim that it was the seat of the soul—the point of interaction between the mind and the brain. He accorded this honour to the pineal gland because it is the only organ in the brain that does not enjoy hemispheric duplication. Since Descartes regarded the soul as simple and indivisible (indeed, non-spatial), he thought it only natural that the conduit between mind and matter should also be undivided—although just how a non-spatial soul could interact with a spatially extended organ was left as a puzzle for future generations of graduate students. Although inventive, Descartes' speculations have not withstood the test of time, and the consensus is that the pineal gland has more to do with the generation of melatonin and the regulation of sleep, temperature, and circadian rhythms than it does with conducting commerce between the body and the mind.

TIM BAYNE

Macchi, M. M. and Bruce, J. N. (2004). 'Human pineal physiology and functional significance of melatonin'. *Frontiers in Neuroendocrinology*, 25.

Zenner, C. (1985). 'Theories of pineal function from classical antiquity to 1900: a history'. In Reiter, R. J. (ed.) *Pineal Research Reviews III*.

positron emission tomography (PET) See FUNCTIONAL BRAIN IMAGING

posterior cingulate See BRAIN

prefrontal cortex See FRONTAL CORTEX

priming One of the scientific approaches developed to investigate consciousness consists in making an exhaustive inventory of the psychological processes that can proceed unconsciously, in order to isolate, by contrast, those that are exclusively restricted to conscious cognition. Within this perspective psychologists devised specific tools to probe unconscious mental processes. Priming is one of the most influential and productive of these tools. Although the priming approach was first devised by psychologists, it now benefits from the powerful combination of behavioural and neurophysiological measures.

1. A tool to probe unconscious cognitive processes
2. Scope of unconscious priming effects
3. Limits of unconscious priming effects
4. Perspectives

1. A tool to probe unconscious cognitive processes

Schvaneveldt and Meyer (1971) performed the first priming experiment using a lexical decision task: on each trial, two chains of letters were simultaneously presented and subjects had to answer 'yes' only if both stimuli were real words. The crucial result was the observation that subjects responded faster to pairs of commonly associated real words (e.g. nurse–doctor) than to unrelated pairs (e.g. bread–doctor). Although the semantic relation between the two words was not explicitly relevant to the task, subjects seemed to implicitly extract this information. The experimental paradigm was then modified in two ways to allow a better assessment of the implicit nature of this process: first, task instructions focused only on one of the two stimuli (e.g. 'Is the target stimulus a real word?'), while the other stimulus (*prime stimulus*) was no longer relevant to the task. Second, the two stimuli were temporally separated, the prime stimulus being presented before the target stimulus in most studies. In this way, any evidence of an influence of the prime–target relationship on responses to the target would demonstrate that implicit processing of the first stimulus occurred and that it *primed* the explicit processing of the target. Many studies using a large range of visual stimuli—not restricted to words—reported such implicit effects. However, such results cannot univocally be interpreted as forms of unconscious processing. Indeed, the non-relevant primes were nevertheless consciously perceptible and subjects may have paid attention to them, and/or could even have used them strategically, at least on some trials. A further step taken in the development of a powerful probe of unconscious cognitive processes consisted in preventing conscious perception of the prime stimuli. This was achieved by using visual *masking procedures to prevent conscious perception of primes. Basically, when the prime is presented for a few tens of milliseconds in between forward and backward mask stimuli, subjects fail to consciously report its presence or identity. This last modification was designed by Marcel (1983), in a seminal study in which he reported an impact of semantic attributes of masked prime words on the conscious processing of unmasked target words. Since then, visual masked priming paradigms still use the same general procedure, but major improvements in assessing the absence of conscious prime perception have been developed in response to major criticisms. A regular priming study now combines both *subjective (conscious reports relative to prime presence, prime visibility, prime identity or category, etc.) and *objective (*signal detection theory parameters such as d′ or indexes) measures to verify the absence of conscious perception of the prime stimuli.

We now focus on the most important properties of unconscious cognitive processes, as revealed through use of visual masked priming paradigms since the 1970s, across different types of experimental research. These results can be grouped in two categories: the scope and limits of unconscious priming effects.

2. Scope of unconscious priming effects

The hierarchical models of neurological evolution proposed in the late 19th century by Herbert Spencer (1820–1903) and J. Hughlings Jackson (1835–1911) shaped the influential conception of unconscious mental life as necessarily primitive, low-level, and restricted to automatic and reflex functions. Masked priming research contributed to a revolutionary transformation of this intellectual landscape. Granted that naturalistic masked visual stimuli such as faces, animals, or emotionally competent stimuli do unconsciously prime behavioural performance and affect neural measures, this seems to also be the case for far more complex and abstract symbolic stimuli such as numbers or words. The story of unconscious semantic processing of masked words nicely illustrates the dialectical mode inherent to research in that field of cognitive psychology. Marcel (1983) first reported evidence for non-conscious access to word semantics in the masked priming paradigm. However, potentially serious flaws in the methodology used to assess the absence of conscious perception of masked words invalidated or qualified most of the first experimental reports (Holender 1986). Subsequently, a set of studies reported behavioural and *functional brain imaging evidence for semantic processing of numbers and words under conditions of demonstrable lack of consciousness of the primes (Greenwald 1996, Dehaene et al. 1998). Again, however, follow-up publications suggested that those non-conscious semantic effects might be entirely accounted for by direct motor specification, i.e. stimulus–response processes by-passing semantic analysis (Abrams and Greenwald 2000). For instance, Abrams and Greenwald asked subjects to evaluate the valence of consciously seen target words as positive or negative. The prior presentation of a masked word, whose valence could be congruent or incongruent with the upcoming target, was used to facilitate or interfere with the subjects' response. This seemed to prove that the masked prime was categorized semantically as positive or negative. Crucially, however, Abrams and Greenwald went on to demonstrate that the priming effect was entirely due to the fact that the prime words were also presented as conscious targets in other trials. When they examined generalization to novel primes that were never seen consciously, priming was obtained only inasmuch as some of their letter fragments matched those of a word from the target list. For instance, after repeated conscious classification of the words 'smut' and 'bile' as negative, the subliminal prime 'smile' primed the negative response, not the positive one. This result suggests that the priming effect, in this particular situation, was not due to a subliminal access to semantics. Rather, subjects had learned to respond rapidly to fragments of the target strings with specific left or right key presses, and this sensorimotor learning generalized to other primes made of the same fragments. Subsequently, a set of convincing reports demonstrated non-conscious semantic processing, including generalization to novel primes, for masked number words (e.g. Naccache and Dehaene 2001a). Beyond this issue of unconscious semantic processing, a set of masked priming studies demonstrated that unconscious processing of masked words and numbers extended to various levels of representation: masked priming effects include visual, morphological, orthographical, and phonological priming codes. Taken together, these results show that masked primes can reach a large variety of representational levels.

In line with this psychological diversity, the recent combination of priming paradigms and functional brain imaging tools revealed a variety of neural *correlates of these unconscious cognitive processes. We will focus in particular on the 'repetition suppression' or 'adaptation' paradigms that proved to be extremely sensitive to detect and define masked priming effects. This approach combines the logic of psychological priming experiments with the recently discovered neurophysiological phenomenon of *repetition suppression* (RS), which provides a possible neural correlate of priming. RS was first described by Desimone and colleagues in *single-cell recordings in the monkey inferotemporal cortex (Miller et al. 1991). They showed that when the same visual stimulus was repeated, neuronal activity evoked in some of the cells was reduced. Importantly, this group also demonstrated that repeating the same object, but changing some stimulation parameter such as its retinal location or its size, still led to a similar reduction in activity. Subsequently, several brain imaging priming experiments in humans, in which subjects were exposed to a prime and then to a target stimulus, reported a decrease in neural activity in many different brain regions, such as occipitotemporal, insular, parietal, prefrontal cortices, and thalamus and basal ganglia structures. RS thus appears to be a general cerebral phenomenon related to neural coding specificity. Examining the conditions which lead to RS using functional brain imaging provides a general method of exploring the neural code in humans. The general logic is first, to isolate a brain area in which repetition of the same exact task conditions leads to RS; second, to then vary the nature of the prime–target relation in order to identify which coding variations are relevant and which are not relevant to obtain the effect. Several previous studies illustrate the value of the priming method, but also underline various important methodological issues. Grill-Spector and colleagues first used the priming method to investigate object recognition processes. Capitalizing on previous work on the role of lateral occipital cortex (LOC) in visual object recognition, they explored the invariance of the neural code in this area using an experimental design based on the fMRI equivalent of RS, named *fMRI adaptation* (Grill-Spector et al. 1999). In a first experiment they presented subjects with blocks of 32 pictures with a variable number of image repetitions and found a reliable decrease in neural activity in LOC when the number of image repetitions increased. They then examined the invariance of this RS phenomenon with regards to variations in object size and position. This led them to distinguish two sub-regions in LOC, a posterior area that showed little or no RS in blocks where images were presented with a variable size or position and a more anterior area where RS persisted across large variations of these parameters. The priming method is greatly improved by adopting an event-related design, in which repeated and non-repeated trials are randomly intermixed. Still, a possible limitation of this study lies in the fact that subjects could have become aware of the presence of word repetitions and could have developed strategies to take advantage of them. These methodological remarks help to define the desirable features of a priming paradigm in which a decrease in a neurophysiological response, if observed, can only be attributed to RS and therefore to properties of the local neural code. Naccache and Dehaene (2001b) proposed using the following strategy: every experimental trial consists of presentation of both a prime and a target. Primes are masked and are not consciously perceived. Subjects perform a constant task on the target throughout the experiment. The relationship between prime and target is varied randomly from trial to trial, thus preventing subjects from shifting their strategy or their attention in advance. In matched subsets of trials, the same primes and the same targets are used, while only their relationship is varied. This can be achieved by using a factorial 2×2 design in which the same stimuli *s1* and *s2* serve both as primes and as targets, thus defining four prime–target pairs: two repeated ones (*s1–s1* and *s2–s2*) and two non-repeated ones (*s1–s2* and *s2–s1*). This design prevents any differential activation to the individual stimuli *s1* and *s2* from contaminating the results. Note that the observation of repetition enhancement rather than suppression does not in itself limit the use of the priming method. Enhancement effects, like suppression effects, can be submitted to priming-based experiments in order to study the level of coding at which they occur (Henson et al. 2000). Using this priming method, an abstract representation of number was detected in the intraparietal sulci as a correlate of repetition priming unaffected by visual format of the numbers (Naccache and Dehaene 2001b). Applied to exploring masked words repetition effects, this method revealed that a physical repetition behavioural priming effect was associated to RS within the occipital cortex, while a more abstract behavioural repetition priming effect unaffected by letter case correlated with RS within the left visual cortex (visual word form area; Dehaene et al. 2001, Devlin et al. 2004).

In the light of these behavioural and brain-imaging studies, it therefore appears that, at present, we cannot easily establish a strict limitation of unconscious processes in terms of representational level and neural locus. Priming effects may involve low-level visual features up to the most abstract forms of visual object representations. Similarly to the diversity of unconscious cognitive representations, neurophysiological recordings of the correlates of visual masked priming effects have been conclusive in almost all neural structures of the visual system. Depending on presentation condition and stimulus type, masked primes may affect the colliculus-mediated subcortical pathway, but they can also enter the geniculate pathway up to occipitotemporal and occipitoparietal regions. Several studies revealed an impact of masked primes in structures related to motor response such as the frontal eye field, supplementary motor area, primary motor cortices, and basal ganglia. Recent studies even reported correlates of the processing of masked primes in small regions of the anterior cingulate and orbitofrontal cortices. It is highly probable that each of the multiple forms of behavioural priming effects might be mapped onto a specific set of neural correlates.

Until recently, most of the traditional cognitive psychology theories have postulated that unconscious processes were necessarily automatic and modular. One of the fundamental criteria of both *automaticity and modular processing is independence from top-down controlled processes. Naccache et al. (2002) first reported strong evidence for a clear dependence of masked priming effects on top-down temporal attention. Several reports replicated and extended this finding to other forms of top-down processes such as endogenous spatial attention, stimulus set, and task instructions. Taken together, these results univocally demonstrate that some forms of unconscious processing are highly sensitive to conscious influences, and strengthen the need for a theoretical revision of the concept of automaticity.

3. Limits of unconscious priming effects

In sharp contrast to their amazingly rich representational content, all unconscious representations probed through masked priming studies share a common limitation: they are short-lived. Greenwald (1996) demonstrated that masked words primed the emotional categorization of target words only at short *stimulus onset asynchronies* (SOAs). As soon as the SOA exceeded 100 ms, primes had no impact on target processing, thereby revealing that unconscious representations at work in short SOAs were no longer active. This crucial result has been replicated many times, and is a cornerstone of unconscious representations. Any long-term effect of masked stimuli over hours, days, or even weeks from stimulus presentation—such as reported in the *mere exposure effect*—is likely to be attributed to neural architecture modifications (synaptic weights, fibre lengths, synaptic contacts) rather than to the active maintenance of unconscious representations.

In spite of being largely influenced by ongoing conscious strategies, intentions and endogenous attention, masked priming effects have a second important limitation in addition to their ultra-short lifespan, i.e. a total inability to exert strategic control. Two seminal experiments nicely illustrate this fundamental result. Merikle et al. (1995) designed a *Stroop paradigm in which masked or unmasked primes predicted target identity. They found that only unmasked visible primes could be used by subjects to generate an original strategy taking advantage of this relevant information and reversing spontaneous priming effects. For masked prime blocks of trials, subjects were unable to use this strategic information and masked priming effects were reduced to automatic associations irrelevant to the current task. More recently, Kunde (2003) showed that a consciously perceived unmasked prime could induce a clear modification of executive control on a single-trial basis, thus affecting subjects' performance on the next trial. Whenever an unmasked prime elicited a response incongruent to the one associated with the upcoming target, subjects increased their level of executive control, as evidenced by a slowing of reaction time and a decrease of priming effect (*Gratton effect*). Crucially, a masked prime could not elicit such a strategical effect on the next trial, while it could still benefit from this top-down effect generated by a consciously perceived unmasked prime on the previous trial.

4. Perspectives

Among the most promising perspectives of priming studies, three deserve special emphasis. First, the elucidation of the neural correlates of the behavioural effects summarized above is the focus of many efforts since the discovery of repetition suppression effects by Miller and Desimone at the single-neuron level. This combination of neurophysiology and behavioural priming paradigms nicely illustrates how neuroscience can help us go beyond raw behavioural measures (such as reaction time) sensitive to the net outcome of many distinct processes, in order to identify the psychological fate of masked primes more specifically. Second, the subtle interplay of conscious top-down processes and unconscious representations should constitute a promising field of research: which of the unconscious processes are sensitive to conscious effects? How are these modulations mediated? Finally, the recent use of auditory masking procedures to probe unconscious auditory representations provides a potential tool to investigate multisensory and *cross-modal unconscious representations through priming paradigms.

See also COGNITION, UNCONSIOUS; GLOBAL WORKSPACE THEORY; MASKING, VISUAL; PERCEPTION; REPRESENTATION

LIONEL NACCACHE

Abrams, R. L. and Greenwald, A. G. (2000). 'Parts outweigh the whole (word) in unconscious analysis of meaning'. *Psychological Science*, 11.

Dehaene, S., Naccache, L. et al. (1998). 'Imaging unconscious semantic priming'. *Nature*, 395(6702).

——, —— et al. (2001). 'Cerebral mechanisms of word masking and unconscious repetition priming'. *Nature Neuroscience*, 4.

Devlin, J. T., Jamison, H. L. et al. (2004). 'Morphology and the internal structure of words'. *Proceedings of the National Academy of Sciences of the USA*, 101.

Greenwald, A. G. (1996). 'Three cognitive markers of unconscious semantic activation'. *Science*, 273.

Grill-Spector, K., Kushnir, T. et al. (1999). 'Differential processing of objects under various viewing conditions in the human lateral occipital complex'. *Neuron*, 24.

Henson, R., Shallice, T. et al. (2000). 'Neuroimaging evidence for dissociable forms of repetition priming.' *Science* 287(5456): 1269–72.

Holender, D. (1986). 'Semantic activation without conscious identification in dichotic listening, parafoveal vision, and visual masking: a survey and appraisal'. *Behavioral and Brain Sciences*, 9.

Kunde, W. (2003). 'Sequential modulations of stimulus-response correspondence effects depend on awareness of response conflict'. *Psychonomic Bulletin and Review*, 10.

Marcel, A. J. (1983). 'Conscious and unconscious perception: experiments on visual masking and word recognition'. *Cognitive Psychology*, 15.

Merikle, P. M., Joordens, S. et al. (1995). 'Measuring the relative magnitude of unconscious influences'. *Consciousness and Cognition*, 4.

Meyer, D. E. and Schvaneveldt, R. W. (1971). 'Facilitation in recognizing pairs of words: evidence of a dependence between retrieval operations'. *Journal of Experimental Psychology*, 90.

Miller, E. K., Li, L., et al. (1991). 'A neural mechanism for working and recognition memory in inferior temporal cortex'. *Science*, 254.

Naccache, L., Blandin, E. et al. (2002). 'Unconscious masked priming depends on temporal attention'. *Psychological Science*, 13.

—— and Dehaene, S. (2001a). 'Unconscious semantic priming extends to novel unseen stimuli.' *Cognition*, 80.

—— —— (2001b). 'The priming method: imaging unconscious repetition priming reveals an abstract representation of number in the parietal lobes.' *Cerebral Cortex*, 11.

privileged access

See INTROSPECTION

problem of other minds

See OTHER MINDS

property dualism See DUALISM

proprioception Though Charles Bell (1774–1842) first described the concept of proprioception, it was Charles Sherrington (1857–1952) who coined the word, which means [bodily] self-awareness. Though conventionally limited to peripheral originating movement and position sensation, a more expansive definition might include visual proprioception (visual information about limb movement, etc.), and other peripherally originating sensations like warmth, fatigue and affiliative or affective touch.

The peripheral receptors underpinning proprioception include muscle spindles and tendon organs informing about limb and body position, and some cutaneous receptors which inform about movement in the face and the hand. They project in the large myelinated sensory nerves and travel via the dorsal column nuclei–medial lemniscus system to the sensory cortex and beyond. Smaller myelinated and unmyelinated nerve fibres, travelling in the spinothalamic tract, underpin the perceptions of fatigue, warmth, and affective touch.

Bell described his 'muscle sense' as the sixth sense, but was very aware that it was often not perceived at all. 'We stand by so fine an exercise of this power, and the muscles from habit directed with so much precision, that we do not know how we stand' (Bell 1833). When the body does what we ask it can appear phenomenologically absent, bringing itself to attention only when the unexpected occurs, or during disease or when the movement is difficult. Though much of the information about movement is fed into the brain at a level below conscious awareness, our perception of movement can be demonstrated by experiments in which joints are moved passively and then, when our attention is focused, we can detect very small movements.

Proprioception can be reduced or removed by a number of pathologies. Diseases of nerve fibres usually involve all fibre types. Selective loss of large fibres alone, affecting touch and proprioception, occurs in less than 5% or so of generalized neuropathies. It is seen in two types of condition. Some toxic agents affect large fibres selectively, e.g. cisplatin and vitamin B_6 toxicity, Friedreich's ataxia, and vitamin E deficiency. In the second group an immune reaction targets the large-fibre nerve's cell bodies close to the cord in the dorsal root ganglia. This appears in some cancers, IgM neuropathy, Sjögren's syndrome, and acute sensory neuronopathy.

The onset of proprioceptive loss can be slow, as in Sjögren's syndrome, or acute and severe, with all large sensory nerve cells being destroyed in days, as in the acute sensory neuronopathy syndrome. In most large-fibre neuropathies cutaneous light touch sensory loss predominates, but in some neuronopathy syndromes uncertain, tremulous movement—ataxia—is the main and presenting symptom, suggesting a selective loss of proprioceptive afferents. Spinal cord damage can also lead to proprioceptive loss, with syphilis being historically important. Strokes, within the thalamus or sensory cortex, can also lead to loss of movement and position sense and of touch.

Although we may think that we know something of blindness, by closing our eyes, the loss of proprioception or touch is not usually imagined. Recently, cases of profound proprioceptive loss have emerged. Studies of these subjects have included both empirical neuroscience and subjective first-person accounts of living without proprioception.

Rothwell et al. (1982) studied a subject with a severe peripheral pansensory neuropathy, with loss of pain and temperature, light touch, and proprioception some months previously. His motor power was almost unaffected. He could produce a wide range of individual finger movements, move his thumb accurately through different distances at different speeds, and produce different levels of force with the thumb. But his hands were relatively useless to him in daily life; he could not grasp a pen to write, fasten his shirt buttons, or hold a cup in one hand. They concluded that his difficulties lay in an inability to sustain constant levels of muscle contraction without visual feedback for more than 1–2 s, and an inability to maintain longer sequences of motor programmes without vision.

Other subjects have been studied with the acute sensory neuronopathy syndrome with complete selective loss of proprioception and cutaneous light touch. G. L. and I. W. are the most studied; each was in their early adult life when affected, and each has now been studied for over 30 years, without evidence of recovery of peripheral nerves. These two individuals show important similarities and intriguing differences in their functional recovery.

G. L., and another subject C. F., have both been largely wheelchair-bound since their illness. Though they can stand and walk with support, walking independently is too difficult. They also remain ataxic, with movements of the arms and hands unsteady and shaky. In contrast, I. W. is able to walk and live independently and does not show ataxia. There are several reasons for these differences. C. F. was 60 when he had the neuronopathy, I. W. 19; G. L. is affected from the lower face down, so that she has no awareness of neck position, whereas I. W. is affected from below the neck (nearly half of the muscle spindles in the body are in the neck, to allow stability of the head, eyes, and vestibular apparatus). So G. L. has to think about maintaining her head position as well as her body posture. Lastly, I. W. was able to spend 17 months in rehabilitation, whereas G. L. had a young family to care for. During that period I. W. spent hours each day thinking about how to dress, feed himself, stand, and walk and seems to have developed an ability to use feed-forward motor programmes which free him from the need to use slow visual feedback to guide movement. These subjects' response to their proprioceptive loss has to be placed not only in a neurological context but also a personal, social one.

Though these cases reveal proprioception underpinning the coordination and control of movement, subjectively the immediate consequence of its loss for IW was a sense of disembodiment (Cole 1995). He took several weeks to realize that he could control movement by looking at and thinking about the moving part. Now, 30 years later, he describes his relation with his body as being normal, *his* normal. G. L. has described herself as being like the captain of a ship, ordering—and acting on—her body as though at one remove.

For I. W., still, most movements require calculation and preparation. Often he will run through movements in his mind before making them, visualizing his solution. Doing something one day does not mean he will be able to do it the next. *Automaticity of movement remains impossible, except possibly for some gestures. A head cold forces him to bed, unable to think enough to coordinate movement. Having said that, he has had some return of—or linking to—previous motor programmes. Walking, on a well-lit, level surface without wind or people to jostle him, now requires round 50% of his mental concentration whereas at first it took 100%. But he still cannot daydream when walking. There are movements that are beyond his ingenuity. He cannot move without light for visual supervision; active touch is impossible, so he cannot get change out of his pocket, and fast complex movements are also impossible; he can walk but not run.

Subjects with sensory neuronopathy still have intact small sensory fibres. Olausson et al. (2002) have found, in both G. L. and I. W., that slow brushing of the hairy skin of the forearm, though leading to no identifiable touch sensation, leads to a sensation of pleasure and to activation of insular cortex without activation of sensory cortex. They ascribe this to a low-threshold unmyelinated CT fibre system, which may underlie some of the pleasure of caress and, in non-human primates, grooming. A similar proprioceptive system remains to be described (but see Cole and Montero 2007).

The role of proprioception in *consciousness is difficult to approach. In theories that consider consciousness an emergent 'bottom-up' phenomenon, proprioception has been considered to make an important contribution at a prelinguistic level to awareness by several workers. Others consider consciousness to have arisen in a more social top-down way, to predict others' behaviour, etc. Then, awareness of movement and position sense might be used to embody intention and so calibrate self. Tsakiris and Haggard (2005) discuss the relations between the acting self and the sensory self. They suggest that, though normally the two are perceived inseparably, intentional action has both a perceptual feel and a modulation of sensory perception of the body which embodies intention and calibrates self. Proprioception could contribute to this both within a movement and an affective dimension.

JONATHAN COLE

Bell, C. (1833/1979). *The Hand: Its Mechanism and Vital Endowments as Evincing Design.*

Cole, J. (1995). *Pride and a Daily Marathon.*

—— and Montero, B. (2007). 'Affective proprioception'. *Janus Head*, 9.

Olausson, H., Lamarre, Y., Backlund, H., et al. (2002). 'Unmyelinated tactile afferents signal touch and project to insular cortex'. *Nature Neuroscience*, 5.

Rothwell, J. C., Day, B. L., Obeso, J. A. et al. (1982). 'Manual motor performance in a deafferented man'. *Brain*, 105.

Tsakiris, M. and Haggard, P. (2005). 'Experimenting with the acting self.' *Cognitive Neuropsychology*, 22.

protocol analysis Protocol analysis is a research method in which verbal reports are elicited from participants and transcribed for qualitative and/or quantitative analysis. It can be used in isolation or jointly with the collection of other process data such as eye movements or keystrokes on a keyboard.

With *concurrent protocols*, participants are requested to think aloud when carrying out a task, for example when solving a problem in physics or in logic, with the explicit instructions to report everything that comes to their mind but not to describe or explain their thoughts. This technique provides useful information with tasks that have a certain duration, say at least a few dozen seconds, but is more limited with visuospatial tasks or tasks that are of short duration. In these cases researchers often use *retrospective* protocols, where participants are asked to report, after completing a task, the thoughts and/or actions that occurred when carrying out the task. For example, participants may be asked first to carry out an arithmetic problem, and then to report the processes that took place. Both concurrent and retrospective protocols must carefully be distinguished from *introspection, where participants, often trained with this purpose in mind, are asked to describe their mental states and theorize about them.

Duncker (1935/1945) was one of the first psychologists to use concurrent protocols, but perhaps the first really influential use of this technique was provided by De

Groot (1946/1965) in his analysis of chess players' thinking processes. De Groot identified an important weakness of protocol analysis; namely, that protocols are often incomplete. There are several reasons for this: some aspects of the thought process do not reach the threshold of awareness; conscious thoughts may be too fast to be verbalized; some thoughts cannot be immediately verbalized; and, finally, participants may suppress some steps of the thought process, e.g. to avoid the embarrassment of reporting mistakes in their thinking. In addition, the reporting of concurrent thoughts may slow down the thinking process itself. In spite of these deficiencies, De Groot concluded that protocols often provide a satisfactory outline of the macro-structure of the thought process, and that their degree of completeness may be assessed by asking participants to which extent the protocol faithfully reproduces this process.

Nisbett and Wilson (1977) argued that retrospective protocols suffer from a number of weaknesses, including the use of general knowledge to fill in gaps in memory, rationalization, and even lack of awareness of critical stimuli. It should be noted that the severity of these weaknesses is affected by the way reports are elicited, and increases with the time lag between the thoughts and their report.

Using Newell and Simon's (1972) information-processing framework, Ericsson and Simon (1980, 1993) provided an extensive discussion of the advantages and disadvantages offered by verbal protocols. The originality of their approach is to validate their analysis with a theoretical model that clearly specifies when protocols will be reliable and when they will not. Their starting point is that people are conscious of only those things that are stored in short-term *memory (STM). When this information is verbal in nature, the action of providing verbal protocols simply amplifies information that is already in STM. When information is non-verbal, talking aloud adds a recoding stage, which slows the process down and introduces translation errors. A consequence of this theory is that retrospective protocols suffer from the fact that information in not in STM any more, in particular when recall occurs a long time after completing the task. Ericsson and Simon's information-processing model also postulates that encoding unfamiliar information into long-term memory (LTM) requires several seconds, which means that only a subset of the thoughts having taken place during the task will be encoded in LTM. Similarly, asking participants to provide explanations of their behaviour requires them to use information that was never in STM, and thus offers little reliability. Hence, retrospective protocols can be recommended only when they are taken a few seconds after the task and when it is plausible to assume that STM cues will enable access to information stored in LTM.

On the basis of their theoretical analysis, Ericsson and Simon offered practical advice as to how collect reliable protocols. Recommendations include giving warm-up tasks to the participants and sitting behind the participants to avoid contaminating the protocols with social interactions. The analysis of verbal protocols is notoriously complex and time consuming, and programs have been developed to facilitate this process. For example, Bhaskar and Simon (1977) describe SAPA, a semi-automatic protocol coding system used in their study of problem solving in thermodynamics.

Verbal protocols have sometimes been used in combination with other process data such as eye movements. For example, Carpenter et al. (1990) used concurrent protocols when participants solved the Raven's Progressive Matrices, a test of intelligence. This and similar studies suggest that the thought contents, as reported verbally in the concurrent protocols, correspond well with the eye-movement data. Similarly, De Groot and Gobet (1996) recorded eye movements in combination with retrospective protocols. Chess players' eye movements were recorded when they looked at a position for five seconds; immediately after, the players attempted to recall where they had focused their attention during those five seconds. Results indicated a fair amount of individual differences, with some players having a remarkable memory of their eye movements, and others displaying poor recollection. An interesting result with respect to the study of consciousness was that, after they had fixated the same square twice or more, players tended to mention only the first fixation in their protocol. This is similar to the *Ranschburg effect* identified in serial recall experiments, where people have difficulty in recalling items that are repeated in the list of stimuli to memorize.

Nowadays, mainstream cognitive psychology has accepted the use of concurrent protocols, but is still reticent about the use of retrospective protocols or introspection. Even critiques of the methodology (e.g. Wilson 1994) agree that concurrent protocols offer a valid means for studying the contents of consciousness. Such protocols offer a high density of micro-data and make it possible to capture the dynamics of sequences of mental states. It is also generally admitted that data gathered from concurrent protocols can be used as any other data to test theories, and some (symbolic) computational process models have in fact been able to reproduce the contents of verbal protocols in great detail (e.g. Newell and Simon 1972).

However, there is also agreement that verbal protocols are ill-suited for studying non-conscious information. In addition, as anticipated by De Groot, there remains the issue of what is missing from the protocols—that is, to what extent non-conscious information plays a key role in the tasks usually studied with this methodology. There is little doubt that such information affects behaviour, even in problem-solving tasks where information is often considered as fairly conscious, as shown for example by the substantial amount of experimental evidence that has been collected in the last decades on subliminal *priming, automatization, and implicit *learning.

Taking into account these strengths and weaknesses, the conclusion is that verbal protocols can offer very useful information for testing theories of human cognition, and that they are best used in conjunction with other methods (either experimental or computational) that ensure cross-validation.

FERNAND GOBET

Bhaskar, R. and Simon, H. A. (1977). 'Problem solving in semantically rich domains: An example from engineering thermodynamics'. *Cognitive Science*, 1.

Carpenter, P. A., Just, M. A., and Shell, P. (1990). 'What one intelligence test measures: A theoretical account of the processing in the Raven progressive matrices test'. *Psychological Review*, 97.

De Groot, A. D. (1946/1965). *Thought and Choice in Chess*.

—— and Gobet, F. (1996). *Perception and Memory in Chess: Heuristics of the Professional Eye*.

Duncker, K. (1935/1945). 'On problem solving'. *Psychological Monographs*, 58.

Ericsson, K. A. and Simon, H. A. (1980). 'Verbal reports as data'. *Psychological Review*, 87.

—— —— (1993). *Protocol Analysis: Verbal Reports as Data*, 2nd edn.

Newell, A. and Simon, H. A. (1972). *Human Problem Solving*.

Nisbett, R. E. and Wilson, T. D. (1977). 'Telling more than we know: verbal reports on mental processes'. *Psychological Review*, 84.

Wilson, T. D. (1994). 'The proper protocol—validity and completeness of verbal reports'. *Psychological Science*, 5.

psychedelic drugs See HALLUCINOGENIC DRUGS

psychogenic fugue See DISSOCIATIVE IDENTITY DISORDER

psychology and the study of consciousness

Views of consciousness within psychology have been animated by several rather grand issues. Most fundamentally, is there a legitimate place for consciousness in the science? If so, are symbolic representations carried by conscious or unconscious states, or both? Are there fully formed and intelligent processes both within and outside consciousness? And can conscious states be causal? Historically and today, the most fundamental meta-theoretical approaches to psychology—the general formulations that imply more specific theories of domains—have taken strong positions on these questions; and those approaches have motivated theory, experiments, and methodological analyses in the more specific research literatures examined in this volume.

1. Historical background that framed the issues
2. The place of consciousness in modern meta-theories
3. Methodology for investigating consciousness
4. Research literatures

1. Historical background that framed the issues

These issues had their origin in a critical episode for the scientific study of consciousness—the establishment of a science of consciousness and the behaviourist rejection of consciousness as a proper subject matter for science.

Structuralism. For Edward B. Titchener (1867–1927), as for his Leipzig mentor Wilhelm Wundt (1832–1920), consciousness was the subject matter of the new science of psychology. The principal aims of the Titchenerian approach were (1) to analyse the structure of a conscious content into its component parts—the sensations, feelings, images, and perhaps imageless thoughts; (2) to determine the laws of their association; and (3) to identify its underlying neural substrate (today's neural *correlates of consciousness, NCC). This was to be a 'mental chemistry', and once we had a table of 'mental elements' we might write 'molecular' formulas for any phenomenal experience, from an insight to an apple-bite. Out of this came Titchener's (1898) *context theory* of meaning and the dimensions on which the elements of consciousness were to be arrayed.

Although Wundt (1896/1907) had earlier described three dimensions of emotion, his view of ideation as an 'apperceptive mass' and his volitional theory of attention went beyond Titchenerian structuralism. For Wundt, consciousness could yield a 'creative synthesis' of conscious elements; it could be causal.

Functionalism. On this view, the aim of psychology should be to understand the way mental activity, including *consciousness, functions in the life of the individual and even in the evolutionary order, e.g. Carr (1930). Functionalists opposed structuralism's analysis of mental contents as too static and its focus on the normal human adult as too narrow. Their position reflected James's (1890) classical *Principles of Psychology* and his theory of the *stream of consciousness, something that represents a variety of objects and relations and is constantly changing while maintaining its personal identity—as 'mine.' In a very real sense, William James (1842–1910) anticipated various subjects of current cognitive psychology, and he positioned them all in this stream of consciousness—attention, concepts, memory, discrimination, reasoning, emotions, and volition. It even included senses of self as the 'me' we know and the personal identity given by that continual sense of possession. With a strong infusion of Darwinian thinking, the University of Chicago and Columbia schools of functionalism came to see mental activity as representing the world in a way that permitted organisms to function more adaptively. Consciousness remained within the subject matter of the science, and it could function causally and symbolically within adaptive mental activity.

Gestalt psychology. It remained for the gestaltists, e.g. Koffka (1935/1963), to emphasize and experimentally examine the configural, or **Gestalt*, qualities of conscious states—most famously in their principles of perceptual organization, insightful learning, transposition effects, and productive thinking of various kinds. The 'whole' of an experience was said to be other than the sum of its parts. Here, too, there was a concern for the neural correlates of consciousness; in fact their general principle of 'psychophysical isomorphism' held that consciously experienced order in space was matched by a functional order of underlying brain processes.

Behaviorism. With the revolutionary emergence of behaviorism, consciousness was vigorously rejected as suitable subject for a science of psychology. As John B. Watson (1878–1958) put it in his Behaviorist Manifesto, 'This suggested elimination of states of consciousness as proper objects of investigation in themselves will remove the barrier from psychology which exists between it and the other sciences' (Watson 1913/1994:253). And why? As he explicitly claimed, reference to consciousness was simply reference to the 'soul' of theology. On a telephone model of the time, the brain was seen as essentially a switchboard for incoming stimuli and outgoing responses. The vocabulary of consciousness was to be redefined by reference to muscular states, and consciousness itself was to be dismissed from science as something non-material to be left to religion.

Clark Hull (1884–1952) developed an influential learning theory describing the relations of prior stimuli, drive states, and reinforcement to measures of behaviour, relations mediated by abstract *intervening variables*—studiously avoiding reference to phenomenal experience. And the famous *cognitive expectancies* and *cognitive maps* of Edward Chase Tolman (1886–1959) were specifically said to lie outside consciousness. The most influential learning theorists of the time shared the central behaviourist dictum, the irrelevance of consciousness to the science, and focused their research on non-linguistic animals unprepared to report anything to the contrary.

With B. F. Skinner (1904–90), whose *radical behaviourism* endures in variants today, 'thinking is behaving,' as he often wrote, but 'This does not mean . . . (and this is the heart of the argument) that what are introspectively observed are the causes of behavior . . . What are introspectively observed are certain collateral products of those histories' (Skinner 1974:17). Behaviour was viewed as under the control of the current environment as well as environmental and genetic histories, all through a brain inadequately accessible to science. And so the experimental enterprise was to determine the laws relating 'respondents' to prior stimuli and 'operants' to reinforcers and discriminative stimuli. What Skinner called 'the inner man' was dismissed from science.

The upshot. The theoretical aims of structuralism were too narrow, and the aims of the functionalists and gestaltists were largely bypassed by the rise of a zealous mainstream behaviourism. In the 1950s–1970s, experimental critiques successfully overturned stimulus–response behaviour theory in the cognitive mainstream. Mandler's (1975) important reminder that consciousness was respectable and probably necessary helped re-open an interest. But running through behaviourism, and continuing in some recent thinking, we see two underlying confusions of the theoretical with the metaphysical: To study and assign causal status to conscious states would grant them a non-material status and commit us to 'free will' in the sense of indeterminism—metaphysical positions generally viewed as unacceptable within the science. Alternatively today, we can place conscious states within theories with causal consequences and causal antecedents, theories entailing no commitment to metaphysical claims of 'free will' or non-material ontology. Theoretical claims may be empirically examined; metaphysical claims are not susceptible to empirical examination in science as we know it.

2. The place of consciousness in modern meta-theories

Although aspects of consciousness have increasingly become a focus of investigation today, we can see this history as influencing theoretical answers to key issues: what is conscious and what not, what is causal and what not, and how symbolic representations are carried. These modern meta-theories are considered here in the order in which they increasingly give roles to consciousness in mental activity.

Computational view. With the emergence of cognitive science and the *computational view of mind*, consciousness once more was given a—limited—place in science. On one part of the computer metaphor of *artificial intelligence (AI), mental activity, like the functioning of a computer, was said to be an instantiation of a universal *Turing machine, and so physical after all. On another part of that metaphor, the so-called *basic analogy*, cognition runs in the brain the way software runs in the hardware of a computer. On the dominant computational view, then, mind has three levels: brain activity, computational cognition, and consciousness—with consciousness acceptable for scientific study so long as it is viewed as an occasional but non-causal emergent of unconscious cognition (e.g. Jackendoff 1987). This has been a monistic emergence of the material from the material, not the dualistic *epiphenomenalism of earlier times on which a material brain was believed to exude a non-material and non-casual consciousness. On one variant of the view from philosophy, *eliminative materialism, psychology should be limited to cognitive-brain science with the vocabulary of consciousness—'belief', 'desire', 'intention'—dismissively consigned to folk psychology. Consciousness was back, in a way, but the real high-level symbolic activity lay outside consciousness: As Gardner (1987:383–4) put it, 'To my mind the major accomplishment of cognitive science has been the clear demonstration of the validity of positing a level of mental representation . . . but this form of representation does not involve processes of which the organism is in any way conscious or aware'.

Information processing view. In the thinking of some, this meta-theory has drawn strongly on the computational view. When Velmans (1991) asked 'Is human information processing consciousness?' his answer essentially was no. For many in the mainstream of psychology, however, consciousness is now given a more significant place, including an important role within causal sequences, by virtue of its identification with an attentional system, e.g. Posner (1994), or with even broader regions of a *working memory.

On another part of the computer metaphor, the organization of a mind's sub-systems is said to be like the organization of a computer's sub-systems—with an attentional sub-system now placed within a causally active working memory thought of as being like the computer's RAM (random access memory) Conscious *attentional states become the consequence of transduction of stimulus energy to a literal representation within a sensory system (input buffer), which in turn accesses long-term memory (hard drive) in activating attentional identification of objects and places and central control of attentional orientation. Consciousness as attention or working memory may then be causal in learning, remembering, thinking, and control of action.

Nevertheless, this systems view of the mind provides a place for symbolic representation not only in consciousness, but also within an unconscious pre-attentional system, a long-term memory system, and even within working memory for high-level intelligent computation such as problem solving. Learning is also said to 'encode' and 'store' symbolic representations in an unconscious long-term memory (LTM), and remembering and recognizing are said to come from 'retrieving' into attention, commonly viewed as an intelligent and unconscious process of search and identification. Indeed, on the information processing view, what has been most emphasized about conscious attention and working memory—from Donald Broadbent and Daniel Kahneman onward—has been limited selectivity, limited capacity for processing information, and limited ability to resist competition for its focus.

**Connectionism*. On its qualitative meta-theory, processing is said to occur within neural networks of units that collect and distribute parallel activation (facilitation or inhibition), to other interconnected units (feedback and feedforward)—most simply with input and output units, and sometimes with intermediate 'hidden' units. Those networks are said to provide for perceiving, learning, or remembering by cycling excitation until a relaxation, a stable state, of the system is achieved. Quantitative models of various domains—from *pattern associators* to *recurrent networks*—then employ specific learning rules, having in common the recursive adjustment of connection weights for that transmission of activation.

Until recently, little more was said of consciousness than that '. . . consciousness consists of a sequence of interpretations—each represented by a stable state of the system', a stability achieved when a processing episode within a neural network is completed (Rumelhart et al. 1986:39). But there has been significance in the view for those enduring conceptual questions about consciousness. O'Brien and Opie (1999) extend the view with their most fundamental claim that phenomenal experience is the exclusive 'vehicle' of symbolic representation, and this occurs when that stable state of a neural network is achieved. Furthermore, connectionism handles learning that establishes associative–activational connections among conscious states, and remembering and immediate judgement may be 'direct' rather than unconsciously deliberative—as in Gluck and Bower's (1988) classical analysis of diagnostic categorization. Inactive memories also become neural networks, not unconscious symbolic representations that have been 'stored' and may be 'retrieved'. Nevertheless, the meta-theory has not successfully handled other conscious phenomena such as higher order representation, sense of possession (agency), degree of belief, or propositions within deliberative processes of inference and decision.

**Global workspace view*. This view (Baars 1997) has probably had more influence than any other in reviving a focus on the scientific study of consciousness. Recognizing the influence of the information processing view, Baars (1997:ix) lays out a theatrical metaphor analogous to the computer metaphor—an analogy that has made the global workspace emphasis on consciousness more acceptable to many cognitivists. Elaborating its visual representation, he wrote that '. . . conscious contents are limited to a brightly lit spot of attention onstage, while the rest of the stage corresponds to immediate working memory. Behind the scenes are executive processes, including a director, and a great variety of contextual operators that shape conscious experience without themselves becoming conscious. In the audience are a vast array of intelligent unconscious mechanisms' (p. 43). The view has inspired extensive work on neural correlates of consciousness, and Baars has proposed that activity of the reticular formation as well as within primary projection areas is necessary for conscious perceptual experience. The view has also led to computational modelling of the theory. As with standard information-processing views, this approach postulates symbolic representation and intelligent computation both within and outside consciousness, operating independently but also exchanging information. But consciousness as a 'global workspace' is now viewed as having broad significance not only in providing 'global access' to what lies beyond, but also providing integrative functions—receiving the metaphoric spotlight at stage centre.

On this view, a central investigative strategy should then be one in which processes of the same general kind—for example, perception, learning, and memory—would be contrasted in conscious and unconscious forms, e.g. Baars (2003). The value of a general contrastive analysis has been widely accepted, and we can see this kind of analysis as leading to research and theory that bears on various current forms of those enduring questions that have occupied the study of consciousness, e.g. Tulving (1985), Cleeremans (2003), Dulany (2004), Block (2007): how should various contrastive findings be interpreted? A dissociation of consciousness and the unconscious? Or alternatively a dissociation within consciousness, between literal and identity awareness or between first-order and higher-order awareness? Or alternatively a dissociation between forms of mental episodes that are deliberative and associative–activational with roles for conscious contents in both? These alternative dissociations are consistent with the mentalistic meta-theory that follows.

Mentalism. This meta-theory has been formalized, e.g. Dulany (1997, 2004), and aspects of the view have been explicitly used, e.g. Carlson (2002), Perruchet and Vintner (2002). Similar but independent thinking has also motivated numerous studies of the roles of conscious states, e.g. Tulving (1985), as well as the many methodological and conceptual critiques of claims for unconscious representation in perception, learning, memory, and volition. On this mentalistic view, it is with conscious states that we symbolically represent the present in perception, a past in remembering, or some possible future in intentions and expectations—a unique capability providing the adaptive value of consciousness. A symbol is functionally specified as a mental content that may be used within propositions, may activate other symbols, and may participate in the control of actions that warrant that special proposition: 'This represents that'. Symbols in awareness can sometimes be only literal and ephemeral but are often an attentional identification of the thing as such.

Viewed more analytically, consciousness is not simply a system, but a succession of states, each the intersection of a set of values on useful and familiar variables: strength of mode (such as belief, perception, intention, fear), strength of a sense of possession, and relation of its symbolic contents to external events. Furthermore, mental episodes—of perceiving, learning, remembering, inferring, deciding—consist of conscious states interrelated by non-conscious operations, which are the brain processes interlinking those underlying the conscious states. Mental episodes may be *deliberative*, in which deliberative operations of inference or decision interrelate propositional forms (e.g. a belief *that* _____), or *evocative*, in which associative–activational operations interrelate sub-propositional forms (e.g. a sense *of* _____). Furthermore, just as first-order awareness may symbolically represent the external world, higher-order awareness may symbolically represent prior states as well as the existence and form of mental episodes—in degree and validity depending upon conditions for memory and inference. Conscious states, therefore, may enter into our causal theories.

There must also be non-conscious neural transducers yielding conscious states from stimulus energy and others yielding muscular action from prior conscious states. In the vernacular, we refer to 'memories', 'beliefs', and 'intentions' when outside consciousness, but in an inactive neural network they lack the functional specification of symbols. Furthermore, in learning, those neural networks are established by association or by deliberative construction, not by 'encoding' or 'storing'; and what is remembered is activated and constructed, not 'retrieved'.

3. Methodology for investigating consciousness

Conscious states can be and are experimentally manipulated in a variety of paradigms—as for example, when instructions in a decision experiment place probabilities and values on possible outcomes. Nevertheless, since subjects bring highly variable histories and capabilities to the laboratory, there is reason to believe that conscious states can often be more strongly related to subjective reports than to manipulations.

The classical introspection of the structuralists employed a *phenomenological data language*, one in which the investigator's data report refers to his/her own conscious states, and so investigator and subject became one—economically called the 'observer'. One reason it failed is that conscious experience is so variable given common stimulus conditions that a fundamental requirement for a data language could not be met: replicability under common experimental stimulus conditions. Today a subject's reports are commonly described in the investigator's *physicalistic data language*—a positive contribution of behaviourism, but in addition the subject's conscious states may then be described in the investigator's *theory language*.

As with any assessment, there are sensitivity and validity conditions to be met. The subject introspectively reports higher-order awareness of a prior conscious state. That representation must therefore be within the subject's memory and verbal limits, and the investigator's controls must minimize reporting bias. Failure to meet those conditions was another reason for the failure of classical introspection—and a common basis for methodological critiques of modern claims for unconscious perception or learning.

Furthermore, on evidence that attention to content is required for establishment of its memory, content of pre-attentive literal awareness may fail to be reported because it lacks the attentional conditions for establishment of its memory. Given these assessment validity conditions, it has been more difficult to establish the absence of a conscious state than reliable, and even strong, relations of strength of the state to other variables.

4. Research literatures

We can see these grander meta-theoretical and methodological views running through many current experimental examinations of conscious phenomena, some now accompanied by *functional brain imaging: Classical perception, our awareness of the current environment—a topic that largely escaped the behaviourists' purge. *Attention—what has been so central to cognitive psychology and the revival of an interest in consciousness. Recollections or only beliefs about a past—and whether correctly or falsely remembered. Source memory and reality monitoring. *Priming, with prime and its target in awareness. Descriptions of the self. Personal narratives. Hypotheses, images, intentions, and feelings. In all of these literatures, investigators examine *contents of consciousness. Many also ask what is conscious and what not in perception, learning, and remembering, bringing to bear contrasting theories and methodological analyses.

DONELSON E. DULANY

Baars, B. J. (1997). *In the Theater of Consciousness.*

—— (2003). 'Introduction: treating consciousness as a variable: the fading of taboo'. In Baars, B. J. et al. (eds) *Essential Sources in the Scientific Study of Consciousness.*

Block, N. (2007). 'Consciousness, accessibility, and the mesh between psychology and neuroscience'. *Behavioral and Brain Science*. 30.

Carlson, R. A. (2002). 'Conscious intentions in the control of skilled mental activity'. *Psychology of Learning and Motivation*, 41.

Carr, H. (1930). 'Functionalism'. In Murchison, C. (ed.) *Psychology of 1930.*

Cleeremans, A. (ed.) (2003) *The Unity of Consciousness: Binding, Integration, and Dissociation.*

Dulany, D. E. (1997). 'Consciousness in the explicit (deliberative) and implicit (evocative)'. In Cohen, J. and Schooler, J. (eds) *Scientific Approaches to Consciousness.*

—— (2004). 'Higher order representation in a mentalistic metatheory'. In Gennaro, R. J. (ed.) *Higher-order Thought Theories of Consciousness.*

Gardner, H. (1987). *The mind's new science: A history of the cognitive revolution.* New York: Basic Books.

Gluck, M. A. and Bower, G. H. (1988). 'From conditioning to category learning: An adaptive network model'. *Journal of Experimental Psychology: General*, 8.

Jackendoff, R. (1987). *Consciousness and the Computational Mind.*

James, W. (1890). *Principles of Psychology.*

Koffka, K. (1935/1963). *Principles of Gestalt Psychology.*

Mandler, G. (1975) 'Consciousness: respectable, useful, and probably necessary'. In Solso, R. (ed.) (2003). *Information Processing and Cognition: The Loyola Symposium.*

O'Brien, G. and Opie, J. (1999). 'A connectionist theory of phenomenal experience'. *Behavioral and Brain Sciences*, 22.

Perruchet, P. and Vinter, A. (2002). 'The self-organizing consciousness'. *Behavioral and Brain Science*, 25.

Posner, M. I. (1994). Attention: The mechanisms of consciousness. *Proceedings of the National Academy of Sciences of the USA*, 91.

Skinner, B. F. (1974). *About behaviorism.*

Rumelhart, D. E., Smolensky, P., McClelland, J. L., and Hinton, G. E. (1986). 'Schemata and sequential thought processes in PDP models'. In McClelland, J. L. and Rumelhart, D. E. (eds) *Parallel Distributed Processing*, Vol. 2.

Titchener, E. B. (1898). 'The postulates of a structural psychology'. *Philosophical Review*, 7.

Tulving, E. (1985). 'Memory and consciousness'. *Canadian Psychology*, 26.

Velmans, M. (1991). 'Is human information processing conscious?' *Behavioral and Brain Sciences*, 14.

Watson, J. B. (1913/1994). 'Psychology as the behaviorist views it'. *Psychological Review*, 20.

Wundt, W. (1896/1907). *Outline of Psychology*, transl. C. H. Judd.

Q

qualia We normally assume that for certain types of mental states, there is 'something it is like' to have them. We suppose, for example, that there is something it is like to see the blue headband of Vermeer's *Girl with a Pearl Earring* or to experience the pain of a dull headache. Contemporary discussions of qualia—that is, of the properties in virtue of which such things are true of some mental states (the qualitative states)—have tended to take such examples and such language ('something it is like' to have them) as definitive of the subject. Not all contemporary uses of 'qualia', however, can be understood in this way.

1. Qualia realism
2. Privileged access
3. The further-fact arguments
4. The problem of other minds
5. Meaning scepticism
6. Alternative approaches to the empirical study of qualia

1. Qualia realism

Some theorists, such as David Rosenthal, use the term in a broad sense that would allow for the existence of unconscious qualia. Others define the term so that only the non-representational properties of mental states count as qualitative properties. Consider a visual experience of two objects viewed at different distances that represents them (correctly) as being the same size. Such a visual experience is an intentional state in that it represents the world as being a certain way and thus has a certain *representational content that can be assessed for accuracy. In this it is normally thought to differ fundamentally from such mental states as pain that are supposed not to represent the world, but simply feel a certain way. But although the visual experience has representational properties in virtue of which the objects are given as being the same size, it will, according to some theorists such as Christopher Peacocke, have non-representational properties as well. These properties (the qualitative content of the experience) include those in virtue of which the closer object seems to occupy a larger area of the observer's subjective visual field. On the characterization of qualia according to which they are necessarily non-representational, only properties of the latter kind would qualify.

In what follows I shall concentrate on the use of 'qualitative state' according to which all that is assumed is that there is something it is like to be in one. The theorists whom I shall call *qualia realists* take it that a state's being conscious, its having qualitative content, and there being something it is like to occupy it go hand in hand. What defines qualia realism is, first, the claim that there are such states and, second, that they are not reducible to any other category of mental state. The first claim contrasts with *eliminativism, according to which science will show not what qualia are, but that they do not exist. And the second claim would entail that a view like George Pitcher's according to which visual perception consists in the acquisition of beliefs would not, by itself, account for its qualitative content. Indeed, this claim would normally be understood to entail the possibility of *zombies—subjects who have all of the same intentional states that we do, but lack any qualitative experience whatsoever. The rationale for this claim is that a reductivist view of qualia that leaves out most of what is intuitively distinctive or essential is not importantly different from eliminativism.

Most qualia realists who are not *dualists also take for granted the truth of *physicalism and scientific realism. Such theorists assume that what exists is what is entailed or presupposed by the truth of the ultimate physical theory of the world. Only those entities exist, it is assumed, that 'pull their weight' in such a causal/explanatory account. And it is assumed that qualitative states are such physical entities. It is a natural further assumption of such non-dualist qualia realists that the scientific study of qualitative states will take place either within the framework of a computational cognitive science or a neurophysiological brain science. Those who favour the first alternative endorse functionalist accounts according to which mental states are internal states defined in terms of their causal relations to inputs, outputs, and other internal states. Such accounts liken mental states to states of a computer program understood in abstraction from their physical realizations in specific machines. Those who reject this alternative hold that some entity might have all the same functional states that we do but fail to have our qualitative states (or indeed any qualitative states at all) because those functional states are not realized 'in the right way' physically.

A final assumption of qualia realists, which is common but often only implicit, is that there is a close connection between the character of our qualitative experience and the relevant organs of perception. In the case of visual perception, this means that what we are given most directly is governed by the nature of the retinal image. Hence it is something not far removed from the apparent colours, shapes, and relative sizes of external objects. In this, their views bear a marked similarity to those of classical empiricists and 20th century sense-datum theorists.

Qualia realism, together with the physicalist and scientific realist background assumptions, has been one of the most important approaches to qualitative experience for the past several decades and is, arguably, the dominant approach today. However, several fundamental problems have emerged.

2. Privileged access

Central-state materialists such as J. J. C. Smart and David Armstrong identified mental states, including qualitative states, with internal physical states of the brain. We generally take it, however, that we have a privileged relation to our own sensations such as pain. We assume, that is, that, necessarily, if we believe that we are in pain we are, and if we are we believe it. We would understand if a doctor, looking at an X-ray film, said we were mistaken in supposing we had a broken arm. It seems unthinkable, though, that the doctor could be justified in dismissing our claim to be in pain on the basis of a brain scan. But it is difficult to see how this feeling of privilege could be supported if the pain and the belief that one is in pain were independently existing physical states, or even independently existing states that were irreducibly mental. Indeed, even the definitional stipulation, suggested by some functionalists, that something is a pain only if it causes a pain belief and vice versa, seems not to capture the intuition that something is a pain in virtue of its intrinsic nature.

3. The further-fact arguments

The attempt to articulate a principled basis for distinguishing between those physical states that are sufficient for qualitative experience and those that are not has met with serious difficulties not directly related to privileged access. In his well-known *knowledge argument, Frank Jackson claims that if the experiences of a subject, Mary, were limited to those inside a black and white room, she might know all the relevant functional and neurophysiological facts about colour perception and yet (since there is no a priori connection) know nothing about the subjective experience involved. For it seems that when she saw her first red object she would learn a further fact—what it is like to see red. If so, it seems that there are facts over and above the physical and functional facts and that such facts are necessary to account for qualitative experience.

Currently there are two important physicalist responses. The first, due to Laurence Nemirow and David Lewis, holds that on seeing a red object for the first time Mary would gain no new knowledge, but only a new skill or ability—a piece of know-how. There are reasons to doubt, however, whether this really disposes of the problem. What could make it intelligible that from her point of view Mary had discovered or learned something new—something that would justify her saying, 'So *this* is what it is like to see red'? Only, it seems, if her new capacity were given as the ability to imagine or visualize red objects, and this ability were understood as itself presupposing an acquaintance with red, would Mary's response be intelligible.

The second response, put forward by Brian Loar and developed by Ned Block, is that on seeing her first red object Mary would gain a new concept—a *phenomenal concept—of the experience of red. Mary would acquire the ability to entertain new propositions and so, in one sense, new propositional knowledge. But on this account she would gain no access to any new facts. How, though, could we characterize the way in which a brain state must present itself to the subject in order to be picked out most naturally by a phenomenal, as opposed to a neurophysiological, concept? Proponents of phenomenal concepts assume that our ordinary relation to our own qualia, when we pick them out ('from the inside') via phenomenal concepts, is direct and demonstrative. Such proponents sometimes put the point by saying that in such cases qualia are their own modes of presentation. If qualia are identical to physical properties, however, this position raises difficulties of its own. For we could have two demonstrative relations to what is by these theorists' lights the same quale—a demonstrative relation to it as the property of being painful, say, and a distinct demonstrative relation to it as a neurophysiological property of a brain state—and we could fail to believe that they were presentations of the same thing. Thus like the earlier response, this threatens to give rise to another version of the same argument.

Since this problem arises for any identity involving the mental that is a posteriori, it raises the same difficulties for most versions of functionalism that it does for physicalist identity theories. Indeed, the problem arises for any reductivist theory with the exception of those that, like analytic functionalism, postulate a conceptual connection between qualia and the properties to which they are reduced. Such general considerations regarding the modes of presentation of qualitative states are currently being explored in the context of discussions of the property dualism argument. The issues of modes of presentation and phenomenal concepts are also crucial to the discussion of what we might call collectively the further-fact arguments—in addition to the knowledge argument and the property dualism argument, Joseph Levine's *explanatory gap argument, which turns on the alleged impossibility of explaining the felt quality of pain by reference to neurophysiology, as well as Saul Kripke's modal argument and David Chalmers' zombie argument. Thus whether the appeal to phenomenal concepts is a promising response to such objections to psycho-physical identity theories is a matter of current dispute.

4. The problem of other minds

As the further-fact arguments indicate, some of the most serious difficulties for non-dualist qualia realists stem from the assumption that mental-physical identities are a posteriori. This assumption generates another set of problems that are arguably even more difficult. Consider a subject who is like us in all the ways that might be supposed to have an a priori connection with consciousness and qualia, but in other ways differs from us significantly—e.g. a subject who has all of our functional states but who differs from us in how they are realized physically. It seems that there is no way in principle of settling the question whether in such a case there is qualitative experience present. Indeed, it seems that nothing could even count as relevant evidence. Since the subject will have the same inputs and outputs that we do, such a subject will claim to have qualitative states (or at least emit sounds as though such a claim were being made). And certainly this subject will make the same discriminations as a normal subject and pass the same behavioural tests. Moreover, looking inside the head will be no help—we already know by hypothesis that we will find that the behaviour is explained by the same functional states that explain our behaviour but that the explanations at the level of the neurophysiology are different. This has been called the problem of DNA physicalist-functionalism (White) and the harder problem of consciousness (Block).

5. Meaning scepticism

The traditional problem of scepticism regarding our knowledge of other minds leads quickly to an even more extreme form of scepticism—meaning scepticism regarding those mentalistic terms with which we ascribe qualitative states to others. If, as the phenomenal concepts view suggests, the only meaning one associates with the term 'pain' is what one gets through acquaintance with the sensation itself, then it seems inconceivable that one could ascribe it to others in the same sense in which one ascribes it to oneself. For if all one has is the ability to recognize pain in the ordinary way when it occurs in one's own case, then one associates nothing with the experience that could, logically, occur without its occurring in oneself. This problem of meaning scepticism, like the epistemological problem of other minds, is as much a problem for dualist versions of qualia as for their physicalist counterparts. These problems are central to the work of Wittgenstein and have been well articulated more recently by Kripke. Qualia realism, then, threatens to make the scientific study of qualia impossible. Such a conclusion would support an eliminativist approach to qualia.

6. Alternative approaches to the empirical study of qualia

In light of the apparent problems for the most prevalent forms of qualia realism, both dualist and non-dualist, it is significant that there exist a variety of other approaches to the scientific and empirical study of qualia. The work of Albert Michotte in investigating the *subjective impression of a causal connection between events and the precise parameters under which it is created has been extended and generalized by contemporary researchers. Their investigations include the subjective impression of *intentionality and of the exercise of meaningful agency, of the manifestation of specific intentions, and of the pursuit of specific goals and purposes. To say these are impressions is to say, for example, that some events are given in perception as actions in the pursuit of goals. Similarly, current research in the tradition of J. J. Gibson credits subjects with perception in which things are given as having functionally relevant properties and presenting the subject with opportunities. Thus things are given not as mere objects having certain sizes and shapes, but as, for example, potential shelters, hiding places, stairs, or bridges. Such topics overlap with those raised by Oliver Sacks. In his work on the brain stemming from the pioneering studies of A. R. Luria, Sacks describes his subjects not by reference to their neurophysiology, but in the terms in which their 'worlds' are given to them. And Sacks' work suggests that the most basic perception of one's own body and the surrounding space is not of objective spatial entities. Instead it is of a subjective space and body image that are mutually determining and themselves determining and determined by one's perception of one's agential possibilities and opportunities.

What grounds the claim of these alternative approaches to being scientific is an empirical methodology capable of generating significant generalizations across subjects. Though the methodology is non-reductive, there are behavioural criteria for the ascription of intentional states to subjects in the Michotte and Gibson paradigms, and/or the formulation of precise characterizations of the physical parameters determinative of the subjects' responses. And in the tradition associated with Luria, there are broad generalizations connecting subjective states with states of the brain, as well as generalizations across subjects. Such generalizations contribute to the empirical investigation of the structure of what might be called the subjects' 'life-worlds'.

Because the perceptual experiences ascribed in these research traditions are rich, they cannot be characterized in terms of such properties as apparent shapes, colours, or relative sizes. We see a person's distress directly, and not in virtue of being given the geometric features of the person's face or body, much less the sorts of apparent shapes and colours that make up some counterpart to the retinal image. The problem of other minds that arose for qualia realism, however, was generated by the lack of a priori or conceptual ties between a subject's qualia and anything to which we might take ourselves to have direct access, such as behaviour or physical states of the brain. If, however, what is given most directly in conscious perceptual experience has the richness attributed to it in these research paradigms, then, there will be such a priori connections between a subject's qualia and intentional states—there will be no describing the qualia of a subject's perceptual experience independently of describing the objects represented, and hence the intentional content. On the side of the subject, then, qualia and intentional states are inextricably tied in a way in which qualia realists—for whom qualia float free of intentional content—evidently cannot allow. Moreover, if our experience is as rich as these traditions would have it, what we are given most directly in our experience of others is not their behaviour, conceived in geometric, spatiotemporal terms, but their actions and their expressions of such things as their hopes and fears. Thus we have in our study of other subjects what the qualia realist cannot supply—a priori or conceptual connections between the qualitative contents of other subjects' perceptual experiences and what we ourselves are given most directly in our experiences of them. Finally, since the theories are non-reductive, there is no conceptual gap of the kind that generates the further-fact problems.

Such non-reductive accounts also have potential implications for the meaning-sceptical version of the problem of other minds. The problem, as we have seen, is that the radical difference in our mode of access to qualitative states in the first- and third-person cases threatened to undermine the assumption that in both cases our mentalistic terms have the same meaning. This points up the importance of the fact that such accounts as Sacks' acknowledge, and depend on, deep connections between perception on the one hand and *action, and hence action theory, on the other. And in the context of action theory, some philosophers have suggested that the notion of joint agency is a conceptual possibility and, arguably, a common occurrence. Such a thesis, could it be sustained, would, in the context of a non-reductive treatment of qualia, bridge the apparent logical gap between our access to our own subjectivity and that of anyone else. And the idea of bridging this gap is supported by the fact that our most fundamental access to our own agency is arguably through our access to affordances and opportunities that are perceived as being in the world and as available to others.

Such theories, in effect, intentionalize the sensational aspects of perceptual experience, at the same time that they make qualia in the form of rich perception of such things as affordances essential to such intentional phenomena as agency. And their doing so allows them to draw on current empirical work to answer the further-fact arguments. Such approaches will not, however, automatically answer the points that threatened to make bodily sensations such as pain immune to empirical investigation. But as some philosophers, such as Michael Tye, have argued, pain and other bodily sensations have many of the supposedly definitive features of such paradigmatically intentional states as visual experiences. Most fundamentally, pain is always located, and hence is part of, and partially constitutive of, a *body image. In such a body image we are given to ourselves as having certain bodily characteristics and so in a way that can be assessed for accuracy or inaccuracy. Thus pain seems to satisfy the basic criterion of an intentional state, and it will be accessible to the same sorts of empirical investigations as perceptual states. Because the approaches are non-reductive, however, there can be no such blatant violations of privileged access as someone's being justified in contradicting one's claim to be in pain on the basis of a brain scan. Thus reductive and non-reductive scientific treatments of qualia, in the context of some philosophical theses currently under investigation, provide very different conceptual contexts within which such problems as those of privileged access, other minds, and meaning scepticism about the mental may be framed and investigated.

See also 'WHAT IT'S LIKE' STEPHEN L. WHITE

Armstrong, D. M. (1969). *A Materialist Theory of the Mind.*

Block, N. (2002). 'The harder problem of consciousness'. *Journal of Philosophy*, 99.

—— (2008). 'Max Black's objection to mind-body identity'. In Alter, T. and Walter, S. (eds) *Phenomenal Concepts and Phenomenal Knowledge: New Essays on Consciousness and Physicalism.*

Chalmers, D. J. (1996). *The Conscious Mind: In Search of a Fundamental Theory.*

Gibson, J. J. (1986). *The Ecological Approach to Visual Perception.*

Jackson, F. (1986). 'What Mary didn't know.' *Journal of Philosophy*, 83.

Kripke, S. A. (1980). *Naming and Necessity.*

—— (1982). *Wittgenstein on Rules and Private Language.*

Levine, J. (1983). 'Materialism and qualia: the explanatory gap'. *Pacific Philosophical Quarterly*, 64.

Lewis, D. (1990). 'What experience teaches.' in Lycan, W. G. (ed.) *Mind and Cognition.*

Loar, B. (1997). 'Phenomenal states'. In Block, N. et al. (eds) *The Nature of Consciousness: Philosophical Debates.*

Luria, A. R. (1972). *The Man with a Shattered World.*

Michotte, A. (1963). *The Perception of Causality.*

Nemirow, L. (1990). 'Physicalism and the cognitive role of acquaintance'. In Lycan, W. G. (ed.) *Mind and Cognition.*

Peacocke, C. (1983). *Sense and Content: Experience, Thought, and Their Relations.*

Pitcher, G. (1971). *A Theory of Perception.*

Rosenthal, D. M. (1997). 'A theory of consciousness'. In Block, N. et al. (eds) *The Nature of Consciousness: Philosophical Debates.*

Sacks, O. (1970). 'Eyes right!' In *The Man Who Mistook His Wife for a Hat and Other Clinical Tales.*

—— (1984). *A Leg to Stand On.*

Smart, J. J. C. (1962). 'Sensations and brain processes'. In Chappell, V. C. (ed.) *The Philosophy of Mind.*

Sperber, D., Premack, D., and Premack, A. J. (1995). *Causal Cognition: A Multidisciplinary Debate.*

Tye, M. (1997). 'A representational theory of pains and their phenomenal character'. In Block, N. et al. (eds) *The Nature of Consciousness: Philosophical Debates.*

White, S. L. (1986). 'The curse of the qualia'. *Synthese*, 68.

—— (2008). 'Property dualism, phenomenal concepts, and the semantic premise'. In Alter, T. and Walter, S. (eds) *Phenomenal Concepts and Phenomenal Knowledge: New Essays on Consciousness and Physicalism.*

Wittgenstein, L. (1953). *Philosophical Investigations.*

qualitative vs quantitative dissociations See PERCEPTION, UNCONSCIOUS

R

readiness potentials and human volition The term 'readiness potential' (*Bereitschaftspotential* in the original German) was first used by Kornhuber and Deecke (1965) to describe a component of the event-related potential preceding voluntary action. In the original experimental design, a volunteer is asked to make simple movements such as a pressing a button or lifting a finger, at a time of their own choosing. The electrical activity of the brain is recorded continuously using scalp electrodes placed at standard locations on the scalp. The *electroencephalograph (EEG) signal around the time of the voluntary movements is subsequently averaged, using the onset of the voluntary movement as a synchronization point. The components of brain activity that are unrelated to the movement are removed by the averaging process, leaving just the brain activity related to the action itself. The characteristic pattern of this action-related component is a gradual ramp-like build-up of negative voltage, beginning around 1 s before the action itself, and reaching a peak around the time of movement onset. This component was given the name *readiness potential.*

Although the spatial resolution of EEG is limited, the principal origin of the readiness potential is thought to be the frontal motor areas, notably the pre-supplementary motor area. The readiness potential is a neural *correlate of voluntary action. Readiness potential amplitudes increase, and onsets begin earlier before action itself, as the action becomes more effortful, and requires more thought. Moreover, no readiness potential is seen when subjects make actions in response to external trigger stimuli.

1. What is voluntary action?
2. Conscious intention and brain activity
3. Experience of urge prior to action
4. Inferring intentions retrospectively from effects

1. What is voluntary action?

Several researchers have tried to use readiness potentials to clarify the processes underlying the internal generation and initiation of action. Where indeed does a voluntary action come from, and what initiates it? Most existing theories have an unsatisfactory dualist or homuncular element. Saying that 'I' or my 'act of will' initiates my voluntary action gives the impression that there is a state or process inside my head which is an uncaused cause. The same problem of regress occurs in neural control as in philosophy of mind. The neural processes measured by the readiness potential may well be the cause of our actions, but what starts the readiness potential?

An important way out of the problem of regress is to begin with a clear definition of a voluntary action. Philosophers of mind typically define voluntary actions counter-factually: my action is voluntary if and only if I could have done otherwise. In contrast, neuroscience defines voluntary actions in a quite different way, in terms of the information that triggers the action. An action is voluntary if it is not a response to an exogenous stimulus. Thus, voluntary actions are considered as the opposite end of a spectrum from a reflex action which is directly specified by an external stimulus. On this view, voluntary actions may simply be 'smart' actions, which go beyond immediately available environmental information. Memory and intelligence therefore probably play a much larger part in volition than normally thought. For example, I may make an action spontaneously, in the absence of any external stimulus, because I remember, i.e. I have internally stored, that it is an appropriate action to make in a given situation. Alternatively, I may make an action which is not obviously driven by a stimulus because it is a useful step towards a longer-range goal. We might well call this a voluntary action, yet it is, interestingly, a key component of classical theories of intelligence based on operant learning (Thorndike 1911).

This view of voluntary action also suggests that a loop is a better model than a hierarchy. A voluntary action does not begin with an 'I', but with a external context for behaviour, and an internal context of memories of previous actions. In that sense, voluntary actions may simply be delayed responses to complex stimuli, rather than instances of magical mind–body interaction. However, this does not dismiss the topic of voluntary action as uninteresting. The ability to initiate actions in the absence of an exogenous stimulus is an important evolved function of the human brain. Moreover, it raises key questions for the study of consciousness.

2. Conscious intention and brain activity
The relation between conscious thought and neural initiation of action has been a particular focus of interest. The term 'intention' is often used to refer to the specific conscious thought that one will perform an action at some time in the future. Most voluntary actions involve both long-range intentions and short-range intentions. Searle (1983) used the term *prior intention* to refer to actions that I plan to do, but which are as yet clearly in the future, such as intending to remove the washing from the machine. He used the term *intention-in-action* to refer to the conscious mental state associated with actually initiating and performing the bodily action itself. Experimental psychology often considers prior intentions as a form of prospective memory, which may be particularly important in executive functions and cognitive task control. In contrast, intention-in-action is normally considered as a cognitive precursor of motor control.

Both prior intention and intention-in-action are thought to precede action itself. But intentions also generally refer to the effect that an action produces. For example, if I intend to cook a meal, the intention seems to anticipate and represent the end-product of the meal on the table. That is, intentions contain an 'urge' component and an 'effect' component. The urge component necessarily precedes action, and could be identified with the readiness potential, as discussed below. The physical effect of an action necessarily follows the action, but the effect may well be represented before the action occurs. Two different views of intention have emerged within psychology, based on the distinction between urge and effect components. One view stresses the importance of urges, reasons, drives, and experiences occurring before action. The second view suggests that intentions are not bona fide mental states at all, but retrospective inferences based on the effects of our actions.

3. Experience of urge prior to action
Conscious intention-in-action corresponds to the experience that one is about to perform an action. The relation between intention-in-action and the readiness potential has been vigorously debated. Causal theories, along with most folk psychology, asserts that intentions cause actions. However, modern neuroscience dislikes this notion, as it seems to attribute a causal role to conscious intentions, and it is unclear how conscious states can cause brain events or body movements. Most neuroscientists believe that conscious intention is a consequence of brain activity, rather than a cause. Indeed, an experiment by Libet and colleagues (1983) appears to provide scientific evidence to confirm this. Libet and colleagues asked people to report the time of their conscious intention preceding voluntary actions. They used readiness potential onset as a measure of the start of neural preparation for action, and related this to the conscious experience of intention. On average, subjects reported experiencing the conscious intention to move around 200 ms before the onset of actual muscle contraction. In contrast, the readiness potential began some 800 ms or more before actual muscle contraction. Since causes cannot precede effects, Libet inferred that the conscious intention could not be the cause of the neural processes that culminate in action. Libet's result is often viewed as invalidating the *dualist view that conscious thoughts are the cause of action.

Libet's experiment has been widely discussed. However, the method has often been criticized (see e.g. responses to Libet 1985). One important concern is the interpretation of a specific numerical value for the time of conscious intention. The argument depends on subjects' reports of the time of conscious intention being unbiased. In fact, however, the reports are based on a cross-modal synchronization process that is known to be extremely prone to biases. Effectively, the subject must judge an event in their own internal stream of consciousness relative to an external stream of clock positions. Synchronization of the two streams depends strongly on which stream one primarily attends to (the *prior entry* phenomenon), and is also very variable across individuals. If the estimate of conscious intention is biased, could the true moment of conscious intention in fact occur before readiness potential onset? Recent further studies have largely replicated Libet's result, and suggest that measurement errors introduced by his method are small relative to the time-gap between readiness-potential onset and conscious intention (Pockett and Miller 2007).

More recent studies have re-examined the link between readiness potentials and conscious intention. First, Haggard and Eimer (1999) found that the time of conscious intention did not correlate well with the time of readiness potential onset. Instead, they found a correlation with the later *lateralization* of cortical activity to the contralateral cerebral hemisphere controlling the hand that subjects chose to move. That is, conscious intention was linked not to a general initiation of action, but to the stage of selection or specification of the precise motor pattern used to achieve the action goal. Second, and as a consequence of the first point: the conscious experiences reported in experiments of this kind relate not to the earliest origin of our actions, but to a relatively late stage in the motor processing chain. This stage might be thought of as the final push towards motor execution. Readiness potentials resemble intentions-in-action, rather than prior intentions.

4. Inferring intentions retrospectively from effects
Finally, some authors have suggested that the experience of willing an action is a retrospective illusion, generated by the association of a prior thought about the action, and its subsequent occurrence. This view has origins in the work of David Hume, but was recently developed by Daniel Wegner (2002). The initial evidence for this view came from experiments in which participants had to attribute an effect either to their own action or to an experimenter (Wegner and Wheatley 1999). When participants had been thinking about making an action, and an appropriate effect occurred soon after, they judged that their own action had caused the effect. Under these conditions under which subjects *judge* that their actions cause external events. However, it remains unclear whether people really have an experience of conscious intention in such situations. A strong version of the theory suggests that an experience of intention is retrospectively inserted into the stream of consciousness, prior to the action that the intention is judged to have caused (Wegner 2002). This view effectively dismisses conscious intentions as fictions, rather than mental states. However, explicit judgements about mental causation are quite different from experiences of control (Synofzik et al. 2008), and it remains unclear whether such situations of agent ambiguity do indeed have the phenomenal feel of one's own actions.

However, in one study neural activity analogous to the readiness potential was induced artificially by directly stimulating the supplementary motor area of awake neurosurgical patients (Fried et al. 1991). When low currents were applied, patients reported an 'urge' to move a particular body part. When the current was increased, the same body part often actually moved. This result suggests that the neural preparation for action is associated with a specific conscious experience. Although the sense of 'urge' experienced by Fried's patients is not described in detail, it appears to have some of the key aspects of intention. Moreover, this experience arises as an intrinsic part of the brain processes that generate the action itself. Characterizing the content of this experience, and describing the necessary and sufficient conditions for it, is an important future task for the scientific study of consciousness. To date, most studies of conscious intention have considered the time of intentions, rather than their content. A second key task is to investigate how the urge aspect of intention, occurring prior to voluntary action, interacts with effect of the action.

See also INTENTIONALITY

PATRICK HAGGARD

Fried, I., Katz, A., McCarthy, G. et al. (1991). 'Functional organization of human supplementary motor cortex studied by electrical stimulation'. *Journal of Neuroscience*, 11.
Haggard, P. and Eimer, M. (1999). 'On the relation between brain potentials and the awareness of voluntary movements'. *Experimental Brain Research*, 126.
Kornhuber, H. H. and Deecke, L. (1965). 'Hirnpotentialänderungen bei Willkürbewegungen und passiven Bewegungen des Menschen: Bereitschaftspotential und reafferente Potentiale'. *Pflügers Archiv*, 284.
Libet, B. (1985). 'Unconscious cerebral initiative and the role of conscious will in voluntary action'. *Behavioural and Brain Sciences*, 8.
——, Gleason, C. A., Wright, E. W., and Pearl, D. K. (1983). 'Time of conscious intention to act in relation to onset of cerebral activity (readiness-potential). The unconscious initiation of a freely voluntary act'. *Brain*, 106.
Pockett, S. and Miller, A. (2007). 'The rotating spot method of timing subjective events'. *Consciousness and Cognition*, 16.
Searle, J. R. (1983). *Intentionality*.
Synofzik, M., Vosgerau, G., and Newen, A. (2008). 'Beyond the comparator model: a multifactorial two-step account of agency'. *Consciousness and Cognition*, 17.
Thorndike, E. L. (1911). *Animal Intelligence*.
Wegner, D. M. (2002). *The Illusion of Conscious Will*.
—— and Wheatley, T. (1999). 'Apparent mental causation. Sources of the experience of will'. *American Psychologist*, 54.

reductionism. *Physicalism about the conscious mind is an ontological thesis, i.e. a thesis about the fundamental nature of reality. It asserts that the mind, including all its conscious aspects, is an entirely physical phenomenon. Since the 1960s a prominent strand in defending physicalism has appealed to *reduction*, which is first and foremost a relationship between representations: theories, concepts, or explanations. The assumed connection is that scientific reductions (or their failures) justify ontological conclusions. So to discover how consciousness relates to physical mechanisms, this approach recommends that we compare features of potential psychology-to-neurobiology reductions with well-known, accomplished cases from the history of science. For example, the accomplished scientific reduction of optics to electromagnetism led to the identity of visible light with electromagnetic radiation with wavelengths of 350–750 nm. The reduction of classical mechanics to special relativity, on the other hand, led to the elimination of mass as classically conceived (as a non-relational property of objects). The failure of electromagnetism to reduce to mechanics, along with the former's acknowledged explanatory successes, led to the ontological autonomy of electricity from basic mechanical properties and relations. Which of these historical reductions (or failures) do potential psychology-to-neurobiology cases appear to resemble most closely? Our answer to this logically prior reduction question will immediately yield a predicted ontological conclusion about the psychological properties, relations, and events involved.

One attractive consequence of this approach for consciousness studies is that hypothesized reductions of consciousness and its features face no unique logical burdens. Perhaps neither current psychology nor neuroscience yet offers robust explanations of conscious phenomena. From this approach, that only means that there is more scientific work to do before we confidently assert any prediction about the outcome of potential reductions. Qualitative properties, *subjectivity, and privileged access, if they exist as genuine phenomena, may prove difficult to explain in physical science. But their detailed nature and their potential physical explanations are jobs first and foremost for empirical research, not armchair speculation. No questions get begged against *dualism. Science's history offers ample examples of sought-after reductions that failed to be achieved. Such an outcome, along with its subsequent conclusion about the autonomy of features of consciousness from those of the physical sciences, remains an open possibility at present.

The principal difficulty facing this promising approach is the lack of a widely accepted account of scientific reduction. In the philosophy of science for roughly the past half-century, scientific reduction has meant *intertheoretic reduction*: the reduction of one scientific theory to another. The most prominent approach in this tradition, especially the one that took root in the philosophy of mind, stems from Ernest Nagel (1961:Ch. 12). According to Nagel, intertheoretic reduction is deduction (logical derivation) of the laws or explanatory generalizations of the reduced theory from those of the reducing. Nagel was aware that this deductive step required additional premises when the reduced theory contained terms not contained in the reducing. For example, the explanatory generalizations of classical thermodynamics contains terms like 'pressure' and 'temperature', which are not contained in the generalizations of statistical mechanics and the kinetic/corpuscular theory of gases. In such 'heterogenous' reductions, the premises of the derivation also contained *bridge principles* that linked terms of the reducing theory to those terms unique to the reduced—for example, a principle linking 'temperature in a gas' with 'mean molecular kinetic energy of constituent molecules'.

Nagel also realized that scientific reductions often correct the reduced theory. To accommodate these cases, he supplemented the premises of the deduction (reducing theory and bridge principles) with counter-to-fact limiting assumptions and boundary conditions on the applications of the reducing theory's generalizations. For example, in the thermodynamics-to-statistical mechanics case, these conditions limit the application of the statistical mechanical principles to idealized situations that are never actually realized: an infinite number of molecules in perfectly random motion, volume of gas indefinitely large in comparison to mean distance between colliding molecules. Only within these limits can the actual laws of classical thermodynamics be derived (Hooker 1981). Hence the required falsity in the premises necessary to validly derive a false conclusion (the reduced theory) could be safely limited to these counterfactual conditions.

Nagel's account was quickly challenged within the philosophy of science, especially as historical cases of actual scientific reductions became described more completely. Numerous revisions, and ultimately replacements, were proposed. (This is a much-told tale; one detailed instance with numerous citations is Bickle 2003:Ch. 1.) Unfortunately, few of these revisions penetrated the philosophy of mind. Proposed psychophysical reductions were assumed to proceed along broadly Nagelian lines.

In the mid-1990s, from 'consciousness studies', there emerged an alternative account of scientific reduction that did not focus directly on inter*theoretic* relations (Levine 1993, Chalmers 1996). Reduction was characterized as a two-step process focusing on concepts. Step 1 involves preparing a concept for reduction by 'functionalizing' it: characterizing it exhaustively in terms of its causes and effects. (This is the step that gave the account its popular name, *functional reduction*.) Step 2 then involves normal empirical science: it is the search for the physical mechanisms that actually play the functional role characterized in step 1. A popular illustration among proponents of functional reduction is that between water and collections of H_2O molecules in liquid state. The causes and effects of water, revealed either by conceptual analysis or pedestrian empirical investigation (such as its boiling point at normal atmospheric pressure), are matched by the structural and dynamic properties of the interacting molecules, as governed by basic mechanical and thermal principles. Anti-reductionists about *qualia have found this account most useful. The well-known philosophical thought experiments are taken to show that qualia forever elude step 1 of a functional reduction—they cannot be exhaustively characterized in terms of their causes and effects. Hence no scientific reduction of them (completing steps 1 and 2) will ever be forthcoming.

Functional reduction differs significantly from intertheoretic reduction. As already mentioned, the primary relata are concepts (not theories). Logical derivation is nowhere involved. Hence no problematic bridge principles across distinct theoretical vocabularies are required to enable a derivation. And falsity in the reduced concept can be captured directly by the extent to which the actual physical mechanism differs in its causes and effects from the functional characterization of the reduced concept.

Despite functional reduction's popularity within recent philosophy of mind, it has not attracted much attention from philosophers of science. This is because it possesses some scientifically suspect features. For example, no proponent of functional reduction has ever analysed the 'Methods' section of a publication in a reputable scientific journal, in order to show that a detailed attempt to wrest experimental predictions from the concepts involved can be adequately described as 'functionalizing' them. This demonstration would seem to be a minimal condition on the account's scientific plausibility—in the same way that accounting for accurately described historical reductions in science has been treated as a minimal condition on the adequacy of accounts of intertheoretic reduction. Is 'functionalization' of concepts really a part of actual reductionistic scientific practice? Is it even an acceptable philosopher's simplification or idealization? Or is it an outright distortion? The case for its being an outright distortion is suggested by the very examples proponents describe to illustrate the account, like the water–H_2O reduction. These examples are drawn neither from recent reductionistic science nor from detailed historical cases: they are drawn rather from elementary school textbooks. They are the cases we use to teach children the rudiments of our scientific world view. This little-noticed fact does not by itself show that functional reduction is a mistaken view. But a very plausible worry is that reductionistic practices in actual, current science might be quite different from those culled from the scientific examples we use to educate children. At the very least, this worry will not be assuaged until proponents of functional reduction show that their account captures essential features of real examples from current reductionistic science.

If functional reduction ultimately is a distortion of actual scientific practice, this generates a serious problem for anti-reductionist arguments about consciousness that rely upon it. Those arguments are then open to the charge that the reduction of consciousness to physical mechanisms might actually be occurring in current scientific practice, but simply are not answering to philosophers' fictions about 'what reduction has to be'.

Lately a more explicitly 'metascientific' approach to characterizing scientific reduction has been advocated (Bickle 2003, Schaffner 2006). It stems from the idea that any analysis of reduction should proceed with actual case studies drawn from an acknowledged 'reductionistic' field of current science. It seeks a description of the experimental practices common to these cases. Bickle draws detailed cases from rodent studies of memory, while Schaffner draws from work on the foraging behaviour of the nematode *C. elegans*. The reductionistic practices central to this work amount to intervening into hypothesized causal mechanisms at increasingly lower levels of biological organization (e.g. individual molecular components of intra- and interneuronal signalling pathways) and then tracking the behavioural effects of these interventions *in vivo* using well-accepted experimental protocols for the cognitive phenomenon under investigation. At present, popular experimental procedures involve intervening into specific gene expression, producing changes in the configuration or amounts of specific proteins. Mostly the measures of the behavioural effects of these molecular interventions have focused on memory consolidation: fear conditioning, memories for particular previously encountered conspecifics, transmission of food preferences, object recognition, and reconsolidation of memory after representation or retrieval of the conditioned stimulus. 'Real reduction', like functional reduction, differs considerably from intertheoretic reduction: theories are not the relata, logical derivation is not an aspect, and there are no problematic bridge principles to interpret. Unlike functional reduction, however, an exhaustive analysis of a reduced concept in terms of its causes and effects is also no part of a reduction. Rather, in keeping with actual scientific practice, reduced concepts are operationalized methodologically, in terms of measures that indicate their occurrences (behavioural measures in the case of psychological concepts), and the effects of the molecular interventions are measured. The necessary experimental controls are extensive, but are widely agreed upon in this field (Silva and Bickle 2008).

This basic reductionistic strategy is being employed increasingly to study the molecular mechanisms of phenomenally conscious states associated with awareness, *arousal, and anxiety level (Bickle 2007). This work is little known within mainstream 'consciousness studies', even among the field's cognitive and systems-level neuroscientists. However, within the broader community of neuroscientists—the 'Society for Neuroscience' crowd, as we might call them—it is important to note how small a number identify themselves as 'cognitive' or 'systems-level' researchers. The vast majority work at the reductionistic levels of cellular and molecular neuroscience. Philosophers, cognitive scientists, and the rest of the 'consciousness studies' community ignore this work at the peril of increasing isolation from the broader community of mainstream neuroscientists.

JOHN BICKLE

Bickle, J. (2003). *Philosophy and Neuroscience: a Ruthlessly Reductive Account*.

—— (2007). 'Who says you can't do a molecular biology of consciousness?' In Looren de Jong, H. and Schouten, M. (eds) *The Matter of the Mind*.

Chalmers, D. (1996). *The Conscious Mind*.

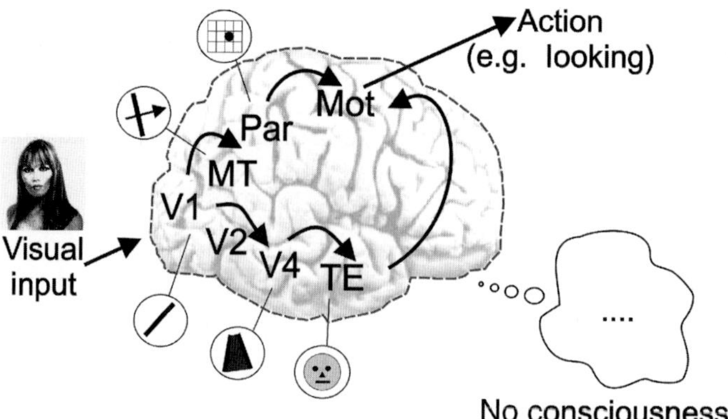

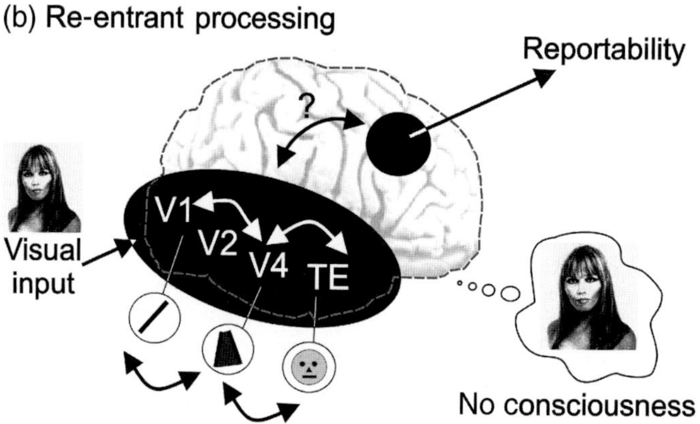

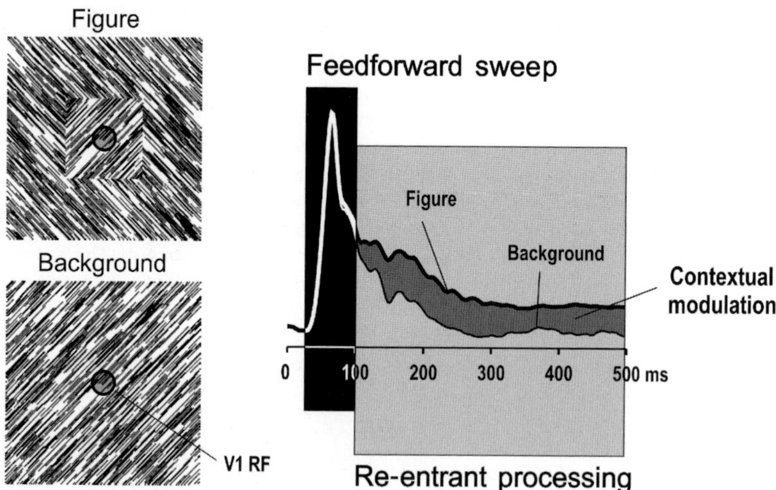

Fig. R1. (a) The feedforward sweep. A visual input will trigger a rapid yet selective activation of cells in successive areas of the sensorimotor hierarchy, which are tuned for increasingly higher-level visual properties. Within 150 ms, a (potential) motor output is activated by the stimulus. The stimulus has not yet evoked conscious experience, however. V1, V2, etc.: visual areas, with icons showing their most

Hooker, C. A. (1981). 'Towards a general theory of reduction. Part I. historical and scientific setting. Part II. Identity in reduction. Part III. Cross-categorial reduction'. *Dialogue*, 20.
Levine, J. (1993). 'On leaving out what it's like'. In Davies, M. and Humphreys, G. W. (eds) *Consciousness: Psychological and Philosophical Essays*.
Nagel, E. (1961). *The Structure of Science*.
Schaffner, K. (2006). 'Reduction: the Cheshire Cat problem and a return to roots'. *Synthese* 151.
Silva, A. J. and Bickle, J. (2008). 'Intimology and the search for the molecular mechanisms of cognitive functions.' In Bickle, J. (ed.) *Oxford Handbook of Philosophy and Neuroscience*.
Society for Neuroscience. www.sfn.org

re-entrant processing Re-entrant processing is a specific mode of operation of the cerebral cortex. Several lines of evidence indicate that without re-entrant processing, there is no conscious experience. It might even be argued that it is the neural equivalent of consciousness. Why is that so? Assuming that the brain generates consciousness, the obvious question is: 'How does it do that?' Hence the quest for the *neural *correlate of consciousness* (NCC), where it is asked what areas, pathways, or neurons dissociate conscious from unconscious information processing. Finding the NCC has been taken to hold great promise for finally really understanding consciousness. But things did not turn out to be that easy. There is no area in the brain that automatically and all by itself produces conscious experience. Conscious vision, for example, uses the same neurons in the same visual areas as unconscious vision does. Intuitively appealing as the idea might be, the NCC thus is not a particular locus in the brain. An alternative approach would be to formulate the NCC as a neural mechanism instead of a locus. The most promising in this respect is the notion of re-entrant processing (also called recurrent or resonant processing).

1. Feedforward, feedback, and horizontal connections
2. Electrophysiological studies
3. Re-entrant processing changes your brain
4. Is re-entrant processing sufficient for consciousness?

1. Feedforward, feedback, and horizontal connections

Recurrent processing is best understood if we first define its counterpart, feedforward processing, e.g. in the domain of vision (Lamme and Roelfsema 2000). We move our eyes about three times per second, and whenever they come to a standstill, a new image is projected on the retina. Information about this image is then rapidly transferred to the visual cortex, where different levels of visual processing can be identified on the basis of feedforward connections from one area to the next. Each level extracts more and more abstract or 'high-level' features from the visual scene, so as to make the information available for action. About every 10 ms a successive stage in this sensorimotor hierarchy is updated, so that in about 100–150 ms the whole brain 'knows' about the new image before our eyes. Not only the speed, but also the level of processing that is achieved by this one-way exchange of action potentials is remarkable. Right away, neurons exhibit complex tuning properties like selectivity for motion, depth, colour, or shape. Even neurons that respond selectively to faces do so from the very first action potentials that are fired. Thus, the *feedforward sweep* enables a rapid extraction of complex and meaningful features from the visual scene (Fig. R1a).

Are we conscious of these features once they are extracted by the feedforward sweep? Do we *see* a face when a face-selective neuron becomes active? It seems not. **Masking* studies, in both humans and monkeys, have shown that masked and therefore unseen visual stimuli activate, throughout the brain, the very

prominent tuning properties. Arrows: direction of information transfer, via feedforward connections.
(b) Re-entrant processing. When neurons, e.g. of temporal cortex (TE), which are selectively responding to faces, engage in re-entrant interactions (bidirectional arrows) with lower-level neurons which are encoding details, colour, depth, motion, etc. of that face, we have a conscious percept of that face. Reportability of that conscious percept depends, independently, on whether the re-entrant interactions include structures necessary for the report, such as motor cortex (or language areas in the case of a verbal report).
(c) Neurophysiology of feedforward sweep and re-entrant processing. Shown is an example of a neurophysiological recording in monkey V1, and the stimuli used to distinguish re-entrant processing signals from feedforward activation. The circle denotes the V1 receptive field, that is 'seeing' a small part of a larger scene, in which a textured square segregates from the background (figure) or not (background). Initially, the neuron responds identically to the two scenes, as it is only activated by its feedforward connections, coming from the RF only, where the information is identical for the two conditions. Later (>100 ms after stimulus onset), re-entrant processing kicks in, and a different response is obtained for the figure as opposed to the background stimulus. This difference (contextual modulation) is a neurophysiological marker for the occurrence of re-entrant processing, and has been used in a variety of studies to investigate the roles of re-entrant vs feedforward processing in conscious vision.

same neurons as visible stimuli do (Lamme et al. 2002). Another intriguing study showed that when faces are presented in opposite colouring to the two eyes, they become invisible to the mind's eye. Nevertheless, they activate face-selective areas of the human brain, i.e. they penetrate deeply into the feedforward sensorimotor hierarchy. Invisible words were even shown to activate the sensorimotor pathways all the way up to motor cortex. In short, no matter what area of the brain is reached by the feedforward sweep, this in itself is not producing conscious experience (Lamme 2003, 2004). The feedforward sweep mediates sophisticated 'cortical reflexes', providing for the translation of visual information into (potential) motor commands, but *unconscious reflexes* they are (Fig. R1a).

The brain is not just a complex reflex machine, however. For almost every feedforward connection, via which signals ascend the sensorimotor hierarchy, there is a feedback connection going in the reverse direction. Also, horizontal connections link neurons within cortical areas to each other, so that neurons 'looking' at different regions of the visual field can exchange information. Together, these feedback and horizontal connections provide for so-called re-entrant (or recurrent, or resonant) processing (Lamme et al. 1998, Grossberg 1999). We have seen that feedforward processing extracts features from the visual scene, and thereby translates visual input into motor outputs. Classical receptive field tuning properties, such as orientation selectivity of *V1 neurons, motion selectivity for MT neurons, or face selectivity in area IT are all a result of feedforward computations. What does re-entrant processing add to that?

2. Electrophysiological studies

Not much, if we are to believe most classic electrophysiological field studies. It has to be noted, however, that this is probably an artefact of the fact that these studies used simple, single stimuli on an otherwise blank screen. If multiple stimuli are present at the same time, as would happen in natural scenes, effects of re-entrant processing start to become noticeable in the electrophysiological recording—or in *electroencephalographic (EEG) or *functional brain imaging (fMRI) measures for that matter. Then it is seen that all sorts of contextual effects arise, typically after some delay with respect to the initial, feedforward response. For example, a neuron may changes its response to a particular stimulus, depending on whether there is another stimulus in the vicinity, and depending on features like distance, similarity, collinearity, etc. (Albright and Stoner 2002). It has proved difficult to interpret these effects. However, given that the modulatory effects often follow rules of **Gestalt principles*, it is most likely that they are a reflection of re-entrant processing mediating the process of *perceptual organization* (or image segmentation), where individual features and elements that make up a scene are combined into coherent objects, segregating from each other and from background (Fig. R1c).

Another way, to more directly measure the occurrence of re-entrant processing, is by recording from (at least) two neurons at the same time. If neurons engage in re-entrant processing, they will mutually influence each other. As a result, they might synchronize their action potentials. Such synchronization does indeed occur. It is typically stronger for neurons that are close by (and that therefore have strong reciprocal connections), but may even occur between neurons that are located in different parts of the brain (Engel and Singer 2001). Experiments have shown that synchrony reflects perceptual organization and attention, but this is controversial (Singer 1999). Various EEG and fMRI methods have been developed to evaluate synchrony at the level of brain regions, instead of individual neurons (Tononi and Edelman 1998, Haynes et al. 2005). Also at that level, synchronization seems to reflect perceptual organization, attention and consciousness.

What about the relation between re-entrant processing, or its neurophysiological manifestations, and consciousness? Given that feedforward processing is not producing conscious experience, it seems logical to conclude that re-entrant processing is necessary for a conscious percept. Moreover, several studies indicate that interfering with re-entrant processing disrupts conscious experience (or vice versa).

Backward masking, i.e. presenting two stimuli shortly after each other, may render the first stimulus invisible. It has been shown that this does not interfere with feedforward tuning properties of neurons, i.e. cells still show selective responses for the unseen, first stimulus. However, the modulations reflecting re-entrant processing (Fig. R1c) are suppressed by it (Lamme et al. 2002). Also, the best predictor of visibility in a backward masking experiment is not the activity evoked in any single area, but the amount of interaction between early and high level visual areas that the masked stimulus evokes (Haynes et al. 2005).

With **transcranial magnetic stimulation (TMS)* the ongoing activity in a particular brain region can be briefly disrupted. Applying TMS to early visual areas (V1) at a latency far beyond the feedforward sweep still renders stimuli invisible, presumably by interfering with re-entrant signals. Other TMS studies showed the necessity of re-entrant processing even stronger: TMS over the motion selective area MT induces motion sensations, unless V1 activity is disrupted at a later moment in time. Since MT is higher in the visual hierarchy than V1, this implies that feedback from MT to V1 is necessary for motion awareness (Pascual-Leone and Walsh 2001).

Feedforward activation of neurons can still be recorded in *anaesthetized* animals, with RF tuning properties that hardly differ from those in the awake animal. Manifestations of re-entrant processing, in particular those contextual modulations that express aspects of perceptual organization, are however fully suppressed under anaesthesia (Lamme et al. 1998). Something similar has been found in awake monkeys as well: a neural correlate of figure–ground segregation, mediated by re-entrant interactions between V1 and extrastriate areas (Fig. R1c), and present when stimuli are seen, is absent when stimuli are not seen (Super et al. 2001; see also below).

There appears to be ample evidence, therefore, that re-entrant processing is at least necessary for conscious (visual) experience (Fig. R1b). Two questions remain, the first being why re-entrant processing would be so special compared to feedforward processing for generating consciousness. After all, in both cases, it is just neurons firing action potentials.

It might simply be a matter of threshold. Re-entrant processing typically causes the neurons that are involved to reach a much higher level of overall activity, due to mutual excitation. Also, neurons engaged in re-entrant processing will remain active for a longer period of time, possibly even after the stimulus has already disappeared. If consciousness depends on neural activity passing a certain threshold, as some have argued, it follows that re-entrant processing is more likely to generate conscious experience than the brisk activation mediated by feedforward connections alone.

Added to this is the tendency of re-entrant processing to behave in a more or less all-or-none fashion. Because of its non-linear dynamics, a tiny core of re-entrant processing will have the tendency to spread like wildfire throughout the brain. If multiple cores exist, a strong competition between them will rapidly resolve into a winner-take-all victory for one or the other, a phenomenon that can be observed at the psychological level in such phenomena as *multistable figures or *binocular rivalry.

3. Re-entrant processing changes your brain

Another, more fundamental difference between feedforward and re-entrant processing emerges when we look at the effects on memory formation. Re-entrant activity, where there is mutual excitation of the neurons involved, creates a condition that satisfies the Hebb rule, where both the pre- and postsynaptic neurons are simultaneously active. This will trigger the activation of NMDA-type receptors and hence the induction of synaptic plasticity processes (Singer 1995). These are the neural basis of *learning and *memory. In other words, stimuli that evoke re-entrant processing evoke learning, i.e. change your brain, while stimuli that evoke only feedforward activation have no lasting impact. The more fundamental reason why re-entrant processing is necessary for conscious experience might therefore very well be that only neural activity that induces synaptic plasticity, or learning and memory, and thus somehow changes the network, produces conscious experience. To put it simply: we need conscious experience to learn (Lamme 2006).

Note, however, that what is termed learning or memory formation here is a very general concept. It includes not only the formation of episodic memory, but also the acquisition of all forms of sensorimotor skills, or in fact any change in response of the system towards future events. Re-entrant processing will change your brain, whether you notice it or not.

4. Is re-entrant processing sufficient for consciousness?

This raises the second remaining issue, which has large philosophical implications. We have seen that there is ample evidence that re-entrant processing is necessary for conscious experience, and we also have neural arguments why this might be the case. But does it follow that re-entrant processing is really producing conscious experience? In other words, is it sufficient for consciousness?

It depends. A variety of studies have shown that re-entrant processing can occur in the absence of a conscious report. For example, re-entrant processes related to perceptual organization evoke specific EEG and fMRI signals in human subjects, that can be recorded when these subjects are aware of the figure–ground organization of the stimuli that are presented. However, these signals can also be recorded when the subjects are in a state of *inattentional blindness, meaning that they cannot report afterwards about what exactly they have seen, because their attention was directed elsewhere (Scholte et al. 2006). The difficulty in interpreting these results lies in the significance of the inattentional blindness paradigm for 'measuring' conscious experience. When subjects do not remember having seen something, does this necessarily imply that they did not see it at the moment of presentation? Or did they just forget (Lamme 2003, 2004, 2006)?

Another study, in monkeys, showed a direct dissociation between reportability and re-entrant processing (Super et al. 2001). Here, contextual modulation of V1 neurons was taken as a measure of the presence or absence of re-entrant processing (see above, and Fig. R1c). The monkeys had to detect the presence or absence of texture-defined squares, presented at random locations. There were also trials in which there was no square at all, and the number of these catch trials was varied in different recording sessions. The monkeys were thus in a classic *signal detection paradigm, where targets (squares) could be either 'seen' (hits) or 'not seen' (missed), and catch trials could be either correctly identified as such (correct rejection), or falsely mistaken for targets (false alarm). The primary finding was that re-entrant signals were present when targets were 'seen', and absent when targets were 'not seen', while feedforward activation of V1 neurons did not differ across these conditions. This stipulated once more the importance of re-entrant processing for conscious detection.

Interestingly, varying the number of catch trials had the effect of changing the decision criterion of the monkey for either giving a 'seen' or 'not seen' behavioural response. With a lot of catch trials, the monkeys gave many more 'not seen' responses on trials where squares where presented, even though nothing changed in the visibility of the squares. At the same time, the perfect correlation between re-entrant signals and report (that was obtained with a low number of catch trials) was lost: Also on 'not seen' trials, re-entrant signals could now be recorded.

This indicates, first of all, that the re-entrant signals are not a direct correlate or reflection of the monkeys' report. So in that sense, there seems to be a dissociation between reportable awareness and re-entrant processing. On the other hand, the data could be perfectly well explained by assuming that the re-entrant signals are a correlate of the subjective visibility of the squares, and by adopting a model where this subjective visibility is fed into a classic signal detection stage, where this 'internal subjective visibility signal' has to surpass a decision criterion threshold for the monkey to give a 'seen' response (Super et al. 2001).

Again, the more or less philosophical question arises, what it means when a monkey (or a human for that matter) says 'not seen', when placed in a situation of sparse signals and high decision criterion. Nothing changes in the stimulus visibility, or in the perceptual apparatus of the receiver. The only difference is that in a situation of high decision criterion, the subject is less inclined to say 'yes, I saw it', than in a situation of low criterion. Is he suddenly 'seeing' less, because he only says 'yes' when he is absolutely sure?

What painfully appears is that we need to make some choices here. If we want to equate conscious experience to the report of that experience (as would those who see consciousness as the broadcasting of information into '*global workspace', or those who believe in inattentional blindness as opposed to inattentional *amnesia), then the conclusion is: re-entrant processing is not sufficient for conscious experience. Advocates of such a conclusion would be in the same camp as those who deny conscious experience to split-brain patients: because, treated with a *commissurotomy, such patient will not report verbally about visual stimuli presented to the right hemisphere. Some take this as evidence that he is really not seeing these stimuli, even though the subject can draw, copy, select and perform cognitive operations on these stimuli. After all, the subjects *says* he is not seeing them. He will know best, won't he?

However, if we accept that some conscious experiences might be too fleeting to remember (in episodic memory, that is), and that reporting about a conscious experience is something else (and requires additional cognitive and neural machinery) than having the conscious experience, the conclusion could be: re-entrant processing is sufficient for conscious experience (Lamme 2004, 2006). Advocates of such a conclusion would grant a split-brain patient conscious experience of what happens in the right hemisphere, even though he cannot speak about it. Philosophers in this camp recognize the difference between seeing and reporting as the difference between *phenomenal consciousness and *access consciousness (Block 2005).

Who is right? For a behavioural chauvinist, the report will be the only true measure of consciousness. For a neural chauvinist, like myself, the neural evidence will put a large weight in the balance (see Lamme 2006 for an elaboration of that point). Re-entrant processing = Consciousness.

VICTOR A. F. LAMME

Albright, T. D. and Stoner, G. R. (2002). 'Contextual influences on visual processing'. *Annual Review of Neuroscience*, 25.

Block, N. (2005). 'Two neural correlates of consciousness'. *Trends in Cognitive Sciences*, 9.

Engel, A. K. and Singer, W. (2001). 'Temporal binding and the neural correlates of sensory awareness'. *Trends in Cognitive Sciences*, 5.

Grossberg, S. (1999). 'The link between brain learning, attention, and consciousness'. *Consciousness and Cognition*, 8.

Haynes, J. D., Driver, J., and Rees, G. (2005). 'Visibility reflects dynamic changes of effective connectivity between V1 and fusiform cortex'. *Neuron*, 46.

Lamme, V. A. F. (2003). 'Why visual attention and awareness are different'. *Trends in Cognitive Sciences*, 7.

—— (2004). 'Separate neural definitions of visual consciousness and visual attention; a case for phenomenal awareness'. *Neural Networks*, 17.

—— (2006). 'Towards a true neural stance on consciousness'. *Trends in Cognitive Sciences*, 10.

—— and Roelfsema, P. R. (2000). 'The distinct modes of vision offered by feedforward and recurrent processing'. *Trends in Neuroscience*, 23.

——, Super, H. and Spekreijse, H. (1998a). 'Feedforward, horizontal, and feedback processing in the visual cortex'. *Current Opinion in Neurobiology*, 8.

——, Zipser, K., and Spekreijse, H. (1998b). 'Figure-ground activity in primary visual cortex is suppressed by anesthesia'. *Proceedings of the National Academy of Sciences of the USA*, 95.
——, Zipser, K., and Spekreijse, H. (2002). 'Masking interrupts figure-ground signals in V1'. *Journal of Cognitive Neuroscience*, 14.
Pascual-Leone, A. and Walsh, V. (2001). 'Fast back projections from the motion to the primary visual area necessary for visual awareness'. *Science*, 292.
Tononi, G. and Edelman, G. M. (1998). Consciousness and complexity. *Science*, 282.
Scholte, H. S., Witteveen, S. C., Spekreijse, H., and Lamme, V. A. F. (2006). 'The influence of inattention on the neural correlates of scene segmentation'. *Brain Research*, 1076.
Singer, W. (1995). 'Development and plasticity of cortical processing architectures'. *Science*, 270.
—— (1999). 'Neuronal synchrony: a versatile code for the definition of relations?' *Neuron*, 24.
Super, H., Spekreijse, H., and Lamme, V. A. F (2001). 'Two distinct modes of sensory processing observed in monkey primary visual cortex (V1)'. *Nature Neuroscience*, 4.

reflexive consciousness See SELF-CONSCIOUSNESS

refrigerator light problem How much are you conscious of at any one point in time? Some (*maximalists*) believe that the *contents of consciousness are rich; others (*minimalists*) believe that the contents of consciousness are sparse. Maximalists argue that their view is supported by *introspection: it *seems* as though the contents of consciousness are rich. Some minimalists reject this claim: they say that the contents of consciousness do not seem to be rich. Other minimalists accept the maximalists' description of how experience seems, but they deny that such descriptions are *true*. These minimalists think that maximalists are seduced by the refrigerator light illusion: just as one might think that the refrigerator light is always on because it is on whenever one checks, so too (the minimalist claims), maximalists assume that consciousness is rich because for any one of a large number of contents, 'checking' suggests that that content is typically conscious. (Are you currently conscious of the positions of your limbs? Have a look—and hey presto!) But—so minimalists hold—this sense of phenomenal plenitude is illusory: much of what we are conscious of we are conscious of only when (and because) we check. Thus, the refrigerator light illusion. Of course, reference to the refrigerator light *illusion* pitches things in favour of minimalism, for maximalists deny that the sense of plenitude that we enjoy *is* illusory. The real issue here is what kind of access we have to consciousness without 'looking'. It is better to call this the refrigerator light *problem*: can we find out whether the light of consciousness is on without opening the refrigerator door?

The refrigerator light problem has an easy solution if—as some argue—it is a conceptual truth that there is no consciousness outside of cognitive accessibility. But there is little to recommend this solution. At this stage of empirical inquiry, it is surely an open question whether phenomenal consciousness might outstrip cognitive accessibility. The question is whether we have—indeed, whether we *could* have—good reason to think that this possibility is realized.

Reflection on refrigerators and their doors suggests a potential line of enquiry. We are not seduced by the refrigerator light illusion because we know how refrigerators work. We know that the refrigerator light is not always on because we know that the light inside a refrigerator is activated by opening and closing the door. In a parallel manner, we might hope to determine whether consciousness exists in the absence of cognitive accessibility by developing a model of consciousness itself. If it turns out that the mechanisms of consciousness demand access (or at least accessibility) to the contents of consciousness, then we have reason to think that the contents of consciousness are likely to be sparse. On the other hand, discovering that the mechanisms of consciousness can operate independently of those of cognitive accessibility would give us reason to think that the contents of consciousness are rich.

The obvious snag with this approach is that we do not have a model of consciousness. Furthermore, any attempt to develop a model of consciousness (at the requisite level of detail) would appear to demand that we take sides on the question of whether phenomenal consciousness might outstrip cognitive accessibility. So we need another line of enquiry. Here is one. Even someone who does not know how refrigerators work might have a pretty good idea of how they have been *designed* to work. Given the use to which we put refrigerators, one might expect them to have been designed with a mechanism that switches the light on only when the door has been opened. Similarly, one might employ a certain conception of the functional role of consciousness in order to argue that consciousness does—or, alternatively, does not—outrun cognitive accessibility.

Unfortunately, this approach faces the same problems as its predecessor, for there is no consensus on the functional role of consciousness—indeed, there is little agreement about what, in the most general terms, an account of the functional role of consciousness might look like. Some theorists take consciousness to be in the business of presenting information to the subject's executive processes—planning, judgement-formation, and the like. On this approach, it is not implausible to suppose that the light of consciousness is on only when one has ready cognitive access to its contents. Other theorists, however, see consciousness as playing a role in certain forms of behavioural control that involve little in the way of executive involvement. Proponents of this approach have reason to allow that the light of consciousness could be on even when the refrigerator door is shut. The refrigerator light problem might not be insoluble, but it is certainly one of the toughest that the science of consciousness faces.

TIM BAYNE

religious experience Contemporary and 20th century philosophical treatments of religious experience are greatly influenced by William James's *The Varieties of Religious Experience* (1902). James (1842–1910) treated religious experience in observational terms, documenting cases in which individuals report an encounter with an unseen supernatural or spiritual reality. While James treated these experiences as ostensible cognitive apprehensions with evidential significance, his conclusions about the nature of this 'spiritual reality' remained unsettled in his published work. Fluctuating between personal theism (in which God is encountered as a person) and what he called *pluralistic pantheism* (in which God turns out to be a 'higher self'), James seemed more convinced of a negative thesis: religious experiences provide some reason to believe there is more to reality than is disclosed in contemporary, scientific naturalism. Subsequent philosophical, and to some extent psychological inquiry has often taken shape in either denying James's conclusion and demonstrating that naturalism can fully account for religious experience, or in a defence of the cognitive value of such ostensible experiences that can, in principle, vindicate a non-naturalist, religious world view.

The naturalist rejoinder to James has drawn on the psychological, sociological, and physiological factors that may explain the occurrence of religious beliefs in a naturalistic framework. The general, overall strategy has been to argue that the kinds of experiences that James took to be cognitively significant would occur in the absence of any transcendent, divine, or sacred object of experience. For example, if there would be reports of ostensible experiences of God even if there is no God, then the ostensible experiences are evidentially empty. Consider an analogy: if you knew there was a powerful yellow light in a room that would make all objects look yellow whether or not they were red or blue, then having an ostensible visual experience of a yellow object in the room would not be evidence that there is a bona fide yellow object in the room. Sigmund Freud (1856–1939) identified primitive guilt, unconscious desires to placate an angry, dead father, and a desire for an allegiance with an all-powerful supernatural ally who would benefit oneself and others, as key causal factors supporting religious experiences and practices. Max Weber (1864–1920) drew on sociological models of control and authority to account for religious, charismatic authority and experience. Today, the naturalist case against James has been advanced in light of recent neurophysiological accounts of religious experience. Andrew Newberg and Eugene D'Aquili seek to account for mystical experiences in terms of the severance of neural inputs into the nervous system. By their lights, the apparent experiential awareness of some transcendent reality is brought about, at least in part, by the effects of the elimination or intervention of sensory nerve impulses (deafferentation).

Throughout the 20th century and today there are leading defenders of the cognitive value of religious experience. Early proponents of a non-naturalist account of religious experiences include Rudolf Otto (1869–1937), Evelyn Underhill (1875–1941), and W. T. Stace (1886–1967). Since the mid-20th century, the prominent defenders of the view that religious experience counts as evidence against naturalism and in favour of some non-naturalist religious world view such as theism include William Alston, H. D. Lewis, Caroline Davis, Jerome Gellman, Gary Gutting, John Hick, Kai Man Kwan, Alvin Plantinga, Richard Swinburne, William Wainright, and Keith Yandell. Common to most of these philosophers is the contention that if one is either undecided between naturalism and, say, some broadly conceived of theism, or one has some independent evidence of theism, then an ostensible experience of God provides prima facie evidence that there is a God in the absence of defeaters. A defeater is an evident belief that undermines the evidence. Using the analogy of visually seeing a yellow object, these philosophers may be read as contending that in the absence of strong reason to believe that there is a yellow light altering our visual experiences, seeing a yellow object is prima facie evidence that the object is indeed yellow. Moreover, Alston has argued that a strong epistemic principle that *the ostensible experience of X is not evidence that X if one would have the experience in the absence of X* can threaten our confidence in all our ordinary perception, for it is possible that all our ordinary perceptions are disordered (e.g. we are brains in vats merely simulated to have the experiences we are having). In place of such strict epistemology, Richard Swinburne has proposed what he calls the *principle of credulity*, according to which if it seems to a subject that X is present, then, in the absence of defeaters, X is probably present.

The current literature seems to support the assessment of religious experiences in light of one's background philosophical framework. Consider the role of neurology again in accounting for religious experience. Newberg and D'Aquili themselves contend that 'tracing spiritual experience to neurological behavior does not disprove its realness... both spiritual experiences and experiences of more ordinary material nature are made real to the mind in the very same way—through the processing powers of the brain and the cognitive functions of the mind' (Newberg et al. 1981:37). In this case, the relevance of the neurological findings will depend on broader, philosophical concerns. If one has good reason independently to adapt naturalism, the appeal to deafferentation could help explain away the apparent cognitive value of religious experience, but if there is independent reason to adopt theism or some alternative, religious world view, deafferentation and other anatomical processes may be taken seriously as reliable ways in which a sacred reality is apprehended on a par with the way in which our sensory and other anatomical processes allow us to experientially apprehend the world.

Recent, new areas of concentrated inquiry include comparative or cross-cultural accounts of religious experience. Huston Smith, Ninian Smart, John Hick, Keith Yandell, and others have offered expansive accounts of religious experience that go beyond the debate between naturalism and theism. There is growing work on Buddhist and monistic Hindu accounts of experiences and arguments over whether these experiences lend evidential weight to Buddhist concepts of the self or Hindu concepts of Brahman. Another arena of new work involves inquiry into the relationship between religious and aesthetic and moral experiences (Douglas Hedley and Mark Wynn).

CHARLES TALIAFERRO

Alston, W. (1991). *Perceiving God.* Cornell University Press.

Bagger, M. C. (1999). *Religious Experience, Justification, and History.*

Davis, C. (1989). *The Evidential Force of Religious Experience.*

Gellman, J. (1997). *Experience of God and the Rationality of Religious Belief.*

—— (2001). *Mystical Experience of God: a Philosophical Inquiry.*

Hedley, D. (2008). *Living Forms of the Imagination.*

Kwan, K. (2003). 'Is the critical trust approach to religious experience incompatible with religious particularism?' *Faith and Philosophy* 20.

Newberg, A., D'Aquili, E., and Rause, V. (2001). *Why God Won't Go Away: Brain Science and the Biology of Belief.*

Otto, R. (1936). *The Idea of the Holy.* Oxford University Press.

Swinburne, R. (2004). *The Existence of God*, 2nd edn.

Wainwright, W. (1981). *Mysticism.*

Wynn, M. (2005). *Emotional Experience and Religious Understanding.*

Yandell, K. (1993). The *Epistemology of Religious Experience.*

REM See SLEEP

representationalism Representationalism is the doctrine that representation plays a central role in philosophical theories of consciousness. For instance, one might say that what makes Jane's fleeting glimpse of a mockingbird conscious is Jane's taking a perspective on, or representing, that glimpse; or one might say that the specific feel of that fleeting glimpse can be understood by saying how things are from Jane's perspective, or how Jane represented things to be (it was to Jane as if a mockingbird flashed by).

Each of these views is attractive: surely we do not think that Jane's glimpse of a mockingbird could be conscious if that glimpse were entirely outside Jane's perspective; and surely we do frequently specify the feel of a conscious mental episode by saying how things were from our perspective in that episode.

1. Philosophical theories of consciousness
2. Representationality
3. Higher-order and first-order representationalism
4. Master cases for representationalism
5. Representationalism and reduction
6. Issues for the higher-order representationalist
7. Issues for the first-order representationalist

1. Philosophical theories of consciousness

A signal fact about psychological states is that some of them are conscious, or feel a certain way. Consider a searing pain, or a fleeting glimpse of a mockingbird: each of these feels some way. Quite plausibly, not all psychological states feel some way: cognitive science posits a series of complex computations by way of which physical stimulus causes conscious awareness, the intermediate stages of which cause consciousness without themselves being conscious. By 'consciousness' contemporary representationalists almost invariably intend phenomenal consciousness (see CONSCIOUSNESS, CONCEPTS OF), where for an episode in the mental life of a subject to be phenomenally conscious (to be an experience) is for there to be something the episode is like for the subject (Nagel 1974; see 'WHAT IT'S LIKE'); and for an episode to be like something for a subject is for there to be some feature or 'property' such that the episode has the feature for the subject. For instance, perhaps, an episode of experiencing pain may be uncomfortable for a subject. In such a case, it is said that the feature (being uncomfortable) is among the (many) *phenomenal characters of the episode; alternatively, the episode has the feature phenomenally (the episode is, phenomenally, uncomfortable). So for an episode to be phenomenally conscious is for it to have some phenomenal character, to be some way phenomenally. This elucidation of consciousness in terms of mental episodes having features for their subjects immediately raises two questions: (1) When an episode is a certain way for a subject, in what further relationship between the episode, the way, and the subject does this consist, if any? (2) What is the possible range of the features which may be phenomenal characters? Theories of consciousness that have been labelled 'representational' have been addressed (somewhat confusingly) to answering each of these questions.

2. Representationality

The notion of perspective is somewhat metaphorical; the representational theory of perspective explicates it in two stages. First, each aspect of a subject's perspective is understood as a taking of an attitude toward a way the world could be. Consider a judgement, or a hope, that Portugal wins the World Cup in 2010. These are both, in a sense, aspects of a subject's perspective on the world. Both fit the mould of being attitudes toward a way the world could be: that Portugal wins World Cup 2010 is a way the world could be—if Portugal does win World Cup 2010, then the world is that way, if it does not, then the world is not that way; the judgement involves taking the attitude of judging toward this way the world could be, while the hope involves taking the attitude of hoping toward this way.

Second, the notion of taking some attitude or other toward a way the world could be is explained in terms of a norm of representational correctness. Which way-the-world-could-be a mental episode is an attitude toward is given by how the world would have to be for that episode to be correct as a representation of the world. A judgement or hope that Portugal wins World Cup 2010 is correct as a representation of the world if Portugal does win World Cup 2010; incorrect as a representation of the world if Portugal does not win World Cup 2010. Correctness as a representation of the world is, like correctness as a use of a salad fork, a *normative* feature, resulting from association with some system of value: in particular, from the system of values associated with representations as such. For a mental episode to be an aspect of a subject's perspective, on the representational theory of perspective, then, is for it to be representational: to be subject to the system of values associated with representations as such. Say that a property like *being correct as a representation just in case such and such* is a 'representational property'. Either stage of the explanation of perspective in terms of representational values may be questioned. Particularly relevant to the study of consciousness are challenges to the first stage: some philosophical theories of consciousness accord a central explanatory role to perspective, but reject the representational theory of perspective (see ACQUAINTANCE; INTENTIONALITY).

3. Higher-order and first-order representationalism

Since the theory of consciousness aims to answer both questions (1) and (2) above, representation may play a role in answering either question. Indeed, philosophers have appealed to representation in answering both questions. A theory which appeals to representation in answering question (1) (Lycan 1996, Rosenthal 2002, Kriegel and Williford 2006) would take the following general form: For a mental episode to be a certain way for its subject is just for the episode to be represented to the subject as being that way: for the subject to undergo some mental episode which is correct as a representation if, and only if, the episode is that way. Such an answer is sometimes referred to as *higher-order representationalism*.

Alternatives to higher-order representationalism are legion. For instance, there is the view that for a mental episode to be a certain way for its subject is: for it just to be that way (assuming, of course, that the feature is a possible phenomenal character in accord with the answer to (2)); or for the episode's being that way to be in a position to play a central role in its subject's cognition (for it to be 'poised': Tye 2000); or for the episode's particular instance of being that way to have a special conscious 'glow' which cannot be understood in more basic terms; or for its being that way to be within the subject's perspective in some way not compatible with the representational theory of perspective.

A theory which appeals to representation in answering question (2) (Siewert 1998, Tye 2000, Byrne 2001, Chalmers 2004) would take something like the following form: A feature may be a phenomenal character only if it is a representational property. Such an answer is sometimes referred to as *first-order representationalism*. Alternatives to first-order representationalism are also legion. For instance, there is the view that any feature which a mental episode can have can be a phenomenal character, assuming it and the episode together meet the condition mandated in the answer to (1); various familiar physicalist and functionalist answers—e.g. that the phenomenal characters are certain special brain features (see FUNCTIONS OF CONSCIOUSNESS); the view that a property is a possible phenomenal character only if that property is of the special conscious type, a type which cannot be understood in more basic terms; and the view, once again, that some non-representational properties characterizing a subject's perspective are phenomenal characters.

First- and higher-order representationalism are compatible. A view answering both questions is that every phenomenal character is a representational property, but that not every representational property is a phenomenal character—to be 'promoted' to phenomenality, such a property must be itself represented (Lycan 1996).

4. Master cases for representationalism

The master case for higher-order representationalism appeals to our inability to make sense of an episode's being some way for its subject despite its being no way at all from the subject's perspective—despite the subject's being utterly blind to the episode (Kriegel and Williford 2006). If this really is incoherent, then if an episode is some way for its subject, it is some way from the subject's perspective. And, granting the representational theory of perspective, if an episode is some way for its subject, it is represented to its subject as being that way. It would then be natural to explain this by holding that what makes the episode be some way for its subject is that it is represented to its subject as being that way. That is what the higher-order representationalist says in answer to (1).

The master case for first-order representationalism stems from introspective or 'phenomenological' study of a variety of phenomenally conscious episodes: to fully characterize what it is like for me to see now I must say that from my perspective, a yellow architect's lamp jitters on its mount (Siewert 1998); to fully characterize my conscious emotions in November 2004 I must mention dejection at election results and concern about the future (Tye 2000)—both aspects of my perspective. (This phenomenological point is one of several made in an attempt to elucidate G. E. Moore's famous discussion of a '*transparency' somehow involved in reflection on experience: Hellie 2006, 2007b.) If this is correct, and if it is granted that the features revealed to phenomenological study are phenomenal characters, this makes a strong case that at least many phenomenal characters of the most important mental states are properties concerning how things are from one's perspective. First-order representationalism follows if we plug in the representational theory of perspective.

5. Representationalism and reduction

Ambitious projects for the *reduction of consciousness to something more basic have been pursued in the hope of locating the place of this richly colourful and flavourful feature of the world in the austere mathematical world of physics (see EPIPHENOMENALISM; EXPLANATORY GAP; HARD PROBLEM OF CONSCIOUSNESS; PHYSICALISM). A number of partial successes in reducing certain varieties of representation to something a bit more austere have suggested the use of representation as a way-station: first, reduce consciousness to some kind of representation; then, reduce that kind of representation to something austere (Tye 2000).

The two-stage reductive strategy faces the difficulty that, in combination, the fact that consciousness seems hard to reduce to the physical and the fact that consciousness seems easy to reduce to a certain variety of representation undermine the view that the variety of representation to which consciousness reduces is the same as that which reduces to physics—a problem especially pressing if representation is to be understood as is standard as involving a variety of value. If the cognitive scientists are correct, not all representation brings about phenomenal character; so perhaps the sort which does is an irreducible sort of conscious representation (Stoljar 2007).

We now turn to some local issues of detail in the development of higher-order and first-order representationalism.

6. Issues for the higher-order representationalist

Much of the literature on higher-order representationalism is devoted to peculiarities of three of its variants: the *higher-order thought (Rosenthal 2002), inner sense (Lycan 1996), and Brentanian (Kriegel and Williford 2006) theories. These views differ along two dimensions.

The first concerns the 'topology' of the 'inner' representation of the episode. On the first two views, this inner representation is other-representation: the representing episode is distinct from the represented episode; while on the third, it is self-representation: the representing episode just is the represented episode. The second of these dimensions concerns the attitude taken toward the inner representation. On the higher-order thought view, the attitude is more like judgement; while on the inner sense view, the attitude is more like perception.

Concerning the latter dimension, it is clear that inner representation is not exactly like ordinary cases of judgement or perception. Against exact resemblance with judgement, babies arguably have experiences without being sophisticated enough to form judgements about them; also, the phenomenal characters of our perceptual experiences seem limitlessly intricate while our judgements seem comparatively crude. Against exact resemblance with perception, whenever one perceives a mockingbird, one has an experience that is distinct from the mockingbird itself; but a conscious perceptual experience of a mockingbird does not seem to involve both a perceptual experience of the mockingbird and a distinct perception of the perception of the mockingbird.

Concerning the former dimension, the motivation for higher-order representationalism extends naturally to the self-representational view. If an episode's being like something for its subject requires that episode's being within the subject's perspective, then shouldn't that perspective also be like something for its subject? Otherwise, it would seem, the whole arrangement would merely take non-conscious representation of a mockingbird, and, as it were, push it inward, resulting in non-conscious representation of representation of a mockingbird—without any additional gain of consciousness. But if so, this would seem to set off an explosion of inner representation without bound. Such an explosion would involve either an infinite chain of distinct other-representing mental episodes, or at some point a circle, in which some episode represents itself. Since, quite plausibly, we have only finitely many mental episodes at once, the former is right out. Hence, consciousness requires, at some stage, self-representation; and why delay the inevitable?

A central question for the higher-order representationalist is whether, always, if an experience is a certain way phenomenally, it is that way in fact. Could it be that, while an experience is unpleasant for its subject, it is in fact pleasant, or at least neutral—or that, while an experience is, for its subject, like seeing a green square, it is in fact like seeing a red octagon? The idea beggars comprehension. And yet the higher-order representationalist seems pressured to accept this possibility. After all, outer representation is fallible: sometimes green squares look like red octagons. Inner representation would certainly be peculiar if it were utterly immune to error.

7. Issues for the first-order representationalist

The literature on first-order representationalism contains extensive discussion of the following three issues.

First, consider the phenomenal contrast between seeing and feeling an X, despite both representing that something X-shaped is before one. The first-order representationalist can explain this difference by appeal to manners of representing, via the 'impure' representational properties (Chalmers 2004) of visually vs tactually representing that something X-shaped is before one. Or consider blurrily seeing an X: first-person reflection arguably reveals the experience to be blurry, but blurriness is also plausibly a manner of representing (Crane forthcoming). The same strategy could perhaps distinguish perceiving from judging that something X-shaped is before one (see PHENOMENOLOGY). Such manners influence how an experience is for its subject, seem to be qualities of the experience (just as a slow run is an episode with slowness as a quality), and fail to be representational properties; so accepting impure representational properties as phenomenal characters requires accepting non-representational phenomenal characters. This involves some departure from the most full-blooded first-order representationalism. Still, these features seem to qualify and depend on the representational features (as the slowness of a run depends on its being a run), so that representational properties still end up fundamental to consciousness.

Second, for some phenomenal characters, the core claim of the phenomenological case for first-order representationalism is not especially contentious: for instance, when one sees an X before one, arguably, first-person reflection on the experience reveals it to be representationally correct if and only if representationally correct if and only if something X-shaped is before one. (Still, this is contested: perhaps first-person reflection reveals only a non-representational visual 'taking in' of or 'acquaintance with' an X; Travis 2004.) By contrast, for other phenomenal characters, the representational theory of perspective does not seem to be a natural fit. A visual experience in which nothing even seems to be seen—such as a visual experience with closed eyes—does not clearly involve any representation of anything; but it may seem to involve a non-representational perspective on something—a field suffused with a sort of 'blackness' (Hellie 2006).

Third, the '*inverted spectrum' threatens first-order representationalism. Very briefly, the issue is this: (1) plausibly, there could be a subject Abnorm who has the same phenomenal character when seeing green as the rest of us have when seeing red, and vice versa. This need not interfere with Abnorm's ability to navigate his environment. But if not, we should assume Abnorm correctly represents the colours of things. But then (2) there need be no difference between the representational properties of the experiences of Abnorm and of a normal subject when seeing certain scene, despite the evident difference in their phenomenal characters. But then it seems that phenomenal character varies independently of representational properties, against first-order representationalism. The literature contains a very extensive discussion of attempts to block (1) (Tye 2000, Lycan 2001) and (2) (Chalmers 2004, Shoemaker 2006).

BENJ HELLIE

Byrne, A. (2001). 'Intentionalism defended'. *Philosophical Review*, 110.

Chalmers, D. J. (2004). 'The representational character of experience'. In Leiter, B. (ed.) *The Future for Philosophy*.

Crane, T. (forthcoming). 'Intentionalism'. To appear in Beckerman, A. and McLaughlin, B. (eds) *Oxford Handbook to the Philosophy of Mind*.

Hellie, B. (2006). 'Beyond phenomenal naiveté'. *Philosophers' Imprint*, 6. www.philosophersimprint.org/006002.

—— (2007a). 'Higher-order intentionalism and higher-order acquaintance'. *Philosophical Studies*, 134.

—— (2007b). 'That which makes the sensation of blue a mental fact'. *European Journal of Philosophy*, 15.

Kriegel, U. and Williford, K. (eds) (2006). *Self-representational Approaches to Consciousness*.

Lycan, W. G. (1996). *Consciousness and Experience*.

—— (2001). 'The case for phenomenal externalism'. *Philosophical Perspectives*, 15.

Nagel, T. (1974). 'What is it like to be a bat?' *Philosophical Review*, 83.

Rosenthal, D. M. (2002). 'Explaining consciousness'. In Chalmers, D. J. (ed.) *Philosophy of Mind: Classical and Contemporary Readings*.

Shoemaker, S. (2006). 'On the ways things appear'. In Gendler, T. S. and Hawthorne, J. (eds) *Perceptual Experience*.

Siewert, C. (1998). *The Significance of Consciousness*.

Stoljar, D. (2007). 'Consequences of intentionalism'. *Erkenntnis*, 66.

Travis, C. (2004). 'The silence of the senses'. *Mind*, 113.

Tye, M. (2000). *Consciousness, Color, and Content*.

representation, problems A representation is anything that is about something. Philosophers call the property of being about something *intentionality. *Intentionality* and *intentional* are technical terms in philosophy; they do not mean a representation was necessarily made 'intentionally' in the everyday sense; just that it is about something. A picture of a tree in your garden is a representation because it is about the tree.

1. Background
2. The representational theory of mind
3. Foundational problems of naturalizing representation
4. Application in sciences

1. Background

When we think, we also think about things, e.g. about my birthday party yesterday, so thoughts are ways of representing. Thoughts are *personal-level representations*; it is the person herself who represents the world a certain way by thinking (or seeing and so on). Psychologists also postulate *sub-personal representations*, where a part of the person does the representing. For example, your auditory system might represent a time difference between sounds that you as a person were not even aware of. Psychologists regularly use representations in their theories: they might say prejudice occurs because of *stereotypes*, or we see the way we do because of the way the visual system *encodes* information. Almost all of psychology refers to personal or sub-personal representations. But how can anything represent? Can we explain the ability of minds to represent in terms of natural science? In short, how is psychology possible?

Representations have a certain anatomy, which we will gloss as *target*, *content*, and *vehicle*. When I think of my birthday party yesterday, the party plays a role in my thought in two distinct ways. On the one hand, there is the actual party I was at yesterday which my current thought is directed at or refers to. This is called the *target* (or *referent*—these terms are not quite synonymous) of the thought. On the other hand, there is how the party is presented in my thought; for example, I may think of it as, 'yesterday's party', or as 'my last birthday party'. These two thoughts have different *contents* because they present the same referent in different ways. If I have a thought with the content, 'my party was yesterday', then the thought is true (target and content match); but if the thought had the content 'my party happened a week ago', the thought would be false. It is because target and content are distinct that thoughts can be true or false (target and content match or mismatch); and that deception, *illusions, and *hallucinations are thus possible. Similarly, the distinction is what allows my boss and my spouses' lover to be thought of as different people (same referent person, different contents); and thus more generally allows people to be at cross-purposes and for life to be interesting. In general, all representations have content, but they need not have a target or referent. If I imagine a horse, there need be no target horse to check the accuracy of my imagination against. Finally, as well as always having content and (sometimes) a target, representations are in general made of something physical, the representational *medium* or *vehicle*. For example, if I write on a blackboard, the vehicle is the chalk and the blackboard. The distinctions between content, target and vehicle may seem obvious, but failure to keep them conceptually separate has lead to mistaken explanations in psychology (see Dennett 1991:Ch. 5–6 and Perner 1991:Ch. 3 for examples).

Representation is a central concept in cognitive science. The fact that some representations are not mental (e.g. photographs) has motivated the idea that understanding simple physical representations might enable understanding the mind in a naturalistic way. Some feel that understanding representation might give us a handle on consciousness itself. Perhaps the goal of psychology in general is precisely to understand to what extent and in what way the mind represents. According to Perner (1991), how children come to understand the mind as representational is central to child development. Further, understanding representation is central to the philosophy of language, of science, and of rationality. Here we will focus just on issues relevant to the nature of mental representation.

2. The representational theory of mind

The claim that people in having mental states can represent an external world is the weakest sense of a *representational theory of mind*. It is bolder to assert the best explanations of the mind will be in terms of representations (a move not all are willing to make, as discussed below). Explaining the mind in terms of representations offers the appeal of having a naturalistic explanation of the mind, if only representations could be understood naturalistically. If a student thinks of a party, then presumably the student has some neural activity (the representational vehicle) that is about the party. There is reason to think we should be able to understand how physical things, like neural activity, could acquire the apparently non-physical relation of aboutness. Computer programs, for example, consist of internal electrical processes that represent things outside the machine. Other familiar physical entities like linguistic inscriptions or pictures are also able to acquire aboutness. For instance, a photograph of the party is a physical object (representational vehicle: piece of paper with patterns of colour) that shows a scene of the party (target) in a certain way (content). Moreover, it seems clear what each of these elements (vehicle, content, and target) is. However, when one asks why the photo shows the scene of the party, the answer defers to the beholders of the photo: they see that scene in it. Similarly for language: the readers understand the linguistic inscriptions in the book, etc. If it is us human users of these representations that determine content, then this makes them useless to explain the origin of intentionality of the mind, because it is only derived from their users' intentionality (*derived intentionality*, see Searle 2005). There is no user endowed with intentionality reading our nervous activity. Philosophers have since made various proposals of how intentionality can be naturalized by explaining how mental representations can have content without the help of an agent imbued with intentionality. A failure to naturalize intentionality pushes one to either adopt *dualism (intentionality is an inexplicable primitive property of minds) or to deny a representational explanation of the mind is possible.

According to the representational theory of mind proposed by Fodor (among others; see Sterelny 1990) a mental state like thinking of a party consists of a mental representation of the party as well as the attitude of thinking, captured by the functional role the representation of the party plays in relation to other mental states. Different functional roles define different attitudes, including wishing, wondering, dreaming and so on (in fact, all the different types of mental states recognized in ordinary language, i.e. as recognized in folk psychology). Some people who endorse explaining the mind in terms of representations nonetheless reject the claim that the folk categories of believing, wanting, etc. are real natural kinds (e.g. Churchland). Fodor's suggestion of a representational theory of mind included the claim that the mental representations were of a special sort, namely symbolic. Others have denied mental representations are symbolic, an issue we also comment on below.

3. Foundational problems of naturalizing representation

Representational content. The content of a representation is how it portrays the world as being. We discuss four main approaches to explaining how the content of a representation is determined. There is no wide agreement yet that any of them has solved the problem.

(a) According to Dennett, there is no fact of the matter as to what the content of a representation is, or even whether it is a representation (a position called *irrealism*). It is sometimes useful for an observer to view a system as an intentional one; in that way the observer takes an *intentional stance*. For example, I might say 'My computer is thinking about the problem', 'My car wants to stop now', if I find this useful in predicting behaviour. In taking this stance one works out what beliefs and desires the system ought to have if it were a rational agent with a given purpose. Hence one can work out what behaviour the system ought to engage in. On other occasions it might be more useful to take a *physical stance*, analysing the system in terms of physical laws and principles, a process that can take considerable effort. What type of stance we take is largely a matter of convenience. Similarly, even the thoughts we seem introspectively to be having are actually interpretations we make: stories we spin about ourselves (e.g. that we are having a certain thought) for which there is no fact of the matter. The account raises a number of issues: Why is the intentional stance so good at making predictions (at least for people) if it fails to describe and explain anything real? How can we as observers make interpretations of ourselves without already having intentionality? And given people are not always optimally rational, how do we constrain the stories that are spun?

The remaining theories are *realist* about representations: they presume there is some fact of the matter as to whether something represents and what its content is.

(b) *Causal/informational theories*, for example Dretske's early work, assume that a neural activity 'cow' becomes a representation meaning COW if it is reliably caused by the presence of a cow, hence reliably carries the information that (indicates) a cow is present. A recognized problem with this approach is that on this theory representations cannot misrepresent. If 'cow' is sometimes caused by the presence of a horse on a dark night then it simply accurately represents the disjunction of COW-OR-HORSE-ON-A-DARK-NIGHT (disjunction problem) instead of misrepresenting the horse as a cow as one would intuitively expect.

(c) *Functional role semantics*, for example Harman's, assume the meaning of a representation is determined by the permissible inferences that can be drawn from it or, in more liberal versions, how the representation is used more generally. 'Cow' means COW because it licenses inferences that are appropriate about cows. The idea can be motivated by considering a calculator. If one inspected the wiring diagram, one could work out which button or state corresponded to the number '3', which to the process of addition, and so on, just by determining how the states were related to each other. To be able to represent the number '3', surely one needs to have appropriate relations between that representation and the one for '2', for the concept of 'successor', etc. And maybe it is just the same for concepts of cows, bachelors, assassins, and so on.

One problem with functional role semantics is how learning anything new, by changing the inferences one is disposed to draw, may change the meaning of all one's representations (a consequence called *holism*). As I am always learning, I can never think the same thought twice. Nor can any two people think the same thought, given their belief structures are different, if only slightly. Does this make it impossible to state useful generalizations concerning mental states and behaviour? How can we respect the difference between changing one's belief involving a concept and changing one's concept? It is also not clear how conceptual role semantics can allow misrepresentation: because the meaning of a representation is determined by its uses, how can a representation meaning one thing be used as if it meant something else? The solution to these problems is to restrict which uses determine meaning, but there is no agreement how in general to do this.

(d) Dretske and Millikan proposed *teleosemantics* as a theory of naturalizing content. Whereas causal/informational theories focus on the input relationship of how external conditions cause representations, and functional role semantics focuses on the output side of what inferences a representation enables, teleosemantics sees representations as midway between input and output and focuses on function as determined by history. Representations do not represent simply because they reliably indicate, or simply because they are used, but because of functions brought about by an evolutionary or learning history, namely a function to indicate. Because of an evolutionary history, a heart is an object with the function of pumping blood. So certain patterns of neural activity may come to have the function of indicating, for example, cows. The basic assumption is that there must be enough covariation between the presence of a cow causing a 'cow' token, so that the token can guide cow-appropriate behaviour often enough that there is a selective advantage without which the cow–'cow' causal link would not have evolved. The 'cow' token *thereby* acquires the function of indicating cows. Just as historically defined function allows a heart to both function and malfunction, a representation can malfunction, making misrepresentation possible. If a horse happens to cause a token naturally selected for indicating cows, then the token misrepresents the horse as a cow. The token still means COW (disjunction problem solved) because the causing of 'cow' by horses was not what established this causal link. Although this theory seems to be the current leading contender, it is far from uncontested (see Neander 2004). For example, it seems conceptually clear that a representation could be adaptive but not accurate, or true but maladaptive to believe. The distinction between accurate and adaptive makes no sense to teleosemantics.

Broad vs narrow content. To the extent the content can be fixed by what happens in our head (same vehicle state implies same content), the content is said to be *narrow*. To the extent that the content can be fixed only by reference to the world as well as the vehicle state, it is said to be *broad* or, equivalently, *wide*. People who believe content is in general narrow are called *internalists*; those who believe content is in general broad are called **externalists*. The two camps have been vigorously debating for some decades now.

Externalism and internalism are motivated by different theories of content. On teleological theories, for example, content is necessarily broad because content is determined by a selection history. Exactly the same neural wiring may constitute a mouse detector or a poteroo detector in different possible worlds in which it was selected for mapping its on/off state onto mice or poteroos, respectively. No amount of examination of the vehicle alone need answer the question of which it represented. Similarly, two different neural wirings may both be poteroo detectors given relevant selection pressures. Conversely, on a strict functional role semantics, content depends on the inferences that could be drawn, so content depends only on what goes on inside the head.

Thoughts about the non-existent. The attempt to naturalize representational content has almost exclusively focused on the use of representations in detecting the state of the environment and acting on the environment. In other words the analysis—in particular of causal and informational approaches—is restricted to cases of real, existing targets. The teleosemantic approach can be extended to the content of desires since these representations can also contribute to the organism's fitness in a similar way to beliefs. Papineau made desires the primary source of representation. However, little has been said on how natural processes can build representations of hypothetical, counterfactual assumptions about the world or even outright fiction. One intuitively appealing step is to copy informative representations (caused by external states) into fictional contexts, thereby *decoupling* or *quarantining* them from their normal indicative functions. Although intuitively appealing, the idea presupposes the standard assumption of symbolic computer languages that symbols exist (but based on derived intentionality) that can be copied and keep their meaning. It remains to be shown how such copying can be sustained on a naturalist theory.

Implicit vs explicit representation. A representation need not make all of its content explicit. David Kirsch proposed that the degree to which information is explicitly encoded in a representation is related to the computational cost of recovering or using the information. According to Dienes and Perner (2002) something is implicitly represented if it is part of the representational content but the representational medium does not articulate that aspect. This can be illustrated with bee dances to indicate direction and amount of nectar. From the placement in space and the shape of the dance, bees convey to their fellow bees the direction and distance of nectar. The parameters of the dance, however, only change with the nectar's direction and distance. Nothing in the dance indicates specifically that it is about nectar (an object which nonetheless plays a causal role in the bees' behaviour). Yet nectar is part of the meaning. It is represented implicitly within the explicit representation of its direction and distance

Bee dances only make the properties of distance and direction explicit. The English sentence 'The nectar is 100 yards south' makes explicit the full proposition that the location is predicated of a certain individual, the nectar. Similarly, if a word, 'butter' is flashed to a person very quickly, they may form an active BUTTER representation, but not represent explicitly that the word in front of them has the meaning butter (subliminal perception). The sentence 'I see the nectar is 100 yards south' or 'I see the word in front of me is "butter" ' makes things even more explicit; namely, the fact that one sees the proposition. Explicit representation is fundamental to consciousness (for the relation between representation and consciousness, see REPRESENTATIONALISM and CONTENTS OF CONSCIOUSNESS).

4. Application in sciences

Despite foundational problems, research in psychology, functional neuroscience, and computer science has proceeded using the notion of representation. The tacit working definition is in most cases covariation between stimuli and mental activity inferred from behaviour or neural processes.

Cognitive neuroscience investigates the representational vehicle (neural structures) directly. The intuitive notion of representation relies heavily on covariation. If a stimulus (including task instructions for humans) reliably evokes activity in a brain region, it is inferred that this region contains the mental representations required to carry out the given task. Particularly pertinent was the success of finding single cortical cells responsive to particular stimuli (*single-cell recording), which led to the probably erroneous assumption that particular features are represented by single cells, parodied as 'grandmother cells'. In the research programme investigating the neural *correlates of consciousness (NCC), conscious contents of neural vehicles are determined by correlating verbal reports with neural activities. Where the NCC are, and if any such thing exists, is an open and active current area of research.

Cognitive psychology assumes that experimental stimuli and task instructions are mentally represented. Theories consist of postulating how the representations are transformed. These representations are modelled and task performance (errors or reaction times) predicted. The quality of predictions provides the evidential basis of mental representations. For the investigation of longer reasoning processes sometimes the introspective verbal report is taken as evidence for the underlying mental representations. The enterprise is predicated on the notion that not only do people represent by having mental states, but thinking, perception and memory in turn can be explained in terms of sub-personal representations. The implicit assumption is that sub-personal intentionality will be naturalized, uniting cognitive psychology with the rest of the sciences.

One extensively argued issue is whether or in what domains thinking is symbolic or non-symbolic (normally *connectionist). A representation is symbolic if a token of it can be copied in different contexts and it retains the same meaning (normally explained by having the 'same shape'). The notion originates from the use of a central processor (CPU) in normal serial computers. Because different tokens of a symbol in different lines of program will only be processed when they pass through the CPU, different tokens can all be treated the same way. It is not clear that the same logic applies to the brain, for which there is no CPU. Nonetheless, Fodor has argued that the symbolic style of representation is the only theory we have for why people think in systematic and infinitely productive ways.

Connectionist networks potentially have two types of qualitatively different representation types: patterns of activation of units and patterns of weight strength between units. Given a teleological theory of content, for example, a learning algorithm may bring it about that a pattern of activation maps onto some external state of affairs so that the rest of the network can do its job. Then the pattern of activation represents that state of affairs. Similarly, the learning algorithm may bring it about that a pattern of weight strengths maps onto enduring statistical structures in the world so that the rest of the network can do its job. Then the pattern of weight strengths represents the external statistical structures. Psychologists naturally think in terms of activation patterns being representational because they naturally think in terms of representations being active or not. In the same way, sometimes they regard weights as non-representational. Weights on a teleological story are representational. They can misrepresent statistical structure in the environment so they can represent it. The process by which knowledge becomes embedded in weights in people is an example of implicit learning, the acquisition of unconscious knowledge.

Cognitive approaches to *perception can be contrasted with ecological and sensorimotor approaches; these latter attempt to do without a notion of representation at all. The anti-representationalist style of argument often goes like this: We need less rich representations than we thought to solve a task; therefore representations are not necessary at all. The premise is a valuable scientific insight; but the conclusion a non sequitur. To take a case in ecological psychology, while people in running to catch a ball do not need to represent the trajectory of the ball, as might first be supposed, they do represent the angle of elevation of their gaze to the ball. The representation is brutally minimal, but the postulation of a content-bearing state about something (the angle) is necessary to explain how people solve the task. There is a similar conflict between cognitive (representational) and dynamical systems (anti-representational) approaches to the mind, e.g. development. For example, how children learn to walk may be best understood in terms of the dynamic properties of legs getting bigger, the muscles getting elastic in certain ways; nothing need change in how the child represents how to walk. The debate has focused people's minds on a very useful research heuristic: try to work out the minimal representations needed to get a task done. Only when such a simple story has been discredited, then increase the complexity of the content of the postulated representations. Finally, note that all accounts must eventually explain how personal level representation is possible, as most people accept that people do represent the world.

**Artificial intelligence.* The traditional approach (symbolic AI, or Good Old Fashioned AI, GOFAI) assumed that the mind can be captured by a program, which is designed to have building blocks with representational content (derived intentionality). The new robotics is a reaction to trying to program explicitly all required information into an AI, a strategy that largely failed. The new strategy is to start from the bottom up, trying to construct the simplest sort of device that can actually interact with an environment. Simplicity is achieved by having the device presuppose as much as possible about its environment by being embedded in it; the aim is to minimize explicit representation where a crucial feature need only be implicitly represented. In fact, the proclaimed aim of new robotics is sometimes to do without representation altogether (see Clark 1997).

ZOLTÁN DIENES AND JOSEF PERNER

Clark, A. (1997). *Being There: Putting Brain, Body and World Together Again.*

Crane, T. (2005). *The Mechanical Mind*, 2nd edn.

Cummins, R. (1996). *Representations, Targets, and Attitudes.*

Dennett, D. (1991) *Consciousness Explained.*

Dienes, Z. and Perner, J. (2002). 'A theory of the implicit nature of implicit learning'. In French, R. M. and Cleeremans, A. (eds) *Implicit Learning and Consciousness: An Empirical, Philosophical, and Computational Consensus in the Making?*.

Greenberg, M. and Harman, G. (2006). 'Conceptual role semantics'. In Lepore, E. and Smith, B. (eds) *Oxford Handbook of Philosophy of Language.*

Kim, J. (2006). *The Philosophy of Mind*, 2nd edn.

Neander, K. (2004). 'Teleological theories of mental content'. In *The Stanford Encyclopedia of Philosophy.*

Perner, J. (1991). *Understanding the Representational Mind.*

Searle, J. (2005). *Mind: a Brief Introduction.*

Sterelny, K. (1990). *The Representational Theory of Mind: An Introduction.*

rubber hand illusion People can be induced to have the experience that a rubber hand is their own hand. This is achieved by brushing a visible rubber hand and synchronously brushing a participant's real hand (Botvinick and Cohen 1998). In the experiment the participant's real hand is hidden out of view (behind a screen), while a realistic life-sized rubber hand is placed in front of the participant. The experimenter uses two small paintbrushes to stroke the rubber hand and the participant's hidden hand, synchronizing the timing of the brushing. After a short period (about 10–30 s in most cases), the majority of people have the experience that the rubber hand is their own hand and that the rubber hand senses the touch of the paintbrush. This *illusion is only evoked if the experimenter applies synchronous brush strokes to the real and fake hand. If the brush strokes are applied asynchronously, the person does not experience any sense of ownership towards the rubber hand. Similarly, the illusion only works well if the rubber hand is aligned with the participant's real hidden hand so that it visually appears to be the real hand. If the rubber hand is rotated 90–180° the illusion is not elicited even if synchronous brush strokes are applied to the two hands. These observations suggest that the illusion of ownership of the fake hand depends on the detection of synchronous visual and tactile events and the match between the seen and perceived orientation of the arm.

The rubber hand illusion is a vivid and strong perceptual illusion that can be evoked in most human participants. However, some people are resistant to the illusion for reasons that have not yet been studied. When a person experiences the illusion, they genuinely feels that the rubber hand is part of their body. For example, people will typically report that they expect the rubber fingers to move when they make a finger movement. Also, people will flinch if the experimenter threatens to injure the rubber hand, but only during the illusion. Such physical threats to the owned rubber hand is associated with increases in skin sweating, which is indicative of autonomic arousal (Armel and Ramachandran 2003), and activation of areas in the emotional system related to anxiety and pain anticipation (Ehrsson et al. 2007). Likewise, after having experienced the rubber hand illusion of their left hand, subjects make a reaching error (toward the location of the rubber hand) when asked to point toward their hidden left hand (Botvinick and Cohen 1998). These observations indicate that the artificial hand becomes incorporated into the body representation during the illusion.

The phenomenon that artificial limbs can be perceived as part of one's own body was probably first observed by Tastevin in 1937. This author reported anecdotally that people tend to attribute proprioceptive sensations to a seen rubber finger when the real finger was out of view (Tastevin 1937). This phenomenon, and the rubber hand illusion as described in modern times (Botvinick and Cohen 1998), belongs to a class of body illusions that are evoked by providing conflicting sensory information to different sensory channels. In the rubber hand illusion the brain has to reconcile the conflicting visual, tactile, and position sense information. This conflict is probably resolved by a recalibration of position sense of the real hand and changes in peripersonal space from the location of the real hand to the rubber hand (Botvinick and Cohen 1998; Ehrsson et al. 2004). This illusion demonstrates the malleability of the *body representation, and how this dynamic representation is continuously updated by the integration and interpretation of sensory information from all modalities.

The rubber hand illusion is important because it provides neuroscientists with a tool to probe the neural mechanisms of body ownership. This illusion suggests that a match between visual, tactile, and proprioceptive signals is sufficient to cause changes in the feeling of ownership of a limb. This is an observation of fundamental importance because it provides empirical evidence for the hypothesis that the self attribution of body parts is mediated by a match between somatosensory and visual information from the body (Bahrick and Watson 1985). Neurophysiological support for this hypothesis was recently obtained by Ehrsson et al. (2004) who used *functional brain imaging (fMRI) to scan the brain activity of participants while they perceived the rubber hand illusion. These authors found that the illusory feeling of ownership of the rubber hand was associated with increases in activity in multisensory brain areas, such as the premotor and parietal cortices, and that this activity correlated with the strength of the illusion.

An interesting question for future studies is how the owned rubber hand differs from hand-held tools. During tool use tactile sensations are projected from fingertips to the tip of the tool (Gibson 1966). You can try yourself when holding a pen and touching a piece of paper! As described above, the rubber hand illusion also involves the projection of touch from the real hand to the rubber hand. So what is the difference? Indeed, it has also been argued that tools becomes incorporated into the body representations after extensive tool use (as say the tennis racket of a professional tennis player), and that this could involve dynamic changes of the receptive field properties of visuo-tactile neurons on multisensory areas (Maravita and Iriki 2004). However, phenomenologically we do not experience tools as part of our own body, and few of us would mistake a hammer for our own hand, or be anxious if it was threatened by a sharp object. Speculatively, the rubber hand illusion involves changes in interoceptive systems such as proprioception and homeostatic emotional areas that do not take place in tool use.

There are also interesting links between rubber hand illusion and *phantom limb phenomena, in particular the treatment of phantom limb pain using so-called *mirror therapy (Ramachandran and Hirstein 1998). Mirror therapy is based on the idea that visual information can change the central proprioceptive representation of a missing limb (the phantom). The amputee puts his stump behind a mirror and places his normal arm in front of the mirror. The amputee then sees the mirror reflection of the intact arm superimposed on the phantom limb, which often elicits an illusory experience of 'seeing the phantom' (Ramachandran and Hirstein 1998). This has been reported to reduce phantom limb pain in pilot trial studies. Relevant for our discussion here is that the rubber hand illusion similarly depends on interactions between vision and proprioception. It might therefore be used in future research on modulation of the phantom limb experience and phantom limb pain.

The feeling of ownership of limbs is a fundamental aspect of human self-consciousness. Although philosophers and psychologists have been discussing the problem of the bodily self for centuries, it is only recently that neuroscientists have begun to study this question. The rubber hand illusion is particularly important in this respect because it provides cognitive neuroscientists with a tool to experiment with the body self in the laboratory setting. The subjective, behavioural, and neuronal correlates of this body-ownership illusion are relevant to the neuroscientific study of the self.

H. HENRIK EHRSSON

Armel, K. C. and Ramachandran, V. S. (2003). 'Projecting sensations to external objects: evidence from skin conductance response'. *Proceedings of the Royal Society of London, Series B: Biological Sciences*, 270.

Bahrick, L. E. and Watson, J. S. (1985). 'Detection of intermodal proprioceptive-visual contingency as a potential basis of self-perception in infancy'. *Developmental Psychology*, 21.

Botvinick, M. and Cohen, J. (1998). 'Rubber hands "feel" touch that eyes see'. *Nature*, 391.

Ehrsson, H. H., Spence, C., and Passingham, R. E. (2004). 'That's my hand! Activity in premotor cortex reflects feeling of ownership of a limb'. *Science*, 305.

——, Weich, K., Weiskopf, N., Dolan, R. J., and Passingham, R. E. (2007). 'Threatening a rubber hand that you feel is yours elicits a cortical anxiety response'. *Proceedings of the National Academy of Sciences of the USA*, 104.

Gibson, J. J. (1966). *The Senses Considered as Perceptual Systems*.

Maravita, A. and Iriki, A. (2004). 'Tools for the body (schema)'. *Trends in Cognitive Science*, 8.

Ramachandran, V. S. and Hirstein, W. (1998). 'The perception of phantom limbs'. The D. O. Hebb lecture. *Brain*, 121.

Tastevin, J. (1937). 'En partant de l'expérience d'Aristote: les déplacements artificiels des parties du corps ne sont pas suivis par le sentiment de ces parties ni pas les sensations qu'on peut y produire [Starting from Aristotle's experiment: the artificial displacements of parts of the body are not followed by feeling in these parts or by the sensations which can be produced there]'. *L'Encephale*, 32.

S

salience See ATTENTION AND AWARENESS

Sapir–Whorf hypothesis See LINGUISTICS AND THE STUDY OF CONSCIOUSNESS

schizophrenia Schizophrenia is a clinically diagnosed psychiatric disorder affecting approximately 1% of people throughout the world. It has been called a psychosis because some of its features can involve loss of contact with reality. The disorder is characterized by so-called *positive* symptoms (positive in so much as they constitute an addition to the 'normal' mental state): certain forms of hallucination (perceptions experienced in the absence of veridical, external stimuli); delusion (abnormalities of belief and inference, out of keeping with the patient's cultural background); thought disorder (manifest as abnormalities of speech, which may be incomprehensible when florid); inappropriate affect (changeable and incoherent emotional expression, classically 'laughing when they should be crying'); and a constellation of *negative* symptoms (themselves reflecting the relative absence of normal functions): lack of speech (alogia), volition (avolition), emotion (so-called 'blunting of affect') and capacity for enjoyment (anhedonia), lack of drive (apathy), and social interaction (asociality). In addition, patients' attention to themselves and their surroundings may be markedly impaired.

In general, an episode of rapid-onset psychosis, arising in apparent response to environmental stressors, and associated with prominent positive symptoms, is thought to carry a better prognosis than an illness marked by slow, insidious decline in social functioning, prominent negative symptomatology, and a family history of the disorder. Schizophrenia is thought to result from an interaction between genetic susceptibilities and toxic environmental factors, e.g. premature and traumatic delivery, urban birth and upbringing, early abuse and familial discord, cannabis use, migration, and membership of an ethnic minority. Neurodevelopmental factors may have been apparent in early life: abnormal movements, speech delay, mixed handedness, and social difficulties (e.g. the child who 'always played alone').

1. Hallucinations
2. Delusions
3. Thought disorder
4. Emotion
5. Movement
6. Consciousness

1. Hallucinations

The characteristic hallucinations of schizophrenia arise most often in the auditory domain: people hear voices, though their voices may have certain recurring qualities: they are heard outside the head, may be more prominent to the right side of space, converse about the person rather than to her (i.e. they are third-person auditory verbal hallucinations) and may be critical and commanding. Particularly distressing may be voices that evince knowledge of the patient's beliefs and desires and that urge her to harm herself or others. Although the cause of such experiences is still unknown, modern brain scanning studies have demonstrated an association between voice-hearing and aberrant activity in the brain's temporal lobes (regions implicated in the normal processing of speech).

2. Delusions

People suffering from schizophrenia often experience other aspects of their subjective space as having been encroached upon by others. Hence, they may report that their thoughts and feelings, speech and movements, are being 'controlled' by external forces: sometimes persecutors known to them, sometimes entities beyond their reach, e.g. God or the Devil. They may feel that their thoughts are literally being sucked out of their minds or else that they are known to others already, via telepathy. When acutely ill, patients should be allowed space and not be touched or crowded inappropriately, for intrusions upon personal space may feel very much like encroachments upon mental space (the so-called *ego boundary* has become porous).

Although in common parlance being paranoid has come to mean feeling picked upon or plotted against, when applied to schizophrenia it has a specific meaning: that the patient is *deluded*. However, delusions need not necessarily be persecutory ('I am being followed, there are recording devices embedded in the walls'); they can be grandiose ('I realized then that I was the Christ'), nihilistic ('My insides are rotting, my brain has turned to stone'), erotic ('The star of the film is in love with me;

he moves his right hand whenever I enter the room'), or of jealousy ('My wife is having an affair; a red car passed me by twice yesterday and twice again today'); what is common is that they involve the sufferer, intimately. The patient will often experience herself as being at the centre of a sequence of events that have acquired special significance or *salience*. Sometimes the illness begins with the feeling that something is going on, there is a strange atmosphere (the so-called *delusional mood*); matters are resolved through an unusual insight: suddenly 'everything makes sense'.

3. Thought disorder

Although termed a disorder of thought, this is really a disorder of speech, as we have no direct insight into another person's thoughts. However, if what someone is saying is incoherent, drifting from topic to topic, and often eliding different themes within the space of a phrase then we may conclude from their objective speech that their subjective thought (their *inner speech*) is similarly disrupted, e.g.

> 'I was talking to the man with the green tie, fish and he said brain in buckets and while I can tinker you believe the sentence was cruel... Took an onion and didn't speak.'

Classically, such disordered speech may be associated with disordered action, so that sufferers can appear disorganized: starting tasks but not finishing them, failing to concentrate on simple procedures, becoming unpredictable or disturbed over short periods of time.

4. Emotion

Generally, our words and the expressions we make with our faces and bodies cohere. The sad person sits hunched, cries, speaks quietly. In schizophrenia this may not be so. The patient may be smiling while she tells us something incredibly painful or frightening, she may cry but not feel sadness, she may notice that there is a disconnection between the emotions she seems to express and the way things feel inside.

Alternatively, what becomes common is a lack of emotional tone. The patient simply feels nothing. He has lost spontaneity, has no interests outside himself, and may not be able to feel emotion towards people he once knew and loved. Such an absence of affect is termed *blunting*. It is a marked negative feature of the disorder, and very difficult to treat.

5. Movement

Someone who is acutely psychotic may exhibit disturbed behaviour, often out of keeping with their premorbid personality; hence, activity may be increased, actions ill-thought out, conduct reckless. However, over the long term, what is more of a problem is lack of initiative, lack of drive and volition. People with severe and persistent schizophrenia may lose their ability to care for themselves, may become homeless and indigent if support is withdrawn, may be subject to exploitation and abuse by others, yet they may not react. These severe features of the disorder probably reflect deficits in frontal lobe function. The prefrontal cortex is intimately involved in the generation of action and can be shown to be hypoactive in people with negative symptoms of schizophrenia. Fortunately, some studies have begun to show that such *hypofrontality* may be reversed with appropriate medication, but there remains considerable room for therapeutic advance.

The movements of a person with schizophrenia may be abnormal in a variety of ways and for a host of reasons: mannerisms may occur when the person performs a purposeful activity in an unusual way, e.g. standing waiting for the bus as if crucified on a cross. Alternatively, movements may lack purpose, and happen involuntarily: abnormal movements of the face and tongue may be consequent upon medication or schizophrenia itself. Looking abnormal is a potent source of stigma. The media add to this by emphasizing the risks that patients pose to others, although in reality they are much more of a risk to themselves, through suicide, self-harm, or misadventure.

6. Consciousness

In terms of consciousness, schizophrenia patients live at a difficult crossroads: on the one hand they experience phenomena that others do not, their bodies and minds feel different at times, they may be acutely aware of social unease and anxiety, they hear things others cannot; porous to the world, they experience what they believe are other people's thoughts, and they believe others can know theirs; on the other hand, patients may lose awareness of aspects of consciousness that others take for granted, both simple and complex: blind to bodily hygiene, lacking plans for the future, bereft of feelings of empathy, trust, and self-worth.

SEAN A. SPENCE

Amador, X. and David, A. (2004). *Insight and Psychosis: Awareness of Illness in Schizophrenia and Related Disorders*, 2nd edn.

Anscombe, R. (1987). 'The disorder of consciousness in schizophrenia'. *Schizophrenia Bulletin*, 13.

Bottoms, G. (2001). *Angelhead: My Brother's Descent into Madness*.

Frith, C. and Johnstone, E. (2003). *Schizophrenia: A Very Short Introduction*.

Leudar, I. and Thomas, P. (2000). *Voices of Reason, Voices of Insanity: Studies of Verbal Hallucinations*.

McKenna, P. and Oh, T. (2004). *Schizophrenic Speech: Making Sense of Bathroots and Ponds that Fall in Doorways*.

Mortimer, A. and Spence, S. A. (2001). *Managing Negative Symptoms of Schizophrenia*.

Ritchie, J., Dick, D., and Lingham, R. (1994). *The Report of the Inquiry into the Care and Treatment of Christopher Clunis.*
Spence, S. A. (1999). 'The screaming man'. *British Medical Journal*, 319.
—— and David, A. S. (2004). *Voices in the Brain: The Cognitive Neuropsychiatry of Auditory Verbal Hallucinations.*
—— and Halligan, P. W. (2002). *Pathologies of Body, Self, and Space.*
Stefan, M., Travis, M., and Murray, R. M. (2002). *An Atlas of Schizophrenia.*
Turner, T. (2003). *Your Questions Answered: Schizophrenia.*

self-consciousness To be self-conscious is to be aware of oneself. This is true but uninformative. To make progress we need to clarify what counts as awareness of the self; what the sources are upon which it is based; and what function it serves in the cognitive economy.

1. Self-consciousness as direct awareness of the self
2. Self-consciousness as propositional awareness of the self
3. Self-consciousness and consciousness of the world

1. Self-consciousness as direct awareness of the self
Direct awareness is one type of awareness. In direct awareness the object of awareness is a particular thing: if I see a car in front of my house then I am directly aware of the car. Direct awareness typically involves some form of perceptual contact with the relevant object. Part of what it is to be directly aware of something is that one can pick it out from its surroundings and that one is thereby in a position to re-identify it were one to encounter it again. Re-identification is not a very sophisticated cognitive ability: I can re-identify something without knowing very much about it, but I do need to have some way of categorizing it. A typical re-identification judgement might be: 'That is the same *F* as I saw yesterday', where *F* is a sortal concept (a concept such as *dog* or *lampshade* that yields criteria for individuating and counting the objects that fall under it—as opposed, say, to concepts such as *water* and *melancholy*).

Self-consciousness would fail to count as a form of direct awareness if selves turned out not to be things in the world at all. Some such view appears to have been held by Wittgenstein in the *Tractatus Logico-Philosophicus*, where he remarks that the self is not in the world but limits it. This view has not had many adherents. Philosophers tend to agree that selves are objects, but to disagree on what type of objects they are. For example, **reductionists* take selves to be complex 'bundles' of psychological events (Parfit 1984), while *animalists* identify selves with biological organisms (Olson 1997).

Another strategy would be to argue that self-consciousness cannot be a form of direct awareness because, although selves are things in the world, they are not the sort of thing to which we can stand in the appropriate perceptual or quasi-perceptual relations. It could be argued, for example, that the idea of re-identifying the self makes no sense. The possibility of re-identification stands or falls with the possibility of misidentification. But does it make sense to assume either that one might perceive the self and fail to realize that it is oneself, or that one might perceive oneself and mistake it for something else? Of course, we can make these types of mistake when we perceive ourselves in mirrors or photographs. But this is not the kind of perception that philosophers typically have in mind when they ask whether we can be directly aware of the self. We can see this by considering David Hume's famous denial that we are ever directly aware of the self. Hume wrote:

> For my part, when I enter most intimately into what I call *myself*, I always stumble on some perception or other, of heat or cold, light or shade, love or hatred, pain or pleasure. I never catch *myself* at any time without a perception, and never can observe anything but the perception. (Hume 1739–40/1978:252)

Hume is talking about *introspection, although he seems to be construing introspection as a form of inward-directed perception. It seems very plausible that there is little sense to the idea of introspectively re-identifying or misidentifying the self—which would allow us to strengthen Hume's introspective report to the stronger claim that direct awareness of the self is impossible.

Philosophers who think that the self is essentially embodied are likely to point out that we do have a form of direct awareness of the body through somatic *proprioception (the complex of systems that give us knowledge 'from the inside' about the configuration and movement of our body parts). Does this stand in the way of what has come to be known as Hume's *elusiveness thesis*? It depends upon whether we can make sense of the notions of re-identification and misidentification in the context of somatic proprioception. There is no clear answer. On the one hand, somatic proprioception provides information only about our own bodies, just as introspection provides information only about our own minds. On the other, this might be just a contingent fact about how our bodies work. It seems incoherent to think that we might have introspective access to minds other than our own, but not so obviously incoherent that we might somatically proprioceive bodies other than our own. Many of these issues are explored in Cassam (1997).

2. Self-consciousness as propositional awareness of the self
Whereas what we are aware of in *direct awareness* is a particular thing; in *propositional awareness* we are aware that a proposition holds or that a state of affairs

is the case. As mentioned in the previous section, direct awareness requires very little by way of categorization or conceptualization of the object of which we are directly aware. Propositional awareness is not like this. I can be aware that a state of affairs holds when it is conceptualized in one way, but be unaware that it holds under a different conceptualization. If 'J. L. B. is propositionally aware that *x* is *F*' is a true report, it will not necessarily remain true if another name that picks out the same object is substituted for *x* and/or a different predicate true of the same objects for *F*. My propositional awareness that a particular state of affairs holds is highly sensitive to how I think about that state of affairs. I might be propositionally aware that Bob Dylan is balding, in virtue of seeing that the person on the stage in front of me is losing their hair and know that that person is Bob Dylan, without being propositionally aware that Robert Zimmerman is balding, since I have no idea that Bob Dylan is Robert Zimmerman.

Propositional awareness *about* the self does not require direct awareness *of* the self. I can be aware that a particular state of affairs holds without being directly aware of one of the constituent objects in that state of affairs (as when the sound of the doorbell makes me aware that Georgina, whom I am expecting, is at the door, even though I have no direct awareness of Georgina), and so I can be aware that the self has certain properties without being directly aware of the self. So the truth or otherwise of the elusiveness thesis is not directly relevant to the possibility of propositional awareness of the self. Nor is it likely that propositional awareness concerning the self will be analysable in terms of, or reducible to, direct awareness of the self. The cognitively mediated character of propositional awareness is an insuperable obstacle to any such reductive or analytic project. Nor is this surprising. An exactly parallel situation holds for ordinary perceptual awareness, where there is no prospect of understanding what it is for me to see *that x is F* in terms of my direct perceptual awareness of *x*.

Propositional awareness of the self is in many ways more interesting than direct awareness of the self (if such there be). Self-consciousness is important because of the role it plays in the cognitive economy. Self-conscious subjects think about, and react to, the world in distinctive and characteristic ways that are not available to non-self-conscious subjects. Self-consciousness makes possible certain types of inference and reflection, and it does this because of the distinctive types of self-conscious thoughts that it makes available. Self-conscious thoughts are thoughts about the person thinking them, but not every thought about the person thinking it counts as a self-conscious thought. If I am thinking about myself without knowing that I am thinking about myself then my thought is not self-conscious. One characteristic of self-conscious thoughts, stressed by philosophers such as Castañeda (1969) and Perry (1979), is that they have immediate implications for action. I may know that the worst-performing philosopher in the department will shortly be ejected from the department, but not until I realize that *I* am the person whose job is on the line will I be galvanized into action. (Here we see, by the way, an illustration of how propositional awareness can be highly sensitive to the way in which a particular situation is being thought about.)

We can say, then, that genuinely self-conscious thoughts are about the thinker of that thought in a way that does not leave any room for the thinker to fail to recognize that the thought concerns her. By extension, we are propositionally aware of the self to the extent that we have genuinely self-conscious thoughts about ourselves. We can distinguish two types of genuinely self-conscious thoughts according to the sources of information that give rise to them. Some sources can provide information *either* about the self *or* about other people. Testimony is a case in point. I can learn facts about myself by being told them by others, in the same way as I might learn facts about anything else. But there are other sources of information about the self that provide information purely about the self. These sources of information are such that, if we know from them that somebody has a particular property, we *ipso facto* know that we ourselves have that property. Introspection is an example. If I know through introspection that someone is currently thinking about self-consciousness then I know that I myself am thinking about self-consciousness. Introspection cannot provide information about anybody other than me. This does not mean that introspection (and other comparable sources of information) cannot be mistaken. They certainly can be mistaken, but there is a certain type of error that they do not permit. Judgements made on the basis of them cannot be mistaken about who it is that has the property in question. Such judgements are *immune to error through misidentification relative to the first-person pronoun* (Shoemaker 1968), an epistemological property that they inherit from the information sources on which they are based.

Here are some prominent and fundamental types of self-conscious thought that have been held to be immune to error through misidentification: (1) thoughts about our own mental states (including our intentions to act in certain ways) gained through introspection; (2) thoughts about our bodily configuration and movement gained through proprioception, kinaesthesia, and joint position sense; (3) thoughts about our personal histories gained through autobiographical memory; (4) thoughts about our location in the world gained through visual perception (in virtue of the fact that the self is the 'origin' of the field of view).

Self-conscious thoughts that are immune to error in this sense (such as the thought that I am in pain, where this is based on information from pain receptors) are clearly more fundamental than those that are not. They reflect ways of finding out about ourselves that are exclusively about the self and that do not require identifying an object *as* the self. Self-conscious thoughts that are not immune to error through misidentification must be analysed in terms of those that are immune, because they will involve identifying an object as the self, and any such identification must be immune to error through misidentification on pain of an infinite regress. For this reason influential accounts of self-consciousness, such as those of Shoemaker (1963, 1968) and Evans (1982), have attributed a fundamental role to the phenomenon of immunity to error through misidentification.

3. Self-consciousness and consciousness of the world
Self-consciousness is essentially a contrastive notion. Subjects are aware of themselves relative to, and as distinct from other members of, a contrast class of either other physical objects or other psychological subjects. In view of this many philosophers have thought that the capacity to think about a mind-independent world is intimately linked with the capacity for self-conscious thought. The claim is not that it would be impossible to be conscious of objects without being self-conscious, but rather that it is impossible to be conscious of the world as objectively structured in certain ways without being self-conscious.

A classic expression of this interdependence thesis is Kant's claim, defended in the section of the *Critique of Pure Reason* entitled 'Transcendental deduction of the categories', that self-consciousness both depends upon and makes possible the perception of a spatiotemporal world composed of continuously existing objects causally interacting in law-like ways. The form of self-consciousness he is discussing (the unity of apperception that he describes in terms of the 'I think' being able to accompany all my representations) is largely formal—essentially the awareness, with respect to each member of a series of thoughts and experiences, that it is one's own. The interdependence emerges from the two-way links between the unity of apperception and the possibility of applying the categorial concepts whose applicability Kant took to define the objectivity of the world. In this sense, Kant's version of the interdependence thesis is closely linked to his claim (the claim of *transcendental idealism*) that the structure of the experienced world is in some sense determined by the conceptual apparatus that we bring to bear on it.

Philosophers such as P. F. Strawson (1966) and Gareth Evans (1982) have more recently attempted to defend a version of the interdependence thesis that is not committed to any form of transcendental idealism. For Strawson and Evans the interdependence thesis holds because the capacity to have a suitably generalized understanding of the first-person pronoun (Evans), or to conceptualize the distinction between experience and what it is experience of (Strawson), requires the ability to formulate judgements reflecting a conception of the embodied self as located within an objective world possessing certain very general features. For Evans, possessing a mastery of the first-person concept that is integrated with thought about the rest of the world in a suitably productive and systematic way requires the ability to conceive of oneself 'from the third-person point of view' as an objective particular in a unified spatiotemporal world. For Strawson, the ability to distinguish appearance from reality within the realm of experience requires the ability to ascribe experiences to oneself as a continuously existing particular.

How broadly can this contrastive notion of self-consciousness be extended? Can we apply the interdependence thesis to non-linguistic and prelinguistic creatures? This is a pressing issue, given that students of animal behaviour and developmental psychologists are increasingly identifying complex abilities to represent the world in animals and young infants. If some form of the interdependence thesis is true then this seems to require being able to attribute primitive forms of self-consciousness to infants and non-linguistic animals.

Some materials for answering this challenge are offered in Bermúdez (1998), where it is shown how primitive non-conceptual and prelinguistic forms of self-consciousness can be appropriately contrastive. Analysing visual perception following the ecological approach of J. J. Gibson (1979) reveals the exterospecific and propriospecific dimensions of visual perception and how the dynamism of visual perception emerges from their interaction. Similarly, somatic proprioception provides a broadly perceptual awareness of the limits of the body as a physical object responsive to the will, and hence as clearly demarcated from all other physical objects. By the same token, it is possible for a creature to have a sense of itself as following a single path through space-time, and hence to possess a (non-conceptual) point of view on the world, as manifested in its memories and navigational understanding of space, rather than in high-level beliefs and judgements.

JOSÉ-LUIS BERMÚDEZ

Bermúdez, J. L. (1998). *The Paradox of Self-Consciousness.*
Cassam, Q. (1994). *Self-Knowledge.*
—— (1997). *Self and World.*

Castañeda, H.-N. (1969). 'On the phenomeno-logic of the I', reprinted in Cassam (1994).
Evans, G. (1982). *The Varieties of Reference.*
Gibson, J. J. (1979). *The Ecological Approach to Visual Perception.*
Hume, D. (1739–40/1978) *A Treatise of Human Nature.*
Olson, E. (1997). *The Human Animal.*
Parfit, D. (1984). *Reasons and Persons.*
Perry, J. (1979). 'The problem of the essential indexical'. *Nous*, 13.
Shoemaker, S. (1963). *Self-knowledge and Self-identity.*
—— (1968). Self-reference and self-awareness. *Journal of Philosophy*, 65.
—— (1986). 'Introspection and the self'. *Midwest Studies in Philosophy*, X.
—— (1996). *The First-Person Perspective and Other Essays.*
Strawson, P. F. (1966). *The Bounds of Sense.*

self, philosophical perspectives While it may seem obvious that there is a close connection between selfhood and consciousness, the precise form of this connection is by no means obvious, and different views as to the nature of both the self and consciousness have very different implications in this regard. We can start to impose some order on the plethora of competing conceptions by distinguishing three different (but interrelated) ways of thinking about the self.

1. Approaches to the self
2. No self?
3. Self and consciousness: three stances

1. Approaches to the self

In the *subject conception*, the self is that which owns (or has) experiences and other mental and/or bodily states. The conception of the self-as-subject derives support from our ordinary talk and thought. My toothache is something I have, it is not something I am, it is not something I could possibly be—or so it seems plausible to say. A very natural way to construe the self–consciousness relationship is to hold that selves are things which have experiences. But what underlies or corresponds to this sort of talk? In order to have a clear idea as to precisely what is involved the ownership of an experience by a self, we need to have an answer to this question: precisely what sort of thing is a self? Matters are further complicated by the fact that the latter question can itself be interpreted in different ways.

One way of construing it is the *identity conception*: the self construed as what a person (or any conscious subject) essentially is. My self is that entity with which I am identical, my irreducible core. The leading identity conceptions can be located on a spectrum. At one extreme is Descartes' view that we are immaterial and essentially conscious substances. While this idea has by no means entirely vanished from the scene, it has certainly fallen out of favour. However, the doctrine that our continued existence essentially requires only the preservation of our *mentality* (in some form or other) can itself flourish in a more naturalistic framework: it is by no means uncommon for contemporary philosophers to hold that our continued existence requires only a functioning brain or nervous system. At the other end of the spectrum, and in a still more wholeheartedly naturalistic vein, the view that we are essentially human organisms also has its staunch defenders (e.g. Olson 1997).

An alternative—and generally complementary—approach, the *threshold conception*, derives from a different general conception of what being a self involves. In this approach, selfhood comes in different forms or levels. To qualify as a self of a particular kind—or possess a particular form of selfhood—an entity must have attained a certain level of cognitive and/or social sophistication, e.g. it must possess one or more of the following: rationality, a distinctive personality, awareness of its own body, the ability to remember its own past experiences, reflect on its own life, use language, interact in a meaningful way with others.

Hence we find Neisser (1988) distinguishing five forms of selfhood: (1) the ecological self, or the self perceived in the context of the physical environment; (2) the interpersonal self, grounded in species-specific (but not necessarily verbal) forms of communication with others; (3) the extended self, rooted in our personal memories and anticipations; (4) the conceptual self, i.e. culturally informed views of the self; (5) the private self, which emerges when we first notice the privileged access we each have to our own experiences. In a related vein, theorists in the *narrative* tradition (e.g. Ricoeur 1985/1988) hold that we create our identities (in one significant sense of the term) by devising narratives in which we ourselves are the central characters.

The threshold and identity conceptions are enshrined in common sense. Most of us have little difficulty in envisaging ourselves surviving the loss of our personal memories, or significant alterations in our personality or cognitive abilities. Hence if we hear someone say 'She has not been the same person since her accident', we know what they mean: the person in question has undergone significant psychological change (in threshold terms they may well no longer be the same kind of self) but only one person is involved—in identity terms, the accident was not fatal. The modes of selfhood described by threshold theorists can often be viewed as phases a typical human subject passes through in the course of their development: newborn children possess few (and perhaps none) of the cognitive abilities required for the higher forms of selfhood. The distinction is sometimes framed thus: theories of the threshold variety strive to tell us *who* we are, whereas theories falling under the rubric of the identity conception purport to tell us *what* we are.

2. No self?

The sheer diversity of competing self-conceptions explains the otherwise puzzling popularity of 'no-self' theories. When an author confidently proclaims the non-existence of the self, rather than denying their own existence, they are typically claiming that some particular conception of the self is either incoherent, or fails to correspond with anything in reality. When Dennett argues that selves are fictitious centres of narrative gravity (1991:418) his target is the view that the stories we tell about ourselves issue from a single unified source point (as some believe), rather than a collection of disparate and often competing neural systems (the position he himself advocates). Metzinger's recent *Being No One* opens with the claim that the 'no such things as selves exist in the world: Nobody ever *was* or *had* a self' (2003:1) But it turns out that what Metzinger is denying is the existence of selves only in the form of 'ontological substances that could in principle exist all by themselves, and as mysteriously unchanging essences that generate a sharp transtemporal identity for persons' (2003:626). Denying the existence of selves in this sense is compatible with recognizing that selves in some other form exist—and Metzinger himself elaborates an alternative in the course of his book.

3. Self and consciousness: three stances

There is no shortage of controversy concerning the proper use of the term 'consciousness'. In the absence of indications to the contrary, in what follows I will use the term to designate **phenomenal consciousness*, understood in the customary manner: a state is phenomenally conscious if there is something it is like to have it. In assessing how these different conceptions of the self relate to consciousness thus construed it will agin prove useful to distinguishing three standpoints: (1) the *essentially conscious self* (ECS)—a self is an entity which is essentially conscious; (2) the *potentially conscious self* (PCS)—a self is an entity which essentially possesses the capacity for consciousness; (3) the *non-experiential self* (NES)—selves typically do possess the consciousness and/or the capacity for it, but they do not need either in order to exist; selves are not essentially experiential beings.

Whereas according to the ECS conception selves enjoy some form of experience at each moment of their existence, the PCS conception is less demanding: selves can lose consciousness without ceasing to exist, provided they retain the ability to have experiences. According to the NES conception not even this much is required for a self to exist. Within the ECS and PCS camps there is room for significant divergences over the kind or level of consciousness—actual or merely potential—that is essential to selfhood. Some hold that selves are essentially self-conscious beings, and hence must be able to think of themselves *as* selves, others hold that beings whose conscious lives are confined to very simple forms of experience should be regarded as selves—and between these extremes there are intermediate positions. Most of the conceptions outlined below are compatible with adopting a range of views on this issue.

It seems safe to assume that most threshold theorists have tacitly adopted the PCS conception. Typical human subjects are not continually conscious—they regularly fall into dreamless sleep—but they have the capacity to be conscious, with different modes of selfhood requiring different modes of consciousness. Neisser's ecological and interpersonal levels of selfhood require only the sort of the non-reflexive perceptual experience and cognitive development that is available to an infant in the first months of life; the private and extended selves, by contrast, only emerge in children of between three and five years of age who have acquired the ability to think about themselves. The latter ability is also a prerequisite of narrative selfhood: a subject must be have a fairly sophisticated level of self-consciousness and access to its own past experiences if it is to construct stories about itself.

Where do things stand with the identity conception? Here we find a broad range of competing views.

Selves as contingently conscious. One popular response to the identity question postulates selves of the NES variety. Van Inwagen (1990) and Olson (1997) are prominent contemporary defenders of the *biological* conception of selfhood. Both fully acknowledge the intuitive pull of Lockean-style imaginary cases which suggest our mental lives (and hence ourselves) can conceivably come apart from our bodies and brains, but drawing on general metaphysical considerations they argue that it would be a mistake to take such fantasies seriously, and so conclude that we (human) persons are essentially human organisms. While such organisms typically possess the capacity for various forms of consciousness, they can also exist (sometimes in perfect health) without possessing the capacity for *any* form of consciousness. Newly fertilized human eggs are human organisms, but it seems unlikely that they possess any capacities for consciousness: these come only later. At the other end of the age range, brain damage can leave an adult human brain incapable of producing even the simplest kinds of experience, even though the brain (and the organism whose autonomic functions it sustains) lives on.

Selves as potentially conscious. The most straightforward way of developing the PCS approach is to hold that the members of any specific kind—human organisms, immaterial substances, Martians—qualify as selves so long as (and only so long as) they possess the capacity for consciousness. Since this approach avoids the introduction of a distinct kind of entity 'selves' in addition to human organisms, Martians, etc., it has the merit of being ontologically economical. But for some PCS theorists it is too restrictive. Unger (1990) holds that we will continue to exist provided the 'physical realizer' of our capacities for consciousness continues to exist. Although these capacities are normally realized in our brains, (in a Lockean vein) Unger argues that most of us believe we could survive if our brains were radically transformed (e.g. into inorganic objects), provided that our capacities for consciousness are preserved throughout.

Those inclined to pursue the PCS approach to (what is arguably) its logical conclusion can take yet a further step: there is also the option of defining existence and persistence conditions of selves solely in terms of *capacities* for consciousness. The obvious way forward is to hold that such capacities belong to a single self only if they can contribute to unified streams of consciousness. Since such capacities can (in principle) be possessed by objects of many different kinds—immaterial objects included, if such exist—an account along these lines constitutes a further step in the direction of maximum generality. See Dainton (2004) for more on this.

Selves as essentially conscious: substances, bundles, chunks. The ECS conception also has its adherents, past and present. Descartes construed selves as immaterial substances possessing consciousness as an essential attribute. Selves such as these are conscious at every moment of their existence. Well aware that this sounds implausible, Descartes argued we remain (dimly) conscious during what we ordinarily take to be periods of unconsciousness, and subsequently forget the experiences we have during such periods (1984:246–7). This position is difficult to refute, but it is speculative to say the least. Contemporary substance dualist John Foster takes a somewhat different stance on this issue, arguing that a self is essentially 'the sort of thing which can possess mental states and perform mental acts' (1991:234). On the face of it, this constitutes a move away from the ECS conception in the direction of the PCS conception.

Some ECS theorists have taken Descartes to task for his commitment to a substance-attribute ontology. Starting from the phenomenological claim that our experience only ever presents us with *experiences*—'... I can never catch *myself* at any time without a perception ... '—Hume argued that we had no warrant for supposing that the self consists of anything other than experiences: 'They are the successive perceptions only, that constitute the mind ... ' (*Treatise* I, IV, §VI). Thus was born the 'bundle' conception of the self as nothing more than a collection of interrelated experiences. According to the 20th century bundle-theorist A. J. Ayer, 'We know that a self, if it is not to be treated as a metaphysical entity, must be held to be a logical construction out of the sense-experiences ... ' (1953:125) The gap between self and experience has now disappeared altogether.

Interruptions in consciousness are as problematic for the bundle theory as they are for substance dualism. It may be legitimate to hold that experiences within uninterrupted streams of consciousness are held together by inter-experiential connections, but on what basis are distinct streams to be assigned to the same subject? In tackling this problem some bundle-theorists have appealed to qualitative similarity and memories (e.g. William James) others to bodily attachment (e.g. Ayer). Although these proposals are by no means problem-free, they do mean that bundle theorists can offer us something akin to the lifespan we take for granted.

Galen Strawson has recently moved in the opposite direction and argued that a typical self has a lifespan that is considerably shorter than a typical stream of consciousness: a matter of a few seconds (1997). Strawson reaches this conclusion by holding that selves are essentially experiential entities, and then arguing that our *streams of consciousness are far less stream-like than is usually assumed. Whether Strawson is right about this is debatable, but there is a further aspect of his position that is distinctive: he is resolutely materialist. Strawsonian selves are chunks of experience, but these chunks of experience are themselves physical things. Conceptions of the self which seem strange by common-sense standards are not confined to the immaterialist school.

Non-phenomenal selves? There may be a further mode of selfhood that is different from any yet mentioned, a mode that is entirely divorced from consciousness (at least of one variety) but which is also very different from the mode of (embryonic or vegetative) non-conscious selfhood recognized by NES theorists such as Van Inwagen and Olson. Suppose you were to contract a novel virus whose effects are limited to subtle changes in your brain chemistry, changes which entirely eliminate your capacities for phenomenal consciousness, but which leave your psychology otherwise unchanged. Although you have been transformed into a **zombie* (of the philosophical variety) your behavioural dispositions are unaltered, likewise the functional organization of your brain. So far as outward appearances are concerned, it is as nothing has happened to you at all: your conversational style is unaffected, likewise your (apparent) intellectual abilities, personality traits, memories, and beliefs. If an entity of this sort is possible—it is not inconceivable that developments in artificial intelligence will approximate it in the not too distant future—there would be prima facie grounds for regarding it as being a *self*, albeit of a non-standard (and non-experiential) kind.

Whether or not a being of this sort really is possible depends on much-disputed foundational issues in the philosophy of mind. *Functionalists and behaviourists will regard such a being as conscious in every sense of the term: theorists in these camps reject the intelligibility of zombies. Those who recognize the distinction between **access consciousness* and *phenomenal consciousness* may well hold that a self of this kind is conscious, albeit in a non-phenomenal manner. While the notion that an entity lacking phenomenal consciousness can nonetheless possess access consciousness is by no means obviously absurd, there are those who are dubious of the very idea of non-phenomenal mentality. Searle (1987) argues that genuinely *mental* states cannot exist in the absence of the capacity for phenomenal consciousness. If so, a zombie would lack anything that could be called a mind or a psychology—it would have at most the appearance of one. If Searle is right, not everything that seems to be a self really is one.

See also DUALISM; SELF, SCIENTIFIC PERSPECTIVES; SELF-CONSCIOUSNESS

BARRY DAINTON

Ayer, A. J. (1953). *Language, Truth and Logic*, 2nd edn.
Dainton, B. (2004). 'The self and the phenomenal'. *Ratio*, 17.
Descartes, R. (1984). *The Philosophical Writings of Descartes* Vol.II, transl. Cottingham et al.
Dennett, D. C. (1991). *Consciousness Explained*.
Foster, J. (1991). *The Immaterial Self*.
Hume, D. (1739/1888). *A Treatise of Human Nature*, ed. L. A. Selby-Bigge.
Locke, J. (1690/1975). *An Essay Concerning Human Understanding*, ed. P. H. Nidditch.
Metzinger, T. (2003). *The Self-Model Theory of Subjectivity*. Cambridge: MIT Press.
Neisser, U. (1988). 'Five kinds of self-knowledge'. *Philosophical Psychology*, 59.
Olson, E. (1997). *The Human Animal: Personal Identity Without Psychology*.
Ricoeur, P. (1985/1988). *Time and Narrative III*, transl. K. Blamey and D. Pellauer.
Searle, J. (1987). 'Indeterminacy, empiricism, and the first person'. *Journal of Philosophy*, 84.
Strawson, G. (1997). 'The self'. *Journal of Consciousness Studies*, 4.
Unger, P. (1990). *Identity, Consciousness and Value*.
Van Inwagen, P. (1990). *Material Beings*.

self-representational theories of consciousness

A theory of consciousness will count as self-representational if, according to it, consciousness essentially involves some sort of invariant reflexive representation, the representation, consciousness, or awareness of itself. On such theories, an episode of consciousness always represents *itself*, whatever else it might also represent.

Different versions of self-representationalism are obtained by varying the interpretation of this central claim and by varying the assessment of its explanatory import. According to **reductive* versions of self-representationalism, states of consciousness are to be identified with those intentional states that self-represent in the right way; and representation itself is to be understood in physicalistically acceptable terms. According to *non-reductive* versions of self-representationalism, consciousness is necessarily self-representational, but this fact does not obviously aid the explanatory project and, according to some, might even make that project impossible. Proponents of both reductive and non-reductive versions agree, however, that consciousness invariably involves some form of self-awareness.

Moreover, all self-representationalists agree that the kind of *self-consciousness or self-representation involved is ubiquitous, accounts for many of the puzzling features of subjectivity, is importantly different from reflective or introspective self-consciousness, is non-attentive or peripheral, and is actual, not merely dispositional. Further, most theorists agree that the thesis is independent of doctrines about the sort of 'self' that is the concern of theories of personal identity. A self may be essential to consciousness in some other way, and one finds self-representational theorists who think so and others who do not. But it is not the direct representation of any such self that is essential to consciousness, rather it is the representation of an episode or *stream of consciousness by *itself*.

The primary motivations for the view are *phenomenological. Most proponents of self-representationalism have maintained that a careful description of consciousness reveals this ever present, non-introspective form of self-consciousness. According to several of them, self-representationalism offers an informative account of the **subjectivity* of consciousness; it purports to explain the obscure, subjectivity, in terms of the less obscure, self-representation.

The view that consciousness always involves some form of self-consciousness or self-representation has a long and illustrious history in both Western and Eastern thought. One finds a version of it in Aristotle (Caston 2002). The thesis was a topic of much debate in Indian and Buddhist philosophy, for example, in Dinnāga, Dharmakīrti, and Mi Pham (Williams 1998). Versions of the view were held by Descartes, Arnauld, Locke, Reid, Kant, and others. It was a major concern of Fichte, Hegel, and the German Idealist tradition and its contemporary heirs, the Heidelberg School philosophers. It was a central component of Franz Brentano's descriptive account of consciousness. Brentano's students—Twardowski, Meinong, Freud, and Husserl—all defended some version of the thesis, sometimes with considerable deviation from the master. But it is in the phenomenological tradition, inaugurated by Husserl, that the view receives its most thorough articulation, and one finds versions of it in Heidegger, Sartre, Merleau-Ponty, Gurwitsch, and many others.

The view was famously attacked by Gilbert Ryle, and, perhaps because of Ryle's influence, it fell out of fashion in analytic philosophy of mind for some time. However, in recent years, the view has seen an impressive comeback as a competitor of the reductive, higher-order representational approach to consciousness. Versions of the view have also had proponents who approach consciousness from more scientific angles, including neuroscientist Antonio Damasio and cognitive scientist Douglas Hofstadter. (For references on all of the above, see Kriegel and Williford 2006.)

Reductive versions of self-representationalism adopt the same basic strategy as reductive versions of *higher-order *representationalism. Both kinds of theories purport to offer accounts of subjectivity, and their proponents find first-order representationalism, according to which consciousness is to be identified with suitably functionally integrated, first-order, or world-directed representations, inadequate for this. Self-representationalism has a few advantages over higher-order representationalism. It seems to embed a better account of the phenomenology of consciousness, and it is not subject to the non-existence problem that plagues the higher-order theory—the possibility that the target, lower-order representation might not exist. Evidently, if something truly self-represents, then it exists.

However, reductive self-representationalism, like its representationalist competitors of both orders, must rely upon a naturalistic, reductive theory of representation. Some such theories, mere causal covariance theories, for example, seem to rule out reflexive representation. Functional role semantics, as developed in this very connection by Peter Carruthers (2000), and teleosemantics can allow for reflexive representation.

However, on both theories something will represent itself only contingently, as a consequence of certain extrinsic, natural-historical relations in the latter case and of a contingent, internal functional economy in the former. Apart from some version of the doctrine of internal relations, according to which the very intrinsic character of the relata of the relevant relations would be dependent on their standing in them, such theories imply that there is nothing intrinsic to the conscious state or episode in virtue of which it represents itself (and is thus conscious). Vary merely its apparently extrinsic relations, and the very same state, identified by its intrinsic properties, passes from being conscious to being unconscious. But this counter-intuitive consequence is common to all varieties of representationalism that assume reductive, naturalistic theories of representation. If one finds this consequence implausible, the ostensible advantages of reductive self-representationalism will hardly matter. If one is willing to accept some version of the doctrine of internal relations, which is no more and no less mysterious than the view that some things are intrinsically representational, then some version of self-representationalism may well be a superior theory of consciousness.

Some have argued, however, that the form of ubiquitous, non-introspective self-consciousness in question cannot be literally identified with a kind of self-*representation* (e.g. Zahavi 1999). They have either held that reflexive representation is impossible or that a representation relation is unable to account for the kind of intimacy with which consciousness primitively knows itself. Accordingly, these theorists maintain that primitive self-consciousness is an irreducible and unanalysable feature of consciousness, and they would be uncomfortable with the appellation 'self-representationalist'. But the claim that reflexive representation is impossible is implausible, and, to date, no compelling arguments for it have been produced. The point about intimacy does merit careful consideration, for, depending on how one construes the representation relation involved, it is far from obvious how its reflexive instantiation could account for subjectivity and, in particular, for the sense that one knows oneself in a direct and primitive way.

Several routinely raised objections apply to all versions of self-representationalism. First, it is often claimed that the view implies that *animals and *infants are not consciousness because they are too unsophisticated to be self-conscious. But the mode of self-consciousness in question is generally held to be primitive and, perhaps, non-conceptual. Moreover, the objection is insensitive to the distinction between introspective and merely marginal self-consciousness. Second, it is sometimes claimed that the view implies either that there is an infinite hierarchy of conscious mental states or that a single conscious mental state has an infinite representational content. But the first suggested regress is, in fact, dispensed with by the theory. Again, the view is that each conscious episode represents *itself*. The second suggested regress presupposes some premise to the effect that each conscious episode represents individually all of its representational properties. But there is no reason to accept that premise. Relatedly, some have thought that the view commits one to the very implausible thesis that one can know one's consciousness infallibly and exhaustively. But an episode of consciousness could represent itself without providing its possessor with such knowledge. Finally, some would argue that the claim involves vicious circularity. This could either be taken to mean that the view is incompatible with a reductive construal or taken to mean that reflexive representation is impossible because it involves some kind of regress. Both claims are false.

Whether or not one is interested in reductive versions of self-representationalism, the phenomenological datum upon which the theory rests is an important one. If the subjectivity of consciousness can indeed be construed in terms of non-introspective, self-representation (of some sort), this will mark an important advance over theories of subjectivity that contain no structural elucidation. If it is true that consciousness involves a form of self-representation, then any structural model of consciousness ought to include this feature. As Hofstadter (1979) and others have argued, this suggests that the conceptual tools useful for understanding self-reference, self-membership, self-application, and other phenomena of the sort, might be useful for modelling and extending our knowledge of consciousness itself. As long as such models provide conceptual clarity, powerful analogies, and, eventually, generate empirically testable predictions, they ought to be explored, even if, as some allege, the proponents of self-representationalism mistake a contingent feature of a good deal of human consciousness for a necessary feature of all consciousness.

See also INTENTIONALITY; PHYSICALISM; REPRESENTATION; SELF, PHILOSOPHICAL PERSPECTIVES

KENNETH WILLIFORD

Carruthers, P. (2000). *Phenomenal Consciousness*.
Caston, V. (2002). 'Aristotle on consciousness'. *Mind*, 111.
Hofstadter, D. R. (1979). *Gödel, Escher, Bach*.
Kriegel, U. and Williford, K. (eds) (2006). *Self-representational Approaches to Consciousness*.
Williams, P. (1998). *The Reflexive Nature of Awareness*.
Zahavi, D. (1999). *Self-awareness and Alterity*.

self, scientific perspectives Over the past decades, significant advances in research methods and experimental designs have enabled the cognitive neurosciences to study the neurocognitive functions that underpin various aspects of selfhood.

The sense of self-identity is both physical and psychological (see Gillihan and Farah 2005). The physical corresponds to the affective and sensorimotor experience of one's own body, while the psychological corresponds to the experience of one's own identity over time, but also to the experience of acting and interacting with the world. The importance of the distinction between the physical and the psychological components of selfhood lies in its applicability in neuroscientific research. Even though the physical and the psychological aspects are not experienced separately, they can be methodologically separated, enabling the empirical investigation of distinct subcomponents of selfhood, such as emotional self-awareness, awareness of one's own body and one's own actions, awareness of one's own identity over time, and awareness of other people.

1. The emotional self
2. The sensorimotor self
3. The self-representing self
4. Future directions in the empirical study of selfhood

1. The emotional self

The concept of an emotional or *core* self is based on the hypothesis that emotions play a positive role in the adaptive functions of the brain, by bringing the current state of the body to conscious awareness. On that view, the brain mediates between compelling demands arising from the internal milieu of the body, on the one hand, and the practical constraints of external reality on the other. Central to this negotiation between the inner and the outer is the neural processing of emotions. Feeling an emotion seems to be a simple matter, consisting of mental images arising from the neural patterns that represent the changes in the body that make up an emotion. However, having consciousness of that feeling might have been the crucial step in the development of human self-consciousness, because awareness of one's own emotions led to environmentally adaptive behaviours that went beyond simple automatic responses.

A primary quality of the self, perhaps its core (Damasio 1999), lies in the awareness of feelings that represent the emotional interaction of one's own body with the environment. This type of awareness can be thought of as an inner sense directed towards one's own body, an idea going back to Locke, Brentano, and James. Interoceptive representations, which provide the content of this inner-consciousness, include distinct feelings originating from the body, such as pain, temperature, itch, sensual touch, muscular and visceral sensations, hunger, and thirst among others. Recent *functional imaging studies have attempted to study the neural *correlates of interoceptive awareness. For example, Critchley and colleagues (2004) measured brain activity while participants judged the timing of their own heartbeat. Brain activity in the right anterior insular cortex predicted the participants' accuracy at detecting their heartbeat. Converging evidence suggests that the insular cortex is responsible for representing interoceptive activity. These interoceptive representations of emotional body states seem to provide the basis for emotional self-awareness.

2. The sensorimotor self

Another principal quality of the self is grounded in the experience of the body as a sensory and motor entity. Two fundamental elements characterize this experience: the sense of body-ownership and the sense of agency (Gallagher 2000).

Body-ownership. The feeling that the body I inhabit is mine and always with me is called body-ownership. Even though in everyday life the link between the body and its self is taken for granted, the cognitive and neural processes by which the body is experienced as linked to the self are far from being fully understood. Clinical cases of abnormal body-awareness aptly demonstrate the need for a neuroscientific account of the bodily self. *Somatoparaphrenia* is a neurological condition, which is usually related to *anosognosia for hemiplegia, and occurs after predominantly right hemispheric lesions. Patients with somatoparaphrenia believe that their limbs contralateral to the side of the lesion belong to someone else, and the disorder is often accompanied by the inability to feel tactile sensations in the 'non-belonging' part of the body. Bottini and colleagues (2002) reported a case of a patient with somatoparaphrenia who thought that her left hand belonged to her niece. Interestingly, the tactile imperceptions on her 'disowned' left hand recovered dramatically when she was verbally instructed to report touches delivered to her niece's hand, rather than to her own hand. This verbal instruction momentarily eliminated the mismatch between her belief about the ownership of the left hand and her ability to perceive touch on it.

Strange feelings of body-ownership can also be elicited in neurologically healthy volunteers. When people are asked to look at a *rubber hand that is being touched by a paintbrush, while at the same time they experience synchronous touches on their own hidden hand, they feel as if the rubber hand is their own hand. This attribution of the rubber hand to one's own body occurs only after synchronous visuo-tactile stimulation, suggesting that correlated multisensory percepts may induce a sense of body-ownership. However, factors other than multisensory integration, such as motor signals and cognitive body-representations, may additionally influence body-ownership.

Developmental psychology has used self-recognition paradigms to explore the onset of bodily self-awareness in infants. Infants, as young as 4 months are able to discriminate between self and other's mirror images, and to detect temporal differences between their movement and the delayed visual feedback of their movement (for a review see Rochat 2003).

Studies on self-recognition of moving body parts in adults have also provided useful insights for body-ownership. Here, self-recognition refers to the process of integrating different sources of information (i.e. intentions, motor signals, and sensory feedback) in order to ascribe an ambiguous visual representation of a moving body part to its proper owner (for a review see Jeannerod 2003). In these studies, participants are asked to perform a movement out of direct view. The online visual feedback is manipulated, and the participants see on a screen either their own hand, or someone else's hand performing the *same* movement, or someone else's hand performing a *different* movement. The task is to give an explicit judgement about the identity of the seen hand. Self-recognition judgements are mostly informed by efferent motor signals when distinctive movements are made (e.g. in the different movement condition), and by afferent sensory signals when action cues are ambiguous (e.g. in the same movement condition). However, when the movements are not voluntary, i.e. in the absence of efferent motor signals, self-recognition performance is severely impaired. Therefore, motor signals may be necessary for the effective distinction between self and other, over and above the processing and integration of multisensory signals.

Agency. The sense of agency is the sense of intending and executing an action, a sense of oneself as an actor who can make things happen. One example taken from the psychiatric literature illustrates how the sense of agency is linked to specific functional and neural processes. *Schizophrenic patients with delusions of control demonstrate a striking failure to experience their own agency over the actions that they execute. The delusion of control is an example of a passivity experience in which a patient feels that his own actions are being created, not by himself, but by an outside force, usually an external agent. The main feature of this symptom is that the intention to act is misattributed to another agent, whereas the ownership of the body part that executes the action is not.

At the neurocognitive level, delusions of control may arise as a result of an abnormal awareness of the predicted consequences of one's own action (Blakemore et al. 2002). An important aspect of agency involves the ability to distinguish actions and effects that are self-generated from those generated by other agents. The ability to distinguish between self-generated and externally generated events is embedded in the function of the motor system. In the case of a self-generated action, intentions and the efference copy of the motor command can be used to predict the consequent visual, auditory, and somatosensory signals produced by one's own movements. An internal **forward model* of the motor system uses the efference copy of the motor command to predict the sensory effects of one's own actions. Once the actual sensory feedback arrives, it is compared to the prediction. If there is no mismatch between the predicted and actual feedback, the action is attributed to the self because the sensory event is recognized as being self-generated. One important implication of this process is that we cannot *tickle ourselves. At the neural level, when there is a match between predicted and actual feedback, there is suppression of activity in regions of parietal cortex where sensations associated with limb movements are processed. In contrast, schizophrenic patients currently experiencing passivity phenomena show heightened activity in parietal cortex (Spence et al. 1997). At the experiential level, this model postulates that the experience of agency is based on action-related processes, such as the awareness of initiating the action and the awareness of the predictive outcome of the action.

The *sensorimotor self seems to be underpinned by implicit representations. Awareness of one's own body and awareness of one's own actions seem to be in the background of mental life. Even though there is an intimate link between the body and the self, the processes by which we control our bodies to generate actions are usually automatic, and the phenomenology of agency is quite thin and elusive, in the sense that we do not constantly represent in an explicit way our agency over every goal-directed movement that we perform. As long as our motor intentions are fulfilled, we have little awareness of any online corrections we make to our movements or of the sensory consequences of those movements.

This lack of awareness can lead to illusions in which the apparent fulfilling of intentions leads to a false sense of agency. As long as an intention is followed by the appropriate outcome, we assume that the intention caused the outcome. Wegner (2004) and colleagues have demonstrated two kinds of *illusion that follow from this. In the first paradigm, participants have a movement intention suggested to them. If the appropriate movement occurs shortly afterwards they will attribute it to themselves even when it is actually made by a confederate. In the second paradigm, which is based on facilitated communication, participants believe that they are sensing the responses made by another person to a series of questions, when in fact they are themselves generating the responses. In this example the participants have the illusion that the other person's intentions are causing the responses.

3. The self-representing self

Our psychological sense of self-identity seems to be grounded in explicit and conceptual representations, such as one's own memories, personality traits, beliefs, and attitudes. A sense of identity over time is given by autobiographical memory. Research on autobiographical memory has not provided a definite answer as to whether autobiographical memory is functionally independent from other *memory systems. Neuropsychological case studies demonstrate that it is possible to have intact autobiographical memory despite severe impairment in semantic memory system. Similarly, the evidence for specific neural correlates of autobiographical memory is inconclusive. The overall pattern across studies suggests that retrieval of autobiographical memories is associated with activations of medial frontal cortex and the left hippocampus (for a review see Maguire 2001). However, many of the studies have failed to control for various confounding factors between autobiographical and other memory systems (for a review see Gillihan and Farah 2005). Importantly, autobiographical memory provides both a sense of continuity over time and a sense of identity. The sense of continuity over time is given by the fact that autobiographical memory provides a template of the past against which new experiences can be assimilated. The sense of identity is generated by the fact that all these experiences are related to me, rather than to someone else. It has been suggested that autobiographical memories are transitory mental constructions that are constantly reshaped on the basis of current self-goals (Conway and Pleydell-Pearce 2000). The interaction between autobiographical memories and self-goals is reciprocal, and it is thought to be essential for the preservation of a coherent self-representation.

Social cognitive neuroscience has focused on the neural circuits that are common to both self- and other-representations, which may be critical for social cooperation and empathy. A meta-analysis of the functional anatomy of action-execution, mental simulation of action, verbal generation of actions, and more importantly observation of other people's actions, showed that for all four processes, overlapping activation was found in supplementary motor area, dorsal premotor cortex, supramarginal gyrus, and superior parietal lobe (Grèzes and Decety 2001). The activation of an overlapping neural network for both the representations of self-generated and observed actions suggests that some representations are agent neutral and shared. More evidence for common representations for self and others comes from the neural substrates of empathy. Bilateral anterior insula, rostral anterior cingulate cortex, brainstem, and cerebellum were activated when participants received pain and also when a loved one experienced pain (Singer et al. 2004). The existence of an overlapping neural network, or *mirror system that underpins both self- and other-representations may support social communication and interaction. This discovery raises the interesting possibility that some aspects of the awareness of self resulted from mechanisms that initially evolved through attempts to predict the behaviour of others through representing their internal states.

However, an explicit self-representation is also necessary for social interaction because it allows for a demarcation of the self from among other people. Several *functional brain imaging studies have looked for the neural substrates of self-representation by manipulating the self–other distinction in various tasks (for a review see Gillihan and Farah 2005). Activation in the right inferior parietal lobe was observed when participants simulated an action from a third-person perspective, and when they attributed an action to someone else. Anterior insula was activated when the action was simulated from a first-person perspective, and when an action was attributed to the self.

A critical distinction between the self and the other concerns differences in point of view and the recognition that two people viewing the same scene from different positions will see, and hence know, different things about that scene. The temporoparietal junction has a critical role in this form of perspective taking; many studies in which participants have to consider another's point of view have observed activity in this region. Furthermore, electrical stimulation of this area can lead to the participant experiencing his or her own body from a third-person viewpoint (Blanke et al. 2005).

4. Future directions in the empirical study of selfhood

The available neurocognitive data suggest that there is no single specialized neural system or a single cognitive function underlying selfhood. Instead, multiple specialized processes underlie distinct aspects of selfhood, such as the affective and sensorimotor self, the autobiographical self, and the social self. These specialized processes operate at a sub-personal level and they may not be accessible to conscious awareness. The cognitive neuroscience of self is faced with the challenge of explaining how these specialized processes interact at the functional and neural level to generate a coherent and conscious sense of self.

Current empirical studies on the sense of self focus on either the physical or the psychological dimension of selfhood. Indeed, there seems to be a real difference between sensorimotor theories of self and most psychopersonal theories of self as regards the continuity of personal identity over time and autobiographical memory. Our sense of embodiment seems to be immediate and transient, while a reflective and autobiographical sense of self seems to be stable over time. Future studies need to address the neurocognitive processes that bridge the physical and the psychological dimensions of selfhood.

MANOS TSAKIRIS AND CHRIS D. FRITH

Blakemore, S. J., Wolpert, D. M., and Frith, C. D. (2002). 'Abnormalities in the awareness of action'. *Trends in Cognitive Sciences*, 6.

Blanke, O., Mohr, C., Michel, C. M. et al. (2005). 'Linking out-of-body experience and self processing to mental own-body imagery at the temporoparietal junction'. *Journal of Neuroscience*, 25.

Bottini, G., Bisiach, E., Sterzi, R., and Vallarc, G. (2002). 'Feeling touches in someone else's hand'. *NeuroReport*, 13.

Conway, M. A. and Pleydell-Pearce, C. W. (2000). 'The construction of autobiographical memories in the self-memory system'. *Psychological Review* 107.

Critchley, H. D., Wiens, S., Rotshtein, P., Ohman, A., and Dolan, R. J. (2004). 'Neural systems supporting interoceptive awareness'. *Nature Neuroscience*, 7.

Damasio, A. (1999). *The Feeling of What Happens: Body and Emotion in the Making of Consciousness*.

Gallagher, S. (2000). 'Philosophical concepts of the self: implications for cognitive sciences'. *Trends in Cognitive Sciences*, 4.

Gillihan, S. J. and Farah, M. J. (2005). 'Is self special? A critical review of evidence from experimental psychology and cognitive neuroscience'. *Psychological Bulletin*, 131.

Grèzes, J. and Decety, J. (2001). 'Functional anatomy of execution, mental simulation, observation, and verb generation of actions: a meta-analysis'. *Human Brain Mapping*, 12.

Jeannerod, M. (2003). 'The mechanism of self-recognition in humans'. *Behavioural Brain Research*, 142.

Maguire, E. A. (2001). 'Neuroimaging studies of autobiographical event memory'. *Philosophical Transactions of the Royal Society of London, Series B, Biological Sciences*, 356(1413).

Rochat, P. (2003). 'Five levels of self-awareness as they unfold early in life'. *Consciousness and Cognition*, 12.

Singer, T., Seymour, B., O'Doherty, J., Kaube, H., Dolan, R. J., and Frith, C. D. (2004). 'Empathy for pain involves the affective but not sensory components of pain'. *Science*, 303.

Spence, S. A., Brooks, D. J., Hirsch, S. R., Liddle, P. F., Meechan, J., and Grasby, P. M. (1997). 'A PET study of voluntary movement in schizophrenic patients experiencing passivity phenomena (delusions of alien control)'. *Brain*, 120.

Wegner, D. M. (2004). 'Precis of the illusion of conscious will'. *Behavioral and Brain Sciences*, 27.

sensation See PERCEPTION

sense data See PERCEPTION; QUALIA

sensitivity criterion See LEARNING, EXPLICT VS IMPLICIT

sensorimotor approach to (phenomenal) consciousness The sensorimotor approach is concerned with elucidating *only one particular* aspect of the problem of consciousness, namely the problem of phenomenal consciousness or *sensory feel*. Phenomenal consciousness is the **what-it-is-like* or *phenomenality* associated with sensory stimulation (most typically visual, auditory, tactile, olfactory, and gustatory sensations). Unlike what the philosopher Ned Block calls **access consciousness*, which seems amenable to analysis in scientific terms, phenomenal consciousness poses a problem for science (the **hard problem*) because one cannot see how biological systems obeying known laws of physics could generate sensory feel: sensory feel seems to be something outside the realm of science (hence the **explanatory gap*).

The sensorimotor approach takes the somewhat counter-intuitive stance that the problem of feel can be solved by adopting the view that for a person to have a feel amounts to (1) the person currently being engaged in exercising a certain sensorimotor skill, and (2) attending to the fact that they are engaged in exercising that skill.

1. Differences in sensory quality
2. Why feels have a quality at all
3. Ineffability
4. How feel is generated by the brain
5. Relation to attention and access consciousness
6. Note on the essential role of skill in the theory
7. Proponents and opponents of the theory

1. Differences in sensory quality

A first example of how this skill-based approach can be applied to the problem of phenomenal consciousness concerns differences in sensory quality. Classically, an explanation for the fact that input in different sensory channels provokes different types of sensation is sought in the different cortical areas that are involved (see *neural *correlates of consciousness*). However, this hypothesis leaves open the question of what exactly it is about these cortical areas or nerve channels that produces the particular sensations. Additional 'linking hypotheses' always have to be made to justify e.g. why particular neurons or neural mechanisms should produce particular sensory qualities, or why particular firing patterns should produce particular modulations in feel. But there would appear logically to be no way of making such a link in a scientifically testable fashion, since neural states are only physical characteristics of the firing patterns of neurons, and have no natural relation to facts of phenomenology. Thus, so claim the proponents of the sensorimotor approach, the search for a neural explanation for sensory quality will logically always fail through lack of such a scientifically testable link. Appealing to mechanisms like *gamma oscillations, *re-entrant processing, or quantum theories of consciousness, or *microconsciousness in particular cortical areas is not a solution, since there is logically no way to link properties of such mechanisms to the different varieties of feel that accompany sensations.

In the sensorimotor theory this logical problem of linking physical mechanisms to experienced feel is, it is claimed, obviated by appealing to the notion of sensorimotor interaction or *skill*. The sensorimotor approach proposes that having a feel involves attending to the fact that one is currently engaged in a particular skill or mode of sensorimotor interaction with one's environment. Taking this definition of feel, the quality of a feel will then be constituted by the particular laws that potentially govern the interaction. Take as analogy the feel of driving a Porsche as compared to driving a Volkswagen: the difference in feel is not generated anywhere in the brain, it is constituted precisely by the different things one can do, potentially (that is, one need not actually be doing them at any moment), when one drives these different cars. And now, it is claimed, there is a way of making a link between the phenomenology and the objective, sensorimotor interaction, because to every aspect of the phenomenology of driving there corresponds an objective physical characteristic of the interaction one has with the car. Of course it is difficult to precisely pinpoint what characterizes the feel of Porsche driving: clearly epithets such as 'invigorating', 'light touch', 'responsiveness', or 'sensitive steering' might be used. But whatever can be said about the feel of Porsche driving will, according to the sensorimotor theory, ultimately boil down to objective facts about the way the car behaves when one acts upon its controls. It is precisely the car's potentialities under our control, that is, the laws that govern our sensorimotor interaction with the car, which, it is claimed, constitute the feel of Porsche driving.

The sensorimotor approach now applies this idea to all sensory feels. By doing this, it provides a way of explaining similarities and differences between different sensations, and so escapes the failings of neural correlate approaches, which had to appeal to arbitrary linking hypotheses between physical mechanisms and different feels. Thus, to understand the felt difference between different sensory modalities, the sensorimotor approach considers the example of seeing and hearing. Seeing is a form of interaction in which blinks, movements of the eyes, of the body, and of outside objects provoke very particular types of change in sensory input. The laws governing these changes are quite different from the laws governing sensory input in the auditory modality. For example, when one sees, moving forward potentially produces an expanding flow-field on the retina, whereas when one hears, the change in sensory input is now mainly an increase in amplitude of the signal. The claim is now that the sum total of these differences constitute precisely what differentiates the sensations of seeing and hearing. (Note that in this explanation, the theory does not require continuous motor involvement.

It suffices that the perceiver should have sufficient information to know, implicitly, that if a movement were made, then particular sensorimotor laws would apply.)

To understand the felt difference between red and pink, for example, the sensorimotor approach notes that when one moves a coloured piece of paper under different illuminants, or when one moves one's eyes on or off the paper, there are precise laws that govern the changes in photon catches made by the three photoreceptor types that humans possess. In the case of red, for example, the changes in photon catches are confined to a single dimension of variation (Philipona and O'Regan 2006), suggesting why red is in some sense a special colour as compared to, say, orange, where three dimensions of variation are observed. In general all differences in experience will, under the sensorimotor approach, be constituted by differences in the sensorimotor laws or dependencies (also called 'sensorimotor contingencies') governing interaction with sensory stimuli.

A notable point about the theory is the way it explains humans' experience of a very rich and continually present visual world. Instead of supposing, as does the classic approach to vision, that this requires continuous activation of a rich internal representation of the world (this, the theory claims, would be to make a confusion between the *vehicle and the *contents of consciousness), the theory says that the experience of richness and continuity can in many cases be due to the fact that a perceiver has immediate *access*, via a flick of attention or an eye movement, to any information about the outside world. The analogy is the *refrigerator light: the light is on every time you open the fridge, so you assume it is on continually. Similar arguments are put forward in the theory to explain the filling in of the blind spot. In both cases, the theory claims it is not necessary for all parts of the visual field to be represented in the brain in order for a person to have the sensation of seeing the whole field.

2. Why feels have a quality at all

Classically in the philosophy of phenomenal consciousness it is said that 'there is something it is like' to have a sensory experience. One of the mysteries of phenomenal consciousness is considered to lie in explaining why the brain processes involved in sensory experiences give rise to this special quality—also referred to as *sensory presence* or *vividness*—while most other brain processes do not possess it.

The sensorimotor approach deals with this problem in the following way. If, as the approach claims, having a feel is precisely attending to the fact that one is engaged in exercising a sensorimotor skill, and if the quality of the feel is *constituted* by the laws of sensorimotor interaction that the skill involves, then by the very definition of feel, the feel must have a quality, namely the quality constituted by exercising the particular sensorimotor law involved.

Then, just as the sensorimotor approach invokes differences in skills to account for differences between sensations, the approach will also invoke differences in skills to account for the difference between experiences involved in perceptual acts and the experiences involved in *mental* activities like thinking, remembering, or deciding. In particular, it is immediately clear that whereas perceptual acts invariably involve, at least potentially, changes caused by motor behaviour, this is not true of mental activities. What we call sensory experience can always potentially (if not actually) be modified by a voluntary motion of the body: sensory input to the eyes, ears, or any other sensory system is immediately changed in a systematic and lawful way by body motions. On the other hand, mental activities like thoughts, memories, and decisions, to the extent that these can be considered as skills, are not skills that intrinsically involve body motions. This then is what makes the skills constituting sensory experiences special as compared to other brain processes: they are by nature sensori*motor*. Even if at any particular moment there need be no motion, they have what the sensorimotor approach calls *corporality* or *bodiliness*.

A second notable characteristic that distinguishes the skills involved in sensory experience from those of mental functions is what is termed *alerting capacity* or *grabbiness*: this is the fact that sensory systems are genetically endowed with the capacity to deflect our cognitive processing. A loud noise or bright flash will automatically, incontrovertibly, attract our attention to the locus of the event. We are thus, in some sense, 'cognitively at the mercy' of sensory input. This is not generally the case for mental activities. If a change occurs in the visual field, e.g. a mouse flitting across the floor, one's attention will immediately be caught by it. But if one has forgotten a word, one only discovers this if one actively tries to recover the word from memory. *Memory, and in general other mental activities, possess no alerting capacity or grabbiness (an exception might be, for example, obsessive thoughts).

Thus: a characterization of the differences in skills associated with sensory acts, as compared to those involved in mental acts, reveals differences which naturally account for the difference in felt quality of sensations as compared to other mental processes. What has been called the 'presence' of sensations seems precisely to consist in the fact that they are both under our control (in that we can modify sensory input by our bodily actions—they have corporality or bodiliness), and also *not* under our control (they can cause uncontrollable alerting reactions that interfere with our normal cognitive processing: alerting capacity or grabbiness).

The sensorimotor approach suggests that this captures the idea of there being 'something it is like' to feel, as opposed to other mental activities. The notions of bodiliness and grabbiness can also be used to account for the particular feel associated with pain (pain has a particularly high degree of grabbiness).

3. Ineffability

In the sensorimotor approach, appealing to skills is also taken to provide a natural way of accounting for the fact that sensations are ineffable. The reason is that the sensorimotor approach claims that while we have mastery of our sensorimotor skills, the mastery we have is implicit: we do not have cognitive access to each and every muscular contraction or change in sensory input that occurs. Indeed, muscular contractions (e.g. the lengths of particular muscle fibres) and sensory inputs (e.g. retinal photoreceptor firings) are not, it is claimed, in themselves things that we can become aware of. The situation is like tying your shoelaces: you know that you are tying your shoelaces, but you cannot say exactly how you are doing it, exactly what are the positions of your fingers, exactly what are the muscle movements involved. You may attend to different ways of tying your shoelaces, like differences occurring when the shoelaces are of different rigidity, length, thickness, etc., but though you can identify that there are these differences, and that these differences provide different feels to the shoelace tying action, you cannot describe in detail what these differences consist in.

Similar considerations, it is claimed, then apply to sensory feels: the sensorimotor dependencies involved in seeing are even less accessible to you than the intricacies of shoelace tying: you know that moving your eyes provokes changes in the information available to you, but you do not know in detail the changes in optic flow that are produced on your retina. You have a notion that when you move coloured surfaces under different lights, changes occur that depend on the particular surface reflectances, but the precise laws that govern those changes are not cognitively accessible to you. Nevertheless, the brain can distinguish between the different laws governing interaction with coloured surfaces, and can classify the associated surfaces as corresponding to different colours—just as you can recognize the feel of driving different cars without being able to cognitively pinpoint what causes these differences. Furthermore the brain structures the similarities and differences between the colour interactions in ways that correspond to the dimensions of brightness, hue, and saturation, and this structure determines the structure of the classifications and colour differences to which we have cognitive access.

4. How feel is generated by the brain

In the sensorimotor approach, this question is considered not to be an appropriate question to ask about feel. The sensorimotor approach considers that the idea that feel might be generated in the brain is a category error similar to the error of thinking that something about the shape of a word might generate its meaning. The idea is that if we think properly about feel, then we realize that feel is not an 'essence' that can be generated: we have a feel when we attend to the fact that we are interacting with our environment in a particular skilful mode. The quality of the feel is constituted by the characteristics of the mode of interaction.

5. Relation to attention and access consciousness

Why do we feel the feels *ourselves*? Whereas the essential ingredient of the sensorimotor approach is the appeal to skill—which provides the basis for an explanation for experienced differences in feel—the theory also stipulates that to experience a feel, one must have cognitive access to the skill that one is exercising. Thus simple sensorimotor automata, e.g. thermostats, missile guidance systems, and presumably insects, cannot, by definition, have feels: it is not sufficient for a system to be exercising a sensorimotor skill, it must in addition have sufficient cognitive capabilities to attend to the sensorimotor contingencies involved. If a system has sufficiently complex capacities for it to make sense to say that it has a *self, then it will be this self that has cognitive access to the ongoing sensorimotor interaction, and thus it will be this self that feels. However, it is claimed that these appeals to cognitive access or attention, and to the notion of self, do not necessitate any scientifically mysterious mechanisms: attention is a notion already widely used in psychology, where it is considered difficult, but not in any way 'magical' or impossible to implement or understand scientifically. The 'self' is a complex construct corresponding to an agent's capacity to reason about its own potential cognitive and social behaviours, but it is also not magical.

To the extent that the sensorimotor approach makes use of the notion of cognitive access and attention, it bears resemblance to theories of consciousness such as the *global workspace theory (see also ATTENTION). Such theories are probably able to provide an acceptable explication of access consciousness. However, it is the addition of the notion of skill which provides the essential element that allows the sensorimotor approach to go further than access consciousness, and to provide insights into what has been considered beyond the reach of functional accounts, namely phenomenal consciousness.

6. Note on the essential role of skill in the theory
The reason that invoking skill in the theory provides help in explaining phenomenal consciousness is that differences and similarities between skills are objective facts about an organism's interaction with the world. Since in the theory the quality of experience is taken to be constituted by the exercise of skills, differences and similarities between qualities are describable in terms of these objective differences in skilful modes of interaction. Making the connection between skill and feel is now easy to do because sensorimotor laws are both describable in terms of objective facts about the perceptible world, and they also have a natural correspondence with what people generally agree characterizes sensory feels as compared to other mental phenomena, in particular their perceptual presence.

In contrast, if the onus of explanation in explaining feel is put on neural states, as is done in the classical 'neural correlate' approach to phenomenal consciousness (cf. neural correlates of consciousness), then there is no natural way of making the connection between similarities and differences of feel and similarities and differences in the neural states. Even something so simple as supposing that increased neural firing should cause increased intensity of feel would require providing an explanation for that particular choice of link between feel and neural activity.

7. Proponents and opponents of the theory
The sensorimotor approach, as set out originally by O'Regan and Noë (2001a, 2001b) and more recently by O'Regan et al. (2006), has also been called the *enactive approach* (Noë 2005). The notion of enaction involves the idea that one can only adequately describe the functioning of the mind in the context of a system with a body acting and sensing in its environment.

However, it should be noted that some other authors have associated the notion of enaction with dynamical systems, and with the idea that re-entrant processing, chaos, and complexity in neural systems might be the key to consciousness. This would be contrary to the sensorimotor approach, which considers that if one thinks carefully about consciousness and feel, one realizes that no appeal to such mechanisms can help to understand why feels feel the way they do.

The sensorimotor approach is sometimes compared to Gibson's ecological approach to perception, with both approaches emphasizing the role of action and sensorimotor dependencies in perception (see ACTION), and both approaches rejecting some senses of the notion of 'internal representation' (see HOMUNCULUS). But the two approaches have very different agendas, with the sensorimotor approach being aimed at solving a problem that Gibson was not concerned with, namely the problem of the origin and nature of phenomenal experience.

Like Gibson's ecological theory, the sensorimotor approach is sometimes labelled as being behaviourist: a relation to behaviourism might lie in the fact that to explain sensations, which are generally thought to be inner states, the theory makes use of the concept of skills, which are sensorimotor dispositions. However, to the extent that the theory invokes cognitive capacities and the concept of attention, it is not behaviourist in the sense of rejecting the causal role of internal mental states.

There are points of similarity between the sensorimotor approach and aspects of the thinking of French philosopher Maurice Merleau-Ponty (see PHENOMENOLOGY), who also wanted to replace the idea of perception as a primarily internal event (involving an iconic replica in the case of vision), with a conception of vision as an active, and further-action-oriented, exploration of the environment. Some of the metaphors used by Merleau-Ponty, such as vision consisting in having a visual grasp on the world, and the analogy between touch and vision, anticipate aspects of the sensorimotor theory. On the other hand, there are clearly points of dissimilarity: the idea that cognitive access or attention is required for consciousness would be rejected by Merleau-Ponty as a piece of 'intellectualist thinking' about the mind.

A different link to behaviourism (and to functionalism and Dennett's *heterophenomenology) might be the attitude of the theory to *qualia: the theory rules out qualia if they are meant to be in principle unobservable and in principle unrelated to behaviour. On the other hand, if qualia are considered to be the phenomenal experiences that are involved in sensation and perception, then far from eliminating qualia (see ELIMINATIVISM), the theory attempts to explain why they are the way they are. The theory claims that compared to other functional approaches, the appeal to skill provides an advantage in accounting for the phenomenology of sensory experience: Sensory feels have a quality rather than no quality because of the bodiliness and grabbiness of sensory systems. The quality of sensation is an objective fact about the way an agent interacts with its environment. For this reason there is also a link with *externalism.

The sensorimotor approach invokes a two-level mechanism to explain phenomenal consciousness: (1) the exercise of a skill, and (2) cognitively accessing the fact that one is exercising the skill. If attending to something can be considered to be a form of cognitive access, the theory might be considered to be related to the *higher-order thought theory of consciousness. Thus it could be said that under the sensorimotor approach, having a feel is having a higher-order thought about the fact of exercising a skill. But the main ingredient of the theory are the skills themselves, since their similarities and differences allow similarities and differences in phenomenal experience (including the difference between feel and no feel) to be explained in a natural way.

An important aspect of the sensorimotor approach is its emphasis on making empirical predictions. The original experiments on *change blindness were motivated by the sensorimotor approach, which is also compatible with the phenomenon of *inattentional blindness. The approach claims to find support in empirical results on *sensory substitution, and in the changes in phenomenal experience caused by sensorimotor adaptation in touch found in the *rubber hand illusion and in *mirror therapy used in reducing *phantom limb pain. A sensorimotor approach to understanding tetrachromacy (see COLOUR VISION, TETRACHROMATIC) and the phenomenal structure of colour space (Philipona and O'Regan 2006) as well as predictions concerning eye movement contingent modifications of colour sensation (Bompas and O'Regan 2006) have also proved successful.

J. KEVIN O'REGAN

Bompas, A. and O'Regan, J. K. (2006). More evidence for sensorimotor adaptation in color perception. *Journal of Vision*, 6.

Noë, A. (2005). *Action in Perception.*

O'Regan, J. K. and Noë, A. (2001a). 'A sensorimotor account of vision and visual consciousness'. *Behavioral and Brain Sciences*, 24.

—— —— (2001b). 'Authors' response. Acting out our experience'. *Behavioral and Brain Sciences*, 24.

——, Myin, E., and Noë, A. (2006). 'Skill, corporality and alerting capacity in an account of sensory consciousness'. *Progress in Brain Research*, 150.

Philipona, D. and O'Regan, J. K. (2006). 'Color naming, unique hues and hue cancellation predicted from singularities in reflection properties'. *Visual Neuroscience*, 23.

sensory substitution We see with the brain, not with the eye. Blindness typically results from the loss of retinal function, but the visual cortex remains intact. Likewise, deafness and bilateral vestibular dysfunction (BVD) usually arises from the loss of transduction processes. Since the cognitive capacity to experience the sensation remains intact, all that is needed restore lost sensory function is an alternative source of sensory data and a human–machine interface to couple the data to the nervous system (Bach-y-Rita 2005).

1. Brain rewiring
2. Vision substitution.
3. Vestibular substitution
4. A curious phenomenon

1. Brain rewiring

In sensory substitution, data from a set of artificial receptors coupled to the sensory cortex via sensory substitution in a form of controlled *synaesthesia that depends on brain plasticity (Hurley and Noë 2003, Bach-y-Rita 2005). This 'rewiring' of the brain has been observed experimentally. Horng and Sur (2006) observe that in response to visual cortex damage the brains of ferrets are rewired to route retinal input to the auditory cortex, and the auditory cortex is remodelled to accommodate visual information.

Although Sur's observations involve the re-routing of information from properly functioning sense organs to a novel cortex to compensate for the loss of function in the normal cortex, the rewiring can occur the other way around. If the flow of information from a sense organ fails while the cortex remains intact, the brain can rewire itself to use the still-functioning cortex to process information from other senses. Positron emission tomography (PET) has been used to study tactile visual sensory substitution (TVSS) in congenitally blind persons (Ptito et al. 2005). The results showed that the visual cortex was activated after, but not before, the one-week training period. No visual cortex activation occurred in blindfolded controls. They concluded that *cross-modal plasticity can occur quickly in the adult brain and that the tongue can act as a portal to convey somatosensory information to the visual cortex. Previously, Bach-y-Rita (2005) had demonstrated the existence of pathways from the skin to the visual cortex.

Many cross-modal sensory substitution schemes are feasible. Bach-y-Rita has done extensive work in TVSS and electrotactile vestibular sensory substitution (EVSS). As another alternative, data from tactile sensors mounted at the fingertips were coupled to skin sensory receptors on the forehead of a leprosy patient. After acclimation, the patient experienced the machine-generated data as if they originated in the fingertips. In addition, various technologies for coupling camera data into the brain via the auditory system have been demonstrated (Meijer 1992).

Hurley and Noë's (2003) model of a sensorimotor cycle appears to be a powerful description of our observations of sensory substitution. One reason for this claim is that our subjects must have motor control and be able to interact with the scene. If not, the electrotactile stimulation is never experienced as anything more than tingling on the tongue. Clark and Eilan (2006) make a rather curious criticism of the model; they do not claim it to be wrong, but suppose it to be 'extreme'. Their objection is that the model fails to accommodate the fractionation of brain function required to support a computational model of the brain. However, our observations lead us to the conclusion that computation does not account for brain function (Kercel et al. 2005) and that Hurley and Noë's model points the way toward a credible alternative paradigm.

2. Vision substitution

The experience of seeing can be partially generated by using an image data from a camera, provided the image data can be coupled to the brain. The camera data are transduced into a form of energy that can be mediated by the skin receptors. The visual information reaches the perceptual levels for cognitive recovery of the image via somatosensory pathways and structures. The most effective strategy for doing so has been found to be electrotactile stimulation of the tongue (Bach-y-Rita 2005).

The question often arises whether blind subjects using TVSS are actually seeing. For the subjects to make sense of the input requires between several hours and several days of training. Successful integration of sensory data depends critically on the subject's ability to manipulate the scene, just as in the case of long-time blind subjects whose vision is restored surgically (see BLINDNESS, RECOVERY FROM). After several hours of training, subjects report experiencing the image in space, rather than on the skin. They make perceptual judgements using visual means of analysis, such as perspective, parallax, looming and zooming, and depth judgements. Even the *illusions that have been tested (e.g. the waterfall effect) are experienced in the same way as vision.

The emotional responses of subjects indicate a recognition that we commonly associate with seeing. In one case, a blind child brightened with genuine and surprised delight upon being shown the flickering flame of a candle via TVSS. In another instance, Eric Weihenmayer, blind since the age of 13, went through several hours of training using TVSS at the age of 32. He described his experience of using TVSS to navigate a corridor as 'seeing.' Although TVSS is not identical to normal seeing, it shares many of the same attributes.

3. Vestibular substitution

BVD produces functional difficulties such as postural wobbling, unsteady gait, and oscillopsia. As a palliative, a vestibular substitution system was developed using a head-mounted accelerometer and an EVSS system (Bach-y-Rita 2005). The accelerometer output provides balance data. Coupling to the brain uses exactly the same transducer for electrotactile stimulation of the tongue as is used in TVSS. The resulting EVSS produces a strong stabilization effect on head–body coordination in BVD patients. Three characteristic and unique head motion features (drift, sway, and long-period perturbations) consistently appear in the head-postural behavior of these patients, but are greatly reduced or eliminated with EVSS.

The greater part of the effect can be seen in a matter of seconds. Subjects who describe themselves as feeling that 'my body is a noodle', and who require help to standing, are able to stand stock-still within five seconds of starting to use EVSS. The subjective experience is much more than simple restoration of balance. Subjects report that using device makes them feel as if a pall of gloom has been lifted from them. Precise measurements of postural stability show that stability improves over a training period of about five days.

4. A curious phenomenon

Another attribute of sensory substitution is the relative ease with which the brain makes the proper substitution. Using tactile stimulation of the skin as the coupling mechanism, subjects experience camera data as vision, fingertip sensor data as touch, and accelerometer data as restoration of balance. In addition, other researchers have successfully demonstrated substitution between many other sensory modes. There appears to be a serious possibility that whatever artificial sensor data are coupled into the brain via the electrotactile transducer, the brain makes proper sense of them, notwithstanding the fact that the same transducer is used in every case.

Why this should be the case is not presently understood. However, the attributes of sensory substitution (such as the necessity of sensorimotor involvement, and the patient's awareness of the *results* of the integration while remaining totally unaware of *how* it occurs) are strikingly similar to those of implicit learning or unconscious integration (UI). UI is largely independent of the learner's awareness of the process of learning and the knowledge ultimately attained (see LEARNING, EXPLICIT VS IMPLICIT). It is closely related to other aspects of unconscious functioning emphasized in contemporary cognitive science, such as (1) blindsight, in which visual information is registered without awareness, (2) implicit memory, in which information is retained and can affect behaviour although the individual is unable to consciously recall or recognize it, and (3) motor or procedural learning, in which the details of actions necessary to produce a fluid motion have become automatic. These processes are, by and large, not available to conscious introspection and they function largely outside the user's awareness.

The similarity between the experiences of sensory substitution patients and those of the subjects of UI experiments suggests the possibility that UI mediates sensory substitution. If so, that might account for the fact that the brain makes proper sense of whatever sensory data are coupled via the electrotactile transducer. Since UI can be indirectly manipulated and influenced, this suggests that sensory substitution could become a much more powerful tool than previously suspected. Instead of merely restoring lost sensory functionality, it introduces a serious possibility of using machine generated data to create entirely new senses.

Research thus far has led to the demonstration of reliable devices that use sensory substitution to restore lost sensory function. There are three paths for future development. First is the development of robust and relatively inexpensive implementations of the technology to make it accessible to a wide range of patients suffering sensory loss. Second, moving beyond the restoration of lost senses, UI may enable of the technology to expand human sensibilities, for example, enabling a diver to use a sonar device to navigate in turbid water. Finally, the technology enables a whole range of non-invasive low-risk experiments with human subjects to gain a deeper understanding of brain plasticity and cognitive processes.

STEPHEN W. KERCEL AND PAUL BACH-Y-RITA

Bach-y-Rita, P. (2005). 'Emerging concepts of brain function'. *Journal of Integrative Neuroscience*, 4.

Clark, A. and Eilan, N. (2006). 'Sensorimotor skills and perception'. *Supplement to the Proceedings of the Aristotelian Society*, 80.

Horng, S. and Sur, M. (2006). 'Visual activity and cortical rewiring: activity-dependent plasticity of cortical networks'. *Progress in Brain Research*, 157.

Hurley, S. and Noë, A. (2003). 'Neural plasticity and consciousness'. *Biology and Philosophy*, 18.

Kercel, S., Reber, A., and Manges, W. (2005). 'Some radical implications of Bach-y-Rita's discoveries'. *Journal of Integrative Neuroscience*, 4.

Meijer, P. B. L. (1992). 'An experimental system for auditory image representations'. *IEEE Transactions on Biomedical Engineering*, 39.

Ptito, M., Moesgaard, S., Gjedde, A., and Kupers, R. (2005). 'Cross-modal plasticity revealed by electrotactile stimulation of the tongue in the congenitally blind'. *Brain*, 128.

sequence learning The ability to generate and comprehend sequences is a significant contributor to human cognitive ability. Sequencing entails using a small number of basic elements and combining them so that they are meaningful when integrated across time. For example, the 26 letters of the English alphabet are combined to generate the approximately 600 000 words in the English language. Sequencing plays a central role in many cognitive abilities, including the perception and production of spoken words and grammatical sentences, keyboarding, dance, and so on. Sequencing is computationally powerful, but it must also be principled; elements are sequenced according to rules.

Introspection indicates that we remain unaware of the rules that govern sequencing in many domains. Although we can use the rules to sequence words grammatically, most people cannot verbalize them. And for some tasks—especially motor skills such as knitting, or hitting a golf ball—we feel that we consciously guide the sequence of action early in training, but with extensive practice we can generate the right sequence without this conscious direction.

Reber (1967) was the first to claim to have observed unconscious sequence learning in the laboratory (see ARTIFICIAL GRAMMAR LEARNING). His subjects were asked to remember letter strings (e.g. APEB) that were generated by an artificial grammar. Later, participants were above chance in determining whether new strings were 'grammatical'. They evinced this knowledge despite an inability to verbalize knowledge of the grammatical rules.

One experimental paradigm, the *serial reaction time task* (Nissen and Bullemer 1987), has been used extensively because the learning is rapid and reliable, the paradigm is open to many variations, and minor variations in the training lead to either conscious (explicit) or unconscious (implicit) learning (see LEARNING, EXPLICIT VS IMPLICIT). The serial reaction time task is a visuomotor skill task. The subject sits before a computer monitor, with the index and middle fingers of each hand poised above four response keys. Four possible stimulus locations (e.g. boxes) are visible on the monitor, arranged in a horizontal line. On each trial a stimulus appears at one of the locations, and the subject is to press the response key directly below the stimulus as quickly as possible, whereupon the stimulus is extinguished, and a new stimulus appears. The stimuli appear in a repeating sequence, usually twelve units long. In other versions, the sequence is probabilistic, meaning that the sequence is not fixed; e.g. the stimulus may be predictable and follow the sequence for only 85% of the time, and unpredictable 15% of the time. Two variants of the task are commonly used. In one, the subject is told that the stimuli are sequenced, and that they should try to learn the sequence so as to speed responses. As one would expect, subjects can do so, faster reaction times ensue, and subjects perform well on standard memory measures such as recall or recognition. In the other task variant, the subject is not told about the sequence. Because the sequence length is beyond working memory capacity (see MEMORY, WORKING), and nothing demarcates its beginning or end, subjects may never become aware of the fact that the stimuli are sequenced—or, more accurately, they may claim to be unaware when queried later. In addition, they perform at chance on recognition or recall measures. Nevertheless, reaction times to the stimuli decrease with training, and increase if the stimulus sequence is changed. This change shows that at least part of the reaction time decrease was due to sequence-specific knowledge. This apparent dissociation between conscious knowledge of the sequence and improved sequence-specific performance led many researchers to conclude that sequence knowledge could be acquired outside of consciousness (Clegg et al. 1998).

A great deal of effort has gone into the evaluation of conscious knowledge in this paradigm. The measurement of conscious report—and in particular, concluding that the subject is unaware of the sequence—is fraught with problems (Shanks and St John 1994). In the typical paradigm, awareness of the sequence is measured after training—the report is retrospective. Hence, it is possible that the subject had some conscious sequence knowledge as they were performing it, but lost that knowledge by the time of the test. Another potential problem is a mismatch between the subject's conscious knowledge and the content of the experimenter's query. Suppose that the experimenter asks 'Was this part of the sequence: 131421?' (with stimulus positions designated 1–4 from left to right). The subject may truthfully feel he has no inkling as to whether or not the stimuli appeared in this sequence. But while performing the task the subject may have consciously thought that the stimulus seemed to appear on the far left quite often. That conscious expectation might have been enough to reduce reaction times, although the recognition test would show the subject to be at chance. More generally, if the subject possesses conscious knowledge that is correlated with, but not identical to, the knowledge for which the experimenter probes, there is a danger of the test failing to detect the subject's conscious knowledge. To avoid this danger, the experimenter might try to make the probe for conscious knowledge as open-ended as possible, e.g. simply asking 'Did you notice a sequence?' But that procedure leaves it to the subject to judge what 'noticing' means. A subject might have conscious knowledge of a fragment of the sequence, but deem it unworthy of report.

Scores of studies have addressed this problem, with variable success. Two varieties of studies provide the most definitive evidence that sequence learning may be unconscious. Some studies have used brief sequences that alternate with random stimuli interleaved in the sequence. With enough training, subjects show the reaction time benefit that characterizes unconscious learning. However, subjects are unable to acquire sequence knowledge even when instructed to do so, making it seem unlikely that learning could be supported by conscious knowledge (Howard and Howard 2001). In another procedure (Shanks and Perruchet 2002) subjects were first trained on the typical SRT task, and were then administered a recognition test in which they responded to sequences as they had done during training, and then rated each sequence as familiar or not. The experimenters observed that recognition was at chance, but response times during the recognition phase were faster for the sequence than for lures. This procedure has two important advantages: the measures of implicit and explicit knowledge are very nearly simultaneous, and the researchers could be relatively confident that they had avoided the problem of the test of conscious knowledge failing to match the subject's conscious knowledge. Whatever knowledge the subject had, it was sufficient to support faster performance in the reaction time task, and so arguably it should have been able to support a simple recognition judgement.

These data have been important to the position that learning and memory are supported by multiple systems. The dissociation of consciousness with different types of learning was a persuasive observation. Also important were data indicating that these two types of learning are neurally independent. Experiments in the 1980s showed that patients with dense anterograde *amnesia due to damage to the medial temporal lobe or diencephalon were severely impaired in the explicit version of the serial reaction time task, but learned the implicit version normally. (Later data indicated that they may be somewhat impaired in learning complex sequences.) Other patient groups—notably those with damage to the cerebellum, or parts of the frontal or parietal cortex—show profound impairment in the implicit version of the task, with only a mild impairment on the explicit version (see BRAIN DAMAGE). *Functional brain imaging studies have supported the dissociation; learning the implicit version depends on secondary motor, posterior parietal, and cingulate cortices, as well as the striatum. Explicit learning depends on dorsolateral prefrontal, secondary motor, and posterior parietal cortices, as well as the medial temporal lobe (Poldrack and Willingham 2006; see MEMORY SYSTEMS, NEURAL BASIS OF). Other researchers, however, believe that a single knowledge source underlies performance on both types of test, and the dissociations are due to differences in retrieval mechanisms.

Efforts to model these phenomena computationally have been successful, but have not led to agreement on how to interpret these findings. Perhaps the most concrete consequence of sequence learning studies has been an expansion of the concept of human learning. Until the 1980s, 'learning' was usually measured by verbal report. Sequencing studies, along with other implicit tasks, have made clear that knowledge may be expressed through other means.

DANIEL T. WILLINGHAM AND JANET P. TRAMMELL

Clegg, B. A., DiGirolamo, G. J., and Keele, S. W. (1998). Sequence learning. *Trends in Cognitive Sciences*, 2.

Howard, D. V. and Howard, J. H. (2001). 'When it *does* hurt to try: adult age differences in the effects of instructions on implicit pattern learning'. *Psychonomic Bulletin and Review*, 8.

Nissen, M. J. and Bullemer, P. (1987). 'Attentional requirements of learning: evidence from performance measures'. *Cognitive Psychology*, 19.
Poldrack, R. A. and Willingham, D. T. (2006). 'Skill learning'. In Cabeza, R. and Kingstone, A. (eds) *The Handbook of Functional Neuroimaging*, 2nd edn.
Reber, A. S. (1967). 'Implicit learning of artificial grammars'. *Journal of Verbal Learning and Verbal Behavior*, 6.
Shanks, D. R. and Perruchet, P. (2002). 'Dissociation between priming and recognition in the expression of sequence knowledge'. *Psychonomic Bulletin and Review*, 9.
—— and St John, M. F. (1994). 'Characteristics of dissociable human learning systems'. *Behavioral and Brain Sciences*, 17.

signal detection theory Signal detection theory (SDT) uses models based on statistical decision theory for assessing performance in psychophysical detection and many other areas, ranging from medical diagnosis to recognition memory to discrimination between ballistic missiles and flocks of birds. When applied to consciousness studies, SDT has had considerable methodological and theoretical influence. This influence is especially strong in the area of unconscious *perception, which often uses weak stimuli for which SDT is particularly suited. It also has the most developed applications of SDT to consciousness and will be the main topic of this entry.

SDT brought two concepts to psychophysics: (1) that the stimulus is not fixed but is imposed on a background of inherent noise, and indeed may itself contain random variability; (2) that perceptual reports are not direct accounts of experience. The report of having seen a stimulus depends on both the signal's discriminability and the decision criterion for a 'yes' applied by the observer.

1. Signal and background noise
2. Sensory thresholds
3. SDT and the dissociation paradigm
4. Greenwald's regression method
5. Final comments

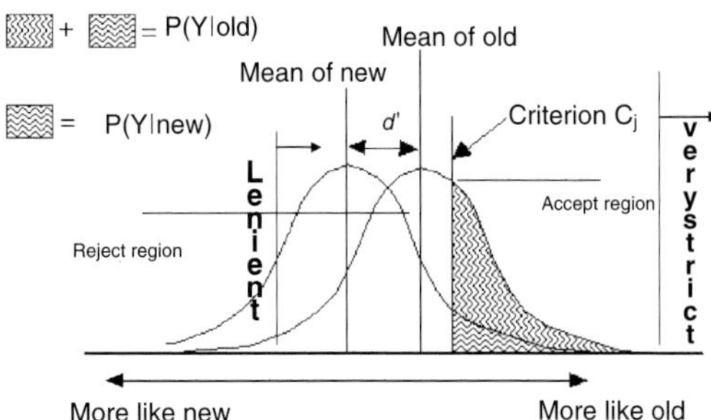

Fig. S1. Gaussian model of SDT. This illustration has equal variance for the signal and noise. Several criteria are shown, from Very Lenient to Very Strict. Operating at the Very Strict criterion would cause the discrimination available in the situation modelled here not to be measured.

1. Signal and background noise

The decision process is illustrated in Fig. S1, which shows the simplest Gaussian SDT model, and is a convenient image for discussion. Signal and noise events are represented as normal distributions. These distributions can be conceived abstractly as summaries of the evidence for a target. If the trial contains only noise, the 'evidence' for a target will be distributed as in the noise distribution. If the stimulus is actually a target, it will be distributed as in the signal distribution. Of course the observer does not know whether signal or noise is presented, only the amount of evidence on a given trial.

The distance between the means is the measure d'. The mean of the noise is the zero point and the standard deviation is the unit of measure. A d' of 1.0 signifies that the mean of the signal distribution is one standard deviation from the mean of the non-signal distribution. When the means of the two distributions coincide, $d' = 0$, and as discriminability improves the distributions separate and d' increases.

Given that the signal and non-signal distributions are continuous, how does the observer decide whether to say yes or no? In most models the observer chooses a point on the x-axis and reports 'yes' if the evidence on a trial is greater than that point and 'no' if it is less. How is this point selected? The weighing of costs and benefits as to whether the stimulus is signal or noise sets the criterion for the amount of evidence needed. Depending on the criterion, detection probability for the target could go from 1.0 (for a criterion at the far left) to 0.0 for the criterion marked Very Strict in Fig. S1.

In Fig. S1 the criterion *Cj* is set at a relatively strict or conservative point: a low false alarm rate (FAR) is imposed, but at the cost of a low hit rate (HR). Such a strict criterion corresponds to a situation in which the cost of a false alarm is considerably greater than the reward for a successful hit. If the reward for a hit were increased, the rational effect would be to move the criterion to the left in the figure. The number of hits then would increase, but so would the number of false alarms. Lowering the cost of a false alarm would also move the criterion to the left. The receiver operating characteristic (ROC) plots the relationship between HR and FAR as the criterion is varied. An example of the ROC produced by the equal-variance Gaussian model as criterion is varied in Fig. S1 is plotted in Fig. S2. The HR and FAR produced by *Cj* and the Lenient criterion in Fig. S1 are marked on the ROC. The Lenient and Very Strict criteria would result in performance very close to (1,1) and (0,0), respectively, and d' would be unmeasurable. Also, with criteria as extreme as this, forced-choice

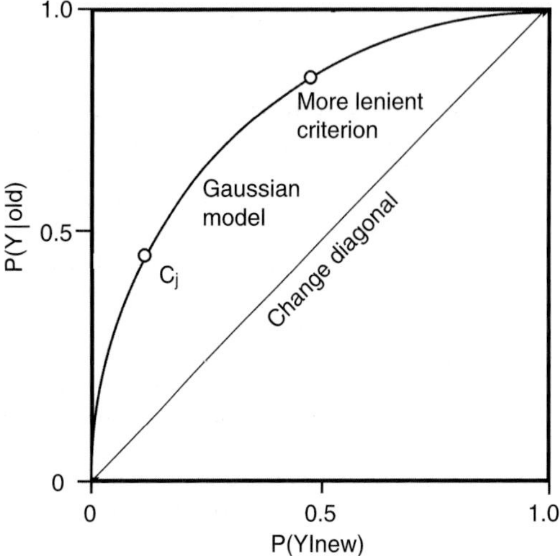

Fig. S2. Receiver operating characteristic (ROC). It plots how Hits and False Alarms covary as the criterion is varied.

responding, which is normally considered to give criterion-free measures, would have performance near chance when d' was otherwise measurable.

In very few cognitive experiments is explicit pay-off used to vary criterion. The pay-off is usually implicit or undefined. Often a difference between experimental conditions can reasonably be attributed to criterial differences, but there is rarely if ever a follow-up test with explicit pay-off to see if the criterial explanation is supported. Several phenomena that seemed to support unconscious perception have been put in doubt when criterion was varied explicitly or measured with confidence ratings (see e.g. Haase and Fisk 2001, and sections below).

A relevant point is that d', though often referred to as a measure of 'strength', does not give an absolute measure of signal strength or visibility or intensity, or in this context, awareness. Rather, it is a measure of discrimination between two stimuli. Even when a forced-choice test shows chance discriminability and hence a d' of 0.0, this is only d' for that discrimination. The target could be paired with a more discriminable foil and yield $d' > 0$. Parametric SDT measures such as d' are interval-scale quantities whose zero point is the mean of the non-target distribution. Change the reference non-target distribution, and the zero point changes—a d' of zero can become a positive or negative number, depending on the distribution from which it is to be distinguished, much as 20 °F is –7 °C.

These points make it clear that while d' is a tool in the study of implicit cognition, it is not itself a measure of consciousness. First, the size of d' measured for a stimulus will be a function of the foil against which it is compared, not of an aspect of the stimulus by itself. Second, d' is a parameter in a model of perceptual decisions. It does not measure awareness but rather the stimulus information used in the decision.

2. Sensory thresholds

Another matter is the idea of a threshold for consciousness, subliminal stimuli, and so on. Swets (1961) presented a compelling case that the sensory threshold concept itself is invalid. Among other evidence for his case is his finding that when an observer is wrong in a four-alternative forced-choice test of detection (one of four intervals contains the target, and the observer must pick one), the second choice is above chance. If there were a threshold of sensation, the second choices would be at chance because the stimulus was not perceived. The second-choice data are predicted very well by a Gaussian model like that in Fig. S1 but with unequal variance of signal and noise distributions.

3. SDT and the dissociation paradigm

The experimental question in unconscious perception is always the same: can some stimulus that falls on our sense organs but is not consciously perceived have a measurable effect of any kind on behaviour? The experimental procedure to answer this question is termed the **dissociation* paradigm. It has two parts: (1) Show that the stimulus is not consciously reportable. A detection measure like d' has a natural application here. Although d' does not measure consciousness, a d' of zero has generally, if not always correctly, been assumed to indicate lack of awareness of the target. (2) Show that the stimulus under conditions where d' was zero nevertheless has an effect on thought, evaluation, memory, recognition, or some cognitive process. This test may be of a direct effect, such as above-chance choice of a word presented so briefly as to be invisible in the dissociation test, or an indirect test, as when associates of the imperceptible word are *primed when it is presented. Detection theory has applications in the second part of the paradigm as well.

Of the two parts of the dissociation paradigm, the first, showing that the stimulus is unconscious, is by far the more difficult to achieve. Part of the problem comes from the general logical difficulty of proving a negative, namely that nothing was seen (Greenwald et al. 1995). There is also a specific problem, the lack of an accepted criterion for consciousness. Below are some of the strategies for dissociation, described and criticized from a signal detection perspective.

Subjective and objective thresholds. Reingold and Merikle (1988, 1990) proposed that unconscious perception effects would be found between two thresholds, the subjective threshold and the objective threshold. The subjective threshold test that the stimulus is unconscious is based on the report by the observer that the stimulus is imperceptible. Assume that stimuli such as words are presented under progressively more and more obscuring conditions. As the duration or contrast decreased, visibility would decline until the observers would report that they could not see the words and could not even tell whether the screen was blank. That point is termed the *subjective threshold*. However, this is still not the *objective threshold*, which would be reached when stimulus information became so meagre that observers forced to guess would perform at chance.

It would be natural to ask what could be more authoritative than a first-person report that something cannot be seen. What effrontery for the experimenter to say, 'yes, you can see it!' However, the matter is not that simple. The subjective threshold is a judgement that reflects criterion as well as perceptibility. Given a brief, murky stimulus, the available information is uncertain, and some criterial cut-off must be chosen for a yes–no decision to be made. It is up to the observer to decide what the criterion will be for declaring that the stimulus cannot be seen. The criterion is entirely the choice of the observer, who may require a very clear view of the stimulus before saying 'yes, I can see it'.

A better test of perception is forced choice. In forced-choice testing there is no yes–no option; two or more stimuli including the target are presented and one of them must be chosen. Finding unconscious perception to be above chance on forced-choice testing after a 'no' in a subjective threshold test seems largely the result of using two different measures. It is much like the case in which 'guessing' on uncertain multiple-choice items results in above-chance performance. However, even in this case criterion could be a factor. If the criterion was at the very strict level in Fig. S1, the difference between the two distributions might be small (say, 0.01% vs 0.0001%) and the observer would choose at random.

Haase and Fisk (2001) demonstrated the importance of the criterial effect in the subjective threshold measurement. They took confidence ratings during the subjective threshold measurement and showed that forced-choice detection correlated well with these ratings. Further, they showed that the identification operating characteristic (IOC) was well predicted by the subjective ratings. The IOC is like an ROC but plots the joint probability of detecting in the subjective rating and identifying in the forced-choice testing.

Some have argued that the objective threshold is the correct measure to use in the dissociation paradigm. Thus, the observer would be tested not for a report of whether the stimulus is perceptible, but for correct identification of the stimulus in a forced-choice test. If identification were at chance with an objective test, the criterion that the presentation be unconscious would seem more likely to be met than with a subjective report.

The objective test is itself the sort of test used to show unconscious perception in subjective threshold experiments. If the stimulus conditions were adjusted to give chance performance in a forced-choice test, it would seem that the possibility of finding any kind of perception, conscious or not, would be eliminated. However, the approach given an objective test for dissociation is to test for unconscious perception with an *indirect* test. The indirect test is a test of the effect of the stimuli on some other measure. For example, Marcel (1983) showed that a word found to be objectively unconscious could still prime the recognition of a related word. Thus, *doctor* presented unconsciously would reduce the time required immediately afterwards to classify *nurse* as an English word, whereas a control word such as *butter* would not prime it. The priming of *nurse* is the indirect measure.

The objective threshold has many problems of its own. The initial research on Marcel's unconscious priming effect was not consistent in replicating it, and the question was whether the objective measure was rigorous (Holender 1986). Reingold and Merikle (1988, 1990) pointed out several rather difficult criteria an objective threshold measure would need to pass to give strong evidence for unconscious perception. First, null sensitivity must be established, meaning that d' must be 0.0 at the objective threshold. Given measurement error, null sensitivity is difficult to establish. A d' of 0.25 would give performance in the range of most unconscious perception effects, but it would take many trials to distinguish a d' of 0.25 from one of 0. With a d' of 0.0 there is still a problem because the spread of the distribution would place 50% of the items above zero and capable of priming on half of the trials.

Given a case in which d' is accepted as zero, there is still the question of *exhaustiveness*, that is, whether the objective discrimination test actually tested the aspects of the stimulus relevant to the indirect effect. Consider that d' is a relative measure. If the comparison and thus the zero point in the objective test is not the same as the zero point for the discrimination relevant to the indirect test, all bets are off. The discrimination relevant for that task might well have a positive d', given that the noise distribution would likely be different.

A third concern is *exclusiveness*, namely the question of whether the dissociation technique eliminates only conscious components of perception or some combination of conscious and unconscious components. The issue comes up in several important places. One is in applications of the exclusion technique to detect unconscious components of perception and memory. It is also an issue in the regression technique of Greenwald et al. (1995). The model of Snodgrass et al. (2004) and Snodgrass and Shevrin (2006) uses detection analyses to get at the separate contributions of conscious and unconscious components of perception.

The *exclusion technique*, introduced by Jacoby (1991) to test for implicit memory, is an ingenious application of opposition logic. The best evidence for unconscious influences, according to this logic, is not detection of or associations to stimuli declared to be invisible, but the *inability to resist their influence on performance*. In the *Stroop task, the conflict in naming the ink colour of a different colour word is good evidence that the word was read despite the participant's best efforts. Now consider words that are presented briefly and reported as not visible. Such reporting is application of a subjective criterion and may result in uncertain perceptions being classified wrongly as unconscious. The exclusion procedure is intended as a better test of unconscious perception. It instructs participants not to use anything that was presented (visible or not!) in a subsequent task. If the invisible words were nevertheless used despite the instructions in, say, stem completion, we would seem to have rather good evidence of unconscious perception of the words. Not only were the words unconsciously perceived but the participants were unable to resist using them. This phenomenon, termed *exclusion failure*, leads to a compelling theory of the role of awareness in perception, namely that material presented out of awareness may be perceived and encoded unconsciously, but awareness adds control over the material.

Further research has demonstrated criterial control of exclusion quantitatively, using SDT methods. See e.g. Banks et al. (1999), Banks (2000), Haase and Fisk (2001), and Fisk and Haase (2006). Given that criterion can determine the degree of exclusion failure, exclusion must be under conscious control, even if the participant claims not to have seen the items excluded. Cognitive control over exclusion does not by itself deny unconscious perception of the items; after all, they could be unconsciously perceived and later become consciously available. However, these findings vitiate the use of exclusion as a qualitative test of unconscious perception (see Merikle and Reingold 1992, Merikle et al. 1995, Fisk and Haase 2006).

4. Greenwald's regression method

Greenwald and his colleagues have developed an innovative method for dissociation and testing for unconscious perception. In this method the participants are first tested for the objective threshold for direct identification of the stimuli, and are then given a second test for an indirect effect of the stimuli. The indirect effect is the test for unconscious perception. For example, in the direct test participants would be required to say whether a briefly presented and masked stimulus word was presented on the left or right side of the display. These were four-letter words such as ALSO and GIRL. In the second test an indirect effect of the stimulus would be measured. Participants would be given the same task, but the letter string LEFT or RIGH would be used rather than position-neutral terms. With presentation conditions that allow easy viewing, there would be a Stroop-like interference such that RIGH would have a bias toward 'right' whichever side it was on, and LEFT would have a bias toward 'left'. If these same biases were found at presentation durations where observers were at chance with the other words, this would be evidence for an indirect effect of unconscious perception of the words.

Simply conducting an experiment with these variables would not overcome the null sensitivity and other problems with objective threshold experiments. However, in this method the d' for the indirect measure (implicit effect) is plotted as a function of the d' for the direct test (dissociative measure). The regression between these two measures is the novel aspect of this method and its advantage over other methods. The intercept of the regression line is an estimate of the size of the indirect effect when the direct effect is at a d' of zero. This estimate does not depend on precise adjustment of the objective threshold on the direct measure at zero.

There may be many questions about this estimate, but it represents a different approach to the null sensitivity problem. A positive intercept is taken as evidence that unconscious perception, as shown by the indirect effects, exists. However, error can still exist in the measures and result in positive intercepts when an error-free measure would give an intercept of zero. Further, because the direct effect has a d' of 0.0, the indirect exists in the absence of the direct effect. The regression line could also test whether direct and indirect effects are independent. In some of these experiments they are correlated, but the slope of the regression function varies from task to task, and no conclusions about independence of conscious and unconscious components can be drawn until the differences are understood. The controversies and statistical issues related to these conclusions are beyond the scope of this article; some of the commentary can be found in a special issue of the *Journal of Experimental Psychology: General*, 127 (1998.)

One surprising result of the regressions is a nonmonotonicity, such that for d' below zero for the direct measure, the indirect measure sometimes increases. This is consistent with the hypothesis of Snodgrass et al. (2004), by which unconscious perceptions are usually over-ridden by conscious ones, but when

$d' < 0$ for the direct measure the unconscious effects can show themselves. Snodgrass et al. (2004) should also be consulted for some uses of multidimensional SDT not covered here.

There are other possible interpretations of this increase in indirect d' once direct d' is negative. It is important to remember that the direct d' is the test of the objective threshold; the regression plots purportedly unconscious effects as a function of the measure of conscious effects. It could be thought that in negative d' territory, the discrimination is taken over by unconscious effects that are contrary to conscious ones. A simpler interpretation is that a negative d' is simply the evil twin of the positive d', that is, the same d' with the responses switched. It takes exactly the same target-noise discrimination to have a positive d' of 0.5 as to have a negative d' of 0.5. Random responding just to be perverse will result in a d' of zero; discrimination of target and noise is needed to achieve a reliably negative d'.

It is possible, then, that the positive d' for the *indirect* task in the negative d' range for the direct task is simply the positive d' given by a subset of the over 2000 participants who got the responses in the *direct* task reversed. If so, the axis should be flipped at the zero point for the direct task. When it is flipped the indirect regression line falls close to the regression line on the positive side.

Snodgrass et al. (2004) have another interpretation, which is that the unconscious effects can be opposed by conscious effects and are seen when the conscious components of perception are eliminated. Their model has many other predictions than this one. Snodgrass et al. (2004; see also Snodgrass and Shevrin, 2006) use a signal detection approach to test their hypothesis that unconscious effects can oppose conscious effects and further can be bidirectional.

5. Final comments

Signal detection analysis has allowed methodology to become far subtler and more complex than when percentage correct was the best measure we had. This improvement in methodology has been accompanied by developments in models of unconscious perception. The overall effect of SDT approaches so far has been to restrict or contradict evidence for unconscious perception many thought was decisive. However, SDT has also allowed tests of ideas simply unapproachable with other methods, for example, that conscious and unconscious influences on perception operate independently and in some cases in contrary directions.

WILLIAM BANKS

Banks, W. P. (2000). 'Recognition and source memory as multivariate decision processes'. *Psychological Science*, 11.

——, Chen, Y-P., and Prull, M. W. (1999). 'Memory and awareness: is memory information stratified into conscious and unconscious components?' In Challis, B. H. and Velichkovsky, B. M. (eds) *Stratification of Consciousness and Cognition*.

Fisk, G. D. and Haase, S. J. (2006). 'Exclusion failure does not demonstrate unconscious perception II: evidence from a forced-choice exclusion task'. *Vision Research*, 46.

Greenwald, A. G., Klinger, M. R., and Schuh, E. S. (1995). 'Activation by marginally perceptible ("subliminal") stimuli: Dissociation of unconscious from conscious cognition'. *Journal of Experimental Psychology: General*, 124.

Haase, S. J. and Fisk, G. D. (2001). 'Confidence in word detection predicts word identifcation: implications for an unconscious perception paradigm'. *American Journal of Psychology*, 114.

Holender, D. (1986). 'Semantic activation without conscious identification in dichotic listening, parafoveal vision, and visual masking: a survey and appraisal'. *Behavioral and Brain Sciences*, 9.

Jacoby, L. (1991). 'A process dissociation framework: separating automatic from intentional uses of memory'. *Journal of Memory and Language*, 30.

Macmillan, N. (1986). The psychophysics of subliminal perception. *Behavioral and Brain Sciences*, 9.

Marcel, A. (1983). 'Conscious and unconscious perception: experiments in visual masking and word recognition'. *Cognitive Psychology*, 15.

Merikle, P. M., Joordens, S., and Stolz, J. A. (1995). 'Measuring the relative magnitude of unconscious influences'. *Consciousness and Cognition*, 4.

Reingold, E. M. and Merikle, P. M. (1988). 'Using direct and indirect measures to study perception without awareness'. *Perception and Psychophysics*, 44.

—— ——. 'On the inter-relatedness of theory and measurement in the study of unconscious processes'. *Mind and Language*, 5.

Snodgrass, M. and Shevrin, H. (2006). 'Unconscious inhibition and facilitation at the objective threshold: replicable and qualitatively different unconscious perceptual effects'. *Cognition*, 101.

——, Bernat, E., and Shevrin, H. (2004). 'Unconscious perception: a model-based approach to method and evidence'. *Perception and Psychophysics*, 66.

Swets, J. A. (1961). 'Is there a sensory threshold?' *Science*, 134.

simultagnosia See BALINT'S SYNDROME AND FEATURE BINDING

single-cell studies: humans Complex networks of interacting neurons are ultimately responsible for our sensory perceptions, our feelings, our behaviour including language, and for consciousness. Consequently, it is essential to understand the responses of single neurons and their interactions within neuronal ensembles and coalitions to be able to understand consciousness at a detailed mechanistic level (Koch 2005). Several non-invasive measurement techniques are available to study brain activity in humans including *electroencephalography (EEG), *magnetoencephalography (MEG), and *functional imaging (such as fMRI and PET). These tools are extremely useful but, currently, they do not provide information at high spatiotemporal resolution about single-neuron activity in the human brain. Therefore, most of our knowledge about the activity of single neurons and neuronal ensembles comes from studies in animal models.

There exists a unique opportunity, however, to invasively monitor the activity of multiple individual neurons in the human brain in the case of patients who are implanted with electrodes for clinical reasons (Engel et al. 2005). The most common conditions where invasive recordings have been used in the human brain are motor disorders such as Parkinson's disease and pharmacologically resistant *epilepsy. In these disorders, the use of invasive monitoring can help in both diagnosis and treatment. For example, in the case of those epileptic patients where pharmacological treatments are ineffective and where non-invasive methods fail to provide concordant data about seizure onset locations, invasive tools can provide important information by carefully mapping the seizure onset foci (Engel 1996). Investigators use microwires, typically with a diameter of about 40 μm and an impedance of about 1 MΩ, which are inserted during brain surgery either unilaterally or bilaterally in multiple brain areas that are of clinical interest. The technique of implanting electrodes in humans, which dates back to the 1940s, allows investigators to monitor broadband activity in the form of local field potentials as well as multi-unit spiking activity. Spike-sorting algorithms can further separate the responses of individual neurons. The electrodes remain implanted while the patients stay in hospital, typically for about 5–10 days (Fried et al. 1999, Engel et al. 2005, Kreiman 2007). In contrast to electrophysiological studies in animals, the recording conditions including the amount of recording time and electrode positions are constrained by clinical criteria. On the other hand, studying single neurons in humans has many advantages over studies in animal models including using complex tasks, rapid training, and the possibility of obtaining feedback from the subjects. Working with humans, as opposed to electrophysiological approaches on animal models, allows investigators to more directly infer the subjective state and contents of consciousness in the subjects under study which may ultimately prove essential to rigorously study consciousness empirically (Crick et al. 2004).

Several single-neuron studies in humans have focused on assessing which brain areas are activated during language production and whether these areas show hemispheric specialization or not (Ojemann and Mateer 1979, Heit et al. 1988). Other human single-neuron studies searched for neuronal signatures for emotional content in the amygdala (Fried et al. 1997, Kawasaki et al. 2001). Many of the experimental studies of consciousness have focused on the visual system given its prominence in primates and its amenability for experimental investigation. In most of the patients with resistant epilepsy, electrodes are implanted in areas of the medial temporal lobe including the hippocampus, the entorhinal cortex, the parahippocampal gyrus, and the amygdala. These multimodal areas receive strong input from the higher stages of visual processing such as the inferior temporal cortex. Evidence from lesions suggests that these areas play a crucial role in the consolidation and storage of explicit memory forms that require awareness for acquisition.

Electrophysiological recordings in the human medial temporal lobe have shown that individual neurons respond in a selective fashion to visual presentation of complex shapes including natural categories of stimuli such as faces, animals, etc. The activity of these neurons parallels several characteristics of human perception, including its invariance to multiple transformations of the images. In a striking example of invariance, investigators observed that individual units responded selectively to several different images of a given famous person (Quian Quiroga et al. 2005). For example, one unit responded to a colour photograph of ex-president Bill Clinton, a black and white caricature of his face and a side view among other people (and the unit did not respond to other faces or other objects). This has been interpreted by some scientists as a revival of the old notion of 'grandmother cells', i.e. the idea that there would be one neuron for each concept. Although these observations are among the most striking demonstrations of sparseness and invariance, care should be taken in the interpretation. First, it is highly unlikely that there is only one neuron for each concept. The simple fact that the investigators could find such neurons probably implies that there are many such neurons. Second, it is not clear that these units respond only to one concept. Theoretical estimates argue that these units could be activated by multiple concepts. Finally, these neurons might be part of a network involved in learning to associate different views of an individual and might not be strictly necessary for visual perception.

An important conceptual paradigm in the empirical studies of consciousness involves the search for the minimal neuronal events that are jointly sufficient to account for the specific contents of consciousness, usually called the neural *correlates of consciousness (Crick and Koch 1990, Koch, 2005). While the whole brain is sufficient for consciousness, the emphasis here is in finding the minimum set of neurons, neuronal assemblies, or networks that can account for consciousness. In this quest, it is important to study ensembles of single neurons in animal models as well as in humans. Processes that do not reach conscious awareness are also represented by neurons. Therefore, in order to empirically investigate and distinguish those neuronal events that are specifically correlated with the contents of consciousness, it is important to be able to empirically separate conscious and unconscious processing while at the same time avoiding other potentially confounding variables. A few paradigms allow investigators to make this dissociation. In the case of the visual system, these paradigms typically involve situations where the visual input to the retinae can be dissociated from perception. Examples of this include the study of visual *dreams, visual *imagery, and *hallucinations where conscious percepts are present in the absence of concomitant visual stimulation.

Visual imagery is perhaps among the most studied of these phenomena; there is abundant work on imagery in philosophy, psychology, and neuroscience. Given the challenges involved in directly studying visual imagery in animals, most empirical efforts have focused on using non-invasive tools in humans including functional imaging and scalp EEG. The study of the responses of single human neurons during visual imagery has shown that (1) individual neurons in the medial temporal lobe selectively modulate their responses during visual imagery of specific objects with eyes closed, and (2) the neuronal selectivity during visual imagery closely matches the selectivity during normal vision. These observations, together with related work in macaque monkeys (Miyashita 1993), suggest that there are common neuronal mechanisms, at least in the higher visual areas, for processing visual input and the volitional creation of mental images in the human medial temporal lobe (Kreiman et al. 2000).

Another important empirical paradigm where visual input and perception can be dissociated has been the study of bistable percepts such as the Necker cube (see MULTISTABLE PERCEPTION). In these stimuli, a constant visual stimulus can be interpreted in more than one possible configuration. A particular instance of bistable percepts is the phenomenon known as *binocular rivalry where two different stimuli are presented to the left and right eyes. Most of the time, subjects perceive a randomly fluctuating alternation between one and the other stimulus (Blake and Logothetis 2002). In spite of the constant stimulus, the contents of conscious perception change with time. Therefore, this phenomenon provides an ideal situation to examine which neurons correlate their activity with these perceptual transitions and which other neurons show responses which are closer to the constant stimulus. Recordings from single neurons in macaque monkeys have shown that there is a progressive increase along the visual hierarchy in the proportion of neurons that respond to the fluctuating percept and do not respond to the constant stimulus (Leopold and Logothetis 1999). Single-neuron studies in the human medial temporal lobe while subjects' perception alternates during this task have shown that the activity of most medial temporal lobe neurons correlate with the subjective percepts (Kreiman et al. 2002). None of these neurons represented the unconscious constant stimulus.

These observations indicate that neurons in the human medial temporal lobe show properties that are close to human perception and correlate their responses with the contents of mental imagery and the contents of subjective perception. The notion that these neurons directly reflect conscious contents supports the prominent role of the hippocampus and related structures in processing declarative information that requires awareness.

In sum, the multiple non-invasive tools to study the human brain currently offer a low spatial and temporal resolution. The spatial averaging over millions of neurons, layers, columns, and neuronal types as well as the temporal averaging over seconds may obscure important aspects of the neuronal correlates of consciousness. Studies in animal models, on the other hand, can overcome these resolution problems but require indirect inferences about the contents of consciousness. Therefore, in spite of the technical difficulties and limitations involved, monitoring the activity of single neurons in humans may provide key mechanistic insights at high spatial and temporal resolution into the functioning of the neuronal coalitions involved in conscious processing of information in the brain.

GABRIEL KREIMAN

Blake, R. and Logothetis, N. (2002). 'Visual competition'. *Nature Reviews Neuroscience*, 3.

Crick, F. and Koch, C. (1990). 'Towards a neurobiological theory of consciousness'. *Seminars in the Neurosciences*, 2.

——, ——, Kreiman, G., and Fried, I. (2004). 'Consciousness and neurosurgery'. *Neurosurgery*, 55.

Engel, A. K., Moll, C. K., Fried, I., and Ojemann, G. A. (2005). 'Invasive recordings from the human brain: clinical insights and beyond'. *Nature Reviews Neuroscience*, 6.

Engel, J. (1996). Surgery for seizures. *New England Journal of Medicine*, 334.

Fried, I., MacDonald, K. A., and Wilson, C. (1997). 'Single neuron activity in human hippocampus and amygdala during recognition of faces and objects'. *Neuron*, 18.

——, Wilson, C. L., Maidment, N. T. et al. (1999). 'Cerebral microdialysis combined with single-neuron and electroencephalographic recording in neurosurgical patients'. *Journal of Neurosurgery*, 91.

Heit, G., Smith, M. E., and Halgren, E. (1988). 'Neural encoding of individual words and faces by the human hippocampus and amygdala'. *Nature*, 333.

Kawasaki, H., Adolphs, R., Kaufman, O. et al. (2001). 'Single-neuron responses to emotional visual stimuli recorded in human ventral prefrontal cortex'. *Nature Neuroscience*, 4.

Koch, C. (2005). *The Quest for Consciousness*.

Kreiman, G. (2007). 'Single neuron approaches to human vision and memories'. *Current Opinion in Neurobiology*, 17.

——, Koch, C., and Fried, I. (2000). 'Imagery neurons in the human brain'. *Nature*, 408.

——, Fried, I., and Koch, C. (2002). 'Single neuron correlates of subjective vision in the human medial temporal lobe'. *Proceedings of the National Academy of Sciences of the USA*, 99.

Leopold, D. A. and Logothetis, N. K. (1999). 'Multistable phenomena: changing views in perception'. *Trends in Cognitive Sciences*, 3.

Miyashita, Y. (1993). 'Inferior temporal cortex: where visual perception meets memory'. *Annual Review of Neuroscience*, 16.

Ojemann, G. and Mateer, C. (1979). 'Human language cortex: localization of memory, syntax, and sequential motor-phoneme identification systems'. *Science*, 205.

Quian Quiroga, R., Reddy, L., Kreiman, G., Koch, C., and Fried, I. (2005). 'Invariant visual representation by single neurons in the human brain'. *Nature*, 435.

single-cell studies: monkey Current understanding of the physiological basis of consciousness is still rudimentary. To fill that gap, researchers look for neuronal events that could yield conscious experiences in the brain of monkeys, who, as our close cousins in evolution, are assumed to have conscious experiences.

1. Two approaches to studying single-cell activity and consciousness
2. Comparing neuronal activity and behavioural measures of perception
3. Different percepts associated with the same physical stimulus
4. Conclusions

1. Two approaches to studying single-cell activity and consciousness

Human subjects can be directly asked about the nature and *content of their conscious experiences, but monkeys cannot verbally report their mental events. To overcome this obstacle, researchers have used two main approaches: First, studies attempt to correlate the activity of individual neurons with behavioural measures of perception. In this approach, a monkey is trained to perform a particular perceptual task, while the activity of single neurons in its brain is being recorded: e.g. a monkey is trained to indicate whether or not a visual stimulus has been presented on a computer screen. Varying the visibility of the stimulus allows researchers to determine the limits of the monkey's perceptual abilities, and to compare them to the activity of individual neurons in the monkey's visual cortex. Neurons whose activity can best account for the observed behavioural performance are assumed to underlie the monkey's perception. This approach led to numerous insights into the locus and nature of neuronal events that support perceptual abilities. However, it suffers from the fact that observed changes in neuronal activity could be due solely to physical changes of the stimulus, and have no or little relation with changes in conscious perception. In such experiments, the link between neuronal events and conscious perception of the stimulus is thus relatively weak.

To ameliorate this situation, researchers have used a second approach: they use stimuli that remain physically constant but yield varying percepts. For example, when presented by different, constant stimuli in the two eyes, the percept alternates between that originating in one and that in the other eye, a condition known as *binocular rivalry. A monkey can indicate (e.g. by pressing one of two buttons) which of the two percepts currently dominates. Neurons whose activity correlates with the monkey's reports must be related to perception, since the activity modulation cannot be attributed to any physical change in the stimulus. Note that this approach also does not prove that the monkey has conscious perception of the stimulus, but at least it rules out the possibility that the observed modulation of neuronal activity is entirely determined by changes in the physical properties of the stimulus.

Although relatively new, these approaches have already produced a large number of studies, which cannot be all reviewed here. Instead, I describe representative examples to illustrate the kind of knowledge gained with each approach.

2. Comparing neuronal activity and behavioural measures of perception

The first approach is to correlate behavioural measures of perception, which is assumed to be conscious, with neural activity in a variety of brain structures. Pioneering work has been performed by W. T. Newsome and his colleagues. In a seminal study (Newsome et al. 1989), monkeys were trained to indicate the direction of motion of an array of dots presented on a display screen. By varying the proportion of dots moving in the same direction, experimenters could modulate the strength of the global motion signal. The responses of individual neurons in the middle temporal (MT) cortical area were shown to correlate highly with the monkey's perception. The results show that the activity of a small number of MT neurons is sufficient to fully account for the monkey's perceptual decisions. Subsequent work (Salzman et al. 1990) showed that electrical stimulation of the same MT neurons could bias the monkey's perceptual decision, further strengthening the notion that MT is part of the neural substrate underlying the conscious perception of the direction of motion. Although the role of MT in the perception of motion direction has been convincingly demonstrated, this is by no mean the only cortical area involved. Indeed, similar experimental protocols showed that other areas such as medial superior temporal (MST) or lateral intraparietal (LIP) are also involved in the generation of those perceptually based decisions.

While the above studies focused on the perception of motion direction, similar studies revealed the cortical areas involved in the perception of other visual attributes such as speed, depth, or colour. In addition, the same comparisons between neuronal responses and behavioural responses allowed researchers to reveal the neural populations underlying perception in the somatosensory domain (Romo and Salinas 2003).

3. Different percepts associated with the same physical stimulus

Another approach to revealing the neural basis of conscious perception is to study whether neural activity correlates with changes in perception when a stimulus remains constant. Alternation of percepts to a constant stimulus has been reported in the situation of binocular rivalry (see above). This perceptual alternation in the absence of a physical change in the stimulus provides a unique opportunity to determine which neural events determine the subject's conscious perception. Leopold and Logothetis (1996) searched for neurons whose activity correlates with a monkey's reported percept, while experiencing binocular rivalry. They found neurons in primary and extrastriate cortex whose time-varying activity strongly correlates with the reported percept.

In addition to binocular rivalry, other stimulus configurations lead to varying percepts in the absence of physical changes in the stimulus. An example of such so-called '*multistable' stimuli is the famous Necker cube. Displaying such multistable stimuli, researchers have found neurons whose activity correlates with one or the other of the percepts. Examples are *structure-from-motion stimuli*. These are made of moving dots, whose two-dimensional motion suggests a three-dimensional object that is rotating in one direction or the other. Observing such a stimulus is known to yield alternating percepts of an object rotating either clockwise or counterclockwise. It was shown that many neurons in area MT, and fewer in primary visual cortex (Grunewald et al. 2002), correlate with the perception of a structure-from-motion stimulus.

4. Conclusions

Using statistical methods to determine the relation between single-neuron activity and perception, or taking advantage of multistable stimuli, neuroscientists have begun to reveal the locus of the neuronal populations responsible for conscious perception. To date, most studies have investigated visual perception, but similar approaches are being developed to study other sensory modalities. The results suggest that conscious perception of a stimulus cannot be attributed to a single neuronal population, but seems to depend on the activity of neurons located in multiple sensory areas. Although these studies provide only indirect evidence for the physiological basis of conscious perception, they are a valuable tool for the development of a neural theory of consciousness.

DANIEL KIPER

Grunewald, A., Bradley, D. C., and Andersen, R. A. (2002). 'Neural correlates of structure-from-motion perception in macaque V1 and MT'. *Journal of Neuroscience*, 22.

Leopold, D. A. and Logothetis, N. K. (1996). 'Activity changes in early visual cortex reflect monkeys' percepts during binocular rivalry'. *Nature*, 379.

Newsome, W. T., Britten, K. H., and Movshon, J. A. (1989). 'Neuronal correlates of a perceptual decision'. *Nature*, 341.

Romo, R. and Salinas, E. (2003). 'Flutter discrimination: neural codes, perception, memory and decision making'. *Nature Reviews Neuroscience*, 4.

Salzman, C. D., Britten, K. H., and Newsome, W. T. (1990). 'Cortical microstimulation influences perceptual judgements of motion direction'. *Nature*, 346.

skin conductance response See ONLINE MEASURES OF NON-CONSCIOUS PROCESSING

sleep From a behavioural perspective, sleep is a normal, reversible, periodically recurring behaviour characterized by a decreased responsiveness to external stimuli, a diminished motor activity, and a characteristic position (in mammals usually, but not necessarily, recumbent with eyes closed). It is often preceded by the active retreat to a safe, secluded place. It is homeostatically regulated in such a way that any extension of the waking period is followed by an increase in sleep depth and (to some extent) duration. In many but not all species, sleep tends to occur at a given circadian period, either during the night (diurnal species) or during the day (nocturnal species). The amount of time spent in sleep differs widely between species. In homeotherms, neurophysiological parameters, in addition to behaviour, allow us to recognize two main sleep states: a *regular sleep*, which shows gradual changes in sleep depth, and a *paradoxical sleep*, which combines nearly complete paralysis of the musculature with elevated brain activity. Paradoxical sleep has also been termed *rapid eye movement (REM) sleep*, because of the large and swift movements of the eyes, which only can be observed in this sleep state. In humans, four to six non-REM/REM sleep cycles with a duration of about 90 min each are usually recorded during one night.

Consciousness is conspicuously modified during sleep. Whereas awareness of the environment is substantially diminished, the content of consciousness can be filled with internally generated mental representations. At sleep onset, as well as during awakening, vivid and complex *hallucinations can occur. These *hypnagogic and hypnopompic hallucinations can be observed in normal individuals and their content seems to depend on previous individual experience. *Dreams exclusively occur during sleep and in every sleep stage, although seldom is deep non-REM sleep. REM sleep has often been called 'dream sleep' because of the frequency of dream reports after awakenings from REM sleep. REM sleep dreams usually consist of highly perceptivo-motor hallucinatory scenarios characterized by their high emotional content and seem to be qualitatively different from non-REM sleep dreams, which are shorter, more static, and less hallucinatory than REM sleep dreams.

Sleep is thought to serve some important, potentially vital, function(s) for two main reasons. First, sleep is conserved in a large number of species, not only in mammals and birds, but also in many other vertebrates and invertebrates. Second, total sleep deprivation irremediably leads rats to death by unspecific failure of immune and endocrine systems and body temperature regulation. Fortunately, no such experiment has been conducted in humans and a single case report shows that a total sleep deprivation of up to 11 days does not produce alarming physiological malfunctions. However, short-term sleep deprivation or restriction can quickly lead to substantial cognitive and metabolic dysfunctions.

Various functions have been proposed for sleep. Each hypothesis is supported by some but not all experimental data, suggesting that sleep might have several functions, which differ depending on the ecological niche of each species. One main function pertains to bodily and cerebral energy balance, energy saving, and thermoregulation. For instance, there is evidence that sleep is intimately related to neuronal energy metabolism (metabolism of adenosine, fatty acids, and glycogen stores). Another potential function of sleep is to restore brain function by detoxifying the cerebral parenchyma from various compounds which accumulate during wakefulness and alter neuronal function (e.g. glutathione, prostaglandin, and a myriad of sleep-inducing compounds). Still another putative function of sleep relates to brain plasticity during development as well as to learning and memory in adulthood. During neurodevelopment, spontaneous neural activity helps to wire the brain appropriately. In adults, sleep has been shown to improve retention of recent declarative memories and protect them from interference. Visual perceptual learning as well motor sequence learning also seems to be improved after sleep. Sleep is beneficial for the lexicalization of new words, helps in the extraction of a general knowledge from learned exemplars, and facilitates insight. The beneficial effect of sleep on *memory could be mediated by different process, such as a synaptic downscaling maintaining synaptic homeostasis or, at the systems level, the replay of firing sequence during post-training sleep, which would help reinforcing synaptic connections established during training.

The regular alternation of sleep and wakefulness is mediated by hypothalamic and brainstem structures which either promote sleep (GABAergic neurons of the ventrolateral pre-optic area) or wakefulness (e.g. histaminergic neurons of the tuberomammillary nucleus, noradrenergic neurons of the locus coeruleus, serotonergic neurons of raphe nuclei, cholinergic neurones of mesopontine nuclei). The alternation of sleep and wakefulness is under the influence of the suprachiasmatic nucleus, the master circadian pacemaker which is synchronized to daylight and is also controlled by posterolateral orexin/hypocretin neurons. Lesions of these various structures can lead to insomnia or hypersomnia (as described by Von Oeconomo after the 1927 influenza epidemics), to unstable sleep/wakefulness cycles (as in narcolepsy), or to coma (see BRAIN DAMAGE; see also ANAESTHESIA AND CONSCIOUSNESS).

In humans, periods of regular or 'non-REM' sleep usually occur first after sleep onset and precede periods of REM sleep. Non-REM sleep is further divided into four sleep stages. *Light sleep* (stages 1 and 2) represents the largest portion of adult sleep and fills in the time between *deep sleep* phases (stages 3 and 4) and REM sleep. Deep sleep occurs mainly during the first hours of sleep, while REM sleep is concentrated mostly in the morning hours. With increasing sleep depth muscle tone is reduced, the awakening threshold increases, and autonomic physiological activity (pulse, blood pressure, breathing) are decreased. Sleep stages are also characterized by specific physiological signs. Stage 1 sleep is a transition between wakefulness and sleep, and occurs mainly at the beginning of sleep. Its main signs are very slow, smooth, non-saccadic eye movements. Brain activity of stage 2 sleep is characterized on *electroencephalographic (EEG) recordings by sleep spindles and K-complexes. The former consist of bursts of crescendo–decrescendo 12–15 Hz oscillations lasting for more than 500 ms. The latter are biphasic slow waves of large amplitude, and a duration of at least 500 ms, and may occur in response to external stimulation. In deep non-REM sleep stages 3 and 4, also known as *slow-wave sleep* (SWS), large-amplitude slow waves progressively become more abundant and eventually constitute the dominant EEG oscillation.

The homeostatic regulation of sleep implies that the need for sleep increases with the duration of the previous waking period. There is supporting evidence that increased neural activity during wakefulness leads to increased generation of slow waves during subsequent sleep, both in humans and in animals. The rising sleep pressure might also be due to the increased production or accumulation of hypnogenic compounds in the brain or in the blood stream. A number of substances have been reported to be related to sleep regulation: cytokines (IL-1, TNF-a), brain-derived neurotrophic factor (BDNF), prostaglandin D_2, glutathione, nitric oxide (NO), adenosine, growth hormone releasing hormone, and a number of other peptides. How these substances interact to generate sleep is not yet precisely known. They seem to interact in complex biochemical cascades that eventually lead to the generation of non REM sleep.

The initiation of non-REM and REM sleep stages at a neuronal level is usually accounted for by the reciprocal-interaction model proposed by Hobson and McCarley (1977). In essence, a bistable equilibrium is established between on the one hand, aminergic REM-off cells from the locus coeruleus (noradrenaline [norepinephrine) and the raphe nuclei (serotonin) and, on the other hand, cholinergic and glutaminergic REM-on cells from the mesopontine tegmentum and the brainstem reticular formation. During non-REM sleep, aminergic activity predominates, but decreases continuously until cholinergic REM-on cells gain the upper hand. These in turn are eventually inhibited by recovering aminergic activity. Recently, GABAergic influences have been involved in the generation of REM sleep, especially in rodents.

Current theories of non-REM sleep generation place a strong emphasis on the activity patterns in thalamocortical loops. Several rhythms and activities coalesce during non-REM sleep: spindles, delta rhythm (4–7 Hz), slow rhythm (<1 Hz) and even fast rhythms (beta, 15–30 Hz; *gamma, 30–80 Hz) coexist or smoothly alternate (spindles and delta rhythm). All these rhythms emerge from complex interactions between reticular thalamic cells, relay thalamic neurons, and cortical networks.

In animals, at sleep onset, thalamic neurons become hyperpolarized because the activating input from brainstem structures progressively decreases. As a result of this hyperpolarization, thalamic neurons change their firing mode from tonic to phasic. First, because of their intrinsic membrane properties, GABAergic cells of the reticular thalamic nucleus burst in the spindle frequency range and entrain thalamocortical neurons in spindle oscillation. As sleep deepens, thalamic neurons become more hyperpolarized and a clock-like delta rhythm emerges in thalamocortical cells, due to their intrinsic membrane properties.

Thalamic oscillations are conveyed to the cortex, which further reorganizes them and modulate their expression by a powerful, cortically generated, slow rhythm (<1 Hz). This slow oscillation has been identified in humans and animals. One of its manifestations is reflected in grouping of other sleep oscillations, e.g. the recurrence of spindles every 2–3 s, observed in animals and in humans. Recordings in vivo and in brain slices have established that this slow rhythm is actively generated in the cortex. It persists in the cerebral cortex after thalamectomy and disappears in the thalamus after decortication. Characteristically, the slow oscillation emerges from the alternation of silent phases of hyperpolarization (often referred to as *down states*) with periods of depolarization characterized by intense neuronal firing and increased neuronal input conductance (*up states*). The up state is related to recurrent excitatory (NMDA) interactions between pyramidal cells and regulated by inhibitory (GABA) interneurons. The long-lasting silent periods of the down state appear to be initiated by a cascade of disfacilitation, related to a progressive depletion of extracellular calcium ions, as well as by a series of potassium ion currents. The down state is characterized by an after-hyperpolarization in pyramidal cells and the withdrawal of synaptic barrages, accompanied by an increase in neuronal membrane input resistance.

The regulation of non-REM sleep oscillations is not yet fully understood. For instance, in humans, spindles are under circadian regulation and slow-wave activity (0.75–4 Hz) is known to be a reliable marker of the homeostatic sleep regulation. On the other hand, recent studies could show that these oscillations are related to previous cognitive activity and that learning can increase local spindle and slow-wave activity.

At the macroscopic level, brain activity as measured by brain energy metabolism and blood flow has been reported to decrease in non-REM sleep. This decrease probably does not reflect a decrease in mean neuronal firing but the adoption of a bursting firing pattern, which implies long periods of silent hyperpolarization. Accordingly, during non-REM sleep, the most deactivated areas are related to generation of non-REM oscillations: dorsal pons, mesencephalon, thalami, and basal forebrain. Cortical areas that are particularly deactivated are the prefrontal cortex, the anterior cingulate cortex, and the precuneus.

REM sleep is characterized in mammals by low-amplitude, relatively high-frequency EEG rhythms, rapid eye movements, complete muscular atonia interrupted by short muscular twitches and neurovegetative instability (e.g. with regard to pulse, blood pressure, and temperature). Penile erections are also frequent during REM sleep.

In general, brain activity during wakefulness and REM sleep are similar, indicating a high level of processing during REM sleep. However, electrophysiological activity of REM sleep has also its specific markers. In cats and rodents, REMs are associated with waves stemming from the pons and transmitted to the lateral geniculate nucleus and the occipital cortex, as well as various other diencephalic and forebrain structures. There is some indirect evidence that these pontine or ponto-geniculo-occipital (PGO) waves also exist in humans. Another type of oscillation occurring during REM sleep in humans is the hippocampal rhythmic slow ,activity in the delta frequency band (1–4 Hz) and the hippocampal theta (4–8 Hz) in rodents. Both might be indications of the same underlying processes, possibly related to memory function.

As a rule, REM sleep is a phase of intense neuronal activity. Neurons adopt a tonic firing mode during REM sleep, similar to the activity recorded during wakefulness. Accordingly, the brain energy metabolism and blood flow are similar during REM sleep and wakefulness. At the forebrain level, in humans, REM sleep is characterized by intense activity in limbic and paralimbic areas (amygdala, hippocampal formation, anterior cingulate cortex) and visual occipital areas whereas prefrontal and parietal are relatively less active. This peculiar distribution of brain activity is thought to explain the main characteristics of dreams.

PIERRE MAQUET, STEFFEN GAIS, MANUEL SCHABUS, AND THANH DANG-VU

Hobson, J. A. and McCarley, R. (1977). 'The brain as a dream state generator: an activation-synthesis hypothesis of the dream process'. *American Journal of Psychiatry*, 134.

Maquet, P., Smith, C., and Stickgold, R. (eds) (2003). *Sleep and Brain Plasticity*.

Meir, H. K., Roth, T., and Dement,W. C. (eds) (2005). *Principles and Practice of Sleep Medicine*.

Saper, C. B., Scammell, T. E., Lu, J. (2005). 'Hypothalamic regulation of sleep and circadian rhythms'. *Nature*, 437.

Sejnowski, T. J. and Destexhe, A. (2000). 'Why do we sleep?' *Brain Research*, 886.

Steriade, M. and McCarley, R. W. (2005). *Brain Control of Wakefulness and Sleep*.

Stickgold, R. (2005). 'Sleep-dependent memory consolidation'. *Nature*, 437.

Tafti, M., Maret, S., and Dauvilliers, Y. (2005). 'Genes for normal sleep and sleep disorders'. *Annals of Medicine*, 37.

Tononi, G. and Cirelli, C. (2006). 'Sleep function and synaptic homeostasis'. *Sleep Medicine Reviews*, 10.

solipsism In the primary, metaphysical, sense of the term, the solipsist believes that only they and their experiences exist. The outer world of shoes, ships, sealing-wax—not to mention other subjects of experience—has been replaced by an internal world consisting only of the self and its conscious states. The solipsistic perspective is eloquently captured in Sylvia Plath's poem 'Soliloquy of the Solipsist':

> I?
> I walk alone;
> The midnight street
> Spins itself from under my feet;
> When my eyes are shut
> These dreaming houses all snuff out;
> Through a whim of mine
> Over gables the moon's celestial onion
> Hangs high.

Metaphysical solipsism is not widely held. (Indeed, there is a sense in which no two solipsists hold the same view, for each denies the other's existence!) Where it does occur, solipsism is a sign of psychiatric disorder rather than philosophical profundity. Individuals with *schizophrenia often cycle between nihilistic and solipsistic moods—when in the grip of nihilism they appear to have lost experiential contact with their very existence, whereas the solipsistic mood brings with it an all-encompassing self that threatens to submerge any awareness of the world as standing over and against them (Parnas and Sass 2001).

Solipsism exerts an influence on consciousness studies in its methodological rather than its metaphysical guise. The methodological solipsist recommends that explanations of psychological states bracket the subject's environment (Fodor 1980). The methodological solipsist does not deny that the subject's environment has a causal influence on their conscious states and processes—how could it not?—she holds only that this causal influence is of no interest to the study of consciousness.

Methodological solipsism has not gone unchallenged, and *externalists of various stripes argue that the sciences of the mind need to take the subject's environment into account. Some content externalists argue that one can have meaningful thoughts and experiences only in the context of a community of thinkers. Others argue that one can have thoughts and experiences about certain types of physical objects and properties only in environments that contain objects and properties of the relevant type. (Roughly, one couldn't have thoughts about cats unless there were cats to think about.) Others—*vehicle externalists*—argue that the vehicles of conscious states extend out into the subject's environment. Whatever their brand, externalists argue that consciousness depends in constitutive—i.e. not merely causal—ways on factors that are external to the subject in question, and that the methodological solipsist's attempt to study experience by bracketing the external is doomed to defeat.

Although externalism has its proponents, it is at present not much more than a promissory note. Few studies of consciousness have made any serious attempt to take environmental variables into account, and the mainstream focus of consciousness science is resolutely 'solipsistic' in its focus on the search for the neural mechanisms underpinning consciousness.

TIM BAYNE

Fodor, J. (1980). 'Methodological solipsism considered as a research strategy in the cognitive sciences'. *Behavioral and Brain Sciences*, 3.

Parnas, J. and Sass, L. A. (2001). 'Self, solipsism, and schizophrenic delusions'. *Philosophy, Psychiatry and Psychology*, 8.

Plath, S. (1981). 'Soliloquy of the solipsist'. In *Collected Poems*.

soul See CONSCIOUSNESS, MODERN SCIENTIFIC STUDY OF

sounds Philosophical work on perceptual consciousness has traditionally focused on vision and visual experience. Considering other varieties of experience, however, reflects the diversity among things and features of which we are conscious. Attention to audition, in particular, has much to contribute to a more comprehensive understanding of perception and sensory awareness. Because they differ in several important respects from visual experiences and their objects, auditory experiences and the nature of sounds hold particular significance for investigating perceptual consciousness.

1. Auditory experiences

What do we hear? Sounds are, in the first instance, what we hear. They are the immediate objects of auditory experience in the following sense: whatever else we might hear, such as ordinary objects (bells, trumpets) and events (collisions, typing), we hear it in virtue of hearing a sound. Sounds are not, however, experienced as private items or sensations akin to pains or nausea. Sounds audibly appear to populate the world beyond our ears. Sounds are, in Moore's sense, 'things to be met with in space'.

What sort of thing is a sound? Science has taught that sounds are waves. Waves, then, are what we hear according to the predominant view of sounds. Philosophers, however, often have grouped sounds, along with colours and tastes, with the sensible or secondary qualities. According to this traditional line of thought, sounds are either dispositions to produce experiences, categorical bases of such dispositions, physical properties, or simple primitive features revealed in experience. The choice depends on one's view of the natures of sensible qualities. According to a third line of thought, it has recently been suggested that sounds are a certain kind of audible event. This view is motivated by several arguments grounded in the phenomenology of auditory experience which indicate that sounds might be neither waves nor sensible qualities.

Where do we hear sounds to be? Hearing, like vision and probably unlike taste, is a spatial modality. We learn through audition not just about whether a sound is high-pitched or loud, but also something about the location of its source. We learn through auditory experience not just the source's direction, but also that it occupies a certain location in egocentric space. Cues to spatial hearing include interaural time and level differences, head- and pinnae-related signal transformations, secondary reflections, and motion-related changes. Sounds furnish information about source locations because sounds audibly seem to be located outside the head in some direction, or *externalized*. Externalization is the sense in which the sound seems in auditory experience to come from or to be located beyond one's ears. Notice, however, that sounds do not ordinarily seem to travel through the surrounding medium. They do not appear to move at all, unless their sources do. The spatial experience of a sound is notably unlike the auditory analogue of experiencing an incoming snowball. So, sounds seem to come from sources only in the sense that sounds seem *generated* or *caused* by their sources.

Are sounds waves? Given the apparent distal locations of sounds, some have argued that the travelling wave view of sounds implies a systematic illusion concerning the experienced locations of sounds. Since the wave travels through the medium, but the sound seems to be located at a distance, we misperceive the spatial locations of sounds if sounds are identical with waves. On the other hand, if location perception is not systematically illusory, then sounds are not waves.

Do sounds have spatial boundaries? Though spatial auditory experience shapes our understanding of the place of sounds in the world, spatial features play a different role in the perceptual individuation of sounds than in the visual individuation of objects. In particular, the spatial boundaries so critical for visual objecthood play a far less important role in audition. For example, spatially distinct sources might seem to make a single sound if they share pitch, and a single source might seem to have multiple sounds that differ in pitch.

The experience of sounds is most notable for its *temporal* characteristics. Sounds are creatures of time. Sounds appear to have durations and to occur, occupy, or unfold through an interval of time. It is difficult, in fact, to conceive of a sound lacking a lifetime: how could there be an instantaneous sound? Sounds not only take time, but also survive and persist through changes to their audible attributes over time. In many examples, such as the sound of a spoken word or a bird's call, the pattern of changes through time is central to the identity of a particular sound. It is intuitively plausible that not all that is required to be a given sound exists at any moment during its lifetime. The auditory experience of a sound in this respect differs from the visual experience of an object.

Sounds as consciously experienced thus are naturally taken as the bearers of audible qualities that persist through time and survive changes. Sounds, therefore, are best understood as particular individuals and not as repeatable properties. But sounds, unlike ordinary objects, are not intuitively wholly present at any moment at which they exist. A view according to which sounds are particular events, and not repeatable properties or object-like particulars, may therefore best capture the temporal characteristics revealed in the experience of sounds.

Is there empirical support for this view? Such a view is in fact vindicated by empirical work on audition. Bregman's (1990) work on *auditory scene analysis* describes perceptual mechanisms for the segregation of distinct *auditory streams* within acoustically complex environments. Auditory scene analysis is the task of individuating sound streams in the presence of interfering signals and background noise. Streams serve as the locus of binding for particular audible qualities, survive changes, persist through masking, and coexist with simultaneous streams.

2. Audible qualities of sounds

Which audible qualities do sounds possess? Sounds as they unfold through time can be distinguished in terms of patterns of pitch, loudness, and timbre. Arguably, other audible attributes of sounds depend upon these basic features. Characterizing these uniquely audible qualities requires confronting both familiar issues and novel questions concerning subjectivity and the sensible qualities. Since the apparent pitch, loudness, and timbre of a sound depend at least upon frequency, intensity, and spectral composition of a sound wave, and since such physical attributes depend upon patterns of movement and pressure variation over time, the audible qualities themselves depend upon temporal characteristics of waves.

What is pitch? Pitch is that attribute in virtue of which sounds can be ordered in respect of 'height' of tone. Among pitched sounds, the apparent pitch of a tone depends upon the tone's fundamental frequency or periodicity, which is determined by the associated pattern of pressure differences through time. Tones heard to match in pitch share fundamental frequency, though they may differ in spectral composition. Nonetheless, the predominant view of pitch among audition researchers holds that pitch is a purely subjective or sensational correlate to frequency. Strictly speaking, on this view, sounds do not have pitch. Conscious experiences have pitch, or else experiences misleadingly present sounds as having pitch. This form of philosophical subjectivism or error theory is motivated by empirical results taken to demonstrate that no straightforward physical attribute of sound waves corresponds to perceived pitch. In particular, it is commonly claimed that physical (fundamental) frequency is not identical with pitch as it is experienced because equal frequency intervals do not translate to equal pitch intervals. Frequencies therefore cannot not capture the structural relations among experienced pitches; if pitch were frequency, subjects would radically misperceive pitch relations. Many auditory researchers, finding no objective physical candidate for pitch, have developed alternative (extensive) pitch scales based upon units of *mels* or *barks* which capture subjective pitch magnitudes.

Is subjectivism mandatory? From a philosophical standpoint, familiar alternatives might avoid the epistemic consequences of the subjectivist and error-theoretic mainstream account while capturing the differences between apparent pitch and frequency. Pitches might be dispositions to produce distinctive pitch experiences, or primitive properties of sounds that depend upon but are not identical with any physical properties of sounds. In fact, the evidence does not even rule out physical pitches. Pitch might be a more complex physical property of sounds that is not identical with (fundamental) frequency, but which nonetheless causes pitch experiences in the appropriate manner. Such complex physical properties would be interesting from an anthropocentric point of view, though perhaps not from the point of view of physical theorizing, which aims for the simplest, most complete characterization of physical reality.

What is loudness? Loudness presents similar difficulties. The consciously experienced loudness of a sound does not vary as a simple function of either the amplitude, intensity, or power of a sound wave. The volume of sound one experiences also depends, for instance, upon aspects of the spectral composition of complex waves. As with pitch, no simple physical correlate to experienced loudness exists.

Are there any reasons to think loudness is objective? Subjects situated at different locations might enjoy different loudness experiences thanks to dampening that occurs with increasing distance from the sources. *Loudness constancy* effects might nonetheless support the claim that loudness is an objective feature of sounds and not a mere conscious sensation by avoiding arguments from variability: though wave attributes upon which experienced loudness depends change with distance from the source, subjects judge little difference in the loudness of a sound despite changes to their distance from the source.

What is timbre? Timbre is difficult to characterize, and has been derisively dubbed 'the psychoacoustician's multidimensional wastebasket category'. Tones that share pitch and loudness might differ in timbre, quality, or 'tone colour', and timbre therefore is critical to recognizing the identities of sound sources in one's environment. As such, it depends at least upon the specific sinusoidal constituents and overall wave shape of a complex signal. It depends, in addition, upon aspects of the attack (onset) and decay (offset) of a signal. Timbre therefore is closely tied to the particular medium-disturbing activity of a sound source. Handel (1995:441) claims that '*no* known acoustic invariants can be said to underlie timbre' and suggests that timbre is best likened to the distinctive look of a face, which remains recognizable across changes to determinate features.

Are sounds all we hear? Awareness of sounds and audible qualities seems to provide awareness of things and events distinct from sounds, such as bells and backfires. In hearing a bang, for instance, we often seem to hear a collision. One view holds that this is mere inference or association. However, *cross-modal illusions and perceptual effects might shed light on how audition grounds genuine awareness of environmental sources of sounds. If explaining illusory interactions among perceptual modalities requires ascribing to them common objects of experience in non-illusory settings, then since sounds are not visible, sounds are not all we hear. Rather, we experience a sound *as* the sound of some significant event that *also* stimulates visual experience. Cross-modal illusions and interactions thus provide fertile ground for future investigation of audition and its relationships to other forms of conscious perceptual experience.

CASEY O'CALLAGHAN

Blauert, J. (1997). *Spatial Hearing: The Psychophysics of Human Sound Localization.*

Bregman, A. (1990). *Auditory Scene Analysis: The Perceptual Organization of Sound.*

Casati, R. and Dokic, J. (2005). 'Sounds'. In Zalta, E. (ed.) *The Stanford Encyclopedia of Philosophy.*

Handel, S. (1995). 'Timbre perception and auditory object identification'. In Moore, B. (ed.) *Hearing.*

O'Callaghan, C. (2007). *Sounds: A Philosophical Theory.*

Pasnau, R. (1999). 'What is sound?' *Philosophical Quarterly*, 49.

Zwicker, E. and Fastl, H. (2006). *Psychoacoustics: Facts and Models*, 3rd edn.

span of apprehension See CAPACITY LIMITS AND CONSCIOUSNESS

spindle cells See VON ECONOMO NEURONS

split brain See COMMISSUROTOMY AND CONSCIOUSNESS

Spock Mr Spock is a character in one of the most popular and enduring American television shows—the so-called 'original' *Star Trek* science fiction series created by Gene Rodenberry in 1964, first shown on the NBC television channel in 1966. *Star Trek* is set in the 23rd century, a time at which humans have united with aliens to form the galaxy-spanning United Federation of Planets. Spock, played by the actor Leonard Nimoy, is half-human and half-Vulcan, and has occupied various military and diplomatic positions in the Federation, mostly as the Science Officer on the vessel *U.S.S. Enterprise.*

The Vulcans are a fictional alien humanoid race who strive to live by reason and pure logic alone, controlling emotions through meditative and self-discipline methods so as to eliminate their influence on decision-making and action. Vulcans are endowed with a number of remarkable abilities, including the 'mind meld'—a form of contact telepathy that makes it possible for Spock to experience the consciousness and memories of someone else through touch—and the 'Vulcan nerve pinch'—a manual grip applied to the base of a subject's neck that renders it unconscious.

While Spock's lack of emotion often provides the opportunity for comic relief in *Star Trek*, it can also prove to be advantageous in some cases, as Spock is able to appreciate problems more objectively than the human personnel of the *U.S.S. Enterprise.*

Spock's character is interesting from the perspective of consciousness studies because he provides a window on what it would be like for an agent to be almost completely devoid of emotions. Spock's lack of emotional responses imbues his personality with the social awkwardness also found in people with *autistic spectrum disorder, and is likewise reminiscent of the features of robotic agents (see MACHINE CONSCIOUSNESS). Finally, the *meditation techniques used by Vulcans to achieve emotional control are inspired by existing Buddhist contemplative traditions, themselves the object of current interest in consciousness studies.

More generally, Spock's character raises the issue of the role that *emotions play in conscious experience. Conscious experience is often bluntly defined as '*what it feels like' for an agent to be that agent (Nagel 1974). What is it like to be Spock, then, if he cannot experience the world and others in such a manner that these experiences are imbued with emotional valence?

Spock's character returned in a somewhat different guise in the later *Star Trek: The Next Generation* (ST:TNG) series, the first episode of which aired in 1987. ST:TNG features an humanoid robot, Commander Data, played by the actor Brent Spiner. Data's astounding computational abilities and personality, or rather lack thereof, are strongly reminiscent of Spock's. Unlike Spock, however, Data suffers from his inability to experience emotion and strives to learn more about how to experience things like a human. In the movie *Star Trek Generations* (Paramount 1994), Data finds himself equipped with an 'emotion chip', the intense activity of which proves so overwhelming that he eventually opts to deactivate it.

ST:TNG interestingly explored the ethical issues entailed by the existence of sentient robots in the episode titled 'The measure of a man', first broadcast in 1989. In the show, a trial is organized to settle the question of whether Data should be considered as an object—the property of Starfleet—or as a conscious, sentient agent with rights equal to those of a human. This question, of course, connects directly with Asimov's explorations of the moral and legal implications of the existence of sentient robots, and, albeit more indirectly, with issues raised by the *Turing test.

Spock and Data both raise interesting questions about the relationships between conscious and unconscious *cognition (see also KNOWLEDGE, EXPLICIT VS IMPLICIT). Specifically, the two are characterized not only by the fact that their decisions are systematically rational, but also by the fact that they both seem be perfectly transparent to themselves, enjoying perfect access to their own bodily and cognitive innards. Except in rare circumstances (which systematically tend to be described as the result of some sort of dysfunction), Data is thus capable of describing in uncanny detail each and every aspect of his internal states: how much force he is applying when attempting to pry open a steel door, how many circuits are currently active in his positronic brain, or the number of times over the last ten years he smelled a particular scent, and in which circumstances he did so, etc. Spock (to some extent) and Data thus both illustrate what it would be like for an agent to enjoy perfect *introspective access to their own cognitive states in that they appear to function in a manner in which whatever knowledge influences their behaviour is always accessible to conscious awareness (see Cleeremans and Jiménez 2002 for further discussion)

Science fiction, like other forms of fiction (see LITERATURE AND CONSCIOUSNESS), provides us with a rich trove of imaginary case studies that are relevant to the study of consciousness. Spock's prominence among popular fictional heroes, and to a lesser extent Data's, can no doubt be traced, rather paradoxically, to their constant struggle with learning how to cope with a most human trait—emotion.

AXEL CLEEREMANS

Cleeremans, A. and Jiménez, L. (2002). 'Implicit learning and consciousness: A graded, dynamic perspective'. In French, R. M. and Cleeremans, A. (eds), *Implicit Learning and Consciousness: An Empirical, Computational and Philosophical Consensus in the Making?*.

Nagel, T. (1974). 'What is like to be a bat?' *Philosophical Review*, 83.

stream of consciousness As a metaphor, the 'stream of consciousness' has meandered over the last century. Although coined by William James, its most conspicuous watershed was neither in philosophy nor psychology, but as a literary style. In the past few decades it has bubbled up again in consciousness studies, recently abetted by discoveries in cognitive neuroscience. However, the contemporary stream of consciousness is quite different from what James imagined.

1. The Jamesian stream
2. The stream in literature
3. The contemporary watershed
4. Conclusion

1. The Jamesian stream

'We now begin our study of mind from within', begins Chapter 9 of James's *Principles of Psychology* (1890). Within the mind we can discern nothing beyond the fact that *'thinking of some sort goes on'* (James's emphasis). Thinking, his stand-in for every form of consciousness, has five important characteristics: (1) every thought is part of personal consciousness, i.e. each is experienced as 'my thought'; (2) thought is always changing; (3) through all its changes thought is nonetheless 'sensibly continuous'; (4) thought 'always appears to deal with objects independent of itself'; (5) thought is 'interested in some parts of these objects to the exclusion of others' (1890:225) The confluence of these characteristics motivates the metaphor:

> Consciousness, then, does not appear to itself chopped up in bits. Such words as 'chain' or 'train' do not describe it fitly as it presents itself in the first instance. It is nothing jointed; it flows. A 'river' or 'stream' are the metaphors by which it is most naturally described. *In talking of it hereafter, let us call it the stream of thought, of consciousness, or of subjective life.* (1890:239)

James's dismissal of other metaphors reflects his ongoing rejection of what he called 'sensationalism', the empiricist attempt to deconstruct the contents of consciousness into atomic sensations, combined into molecular ideas. Simple introspection reveals that no one has ever experienced a sensation as such. Instead, every thought is a shifting pool reflecting not just objects before the mind, but all their relations, tendencies, nuances, and overtones. (James would have dismissed *qualia as well.)

James used the stream to enliven his five characteristics of consciousness. Like a stream, thought changes continuously; no thought is static, nor ever recurs in exactly the same form. Changes in consciousness are never abrupt. Each thought shades into the next, and each includes intimations of upstream and downstream thoughts. The rate of flow varies as well, giving rise to a further metaphor for the stream of consciousness: 'Like a bird's life, it seems to be made of an alternation of flights and perches' (James 1890:243). That is, relatively stable thoughts alternate with transitory passages. These two elaborations on the role of context condense in a further distinction between the relatively stable 'nucleus' of a momentary thought and its evanescent 'fringe'. The *fringe is nonetheless part of consciousness, both as feelings of flight and as traces of context felt during the more stable perching. According to James, denying the phenomenal reality of the fringe is a defect shared by both empiricist and rationalist philosophers.

For James, it seems that the streaming flights and perches are contingent properties of consciousness, but always present. He defends his *phenomenology through numerous examples and exhortations, and promotes it as a consequence of neurology. (His neurological arguments have a contemporary feel, closely resembling main themes in *connectionism in its renaissance in the 1980s.) Meanwhile, both stream and fringe were prominent in the phenomenology of Edmund Husserl (1964). In lectures originally delivered in 1905, Husserl described consciousness as a 'flow', and throughout his work one finds an emphasis on nonsensory 'apprehension' (also called 'fringe' and 'halo'). For Husserl, however, both flow and fringe were essential determiners of the contents of consciousness, and defended by arguments reminiscent of Kant.

2. The stream in literature

Since James defended his metaphor through appeals to introspection and brain science, it is not surprising that with the rise of behaviourism the stream would dry up in mainstream psychology. (Nor is its flow easy to accommodate in classical cognitive science, resting on computation involving discrete states comprising symbols with fixed meaning.) But the metaphor could not be dammed, appearing next as a form employed by some of the literary titans of modernism. It would be tempting to surmise that William James's ideas of the stream would influence the novels of his younger brother Henry, who was also an acute observer of human psychology. However, the brothers each professed incomprehension toward the other's published work and an implied disdain for each other's calling. Henry James mastered the narrative style of free indirect discourse, that is, the interpenetration of third-person narrative with the diction, style, and psychology of a character's thoughts, but this had been a characteristic of earlier novels. 'Stream of consciousness', in contrast, came to denote pure interior monologue, completely without interventions by narrators other than the speaking/thinking character, and shorn of any supposed auditors—talking to oneself alone. The popular feminist novelist May Sinclair first employed the phrase in 1918 to describe the fiction of Dorothy Richardson, marking Richardson's *Pilgrimage* (1915) as the first 'stream of consciousness' novel in English. Virginia Woolf, Katherine Anne Porter, William Faulkner, and James Joyce developed variants of stream of consciousness fiction. Perhaps the summit of the form is Joyce's *Ulysses*. In that novel, stream of consciousness style varies among characters; the book concludes with a long monologue interior to Molly Bloom:

> ... O and the sea the sea crimson sometimes like fire and the glorious sunsets and the figtrees in the Alameda gardens yes and all the queer little streets and pink and blue and yellow houses and the rosegardens and the jessamine and geraniums and cactuses and Gibraltar as a girl where I was a Flower of the mountain yes when I put the rose in my hair like the Andalusian girls used or shall I wear a red yes and how he kissed me under the Moorish wall and I thought well as well him as another and then I asked him with my eyes to ask again yes and then he asked me would I yes to say yes my mountain flower and first I put my arms around him yes and drew him down to me so he could feel my breasts all perfume yes and his heart was going like mad and yes I said yes I will Yes. (*Ulysses*, final lines.)

The liaison with literature changed the meaning of the metaphor in two ways. First, as interior monologue, the streaming consciousness came to be identified with an inner voice that comments on experience, rather than with the flow of experience itself. As commentary, the inner voice presupposes the monologist's activity and sensory experience, obviating their description. Yet the reader needs at least some of this information to comprehend the narrative. These difficulties led to the second re-channelling of the metaphor: if plot and setting are difficult to convey through interior monologue, then it is best used when the exterior dynamics of the story pause. Joyce's monologue is successful, and canonical, in part because Molly's mind wanders in the midnight of her insomnia, without tasks and intrusions. The literary stream of consciousness thus became the soliloquizing expression of idle daydreaming.

3. The contemporary watershed

Although the literary stream of consciousness flowed at its deepest during the first half of the 20th century, it remains among the stylistic options for contemporary writers. Accordingly, as consciousness returned to respectability as a target of philosophical and scientific study, the stream of consciousness surfaced again, needing no special introduction. Or, when philosophers do explicate the metaphor, they cite James. The literary stream occasionally intermixes with this Jamesian revival. In Daniel Dennett's *Consciousness Explained*, for example, we read that the brain's widely distributed 'multiple drafts' can form 'something *rather like* a narrative stream or sequence' (Dennett 1991:113; also p. 135). Narrative, however, was not a characteristic of the Jamesian stream. Dennett's literary source appears later in the book, as consciousness is recast as a 'Joycean virtual machine,' implemented by massively parallel neural operations.

Dennett's Joycean machine and most other *fin de siècle* treatments of the stream of consciousness imagine it within the framework of functionalism: the stream has been seen as a high-level flow of contents, possibly epiphenomenal but in any case independent and remote from the details of neural implementation. So it is surprising to find that cognitive neuroscience has returned to James's metaphor to characterize the discovery of the *default mode* (DM) network in the brain. The DM network comprises brain areas (posterior cingulate cortex, inferior parietal lobes, and medial prefrontal cortex, among others) that deactivate during a wide variety of cognitively demanding tasks. That is, the DM network is consistently most active in 'rest' conditions between tasks, or when 'task-unrelated thoughts' intrude on the experimental task at hand. The default mode was first described by Raichle et al. (2001), but not yet linked to the stream of consciousness. Subsequent reports have cited James, however. The cognitive role of the DM network has been elusive. For example:

> ... Included in the list of possible resting activities is the ongoing internal 'thought' processing that humans experience during resting consciousness, sometimes referred to as 'stream of consciousness' (James 1890). Since these 'thought' processes are generally self-initiated and self-referential and not related to specific exogenous task demands we use the term 'task-unrelated thoughts' (TUTs) to describe them. ... This term is comparable to others such as 'stimulus independent thoughts' (SITs) ... and 'free association' (McKiernan et al. 2006).

> Language becomes imprecise at this stage, but one is tempted to describe this passive task as 'mindless' except in certain subjects. ... In this view, the default-mode network—free-flowing until interrupted by an external task—emerges as a reasonable candidate for the neural correlate of James's (1890) stream of consciousness. (Greicius and Menon 2004)

> We believe that these events, such as episodic memory, planning for the future, inner speech or simulation of behaviour reflect thoughts or the 'streams of consciousness' (James 1890) of which we are aware, when overt task performance is absent. (Fransson 2006)

But which stream of consciousness is this? James's original characterization, cited above, applies the metaphor to *all* consciousness, and his many examples of streaming consciousness include several that show up regularly in experimental tasks in *functional neuroimaging. The daydreaming of the DM network is the stream of consciousness mainly in the literary sense. Its affiliation with rest between tasks or stimuli suggests a more accurate citation: not James (1890) but Joyce et al. (1922 ff.)

Nonetheless, the interest in default mode thinking brings cognitive neuroscience closer to the Jamesian stream. The emerging brain is not a task machine, dormant until prodded. Rather, it ever flows among complex patterns of activity, continuous and seamless. This totality, the stream of neural processing, is very much what William James had in mind. If James set the stage for Joyce, Joyce and his colleagues have returned the favour.

4. Conclusion

Elaborated by psychology, philosophy, and literature, the concept of consciousness expanded in the late 19th and early 20th centuries. The new mind of the gilded age found its perfect metaphor, the stream. After the behaviourist lull, cognitive science, consciousness studies, and finally cognitive neuroscience have recognized that William James and his literary stepchildren described one ubiquitous aspect of all lived experience. The stream of consciousness is thus reflected, though in slow motion and large scale, in the stream of consciousness science.

DAN LLOYD

Dennett, D. (1991). *Consciousness Explained*.

Fransson, P. (2006). 'How default is the default mode of brain function? Further evidence from intrinsic BOLD signal fluctuations'. *Neuropsychologia*, 44.

Greicius, M. D. and Menon, V. (2004). 'Default-mode activity during a passive sensory task: uncoupled from deactivation but impacting activation'. *Journal of Cognitive Neuroscience*, 16.

Husserl, E. (1964). *Phenomenology of Internal Time Consciousness*, trans. J. S. Churchill.

James, W. (1890). *Principles of Psychology*.

McKiernan, K. A., D'Angelo, B. R., Kaufman, J. N. and Binder, J. R. (2006). 'Interrupting the "stream of consciousness": an fMRI investigation'. *Neuroimage*, 29.

Raichle, M. E., MacLeod, A. M., Snyder, A. Z., Powers, W. J., Gusnard, D. A., and Shulman, G. L. (2001). 'A default mode of brain function'. *Proceedings of the National Academy of Sciences of the USA*, 98.

Stroop effect Over 70 years ago, John Ridley Stroop (1935) published a dissertation that provided the point of origin for one of psychology's best known and most enduring phenomena.

1. The phenomenon
2. What causes interference?
3. Stroop and consciousness

1. The phenomenon

The Stroop effect is simultaneously deceptively simple yet compelling. When naming aloud the print colour of an incongruent colour word (e.g. saying 'red' to the word 'green' printed in red), people are much slower and more error prone than they are when naming aloud the colour of a neutral letter string (e.g. saying 'red' to the string 'xxxxx' in red) or of a non-colour word (e.g. saying 'red' to the word 'table' in red). This is illustrated in Fig. S3. The difficulty experienced in ignoring the task-irrelevant printed word when trying to name the colour is called *interference*, and it is a highly robust and replicable result. Many hundreds of studies have explored the sources of this interference, and many more have used the task to investigate aspects of cognitive processing (see MacLeod 1991 for a review).

The Stroop task has spawned numerous versions of interference tasks. Among these are the *picture–word interference task*, where naming a picture in which an incompatible word is embedded (e.g. saying 'house' to a picture of a house with the word 'sheep' printed inside it) is slowed relative to a suitable control (e.g. a picture of a house with 'xxxxx' inside it), and the *flanker task*, where responding to a central letter is slowed when peripheral letters on both sides conflict (e.g. say 'h' to 'DHD') as opposed to when the peripheral letters match the central letter (e.g. 'HHH') or to when there are no peripheral letters (e.g. '*H*').

Hundreds of interference tasks have been developed, but the Stroop task remains the best known and most often used. It is routinely used in neuropsychology as an index of *attention and attentional disorders, and it is now often used throughout psychology as an index of the relative activation of the to-be-ignored words. Thus, for example, a spider-phobic individual shows greater interference in colour naming from irrelevant words if those words are spider-related than if they are neutral with respect to the individual's phobia (see Williams et al. 1996 for a review). The assumption is that the spider-related words are already highly activated in the phobic individual's mind, and therefore compete more strongly with the colour, in terms of winning control of the overt response, than do unrelated words. This is seen as evidence of *chronic priming*, analogous to the more fleeting *priming—and hence amplified interference—seen when a to-be-ignored word is pre-activated (e.g. the response 'red' is slower to 'table' in red when the colour-naming trial is preceded by a related word such as 'chair' or 'table' itself, as opposed to an unrelated word such as 'horse').

Fig. S3. Stroop task and its experimental conditions. The effect is quite readily experienced: for each column, name aloud the eight colours as rapidly as possible, ignoring the printed characters. To measure performance, start a stopwatch, then name aloud the eight colours in a column, then stop the stopwatch. Record the time and do the same for the remaining columns. The conditions are (a) colour patch neutral, (b) non-word neutral, (c) word-neutral, (d) incongruent, and (e) 'super' incongruent. Stroop himself used the colour patch neutral condition; most researchers today use either the non-word or the word-neutral condition. Stroop interference is the time difference between the incongruent condition and any of the neutral conditions, a cost due to the word's incompatibility with the colour to be named. The three neutral conditions will not differ much from each other in response time (although the word neutral usually will be a little slower) but the incongruent condition will be substantially slower. Condition (e) is a special case of the incongruent condition in which each successive colour names the word that had to be ignored in the preceding stimulus. This version of the incongruent condition ordinarily produces the most interference, combining standard Stroop interference with *negative priming*, the incremental cost in responding with a colour name that has just been ignored (permitting colour naming to be accomplished on the preceding trial). (See Colour Plate 12.)

2. What causes interference?

Stroop's own account of his interference effect relied on differential practice. Word reading is a highly practised skill, perhaps carried out automatically, without intention and even beneath awareness. Colour naming is less practised, requiring more effort and attention to accomplish. For this reason, word reading disrupts colour naming even when the goal is to ignore the printed words. This is nicely illustrated by Stroop's other key finding—that incompatible colour information does not interfere with reading the word. Modern explanations that rely on relative *automaticity—or degree of practice-based learning—trace their origins to Stroop's practice account and to the asymmetry of interference.

Another way to explain this asymmetry is in terms of a serial processing view, sometimes called a 'horse race' explanation because interference is based on the relative speed of processing each of the two dimensions (word and colour). Such explanations were popular for about a quarter century from the mid-1960s to the early 1980s. Here, the faster process (word reading) interferes with the slower process (colour naming)—but not vice versa—because the faster process always reaches the limited-capacity bottleneck in the system first. Interference is thus located at this bottleneck, often thought to be response preparation and production. There has been increasing evidence against such serial processing accounts providing a complete explanation of the Stroop effect.

More recently, the parallel view has supplanted the serial view. Here, processes involved in colour naming and those involved in word reading are seen as being carried out in parallel, despite instructions to ignore the word. Thus, interference can happen throughout the course of processing, as the two streams of processing repeatedly 'bump into' each other; there is not necessarily a single locus of interference. This view is captured in *connectionist (neural net) models where relative strengths of pathways are adjusted with practice (e.g. Cohen et al. 1990) or in models where interactions occur during language production (e.g. Roelofs 2003).

3. Stroop and consciousness

How does the Stroop effect inform our understanding of consciousness? When the task is to name the colour, processing of the word is nevertheless carried out, otherwise interference would not occur. By implication, if there is no intention to read the word, then it is tempting to think of it as necessarily having been read unconsciously. Such a perspective is bolstered by studies showing that even very briefly presented and masked (covered) words—which subjects report not even having seen—nevertheless influence time to name an immediately following patch of colour (e.g. Cheesman and Merikle 1986). This suggests that the word can be processed unconsciously and still produce Stroop interference. There is, however, continuing debate about the interpretation of self-reported failure to see the word: Is this a good index of unconsciousness?

Perhaps the most striking demonstration of the relation between the Stroop effect and consciousness appears in the recent work of Raz and his colleagues (e.g. Raz et al. 2002). They have used *hypnosis as a tool to explore the processes underlying interference. Most notably, they have shown that a posthypnotic suggestion to highly hypnotizable subjects that they will be unable to read eliminates Stroop interference. This result leads to the inference that word reading is not completely automatic, because it can be turned off, and suggests that manipulation of consciousness via hypnosis can affect even a very robust, otherwise always seen, phenomenon such as Stroop interference.

Research using the Stroop effect is pushing into new frontiers, most notably into the domain of cognitive neuroscience (see MacLeod and MacDonald 2000), where the brain mechanisms supporting the cognitive performance are being investigated. Brain mechanisms of consciousness are also under very active exploration, so it is highly likely that in the not-too-distant future these research tracks will converge, helping us to understand cognitive processing, both conscious and unconscious. As it has for so long, the venerable Stroop task will provide an important tool in this work.

COLIN M. MACLEOD

Cheesman, J. and Merikle, P. M. (1986). 'Distinguishing conscious from unconscious perceptual processes'. *Canadian Journal of Psychology*, 40.

Cohen, J. D., Dunbar, K., and McClelland, J. L. (1990). 'On the control of automatic processes: a parallel distributed processing account of the Stroop effect'. *Psychological Review*, 97.

MacLeod, C. M. (1991). 'Half a century of research on the Stroop effect: an integrative review'. *Psychological Bulletin*, 109.

—— and MacDonald, P. A. (2000). 'Inter-dimensional interference in the Stroop effect: uncovering the cognitive and neural anatomy of attention'. *Trends in Cognitive Sciences*, 4.

Raz, A., Shapiro, T., Fan, J., and Posner, M. I. (2002). 'Hypnotic suggestion and the modulation of Stroop interference'. *Archives of General Psychiatry*, 59.

Roelofs, A. (2003). 'Goal-referenced selection of verbal action: modeling attentional control in the Stroop task'. *Psychological Review*, 110.

Stroop, J. R. (1935). 'Studies of interference in serial verbal reactions'. *Journal of Experimental Psychology*, 18.

Williams, J. M. G., Mathews, A., and MacLeod, C. (1996). 'The emotional Stroop task and psychopathology'. *Psychological Bulletin*, 120.

subitizing vs counting See CAPACITY LIMITS AND CONSCIOUSNESS

subjective confidence See METACOGNITION

subjectivity In the study of consciousness, subjectivity is arguably part of the explanandum and consequently something that requires closer investigation. As Shoemaker puts it,

> it is essential for a philosophical understanding of the mental that we appreciate that there *is* a first person perspective on it, a distinctive way mental states present themselves to the subjects

whose states they are, and that an essential part of the philosophical task is to give an account of mind which makes intelligible the perspective mental subjects have on their own mental lives (Shoemaker 1996:157).

Whereas others must rely on what I say and do in order to know what I think or feel, my access to my own psychological states is not exclusively based on behavioural evidence. A satisfying account of consciousness should respect and acknowledge this epistemic asymmetry. It must take the first-personal or subjective givenness of consciousness seriously, since an important and non-negligible feature of consciousness is the way in which it is experienced by the subject.

To discuss the subjectivity of consciousness is to address issues pertaining to the structures and features of experiential life, rather than the various sub-personal mechanisms that might underlie it. However, there is more to the subjectivity of experience than the fact that a range of conscious mental states have subjectively accessible qualitative features or that '*what it is like' to perceive a black triangle is subjectively distinct from what it is like to perceive a red circle (cf. Nagel 1974). In focusing on the qualitative character of what we experience, we should not overlook the subjective nature of the mental acts that enables us to experience what we experience. We are never conscious of an object simply as an object, but always of the object as appearing in a certain way, say, as judged, seen, feared, remembered, smelled, anticipated, tasted, etc. The redness of the cherry is present to me through my seeing it; the hardness of the table is present to me through my touching it. In fact, the very same object, with the exact same worldly properties, can present itself in a variety of manners. It can be given as perceived, imagined, or recollected, etc.

When I consciously imagine a unicorn, desire an ice cream, anticipate a holiday, or reflect upon an economic crisis, all of these intended objects are given in correlation to a variety of subjectively distinct intentional experiences. The reason why these experiences are said to be subjective is not only because they are accessible in a unique way from the very same first-person perspective they themselves help constitute. Rather, it is also because such experiences are characterized by a subjective mode of existence in the sense that they necessarily exist for a subject, they necessarily feel like something for somebody. With the possible exception of certain pathological states, experiences that are given from the first-person perspective, are given (at least tacitly) as my experiences, as experiences I am undergoing or living through. It has in this connection become customary to speak of a *sense of ownership*: When I think about Paris, smell crushed mint leaves, listen to Prokofiev's *Romeo and Juliet* or move my left arm, all these various experiences seem to share a certain feature; they are all felt as mine (cf. Gallagher 2000). Thus, in addition to addressing the issue of phenomenality, a discussion of subjectivity must also touch upon the issues of first-personal self-reference, the experience and status of self, the unity and continuity of conscious experience, and arguably include analyses of such further issues as individuality, personality, agency and (moral) responsibility. Why do all these topics involve subjectivity? Because they all have something in common, they all involve a *first-person perspective*, a reference to how things are for me.

Ultimately, what we need is an account of subjectivity that (among other things) addresses its significance (the role it plays), describes its structure, specifies the kind of epistemic access we have to it, delineates the methodology that we should employ when investigating it, and finally clarifies its ontological or metaphysical status. It is part of the current state of affairs that any attempt to provide an answer to these questions is bound to be controversial.

The claim that a scientifically respectable account of consciousness must include a thorough investigation of subjectivity has, for instance, not gone unchallenged. Watson famously demanded that behaviourist should drop from their scientific vocabulary all subjective terms such as sensations, perception, image, desire, purpose, and even thinking and emotion as they are subjectively defined (Watson 1924:5–6). Even after the official demise of behaviourism, scepticism concerning the issue of subjectivity has continued to prevail in many circles, be it because it is thought to be *epiphenomenal, non-existent, or simply unsuitable for scientific investigation due to its subjective nature. Thus, for a number of years it has been argued that a serious investigation of consciousness should focus on its various computational, functional, or systemic properties and that it could safely ignore the subjective dimension.

The more overarching theoretical implications are also highly contested. Whereas some have argued that the subjective character of experience is a decisive challenge for any thoroughgoing reductionism and that a careful investigation of subjectivity requires the rehabilitation of introspective evidence and even the development of a first-person science since a third-person science by treating consciousness as an object will inevitably miss it as a subject (cf. Varela and Shear 1999, Jack and Roepstorff 2003), others have argued that any science of consciousness must be based on data that are available from the third-person scientific perspective, that such a third-person scientific perspective can do justice to the most ineffable subjective experiences, and that the very idea of a first-person science is a fantasy (Dennett 1991).

Even the descriptive findings are contested. Some have argued that the positing of a conscious subject is descriptively unwarranted and that experiences are anonymous mental events that simply occur without being states or properties of anyone. To claim that each of my experiences are given as mine, to claim that every episode of experiencing necessarily includes a reference to a subject of experience, has consequently been taken to be a post-hoc fabrication, the result of a subsequent theorizing. In the contemporary debate, such a view is for instance defended by those who argue that the self-ascription of actions and experiences is a *metacognitive operation that involves conceptual and linguistic resources (Carruthers 1996). This idea has gained a certain prominence not only in recent neuroscience, but also in German and French post-war philosophy, where it was argued—partly as a showdown with Husserlian phenomenology—that subjectivity rather than being a given, something innate and fundamental, was a cultural and linguistic construction. That is, subjectivity was considered the result of a discursive or narrative praxis; it was something that could only be acquired by participating in a linguistic community that employed the personal pronoun 'I' (Kerby 1991).

One of the reasons for all this controversy has to do with the problem of demarcation and limitation. The concept of subjectivity has been used in a variety of disciplines (including philosophy, developmental psychology, psychiatry, anthropology, and sociology) to denote somewhat different issues. Moreover, it is a concept with a long history, and it has been used with different connotations at different times and in different philosophical traditions. Thus, although neuroscience has only recently started to consider the subjective dimension of consciousness a topic worthy of scientific investigation, subjectivity is by no means a *terra incognita* to those familiar with the tradition. Since Descartes, and in particularly since Kant, subjectivity has for instance been of ongoing concern to many philosophers working within the German and French tradition. In the period from Kant to Hegel, occasionally labelled as the reign of the *philosophy of subjectivity*, subjectivity was even considered to constitute if not the most, then at least one of the most important themes and principles of philosophy. In 20th century philosophy, this theoretical orientation probably found its most significant continuation in Husserlian *phenomenology (cf. Carr 1999, Zahavi 2003). It is no coincidence that whereas there is no entry on subjectivity in the *Oxford Companion to the Mind* or the *Routledge Encyclopedia of Philosophy*, the term rates a 9000-word entry in the German *Historisches Wörterbuch der Philosophie*.

Much of the recent debate has centred on the question of whether or not it is possible to naturalize subjectivity. But it should be realized that there are many other questions that remain in need of answers (see Zahavi 2005). To mention a few examples: (1) What is the relation between *intentionality and subjectivity? Does real (in contrast to derived) intentionality presuppose subjectivity, or is it rather the case that the subjectivity of experience might be amenable to a representationalist analysis in the same way the phenomenal features of experience are claimed to be? (2) Is the unity and continuity of the *stream of consciousness guaranteed by a subject of experience understood as some formal principle of identity or is the owner or bearer of the various experiences rather the concrete creature or organism? (3) What is the link between subjectivity and *temporality? What temporal form or structure, if any, does subjectivity possess? (4) If subjectivity is a first-person phenomenon *par excellence*, do we then only have experiential access to our own subjectivity? Is the subjectivity of others hidden from us, and are we consequently condemned to some form of *solipsism? Or should one on the contrary insist that subjectivity reveals itself in meaningful and expressive behaviour, and that it would be a mistake to equate the subjective with the purely private? (5) What is the link between subjectivity and intersubjectivity? To what extent are the structures of subjectivity transformed by language use and social interaction? (6) Do all conscious states and experiential episodes exhibit the same degree of subjectivity? How do, say, the experience of scrutinizing a menu written in French, of being hit by a snowball, and of deciding to climb up a rock face compare to each other? (7) How do conditions like *dementia, infantile *autism, or *schizophrenia affect subjectivity? Do such pathologies diminish, distort, or even completely eliminate the subjectivity of consciousness?

Despite all the controversy surrounding the issue of subjectivity, when all is said and done, the notion has enjoyed a renaissance in recent years. This is the case not only in empirical science, but also in both analytical and continental philosophy. One reason for this change is surely the perceived shortcomings of neo-behaviourist models—to ignore the issue of subjectivity when investigating consciousness is like seeking to 'explain' consciousness by defining it away, it is like 'solving' a problem by ignoring the part of it that makes it difficult—but another reason probably has to do with the growing realization that one should not throw the baby out with the bathwater. One can reject the notion of an isolated, self-contained, autonomous, worldless, self-transparent soul substance and still retain a significant and legitimate concept of subjectivity. Recently there has even been a growing recognition of the fact that there is still much to learn from earlier accounts of subjectivity, say, those of Kant, Hegel, Kierkegaard, Brentano, James, Dilthey, Husserl, Sartre, and Merleau-Ponty, and that many of these figures in addition to offering painstakingly detailed analyses of subjectivity were already emphasizing its embodied and embedded nature (see Zahavi 2004).

DAN ZAHAVI

Carr, D. (1999). *The Paradox of Subjectivity: The Self in the Transcendental Tradition.*

Carruthers, P. (1996). *Language, Thoughts and Consciousness: An Essay in Philosophical Psychology.*

Dennett, D. C. (1991). *Consciousness Explained.*

Gallagher, S. (2000). 'Philosophical conceptions of the self: implications for cognitive science'. *Trends in Cognitive Sciences*, 4.

Jack, A. I. and Roepstorff, A. (eds) (2003). *Trusting the Subject? Volume I: The Use of Introspective Evidence in Cognitive Science.*

Kerby, A. P. (1991). *Narrative and the Self.*

Nagel, T. (1974). 'What is it like to be a bat?' *Philosophical Review*, 83.

Shoemaker, S. (1996). *The First-Person Perspective and Other Essays.*

Varela, F. J. and Shear, J. (1999). *The View from Within: First-Person Approaches to the Study of Consciousness.*

Watson, J. B. (1924). *Behaviorism.*

Zahavi, D. (2003). *Husserl's Phenomenology.*

—— (2004). *The Hidden Resources: Classical Perspectives on Subjectivity.*

—— (2005). *Subjectivity and Selfhood: Investigating the First-Person Perspective.*

subliminal perception See PERCEPTION, UNCONSCIOUS

subliminal tapes In September 1957 public outrage followed the disclosure that film audiences had been covertly manipulated by invisible messages exhorting them to 'Drink Coca-Cola' and 'Eat popcorn'. Minds had been 'broken and entered' said the *New Yorker*. Although there was never any good evidence for these claims of surreptitious control, the myth of subliminal persuasion proved very durable. In the 1980s self-help audio tapes that promised to induce dramatic improvements in mental and psychological health began to appear in bookshops. These tapes were widely advertised as being able to produce many desirable effects, including weight loss, breast enlargement, improvement of sexual function, and relief from constipation. The tapes shared a common format in that the only consciously perceivable sounds on the tapes consisted of music, ocean waves, and the occasional bird cry. The intended therapeutic effects were purportedly brought about by the unconscious (i.e. 'subliminal') *perception of messages and directives contained on the tapes.

Subliminal tapes represented a change in modality from visual to auditory, and they were ostensibly being exploited for more noble purposes, inasmuch as they were being touted as a form of psychotherapy—clearly a less crass objective than that of covert advertising. Regrettably, however, there is no scientific evidence to support their utility.

Two methods have been used for testing the efficacy of subliminal tapes. Since the tapes are designed to bring about improvements of various kinds, the most obvious means of appraising effectiveness was to look for evidence of improved functioning or enhanced performance. In an innovative study by Pratkanis et al. (1994) participants listened daily for five weeks to tapes designed to improve either self-esteem or memory. Without the subjects' knowledge, half of them received tapes that were mislabelled. That is, half the subjects with self-esteem tapes actually listened to tapes designed to improve memory. Similarly, half the subjects who thought they had memory tapes were really listening to self-esteem tapes. Pre- and post-test measures of both self-esteem and memory revealed that no improvements in either domain of functioning were achieved by using the tapes. Interestingly, participants *believed* that they had benefited from the tapes in a manner consistent with the tapes' labels (and with the manufacturers' claims), even though objective measures showed no such improvements. The investigators thus obtained what they called an *illusory placebo effect*. Participants' expectations of improvement appear to have created the illusion of improvement, even though there was no actual improvement.

Merikle and Skanes (1992) evaluated subliminal weight-loss tapes by recruiting overweight subjects who had a desire to lose weight, and who also believed that such tapes could help. Some participants were assigned to a placebo condition in which tapes identical to those in the weight-loss condition were used, with the exception that the subliminal affirmations pertained to dental anxiety as opposed to weight loss. The appearance, packaging, and supraliminal materials on the placebo tapes were otherwise indistinguishable from the weight-loss tapes. Another group of subjects were assigned to a 'wait list control' condition. All subjects were weighed once a week for five weeks. Subjects in all three groups lost about a pound over the five weeks, with no evidence of subliminal influences or of placebo effects. It is possible that simply participating in the study made subjects more conscious of weight-related issues. Other investigators have found no evidence that subliminal tapes can improve study skills or reduce anxiety.

Another means of appraising the scientific validity of these devices entails an assessment of the nature of the subliminal auditory signal they contain. Proponents seem to have assumed that for obtaining subliminal effects one modality is as good as another. Claims about the utility of subliminal tapes are thus essentially claims about the subliminal perception of speech. It is not obvious what the analogue to visual *masking is for a speech signal. Masking, in the visual domain, is procedurally defined with relative precision. The mask does not impair or change the target stimulus, it simply limits the time available for processing the preceding target. In the absence of the mask, the target is easily perceived.

The target messages on subliminal tapes (assuming that they are present at all) are reduced in volume and further attenuated by the superimposition of other supraliminal material. The problem is that in the process of prohibiting conscious awareness of the signal, the signal itself can easily become mutilated, if not eradicated. Sometimes the subliminal 'message' is accelerated or compressed to such a degree that the message would be unintelligible even if it were clearly audible.

One study showed that there was no spectrographic evidence of any speech signals on the tapes from one of the subliminal tape companies. Another study showed that listeners were unable to distinguish a subliminal tape from a placebo control in a forced-choice task. This presence/absence discrimination required a 'placebo' tape which was identical to its companion subliminal tape but without any subliminal message. Similarly, Moore (1995) used matched pairs of audiotapes from three different manufacturers. Tapes in each pair were identical, except for the nature of the ostensible subliminal messages they contained. In the course of 400 forced-choice trials, subjects could not discriminate between tapes containing allegedly different subliminal messages. Taken together, these data show that little or no perceptual activity is triggered by the subliminal content of the tapes tested. It should not, therefore, surprise us that no therapeutic effects have been obtained by any of the evaluation studies mentioned above. Moreover, the *signal detection data suggest that there could *never* be therapeutic benefits from such devices because they do not appear to contain a signal that is capable of triggering the requisite semantic processing that practical benefits would require. Recent research (Kouider and Dupoux 2005) has shown that speech perception in the absence of conscious awareness is possible, although the nature of the effect did not extend to semantic activation. Semantic *priming was achieved only when the prime stimuli were available to consciousness.

Psychological self-help is big business, and many psychologists rush to market with exaggerated product claims. Subliminal tapes constitute a paradigmatic example. Not all proponents of these devices were unabashed quacks, but advocates were almost invariably associated with their sale. Because semantic activation without conscious awareness was a well-established phenomenon, some observers apparently jumped to the conclusion that subliminal stimulation provided relatively direct access to the systemic unconscious. They assumed that there was a pipeline to peoples' internal motives. Unconscious perceptual processes were thought to provide the means by which therapeutic directives could be smuggled into the unconscious through the back door. Scientific studies have made it clear that this assumption has neither theoretical nor empirical support. Notwithstanding their scientifically dubious status, subliminal audio tapes can still be found, although their presence in the marketplace is now largely confined to mail order and internet sales. The scientific community can take some credit for their demise and for placing unfounded claims in proper perspective.

TIMOTHY E. MOORE

Kouider, S. and Dupoux, E. (2005). 'Subliminal speech priming'. *Psychological Science*, 16.

Merikle, P. M. and Skanes, H. (1992). 'Subliminal self-help audiotapes: a search for placebo effects'. *Journal of Applied Psychology*, 77.

Moore, T. E. (1995). 'Subliminal self-help auditory tapes: an empirical test of perceptual consequences'. *Canadian Journal of Behavioral Science*, 27.

Pratkanis, A. R., Eskanazi, J., and Greenwald, A. G. (1994). 'What you expect is what you believe (but not necessarily what you get): a test of the effectiveness of subliminal self-help audiotapes'. *Basic and Applied Social Psychology*, 15.

substance dualism See DUALISM

superblindsight See FUNCTIONALIST THEORIES OF CONSCIOUSNESS; HELEN, 'A BLIND MONKEY WHO SAW EVERYTHING'; ZOMBIES

supervenience See EMERGENCE

synaesthesia Synaesthetes taste what we taste, hear what we hear, and see what we see, but when they engage in these perceptual acts they also experience something extra. Tastes can be accompanied by feelings of texture, sounds by tastes, and in the most common form of synaesthesia, ordinary black letters and digits induce experiences of colour. As one synaesthete relates 'I know the letters are black, but I also see a colour above the black letter'. It is these 'extra' perceptions that distinguish a synaesthete's perceptual world from our own (see Cytowic 2002 for these and other examples of synaesthesia). Unlike extra perceptions that can be temporarily experienced under the influence of certain drugs (LSD) or under hypnotic suggestion, for people with true, developmental synaesthesia, their synaesthetic experiences have coloured their cognition for as long as they can remember.

The inducers of synaesthetic experiences can be relatively simple (a tone, the letter K), or more complex (the word January). For *time–space synaesthetes*, July is not only pink, but occupies a discrete location in space (e.g. 45° to the right of midline). For P. D., each month has a different colour, and the months are located in discrete positions that surround her body.

Although synaesthetes can experience a variety of synaesthetic concurrents (taste, touch, sound) colour is by far the most common synaesthetic experience. Synaesthetes describe colours that range from the ordinary (colours that they can match to those on a colour palette) to the extraordinary—colours that they claim never to have seen in the real world (Ramachandran and Hubbard 2001). Intriguingly, for some synaesthetes, colour words like 'red' can induce colours different from that referenced by the word (e.g. when shown 'red', they experience blue). This so-called *alien colour effect* suggests that synaesthetic colours are not simply the result of associative learning (Gray 2005).

Consistency is a hallmark of developmental synaesthesia. For *grapheme–colour synaesthetes*, if K induces yellow during initial testing, it almost invariably induces yellow when assessments are repeated at a later time. Indeed, a number of laboratories have used consistency to 'diagnose' synaesthesia. In a typical consistency assessment, grapheme–colour synaesthetes are presented a series of graphemes and asked to select from a colour palette the colour that best matches their synaesthetic experience. When this task is repeated later, the typical finding is that those with synaesthesia are far more consistent in their colour selections than non-synaesthetic controls who have been asked to generate associations between graphemes and colours. Consistency has also been used to investigate time–space synaesthetes for whom months occupy discrete spatial locations. Synaesthetes are asked to use a laser pointer mounted on a 360° compass to point to the middle of the space occupied by the each month. They do this on two separate occasions. Time–space synaesthetes are more consistent in their laser pointing than controls instructed to act 'as though' time units occupied discrete spatial locations (Smilek et al. 2007).

Demonstrations of consistency are often only the starting point for more fine-grained investigations into the nature of this fascinating condition. Such experiments have revealed a second hallmark of synaesthesia, i.e. that synaesthetic experience cannot be turned on or off by an act of conscious volition. Grapheme–colour synaesthetes often describe how as soon as they see a grapheme they 'automatically' experience their synaesthetic colour. Prompted by these descriptions, researchers have devised a synaesthetic variant of the *Stroop task in which coloured graphemes are presented on a computer monitor and synaesthetes are required to name, as quickly as they can, the video colour that they see while ignoring the synaesthetic colour that is induced by the grapheme. Consistent with their self-reports, numerous laboratories have shown that when the video colour synaesthetes must name is incongruent with the synaesthetic colour that the grapheme induces, synaesthetes' response times are significantly slowed relative to conditions in which the video colour and the synaesthetic colour are congruent. Such findings suggest that for synaesthetes black graphemes 'automatically' induce colour experiences.

Interestingly, neither high consistency levels, nor large synaesthetic Stroop effects, 'prove' the perceptual reality of synaesthetic colours. One can train people to associate shapes with colours, and with enough training they will be highly consistent in generating colour associations to that shape, and even show large Stroop-type effects. What sets synaesthetes apart from these trained participants is (1) the absence of an external training regimen and (2) that synaesthetes 'see' yellow rather than just 'knowing' that yellow is linked to the digit 7. Indeed, it is these descriptions of these vivid experiences of colour induced by achromatic stimuli that have prompted a large number of studies devoted to demonstrating the 'perceptual reality' of synaesthetic colours. The synaesthete C., for example, relates how she experiences her colours 'out there, on the page' as coloured overlays above the graphemes she is viewing. To demonstrate the perceptual reality of such synaesthetic colours, researchers have adapted a number of tasks in which video colours influence participants' performance in known and predictable ways. The tasks are modified and used to assess whether synaesthetic colours could induce analogous patterns of behaviour. For instance, it is well known that during visual search, a target number (e.g. 2) is easier to find in an array of distracting digits (e.g. 5s) when the target and distractors are presented in different video colours than when they are presented in the same colour. Synaesthesia researchers have adapted these tasks using carefully chosen achromatic targets and distractors. When the target and distractors elicit the same synaesthetic colour, search is more difficult than when the targets and distractors elicit different synaesthetic colours (Blake et al. 2005). Synaesthetic colours have been found to influence a number of other perceptual tasks including perceptual grouping and perceptual crowding tasks (Ramachandran and Hubbard 2001). Furthermore, the synaesthetic colours induced by staring at specially aligned achromatic graphemes have even been reported to induce the McCullough effect—orientation-contingent colour *after-effects (Blake et al. 2005). Thus it would appear that at least for some synaesthetes, synaesthetic colours are 'perceptually real' entities.

Of course we should be cautious not to push the analogy between our experience of physically coloured stimuli and the synaesthete's experience of synaesthetic colours too far. Although synaesthetic colours may influence the efficiency of visual search in appropriately constructed displays, there is no data to suggest that they do so to the same degree as physically coloured stimuli. Indeed, one should interpret with caution claims of synaesthetic colours that 'pop out' of displays of carefully constructed graphemes. In many cases the empirical data point to important differences between the perception of physically coloured objects and synaesthetically coloured objects. This should come as no surprise. Physically coloured objects have different reflectance properties than achromatic objects, hence the inputs to the visual system are different. When synaesthetes and non-synaesthetes view black letters the inputs into the visual system are presumably identical, yet somewhere in the processing of these achromatic graphemes synaesthetes construct the experience of colour.

The neural architecture involved in this constructive process is a matter of debate. One suggestion is that brain areas that process the form and areas that process colour are cross-wired. Another suggestion involves a more complex circuit connecting areas that process form, meaning, and colour. That meaning plays a role is suggested by the fact that identical forms can induce markedly different synaesthetic colours (see Fig. S4). These findings suggest an architecture in which brain areas that process form activate brain areas that process meaning, which in turn back-activate earlier areas that process colour. Of course different types of synaesthetic experience will necessitate different architectures to explain them—the neural circuits that explain sound–taste synaesthesia will be different from the architectures used to explain grapheme–colour synaesthesia.

A question of interest is how these unusual neural circuits come to be. One suggestion is that the infant brain initially has massive interconnectivity and during development many of these connections are pruned back to form the modules for processing form, colour, sound, gustatory sensations, etc. (Maurer 1997). A failure of this pruning process could lead to synaesthesia. Others suggest that these connections between modules are intact but in most people are inhibited (except under unusual circumstances such as after taking LSD). Thus synaesthesia may result from a failure to inhibit these connections (Grossenbacher and Lovelace 2001).

Explorations of the genetics of synaesthesia have been complicated by potential reporting biases among males and females. Early reports suggesting that there were six female synaesthetes for every male synaesthete (suggesting that synaesthesia was an X-linked trait) have not been supported by a recent large-scale study that controlled for these biases (Simner et al. 2007).

One of the main reasons it has been difficult to isolate the neural mechanisms of synaesthesia and to identify possible genetic causes of synaesthesia is the myriad of individual differences among synaesthetes. Even among grapheme–colour synaesthetes there are marked differences in the manner in which they perceive their synaesthetic colours. Some, like C., perceive their colours as coloured overlays bound to the form of the graphemes. For others, the colours are not perceived in external space, but rather in 'the mind's eye'. Still others have difficulty conveying exactly how their colours are perceived and resort to various analogies that make any type of classification difficult. Importantly, such differences in the nature of their synaesthetic experience may markedly impact the way they perform various cognitive tasks such as the synaesthetic Stroop task (Dixon et al. 2004). Only recently have researchers begun to attend to these important individual differences—differences that must be understood before advances can be made in understanding the genetics of synaesthesia, and the neural architectures that underlie this fascinating condition.

MICHEAL J. DIXON AND DANIEL SMILEK

Blake, R., Palmeri, T. J., Marois, R., and Kim, C-Y. (2005). 'On the perceptual reality of synesthetic color'. In Robertson, L. and Sagiv, N. (eds) *Synesthesia: Perspectives from Cognitive Neuroscience*.

Cytowic, R. E. (2002). *Synesthesia: A Union of Senses*, 2nd edn.

Dixon, M. J., Smilek, D., and Merikle, P. M. (2004). 'Not all synaesthetes are created equal: projector vs associator synaesthetes'. *Cognitive, Affective and Behavioral Neuroscience*, 3.

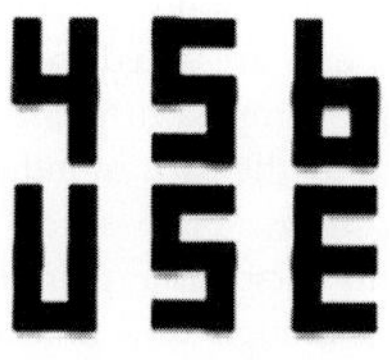

456
USE

Fig. S4. The middle grapheme in '456' and the middle grapheme in 'USE' elicit markedly different synaesthetic colours despite having exactly the same form.

Gray, J. (2005). 'Synesthesia: a window on the hard problem of consciousness'. In Robertson, L. and Sagiv, N. (eds) *Synesthesia: Perspectives from Cognitive Neuroscience*.

Grossenbacher, P. G. and Lovelace, C. T. (2001). 'Mechanisms of synaesthesia: cognitive and physiological constraints'. *Trends in Cognitive Sciences*, 5.

Maurer, D. (1997). 'Neonatal synaesthesia: Implications for the processing of speech and faces'. In Baron-Cohen, S. and Harrison, J. E. (eds) *Synesthesia: Classic and Contemporary Readings*.

Ramachandran, V. S. and Hubbard, E. M. (2001). 'Psychophysical investigations into the neural basis of synaesthesia'. *Journal of Consciousness Studies*, 10.

Simner, J., Sagiv, N. Mulvenna, C. et al. (2007). 'Synaesthesia: the prevalence of atypical cross-modal experiences'. *Perception*, 35.

Smilek, M., Callejas, A., Dixon, M. J., and Merikle, P. M. (2007). 'Ovals of time: time-space associations in synaesthesia'. *Consciousness and Cognition*, 16.

T

task switching See WORKING MEMORY

temporality, philosophical perspectives Our experience of time over days, months, and years can involve complexities (as readers of Proust will be aware) but the principal psychological elements involved are not particularly mysterious. Our relationship with the medium-to-long term past depends heavily on memories and beliefs, whereas our relationship with the future is forged by expectations, anticipations, hopes, fears, intentions and the like. It is otherwise with the short term. Consider:

(1) Our immediate experience is confined to the present.

We can remember the past and anticipate the future, but our immediate experience is confined to the present. It seems obvious that we are only directly aware of what is happening *now*.

(2) The present is instantaneous.

This too looks very plausible. Although we often talk of the 'present century' or the 'present day', the contention that the present does have some duration quickly runs into difficulties: since some parts of such a duration will occur earlier than others, some parts must lie in the *past* with respect to others, so how can all parts be present? This familiar reasoning suggests that the present is the durationless boundary separating the past from the future. Now consider:

(3) We can directly experience change, succession, and persistence.

Some changes happen too quickly for us to perceive (e.g. a bullet in flight), others happen too slowly (e.g. the growth of an oak tree), but some changes can be perceived: we cannot see a tree growing, but we can certainly see its branches swaying in the wind—just as we a car moving along the street, or hear the whirr of a drill, or feel the ebb and flow of a throbbing toothache. In such cases we seem to be aware of a continuous flow of sensory content.

Clearly, construed as a purely phenomenological claim (3) seems very plausible. Unfortunately, it difficult to reconcile with (1) and (2). Given that change and persistence both possess temporal extension, how can we directly experience them if our immediate experience is confined to a durationless instant?

This apparent paradox gave rise to the doctrine that the present as it features in our experience—the so-called 'specious present'—is not instantaneous, but rather has some temporal depth. William James refers to it as 'the short duration of which we are immediately and incessantly sensible' (1890:631). If change and persistence feature in our immediate experience in the way they appear to, then we may well need to appeal to the specious present to explain how this is possible. But precisely how should the specious present be conceived? Much hangs on this question—not least for our understanding of the general structure of consciousness—but there is little agreement on how it should be answered. Opinions have tended to divide into two main camps: on the one hand, there are those who hold that our consciousness really does extend some short distance through time, on the other there are those who hold that it merely seems to. In the absence of any widely agreed terminology, let us call the latter approach the *retention theory* (here following Kelly 2004) and the former the *duration theory*.

1. Retention theories
2. Duration theories
3. Contents and vehicles
4. Psychophysical findings

1. Retention theories

The retention approach is rooted in a widely accepted (perhaps ultimately Kantian) thesis that is then developed in a particular direction. In James's words, the relevant thesis is that 'A succession of feelings, in and of itself, is not a feeling of succession.' (1890:628) It is easy to see what James means. Suppose you hear a succession of notes C, D, E, and that when you hear D you have no recollection whatsoever of having heard C, and similarly, by the time you hear E you have no recollection of having heard D (or C). You would experience the tones in sequence, but you would have no awareness of the sequence. Evidently, to experience a succession as a succession a sequence of experiences must be unified in some manner. It is here that retention theorists introduce a more contentious assumption:

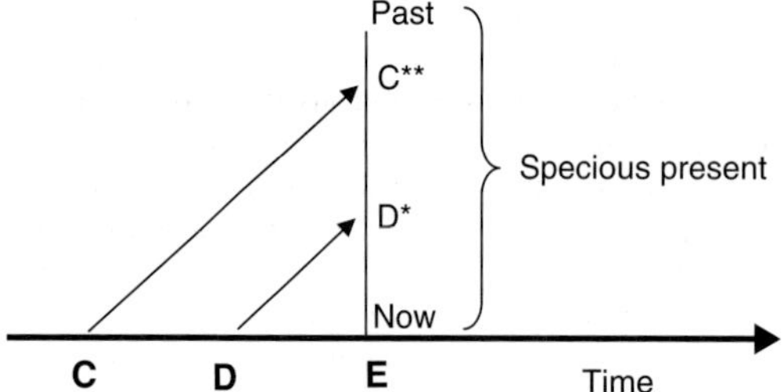

Fig. T1. Hearing the succession C–D–E.

they hold that for a succession of contents to be unified in experience they must be apprehended together simultaneously, in a single momentary apprehension. Following Miller (1984), let us call this the *principle of simultaneous awareness* (PSA). Accordingly, when we hear the succession C–D–E as a succession we first hear C and then hear D accompanied by a representation (or in Husserl's terminology, a *retention*) of C which places it in the very recent past, and then we hear E accompanied by a representation of D as 'just past' and C as 'more past' (Fig. T1). The simultaneous awareness of present and just-past phases of our *stream of consciousness underpins the experience of succession in such cases: when we hear the later note the earlier ones have not entirely vanished from our consciousness.

C. D. Broad (1938) expounded an account along these lines in more detail, and a yet more sophisticated—though at times obscure—account (or succession of accounts) had already been developed by Husserl, in his various writings on the topic. The relevant Husserlian texts can be found in Husserl (1991); see Miller (1984) for a useful exposition.

The retention approach faces two particularly pressing problems. The first concerns the relationship between neighbouring specious presents. The vertical line in Fig. T1 depicts just one specious present; in reality (if the retention theory were correct) it would be surrounded on each side by other specious presents, each with a slightly different content. If each specious present consists of an entirely self-contained phase of experience, it is by no means obvious how they can combine to form a continuous stream of consciousness of the sort we typically enjoy. The second difficult lies with the retentions themselves: how is that a collection of simultaneously occurring momentary contents can appear to be spread through time? Returning to Fig. T1, why is it that E, D*, and C** are apprehended as a succession rather than as a chord?

Husserl was well aware of both these potential pitfalls. He appreciated that successive stream-phases had to be connected, and postulated a level of 'absolute time-consciousness' to accomplish this. He also saw that if retentions were akin to ordinary memory-impressions they would not appear spread through time. He thus stipulated that retentions function in a different way: they directly present the past *as* past. Opinion remains divided over whether Husserl solved these problems, or merely appreciated what a successful solution would look like. (Dainton 2003, Gallagher 2003).

Despite these difficulties (and obscurities), the retention theory in its Husserlian guise has inspired work in cognitive science and neuroscience: see Van Gelder (1996), Varela (1999), Grush (2005).

2. Duration theories

Whereas the retention approach confines our immediate experience to momentary slices, duration theorists hold that it extends a short distance through time, and hence is well suited to embrace temporally extended events. When it comes to spelling out the precise manner in which our consciousness extends through time, opinions diverge.

In his earlier writings on time-perception in his *Scientific Thought*, Broad (1923) combined the thesis that our consciousness is temporally extended with PSA: he accomplished this by holding that we are at each moment aware of a short stretch of the recent past, in the manner depicted in Fig. T2. Only three momentary acts of awareness are shown here—A1, A2, A3—on Broad's view such acts form a dense succession.

This theory certainly allows us to see how the specious present could be 'the short duration of which we are immediately and incessantly sensible', but in other respects it is problematic. Since the contents of neighbouring awarenesses (such as A1 and A2) overlap, will not the same occurrences be experienced several times over? There is a further, and more general worry. If Broad's theory is correct, we are at each moment directly aware of what has been and gone. How plausible is this?

An alternative (and perhaps less problematic) form of the duration theory emerges if the commitment to PSA is dropped. Rather than supposing that the different phases of temporal spread of content are unified by being presented *simultaneously* to a momentary

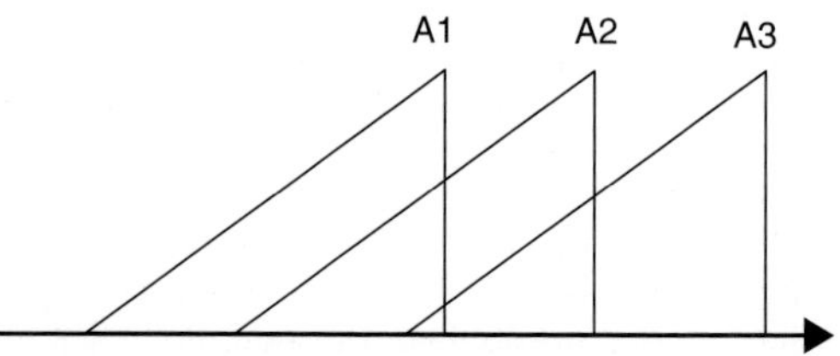

Fig. T2. Momentary acts of awareness.

awareness, we recognize that the relationship of 'experienced togetherness' (or *co-consciousness*) comes in synchronic and diachronic forms: co-consciousness can obtain at a time, but it can also obtain over (brief) intervals of time. When it does, the contents so unified have the form of what James termed a 'duration-block', i.e. a temporal spread that is apprehended as a temporally extended whole, a whole whose parts are connected by the relationship of diachronic co-consciousness. Since PSA has been abandoned, it is no longer being assumed that the successive phases of a duration-block are apprehended simultaneously at any one point in time: at the phenomenal level they exist only as a succession. Wholes of this kind are not fully experienced as such at each moment of their duration, rather they are experienced as wholes *over* the full course of their duration. (There may be a sense in which James's talk of a 'block' in this context is misleading: these units of experience are no means *static* or *frozen*, they typically contain change and movement.)

How do duration-blocks, thus conceived, combine to form a stream of consciousness? Since from a *phenomenological perspective our experience is typically continuous, not packaged into discrete pulses, it is not a (phenomenologically) viable option to hold that they are laid end to end, in the manner of a row of bricks. Continuity can be secured if neighbouring blocks *overlap*, by sharing common parts, in the manner shown in Fig. T3. Hence, and recalling our earlier example, if a subject hears a succession of tones C–D–E, this might take the form of two specious presents, one consisting of the succession C–D, the other D–E, where the experiencing of D in the latter is numerically identical with the experiencing of D in the former. If successive specious presents overlap in this manner, the repetitions which plagued Broad's version of the duration theory are eliminated.

This 'overlap' version of the duration approach circumvents some problems, but it also faces difficulties of its own. How is the apparent direction of experienced time to be explained on this view? Can phenomenal unity be spread through time in the way envisaged? For further discussion see Dainton (2000) and Kelly (2004).

3. Contents and vehicles

A signpost bearing the message 'I weigh a ton' need not itself weigh a ton, and what goes for signposts goes for thoughts and utterances and other modes of representation. Quite generally we need to distinguish between the *vehicle* of a representation and its *content*: the latter is the state of affairs represented, the former is what carries the representation. Although it is possible for vehicles to possess the properties represented by their contents—some signposts saying 'I weigh a ton' *do* weigh a ton—there is no need for them to do so: it may well be the case that no conscious thoughts carrying this content weigh anything like a ton.

Experiences have temporal features (they can extend through time) but they also have contents which represent temporal features. How do the temporal features of experiences which are the vehicles of such contents relate to the contents themselves? Since experiential contents can be classified in different ways this is potentially a complex issue, but some basic observations can be made. It is obvious that in the case of conscious thoughts there can be a wide discrepancy between vehicle-properties and content-properties: it can take almost no time at all to think 'This has been going on for hours'. In the case of perception, the time-lags created by the finite speed of signal transmission and neural processing mean we perceive events some time after they actually occur (millions of years in the case of distant stars). Discrepancies of this kind can be eliminated by construing 'content' in a narrow way, so as to refer only to the phenomenal features of our experiences, rather than their usually distant causes. Even when content is thus construed, on the retention model there remains a difference, of a systematic kind, between content- and vehicle-properties. The relevant vehicles are momentary (or very brief) experiences, but the phenomenal contents of these experiences are typically *not* momentary: the content of the momentary experience depicted in Fig. T1 is the sequence of phenomenal tones C–D–E. This divergence coexists with a correlation, in that there is no discrepancy between the order in which experiences occur and the order in which they are represented as occurring. Duration theorists agree that the latter correlation obtains but posit a still stronger one. The experience which carries the content C–D–E is itself extended over time. Indeed, if this content is construed narrowly (as denoting purely phenomenal items, as opposed to their environmental causes) the duration of the experiential vehicle and its content perfectly coincide.

Dennett moves in the opposite direction. He argues that (over quite brief time scales) there need be no correspondence between the order in which we represent events as occurring and the order in which these

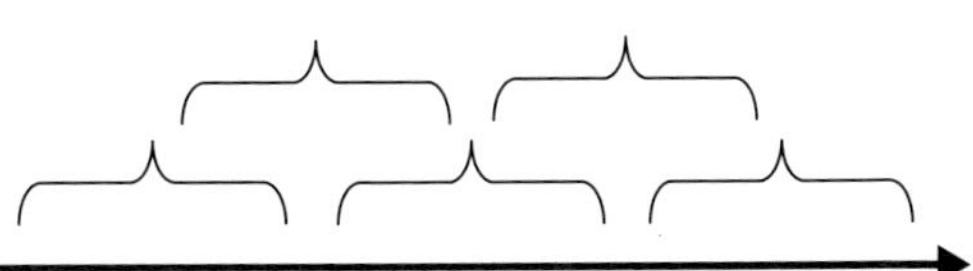

Fig. T3. Continuity secured by overlapping blocks.

events are apprehended: 'what matters is that the brain can proceed to control events 'under the assumption that A happened before B' whether or not the information that A has happened enters the relevant system of the brain and gets recognized as such before or after the information that B has happened.' (Dennett 1991:149) It is not obvious (to say the least) that this degree of dissociation is compatible with the phenomenology of temporal perception: when I directly perceive a succession C–D, it is hard to believe that my hearing of C occurs later than my hearing of D. But Dennett's propounds this view in the context of his *multiple drafts model, according to which there is no fact of the matter as to the precise moment at which a subject becomes conscious of a given stimulus. For Dennett, the project of attempting to discover the temporal microstructure of phenomenal consciousness is misconceived, and our consciousness does not possess the continuity writers such as James attribute to it—and in line with this Dennett often prefers to speak of 'informational vehicles' rather than 'experiences'. It goes without saying that Dennett's operationalist conception of consciousness—'There is no reality of conscious experience independent of the effects of the various vehicles of content on subsequent action' (1991: 132)—is itself contentious.

4. Psychophysical findings

If the specious present does exist (in one or other of the forms just outlined), what is its duration? Since there may well be intersubjective differences—and even in the case of a single subject, it may be different at different times—there may well be no one answer to this question. Nonetheless, we are all in a position to make our own rough estimations. If I clap my hands twice in a row, I am no longer experiencing the first clap when I hear the second, so an answer of 'a few seconds at most' has some plausibility, at least in the auditory case. James estimated that it typically extended to a dozen or so seconds, and sometimes more. Most commentators have found been baffled by James's opting for an estimation of this magnitude, and more recent experimental work (e.g. Rühnau 1995) suggests a far shorter duration.

Experimental evidence has given rise to further puzzles. One such derives from Libet's work on how long it takes our brains to turn a perceptual stimulus into a conscious experience (Libet 2004). Libet concluded that the delay is typically of the order of a full half-second. If this is correct the implications are potentially significant: since we frequently react to events in less than half a second, it seems that our conscious decision-making is often nothing more than an epiphenomenal after-effect. For critical discussion of Libet see Dennett (1991:Chs 5–6) and Pockett (2000).

For further relevant psychophysical results and discussion see TEMPORALITY, SCIENTIFIC PERSPECTIVES.

BARRY DAINTON

Broad, C. D. (1938). *An Examination of McTaggart's Philosophy.*

Dainton, B. (2000). *Stream of Consciousness.* London: Routledge.

Dainton, B. (2003). 'Time in experience: reply to Gallagher'. *Psyche,* 9.

Dennett, D. (1991). *Consciousness Explained.*

Gallagher, S. (2003). 'Syn-ing in the stream of experience: time-consciousness in Broad, Husserl, and Dainton'. *Psyche,* 9.

Grush, R. (2005). 'Brain time and phenomenological time'. In Brook, A. & Atkins, K. (eds) *Cognition and the Brain: The Philosophy and Neuroscience Movement.*

Husserl, E. (1991). *On the Phenomenology of the Consciousness of Internal Time* (1893–1917), ed. and transl. J. B. Brough.

James, W. (1890/1950) *The Principles of Psychology.*

Kelly, S. (2004). 'The Puzzle of Temporal Experience'. In Brook, A. and Atkins, K. (eds) *Philosophy and Neuroscience,* Cambridge: Cambridge University Press.

Libet, B. (2004). *Mind Time.*

Miller, I. (1984). *Husserl, Perception, and Temporal Awareness.*

Pockett, S. (2000). 'On subjective back-referral and how long it takes to become conscious of a stimulus: A reinterpretation of Libet's data'. *Consciousness and Cognition,* 11.

Rühnau, E. (1995). 'Time gestalt and the observer'. In Metzinger T. (ed.) *Conscious Experience.*

Van Gelder, T. (1996). 'Wooden iron? Husserlian phenomenology meets cognitive science'. *Electronic Journal of Philosophy,* 4.

Varela, F. (1999). 'Present-time consciousness'. *Journal of Consciousness Studies,* 6.

temporality, scientific perspectives Most of the actions that brains carry out on a daily basis—such as perceiving, speaking, and driving a car—require exact timing on the scale of tens to hundreds of milliseconds. Although this timing may seem effortless, brains in fact have a difficult problem to solve: signals from different modalities are processed at different speeds in distant neural regions. To be useful for a unified conscious impression of 'what just happened', signals must become aligned in time and correctly tagged to outside events. Understanding the timing of events—such as a motor act followed by a sensory consequence—is critical for moving, speaking, determining causality, and decoding the barrage of temporal patterns at our sensory receptors.

Scattered confederacies of investigators have been interested in time for decades, but only in the past decade has a concerted effort been applied to old problems. Now, experimental psychology is striving to understand how animals perceive and encode temporal intervals, while electrophysiology and neuroimaging unmask how neurons and brain regions underlie temporal computations. The questions being addressed include: How are signals entering various brain regions at varied times coordinated with one another for a unified conscious experience? What is the temporal precision with which perception represents the outside world? How are intervals, durations, and orders coded in the brain? What factors (causality, attention, adrenaline [epinephrine], eye movements) influence temporal judgements, and why? Does the brain constantly recalibrate its time perception?

Most of what we know about time in the brain comes from psychophysical experiments. One class of studies involves ways in which duration perception distorts—for example, observers can misperceive durations during rapid eye movements (saccades), or after adaptation to flickering or moving stimuli. More dramatically, during brief but dangerous events such as car accidents and robberies, many people report that events seem to have passed in slow motion, as though time slowed down. To test this sort of conscious experience, Stetson et al. (2007) dropped participants in free fall from a tower 150 feet (46 m) high (they were caught in a net below). During this 3 s psychophysical experiment, changes in the speed of visual processing were measured by a wristwatch-like display strapped to the participant's wrist. The surprising result: although participants retrospectively estimated (with a stopwatch) the duration of their own fall to be 35% longer than others' falls, they did not gain increased temporal resolution—in other words, they could not actually see the world in slow motion. This result illustrates that conscious 'time' is not a unified experience in the brain, but instead that aspects of it (e.g. durations) can change with no concomitant change in other aspects (e.g. flicker rate).

Safer experiments in the laboratory have confirmed this same conclusion. For example, when many stimuli are shown in succession, an unpredicted 'oddball' stimulus in the series appears to last subjectively longer than the repeated stimuli when they are presented for the same objective duration (Tse et al. 2004). This illusion was originally described as the 'subjective distortion of time', but we now know that it is only duration, not time in general, that is distorted: even during the perceptually expanded oddball, flicker rates do not change and auditory pitches do not lower.

It now seems likely that the story of time will emerge in the same manner as the story of vision. Although vision seems like an effortless, unified experience, it is underpinned by a motley crew of different neural mechanisms. The same applies in the temporal domain. Varied judgements—such as simultaneity, duration, flicker rate, order, and others—are underpinned by separate neural mechanisms that usually work in concert but are increasingly separable in the laboratory—demonstrating that their cooperation is typical but not necessary. The word 'time' is currently loaded with too much semantic weight; future experiments will be forced to be more specific about which aspect of time they are exploring, abandoning the naive assumption that time is a single, unified experience.

Another illustration that time perception is a construction of the brain comes from examples of its dynamic recalibration. Judging the order of action and sensation is essential for determining causality. Accordingly, the nervous system must be able to recalibrate its expectations about the normal temporal relationship between action and sensation in order to overcome changing neural latencies. A novel illusion in this domain shows not only that the perceived time of a sensation can change, but also that temporal order judgements of action and sensation can become reversed as a result of a normally adaptive recalibration process. When a fixed delay is consistently injected between the participant's keypress and a subsequent flash, adaptation to this delay induced a reversal of action and sensation: flashes appearing at delays shorter than the injected delay were perceived as occurring *before* the keypress (Stetson et al. 2006). This illusion appears to reflect a recalibration of motor-sensory timing, which results from a neural prior expectation that sensory consequences should follow motor acts with little delay.

Another clue in our search for understanding time in the brain is the basic temporal limits on perceiving various aspects of the visual world. Specialized processors in our visual system allow us to perceive certain changes rapidly, on timescales of a few dozen milliseconds or less. But when a specialized detector is not available for a visual timing judgement, the brain shows very poor temporal resolution (e.g. six changes per second; Holcombe and Cavanagh 2001). There is no single speed at which the brain processes information, consistent with the emerging picture that a diverse group of neural mechanisms mediates temporal judgements.

We have so far highlighted psychophysical findings which demonstrate that time judgements can distort, recalibrate, reverse, or have a range of resolutions depending on the stimulus and on the state of the viewer. But the theoretical details of the neural mechanisms are in debate. For the experience of duration, at least at short time scales, some have proposed a simple 'counter' model, in which one part of the brain provides the ticking of a pacemaker, and another mechanism acts like a counter. In this framework, distortions of time perception are thought to be the result of a speeding or slowing pacemaker. If the brain's assessment of duration is the result of the output of such a counter, it would come to the wrong conclusion that more objective time had passed.

The counter model has lost momentum, however, largely because no good evidence has emerged to support it. In contrast to a counter which integrates events, a 'state-dependent' network model proposes that the way network patterns evolve through time can code for time itself (Mauk and Buonomano 2004). In other words, as patterns of neural activity unfold through time, a snapshot of the pattern at every moment can encode how long it has been since the original event happened. This framework suggests that temporal processing is distributed throughout the brain rather than relying on a centralized timing area. Further experiments are needed to cleanly separate the domains of integrator models and state-dependent network models, and understanding the difference will be critical to our search for how brains tell time.

At the level of the behaving animal, experiments in monkeys have shown that neurons in the posterior parietal can encode signals related to the passage of time. In humans, *functional brain imaging studies such as PET and fMRI are identifying brain regions (including the posterior parietal area) that are involved in various sorts of temporal judgements.

Over the last decade researchers have come to view certain disorders—e.g. aphasias and dyslexias—as potentially being disorders of timing rather than disorders of language. Other deficits in time perception are found in a variety of disorders such as Parkinson's, attention deficit hyperactivity disorder (ADHD), and *schizophrenia. Ongoing studies of time in the brain are expected to uncover other contact points with clinical neuroscience.

DAVID M. EAGLEMAN

Buhusi, C. V. and Meck, W. H. (2005). 'What makes us tick? Functional and neural mechanisms of interval timing'. *Nature Reviews Neuroscience*, 6.

Holcombe, A. O. and Cavanagh, P. (2001). 'Early binding of feature pairs for visual perception'. *Nature Neuroscience*, 4

Mauk, M. D. and Buonomano, D. V. (2004). 'The neural basis of temporal processing'. *Annual Review of Neuroscience*, 27.

Stetson, C., Cui, X., Montague, P. R., and Eagleman, D. M. (2006). 'Motor-sensory recalibration leads to an illusory reversal of action and sensation'. *Neuron*, 51.

——, Fiesta, M. P., and Eagleman D. M. (2007). 'Does time really slow down during a frightening event?' *PLoS ONE*, 2.

Tse, P. U., Intriligator, J., Rivest, J., and Cavanagh, P. (2004). 'Attention and the subjective expansion of time'. *Perception and Psychophysics*, 66.

theory of mind and consciousness The human theory of mind (ToM) encompasses the cognitive and conceptual tools with which people grasp the mental states of others.

1. What ToM is and is not
2. The importance of ToM in social functioning
3. Research topics
4. ToM and consciousness

1. What ToM is and is not

The 'theory of mind' label is often used synonymously with terms such as *naive theory of action, folk psychology*, or *mind-reading*. Most fundamentally, ToM refers to the network of concepts and assumptions people make about what 'minds' are and how they relate to behaviour (Wellman 1990). Central elements in this network include the concepts of agency and intentionality, the distinction between observable behaviour and unobservable mental states, and distinctions among a number of specific mental states, such as belief, desire, intention, and various emotions (Malle 2005). Some scholars also include within the ToM label the cognitive mechanisms by which people come to represent others' mental states. But theorists disagree on which mechanisms are most central, and there are in fact many such mechanisms, such as rule-based inferences, stereotypes, simulation (e.g. grasping the other's mental states by running a 'model' composed of one's own mental states), emotional contagion (e.g. the mere presence of a joyful person makes another person joyful as well), and so on.

In addition to clarifying what ToM is, it is also important to clarify what it is not. ToM is not a set of cultural beliefs about mind and behaviour. Rather, it comprises a conceptual framework, a set of fundamental distinctions, requisite for developing any cultural beliefs about how minds and behaviour work. ToM is also not a set of social norms or obligations that can be adhered to or disregarded. A social norm might be to punish unintentional behaviours less than intentional ones, but the intentional–unintentional distinction itself is not a cultural norm. Strictly, ToM should also be distinguished from the *ability* to understand other minds. ToM provides the conceptual assumptions and distinctions on which a variety of psychological processes (inference, simulation, empathy, etc.) rely, and concepts and processes together constitute the person's ability to grasp mental states.

2. The importance of ToM in social functioning

Ubiquitous in social interaction, ToM is often taken for granted by ordinary people and scientists alike—after all, fish are usually the last to notice the water. But the importance of ToM in successful social functioning cannot be overstated, as people who appear to lack ToM often have tremendous difficulties in everyday social situations. Consider a man leaving a tip at a restaurant. Without a ToM, one could give a mechanistic account of this behaviour: 'The man left the money on the table because something forced his hand to grab his wallet, remove some money from it, and set the money on the table.' How would people with a ToM account for this behaviour? They would refer to beliefs, desires, and the agent's decision to act (Dennett 1987). For example, 'He left a tip because he wanted the waiter to know he appreciated the service'; or 'Because he thought that tipping is expected in this country'; or 'Because he had decided to become a more generous person and thought this was good opportunity to start.' For organisms with a ToM, these explanations not only clarify what caused the behaviour but how one can *make sense* of it as an interplay between the person's mental states and observable behaviour.

3. Research topics

Recent research on the human ToM has focused on a variety of topics: ToM's rapid development from infancy into the early school years; the possible absence of a genuine ToM even in our closest primate relatives (they appear to be excellent behaviour readers but apparently not mind-readers); the relationship between ToM and other faculties, such as executive functioning and language; the grounding of ToM in specific brain mechanisms; and the severe challenges for people who seem to lack ToM capacities—primarily *autistic individuals and perhaps some with *schizophrenia (Baron-Cohen et al. 2000).

4. ToM and consciousness

An emergent topic is the question of whether ToM is employed primarily consciously or unconsciously. If ToM is the conceptual framework on which a number of different psychological tools rely, then the answer is twofold. As a conceptual framework, ToM is normally unconscious (though it can be made conscious by specifically asking people about their conceptual assumptions). Among the cognitive mechanisms that operate on those concepts, some are conscious, some are not. Among the conscious ones, we can list active simulation of the other's mental states, search for prior knowledge about the behaviour, the agent, or the context, and specific attempts to detect subtle signs in the agent's outward behaviour that might reveal inward states. The list of unconscious processes is longer: tracking gaze and body orientation, parsing the behaviour stream into intention-relevant units, empathy by emotional contagion, reading of facial and body expressions that transparently indicate the underlying mental state, and projection of one's own beliefs and perceptions onto another person. For some of these unconscious processes, the perceiver may not literally represent a mental state, making them precursors or facilitators of ToM. Many of these processes have indeed been found operative at a very early age and some among other primates. Several researchers assume that a conscious grasp of mental states requires the prior operation, both ontogenetically and phylogenetically, of many of these unconscious processes.

Even unconscious ToM mechanisms can confer powerful adaptive advantages on the individual. Parsing others' intentional actions, recognizing their goal-directedness, and sensing in one's own affective system the affect of others both facilitates social coordination and opens opportunities for influence and manipulation. In addition, processes like emotional contagion may select for prosocial behaviours because making others feel good has the attractive consequence that, due to the automatic empathy with others' states, one feels good oneself. Indeed, there is experimental evidence that prosocial behaviour can produce positive mood in the helper.

If ToM has evolved from a more automatic and unconscious to a more deliberate and conscious variety, one might ask whether the evolution of ToM can tell us something about the evolution of consciousness. What might precipitate the emergence of conscious processes in social perception? Automatic processes are sufficient as long as the input stimuli fall within the sensitivity range of the response mechanism, such as prototypical facial expressions, coordinated gaze and body orientation, repeated behaviour patterns, and the like. However, when the input stimuli lie outside these ranges (e.g. because they are novel or ambiguous), the organism must respond with a more flexible system. Conscious processing appears to provide two distinct advantages: it slows down processing to gain time for 're-computing' the input stimuli, and it allows, in service of this re-computation, an open search for and consideration of any potentially relevant information, be it in the immediate situation or stored in memory. Thus, the organism interrupts a normally fast and fixed stimulus–response linkage and takes time to build a creative new link, holding and experimenting with several pieces of information simultaneously. The early origins of such conscious processing can be seen in the infant's longer looking times towards objects or scenes that violate the infant's assumptions; longer looking presumably equates here to a slowing and re-computing of information.

The slowing and creative re-computation as one aspect of consciousness both points to consciousness' important problem-solving function and makes intelligible why, as is assumed by many scholars, the evolution of ToM may have resulted from a ratcheting-up process in which humans had to become more sophisticated in order to make sense of ever more sophisticated conspecifics. Organisms with consciousness, who act upon novel stimuli with novel solutions, are less predictable than stimulus–response creatures. Such conscious organisms in turn pose new complex and surprising stimuli for their conspecifics, who have to consciously re-compute them and therefore show yet another level of novel responses, which figure as yet another layer of novel stimuli, and so on. Thus emerges an escalation between humans' complexity in behaviour and their complexity in perception. Interestingly, the perception of others as complex, creative, and unpredictable in response to novel situations may have given rise to the central assumption of ToM that humans are intentional agents who can make free choices. Conversely, humans' actual slowing and creative recomputation of stimuli may very well define the nature of free will.

Another aspect of the relationship between ToM and consciousness concerns conscious vs unconscious mental states as the *objects* of social perception. Perhaps the most remarkable mental states that organisms with a ToM represent are another's *conscious reasons* to act. Reasons, typically beliefs and desires, are seen as motivating and rationalizing an intention, which in turn constitutes perceived free will. In our times, humans additionally make inferences about unconscious motives. It is not clear whether these inferences occur in all cultures, or existed even 500 years ago. The conscious/unconscious distinction may represent merely a culturally bound application of the ToM framework to a new domain. Indeed, the domain of the unconscious is understood with the same concepts that apply to the mental domain in general: it contains specific states (e.g. beliefs, desires) that are not under the person's intentional control and are, in a sense, unobservable even to the person him- or herself.

Future ToM research will attempt to provide a coherent theory of how early infant cognition of behaviour develops into full-fledged adult inferences of mind; outline a similar progression at the evolutionary level; illuminate ToM deficits in some individuals and what might be done to ameliorate them; and document in more detail the social functions and adaptations afforded by a ToM. There will also be attempts to identify brain mechanisms that underlie ToM capacities, but because of the involvement of specific concepts and the breadth of the encompassed cognitive processes, the research will not provide a specific location but perhaps a better understanding of the interplay of all the elements that go into the complex phenomenon of a ToM.

See also AUTOMATICITY; COGNITION, UNCONSCIOUS; FUNCTIONS OF CONSCIOUSNESS;

BERTRAM F. MALLE AND JESS SCON HOLBROOK

Baron-Cohen, S., Tager-Flusberg, H., and Cohen, D. (eds) (2000). *Understanding Other Minds: Perspectives From Developmental Cognitive Neuroscience.*

Dennett, D. C. (1987). *The Intentional Stance.*

Malle, B. F. (2005). 'Folk theory of mind: conceptual foundations of human social cognition'. In Hassin, R. et al. (eds) *The New Unconscious.*

Wellman, H. (1990). *The Child's Theory of Mind.*

third person See FIRST PERSON/THIRD PERSON

threshold, objective vs subjective See DISSOCIATION METHODS

tickling Tickling is a pleasure that 'cannot be reproduced in the absence of another', as psychoanalyst Adam Phillips wrote (Phillips 1994). Why can't you tickle yourself? Evidence suggests that the sensory consequences of some self-generated movements are perceived differently from identical sensory input when it is externally generated. An example of such differential perception is the phenomenon that people cannot tickle themselves (e.g. Weiskrantz et al. 1971). We carried out a series of experiments to investigate why this is the case.

In the first set of experiments, subjects were asked to rate the sensation of a tactile stimulus on the palm of their hand when the correspondence between self-generated movement and its sensory consequences was altered. Subjects moved a robotic arm with their left hand and this movement caused a second foam-tipped robotic arm to move across their right palm. By using this robotic interface so that the tactile stimulus could be delivered under remote control by the subject, delays of 100, 200, and 300 ms were introduced between the movement of the left hand and the tactile stimulus on the right palm. The result is that the sensory stimulus no longer corresponds to what is predicted, so as the delay is increased the sensory prediction becomes less accurate. The results showed that subjects rated self-produced tactile stimulation as being less tickly, intense, and pleasant than an identical stimulus produced by the robot (Blakemore et al. 1999). Furthermore, subjects reported a progressive increase in the tickly rating as the delay was increased. These results suggest that the perceptual attenuation of self-produced tactile stimulation is due to precise sensory predictions. When there is no delay, a forward model correctly predicts the sensory consequences of the movement, so no sensory discrepancy ensues between the predicted and actual sensory information, and the motor command to the left hand can be used to attenuate the sensation on the right palm. As the sensory feedback deviates from the prediction of the model (by increasing the delay) the sensory discrepancy between the predicted and actual sensory feedback increases, which leads to a decrease in the amount of sensory attenuation.

In the second series of experiments, we investigated the neural basis of this phenomenon. In an fMRI study, subjects experienced tactile stimulation on their palm that was produced either by the subject himself, or by the experimenter. The results showed an increase in activity of the secondary somatosensory cortex (SII) and the anterior cingulate cortex (ACC) when subjects experienced an externally produced tactile stimulus relative to a self-produced tactile stimulus. The reduction in activity in these areas in response to self-produced tactile stimulation might be the physiological correlate of the reduced perception associated with this type of stimulation. While the decrease in activity in SII and ACC might underlie the reduced perception of self-produced tactile stimuli, the pattern of brain activity in the cerebellum suggests that this area is the source of the SII and ACC modulation. In SII and ACC, activity was attenuated by all movement: these areas were equally activated by movement that did and that did not result in tactile stimulation. In contrast, the right anterior cerebellar cortex was selectively deactivated by self-produced movement which resulted in a tactile stimulus, but not by movement alone, and significantly activated by externally produced tactile stimulation. This pattern suggests that the cerebellum differentiates between movements depending on their specific sensory consequences. A further experiment supported this hypothesis. When delays were introduced between the movement and its tactile consequences, cerebellar activity increased (Blakemore et al. 2001). The higher the delay, the higher was activity in the cerebellum. We suggest that the cerebellum is involved in signalling the discrepancy between predicted and actual sensory consequences of movements.

SARAH-JAYNE BLAKEMORE

Blakemore, S.-J., Wolpert, D. W., and Frith, C. D. (1998). 'Central cancellation of self-produced tickle sensation'. *Nature Neuroscience* 1.

——, Frith, C. D., and Wolpert, D. W. (1999). 'Spatiotemporal prediction modulates the perception of self-produced stimuli'. *Journal of Cognitive Neuroscience*, 11.

——, Frith, C. D., and Wolpert, D. W. (2001). 'The cerebellum is involved in predicting the sensory consequences of action'. *NeuroReport*, 12.

Phillips, A. (1994). *On Kissing, Tickling, and Being Bored. Psychoanalytic Essays on the Unexamined Life.*

Weiskrantz, L., Elliot, J., and Darlington, C. (1971). 'Preliminary observations of tickling oneself'. *Nature*, 230.

tip of the tongue See FEELING OF KNOWING

touch Touch is the most ill-defined sense modality. As Aristotle said 'It is a problem whether touch is a single sense or a group of senses . . . we are unable clearly to detect in the case of touch what the single subject is which . . . corresponds to sound in the case of hearing.' (Aristotle, *De Anima* 422b20–24).

1. What is touch?
2. Touch and reality
3. Touch and the body

1. What is touch?

If sensory modalities are to be individuated by their proper objects, there seems to be no single modality of touch, for there are too many proper objects: texture, temperature, solidity, humidity, contact, weight, pressure, force, material bodies. Other individuating criteria are equally problematic. There is no obvious proper organ for touch. The hands are too restrictive, but neither the skin nor the whole body is restrictive enough, for each contains other sensory organs. Looking for more specific organs, one faces the multiplicity of receptors involved in touch: nociceptors, thermoceptors, and mechanoreceptors (which themselves divide into Meissner and Pacinian corpuscles, Ruffini organs, Merkel discs, hair receptors, and bare nerve endings). Neuroscience textbooks often define touch extensionally as the sense mediated by cutaneous mechanoreceptors (except mechanical nociceptors), but this definition seems to be ad hoc.

A third option is to individuate senses by their **introspectible* character. Here again, it is not obvious what *qualia experiences of heat, weight, and humidity might have in common. One might argue that they all involve bodily feelings, but if so, pain, itches, tickles, experiences of taste, and proprioception should be considered as instances of tactile perception as well.

In response to these difficulties many theorists attempt to find a happy medium between splitting the sense of touch into multiple senses and reducing some proper objects to others. With respect to the first option, most people agree that touch differs from *senses of the body* (e.g. *proprioception, kinaesthesis, nociception, hunger, thirst). Likewise, the *sense of temperature* and the *sense of force* (or pressure) are widely held to be distinct (Weber 1846). More controversially, Katz (1925) distinguishes a specific *vibration sense*. With respect to the second option, one might reduce the felt properties of (a) hardness, solidity, weight, texture, and vibration to spatiotemporal patterns of pressures; (b) humidity, liquidity, and clamminess to complexes of felt pressures and temperatures; and, more controversially, (c) pressure to spatial properties of the body (Armstrong 1962, who has since abandoned this view).

There are, however, more radical responses to the problem of defining the sense of touch. The first holds that touch is not a sense, by denying the intentionality of tactile sensations. According to this view, experiences of touch are merely subjective feelings, contingently associated with physical contacts. The second strategy, attributed to Democritus by Aristotle, claims that all sensory modalities are forms of touch. Both strategies rely on a reduction of tact to mere physical contact.

If a definition can be given, one has still to distinguish between different types of touch. An influential distinction is between *passive touch*, which is static and merely cutaneous, and *active touch* (or haptics), which involves exploratory movements. However, this influential distinction suffers from several problems. First, not all movements are exploratory. The notion of active touch confuses the notions of kinaesthesis and motor control. When the subject's hand is moved by the experimenter, only kinaesthesis comes into play. Moreover, even when the body does not move, one may still distinguish between static touch (the pressure of the cat on your knees) and cinematic touch (the motion of the beetle on your arm). Second, there are different types of exploratory movements. One can follow the contours of an object, or one can grasp, lift, wield, and manipulate it with muscular effort. The latter has been called *effortful* or *dynamic* touch (Turvey and Carello 1995, Gibson 1966).

2. Touch and reality

Touch has often been claimed to play a special role in the origin and justification of our belief in the external world. In this respect, we might say that touch is the most objective of the senses because, unlike other sensory modalities, it is needed for common-sense realism. There are two main versions of this view.

(a) Kant suggested that the sense of touch is the most *reliable* sense because it puts us in direct contact with the world, leaving no room for distortion of the information coming from the object. Optical phenomena such as refraction or perspective distortions appear to have no tactual counterpart. Consequently, there is no need to postulate mental intermediaries, tactile sense-data, between us and the world (O'Shaughnessy 1989). Insofar as this view attempts to overcome the argument from illusion by denying the possibility of tactile illusions, it is probably false. Indeed, tactile illusions are possible because (1) one is not necessarily in direct contact with the touched object (e.g. prosthetic touch) and (2) even if one is in direct contact, the presence of other types of information like visual information may influence and distort tactile sensations. There is still room for misrepresentation after transduction, resulting in physiological and psychological illusions. There is no reason why those internal processes would be more reliable in the case of touch.

(b) The sense of touch is not necessarily more reliable than the other senses, but it is the only one to provide access to certain essential properties of physical bodies. This proposal has been developed in two rather different ways.

According to Berkeley, touch is the only sense that informs us about the third spatial dimension, in contrast with sight, which is only two-dimensional. However, one might respond that touch, on the contrary, is essentially a sequential and temporal sense that does not allow for direct perception of spatial properties (see Evans 1985). Another response is to question the assumption that vision is two-dimensional.

By contrast, Locke argued that touch is the only sense to provide us with perceptual access to the impenetrability of objects. This form of access involves both passive and active touch. Passive touch provides exclusive access to causal relationships of *forces* via cutaneous sensations of pressure. Active touch enables us to experience the *resistance* of objects to our will, which is often held to be at the origin of our belief in the external world (Katz 1925, Baldwin 1995).

3. Touch and the body

The second distinctive feature of touch is that it seems to be closely tied to the body (Katz 1925, O'Shaughnessy 1989, Martin 1992). However, since all sensory modalities somehow depend on bodily information, the challenge is to explain the uniqueness of the dependency between touch and bodily awareness. Are bodily sensations just a subjective *epiphenomenon, as Reid claimed, or do they constitutively calibrate touch?

O'Shaughnessy (1989) and Martin (1992) suggest that the body functions as a *template* for tactile perception, i.e. tactile perception of spatial properties of the object relies on the experience of similar properties of one's body. This is particularly salient for *shape* in active touch: we feel the circularity of a glass because we feel the circularity of the motion of our hand. Even in passive touch, the experience of the shape of objects might mirror the feeling of the concavities of the flesh. As to *size*, an object feels bigger if the touched body part feels temporarily elongated because of kinaesthetic illusions. This template function also holds for the experience of *location*: tactile properties are ascribed to a location within a spatial representation of the body. More precisely, the experimental literature has distinguished between two kinds of tactile localization depending on the context. Actions directed toward the location of tactile stimuli are based on a sensorimotor map. Judgements about their location are based on a visuospatial map. This distinction is illustrated by patients with numbsense who can point to the touched body part though they cannot identify it, while deafferented patients show the reverse dissociation.

We can highlight two kinds of difficulties for the template theory (Scott 2001). First, veridical tactile perception does not necessarily match proprioceptive sensations, as in extrasomatic touch. While scanning the outline of an object with a stick, the shape of the hand movement differs from the shape of the object. However, the template theory can reply that extrasomatic touch is prosthetic. Bodily awareness integrates tools as appendices of body.

Second, tactile *illusions are not necessarily linked with proprioceptive illusions. A stick that is seen curved also feels curved, despite the fact that the exploratory movement is straight. There seems to be a predominance of vision on touch over proprioception. However, the template theory can reply that in this illusion vision also influences proprioception. Here are some more illusions. If one places an object between one's fingers while they are crossed, one will feel two objects (Aristotle, *Metaphysics*). There is a mismatch between one's proprioceptive awareness of the crossed fingers and the tactile processing which does not take the fact that one's fingers are crossed into account. Similarly, if one rotates one's tongue by 90°, one will not perceive the orientation of a tactile stimulus applied to one's tongue as identical to the orientation of the tongue itself. Furthermore, if one crosses one's hands, one will have difficulty judging the temporal order of tactile stimulations delivered on the crossed hands due to conflict between the body-centred and the external frames of reference. The template of touch is not only proprioceptive, but also visual. These illusions raise a more important worry for the template theory: although they do not show that touch is completely independent of bodily awareness, they do point toward some possible dissociations between them.

The template theory can account for the privileged relations between touch and the body, at the cost of forbidding the possibility of mismatch between touch and proprioception. It is far from obvious that it can provide a homogeneous account of the different ways proprioception calibrates touch. To cope with these difficulties, one might claim that the proper objects of touch are perceived *relations* between the body and the world (Armstrong 1962).

Many questions still remain open about the dependency of touch on proprioception. Is it reciprocal, or is there a priority of proprioception over touch (O'Shaughnessy 1989)? Does proprioceptive information merely play a causal role or does it plays an epistemic role? Is the specific contribution of proprioception to touch part of the phenomenology of touch?

FRÉDÉRIQUE DE VIGNEMONT AND OLIVIER MASSIN

Armstrong, D. M. (1962). *Bodily Sensations*.
Baldwin, T. (1995). 'Objectivity, causality, and agency'. In Bermùdez, J. L. et al. (eds) *The Body and the Self.*
Evans, G. (1985). 'Molyneux's question'. In *Collected Papers*.
Gibson, J. J. (1966). *The Senses Considered as Perceptual Systems*.
Katz, D. (1925/1989). *The World of Touch*, trans. L. E. Krueger.
Martin, M. G. F. (1992). 'Sight and touch'. In Crane, T. (ed.) *The Contents of Experience*.
O'Shaughnessy, B. (1989). 'The sense of touch'. *Australasian Journal of Philosophy*, 67.
Scott, M. (2001). 'Tactual perception'. *Australasian Journal of Philosophy*, 79.
Turvey, M. T. and Carello, C. (1995). 'Dynamic touch'. In Epstein, W. and Rogers, S. (eds), *Handbook of Perception and Cognition: Vol. 5. Perception of Space and Motion*.
Weber, E. H. (1846/1996). 'Tastsinn und Gemeingefühl'. In Ross, H. E. and Murray D. J. (trans.) *E. H. Weber on the Tactile Senses*.

transcranial magnetic stimulation There are many ways of attempting to capture the scientific essence of consciousness. One can record brain activity that correlates with states of awareness (see CORRELATES OF CONSCIOUSNESS, SCIENTIFIC PERSPECTIVS; ELECTROENCEPHALOGRAPHY), study patients who have lost aspects of awareness (see BLINDSIGHT), or manipulate awareness by using psychological techniques (see CHANGE BLINDNESS). One can also directly interfere with states of awareness by stimulating neurologically intact brains. This is achieved by transcranial magnetic stimulation (TMS).

TMS operates by placing an electrical coil on the scalp of an experimental subject. A brief electrical current is passed through this coil and induces a magnetic field which passes through the scalp of the subject. The magnetic field in its turn induces an electrical field in the region of the brain underneath the coil and this electrical change stimulates neurons (see Walsh and Pascual-Leone 2003). The duration of a single magnetic pulse is less than 1 ms and it is therefore possible to interfere with brain processes at very fine levels of temporal resolution. Figure T4 shows a timeline of a sequence of events in a typical TMS application.

Because TMS can interfere with local brain processes with fine temporal resolution, it presents us with two powerful ways of making inferences about consciousness and other processes. It has been used most successfully in studies of visual awareness. Cowey and Walsh (2000) and Pascual-Leone and Walsh (2001) used TMS to explore the cortical connectivity and timing of interactions between brain areas necessary for visual awareness. By applying TMS to a region of the brain containing many movement-sensitive cells, Pascual-Leone and Walsh caused subjects to experience visual movement. By applying a second pulse of magnetic

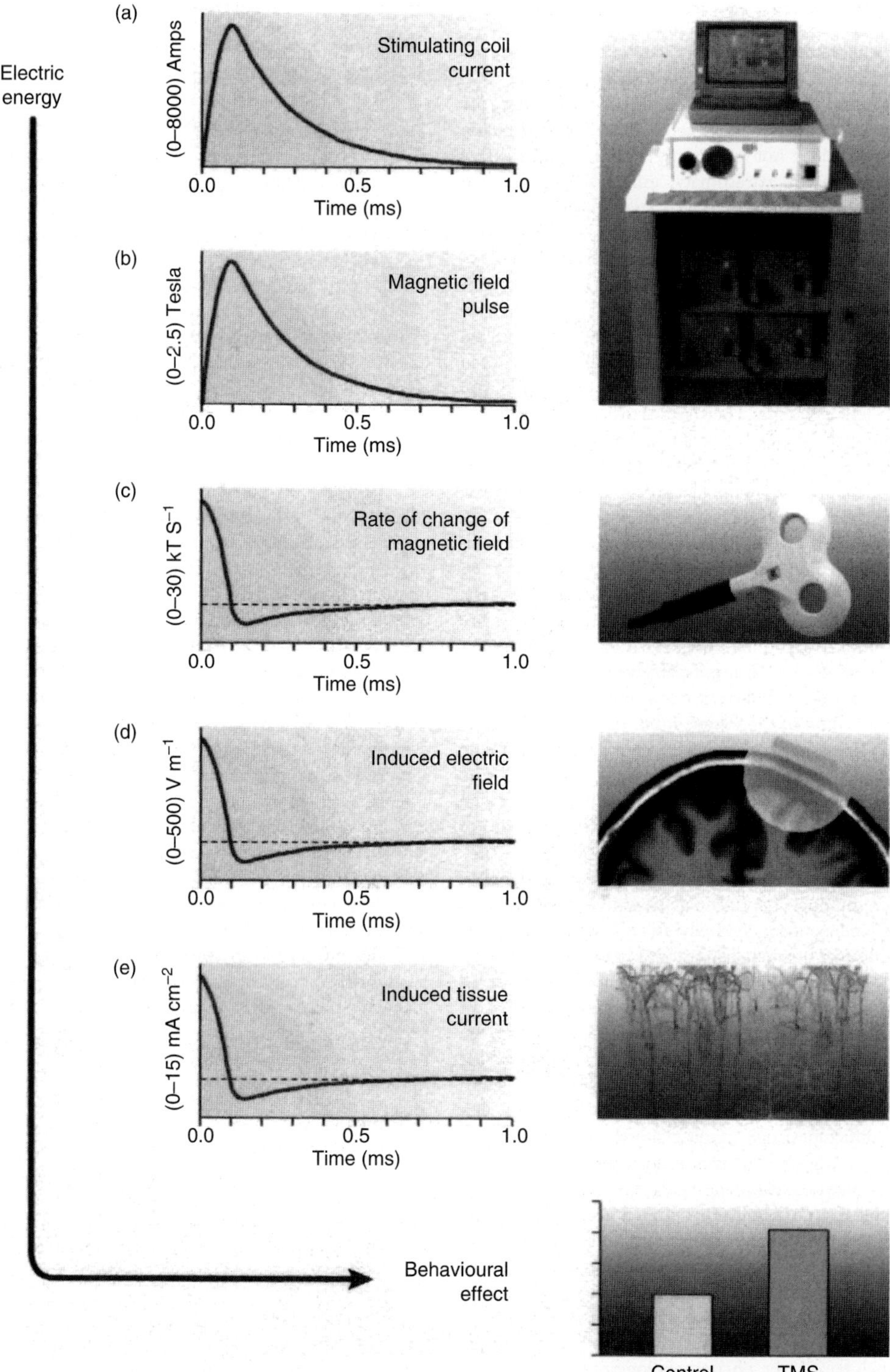

Fig. T4. Cycle of events in the application of a magnetic stimulation pulse. An electrical current is generated by the TMS stimulating unit and discharged into a circular or figure-of-eight shaped coil. Note the short rise time and duration of the pulse (a). The current generates a magnetic field pulse (b) which in turn induces a field in the brain and subsequent current changes in the underlying brain tissue (panels (c)–(e)).

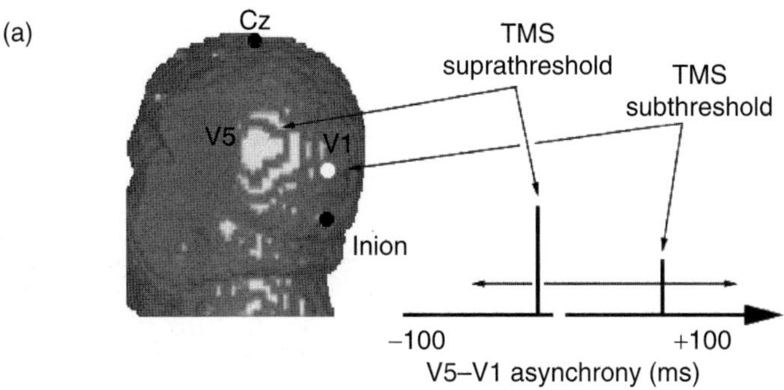

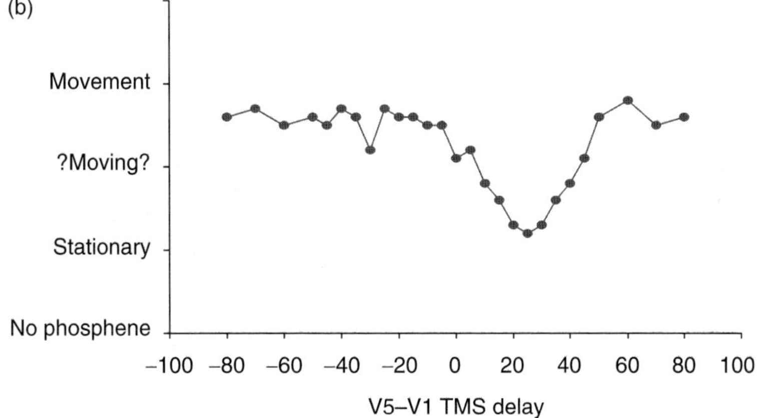

Fig. T5. An example of using the temporal resolution of magnetic stimulation, the differential effects of high and low intensity stimulation, and double coil stimulation to examine cortical connectivity. (a) Schematic of the experiment by Pascual-Leone and Walsh (2001). TMS was delivered over MT/V5 to induce the perception of movement and either preceding or following this pulse a single pulse of sub-threshold TMS was applied over V1. (b) The results show that the perception of movement was degraded or abolished when V1 stimulation post-dated V5 stimulation by approximately 15–40 ms. (after Pascual-Leone and Walsh 2001).

stimulation over the primary visual cortex (*V1) they were able to degrade and, depending on the timing of stimulation, abolish the sensation of visual movement. The effect of stimulating primary visual cortex was greatest when it occurred between 15 and 45 ms after the stimulation of the movement sensitive neurons. Figure T5 shows the sequence of events in this experiment. This experiment showed that our awareness of activity in parts of the brain that are responsive to visual stimulation is dependent on back-projections to V1.

TMS can also be used to control the level of stimulation in brain areas. Silvanto et al. (2005) exploited this to explore whether the level of activity in V1 was important in determining whether activity in other regions of the visual cortex reached awareness. In this experiment a region of the visual cortex containing movement-sensitive cells received TMS at a level of intensity sufficient to stimulate the neurons but not sufficient to induce an experience of visual movement. Within a few milliseconds of this stimulation TMS was also delivered over V1 at one of two levels of intensity: a level sufficient to induce a visual percept (a *phosphene*) or a lower level sufficient to stimulate the underlying neurons but not to induce a visual experience. Remarkably, when the level of V1 stimulation was high enough to induce a visual percept, the percept acquired characteristics of the neurons in the subliminally stimulated region of cortex containing visual movement-sensitive neurons. These perceptual characteristics could only have been carried by back projections from movement-sensitive neurons to V1. Thus TMS has established the necessity of V1 in visual awareness (Cowey and Walsh 2000, Pascual-Leone and Walsh 2001) and the fact that the level of activity in V1 gates access to visual experience (Silvanto et al. 2005). These findings are taken to speak very strongly against the *microconsciousness view of visual awareness, which predicts that activity in the movement-sensitive neurons would be sufficient for visual experience irrespective of V1 activity. They are more in line with the *re-entrant view of awareness.

TMS can be used in a simpler way to directly test whether a brain region is necessary for awareness. Any theory which proposes that a particular brain region is a necessary part of the circuits supporting consciousness must meet what might be called the 'lesion challenge': i.e. if a region of the brain is said to be important, then interfering with the normal processes of that region should also interfere with awareness. This is a test that has so far not been passed by any other region of cortex as impressively as V1, but there interesting suggestions that stimulating the right parietal cortex may affect awareness (see Walsh and Pascual-Leone 2003).

The phosphenes evoked by TMS in these and other studies are interesting in the context of consciousness and they have been evoked by electromagnetic stimulation for some time (see Fig. T6). When TMS is used to stimulate the regions of the brain responsible for hand movement, parts of the hand will twitch because TMS has introduced a disorganized pattern of firing into one of the motor areas of the brain. When TMS is applied to visual regions of the brain, the disorganized pattern of activity may be expressed as flash of light or a sensation of shimmering light. These light percepts are called phosphenes and their value lies in them as a means of activating the visual areas of the brain by bypassing the eye and pathways between the eye and the cortex. Cowey and Walsh (2000) used phosphenes to good effect to resolve a dispute about the patient G. Y. who has blindsight. There had been a long debate concerning whether G. Y.'s ability to accurately guess about the presence and even location of stimuli of which he was not aware was due to stray light in the retina. Cowey and Walsh were able to excite parts of G. Y.'s visual cortex without stimulating the eye and therefore avoiding stray light.

Phosphenes are intriguing in their own right. They tend to be colourless, but colours can be induced if subjects have adapted before TMS is applied. They tend to indistinct in form—'blurry, jagged edges, uneven brightness' are the kinds of comments subjects make, rather than reporting anything organized such as a face or an object. Much remains to be discovered about phosphenes and they promise to continue to provide an important method of parsing visual awareness. Figure T7 shows some examples of phosphenes drawn by subjects.

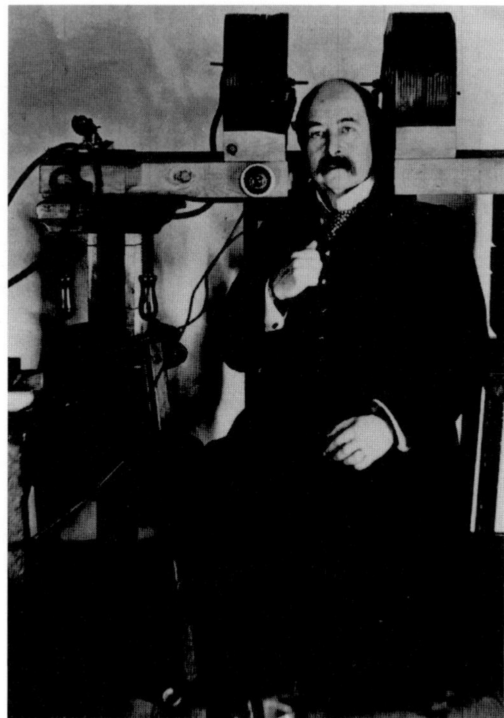

Fig. T6. Sylvanus P. Thompson (*c.*1910), one of the pioneers of brain stimulation.

We are of course not only aware of external events but are also aware of ourselves and TMS has been used to test whether brain activity related to self-awareness seen in *functional brain imaging (fMRI) studies is an essential for this experience. Keenan and colleagues (2001) applied repetitive pulses of TMS over the right prefrontal cortex and observed that subjects were less aware of their own faces than without stimulation. This is consistent with several other studies implicating the right prefrontal cortex in self-recognition. Keenan's finding is also important because it is indicative of different brain networks for different aspects of consciousness. Even severe damage to the prefrontal cortex or repetitive TMS over the left and right prefrontal cortex simultaneously does not interfere with visual awareness (Cowey and Walsh 2000).

The advantages of TMS, then, are in its temporal accuracy and the potential to study the necessity of a brain region's contribution to awareness. Future advances may depend on the integration of TMS with

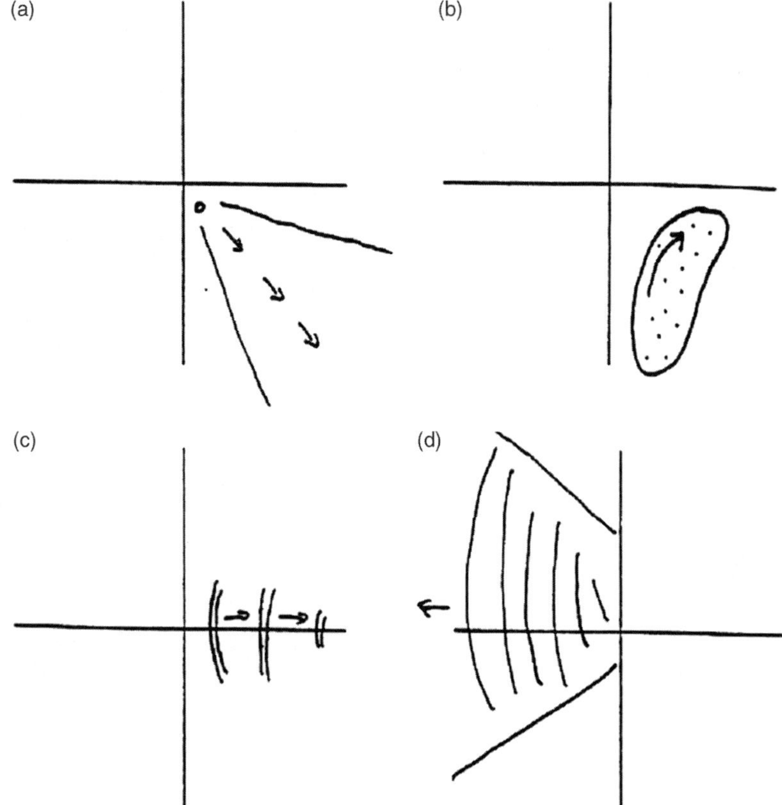

Fig. T7. Some examples of phosphenes drawn by subjects when TMS was applied over a region of the brain containing movement-selective cells. The arrows indicate the direction of perceived movement.

other techniques and in particular with electroencephalography (EEG) and fMRI. If brain activations are postulated to be necessary for awareness it should be possible to stimulate these or other connected brain regions prior to recording brain activity with EEG or fMRI and determine whether the brain activity under examination is modulated by different levels of awareness.

VINCENT WALSH

Cowey, A. and Walsh, V. (2000). Magnetically induced phosphenes in sighted, blind and blindsighted observers. *NeuroReport*, 11.

Keenan, J. P., Wheeler, M. A., Gallup Jr, G. G., and Pascual-Leone, A. (2001). Self recognition and the right prefrontal cortex. *Trends in Cognitive Sciences*, 4.

Pascual-Leone, A. and Walsh, V. (2001). Fast backprojections from the motion area to the primary visual area necessary for visual awareness. *Science*, 292.

Silvanto, J., Cowey, A., Lavie, N., and Walsh, V. (2005). Striate cortex (V1) activity gates awareness of motion. *Nature Neuroscience*, 8.

Walsh, V. and Pascual-Leone, A. (2003). *Transcranial Magnetic Stimulation: A Neurochronometrics of Mind.*

transitive consciousness See CONSCIOUSNESS, CONCEPTS OF

transparency Yesterday, turning my head from the computer in my office to the window, I caught sight of the sulphur crest of a cockatoo sitting in a branch opposite; I had, as philosophers say, a visual experience *as of* the sulfur crest. Later (having nothing better to do) I indulged in some *introspection. I reflected on this experience, asking myself how it might have been different had circumstances been otherwise: what if I had been wearing dark glasses, for example, or if it were later in the evening? This kind of reflection is often characterized as being directed inward, as being focused on my psychological states and how they might have been different. Indeed, the word 'introspection' itself suggests this sort of orientation. But if you think about what actually happens in this sort of case—on what we do when we do what is called 'introspection'—the opposite seems true. In the course of such reflection, my attention seems to be occupied, not on some psychological fact about myself, but completely on the sulfur crest. For if had been wearing dark glasses, it is the sulfur crest itself that would have looked different. This fact or seeming fact—that my attention is directed outward to the sulfur crest, rather than inward to my experience—is the so-called transparency of experience: in introspection, one apparently looks *through* the experience *to* the world, just as if the experience itself were transparent. The transparency of experience is sometimes known as the 'diaphanousness' of experience—the latter being the word the English philosopher G. E. Moore used in 'The refutation of idealism', the paper to which the original insight is often credited (see Moore 1903). The word 'diaphanousness' is cumbersome, and this is no doubt one reason that 'transparency' is commonly used. But 'transparency' has the disadvantage that it already has a number of established uses in philosophy for phenomena that have little to do with the fact about introspection at issue here. For example, in philosophy of language, a *transparent* linguistic context is one that permits substitution of coextensive terms *salva veritate*. This idea is quite unrelated to the transparency of experience, since here we are talking about experience, not bits of language. And 'transparent' is sometimes used in epistemology for the apparent *privileged access* of psychological states, the fact that at least some psychological states are such that if one is in them, one thereby bears knows or is in a position to know various facts about those states—that one is having it, for example, or various essential features of it. Privileged access is closer to transparency as intended here, but still different. When Moore and others talk about transparency, they are talking about what the focus of introspection is; they are not talking about any epistemological property of the experience.

The transparency of experience has played a significant role in philosophy of mind in the last hundred years or so. Moore himself drew attention to it in the course of arguing against *idealism, the view that reality is in some fundamental sense spiritual or mental—strange as now seems, a very influential doctrine in philosophical circles at the end of the 19th century. Idealists, in Moore's view, failed to distinguish between the act of having a sensation, on the one hand, and the object of the sensation, on the other: the sensing of something blue, and the something blue that one senses. Moore offered the transparency of experience as part of a psychological explanation of why idealists commit this mistake (assuming they do).

But Moore's point was almost immediately recognized as having a bearing on philosophy of mind more specifically. Writing only a year after Moore, William James (1904), the American philosopher and psychologist, argued that Moore did not go far enough. In his original paper, Moore says that when 'we try to introspect the sensation of blue, all we can see is the blue; the other element is as if it were diaphanous'. But he added: 'Yet it can be distinguished, if we look attentively enough, and know that there is something to look for.' For James, there is nothing 'as if' about it. Consciousness cannot be found, James thinks, for the simple reason it does not exist—at any rate, not if one means by 'consciousness' or 'experience' an object that might be the target of some perceptual like process. What we see in James is an example of certain style of philosophical reasoning often exhibited by discussions of transparency. It is alleged that ordinary thought about consciousness or experience implicitly supposes that there are objects called 'experiences' and that such objects can be seen by an act of inner perception. Transparency is then brought in to destroy this implicit supposition, often with the accompanying implication that, if one corrects for it, one would likewise be in a position to defuse the central metaphysical puzzles about the nature of experience, in particular, whether the existence of experience is compatible with a complete physical or scientific or objective theory of the world.

Later philosophers (at least in the analytic tradition) continue this tendency of discussing transparency in the context of the question of whether ordinary thought about experience embodies a mistake. C. D. Broad, a philosopher deeply influenced by Moore, is one who takes himself to be defending the picture. In *Mind and Its Place in Nature* (1925), he argues against those who appeal to transparency by drawing a distinction between introspection and inspection: one inspects the penny but introspects one's sensing the penny. And B. A. Farrell (1950), writing in the heyday of ordinary language philosophy, took himself to be attacking the idea of experience as an object, a position he summarized by saying that experience is featureless.

In contemporary philosophy, the idea that there is some conceptual mistake or confusion associated with various positions in philosophy of mind is less influential than it once was—in part because the underlying conception of philosophy as the removal of conceptual blockages to science is less influential. But the transparency of experience nevertheless continues to play an important role, particularly in the debate between *representationalists (or *intentionalists) and anti-representationalists (anti-intentionalists) in philosophy of mind. In this debate, the representationalist position says that the most basic fact about the mind is its ability to represent things as being thus and so. If that is so, then every difference in experience must at the end of the day be explained in terms of a representational difference. Transparency is often appealed to as a datum that supports this view. For example, transparency is sometimes said to support the premise that in introspection one has access only to the properties *represented in* one's experience and not to *properties of* one's experience. From this premise it is concluded that representationalism is true. Indeed representationalists often leave the strong impression that in their view the transparency point provides a very powerful, and perhaps decisive, argument in favour of representationalism (see Harman 1990).

How successful is the argument from transparency for representationalism? At the time of writing there is no consensus on this issue. But what a number of philosophers have argued is that the argument here is much less decisive and crisp than it might have seem (see Stoljar 2004). For one thing, the idea that one only has access to properties represented in experience is, if taken quite literally, false. Take the property of having an experience as opposed to imagining having an experience. It seems clear enough that we can distinguish these in introspection, at least in clear cases. But then it cannot be that we *only* have access to represented properties, for an experience and an imagined experience might represent precisely the same properties. Moreover, it is quite unclear that the phenomenology of introspection supports the claim (ignoring for the moment whether it is true) that one *only* has access to represented properties. The phenomenology seems to be a about where one's attention is primarily occupied; it does not seem to entail a negative thesis about what one has access to.

What all of this seems to indicate is that the transparency point is of limited value when it comes to deciding large-scale issues in philosophy of mind. On reflection, however, this is unsurprising. For just below the surface here is a more general epistemological question about the extent to which abstract theories may be viewed as being confirmed by relatively unadulterated reports of experience. The problem is that the theories themselves seem to recast the reports in their own image. Whether this is true in general is a big issue, but it certainly seems true in this part of philosophy of mind: representationalists tend to construe transparency in such a way that it supports their view; *mutatis mutandis* the anti-representationalists. DANIEL STOLJAR

Broad, C. D. (1925). *The Mind and Its Place in Nature.*

Farrell, B. A. (1950). 'Experience'. *Mind*, 59.

Harman, G. (1990). 'The intrinsic quality of experience'. *Philosophy of Mind and Action Theory: Philosophical Perspectives*, 4.

James, W. (1904). 'Does "consciousness" exist?' *Journal of Philosophy, Psychology and Scientific Method*, I.

Moore, G. E. (1903/1922). 'The refutation of idealism'. In Moore, G. E. *Philosophical Papers.*

Peacocke, C. (1983). *Sense and Content.*

Stoljar, D. (2004). 'The argument from diaphanousness'. In Ezcurdia, M. et al. (eds) *New Essays in The Philosophy of Mind and Language (Canadian Journal of Philosophy Supplementary Volume 30).*

Turing test The underlying idea of the Turing test is that whatever *acts* as if it is sufficiently intelligent *is* intelligent. 'If it walks like a duck and quacks like a duck, it probably is a duck.' So goes a pithy observation, undoubtedly as old as English itself, that provides a quick-and-dirty way to recognize ducks. This little maxim constitutes an operational means of duck identification that, for better or for worse, sidesteps all the thorny issues associated with actually explicitly defining a set of features allowing us to identify a duck (e.g. has feathers, can fly, weighs less than 5 kg, has webbed feet, swims well, has nucleated red blood cells, has a four-chambered heart, has a flat bill, etc.). What folk wisdom did for ducks, Alan Turing did for intelligence. He was the first to suggest an operational means of identifying intelligence that has come to be called the Turing test (Turing 1950). The underlying idea of his test is the same as our folk means of duck identification. Translated into the vernacular of modern electronic communication, the Turing test says that if, by means of an extended computer-mediated conversation alone, you cannot tell whether you are chatting with a machine or a person, then whomever or whatever you are chatting with is intelligent.

Since it first appeared nearly six decades ago, Turing's article has become the single most cited article in artificial intelligence. In fact, few articles in any field have caused so much ink to flow. References to the Turing test still appear regularly in artificial intelligence journals, philosophy journals, technical treatises, novels, and the popular press. Type 'Turing test' into any Internet search engine and there will be, literally, thousands of hits.

1. How the Turing test works
2. Commentary on the Turing test: two lines of argument

3. The Turing test as a graded measure of human intelligence and consciousness

1. How the Turing test works

Turing's original description of his 'Imitation Game' was somewhat more complicated than the simpler version that we describe below. However, there is essentially universal agreement that the additional complexity of the original version adds nothing of substance to its slightly simplified reformulation that we refer to today as the Turing test.

The Turing test starts by supposing that there are two rooms, one of which contains a person, the other a computer. Both rooms are linked by means of text-only communication to an Interrogator whose job it is, by means of questioning the entities in each room, to determine which room contains the computer and which the person. Any and all questions that can be transmitted via typed text are fair game. If after a lengthy session of no-holds-barred questions, the Interrogator cannot distinguish the computer from the person, then the computer is declared to be intelligent (i.e. to be thinking). It is important to note that *failing the Turing test proves nothing*. It is designed to be a sufficient, but not necessary, condition for intelligence.

2. Commentary on the Turing test: two lines of argument

There have been numerous approaches to discussing the Turing test (see French 2000, Saygin et al. 2000, Shieber 2004 for reviews.) The first, and by far the most frequent, set of commentaries on the Turing test attempt to show that if a machine did indeed succeed in passing it, that this alone would not necessarily imply that the machine was intelligent (e.g. Scriven 1953, Gunderson 1964, Purtill 1971 and more recently Searle 1980, Block 1981, Copeland 2000 who argue against the 'behaviouristic'—i.e. input/output (I/O) only—nature of the Turing test). Numerous authors (e.g. Millar 1973, Moor 1976, Dennett 1985, Hofstadter and Dennett 1981) argued, on the contrary, that passing the test would indeed constitute a sufficient test for intelligence. Certain authors (e.g. Dennett 1985, French 1990, Harnad 1991) also emphasized the enormous, if not insurmountable, difficulties a machine would have in actually passing the test.

The I/O-only nature of the Turing test has been the basis of several important criticisms (see, in particular, Block 1981, Copeland 2000, and the *Chinese room argument of Searle 1980 and Harnad 1991). Just as critics of behaviourism, arguably beginning with Tolman (1948), have repeatedly demonstrated that there is more to cognition than mere behaviouristic I/O, the 'behaviourism' critics of the Turing test contend that there is more to human intelligence than could ever be elicited by an typewritten I/O exchange with a machine. Consequently, they claim, a machine might well pass the I/O-alone subset of human cognition that the Turing test is capable of testing for, but, since that is only a subset of cognition, passing the Turing test would be insufficient to demonstrate real human intelligence. In short, the Turing test tests only for 'I/O cognition,' not full cognition, and, as such, is not testing for full human intelligence.

Various authors take another tack and emphasize the test's extreme difficulties. French (1990), for example, takes issue with Turing's assumption that a disembodied machine that had not experienced the world as we humans had could ever actually pass the Turing test. In French's argument the Interrogator relies on the vast web of 'sub-cognitive' (i.e. unconscious) associations that we humans develop over the course of a lifetime of interacting with the world. He has the Interrogator go out prior to the start of the Turing test and ask a large number of randomly chosen people questions that derive from their interactions with the world over the course of their lifetime, such as: On a scale of 1 to 10, rate kisses as medicine, billiard balls as Christmas ornaments, credit cards as banana peels, etc. He asks them questions that derive from the fact that humans have bodies that are designed in a very particular way, e.g. 'Is holding a gulp of Coke in your mouth more like having pins and needles in your feet or having cold water poured on your head?' The Interrogator then collects all the responses and calculates the distribution of answers for each question. Then he puts the same set of questions to the entities in both rooms. The entity whose set of answers is farthest from those of people is the computer.

Crucially, all of the replies to these sub-cognitive questions are based, not on logic or reasoning or memorized facts, but, rather, on having a human body and on having experienced the world as we have. Not having either a human body or benefiting from human experience, any computer now, or in the foreseeable future, would have immense—arguably insurmountable—difficulties answering questions of this kind as humans do. In other words, the Turing test is not actually testing for (general) intelligence, but is rather a test for intelligence in humans, with human bodies, having experienced life as a human being.

3. The Turing test as a graded measure of human intelligence and consciousness

The Turing test is a discrete pass/fail test. Machines that pass a no-holds-barred Turing test are said to be intelligent; as for those that do not, we withhold judgement. But what if a machine *almost* passed the test? Let us assume that only after an hour of intense questioning with sub-cognitive questions does the Interrogator even begin to suspect that the entity in, say, Room 1 might be the computer. It then takes another full hour for him to correctly identify the computer. Would we not be willing to grant that this machine has a higher degree of intelligence than one for which the same conclusion (i.e. correctly deciding that it was a machine) had been reached in a single minute of questioning? Most likely.

The idea then is that we could use the Turing test as a way of providing a *graded* assessment, rather than an all-or-nothing decision, on the intelligence of the machine. Thus, the further the machine's answers were from average human answers, the less intelligent it would be.

In like manner, the Turing test could potentially be adapted to provide a graded test for human consciousness. The Interrogator would draw up a list of sub-cognitive question that explicitly dealt with subjective perceptions, like the question about holding Coca-Cola in one's mouth, about sensations, about subjective perceptions of a wide range of things, etc. As before, the Interrogator would pose these questions to a large sample of randomly chosen people. And then, as for the graded Turing test for intelligence, the divergence of the computer's answers with respect to the average answers of the people in the random sample would constitute a 'measure of human consciousness' with respect to our own consciousness. In short, the Turing test, with an appropriately tailored set of questions, given first to a random sample of people, could be used to provide an operational means of assessing consciousness.

ROBERT M. FRENCH

Block, N. (1981). 'Psychologism and behaviourism'. *Philosophical Review*, 90.

Copeland, B. J. (2000). 'The Turing test' *Minds and Machines*, 10.

Dennett, D. (1985). 'Can machines think?' In Shafto, M. (ed.) *How We Know*.

French, R. M. (1990). 'Subcognition and the limits of the Turing test'. *Mind*, 99.

——. 'The Turing test: the first 50 years'. *Trends in Cognitive Sciences*, 4.

Harnad, S. (1991). 'Other bodies, other minds: a machine incarnation of an old philosophical problem'. *Minds and Machines*, 1.

Hofstadter, D. and Dennett, D. (1981). 'Reflections on "Minds, Brains, and Programs"'. In *The Mind's I*.

Millar, P. (1973). 'On the point of the Imitation Game'. *Mind*, 82.

Moor, J. (1976). 'An analysis of the Turing test'. *Philosophical Studies*, 30.

Purtill, R. (1971). 'Beating the imitation game'. *Mind*, 80.

Saygin, A. P., Cicekli, I., and Akman, V. Turing test: 50 years later. *Mind and Machines*, 10.

Scriven, M. (1953). 'The mechanical concept of mind'. *Mind*, 62.

Searle, J. (1980). 'Minds, brains and programs'. *Behavioural and Brain Sciences*, 3.

Shieber, S. M. (2004). *The Turing Test. Verbal Behavior as the Hallmark of Intelligence*.

Tolman, E. C. (1948). 'Cognitive maps in rats and men'. *Psychological Review*, 55.

Turing, A. (1950). 'Computing machinery and intelligence'. *Mind*, 59.

Twin Earth See FUNCTIONALIST THEORIES OF CONSCIOUSNESS; INVERTED SPECTRUM

U

unity of consciousness At any one point in time we typically enjoy a rich phenomenal perspective. I can currently hear the music of Charles Mingus, see these words on my computer monitor, taste and smell the olives that I am eating, and sense a slight ache in my shoulders. Arguably, each of these experiences (and more) contributes to my overall conscious state—each experience plays a role in fixing what it is currently like to be me (see 'WHAT IT'S LIKE'. These experiences are not merely had by me, they are had by me in a certain kind of way: as unified with each other in a single phenomenal perspective.

The issues raised by the unity of consciousness cluster around three headings. What forms can the unity of consciousness take? To what degree is consciousness unified? How might we explain the unity of consciousness?

1. The varieties of unity
2. To what extent is consciousness unified?
3. Explaining the unity of consciousness

1. The varieties of unity

Although it is common to speak of *the* unity of consciousness, there are in fact a variety of ways in which experiences can be unified. This section surveys some of the central forms of unity to be found within consciousness. I focus here on the unity of consciousness at a single time and leave to one side the unity of consciousness as it holds across time—that is, its continuity.

One form of the unity of consciousness concerns the fact that conscious states are had by subjects of experience. Let us describe conscious states that are had by the same subject of experience as *subject unified*. Your visual and auditory experiences are subject unified with each other, but neither of these experiences is subject unified with my visual or auditory experiences. What precisely subject unity amounts to depends to a large degree on what subjects of experience are, but we can agree that subject unity plays an important role in structuring consciousness without agreeing on how to conceive of subjects of experience. Closely related to subject unity is the sense that self-conscious subjects have of being a single subject of experience (Rosenthal 2003). We might think of this as the unity of subjectivity.

A second kind of unity to be found within consciousness concerns its representational content. It is a matter of some controversy whether all conscious states have representational content, but certainly many do. One's visual experience might represent a black dog standing in front of a cluster of trees, one's auditory experience might represent the barking of the dog and the approach of a police car, and one's bodily experience might represent one's hands as being raised above one's head. The representational content of consciousness involves both what we might call *object unity* and *spatial unity*. Experiences are object unified insofar as they represent objects as unified entities. For example, my visual experience of the dog and my auditory experience of the dog are object unified in so far as they are directed at one and the same object. My visual and auditory experiences are spatially unified in that their intentional objects are presented as occurring within a common space; for example, I might experience the ambulance as moving towards the dog. More generally, one sees, hears and feels objects as bearing determinate spatial relations to each other and to oneself.

The *contents of consciousness are typically available to a range of consuming systems—systems that drive belief-formation, voluntary agency, verbal report, memory consolidation, and so on. For any set of conscious states, we can ask whether the contents of those states are available to the same consuming systems. Let us say that conscious states are *access unified* when, and only when, their contents are available to the same consuming systems. If a pain experience is access unified with an olfactory experience, then any consuming system that has access to the content of the experience of pain will also have access to the content of the olfactory experience and vice versa.

Each of the unity relations described thus far captures an important sense in which consciousness is unified, but there is a fundamental sense of unity within consciousness that we have not yet identified. As we noted in the introduction, a person's simultaneous conscious states are typically contained within an overall phenomenal 'perspective' or 'field'. My experiences of hearing the music of Mingus, seeing words on a computer monitor, and tasting olives do not occur in isolation from each but occur together, as components of a phenomenal whole. States that are unified in this way are said to be *co-conscious* or *phenomenally unified*.

Although the notion of co-consciousness is often left unanalysed, a number of theorists have attempted to give accounts of it (see Tye 2003, Dainton 2006). One such analysis proceeds in terms of a subsumption relation between conscious states (Bayne and Chalmers 2003). This analysis holds that conscious states *e1* and *e2* are co-conscious exactly when there is a conscious state (*e3*) that subsumes them both. The subsumption relation can itself be understood in various ways, but at a minimum we should suppose that *e3* captures the phenomenology of both *e1* and *e2*: what it is like to be in state *e3* guarantees what it is like to be in *e1* and *e2*. On this approach, we might think of unified conscious states as parts, aspects, or components of those states that subsume them. It is an open question whether the subsumptive analysis can itself be understood in more primitive terms. Some theorists have argued that co-consciousness must be taken as a primitive unity relation (Dainton 2006). Others have argued that co-consciousness can be analysed in representational terms—that it goes together with the closure of conscious content under co-instantiated conjunction (Tye 2003, Hurley 1998). Exactly how best to understand co-consciousness is a matter of ongoing debate.

A second issue raised by co-consciousness concerns its logical structure. Here, the literature has focused on whether co-consciousness is a transitive relation, at least where simultaneous states are concerned. (A relation *R* is transitive when it is such that *aRb* and *bRc* entails *aRc*.) Take three particular experiences, *e1*, *e2*, and *e3*: if *e1* and *e2* are each co-conscious with *e3*, must *e1* and *e2* be co-conscious with each other? Some theorists answer this question in the affirmative (Dainton 2006), others in the negative (Lockwood 1989). The resolution of this debate has important implications, both for our understanding of co-consciousness and for the question of whether consciousness is necessarily unified. To that topic we now turn.

2. To what extent is consciousness unified?

There is little consensus as to how much unity there is within consciousness. Some theorists hold that consciousness is rarely unified to any considerable degree, others hold that although consciousness is typically unified (in humans at least) this unity can break down in the context of pathologies of consciousness, and still others hold that there is some sense in which consciousness is necessarily unified. Although there are substantive disagreements here, it is difficult to disentangle them from terminological disagreements, for even a cursory glance at the literature reveals that a large number of things have been meant by the claim that consciousness is or is not unified. Some forms of unity can clearly be lost from consciousness, but other forms of unity may be deep, and perhaps even necessary, features of consciousness.

Let us begin with subject unity. There is a sense in which subject unity itself cannot be lost, for conscious states must always be the states of a particular subject of experience. However, there are various pathologies of consciousness in which the subject's *sense* of being a unified subject of experience is disrupted. For example, patients suffering from the *schizophrenic disorder of thought insertion will describe thoughts as being put into their mind by an alien agency. Certain aspects of the sense of being a unified subject of experience may also be undermined in the depersonalization syndrome, in which patients often report that it is *as if* their experiences are no longer their own.

Pathologies of consciousness also provide us with examples in which aspects of the representational unity of consciousness are compromised. In apperceptive *agnosia, the normal experience of objects as unified wholes is lost. Patients experience the various features of visually presented objects, but are unable to synthesize those features into representations of unitary objects. In certain types of *out-of-body experience perception may lose the spatial unity that it normally has, for subjects report that they experience the world from discontinuous spatial locations.

What about access unity? Many theories of consciousness take access unity as a kind of theoretical ideal, assuming that once performance limitations of various kinds are taken into account the contents of consciousness will be equally available for cognitive and behavioural consumption. It is very much an open question whether this assumption is justified. At the very least, certain experimental findings put pressure on it. We have space here to mention only Marcel's (1993) results. Marcel presented subjects with a light for 200 ms, and required subjects to report the onset of the light in three ways at once: by blinking, by pressing a button, and by saying yes. Surprisingly, he found that subjects often gave inconsistent responses: e.g. a subject's positive button-pressing response might be at odds with his negative verbal response.

Perhaps the most intense debate regarding the question of whether consciousness is unified has concerned the relationship between subject unity and co-consciousness. According to one conception of the unity of consciousness, it is not possible for a subject to have simultaneous conscious states that are not co-conscious. Bayne and Chalmers (2003) call this the *unity thesis*. Let us examine some objections to the unity thesis. In order to simplify discussion I will assume that subjects of experience are organisms.

Many objections to the unity thesis involve dissociative phenomena, such as automatic writing, fugue states and multiple personality (now known as *dissociative identity disorder). These phenomena received detailed examination by Alfred Binet, William James, and Morton Prince in the 19th century, and were commonly thought to show that 'in certain persons, at least, the total possible consciousness may be split into parts which coexist but mutually ignore each other' (James 1890:206). The tradition of appealing to dissociative phenomena as evidence against the claim that consciousness is necessarily unified continued into the 20th century, with Ernest Hilgard arguing that the unity of consciousness is lost under hypnosis. However, the interpretation of these syndromes is extremely challenging (see Braude 1995). It is clear that dissociation involves various kinds of representational and access disunities, but it is debatable whether it ever involves the simultaneous existence of two separate *streams of consciousness in a single subject (Bayne 2007).

Since the 1970s, discussion of the unity of consciousness has been dominated by the *commissurotomy (or split-brain) syndrome. Commissurotomy involves sectioning the corpus callosum in order to treat *epilepsy. Although the procedure has little impact on cognitive function in everyday life, carefully controlled research seems to show that commissurotomy patients have a divided consciousness, at least in certain environments. In an example of a typical split-brain experiment, the word 'keyring' might be presented so that 'key' falls within the patient's left visual field and 'ring' falls within the patient's right visual field. The contralateral structure of the visual system ensures that stimuli projected to the left visual field are processed in the right hemisphere and vice versa. When asked to report what she sees the patient will say that she sees only the word 'ring', yet, with her left hand the patient may select a picture of a key, ignoring pictures of a ring and a keyring.

Many theorists endorse the two-streams model of the split brain, according to which split-brain patients have two streams of consciousness, one in each hemisphere (e.g. Marks 1981, Sperry 1984, Tye 2003). It is this duality of consciousness which is thought to explain: (1) why the patient appears to have a conscious representation of 'key' and 'ring' but no representation of 'keyring'; and (2) why the patient's representations of 'key' and 'ring' are available to different consuming systems. Two-streams accounts of the split brain are well-equipped to explain the behavioural disunity that patients exhibit in laboratory conditions, but they struggle to account for the unity that split-brain patients exhibit in everyday situations. Some two-stream theorists attempt to explain this unity by adopting the 'duplication gambit', according to which the commissurotomy patient has behavioural integrity because their two streams of consciousness have the same contents. Other two-streamers hold that the patient's stream of consciousness is normally unified and divides into two only in laboratory conditions.

Another model of the split brain holds that such patients have a fragmented stream of consciousness, in that they have triples of conscious states (*e1*, *e2*, and *e3*) such that *e1* and *e2* are each co-conscious with *e3* but not with each other (Lockwood 1989). This model attempts to account for both the unity and disunity exhibited by commissurotomy patients. However, as we noted above, it is controversial whether consciousness *can* fragment in this way.

A third model of the split brain holds that consciousness in the split brain switches between hemispheres (Bayne 2008). A central line of evidence for this approach derives from research conducted by Levy and Trevarthen involving chimeric stimuli (i.e. similar stimuli joined at the vertical midline; Levy 1977). Since each hemisphere receives information about a different stimulus one would expect the subject to produce conflicting responses if both left-hemisphere and right-hemisphere representations were conscious, but no such conflict was observed. Patients gave one response on the vast majority of competitive trials, and the non-responding hemisphere gave no evidence that it had any conscious perception at all. In light of these findings, one might suppose that consciousness in the split brain switches between hemispheres, and that at any one time the split-brain patient has but a single stream of consciousness. If this model is correct, then perhaps consciousness is always unified, even in those human beings in whom the corpus callosum has been severed.

3. Explaining the unity of consciousness

Of the many complex issues surrounding the unity of consciousness, explanatory issues are arguably the most obscure. Perhaps the only point that is clear is that we should not be looking for a single explanation of the unity of consciousness: not only are there different forms of the unity of consciousness, particular types of unity might each demand a variety of explanations. As Hurley points out, the unity of consciousness might demand both personal and sub-personal levels of explanation (Hurley 1998).

The task of explaining object unity has been pursued under the heading of the *binding problem: what is it that binds the various experiential features of an object together into a representation of a unitary object? There is at present no consensus as to how the binding problem ought to be solved; indeed, there is little consensus about the nature of the problem. It is also controversial whether the binding problem might be related to wider questions concerning consciousness. Although it has often been assumed that the mechanisms of object binding are intimately related to the mechanisms responsible for consciousness itself, convincing arguments for this claim are rather thin on the ground.

What about co-consciousness? How might we explain why it is that a person's simultaneous experiences are usually (if not always) mutually co-conscious? Here it is useful to contrast atomistic theories of consciousness with holistic theories of consciousness. Current theories tend to take an atomistic or 'building block' (Searle 2000) approach to consciousness. Rather than account for the subject's entire phenomenal field at once, they account for particular conscious states—a pain, a visual experience, a conscious thought—on a case-by-case basis. Atomistic accounts of consciousness posit one mechanism responsible for making mental states conscious and another for making them co-conscious. There is no shortage of proposals for what the first mechanism might be, but theorists have been noticeably reluctant to tackle the question of what might bind experiential states together. Note, importantly, that this kind of binding problem is distinct from the content-based binding problem discussed in the previous paragraph.

Instead of positing one mechanism responsible for consciousness and another that is responsible for the unity of consciousness, holistic theorists invoke a single mechanism responsible for both making mental states conscious and putting them together into a single phenomenal field. According to such models, consciousness is created as a single global state of which the various conscious states—bodily sensations, thoughts, perceptual states, affective states, and so on—are components or abstractions. There are various ways in which this holistic approach might be developed. Accounts of consciousness that posit some form of centralized consciousness module or workspace are most naturally understood in holistic terms. One particularly appealing approach looks to the domain-general enabling mechanisms that are involved in mediating the transition from unconsciousness to consciousness. Perhaps such systems not only enable the creature to be consciousness but also play a role in ensuring that the conscious creature has a single phenomenal field.

The debate between atomistic and holistic approaches to consciousness is very much a live one. The plausibility of each approach depends to some degree on just how common breakdowns in co-consciousness are. Atomism would be buoyed if such breakdowns are common, for holistic approaches struggle to explain how a subject's conscious states could be conscious without being conscious together. On the other hand, the prospects of holism would be advanced if such breakdowns do not occur (or are exceedingly rare), for the absence of phenomenal disunity is precisely what one would expect were consciousness to have a fundamentally holistic structure. Not surprisingly, debates about how best to explain the unity of consciousness cannot be separated from debates about the degree to which consciousness is unified.

TIM BAYNE

Bayne, T. (2007). Hypnosis and the unity of consciousness. In Jamieson, G. (ed.) *Hypnosis and Conscious States: The Cognitive Neuroscience Perspective.*

—— (2008). 'The unity of consciousness and the split-brain syndrome'. *Journal of Philosophy*, 105.

—— and Chalmers, D. (2003). 'What is the unity of consciousness?' In Cleeremans, A. (ed.) *The Unity of Consciousness.*

Braude, S. E. (1995). *First Person Plural: Multiple Personality and the Philosophy of Mind*, 2nd edn.

Dainton, B. (2006). *Stream of Consciousness: Unity and Continuity in Conscious Experience*, 2nd edn.

Hurley, S. (1998). *Consciousness in Action.*

James, W. (1890). *Principles of Psychology.*

Levy, J. (1977). 'Manifestations and implications of shifting hemi-inattention in commissurotomy patients'. *Advances in Neurology*, 18.

Lockwood, M. (1989). *Mind, Brain and the Quantum: The Compound 'I'.*

Marcel, A. (1993). 'Slippage in the unity of consciousness'. In Bock, G. R. and Marsh, J. (eds) *Experimental and Theoretical Studies of Consciousness.*

Marks, C. (1981). *Commissurotomy, Consciousness and Unity of Mind.*

Rosenthal, D. (2003). Unity of consciousness and the self. *Proceedings of the Aristotelian Society*, 103.

Searle, J. (2000). Consciousness, *Annual Review of Neuroscience*, 23.

Sperry, R. W. (1984). Consciousness, personal identity, and the divided brain, *Neuropsychologia*, 22.

Tye, M. (2003). *Consciousness and Persons.*

V

V1 and visual consciousness Of the forty or so cortical visual areas that comprise the primate visual system, the primary visual cortex (V1) occupies a unique position—arguably at the bottom or the top of a hierarchically arranged, densely interconnected network. More is known about the physiological, anatomical, and functional properties of V1 than just about any region of the cerebral cortex, yet much remains to be learned about its functional role in visual consciousness. Does V1 have a direct role in representing information in visual awareness? Or does this region simply provide the necessary input to higher visual areas that support awareness?

1. Theories about V1's role in awareness
2. V1 lesions and blindsight
3. Neural correlates of consciousness in V1
4. Constructive perception and filling-in
5. V1 and voluntary cognitive processes

1. Theories about V1's role in awareness

Since the groundbreaking work of Hubel and Wiesel, it has been known that V1 is the first stage of visual processing to show robust selectivity for fundamental visual features such as orientation, motion direction, and binocular disparity. However, only within the last decade or so have there been major advances regarding the relationship between V1 activity and visual awareness across a variety of ambiguous viewing conditions (Tong 2003).

Damage to V1 leads to loss of conscious vision in the corresponding part of the visual field—what is known as a *scotoma*. In comparison, selective lesions of extrastriate visual areas lead to more subtle or specific perceptual impairments. The devastating effects of V1 lesions could either indicate that V1 has a direct role in representing conscious visual experiences or that higher visual areas are responsible for awareness but have been deprived of their normal input. In primates, about 90% of the projections from the eye are channelled through the lateral geniculate nucleus (LGN) and onward to the primary visual cortex. Area V1, in turn, has strong reciprocal connections with most extrastriate visual areas, including areas V2, V3, V3A, V4V, and MT. Thus, V1 is the primary source of visual information to higher visual areas, and constitutes the major gateway by which feedforward signals reach the cortex.

According to hierarchical theories of visual consciousness, V1 provides the necessary input to the rest of the visual system, just as the eyes do, but its activity is not directly linked to the neural *correlates of consciousness (Rees et al. 2002). Instead, awareness is believed to be linked to activity in higher areas where more abstract and invariant aspects of the stimulus are analysed. Some have further proposed that a visual area must have direct projections to the frontal cortex to contribute directly to awareness, since awareness is argued to depend on the observer's ability to report perceptions via planned motor acts. V1 lacks such direct projections to frontal cortex, so its role in conscious perception is considered to be indirect. Hierarchical models consider V1 as the bottom of the visual hierarchy, emphasizing its role in feedforward stimulus-driven processing. Its primary function is to provide a local analysis of the physical input and to relay this information to higher areas. These theories predict that V1 activity should primarily reflect the properties of the physical stimulus rather than the observer's perceptual state.

However, V1 is not dedicated to feedforward processing alone. In fact, most synaptic connections within V1 are intracortical, and the detailed arrangement of these excitatory and inhibitory connections could allow for complex neuronal interactions to take place, leading to the emergence of more global representations. There are also extensive feedback projections from extrastriate areas to V1, which serve to modulate, select or fine tune the activity patterns emanating from V1, thereby further shaping the incoming pattern of feedforward activity. If feedback to V1 is important for conscious perception, then this late component of activity would reflect the final stages of visual processing in which V1 is positioned at the top of this visual hierarchy.

According to interactive theories of visual consciousness, V1 is believed to have a direct and integral role in awareness for several reasons (Pollen 1999, Lamme and Roelfsema 2000). First, V1 provides high-resolution feature maps of the visual array, which may be essential for fine-scale visual perception. Second, considerable intracortical processing takes place within V1, and these inhibitory and excitatory interactions could contribute to selective and constructive aspects of perception, respectively. Finally, V1 is the primary distributor of visual information to higher extrastriate areas and has strong reciprocal connections with these areas. As a consequence, V1 might be inextricably linked to awareness, since the reliability of visual signals in V1 might be closely associated with the reliability of signals in higher areas. In particular, extrastriate areas may send feedback signals to V1 for the purposes of selecting or biasing perceptual signals, confirming the reliability of the signals they receive, or fine-tuning their own responses based on the high-resolution feature information available in V1. Some interactive models emphasize that reciprocal connections between V1 and extrastriate areas lead to the formation of temporary circuits of recurrent activity. Such recurrent activity would prolong the neural representation of a stimulus for durations well beyond the initial feedforward sweep, which could be essential for maintaining the representation of a visual stimulus in awareness (see also *re-entrant processing). Taken together, interactive models favour the notion that recurrent interactions, between high-level areas with coarse-resolution maps and V1 with its high-resolution feature maps, are important for sustaining a visual representation in awareness.

2. V1 lesions and blindsight

Some evidence in favour of the interactive model comes from patients with V1 lesions who show evidence of *blindsight, that is residual visual function despite a loss of perceptual experience (Stoerig and Cowey 1997). In forced-choice tasks, patients with blindsight may be able to discriminate the presence, location, orientation, wavelength, or motion direction of a target stimulus presented in their scotoma at levels well above chance, despite the fact that they report no awareness of seeing these stimuli. Monkeys with unilateral V1 lesions also show evidence of blindsight. In detection tasks, these animals fail to report stimuli presented to the impaired hemifield, though they can accurately discriminate the properties of such stimuli under forced-choice conditions.

What brain areas are responsible for residual visual function in blindsight, and why is this neural activity insufficient to support normal awareness? Neurophysiological and neuroimaging studies indicate that some extrastriate areas, including MT and V4, are activated by the presentation of unseen stimuli in the damaged hemifield. Although most visual inputs reach the cortex via the geniculostriate pathway, a minority of retinal ganglion cells (about 10%) project to various subcortical structures, some of which, in turn, project to extrastriate areas. With V1 damaged, extrastriate activity alone appears to be insufficient to support awareness though it can still support forced-choice discriminations in blindsight. These findings are consistent with interactive models, which propose that feedback signals from extrastriate areas to V1 are necessary to maintain a representation in awareness. However, the results are also consistent with the notion that extrastriate activity is degraded after damage to V1, thereby leading to impairments in conscious vision.

Some evidence that directly favours the interactive model comes from studies employing *transcranial magnetic stimulation (TMS). TMS can temporarily induce or disrupt activity in a small patch of cortex, non-invasively. In one study, TMS was applied to motion-selective area MT to elicit a motion *phosphene*, a brief impression of a streak of motion. A second TMS pulse was applied to either V1 or MT at various times before or after the phosphene-eliciting pulse. Perception of the motion phosphene was selectively impaired when V1 stimulation occurred shortly after MT stimulation (10–40 ms later) but not beforehand. The fact that V1 had to be stimulated at a later point in time to achieve this effect is consistent with the notion that feedback interactions, from MT to V1, underlie this electrically induced experience of motion. From these findings, it was concluded that activity in area MT alone is insufficient to support awareness of motion, and that feedback from MT to V1 may be necessary for visual awareness (Pascual-Leone and Walsh 2001). In a follow-up study, subjects received a sub-threshold TMS pulse to area MT, which alone was too weak to elicit a motion phosphene. However, when this pulse was shortly followed by a suprathreshold TMS pulse to V1 (which alone would elicit the impression of a stationary phosphene), dual stimulation of MT followed by V1 elicited the impression of a *moving* phosphene. Thus, it appears that rapid feedback interactions can take place between MT and V1, and these can have a strong impact on awareness.

3. Neural correlates of consciousness in V1

Whereas the disruptive effects of lesions or TMS can reveal whether V1 is necessary for awareness, correlational measures allow for more detailed investigation of the functional role of V1. Studies of the neural correlates of consciousness rely on compelling illusions or task-related manipulations to investigate whether activity in a given cortical area reflects the observer's perceptual state, independent of changes in the physical stimulus.

Visual experience can differ from the physical patterns of light that strike the retina in several important ways. Visual perception is highly selective; only a subset of the information processed by the retina ultimately reaches awareness. Perception is also constructive in nature. For example, vivid impressions can occur in regions of the visual field that lack direct stimulation. Finally, one's experience can be shaped by voluntary control. A person can pay attention to a particular feature or object at the expense of other neighbouring items (see also ATTENTION AND AWARENESS) or imagine an object in its absence (see also IMAGERY, SCIENTIFIC PERSPECTIVES). Might activity in V1 reflect selective and constructive aspects of perception, or aspects of awareness that are under voluntary control?

One of the most striking examples of selective perception can be witnessed during *binocular rivalry (Fig. V1a). When conflicting monocular images are presented to corresponding locations in the two eyes, observers fail to perceive a stable fused image; instead, perception spontaneously alternates between one monocular image and the other image every few seconds. Because the observer's conscious state is continually in flux while the visual stimulus remains invariant, the multistage phenomenon of binocular rivalry provides an effective means for isolating the neural correlates of visual awareness (Blake and Logothetis 2002). *Functional brain imaging studies have found robust modulations in human V1 that closely reflect the observer's perceptual state during rivalry (Tong et al. 2006). For example, when a high-contrast pattern is suppressed from awareness by a low-contrast pattern, activity levels decline in V1, and these activity changes closely follow the spatiotemporal dynamics of rivalry. The cortical representation of the blind spot, an exclusively monocular region of V1, also shows activity changes tightly linked to conscious perception, suggesting that binocular rivalry involves direct neural competition between monocular neurons in the visual system. Such suppressive effects could arise from lateral inhibition between left- and right-eye columns within V1. Rivalry modulations have even been reported in the human lateral geniculate nucleus, a structure that consists entirely of monocular neurons. These findings support feedback theories of interocular competition, which propose that feedback inhibition from V1 to monocular layers of the LGN accounts for visual suppression during rivalry. Consistent with these low-level suppressive effects, recent psychophysical studies indicate that rivalry suppression attenuates adaptation to low-level visual properties including colour, orientation, and motion. It is generally agreed that rivalry involves competition at multiple levels of the visual hierarchy, though it remains an open question as to why human neuroimaging studies have revealed more pronounced effects of rivalry in human V1 than neurophysiological recordings in area V1 of the monkey (Blake and Logothetis 2002, Tong et al. 2006). Nonetheless, current evidence indicates a close correspondence between population measures of V1 activity and selective perception during rivalry.

V1 activity has also been linked to selective perception under near-threshold conditions. One neuroimaging study found that V1 shows positive responses on trials when observers successfully detect the appearance of a faint visual pattern in noise, but not when that pattern fails to be detected (Ress and Heeger, 2003). Interestingly, these areas also show greater activity on 'false alarm' trials when subjects mistakenly report perceiving a target when no stimulus was presented. It appears that random fluctuations in spontaneous activity at early visual sites might account for the illusory impression of seeing a stimulus in near-threshold experiments. Neurophysiological recordings in alert monkeys have found that the late component of V1 activity, starting about 80–100 ms after response onset, is also linked to successful detection of a target against a similar background. These neurons show enhanced responses if their receptive field lies on a large figure that can be perceptually segregated from the background on the basis of orientation, texture, disparity, or colour cues (Lamme and Roelfsema 2000). Critically, enhanced V1 responses are found only when the monkey successfully perceives the target; no enhancement occurs when the target is missed, indicating that these neural modulations are linked to the monkey's perception of the target. The late enhancement of V1 responses is consistent with the proposal that delayed feedback interactions with V1 are important for visual awareness.

It should be noted that stimulus-driven activity can often be found in V1 and extrastriate areas, despite lack of awareness. Neural responses can sometimes be observed for visually masked stimuli or rapid unperceived flicker, and are commonly observed during anaesthesia. Thus, activity in V1 alone is insufficient for awareness, as is true for extrastriate areas. Both hierarchical and interactive models agree that the feedforward component of V1 activity appears to be stimulus-driven and largely unconscious. Unique to interactive models is the proposal that the feedback component of V1 activity is strongly associated with awareness.

4. Constructive perception and filling-in

The strong correlations found between V1 activity and various forms of selective perception could either indicate a direct relationship between V1 and awareness, or the suppression of visual signals from reaching higher areas. Studies of constructive perception provide converging evidence in favour of a direct relationship. Though most V1 neurons have small receptive fields that are driven by punctate stimuli, these neurons can integrate information over several degrees of visual space to support contour integration and perceptual grouping. For example, V1 neurons show enhanced responses to a bar presented within their receptive field if collinear bars appear outside of the classical receptive field (Kapadia et al. 1995). Lateral excitatory interactions or possibly feedback interactions between neurons with common orientation preferences could account for these effects. Organized connections between V1 neurons may be important for perceptual segmentation and grouping, allowing the visual system to pick out coherent contours, perceptual groups and candidate objects.

Perceptual *filling-in leads to vivid impressions in regions of the visual field that lack direct stimulation, and also appears to depend on constructive visual mechanisms. Scientists and philosophers have debated whether the brain must actively fill in these gaps in the visual field or whether it can simply ignore the absence of information from these regions. Filling-in can occur in a variety of circumstances, across the blind spot, in the gap between two collinear contours, as a uniform surface fades against a textured background, or when discrete changes in object position lead to an impression of smoothly interpolated motion. Early studies found effects of filling-in primarily in extrastriate areas, but more recent studies implicate V1 in multiple forms of filling-in (Komatsu 2006).

Although there are no photoreceptors in the blind spot itself, some neurons in the corresponding region of V1 respond well to stimuli that encompass or traverse the blind spot. Neurons that show evidence of filling-in have large receptive fields that span several degrees, and tend to be located in the deep layers of V1. This raises the intriguing possibility that a sub-population of V1 neurons with large receptive fields may support visual completion across the blind spot. Related studies indicate that bilateral retinal lesions can dramatically alter the receptive field structure of V1 neurons. Receptive fields that previously occupied the lesioned zone may shift or extend away from the scotoma to adjacent locations within minutes after the lesion, with further plasticity effects occurring over several months.

Collinearity is crucial for many forms of perceptual filling-in. Some V1 neurons show non-linear summation when collinear bars are presented on opposite sides of the blind spot simultaneously, as compared to sequentially. This might be due to facilitatory lateral interactions within V1 or integration of feedback signals to V1. In the intact visual field, subjective contours can lead to the impression of a filled-in surface lying in front of collinear inducers (Fig. V1b). Neural responses to subjective contours are commonly found in V2, but more recent studies have found similar effects in V1, especially after perceptual training. Amodal completion can also lead to filling-in responses in foveal V1 neurons; two bars presented outside of the receptive field may evoke a response if they appear to be connected behind an occluder positioned in front of the bars (Fig. V1c). Activity in V1 and V2 has also been linked to the perception of visual phantoms. Collinear low-contrast gratings, separated by a gap, can lead to the ghostly impression of a grating extending through the blank gap (Fig. V1d). Activity in V1/V2 is found in the gap region, even when subjects must attend to stimuli presented elsewhere, suggesting that neural filling-in of visual phantoms occurs automatically and pre-attentively. Interestingly, when observers are shown a rivalry display consisting of collinear phantom-inducing gratings presented to one eye and orthogonal gratings presented to the other eye, activity in V1/V2 is strongly correlated with spontaneous fluctuations in the phenomenal visibility of the visual phantoms (Meng et al. 2005).

The above studies suggest that V1 provides an appropriate medium for excitatory lateral or feedback interactions to take place between orientation-selective neurons, allowing for filling-in to occur between collinear inducers across a variety of viewing conditions. Some important questions for future research include the following. Does a common mechanism in V1 support these varieties of filling-in, which all depend on collinearity cues? Is V1 involved in other forms of filling-in?

Some studies of surface filling-in, involving the Cornsweet illusion or artificial scotomas, have found reliable effects in extrastriate areas but not in V1. However, a recent fMRI study of neon-colour spreading provides novel evidence of surface filling-in effects in V1 (Fig. V1e). In this variant of the subjective contour illusion, the colour or luminance of the inner component of the inducers appears to spread beyond its immediate borders, leading to the impression of a transparent surface lying in front of a dark background. V1 shows enhanced responses in the region of neon colour spreading, even when subjects must attend to other stimuli, again suggesting that neural filling-in of implied surfaces can occur automatically.

Real-time optical imaging with voltage-sensitive dyes has also revealed V1's role in motion filling-in (Jancke et al. 2004). In the line motion illusion, a small rectangle is displayed, followed by a bar that is elongated in one direction (Figure 1f). This two-frame display leads to a vivid impression that the elongated bar is shooting out of the preceding rectangle. Real-time imaging indicates that neural activity emerges first at the location corresponding to the small rectangle, and then spreads rapidly across the cortex. Similar responses are found for the actual motion of a physically lengthening bar. Thus, activity in V1

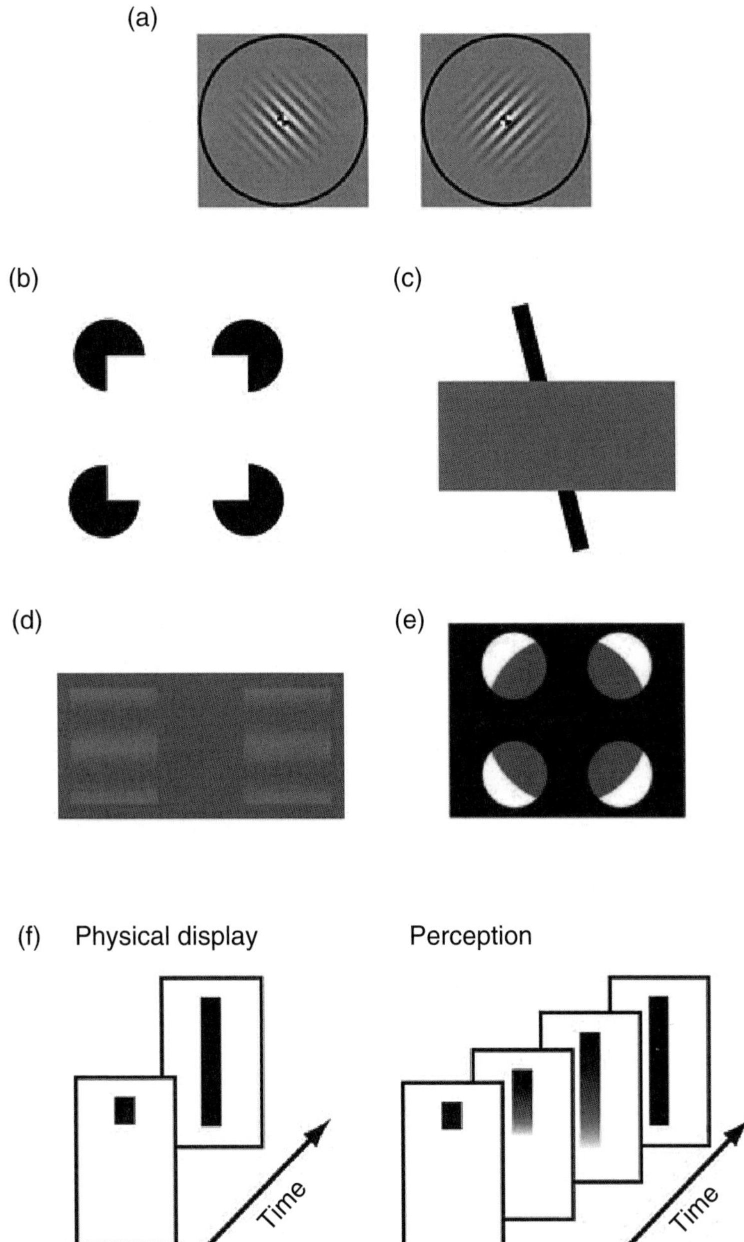

Fig. V1. Examples of visual displays used to investigate the neural correlates of conscious perception. (a) Binocular rivalry display with different oriented patterns presented to the two eyes. Readers can experience rivalry by crossing their eyes to fuse the left and right images, so images are aligned. (b) Subjective contours may be perceived between the four 'pacman' inducers, leading to an overall impression of an illusory white square lying in front of four circles (i.e. modal completion). (c) Amodal completion of a black bar behind a grey occluder. Here, there is no perception of illusory contours but still an impression of connectedness. (d) Visual phantoms can be perceived in the blank gray region between the two collinear gratings. (e) Example of neon colour spreading. An illusory impression of a transparent grey circle lying in front may be perceived, which extends across the physically uniform black region. (f) Two-frame display used to evoke illusory line motion, and the associated perception of such displays.

seems to mirror the spatiotemporal dynamics of motion filling-in.

5. V1 and voluntary cognitive processes

Perception not only depends on the operation of automatic selective and constructive mechanisms, it is also influenced by voluntary cognitive processes such as attention and mental imagery. Spatial attention directed to a visual location leads to enhanced activity in corresponding regions of retinotopic visual cortex, including V1. Enhanced activity can be observed even before the appearance of a stimulus, indicating that baseline activity can be modulated in the absence of visual stimulation. Related studies of mental imagery have also found that imagining a stimulus in a particular location or with a certain spatial extent can activate V1 in a retinotopically specific manner (Kosslyn et al. 2001). Interestingly, TMS applied to the occipital pole can interfere with visual imagery, suggesting a causal role for V1.

V1 may also be important for the attentional selection of overlapping visual features and objects. In neurophysiological studies of mental line tracing, monkeys had to report which of two overlapping curved lines was connected to a dot shown at fixation by making an eye movement to the end-point of the target line (Roelfsema et al. 1998). Longer path lengths and intersections between the two lines led to longer response times, suggesting that the animal was mentally tracing through the path. Activity in V1 was greater on trials when the neuron's receptive field was positioned on the target curve rather than the distractor curve. Moreover, the latency of these modulation effects was correlated with the time required to perform the task. Thus, V1 activity reflects the time required for the animal to mentally trace through the path formed by these lines.

Functional imaging studies of feature-based attention also suggest a role for V1. Orientation-selective activity patterns, revealed by neural decoding methods, can reliably predict which of several different orientations a subject is viewing (Kamitani and Tong 2005). When observers are presented with an ambiguous plaid stimulus and must attend to one of the two overlapping orientations, attention strongly biases orientation-selective responses in favour of the attended pattern. In effect, it is possible to predict which orientation is being attended to based on the activity patterns observed in V1, with accuracy levels matching that of higher areas. Related neuroimaging studies of motion processing have also found evidence of feature-based attention in areas MT and also V1. These findings support theories of early attentional selection, which propose that attention modulates neural responses at very early stages of processing to filter out task-irrelevant information.

Mental imagery, mental line tracing, and the attentional selection of locations, features and objects, are all examples of goal-directed behaviour. Activity modulations found in V1 during these tasks are best understood in terms of top-down feedback. Why does the brain spend so much metabolic energy to send feedback signals to V1? V1 may provide the necessary spatially organized feature maps for cognitive operators to act upon, and serve as an information-dense representational medium to allow for detailed neural computations to take place. Lateral and feedback interactions can have strong influence on the signals that ultimately propagate from V1 to higher areas. It appears that much of the activity in V1 reflects complex neuronal interactions that are closely linked to visual awareness.

FRANK TONG

Blake, R. and Logothetis, N. K. (2002). 'Visual competition'. *Nature Reviews Neuroscience*, 3.

Jancke, D., Chavane, F., Naaman, S., and Grinvald, A. (2004). 'Imaging cortical correlates of illusion in early visual cortex'. *Nature*, 428(6981).

Kamitani, Y. and Tong, F. (2005). 'Decoding the visual and subjective contents of the human brain'. *Nature Neuroscience*, 8.

Kapadia, M. K., Ito, M., Gilbert, C. D., and Westheimer, G. (1995). 'Improvement in visual sensitivity by changes in local context: parallel studies in human observers and in V1 of alert monkeys'. *Neuron*, 15.

Komatsu, H. (2006). The neural mechanisms of perceptual filling-in. *Nature Reviews Neuroscience*, 7.

Kosslyn, S. M, Ganis, G., and Thompson, W. L. (2001). 'Neural foundations of imagery'. *Nature Reviews Neuroscience*, 2.

Lamme, V. A. and Roelfsema, P. R. (2000). 'The distinct modes of vision offered by feedforward and recurrent processing'. *Trends in Neuroscience*, 23.

Meng, M., Remus, D. A. and Tong, F. (2005). 'Filling-in of visual phantoms in the human brain'. *Nature Neuroscience*, 8.

Pascual-Leone, A. and Walsh, V. (2001). 'Fast back-projections from the motion to the primary visual area necessary for visual awareness'. *Science*, 292.

Pollen, D. A. (1999). 'On the neural correlates of visual perception'. *Cerebral Cortex*, 9.

Rees, G., Kreiman, G., and Koch, C. (2002). 'Neural correlates of consciousness in humans'. *Nature Reviews Neuroscience*, 3.

Ress, D. and Heeger, D. J. (2003). 'Neuronal correlates of perception in early visual cortex'. *Nature Neuroscience*, 6.

Roelfsema, P. R., Lamme, V. A., and Spekreijse, H. (1998). 'Object-based attention in the primary visual cortex of the macaque monkey'. *Nature*, 395(6700).

Stoerig, P. and Cowey, A. (1997). 'Blindsight in man and monkey'. *Brain*, 120.

Tong, F. (2003). 'Primary visual cortex and visual awareness'. *Nature Reviews Neuroscience*, 4.

—— Meng, M., and Blake, R. (2006). 'Neural bases of binocular rivalry'. *Trends in Cognitive Science*, 19.

vehicles of consciousness Despite its puzzling and elusive nature, contemporary theories almost universally associate consciousness with the vehicles that are used to represent information in the brain. To understand this tactic one must appreciate the connection between a widespread intuition about consciousness, on the one hand, and the computational approach to cognition, on the other.

The pertinent intuition is that conscious experiences are typically 'about something'. Right now, for example, you are aware of the shapes and meanings of these words. But you can easily shift your attention to ambient sounds, the position of your legs, or your plans for the rest of the day. In each case, your conscious experience is directed at some feature of the world, your body, or yourself. One natural way to characterise this intuition is to say that conscious experiences are *representations in that they always convey information of some kind.

Cognitive science treats cognitive processes as computations. To explain cognition is thus to model the information processing going on in the brain. For information to be processed it must take some physical form, i.e. a computational system must contain *representing vehicles*: physical states that carry information in or to the system (commonplace examples of representing vehicles include speech sounds, text, and photographs). Put in these terms, the foundational claim of cognitive science is that cognitive processes are disciplined operations over representing vehicles of some kind.

There is an obvious confluence between the intuition and the computational framework. Conscious experiences are representations—they are information bearers. Cognition, according to cognitive science, consists of processes defined over representing vehicles. It is thus natural to suppose that conscious experiences are somehow associated with the representing vehicles on which cognitive processes operate, and that the *contents of consciousness are part of the information carried by those vehicles.

Regarding this much there is some consensus, but when it comes to formulating a detailed theory of consciousness two quite distinct strategies have emerged. One approach focuses on the computational processes in which representing vehicles engage (call these *process* theories), the other on structural or dynamical properties of the representing vehicles themselves (call these *vehicle* theories).

Process theories currently dominate the theoretical landscape. According to the most popular of these, informational contents enter consciousness when they gain competitive access to a *global workspace, permitting them to be broadcast throughout the brain (Baars 1997). On the alternative *higher-order thought (HOT) theory, the content of a representing vehicle becomes conscious when it gives rise to a second-order representation directed at itself (Rosenthal 1997). The common thread here is that, of all the representing vehicles present in the brain, only those caught up in specific kinds of computational processes—such as global broadcasting or internal monitoring—contribute to conscious experience.

Process theories focus on what representing vehicles do, rather than what they are. A process theory thus presupposes metaphysical functionalism about consciousness: conscious states occur when representing vehicles enter into certain causal (i.e. computational) relations, without regard to the physical structure or internal dynamics of those representations. A vehicle theory, by contrast, is overtly non-functionalist, because vehicle theorists identify conscious experiences with intrinsic properties of the brain's representing medium.

In accounting for the rich structure of experience, vehicle theorists can avail themselves of the full range of properties revealed by neurobiology and biophysics. For example, it has been conjectured that the phenomenal unity of perceptual objects arises from the dynamic binding of feature-specific cells via the transient synchronization of their discharges (Singer 2001), and that the intensity or 'degree' of some kinds of experience may be determined by the size of dynamic, large-scale neuronal assemblies (Greenfield and Collins 2005). Such hypotheses are not available to process theorists because their medium-neutral models are necessarily couched in terms of causal-cum-computational relations among mental representing vehicles.

A problem for vehicle theorists is that, in the absence of a fully fledged account of cognition, it is extremely difficult to identify which of the various kinds of physical states in the brain are in the representing business. One way forward is offered by *connectionism, a computational theory of cognition grounded in specific claims about the nature of the brain's representing vehicles. Connectionists draw a distinction between information encoded in the synaptic connections between neurons (or more generally, in the organization of the brain), and information transiently encoded in patterns of neural firing activity. Such patterns are presumed to represent only a fraction of the information tied up in the long-term structure of the brain, and some theorists have suggested that the contents of consciousness correspond to information encoded in this way (Lloyd 1991, O'Brien and Opie 1999).

GERARD O'BRIEN AND JON OPIE

Baars, B. J. (1997). 'In the theatre of consciousness: global workspace theory, a rigorous scientific theory of consciousness'. *Journal of Consciousness Studies*, 4.

Greenfield, S. A. and Collins, T. F. T. (2005). 'A neuroscientific approach to consciousness'. In Laureys, S. (ed.), *Progress in Brain Research*, 150.

Lloyd, D. (1991) 'Leaping to conclusions: Connectionism, consciousness, and the computational mind'. In Horgan, T. and Tienson, J. (eds) *Connectionism and the Philosophy of Mind*.

O'Brien, G. and Opie, J. (1999) 'A connectionist theory of phenomenal experience'. *Behavioral and Brain Sciences*, 22.

Rosenthal, D. (1997) 'A theory of consciousness'. In Block, N. et al. (eds) *The Nature of Consciousness: Philosophical Debates*.

Singer, W. (2001) 'Consciousness and the binding problems'. *Annals of the New York Academy of Sciences*, 929.

ventral stream See VISUAL STREAMS: WHAT VS HOW

visual streams: what vs how For most of us, visual consciousness forms an overwhelming part of our everyday mental life. We depend on vision, more than on any other sense, to perceive the world of objects and events beyond our bodies. At the same time, however, we also use vision to move around that world and to guide our goal-directed actions. Over the last two decades, it has become increasingly clear that the visual pathways that underlie our perception of the world are quite distinct from those that underlie the control of our actions. Indeed, this distinction between 'vision-for-perception' and 'vision-for-action' has emerged as one of the major organizing principles of the visual brain, particularly with respect to the visual pathways in the cerebral cortex (Milner and Goodale 1995/2006, Goodale and Milner 2004).

Our reliance on vision is reflected in the large amount of brain in humans (and in our primate cousins) that is devoted to visual processing. Beyond primary visual cortex, the ascending visual pathways convey information to a patchwork quilt of visual areas in the primate cerebral cortex. Although these areas have a complex pattern of interconnections, two broad 'streams' of projections arising from primary visual cortex in the macaque monkey have been identified: a ventral stream projecting eventually to the inferotemporal cortex and a dorsal stream projecting to the posterior parietal cortex (Ungerleider and Mishkin 1982, Van Essen 2005). These streams also receive inputs from a number of subcortical visual structures, including the superior colliculus, which sends prominent projections to the dorsal stream via the thalamus. A schematic diagram of these pathways can be found in Fig. V2. While some caution must be exercised in generalizing from the monkey to the human brain, a decade or more of neuroimaging evidence now suggests that the visual projections from primary visual cortex to the temporal and parietal lobes in the human brain form distinct ventral and dorsal streams broadly similar to those seen in the monkey (Culham and Kanwisher 2001).

1. 'What vs where' or 'what vs how'?
2. Studies of neurological patients
3. How the dorsal and ventral streams operate
4. Teasing the two streams apart in healthy subjects
5. Consciousness and the two visual streams

1. 'What vs where' or 'what vs how'?

In what was to become one of the most influential theories in behavioural neuroscience, Ungerleider and Mishkin (1982) initially proposed that the ventral stream mediates *object vision*, enabling the monkey to identify an object, while the dorsal stream mediates *spatial vision*, enabling the monkey to locate the object. In other words, a partition was drawn between two classes of sensory input, with one stream handling information about an object's features (the 'what' pathway) and the other handling information about its location (the 'where' pathway). This distinction between 'what and where' resonated not only with psychological accounts of perception, but also with nearly a century of Anglo-Saxon neurological thought about the functions of the temporal and parietal lobes in vision. Within 10 years, however, the 'what vs where' story had begun to unravel. New evidence began to accumulate from work with both monkeys and neurological patients, showing that a purely input-based distinction simply would not work. It soon became apparent that the only way to make sense of these new findings was to consider the different *outputs* of the two streams—and to work out how visual information is eventually transformed to suit the demands of these outputs.

According to our current understanding, processing in the ventral stream serves to construct the rich and detailed representation of the world that serves as a perceptual foundation for cognitive operations, allowing us to recognize objects, events and scenes, attach meaning and significance to them, and infer their causal relations. Such operations are essential for accumulating a knowledge base about the world. In contrast, the transformations carried out by the dorsal stream deal with the moment-to-moment information about the location and disposition of objects with respect to the observer's limbs, and thereby provide the necessary visual control of skilled actions, such as manual prehension, directed at those objects. Thus, the dorsal stream can be regarded as a cortical extension of the dedicated visuomotor modules in the midbrain and brainstem that mediate visually guided movements in all vertebrates. Of course, even though the two streams have different functions and operating principles, in everyday life they have to work together. The perceptual networks of the ventral stream interact with various high-level cognitive mechanisms and enable an organism to select a goal and an associated course of action, while the visuomotor

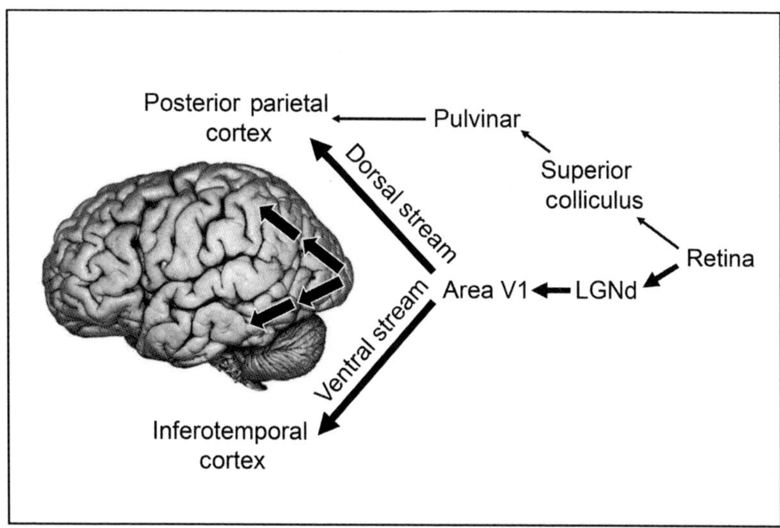

Fig. V2. The two streams of visual processing in human cerebral cortex. The retina sends projections to the dorsal part of the lateral geniculate nucleus (LGNd), which projects in turn to primary visual cortex. Within the cerebral cortex, the ventral stream arises from early visual areas and projects to the inferotemporal cortex. The dorsal stream also arises from early visual areas but projects instead to the posterior parietal cortex. The posterior parietal cortex also receives visual input from the superior colliculus via the pulvinar.

networks in the dorsal stream (and their associated cortical and subcortical pathways) are responsible for the programming and online control of the particular movements that action entails.

2. Studies of neurological patients

The division of labour between the two streams is most clearly evident in the pattern of deficits and spared visual abilities seen in neurological patients with selective damage to the dorsal or ventral stream. Thus, patients with lesions in the superior regions of the posterior parietal cortex, the major terminus of the dorsal stream, typically have problems using vision to direct a grasp or aiming movement towards the correct location of a visual target placed in different positions in the visual field, particularly the peripheral visual field. This particular deficit, typically caused by stroke, is known as *optic ataxia*. But this failure to locate an object with the hand does not constitute a problem in spatial vision per se; many of these patients, for example, can describe the relative position of the object in space quite accurately, even though they cannot direct their hand towards it. At the same time, these patients typically have no difficulty using input from other sensory systems, such as *proprioception or audition, to guide their movements. Furthermore, the visuomotor impairment in these patients extends to other visual domains beyond the spatial. Many of them are unable to use visual information to rotate their hand, scale their grip, or configure their fingers properly when reaching out to pick up objects, even though they have no difficulty describing the orientation, size, or shape of those objects (see Fig. V3, right). All of this confirms the critical role that the dorsal stream plays in the visual control of skilled actions. The patients exhibit neither a purely visual nor a purely motor deficit, but instead a selective deficit in visuomotor control.

The opposite pattern of deficits and spared abilities has been described in patients with damage to the ventral stream. The best-documented case is patient D. F., a young woman who developed a profound visual form *agnosia following carbon monoxide poisoning (Milner et al. 1991). Structural MRI showed evidence of diffuse damage, as is usual following hypoxia, but also dense lesions in ventrolateral regions of the occipital cortex, largely sparing primary visual cortex (James et al. 2003). Even though D. F.'s contrast sensitivity and other low-level visual abilities remain reasonably intact, she can no longer recognize everyday objects or the faces of her friends and relatives; nor can she identify

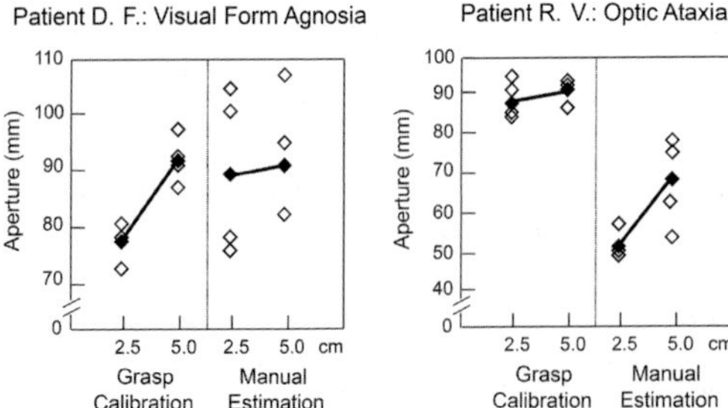

Fig. V3. Comparison between grasping and perceptual judgements in patients D. F. (visual form agnosia) and R. V. (optic ataxia). The graph on the left shows the maximum size of the aperture between D. F.'s index finger and thumb during object-directed grasping and manual estimates of object width. Her maximum grip aperture in flight (individual trials shown as diamonds) was sensitive to the size of the target object, opening wider for a 50 mm wide object than for a 25 mm wide object. Her manual estimates of the width of the two objects, however, were grossly inaccurate and show enormous variability from trial to trial. The graph on the right shows a converse pattern, whereby patient R. V. opened her hand widely and indiscriminately for objects of different widths, while retaining the ability to make good perceptual estimates of width.

or copy line drawings of common objects or even simple geometric shapes. (If an object is placed in her hand, however, she has no difficulty identifying it using touch.) Despite this profound impairment, D. F. shows strikingly accurate guidance of her hand movements when she attempts to pick up the very objects she cannot identify (see Fig. V3, left). For example, when she reaches out to grasp objects, her hand opens wider on the way towards larger objects than towards smaller ones, just as in people with normal vision (Goodale et al. 1991). She also automatically takes into account the position of potential obstacles in the vicinity of a goal object to which she is reaching. Similarly, she rotates her hand and wrist quite normally when she reaches out to grasp objects in different orientations, and she places her fingers correctly on the surface of objects of different shapes. Yet at the same time, she is quite unable to distinguish between any of these objects when they are presented to her in simple discrimination tests. She even fails in manual 'matching' tasks in which she is asked to show how wide an object is by opening her index finger and thumb a corresponding amount. In short, a profound loss of form perception coexists in D. F. with a preserved ability to use information about the form of objects to guide a broad range of actions. The contrast between what D. F. can and cannot do is what one would expect in someone with a damaged ventral 'perception' stream but a functionally intact dorsal 'action' stream.

This formulation also sheds light on the well-known phenomenon of *blindsight, where certain kinds of 'unconscious' visual function can survive damage to the primary visual cortex or its subjacent white matter, despite the loss of conscious perception in the affected parts of the visual field. Crucially, physiological evidence from non-human primates has shown that ventral stream neurons become completely silent to visual stimulation following primary cortical damage or deactivation, whereas the dorsal stream remains surprisingly responsive to visual stimuli (Bullier et al. 1994). The model would predict from the observed lack of ventral-stream activity, precisely the global loss of conscious vision that is seen in blindsight patients. At the same time, however, the dorsal stream's continued processing of visual information (received through secondary subcortical routes), would permit them to detect and respond to visual information. On this interpretation, the preservation of dorsal-stream processing in patient D. F. could be regarded as a specialized form of blindsight. It is important to note, however, that D. F.'s spared primary visual cortex provides a far more efficient visual route to the dorsal stream than the secondary input pathways available in blindsight. (For fuller discussions of blindsight, see Milner and Goodale 1995/2006 and Danckert and Rossetti 2005.)

3. How the dorsal and ventral streams operate

The existence of two separate cortical visual pathways reflects the fact that perception and action each require their own particular transformations to be carried out on the incoming visual information. To be able to grasp an object successfully, for example, it is essential that the brain compute the object's actual (absolute) size, orientation, and position with respect to the observer. Moreover, information about the orientation and position of the object needs to be computed in egocentric frames of reference that take into account the orientation and position of the object with respect to the effector that is to be used to perform the action. The time at which these computations are performed is also critical. Observers and goal objects rarely stay in a static relationship with one another, and as a consequence the egocentric coordinates of a target object can typically change dramatically from moment to moment. For this reason, it is essential that the brain compute the parameters specifying a given movement immediately before the action is initiated. For the same reason, it would be of little value for these parameters (or the resulting motor programmes) to be stored in memory. In short, the vision-for-action systems in the dorsal stream need to work in an online mode.

The situation is quite different for perception, both in terms of the frames of reference used to construct the percept and the period of time over which that percept (or the information it provides) can be accessed. Vision-for-perception appears not to rely on computations about the absolute size of objects or their egocentric locations. Instead, the perceptual system in the ventral stream computes the size, location, shape, and orientation of an object primarily in relation to other objects and surfaces in the scene. Encoding an object in such a scene-based frame of reference provides a perceptual representation that preserves information about the location, size, and disposition of the object relative to its surroundings, while discarding any information specific to the viewpoint of the observer. In contrast, the visuomotor system needs to have information coded in absolute metrics (e.g. in order to calibrate the size of a hand grasp) and in egocentric coordinates (in order to reach precisely in space with the hand suitably oriented).

The products of perception also need to be available over an indefinite time scale. We can still recognize objects and places that we last saw minutes, hours, days, or even years previously. To achieve this, the coding of the visual information has to be somewhat abstract, transcending particular viewpoints and viewing conditions. By working with perceptual representations that are object- or scene-based, we are able to maintain the constancies of size, shape, colour, lightness, and relative location over time and across different viewing conditions. There is much debate in the object recognition literature about how this is accomplished. Some of the mechanisms underlying object perception may use a network of viewer-centred representations of the same object; others may use an array of canonical representations; still others may be truly 'object-centred'. But whatever the nature of the coding might be, it is the identity of the object and its location within the scene, not its disposition with respect to the observer, that is the primary concern of the perceptual system. It enables us to recognize objects we have seen before, even though the position of those objects with respect to our body may have changed considerably since the last time we saw them.

One way of studying the role of the ventral stream in memory is to present a visual object briefly, and then a few seconds later ask the subject to perform a 'pantomimed' action, as if the object were still there. Remarkably, D. F. failed completely in this task. Unlike her behaviour in the normal task of reaching to grasp a visible object, she no longer showed any scaling of her finger–thumb separation as she reached out and pretended to pick it up (Goodale et al. 1994). Evidently she had no working memory of the object—not because her memory per se was not working properly, but because she had not perceived the dimensions of the object in the first place.

Of course healthy subjects have no problem in performing pantomimed acts, indicating that the visual representations generated in the normal ventral stream are not only available for mediating recognition of previously encountered objects: they can also guide our movements when we are working in offline mode. In fact it has recently been found that optic ataxic patients, who often have a spared ventral stream, show exactly the converse pattern to that seen in D. F. They show no sign of tailoring their handgrip to the size of objects in real time, but when asked to perform the delayed pantomime task, they perform just like healthy subjects (Milner et al. 2003). They even do this when the object is re-presented at the end of the delay, i.e. when the task no longer requires pantomiming 'as if' grasping. Evidently, once the healthy ventral stream has a chance to become involved, it tends to dominate the patient's actions even when she is subsequently faced with a visible object to respond to. In one study, the experimenters probed this by covertly switching between different-size objects during the delay on some trials. The patient's hand opened widely when she had previewed a large object even though a small one was actually presented for grasping.

4. Teasing the two streams apart in healthy subjects

It has been very difficult for many people to accept the notion that what we experience in our visual perception is not what is in direct control of our visually guided actions. The idea seems to fly in the face of common sense: after all, our actions are usually voluntary, under the direct control of the will; and the will seems intuitively to be governed by what we consciously experience. And of course we normally are conscious of the objects to which we direct our actions. So when it was reported that a visual *illusion of object size (the Ebbinghaus illusion) did not deceive the hand when people reached out to pick up objects that appeared to be larger or smaller than they really were (Aglioti et al. 1995), vision scientists around the world embarked on a series of experiments to prove that this could not possibly be true.

Of course, the 'what vs how' model does not predict that all actions are immune to all visual illusions. Some illusions, after all, arise so early in visual processing that they would be expected to affect both perception and action. This prediction has been specifically confirmed using two different illusions of visual tilt (Dyde and

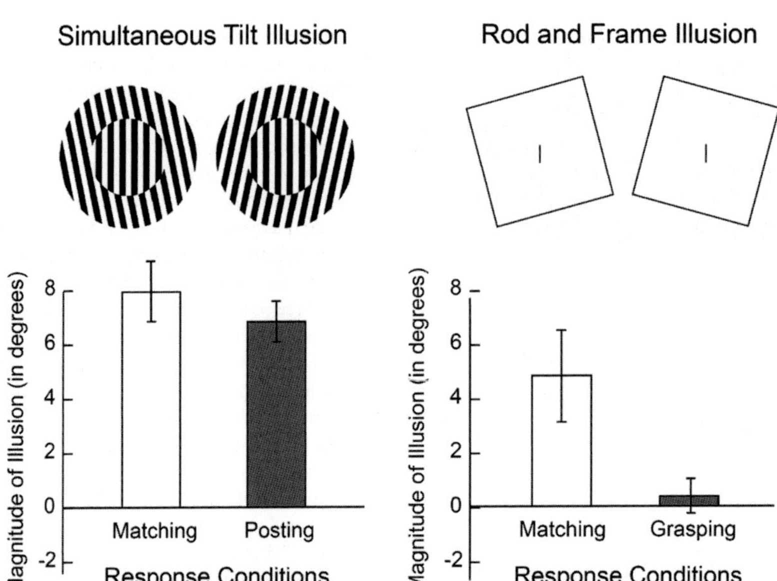

Fig. V4. Two different illusions of visual orientation: the simultaneous tilt illusion (STI) and the rod-and-frame illusion (RFI). The STI (left) is generally believed to originate in the lower levels of the cortical visual system, probably in primary visual cortex. As well as being manifest in a perceptual task (e.g. rotating a plastic card to match the apparent orientation of the central grating pattern) the STI is equally apparent when subjects are asked to move the card towards the central pattern as if 'posting' it through the bars of the grating. In contrast, the RFI, which affects perceptual judgements to a similar extent, has no effects on movements to grasp the central rod (or to 'post' a card toward a small central grating pattern).

Milner 2002: see Fig. V4). Nonetheless, the model does predict that some illusions, those that arise deep in the ventral stream, should not directly affect visuomotor processing. Whenever this dissociation does appear, as it often does, it dramatically illustrates the claim that what we see is not necessarily what controls our actions.

One recent example of this dissociation between perception and action is particularly striking. In the powerful 'hollow face' illusion, knowledge of what faces look like impels observers to see the inside of a mask as if it were a normal protruding face (Kroliczak et al. 2006). Despite the fact that observers could not resist this compelling illusion, actions that they directed at the face were not deceived. Thus, when they were asked to flick off a small ('bug-like') target stuck on the face, they unhesitatingly reached out to the correct point in space (see Fig. V5). This striking dissociation between what you see and what you do provides a dramatic demonstration of the simultaneous engagement of two parallel visual systems, each constructing its own version of reality.

5. Consciousness and the two visual streams

There is indirect evidence from various sources that the contents of ventral stream processing can enter our visual awareness, whereas those of dorsal stream processing cannot (although we might well be fully conscious of the *action* we are performing under dorsal stream guidance). D. F., after all, is unable to describe or indicate manually the appearance of visual shapes, and even simple visual properties like width or orientation, while still being able to use these properties to guide her movements. These facts are directly mirrored by the bilateral damage in her ventral stream (mainly restricted to the lateral occipital area, LO), and by observations using *functional brain imaging (fMRI) of zero net ventral stream activity when she views intact vs scrambled line drawings, but yet spared dorsal stream activation during a visual grasping task (James et al. 2003). Visual illusions provide a second line of argument: although they do not speak to the anatomical systems involved, they do show that the normal brain can simultaneously generate conscious percepts and visually guided acts that are mutually contradictory.

More direct evidence comes from fMRI studies of *binocular rivalry, for example when subjects are presented simultaneously with a picture of a house to one eye and a face to the other. Subjects experience alternating perceptions of either the house or the face, but almost never both at once. Tong and colleagues (1998) found that whenever the subject reported seeing

(a)

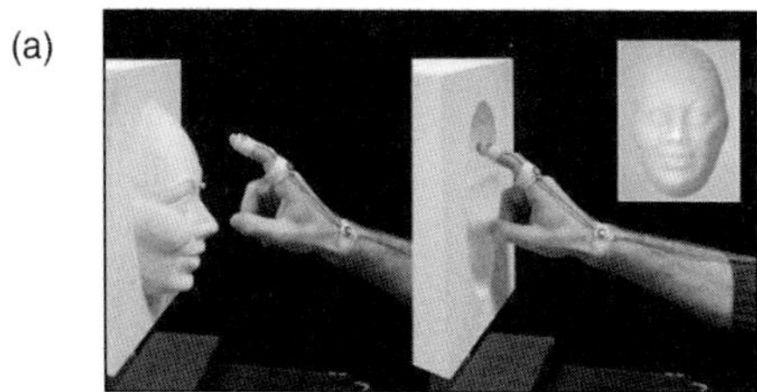

(b)

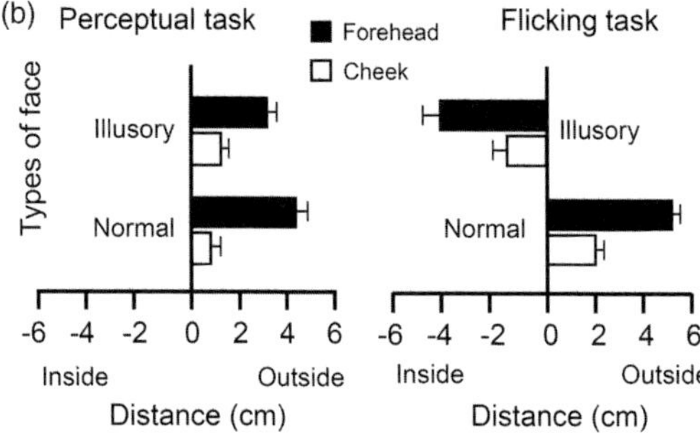

Fig. V5. Perceptual judgments and visuomotor control with the hollow face illusion. (a) A small magnet was placed on either the cheek or forehead of a normal three-dimensional face (left) or a hollow mask (right). The inset shows a photograph of the bottom-lit hollow face, clearly revealing the illusion of a normal convex face. Participants were required either to flick the magnet from the normal or illusory face, or to estimate its distance psychophysically. (b) The left-side histogram gives the mean perceptual judgements of the apparent position of the magnets on the illusory (upper bars) and normal face (lower bars) with respect to the reference plate, confirming that subjects perceived the hollow face as protruding forwards just like the normal face. The right-side data show the mean distance of the hand as the subject attempted to flick the target off each face. In the case of the illusory face (upper bars), the flicking movements corresponded to the actual distances of the targets, not to the consciously seen distances.

the face there was more activity in a part of the ventral stream associated with face perception (area FFA), but when they reported seeing the house, there was more activity in a different area, that associated with the perception of places or buildings (area PPA). In other words, the activity in FFA and PPA reflected what the subjects consciously perceived, not what was on their retina. In agreement with this, a more recent fMRI study, using a slightly different interocular suppression technique, showed that area LO in the ventral stream showed differential activation according to whether an object was or was not consciously perceived. Strikingly, however, the dorsal stream did not: it responded just as strongly to images of objects when they were 'invisible' as when they were 'visible' (Fang and He 2005).

Two recent studies of a patient with visual extinction provide direct confirmation that the dorsal stream uses unconscious visual information to carry out its visuomotor computations. This patient (V. E.) successfully guided his hand while reaching between two potential obstacles (thin vertical poles) even when they were visible for only 500 ms, which often induced perceptual extinction of the left pole. His reach trajectories were the same on trials when he reported seeing only the right pole as on those when he saw both. Separate evidence that the dorsal stream was mediating this unconscious visual processing is provided by patients with optic ataxia: they are severely impaired on tests of implicit obstacle avoidance, even though well able to bisect the space between two potential obstacles. In a further study of patient V. E. by Schenk and colleagues (2005), it was found that he was able to benefit just as well from visual feedback from his hand while reaching for a target when he was conscious of the feedback as when he was not (i.e. on trials when the target LED caused extinction of the LED on his hand).

In conclusion, a variety of converging sources of evidence support the idea that the computations performed by the dorsal stream during the online guidance of behaviour are performed on visual information that is not conscious. Of course, it is not denied that most of the time the *observer* would be visually conscious of the target object, his moving hand, and indeed of non-target objects in our environment. The point is that the brain activity underlying this conscious perception is going on somewhere else: presumably in the ventral stream and beyond.

DAVID MILNER AND MELVYN A. GOODALE

Aglioti, S., Goodale, M. A., and DeSouza, J. F. X. (1995). 'Size-contrast illusions deceive the eye but not the hand'. *Current Biology*, 5.

Bullier, J., Girard, P., and Salin, P.-A. (1994). 'The role of area 17 in the transfer of information to extrastriate visual cortex'. In Peters, A. and Rockland, K. S. (eds) *Cerebral Cortex, Volume 10: Primary Visual Cortex in Primates*.

Culham, J. C. and Kanwisher, N. G. (2001). 'Neuroimaging of cognitive functions in human parietal cortex'. *Current Opinion in Neurobiology*, 11.

Danckert, J. and Rossetti, Y. (2005). 'Blindsight in action: what can the different sub-types of blindsight tell us about the control of visually guided actions?' *Neuroscience and Biobehavioral Reviews*, 29.

Dyde, R. T. and Milner, A. D. (2002). 'Two illusions of perceived orientation: one fools all of the people some of the time, but the other fools all of the people all of the time'. *Experimental Brain Research*, 144.

Fang, F. and He, S. (2005). 'Cortical responses to invisible objects in the human dorsal and ventral pathways'. *Nature Neuroscience* 8.

Goodale, M. A. and Milner, A. D. (2004). *Sight Unseen: An Exploration of Conscious and Unconscious Vision.*
——, Milner, A. D., Jakobson, L. S., and Carey, D. P. (1991). 'A neurological dissociation between perceiving objects and grasping them'. *Nature*, 349.
——, Jakobson, L. S., and Keillor, J. M. (1994). 'Differences in the visual control of pantomimed and natural grasping movements'. *Neuropsychologia*, 32.
James, T. W., Culham, J., Humphrey, G. K., Milner, A. D., and Goodale, M. A. (2003). 'Ventral occipital lesions impair object recognition but not object-directed grasping: a fMRI study'. *Brain*, 126.
Kroliczak, G., Heard, P., Goodale, M. A., and Gregory, R. L. (2006). 'Dissociation of perception and action unmasked by the hollow-face illusion'. *Brain Research*, 1080.
Milner, A. D. and Goodale, M. A. (1995/2006). *The Visual Brain in Action.*
—— and McIntosh, R. D. (2004). Reaching between obstacles in spatial neglect and visual extinction. *Progress in Brain Research*, 144.
——, Perrett, D. I., Johnston, R. S. et al. (1991). 'Perception and action in "visual form agnosia" '. *Brain*, 114.
——, Dijkerman, H. C., McIntosh, R. D., Rossetti, Y., and Pisella, L. (2003). 'Delayed reaching and grasping in patients with optic ataxia'. *Progress in Brain Research*, 142.
Schenk, T., Schindler, I., McIntosh, R. D., and Milner, A. D. (2005). 'The use of visual feedback is independent of visual awareness: evidence from visual extinction'. *Experimental Brain Research*, 167.
Tong, F., Nakayama, K., Vaughan, J. T., and Kanwisher, N. (1998). 'Binocular rivalry and visual awareness in human extrastriate cortex'. *Neuron*, 21.
Ungerleider, L. G. and Mishkin, M. (1982). 'Two cortical visual systems'. In Ingle, D. J. et al. (eds) *Analysis of Visual Behavior*.
Van Essen, D. C. (2005). 'Corticocortical and thalamocortical information flow in the primate visual system'. *Progress in Brain Research*, 149.

volition See PHENOMENOLOGY

Von Economo neurons The Von Economo neurons (VENs) are large, bipolar cells located in layers 3 and 5 of anterior cingulate (ACC) and frontoinsular (FI) cortex. They are distinguished from pyramidal cells because they have only a single large basal dendrite whereas pyramidal cells have an array of smaller basal dendrites extending from the cell body. They were carefully described and mapped in humans by Von Economo and Koskinas (1925). My colleagues and I found that the VENs are present in primates only in humans and great apes and are far more abundant in humans than in apes (Nimchinsky et al. 1999). The VENs are thus a phylogenetic specialization that has arisen within the last 15 million years in hominoids and has proliferated greatly within the human line of descent. Because of their late emergence in phylogeny, the force of natural selection has had only a relatively short time to shape their functioning and integration with other cell populations. Consequently the VENs may be particularly vulnerable to dysfunction, in a manner analogous to the propensity of humans to suffer lower back, hip, and knee disorders as a consequence of the recent evolution of bipedal posture. William Seeley and I together with our colleagues have found that the VENs are selectively vulnerable to degeneration in frontal temporal dementia (FTD) and appear to be the prime early target of this disease (Seeley et al. 2006). FTD causes a severe breakdown of social functioning and disintegration of personality. The capacity for empathy is particularly disrupted in FTD when it attacks the right hemisphere. The VENs are spared in Alzheimer's dementia, and empathy is preserved as well. Jason Kaufman and I together with our collaborators have found that the number of VENs is greatly reduced in a congenital disorder in which the corpus callosum fails to form normally. The loss of the VENs in this disorder is not a direct consequence of the failure of the corpus callosum to develop but rather is an associated defect that probably arises from a common cause. Agenesis of the corpus callosum is also associated with abnormal social behaviour.

The VENs develop late in ontogeny as well as phylogeny. They first appear in small numbers in week 35 of gestation and at birth only about 15% of the mature number are present. There is a rapid increase in their numbers during the first postnatal year followed by a slow pruning back during the next decade. This postnatal increment in VEN population may arise by differentiation from some pre-existing cell type or by migration from a potentially proliferative zone in the ventricles. Whether the VENs emerge by differentiation or migration, there is the possibility that their emergence might be disrupted during postnatal development with dysfunctional consequences related to neuropsychiatric disorders. In all of the great ape and postnatal human brains I have studied, the VENs are more numerous in the right hemisphere than in the left. However, at birth there are about the same number in both hemispheres. Thus the predominance of VENs in the right hemisphere emerges postnatally. The fact that this right preference is consistent across postnatal humans and apes suggests that this specialization arose in the common ancestor of humans and apes before the advent of language. This right-hemisphere predominance in VENs may be related to an asymmetry between the hemispheres in which the right hemisphere is preferentially related to the functions of the sympathetic nervous system and the left hemisphere to the parasympathetic system, a lateralization which is widespread in vertebrates. Thus the functioning of the expanded VEN population in the right hemisphere may be related to intense and powerfully arousing emotions, particularly in the social domain.

The dendritic architecture of neurons reflects the way in which they integrate information. The apical dendrites of VENs are very similar to those of the apical dendrites of neighbouring pyramidal cells. However, the basal dendritic pattern of the VENs is much simpler than that of the pyramids. The large soma size and the fact that they contain an abundance of non-phosphorylated neurofilaments suggest that they bear large, rapidly conducting axons, which are characteristic of big neurons in layer 5 throughout the cortex. Lipophilic dye injected into the anterior part of the cingulum bundle backfills VENs in ACC, thus indicating that they are projection neurons. The radial orientation and narrow width of the dendritic arborization indicate that the VENs sample a sharply circumscribed cylinder of cortex possibly corresponding to a minicolumn. They may thus constitute a fast fire output from minicolumns that provides a rapid relay to other parts of the brain.

VEN functions are revealed by immunocytochemical staining with antibodies to neurotransmitter receptors. The VENs are strongly labelled with antibodies to the dopamine D3 receptor, which may signal the expectation of reward under uncertainty. The activation of FI and ACC increases with the degree of uncertainty. FI is activated by negative feedback in tasks that involve a high degree of uncertainty. FI and ACC activity is coupled to situations in which the subject sustains a gambling loss (punishment) and then switches to a different behavioural strategy, implying that in normal subjects these areas are involved in adaptive decision-making and cognitive flexibility. Right FI is also activated in situations in which the subject is asked to stop an ongoing activity.

The destruction of right FI in FTD is associated with poor appetite control and continued food consumption even when the patient reports that their stomach feels full. I propose that forms of social cognition performed in the VEN-containing areas are ultimately derived from neural circuitry involved in the ingestion of food and the rejection toxins, which are key functions of the insular cortex. This regulation of food intake is expressed in the primordial opposed emotions of lust and disgust: the consumption of the nutritious and the spitting out or vomiting of the toxic. The neural circuitry for lust–disgust served as the evolutionary template for complex social emotions that tend to occur in polar opposites such as love–hate, gratitude–resentment, self-confidence–embarrassment, humour–obliviousness, trust–distrust, empathy–contempt, approval–disdain, pride–humiliation, truthfulness–deception, and atonement–guilt. The first of each of these pairs generally favours the formation of social bonds (prosocial) and the second tends to disrupt bonds (antisocial). Most of these complex social emotions activate FI and ACC and lesions of these structures disrupt them. The negative (antisocial) member of each of these pairings may be preferentially related to the right VEN populations in FI and ACC and the positive (prosocial) members to the VEN populations in the left hemisphere. The more numerous VEN populations in FI and ACC in the right hemisphere may be related to the computationally greater demands associated with sympathetic arousal than to parasympathetic quietude. The VENs can thus be seen as part of a suite of adaptations that support the increased complexity of hominoid and especially human social networks.

J. ALLMAN

Allman, J., Katson, K., Tetreault, N., and Hakeem, A. (2005). 'Intuition and autism: a possible role for Von Economo neurons'. *Trends in Cognitive Science*, 9.

Aron, A. and Poldrack, R. (2006). 'Cortical and subcortical contributions to stop signal response inhibition'. *Journal of Neuroscience*, 26.

Craig, A. (2002). 'Forebrain emotional asymmetry: a neuroanatomical basis?' *Trends in Cognitive Science*, 9.

Nimchinsky, E., Gilissen, E., Allman, J., Perl, D., Erwin, J., and Hof, P. (1999). 'A neuronal morphotype unique to humans and great apes'. *Proceedings of the National Academy of Sciences of the USA*, 96.

Rankin, K., Gomo-Tempini, K., Allison, S., Stanley, C., Glenn, S., Weiner, M., and Miller, B. (2005). 'Structural anatomy of empathy in neurodegenerative disease'. *Brain*, 129.

Rogers, L. and Andrew, R. (2002). *Comparative Vertebrate Lateralization*.

Seeley, W., Carlin, D., Allman, J., Macedo, M., Bush, C., Miller, B., and DeArmond, S. (2006). 'Early frontotemporal dementia targets neurons unique to apes and humans'. *Annals of Neurology*, 60.

Ullsperger, M. and von Cramon, Y. (2003). Error monitoring using external feedback, Journal of Neuroscience 23:4308–4314.

Von Economo, C. and Koskinas, G. (1925). *Die Cytoarchitectonik der Hirnrinde des erwachsene Menschen*.

Watson, K., Matthews, B., and Allman, J. (2006). 'Brain activation during sight-gags and language-dependent humor.' *Cerebral Cortex*, 17.

Wooley, J., Gorno-Tempini, M., Seeley, W., Rankin, K., Lee, S., Matthews, B., and Miller, B. (2007) 'Binge eating is associated with right orbito-frontal-insular-striatal atrophy in frontotemporal dementia'. *Neurology*, 69.

W

'what it's like' Introduced into the consciousness literature by Brian Farrell (1950) in his paper 'Experience', the phrase 'what it's like' is typically used to elucidate the notion of phenomenal consciousness: *phenomenal states—and only phenomenal states—are said to possess or bring with them a 'what it's likeness'. There is something distinctive that it is like to have a headache, to taste burnt butter, and to listen to the opening bars of Keith Jarrett's Köln concert. Phenomenal states have phenomenality in common—there is something it is like to be in each of them—and they are distinguished from each other by their phenomenal characters—what exactly it is like to be in each of them. In one sense of that multiply used term, 'what it's likenesses' can be identified with *qualia. We can also use the notion of 'what it's likeness' to explicate one (note: not the only) notion of creature consciousness, for we can say that a creature is conscious when, and only when, there is something it is like to be it. By definition, there is nothing that it is like to be a *zombie.

Although the notion of 'what it's likeness' plays a central role in some of the most fundamental problems associated with consciousness, it is far from clear that there is a uniform conception of 'what it's likeness' at work in the literature on consciousness (Byrne 2004). Certainly theorists give wildly different accounts of the kinds of mental states that possess a distinctive 'what it's likeness'. Suppose that you are looking at a yellow vehicle weaving in and out of traffic. You recognize it as a Volvo GL240. What is it like for you to have this kind of visual experience? All hands are agreed in holding that there is something distinctive that it is like to see the car as yellow, as shaped a certain way, and as moving; but consensus ends around about here. Some theorists hold that as far as visual experience is concerned, 'what it's likeness' attaches only to low-level properties such as these. Other theorists hold that 'what it's likeness' attaches to a much-wider range of properties—that there might be something distinctive that it is like to see the car as a car, as a Volvo, or, indeed, as a Volvo GL240. We might call theorists of the former persuasion 'phenomenal conservatives' and those of the latter persuasion 'phenomenal liberals'. A typical conservative might allow that there is a 'what it's likeness' associated with bodily sensations (aches, pains, orgasms), low-level perceptual states (seeing yellow, tasting sourness, hearing something as approaching), and various affective states (anger, fear, elation), but that's about it as far as 'what it's likeness' extends. A phenomenal liberal, by contrast, might hold that the range of 'what it's likeness' includes not only high-level perception (such as seeing an object as a specific type of car) but also includes such cognitive states as judging that it would be a good idea to go to the south of France in April, wondering whether whales are mammals, and hoping that New Zealand will win the cricket. The debate between conservatives and liberals is a puzzling one: whether or not (say) high-level perception possesses a distinctive 'what it's likeness', should this fact not be apparent (indeed: readily apparent!) to all parties to the debate? The fact that it is not suggests that conservatives and liberals may not have a shared understanding of the phrase 'what it's likeness'.

Much of the debate surrounding 'what it's likeness' concerns epistemic status. Whereas one can know what it is to be in a particular physical state without being in the state in question, a number of theorists have argued that one cannot know what it is to be in a particular phenomenal state without having been in it (or one of its near relatives). Indeed, the 'what it's like' locution is most closely associated with a paper whose central purpose is to make such claims vivid. In his paper 'What it is like to be a bat?' Thomas Nagel (1974) argues that we face profound challenges in grasping alien experiential perspectives, such as those possessed by the bat. The epistemic challenges posed by 'what it's likeness' are also to the fore in Frank Jackson's *knowledge argument. Jackson claims, with some plausibility, that Mary learns something new when she first sees red—something that she could not have learnt without seeing red. Again, many take an upshot of Jackson's argument to be that one cannot know what it is like to instantiate a certain phenomenal property without having instantiated that property (or, at least, a very similar property). When it comes to knowing what it's like—so the claim goes—there is no substitute for experience.

A related sort of epistemic challenge posed by the 'what it's likeness' of consciousness concerns our inability to grasp how it might be explained. This is

Joseph Levine's famous *explanatory gap. There seem to be principled difficulties in explaining both why there should be anything it is like to be in certain mental states, and why particular conscious states have the 'what it's likeness' that they do. Although the explanatory gap is often put in terms of a gap between phenomenal properties and physical (or functional) properties, it is actually much broader than that. The problem, in a nutshell, is that we do not have a good grip on how to explain facts about 'what it's likeness' in any terms.

But perhaps there are no such facts—at least, perhaps there are no such facts over and above facts about discriminatory responses. Dennett invites us to consider two coffee tasters, Mr Chase and Mr Sanborn (Dennett 1988). Chase and Sanborn no longer like a certain coffee that they both once liked, but they give different accounts of why they no longer like it. Chase says that the flavour of the coffee has not changed, it is just that he no longer likes that flavour; Sanborn says that he still likes that flavour, the problem is just that the coffee does not taste the way that it used to. Dennett suggests that although Chase and Sanborn describe their predicaments in different ways, there may in fact be only a verbal difference here, and that what it's like for a subject to enjoy a certain phenomenal state cannot be prised apart from the various discriminatory responses that the state facilitates. Dennett's deflationism is attractive, for it promises to dissolve some of the thorniest problems posed by consciousness. But is it right? Is it true that all that needs to be explained when one listens to the opening bars of Keith Jarrett's Köln concert is a cluster of discriminatory responses? Believe it if you can.

TIM BAYNE

Byrne, A. (2004). 'What phenomenal consciousness is like'. In R. Gennaro (ed.) *Higher-Order Theories of Consciousness*.

Dennett, D. (1988). 'Quining qualia'. In Marcel, A. and Bisiach, E. (eds) *Consciousness in Contemporary Science*.

Farrell, B. (1950). 'Experience'. *Mind*, 49.

Nagel, T. (1974). 'What is it like to be a bat?'. *Philosophical Review*, LXXXIII.

wine and consciousness Of all the consciousness-modifying substances developed by human civilizations, wine is the most ancient (traceable at least back to 5000 BC) and the most widespread (produced in at least 65 of the world's countries). It is also the substance most rich in meaning and significance in western European civilizations, widely used for ritual and celebratory purposes.

Wine (in this sense) is the product of the fermentation of crushed grapes, their natural sugars turned to alcohols by the activity of naturally occurring, or added, yeasts. Ethanol is the characteristic alcohol in wine, but various acids, esters, acetates, and lactates are also contained in the final product (see Goode 2005).

Alcohol is classified as a depressant in the sense that it suppresses the reactions of the central nervous system. A significant effect of wine upon consciousness is, of course, intoxication by alcohol. Since the earliest stories of wine drinking—e.g. the story of Noah in the biblical book of Genesis—wine's capacity to intoxicate has been a source of its value and also of its power over people.

But wine is also valued for its effects that fall short of intoxication. Wine is thought to encourage conviviality, conversation, and romance. Plato recommended that middle-aged men drink wine 'to renew their youth, and that, through forgetfulness of care, the temper of their souls may lose its hardness and become softer and more ductile'. And Immanuel Kant believed that when drinking wine 'we forget and overlook the weaknesses of others' (see Crane 2005 for details).

Wine differs from other consciousness-modifying substances in at least two ways. The first is in its meaning or significance. Intoxication through wine-drinking was an important part of ancient Greek religions, such as the Dionysian cults, and it still has a ritual and religious function in many contemporary Western societies, notably in Jewish and Christian rituals. In the Jewish tradition, wine is drunk during the Kiddush, a blessing said before eating on the Sabbath; and at the Passover meal the drinking of wine is obligatory. The main place of wine in Christian ritual is in the sacrament of the Eucharist. Roman Catholics and many other Christians believe that in this ritual wine is transformed into (or in some other way comes to symbolize) the blood of Christ.

The second difference lies in the amount of attention that has been given by writers to the effects of wine on consciousness. Many poets (Keats, Shakespeare, out of many other examples) have discussed the intoxicating effects of wine and its effects on other human appetites. But there is also a long tradition of writing about the extraordinary variety of tastes contained in the world's different wines. Much of what is written aims to describe precisely the sensory qualities of the experience of drinking wine. Wine writing therefore serves as an excellent source of *phenomenological descriptions of experience, ranging from the simple ('sour', 'sweet', 'fruity', etc.) through the imaginative and comparative ('velvet', 'tar', 'tobacco') to the extravagant and simply incomprehensible ('wet slate').

TIM CRANE

Crane, T. (2005). 'Excess'. *The World of Fine Wine*, 4.

Goode, J. (2005). *Wine Science*.

Johnston, H. (2004). *The Story of Wine*, 2nd edn.

Smith, B. C. (ed.) (2007). *A Question of Taste*.

working memory Working memory refers to online processing and temporary storage of information in the service of ongoing tasks. It is the system that supports moment-to-moment monitoring and updating, helping us keep track of what we have just done, what we are doing now, and what we plan to do in the very near future. While it would seem to have much to do with conscious experience, direct tests of this link have been relatively rare, and have tended to focus on conscious experience of mental visual images.

Working memory also refers to a group of theories that have been developed largely from empirical findings to account for the functioning of what might be viewed as a mental workspace. Broadly, these theories ascribe similar characteristics to the concept of working memory, namely that it is limited both in the amount of information that can be held at any one time, and in the time for which specific information can be held. This limited capacity supports temporary storage of details of recently viewed objects or scenes as well as sequences of numbers, letters, or words recently read or heard, and current goals and intentions. It also supports manipulation of the information that it stores, hence the concept is of something more than just a passive memory system. However, the theories differ as to precisely how working memory is organized and how its functions are provided, and few directly refer to consciousness.

Finally, working memory refers to a neurobiological network in the brain, but the mapping between the neurobiology and the conceptual theories is the subject of debate. Some researchers argue that working memory comprises simply the currently activated aspects of long-term memory. Others argue that working memory relies on a different (but overlapping) neuroanatomical network from long-term memory, and that selective brain damage can damage working memory function but leave long-term memory intact and vice versa. This entry cannot be comprehensive but will focus on empirical approaches to the link between working memory and consciousness. Detailed reviews of the different theories of working memory are given in Miyake and Shah (1999), and more recent research on the topic is described in Osaka et al. (2007).

There have been four broad approaches to the topic. One of these has examined the cognitive processes and particularly working memory functions that appear to correlate, or do not correlate, with conscious experience such as mental *imagery. A second involves experimental manipulations that appear to disrupt the vividness of conscious experience in healthy individuals. A third draws on studies and observations of individuals who report having no experience of mental visual images or have lost this experience following *brain damage. The fourth offers a more theoretical and philosophical treatment. In all cases, while there is the generally agreed broad definition of working memory given above, it is not clear that there is an equivalent generally agreed definition of *consciousness. For the purpose of this entry, a conscious experience is assumed if the participant reliably and consistently reports such an experience. The focus will be primarily, but not exclusively, on visual mental images because this is the topic that has received the most attention in the experimental psychology literature on working memory and conscious experience. Further, there will be two recurring questions throughout the article: (1) Does conscious experience necessarily reflect the function of working memory? (2) Are working memory functions necessarily available to conscious inspection?

1. Self-report of mental imagery and working memory
2. Experimental manipulation of vividness
3. Working memory, conscious experience, and brain damage
4. Theoretical and philosophical issues
5. Summary and conclusion

1. Self-report of mental imagery and working memory

One way to study conscious mental experience experimentally is to investigate what factors might affect the vividness of that mental experience. Self-report of the vividness of the conscious experience of mental images can be traced back to the work of Francis Galton in the late 19th century, who asked his colleagues and friends to imagine and then to report the vividness and clarity of their mental recollection of the details of their breakfast table, of light and colour in a cloudy sky, of familiar sounds, smells, taste, touch, hunger, cold, and so on. He observed that people varied dramatically in whether or not they reported having any phenomenal experience of this kind in the absence of the object, scene, or other relevant stimulus.

One of the most common self report measures in use today is the Vividness of Visual Imagery Questionnaire (VVIQ) originally developed by Marks (1973). It is similar to the original Galton questionnaire in that it asks individuals to give a rating of how vivid are their conscious mental experiences when recollecting a sunrise, a close relative or friend, and a familiar shop or landscape. The advantage to the latter questionnaire is that it has been used very widely. As a result, it is known to generate a spread of scores in the normal population, to be reliable on test–retest with the same individuals, and to correlate with other measures of visual imagery experience. It also appears to be sensitive to loss of visual imagery ability following brain damage. However, studies from the 1970s showed strong correlations between subjectively rated mental imagery and social desirability, raising doubts about whether the VVIQ was measuring mental imagery experience, or was measuring a tendency to give a socially desirable answer. Also, Reisberg et al. (2003) reported that researchers who rated themselves as having highly vivid imagery also were more likely than low-scoring researchers to feel that research on mental imagery was an important phenomenon and worth pursuing. Moreover, the VVIQ does not correlate highly with *objective performance measures of visual working memory, such as the ability to recall or recognize novel, abstract patterns presented a few seconds earlier. These and other results point to the suggestion that there might not be a causal link between the phenomenal conscious experience of mental imagery and the functioning of visual working memory. In other words, what people report of their conscious experience of mental images might not reflect any functional aspects of working memory.

A more positive link between conscious visual images and memory came from research showing that lists of words that are rated as being easy to image are remembered much more readily than are lists of words that are low in imagery (e.g. Paivio 1971). Moreover, creating bizarre or unusual images is well known as a technique for improving memory for words. Therefore, there appears to be an advantage in memory for words that are easy to associate with a conscious image for most people. However, these conscious images are generated from information held in long-term memory, and it may be that generation of a conscious image reflects the temporary activation of long-term memory, and not the functioning of working memory. In contrast working memory might be more focused on the retention and manipulation of recently experienced novel material. Indeed, one primary function of working memory might be to deal with novel information that has few, if any associations in long-term memory (for a detailed discussion see Logie 2003).

2. Experimental manipulation of vividness

A possible reason for the lack of a relationship between rated conscious experience of an image and memory performance is the problem of inter-rater calibration of *subjective ratings; one person might rate a particular conscious experience as being highly vivid, but a similar experience might be rated as less vivid by someone else. As such, rating scales for visual mental images might be poor measures of individual differences in the phenomena being rated, even if they are robust and reliable measures within one individual tested on different occasions.

Baddeley and Andrade (2000) approached this problem by examining how subjective ratings of mental images within the same individuals are affected by experimental manipulations. They asked their participants to generate mental images while they performed another task, such as tapping the keys on a 4×3 keypad or watching irrelevant random dot patterns. Rated vividness of visual images was reduced by concurrent tapping and by watching random dot patterns. In contrast, memory performance was affected by concurrent tapping but not by random dot patterns.

The disruptive effects of the secondary tasks on rated vividness of imagery were more evident for imaging novel patterns (using working memory) than they were for familiar scenes such as cows grazing, a game of tennis, or a sleeping baby (using long-term memory). This points towards a more direct link between working memory and conscious experience, and because each participant is being compared with themselves, there is not a problem of differences between individuals in the criteria that they use for their vividness rating. However, because memory performance and rated vividness are affected differently by secondary tasks, the suggestion is that conscious experience of visual images might not draw on the same aspects of working memory that are used for temporary visual memory.

One potential problem remains, and that is the possible expectation by the participants that a secondary distractor task will affect their mental operations. Hence, they rate their visual mental images as being less vivid when performing a secondary visual task because they expect their images to be affected in this way. Subtle, unintentional hints from the experimenter in how the instructions are presented could reinforce this expectation. However, participants' expectations should apply equally for imagery involving long-term memory and imagery involving working memory, given that conscious images are reported in both cases. It was clear from the experiments that the strongest effects appeared for the working memory tasks, and this differential effect for working memory and for long-term memory is less easy to explain in terms of participant expectations, giving more confidence to the conclusion that the experimental manipulations did indeed affect the conscious experience.

3. Working memory, conscious experience, and brain damage

Individuals who suffer from a dense anterograde *amnesia appear unable to retain new information for more than a few minutes, and several such patients have described their experience as 'continually waking from a dream'—their awareness of real events appears to fade in the same way that dreams fade a few moments after we wake in the morning. Such individuals appear to have largely intact working memory functions, and to be aware of what is happening moment to moment. This suggests that whatever is affecting their ability to remember their immediate and more remote past, affects neither their working memory function nor their awareness of what the 19th century philosopher and psychologist William James referred to as 'the specious present'. Other brain-damaged patients with a rather different cognitive impairment, namely unilateral spatial neglect, appear unaware of one half of their environment (usually on the left) and they also appear to have impairments of visual working memory performance.

Both of the above examples suggest that the functioning of working memory is associated with conscious awareness—current awareness and working memory are both intact in the face of severe amnesia, and damage to working memory function is associated with loss of awareness. However, these are associations, not causal links, and some other cases suggest that the association is less clear: for example, with individuals who report having lost, or never having had the ability to generate mental images. These individuals report being unable to experience any kind of visual mental experience such as imaging the appearance of characters in a radio play, or the visual appearance of a familiar scene or face. They can nevertheless perform well on tests of visual working memory, such as recognizing unfamiliar patterns that they have seen a few moments before, recalling the layout of objects or scenes, or navigating their way around the world (e.g. Botez et al. 1985). That is, memory for visual and spatial information does not necessarily rely on having phenomenal awareness of the visual characteristics of that information.

4. Theoretical and philosophical issues

One influential theory of working memory proposes that there are separate components, each with different roles, and there is now a large body of experimental evidence for the characteristics of these components (reviewed in Logie 2003, Baddeley 2007). One of these components, the *phonological loop*, is thought to support inner speech and the ability to remember and repeat verbal sequences in the correct order, such as a new, multisyllabic word, or a telephone number. A second component, the *visual cache*, is thought to retain the visual appearance and spatial layout of objects or scenes, allowing us to remember where things are or what they look like, while another component, the *inner scribe*, helps us remember sequences of movements. A fourth component, referred to as the *episodic buffer*, is thought to act as a temporary store for integrated information from several modalities and to include semantic information. A fifth consists of what is sometimes referred to as the *central executive*, now thought to be a collection of 'executive' functions, including the control of *attention, of multitasking and task switching, encoding and retrieval strategies, along with higher-order functions such as reasoning and problem solving. The formation of visual images are also seen as executive functions. In a previous version of this framework, a 'visuospatial sketch pad' was thought to support visual and movement memory as well as imagery. But it has become clear that the temporary memory (visual cache and inner scribe) and imagery functions are quite distinct. An illustration of a current version of this theory is shown in Fig. W1.

Given the characteristics of these components, the executive functions might, at first glance, be seen as serving consciousness. However, we can also be conscious of repeating numbers to ourself; a function of the phonological loop, not of the central executive. So this is clearly not the whole story. A second possibility is that working memory as a whole offers a cognitive theory of consciousness. However, this too does not quite fit: when we are mentally rehearsing numbers, we are

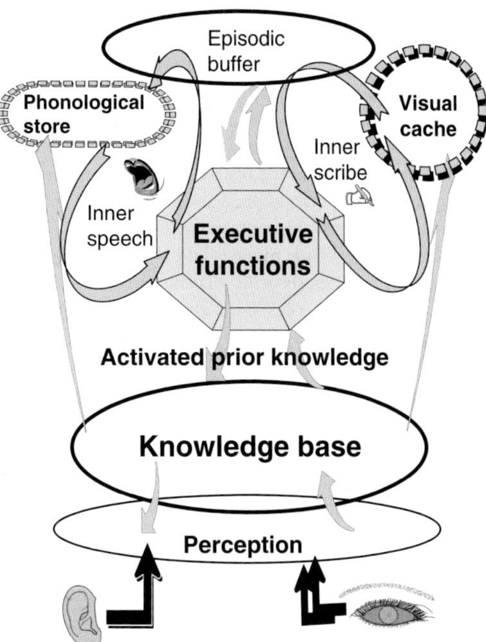

Fig. W1. Schematic view of the multicomponent model of working memory. Adapted from Logie (2003).

conscious only of the number that we are currently rehearsing, while others in the sequence are held in some non-conscious form, but in a 'state of readiness' until they are rehearsed in turn.

Baars (1997) has argued that the concept of working memory can be considered as a 'workspace of the mind' using the metaphor of a theatre in which the main actor is under a spotlight, to illustrate the focus of attention or of consciousness, while other actors, props, etc. are in the immediate background ready to move into the spotlight when their turn arises. This presumably contrasts with props that are held in the storeroom or possible actors who have not been cast for this play, so are not readily available or needed in the immediate future. This last category of props and actors would offer a metaphor for the vast amount of information held in some form of longer-term memory that would require some effort to retrieve and that is not needed for the current task. Cowan (2005) has demonstrated that the spotlight or focus of attention might be limited to around four items at any one time.

Baars (2002) argued further that consciousness offers a means to integrate information across independent brain functions, by focusing the attentional spotlight on quite different kinds of information from different sources. Evidence for this last conjecture is derived from the now large literature on the use of *functional brain imaging techniques, and Baars (2002) reviews several studies demonstrating that conscious activity appears to be associated with relatively widespread activation across the cortex (hence allowing for integration across these different areas) compared with non-conscious activity. In contrast, studies specifically of working memory components are associated with more focused patterns of activation, for example the operation of the phonological loop is linked with activation in the speech areas (primarily Broca's area and the supramarginal gyrus) in the left hemisphere. The visual cache is linked with activation in the posterior parietal cortex (Todd and Marois 2004). Executive functions appear to be linked with specific areas in the prefrontal cortex. For example, the ventrolateral prefrontal cortex appears to be associated with updating and maintaining the contents of working memory while the dorsolateral prefrontal cortex is associated with selecting, manipulating and monitoring the contents of working memory (Fletcher and Henson 2001).

5. Summary and conclusion

The concept of working memory appears to offer a prime candidate for providing a cognitive theory of consciousness. There is evidence for an association, with, for example phenomenal experience of vividness of mental images and immediate memory for unfamiliar visual patterns being affected by some, but not all, of the same experimental manipulations. However, there is relatively limited empirical evidence demonstrating any causal link, and individual differences in subjective ratings of the vividness of visual mental images do not correlate with visual working memory performance. Moreover, some studies have shown that visual working memory can function adequately when participants report having little or no visual phenomenal experience.

Although only a limited range of literature can be reviewed here, it seems clear that working memory cannot be viewed simply as currently activated long-term memory, but is a multi-component system that deals with novel material and can carry out a range of operations including updating, inhibition, transformation, and formation of new associations including mental images, as well as supporting temporary memory. The findings alluded to here illustrate that the possible link between conscious experience and working memory can be studied empirically. Although this link remains unclear, we can at least provide a response to the two questions raised at the start: working memory might fulfil a necessary, but not sufficient prerequisite for consciousness, but consciousness is not a necessary prerequisite for all of working memory function.

ROBERT H. LOGIE

Baars, B. J. (1997). *In the Theater of Consciousness: The Workspace of the Mind.*

—— (2002). 'The conscious access hypothesis: origins and recent evidence'. *Trends in Cognitive Sciences*, 6.

Baddeley, A. D. (2000). 'The episodic buffer: a new component of working memory?' *Trends in Cognitive Sciences*, 4.

—— (2007). *Working Memory, Thought and Action.*

—— and Andrade, J. (2000). 'Working memory and the vividness of imagery'. *Journal of Experimental Psychology: General*, 129.

Botez, M. I., Olivier, M., Vézina, J-L., Botez, T., and Kaufman, B. (1985). 'Defective revisualization: dissociation between cognitive and imagistic thought. Case report and short review of the literature'. *Cortex*, 21.

Cowan, N. (2005). *Working Memory Capacity.*

Fletcher, P. and Henson, R. (2001). 'Frontal lobes and human memory: insights from functional neuroimaging'. *Brain*, 124.

Logie, R. H. (2003). 'Spatial and visual working memory: a mental workspace'. In Irwin, D.and Ross, B. (eds) *Cognitive Vision: The Psychology of Learning and Motivation*, Vol. 42.

Marks, D. (1973). 'Visual imagery differences in the recall of pictures'. *British Journal of Psychology*, 64.

Miyake, A. and Shah, P. (1999). *Models of Working Memory.*

Osaka, N., Logie, R.H., and D'Esposito, M. (eds) (2007). *The Cognitive Neuroscience of Working Memory.*

Paivio, A. (1971). *Imagery and Verbal Processes.*

Reisberg, D., Pearson, D., and Kosslyn, S. (2003). 'Intuitions and introspections about imagery: the role of imagery experience in shaping an investigator's theoretical views'. *Applied Cognitive Psychology*, 17.

Todd, J. J. and Marois, R. (2004). 'Capacity limit of visual short-term memory in the human posterior parietal cortex'. *Nature*, 428.

Z

zombies The zombie is a philosophical fiction: a creature exactly similar to a conscious being in all respects except that it lacks consciousness. Zombies are members of a family of philosophical denizens that are stipulated to be similar to ordinary conscious creatures in certain ways but differ in their consciousness by having missing, inverted or otherwise unusual qualitative mental states. In the case of zombies, consciousness is stipulated to be altogether absent. While the general idea has independently arisen many times throughout history, the term 'zombie' was introduced into the philosophical literature by Robert Kirk (1974; see also Kirk 2005).

Zombies find their way into philosophical debates in two ways. They may figure in arguments for or against *theories of consciousness, as when it is asserted that a variety of zombie is possible and that any theory which contravenes that datum is therefore unacceptable. In the current literature, David Chalmers (1996) is perhaps the leading advocate of this tactic. He argues that the possibility of zombies reveals that physicalist theories of consciousness are inadequate. On the other hand, zombies may simply be a way of exploring the consequences of a theory of consciousness to which one is already committed. Fred Dretske (1995), for example, concludes that his own teleofunctional theory of consciousness admits the possibility of zombies. Philosophical disputes over zombies concern the relevant kind of similarity, the strength of the possibility claim, the answer to the question of whether they are possible, and the consequences of that answer for theories of the nature of consciousness.

To ask whether some kind of zombie is possible is to ask whether it is indeed possible for two creatures to be exactly similar in some particular respects but differ in that one has conscious experiences and the other has none.

The first dispute concerns the ways in which two things may be similar or different. Two creatures may, for example, be exactly similar in their behaviour. (Behaviour is here thought of in terms of mere movement, not as intentionally characterized.) On the other hand, two creatures may be exactly similar in their fundamental physical composition—quark-for-quark, string-for-string, or whatever the fundamental physics turns out to be. Physically identical creatures would also be behaviourally identical, on the assumption that behaviour is determined by physical arrangement. But there are indefinitely many ways that two creatures may be similar with respect to their internal mechanical structure that fall short of exact physical similarity. It is common to think of these intermediate kinds of similarity in terms of the relations between variously characterized inputs and outputs, and thus to think of them as kinds of functional similarity. Like the physically identical creatures, functionally identical creatures would be behaviourally identical to one another on the assumption that internal structure determines behaviour. Yet functional similarity involves structures whose commonalities are more abstract or general than physical similarity. Coarsely put, then, zombies may be stipulated to be behaviourally, functionally, or physically identical to conscious creatures.

The second dispute involves the strength of the modal claim about possibility. For the sake of exposition let us consider creatures that are physically identical to one another, rather than functionally or behaviourally identical to one another. One question we might ask is: is it physically or nomologically possible that two creatures be physically identical to one another but differ with respect to their consciousness? Here the variety of possibility under consideration concerns compatibility with the facts or laws of physics, or natural laws more generally. (As a matter of fact, most philosophers agree that consciousness is at least nomologically determined by the physical composition of things, and thus that physically identical zombies are not nomologically possible. This is not a radical claim, because it is compatible with versions of substance *dualism, property dualism, emergentism, and *physicalism. Still, there are dissenters.) On the other hand, we might wonder whether it is logically or conceptually possible that two creatures be physically identical to one another but differ with respect to their consciousness. Here the possibility concerns whether the conjunction of physical sameness and difference in consciousness is a formal contradiction, or is a conceptual impossibility in virtue of contravening an analytic truth. Finally, we might be interested in whether it is metaphysically possible that two creatures be physically identical to one another but differ with respect to whether each has consciousness. Metaphysical possibility is usually thought of in terms of the constraints of individual and kind essences, along the lines of the impossibility that water could fail to be H_2O or the impossibility that I could have a different mother than I in fact have. But there is some dispute over whether there is a variety of metaphysical possibility that is weaker than logical or conceptual possibility and yet stronger than nomological possibility, or whether all such possibilities reduce to logical, conceptual, or nomological possibilities (Jackson 1998, Block and Stalnaker 1999, Chalmers and Jackson 2001). So leaving open the chance that metaphysical possibility is a redundant category, zombies may be said to be nomologically, metaphysically, or logically/conceptually possible.

The remaining disputes concern whether some sorts of zombies are possible after all, and what consequences if any such possibilities or impossibilities bear for theories of consciousness. Consider the theory that consciousness is analytically defined in terms of syndromes of behavioural dispositions: to be in pain simply is to exhibit a distinctive pattern of behaviours and behavioural dispositions; and similarly for other conscious states or processes. On this view, it will be logically or semantically impossible for two things to have exactly the same behaviours and behavioural dispositions but differ with respect to consciousness. One can run the argument in either direction: if this sort of behaviourism is correct, then behaviourally identical zombies are not logically possible. Or: if behaviourally identical zombies are logically possible, then analytic behaviourism about consciousness is not correct.

Theorists have not been much interested in the possibility of behavioural zombies, creatures that are exactly similar to conscious creatures in their behaviour but which lack consciousness. This is because almost all of the contending theories of consciousness admit that it is even nomologically possible that two things could be behaviourally identical and yet differ in their states of consciousness. Only a few theories, such as the analytic behaviourism described above, would deny this possibility. But the example illustrates the connection between questions about zombies and questions about theories of the nature of consciousness.

Rather than discussing behavioural zombies, philosophers have typically been concerned about functional or physical duplicates. Until recently, philosophers of mind have tended to be concerned with the metaphysical possibility of zombies that are functionally identical to conscious creatures, as a litmus test for the adequacy of functionalism as a theory of consciousness (Dretske 1995, Polger 2004). In this debate, zombies figure in the same role as *inverted spectrum examples: they are used to show that the functionalist theory is incomplete. But of late the metaphysical possibility of physically identical zombies has been taken to figure into the evaluation of physicalism as a general metaphysical commitment about the world in general. Consciousness is taken to be a central test case of a general metaphysical view, thus making zombies broadly relevant to metaphysics and philosophy of language (Chalmers 1996). For example, this dispute has given zombies a place in the debate over whether there is a kind of metaphysical necessity that is distinct from logical or conceptual necessity (Jackson 1998, Chalmers and Jackson 2001).

Many philosophers find that zombies can be a colourful tool for illustrating and testing theories of consciousness. But not everyone accepts that zombies are even a useful theoretical device. Daniel Dennett (1991, 1995, 2005) has been increasingly critical of this particular intuition pump. His worry seems to stem from concerns about the epistemic and methodological problems of distinguishing conscious from non-conscious creatures if zombies were possible. He argues that the very idea of mechanically identical creatures that differ with respect to consciousness presupposes a preposterous *epiphenomenalist notion of consciousness. Dennett's conclusion, however, is the minority opinion; and there are reasons to question his diagnosis (Polger 2004).

Zombies appear to be well ensconced in the philosophical literature. They vividly illustrate the differences among various theories of consciousness. And their mobilization in arguments about consciousness has instigated a renewed interest in metaphilosophical questions about the relationships between conceivability and possibility (e.g. Block and Stalnaker 1999, Chalmers and Jackson 2001).

THOMAS W. POLGER

Block, N. and Stalnaker, R. (1999). 'Conceptual analysis, dualism, and the explanatory gap'. *Philosophical Review*, 108.

Chalmers, D. (1996). *The Conscious Mind: In Search of a Fundamental Theory*.

—— and Jackson, F. (2001). 'Conceptual analysis and reductive explanation'. *Philosophical Review*, 110.

Dennett, D. (1991). *Consciousness Explained*.

—— (1995). 'The unimagined preposterousness of zombies'. *Journal of Consciousness Studies*, 2.

—— (2005). *Sweet Dreams: Philosophical Obstacles to a Science of Consciousness*.

Dretske, F. (1995). *Naturalizing the Mind*.

Jackson, F. (1998). *From Metaphysics to Ethics: A Defense of Conceptual Analysis*.

Kirk, R. (1974). 'Zombies v. materialists'. *Proceedings of the Aristotelian Society*, 48 (suppl.).

—— (2005). *Zombies and Consciousness*.

Polger, T. (2004). *Natural Minds*.